You Be the Subject figures allow students to be their own research subjects and to experience the methods of social psychology.

FIGURE 10.3 You Be the Subject: The Mere Exposure Effect

Which image do you prefer, the one on the left or the one on the right?

Results: People prefer true photos of others, but mirror-image photos of themselves. (The one on the right is the true image.)

Explanation: People see themselves when they look in the mirror, which means that they are familiar with a reverse image of themselves—and this is the image they generally prefer. They see others, however, as they truly are and usually prefer this true image to a mirror image.

Social Psychology

SECOND EDITION

Social Psychology

SECOND EDITION

Thomas Gilovich
Cornell University

Dacher Keltner
University of California, Berkeley

Richard E. Nisbett
University of Michigan

W. W. NORTON & COMPANY • NEW YORK • LONDON

W. W. Norton & Company has been independent since its founding in 1923, when
William Warder Norton and Mary D. Herter Norton first published lectures delivered
at the People's Institute, the adult education division of New York City's Cooper Union.
The firm soon expanded its program beyond the Institute, publishing books by celebrated
academics from America and abroad. By midcentury, the two major pillars of Norton's
publishing program—trade books and college texts—were firmly established. In the 1950s,
the Norton family transferred control of the company to its employees, and today—with
a staff of 400 and a comparable number of trade, college, and professional titles published
each year—W. W. Norton & Company stands as the largest and oldest publishing house
owned wholly by its employees.

Editor: Sheri Snavely
Associate Editor: Sarah England
Editorial Assistant: Josh Bisker
Managing Editor, College: Marian Johnson
Associate Managing Editor, College: Kim Yi
Copy Editor: Janet Greenblatt
Supplements Editor: Matthew Freeman
E-Media Editor: Dan Jost
Marketing Manager: Amber Chow
Senior Production Manager: Benjamin Reynolds
Art Director: Hope Miller Goodell
Designer: Lisa Buckley
Photo Editor: Junenoire Mitchell
Photo Researcher: Elyse Rieder
Composition: Cadmus
Page layout: Brad Walrod/Kenoza Type
Art file manipulation: Jay's Publishers Services
Figure art: Dragonfly Media Group
Manufacturing: Worldcolor—Versailles, KY

Library of Congress Cataloging-in-Publication Data
Gilovich, Thomas.
  Social psychology/Thomas Gilovich, Dacher Keltner, Richard E. Nisbett.—2nd ed.
    p. cm.
  Includes bibliographical references and index.
  ISBN 978-0-393-93258-4 (hbk.)
  1. Social psychology.   I. Keltner, Dacher.   II. Nisbett, Richard E.   III. Title.
HM1033.G52 2010
302—dc22   2009033806

ISBN: 978-0-393-93258-4

W. W. Norton & Company, Inc., 500 Fifth Avenue, New York, NY 10110
www.wwnorton.com

W. W. Norton & Company Ltd., Castle House, 75/76 Wells Street, London W1T 3QT
1 2 3 4 5 6 7 8 9 0

About the Authors

THOMAS GILOVICH is Professor of Psychology and Co-Director of the Center for Behavioral Economics and Decision Research at Cornell University. His research focuses on how people evaluate the evidence of their everyday experience to make judgments, form beliefs, and decide on courses of action. He is the recipient of the Russell Distinguished Teaching Award for teaching social psychology, statistics, and human judgment at Cornell. He is a fellow of the American Psychological Society, the American Psychological Association, the Society for Personality and Social Psychology, the Society of Experimental Social Psychology, and the Committee for Skeptical Inquiry. His other books include *How We Know What Isn't So: The Fallibility of Human Reason in Everyday Life, Why Smart People Make Big Money Mistakes—and How to Correct Them* (with Gary Belsky), and *Heuristics and Biases: The Psychology of Intuitive Judgment* (with Dale Griffin and Daniel Kahneman).

DACHER KELTNER is Professor of Psychology and the Director of the Greater Good Science Center at the University of California at Berkeley. His research focuses on the prosocial emotions, such as love, sympathy, and gratitude, morality, and power. He is the recipient of the Western Psychological Association's award for outstanding contribution to research, the Positive Psychology Prize for excellence in research, the Distinguished Teaching Award for Letters and Sciences (for his teaching of Social Psychology for the past 15 years), and the Distinguished Mentoring Award at UC Berkeley, and is a fellow of the American Psychological Association, the American Psychological Society, and the Society for Personality and Social Psychology. In 2008, the *Utne Reader* listed Dacher as one of the 50 visionaries changing the world. He is the author of three other books, including *Born To Be Good: The Science of a Meaningful Life* and *The Compassionate Instinct*.

RICHARD E. NISBETT is Theodore M. Newcomb Distinguished University Professor of Psychology at the University of Michigan and Research Professor at Michigan's Institute for Social Research. His research focuses on how people from different cultures think, perceive, feel, and act in different ways. He has taught courses in social psychology, cultural psychology, cognitive psychology, and evolutionary psychology. He is the recipient of the Distinguished Scientific Contribution Award of the American Psychological Association and the William James Fellow Award of the American Psychological Society and is a member of the National Academy of Sciences and the American Academy of Arts and Sciences. His other books include *Intelligence and How to Get It, The Geography of Thought: How Asians and Westerners Think Differently . . . and Why, Human Inference: Strategies and Shortcomings of Social Judgment* (with Lee Ross), *The Person and the Situation* (with Lee Ross), and *Culture of Honor: The Psychology of Violence in the South* (with Dov Cohen).

Contents in Brief

Contents

What made
Gandhi
Gandhi.

SOUL
Pass It On.
VALUES.COM

CHAPTER 6   Attitudes, Behavior, and Rationalization   196

CHAPTER 7   Emotion   234

PART THREE   Influencing Others   272

CHAPTER 8   Social Influence   274

PART FOUR   Social Relations   352

CHAPTER 10   Attraction   354

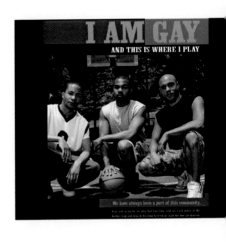

CHAPTER 14 Groups   532

CHAPTER 15 Healthy, Wealthy, and Wise: Social Psychology Applied   568

Preface

A FRESH PERSPECTIVE IN SOCIAL PSYCHOLOGY

Social psychology illuminates and clarifies the nature of human beings and their social world. It is a science that offers novel insights into the foundations of moral sentiments, the origins of violence, and why people fall in love. It offers basic tools for understanding how people persuade one another, why people are so prone to mass phenomena, and how people rationalize their undesirable actions. It offers science-based answers to questions humans have been thinking about since we started to reflect upon who we are: Are we rational creatures? How can we find happiness? What is the proper relationship of the individual to the larger society?

After decades of collective experience teaching social psychology, we decided in 2000 to put pen to paper (or fingers to keyboard) and write our own vision of this fascinating discipline. It was a great time to do so. Many new developments in the field were reshaping social psychology. Ten years of study had revealed how different kinds of culture—country of origin, regional culture, social class—shape human thought, feeling, and action. Insights from evolutionary theory were increasingly guiding how social psychologists study things such as homicide and cooperation. Social psychologists were making inroads into the study of the brain. Specific areas of interest to us—judgment and decision making, emotion, and relationships—had emerged as well-defined areas deserving full treatment. And the findings of social psychology had become recognized as more relevant than ever before. Social psychological studies were making their way into best sellers, written by journalists such as Malcolm Gladwell and psychologists such as Dan Ariely and Dan Gilbert. Social psychology had begun to shape political campaigns and is currently having an influence on the policies of the current U.S. administration (for example, through the social psychological ideas advanced in the book *Nudge*).

The lure of writing a textbook, and the challenge in doing so, was to capture all of these new developments and integrate them with the timeless classics of social psychology that make it such a captivating discipline. We also wanted to convey to the student that social psychology is a productive *scientific* enterprise. Much of the subject matter of social psychology—attraction, conformity, prejudice—readily engages the student's attention and imagination. The material sells itself. But in most textbook summaries of the field, the presentation comes across as a list of unconnected topics—as one fun and intriguing fact after another. As a result, the students often come away thinking of social psychology as all fun and games. That's fine up to a point. Social psychology *is* fun. But it is much more than that, and we have tried to show how the highlights of our field—the classic findings and the exciting new developments—are part of a scientific study of human nature that can sit with pride next to biology, chemistry, and physics and that is worthy of the most serious-minded student's attention.

For all of these reasons, we jumped at the chance to work together on this new edition you hold in your hands. It has been deeply rewarding to have our fascination with the field, and our pride in being a part of it, rekindled and magnified. It is all the more gratifying to have this book reach the minds of the next generation of social psychology students.

CULTURE, EVOLUTION, AND CUTTING-EDGE DISCOVERIES

Social psychology covers a breathtaking array of areas—group dynamics, self-esteem and self-deception, revenge and forgiveness, the perception of risk, conformity, and persuasion to name just a few. This is what makes the field so interesting—and so challenging as well. What broad theoretical ideas can unify these vastly different phenomena? What core concepts should the student take away from the study of social psychology?

Any serious attempt to integrate these diverse phenomena must draw on two important facts. First, we are evolved creatures shaped by hundreds of thousands of years of evolution to function in our social environment. And second, we are powerfully influenced by rich, and sometimes very different, cultural contexts. It is a remarkable quirk of the history of social psychology that until recently, it was possible to summarize what social psychologists were thinking about and working on in their labs without making any reference to these two important facts. It is no longer possible—or at least no longer defensible—to do so. We therefore devote a great deal of attention to these two recent arrivals to the theoretical development of our field. Any student of human behavior cannot help but be struck by how variable people are around the world, yet at the same time how profoundly similar we all are. In all corners of the world, people manage to get nourishing food into their bodies, and yet, how we eat—be it with our hands or with forks and knives, in a crowd or by ourselves, lying on a hammock or wolfing down fast food in the car—varies enormously from one part of the world to another. The rules that govern how women and men interact in public also vary dramatically: in some cultures, public displays of affection, such as a kiss, cause moral outrage; in other cultures, such displays are commonplace. Yet at the same time, when you look closely enough, people flirt and fall in love in strikingly similar ways, no matter where they are or in what culture they were raised.

Although people sometimes think that evolutionary and cultural approaches are at odds with one another, we have a different view. We present an emerging consensus that human behavior is shaped by both culture and evolution and that these two traditions offer *complementary* insights into everyday social behavior. Reflecting how an evolutionary theorist would think about some of the basic phenomena of social psychology, we frequently report animal behavior that is analogous to what we see in humans, and we discuss how behavior that is uniquely human is understandable in terms of the early challenges to survival and reproduction faced by our ancestors. But we also discuss how cultural adaptations to unique circumstances may have taken some originally universal tendencies in utterly different directions.

We take a particularly close look at how different kinds of culture shape behavior in profound ways. We look at the influence of gender on emotion, relationships, and altruism. We consider fascinating regional variations in aggression. And throughout the book, we look at two quite different ways of being human (and all sorts of blends and variants in between). One of these is the Western way—studied almost exclusively by psychologists for the first 100 years that psychology could be called a science. In this mode of existence, relationships are seen as informal, role relations are relatively unscripted, and the self is experienced as existing independently of groups. The other way is the Eastern way (probably more characteristic of most of the world's people), in which relationships and role constraints are seen as more structured, and the self as fundamentally enmeshed in groups. We spend a great deal of time attempting to convince the student that there really are two such very different ways of being human, and we explore many of the social, perceptual, and cognitive consequences of these different ways of being.

We rely on our integration of culture and evolution to profile new developments in social psychology. New empirical literature has emerged that has led us to write chapters both dear to our hearts and important to our field—chapters that wouldn't have been written even a decade or so ago. Early on we have a chapter on emotion that brings together the new discoveries of that field, ranging from studies of emotional communication through facial expression and touch to the new neuroscience of trust and happiness to the role of emotion in moral judgment. Another chapter integrates studies of judgment and decision making with mainstream research on social cognition. In this chapter, we delve into the studies of human judgment that led Daniel Kahneman to win the Nobel Prize and explore how people sometimes go with their gut instincts and other times follow the dictates of more rational analyses. We have a chapter on relationships, a field of great (and obvious) appeal to students and one that has exploded with new discoveries, such as what makes for a healthy marriage and why people in power so often act like fools. Throughout these chapters, and in all the others as well, the student will learn to look at different phenomena through the lenses of evolution and culture.

Throughout the book, we worked especially hard to present contemporary thinking about culture and evolution in a way that fits with social psychology's classic findings and enduring ideas. One such enduring idea is the recognition of the extraordinary power that situations can have over people's behavior. Time and time again, social psychologists such as Milgram, Asch, Darley, and many others have been able to shed light on how subtle changes in the social context dramatically alter people's actions.

A second central idea of social psychology involves the role of a person's "construal" of stimuli and prevailing situations—that is, the degree to which a person's understanding of the world is an interpretation that might or might not be shared by others. Over and over, social psychologists have illuminated how it is the person's interpretation of situations that influences behavior, not the objective events or circumstances themselves.

A third theme is related to the first two and makes them comprehensible: much of our understanding of the world and of the reasons for our behavior are hidden from us. We humans take our conscious, controlled processing to be the whole of what governs our understanding and behavior and are often blind to the subterranean forces of situational constraints and unconscious construal. We explore these forces in considerable detail throughout the book, but we also strive to ensure that the student comes away knowing that people are anything but empty vessels controlled by stimuli of which they can never be aware and by situations too powerful to overcome or modify. Accordingly, we emphasize how people's conscious thoughts interact with more automatic psychological processes and how reflection can help us actively and purposefully construe the stimuli we encounter and guide our behavior by goals and plans of our own choosing.

THE STORY OF OUR SCIENCE

Whether students end up as teachers, salespeople, or talent agents, or as software designers, forest rangers, or copy editors, other people are going to be the center of their lives. We grow up dependent on the members of our nuclear family (and in many cultural contexts a larger extended family), we go through adolescence obsessed with our social standing and intensely focused on the prospects for romance and sexuality, and as adults we seek out others in the workplace, at clubs, in places of worship, and on holidays. Social psychologists spend their professional lives studying this intense sociality, examining how we act, think, and feel in all of these social encounters—and why we act, think, and feel that way. Above all else, we wanted our book to capture the fundamentally social nature of human life and to present the clever, informative, and sometimes inspiring methods that social psychologists have used to study and understand the social life around us.

In our teaching, we have found that so many great studies in social psychology are simple narratives: the narrative of the person who felt trapped into harming another person in the name of science, the narrative of the clergyman who did not help someone in need because he was in a hurry, the narrative of the Southerner whose blood pressure (and testosterone level) rose when insulted in a hallway, the story of the young researcher who lived among hunter-gatherers in New Guinea to discover universal facial expressions. This is why, in our experience, teaching social psychology can bring so many laughs and "Aha!" moments—because the studies of our field are so often stories that are embedded in—and that inspire—our science.

To make sure that students gain an understanding of the scientific process—and to ensure that they hone their critical thinking skills—we approach the subject of research methods in two ways. A new chapter, "The Methods of Social Psychology," provides an overview of the most important elements of conducting research in social psychology. It ties the methods of social psychology together by showing how many of them can be applied to a single problem—the nature of the "culture of honor." That chapter, and much of the rest of the book, is oriented toward providing the critical thinking skills that are the hallmark of social psychology. We show how the tools of social psychology can be used to critique research in the behavioral and medical sciences that the student reads about on the Web and in magazines and newspapers. More important, we show how the methods of social psychology can be used to understand everyday life, including ways to figure out how to navigate new situations. We then embed the discussion of methodological issues throughout the book, in the context of pertinent lines of research, melding the content of social psychology together with the means of discovering that content and showing how the principles that underlie research can be used to understand ordinary events in people's lives.

The new graphics of the book—annotated figures and Scientific Method figures highlighting the details of particularly informative experiments—bring the parables of social psychology to visual life, as do You Be the Subject figures that help the student get an insider's view of experimentation in social psychology and how it all works. We believe that students understand methodological issues best when they see them applied to questions that capture their interest. We have tried to make sure that all of our field's varied methods—for example, archival analyses, semantic and affective priming, neuroimaging, and participant observation—are discussed in sufficient depth to give the reader an understanding of how they work and what their strengths and weaknesses are. Throughout the text, we provide Focus On boxes that concentrate on two new developments in our field—neuroscientific approaches to the social brain and the study of happiness, or positive psychology. These boxes allow the student to get a flavor of these new trends in our field and can be elaborated on as the instructor sees fit.

THE APPLICATION OF SOCIAL PSYCHOLOGY TO EVERYDAY LIFE

Possibly the easiest part of writing a social psychology textbook is pointing out to the student the enormous applied implications of what the field has to offer. We do a lot of that pointing throughout the text. We begin each chapter with events in the real world that drive home the themes and wisdom of social psychology. For example, we begin the chapter on altruism, aggression, and cooperation with the story of Paul Rusesabagina, the Hutu in Rwanda who rescued hundreds of Tutsis, risking his own life and the lives of his children during the tragic genocide in that country in 1996. What better way for the student to ponder the findings of social psychology than relying on them to understand current events. Many of our Focus On boxes profile real-world applications of the wisdom of social psychology—for example, in understanding how black uniforms make professional athletes more aggressive or how meditation might shift the reader's brain chemistry.

But to bring into sharper focus the relevance of social psychology to daily living, we have added an applied chapter at the end of the book. This chapter brings science-based insight to bear on three areas of great importance to just about everyone: the latest findings on health and how science-based, practical techniques help us transcend stress during difficult times; the new science of behavioral economics and how it can help us lead more financially stable and rewarding lives; and the latest discoveries in the study of human intelligence and education. In many ways, social psychology is only as good as the relevance of its findings to advancing human welfare and society. We believe that these three sections of our applied chapter illustrate past successes and future promise of our field.

WHAT'S NEW IN THE SECOND EDITION

The cumulative nature of science requires revisions that do justice to the latest discoveries and evolving views of the field. Our Second Edition has much to offer in this regard. The student will learn about a great many new discoveries in our field. Here is a small sampling:

In the chapter on the self, we cover new findings on the costs of exerting the will, gender differences in self-construal, and striking evidence that cultural differences in the self are related to different kinds of activation in the brain.

In the chapter on emotion, we present new findings related to culture and pride, ideal emotions in different cultures, touch, intergroup emotions, and the cultivation of happiness.

In the chapter on persuasion, the student will read up on the latest in social psychological approaches to political ideology, on lying and the television show *Lie to Me*, and the role of genetics in shaping voting behavior.

In the chapter on altruism, aggression, and cooperation, the student will read about the origins of volunteerism, how the greening of urban neighborhoods promotes cooperation, and how cooperation activates reward-related regions of the brain.

In the chapter on relationships, the student will learn about the powerful effects of social rejection and solitary confinement, about how we get and retain power, and the latest scientific findings on what makes romantic relationships work.

In the chapter on attitudes, behavior, and rationalization, the student will be presented with an extensive treatment of terror management theory and with research on people's need to justify the broader social and political systems of which they are members.

The student will learn about the important role of the experience of fluency in aesthetic judgments in the chapter on attraction and fluency's broader influence on judgment in the chapter on social judgment.

In Chapter 4, the student will learn about recent work on people's snap judgments—and the accuracy of those judgments.

In addition to these new areas of coverage, we worked hard to produce a new organization to our text to accommodate the different approaches to our field that an instructor might take. There are many ways to teach social psychology. One can approach the field historically and start where it began—in the study of groups and persuasion. One can approach the field by looking at the different elements of being human, as psychologists often do, and organize the course accordingly—examining, say, thought, feeling, and action. Or one can take the approach that we do, which is to begin within the individual and then move outward to how people influence one another and from there to relationships and groups.

All are excellent ways to approach our field. To honor these different approaches, we have written each chapter so that it can stand alone and so that the chapters can be read in any order. We have done so stylistically by writing chapters that are complete narratives in their own right. Our chapters stand on their own theoretically as well, being organized around the central concepts of culture and evolution and around social psychology's emphasis on situationism, construal, and automaticity.

ACKNOWLEDGMENTS

No book is written in a vacuum. Many people have helped us in the course of writing this text, starting with our families. Karen Dashiff Gilovich was her usual bundle of utterly lovable qualities that make the sharing of lives so enjoyable—and the difficulties of authorship so tolerable. Mollie McNeil was a steady source of kindness, enthusiasm, and critical eye and ear. Sarah and Susan Nisbett were sounding boards and life support systems. Mikki Hebl, Dennis Regan, and Tomi-Ann Roberts went well beyond the call of collegial duty by reading every chapter and providing us with useful commentary. In addition to giving us the considerable benefit of their good judgment and good taste, they also pointed out a few of our blind spots and saved us from an occasional embarrassing error.

We are also grateful to Jon Durbin, Vanessa Drake-Johnson, and Paul Rozin for bringing us together on this project and getting it all started. We have had a great deal of fun working together and have enjoyed the opportunity to think and write about the broad discipline that is social psychology. Thanks. We would also like to extend our deeply felt thanks to Sheri Snavely, whose positive spirit and exquisite taste make her a dream editor. We also owe a great deal to our tireless project editor Kim Yi, art development editor Sarah England, photo researcher Elyse Rieder, photo editor Junenoire Mitchell, production manager Ben Reynolds, and developmental editor Beth Ammerman. We also are grateful for the marketing efforts of Amber Chow and the Norton travelers who have worked to make this book a success.

Our thanks to the following for their helpful suggestions and close reading of various chapters in the first and second editions of the book.

Reviewers for the First Edition

Glenn Adams, *University of Toronto*; Craig Anderson, *Iowa State University*; Elliott Beaton, *McMaster University*; Susan Boon, *Calgary University*; Tim Brock, *Ohio State University*; Susan Cross, *Iowa State University*; George Cvetkovich, *Western Washington University*; Dan Dolderman, *University of Toronto*; Richard Eibach, *Yale University*; Eli Finkel, *Northwestern University*; Marcia Finkelstein, *University of South Florida*; Azenett Garza-Caballero, *Weber State University*; Jon Haidt, *University of Virginia*; Lora Haynes, *University of Louisville*; Steve Heine, *University of British Columbia*; Andy Karpinski, *Temple University*; Marc Kiviniem, *University of Nebraska, Lincoln*; Ziva Kunda (deceased), *Waterloo University*; Marianne LaFrance, *Yale University*; Alan Lambert, *Washington University*; Jeff Larsen, *Texas Tech University*; Norman Li, *University of Texas, Austin*; Doug McCann, *York University*; Daniel Molden, *Northwestern University*; Gerrod Parrott, *Georgetown University*; Ashby Plant, *Florida State University*; Deborah Prentice, *Princeton University*; Jane Richards, *University of Texas, Austin*; Jennifer Richeson, *Northwestern University*; Alex Rothman, *University of Minnesota, Twin Cities Campus*; Darcy Santor, *Dalhousie University*; Jeff Sherman, *Northwestern University*; Colleen Sinclair, *University of Missouri, Columbia*; Jeff Stone, *University of Arizona*; Warren Thorngate, *Carleton University*; Zakary Tormala, *Indiana University, Bloomington*; David Wilder, *Rutgers University*; Connie Wolfe, *Muhlenberg College*; Joseph Vandallo, *University of South Florida*; Leigh Ann Vaughn, *Ithaca College*; Randy Young, *Bridgewater State University*; Jennifer Yanowitz, *University of Minnesota, Twin Cities Campus*.

Reviewers for the Second Edition

Leonard Berkowitz, *University of Wisconsin—Madison*
Nicholas Christenfeld, *University of California, San Diego*
Eric Cooley, *Western Oregon University*
Chris Crandall, *University of Kansas*
Deborah Davis, *University of Nevada, Reno*
Chris De La Ronde, *Austin Community College*
Rachel Dinero, *Cazenovia College*
John Dovidio, *Yale Univserity*
Richard P. Eibach, *University of Waterloo*
Naomi Eisenberger, *University of California, Los Angeles*
Daniel Gilbert, *Harvard University*
Lisa Harrison, *California State University, Sacramento*
Todd Hartman, *Appalachian State University*
Edward Hirt, *Indiana University*

Matthew I. Isaak, *University of Louisiana at Lafayette*
Kareem Johnson, *Temple University*
Iva Katzarska-Miller, *University of Kansas*
Catalina E. Kopetz, *University of Maryland*
Alan Lambert, *Washington University*
Debra Lieberman, *University of Hawaii*
Batja Mesquita, *University of Leuven*
Angela J. Nierman, *University of Kansas*
Bernadette Park, *University of Colorado*
Emily Pronin, *Princeton University*
Denise Reiling, *Eastern Michigan University*
Neal Roese, *University of Illinois at Urbana-Champaign*
Constantine Sedikides, *University of Southampton*
Gregory P. Shelley, *Kutztown University*
Elizabeth R. Spievak, *Bridgewater State College*
Emily Stark, *Minnesota State University, Mankato*
Lauren A. Taglialatela, *Kennesaw State University*
Jeanne Tsai, *Stanford University*
Marcellene Watson-Derbigny, *Sacramento State University*
Nancy Yanchus, *Georgia Southern University*

T.G.
D.K.
R.E.N.
January 2010

MEDIA & PRINT RESOURCES FOR INSTRUCTORS AND STUDENTS

For Instructors

Instructor's Manual

By Karen Wilson (College of Staten Island/CUNY)

Providing a wealth of suggestions on how to enhance lectures using *Social Psychology, Second Edition*, this Instructor's Manual includes detailed chapter outlines with lecture suggestions, discussion questions to engage the student in lecture or recitation, demonstrations and activities to draw the student in and reinforce concepts, suggested films for in-class presentation, and classroom lectures by Thomas Gilovich and Dennis Regan, with tables and figures from the text.

Test Bank

By Emily N. Stark (Minnesota State University, Mankato)
Joseph L. Etherton (Texas State University, San Marcos)
Matt Canham (Portland, Oregon)

As an aid in constructing an in-class quiz, midterm, or final exam, the Test Bank contains a flexible pool of questions for each chapter that allows instructors to create a quiz or test that meets their individual requirements. Revised and expanded for the second edition, each chapter of the Test Bank includes a concept map and consists of three question types classified according to a taxonomy of educational objectives:

1. *Factual* questions test the student's basic understanding of facts and concepts.
2. *Applied* questions require the student to apply knowledge in the solution of a problem.
3. *Conceptual* questions require the student to engage in qualitative reasoning and to explain why things are as they are.

Questions are further classified by section and difficulty, making it easy to construct tests and quizzes that are meaningful and diagnostic. The question types are multiple-choice, true–false, and short answer/essay.

Test Bank is available in print, PDF, Word RTF, and ExamView® Assessment Suite formats.

NEW *Social Psychology* Video Clip DVD

Ideal for introducing key social psychological concepts to your students, this DVD offers lecture-ready video clips focusing on real-world research in action. For the second edition, the DVD has been updated to provide the latest profiles of research in the field.

Instructor's Resource DVD

The Instructor's Resource Disc provides an array of resources for instructors to create easy and effective lecture presentations:

- Lecture PowerPoint slides with clicker questions
- Art PowerPoint slides
- Image Gallery of all of the art from the text
- BlackBoard/WebCT coursepack
- BlackBoard/WebCT Web quizzes and Test Bank
- Computerized Test Bank

Instructor's Resource Site

The Instructor's Resource Site is an online source of instructional content for use in lectures, modified classrooms, and distance education courses. The site includes:

- Lecture PowerPoint slides
- Clicker questions in PowerPoint format
- Art PowerPoint slides
- Image Gallery of all of the art and photos from the text
- BlackBoard/WebCT coursepack
- BlackBoard/WebCT Web quizzes and Test Bank
- Computerized Test Bank and ExamView® Assessment Suite Software

For Students

 StudySpace

wwnorton.com/studyspace

This free student Web site provides a rich array of multimedia resources and review materials within a proven, task-oriented study plan. Each chapter is arranged in an effective Organize, Learn, and Connect structure, with review materials such as chapter outlines, flashcards, quizzes, and ebook links. The Norton Quiz+ Assessment Program gives the student customized chapter-by-chapter study plans that target specific content areas for review. The StudySpace also offers:

- Updated Apply It! Exercises that provide the student with exercises to learn about and use online social psychology resources.
- Author Insights video podcasts that present firsthand discussions by the text authors on core social psychology topics and current research trends.
- Drag-and-Drop Labeling Exercises that use the line art from the text to help the student understand key diagrams and complex structures.
- Visual Quizzes that integrate the revised art program from the text to help the student review the details of important figures and diagrams.
- A regularly updated Social Psychology in the News feed.

 Ebook

nortonebooks.com

Same great content, half the price!

The ebook links to StudySpace and offers many useful electronic tools, such as highlighting and sticky notes.

Study Guide

By Connie Wolfe (Muhlenberg College)

This Study Guide helps the student achieve an even greater understanding of the material covered in lecture and the text by providing additional self-testing opportunities and resources for further study. Each chapter includes an annotated (fill-in-the-blank) chapter outline with answers, chapter goals, multiple-choice and essay-type review questions, critical thinking exercises for testing in-depth understanding, and social psychology references in popular media such as books, films, and Web sites.

Social Psychology

SECOND EDITION

PART ONE

The Science of Social Psychology

Social psychology is the one branch of psychology that deals primarily with the important fact that we live our lives connected to others. We originate in families, we seek out friendship and romance, and we spend a great deal of our waking moments in groups of various sorts—in classes, on the job, in a place of worship, or with those who share our hobbies and enthusiasms. In Chapter 1, we present a quick tour of what the field of social psychology is all about and the themes and perspectives that are most helpful in gaining insight into human social behavior. Then, in Chapter 2, we discuss the different methods that can be used to achieve a true understanding of the many topics that make up the field of social psychology.

An Invitation to Social Psychology

WHEN ONE OF THE AUTHORS of this book was a teenager, the buses in the southwestern city where he lived had signs over a row of seats reading "colored section." Around the same time, one of today's most distinguished social psychologists —the African-American Claude Steele—was prohibited from swimming in the public pools of Chicago (except on Wednesdays) because of his race. Meanwhile, black men with PhD's were stuck in low-status jobs—often as sleeping car porters or post office clerks. These injustices were accepted by white people who were not monsters—in fact, many were kind, often religious people who might be models of human decency in their conduct, even toward individual black people. Indeed, if you are white, it is entirely likely that your grandparents were among the decent white people who would not have thought of protesting public policies that strike the great majority of Americans today as appalling.

In the late 1950s and early 1960s, black people in the South began to demand the right to vote without harassment as well as the right to use public accommodations such as restrooms and restaurants. The initial reaction on the part of a great many whites, in both the South and the North, was to regard these demonstrations as improper disturbances of the peace and to view the demonstrators as mere troublemakers.

But then newspapers and television began showing civil rights demonstrators being humiliated and set upon by dogs and fire hoses. And when a black church in Birmingham was firebombed, four little girls were killed. Almost overnight, public opinion in the non-South, and in much of the South as well, turned in favor of the demonstrators. People who, a very few years before, would have rejected the idea of changing the nation's "Jim Crow" laws were now in favor of civil rights. And laws on voting and public accommodations proposed by a president from Texas were overwhelmingly passed by Congress.

Flash forward a few decades. Black people have now served as the CEOs of multibillion-dollar corporations, including the largest communications company in the world, one of the largest financial services companies in the world, one of the largest wholesale food companies, and the largest mortgage finance corporation in the country. Blacks are presidents of major universities. A black man has been the highest military officer in the land. The most bankable movie actor is a black man. A black woman who grew up at the same time as the little girls who were killed in the church fire in Birmingham—and in a nearby neighborhood—has been secretary of state. Her successor was appointed by a president of African descent.

The Roots of Social Behavior
In the pre-civil rights era of the American South it was common for public facilities, including water fountains, restrooms, railroad cars, and sections of buses, to be segregated by race.

The history of race relations in the United States is full of disturbing episodes and also moments of great uplift. But for social psychologists especially, it is also full of fascinating questions. How could one of the founders of the country, a beacon of eighteenth-century enlightenment, write that it is self-evident that all men are created equal—yet keep scores of slaves? Why would millions of Southerners risk civil war to ensure that slavery would be legal in the new states in the West? Why were the Northern states not more magnanimous in their treatment of the defeated South after the end of the Civil War? Why did blacks, who were rated by Northerners as more acceptable neighbors and more desirable employees than the Irish at the beginning of the twentieth century, fail to thrive economically or politically as much as the Irish did later in the century? Why did white Northerners accept laws allowing segregation in public facilities? Why did a dramatic social revolution in the South, overthrowing practices that were deeply engrained in the society, not produce a blood bath? How could countless white people move in a matter of a few years from acceptance of segregation to moral revulsion toward it? Why did the crashing of every barrier to black success leave millions of blacks mired in abject poverty?

In this book, you will read about theories and research findings that shed light on many of these questions. You will read about persuasion and attitude change, about people's seemingly limitless capacity for self-deception, about the economic roots of social behavior, about the force of culture, about the origins and antidotes to racial prejudice, and about the sources of violence and the forces that can counter violence. You will also learn about the tools with which social psychologists address these questions—the scientific methods that allow them to supplement historical analysis, anthropological inquiry, and common sense. We hope that exploring these theories, findings, and tools will both challenge you intellectually and give you the resources you will need to understand social relations and social psychology in the everyday world.

In this chapter, we explain what social psychology is and what social psychologists study. We also present some of the basic concepts of social psychology, especially the surprising degree to which social situations can influence behavior; the role of construal, that is, the interpretive processes people use to understand situations; and how two different kinds of thinking—one rapid, intuitive, and unconscious and the other slower, analytical, and conscious—contribute in tandem to understanding what is happening in social situations. We also describe some recent developments in social psychology that are beginning to change the field—namely, the application of evolutionary concepts to human behavior and the discovery of some significant differences in human cultures that frequently lead people in different societies to respond to the "same" situation in very different ways.

CHARACTERIZING SOCIAL PSYCHOLOGY

People have long sought explanations for human behavior. They have wondered about such things as why people are inclined to stereotype members of different groups, why people risk their lives to help others, why some marriages flourish and others fail, and why crowds can turn into violent mobs. Stories and parables have attempted to explain human behavior for millennia. Folk wisdom has been passed from generation to generation through lore, jokes, and admonitions, explaining why people do what they do and prescribing behaviors to avoid or follow. Social psychologists go beyond folk wisdom and try to establish a scientific basis for understanding human behavior by conducting studies and setting up experiments. **Social psychology** can be defined as the scientific study of the feelings, thoughts, and behaviors of individuals in social situations.

social psychology The scientific study of the feelings, thoughts, and behaviors of individuals in social situations.

Explaining Behavior

In April 2004, more than a year after the start of the war in Iraq, CBS broadcast a story on *60 Minutes II* that exposed American atrocities against Iraqi prisoners in the Abu Ghraib prison near Baghdad. CBS showed photos of naked prisoners with plastic bags over their heads, stacked up in a pyramid and surrounded by jeering and laughing male and female American soldiers. Other photos showed hooded prisoners who were standing on narrow pedestals with their arms stretched out and electric wires attached to their bodies. CBS also reported that prisoners had been required to simulate sexual acts.

Most Americans were appalled at the abuse and ashamed of the behavior of the U.S. soldiers. The reaction on the part of many Iraqis and others in the Arab world was to regard the acts as evidence that the United States had malevolent intentions toward Arabs (Hauser, 2004). The United States dropped yet further in the esteem of the world.

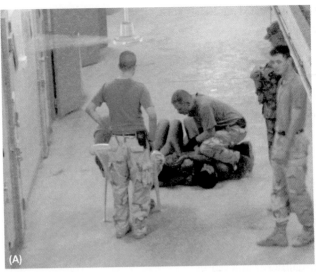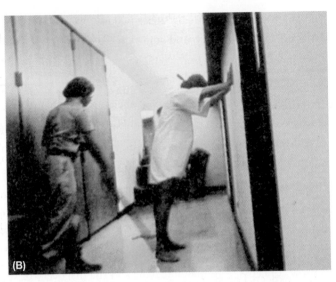

Prison Situations and Intimidation (A) Military guards at the Abu Ghraib prison in Iraq used torture, humiliation, and intimidation to try to obtain information from the prisoners. This included stripping them and making them lie naked in the prison corridors, as shown here, or stacking them naked in a pyramid, as in the image shown on *60 Minutes II*. Such degradation echoes what happened in the Zimbardo prison study, as shown in (B) a photo of a "guard" seeking to humiliate one of his prisoners at the simulated prison.

The assumption—or hope—of many Americans was that the soldiers who had perpetrated these acts were rotten apples—exceptions to a rule of common decency prevailing in the military. But social psychologists were not so quick to reach such a conclusion.

Thirty years before the atrocities at Abu Ghraib, Philip Zimbardo and his colleagues paid 24 Stanford University undergraduate men, chosen for their good character and mental health, to be participants in a study of a simulated prison (Haney, Banks, & Zimbardo, 1973). By the flip of a coin it was determined who would be a "guard" and who would be a "prisoner." The guards wore green fatigue uniforms and reflective sunglasses. The prisoners wore tunics with nylon stocking caps and had a chain locked around one ankle. The "prison" was set up in the basement of the psychology department, and the researchers anticipated the study lasting for two weeks. But the guards quickly turned to verbal abuse and physical humiliation, requiring the prisoners to wear bags over their heads, stripping them naked, and requiring them to engage in simulated sex acts. The study had to be terminated after six days because the behavior of the guards produced extreme stress reactions in several of the prisoners.

Zimbardo today maintains that the balance of power in prisons is so unequal that they tend to be brutal places unless heavy constraints are applied to curb the guards' worst impulses. Thus, at both Abu Ghraib and Stanford, "It's not that we put bad apples in a good barrel. We put good apples in a bad barrel. The barrel corrupts anything that it touches" (quoted in Schwartz, 2004).

It might be contended that the soldiers in Iraq were only following orders and that, left to their own devices, they would not have chosen to behave as they did. This may be the case, but it only pushes the question back one step: Why did they follow such orders? Social psychologists seek to find answers to just such questions.

Social psychologists study situations in which people (real or imagined, today or in the past, face-to-face or through television or the Internet) exert influence over one another, and they study how people respond to influence attempts of various kinds. Social psychologists are also interested in how people make sense of their world—how they decide what and whom to believe, how they make inferences about the motives, personalities, and abilities of other people, and how they reach conclusions about the causes of events. Social psychologists address questions like the following: Why might people assigned to play the role of guards abuse those who are assigned to be prisoners? Why do roles like prison guard, football fan, or class clown exert such powerful influences on social behavior? Does the presence of others affect how people perceive a situation or their ability to solve a difficult problem? What is the best way to persuade others to change their opinions or to do something they might not do under normal conditions? When people are led to say something they don't believe, do their beliefs normally move in the direction of what they've said, or do they more typically become even more firmly entrenched in their initial beliefs?

These sorts of questions lie at the heart of social psychology. There are answers to all of them—answers hard won by research. Some of the answers surprised even the social psychologists who conducted the research, because they commonly have the same sorts of expectations that nonpsychologists have, based on folk theories about human behavior. Such findings are counterintuitive—not what most people would expect. For example, we would not expect ordinary undergraduates to treat people badly just by virtue of being assigned the role of prison guard. On the other hand, some folk theories are right on the money. For example, we tend to like people who like us, and the people we like generally have interests that are similar to ours. When experimental findings reflect what our intuitions and folk wisdom say will happen, social psychologists elaborate that folk wisdom—they seek to discover when it applies and what lies behind the phenomenon in question. Yet, we will demonstrate numerous times in this book that many of our most strongly held folk theories or intuitions fail to give complete answers to many important questions. And others are just plain wrong. Thus, social psychologists need to test intuitions by devising studies and crafting experiments that successfully isolate the causes of behavior in social situations.

Much of what social psychologists know about human behavior is invaluable. Social psychology now forms a significant part of the curriculum in many schools of business, public health, social work, education, law, and medicine. Social psychological research on such topics as judgment and decision making, social influence, and how people function in groups are relevant to all those fields. Social psychologists apply their knowledge to important questions regarding individuals and society at large, studying how to reduce stereotyping and prejudice in the classroom and workplace; how to

Explaining Situations Social psychologists seek to understand how individuals act in relation to others in social situations. Why might some people on line ignore everyone else (and be left alone by everyone), whereas others talk to anyone who will listen to them? Are they more willing to wait because they are with other people? Does their behavior change based on the number of people present or the length of the wait?

make eyewitness testimony more reliable; how physicians can best use diverse sources of information to make a correct diagnosis; what goes wrong in airplane cockpits when there is an accident or near-accident; and how businesses, governments, and individuals can make better decisions.

Research by social psychologists regularly influences government policy. For example, research on the effects of different kinds of welfare programs is used in shaping government assistance policies. Research also affects decisions by the courts. The landmark 1954 *Brown v. Board of Education* ruling that struck down school segregation in the United States drew heavily on social psychological research, which had indicated that segregated schools were inherently unequal in their effects (and thus unconstitutional). By the time you have finished this book, you will have acquired a great deal of knowledge used by educators, businesspeople, and the government. We believe that this knowledge will give you a greater understanding of yourself and others and make you more effective and satisfied in both your personal and professional life.

Comparing Social Psychology with Related Disciplines

The events at Abu Ghraib, like so many other telling events, can be studied from many viewpoints, including those of politicians, criminologists, sociologists, and personality psychologists. Each type of professional takes a different approach to what happened and offers different kinds of explanations.

Personality psychology is a close cousin of social psychology, but it stresses individual differences in behavior rather than the social situation. Thus, social psychologists would examine the general situation at Abu Ghraib, in which orders were not clear but pressures were brought to bear on the guards to "soften up" the prisoners to get information about other insurgents and future attacks. Personality psychologists would instead look at whether certain traits and dispositions—for example, sadism or hostility—would predict cruel behavior across a range of situations. Personality psychologists try to find a consistent pattern in the way an individual behaves across situations—to find an individual's position on a trait dimension. For example, everyone has a location on the dimension of extraversion (outgoingness) to introversion (shyness). Some people behave more or less consistently in an extraverted or introverted fashion across a wide range of situations. Others—the great majority, actually—are harder to predict, so that consistency typically comes in the form of situation-specific consistency: in situation X they behave in extraverted fashion; in situation Y, in more introverted fashion (Mischel, 2004; Mischel, Shoda, & Mendoza-Denton, 2002).

Social psychology is also related to cognitive psychology, the study of how people perceive, think about, and remember aspects of the world. In fact, many psychologists call themselves cognitive social psychologists. They differ from cognitive psychologists primarily in that the topics studied are usually social—perceptions and beliefs about other people. Cognitive psychologists would be more likely to study categorization or memory for words or objects.

Sociology is the study of behavior of people in the aggregate. Sociologists study institutions, subgroups, bureaucracies, mass movements, and changes in the demographic characteristics of populations (for example, age, gender, socioeconomic status). Sociologists might ask about the religious and social backgrounds of the insurgents in Iraq, whether they are part of a mass movement, and whether imprisonment and torture of insurgents would be a successful strategy to stop further attacks against American forces and the new Iraqi government and police force. Social psychologists sometimes do sociological work themselves, although they are likely to bring an interest in individual behavior to the study of aggregates. A sociologist might study how economic or government policy influences marriage and divorce rates in a population, whereas a social psychologist would be more likely to study why individuals fall in love, get married, and sometimes get divorced.

Proximal and Distal Influences in Social Psychology

Fifteen years ago, social psychologists would have said that their field deals primarily with the "proximal" factors influencing behavior—that is, factors that exist in the here and now or that immediately precede what the individual does. This would include the situation itself, how the individual perceives the situation, and the processes—conscious and unconscious—of perceiving and reacting to situations. But things have changed. In recent times, two important "distal" factors—that is, factors that are more removed in time from a given context or episode—have greatly influenced the field of social psychology. One such distal factor is evolution. Psychologists can apply evolutionary theory to an understanding of human behavior. Using the evolutionary approach, psychologists seek primarily to understand the ways in which all, or nearly all, humans behave in similar fashion, and they try to explain these commonalities in terms of adaptation. Another distal factor is culture. Using the cultural approach, psychologists attempt to understand the deep cultural differences that exist between different societies and how they lead people to behave quite differently in situations that on the surface appear to be the same.

Social psychology (and psychology as a whole) differs from all other social sciences, including anthropology, political science, and economics, in that its chief investigative tool is the experiment. We will now discuss some of the most important influences on social behavior and how social psychologists use research—typically *experimental* research—to gain greater understanding of how people act in social contexts and why they act that way. We begin our discussion of important influences by considering the proximal factors.

THE POWER OF THE SITUATION

Are we all capable of acts of brutality? The philosopher Hannah Arendt in 1963 suggested as much in her controversial book *Eichmann in Jerusalem*. Arendt described the trial of Adolf Eichmann, the notorious architect of Hitler's plan to exterminate the Jews in Nazi-occupied Europe. Advancing a very controversial thesis, Arendt described Eichmann as little more than a bureaucrat doing his job. While not condoning his actions (Arendt herself was Jewish), Arendt argued that Eichmann was not the demented, sadistic personality everyone expected (and that the prosecutor claimed), but instead a boring, unimaginative, uncaring cog in a machine that he served, not with glee, but with a resigned (if nevertheless perverse) sense of duty. Perhaps even more disturbing, the logical conclusion of Arendt's theory is that any one of us is capable of performing acts of brutality. Look at the person sitting closest to you right now. Do you think that he or she is capable of atrocities? Do you think that any situation could be so powerful that even you or the person next to you could act as Eichmann did in Nazi Germany or as the prison guards behaved at Abu Ghraib?

Arendt's book created a firestorm of indignant protests, and she was denounced for what many regarded as her attempt to exonerate a monster. But as we will see, research has supported Arendt's heretical views. In examining this research, we need to ask another question, one that is central to the study of social psychology: How does the situation that people find themselves in affect their behavior?

Kurt Lewin, the founder of modern social psychology, was a Jewish Berliner who fled Nazi Germany in the 1930s and became a professor at the University of Iowa and then at MIT. Lewin was a physicist before becoming a psychologist, and he applied a powerful idea from physics to an understanding of psychological existence. He believed that the behavior of people, like the behavior of objects, is always a function of the *field of forces* in which they find themselves (Lewin, 1935). To understand how fast a solid object will travel through a medium, for example, we must know such

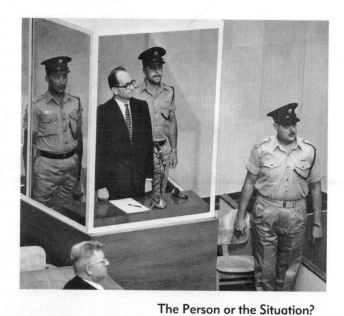

The Person or the Situation?
Adolf Eichmann was apprehended in Argentina, where he had escaped after the end of World War II, and taken to Israel to stand trial for the murder of 6 million Jews. Here he stands with Israeli police in a bulletproof glass cage during his trial. Was Eichmann a brutal murderer or simply a bureaucrat following the orders of his superiors?

Kurt Lewin A pioneer of modern social psychology, Lewin stressed the importance of the field of forces, including the social situation, in affecting a person's behavior.

things as the viscosity of the medium, the force of gravity, and any initial force applied to the object. In the case of people, the forces are psychological as well as physical. Of course, the person's own attributes are also important determinants of behavior, but these attributes always interact with the situation to produce the resulting behavior.

The social equivalent of Lewin's concept of the field of forces is the role of the situation, especially the social situation, in guiding behavior. The main situational influences on our behavior, influences that we often misjudge or fail to see altogether, are the actions—and sometimes just the mere presence—of other people. Friends, romantic partners, even total strangers can cause us to be kinder or meaner, smarter or dumber, lazier or more hardworking, bolder or more cautious. They can produce drastic changes in our beliefs and behavior by what they tell us, by modeling through their actions what we should think and do, by subtly implying that our acceptability as a friend or group member depends on adopting their views or behaving as they do, or even by making us feel that our freedom is being encroached upon by their influence attempts, which may lead us to actually move in the opposite direction. We rely on other people for clues about what emotions to feel in various situations and even to define who we are as individuals. All this has been shown in numerous studies that have demonstrated the power of the situation.

The Milgram Experiment

In the same year as the publication of Arendt's book, Stanley Milgram (1963, 1974) published the results of a now-classic experiment on social influence. Milgram advertised in the local newspaper for men to participate in a study on learning and memory at Yale University in exchange for a modest amount of money. (In subsequent experiments, women also participated, with similar results.) When the volunteers—a mix of laborers, middle-class individuals, and professionals ranging in age from their 20s to their 50s—arrived at the laboratory, a man in a white lab coat told them that they would be participating in a study of the effects of punishment on learning. There would be a "teacher" and a "learner," with the learner trying to memorize word pairs such as "wild/duck." The volunteer and another man, a somewhat heavyset, pleasant-looking man in his late 40s, drew slips of paper to determine who would play which role. But things were not as they seemed: the pleasant-looking man was actually an

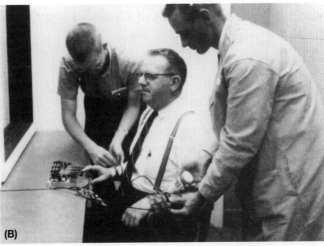

The Milgram Study To examine the role of social influence, Stanley Milgram set up a study in which participants believed they were testing a learner (actually a confederate) and punishing him with shocks when he gave the wrong answer. (A) Milgram's "shock machine." (B) The participant and experimenter attaching electrodes to the "learner" before testing begins.

accomplice of the experimenter, and the drawing was rigged so that he was always the learner.

We describe Milgram's study in more detail in Chapter 8. For now, suffice it to say that the "teacher" was instructed to administer shocks—from 15 to 450 volts—to the "learner" each time he made an error. Labels under the shock switches ranged from "slight shock" through "danger: severe shock" to "XXX." The experimenter explained that the first time the learner made an error, the teacher was to administer a shock of 15 volts; the next time the learner made an error, 30 volts; and so on, in ascending 15-volt magnitudes. The teacher was given a 45-volt shock so that he would have an idea of how painful the shocks would be. What he didn't know was that the learner, who was in another room, was not actually being shocked.

Despite groans, pleas, screams, and eventually silence from the learner as the intensity of the shocks increased, 80 percent of the participants continued past the 150-volt level—at which point the learner had mentioned that he had a heart condition and had screamed, "Let me out of here!" Most participants became concerned as the shock levels increased and turned to the experimenter to ask what should be done. But the experimenter insisted they go on. The first time the teachers expressed reservations, they were told, "Please continue." If the teacher balked, the experimenter said, "The experiment requires that you continue." If the teacher continued to be recalcitrant, the experimenter said, "It's absolutely essential that you continue." If necessary, the experimenter escalated to, "You have no other choice. You must go on." If the participant asked if the learner was liable to suffer permanent physical injury, the experimenter said, "Although the shocks may be painful, there is no permanent tissue damage, so please go on."

In the end, 62.5 percent of the participants went all the way to the 450-volt level, delivering everything the shock generator could produce. The *average* amount of shock given was 360 volts, *after* the point at which the learner let out an agonized scream and became hysterical. Milgram and other experts did not expect so many participants to continue to administer shocks as long as they did (a panel of 39 psychiatrists predicted that only 20 percent of the participants would continue past the 150-volt level and that only 1 percent would continue past the 330-volt level).

At first, some researchers expressed suspicion as to whether Milgram's participants really believed that they were shocking the learner. To prevent the scientific community from having to rely on his own assertions about whether his participants took the situation seriously, Milgram invited social scientists to observe his experiments from behind a one-way mirror. The observers could scarcely believe what they were seeing. One of them reported:

> I observed a mature and initially poised businessman enter the laboratory smiling and confident. Within twenty minutes he was reduced to a twitching, stuttering wreck, who was rapidly approaching a point of nervous collapse. He constantly pulled on his earlobe and twisted his hands. At one point he pushed his fist into his forehead and muttered: "Oh God, let's stop it." And yet he continued to respond to every word of the experimenter and obeyed to the end. (Milgram, 1963, p. 377)

What made the participants in Milgram's study engage in behavior that they had every reason to believe might seriously harm another person? Milgram's participants were not monsters. Instead, the situation was extraordinarily effective in getting them to do something that most people would predict only heartless fiends would do. For example, the experiment was presented as a scientific investigation—an unfamiliar situation for most participants. In all probability, the participants had never been in a psychology experiment before, they had never been in a situation in which they

"Evil is obvious only in retrospect."

—Gloria Steinem

could be doing serious physical damage to another human being, and they had no means by which they could readily step out of the vaguely defined role the experimenter had placed them in. The experimenter explicitly took responsibility for what happened (a frequent pledge by Adolf Hitler during the years he marched his nation over a precipice). Moreover, participants could not have guessed at the outset what the experiment involved, so they weren't prepared to have to resist anyone's demands. And as Milgram stressed, the step-by-step nature of the procedure was undoubtedly crucial. If the participant didn't quit at 225 volts, then why quit at 255? If not at 420, then why at 435?

Seminarians as Samaritans

A classic experiment by John Darley and Daniel Batson (1973) shows the importance of the situation in even simpler fashion. These investigators asked students at the Princeton Theological Seminary about the basis of their religious orientation to determine whether particular students were primarily concerned with religion as a means toward personal salvation or were more concerned with religion for its other moral and spiritual values. After determining the basis of their religious concerns, the psychologists asked each young seminarian to go to another building to deliver a short sermon. The seminarians were told what route to follow to get there most easily. Some were told that they had plenty of time to get to the building where they were to deliver the sermon, and some were told that they were already late and should hurry. On the way to deliver their sermon—on the topic of the Good Samaritan, by the way—each of the seminarians passed a man who was sitting in a doorway and had his head down while he was coughing and groaning. It turned out that the nature of religious orientation was of no use in predicting whether or not the seminarians would help. But as can be seen in **Figure 1.1**, whether seminarians were in a hurry or not was a very powerful predictor. The seminarians, it turned out, were pretty good Samaritans as a group—but only so long as they weren't in a rush.

Channel Factors

channel factors Certain situational circumstances that appear unimportant on the surface but that can have great consequences for behavior, either facilitating or blocking it or guiding behavior in a particular direction.

Kurt Lewin (1952) introduced the concept of **channel factors** to help explain why certain circumstances that appear unimportant on the surface can have great consequences for behavior, either facilitating or blocking it. The term is also meant to reflect the fact that such circumstances can sometimes guide behavior in a very particular direction by means of making it easier to follow one path rather than another. Consider a study by Howard Leventhal and others on how to motivate people to take advantage of health facilities' offerings of preventive care (Leventhal, Singer, & Jones, 1965). They attempted to persuade Yale seniors to get tetanus inoculations. To convince them that this was in their best interest, they had them read scary materials about the number of ways one could get tetanus (in addition to the proverbial rusty nail you undoubtedly know about). To make sure they had the students' attention, they showed them photos of people in the last stages of lockjaw. But not to worry—they could avoid this fate simply by going to the student health center at any time and getting a free inoculation. Interviews showed that most participants formed the intention to get an inoculation. But only 3 percent did so. Other participants were given a map of the Yale campus with a circle around the health center and were asked to review their weekly schedule and decide on a convenient time to visit the center and the route they would take to get there. Bear in mind that these were seniors who knew perfectly well where the health center was. So we might assume that this condescending treatment

FIGURE 1.1 Scientific Method: The Power of the Situation and Helping

Hypothesis: A major cause of offering help to another person is whether one is in a hurry or not.

Research Method:

1 Participants were chosen who were expected to be helpful, (seminary students). They were primed to think about helping by being asked to prepare a talk on the Good Samaritan.

2 Some participants were told they had to rush, while others were told they had plenty of time to prepare.

3 Participants then passed by a "victim" in obvious need of help.

Results:

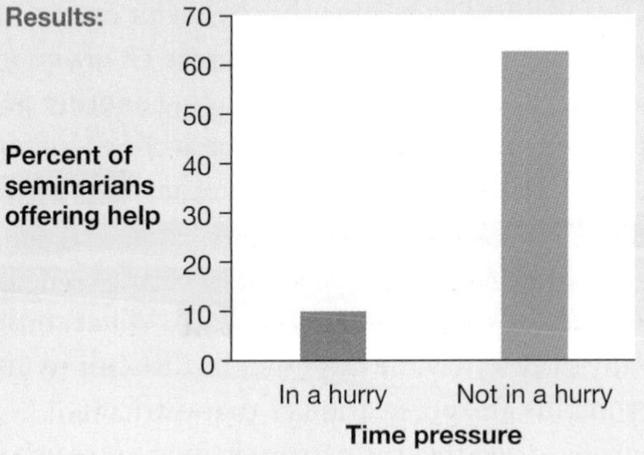

Percent of seminarians offering help (y-axis: 0 to 70)

In a hurry: ~10
Not in a hurry: ~63

Time pressure (x-axis)

Conclusion: The mundane fact of being in a hurry is such a powerful situational factor that it overrides people's good intentions.

Source: Darley & Batson (1973).

would produce little more than annoyance. In fact, it increased the percentage of students getting an inoculation ninefold, to 28 percent.

The channel factor in this case was the requirement to shape a vague intention into a concrete plan. A similar channel factor accounts for the use of public health services more generally. Attitudes about health, personality tests, demographic variables such as age, gender, and socioeconomic status, and other individual differences don't do a very good job predicting who will use these services. The most powerful determinant of usage yet discovered is the distance to the closest facility (Van Dort & Moos, 1976).

The Fundamental Attribution Error

People are thus governed by situational factors—such as whether they are being pressured by someone or whether or not they are late—more than they tend to assume. You are likely to be surprised by many of the findings reported in this book because most people underestimate the power of external forces that operate on the individual and tend to assume, often mistakenly, that the causes of behavior can be found mostly within the person.

Psychologists call internal factors **dispositions**—that is, beliefs, values, personality traits, or abilities, real or imagined. People tend to think of dispositions as the underlying causes of behavior. Seeing a prison guard humiliating a prisoner, we may assume that the guard is a cruel person. Seeing a stranger in the street behave in an angry way,

dispositions Internal factors, such as beliefs, values, personality traits, or abilities, that guide a person's behavior.

we may assume that the person is aggressive or ill-tempered. Seeing an acquaintance being helpful, we may assume that the person is kinder than we had realized. Such judgments are valid far less often than we think. Seeing an acquaintance give a dollar to a beggar may prompt us to assume that the person is generous; but subsequent observations of the person in different situations may negate that assumption.

The failure to recognize the importance of situational influences on behavior, together with the tendency to overemphasize the importance of dispositions, or traits, was labeled the **fundamental attribution error** by Lee Ross (1977). Many of the findings in social psychology can be viewed as a warning to look for situational factors that might be affecting someone's behavior before assuming that the person has dispositions that match the behavior. As you read this book, you will become more attuned to situational factors and less inclined to assume that behavior can be fully explained by characteristics inherent in the individual. To paraphrase an oft-quoted American Indian adage, we should exercise extreme caution in judging another person until we have walked a mile in that person's moccasins—and hence attained a clear understanding of the situational forces compelling one action or another. The ultimate lesson of social psychology, we believe, is thus a compassionate one. It encourages us to look at another person's situation—to try to understand the complex field of forces acting on the individual—to fully understand the person's behavior. What to think and how to act effectively and morally in everyday life can often be difficult to discern, but the study of social psychology instills an appreciation of that difficulty.

We doubt that we've convinced you that the person sitting next to you in class would have delivered a lot of shock in the Milgram experiment; we're confident we haven't convinced you that *you* would have. We hope, however, that by the time you complete this course, you will regard it as a serious possibility that you might have acted as Milgram's participants did, recognizing that situations can be extraordinarily powerful, and character can sometimes be of little use in predicting what people will do.

 We have seen that situations are often more powerful in their influence on behavior than we realize. Whether people are kind to others or not, whether they take action in their own best interest or not, can be dependent on subtle aspects of situations. Such situational factors are often overlooked when we try to understand our own behavior or that of others, and behavior is often mistakenly attributed to presumed traits, or dispositions (the fundamental attribution error). The cognitive processes that we use to understand situations and behavior are the topic of the next section.

THE ROLE OF CONSTRUAL

In his study of obedience, Milgram manipulated his participants' understanding of the situation they found themselves in by lulling them with soothing interpretations of events that were designed to throw them off the scent of anything that could be regarded as sinister. A "study participant" who had "chosen" to be in the "experiment" was "learning" a list of words with "feedback" that was given by the real participant in the form of electric shock.

A "participant" is someone who is acting freely; "learning" is a normal activity that often depends on "feedback"—a usually innocuous form of information. All this takes place in an "experiment"—a benign activity carried out by trustworthy scientists. Our **construal** of situations and behavior refers to our interpretation of them

fundamental attribution error The failure to recognize the importance of situational influences on behavior, together with the tendency to overemphasize the importance of dispositions or traits on behavior.

construal Interpretation and inference about the stimuli or situations we confront.

and to the inferences—often unconscious—that we make about them. Whether we regard people as free agents or victims, as freedom fighters or terrorists, will affect our perceptions of their actions. And our perceptions drive our behavior toward them.

Interpreting Reality

Look at **Figure 1.2**. Do you see a white triangle? Most people do. But in fact there is no white triangle. We construct a triangle in our mind out of the *gaps* in the picture. The gaps are located just where they would be if a triangle were laid over the outlined triangle and a portion of each of the three circles. That makes a good, clear image, but it's entirely a creation of our perceptual apparatus and our background assumptions about the visual world. These assumptions are automatic and unconscious, and they can be almost impossible to override. Now that you know the triangle is in your mind's eye and not on the page, do you still see it? Now look at **Figure 1.3**, a painting by surrealist artist Salvador Dalí. Dalí was a master at using the mind's tendency to construct meaningful figures from the gaps in an image. He created a number of well-known double images—paintings that could be perceived in two different ways, as in this painting.

Our perceptions normally bear a resemblance to what the world is really like, but perception requires substantial interpretation on our part and is subject to significant error under certain conditions. German psychologists in the early part of the twentieth century convincingly argued for this view in the case of visual perception. The theoretical orientation of those psychologists centered on the concept of gestalt. The word *gestalt* is German for "form" or "figure." The basic idea of **Gestalt psychology**

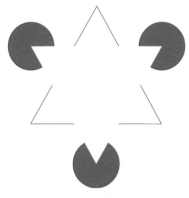

FIGURE 1.2 Gestalt Principles and Perception When viewing the above figure, known as the Kanizsa triangle, we fill in the empty spaces in our mind and perceive a triangle.

Gestalt psychology Based on the German word, *Gestalt*, meaning "form" or "figure," this approach stresses the fact that objects are perceived not by means of some automatic registering device but by active, usually unconscious, interpretation of what the object represents as a whole.

FIGURE 1.3 Gestalt Principles in Art In his *Slave Market with Disappearing Bust of Voltaire*, Salvador Dalí confronts the viewer with the bust of the French philosopher Voltaire (at center of painting). But on closer inspection, the bust is largely the product of the gap in the wall behind the two merchants. Their faces form Voltaire's eyes, and their collars form his nose and cheeks. The same gestalt principles are also at work in a less celebrated portion of the painting. Notice the sloping hill off to the right and how it forms the pear in the fruit dish on the table where the woman (Dalí's wife Gala) is sitting.

is that objects are perceived not by means of some passive and automatic registering device, but by active, usually unconscious interpretation of what the object represents (as when we see a triangle from the gaps in a picture, or a bust of Voltaire from the gaps between the two merchants in Dalí's painting). What we see is not necessarily what is actually there but what is plausible—what makes a good, predictable "figure" in light of stored representations we have of the world and what makes sense in light of the context in which we encounter something.

What's true for perception is even more true for judgments about the social world. Judgments and beliefs are constructed from perceptions and thoughts, and they are not simple readouts of reality. A study conducted by Liberman, Samuels, and Ross (2002) showed in a concrete way how construal could operate to define a situation and dictate behavior. The investigators asked Stanford University dormitory resident assistants to identify students in their dorms who they thought were particularly cooperative or competitive. Both types of students were then recruited to participate in a psychology experiment in which they would play a game that offered them the opportunity to pursue either a competitive or a cooperative strategy.

The game they played is called the **prisoner's dilemma** (discussed in greater detail in Chapter 13). The game gets its name from the dilemma that would confront two criminals who were involved together in a crime, were apprehended, and were being held and questioned separately. Each prisoner could behave in one of two ways: confess the crime, hoping to get lenient treatment by the prosecutor, or deny the crime, hoping that the prosecutor would not bring charges or would fail to persuade a jury of his guilt. But of course the outcome that would result from the prisoner's choice would be dependent on the other prisoner's behavior. If both denied the crime—a "cooperative strategy"—both would stand a good chance of going free. If one denied the crime and the other admitted it—a "defecting strategy"—the prisoner who admitted the crime would get treated leniently, and the denying prisoner would get the book thrown at him. If both admitted the crime, then both would go to prison.

It is possible to play the game with monetary payoffs rather than prison time. The particular payoffs that Liberman and his colleagues used are shown in the matrix in **Figure 1.4**. If both cooperate (deny the crime) on a given trial, they both make some money; if both defect (admit the crime), neither gets anything. If one defects and the other doesn't, the defector wins big and the cooperator loses a small amount. As we discuss in greater detail in Chapter 13, each player does better by defecting, no matter what the other player does (win 80 cents rather than 40 cents if the other player cooperates, get nothing rather than lose 20 cents if the other player defects). And yet if each player follows the logic of defecting and acts accordingly, both players are worse off (they each get nothing) than if they had both cooperated (they each would have gotten 40 cents).

The researchers employed two experimental conditions that differed from each other in a way that seems trivial on the surface: for half the participants the game was described as "the Wall Street game" and for the other half as "the community game." **Figure 1.5** shows how construal affected the results: the majority of students who played the Wall Street game played it in a competitive fashion; the majority of students who played the community game played it in a cooperative fashion. It seems reasonable to infer that the terminology that was used prompted different construals: the name Wall Street conjures up images of competitors struggling against one another for monetary advantage. The word *community* stirs up thoughts of sharing and cooperation. Whether the participants had been identified as highly competitive or highly cooperative was of no use in predicting their behavior. The

prisoner's dilemma A situation involving payoffs to two people in which trust and cooperation lead to higher joint payoffs than mistrust and defection. The game gets its name from the dilemma that would confront two criminals who were involved in a crime together and are being held and questioned separately. Each must decide whether to "cooperate" and stick with a prearranged alibi or "defect" and confess to the crime in the hope of lenient treatment.

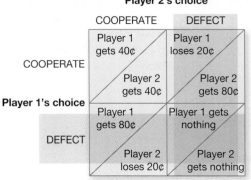

FIGURE 1.4 The Payoff Matrix for the Prisoner's Dilemma Payoffs differ based on whether both players cooperate, both players defect, or one cooperates and the other defects.

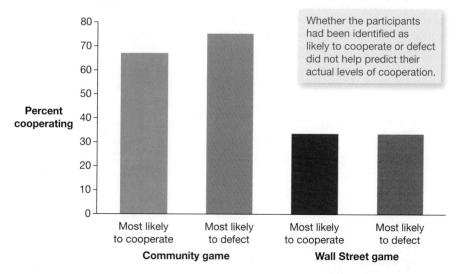

Whether the participants had been identified as likely to cooperate or defect did not help predict their actual levels of cooperation.

FIGURE 1.5 Construal and the Prisoner's Dilemma Percentage of Stanford University students who cooperated playing "the Wall Street game" versus "the community game," their resident adviser having previously picked them as being either most likely to cooperate or most likely to defect (compete). (Source: Liberman, Samuels, & Roth, 2002.)

situation exerted its influence through its effect on the way participants interpreted the meaning of the activity they were performing. And once again, the presumed dispositions of people were of no use in predicting behavior.

Schemas

How do we know how to behave in different kinds of situations? For example, if we are riding on an uncrowded train and someone asks us to give up our seat so he or she can sit, what prompts us to respond in a particular way? For that matter, how do we know how to behave in even the most ordinary situations, such as attending a college seminar? Although it usually seems as if we understand social situations immediately and directly, we actually depend on elaborate stores of systematized knowledge to understand even the simplest and most "obvious" situation. These knowledge stores are called **schemas**—generalized knowledge about the physical and social world, such as what kind of behavior to expect when dealing with a minister, a sales clerk, a professor, or a panhandler and how to behave in a seminar, at a funeral, at a McDonald's or a four-star restaurant, or when riding on a crowded or empty subway. There is even a schema—alleged to be universal—for falling in love.

Schemas capture the regularities of life and lead us to have certain expectations we can rely on so that we don't have to invent the world anew all the time. We have a schema for "a party," for example. We expect people to act cheerful, excited, and maybe a little silly, and if it's a party attended by young people, there may be loud music, dancing, and a certain amount of rowdiness. (We miss those parties ourselves; our most frequently activated party schema now centers on standing around with a drink wondering whether we're boring the person we're talking to.)

An early experiment by Solomon Asch (1940), another of the great German founders of social psychology who immigrated to the United States in the 1930s, shows that schemas can sometimes operate very subtly to influence judgments. Asch asked two groups of undergraduates to rank various professions in terms of prestige. One of the professions was "politician." Before they gave their own ratings, the participants

schemas Generalized knowledge about the physical and social world and how to behave in particular situations and with different kinds of people.

Schemas   Our schemas—generalized knowledge about the physical and social world—help us to know what is expected of us and how to behave in particular situations. (A) Our schema of a pizza shop leads us to order at a counter, wait for the pizza to be ready, and then either take it to a bare table or take it home to eat. (B) But our schema of a high-end restaurant leads us to be seated at a table with silverware, glasses, and a tablecloth, to choose what we want from a menu, to order at the table, and to be served food and wine by a waiter.

in one group were told that a sample of fellow students had previously ranked politicians near the top in prestige, whereas the participants in the other group were told that their fellow students had ranked politicians near the bottom. This manipulation affected the participants' judgments substantially, but not because it changed their minds about politicians or because they were trying to conform. Asch was able to show that participants in the first group took the term *politician* to refer to statesmen of the caliber of Thomas Jefferson and Franklin D. Roosevelt. Participants in the second group were rating something closer to corrupt political hacks. It wasn't that the participants were blindly going along with the ratings of their peers, but rather that their peers' ratings served to define just what it was that was being judged via the different schemas that their ratings suggested. Many of the persuasion attempts we are exposed to in the media have the goal not so much of "changing the judgment of the object" but rather of "changing the object of judgment." Pro-abortion advocates try to call up schemas related to *freedom*, and anti-abortion activists try to activate schemas related to *murder*. Affirmative-action advocates encourage schemas related to *diversity*, and those opposed to affirmative action try to activate schemas related to *fairness*.

Stereotypes

stereotypes Schemas that we have for people of various kinds that can be applied to judgments about people and decisions about how to interact with them.

Much work in social psychology has been dedicated to the study of **stereotypes**—schemas that we have for people of various kinds. Research on stereotyping examines the content of these person schemas and how they are applied and sometimes misapplied so as to facilitate, and sometimes derail, the course of interaction. We tend to judge individuals based on particular person schemas we have—stereotypes about a person's nationality, gender, religion, occupation, neighborhood, or sorority. Such summaries may be necessary to function efficiently and effectively. But they can be wrong, they can be applied in the wrong way and to the wrong people, and they can be given too much weight in relation to more specific information we have about a particular

Stereotypes and Construal How observers interpret reality affects their reaction to what is going on. These Iraqi boys look at wall paintings showing the U.S. Statue of Liberty administering shock to an Iraqi prisoner. Their stereotypes about Americans as occupiers rather than rescuers are most likely reinforced through such paintings and affect how they regard Americans.

person (or would have if we didn't assume that the stereotype is all we need to know). The frequently pernicious role of stereotypes is the subject of an entire chapter of this book (Chapter 12).

 We have seen that although it often seems as though our understanding of situations is the result of a direct, unmediated registration of meaning, our comprehension of even the simplest physical stimulus is the result of construal processes that make use of well-developed knowledge structures. Such structures are called schemas when they summarize commonly encountered situations, and they are called stereotypes when they describe different types of people. Next we consider just how accessible to consciousness our construal processes usually are.

AUTOMATIC VERSUS CONTROLLED PROCESSING

How would you react if you saw a stranger at an airport carrying a backpack, looking agitated, and sweating profusely? In the post-9/11 world, you might fear that such a person might be carrying a bomb and that you could become a victim of a terrorist attack. The mind processes information in two different ways when you encounter a social situation: one is automatic and unconscious, often based on emotional factors, and the other is conscious and systematic and more likely to be controlled by careful thought. Often, emotional reactions to people occur before conscious thought takes over. Thus, your fearful reaction to the person with the backpack might automatically kick in without any special thought on your part. But when you start thinking systematically, you might realize that he might have just come in from the summer heat,

Automatic Processing People often react quickly to frightening situations so that they can take immediate actions to save themselves from danger if necessary. The boy is handling the snake under the supervision of his teacher, but an automatic reaction is still visible. If the boy were to come across a snake in the grass, he would likely have a stronger automatic fear reaction.

that he might be agitated because he is late for his plane, and that there is no reason to suspect that he might be carrying a bomb or threatening your safety in any other way.

Research by Patricia Devine and her colleagues has shown how automatic and controlled processing can result in incompatible attitudes in the same person toward members of outgroups (Devine, 1989a, 1989b; Devine, Monteith, Zuwerink, & Elliot, 1991; Devine, Plant, Amodio, Harmon-Jones, & Vance, 2002). People with low expressed prejudice toward an outgroup may nevertheless reveal feelings toward people in the outgroup that are almost as prejudiced as those of people who confess to explicit disliking of the group. For example, when white participants read words reminiscent of African-Americans and then were asked to make judgments about whether a particular individual whom they read about was hostile or not, they were more likely to report that the individual was hostile than if they hadn't read such words. And this was true whether they were willing to express antiblack attitudes in a questionnaire or not. The judgments of the "unprejudiced people" could thus be shown to be prejudiced when studied by a technique that examines unconscious processing of information. Furthermore, Anthony Greenwald and his colleagues showed that the great majority of white people take longer to classify black faces with pleasant stimuli than to classify white faces with pleasant stimuli (Greenwald, McGhee, & Schwartz, 1998). This was true even for participants who showed no overt prejudice when asked about their attitudes. In general, automatic processes give rise to *implicit* attitudes and beliefs that cannot be readily controlled by the conscious mind; and controlled, conscious processing results in *explicit* attitudes and beliefs of which we are aware—though these may become implicit or unconscious over time.

Types of Unconscious Processing

The unconscious mind plays an important role in producing beliefs and behaviors even when there is no reason to hide what is going on in our mind. There are two major types of unconscious processing that have been identified. The great psychologist William James identified one type that has given rise to the study of what is called "skill acquisition." If you have ever driven a car and realized that you haven't a clue as to what you have been doing—even what you have seen—for the last few minutes, you know about this type of automatic mental processing. As skills are learned and then overlearned, they can be carried out without our awareness. They also can be performed without distracting us from other, conscious thoughts and processing.

The other type of automatic mental processing (associated with Sigmund Freud but with roots going well back into the nineteenth century) concerns the production of beliefs and behaviors without our awareness of the cognitive processes that have generated them. Sometimes in solving problems we are well aware of the relevant factors we are dealing with and the procedures we are using to work with them. This is often true when we solve mathematical problems—for example, "Take half the base, multiply it by the height and . . . ." But these sorts of cognitive processes—where most of what is going on is visible to our consciousness—are rarer than you might think. For many cognitive processes, it seems, we cannot accurately describe what is going on in our head (Nisbett & Wilson, 1977; Wegner & Bargh, 1998; Wilson, 2002).

This applies to our guesses about how we make judgments about other people, to our understanding of the causes of physical and social events, and even to how we come to choose one applicant versus another for a job (or one romantic partner over another). Often we cannot even consciously identify some of the crucially important factors that have affected our beliefs and behavior. We know this in part from experiments that present visual stimuli so rapidly that people cannot even report having seen them, and yet their beliefs and behavior are affected by them.

Functions of Unconscious Processing

Why is our mind designed so that so much takes place outside of awareness? It is because conscious processes are generally slow and can run only serially—one step or one problem at a time. Automatic processes are typically much faster and can operate in parallel. When we recognize a face as belonging to a fourth-grade classmate, we have done so by processing numerous features (forehead, eyes, chin, coloring, and so on) at the same time. Doing all of this one step at a time would leave us hopelessly mired in computation. And it's quite handy to be able to drive on autopilot while enjoying the scenery or carrying on a conversation. (Just make sure that the conversation is with someone physically in the car with you. Talking on a cell phone seems to be a completely different type of activity that substantially increases your risk of having an accident.)

Because much of what goes on in our head is not available to us consciously, we are unable to figure out exactly what factors influence us, and to what degree, and we experience the world as being manifest to us as it is, without any real cognitive work on our part. This is one reason why scientific research on human behavior is so essential. We can't simply ask people what caused them to behave as they did, because often they do not know. Instead, social psychologists must craft experiments to isolate the true causes of people's behavior.

Some examples should make these points clearer. When a person encounters novel stimuli while the arm is flexed (bent back toward the shoulder), attitudes toward the stimuli tend to be favorable (Cacioppo, Priester, & Berntson, 1993). But when a person encounters novel stimuli while the arm is extended away from the body, the person tends to form more negative attitudes. This is because the muscular feedback from the arm positions gives "information" about whether the object is desirable or undesirable (based on a lifetime's experience embracing positive stimuli and pushing away negative stimuli). But people are completely unaware that they have incorporated this bodily information into their judgments (and in many experiments become annoyed when asked if such "irrelevant" information played any role in their judgments!).

Or consider social categories. Easily discriminable personal features, such as gender, race, and age, tend to trigger stereotypes that play a role in forming judgments about people, even when the individual is unaware that these social categories have influenced the judgment in question (Blair, Judd, & Fallman, 2004; Brewer, 1988; Macrae, Stangor, & Milne, 1994). And even behavior can be unconsciously influenced by social categories. Bargh, Chen, and Burrows (1996) have found that just mentioning words that call to mind the elderly ("cane," "Florida") causes college students to walk down a hall more slowly. And others have found that activating the concept of "professor" actually makes students do better on a trivia test (Dijksterhuis & van Knippenberg, 1998)!

The concepts of automatic and unconscious processing of information help us to understand why we are often blind to the role of many important situational factors and why the processes underlying construal may be hidden from us. We refer to these concepts throughout the book and frequently distinguish those social behaviors that

William James   One of the founding fathers of psychology, James wrote about attention, memory, and consciousness, asking how unconscious processing affects behavior.

appear to be the result of effortful, deliberate, and conscious processing from those that appear to be the result of effortless, automatic, and unconscious processing.

We have seen that much behavior and many kinds of construal processes are carried out without awareness, sometimes without awareness of even the stimuli to which we are responding. We overestimate the degree to which our mental processes are accessible to consciousness. In the next two sections, we will examine the distal influences on behavior—our evolutionary history and the cultural circumstances in which we find ourselves.

EVOLUTION AND HUMAN BEHAVIOR: HOW WE ARE THE SAME

Why do human beings generally live in family groups, assign roles to people on the basis of age, adorn their bodies, classify flora and fauna, and have rites of passage and myths? Evolution may explain such behaviors (Conway & Schaller, 2002).

Evolutionary theory has been around for about 150 years, ever since Charles Darwin's famous voyage to the Galápagos Islands and the discoveries he made about the modifications in animal and plant characteristics that had occurred over time. The theory has proved invaluable in understanding why (and how) organisms of all kinds have the properties they do. The key idea is that a process of **natural selection** operates on animals and plants so that traits that enhance the probability of survival and reproduction are passed on to subsequent generations. Organisms that will die before they reproduce either have bad luck or possess characteristics that are less than optimal in the environments in which they find themselves. And organisms that don't reproduce don't pass on their characteristics (through their genes) to a new generation. Those that do reproduce give their genes a chance to live on in their offspring, with the possibility that their characteristics will be represented in at least one more generation. Disadvantageous characteristics are selected against; characteristics better adapted to the environment are selected for.

Darwin himself assumed that natural selection is important for behavioral inclinations just as it is for physical characteristics such as size, coloring, or susceptibility to parasites. And the number and importance of things that are universally true about humans is certainly consistent with the idea that much of what we share is the result of natural selection and is encoded in our genes. These ideas were generally accepted by scientists until the 1920s. But the approach fell into disrepute because of misplaced claims that Darwin's ideas justified the struggle of some groups of people to achieve supremacy over others, with might justifying right. The movement approvingly espoused "the survival of the fittest"—which was incorrectly taken to mean the survival of one human group over another. This movement, called social Darwinism, was a distorted application of Darwin's theory, but it drew adherents nevertheless. A rogue version of Darwin's theory was also used by some to justify fascism and the ruthless domination of the weak by the strong. Some in the scientific community overreacted to these misappropriations by rejecting the notion that evolution has played a role in shaping human behavior. Not wishing to fight about it, other scientists simply dropped the subject. But toward the end of the twentieth

natural selection An evolutionary process that molds animals and plants such that traits that enhance the probability of survival and reproduction are passed on to subsequent generations.

century, developments in evolutionary theory and comparative biology, together with anthropological findings and studies by psychologists, convinced many that the theory of evolution can be quite helpful in explaining why people behave as they do.

Human Universals

One theme that emerges from evolutionary theory is that many human behaviors and institutions are universal, or very nearly so. This would follow clearly from evolutionary reasoning (Schaller, Simpson, & Kenrick, 2006). In the process of human evolution, we have acquired basic behavioral propensities—much as we have acquired physical features like bipedalism—which help us adapt to the physical and social environment. **Table 1.1** contains a list of these reputed universals. Two things should be

> "There is grandeur in this view of life . . . whilst this planet has gone cycling on according to the fixed law of gravity, from so simple a beginning endless forms most beautiful and most wonderful have been, and are being, evolved."
>
> —Charles Darwin

TABLE 1.1 Universal Behaviors, Reactions, and Institutions

This is a sampling of some of the behaviors and characteristics that anthropologists believe hold for all human cultures, grouped into categories to show general areas of commonality.

Sex, Gender, and the Family

Copulation normally conducted privately	Rape	Rape proscribed
Live in family (or household)	Sexual jealousy	Sexual regulation
Sexual modesty	Marriage	Husband usually older than wife
Males dominate public realm	Division of labor by gender	Males more physically aggressive
Females do more child care	Mother-son incest unthinkable	Incest prevention and avoidance
Preference for own kin	Sex differences in spatial cognition	

Social Differentiation

Age statuses	Classification of kin	
Ingroup distinguished from outgroup	Division of labor by age	Leaders

Social Customs

Baby talk	Pretend play	Group living
Dance	Rites of passage	Law (rights and obligations)
Dominance/submission	Tabooed foods	Feasting
Practice to improve skills	Body adornment	Property
Hygienic care	Death rites	Rituals
Magic to sustain and improve life	Etiquette	Tabooed utterances
Magic to win love	Gossip	Toys
Nonbody decorative art	Food sharing	

Emotion

Childhood fear of strangers	Wariness around snakes	Rhythm
Facial expressions of fear, anger, disgust, happiness, sadness, and surprise	Envy	Melody

Cognition

Aesthetics	Anthropomorphism of animals	Myths
Belief in supernatural, religion	Medicine	Taxonomy
Classification of flora and fauna	Language	Narrative

Source: Compiled by Donald Brown (1991), appearing in Pinker (2002).

Universal Facial Expressions Chimpanzees and humans express dominance and submission, anger and fear, through similar facial expressions. (A) The screaming chimp and (B) basketball coach Bobby Knight yelling during a game both have their mouths open and show their teeth in an aggressive display of dominance.

noted about the practices and institutions cited in Table 1.1, aside from their alleged universality. One is that we share some of these practices with other animals, especially the higher primates. These include facial expressions (almost all of which we share with chimpanzees and some other animals), dominance and submission, food sharing, group living (true of all primates except orangutans), greater aggressiveness on the part of males (true of almost all mammals), preference for own kin (true of almost all animals), and wariness around snakes (true of all the large primates, including humans). The other, even more striking aspect of Table 1.1 is that the number of universals we share with other animals is (so far as we know) quite small. The bulk of Table 1.1 represents a large number of behaviors and institutions that would appear to be effective adaptations for highly intelligent, group-living, upright-walking, language-using animals that are capable of living in almost any kind of ecology. These latter universals are compatible with an evolutionary interpretation (we are a particular kind of creature qualitatively different from any other, with many adaptations so effective that they have become wired into our biology). But some theorists believe that the commonalities can be accounted for as simply the result of our species' superior intelligence. For example, every human group figures out for itself that incest is a bad idea and that classification of flora is useful.

Group Living, Language, and Theory of Mind

Group living contributed to survival in ages past, as groups provided protection from predators, greater success in finding foraging areas, access to mates, and other adaptive functions. The ability to produce and understand language has facilitated the ability to live in groups and to convey not only emotions and intentions to others, but also beliefs and attitudes and complex thoughts. The claim is made that infants are born prewired to acquire language, perhaps because of its importance to humans living together in groups (Pinker, 1994). Language is learned by all normal children at developmental stages that are almost identical from one culture to another. All infants are born with the full range of possible sounds (phonemes) that exist in the totality of languages spoken anywhere on earth, and they babble all these sounds in the crib. Language acquisition consists of dropping all the "wrong" phonemes that are not used by the child's particular language. Thus, children can learn to speak any language, depending on where they grow up; they can learn to speak their native language perfectly well even if they grow up with deaf parents who never speak at all; and twins can sometimes develop their own unique language in the crib, a language that follows rules of grammar in the same way as formally recognized languages (Pinker, 1994, 2002). So there are general, inherited propensities to develop grammatical language.

Just as evolution has prepared humans to live together in groups and to be able to communicate to promote survival and reproduction, it also may have provided humans with a **theory of mind**—the ability to recognize that other people have beliefs and desires. The implications for group living are profound, as it may prevent misunderstandings that could lead to aggression and even death. Children recognize before the age of 2 that the way to understand other people's behavior is to recognize what their beliefs and desires are (Asch, 1952; Kuhlmeier, Wynn, & Bloom, 2003; Leslie, 2000). This is just the recognition that people do what they do because they want to achieve some goal and because they believe that the behavior in question will produce the desired result. By the age of 2, children can recognize "pretend" games, as when the mother holds a banana to her ear and pretends it's a telephone. By the age of 3 or 4, children's theory of mind is sophisticated enough that they can recognize when other people's beliefs are false (Wellman, 1990). It seems highly unlikely to some psychologists that theory of mind has been learned. Instead, like theories about the physical world, it seems plausible that evolution has provided us with information that is too universally essential to leave to chance or laborious trial-and-error learning. Given the importance of accurately understanding other people's beliefs and intentions, it would not be surprising that a theory of mind comes prewired.

> **theory of mind** The understanding that other people have beliefs and desires.

Some of the most powerful evidence for a theory of mind comes from the study of people who, through a genetic defect or physical or chemical trauma before or after birth, seem not to have one or to have only a weak version of one. Such a claim has been made about people with *autism*. Individuals with autism have deeply disordered abilities for interacting and communicating with others. They do not seem able to comprehend the beliefs or desires of others, including that the beliefs of others can be false (Perner, Frith, Leslie, & Leekam, 1989). Autistic children can have normal or even superior intellectual functioning but have less comprehension of people's beliefs and desires than children with Down syndrome, whose general intellectual functioning is far below normal.

Theory of Mind Because autistic children lack a theory of mind, they do not recognize or understand the beliefs and desires of others. Because of this deficit, they have difficulty communicating and interacting with other people, as shown by the boy who is ignoring the man working with him.

The standard method of showing that most children can recognize false beliefs is to show them a candy box and ask them what is in it. Naturally, the children say that candy is in it. The children are then shown that pencils or some other objects are in the box. In other words, the children are shown that their former belief was false. Then the box is sealed up, and the children are told that a friend of theirs is about to come in and will be asked what is in the box. Children are asked to predict what the friend will say. In one study, almost all normal children with a mental age of 4 correctly said that the friend would guess that candy was in the box, showing that they were aware that the friend would be misled by the box. In contrast, only a small minority of children with autism (including those with a much higher mental age) correctly guessed that the friend would have a false belief. Such children may be able to solve problems about the physical world at a very high level, but understanding the beliefs and desires of other people is extremely difficult for them.

The evidence that a theory of mind is universal among nonimpaired children comes from studies of children in socities very different from those in the industrialized world. Avis and Harris (1991), for example, studied theory of mind in BaAka children. The BaAka are a pygmy people who live in the rain forests of Cameroon. They are hunter-gatherers, and they are illiterate. Using a task conceptually the same as that used with Western children (Perner, Leekam, & Wimmer, 1987), Avis and Harris found that BaAka children typically learn by the age of 4 or 5 to predict a person's behavior on the basis of the person's beliefs.

Evolution and Gender Roles

Why do men so often choose to marry younger women? Why do women often look for husbands who will be able to support them and their children? The evolutionary approach provides a possible answer to these questions in its theory of **parental investment.** In almost all mammalian species, the two sexes typically have different costs and benefits associated with the nurturing of offspring. This has to do with the fact that the number of offspring a female can have over the course of her lifetime is highly limited. The value of each child to her is therefore relatively high, and it is very much in the interest of her genes to see to it that each infant grows to maturity. For males, however, a nearly unlimited number of offspring is theoretically possible because so little energy is involved in creating them. A male can walk away from copulation and never see his mate or offspring again. Indeed, this is just what the males of many mammalian species do (as well as some individual human beings). Even if the male stays with the female and their offspring, however, his investment in the offspring is less than that of the female. As we discuss in Chapter 10, many apparent differences between males and females are consistent with the implications that follow from this asymmetry. Evolution thus provides one way of looking at many seemingly universal tendencies related to sex, gender, and child rearing.

Avoiding the Naturalistic Fallacy

Evolutionary theory as applied to human behavior is controversial—sometimes for sound reasons and sometimes for reasons that are less so. The claim that there are biologically based differences between men and women in behaviors related to mate choice is particularly objectionable to some people. Such claims are controversial in part because they follow a long and embarrassing history of faulty assertions about biological differences that have been used to legitimize and perpetuate male privilege (Bem, 1993). Even more objectionable, evolutionary theory has been invoked as justification for viewing the different human "races" almost as separate subspecies. But the fact that a theory can be misused is no reason to reject the theory itself in all its aspects.

Claims about biological shaping of human behavior can also be controversial because of a mistaken tendency for people to think that such evolutionary claims imply that biology is destiny—that what we are biologically predisposed to do is what we inevitably *will* do and perhaps even *should* do. Not so. There are many things we are predisposed to do that we readily overcome. The tendency for eyesight to fail with advancing age is genetically determined, but it is easily dealt with by corrective lenses. The tendency for people to lash out when they are frustrated is (less easily) dealt with by teaching children that aggression is not an appropriate response to frustration. The claim that the way things *are* is the way they *should be* is known as the **naturalistic fallacy,** and it has no logical foundation. Civilization can be regarded

parental investment The evolutionary principle that costs and benefits are associated with reproduction and the nurturing of offspring. Because these costs and benefits are different for males and females, one sex will normally value and invest more in each child than will the other sex.

naturalistic fallacy The claim that the way things *are* is the way they *should be.*

as the never-ceasing attempt to modify much of what comes naturally. With some notable and depressing exceptions, it has been highly successful in reducing the extent to which human life, as seventeenth century philosopher Thomas Hobbes wrote, is "poor, nasty, brutish, and short."

Nevertheless, people frequently commit the naturalistic fallacy. Pundits and politicians (and ordinary laypeople) sometimes excuse practices such as male dominance by appealing to evolutionary claims about the basis of gender differences. Indeed, one hears increasing amounts of nonsense from armchair evolutionists about these and other alleged biologically determined aspects of human behavior. That being the case, we must take care to separate the wheat from the chaff. We must be sure that claims about inherited behavior and preferences rest on a solid scientific foundation. Caution about evolutionary claims is called for. What is not called for, however, is a rejection of evolutionary ideas out of hand.

Social Neuroscience

Evolutionary approaches to the study of social behavior alert us to the fact that everything that humans do or think takes place on a biological substrate. In recent years, social psychologists have begun to examine the nature of that substrate— the brain—and have come to some intriguing conclusions about the areas of the brain that function most when we are feeling angry, fearful or amorous (Heatherton, Macrae, & Kelley, 2004; Ochsner & Lieberman, 2001). The research is also showing us the regions of the brain that operate when we are solving various kinds of cognitive and social problems. Scientists are able to find out which brain regions mediate various feelings and behaviors by taking pictures of the brain while the person is experiencing different emotions or solving various problems. Blood flows to the areas of the brain that are active, and this blood flow is detected by functional magnetic resonance imaging (fMRI).

Neuroscience provides a window into the development of social behavior. For example, it turns out that a region of the brain that alerts people to danger is poorly developed until early adulthood. This late development of an important brain region may help explain why adolescents take greater risks (in how they drive, for instance) than people in their mid-20s and beyond. Neuroscience is also revealing important facts about the other end of life. The elderly find it more difficult to learn than do young people because the brain regions that mediate learning, notably the prefrontal cortex, decay particularly rapidly with increasing age (Raz et al., 1997).

Neuroscience not only tells us which areas of the brain function most when certain kinds of activities are taking place, but also informs us about how the brain, the mind, and behavior function as a unit and how social factors influence each at the same time.

 We have seen that evolutionary theory informs our understanding of human behavior just as it does our understanding of the physical characteristics of plants and animals. The many universals of human behavior suggest that many of these behaviors may be prewired—especially language and theory of mind. We have noted that differential parental investment of males and females may help us understand certain differences between men and women. Nonetheless, we have also warned against the naturalistic fallacy, the assumption that the way things *are* is the way they *should* be. As we are about to see, the most important legacy of evolution for human beings is the great flexibility it allows for adaptation to distinctive circumstances.

CULTURE AND HUMAN BEHAVIOR: HOW WE ARE DIFFERENT

Despite the existence of universal human tendencies to have various emotions, customs, and forms of social organization, there is great flexibility among humans in the particular expression of these tendencies. The enormous behavioral flexibility of humans is tied to the fact that—together with rats—we are the most successful of all the mammals in our ability to live in virtually every type of ecology. Our adaptability and the range of environments we have evolved in have resulted in extraordinary differences between human cultures. Depending on the prevailing culture, humans may be more or less likely to cooperate with each other, to divide the roles of men and women, or to try to distinguish themselves as individuals.

Cultural Differences in Self-Definition

Until recently, psychologists regarded cultural differences as being limited primarily to differences in beliefs, preferences, and values. Some cultures regard the world as having been created by a supernatural force, some by impersonal natural forces, and some don't ponder the question much at all. The French like to eat extremely fatty goose liver, the Chinese like to eat chicken feet, and the Americans like to eat cotton candy—tastes that each finds incomprehensible in the others. These differences, while interesting, are not the sort of thing that would make anyone suspect that fundamentally different psychological theories are needed to account for the behavior of people in different societies.

But recent work shows that cultural differences go far deeper than beliefs and values. In fact, they extend all the way to the level of fundamental forms of social existence and self-conceptions and even to the perceptual and cognitive processes used to develop new thoughts and beliefs (Henrich, Heine, & Norenzayan, in press). We discuss many of these differences throughout the book, but one set of interrelated dimensions is particularly central, and we introduce it at some length here. But before you continue, see **Figure 1.6** below.

FIGURE 1.6 You Be the Subject: Self-Definition

Before you begin reading about these dimensions, write down ten things that describe who you are. No, really do this. You'll get much more out of the discussion if you do.

1. I am _____
2. I am _____
3. I am _____
4. I am _____
5. I am _____
6. I am _____
7. I am _____
8. I am _____
9. I am _____
10. I am _____

How plausible do you find the following propositions?

- People have substantial control over their life outcomes, and they much prefer situations in which they have choice and control to those in which they do not.
- People want to achieve personal success. They find that relationships with other people can sometimes make it harder to attain their goals.
- People want to be unique, to be different from other people in significant respects.
- People want to feel good about themselves. Excelling in some ways and being assured of their good qualities by other people are important to personal well-being.
- People like their relations with others to be on a basis of mutuality and equality, but if some people have more power than others, their preference is to be in the superior position.
- People believe that the same rules should apply to everyone—individuals should not be singled out for special treatment because of their personal attributes or connections to important people. Justice is—or should be—blind.

There are hundreds of millions of people who are reasonably well described by those propositions, but they tend to be found in particular parts of the world, namely, Europe and many of the present and former nations of the British Commonwealth, including the United States, Canada, and Australia. Westerners are highly **independent,** or **individualistic** (Fiske, Kitayama, Markus, & Nisbett, 1998; Hofstede, 1980; Hsu, 1953; Markus & Kitayama, 1991; Triandis, 1995). They think of themselves as distinct social entities, tied to each other by bonds of affection and organizational memberships to be sure, but essentially separate from other people and having attributes that exist in the absence of any connection to others. They tend to see their associations with other people, even their own family members, as voluntary and subject to termination once those associations become sufficiently troublesome or unproductive (see **Table 1.2**).

independent (individualistic) cultures Cultures in which people tend to think of themselves as distinct social entities, tied to each other by voluntary bonds of affection and organizational memberships but essentially separate from other people and having attributes that exist in the absence of any connection to others.

TABLE 1.2 Independent versus Interdependent Societies

People in independent (individualistic) cultures have different characteristics than people in interdependent (collectivistic) cultures, as shown by the difference in emphasis on the individual and on the group.

Independent Societies	Interdependent Societies
Conception of the self as distinct from others, with attributes that are constant	Conception of the self as inextricably linked to others, with attributes depending on the situation
Insistence on ability to act on one's own	Preference for collective action
Need for individual distinctiveness	Desire for harmonious relations within group
Preference for egalitarianism and achieved status based on accomplishments	Acceptance of hierarchy and ascribed status based on age, group membership, and other statuses
Conviction that rules governing behavior should apply to everyone	Preference for rules that take context and particular relationships into account

But these characterizations describe other people less well. In fact, they provide a poor description of most of the world's people, particularly the citizens of most East Asian countries, such as the Chinese (Triandis, McCusker, & Hui, 1990), the Japanese (Bond & Cheung, 1983), the Koreans (Rhee, Uleman, Lee, & Roman, 1995), people from other Asian countries such as India (Dhawan, Roseman, Naidu, Thapa, & Rettek, 1995) and Malaysia (Bochner, 1994), and people from many Latin American countries. People in these societies are more **interdependent,** or **collectivistic,** in their orientation than are Westerners (see Table 1.2). They do not have as much freedom or personal control over their lives, and they do not necessarily want or need these things (Sastry & Ross, 1998). **Figure 1.7** is designed to illustrate some of the fundamental differences between people in independent (individualistic) and interdependent (collectivistic) societies.

This difference in self-definition between people in independent and interdependent societies has important implications for the nature of their personal goals and strivings, values and beliefs (see **Table 1.3**). Success is important to East Asians, but in good part because it brings credit to the family and other groups to which they belong rather than merely as a reflection of personal merit. Personal uniqueness is not very important to interdependent peoples and may in fact even be undesirable. In a clever experiment by Kim and Markus (1999), Korean and American participants were offered a pen as a gift for being in a study. Several of the pens were of one color and one pen was of another color. Americans tended to choose the unique color and Koreans the common color. There is a saying frequently heard in East Asia: "The nail that stands out is hammered down." Being better than others is not such a necessity in order for interdependent people to feel good about themselves, and feeling good about themselves is itself not as important a goal as it is for Westerners and other independent peoples (Heine, Lehman, Markus, & Kitayama, 1999). Interdependent people tend not to expect or even value mutuality and equality in relationships; on the contrary, they are likely to expect hierarchical relations to be the rule (Hsu, 1953;

interdependent (collectivistic) cultures Cultures in which people tend to define themselves as part of a collective, inextricably tied to others in their group and having relatively little individual freedom or personal control over their lives but not necessarily wanting or needing these things.

(A) Independent view of self

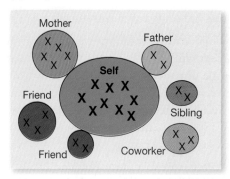

(B) Interdependent view of self

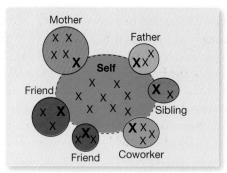

FIGURE 1.7 **Self and Other in Independent and Interdependent Cultures**
(A) People in independent cultures think of themselves as having attributes—attitudes, abilities, personality traits—that exist in all social settings, as indicated by the bold Xs (representing different attributes) internal to the self. Other people have varying degrees of closeness to them, but they are separate from them. The boundary around the self is thick to indicate that the self exists apart from its relationships to others. (B) People in interdependent cultures think of some of their most important attributes as entirely social, existing only in relationships with others, as indicated by the bold Xs that exist simultaneously in the self and another person. The boundary around the self is thin to indicate that others are a part of the conception of who the self is. (Markus & Kitayama, 1991.)

TABLE 1.3 Values and Beliefs of Independent and Interdependent Cultures

People in independent (individualistic) and interdependent (collectivistic) cultures tend to have different values and beliefs, as can be seen below in what people in independent cultures tend to want and believe and what people in interdependent cultures tend to want and believe.

Independent Cultures	Interdependent Cultures
Want to get the recognition they deserve when they do a good job	Want the employer to have a major responsibility for their health and welfare
Want to have considerable freedom to adopt their own approach to the job	Want to work in a congenial and friendly atmosphere
Want to fully use their skills and abilities on the job	Want to be completely loyal to their company
Want to work in a department that is run efficiently	Believe that knowing influential people is more important than ability
Believe that decisions made by individuals are better than those made by groups	Believe that the better managers are those who have been with the company the longest time

Source: Hofstede, 1980.

Triandis, 1989, 1995). They tend not to be universalists in their understanding of social norms; instead, they believe in different strokes for different folks. Justice should keep her eyes wide open, paying attention to the particular circumstances of each case that comes before her.

Individualism versus Collectivism in the Workplace

The distinction between independence and interdependence as cultural predilections is so important that we develop it throughout this book, but we present some representative findings now so that the concept will be well grounded at the outset. One of the first social scientists to measure the dimension of independence (or individualism) versus interdependence (or collectivism) was Geert Hofstede (1980), who surveyed the values of tens of thousands of IBM employees around the world. Table 1.3 shows the sorts of values and beliefs that Hofstede examined and the differences he observed in individualistic versus collectivistic cultures. **Figure 1.8** displays these results geographically, showing the degree of individualism expressed on average by the citizens of 67 countries. You can see that the countries of British heritage are the most independent, followed by the countries of continental Europe, South Asia, Asia Minor, and Latin America.

Although Hofstede himself studied few East Asian societies, we now have a great deal of evidence about them. The research to date indicates that those cultures are turning out to be very different from the Western cultures. In a survey similar to Hofstede's, two professors in a business school in the Netherlands, Charles Hampden-Turner and Alfons Trompenaars, examined independence and interdependence among 15,000 middle managers from the United States, Canada, Great Britain, Australia, Sweden, the Netherlands, Belgium, Germany, France, Italy, Japan, Singapore,

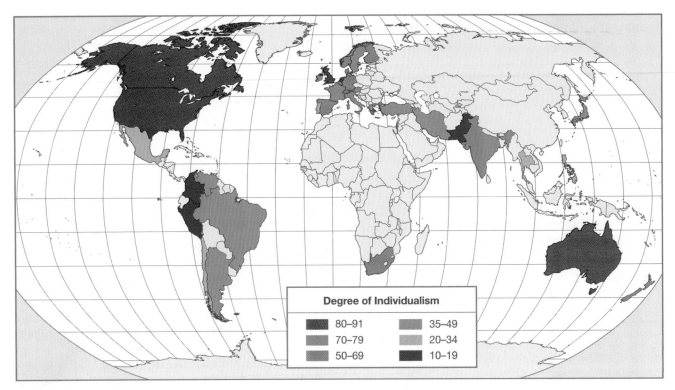

FIGURE 1.8 Individualism and Collectivism The map shows the degree of individualism and collectivism among IBM employees around the world, indicating greater individualism in Great Britain and in the United States, Canada, Australia, and New Zealand, all former British colonies. People in the countries represented by the tan color were not surveyed by the researchers. (Source: Sabini, 1995, p. 261; based on data from Hofstede, 1980.)

and Korea (Hampden-Turner & Trompenaars, 1993). They presented these managers, who were attending seminars conducted by the investigators, with dilemmas in which individualistic values were pitted against collectivistic values. In line with Hofstede's results, they found that managers from East Asia valued collectivistic values, managers from British and former British colonies valued individualism, and managers from continental European nations valued a mix of individualism and collectivism. A sampling of the researchers' questions can be found in **Box 1.1**.

Dick and Jane, Deng and Janxing

The first page of a reader for American children from the 1930s shows a little boy running with his dog. "See Dick run," the primer reads. "See Dick run and play." "See Spot run." The first page of a Chinese reader from the same era shows a little boy sitting on the shoulders of a bigger boy. "Big Brother loves Little Brother" reads the text. "Little Brother loves Big Brother." The difference between what the American child and the Chinese child of the 1930s were exposed to on the first day of class says much about the differences between their worlds. The American child is taught to orient toward action and to be prepared to live in a world where control and individual choice are possible. The Chinese child is more likely to be taught to be attuned to relationships. To the Westerner, it makes sense to speak of the existence of the person apart from any group. To East Asians (for example, Chinese, Japanese, and Koreans) and to many of the world's other peoples, the person really exists only as a member of a larger collective—family, friends, village, corporation. People are related to one another like ropes in a net—completely interconnected and having no real existence without the connections (Munro, 1985).

BOX 1.1 **FOCUS ON CULTURE**

Individualism or Collectivism in Business Managers

Charles Hampden-Turner and Alfons Trompenaars (1993) studied individualism versus collectivism in thousands of business managers. To examine the value placed on individual distinctiveness and accomplishment versus harmonious relations within the group, they asked the business managers in their seminars whether business managers preferred

jobs in which personal initiatives are encouraged and individual initiatives are achieved.

or

jobs in which no one is singled out for personal honor, but in which everyone works together.

To examine the acceptance of ascribed status (for example, age, family, religious background) as a basis for rewarding employees, Hampden-Turner and Trompenaars asked the business managers whether they agreed with the following sentiment:

It is important for a manager to be older than his subordinates. Older people should be more respected than younger people.

To see whether their respondents felt there should be universal rules governing employer-employee relations or whether instead circumstances and specific situations should be taken into account, the investigators asked the business managers how they thought one should deal with an employee who had performed well for 15 years, but had recently become unproductive. If circumstances indicate it's unlikely that performance will improve, should the employee be dismissed on the grounds that

job performance should remain the grounds for dismissal, regardless of the age of the person and his previous record.

or

[it is] wrong to disregard the 15 years the employee has been working for the company. One has to take into account the company's responsibility for his life.

The cultures studied fell into three major clusters. The East Asian managers were by far the most interdependent, or collectivistic, in their expressed values; the managers from the British and former Commonwealth nations were the most independent, or individualistic (with the United States and Canada being the most extremely independent); and the managers from continental Europe were in between. There was also an interesting difference within Europe. The researchers found that the people from the northwestern European nations of Sweden, the Netherlands, and Belgium were more individualistic than the people from the more southern European nations of France, Italy, and Germany.

Who Are You?

Westerners' belief that they are self-contained is revealed by simply asking them to describe themselves. Kuhn and McPartland (1954) invented a simple "Who Am I" test that asks people to list 20 statements that describe who they are. (Remember that we asked you to list ten statements that describe who you are at the beginning of this section. If you didn't do it then, do it now if you want to get the most out of this section.) Americans' self-descriptions tend to be context-free answers referring to personality traits ("I'm friendly," "hardworking," "shy") and personal preferences ("I like camping"). When more interdependent participants respond to this little test, however, their answers tend to refer to a relationship with some other person or group ("I am Jan's friend") and are often qualified by context ("I am serious at work," "I am fun-loving with my friends") (Cousins, 1989; Ip & Bond, 1995; Markus & Kitayama, 1991). You might want to look back at your own answers on the ten-question "Who Am I" test you took at the beginning of this section and see what type of characterizations you emphasized.

Social psychologists Vaunne Ma and Thomas Schoeneman (1997) administered the "Who Am I" test to American university students and to four different groups

"Culture is an inherited habit."

—Francis Fukuyama

Attention to Action versus Relationships (A) The Dick and Jane readers of the United States emphasize action and individualism, as shown on this page with the drawing of Dick running and the words, "See Dick. See Dick run." (B) Japanese and Chinese readers are more likely to emphasize relationships, as seen in this Chinese reader in which two boys walk down the street with their arms around each other. The text says, "Xiao Zhiang is a very nice boy. He is my best friend. We always study together and play together. We have a lot of fun together."

living in Kenya—university students, workers in Nairobi (the capital city), and traditional Masai and Samburu herding peoples. Kenya was for decades a colony of Great Britain, and city dwellers, especially those who are educated, have had a great deal of exposure to Western culture. Kenyan students have been exposed still more to Western culture and are being educated in a Western tradition. In contrast, traditional African tribespeople are reputed to have little sense of themselves as individuals. Rather, their sense of self is defined by family, property, and position in the community. Tribespeople are constantly made aware of their roles and status in relation to family and other groups (Mwaniki, 1973).

Figure 1.9 shows how differently these four African groups view themselves. Traditional Masai and Samburu characterize themselves in terms of roles and group memberships, whereas Kenyan students are far more likely to mention personal characteristics. Kenyan students, in fact, differ only slightly from American students. Workers in Nairobi are in between the tribespeople and the students. This pattern of evidence, when considered in relation to the very large differences typically found between East Asian and Western students, suggests that modernization by itself does not produce substantial differences in self-conceptions. Rather, it is a Western orientation that seems essential to an independent conception of the self.

> Among traditional Kenyan tribespeople, the individualist is "looked upon with suspicion. . . . There is no really individual affair, for everything has a moral and social influence."
>
> —Jomo Kenyatta (1938), first president of independent Kenya

Culture and Gender Roles

Earlier, we focused on some aspects of gender roles that are—or were—universal. But gender roles vary greatly around the world and even within subcultures in the same country. Male dominance is one of the most variable aspects of gender roles. Traditional, preliterate peoples, living lives much like those of people during the thousands of years of recent human evolution, are hunter-gatherers. The male role is to hunt; the female role is to gather plants. Despite the sharp demarcation of gender roles, such societies are relatively gender egalitarian. Indeed, the social structures are characterized by weak hierarchies in general, with leaders having little power over others. Modern Western cultures are also relatively gender egalitarian, especially Scandinavian countries. Women constitute almost half the membership of the Parliament in Sweden. The Scandinavians, incidentally, have been relatively gender egalitarian for 1,000 years. The helmeted Viking woman of operas and cartoons was a reality.

There is even greater divergence in gender roles among Muslim cultures. Some Muslim countries have relatively gender-egalitarian societies. Indeed, several have had women as prime minister or president. But still today in some fundamentalist Muslim subcultures, women occupy a position not much different from chattel slaves.

The kinds of sexual relations that are considered normal and appropriate also vary enormously. Overwhelmingly, polygamy, in which one man has several wives, and serial monogamy are the most common expectations among the world's subcultures—and that may have been the case for thousands of years. The traditional U.S. standard of lifetime monogamy is a rarity, and serial monogamy is now a common pattern. The United States is considered decidedly prudish by many Western Europeans. In some European subcultures, extramarital affairs are expected. The funeral of a recent president of France was attended by his wife and his mistress standing side by side. Homosexuals are permitted to serve in many European armies without disguising their sexual orientation. In stark contrast, in some cultures women (and sometimes even men) who are suspected of having extramarital affairs are put to death. Indeed, in some of those cultures, a woman who is raped is expelled from the family circle or even killed. Homosexuals may be sentenced to prison or worse.

It is a matter of some disagreement among social scientists whether the different sexual mores (norms) that characterize different cultures are merely arbitrary or whether there are economic or other practical roots to most of them. For example, some farmers in Nepal and Tibet practice polyandry—one wife with many husbands who are brothers. This serves the economic goal of keeping land in one family, with just one set of related heirs per generation. A similar purpose was served by primogeniture, a common rule in Western Europe that only the firstborn male could inherit land. Otherwise, estates would be broken up into ever smaller units and the original power of the landowning family would dwindle away to the status of ordinary peasants.

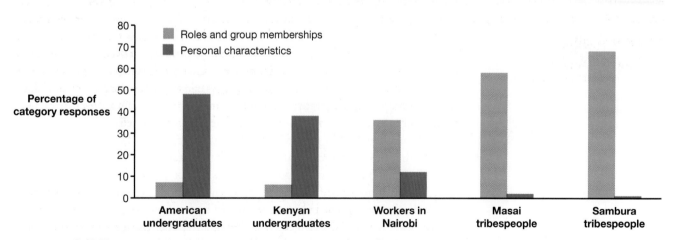

FIGURE 1.9 **Self-Characterization** The graph shows the percentage of "role and group membership" and "personal characteristics" responses on the "Who Am I" test by American undergraduates, Kenyan undergraduates, workers in Nairobi, Masai tribespeople, and Sambura tribespeople. (Source: Ma & Schoeneman, 1997.)

Some Qualifications

Societies differ in many ways, and it's not possible to put each society entirely in one box or the other and say that some are independent in all respects and others are interdependent in all respects. Moreover there are regional and subcultural differences within any large society. The U.S. South, for example, is more interdependent than much of the rest of the country in the sense that family connections and community ties tend to be more important (Vandello & Cohen, 1999). On the other hand, the South has been described as more tolerant of character quirks and various kinds of social deviance than other regions of the country—clearly individualistic tendencies (Reed, 1990).

Moreover, the socialization within a given society of particular individuals or particular types of individuals may be oriented more toward independence or more toward interdependence. Gender socialization in our society is a good example of this (Kashima et al., 1995). While Dick is depicted in children's readers as running and playing (being independent), Jane is often shown caring for her dolls and cooking for others (being interdependent). So there are differences within each culture. In addition, the same person can have a relatively independent orientation in some situations (for example, competing in a debate tournament) and a relatively interdependent orientation in others (for example, singing in a choir) (Gardner, Gabriel, & Lee, 1999; Kühnen & Oyserman, 2002; Trafimow, Triandis, & Goto, 1991).

Nevertheless, the broad generalizations we have made about different cultures hold fairly well, as you will see in later chapters. Some cultures are much more concerned than others with issues of individuality, freedom, personal achievement, and universally applicable rules. Others are more concerned with harmony within the group, achievement as it serves collective goals, and social rules that take particular relationships and context into account. Many of the most important findings in social psychology turn out to be much more descriptive of Western cultures than of many other cultures (Henrich, Heine, & Norenzayan, in press), as we will point out repeatedly in this book.

Culture and Evolution as Tools for Understanding Situations

As we have seen, both culture and evolution affect how people see the world and behave within it. It may be useful to look at both culture and evolution as ways of understanding extremely broad situations and how people process and react to those broad situations. The situations confronting humans for their first several hundred thousand years concerned the necessities of surviving, reproducing, and nourishing their young in a fundamentally social environment. Within such an environment, humans had to learn to deal with competition, social influence, and dominance relations. Such challenges may have resulted in the evolution of prewired inclinations to formulate theories and schemas and to behave in certain ways in reaction to certain social situations. But such inclinations are tools that can be applied flexibly or not at all. And many, if not most, of these tools are highly modifiable by culture (Sperber, 1996). Indeed, they *required* culture of some sort to develop naturally. Different ecologies and economies led people to constantly encounter certain kinds of situations that differed markedly from those that confronted other peoples and in turn produced different social systems and practices.

Evolution has given us all the capacity for an astonishingly wide range of behaviors. But whether we develop a particular prewired option or not may depend on how adaptive the behavior is for the circumstances that confront the society (Sperber, 1996). For example, all infants have the capacity to utter every known phoneme, and indeed they do so while lying in the crib babbling away. But Japanese-speaking adults find it hard to distinguish *r* from *l*, French-speaking adults find it hard to distinguish *te* from *the*, and English-speaking adults find it hard to distinguish *dew* from the German *dü*. Inherited potentials provide the options, but societies select those that are valuable to retain and allow the others to wither away. Nature proposes but culture disposes. Far from making us rigidly programmed automatons, evolution has equipped us with a large repertoire of tools for dealing with the enormous range of circumstances that humans confront. Cultural circumstances and our high intelligence determine which tools we develop and which tendencies we try to override.

 LOOKING BACK We have seen that people in Western societies tend to be individualistic, or independent, whereas people in other societies are more likely to be collectivistic, or interdependent. Westerners tend to define themselves as having attributes that exist apart from their relations with other people. Non-Westerners tend to define themselves in terms of their relations with others. These differences have important implications for many of the most important phenomena of social psychology. Gender roles and sexual mores are examples of behaviors that differ widely from one culture to another. Evolution and culture each make important contributions to understanding human social behavior, with evolution predisposing us to certain behaviors, but culture determining which behaviors are likely to be developed in particular situations.

Summary

Characterizing Social Psychology

- *Social psychology* is the scientific study of the feelings, thoughts, and behaviors of individuals in social situations.

The Power of the Situation

- Social psychology emphasizes the influence of *situations* on behavior. People often find it difficult to see the role that powerful situations play in producing their own and others' behavior, and they are inclined to overemphasize the importance of personal dispositions in producing behavior. The two tendencies together are called the *fundamental attribution error.*

The Role of Construal

- Social psychology also focuses on the role of *construal* in understanding situations. People often feel that their comprehension of situations is direct, without much mediating thought. In fact, even the perception of the simplest objects rests on substantial inference and the existence of complex cognitive structures for carrying it out.

- The primary tool people use for understanding social situations, and physical stimuli for that matter, is the schema. Schemas are the stored representations of numerous repetitions of highly similar stimuli and situations. They tell us how to interpret situations and how to behave in them. Stereotypes are schemas of people of various kinds—police officers, Hispanics, yuppies. Stereotypes serve to guide interpretation and behavior, but they can often be mistaken or misapplied, and they can lead to damaging interactions and unjust behaviors.

Automatic versus Controlled Processing

- People's construals of situations are often largely automatic and unconscious; as a consequence, people are sometimes in the dark about how they reached a particular conclusion or behaved in a particular way.

Evolution and Human Behavior: How We Are the Same

- The *evolutionary perspective* focuses on practices and understandings that are universal and that seem to be indispensable to social life. This leads to the suspicion that we are prewired to engage in those practices. Some evolutionary theorists have argued that differences between males and females may be explained by the fact that the two sexes have differential *parental investment.* They also talk about other universal characteristics that are more cognitive in nature, including *language*, which appears in almost identical fashion and at the same stage of development in all cultures, as well as a *theory of mind*, which also appears very early in normal people in all cultures.

Culture and Human Behavior: How We Are Different

- Behaviors and meanings can differ dramatically across cultures. Many of these differences involve the degree to which a society is *interdependent,* or *collectivistic*, in its social relations (having many relationships of a highly prescribed nature) versus *independent,* or *individualistic* (having fewer relationships of a looser sort). These differences influence conceptions of the self and the nature of human relationships and even basic cognitive and perceptual processes.

- Gender roles and sexual mores differ enormously across cultures. Even within the West, gender and sexual practices diverge significantly. Theorists differ in the extent to which they believe this variability is arbitrary versus rooted in economic factors or some other aspect of the objective situation confronting the culture.

Key Terms

channel factors (p. 14)
construal (p. 16)
dispositions (p. 15)
fundamental attribution error (p. 16)
Gestalt psychology (p. 17)

independent (individualistic) culture (p. 31)
interdependent (collectivistic) culture (p. 32)
naturalistic fallacy (p. 28)
natural selection (p. 24)

parental investment (p. 28)
prisoner's dilemma (p. 18)
schemas (p. 19)
social psychology (p. 7)
stereotypes (p. 20)
theory of mind (p. 27)

Further Reading

Darley, J. M., & Batson, C. D. (1973). From Jerusalem to Jericho: A study of situational and dispositional variables in helping behavior. *Journal of Personality and Social Psychology, 27,* 100–119. A classic experiment showing the power of "small" situational factors.

Doris, J. M. (2002). *Lack of character: Personality and moral behavior.* New York: Cambridge University Press. A philosopher shows the importance for the field of ethics of the fact that situational factors influence so powerfully behaviors that we consider moral or immoral.

Henrich, J., Heine, S. J., & Norenzayan, A. (in press). The Weirdest people in the world. *Behavioral and Brain Sciences.* A documentation of the scores of important ways that people of European cultures differ from people of other cultures.

Ross, L., & Nisbett, R. E. (1991). *The person and the situation: Perspectives of social psychology.* New York: McGraw-Hill. A brief text reviewing some of the basic principles of social psychology.

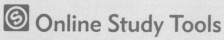 Online Study Tools

StudySpace

Go to StudySpace, wwnorton.com/studyspace, to access additional review and enrichment materials, including the following resources for each chapter:

Organize

- Study Plan
- Chapter Outline
- Quiz+ Assessment

Learn

- Ebook
- Chapter Review
- Critical-Thinking Questions
- Visual Quizzes
- Vocabulary Flashcards

Connect

- Apply It! Exercises
- Author Insights Podcasts
- Social Psychology in the News

The Methods of Social Psychology

BUSINESS OWNERS ACROSS the Northern and Southern United States were sent the following letter from a job applicant who described himself as a hardworking, 27-year-old man who was relocating to the letter recipient's area from Michigan (Cohen & Nisbett, 1997). Among a set of appropriate qualifications listed in the letter, the applicant described one rather striking blemish:

> There is one thing I must explain, because I feel I must be honest and want no misunderstandings. I have been convicted of a felony, namely manslaughter. You will probably want an explanation for this before you send me an application, so I will provide it. I got into a fight with someone who was having an affair with my financée. I lived in a small town, and one night this person confronted me in front of my friends at the bar. He told everyone that he and my fiancée were sleeping together. He laughed at me to my face and asked me to step outside if I was man enough. I was young and didn't want to back down from a challenge in front of everyone. As we went into the alley, he started to attack me. He knocked me down, and he picked up a bottle. I could have run away and the judge said I should have, but my pride wouldn't let me. Instead I picked up a pipe that was laying in the alley and hit him with it. I didn't mean to kill him, but he died a few hours later at the hospital.

Some of those contacted replied to the letter. The investigators measured how cooperative they were in complying with the "applicant's" requests—whether they included an application, gave the name of a contact person, provided a phone number to call, sent a note with their response, and so on. If there was a note, the investigators rated how sympathetic it seemed—how encouraging it was, how personal it was, and whether it mentioned an appreciation for the applicant's candor.

Defending One's Honor
Duels such as the one depicted here, between Aaron Burr and Alexander Hamilton, were practiced in the United States well into the nineteenth century.

Retailers from the South complied with the applicant's requests more than the retailers from the North did; for example, they were more likely to send an application or give the name of a contact person. And the notes from Southern businesses were much warmer and more sympathetic than those from the North. One Southern retailer wrote the following in her letter:

> As for your problem of the past, anyone could probably be in the situation you were in. It was just an unfortunate incident that shouldn't be held against you. Your honesty shows that you are sincere. . . .
>
> I wish you the best of luck for your future. You have a positive attitude and a willingness to work. Those are the qualities that businesses look for in an employee. Once you get settled, if you are near here, please stop in and see us.

No letter from a Northern employer was remotely as sympathetic toward the applicant. Why do you suppose that is? Why were the Southerners seemingly so accepting of murder? You will find out in this chapter. More importantly, you will find out how the investigators found out. They employed most of the methods at the disposal of social psychologists—methods that deepen our understanding of human behavior and help us improve many types of social outcomes.

WHY DO SOCIAL PSYCHOLOGISTS DO RESEARCH (AND WHY SHOULD YOU WANT TO READ ABOUT IT)?

Social psychologists have an enviable job. They get to study interesting behavior under controlled conditions in which it is possible to reach scientifically justified conclusions about some aspect of human nature. They then get to communicate these conclusions to their colleagues and their students.

For the most part, we can get along perfectly well in everyday life without the benefit of findings from social psychology. Daily life tells us what to expect of people's behavior in most situations. The world is a reasonably predictable place: most of the situations we find ourselves in are similar to other familiar situations, and our observations about how people behave in those situations are accurate enough to allow us to navigate through the world with some confidence in the correctness of our predictions.

But many situations—interviews, initiations, dating—can contain surprises and pitfalls that social psychological research can help us anticipate and avoid. And our opinions about how people tend to behave, even in situations that we have encountered before, can be mistaken. We have stereotypes about how people are likely to behave in particular situations or how particular people would behave in those situations, and we may use those stereotypes to anticipate what we think we're going to observe and to interpret what we do in fact observe. Chapters 4, 5, and 12 describe some of these stereotyped but mistaken beliefs about social behavior and how those beliefs get formed.

Our opinions about *why* we behave as we do can also be mistaken. You might think that your ideas about why you yourself behave the way you do can be an accurate guide as to why other people behave the way they do. But even some of our strongest convictions about why we behave as we do can be mistaken (Nisbett & Wilson, 1977). (Chapter 1 provides some of the reasons for our mistaken beliefs about the causes of our own behavior.) Many of the factors that influence our behavior are in fact hidden from us: they aren't represented in conscious, verbal forms but in nonconscious, non-verbal forms that aren't accessible to introspection. Fortunately, social psychology can tell us about the reasons not just for other people's behavior but for our own as well.

Some of the things that social psychologists are interested in we don't encounter in daily life at all. Why were lynchings common in the years between the end of the U.S. Civil War and the beginning of World War II? What are the conditions that encourage riots? We need social psychological research and theory to help us understand such historical events and social problems.

To see why social psychological research is needed to examine even ordinary aspects of human behavior and its causes, take a look at **Box 2.1**. Make your own guesses about the outcomes of the research described and then see how accurate those guesses are by looking at p. 47. When you have to predict the results of studies and *then* find out what they were, you avoid the **hindsight bias**, which refers to people's tendency to be overconfident about whether they could have predicted a given outcome (Bradfield & Wells, 2005; Fischhoff, Gonzalez, Lerner, & Small, 2005; Guilbault, Bryant, Brockway, & Posavac, 2004). When people read about how some historical event turned out or what happened to someone in a newspaper story or what some scientific finding is, they tend to believe that they could have predicted the outcome when in fact they could not have (which we know by asking people who are ignorant of the outcome to predict it). Matching your predictions about Box 2.1 with the actual findings should serve as an antidote against thinking that social psychology findings are obvious. They are often obvious only in hindsight and not in foresight.

hindsight bias People's tendency to be overconfident about whether they could have predicted a given outcome.

We have seen that social psychology shows us that some of our stereotypes about how people behave are mistaken, and shows us how such beliefs are formed with sometimes faulty procedures. Our beliefs about the reasons for our own behavior can also be mistaken. Social psychology also has much to tell us about things that don't touch our daily lives at all but are nevertheless valuable to understand, such as the reasons for historical events. Social psychological findings sometimes seem obvious, but that is often only after we know what they are. Hindsight mistakenly tells us that we knew about those findings all along.

BOX 2.1 **FOCUS ON INTUITIVE SOCIAL PSYCHOLOGY**

Predicting the Results of Social Psychology Studies

Predict how people would behave in each of the situations below. (See p. 47 for answers.)

1. Does familiarity breed liking or contempt? Would you be likely to prefer a song you had heard many times on the radio or one you had heard less often?

2. Suppose someone were persuaded to lie about his or her beliefs about some matter. Would that person be more inclined to move his or her beliefs in the direction of the lie if paid a small amount of money, a large amount of money, or no money at all?

3. Suppose you knew that an acquaintance wanted a favor from you. Would you like the person better if (a) the person refrained from asking you the favor, (b) the person asked you to do the favor and you complied, or (c) the person asked you to do the favor and you turned the person down?

4. Suppose you got someone to think seriously for a few minutes about the inevitability of death. Would that be likely to make the person feel (a) more helpless, (b) less favorably inclined toward their fellow human beings, or (c) more patriotic?

5. Suppose a person endured a painful medical procedure. Would the person be less willing to undergo the procedure again if (a) the pain lasted for a long time, (b) the pain at its peak was particularly intense, (c) the first phase of the procedure was particularly painful, or (d) the final phase of the procedure was particularly painful?

6. Suppose male college students were asked to grade an essay written for an English class, and a picture of the female student who allegedly wrote the essay were attached to the essay. Would the grade be higher if (a) the student was very pretty, (b) the student was average looking, (c) the student was quite plain looking, or (d) the student grading the essay was about as good looking as the person who allegedly wrote the essay?

7. Suppose people were asked what a person should choose if one choice meant that there was a substantial potential gain but also substantial risk and the other choice entailed less potential gain but also less risk. Would people be more likely to recommend the risky choice if (a) they considered the choice by themselves or (b) they considered the choice in discussion with a small group—or (c) would it make no difference?

8. Suppose you asked one group of people to give their opinion about an issue after very brief consideration and asked another group to spend several minutes thinking about as many aspects of the issue as possible and then give their opinion. Which group do you think would have more extreme views on the topic: (a) the group asked immediately about their opinion or (b) the group asked to ponder a while before answering—or (c) would the amount of time thinking about the question make no difference?

9. Suppose you offered an award to some nursery school children if they would draw with magic markers, and all the children who were offered the award drew with them. Would these children be (a) more likely to play with the magic markers at a subsequent time than children never offered the award, (b) less likely, or (c) would it make no difference?

10. Suppose you asked a group of people to report 6 instances in which they behaved in an assertive fashion, another group to report 12 instances in which they behaved in an assertive fashion, and a third group to report 6 instances of some other behavior altogether, such as instances of introverted behavior. Which group would later report that they were most assertive: (a) the group asked for 6 instances of assertive behavior, (b) the group asked for 12 instances of assertive behavior, (c) the group asked about some other behavior—or (d) would it make little difference what the group was asked?

HOW DO SOCIAL PSYCHOLOGISTS TEST IDEAS?

Social psychologists use a wide variety of methods to test hypotheses about human behavior. As you read about these methods in this chapter and see them applied elsewhere in the book, keep in mind that the logic that underlies these methods is crucial for getting at the likely truth of propositions about social behavior. Even if you can't do a study to test a particular proposition, thinking through how you *would* test a given idea can lead you to new hypotheses that, on reflection, might seem preferable to your initial speculation. And just thinking about how you might apply the methods can be a useful check on overconfidence, which can be a source of serious mistakes in life. We tend to be more confident about the truth of our beliefs than is justified. For example, people overestimate the accuracy of their beliefs about matters of fact—what continent grows the most coffee, whether Madison was president before Jefferson, or how long the secretary of defense said the war in Iraq would last (Lichtenstein, Fischhoff, & Phillips, 1982).

Observational Research

At the simplest level, research can be a matter of merely looking at a phenomenon in some reasonably systematic way with a view to understanding what is going on and coming up with hypotheses about why things are happening as they are. Charles Darwin was first and foremost a great observer of natural life, and these observations led to his theory of evolution by natural selection. Social psychologists themselves learn a great deal from observations.

One method of social psychological research, called *participant observation*, is shared with the field of cultural anthropology. A good way of understanding some phenomenon is to observe it at close range. Anthropologists may live with a group of people for a long time, just noting what they do and coming up with guesses—sometimes inspired by conversations with the people they are studying—about why they do certain things or have certain beliefs. In the 1970s, for example, cultural anthropologist Shirley Brice Heath used participant observation to study preparation for schooling by middle-class and working-class families in a North Carolina town. She found remarkable differences between these two groups by living with them for lengthy periods. The middle-class families read to their children a great deal, included them in dinner-table conversations, used the printed word to guide their behavior (recipes, game rules), and taught them how to categorize objects, how to answer "why" questions, and how to evaluate and make judgments about things. The working-class families didn't do those things as much, and although their children were reasonably well prepared for the early grades of school, their lack of preparation showed up in later grades, when they faced more complex tasks involving categorization and evaluation.

Social psychologists often observe social situations in a semiformal way, taking notes and interviewing participants; but unlike anthropologists, social psychologists typically design additional research to verify the impressions they get from participant observation. As you will see repeatedly in this book, we are often misled by what we observe, and so any tentative conclusions gleaned from observation should ideally be tested with other methods. It is through these methods that social psychological research adds extra dimensions to our understanding of cultural differences.

Archival Research

One type of research can be conducted without ever leaving the library (or the laptop). This method looks at evidence that can be found in archives of various kinds—record

"The scientific method itself would not have led anywhere, it would not even have been born without a passionate striving for clear understanding."

—Albert Einstein,
Out of My Later Years

How accurate were your predictions? (See Box 2.1 on p. 46.)

1. Familiarity, in general, breeds liking. The more we have been exposed to a stimulus, within broad limits, the more we like it. See Chapter 10.

2. People are more persuaded by the lies they tell if they are paid nothing or a small amount than if they are paid a lot. See Chapter 6.

3. We like people more if we do them a favor. See Chapters 6 and 9 .

4. When people are reminded of their own mortality, they focus on the values they hold most dear, such as religion and love of country. See Chapter 6.

5. The duration of pain has little effect on people's willingness to experience a procedure again. See Chapter 7.

6. Males give higher grades to females who are good looking. See Chapter 10.

7. In general, group discussion shifts people toward more risky choices. See Chapter 14.

8. Thinking more about an issue makes people's opinions about the issue more extreme. See Chapter 8.

9. Rewarding children for doing something they would do anyway makes them less interested in doing it. Contracts turn play into work. See Chapter 6.

10. People report that they are more assertive if they are asked to think of a few instances of assertiveness rather than if they are asked to think of many. It's easier to come up with a few instances than many, and people use the effort they expend as an indicator of what they are really like. See Chapter 5.

Observational Methods The evolutionary psychologist and human behavioral ecologist Lawrence Sugiyama is shown here, with bow and arrow, involved in a particularly active form of participant observation.

books, police reports, sports statistics, newspaper articles, and databases containing ethnographic (anthropological) descriptions of people in different cultures. For example, Nisbett and his colleagues (1993) studied FBI reports of homicides and found, as they had anticipated, that homicides were more common in the South than in the North. The reports also provided a clue about the reason for the regional difference. FBI reports of homicide include the circumstances under which the homicide takes place— murders conducted in the context of another felony (for example, while robbing a convenience store) versus murders that are crimes of passion (for example, during a heated argument between neighbors or in the context of a lovers' triangle). Nisbett and colleague Dov Cohen analyzed the various types of murders and discovered that the kinds of homicide that were most common in the South were those involving an insult of some kind—for example, barroom quarrels and cases in which a man's girlfriend or wife was "stolen" by another man ((Nisbett & Cohen, 1996). Other kinds of homicides are actually less common in the South than in the North, which led one researcher to say that as long as a Southerner stays out of the wrong bars and bedrooms, he's safer than Northerners (Reed, 1981). The observation that insult-related homicides are more common in the South led Cohen and Nisbett to begin a research program to study whether it is really the case that insults are responded to with more aggression in the South.

Surveys

One of the most common types of study in social psychology involves simply asking people questions. This can be done either with interviews or with written questionnaires. The participants can be a small, haphazard collection of students or a large national survey. When the investigator is trying to discern the beliefs or attitudes of some group of people—freshmen at a particular university, Hispanics living in California, or the population of the United States as a whole—it is important that the sample of people in the survey be a *random sample* of the population as a whole. The only way to do this is to give everyone in the population an equal chance of being chosen to be in the sample. If the university has a directory of students, a random sample can be obtained by finding out the total number of freshmen—say, 1,000—deciding how many to interview—say, 50—and then selecting every 20th name from the directory and asking them to participate in the survey (**Figure 2.1**).

A haphazard sample, obtained, for example, by contacting people as they enter the library or e-mailing fraternity and sorority members, runs the risk of being *biased* in some way—that is, of including too many of some kinds of people and too few of other kinds of people. Information based on biased samples is sometimes worse than no information at all. For example, a survey by the *Literary Digest*, based on more than a million respondents, erroneously predicted that the Republican Alf Landon would defeat FDR in the 1936 presidential election. In fact, the election was one of the biggest landslides in history: Landon carried only two states. The problem with the survey was that the sample was drawn from telephone directories and automobile registrations. In 1936, well-heeled people were more likely to own phones and cars than poorer people, and the well-heeled were more likely to be Republicans.

You have probably read about the results of lots of surveys of readers of various magazines. Two-thirds of *Cosmopolitan* readers who went on a vegan diet say that they lost weight. Three-quarters of the readers of *Outside* magazine say that sex is more enjoyable outdoors. Sixty percent of respondents in a *Readers Digest* poll claim they are happier after going to church instead of watching a football game on Sunday. Actually, we made up all three results and you should ignore each claim. But you should ignore claims like these even if we hadn't made them up. The people who take the time to respond to such polls are likely to be different from those who do not respond and therefore unlikely to represent the population as a whole. *Cosmo* readers who lost weight are more likely to respond to a survey about weight loss than those who did not lose weight. The criterion that everyone is equally likely to be in the sample is clearly not met, upping the odds that the survey results are misleading.

People often assume that you need very large numbers of people to be able to make inferences about large populations. But in fact, the number of people needed to get a reasonably accurate bead on some question—presidential preference, for example—is essentially independent of the size of the population in question. A sample of about 1,200 people from the entire adult population of the United States is sufficient to estimate the population value to a degree of accuracy of + or − 3 percent and to be 95 percent confident that the true value is within that range. The major national polls taken just before the presidential election generally come within 2 percent of the actual vote.

The use of surveys to pursue a social psychological question is demonstrated in a study by Cohen and Nisbett concerning attitudes toward violence (Nisbett & Cohen, 1996). One guess about why Southerners are more likely to commit homicide is that Southern attitudes might be more accepting of violence. But when Cohen and Nisbett looked at published national surveys of attitudes toward violence, they found few regional differences. For example, Southerners were no more likely than Northerners to agree with the sentiment that "an eye for an eye" is a justified retaliation, and Southerners were actually more likely to agree that "when a person harms you, you should turn the other cheek and forgive him." But they found that Southerners were more likely to favor violence in response to insults, to think that it would be all right for a man to fight an acquaintance who "looks over his girlfriend and talks to her in a suggestive way." Southerners were also more likely to approve of violence in response to threats to home and family, thinking, for example, that "a man has a right to kill a person to defend his house." They also found that Southerners were more approving of violence in the socialization of children: they were more likely to say that spanking was a reasonable way to handle a child's misdeeds and more likely to say that they would encourage a child to beat up someone who was bullying him (**Figure 2.2**).

In trying to explain this pattern of highly targeted acceptance of violence, Cohen and Nisbett sought out anthropologists and historians. Several sources suggested that the South might be a "culture of honor". The U.S. North was settled by farmers from England, Holland, and Germany. The U.S. South was settled by herding peoples from the edges of Britain—Scottish, Irish, and Scotch-Irish from Ulster. Herding peoples throughout the world are tough guys. They have to be because they can lose

Population
Group you want to know about
(e.g., U.S. college students)

Random sample
Taken at random from the population (e.g., giving every student in the country an equal chance to be in the sample)

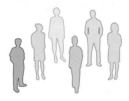

Convenience sample
Taken from some available subgroup in the population (e.g., students questioned as they come into the Student Union)

FIGURE 2.1 Sampling

FIGURE 2.2 You Be the Subject: Attitude toward Violence

Sometimes conflicts are resolved through fighting, and other times they are resolved nonviolently.

Imagine that a man named "Fred" finds himself in the following situations. In these situations, please indicate whether Fred starting a fight would be extremely justified, somewhat justified, or not at all justified.

1 Fred fights an acquaintance because that person looks over Fred's girlfriend and starts talking to her in a suggestive way.

2 Fred fights an acquaintance because that person insult's Fred's wife, implying that she has loose morals.

3 Fred fights an acquaintance because that person tells others behind Fred's back that Fred is a liar and a cheat.

On occasion, violent conflict involves shooting another person. Imagine that a man named "Fred" finds himself in the following situations. In these situations, indicate whether Fred shooting another person would be extremely justified, somewhat justified, or not at all justified.

4 Fred shoots another because that person steals Fred's wife.

5 Fred shoots another because that person sexually assaults Fred's 16-year-old daughter.

Results: Turn to p. 52 to see what your answers indicate.

their livelihood—their herd—in an instant. They cultivate a stance of being ready to commit violence at the merest hint that they might not be able to protect themselves, their homes, and their property. Insults must be prevented or retaliated against for a person to establish that he is not to be trifled with. Children are raised not to fear violence, to know how to protect themselves. This historical hypothesis guided the rest of Cohen and Nisbett's research.

Correlational Research

correlational research Research in which there is not random assignment to different situations, or conditions, and from which psychologists can just see whether or not there is a relationship between the variables.

experimental research In social psychology, research in which people are randomly assigned to different conditions, or situations, and from which it is possible to make very strong inferences about how these different conditions affect people's behavior.

In dealing with different types of research methods, the most important distinction we can make is between correlational and experimental research. In **correlational research**, there is no random assignment to different situations or conditions, and psychologists simply determine whether or not there is a relationship between two or more variables. In **experimental research**, people are randomly assigned to different situations (conditions), and it is possible to make very strong inferences about how these different situations or conditions affect people's behavior.

Most branches of social science make use only of correlational data, in which the natural association between two or more variables is examined. Correlations are important places to begin a line of inquiry. For example, in Chapter 11 we see that people who are very anxious, who get married at a younger age, and who are of lower socioeconomic status are more likely to divorce. These correlations are all interesting but beg for further exploration. That's because in correlational research, where by definition there is no manipulation of variables, we can never be sure about causality. Does variable *A* causally influence variable *B*, or is it the other way around? Or is it some third variable that influences both? For example, *Time* magazine (February, 2004) published a cover story devoted to the proposition that love and sex are good for physical and mental health. The magazine was able to quote statistics showing that married people are happier than unmarried people. But this leaves open a number of questions that should make us skeptical of the magazine's causal claims. Happier people may be more appealing to others and more likely to be married for that reason, so it could be that happiness causes marriage rather than marriage causing happiness. Or perhaps good physical and mental health lead both to greater likelihood of marriage and greater likelihood of being happy.

In correlational research, we look at the degree of relationship between two or more variables. Strength of relationship can range from 0, meaning that there is no relationship at all between the variables, to 1, meaning that the covariation is perfect—the higher the level on one variable, the higher the level on the other—without exception. (In the latter case, the correlation is +1. If it were the case that being higher on one variable was perfectly associated with being lower on the other, the correlation would be −1.) By convention, a correlation of .2 indicates a slight relationship, a correlation of .4 a moderately strong relationship, and a correlation of .6 or higher a very strong relationship. **Figure 2.3** shows what are called scatterplots. Variable *A* is on the *x*-axis, and variable *B* is on the *y*-axis. Each dot represents a case—for example, a study participant for whom you have a score on variable *A* and a score on variable *B*.

Panel B in Figure 2.3 shows a correlation of .3, which corresponds, for example, to the correlation between the degree to which an individual is underweight, average, or overweight and the degree of incipient cardiovascular illness. Both the marked spread of the dots (their scatter) and the relatively shallow slope of the line that best fits the scatterplot show that that association is relatively weak. Consider the causal possibilities for the relationship in panel B. It is possible that something about being overweight causes cardiovascular illness. But it is also possible, for example, that people who are under stress tend to gain weight and also to develop cardiovascular symptoms. And it is possible that some underlying syndrome makes people both overweight and prone to cardiovascular illness. In either case, being overweight might play no causal role in cardiovascular illness. This point is important, because if you are a physician and you believe that being overweight is a cause of cardiovascular illness, you're likely to try to get your patients to lose weight. But in fact, people who lose a large amount of weight are likely to gain it back at some later point, and some scientists believe that "yo-yoing" between weight levels is actually a cause of cardiovascular disease (Jeffery, 1996).

Panel C in Figure 2.3 shows a correlation of .5, which is approximately the degree of association between height and weight. This correlation helps us understand the ambiguity of correlational findings. Height predicts weight, and weight predicts height, but you wouldn't want to say that one *causes* the other. Rather, a wide range of genetic and environmental factors causes both. Some of those factors undoubtedly make some people larger than others—influencing both height and weight. But some factors

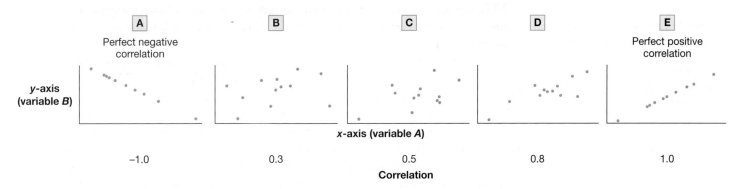

FIGURE 2.3 Scatterplots and Correlations

influence weight more than height and vice versa. In any case, height does not cause weight, nor does weight cause height.

Panel D in Figure 2.3 shows a correlation of .8. This is about the degree of correlation that you would find between two scores on the Scholastic Aptitude Test obtained about a year apart. The association is quite strong, as indicated by the relatively slight scatter of the points around the line fitting the scatterplot and the relatively steep slope of that line. But it would be odd to say that the SAT score on the first occasion caused the score on the second occasion. Instead, we would say that an underlying and undoubtedly highly complex set of factors involving genetics and social variables caused both scores to be similar for a given individual.

Correlational studies can be very helpful in alerting us to various possibilities for valid causal hypotheses about the nature of the world, but they don't tell us about the direction of causality, and they don't tell us whether some "external" variable is driving the association between the two variables of interest. Consider two examples.

1. *People who watch the local evening news—with its murders, fires, and other newsworthy mayhem—see more danger in the world than people who do not.* The most obvious explanation is that watching dangers on TV makes people feel more at risk. But mightn't it be the case that people who are anxious watch local TV in order to justify their fearfulness? Or is it some third variable? For example, elderly people may have more anxiety about their lives and may have more time to watch TV. Note that we can refine this study and potentially rule out the latter hypothesis. For example, it may not in fact be the case that the elderly are more likely to watch TV than younger people, and the elderly may be no more anxious about their lives than are younger people. This still leaves a myriad of as yet unimagined factors that might produce the relationship. Nevertheless, clever analysis of correlational data can sometimes be quite persuasive about the meaning of the relationship.

2. *People who watched a great deal of violent TV when they were 8 years old are more likely to be incarcerated for violence and other criminal behavior in adolescence and adulthood.* At first blush, it seems obvious that watching violent TV would tend to make people more violent. On the other hand, it also seems obvious that people with more violent temperaments would be more likely to want to watch violent TV when younger and more likely to engage in criminal behavior when older. Note, however, that such a **longitudinal study** (in which people are studied at two points in time) rules out the opposite direction of causality: nothing that happens when a person is 30 can affect anything the person did when younger. And again, clever analysis of data such as these, as discussed in Chapter 13, can make some interpretations much less plausible than others.

longitudinal study A study conducted over a long period of time with the same population, which is periodically assessed regarding a particular behavior.

self-selection A problem that arises when the participant, rather than the investigator, selects his or her level on each variable, bringing with this value unknown other properties that make causal interpretation of a relationship difficult.

The problem with correlational research is that it suffers from **self-selection**—that is, the investigator has no control over the degree of a particular participant's score on a given variable (such as degree of overweight or opinions toward violence). In effect, the participant has "chosen" the level of *all* variables—both those that are measured and those that are not. For example, the investigator does not choose whether a given 8-year-old watches a lot of television or only a little. The child chooses the level of TV watching. And the investigator can't know what other qualities the child brings with high or low TV watching. These various qualities are self-selected as opposed to investigator-selected.

Box 2.2 presents the results of numerous correlational studies for which scientists or the media have implied a clear causal connection. To be a good consumer of correlational research, you want to be able to "argue back" against such strong interpretations of causality. Try your hand at interpreting the correlational results in Box 2.2. (Our responses to those causality claims are presented on p. 55.) For each of the correlational findings listed, see if you can think of ways that the causal hypothesis could be tested in an experiment.

Experimental Research

The best way to be sure about causality is to employ the experimental method. In experimental research, there is an independent variable and a dependent variable. The **independent variable** is the variable that is manipulated and that is hypothesized to be the cause of a particular outcome. The **dependent variable** is the variable that is measured (as opposed to manipulated) and is hypothesized to be the outcome of a particular causal process. In experiments, the researcher determines what will be the independent variable and what levels there will be for that variable. In an experiment by John Darley and Daniel Batson (1973; see Chapter 1), the researchers found that seminary students in a hurry were less likely to offer aid to a victim. In that experiment, one of the independent variables was whether or not the student was in a hurry. The dependent variable was whether or not the student stopped to help the victim. Dependent variables can be measured in many different ways—by verbal reports (such as statements about degree of anger or anxiety), behavior (helping or not; getting an inoculation or not), or physiological measures (heart rate, sweating, stress measures such as cortisol level).

The great power of experiments comes from the fact that participants are allotted their positions on the independent variable by **random assignment**. This means that participants are as likely to be assigned to one condition as to another and that, on average, except for the manipulation of the independent variable, there should be no differences across experimental groups. This serves to rule out the possibility of selection biases in samples (which we referred to earlier). Also critical to experiments is a carefully crafted **control condition**, which is comparable to the experimental condition in every way except that it lacks the one ingredient that is hypothesized to produce the expected effect on the dependent measure. For example, it is possible to expose a group of young children to violent TV for a couple of hours while exposing a control group to innocuous programs that are emotionally vivid but not violent and see whether the "violent TV" group behaves in a more violent fashion subsequently. They do indeed, which buttresses the hypothesis that violent TV leads to violence in later life (see Chapter 13). In the Darley and Batson study, the seminary students were randomly assigned to be either in the "late" condition or the control condition. This ensured that participants in the two conditions were, on average, the same kind of people and that something having to do with being late is what caused such a large proportion of seminarians in the "late" condition to fail to help the apparent victim.

Experimental research can sometimes answer the causality questions that are left unclear by purely correlational research. This is not always true, though. We wouldn't want to assign 10-year-old children to watch lots of violent TV over a long period of time. It wouldn't be possible and certainly wouldn't be ethical. And we couldn't randomly assign some people to be married and others to remain single. However, it is possible to take advantage of **natural experiments**, in which events occur that the

Longitudinal Studies Three participants in the *UP* series of documentary films by Michael Apted. The films are an ongoing longitudinal study that has traced the development of 14 British people from various socioeconomic backgrounds since 1964.

independent variable In experimental research, the variable that is manipulated and that is hypothesized to be the cause of a particular outcome.

dependent variable In experimental research, the variable that is measured (as opposed to manipulated) and that is hypothesized to be affected by manipulation of the independent variable.

random assignment Assigning participants in experimental research to different groups randomly, such that they are as likely to be assigned to one condition as to another.

control condition A condition comparable to the experimental condition in every way except that it lacks the one ingredient hypothesized to produce the expected effect on the dependent variable.

natural experiments Naturally occurring events or phenomena having somewhat different conditions that can be compared with almost as much rigor as in experiments where the investigator manipulates the conditions.

BOX 2.2 **FOCUS ON SCIENTIFIC METHOD**

Thinking about Correlations

Determine the nature of the correlation for each of the situations below. (See p. 55 for answers.)

1. *Time* magazine (June 23, 2008, p. 102) reported that if parents try to control the portions that their children eat, this can cause them to become overweight. If the parents of overweight children stop controlling their portions, will the children get thinner?

2. Countries with higher average IQs have higher average wealth measured as gross domestic product (GDP). Does being smarter make a country richer?

3. People who attend church have lower mortality rates than those who do not (Schnall et al., 2008). Does this mean that religion makes people live longer?

4. People who have a dog are less likely to be depressed. If you give a dog to a depressed person, will the person get happier?

5. States with abstinence-only sex education have higher homicide rates. Does abstinence-only sex education cause aggression? If you give more informative sex education to students in those states, will the homicide rate go down?

6. Intelligent men have better sperm—more sperm and more mobile sperm (Arden, Gottfredson, Miller, & Pierce, 2008). Does this suggest that attending college, which improves intelligence, would also improve sperm quality?

7. People who smoke marijuana are subsequently more likely to use cocaine than people who do not smoke marijuana. Does marijuana use cause cocaine use?

---

investigator assumes has causal implications for some outcome. For example, we might measure people's happiness before and after they get married. And indeed, it turns out that people are happier after marriage than they were before (Argyle, 1999). This is scarcely decisive, but it strongly suggests that married people are happier *because* they are married—rather than being married because they are cheerful. When television was first introduced in the United States, it was not broadcast to all communities across the country. Some communities had TV and others didn't. And whether or not a community received television was not determined by self-selection. This natural experiment therefore allowed investigators to draw relatively strong conclusions about the impact of television on people's habits and opinions.

In this book, you will see many illustrations of the different types of inferences that can be drawn from correlational and experimental studies as well as some of the clever ways that social psychologists have managed to circumvent the problems characteristic of correlational research.

Recall the finding that Southerners are more likely to commit homicide in situations where there has been an insult, and recall the finding that Southerners are more likely to believe that violence is an appropriate response to an insult. Both of these findings are correlational: Southernness is associated with insult-related homicides, and Southernness is associated with the belief that violence is an appropriate response to an insult. But the correlations do not tell us that Southerners actually react more aggressively to an insult. It might just be that Southerners have more access to guns and are more likely to commit homicide for that reason. It might also be that Southerners express the view that violence is a reasonable response to an insult because they are poorer than Northerners in general and poorer people are more likely to endorse violence. Both are true, incidentally: Southerners are poorer on average than Northerners, and poorer people are more likely to endorse violence in response to an insult. But it might be the case that nothing about Southernness per se causes more violent responses to insults.

"Science walks forward on two feet, namely theory and experiment. Sometimes it is one foot which is put forward first, sometimes the other, but continuous progress is only made by the use of both . . ."

—Robert Millikan, Nobel Prize in Physics, 1946

To find out whether insults really do bring violence to the fore for Southerners more than for Northerners, and that it is the region of the country that is important rather than just social class, Dov Cohen and his colleagues performed a series of experiments (Cohen, Nisbett, Bowdle, & Schwarz, 1996). The participants in their studies were all middle-class students at the University of Michigan, some of whom were Southerners and some of whom were Northerners. They were asked to participate in a study on the effects of time constraints on judgments of various kinds. After filling out a questionnaire, they were asked to take it down a long, narrow hallway lined with filing cabinets and leave it on a table at the end. For some participants, a nasty surprise awaited near the end of the hallway. Another student stood in the hallway with a drawer pulled out. For the participant to pass by, it was necessary for the student to push the file drawer in and move out of the way. Then, moments later when the participant started back down the hall, the student had to get out of the participant's way again. This time the student slammed the file drawer shut, pushed into the participant's shoulder, and said, "asshole." (He then quickly exited behind a door labeled "Photo Lab" to avoid a physical confrontation. One participant actually ran after the student and rattled the door knob trying to get at him. Would you care to guess the region of the country that participant was from? See **Figure 2.4**.) Subjects in a control condition simply left the questionnaire on the table without incident.

There were several dependent variables that were examined after the insult either took place or didn't. First, observers were stationed in such a way that they could see the participant immediately after he was insulted. Insulted Southerners usually showed a flash of anger; insulted Northerners were more likely to shrug their shoulders or to appear amused. Second, participants were asked to read a story in which a man made a pass at another man's fiancée. Participants were asked to provide an ending for the story. Southerners who had been insulted were much more likely to provide a violent ending to the story than were Southerners who had not been insulted, whereas the endings provided by Northerners were unaffected by the insult. Third,

---

FIGURE 2.4 Scientific Method: Honor Experiments

Hypothesis: Members of a culture of honor, such as U.S. Southerners, will respond with more anger and aggression when insulted than will other people such as U.S. Northerners.

Research Method:

1. Participants were asked to fill out a questionnaire and take it down a long, narrow hallway lined with filing cabinets and leave it on a table at the end.

2. Some participants had to pass another student in the hall with a drawer pulled out. This student would have to close the drawer and move out of the way each time the participant passed. When the participant passed the student for the second time, the student slammed the file drawer shut, pushed into the participant's shoulder, and said, "asshole."

Results: Insulted Southerners responded with more facial and bodily expressions of anger when insulted than did Northerners and their testosterone level increased, whereas that of Northerners did not.

Conclusion: Southerners do indeed experience more anger when insulted and are more biologically prepared for aggression.

Source: Cohen, Nisbett, Bowdle, & Schwarz (1996).

Possible Answers to Questions about Correlations (See Box 2.2 on p. 54.)

1. It could be that parents try to control the portions that children eat if they are overweight. If so, the direction of causation runs opposite from *Time* magazine's hypothesis. It could also be the case that less happy, more stressful families have more controlling parents and more overweight children, but there is no causal connection between the two.

2. It could be that richer countries have better education systems and hence produce people who get higher IQ scores. In that case, it's wealth that causes intelligence rather than the other way around. It's also possible that some third factor, like physical health, influences both variables.

3. It could be that healthier people engage in more social activities of all kinds, including going to church. If the so, the direction of causation runs opposite of the one implied. Or it could be that good social adjustment causes people both to engage in more social activities and to be healthier.

4. It could be that people who are depressed are less likely to do anything fun, like buying a pet. If so, the direction of causation is opposite to the one implied. (But in fact, giving a pet to a depressed person does improve the person's mood.)

5. It could be that states that are poorer are more likely to have higher homicide rates and states that are poorer are more likely to have abstinence-only sex education. Indeed, both are true. So there may be no causal connection at all between sex education and homicide. Rather, poverty or something associated with it may be causally linked to both.

6. It could be that greater physical health helps people to be smarter and helps sperm to be of better quality. Or some factor could be associated with both intelligence and sperm quality, such as drug or alcohol use. So there might be no causal connection between intelligence and sperm quality.

7. It could be that people who take any kind of drug are more sensation seeking than other people and therefore engage in many kinds of stimulating behavior that are against the law. Smoking marijuana may not cause cocaine use and cocaine use may not cause marijuana use. Rather, some third factor may influence both.

the participants' level of testosterone, which mediates aggression in males, was tested both before and after the insult. The level of testosterone increased for Southerners who had been insulted but not for Southerners who had not been insulted nor for Northerners, whether insulted or not. Fourth, as the participant walked back down the narrow hallway, another assistant to the experimenter walked toward him. This assistant was 6 feet 3 inches tall and weighed 250 pounds, and his instructions were to walk down the middle of the hall, forcing the participant to dodge out of his way. The dependent measure was how far away the participant was when he finally swerved out of the assistant's way. The investigators thought that the insulted Southerners would be put into such an aggressive mood that they would play "chicken" with the assistant, waiting till the last moment to swerve aside. And this is what happened. Northerners, whether insulted or not, swerved aside at a distance of about 5 feet from the assistant. Southerners, who have long been known for their politeness, stood aside at 9 feet if not insulted, but bulled ahead until 3 feet away if insulted.

The experiment by Cohen and colleagues is not an experiment in the full sense. Only one of the independent variables was created by random assignment, namely, whether the participant was insulted or not. The other independent variable was status as a Southerner or Northerner. Thus, technically, the Cohen study is correlational. The basic finding is that something about Southernness predisposes college men to respond with aggression to insults. The study can't tell us what the causally relevant aspect of Southernness is.

 We have seen that social psychologists study phenomena by observational methods (though usually this is to get an intuitive understanding with a view toward applying other methods), archival research involving records of various kinds, and surveys in which people are asked questions. It is usually essential to the validity of surveys that respondents be randomly sampled from the population they represent. Correlational research, in which the investigator establishes whether there is a relationship between two variables, suffers from the problem of self-selection: the individuals being studied have "chosen" their level on each variable rather than being assigned a level by the investigator. Experimental research manipulates an independent variable and observes the effects of the manipulation on a dependent variable.

SOME OTHER USEFUL CONCEPTS FOR UNDERSTANDING RESEARCH

To round out our discussion of research methods, we next present several concepts that are particularly relevant to social psychology experiments—namely, types of validity (and invalidity) in experiments, as well as types of reliability and validity that are relevant to the scientific method in all the behavioral sciences, that is, reliability and validity of measurement and the concept of statistical significance.

External Validity in Experiments

We've pointed out the weaknesses in correlational studies, but there are weaknesses in experimental studies as well. Sometimes experiments are a bit sterile and so removed from everyday life that it can be hard to know how to interpret them (Aronson, Ellsworth, Carlsmith, & Gonzalez, 1990). When we don't know how to generalize the results obtained in an experiment to real-life situations, we say we have poor **external validity**. Experiments have poor external validity when the basic situation the participants are put into bears little resemblance to any real-life situation. The Milgram study of obedience discussed in Chapters 1 and 9 has poor external validity inasmuch as most people in our society are almost never placed in a situation in which they are being commanded by an authority figure to harm another person. On the other hand, such things have happened in the world and will happen again.

Poor external validity is not always fatal; in fact, investigators sometimes deliberately strip down a situation to its bare essentials to make a theoretical point that would be hard to make with real-world materials. For example, to find out how much familiarity with a stimulus affects its attractiveness, Robert Zajonc and his colleagues presented Turkish words to Americans over a headset, presenting some of them many times and some of them only a few times. The experiment has poor external validity in that the situation is not like one ever encountered in real life. On the other hand, the simplicity of the situation and the complete initial unfamiliarity of the Turkish words make it possible to be sure that it is the sheer number of repetitions of the words that affects their attractiveness and not something else about the stimuli, such as how much they were liked beforehand. When the purpose of the research is to generalize the results of an experiment directly to the outside world, external validity is critical. But when the purpose of the research is to clarify a general idea or theory, such as in the Zajonc experiments on familiarity, external validity is not essential.

One of the best ways to ensure the external validity of an experiment is to do a **field experiment**. These resemble laboratory experiments conceptually, but they take place in the real world, usually under circumstances in which the participants are not aware that they are participating in a study. An example would be an experiment in which researchers study the reactions of people who are asked to give up their seats on an uncrowded bus or train.

We also described a field experiment at the very beginning of this chapter. Cohen and Nisbett (1997) examined Southern and Northern merchants' reactions to a letter allegedly written by a man applying for a job at a restaurant, motel, or retail outlet. There were actually two versions of the letter. In both versions, the writer described himself as being a high school graduate in his late 20s who was applying for a job as an assistant manager. In a paragraph near the end, he stated that he had to confess that he had been convicted of a felony. The felony in question was either a motor vehicle theft or a homicide in the context of a love triangle (which is the version you read). The dependent variable was the degree of responsiveness to the applicant's letter, ranging from no response at all to sending an encouraging letter and an application form. Southern businesses were much more encouraging of the man convicted of homicide than were Northern businesses. The experiment provides, in a field setting, evidence that Southern norms concerning violence in response to an insult are more accepting than Northern norms. We know that it isn't just that Southerners are more forgiving of crimes generally because there was no difference in the reactions of Southerners and Northerners to the letter that mentioned a theft. Thus, the theft letter constitutes a control condition in this field experiment.

Internal Validity in Experiments

Whatever use we want to make of an experiment, **internal validity** is essential. Internal validity is achieved when we know that it is the manipulated variable only that could have produced the results. The experimental situation is held constant in all other respects, and participants in the various experimental conditions don't differ on average in any respect before they come to the laboratory. In the Cohen insult experiment, if insulted

external validity An experimental setup that closely resembles real-life situations so that results can safely be generalized to such situations.

field experiment An experiment set up in the real world, usually with participants who are not aware that they are in a study of any kind.

internal validity In experimental research, confidence that it is the manipulated variable only that could have produced the results.

Southerners had differed from noninsulted Southerners in some additional way, then we couldn't conclude that it was the insult that caused the different behavior. It could have been something associated with the difference between the two groups before they ever arrived at the lab. Fortunately, there is an easy way to rule out such a possibility. This is achieved by random assignment of participants to experimental conditions, which can be done by flipping a coin to determine what condition the participant will be in or by consulting a random number table and assigning the participant to the experimental condition if the next number is odd and to the control condition if the next number is even. When this is done, we can be reasonably sure that the participants in one condition are not different, on average, from the participants in the other conditions. They will have the same average height, the same average degree of extraversion, the same attitudes (on average) toward capital punishment, and so on.

Internal validity also requires that the experimental setup seem realistic and plausible to participants. If it is implausible, if participants don't believe what the experimenter tells them, or if participants don't understand something crucial that is said to them, then internal validity is lacking and we can have no confidence in the results. In such cases, participants weren't responding to the independent variable as conceptualized by the experimenter but to something else entirely. Experimenters can help ensure that they pass the various criteria of internal validity by **debriefing** participants in preliminary versions of the experiment—that is, by asking them straightforwardly if they had understood the instructions, found the setup to be reasonable, and so forth. Pilot study participants are generally told the purpose of the experiment and what the experimenters expected to find. Pilot participants can often provide useful information about how well the experiment is designed when they are brought in as consultants, so to speak, in the debriefing. Debriefing participants is also routine even once the experimental setup is finalized. This is done for the purpose of education— to let the participants know what questions were being studied, how the experiment speaks to those questions, and why the results might have social value.

debriefing In preliminary versions of an experiment, asking participants straightforwardly if they understood the instructions, found the setup to be reasonable, and so forth. In later versions, debriefings are used to educate participants about the questions being studied.

Reliability and Validity of Tests and Measures

Reliability concerns the degree to which the particular way we measure a given variable—for example, intelligence or ratings of a person's charisma—is likely to yield consistent results. If you take an IQ test twice, do you get roughly the same score? Do two observers agree in their ratings of the charisma of world leaders or fellow fraternity members? Reliability is typically measured by correlations between 0 and 1. As a rule of thumb, ability tests are expected to have reliability correlations of about .8. Personality tests, such as measures of introversion, are expected to have that level of correlation or a little lower. People's degree of agreement about the kindness or charisma of another person would be expected to show a correlation of at least .5.

reliability The degree to which the particular way we measure a given variable is likely to yield consistent results.

Measurement validity refers to the correlation between some measure and some outcome that the measure is supposed to predict. For example, IQ test validity is measured by correlating IQ scores with grades in school and with performance in jobs. Such validity coefficients, as they are called, typically do not exceed .5. It is rare for personality tests to correlate with behavior in a given situation better than about .3. This is surprising to most people. They expect that a measure of extraversion or aggression should predict quite well a person's behavior at a party or a hockey game.

measurement validity The correlation between some measure and some outcome that the measure is supposed to predict.

Statistical Significance

When we have an empirical result such as the finding that there is a correlation between two variables or the finding that some independent variable affects a dependent variable in an experiment, we can test the **statistical significance** of the relationship. A finding has statistical significance if the probability of obtaining the finding by chance is less than some quantity. By convention, this quantity is usually set at 1 in 20, or .05, but probabilities can of course go much lower than that, sometimes by orders of magnitude. Statistical significance is primarily due to (1) the size of the difference between groups in an experiment or the size of a relationship between variables in a correlational study and (2) the number of cases the finding is based on. The bigger the difference or relationship and the larger the number of cases, the greater the statistical significance. We will not mention the concept of statistical significance again because all of the findings we report in this book are statistically significant (though not all are based on large effects).

 We have seen that external validity refers to the extent to which an experimental setup resembles what we find in the real world. Internal validity refers to the extent to which we know that it is only the manipulated variable that could have produced the results. Reliability of measures refers to the degree to which different instruments or the same instrument at different times produce the same values for a given variable. Measurement validity refers to the extent to which a measure predicts outcomes that it is supposed to measure.

BASIC AND APPLIED RESEARCH

Science is of two broad types: basic science and applied science. **Basic science** isn't concerned with any particular real-world problem, but with trying to understand some phenomenon in its own right, with a view toward using that understanding to build valid theories about the nature of some aspect of the world. **Applied science** is concerned with solving some real-world problem of importance. Social psychologists who study the obedience of people to an authority figure in the laboratory are doing basic science—trying to understand the nature of obedience and the factors that influence it. They are not trying to find ways to make people less obedient to dubious authorities, which would be applied research, though they may hope that their research is relevant to such real-world problems. Social psychologists who study the effect of being in a hurry on helping another person are interested in how situational factors affect people's behavior. They may also be interested in comparing the power of a particular situation with some other variable, such as a personality trait that is thought to influence the behavior in question. They are not trying to find ways to make people more inclined to help people in need, though they may hope that their research would be relevant to such a goal.

Applied research in social psychology is concerned with solving particular social problems. For example, some social psychologists study how they can make preteens less susceptible to cigarette advertising. (One way is to make them aware of the motives of tobacco companies and of their cynical desire to make chumps of kids by getting them to do something that is not in their best interest.) And other social psychologists try to convince people to use condoms to prevent the spread of sexually transmitted diseases (STDs). (One way is to have characters in soap operas talk about the use of condoms—a form of product placement, as it's known in the advertising industry (Bandura, 2004).

There is a two-way relationship between basic and applied research. Basic research can give rise to theories that are the basis of **interventions**, or efforts to change

statistical significance A measure of the probability that a given result could have occurred by chance.

basic science Science concerned with trying to understand some phenomenon in its own right, with a view toward using that understanding to build valid theories about the nature of some aspect of the world.

applied science Science concerned with solving some real-world problem of importance.

interventions Efforts to change people's behavior.

people's behavior. This happens fairly often. For example, social psychologist Carol Dweck found that some people believe that intelligence is a matter of hard work (Dweck, Chiu, & Hong, 1995). In Dweck's terms, such people are "incrementalists." Incrementalists work harder in school and get better grades than people who believe that intelligence is a matter of genes. In Dweck's terms, the latter hold "entity theories"; they believe that intelligence is an entity that you either have a lot of or a little of and isn't much influenced by anything you might do to change it. Her basic research on the nature of beliefs about intelligence and their relationship to work in school prompted her to design an intervention with minority junior high students. She told some of them that their intelligence was under their control and gave them information about how working on school subjects actually changes the physical nature of the brain (Blackwell, Trzesniewski, & Dweck, 2007; Henderson & Dweck, 1990). Such students worked harder and got better grades than did students who were not given such information. Joshua Aronson and his colleagues have obtained similar results (Aronson, Fried, & Good, 2002; Good, Aronson, & Inzlicht, 2003).

The direction of influence can also go the other way: Applied research can produce results that feed back into basic science. For example, the applied research during World War II on how to produce effective propaganda led to an extensive program of basic research on attitude change. That program in turn gave rise to theories of attitude change and social influence that continue to inform basic science and to generate new techniques of changing attitudes in applied, real-world contexts.

Applied Research Tobacco companies spend a lot of money on advertising to encourage people to buy their cigarettes. Social psychologists can study how to counter that effect, as this public service advertisement by the California Department of Health Services is trying to do.

 LOOKING BACK We have seen that basic science attempts to discover fundamental prinicples; applied science attempts to solve real-world problems. But there is an intimate relationship between the two: basic science can show the way to solve real-world problems, and science solving real-world problems can give rise to the search for basic principles that explain why the solutions work.

ETHICAL CONCERNS IN SOCIAL PSYCHOLOGY

Whether you would want to conduct research geared to changing people's attitudes about some issue would depend on whether you think the direction of change is for the better. You wouldn't care to support, or even to allow, research that might have the effect of encouraging people to take LSD. Research conducted at universities has to go before an **institutional review board (IRB)**, which examines research proposals and makes judgments about the ethical appropriateness of the research. Such boards must include at least one scientist, one nonscientist, and one person who is not affiliated with the institution. If some aspect of the study procedures is deemed overly harmful, that procedure must be changed before the research can be approved.

The key to the previous sentence is the word *overly*. Research may be allowed even if it does make people uncomfortable or embarrassed or cause physical pain, so long as the research is deemed sufficiently likely to yield scientific information of significant value and the discomfort or harm to the participants is not too great. For example, although it was conducted before IRBs came into existence, Milgram's research on

institutional review board (IRB) A university committee that examines research proposals and makes judgments about the ethical appropriateness of the research.

obedience would be sure to get a thorough examination by an IRB, and it's not clear that it would be approved today. There is no question that some participants were made to be uncomfortable in the extreme; their psychological distress was manifest to observers. On the other hand, many (if not most) people would consider the knowledge gain to be enormous. It's not possible to think about Nazi Germany in the same way after knowing the results of the Milgram studies. Nor can we think the same way about the behavior of the American soldiers involved in torturing Iraqi prisoners once we know about the studies. Social planners can no longer blithely assume that ordinary, decent people would refuse to obey commands that are patently harmful. Different IRBs would undoubtedly reach different conclusions about the admissibility of the Milgram experiments today. What do you think? Would you permit research like that to be conducted?

In medical research, which is also governed by IRBs, there is a principle that governs acceptability of research called **informed consent**. Even if a given procedure is not known to be beneficial—indeed, even if there is a possibility that it will be less beneficial than other procedures or actually harmful in the short term—IRBs will allow the research to be conducted if the knowledge gain relative to the risk is deemed great enough. But participants must give their informed consent, which is their willingness to participate in light of their knowledge about all relevant aspects of the procedure. This same practice is followed for most psychological research.

But for some research—namely, **deception research**—informed consent is not possible. It would not have been possible for John Darley and his colleagues to have told their seminary participants that they were doing a study on the effects of being in a hurry on the likelihood of helping someone in apparent need, that the reason given for the hurry was bogus, and that the apparent victim was actually a stooge for the experimenter who was merely playacting. Informed consent would have destroyed the experiment. So exceptions are made for deception research. If there is a good reason to deceive, it will generally be allowed by IRBs. An IRB, for example, gave permission for Cohen and his colleagues to deceive their Southern and Northern participants and even to shove them and call them a dirty name. Some psychologists are made uncomfortable by allowing deception and minor harm to participants. But it is important to know that participants themselves, when asked their opinion about what they were put through, are generally understanding of the reasons for it and often say they learned more, and enjoyed the study more, than subjects who were not deceived or made uncomfortable (Smith & Richardson, 1983). For example, participants in the Cohen et al. study (1996) actually reported that they learned more and enjoyed themselves more if they were in the insult condition than if they were in the control condition.

The debriefing procedure is particularly important when participants have been deceived or made uncomfortable. Experimenters owe them a full accounting of what was done, what aspects of the procedure involved deception, why they were made uncomfortable, what the experiment was intended to examine, and what the potential is for valuable social contributions based on the research.

The concepts discussed in this chapter are vital to the studies described in this book, and it will be useful to keep them in mind. For example, when you read about an experiment, it will be helpful to identify the independent and dependent variables and to think about whether the experiment has good external validity. But most important, we hope you will keep these methods in mind when you read about scientific findings in magazines and newspapers and on the Internet, as well as when you think about reasons for your own behavior or that of others. We can assure you that much science reporting is dubious on methodological grounds. We believe also that understanding these methodological principles is helpful in understanding other people's behavior and in guiding your own.

informed consent Participants' willingness to participate in a procedure or research study after learning all relevant aspects about the procedure or study.

deception research Research in which the participants are misled about the purpose of the research or the meaning of something that is done to them.

We have seen that ethical concerns about research are dealt with by institutional review boards.. For research not involving deception, the procedures and purposes of experiments are explained to potential participants, and their informed consent is requested. Deception and even minor harms to participants are sometimes allowed when the potential gain to knowledge is considered to be great enough.

Summary

Why Do Social Psychologists Do Research (and Why Should You Want to Read about It)?

- Social psychological research teaches us how to interpret and predict the outcomes of various social experiences and helps us to understand our own behavior and that of others. It also helps us to understand the reasons for rare events and historical occurrences.

How Do Social Psychologists Test Ideas?

- Social psychologists often use participant observation, in which they place themselves in real situations to understand some social phenomenon better and to help them plan research that will test the hypotheses developed in observational settings.

- Social psychologists go to archives of various kinds to find information that helps them understand social phenomena. Such records include census reports, police reports, newspaper accounts, and historical and ethnographic records.

- Surveys ask people questions. Random assignment is essential for describing accurately the attitudes or behavior of people of a particular population: students at X university, the people of town Y, or the population of a country as a whole.

- Correlational research describes relationships between variables—for example, between age and support for welfare reform. Correlations can vary in strength from −1 to +1.

- Self-selection is a particular problem in correlational research, where the investigator is unable to choose the level of any variable for participants. Consequently, it's impossible to know if something associated with one of the measured variables is causing the correlation between two variables or if one of the variables is causing the other. *Confound*

- In experimental research, the investigator manipulates different levels of the independent variable (the variable about which a prediction is made) and measures the effect of different levels on the dependent variable.

Some Other Useful Concepts for Understanding Research

- External validity refers to the degree to which the experimental setup resembles real-life situations. The greater the external validity, the more it is possible to generalize from the results obtained to real-life settings.

- Field experiments test hypotheses experimentally in real-life situations as opposed to the laboratory. Field experiments automatically have external validity.

- Internal validity refers to whether the experimenter can be confident that it is the manipulated variable only that accounts for the results rather than some extraneous factor, such as participants' failure to understand instructions.

- Participants in studies are normally debriefed; that is, the purpose of the experiment and the likely knowledge gain are communicated to them.

- Reliability refers to the extent to which participants receive the same score when tested with a conceptually similar instrument or when tested at different times.

- Measurement validity refers to the degree to which some measure predicts what it is supposed to, such as the degree to which an IQ test predicts school grades.

Basic and Applied Research

- Basic research is intended to test theory. Applied research is intended to solve some real-world problem.

Ethical Concerns in Social Psychology

- Institutional review boards are committees set up to review research procedures to make sure that participants' privacy and safety are protected.

- Informed consent refers to the willingness of participants to take part in a study based on information presented to them before the study begins, informing them of the procedures they will undergo and any possible risks. Informed consent is not always possible, as when an experiment involves deception, where participants are misled about the purposes of a study.

Key Terms

applied science (p. 59)
basic science (p. 59)
control condition (p. 53)
correlational research (p. 50)
debriefing (p. 58)
deception research (p. 61)
dependent variable (p. 53)
experimental research (p. 50)

external validity (p. 57)
field experiment (p. 57)
hindsight bias (p. 45)
independent variable (p. 53)
informed consent (p. 61)
institutional review board (IRB)
   (p. 60)
internal validity (p. 57)

interventions (p. 59)
longitudinal study (p. 52)
measurement validity (p. 58)
natural experiments (p. 53)
random assignment (p. 53)
reliability (p. 58)
self-selection (p. 52)
statistical significance (p. 59)

Further Reading

Aronson, E., Ellsworth, P. C., Carlsmith, J. M., & Gonzales, M. H. (1990). *Methods of research In social psychology* (2nd ed.). New York: McGraw-Hill. An excellent source of information about how to conduct research in social psychology.

Gilbert, D. T., Fiske, S. T., & Lindzey, G. (1998). *The handbook of social psychology* (4th ed., Vols. 1 and 2, part 2). New York: Oxford University Press. Advanced treatment of methods of research in social psychology.

Ⓢ Online Study Tools

StudySpace

Go to StudySpace, wwnorton.com/studyspace, to access additional review and enrichment materials, including the following resources for each chapter:

Organize

- Study Plan
- Chapter Outline
- Quiz+ Assessment

Learn

- Ebook
- Chapter Review
- Critical-Thinking Questions
- Visual Quizzes
- Vocabulary Flashcards

Connect

- Apply It! Exercises
- Author Insights Podcasts
- Social Psychology in the News

The Individual in the Social World

In Part Two, we examine essential psychological processes that take place inside each of us as we try to get along effectively in the social world. Chapter 3 starts with the fact all social groups consist of individuals and explores the nature of the individual "self." Although the self might seem to be an element of social psychology that stands apart from other people, social psychologists have discovered that it is something that is created and sustained in our interactions with others. We thus explore many of the causes and consequences of the fundamentally social nature of the self. To be effective in the social world, each of us must be able to anticipate and understand the behavior of others. Chapter 4 therefore examines how we make inferences about what others are like and what caused their behavior. Whether a smile is seen as friendly or manipulative has considerable impact on how it makes us feel and how we act toward a person, and we explore how such judgments are made. In Chapter 5, we examine judgment more broadly. How do people understand others, comprehend the past, and predict the future? In pursuing these questions, we also discuss some of the most common sources of error in people's judgments. In Chapter 6, we discuss how our thoughts and judgments influence our behavior and how, in turn, our behavior influences our thoughts and feelings. Much of the chapter is devoted to examining the pressures we feel to make sure our thoughts, attitudes, and actions are aligned; the chapter further explores how these pressures give rise to the rationalization and justification of what we've done and of the broader social entities of which we are a part. We end Part Two with Chapter 7, an examination of the nature of emotions and the important role they play in regulating social behavior.

The Social Self

On February 4, 1974, 19-year-old Patricia Hearst was enjoying a quiet evening in her Berkeley, California, apartment when there was a knock on the door. When she went to answer, three members of the Symbionese Liberation Army (SLA), a self-styled revolutionary vanguard group, pushed their way in. The three beat up Patricia's fiancé, Steven Weed, and bound, blindfolded, and gagged Ms. Hearst before forcing her into the trunk of a car. The long and strange tale of the kidnapping of Patty Hearst had begun.

Days later, a tape was delivered to a local radio station demanding that Patty's father, Randolph Hearst, son of newspaper magnate William Randolph Hearst (the inspiration for the film classic *Citizen Kane*), distribute millions of dollars of food to the needy throughout the Bay Area. Hearst eventually complied, but his daughter was not released. Instead, two months after her kidnapping, a second tape was released in which Patty stated that she had joined the SLA and fully and freely embraced their cause of helping "all oppressed people." She took on the *nom de guerre* Tania, after Che Guevara's revolutionary comrade, and stated that she would "never choose to live the rest of my life surrounded by pigs like the Hearsts."

On April 15, she was videotaped wielding an M1 rifle while she and her revolutionary comrades robbed a branch of the Hibernia Bank in San Francisco. Although two passersby were shot and killed, the robbery was successful. One month later, Patty was waiting outside in a car while two fellow SLA members entered Mel's Sporting Goods store in Los Angeles to steal some ammunition. When a tussle broke out in the parking lot between the SLA members and store employees who had witnessed the shoplifting, Patty fired 32 shots from her rifle, spraying the façade of the store and a concrete divider in the middle of the road.

After this event, the heat on the SLA intensified and nothing was heard from Patty until 17 months later, when she was arrested in an apartment she was renting in San Francisco. Her trial, predictably, was a battle between the defense's

The Nature of the Self Patty Hearst came from a wealthy family and was quite conventional until kidnapped by a radical group. With them she seemed to transform into a gun-wielding radical. Now, over 35 years later, she's a contented mother of two. Who is the real Patricia Hearst?

"A man has as many social selves as there are individuals who recognize him. As many different social selves as there are distinct groups about whose opinions he cares."

—William James

claim that she was an innocent victim of a violent kidnapping who had been brainwashed to act as she did and the prosecution's claim that she had had numerous opportunities to escape and neglected to do so and that she genuinely took up the cause of the SLA. The jury sided with the prosecution, finding Patty guilty of bank robbery. She was sentenced to 35 years in prison, but her sentence was commuted by President Jimmy Carter after she had served 22 months, and she was granted a full pardon by President Bill Clinton in 2001. After her release from prison, she married her former bodyguard, Bernard Shaw, with whom she has two children.

The saga of Patty Hearst raises important questions about the nature of the self. Was she a different person as the gun-toting Tania than she was before, or is it more accurate to say that different sides of her were brought out by the kidnapping and her life with the SLA? Could she really "go back" to her old self after this long and trying ordeal? Do we have one Patricia Hearst here or two? Or three?

To even attempt to answer questions such as these, we must understand the nature of the self, the subject of this chapter. As you will see, although the self can seem like the most individual, basic, and set-apart element of social life, it is a social entity through and through. And that is why we titled this chapter "The *Social* Self." Our sense of who we are is forged in our interactions with others, shaping, in turn, how we interact with others and influence *their* sense of *them*selves.

To explore the self and understand its inextricable links to social life, we will focus on four approaches that psychologists have taken on the nature of the self. First, we will explore the nature and origins of the social self by examining how the social self is shaped by evolutionary processes, culture, current situations, and construal processes. Second, we will examine the nature of self-knowledge and how it provides coherence and order to our perception of other people's behavior and guidance for our own. We will see that self-conceptions vary dramatically from one culture to another. Third, we will take a look at self-evaluation—our assessments of our virtues and flaws. We will focus in particular on self-esteem—the value we place on ourselves—and what affects self-esteem, how it varies across different cultures, and what the risks are of having too much self-esteem. Finally, we will discuss the social self as the "director" of a dramatic performance. This notion will guide the last section of this chapter, which focuses on self-presentation and the different facets of the social self that are realized in the drama of social life.

NATURE OF THE SOCIAL SELF

The search for our sense of self is one of life's great quests. Socrates urged his fellow Athenians to examine the self, to find its essential and distinctive characteristics. Buddhist thought counsels us to transcend the material graspings of the self and its desires, illusions, and frustrations. Where do you think *your* core self comes from? A social psychological answer relies on the time-honored ideas of the field: your social self is shaped by evolved traits and family dynamics, your culture of origin, your current situation, and the way you construe your behavior in relation to that of other people.

Evolution of the Social Self

When you wrote your essay for your college application, you probably mentioned certain traits that characterize who you are. Your **traits** are the characteristic ways that you think, feel, and act that mark you as different from others. Perhaps you said that you're often contemplative, sensitive, and shy. You probably also mentioned the particulars of your family—your mother and father, your relationship with your siblings—and how your family shaped who you are. Our traits and family background are critical components of who we are, and our understanding of each can be advanced by taking an evolutionary approach to the social self.

traits Consistent ways that people think, feel, and act across classes of situations.

Biological Dispositions According to the **five-factor model** of personality, five traits lie at the core of the social self (Costa & McCrae, 1995; John, 1990; John & Srivastava, 1999; John, Naumann, & Soto, 2008). **Table 3.1** presents descriptors of these traits—the Big Five—which go by the helpful acronym OCEAN. People who are *open to experience* are imaginative, curious, and artistic. They tend to score high on creativity tests and get advanced degrees, and they are less likely to endorse conservative political attitudes. Highly *conscientious* people are efficient, achievement oriented, and organized; not surprisingly, they achieve higher GPAs, and they are less likely to suffer poor health from smoking or poor diets. *Extraverts* are the proverbial social butterflies—sociable, energetic, and enthusiastic. Their social relationships reflect this disposition: extraverts tend to enjoy high status in groups and have many friends and acquaintances. *Agreeable* people are warm, friendly, and kind. They fare

five-factor model Five personality traits (openness, conscientiousness, extraversion, agreeableness, and neuroticism) that psychologists believe are the basic building blocks of personality.

TABLE 3.1 Descriptors of the Five-Factor Model of Personality

Five traits are believed to lie at the core of self-definitions. The five-factor model of personality is based on whether people are high or low on each of these "Big Five" personality traits.

Trait	High	Low
Openness to experience	Wide interests, imaginative, intelligent	Narrow interests, simple, commonplace
Conscientiousness	Organized, thorough, planful	Careless, disorderly, irresponsible
Extraversion	Sociable, assertive, active	Reserved, shy, withdrawn
Agreeableness	Sympathetic, appreciative, affectionate	Cold, unfriendly, quarrelsome
Neuroticism	Tense, anxious, moody	Stable, calm, unemotional

well in work groups and in their cardiovascular health. And *neurotic* people are anxious, tense, and emotionally volatile. Neurotic individuals often enjoy less satisfaction in their intimate relations and often struggle with burnout in their work.

From an evolutionary perspective, these five traits are thought of as strategies that enable the individual to adapt to the social environment and enhance the chances of survival and reproductive success (Buss, 1989). Extraversion, for example, enables people to connect with others and rise in status, as we point out in Chapter 11. Agreeableness, by contrast, is a disposition that enables us to care for others—a capacity with many obvious evolutionary benefits. Even neuroticism can confer evolutionary benefits—a fight-or-flight vigilance to threat and danger.

Several lines of evidence lend further credence to the notion that these traits have been shaped by evolution. First, like many evolved adaptations, these five traits are *universal*. When researchers have asked people in various countries—including China, the Philippines, Japan, Germany, and Spain, for example—to describe themselves and other people in their own language, they do so with terms related to these five traits (John & Srivastava, 1999). Indeed, these trait dimensions are even more universal than that: animals of many other species, especially primates, appear to differ from one another in their degree of extraversion and neuroticism (Gosling, Kwan, & John, 2003).

Additional evidence of the evolutionary origins of the Big Five is that people's levels of openness to experience, conscientiousness, extraversion, agreeableness, and neuroticism are partly *heritable*—that is, these traits are shaped by genetic tendencies that we inherit from our parents (Loehlin, 1992; Plomin & Caspi, 1998). To determine the **heritability** of personality traits—that is, the degree to which they are determined by genes—researchers have assessed the personalities of identical twins

heritability The degree to which traits or physical characteristics are determined by genes and hence inherited from parents.

Heritability in Identical Twins   Identical twins raised apart typically share many basic personality traits and often have in common many unusual habits and interests. Jim Springer (left) and Jim Lewis (right) are identical twins who were adopted into different families when they were 4 weeks old and did not see each other again for 39 years. When they rediscovered each other, they found that they enjoyed the same cigarettes (Salems), beer (Miller Lite), cars (blue Chevrolets), hobbies (woodworking), and interests (stock-car racing). They both stood the same way, held their hands the same way, and suffered from migraine headaches and slightly high blood pressure. Both had built circular benches around trees in their backyards, had had first wives named Linda, second wives named Betty, a son named James (James Alan and James Allan), and a dog named Toy. Moreover, when given personality tests, their scores on measures of tolerance, conformity, flexibility, self-control, and sociability were almost identical.

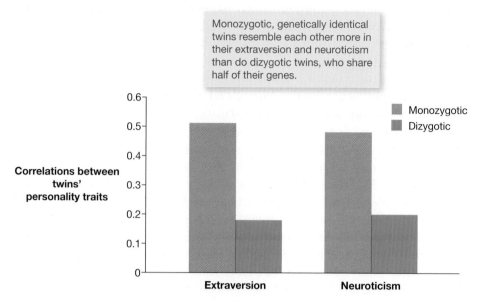

Monozygotic, genetically identical twins resemble each other more in their extraversion and neuroticism than do dizygotic twins, who share half of their genes.

FIGURE 3.1 Heritability of Traits (Source: Adapted from Loehlin, 1992.)

and fraternal twins raised in the same family environment. Identical, or **monozygotic**, twins originate from a single fertilized egg that splits into two exact replicas that then develop into two genetically identical individuals. Fraternal, or **dizygotic**, twins arise when two different eggs in the female reproductive tract are fertilized by different sperm cells. Fraternal twins, like ordinary siblings, share on average half of their genes. Studies consistently find that the personalities of identical twins tend to be more similar than the personalities of fraternal twins (Plomin & Caspi, 1999). For example, Loehlin (1992) found that across 23,000 pairs of twins, monozygotic twins resembled each other more in terms of extraversion and neuroticism than did dizygotic twins (see **Figure 3.1**).

Finally, there are *specific biological processes* associated with each of the Big Five. For example, extraversion is associated with elevated levels of the neurotransmitter dopamine, which promotes approach-related behavior, enthusiasm, and receptiveness to rewards (DePue, 1995). Highly agreeable individuals tend to have higher baseline activation in a bundle of nerves known as the vagus nerve, which calms heart rate, deepens breathing, and stimulates muscles involved in vocalizations and head nods, all of which help people to connect with others (Oveis et al., 2009). And highly neurotic individuals experience chronically higher levels of sympathetic autonomic nervous system activity—increased heart rate, shallow breathing, and sweaty palms, for example—that in part account for their elevated stress and tension (Zuckerman, 1996, 1998).

Evolution, then, has crafted different genetically based traits that shape who we are. Why, then, do people vary in these traits? Why doesn't everyone have the optimal level of each trait? One answer has to do with the particular way that your parents' chromosomes combined to produce variations on the Big Five that in part define who you are. Another answer is a situationist one: there is no overall optimal level of each of these traits. Different levels of certain traits are well suited to different situations, and so individuals who frequently experience those situations will likely develop higher levels of those traits. For example, individuals who encounter high levels of threat and danger in their lives will score higher on neuroticism because of that trait's suitability for that recurrent life circumstance. This thinking in part anticipates how older and younger siblings' personalities differ on the Big Five, as you will now see.

monozygotic (identical) twins Twins who originate from a single fertilized egg that splits into two exact replicas that then develop into two genetically identical individuals.

dizygotic (fraternal) twins Twins who originate from two different eggs fertilized by different sperm cells; like ordinary siblings, they share on average half of their genes.

Family Influence and Sibling Dynamics What do most U.S. presidents, English and Canadian prime ministers, Oprah Winfrey, Bette Davis, and all of the actors who have portrayed James Bond (except Daniel Craig) have in common? What do Virginia Woolf, Ben Franklin, Charles Darwin, Mohandas Gandhi, Vincent Van Gogh, and Madonna have in common? The first group are firstborns. The second are later-borns.

What does birth order have to do with our sense of self? According to Frank Sulloway (1996, 2001), a great deal. Sulloway has looked at sibling dynamics from an evolutionary perspective and arrived at his "born-to-rebel" hypothesis. His theory is as follows. Across species, sibling conflict—particularly when resources are scarce—is frequent, widespread, and on occasion deadly. Sand sharks devour one another prior to birth in the oviducts of the mother until one well-fed young shark emerges. Once a blue-footed booby drops below 80 percent of its body weight, its siblings exclude it from the nest, or worse, peck it to death. Infant hyenas are born with large canine teeth, which they often turn to deadly effect upon their newly born siblings. Even in humans, young siblings engage in frequent conflict, up to one fracas every 5 minutes (Dunn & Munn, 1985), often to the chagrin of parents a bit too tired to mediate yet another struggle. (You may remember long car trips in which the chief entertainment was sibling baiting.)

Humans have evolved adaptations, or solutions, to threats to survival, and one such adaptation involves a means of resolving sibling conflict. According to the principle of **diversification**, siblings develop into quite different people so that they can peacefully occupy different niches within the family environment. Just as different plant species will coexist alongside one another in different areas of a creek-bed ecosystem, siblings diversify by developing different traits, abilities, and preferences, thereby occupying different identities within the family.

So what identities do older and younger siblings take on? Throughout most of development, older siblings are bigger, more powerful, and often act as surrogate parents. They are invested in the status quo, which, not coincidentally, benefits them.

diversification A principle that maintains that siblings develop into quite different people so that they can peacefully occupy different niches within the family environment.

Shared Genes and Environments in Families Genes and environment interact to create dispositions and interests. The Kennedy men were charming, charismatic, competitive, and adventurous (sometimes to the point of foolhardiness). (A) Joe Kennedy Sr. surrounded by sons Joe Jr. (left) and John (right). (B) The next generation of Kennedys also shared good looks, charm, and a competitive streak that led many of them into positions of power. Pictured here is John's son, John F. Kennedy Jr.

Sibling Conflict Sibling conflict is frequent and widespread and based on competition over resources such as food, space, and parental attention. (A) Blue-footed booby chicks fight with each other. (B) A spotted hyena bites its sibling.

("Things were fine until you came along.") In contrast, younger siblings, with the "establishment" niche already occupied by their older sibling, are born to rebel. They develop in ways that make them inclined to challenge the family status quo. In a review of 196 studies of personality and birth order, Sulloway found that older siblings tend to be more assertive and dominant and more achievement oriented and conscientious. This is consistent with their more assertive, powerful role in the family. In contrast, younger siblings tend to be more agreeable, and they are likely to be more open to novel ideas and experiences. This social self emerges as younger siblings learn to coexist with their more dominant older siblings—which accounts for their elevated agreeableness—and as they think of imaginative ways to carve out their own niche in the world—which maps onto their increased openness to experience.

To further test his hypotheses regarding birth order and personality, Sulloway examined the personalities of 3,400 different scientists involved in 28 scientific revolutions. Who do you think would be more open to revolutionary scientific ideas, such as Copernicus's thesis that the earth revolves around the sun or Darwin's theory of evolution, which argues that humans are not designed by God but instead evolved through a gradual process of natural selection? The answer is younger siblings, which is consistent with the personality finding that they are more open to novel ideas. For example, after Darwin published *On the Origin of Species* in 1859, 100 percent of the younger-sibling scientists in Sulloway's sample endorsed the theory, whereas only 50 percent of the older-sibling scientists did. Before you younger siblings start taunting your older kin about their narrow-minded and outdated ideas, however, take note: younger siblings are also more likely, given their openness to experience, to endorse radical but misguided pseudoscientific ideas, such as phrenology, the thoroughly discredited theory of how personality types relate to bumps on the head.

Also consistent with the notion that younger siblings are more open to novel ideas, later-born scientists were more likely than firstborns to excel in numerous scientific disciplines. And younger-sibling scientists were more likely to travel to faraway lands, often risking their own lives, in the pursuit of novel ideas. Charles Darwin is an excellent case study for Sulloway's hypothesis. The fifth of six children, Darwin developed perhaps the most revolutionary scientific theory in human history, one that challenged religious ideas about the creation of life on earth. He excelled in five

Sibling Dynamics First-borns like Prince William (right) are often more responsible and more likely to support the status quo than younger siblings like Prince Harry (left), who often are more mischievous, open to novel experiences, and more likely to rebel against authority.

scientific areas: geographic exploration, geology, zoology, botany, and psychology. And he circumnavigated the globe on the ship *The Beagle*, often facing great dangers as he collected evidence that led to his original, paradigm-shifting theory of evolution.

Culture, Gender, and the Social Self

The American Declaration of Independence and the *Analects* of the Chinese philosopher Confucius have shaped the lives of billions of people. Yet they reflect radically different ideas about the social self. The Declaration of Independence prioritized the rights and freedoms of the individual, and it protected the individual from having those rights and liberties infringed on by others. Confucius emphasized the importance of knowing one's place in society, of honoring traditions, duties, and social roles, and of thinking of others before the self.

These documents reflect significant cultural differences in views of the self, differences that run deep in the cultures we inhabit. In Western societies, people are concerned about their individuality, about freedom, and about self-expression. Our adages reflect this: "The squeaky wheel gets the grease." "If you've got it, flaunt it." In Asian cultures, the homilies and folk wisdom encourage a different view of the self: "The empty wagon makes the most noise." "The nail that stands up is pounded down." Psychologists Hazel Markus, Shinobu Kitayama, and Harry Triandis have offered far-reaching theories about how cultures vary in the social selves they encourage and how these different conceptions of the self shape the emotions we feel, the motivations that drive us, and our ways of perceiving the social world (Markus & Kitayama, 1991; Triandis, 1989, 1994, 1995).

The independent self is widespread throughout much of the West, especially in northwestern Europe and North America. In cultures that promote independent self-construals, the self is an autonomous entity that is distinct and separate from others. The imperative is to assert uniqueness and independence. The focus is on internal causes of behavior. Together, these forces lead to a conception of the self in terms of traits that are stable across time and social context.

In contrast, in cultures that foster interdependent self-construals, the self is fundamentally connected to, even intermixed with, other people (see **Figure 3.2**). The imperative is for a person to find his or her status and roles within the community and other collectives—for example, within families and organizations. The focus is on

> "We hold these truths to be self-evident, that all men are created equal, that they are endowed by their Creator with certain inalienable rights, that among these are Life, Liberty, and the pursuit of Happiness."
>
> —Declaration of Independence

> "A person of humanity wishing to establish his own character, also establishes the character of others."
>
> —Confucius

(A) Independent view of self

(B) Interdependent view of self

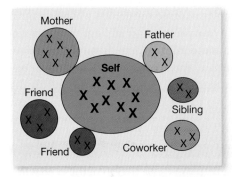
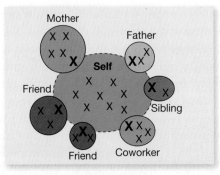

FIGURE 3.2 Views of the Self   In the independent view of the self (A), the self is construed as a distinct, autonomous entity, separate from others and defined by distinct traits and preferences. In the interdependent view of the self (B), the self is construed as connected to others, and defined by duties and roles and shared preferences and traits.

how the social context and the situation influence current behavior. And together these forces lead to a self-conception in which the self is embedded within social relationships, roles, and duties. As we emphasize in Chapter 1, this kind of self-construal is prevalent in many Asian cultures, as well as in many Mediterranean, African, and South American cultures.

Some aspects of Eastern language capture the interdependent self. In Japanese, the word for "I"—meaning the person who is the same across situations and in relation to everyone—is almost never used. Instead, a Japanese man would use different words for "I" when talking with a colleague (*watashi*), his child (*tochan*), old college pals (*ore*), and close female friends (*boku*). Sometimes when referring to themselves the Japanese use the word *jibun*, which originally meant "my portion"—reflecting the sense of self as a part of the whole—and which now would be translated "shared life space." Throughout this chapter, you will see that culture-based self-construals also influence the different elements of the social self—self-knowledge, self-evaluation, and concerns about how we present ourselves in public (see **Table 3.2**).

As you read about independent and interdependent self-construals, you may have wondered about the relationship between gender and the self-concept. A great many social and personality psychologists have thought about this as well. In their

Culture and Self-Concept

In interdependent cultures, the social relationships you have with other people are crucial in determining how you behave toward them. These Japanese businessmen want to fit in with Western business associates. They attend a smile workshop to learn how to smile and behave as Western businessmen would expect so that their reactions won't be misconstrued by their Western associates.

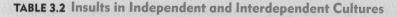

TABLE 3.2 Insults in Independent and Interdependent Cultures

Noting that southern Italy is more collectivist, or interdependent, than northern Italy, Semin and Rubini asked people from both regions to list insults that they knew. They found that insults in northern Italy tended to be directed toward the individual, whereas insults in southern Italy were much more likely to be directed at people with whom the person had relationships.

Individualistic Insults	Relational Insults
Negative physical features	**Relational sexual insults**
Bruttone.	Vaffanculo te a 36 dei tuoi parente.
(You are incredibly ugly.)	($#@% you and 36 of your relatives.)
Ill omens	Tua madré puttana.
Che ti venga un cancro.	(Your mother is a whore.)
(I wish you a cancer.)	
Animal analogies	**Relatives equated with animals**
Porco.	Figlio di troia.
(Swine.)	(Your mother is a breeding sow.)
References to excretia	**Bad wishes to target's relatives**
Stronzo.	A li mortaci tuoi.
(Pile of shit.)	(Go to your @#$! dead relatives.)
Individual sexual insults	
Segaiolo.	
(Male organ.)	

Source: Semin & Rubini (1990).

review of the literature on the self-concept and gender, for example, Susan Cross and Laura Madson (1997) marshaled evidence indicating that women in the United States tend to construe the self in interdependent terms—that is, in terms of connection to others. In contrast, men in the United States tend to construe the self in more independent terms—that is, by prioritizing difference and uniqueness. The same gender differences are found among the Japanese (Kashima, Siegal, Tanaka, & Kashima, 1992).

The evidence for these basic differences in self-construal is manifold. When women define themselves, they are more likely than men to refer to social characteristics and relationships (Maccoby & Jacklin, 1974). When asked to select photographs that are most revealing of who they are, women are more likely than men to select photos that include other people, such as friends and family members (Clancy & Dollinger, 1993). In social interactions, women report more thoughts about their partners (Ickes, Robertson, Tooke, & Teng, 1986), and women tend to be more empathic and better judges of other people's personalities and emotions (Ambady, Hallahan, & Rosenthal, 1995; Bernieri, Zuckerman, Koestner, & Rosenthal, 1994; Davis, 1980; Davis & Franzoi, 1991; Eisenberg & Lennon, 1983; Hall, 1984). Men tend to be more attuned to their own internal responses, such as increased heart rate, whereas women are more attuned to situational cues, such as other people's reactions (Pennebaker & Roberts, 1992; Roberts & Pennebaker, 1995).

Where do these gender-related differences in self-construal come from? There are many agents of socialization that guide women and men into these differing self-construals. The media portray women and men differently, typically portraying men in positions of power and agency. Cultural stereotypes lead teachers to have different expectations of women and men (see Chapter 12). Our family context plays a role as well. Parents raise girls and boys differently. For example, parents tend to talk with girls more about emotions and being sensitive to others (Fivush, 1989, 1992). The friendships and groups we form from the earliest ages also affect gender differences in self-construal. Starting at age 3 and continuing through the primary school years, girls and boys tend to play in gender-segregated groups that reinforce and amplify the differences in self-construal (Maccoby, 1990). Girls' groups tend to focus on cooperative games that are oriented toward interpersonal relationships (for example, mother and child). Boys' groups tend to emphasize competition, hierarchy, and distinctions among one another. As adults, gender-specific roles further amplify these differences. For example, even today, women take on most of the responsibilities of raising children, which calls on interdependent tendencies.

In other chapters, we discuss how certain gender differences in the social self may have originated in our evolutionary history. For now, we simply note that men were equipped physically and psychologically for hunting and aggressive encounters with other groups, whereas women were equipped physically and psychologically for the nurturance of the young. Thus, an independent self-construal fits the roles largely fulfilled by males in our evolutionary history, and an interdependent self-construal is better tailored to the caregiving demands that fell disproportionately to females. And yet, different cultures have very different ways of dealing with gender, and we have witnessed enormous changes in gender roles in the past several generations. Clearly, there are sharp limits to any evolutionary account of gender differences.

Situationism and the Social Self

In the film *Zelig*, Woody Allen plays a character who unwittingly takes on the appearance of the people around him. Surrounded by a group of African-Americans, he begins to look black; in the presence of a group of elderly Greeks, he takes on their

Context and the Sense of Self In *Zelig*, Woody Allen takes on the appearance of those with whom he interacts, providing a dramatic illustration of how we often express different traits and characteristics when in different social contexts. (A) Zelig looks Chinese when he is next to a Chinese man. (B) Zelig takes on African-American features when he stands between two African-American men.

Mediterranean appearance. The humor of the film stems from how it makes light of a deeper truth: that our social self shifts dramatically according to the situation in which we find ourselves. Outspoken with our close friends, we become shy and inhibited in a group of new acquaintances. Students who are rebellious and free-spirited in the dorm will shift to a more sober and conventional demeanor around parents or professors. The sense of self is shaped by the current situation.

Social Context The notion that the social self changes in different contexts is consistent with the principle of situationism and is supported by abundant empirical evidence. In Chapter 11, we discuss how our sense of self shifts dramatically according to whether we are interacting with someone who reminds us of a positive or negative significant other in our life. In interactions with subordinates, we feel empowered and act authoritatively, but we shift to a more easygoing style with equal-status peers (Moskowitz, 1994). When we fall into a dark mood, the more peripheral aspects of our social self—that is, the parts of our self that are not central to our identity—will seem more negative (Sedikides, 1995). We should take heart in the finding that the more central dimensions to our social self—where we fall on the Big Five, for example—are not swayed by momentary feelings, because these are stable features of who we are. Moreover, momentary failures—for example, on exams or interpersonal tasks—increase our feelings of self-criticism and self-doubt (Brown, 1998).

Distinctiveness William McGuire and Alice Padawer-Singer (1978) have proposed a rather general perspective on the effects of the current situation on our social self. According to their **distinctiveness hypothesis**, we identify what makes us unique in each situation, and we highlight that in our self-definition. To test this hypothesis, sixth graders at different schools spent 7 minutes describing themselves. On average, children wrote 11.8 statements, and these statements referred to their recreational activities, attitudes, friends, and school activities. (The children, incidentally, were more likely to refer to their dog when defining themselves than to all other family members combined!)

distinctiveness hypothesis The hypothesis that we identify what makes us unique in each particular context, and we highlight that in our self-definition.

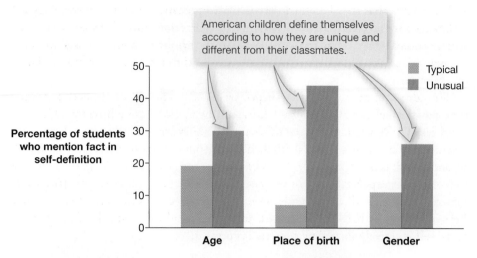

American children define themselves according to how they are unique and different from their classmates.

FIGURE 3.3 **Distinctiveness and the Sense of Self** (Source: Adapted from McGuire & Padawer-Singer, 1978.)

McGuire and Padawer-Singer examined these descriptions to see whether children defined themselves according to how they differed from their classmates. Indeed, they did (see **Figure 3.3**). Thirty percent of children who were especially young or old compared with their classmates (that is, 6 months from the most common age of their classmates) mentioned their age in their self-definition, whereas only 19 percent of the other children did. Forty-four percent of children who were born outside of the United States mentioned this biographical fact, whereas only 7 percent of those born in the United States mentioned that fact about themselves. Twenty-six percent of children in the minority gender in their class mentioned their gender as part of their self-definition compared with 11 percent of children in the majority gender (see also Cota & Dion, 1986). In the West, at least, what is distinct about who you are is also most central to your identity.

Construal Processes and the Social Self

Walt Whitman, the great American poet, began his well-known poem "Song of Myself" as follows:

> I celebrate myself
> And what I assume you shall assume,
> For every atom belonging to me as good belongs to you.

This three-line stanza brings into focus several important themes—the American celebration of individuality in the first line, a commitment to the belief in common humanity in the third. And Whitman also hints at the theme of this section: that the social self is shaped by construal processes. When he declares "what I assume you shall assume," he is not only saying that we share common beliefs about who we are; he is also saying that those beliefs are part of our social selves, or, in his more poetic phrasing, the "Song of Myself."

This notion, that the social self is created by acts of construal, was a central point made by one of Whitman's admirers and a founding figure in psychology, William James. James described different perspectives on the social self. The "I" self actively perceives and interprets the social self; the "me" self is the shifting collection of traits and attributes that the "I" self construes. An important movement in sociology led by George Herbert Mead, known as symbolic interactionism, elaborated on the construal processes that create the social self. For the symbolic interactionists, we come to know our social selves within social interactions through an understanding of how others see us.

This idea that the social self is shaped by construal processes yields two insights that run throughout this chapter (and social psychology more broadly). The first insight is that we actively construe who we are within particular situations. As we have just seen, for example, our social self is shaped by our current situation and culture. A second insight is that the social self can be thought of as a rich knowledge structure—a web of beliefs, expectations, motives, and goals—that guides how we construe social information. We will consider this notion in depth in our section on self-knowledge. Let's now consider three areas of research that are in keeping with the claim that the social self is actively shaped by construal processes.

Social Comparison One way that we actively construe the social self is by comparing ourselves with other people, the central tenet of **social comparison theory**, an influential and enduring theory in social psychology put forward by Leon Festinger (Festinger, 1954; see also Suls & Wheeler, 2000; Wood, 1996). The essence of the theory is that when people have no objective standard that they can use to define their abilities or traits, they do so in large part by comparing themselves with others. How can you know how good you are at tennis or physics, for example, or how conscientious you are, without comparing yourself with other relevant people? Festinger noted, however, that there is no point in comparing yourself with Serena Williams or Albert Einstein, nor is it very helpful to compare yourself with total novices. To get a sense of how good you are at something, you must compare yourself with people who have approximately your level of skill. Numerous experiments have demonstrated that people are particularly drawn to comparisons with others roughly similar to themselves (Kruglanski & Mayseless, 1990; Suls, Martin, & Wheeler, 2002; Suls & Wheeler, 2000).

But we like to feel good about ourselves, so our search for similar targets of comparison tends to be biased toward people who are slightly less able than ourselves. All of this is a bit ironic because it leaves us in the position of saying, "Compared with people who are slightly worse at tennis than I am, I'm pretty good!" or "Compared with people who are almost as conscientious as I am, I'm pretty darn conscientious!" These sorts of *downward social comparisons* help us to define ourselves rather favorably, giving a boost to our self-esteem (Aspinwall & Taylor, 1993; Helgeson & Mickelson, 1995; Lockwood, 2002). But don't these sorts of biased social comparisons come at a cost? After all, we can learn a lot from people who are better than we are in various domains of life, and we sacrifice important opportunities for improvement if we only engage in downward social comparison. One influential study of breast cancer patients identified a strategy people use to get the emotional benefits of favorable comparisons without forfeiting the opportunity to learn from those who are better off (Taylor & Lobell, 1989). They do so by *comparing* themselves with those who are worse off ("I only had to have one set of lymph nodes removed") but initiating contact with those who are better ("She seems to be in good spirits all the time and I'd like to ask her over for lunch to find out how she does it"). And although downward social comparison may be more common, it is not the case that people never engage in *upward social comparison*. We are particularly inclined to do this when we aspire to be substantially better at some skill or when we wish to improve some component of our character or personality (Blanton, Pelham, De Hart, & Kuyper, 1999). Note, however, that whether we seek to compare ourselves with those

social comparison theory The hypothesis that we compare ourselves to other people in order to evaluate our opinions, abilities, and internal states.

"It is not enough to succeed. Others must fail."

—Gore Vidal

who are superior or those who are inferior, we are relying on others to help define the self.

The Social Self as a Narrative The most systematic statement about the role of construal in the social self is Dan McAdams's recent writings on the narrated self (McAdams, 2008). McAdams's central argument is that we are continually telling a particular story about our social self as we live our lives. Like a good novel, this narrated self has settings (where you grew up), characters (a generous mentor), plot twists and turns (your parents' divorce), dramatic themes (the quest for justice), and vivid images and scenes (when your girlfriend/boyfriend dumped you for your best friend). We tell these self-narratives, McAdams maintains, to important people in our lives—for example, your father, a best friend, or some adversary who always doubted you. And we tell them in part to integrate our many goals, to make sense of conflict, and to explain how we change over time. Your narrated self right now, for example, might involve plot twists and scenes revealing how you are in the process of choosing a particular life path—a career pursuit, a romantic partner, particular values— that differs from your parents' aspirations. In his research, McAdams has found that self-narratives often involve powerful scenes of redemption and connecting to those who suffer. More vivid and engaging self-narratives, McAdams also finds, enable people to feel happy and fulfilled as they age.

Cross-cultural research finds that self-narratives vary across societies in intriguing ways. Dov Cohen and Alex Gunz (2002) asked Canadian and Asian students (a potpourri of students from Hong Kong, China, Taiwan, Korea, and various South and Southeast Asian countries) to tell stories about ten different situations in which they were the center of attention—for example, "being embarrassed." Canadians were more likely than Asians to reproduce the scene from their original point of view, looking outward from their own perspective. Asians were more likely to imagine the scene as an observer might, describing it from a third-person perspective. You might say that Westerners experience and recall events from the inside out—with themselves at the center, looking out at the world. Easterners are more likely to experience and recall events from the outside in—starting from the social world, looking back at themselves as an object of attention (see also Chua, Leu, & Nisbett, 2005).

Construal Processes and Self-Assessment As you will see shortly, people—at any rate, most Westerners—tend to have a positive view of themselves, and on average, their level of self-esteem is rather high. In fact, when you ask people to state how they think they compare with people in general on various traits and abilities, you consistently observe a pronounced *better-than-average effect*. That is, people tend to think they are decidedly above average (Alicke & Govorun, 2005). The majority of people think they are above average in popularity, kindness, fairness, leadership, and the ability to get along with others, to name just a few characteristics. And it will surely be no surprise to you that most people think they are above average drivers (Svenson, 1981). Indeed, a majority of drivers interviewed *while hospitalized for being in an automobile accident* rated their driving skill as closer to "expert" than "poor" (Preston & Harris, 1965).

Why are people so upbeat about their talents and dispostions? Part of the answer has to do with how people interpret what it means to be kind, fair, athletic, or even a good driver. If people tend to construe particular trait or ability dimensions in terms of those things at which they excel, then most people will end up convinced that they are above average. Indeed, construed in such self-serving ways, most people *are* above average. As Nobel Prize–winning economist Thomas Schelling once put it, "Everybody ranks himself high in qualities he values: careful drivers give weight to care, skillful

"Very early, I knew that the only object in life was to grow."

—Margaret Fuller

drivers give weight to skill, and those who think that, whatever else they are not, at least they are polite, give weight to courtesy, and come out high on their own scale. This is the way that every child has the best dog on the block" (Schelling, 1978, p. 64).

David Dunning and his colleagues have shown that people engage in just this sort of self-serving construal of what it means to be, say, artistic, athletic, or agreeable and that such construals are an important part of the better-than-average effect. They have found, for example, that much stronger better-than-average effects are observed for ambiguous traits that are easy to construe in various ways (artistic, sympathetic, talented) than for unambiguous traits that are not (tall, punctual, muscular). Also, when people are given precise instructions about how they should interpret what it means to be artistic or athletic, for example, before they are asked to rate themselves, the magnitude of the better-than-average effect diminishes dramatically (Dunning, Meyerowitz, & Holzberg, 1989).

 We have seen that the social self is shaped by four processes that lie at the heart of social psychology. Evolution has crafted biologically based traits that define who we are. Sibling dynamics lead firstborns to be more assertive and achievement oriented and later-borns to be more agreeable and open to new, and at times radical, ideas. A person's culture of origin shapes the social self in profound ways: People from Western cultures—especially men in these cultures—define the self in independent terms, emphasizing uniqueness and autonomy, whereas people from East Asian cultures, and women in many cultures, define the self in interdependent terms, emphasizing connection to others. The current situation matters as well: the social self shifts from one situation to another. Finally, the social self is shaped by broad construal processes, including the tendency to compare ourselves to others, to construct stories about our lives, and to construe the meaning of traits and abilities in ways that favor our own particular strengths.

SELF-KNOWLEDGE

In his treatment of patients suffering from various neurological disorders, Oliver Sacks worked with one fascinating patient, William Thompson, who suffered from Korsakoff's syndrome (Sacks, 1985). Often the result of long years of alcohol abuse, Korsakoff's syndrome destroys memory structures in the brain. Thompson was unable to remember things for more than a second or two. As a result, in each new situation, he would create false identities for the people he encountered, and his social self would move quickly from one identity to the next. Here is one exchange in which Thompson attributes a variety of identities to Oliver Sacks:

> "What'll it be today?" he says, rubbing his hands. "Half a pound of Virginia, a nice piece of Nova?"
> (Evidently he saw me as a customer—he often would pick up the phone on the ward, and say "Thompson's Delicatessen.")
> "Oh Mr. Thompson!" I exclaim. "And who do you think I am?"
> "Good heavens, the light's bad—I took you for a customer. As if it isn't my old friend Tom Pitkins. . . . Me and Tom" (he whispers in an aside to the nurse)
> "was always going to the races together."
> "Mr. Thompson, you are mistaken again."

"So I am," he rejoins, not put out for a moment. "Why would you be wearing a white coat if you were Tom? You're Hymie, the kosher butcher next door. No bloodstains on your coat though. Business bad today? You'll look like a slaughterhouse by the end of the week!" (Sacks, 1985, p. 108).

What is clear in this exchange is that Thompson is utterly at sea in identifying the people who come into his world. He constructs identities for them that seem to have some plausibility at the moment but which are only loosely connected to any memories he might have about other people. Thompson's own social self also shifts with disorienting rapidity: one second he's in his role at Thompson's deli, and seconds later he's ready to go off galavanting with his friend Tom.

This case study reveals that our social selves depend on our ability to remember, to know who we and other people are, as well as other kinds of more general knowledge. And the literature on self-knowledge that we are about to explore reveals that our knowledge about ourselves, in the form of beliefs, schemas, stories, and expectations, helps organize how we behave in the strikingly diverse situations and relationships that make up our daily lives (Sedikides & Skowronski, 1997).

Central to our self-knowledge are our self-beliefs (Brewer & Gardner, 1996; Brown, 1998; Deaux, Reid, Mizrahi, & Ethier, 1995; Kihlstrom & Cantor, 1984). **Personal beliefs** refer to our understanding of our own personality traits, like the Big Five, as well as our beliefs about other abilities and attributes, and our preferences, tastes, and talents. Our **social self-beliefs** concern the roles, duties, and obligations we assume in groups—for example, at work, on sports teams, or in community organizations. **Relational self-beliefs** refer to our identities in specific relationships—for example, as doting husband or black sheep of the family. Finally, we have **collective self-beliefs,** referring to our identity with the social collectives to which we belong—for example, Irish-Canadian, Episcopalian, Libertarian, weekend trainspotter, or member of Red Sox Nation (Chen, Boucher, & Tapias, 2006). In Chapter 1, we discuss how self-beliefs vary according to a person's culture of origin (Dhawan, Roseman, Naidu, Thapa, & Rettek, 1995; Heine et al., 2001; Kitayama, Markus, Matsumoto, & Norasakkunkit, 1997). In one study, American college students defined themselves primarily in terms of personal attributes (traits), whereas Japanese students were three times more likely than American students to define themselves in terms of social roles and relationships (Cousins, 1989).

"I don't know anybody here but the hostess— and, of course, in a deeper sense, myself."

personal beliefs Beliefs about our own personality traits, abilities, attributes, preferences, tastes, and talents.

social self-beliefs Beliefs about the roles, duties, and obligations we assume in groups.

relational self-beliefs Beliefs about our identities in specific relationships.

collective self-beliefs Our identity and beliefs as they relate to the social categories to which we belong.

The Organizational Function of Self-Knowledge

In an influential essay, Anthony Greenwald characterizes self-knowledge as a "totalitarian ego" (Greenwald, 1980). Totalitarian political regimes, like those in the former Soviet Union or in Saddam Hussein's Iraq, suppress dissent, rewrite history to fit political ideologies, and tolerate little or no contradiction. Self-knowledge, Greenwald contends, operates in a similar fashion. We actively construe current situations, view other people's actions, and revise our personal histories to fit our preexisting beliefs about the self. This organizational function of self-knowledge is in keeping with a broad theme in this book: that our social knowledge generally—our attitudes,

BOX 3.1 **FOCUS ON CULTURE AND NEUROSCIENCE**

The Social Self in the Brain

When participants are asked to judge the self with respect to various trait dimensions, which gives rise to the self-reference effect, a certain region of the brain known as the medial prefrontal cortex is particularly active (Heatherton et al., 2006). This suggests that this part of the frontal lobe is involved in processes that represent self-knowledge. Ying Zhu and colleagues conducted a study using an interesting twist on this paradigm to ascertain whether many of the cultural differences in self-construal we have discussed would be reflected in differences in neural activation (Zhu, Zhang, Fan, & Han, 2007). They had Chinese participants and Western Europeans rate the applicability of different traits with respect to the self, another person, and their mothers. For members of both cultures, these assessments of self-trait similarity produced activation in the medial prefrontal cortex. But for Chinese participants, activation in this same region was also observed when participants were making the trait-mother comparisons. For the Westerners, in contrast, there was, if anything, a relative deactivation of the medial prefrontal cortex when thinking about their mothers. This seems to suggest that for people with interdependent self-construals, the same region of the brain represents the self and mother; they are merged within the brain. In contrast, for those with independent self-construals, the self and mother are quite distinct, all the way down to the neurons in the brain.

stereotypes, expectations, and so on—organizes how we construe our social world. Relevant research lends credence to Greenwald's dramatic claims and suggests that we are more likley to remember, attend to, and construe social information in a fashion that is consistent with our self-knowledge.

Memory and the Self-Reference Effect We have seen that our self-knowledge involves a rich network of beliefs. This self-knowledge helps us remember information we encounter. The tendency to elaborate on and recall information that is integrated into our self-knowledge is called the **self-reference** effect (Klein & Kihlstrom, 1986; Klein & Loftus, 1988). It is explained by a powerful principle in the study of memory: information that is integrated into preexisting knowledge structures, such as the beliefs that we have about ourselves, is more readily recalled. It also appears to involve specific regions of the frontal lobes (see **Box 3.1**).

In one of the first studies to document the self-reference effect, participants were presented with 40 different trait adjectives (Rogers, Kuiper, & Kirker, 1977). For 10 of the adjectives, participants answered structural questions about the words—for example, whether the font was big or small. For another 10 adjectives, participants answered phonemic questions, addressing whether a given adjective rhymed with a target adjective. For an additional 10 adjectives, participants answered a semantic question, addressing whether each adjective was a synonym or an antonym of a target word. And finally, for still another 10 adjectives, participants answered yes or no as to whether the word described the self, thus integrating the adjective into their self-knowledge. An hour later, after a few filler tasks, participants were asked to recall the original 40 traits.

Figure 3.4 presents the results. When information is integrated into our self-knowledge, we remember it better. This is the self-reference effect. It is also interesting to note that in this study, it took participants more time to assess whether a trait was like or not like the self than it took to answer the questions about structure, sounds, or semantics, which suggests that people were using rather elaborate knowledge about

self-reference effect The tendency to elaborate on and recall information that is integrated into our self-knowledge.

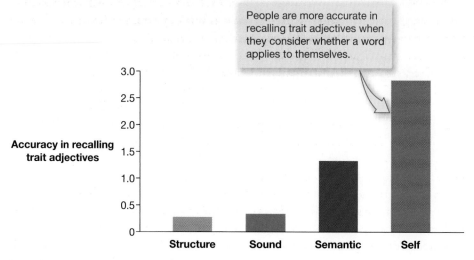

FIGURE 3.4 **The Self-Reference Effect** People are more accurate in recalling trait adjectives when they consider whether a word applies to themselves than when they process the words according to their font style (structure), sound, or semantic meaning. (Source: Adapted from Rogers, Kuiper, & Kirker, 1977.)

the self to answer the question about whether the adjective was similar to the self. Studies of the self-reference effect indicate that to the extent that you personalize how you perceive and understand events and objects in the environment—scenes of sunsets, statements by political leaders, outcomes of athletic competitions, passing remarks made by some authority figure—you will be more likely to think about and remember that information. Self-knowledge shapes what we remember.

Self-Schemas and Self-Understanding Self-knowledge also shapes what we attend to in our social environment—an important thesis explored by Hazel Markus (1977). Her particular concern was **self-schemas,** which she defined as knowledge-based summaries of our feelings and actions, others' beliefs about our social selves, and beliefs that are particularly relevant to the individual's sense of self. Markus argued that people with specific self-schemas—for example, self-schemas about extraversion or intellectual curiosity—should process information in that domain more quickly, retrieve evidence consistent with that self-description more rapidly, and more strongly resist information that contradicts that self-schema.

To test these hypotheses, Markus identified participants who labeled themselves as either quite dependent or quite independent, whom we will call "schematic" participants. She also identified "aschematic" participants; these were participants for whom dependence/independence was not important to their self-definition. Participants returned to the laboratory three to four weeks later and rated how well they were described by a series of traits presented on a computer screen. The schematic participants judged schema-relevant traits as true or not true of themselves much more quickly than aschematic participants, suggesting that we are particularly attuned to information that maps onto the self-schema. The schematic participants generated many more behaviors consistent with the schema-relevant traits, suggesting that past actions and experiences supporting the self-schema come readily to mind. And the schematic participants were faster to refute feedback from a personality test that gave them counterschematic information—for example, refuting feedback that told the independent participants that the results of the test indicated that they were actually dependent.

self-schemas Knowledge-based summaries of our feelings and actions and how we understand others' views about the self.

Now let's consider the relevance of the self-reference effect and self-schemas to an important property of the social self: that it is stable. Certain traits that define our social selves—such as our standing on the Big Five personality dimensions—are quite stable over time (Caspi & Roberts, 2001; Roberts & DelVecchio, 2000). Children identified as shy and inhibited as early as age 2 tend to be more hesitant to enter into social interactions at age 8 (Kagan, 1989), and they take more time to enter into marriage and intimate bonds later in life (Caspi, Elder, & Bem, 1988). Explosive children identified by the severity of their temper tantrums at age 8 have greater difficulties in school and in the workforce, and they are twice as likely to divorce (Caspi, Elder, & Bem, 1987). What we are like early in life—whether we are kind, outgoing, impulsive, or demure—tends to resemble what we are like later in life.

Studies of the self-reference effect and of self-schemas point to likely sources of the stability of the self (as do biological accounts of these traits, which we considered earlier). Once we form beliefs about ourselves, probably quite early in life, we are likely to remember information that is consistent with those self-beliefs. Our self-beliefs lead us to attend to events and experiences that confirm our prior beliefs. They lead us to look back on the past in ways that support our current self-schema (Ross, 1989). And they lead us to resist information that might reveal some new, surprising facet to the self. The self does seem to be organized in a totalitarian fashion, just as Greenwald maintained.

The Self as a Standard in Social Perception Thus far, we have seen that our self-knowledge improves our memory of self-relevant information, and it guides what we attend to. Our self-knowledge also plays an important role in how we evaluate other people. The social self, in effect, is a standard that guides our judgments of others.

For example, the **self-image bias** refers to the tendency to judge other people's personalities according to their similarity or dissimilarity to our own (Lewicki, 1983). To capture this bias, Pavel Lewicki had participants rate themselves on 20 traits, such as "warm," "demanding," "fearful," and "impractical," and then rate the personalities of 20 other individuals, including mom and dad, a best friend, the most unusual person ever met, and even a most disliked teacher. For each participant, Lewicki created a measure of how desirable the participant considered each trait to be and a measure of how important the trait was in the participant's judgment of the 20 other individuals. Lewicki found that the traits that participants rated themselves most positively on were also the most important in their judgments of other people. For example, if you value your practicality or your bravery, you will judge others according to their practicality (or lack of it) and their tendency to be fearful or brave. Thus, the most valued aspects of yourself guide your construction of others people's personalities.

Research by David Dunning and his colleagues suggests that people rely on their self-knowledge to define what it means to have particular traits and abilities and to belong to particular social categories (Dunning et al., 1989; Dunning, Perie, & Story, 1991). We have already seen how this tendency leads to the kinds of favorable self-assessments that give rise to the better-than-average effect. But the self-based ways that we define particular categories have implications beyond our evaluations of ourselves: they also influence how we understand and evaluate others. In one telling study of egocentric social construal, participants first reported their own SAT scores, how many hours a week they studied, and their weekly athletic activities (Dunning & Cohen, 1992). Several weeks later, in the context of another experiment, participants indicated the kind of performance that they thought would define studiousness and athleticism. What defines a smart, studious, or athletic individual? Not surprisingly, how smart, studious, or athletic you yourself are.

self-image bias The tendency to judge other people's personalities according to their similarity or dissimilarity to our own personality.

So far, the evidence we have reviewed suggests that people use their self-knowledge in an egocentric fashion as a guide in judging other people and in judging important abilities. But should we expect people who construe themselves in interdependent terms to use the self as a standard? Probably not. Embedded within the interdependent self-construal is a greater focus on others, on fitting into relationships and groups, and on fulfilling others' expectations. In light of these tendencies, we might expect people from interdependent cultures to rely on other people, rather than the self, as a standard for social judgment.

To understand one way in which this seems to be the case, consider the following questions, far removed from the subject of the self. Is Cincinnati more similar to Chicago, or is Chicago more similar to Cincinnati? Is Belgium more similar to France, or is France more similar to Belgium? Although it might seem that any object A must be as similar to object B as object B is to object A, for any actual concrete judgment, one object—usually the more "important" or salient—is implicitly the standard against which the other object is compared (Tversky, 1977). Thus, large, salient Chicago is the implicit standard against which the smaller Cincinnati is compared, and the larger France is the standard against which the smaller Belgium is compared.

This asymmetry in similarity judgments applies to people, too. For example, is Denzel Washington more similar to Jamie Foxx or Jamie Foxx more similar to Denzel Washington? You would probably say that the person more frequently pictured on magazine covers and discussed in tabloids (Denzel Washington) would be the person to whom someone who is not as frequently in the news (Jamie Foxx) would be compared. Taking this one step further, we can ask what the standard of comparison is when people are comparing themselves to other people. When asked to make such a comparison, university students in the United States consistently say that other people are more similar to themselves than they are to other people, whereas Asian students are more likely to say that they are more similar to other people than other people are similar to them (Markus & Kitayama, 1991; see also Satterwhite, Feldman, Catrambone, & Dai, 2000). Thus, for the typical independent U.S. college student, the self is the standard of comparison.

The Motivational Function of Self-Knowledge

A second function of self-knowledge is that it helps motivate behavior (Carver & Scheier, 1982; Higgins, 1999; Scheier & Carver, 1977; Wicklund, 1975). Self-beliefs, schemas, and narratives serve as standards that motivate certain kinds of actions and prevent us from acting in inappropriate ways (Gollwitzer, Fujita, & Oettingen, 2004). For example, as we get older, we develop beliefs about our **possible selves,** which refer to the kinds of people we hope to be in the future (Cross & Markus, 1991; Markus & Nurius, 1986). For example, you might imagine yourself ten years from now as an environmental scientist or as a lawyer seeking to redress injustice. This kind of self-knowledge motivates present actions—learning organic chemistry or studying for the LSATs—that will help you get closer to your possible selves. Hazel Markus has found that people who have rich ideas about possible selves are more optimistic and energetic and are less vulnerable to depression (Markus & Nurius, 1986).

Another perspective on how self-knowledge motivates and guides productive action is provided by Tory Higgins's **self-discrepancy theory** (Higgins, 1987). The theory is based on the idea that we all have an **actual self**—that is, who we truly believe ourselves to be—and that frequently we compare our actual self with two other selves, comparisons that have important motivational implications (Higgins, 1999). The first

possible selves Hypothetical selves we aspire to be in the future.

self-discrepancy theory A theory that appropriate behavior is motivated by cultural and moral standards regarding the ideal self and the ought self. Violations of those standards produce emotions such as guilt and shame.

actual self The self we truly believe ourselves to be.

FIGURE 3.5 You Be the Subject: Possible Selves

Write down some of your possible selves, that is, who you imagine being in the future.

_____

_____

_____

_____

_____

Think about the extent to which the possible selves you describe are ideal selves you hope to achieve or ought selves you feel obligated to achieve.

Results: The more you envision these possible selves, research suggests you will fare better in life, because these possible selves are such strong sources of motivation. In more specific terms, a focus on how you are moving toward your ideal self can trigger positive affect, whereas too great a focus on how you differ from your ought self can trigger anxiety.

---

of these additional selves is an **ideal self**, which represents the wishes and aspirations we have about ourselves (**Figure 3.5**). When primed (subtly reminded, often out of awareness) to think about our ideal self, we experience what Higgins calls a **promotion focus,** which includes a sensitivity to positive outcomes, approach-related behavior, and cheerful emotions if we are living up to our ideals and aspirations. The second additional self is the **ought self,** which refers to the duties, obligations, and external demands we feel compelled to honor. When primed to think about our ought self, we experience a **prevention focus,** which involves a sensitivity to negative outcomes, an avoidance motivation, and agitated emotions such as guilt or anxiety when we fail to live up to our sense of what we ought to do.

Experimental evidence supports Higgins's account of how self-knowledge can have these different motivational consequences. When people are subtly induced to think about how they might approximate their ideal self—for example, by reading trait terms that capture their ideal self—they generally show elevated cheerful affect (Higgins, Shah, & Friedman, 1997; Shah & Higgins, 2001) and heightened sensitivity to positive outcomes (Brendl, Higgins, & Lemm, 1995). But if they think they will never become their ideal self, they will experience dejection-related emotions such as depression and shame and will show reduced physiological arousal. Similarly, a prevention focus, triggered by associations regarding the ought self and any deviation from it, will activate agitated affect (guilt, anxiety, terror, panic), elevated physiological arousal, avoidant behavior, and sensitivity to negative outcomes (Strauman & Higgins, 1987).

Acting in socially appropriate ways and trying to act in accordance with our ideal and ought selves can be hard work. In fact, such acts of self-control can be downright exhausting. Roy Baumeister, Kathleen Vohs, and their colleagues argue that when we attempt to control our behavior to live up to important standards and requirements, we often experience something known as **ego depletion** (Baumeister, Vohs, & Tice, 2007). Much as physical exercise can exhaust our muscles, self-control can exhaust us psychologically. This claim is based on the idea that self-control draws on a limited psychological resource (Muraven & Baumeister, 2000). When we exercise self-control, we use up that precious resource, and less of it is available to sustain further acts of self-control. In one study that illustrates this important feature of self-control, participants were asked to rein in their emotions while watching an evocative film clip. Afterward, they were able to squeeze a hand grip less powerfully

ideal self The self that embodies the wishes and aspirations we and other people maintain about us.

promotion focus A sensitivity to positive outcomes, approach-related behavior, and cheerful emotions that result if we are living up to our ideals and aspirations.

ought self The self that is concerned with the duties, obligations, and external demands we feel we are compelled to honor.

prevention focus A sensitivity to negative outcomes often motivated by a desire to live up to our ought self and to avoid the guilt or anxiety that results when we fail to live up to our sense of what we ought to do.

ego depletion A state produced by acts of self-control, where we don't have the energy or resources to engage in further acts of self-control.

than control participants. In another study, participants who exercised their will by eating healthy radishes instead of delicious-smelling cookies later gave up on an unsolvable puzzle faster than participants who did not exercise such control and who were lucky enough to eat the cookies (Baumeister, Bratslavsky, Muraven, & Tice, 1998).

Illusions and Biases about the Self

It is widely assumed that a hallmark of mental health and happiness is an honest understanding of who you really are. Self-knowledge should be accurate. For example, many important movements in psychology, like the humanistic movement of Abraham Maslow and Carl Rogers, encourage us to accept our weaknesses, foibles, and flaws. In a controversial line of work, Shelley Taylor and Jonathon Brown have challenged this position. They argue that self-knowledge often includes illusions about ourselves—for example, that we are funnier, smarter, or warmer than we really are—and that illusions about the self, far from being detrimental, actually enhance personal well-being (Taylor & Brown, 1988, 1994; see also Taylor, 1989). Dozens of studies, carried out with Europeans and North Americans, find that people who are well adjusted are more prone to various illusions about the self than those who suffer from low self-esteem and unhappiness.

First, people who are well adjusted have *unrealistically positive views about the self.* They tend to believe that positive personality traits describe themselves better than negative traits. Moreover, they falsely assume consensus (universality) when it comes to their negative traits and actions: "Look, everyone lies to their friends every now and then." And they assume uniqueness for their positive traits: "Unlike most people, I try to express gratitude whenever someone does me a favor."

People who are happy and well adjusted also have *exaggerated perceptions of control.* If you're rolling dice and need to throw a small number, you're likely to throw the dice in a restrained, gentle fashion; if you need to throw a large number, you'll probably throw more vigorously, as if you can control the outcome with the way you throw. More generally, people think they can control events that they in fact can't influence. Ellen Langer examined the illusion of control among participants who were entered in a lottery (Langer, 1975). They were either given a ticket (from a set of 227 tickets, each with the photograph and name of a different famous football player) or allowed to choose their own ticket from the batch of cards. When later asked if they would be willing to sell back their ticket, those who were given the ticket asked for $1.96 on average, whereas those who had "had control" and chosen their own ticket held out for close to $9! So does anyone understand that they don't have control over random events such as lotteries? It turns out that depressed people do. In general, depressed people tend to have more accurate appraisals of their control of environmental events than do other people (Abramson, Metalsky, & Alloy, 1989).

Finally, *optimism*—the sense that the future offers the promise of happiness and success—is a hallmark of well-being (Aspinwall & Brunhart, 1996; Scheier & Carver, 1987; Seligman, 1991). Many people from Western backgrounds are prone to unrealistic optimism. When asked to indicate the likelihood that various positive events or negative events will happen to them and to other college students, most college students think that positive events are more likely to happen to them than to others, and negative events are less likely to happen to them than to others (Weinstein, 1980; see **Table 3.3**). Of course, unusually positive and problem-free futures are not going to be enjoyed by more than half of all participants. Work by Justin Kruger has

"Lord, I thank thee that I judge not—as others do."

—Puritan prayer

TABLE 3.3 Evidence of Unrealistic Optimism

Researchers asked college students to indicate the likelihood that various positive and negative events would happen to them and to others. Positive scores indicated that they believed that their own chances of the event were greater than those of others; negative scores indicated the belief that others were more likely to experience the event. Estimates were made on the following scale: 0 = won't happen; 100 = absolutely certain will happen. Most Western students thought that positive events were more likely to happen to them than to others, but that negative events were more likely to happen to others than to themselves.

Life Event	Comparative Judgment of Own Versus Others' Chances
Like postgraduation job	50.2
Own your own home	44.3
Travel to Europe	35.3
Work recognized with award	12.6
Live past 80	11.3
Have a mentally gifted child	6.2
Weight constant for 10 years	2.0
Have drinking problem	−58.3
Attempt suicide	−55.9
Divorce after a few years of marriage	−48.7
Heart attack before age 40	−38.4
Contract venereal disease	−37.4
Become sterile	−31.2
Develop gum problems	−12.4

Source: Weinstein (1980).

shown that although such comparative optimism is common, it is not inevitable, and predictable instances of comparative *pessimism* occur as well. Kruger's work indicates that comparative optimism stems from people's egocentrism—their tendency to focus on themselves (and whether an event is likely or unlikely to happen to them) and to simply ignore what happens to comparison "others" (Kruger & Burrus, 2004). This results in people being overly optimistic about common positive events ("yep, that'll happen to me") and rare negative events ("no way"). But it also results in overly *pessimistic* assessments about rare positive events ("I'll never be that lucky") and common negative events ("there's no escaping it"). Nonetheless, evidence of the more pervasive optimism described by earlier researchers has been obtained when people's assessments of what is likely or unlikely to happen to them is compared with what actually transpires (Buehler, Griffin, & Ross, 1994; Hoch, 1985; Shepperd, Ouellette, & Fernandez, 1996).

Taylor and Brown believe that unrealistically positive views of the self, exaggerated perceptions of control, and unrealistic optimism promote elevated well-being in three ways: (1) they elevate positive mood and reduce negative mood, (2) they foster healthier social bonds by making people more altruistic and magnanimous, and (3) they promote goal-directed behavior. When we believe that we are highly able and in control and we expect positive outcomes, we are more likely to persist in pursuing goals central to life—at work, at play, or in love. Taylor and Brown's controversial thesis has been critiqued on several grounds (Colvin & Block, 1994). Consider the research on narcissists, who are prone to extreme versions of these self-enhancing illusions (John & Robins, 1994; Raskin & Terry, 1988; Twenge, Konrath, Foster, Campbell, & Bushman, 2008). True narcissists, for example, have no trouble endorsing the thesis that the world would be a better place if they were in charge. Narcissists have been shown to make good first impressions but to be rather unpopular in the long run (Paulhus, 1998). People are charmed by narcissists' charisma initially, but eventually tire of their self-promotion. Thus, it's hard to argue that such a tendency is ultimately beneficial.

In addition, recent longitudinal evidence has identified an important downside of one particular kind of self-enhancement: the overestimation of academic talents (Robins & Beer, 2001). College students who at the start of their college careers overestimated their academic abilities exhibited deteriorating academic performance over time, became disengaged with school, and experienced a drop in their self-esteem. Thus, self-enhancement may prove detrimental, at least in certain domains (Colvin, Block, & Funder, 1995).

Perhaps the greatest challenge to Taylor and Brown's thesis about the benefits of self-illusions comes from cross-cultural research. This work strongly suggests that East Asians are less likely to endorse positive illusions about the self than are Westerners (Heine, Lehman, Markus, & Kitayama, 1999; Kitayama, Markus, et al., 1997). For example, survey research on 42 nations found that Asians, compared with non-Asians, were less likely to report feeling they had "complete free choice and control over their lives" and that perceived lack of control was only associated with lower well-being for the non-Asian participants (Sastry & Ross, 1998). Japanese college students are less likely than American students to assume that they are better than average in important abilities, such as academic talent (Markus & Kitayama, 1991). Students in Japan are also less likely to show evidence of unrealistic optimism than students in Canada (Heine et al., 2001; Heine & Lehman, 1995).

The cultural evidence suggests that self-illusions do not automatically enhance well-being. They often do so for Westerners because optimism, a positive view of the self, and a sense of control over outcomes are cherished values. In contrast, personal well-being for East Asians appears to be more closely tied to interdependent values. For example, Mark Suh, Ed Diener, and their colleagues have found that the well-being of East Asians is more dependent on fulfilling social roles and expectations, consistent with an interdependent self-construal (Suh, Diener, Oishi, & Triandis, 1998).

 We have seen that self-knowledge serves as an important foundation for organizing, understanding, and acting in the social world. The self-reference effect leads us to remember particularly well information that is integrated into our self-knowledge. Our self-schemas—knowledge-based summaries of our traits, abilities, feelings, and others' views of us—guide our understanding of ourselves and others. Our self-knowledge also serves as a standard by which we judge other people and social categories. There are several possible selves, including our actual self, our ideal self, and our ought self, which help motivate socially appropriate behavior. Exercising self-control to bring our actual self in line with our ideal and ought selves can produce ego depletion. It would seem that for people in the West, illusions about the self can promote enhanced well-being.

"There is no human problem which could not be solved if people would simply do as I advise."

—Gore Vidal

SELF-EVALUATION

In 1987, California Governor George Deukmejian signed Assembly Bill 3659 into law. The bill allocated an annual budget of $245,000 for a self-esteem task force, charged with understanding the effects of self-esteem on drug use, teenage pregnancy, and high school dropout rates and elevating schoolchildren's self-esteem. The initiative was based on the assumption that elevating self-esteem would help cure society's ills. Several findings offer support for this assumption. People with low self-esteem are less satisfied with life, more hopeless, and more depressed (Crocker & Wolfe, 2001), and they are less able to cope with life challenges, such as loneliness at college (Cutrona, 1982). They tend to disengage from tasks following failure (Brockner, 1979), and, most important, they are more prone to antisocial behavior and delinquency (Donnellan, Trzesniewski, Robins, Moffitt, & Caspi, 2005). Raising self-esteem, the thinking was, just might produce healthier, more resilient children and a better society in the long run.

By now, such a legislative act should strike you as something that could only happen in a Western culture (or perhaps California more specifically!). Indeed, later in this section, we will examine the rather pronounced cultural differences in self-esteem. For the moment, however, let's fully consider the premise of the California task force—that elevating self-esteem is likely to yield numerous benefits to society. To do so, we need to know what self-esteem is and where it comes from.

Trait and State Self-Esteem

Self-esteem refers to the positive or negative overall evaluation we have of ourselves. Researchers usually measure self-esteem with simple self-report measures like that in **Table 3.4**. As you can see from this scale, self-esteem concerns how we feel about our attributes and qualities, our successes and failures, our self-worth. People with

self-esteem The positive or negative overall evaluation that we have of ourselves.

TABLE 3.4 Self-Esteem Scale

Indicate your level of agreement with each of the following statements by using the scale below.

0	1	2	3
Strongly Disagree	Disagree	Agree	Strongly Agree

—— 1. At times I think I am no good at all.
—— 2. I take a positive view of myself.
—— 3. All in all, I am inclined to feel that I am a failure.
—— 4. I wish I could have more respect for myself.
—— 5. I certainly feel useless at times.
—— 6. I feel that I am a person of worth, at least on an equal plane with others.
—— 7. On the whole, I am satisfied with myself.
—— 8. I feel I do not have much to be proud of.
—— 9. I feel that I have a number of good qualities.
—— 10. I am able to do things as well as most other poeple.

To determine your score, first reverse the scoring for the five negatively worded items (1, 3, 4, 5, & 8) as follows; 0 = 3, 1 = 2, 2 = 1, 3 = 0. Then add up your scores across the 10 items. Your total score should fall between 0 and 30. Higher numbers indicate higher self-esteem.

Source: Rosenberg (1965).

Elevated Self-Esteem　People in the self-esteem movement feel that it is important that all children have high self-esteem so that they will be happy and healthy. They have encouraged teachers to make every child a VIP for a day and coaches to give trophies to every child who plays on a team, whether the team wins or loses. Every child on this ice hockey team was awarded a trophy.

trait self-esteem The enduring level of confidence and regard that people have for their defining abilities and characteristics across time.

state self-esteem The dynamic, changeable self-evaluations that are experienced as momentary feelings about the self.

high self-esteem feel quite good about themselves. People with low self-esteem feel ambivalent about themselves; they tend to feel both good and bad about who they are. People who truly dislike themselves are rare and are typically found in specific clinical populations, such as severely depressed individuals.

　Trait self-esteem is the enduring level of regard that we have for ourselves across time. Studies indicate that trait self-esteem is fairly stable: people who report high trait self-esteem at one point in time tend to report high trait self-esteem many years later; people who report low trait self-esteem tend to report low trait self-esteem many years later (Block & Robins, 1993).

　There is also **state self-esteem,** the dynamic, changeable self-evaluations that are experienced as momentary feelings about the self (Heatherton & Polivy, 1991). Your state self-esteem rises and falls according to transient moods and specific construal processes that arise in different situations. For example, your current mood, either positive or negative, will shift your self-esteem up or down (Brown, 1998). When people experience a temporary setback—especially those with low self-esteem to begin with—their self-esteem frequently takes a temporary dive (Brown & Dutton, 1995). When college students watch their beloved college football team lose, their feelings of personal competence often drop (Hirt, Zillman, Erickson, & Kennedy, 1992). And children of average intelligence have lower self-esteem when they are in a classroom with academically talented children rather than with children who have lower academic abilities (Marsh & Parker, 1984). Comparing themselves with highly talented children makes them feel less able. Self-esteem also shifts during different stages of development. As males move from early adolescence (age 14) to early adulthood (age 23), self-esteem tends to rise. During the same period, females' self-esteem tends to fall (Block & Robins, 1993). Clearly, then, while one part of your self-esteem is quite stable, another part of it shifts in response to your current situation and broader life context.

Contingencies of Self-Worth

Let's think a bit more systematically about how your self-esteem is related to specific situations and life domains that matter to you. Some of you may rest your feelings of self-worth and self-esteem on your academic achievements. For others, your self-esteem may be more closely tied to your physical fitness, being up on cultural trends, or religious values.

To account for how self-esteem relates to different life domains, Jennifer Crocker and Connie Wolfe have proposed a **contingencies of self-worth** account of self-esteem (Crocker & Wolfe, 2001; Crocker & Park, 2003). Their model is based on the premise that self-esteem is contingent on—that is, rises and falls with—successes and failures in domains on which a person has based his or her self-worth. They have focused on several domains that account for fluctuations in self-esteem among college students in particular: family support, school competence, competition, virtue, social approval, physical appearance, and God's love, or what might be called religious identity (see also Crocker, Luhtanen, Cooper, & Bouvrette, 2003). A sample item measuring the domain of academic competence is "My self-esteem gets a boost when I get a good grade on an exam or paper." An item measuring the domain of others' approval is "I can't respect myself if others don't respect me." Which domains are most important to self-esteem varies from person to person. Similarly, cultures and subcultures also vary as to which domains are considered most important. For example, the experience of God's love is much more important to the self-esteem of African-Americans than to the self-esteem of either European-Americans or Asian-Americans.

We are hostages to our contingencies of self-esteem. If things are going well in domains that are important to us, our self-esteem will be high, but if they are going badly in these domains, then our self-esteem will plummet. Jennifer Crocker, Samuel Sommers, and Riia Luhtanen (2002) studied the self-esteem of University of Michigan students who had applied to graduate school. The researchers created a Web page that contained an online questionnaire measuring self-esteem. They asked students to go to the Web site and fill out the questionnaire every day that they received a response from a graduate school—either an acceptance or a rejection. Needless to say, students in general had higher self-esteem on days when they received an acceptance and lower self-esteem on days when they received a rejection, but these effects were much larger for those students whose self-esteem was heavily contingent on academic competence.

This work on the contingencies of self-worth offers important lessons about cultivating higher self-esteem. One lesson is that to the extent that we can create environments that allow us to excel in domains that comprise our specific contingencies of self-worth, we will enjoy elevated self-esteem and its numerous benefits. A second is that it is also important to derive a sense of self-worth from many domains. Patricia Linville and her colleagues refer to the tendency to define the self according to multiple life domains as **self-complexity** (Linville, 1987; Showers, 1992). Linville finds that people who define the self according to multiple areas of interest experience smaller drops in self-esteem when they suffer a setback. Having multiple areas of self-definition acts as a buffer against difficulties in one particular domain and gives us strength and a sense of purpose when times are hard.

Social Acceptance and Self-Esteem

In Crocker and Wolfe's research on contingencies of self-worth, several of the domains that define people's self worth—social approval, virtue, even competition—are social in nature. Mark Leary's **sociometer hypothesis** offers a broad account of how self-esteem reflects our standing with others. According to this view, self-esteem is an internal, subjective index or marker of the extent to which we are held in high regard by others and hence likely to be included or excluded by them (Leary, Tambor, Terdal, & Downs, 1995). His argument is an evolutionary one that we discuss further in Chapter 11, where we deal with the pain of social rejection. Leary reasons that as the most social of

contingencies of self-worth An account of self-esteem maintaining that self-esteem is contingent on successes and failures in domains on which a person has based his or her self-worth.

self-complexity The tendency to define the self in terms of many domains and attributes.

sociometer hypothesis A hypothesis that maintains that self-esteem is an internal, subjective index or marker of the extent to which we are included or looked on favorably by others.

"So, when he says, 'What a good boy am I,' Jack is really reinforcing his self-esteem."

animals, we thrive when we are in healthy social relationships. Our feelings of state self-esteem provide a rapid assessment of how we are doing in our social bonds. Leary notes that those things that make us feel good about ourselves—feeling attractive, competent, likable, and morally upright—are precisely those things that make others want to accept or reject us—how attractive, competent, likable, and moral we are. Elevated self-esteem indicates that we are thriving in our relationships; low self-esteem suggests that we are having interpersonal difficulties—or that we are in danger of that. In this sense, low self-esteem is not something to be avoided at all costs; rather, it provides useful information about when we need to attend to our social relations or strengthen our social bonds.

As a test of this sociometer hypothesis, Leary and his colleagues led participants to believe that they were to perform a group task (Leary, Tambor, Terdal, & Downs, 1995). Prior to the task, each participant had written an essay about "what it means to be me" and "the kind of person I would most like to be." The experimenter then gave each person's often quite revealing essay to other participants (in another location), who indicated who they would like to work with in the group setting. The experimenter ignored the participants' actual preferences and randomly assigned some participants to a condition in which they had supposedly been passed over completely by the others and had to work alone, and other participants to a condition in which they were in high demand by others and got to work with a group. Participants in the work-alone condition, who believed they had been excluded, reported lower levels of self-esteem than those included by the group. Our momentary feelings of self-worth strongly track the extent to which others approve of us and include us (Baumeister, Twenge, & Nuss, 2002).

Motives for Self-Evaluation

Beyond the need to monitor our standing with others, psychologists who study the self have argued that the process of self-evaluation is guided by two conflicting motivations. One is the desire to feel good about ourselves. The other is the desire to know the truth about ourselves.

The Motive to Elevate Self-Esteem Having elevated self-esteem is a high priority in Western cultures—so much so, in fact, that the desire to maintain high self-esteem shapes our friendships. According to Abraham Tesser's **self-evaluation maintenance model,** we are motivated to view ourselves in a favorable light, and we do so through two processes: reflection and social comparison (Tesser, 1988). First, through *reflection*, we flatter ourselves by association with others' accomplishments. When our college football team wins, for example, we are more likely to wear school colors the following Monday and to use the pronoun "we" when describing the game-winning drive or decisive goal-line stand, presumably because our association with our team reflects favorably on the self (Cialdini et al., 1976). Basking in the reflected glory of another's accomplishments is especially likely to boost our self-esteem when the other person is close to us and the person's success is in a domain that is *not* important to our own self-esteem.

Second, we flatter ourselves through *social comparison*, strategically noting how our own performance compares favorably with that of others, especially when the domain is important to our self-concept. Putting reflection and social comparison together,

self-evaluation maintenance model A model that maintains that we are motivated to view ourselves in a favorable light and that we do so through two processes: reflection and social comparison.

Tesser maintains that we tend to select friends who are not our equal in domains that matter to us (thus leading to favorable social comparisons), but that we seek out people who excel in domains that are not our own (thus leading to opportunities for esteem-enhancing reflection).

In one study of reflection and social comparison, Tesser and Smith documented the ways friends aid or undermine each other in the service of maintaining their self-esteem (Tesser & Smith, 1980). Two pairs of friends, seated in four individual booths, played a word game with one another. Each participant had to guess four different words based on clues provided by the three other participants. Each participant chose clues from a list of ten clues clearly marked in terms of level of difficulty, and these clues were conveyed by the experimenter, which prevented participants from knowing the source of the clue. In the high-relevance condition, the task was described as a measure of verbal skills. In the low-relevance condition, the task was presented as a playful game. Thus, in the high-relevance condition, participants would presumably be a bit worried by their friend's possible success, to which they might compare their own performance unfavorably, and thus they might give harder clues. In the low-relevance condition, a friend's success would reflect positively on the participant and presumably would motivate the participant to provide easier clues.

As you can see in **Figure 3.6**, when the word game was not relevant to self-esteem (that is, when it was described as a playful game), participants provided easier clues

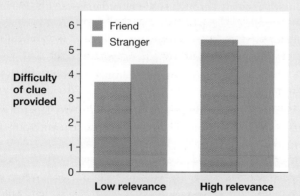

FIGURE 3.6 Scientific Method: Comparison and Self-Esteem

Hypothesis: Individuals will enable their friends' success in domains not relevant to them, but undermine their friends' performance in domains important to their self-esteem.

Research Method:

1 Two pairs of friends, seated in four individual booths, played a word game with one another in which each participant had to guess words based on clues provided by the three other participants.

2 Each participant chose clues from a list of ten clues clearly marked in terms of level of difficulty.

3 In the high-relevance condition, the task was described as a measure of verbal skills. In the low-relevance condition, the task was presented as a playful game.

Results: In the high-relevance condition, participants provided clues to a friend that were every bit as hard as the clues they provided to a stranger. In the low-relevance condition (when the word game was described as a playful game), participants provided easier clues to a friend than to a stranger.

Conclusion: Friends bask in their friends' successes in domains not relevant to their self-esteem, but seek to outperform their friends in domains important to their self-esteem.

Source: Tesser & Smith (1980).

to a friend than to a stranger, presumably to elevate their friend's performance and, by association, their own self-regard. (Of course, participants may also have been motivated to provide easier answers so as to make their friend feel good.) Matters were quite different, however, when the word game was relevant to participants' self-concept. In this condition, participants provided clues to a friend that were every bit as hard as the clues they provided to a stranger. They did so, the theory goes, out of fear that a stellar performance on the part of the friend would reflect badly on themselves.

Recall the key implication of Tesser's theory—that we should choose friends whom we outperform in domains relevant to our self-concept but who are talented in domains that are not relevant to the self. To test this hypothesis, Tesser and his colleagues had 270 fifth and sixth graders identify their closest friends, the most and least important activities relevant to their self-concept (for example, sports, art, math), and their friends' performance in those domains (Tesser, Campbell, & Smith, 1984). As evidence of self-enhancing comparison processes, students rated their own performance as better than that of their friends in the self-defining activities. Evidence of reflection processes was also observed: students rated their friends' performance as equal to their own in the least important domain. For example, if a student greatly valued athletics and had little interest in art, his closest friends tended not to be as good at athletics but to be skilled in art. Teachers' ratings further revealed how self-enhancement shapes friendships. Students overestimated their performance relative to teachers' ratings on their most important activities, and they overestimated their friends' performance, again relative to the teacher's ratings, in the least important domain.

The tendency to remain close to people whom we outperform in domains relevant to the self holds within families as well. For example, eminent scientists reported feeling closer to fathers who pursued different occupations from their own than did scientists whose fathers were engaged in similar occupations (Tesser, 1980). Participants who are within three years of age of a sibling feel closer to that sibling when they feel they outperform the sibling in self-relevant domains, but less close to the sibling when they feel the sibling outperforms them. These kinds of comparison processes are another reason why siblings could be expected to develop different talents, abilities, and traits within the same family setting—a theme we explored in discussing Frank Sulloway's research on the born-to-rebel hypothesis.

The Motive to Find Out the Truth about the Self Tesser's work shows that the motive to boost self-esteem is a powerful force in our social lives. But we do not seek to look at ourselves solely through rose-colored glasses. The truth also matters. **Self-verification theory** holds that we strive for stable, accurate beliefs about the self because such beliefs give us a sense of coherence (Cooley, 1902; Mead, 1934; Swann, 1992) and make us more predictable to ourselves and others (Goffman, 1959). Accuracy also tells us which endeavors to pursue (because success is likely) and which to avoid (because failure is likely).

We gather truthful information about ourselves in two general ways. First, we selectively attend to and recall information that is consistent with our self-views, even when that information is not flattering. People with negative self-views, for example, spend more time studying negative rather than positive feedback about themselves, remember negative feedback better, and prefer to interact with other people who are likely to provide negative rather than positive feedback (Swann & Read, 1981; Swann, Wenzlaff, Krull, & Pelham, 1992).

Second, we create self-confirmatory social environments through our behavior. Our **identity cues**—such as our customary facial expressions, posture, gait, clothes,

self-verification theory A theory that holds that we strive for stable, accurate beliefs about the self because such beliefs give us a sense of coherence.

identity cues Customary facial expressions, posture, gait, clothes, haircuts, and body decorations, which signal to others important facets of our identity and, by implication, how we are to be treated and construed by others.

Identity Cues and Self-Construal   We create self-confirmatory social environments through the clothes we wear, hairstyles, jewelry, tattoos, and other identity cues. (A) Musician Pete Wentz dons identity cues of the emo social category. (B) Shirts signaling an interest in green matters and recycling have become commonplace with rising concerns about climate change.

haircuts, and body decorations—signal to others important facets of our identity and, by implication, how we are to be treated and understood by others. Wearing a simple T-shirt conveys information about our political affiliations, our music preferences, the clubs we belong to, the holidays we take, our university, even our sexual attitudes. And Samuel Gosling and his colleagues have found that college students' dorm rooms—including the way clothes are folded (or not, as the case may be), the way books are arranged, and what is hanging on the walls—convey valid information about their social selves (Gosling, Ko, Mannarelli, & Morris, 2002). For example, really conscientious individuals have tidy rooms with little clutter. Students who are open to experience have rooms decorated with wild art and littered with stacks of different kinds of books and CDs. Even the music we choose to listen to reveals our social selves (Rentfrow & Gosling, 2003). Extraverted individuals tend to prefer either upbeat, conventional songs characteristic of pop and country or energetic songs typical of hip hop and electronica. Students who are open to experience tend to prefer music that is reflective and complex, found in jazz and classical music, and rebellious music more typical of alternative rock.

As many novels so vividly portray, people also choose to enter into relations that maintain consistent views of the self, even when those views are dark, ruinous, and tragic. These sorts of preferences guarantee that our personal lives will likely confirm our views of the self. In a study of intimate bonds, romantic partners who viewed each other in a congruent fashion—that is, whose perceptions of each other were in agreement—reported more commitment to the relationship, even when one partner viewed the other in a negative light (Swann, De La Ronde, & Hixon, 1994).

How might we integrate the self-enhancement and self-verification perspectives? One answer is that these two motives guide different processes related to self-evaluation. Self-enhancement seems to be most relevant to our emotional responses to feedback about the self, whereas self-verification determines our more cognitive assessment of the validity of the feedback (Swann, Griffin, Predmore, & Gaines, 1987). To test this hypothesis, Swann and colleagues gave participants with negative or positive self-beliefs negative or positive feedback. In terms of participants' evaluations of the accuracy and competence of the feedback—that is, the quality of the information—truth prevailed. Namely, participants with negative self-beliefs found

"Every time a friend succeeds, I die a little."

—Gore Vidal

the negative feedback most diagnostic and accurate, whereas participants with positive beliefs rated the positive feedback higher on these dimensions. All participants, however, felt good about the positive feedback and disliked the negative feedback. Our quest for truth, then, guides our assessment of the validity of self-relevant information. Our desire to think favorably about ourselves guides our emotional reactions to the same information.

Culture and Self-Esteem

East Asian languages have no word that captures the idea of feeling good about oneself. The Japanese have a term now, but like the Japanese rendering for *baseball*—namely, *beisoboru*—the term for *self-esteem* is simply borrowed from English: *serufu esutiimu*. That it was Westerners who invented the term *self-esteem* reflects a long-standing concern in the West with the value of the individual. During the Enlightenment, in the seventeenth century, people in Western Europe began to prioritize individuality, freedom, and rights, ideas that would weave their way into the Constitution of the United States (Baumeister, 1987; Seligman, 1988; Twenge, 2002). Nineteenth-century "transcendentalist" writers, including Ralph Waldo Emerson, Henry David Thoreau, and Margaret Fuller, continued in this tradition and emphasized the dignity and power of the individual. Today, the emphasis on self-esteem in the West is at an apex. Bookstores are filled with children's books about the importance of having a strong sense of self-worth. American parents today seek to raise independent and confident children—not the obedient children of 50 years ago (Remley, 1988). It comes as little surprise, then, that between 1968 and 1984, American college students increased greatly in their reported self-esteem (Twenge & Campbell, 2001).

Anecdotally, it seems that independent cultures foster higher levels of self-esteem than interdependent cultures. Empirical data dovetail with these observations. Compared with the world's more interdependent peoples—from Japan to Malaysia to India to Kenya—Westerners consistently report higher self-esteem and a more pronounced concern with evaluating the self (Dhawan et al., 1995; Markus & Kitayama, 1991). It's not that Asians and other non-Westerners feel bad about themselves; rather, they are more concerned with other ways of feeling good about themselves; for example, they are motivated toward self-improvement and commitment to collective goals (Heine, 2005; Crocker & Park, 2004; Norenzayan & Heine, 2004; Pyszczynski, Greenberg, Solomon, Arndt, & Schimel, 2004). Perhaps more dramatically, as people from interdependent cultures gain greater exposure to the West, this emphasis on self-worth rubs off on them, and their self-esteem rises. As you can see in **Figure 3.7**, as Asian individuals experience increasing contact with Canada, they become more like Canadians with respect to self-esteem (Heine & Lehman, 2003).

So what is it about independent and interdependent cultures that creates these differences in self-esteem? We hope your first hypothesis would be a situationist one, that people from Western cultures create social interactions that enhance self-esteem. Consistent with this notion, empirical studies find that situations described by Japanese as common in their everyday experience are regarded as less enhancing of self-esteem—by both Japanese and Americans—than situations common in the United States (Kitayama, Markus, et al., 1997). For example, Japanese are much more often encouraged to engage in "assisted" self-criticism than are Americans. Japanese math teachers and sushi chefs, for example, critique themselves in sessions with their peers—not the sort of activities that would operate to build self-esteem, however beneficial they might be to skill development. Situations reported by Americans as common in their country, by contrast, are regarded by both Americans and Japanese

"Whoso would be a man must be a nonconformist. Hitch your wagon to a star. Insist on yourself; never imitate. The individual is the world."

—Ralph Waldo Emerson

"Independence is happiness."

—Susan B. Anthony

"Men resemble the times more than they resemble their fathers."

—Arab proverb

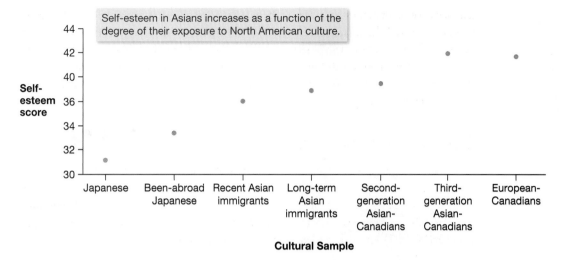

FIGURE 3.7 Cultural Change and Shifts in Self-Esteem   The figure shows self-esteem for Japanese who live in Japan; for been-abroad Japanese (those who have spent time in a Western culture); for recent Asian Immigrants (those who have moved to Canada within the last 7 years); for long-term Asian immigrants (those who have lived in Canada for more than 7 years); for second-generation Asian-Canadians (those who were born in Canada but whose parents were born in Asia); for third-generation Asian-Canadians (those who were born in Canada, whose parents were born in Canada, but whose grandparents were born in Asia); and for European-Canadians (Canadians whose ancestors were Europeans). (Source: Adapted from Heine & Lehman, 2003.)

as more esteem-enhancing than situations common in Japan. For example, Americans are much more often praised for their achievements than are Japanese.

These cultural differences in promoting self-esteem versus working to improve the self have important consequences for how people respond to failures and setbacks (Heine et al., 2001). For example, Steven Heine and colleagues asked Canadian and Japanese students to take a so-called "creativity test" and then gave them false feedback about their performance. Some were told they had performed very well, and others were told they had performed very badly. The experimenter then gave the participants the opportunity to work on a similar task. The Canadians worked longer on the task if they had succeeded at it; the Japanese worked longer if they had failed. Canadians thus avoided being reminded of failure, and Japanese used the occasion to improve.

Possible Dangers of High Self-Esteem

Self-esteem appears to be an increasingly central part of personal identity in many parts of the world. The benefits of elevated self-esteem suggest that this is a positive development. But perhaps we are taking this too far. Roy Baumeister and his colleagues have highlighted some compelling dangers of elevated self-esteem (Baumeister, Smart, & Boden, 1996). Many people with self-esteem may think they are superior to others and as a result may be especially sensitive to threats, insults, and challenges. This may be because high self-esteem is often just inflated egotism—high self-regard that is not really warranted and hence is rather tenuous and insecure. Inflated egotists often react volatilely to threats to their self-esteem, using violent action to reassert their superiority and dominate those who challenge them. Thus, elevated self-esteem mixed with threats to the ego may lead to violence.

There is diverse evidence for this thesis, and it challenges the widespread assumption that depressed self-esteem is the cause of violence. In self-report studies, people

"America is a vast conspiracy to make you happy."

—John Updike

Dangers of High Self-Esteem
Narcissus was a mythological figure who was famously attractive and cruel to others. He fell in love with his own reflection so powerfully that he was unable to leave it, dying because he was unable to look away.

who report elevated self-esteem and grandiosity also report greater aggressive tendencies (Wink, 1991). Hare (1993) has observed that psychopaths, who he estimates might be responsible for 50 percent of serious crimes, have grossly inflated views of their self-worth, and at the same time they are highly sensitive to insults and threats. Alcohol tends to elevate people's self-esteem and to increase the likelihood of aggression (Banaji & Steele, 1989). Interview and questionnaire studies of murderers, bullies, and rapists find that they are not depressed and insecure; instead, they tend to have inflated views of themselves. Members of violent youth gangs tend to be assertive, defiant, and narcissistic, and violence often occurs when they are disrespected or threatened. Baumeister and his colleagues even go so far as to suggest, drawing on historical scholarship, that slavery, terrorism, and genocide are products of the dangerous mixture of feelings of superiority and threats to the ego.

Baumeister and his colleagues' provocative thesis serves as a caveat for the faith that Westerners place on raising people's self-esteem. Certainly, there are many benefits to modesty and humility, and there appear to be risks associated with raising self-esteem.

 We have seen that self-esteem involves how people feel about their traits and abilities, successes and failures, and overall self-worth. Trait self-esteem is fairly stable, generally enduring from childhood into adulthood. In contrast, state self-esteem is changeable, fluctuating in different situations and different stages of development. We have seen that people have different contingencies of self-worth, with some people more invested in intellectual ability, others in religious orientation, still others in sociability. We seek to maintain and elevate self-esteem, both through basking in reflected glory and comparing ourselves with others. We are also motivated to gather truthful information about ourselves, paying attention to information consistent with our self-views and creating self-confirmatory social environments. We have discussed how culture affects self-esteem: people of non-Western cultures are less concerned with feeling positively about their attributes than are modern Westerners, and non-Westerners are more likely to seek out opportunities for self-criticism. Though high self-esteem is probably beneficial for the most part, it appears that there is such a thing as too much of it.

SELF-PRESENTATION

Alexi Santana entered Princeton University as a member of the class of 1993. He excelled in his classes, was a star of the track team, and was admitted to one of Princeton's most exclusive eating clubs. He dazzled his dormmates with his tales of being raised on a sheep farm in the wild canyons of southern Utah and his almost otherworldly habits—for example, he routinely arose at dawn and preferred to sleep on the floor.

The only trouble was that Alexi Santana was a fictitious identity. Santana was actually James Hogue, a 34-year-old drifter and former track star from Kansas City. Hogue had been convicted and served time for various crimes, including check forging and bicycle theft. He had gotten into Princeton thanks to a fraudulent application and had won the intense admiration of his peers based on a completely fabricated identity.

Hogue's story (or is it Santana's) is an extreme version of a basic truth: our social self is often a dramatic performance in which we try to project a public self that is in keeping with our hopes and aspirations. This public self is one that we actively create in our social interactions and that is shaped by the perceptions of other people and the perceptions we want others to have of us (Baumeister, 1982; Mead, 1934; Schlenker, 1980; Shrauger & Schoeneman, 1979). The public self is concerned with **self-presentation**—that is, presenting who we would like others to believe we are—in Hogue's case, a brilliant track star. Another term for this is **impression management,** which refers to how we attempt to control the beliefs other people have of us.

Sociologist Erving Goffman inspired the study of self-presentation with his striking observations about how we stake out our identity in the public realm, something James Hogue had mastered (Goffman, 1959, 1967). Rather than doing controlled experiments, Goffman relied on naturalistic observations of how people behave in public settings. He spent time in mental institutions, noting the almost comical ways that patients violate basic rules of politeness. Patients would tell the staff in all too frank terms things we don't often say to others—for example, that they had gained weight or were the recipients of an unflattering haircut. The deeper lesson is that smooth interactions require that we cooperatively participate in the presentation of

self-presentation Presenting who we would like others to believe we are.

impression management Attempting to control the beliefs other people have of us.

Self-Presentation   James Hogue attended Princeton University on an academic scholarship under the assumed name of Alexi Santana. He constructed a false identity for himself at Princeton, and everyone believed that he was the self-educated 18-year-old from Utah that he presented himself as. He was a member of Princeton University's track team and was admitted to the most selective of Princeton's private eating clubs. In a documentary called *Con Man,* Jessie Moss showed that Hogue had had a pattern of assuming false identities. Hogue is shown (A) competing for Palo Alto High School under another assumed name and (B) under arrest for forgery, wrongful impersonation, and falsifying records at Princeton.

Public and Private Face People may present themselves differently in public and private. (A) Nick Nolte is not showing a carefully constructed public face when he is arrested on suspicion of driving under the influence, but (B) he does present a public face when he arrives at a screening of one of his movies.

our own and others' public selves. Goffman wrote an entire chapter on what he called response cries, like "Oops," which we resort to when we have committed social gaffes and feel deeply embarrassed. These linguistic acts help reestablish social order when we have violated the rules of self-presentation and show how committed we are to the public self.

From these observations, Goffman arrived at what has been called a dramaturgic perspective on the social self: social interaction can be thought of as a drama of self-presentation, in which we attempt to create and maintain an impression of ourselves in the minds of others (Baumeister, 1982; Brown, 1998; Goffman, 1959; Leary & Kowalski, 1990; Schlenker & Leary, 1982). Critical to this drama, in Goffman's terms, is **face,** which refers to the public image of ourselves that we want others to believe. We may want others to think we are gifted but temperamental artists, that we have intellectual gifts that allow us to excel without studying, or that we are the object of many romantic interests. Social interactions are the stage on which we play out these kinds of claims, regardless of how true they are. Much like a play, the social drama of self-presentation is highly collaborative. We depend on others to honor our desired social identities, and others likewise depend on us to honor their face claims. Goffman's insights have shaped the study of the self in several lasting ways.

face Who we want others to think we are.

Ideas about the Public Self

Furthering Goffman's analysis of face, researchers differentiate between public and private self-consciousness (Fenigstein, Scheier, & Buss, 1975). **Public self-consciousness** refers to our awareness of what other people think about us—very much akin to Goffman's concept of face, or public identity. **Private self-consciousness** refers to our awareness of our interior lives—our private thoughts, feelings, and sensations. In general, people who attend a great deal to their public self—who are high in public self-consciousness—overestimate the extent to which

public self-consciousness Our awareness of what other people think about us—our public identity.

private self-consciousness Our awareness of our interior lives—our private thoughts, feelings, and sensations.

others attend to them (Fenigstein, 1984), and they define their social self more in terms of social attributes, such as popularity and attractiveness. In contrast, people who attend more to their private self define their social self more in terms of their interior thoughts and feelings.

The concept of self-monitoring also derives in part from Goffman's analysis of strategic self-presentation (Gangestad & Snyder, 2000; Snyder, 1974, 1979). **Self-monitoring** refers to our tendency to monitor our behavior in such a way that it fits the demands of the current situation. High self-monitors carefully scrutinize situations, and they shift their self-presentation and behavior to fit the prevailing context. James Hogue was off the charts in terms of being a high self-monitor. Low self-monitors act in accordance with their internal inclinations, impulses, and dispositions, independent of the social context. High self-monitors are like actors, changing their behavior according to the people they are with. In contrast, low self-monitors are more likely to behave in accordance with their own traits and preferences, which suggests admirable candor and honesty. On the other hand, patients in a psychiatric hospital scored low on a self-monitoring scale, consistent with Goffman's early observations and his thesis that effective social functioning requires that we participate in strategic self-presentation (Snyder, 1974).

self-monitoring The tendency for people to monitor their behavior in such a way that it fits the demands of the current situation.

Self-Monitoring An audience watches the 2008 vice-presidential debate. During their debate, Sarah Palin and Joseph Biden exchanged heated words. This split screen close-up shows Biden reacting to some of Palin's claims, clearly monitoring his behavior in ways to show what she is saying should not be taken seriously.

Self-Handicapping: Protecting Your Own Face

No doubt the public self is a real and powerful part of our identity. One of the complexities of strategic self-presentation is that we often don't live up to the public self we are trying to portray. For example, your claim about being the next great American writer will eventually be put to the test when you submit your prose for publication. Your claim about being the next great triathlete will eventually face the truth of the stopwatch and other competitors. The obvious risk of the public self is that we might not live up to it, and we risk embarrassing ourselves when that happens. To protect the self in these circumstances, we engage in various self-protective behaviors (see **Box 3.2**).

One such behavior is **self-handicapping**, the self-defeating behaviors we engage in to protect our public self and to prevent others from drawing unwanted attributions from poor performance (Arkin & Baumgardner, 1985; Deppe & Harackiewicz, 1996; Hirt, McRea, & Kimble, 2000). Think of how often people engage in self-destructive behaviors when their public selves are on the line. Students will irrationally put too little effort into studying for an exam. Athletes party all night before the championship game. You may act too casually at a job interview or say shockingly inappropriate things on a first date. Why do we engage in such self-defeating behaviors? In Goffman's view, these actions provide an explanation for possible failure, thus maintaining the desired public self. If you don't perform as well as expected on an exam that you didn't prepare for, there is no threat to the claim you would like to make about your academic talents. Of course, people sometimes claim "self-handicaps" they have not experienced. Classrooms are filled with students who act as though they haven't studied terribly hard when in fact they did. The phenomenon is so common that

self-handicapping The tendency to engage in self-defeating behaviors in order to prevent others from drawing unwanted attributions about the self as a result of poor performance.

BOX 3.2 **FOCUS ON HEALTH**

Dying to Present a Favorable Self

Thus far, you might think that self-presentation is a good thing. Erving Goffman himself wrote about how our strategic self-presentation and how our honoring others people's public claims are essential ingredients of harmonious communities. But our worries about our public image and the means by which we are guided by self-presentational concerns may be dangerous to our health (Leary, Tchividjian, & Kraxberger, 1994). Many practices that promote health are awkward or embarrassing and pose problems for our public identity. As a consequence, we avoid them.

We sacrifice physical health to maintain a public identity defined by composure and aplomb. For example, between 30 and 65 percent of respondents reported embarrassment when buying condoms (Hanna, 1989). This embarrassment may deter sexually active teenagers from buying and using condoms, which of course increases their risk of sexually transmitted diseases and unwanted pregnancies. Similarly, the fear of embarrassment at times prevents obese individuals from pursuing physical exercise programs or taking needed medications (Bain, Wilson, & Chaikind, 1989).

In other instances, we engage in risky behavior to enhance our public image and identity. Concerns about others' impressions and our own physical appearance are good predictors of excessive sunbathing, which increases the likelihood of skin cancer (Leary & Jones, 1993). Moreover, adolescents typically cite social approval as one of the most important reasons for why they start to drink alcohol and smoke (Farber, Khavari, & Douglass, 1980). And the same need for an enhanced public image motivates many cosmetic surgeries, which carry with them a variety of health risks.

students on at least one campus, Dartmouth College, have given the people who do it a name—"sneaky bookers."

In one of the first studies of self-handicapping, male participants were led to believe either that they were going to succeed or that they were going to have difficulty on a test they were scheduled to take (Berglas & Jones, 1978). Participants were then given the chance to ingest one of two drugs: the first would enhance their test performance; the second would impair it. Participants who felt they were likely to fail the test

Self-Handicapping In the animal kingdom, self-handicapping behaviors or traits may signal superior genes to potential mates. (A) The peacock's tail makes quick flight difficult, and (B) the stag's antlers also make some movements difficult.

preferred the performance-inhibiting drug, even though it would seem to diminish their chances of success. Apparently, people would sometimes rather fail and have a good reason for it than to go for success and have no excuse for their failure.

One view of self-destructive behaviors, then, is that they protect our public identity in the event of failure. An evolutionary theory of self-handicapping contends that such behaviors sometimes signal superior genes to potential mates (Zahavi & Zahavi, 1997). In numerous species, males have evolved physical traits that handicap survival-related behavior. Male peacocks have elaborate tails that make quick flight difficult. Certain male swallows have unusually long tails that hinder flight. Adult male orangutans have fleshy pads surrounding their eyes that narrow their field of vision and significantly restrict their ability to see—no doubt a hindrance in aggressive encounters. The heavily branched antlers of some male deer prevent certain physical movements and have been shown to be maladaptive in combat. All of these physical traits require the expenditure of valuable energy and resources, and they often hinder the very actions important to survival. At the same time, these traits have important signal value to potential rivals and mates: only an individual with superior genes can afford them. Thus, any success a handicapped organism enjoys must be the product of great talent and genes—the same thing you hope your friends will think when you get an A after (allegedly) not having cracked a book.

Self-Presentation, Flirtation, and Teasing

In many parts of the world, honesty is a virtue. We encourage it in our children and cherish it in our intimate relationships. Honesty is the best policy. Or is it? In Goffman's world of strategic self-presentation, honesty can be downright dangerous; it can threaten other people's attempts to present their desired public selves. Imagine that your best friend is in a band, and he thinks they're on the verge of making it big. When you first hear their music, it sounds clichéd and corny. Do you tell him so? Probably not directly if you want to preserve your friendship. Instead, you might resort to polite white lies or some indirect suggestions. Honest language, especially of a critical nature, threatens the public self that the individual (your friend in our example) is trying to project, and it makes the honest speaker (you) come across as impolite and inconsiderate.

These ideas about protecting the public self have led to insightful analyses of language, flirtation, and teasing. Linguists Penelope Brown and Steven Levinson (1987) propose that there are two levels of communication. On-record communication refers to the statements we make that we intend to be taken literally. **On-record communication** tends to follow the rules of honest communication; it is direct, relevant, and delivered in sincere, straightforward fashion (Clark, 1996; Grice, 1975). When a doctor delivers a dire prognosis or a financial advisor announces the loss of a family fortune, the doctor and financial advisor adhere to the rules of on-record communication like priests following scripture.

When we need to deliver a message that threatens our public self or that of someone we like, we resort to off-record communication. **Off-record communication** is indirect and ambiguous; it allows us to hint at ideas and meanings that are not explicit in the words we utter. Off-record communication violates the rules of direct, honest communication with a variety of tactics, including rhetorical questions, exaggeration, understatement, or intentional vagueness, suggesting alternative interpretations of what is being said. Let's return to our hypothetical example of having to comment on your friend's music. Direct, on-record criticism threatens your friend's public self and your image as a kind friend. Instead of being direct ("To be honest, you should

on-record communication The statements we make that we intend to be taken literally.

off-record communication Indirect and ambiguous communication that allows us to hint at ideas and meanings that are not explicit in the words we utter.

think of another career"), self-presentation concerns are likely to lead you to off-record forms of communication. You might politely resort to obvious exaggeration ("Omigod, you're the next Bono"), vagueness ("Some of the rhythms are really interesting"), or jokey obliqueness ("You guys would be off the charts in Estonia"). In the drama of self-presentation, we break the rules of sincere communication to protect other people's public selves.

Let's apply these ideas of on- and off-record communication to how we flirt. Think of the last time you expressed your initial attraction to someone. We suspect you did not initially do so with on-record communication. You probably did not declare, "You are the second most attractive person in this room and my best shot at a good date here, and I could envision a long-term relationship with you because of your keen wit, kindness, and beauty and would like to go home with you tonight." Such a direct expression of affection would jeopardize your public self as a cool and composed player in the dating scene, and it would risk embarrassing the object of your affection. Instead, we flirt in indirect and off-record ways. For example, we often express our initial interest in the form of teasing ("I'd never go out with someone like you"). Here our words say one thing that is on-record, but what is implied, or off-record, is actually the opposite—that we would like to go out with the person. Many of the nonverbal actions of flirtation have the strategic indirectness that so interested Goffman. For example, people flirt with silly behaviors—playful wrestling, shoulder nudges, tongue protrusions, keep-away games—that allow them to come into physical contact with one another without laying it on the line (Grammer, 1990; Moore, 1985).

Let's look at an even more complex behavior—teasing—through the lens of Goffman's ideas about face and off-record communication. There is, to be sure, a dark side to teasing. The wrong kind of teasing can humiliate in offensive and damaging ways (Georgeson, Harris, Milich, & Young, 1999). Yet very often people rely on teasing as a playful, indirect way of commenting on other people's inappropriate behavior (Keltner, Capps, Kring, Young, & Heerey, 2001). Teasing involves an intentional provocation—a tickle, poke, nickname, or comment—but the provocation is softened by accompanying nonverbal actions that signal that the tease is off-record. We use our voice to signal we don't mean what we say when we tease, using exaggerated pitch and pacing. Daughters mock their obtuse fathers with slow, low-pitched mimicry. The face is its own source of off-record commentary. Preteens tease their parents with exaggerated facial expressions of anger, fear, or surprise, to satirize their parents' outdated moral indignation. Inappropriate actions and conflicts are inevitable parts of enduring relationships. Direct commentary on them can threaten the public self of others, so we resort to teasing.

Consider the role of teasing in romantic relationships. Conflicts and differences are part of long-term romantic bonds; romantic partners must negotiate different preferences, work lives, housework, opinions about friends, and finances. As relationships develop, partners develop teasing nicknames for each other, which they use to playfully comment on each other's quirks and foibles. And in fact, happier relationships have a richer vocabulary of insulting nicknames (Baxter, 1984). You may also be interested to know that couples who resort to lighthearted teasing rather than direct, honest criticism tend to negotiate conflicts in more cooperative fashion and that people (including children) who have many warm relationships tend to be very skilled at playful teasing (Keltner, Young, Heerey, Oemig, & Monarch, 1998).

 LOOKING BACK We have examined self-presentation—how we hope to seem to others. Researchers have distinguished between public self-consciousness, which refers to our awareness of what others think of us, and private self-consciousness, which refers to our private thoughts, feelings, and sensations. Some people are high self-monitors, and they change their behavior based on the situation in which they find themselves. Others are low self-monitors, and they attend more to their own preferences and dispositions, with little regard for the situation or what others think. People may self-handicap, or engage in self-defeating behaviors, in order to "save face" for possible failures. They may also engage in off-record communication, merely hinting at disagreement or disapproval to avoid possible rejection by others.

Summary

Nature of the Social Self

- There are several different foundations of the social self. The self originates in part from evolved, biologically based dispositions inherited from parents, as well as from family birth order. Firstborns tend to be more assertive and achievement oriented; later-borns tend be more open to experience and cooperative.

- The self is profoundly shaped by whether people live in independent or interdependent cultures.

- Gender also affects how people define themselves, with women generally emphasizing their relationships and defining themselves in an interdependent way and men generally emphasizing their uniqueness and construing themselves in an independent way.

- The social self is shaped by the current situation in many ways. For example, according to the *distinctiveness hypothesis*, people in Western cultures tend to define themselves according to what is unique about themselves compared with others in the social context.

- The social self is shaped by construal processes. People rely on *social comparison* to learn about their own abilities, attitudes, and personal traits. The social self can also be thought of as a *narrative*, or story, that we tell to make sense of our goals, conflicts, and changing identities.

Self-Knowledge

- There are several forms and functions of *self-knowledge*. Self-knowledge can take the form of beliefs, images, memories, and stories we tell about our lives. This self-knowledge helps guide construal of social information through memories and self-schemas, typically reinforcing preexisting beliefs about the self. In independent cultures, people use their self-knowledge as standards in judging others.

- Self-knowledge serves an important motivational function embodying cultural and moral standards and motivating appropriate behavior. *Self-discrepancy theory* investigates how people compare their actual self to both their ideal and ought selves.

- Self-control can produce a state of ego depletion, which makes it harder to carry through additional acts of self control.

- People tend to have unrealistically positive beliefs about themselves, an illusion of control, and unrealistic optimism, which all enhance their sense of well-being. This is particularly true in independent cultures.

Self-Evaluation

- There are two kinds of self-esteem: *trait self-esteem*, which tends to be a stable part of identity, and *state self-esteem*, which changes according to different contextual factors, such as personal failure or the poor performance of a beloved sports team.

- Our self-esteem is defined by particular domains of importance, or contingencies of self-worth, and by our being accepted by others. More complex self-representations enable us to be more resilient in response to stress.

- The motivation to have elevated self-esteem guides the formation of friendships that allow us to engage in favorable social comparisons and esteem-enhancing pride taken in the friend's successes.

- Self-esteem is more important and elevated in Western than in East Asian cultures.

- There are perils of high self-esteem, and studies have linked various forms of antisocial behavior with narcissistic levels of self-esteem.

Self-Presentation

- *Self-presentation theory* considers the self to be a dramatic performer in the public realm. People seek to create and maintain a favorable public impression of themselves. *Face* refers to what people want others to think they are.

- Researchers now distinguish between *private* and *public self-consciousness*. They have shown that people engage in *self-monitoring* to ensure that their behavior fits the demands of the social context.

- People protect their public self through *self-handicapping behaviors*, which are self-defeating behaviors that can explain away possible failure.

- Face concerns and self-presentation shape social communication. *On-record communication* is direct; *off-record communication*, like flirtation and teasing, is indirect and subtle.

Key Terms

actual self (p. 86)
collective self-beliefs (p. 82)
contingencies of self-worth (p. 93)
distinctiveness hypothesis (p. 77)
diversification (p. 72)
dizygotic (fraternal) twins (p. 71)
ego depletion (p. 87)
face (p. 102)
five-factor model (p. 69)
heritability (p. 70)
ideal self (p. 87)
identity cues (p. 96)
impression management (p. 101)
monozygotic (identical) twins (p. 71)
off-record communication (p. 105)

on-record communication (p. 105)
ought self (p. 87)
personal beliefs (p. 82)
possible selves (p. 86)
prevention focus (p. 87)
private self-consciousness (p. 102)
promotion focus (p. 87)
public self-consciousness (p. 102)
relational self-beliefs (p. 82)
self-complexity (p. 93)
self-discrepancy theory (p. 86)
self-esteem (p. 91)
self-evaluation maintenance model (p. 94)

self-handicapping (p. 103)
self-image bias (p. 85)
self-monitoring (p. 103)
self-presentation (p. 101)
self-reference effect (p. 83)
self-schemas (p. 84)
self-verification theory (p. 96)
social comparison theory (p. 79)
social self-beliefs (p. 82)
sociometer hypothesis (p. 93)
state self-esteem (p. 92)
traits (p. 69)
trait self-esteem (p. 92)

Further Reading and Films

Allen, W. (1983). *Zelig.* "Human chameleon" Leonard Zelig (Woody Allen) soars to celebrity in the 1920s and '30s with his unexplained ability to transform himself into anyone he meets. Allen's "mockumentary" finds Zelig in the unlikeliest of places—from the intensity of a New York Yankees dugout to the frenzy of a Nazi rally.

Dennis, N. F. (1955/2002). *Cards of identity.* Normal, Il: Dalkey Archive Press. A very entertaining novel about a group of people (psychologists?) who find individuals with identities that are making them miserable and change their identities by surrounding them with people and evidence supporting the new identity. If you're confident that it couldn't happen to you, finish this text before reading Dennis's book.

Higgins, E. T. (1987). Self discrepancy: A theory relating self and affect. *Psychological Review, 94,* 319–340. A classic paper showing how the "ought self" and the "ideal self" are different not only from the "actual self" but from each other.

Taylor, S. E. (1989). *Positive illusions: Creative self-deception and the healthy mind.* New York: Basic Books. A recounting of the ways in which psychologically healthy people hold various illusions about themselves and the nature of the world. Who says wishful thinking is dangerous? (Actually, several of the author's critics—but she has interesting answers.)

ⓢ Online Study Tools

StudySpace

Go to StudySpace, wwnorton.com/studyspace, to access additional review and enrichment materials, including the following resources for each chapter:

Organize
- Study Plan
- Chapter Outline
- Quiz+ Assessment

Learn
- Ebook
- Chapter Review
- Critical-Thinking Questions
- Visual Quizzes
- Vocabulary Flashcards

Connect
- Apply It! Exercises
- Author Insights Podcasts
- Social Psychology in the News

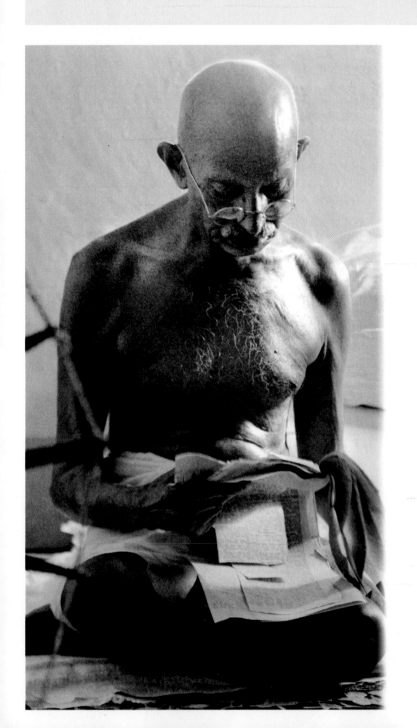

What made Gandhi Gandhi.

SOUL

Pass It On.

VALUES.COM THE FOUNDATION FOR A BETTER LIFE®

Understanding Others

IT CAN BE A BIT SHOCKING to those who've known Mickey Mouse as the endearing, iconic host of Disney's Magic Kingdom to learn that he wasn't always so sweet or kind. In such early cartoons as *The Karnival Kid* and *Steamboat Willie*, he comes across as a bit of a scamp, often more like a rat than a mouse. He torments a cat by pulling its tail, pounds on the teeth of a cow to create a makeshift xylophone, and treats a goat's tail like the crank of a barrel organ. This can be jarring to those who've only known the contemporary Mickey, because these actions just don't seem like him. Someone that cute wouldn't do those sorts of things, would he?

No he wouldn't—and he didn't. That is, Mickey of the 1920s and '30s did do a number of unkind things on-screen. But he didn't look the way he does now (Finch, 1975). His eyes were smaller (and had no iris), his head was smaller, and the distance between his eyes and hairline was narrower. In short, he looked nastier, making his occasional acts of hard-edged mischief seem more fitting. But despite his appearance and his occasional misdeeds, Mickey quickly became an audience favorite, so much so that fans would write and complain whenever he was depicted doing something mean. So Walt Disney and his animators soon banished all unpleasantness from Mickey's behavioral repertoire and began to draw him in the kinder, gentler fashion that we see today.

The fit between appearance and behavior that Disney fans have been exposed to over the years has been echoed over and over in all visual media. Innocent characters are cast, drawn, or made up to look like innocents; villains to look like villains; leaders to look like leaders; and cowards to look like cowards.

In this chapter, we'll examine the sorts of facial cues that suggest particular personal dispositions and, more broadly, how people form impressions of others on the basis of the information they have before them. Fair or unfair, right or wrong, people make inferences about others based on their appearance. People don't stop there, of course. People also draw inferences about others based on their behavior.

But the true meaning of an action may not be clear. Was Robert kind to his new employer because he's a genial person or because he was just currying favor? Did the congresswoman visit the new senior citizens' center because she has a real interest in the elderly, or was she just trying to win votes? In this chapter, we will also examine how people resolve these ambiguities and decide whether someone's behavior is a telling sign of the person's true, underlying dispositions or whether it is a reflection of compelling constraints or incentives. This is the concern of **attribution theory,** or the study and analysis of how people understand the causes of events.

attribution theory An umbrella term used to describe the set of theoretical accounts of how people assign causes to the events around them and the effects that people's causal assessments have.

FROM PHYSICAL APPEARANCE TO INFERENCES ABOUT PERSONALITY TRAITS

One of the most interesting things about the inferences we make about people based on their appearance is how quickly we make them. The term *snap judgment* exists for a reason. In a telling empirical demonstration of this fact, Janine Willis and Alex Todorov (2006) showed participants a large number of faces and had them rate how attractive, aggressive, likable, trustworthy, and competent each person seemed. Some participants were given as much time as they wanted to make each rating, and their estimates were used as the standard of comparison—as the most informed impressions one could form based solely on photographs. Other participants were asked to make the same ratings, but only after seeing each face for a second, half a second, or a tenth of a second. How well did these hurried judgments correspond with the more reflective assessments? As you can see in **Table 4.1**, remarkably well. A great deal of what we conclude about people based on their faces is determined almost instantaneously.

What is it that people so quickly think they see in another's face? To find out, Todorov and his colleagues (Todorov, Said, Engell, & Oosterhof, 2008) had participants rate a large number of photographs of different faces, all with neutral expressions, on the personality dimensions people most often spontaneously mention when describing faces. When he looked at how all these judgments correlated with one another, he found that two dimensions tend to stand out. One is a positive/negative dimension, involving such

TABLE 4.1 Correlations between Time-Constrained Trait Judgments Based on Facial Appearance and Judgments Made in the Absence of Time Constraints

Trait judgment	Exposure time		
	100 ms	500ms	1,000ms
Trustworthiness	.73	.66	.74
Competence	.52	.67	.59
Likability	.59	.57	.63
Aggressiveness	.52	.56	.59
Attractiveness	.69	.57	.66

Note: All correlations were significant. $p < .001$.

assessments as whether someone is seen as trustworthy or untrustworthy, aggressive or not aggressive. The other dimension centers around power, involving such assessments as whether someone seems confident or bashful, dominant or submissive. It appears, then, that people are attuned to making highly functional judgments about others—whether they should be approached or avoided (dimension 1) and where they are likely to stand in a status or power hierarchy (dimension 2). Todorov has utilized computer models to generate faces that occupy various points in the space defined by the traits that comprise these two dimensions, including faces that are more extreme on each trait dimension than you would ever encounter in real life (see **Figure 4.1**). From these faces, we can see the hypermasculine features, such as a very

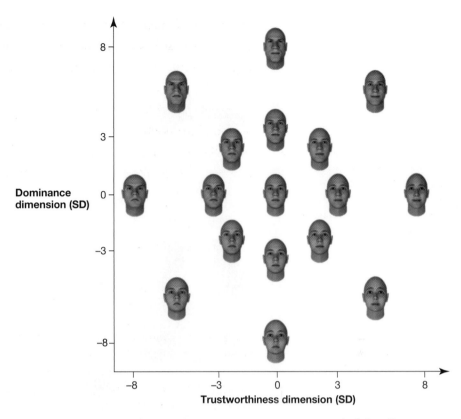

FIGURE 4.1 Judging Faces
Computer-generated faces showing variation on the two independent dimension of trustworthiness (*x*-axis) and dominance (*y*-axis).

pronounced jaw, that make someone look dominant and the features, such as the shape of the eyebrows and eye socket, that make someone look trustworthy.

If you look at the faces that are seen as trustworthy and not dominant, you'll notice something else that people pick up on when judging faces—the trustworthy, nondominant faces tend to look rather youthful. They're baby faces. Note that babies are anything but dominant, and they don't have the capacity to be very deceitful. Perhaps, then, we overgeneralize these facts and consider even adults with baby-faced features to be relatively harmless and helpless. Theoretically, it makes sense. The renowned ethologist Konrad Lorenz (1950) wondered why people consider the young of many mammalian species to be so cute, and he speculated that it reflects a hardwired, automatic reaction that helps to ensure that adequate care is given to the young and helpless. The automatic nature of our response to infantile features makes it more likely that we would indeed overgeneralize and come to see even adults with such features as trustworthy and friendly.

Extensive research by Leslie Zebrowitz and her colleagues has shown that adults with such baby-faced features as large round eyes, a large forehead, high eyebrows, and a rounded, relatively small chin are indeed assumed to possess many of the characteristics associated with the very young (Berry & Zebrowitz-McArthur, 1986; Zebrowitz & Montepare, 2005). They are judged to be relatively weak, naive, and submissive, whereas those with small eyes, a small forehead, and an angular, prominent chin tend to be judged as strong, competent, and dominant (see **Figure 4.2**). These assessments have dramatic implications: baby-faced defendants receive more favorable treatment in court (Zebrowitz & McDonald, 1991) but have a harder time being seen as appropriate for "adult" jobs such as banking (Zebrowitz, Tenenbaum, & Goldstein, 1991).

Recall our earlier discussion of how Disney's artists changed their depictions of Mickey Mouse. To make him look warmer, nicer, and friendlier, they gave him the features associated with the young—larger eyes, a bigger head, and a bigger forehead (Gould, 1982). We see these features and we automatically think of Mickey as warm,

FIGURE 4.2 You Be the Subject: Personality Ratings Based on Appearance

Review these photos and circle where you think they fall on the personality scales below

Personality Rankings

Weak	1	2	3	4	5	6	7	8	9	10	Strong
Naive	1	2	3	4	5	6	7	8	9	10	Competent
Submissive	1	2	3	4	5	6	7	8	9	10	Dominant
Weak	1	2	3	4	5	6	7	8	9	10	Strong
Naive	1	2	3	4	5	6	7	8	9	10	Competent
Submissive	1	2	3	4	5	6	7	8	9	10	Dominant

Results: If you are like most people, you judged the top photo (which is more "babyish" according to the criteria used by Zebrowitz, et al.) to be lower on these personality dimensions, and the bottom photo to be higher.

honest, and kind—and we have the same nurturing impulses when we see a fawn, a lion cub, or a baby human.

The Accuracy of Snap Judgments

How accurate are the snap judgments we make of people based on their appearance or upon witnessing very brief samples of their behavior? It depends on what is meant by "accurate," or what our snap judgments are meant to predict. Sometimes what is important to predict is what other people think. In these cases, the pertinent question boils down to how well snap judgments predict more considered consensus opinion. And the evidence indicates that they predict rather well. For example, in one study, participants were shown, for 1 second, pictures of the Republican and Democratic candidates in U.S. congressional elections and asked to indicate which ones looked more competent. The candidates judged to be more competent by a majority of the participants won 69 percent of the races (Todorov, Mandisodza, Goren, & Hall, 2005). The person judged to be more competent might not actually be more competent, but what matters in predicting the outcome of elections is not what is really true, but what the electorate believes to be true.

In another line of research, participants were shown "thin slices" of professors' performance in the classroom (that is, three 10-second silent video clips) and asked to rate the professors on a variety of dimensions, such as how anxious, competent, active, professional, and warm they seemed. A composite of these relatively quick assessments correlated significantly with students' evaluations of their professors at the end of the semester (Ambady & Rosenthal, 1993). Again, we don't know whether individual professors who are quickly sized up as warm and competent actually are warm and competent, but those who are thought to be warm and competent by their students are likely to receive more favorable course evaluations.

But what if the task is to predict not what other people will think but what really is the case? Are people with baby-faced features, for example, really more likely to be weak or submissive? It's easy to imagine how being treated by others as weak and submissive might encourage something of a dependent disposition. It's also easy to imagine how a strong jaw might elicit deference from others, thereby encouraging a forceful, dominant stance toward the world. So, are the facial features people associate with different personality traits valid cues to those traits?

That is a question that awaits a fully satisfactory answer. The current evidence is mixed. Some investigators report moderately high correlations between the judgments made about people based on their facial appearance and those individuals' own reports of how approachable, extraverted, and powerful they are (Berry, 1991; Berry & Brownlow, 1989; Penton-Voak, Little, & Perrett, 2006). But similar studies have found no connection between judgments based on facial appearance and self-reports of agreeableness and conscientiousness (Pound, Penton-Voak, & Brown, 2007). And when behavioral observation rather than self-ratings are used as the criterion of accuracy, evidence that people can accurately assess people's personalities based on facial appearance alone is even harder to find (Zebrowitz, Andreoletti, Collins, Lee, & Blumenthal, 1998; Zebrowitz, Voinescu, & Collins, 1996). Perhaps the fairest summary of current research in this area is that there may be a kernel of truth to people's snap judgments about facial appearance, but it is a very small kernel. It seems that our ability to make such judgments, and to agree with one another when we do so, mostly stems from an automatic tendency to overgeneralize from facial features typical of youth (for example, large eyes) or typical of particular emotions (for example, the slight squint of the eyes associated with anger) and to conclude that adult faces with such features reflect such dispositions as naivete or dominance, respectively.

FROM ACTS TO DISPOSITIONS: THE IMPORTANCE OF CAUSAL ATTRIBUTION

In class one day, you listen as a student gives a long-winded answer to a question posed by your professor. When the student is finally finished, your professor says, "Good point" and then proceeds to expand on the topic. You can't help but wonder, "Did she really think it was a good point or was she just trying to encourage student participation? Or was she trying to boost her standing on rateyourprofessor.com?" You are especially likely to ask yourself these questions if you yourself were not so impressed with your classmate's comments. The answer that you give yourself to these questions not only explains this particular action by your professor but helps make sense of many of her other actions in the course (such as whether she calls on this student often or whether she seems consistently solicitous of student opinion).

Causal attribution is the process by which we explain both our own behavior and that of others. Understanding causal attributions is crucial to understanding much of everyday social behavior because we all make causal attributions many times a day, and the attributions we make greatly affect our thoughts, feelings, and future behavior.

causal attribution Linking an instance of behavior to a cause, whether the behavior is our own or someone else's.

The Pervasiveness and Importance of Causal Attribution

When you get back an exam, you are not simply happy or sad about the grade you received. You make an attribution. You decide that you are smart and hardworking or that the test was unfair. Or when you ask someone out for a date but are rebuffed

("No thanks, I have a cold"), you do not simply take the response at face value. You wonder, "Does she really have a cold or am I getting the brush-off?" Attributions are a constant part of mental life. You may ask yourself such questions as: "Did John McCain really believe that Sarah Palin was qualified to assume the duties of president, or was he trying to shore up his connections to the conservative base of the Republican Party?" "Why was my interview so short? Did the interviewers conclude that I obviously have what it takes, or were they just not interested?" "Why does everything work out so well for my roommate, while I have to struggle to get by?"

The causes people cite have tremendous significance. They matter. The belief that Senator McCain's choice of Sarah Palin as his running mate resulted from a sincere conviction about her qualifications leads to certain thoughts and feelings about him; the belief that his actions reflected a narrower political calculation leads to a very different set of reactions.

Likewise, concluding that someone won't go out with you because she's sick leads to an entirely different set of emotional reactions than concluding that she does not find you appealing. And attributing a bad grade on an exam to a lack of ability leads to unhappiness and withdrawal, whereas attributing failure to a lack of effort often leads to more vigorous attempts to study harder and more effectively in the future.

Systematic research on causal attribution has shown that people's explanations have tremendous consequences in a number of domains, with the most widely studied being health and education. In the educational sphere, setbacks are experienced by even the best students (a lost set of notes, a mystifying lecture, a failed quiz), and the attributions made about those setbacks are related to how well a student tends to perform in school.

Explanatory Style and Attribution

One group of investigators, led by Chris Peterson and Martin Seligman, has examined the impact of attributions on academic success by relating a person's explanatory style to long-term academic performance. **Explanatory style** refers to a person's habitual way of explaining events, and it is assessed along three dimensions: internal/external, stable/unstable, and global/specific. To assess explanatory style, researchers ask respondents to imagine six different good events that might happen to them ("You do a project that is highly praised") and six bad events ("You meet a friend who acts hostilely toward you") and to provide a likely cause for each. Respondents are then asked if each cause (1) is due to something about them or something about other people or circumstances (internal/external), (2) will be present again in the future or not (stable/unstable), and (3) is something that influences other areas of their lives or just this one (global/specific). An explanation that cites an *internal* cause implicates the self ("There I go again"), but an *external* cause does not ("That was the pickiest set of questions I've ever seen"). A *stable* cause implies that things will never change ("I'm just no good"), whereas an *unstable* cause implies that things may improve ("The cold medicine I was taking made me groggy"). Finally, a *global* cause is something that affects many areas of life ("I'm stupid"), whereas a *specific* cause applies to only a few ("I'm not good with names").

In the research by Seligman, Peterson, and their colleagues, the three dimensions of internal/external, stable/unstable, and global/specific are combined to form an overall explanatory style index, which is then correlated with an outcome variable of interest, such as students' GPAs. A tendency to explain negative events in terms of stable, global, and internal causes is considered a pessimistic explanatory style and it is related to a variety of undesirable life outcomes. For example, students with a pessimistic

explanatory style A person's habitual way of explaining events, typically assessed along three dimensions: internal/external, stable/unstable, and global/specific.

explanatory style tend to get lower grades than those with a more optimistic style (Peterson & Barrett, 1987).

Petersen and Seligman have also studied the impact of different explanatory styles on health. In one study, for example, they examined whether a person's explanatory style as a young adult could predict physical health later in life (Peterson, Seligman, & Vaillant, 1988; see also Peterson, 2000). The study took advantage of the fact that members of Harvard's graduating classes from 1942 to 1944 took part in a longitudinal study that required them to complete a questionnaire every year and submit medical records of periodic physical examinations. Each person's physical health was assessed by having judges score the medical records on a 5-point scale, with "1" meaning the person was in good health and "5" meaning the person was deceased. This was done for all participants when they reached the ages of 25, 30, 35, and so on.

Their physical health at each of these ages was then correlated with their explanatory style as young men, which was assessed by having judges score their descriptions of their most difficult experiences during World War II—a question they had been asked in 1946, when they were all recent college graduates. These correlations, after statistically controlling for the respondents' initial physical condition at age 25, are reported in **Table 4.2**. As a quick glance at the table indicates, explanatory style during young adulthood is a significant predictor of physical health in later life. (The fact that it does not correlate with health at ages 30 to 40 is most likely due to the fact that nearly all of the respondents were in generally good health at those ages, and so there was nothing to predict. In similar fashion, explanatory style—or anything else, for that matter—is unlikely to be related to physical health at age 100 because at that age, nearly everyone, regardless of explanatory style, is dead.) So in terms of one of the most important outcomes there can be—whether we are alive or dead, vigorous or frail—our causal attributions matter. The tendency to make external, unstable, and specific attributions for failure presumably makes us less prone to despair and encourages more of a "can do" outlook that promotes such behaviors as flossing our teeth, exercising, and visiting the doctor—behaviors that can lead to a longer, healthier life.

A second group of researchers, led by Bernard Weiner and Craig Anderson, has conducted research that reinforces the idea that people's attributional tendencies

"A pessimist sees the difficulty in every opportunity; an optimist sees the opportunity in every difficulty."

—Sir Winston Churchill

TABLE 4.2 Does Explanatory Style Early in Life Predict Later Physical Health?	
The correlation between explanatory style at age 25 and physical health at seven points in life, with earlier physical health controlled statistically.	
Age	**Correlation**
30	.04
35	.03
40	.13
45	.37*
50	.18
55	.22*
60	.25*

*Denotes statistically significant correlation.
Source: Peterson, Seligman, & Vaillant (1988).

Attribution and Control
Christopher Reeve was paralyzed in a riding accident, but he continued to believe that his efforts mattered and that he could control some aspects of his life. He did what he could to exercise his muscles, to campaign for further research on spinal cord injuries, and to help other disabled people. He is pictured here with his wife, Dana Reeve, and with Meryl Streep after accepting an award from an association of disabled people.

have a powerful effect on their long-term outcomes, but these investigators emphasize whether an attribution implies that an outcome is controllable, not whether its consequences are global or specific. Attributions for failure that imply controllability—for example, a lack of effort or a poor strategy—make perseverance easier because we can always try harder or try a new strategy (Anderson, 1991; Anderson & Deuser, 1993, Anderson, Krull, & Weiner, 1996). If outcomes are viewed as beyond one's control, on the other hand, it's tempting to simply give up—indeed, it's often rational to do so. The importance of controllability is also apparent in the impact of a person's attributions in judging someone else's behavior. People who are opposed to a gay lifestyle, for example, express more sympathetic attitudes toward gays if they consider homosexuality an inescapable result of a person's biology rather than a lifestyle choice (Whitely, 1990). And when a person offers an excuse for problematic behavior, it typically yields more pity and forgiveness if it involves something out of the person's control ("I had a flat tire") than if it involves something controllable ("I needed to take a break") (Weiner, 1986).

Research inspired by these findings has shown that people can be trained to adopt more productive attributional tendencies (especially to attribute failure to a lack of effort) and that doing so has beneficial effects on subsequent academic performance (Dweck, 1975; Forsterling, 1985). The effects are both substantial and touching. Blackwell, Dweck, and Trzesniewski (2004) report tough junior high school boys crying when made to realize that their grades were due to a lack of effort rather than a lack of brains. Making people believe that they can exert control over events that were formerly thought to be outside of their control restores hope and unleashes the kind of productive energy that makes future success more likely (Crandall, Katkovsky, & Crandall, 1965; Dweck & Reppucci, 1973; Peterson, Maier, & Seligman, 1993; Seligman, Maier, & Geer, 1968).

This type of training might be put to good use, we should note, to undo some inadvertent attributional training that takes place in elementary school classrooms across the United States, a type that appears to give rise to a troubling gender difference in attributional style. That is, boys are more likely than girls to attribute their failures to lack of effort, and girls are more likely than boys to attribute their failure to lack of ability. Carol Dweck and her colleagues have found that this difference results in part from boys and girls being subtly taught different ways to interpret both their successes and their failures (Dweck, Davidson, Nelson, & Enna, 1978). They observed teachers' feedback patterns in fourth- and fifth-grade classrooms and found that despite the fact that girls, on average, outperform boys in school, negative evaluations of girls' performance were almost exclusively restricted to intellectual inadequacies ("This is not right, Lisa"). In contrast, 45 percent of the criticism of boys' work referred to nonintellectual factors ("This is messy, Bill"). Positive evaluation of girls' performance was related to the intellectual quality of their performance less than 80 percent of the time; for boys, it was 94 percent of the time. Dweck and her colleagues argue from these data that girls learn that criticism means they lack ability, whereas boys learn that criticism means they haven't worked hard enough or paid enough attention to detail.

To nail this down, Dweck and her colleagues performed an experiment in which they gave students feedback of the kind girls typically receive in the class or the kind boys typically receive. They found that both boys and girls receiving the comments typically given to girls were more likely than those receiving feedback typically given to boys to view subsequent failure feedback as reflecting their ability. So, whatever other reasons there may be for boys crowing about their successes and dismissing their failures, they are aided in this pattern by the treatment they receive in the classroom. And whatever motivational factors operate for girls, their more modest attributions are likewise shaped by the feedback they receive in school.

LOOKING BACK We have noted that causal attribution goes on all the time in our lives and that there are substantial individual differences in explanatory style. That is, people differ in whether they tend to make attributions that are external or internal, stable or unstable, global or specific. Attributional style has been shown to predict academic success as well as health and longevity. Belief in the controllability of outcomes is important, and beliefs about the controllability of academic outcomes can be altered by training. Boys and girls learn different attributional beliefs about academic outcomes, with boys receiving feedback that success is due to ability and failure is due to insufficient effort or to incidental factors, and girls receiving feedback indicating the reverse.

THE PROCESSES OF CAUSAL ATTRIBUTION

Does she really like me, or is she just acting that way because I'm rich and famous? Does that candidate really believe what she is saying, or is she just saying that to win votes? Is he really a jerk, or is he just under a lot of pressure? These types of questions run through our head on a daily basis. Before we explore how people might answer these questions, we should note that people's assessments of the causes of observed or reported behavior are not capricious; rather, they follow rules that make them predictable. Much of this chapter is devoted to examining the most important of these rules, which have evolved to serve many functions—namely, to understand the past, illuminate the present, and predict the future. It is only by knowing the cause of a given event that we can grasp the true meaning of what has happened and anticipate what is likely to happen in the future.

A particularly important focus of people's attributional analysis is determining whether an outcome is the product of something internal to the person (that is, an internal, or "dispositional," cause) or a reflection of something about the context or circumstances (that is, an external, or "situational," cause). Ever since Kurt Lewin (see Chapter 1) pointed out that behavior is a function of both the person and the situation, all theories of attribution have been concerned with people's assessments of the relative contributions of these two types of causes (Heider, 1958; Hilton & Slugoski, 1986; Hilton, Smith, & Kim, 1995; Jones & Davis, 1965; Kelley, 1967; Medcoff, 1990). If behavior is a function of both the person and the situation, how do we figure out whether someone acted a certain way primarily because that's who he is or because of the dictates of the situation?

Frequently, the distinction between internal and external is straightforward. You might win the pot in your weekly poker game because you're a better player than everyone else (internal cause), or you may have simply been lucky and gotten the best cards (external cause). Knowledge and skill clearly reside inside a person, and luck is something completely beyond a person's influence; the internal/external dichotomy is unambiguous. In other contexts, however, the distinction isn't so clear. We might

"If we're being honest, it was your decision to follow my recommendation that cost you money."

say that someone became a rock n' roll guitarist because of a deep love of the instrument (internal cause) or because of the desire for fame and fortune (external cause). But aren't love and desire both inner states? And if so, why is the love of playing the guitar considered an internal cause, whereas the desire for fame and fortune is considered an external cause? The answer is that loving to play the guitar is not something shared by everyone, or even most people, and so it tells us something individuating and informative about the person. It thus makes sense to refer to the cause as something personal or internal. Most people, however, find the prospect of fame attractive (why else would there be so many reality TV shows?), and even more find the prospect of wealth attractive. Doing something to achieve fame and fortune, then, tells us nothing about the person in hot pursuit of either. It therefore makes sense to refer to the cause in this case as something impersonal or external. This implies, then, that determining whether certain actions are the product of internal versus external causes requires assessments of what most people are like and what most people are likely to do, a topic to which we now turn.

Attribution and Covariation

When scientists try to nail down the cause of some phenomenon, they try to isolate the one cause that seems to make a difference in producing the effect. That is, they try to identify the cause that seems always to be present when the effect or phenomenon occurs and always seems to be absent when the phenomenon does not occur. For example, to determine whether ulcers are caused by a bacterium, a medical researcher might determine whether individuals who are given the bacterium develop ulcers and whether individuals who have ulcers improve after taking a suitable antibiotic.

To a considerable degree, we assess causality in our everyday lives much the way scientists do in their professional lives (Cheng & Novick, 1990; Fiedler, Walther, & Nickel, 1999; Forsterling, 1989; Hewstone & Jaspers, 1987; Kelley, 1973; Nisbett & Ross, 1980; White, 2002). When your friend states that she likes her statistics class, you automatically try to figure out why ("Is she a math nut?" "Is it taught by a gifted teacher?") by identifying what seems decisive. What does your friend have to say about other math classes or about her classes in general? What do other students in her statistics class have to say about it?

In considering these questions, people use what attribution theorists have dubbed the **covariation principle** (Kelley, 1973). That is, we try to determine what causes—internal or external; symptomatic of the person in question or applicable to nearly everyone—"covary" with the observation or effect we are trying to explain. There are three types of covariation information that psychologists believe are particularly significant: consensus, distinctiveness, and consistency. **Consensus** refers to what most people would do in a given situation—that is, does everyone behave the same way in that situation, or do few or no other people behave that way? Is your friend one of a precious few who likes her statistics class, or do most students like the class? All else being equal, the more an individual's reaction is shared by others (that is, when consensus is high), the less it says about that individual and the more it says about the situation. **Distinctiveness** refers to what an individual does in different situations—that is, whether a behavior is unique to a particular situation or occurs in all situations. Does your friend claim to like all math classes, or even all classes in general, or does she just like her statistics class? The more someone's reaction is confined to a particular situation (that is, when distinctiveness is high), the less it says about that individual and the more it says about the specific situation. **Consistency** refers to what an individual does in a given situation on different occasions—that is, whether the behavior is the

"The logic of science is also that of business and life."

— John Stuart Mill

"The whole of science is nothing more than refinement of everyday thinking."

—Albert Einstein

covariation principle The idea that we should attribute behavior to potential causes that co-occur with the behavior.

consensus Refers to what most people would do in a given situation—that is, whether most people would behave the same way or few or no other people would behave that way.

distinctiveness Refers to what an individual does in different situations—that is, whether the behavior is unique to a particular situation or occurs in all situations.

consistency Refers to what an individual does in a given situation on different occasions—that is, whether next time under the same circumstances, the person would behave the same or differently.

TABLE 4.3 Covariation Information

Putting covariation information to work by using consensus, distinctiveness, and consistency information. How do we explain a friend's enthusiastic comments about her statistics class? Does she have idiosyncratic tastes (internal attribution), or is the class a gem (external attribution)?

Attribution	Consensus	Distinctiveness	Consistency
An **external attribution** is likely if the behavior is:	High in **consensus**: Everyone raves about the class.	High in **distinctiveness**: Your friend does not rave about many other classes.	High in **consistency**: Your friend has raved about the class on many occasions.
An **internal attribution** is likely if the behavior is:	Low in **consensus**: Hardly anyone raves about the class.	Low in **distinctiveness**: Your friend raves about all classes.	High in **consistency**: Your friend has raved about the class on many occasions.

same the next time or whether it varies. Does your friend have favorable things to say about her statistics class today only, or has she extolled its virtues all semester? The more an individual's reaction is specific to a given occasion (that is, when consistency is low), the harder it is to make a definite attribution either to the person or the situation. The effect is likely due to some less predictable combination of circumstances.

Putting the three sources of information together, a situational attribution is called for when consensus, distinctiveness, and consistency are all high (see **Table 4.3**). When everyone likes your friend's statistics class, when she claims to like no other math class, and when she has raved about the class all semester, there must be something special about that class. In contrast, a dispositional attribution is called for when consensus and distinctiveness are low but consistency is high. When few other students like her class, when she claims to like all math classes, and when she has raved about the course all semester, her fondness for the course must reflect something about her.

To verify that people do indeed use covariation information in these ways, attribution researchers have presented participants with statements such as: "John laughed at the comedian. Almost everyone who hears the comedian laughs at him (indicating consensus). John does not laugh at many other comedians (indicating distinctiveness). In the past, John has almost always laughed at the same comedian (indicating consistency)." The participants are then asked to indicate whether they think the event (John's laughing) was due to the person (John), the situation (the comedian), the circumstances (the details surrounding the performance that particular day), or some combination of these factors.

These studies have revealed consistent use of the logic of covariation (Forsterling, 1989; Hewstone & Jaspers, 1983; Hilton et al., 1995; McArthur, 1972; White, 2002). Participants tend to make situational attributions when consensus, distinctiveness, and consistency are high and to make dispositional attributions when consensus and distinctiveness are low but consistency is high. The only mildly surprising finding in these studies is that participants are sometimes only modestly influenced by the consensus information. They respond to whether or not everyone laughed at the comedian, but rather mildly. As we shall see, this reflects a common tendency to focus more on information about the person (here, distinctiveness and consistency, or what this person has done on other occasions and in other contexts) at the expense of information that speaks to the influence of the surrounding context (here, consensus, or what other people have done in this situation).

Covariation and Attribution
A person in the audience watching Robin Williams perform a comedy routine, as here, may be laughing because of his own disposition or the situation. If we can observe the person on a number of occasions at comedy clubs and find that he always laughs at Robin Williams's routines (high consistency), that he rarely laughs at other comedians' jokes (high distinctiveness), and that most people laugh when Williams performs (high consensus), covariation principles will lead us to attribute the person's laughter to the situation rather than to his disposition.

Attribution and Imagining Alternative Actors and Outcomes

The observations that serve as grist for the attributional mill are not limited to what we know actually happened; sometimes they are derived from what we *imagine* would happen under different situations or if a different individual were involved. For example, in trying to fathom the high rates of obedience in Stanley Milgram's experiments (see Chapters 1 and 8), people imagine what they would do if they were a participant. Because people have difficulty imagining that they themselves would administer so much electric shock to the victim, they believe that a change in the participant (in this case, themselves instead of the typical Milgram participant) would lead to a change in the outcome. Hence, they conclude that it must have been the person, not the situation, that was responsible for the behavior.

The Discounting and Augmentation Principles Sometimes the information available to us suggests that either of two (or more) causes might be responsible for a given behavior. Someone interviews for a job and seems quite personable. Is that the way she really is, or is she just putting on a good face for the interview? We are particularly likely to be in such an attributional quandary when we haven't had the opportunity to see how this person behaves in other situations or we haven't been able to witness how other people behave in exactly the same situation.

Note that we're rarely stymied in these situations. To the contrary, we typically use our general knowledge about the world to infer how most people would behave in the situation in question, and we combine that knowledge with a bit of logic to arrive at an attribution. The logic is known as the **discounting principle**, according to which a person's confidence that a particular cause is responsible for a given outcome must be reduced (discounted) if there are other plausible causes that might have produced it (Kelley, 1973). Either a sunny disposition or the desire to land a job is sufficient to make someone act personally in an interview. By pure logic, then, a confident attribution cannot be made. But we supplement the pure logic with our knowledge of people. That knowledge tells us that nearly everyone would act in a personable manner to get the job offer, but what we can't be confident of is the sunny disposition. We thus discount the possibility that what we've seen (a personable demeanor) tells us something about the person involved (she's personable) because we imagine that nearly everyone would act similarly in that context. More generally, we cannot be sure that someone's actions are a reflection of the person's true self if the circumstances are such that those actions are likely to occur anyway. For example, you cannot believe what someone says under the threat of torture because the threat is sufficient to get most people to say almost anything; you discount the internal cause (the person is honestly confessing) because the external cause (the threat of punishment) is sufficient to explain the behavior.

Extending the logic just a bit leads to a complementary **augmentation principle**, by which we can have great (augmented) confidence that a particular cause is responsible for a given outcome if there are other causes present that we imagine would produce the *opposite* outcome. Once again, this typically means that we can be sure that a person's actions reflect what that person is really like if the circumstances would seem to discourage such actions. If someone advocates a position despite being threatened with torture for doing so, we can safely conclude that the person really and truly believes in that position.

One important derivation of the discounting and augmentation principles is that it can be difficult to know what to conclude about someone who behaves "in role," but easy to figure out what to think about someone who acts "out of role." One of the

discounting principle The idea that we should assign reduced weight to a particular cause of behavior if there are other plausible causes that might have produced it.

augmentation principle The idea that we should assign greater weight to a particular cause of behavior if there are other causes present that normally would produce the opposite outcome.

earliest attribution studies makes this point quite clearly (Jones, Davis, & Gergen, 1961). The participants witnessed another person present himself in either an extraverted or introverted manner during an interview. Half of the participants were led to believe he was interviewing for a job as a submariner, a position that required close contact with many people over a long period of time and thus favored extraverted personalities. The other participants thought he was interviewing for a job as an astronaut, which involved long periods of solitude and thus favored an introverted personality. (Note that this study was published in 1961, when space flight involved a single astronaut in a tiny capsule.)

In short, half the participants witnessed behavior that conformed to the dictates of the situation—someone who exhibited extraversion for the submariner job or introversion for the astronaut job. Because the behavior fit the situation in these instances, it should be difficult to judge whether the behavior was a true reflection of the person being interviewed. In contrast, the other participants witnessed behavior that defied the dictates of the situation—someone who exhibited introversion for the submariner assignment or extraversion for the astronaut job. Because the behavior was at variance with what is called for in the situation, it should be seen as a clear reflection of the interviewee's true self.

When the participants subsequently rated the interviewee on a host of trait dimensions dealing with introversion/extraversion, their judgments closely followed the logic of the discounting and augmentation principles. As shown in **Figure 4.3**, in-role behavior prompted rather mild inferences (see the middle two bars), whereas out-of-role behavior prompted more extreme judgments (see the two outer bars). Someone who acts outgoing when he should be subdued is assumed to be a real extravert;

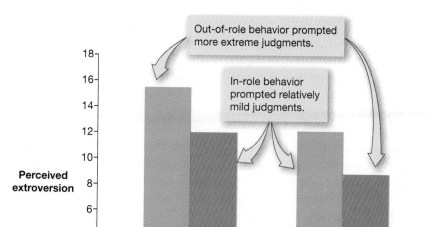

FIGURE 4.3 **Discounting and Augmentation** Out-of-role behavior is seen as more informative of a person's true self than in-role behavior. The figure shows the perceived extraversion of a person who acted in an introverted or extraverted manner while interviewing for a position that favored introversion (astronaut) or extraversion (submariner). (Source: Adapted from Jones, Davis, & Gergen, 1961.)

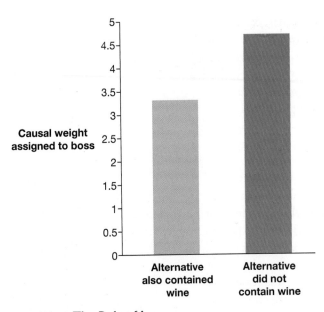

FIGURE 4.4 The Role of Imagined Outcomes in Causal Attribution The causal significance of the boss's choice of meals as seen by participants who read that the boss almost ordered a different dish that did or did not also contain wine. (Source: Adapted from Wells & Gavanski, 1989.)

counterfactual thoughts Thoughts of what might have, could have, or should have happened "if only" something had been done differently.

emotional amplification A ratcheting up of an emotional reaction to an event that is proportional to how easy it is to imagine the event not happening.

likewise, someone who acts withdrawn when he should be outgoing is assumed to be a real introvert. A person's traits are discounted as a likely cause of behavior if the behavior goes with the flow of the situation. In contrast, a person's traits are augmented as a likely cause if the behavior goes against the flow of the situation.

To employ the discounting and augmentation principles properly, each of us needs to be something of a psychologist and have an accurate understanding of how most people are likely to act in particular contexts (Kelley, 1973). We must recognize, for example, that people tend to seek pleasure and avoid pain, that people are embarrassed if attention is called to their shortcomings, and that people typically try to "fit in" to the situations in which they find themselves.

The Influence of What Almost Happened Another way in which we perform what are essentially thought experiments when making causal assessments is to consider whether a given outcome would likely have happened if the circumstances were slightly different. Consider, for example, an experiment in which participants read about a woman who went to lunch with her boss to celebrate her promotion (Wells & Gavanski, 1989). The woman's boss ordered for her, but not knowing she suffered from a rare allergy to wine, he ordered a dish made with a wine sauce. The woman fell ill shortly after the meal, went into convulsions, and died en route to the hospital. Some participants read a version of this story in which the boss had considered ordering a different dish that did not contain wine. The others read a version in which the alternative dish her boss had considered also contained wine. The participants were then asked several questions about the cause of the woman's death.

The investigators predicted that the participants' attributions would be influenced not only by what happened in the scenario but by what *almost* happened. Those who read that the woman's boss almost ordered a dish without wine would readily imagine a chain of events in which she was just fine, and thus they would come to view the boss's choice of meals as causally significant. In contrast, if the dish the boss almost ordered also contained wine, the participants would not readily imagine a different outcome, and so they would likely see the boss's choice of meals as less causally significant. As **Figure 4.4** indicates, that is exactly what happened.

Our attributions are thus influenced not only by our knowledge of what has actually happened in the past, but also by our **counterfactual thoughts** (or thoughts *counter to the facts*) of what might have, could have, or should have happened "if only" a few minor things were done differently (Johnson, 1986; Kahneman & Tversky, 1982a; Roese, 1997; Roese & Olson, 1995; Sanna, 2000). "If only I had studied harder" implies that a lack of effort was the cause of a poor test result. "If only the Republicans had nominated a different candidate" implies that it was the candidate, not the party's principles, that was responsible for defeat.

Because our attributions influence our emotional reactions to events, it stands to reason that our counterfactual thoughts do as well. Our emotional reaction to an event tends to be amplified if it almost did not happen—a phenomenon known as **emotional amplification**. In particular, the pain or joy we derive from any event tends to be proportional to how easy it is to imagine the event not happening.

Consider a news account of a father who took his young daughter to Detroit's Metropolitan Airport for a flight to visit her grandparents in Arizona. As the father tried to say goodbye near the boarding area, his daughter began to cry and say she did not want to go. The father did what most parents would do under the circumstances. He tried to reassure her that everything would be all right ("Don't worry, the flight attendants will look after you the whole way and grandma and grandpa will be there at the gate to meet you"), and he insisted that she go. She did, and the plane crashed en route, ending her brief life (cited in Sherman & McConnell, 1995). It is impossible to consider that story without experiencing tremendous compassion for the father. Besides his agonizing grief at losing a child, the father is certain to be tormented by the thought, rational or not, that he caused his daughter's death—that if he had only listened to his daughter, she would still be alive. Because it is so easy to imagine how her fate could have been avoided, his pain is bound to be all the more intense.

Given that our thoughts about "what might have been" exert such a powerful influence on our reactions and attributions, a key question becomes what determines whether a counterfactual event seems like it "almost" happened. The most common determinants, certainly, are time and distance. Suppose, for example, that someone survives a plane crash in a remote area and then tries to hike to safety. Suppose he hikes to within 75 miles of safety before dying of exposure. How much should the airline pay his relatives in compensation? Would your estimate of the proper compensation change if the individual made it to within ¼ mile of safety? It would for most people. Those led to believe he died ¼ mile from safety recommended an average of $162,000 more in compensation than those who thought he died 75 miles away (Miller & McFarland, 1986). Because he almost made it (within ¼ mile), his death seems more tragic and thus more worthy of compensation.

This psychology of coming close leads to something of a paradox in Olympic athletes' emotional reactions to winning a silver or bronze medal. An analysis of the smiles and grimaces that athletes exhibited on the medal stand at the 1992 summer Olympics in Barcelona, Spain, revealed that silver medalists, who finished second, seemed to be less happy than the bronze medalists, or third-place finishers, they had outperformed (Medvec, Madey, & Gilovich, 1995; see **Figure 4.5**). This finding was replicated in the 2004 Olympic Games in Athens, Greece (Matsumoto & Willingham, 2006). This effect appears to result from silver medalists being consumed by what they did not receive, the coveted gold medal, whereas bronze medalists focus on what they did receive—a medal. (Those who finish fourth in Olympic competition receive no medal at all.) Indeed, analyses of the athletes' comments during postevent interviews confirmed the suspected difference in their counterfactual thoughts. Silver medalists were more focused on how they could have done better "if only" a few things had gone differently, whereas bronze medalists were more inclined to state that "at least" they received a medal. Second place can thus be a mixed blessing. The triumph over many can get lost in the defeat by one.

The Influence of Exceptions versus Routines Another determinant of whether it is easy to imagine an event not happening is whether it resulted from a routine action or a departure from the norm. Would you feel worse, for example, if someone you loved died in a plane crash after switching her assigned flight at the last minute or after sticking with her assigned flight? Most people say that a last-minute switch would make everything harder to bear because of the thought that it "almost" did not happen. In one study that examined this idea, participants read about a man who had been severely injured when a store he happened to be in was robbed. In one version of the story, the robbery took place in the store in which he most often shopped. In

Emotional Amplification If you are watching a film and an appealing character utters something like, "I'm quitting the force" or "This is my last mission," you had better emotionally disinvest in that character or break out a tissue because the character has been handed a death sentence. Steven Spielberg used this phenomenon of emotional amplification in his film *Saving Private Ryan*, in which the death of Captain Miller (played by Tom Hanks as shown here) at the end of the film is made to feel even more painful because it almost did not happen—he was scheduled to go home at the end of the mission.

FIGURE 4.5 Scientific Method: Counterfactual Thinking among Olympic Medalists

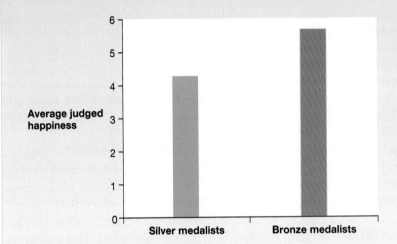

Hypothesis: People's emotional responses to events are influenced by their thoughts about "what might have been."

Research Method:

1. Researchers videotaped all televised coverage of the 1992 summer Olympic games in Barcelona, Spain.

2. They had college students who didn't know anything about the athletes examine their smiles and grimaces and rate how happy each athlete appeared.

3. The students rated the athletes shown immediately after finishing their events and when shown on the podium.

Results: Silver medalists, who finished second, seemed to be less happy than the bronze medalists they had outperformed.

Conclusion: People react to events based not only on what they are, but also on what they are not. Silver medals are often experienced as *not* a gold medal, and so may be enjoyed less than bronze medals, which are often experienced as *not* an also-ran.

Source: Medvec, Madey, & Gilovich (1995).

---

another version, the robbery took place in a store he decided to visit for "a change of pace." When asked how much the victim should be compensated for his injuries, those who thought they were sustained in an unusual setting recommended over $100,000 more in compensation than did those who thought they were sustained in the victim's usual store (Miller & McFarland, 1986). The injuries were presumably more tragic because it was so easy to see how they could have been avoided.

This reasoning helps explain why those who put themselves in considerable danger, such as bullfighters and fighter pilots, often have informal rules against changing places with someone else. Changing places is thought to be asking for trouble. The death some years ago of the Spanish matador Yiyo was accompanied by unusual anguish, in part because he violated the unwritten code of his profession and served as a last-minute replacement for another matador (cited in Miller & Taylor, 1995). The extra anguish that accompanies such tragedies may make them particularly

The Anguish of What Might Have Been It is especially upsetting when someone dies who was not supposed to be in a particular situation. (A) The bullfighter José Cubero, known as Yiyo, died in the bullring after substituting at the last minute for another bullfighter. (B) In the Israeli army, soldiers are forbidden to trade missions, no matter how compelling the circumstances. This is because if a soldier dies on a mission that he was not supposed to go on, the family will feel even greater anguish at his "needless death," and the soldier who should have gone will feel enormous guilt at still being alive.

memorable and therefore lead to the superstition that switching spots somehow increases the chances of disaster by "tempting fate" (Risen & Gilovich, 2007, 2008). In less ominous circumstances, we see the same processes at work in the belief that you should never change lines at the grocery store or depart from your initial hunch on a multiple-choice test. Because we "kick ourselves" when our new line slows to a crawl or when our initial hunch was right, such occasions may be particularly memorable, and we may overestimate how often a change of heart leads to a bad outcome (Kruger, Wirtz, & Miller, 2005; Miller & Taylor, 1995).

 LOOKING BACK We have seen that one of the most important elements of causal attribution involves an assessment of how much the person or the situation is responsible for a given event. We make such assessments by employing the logic of covariation. We consider the distinctiveness and consistency of a person's behavior, as well as whether other people would have behaved similarly. When the person's behavior is not unique to a particular situation, when the person behaves consistently in those circumstances, and when not everyone behaves in that way, we feel confident that it is something about the person that caused the behavior. When behavior is distinctive and consistent and most people behave in the same way as the person, we tend to attribute the behavior to the situation. We also rely on our psychological acumen to make attributions. When someone stands to gain from a particular behavior, we attribute the behavior to what the person stands to gain and not to the person's underlying disposition; but when someone behaves in a way that conflicts with self-interest, we are inclined to attribute the behavior to the person's dispositions. Moreover, counterfactual thoughts about events that "almost" occurred influence our causal attributions and emotional reactions to events that did occur.

ERRORS AND BIASES IN ATTRIBUTION

If a student won a coveted prize, would you make the same attribution for the accomplishment whether it was your best friend or your most hated enemy who had won it? Do you tend to make the same attributions for your own behavior as you do for the behavior of others? These questions highlight the possibility that the attributions we make may sometimes be less than fully rational. Our hopes and fears sometimes color our judgment; we sometimes reason from faulty premises; and we are occasionally seduced by information of questionable value and validity. Thus, it's safe to assume that our causal attributions are occasionally subject to predictable errors and biases. Indeed, since the initial development of attribution theory in the late 1960s and early 1970s, social psychologists have expended considerable effort trying to understand some of the problems and pitfalls of everyday causal analysis.

"There might have been some carelessness on my part, but it was mostly just good police work."

self-serving bias The tendency to attribute failure and other bad events to external circumstances, but to attribute success and other good events to oneself.

"We permit all things to ourselves, and that which we call sin in others, is experience for us."

—Ralph Waldo Emerson, *Experience*

The Self-Serving Bias

One of the most consistent biases in causal assessments is one you have no doubt noticed time and time again: people are inclined to attribute failure and other bad events to external circumstances, but to attribute success and other good events to themselves—that is, they are subject to a **self-serving bias** (Carver, DeGregorio, & Gillis, 1980; Greenberg, Pyszczynski, & Solomon, 1982; Mullen & Riordan, 1988). Think for a moment about two of your classes, the one in which you've received your highest grade and the one in which you've received your lowest. In which class would you say the exams were the most "fair" and constituted the most accurate assessment of your knowledge? If you're like most people, you'll find yourself thinking that the exam on which you performed well was the better test of your knowledge (Arkin & Maruyama, 1979; Davis & Stephan, 1980; Gilmour & Reid, 1979). Students tend to make external attributions for their failures ("The professor is a sadist," "The questions were ambiguous") and internal attributions for success ("Man, did I study hard," "I'm smart"). Research has shown that professors do the very same thing when their manuscripts are evaluated for possible publication (Wiley, Crittenden, & Birg, 1979). (Although your textbook authors' papers are of course only rejected because of theoretical bias, unfair evaluation procedures, and the simple narrow mindedness of reviewers.)

Or consider your favorite athletes and their coaches. How do they explain their wins and losses, their triumphs and setbacks? Richard Lau and Dan Russell (1980) examined newspaper accounts of the postgame attributions of professional athletes and coaches and found that attributions to one's own team were much more common for victories than for defeats. In contrast, attributions to external elements (bad calls, bad luck, and so on) were much more common for defeats than for victories. Overall, 80 percent of all attributions for victories were to aspects of one's own team, but only 53 percent of all attributions for defeats were to one's own team. Only 20 percent of attributions for victories were to external elements, whereas 47 percent of attributions for defeats were to external elements (see also Roesch & Amirkhan, 1997).

You no doubt have observed this tendency to attribute success internally and failure externally (see **Box 4.1**), and you no doubt can readily explain it: people exhibit a self-serving bias in their attributions because doing so makes them feel good about themselves (or at least prevents them from feeling bad about themselves). The self-serving attribution bias, then, is a motivational bias. What could be simpler?

 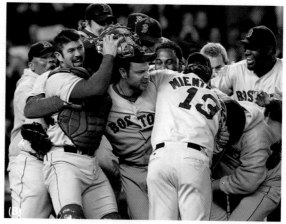

Self-Serving Bias   Athletes often attribute victory to their own skills and defeat to external factors. (A) When the Boston Red Sox were defeated by the New York Yankees, they may have attributed their defeat to external factors, such as bad calls or even the "Curse of the Bambino" (Babe Ruth's revenge after the Red Sox sold his contract to the Yankees). (B) When the Red Sox defeated the Yankees in game 7 of the American League Championship in 2004 and went on to win the World Series that year, they most likely attributed their victories to their personal qualities and skills.

Actually, things are not so simple. Although attributing success to oneself but blaming failure on someone or something else *may* result from a desire to feel good about oneself, it could also result from more dispassionate processes. Even a perfectly rational person might make the same pattern of attributions and be perfectly justified in doing so (Wetzel, 1982). After all, when we try to succeed at something, any success is at least partly due to our efforts and thus warrants some internal attribution credit. Failure, on the other hand, usually occurs *in spite of* our efforts and therefore requires looking elsewhere, perhaps externally, for its cause. A fully rational individual, then, might exhibit a self-serving pattern of attribution because success is generally so much more tightly connected than failure to our intentions and effort.

To see this more clearly, consider an experimental paradigm that reliably elicits the self-serving attributional bias (Beckman, 1970). Participants in these studies

> "Success has a hundred fathers; failure is an orphan."
>
> —Old saying

BOX 4.1   FOCUS ON DAILY LIFE

Self-Serving Attributions

The magnitude of the self-serving bias can be seen in various public documents. When corporations send end-of-year letters to their shareholders, how do you think they account for their corporation's triumphs and tribulations? One study found that chief executive officers (CEOs) claimed credit for 83 percent of all positive events and accepted blame for only 19 percent of all negative events (Salancik & Meindl, 1984). Or consider the accident reports motorists file with their insurance companies after being involved in an auto accident. The externalizing here can be downright comic. "The telephone pole was approaching; I was attempting to swerve out of its way when it struck my car," was how one motorist explained his mishap. "A pedestrian hit me and went under my car" stated another (MacCoun, 1993). These data, of course, require a disclaimer. Unlike the more controlled laboratory studies of the self-serving bias, the corporate reports and insurance forms are for public consumption. It may be, then, that the authors of these reports don't really believe what they are saying; they're just hoping others will swallow it. These examples should thus be taken as illustrations of the self-serving bias, not as solid evidence for it. The real evidence comes from the more carefully controlled studies described in the text.

are required to tutor a student having difficulty mastering some material. (The participants in some of these studies are real teachers and in others they are college students.) After an initial round of tutoring, the student is assessed and found to have done poorly. A second round of tutoring ensues, and then an additional assessment is made. For half the participants, the student's performance on the second assessment remains poor; for the other half, the student shows marked improvement. What is typically observed in such studies is that the teachers tend to take credit if the student improves from session to session, but they tend to blame the student if the student continues to perform poorly. In other words, people make an internal attribution for success (improvement) but an external attribution for failure (continued poor performance).

It may seem as if the teachers are trying to feel good about themselves and are making less than rational attributions to do so. But that is not necessarily the case. Suppose we programmed a computer, devoid of any feelings and hence having no need to feel good about itself, with software that allowed it to employ the covariation principle. What kind of attributions would it make? It would receive as inputs: (1) the student did poorly initially, (2) the teacher redoubled his or her efforts or changed teaching strategy (as most people do after an initial failure), and (3) the student did well or poorly in the second session. The computer would then look for a pattern of covariation between the outcome and the potential causes that would tell it what sort of attribution to make. When the student failed both times, there would be no correlation between the teacher's efforts and the student's performance (some effort at time 1 and poor performance on the part of the student; increased effort at time 2 and continued poor performance). Because an attribution to the teacher could not be justified, the attribution would be made to the student. When the student succeeded the second time, however, there would be an association between the teacher's efforts and the student's performance (some effort at time 1 and poor performance; increased effort at time 2 and improved performance). An attribution to the teacher would therefore be fully justified.

As this example indicates, we shouldn't be too quick to accuse others of self-serving bias. It can be difficult to tell from the pattern of attributions alone whether someone has made an attribution to protect self-esteem; such a pattern could be the result of a purely rational analysis.

Does that mean that the self-serving bias is always rational—that it is not the result of people trying to feel good about themselves? Not at all. More extensive research has demonstrated that such motives often are at work, for example by showing that the self-serving bias is particularly strong when people's motivation to feel good about themselves is particularly high (Klein & Kunda, 1992; Miller, 1976; Mullen & Riordan, 1988).

As a final thought about the self-serving bias, consider how it might play out in the attributions people make about their most intimate partners. Do married couples make attributions about each other's behavior that resemble the attributions they make about themselves? They do and they don't. That is, those in happy marriages attribute their partner's behavior in the same way they attribute their own behavior, but those in unhappy marriages do not. As we discuss in Chapter 11, happy couples explain each other's positive actions internally ("That's just the way he is") and negative actions externally ("He's just so busy providing for all of us that he doesn't have the time"). Unhappy couples tend to do the opposite. They attribute their partner's positive behavior externally ("He just wanted to look good in front of our guests"), but they blame their partner's negative behavior on internal causes ("He just doesn't care"). Whatever conflicts or disappointments unhappy couples might have suffered, such a pattern of attributions can only poison the atmosphere further and make things worse (Fincham, 1985; Fincham, Bradbury, Arias, Byrne, & Karney, 1997; Karney & Bradbury, 2000; Miller & Rempel, 2004).

The Fundamental Attribution Error

Try to recall your initial thoughts about the individuals who delivered the maximum level of shock in Milgram's studies of obedience (see Chapters 1 and 8). The participants were asked to deliver more than 400 volts of electricity to another person, over the victim's protests, as part of a learning experiment. Nearly two-thirds of all participants did so. If you are like most people, you formed a rather harsh opinion of the participants, thinking of them as unusually cruel and callous, perhaps, or as unusually weak. And in doing so, your judgments reflected a second way in which everyday causal attributions often depart from the general principles of attributional analysis. There seems to be a pervasive tendency to see people's behavior as a reflection of the kind of people they are, rather than as a result of the situation in which they find themselves. Note that a straightforward application of the covariation principle would lead to a situational attribution in this case and not an inference about the participants' character or personalities. Because virtually all of these participants gave huge amounts of shock in the face of protests by the "learner," and nearly two-thirds were willing to deliver everything the machine could produce, their behavior doesn't say much about the individual people involved, but rather speaks to something about the situation that made their behavior (surprisingly) common.

The tendency to locate the causes of behavior in elements of a person's character or personality even when there are powerful situational forces acting to produce the behavior is known as the **fundamental attribution error** (Ross, 1977). It is called that both because the problem people are trying to solve (figuring out what someone is like from a sample of behavior) is so basic and essential and because the tendency to think dispositionally (to attribute behavior to the person while ignoring important situational factors) is so common and pervasive.

fundamental attribution error The tendency to believe that a behavior is due to a person's disposition, even when there are situational forces present that are sufficient to explain the behavior.

Experimental Demonstrations of the Fundamental Attribution Error Social psychologists have devised a number of experimental paradigms to examine the fundamental attribution error more closely (Gawronski, 2003; Gilbert & Malone, 1995; Lord, Scott, Pugh, & Desforges, 1997; Miller, Ashton, & Mishal, 1990; Miller, Jones, & Hinkle, 1981; Vonk, 1999). In one of the earliest studies, students at Duke University were asked to read an essay about Fidel Castro's Communist regime in Cuba (Jones & Harris, 1967). Half of the participants read a pro-Castro essay, and half read an anti-Castro essay, supposedly written in response to a directive to "write a short, cogent essay either defending or criticizing Castro's Cuba as if you were giving the opening statement in a debate." Afterward, the participants were asked to rate the essayist's general attitude toward Castro's Cuba. Because the essayist was thought to have been free to write an essay that was either supportive or critical of Castro's Cuba, it is not surprising that those who read a pro-Castro essay rated the writer's attitude as much more favorable toward Cuba than those who read an anti-Castro essay (see **Figure 4.6**).

There is nothing noteworthy in these results. But the results from other participants in this experiment are surprising. These participants read the same essays, but they were told that the stance taken (pro- or anti-Castro) had been assigned, not freely chosen. When these participants rated the essayist's true attitude, their judgments were less extreme, but they nevertheless drew inferences about the essayist's attitude:

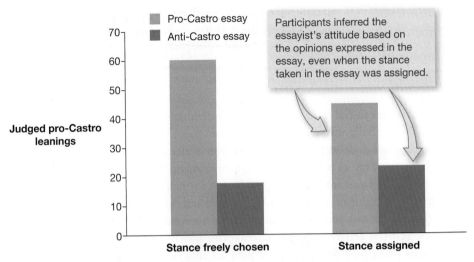

FIGURE 4.6 The Fundamental Attribution Error Participants' ratings of the essayist's true attitude toward Castro's Cuba, with higher numbers indicating more of an assumed pro-Castro attitude. (Source: Adapted from Jones & Harris, 1967.)

those who read a pro-Castro essay thought the author was relatively pro-Castro, and those who read an anti-Castro essay thought the author was relatively anti-Castro (see the rightmost portion of Figure 4.6). From a purely logical perspective, these inferences are unwarranted. If individuals are assigned to write on a given topic, what they write cannot be taken as an indication of what they really believe. That participants nonetheless thought that the essays were informative of what the authors were like is thus a reflection of the fundamental attribution error.

You might object to this conclusion and question how much support such studies provide for the fundamental attribution error. After all, participants were given essays to read, and they were asked to infer what the essayist was like. If the experimenter is to maintain that nothing can be inferred, why did the experimenter ask for an inference? In addition, when people are compelled to say something that is inconsistent with their beliefs, they normally "distance" themselves from their statements by subtly indicating that they do not truly believe what they are saying (Fleming & Darley, 1989). But there were no distancing cues present in the essays, and so participants may have legitimately inferred that the essays reflected something of the essayists' true attitudes.

Other demonstrations of the fundamental attribution error get around these problems by allowing plenty of room for such distancing behaviors. In the paradigm used in these studies, participants are randomly assigned to one of two roles: questioner or responder (Gilbert & Jones, 1986; Van Boven, Kamada, & Gilovich, 1999). The questioner's job is to read a series of questions over an intercom to the responder, who then answers with one of two entirely scripted responses. Thus, the responders' answers are not their own and should not be considered informative of their true personalities. The added twist in this study is that after reading each question, the questioners themselves—with instructions from the experimenter—indicate to the responder which of the two responses he or she is to make. Thus, the questioners themselves constrain the responder's behavior. For example, in response to the question, "Do you consider yourself to be sensitive to other people's feelings?," the questioner signals to the responder which of these two answers to give: "I try to be sensitive to others' feelings all the time. I know it is important to have people one can turn to for sympathy and understanding. I try to be that person whenever possible" (altruistic response)

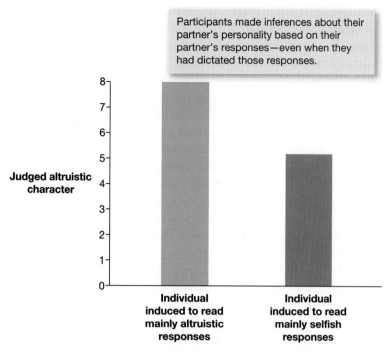

Participants made inferences about their partner's personality based on their partner's responses—even when they had dictated those responses.

Judged altruistic character

Individual induced to read mainly altruistic responses

Individual induced to read mainly selfish responses

FIGURE 4.7 The Perceiver-Induced Constraint Paradigm Participants' average trait ratings of individuals that *they themselves* had directed to respond in an altruistic or selfish manner. Higher numbers indicate greater assumed altruism. (Source: Adapted from Van Boven, Kamada, & Gilovich, 1999.)

or "I think there are too many sensitive, 'touchy-feely' people in the world already. I see no point in trying to be understanding of another if there is nothing in it for me" (selfish response).

After reading a list of these questions to the responder and eliciting a particular response, the questioners in one such study were asked to rate the responder on a set of personality traits (trustworthiness, greediness, kindheartedness). What the investigators found was that the questioners drew inferences about the responders even though they had directed the responders to answer as they did! Responders led to recite mainly altruistic responses were rated more favorably than those led to recite mainly selfish responses (see **Figure 4.7**). Note also that this occurred even though the responders could have (and may have) tried through tone of voice to distance themselves from the responses they were asked to give (Van Boven et al., 1999).

The Fundamental Attribution Error and Perceptions of the Advantaged and Disadvantaged An inferential problem we all face in our daily lives is deciding how much credit to give to those who have been successful in life and how much blame to direct at those who have been unsuccessful. How much praise and respect should be directed at successful entrepreneurs, film stars, and artists? And to what degree should the impoverished among us be held accountable for their condition? What we have seen thus far about the fundamental attribution error suggests that people tend to assign too much responsibility to the individual for great accomplishments and not enough responsibility to the particular situation, broader societal forces, or pure dumb luck.

An ingenious laboratory experiment captured the essence of this inferential problem (Ross, Amabile, & Steinmetz, 1977). The study showed that people are indeed quick to commit the fundamental attribution error. From a broader perspective, it also suggested that we often fail to see the inherent advantages that some people enjoy in life and the inherent disadvantages that others must overcome. In the study, participants took part in a quiz-game competition much like the television show *Jeopardy*. Half the participants were assigned the role of questioner and the other half the role of contestant. The questioner's job was to think of challenging but not impossible general-knowledge questions ("Who were the two coinventors of calculus?" "Who played the role of Victor Laslo in the film *Casablanca*?"), and the contestant was to answer the questions (see answers on the next page).

From a self-presentation standpoint, the questioners had a tremendous advantage. It was relatively easy for the questioners to come off well because they could focus on whatever idiosyncratic knowledge they happened to have and could ignore their various pockets of ignorance. Everybody has *some* expertise, and the questioners could focus on theirs. The contestants, however, had no such luxury. They suffered from the disadvantage of having to field questions about the questioners' store of arcane knowledge, which typically did not match their own.

If people were not so dispositionist in their thinking, they would correct appropriately for the relative advantages and disadvantages enjoyed by the questioners and contestants, respectively. Thus, if asked to rate the questioners' and contestants' general knowledge and overall intelligence, anyone watching the quiz show should be reluctant to make any distinction between the participants in these two roles: any difference in their *apparent* knowledge and intelligence could so easily be explained by their roles. But that was not what happened. Predictably, the unfortunate contestants did not answer many of the questions correctly. The contestants came away quite impressed by the questioners' abilities, rating them more highly than their own. And when the quiz game was later reenacted for a group of observers, they, too, rated the questioners' general knowledge more highly than that of the contestants (see **Figure 4.8**). Notice that the only people not fooled by the questioners' performance were the questioners themselves, who rated their own general knowledge and intelligence as roughly equal to the average of the student body. This aspect of the results is almost certainly due to the fact that the questioners knew they had skipped over yawning

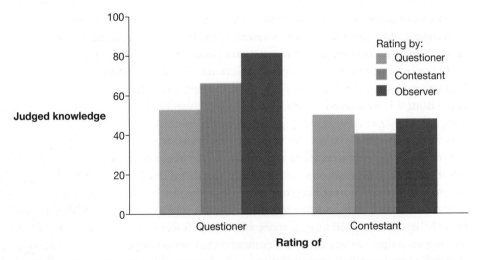

FIGURE 4.8 Role-Conferred Advantage and Disadvantage The bars show ratings of the general knowledge of the questioner and contestant in the quiz-show experiment. Participants thought the questioners were more knowledgeable than the contestants even though they knew they had been randomly assigned to their roles and that the questioners had a much easier task. (Source: Adapted from Ross, Amabile, & Steinmetz, 1977.)

gaps in their knowledge base in order to come up with whatever challenging questions they could offer.

Answers to quiz-show game questions on the previous page: Isaac Newton and Gottfried von Leibnitz; Paul Henreid.

This experiment serves as a caution about the inferences we draw in our everyday lives. On average, the very successful among us have worked harder and exercised more talent and skill than the unsuccessful. The successful thus deserve our admiration—on average. But this experiment teaches us not to lose sight of the invisible advantages that many people enjoy and the equally invisible disadvantages that others must struggle to overcome. By dint of birth and connections, for example, some people start out in life with considerable financial resources, and for them, making even more money is not terribly difficult because they already have a sizable stake. Conversely, few things are as challenging as making money when you must start from scratch and make it entirely on your own. Thus, our attributions for success and failure in life, and the traits we infer as a result, should reflect the relative advantages and disadvantages to which different individuals have been subject.

The popular science writer Malcolm Gladwell has written a book about highly successful people called *Outliers*. He presents case after case of people we think of as extraordinarily accomplished, such as Bill Gates, and shows how they had extraordinary advantages. Gates, for example, was one of a tiny number of junior high school students in the country who had unlimited access to a high-powered computer shortly after computers were developed. He was able to get thousands of hours of precious computer time acquiring skills that made possible his achievements a few years later. Gates was talented, to be sure—but he was also extremely lucky.

Causes of the Fundamental Attribution Error

Why are people so quick to see someone's actions as reflective of the person's inner traits and enduring character? Precisely because this tendency is so strong and so pervasive, it's a good bet that it's not due to a single cause, but is more likely the result of several causes acting jointly. Indeed, social psychologists have identified several psychological processes that appear to be responsible for the fundamental attribution error.

Motivational Influence and the Belief in a Just World One reason we are likely to attribute behavior to people's traits and dispositions is that dispositional inferences can be comforting. The twists and turns a life can take can be unsettling. A superbly qualified job candidate may be passed over in favor of a mediocre applicant with the right connections. A selfless Good Samaritan may be stricken with cancer and experience a gruesome death. A well-loved valedictorian may be murdered by a complete stranger a week after graduation. The anxiety that these events produce tempts us to think that it couldn't happen to us. There are a number of ways we can minimize the perceived threat to ourselves, and one of them is to attribute people's outcomes to something about them rather than to fate, chance, or pure dumb luck (Burger, 1981; Walster, 1966). More broadly, by thinking that people "get what they deserve," that "what goes around comes around," or that "good things happen to good people and bad things happen to bad people," we can reassure ourselves that nothing bad will happen to us if we are the right kind of person living the right kind of life. Thus, people tend to attribute behavior and outcomes to dispositions in part because they are *motivated* to do so.

"The employees have to assume a share of the blame for allowing the pension fund to become so big and tempting."

just world hypothesis The belief that people get what they deserve in life and deserve what they get.

Social psychologists have studied this impulse as part of their examination of the **just world hypothesis**—the belief that people get what they deserve in life and deserve what they get (Lambert, Burroughs, & Nguyen, 1999; Lerner, 1980; Lipkus, Dalbert, & Siegler, 1996). Victims of rape, for example, are often viewed as responsible for their fate (Abrams, Viki, Masser, & Bohner, 2003; Bell, Kuriloff, & Lottes, 1994), as are victims of domestic abuse (Summers & Feldman, 1984). This insidious tendency reaches its zenith in the claim that if no defect in a victim's manifest character or past actions can be found, the tragic affliction must be due to some flaw or transgression in a "past life." Thus, for example, it has been argued that children who have been sexually abused are likely to have been sex offenders themselves in a past life (Woolger, 1988). Such beliefs show the extent to which people will go to find justification, however far-fetched, for their belief in a just world. Research in this area has also shown that people tend to "derogate the victim"—that is, they rate unfavorably the character of those who suffer unfortunate outcomes that are completely beyond the victims' control (Jones & Aronson, 1973; Lerner & Simmons, 1966; Lerner & Miller, 1978).

The Differential Salience of People and Situations An outcome can only be attributed to those causes that spring to mind as possible causal candidates. Causes never considered cannot receive any attributional weight. But what influences whether or not a potential cause springs to mind or how readily it springs to mind? One important determinant is how much it stands out perceptually, or how *salient* it is (Lassiter, Geers, Munhall, Ploutz-Snyder, & Breitenbecher, 2002; Robinson & McArthur, 1982; Smith & Miller, 1979). Those elements of the environment that more readily capture our attention are more likely to be seen as potential causes of an observed effect. And because people are so dynamic, they tend to capture our attention much more readily than other aspects of the environment. Situations, if attended to at all, may be seen as mere background to the person and his or her actions. This is particularly true of various social determinants of a person's behavior (customs, social norms) that are largely invisible. Attributions to the person, then, have an edge over situational attributions in everyday causal analysis.

Perceptual Salience and Attribution The fundamental attribution error is made in part because people are more salient than situations. If the people in this photo were to engage in a particular behavior—say, break out in song, tell embarrassing anecdotes, or complain about the weather—observers would be likely to assume that the behavior in question reflects the disposition of the woman in the center more than it reflects the others' dispositions because her red clothing and her uncovered face make her stand out.

The importance of perceptual salience in our attributions has been demonstrated in many ways. In one study, participants watched a videotape of a conversation between two people. Some participants saw a version of the tape that allowed them a view of only one of the individuals; others saw a tape that allowed them to see both individuals equally well. When asked to assign responsibility for the thrust of the interaction, those who could see only one individual assigned more responsibility to that individual than did those who could see both equally well (Taylor & Fiske, 1975). In another set of studies, one person in a videotaped conversation was made highly salient by being brightly lit on camera or by wearing a dramatically striped shirt. Those who witnessed the videotaped conversation made more dispositional attributions for the behavior of the salient individual than they did for the behavior of the nonsalient individual (McArthur & Post, 1977).

The Cognitive Mechanics of Attribution Perceptual salience explains some instances of the fundamental attribution error better than others. It explains the results of the quiz-show study, for example, because the decisive situational influence—that the questioner could avoid areas of ignorance but the contestant could not—was invisible and therefore had little impact on people's judgments. But what about the attitude attribution studies in which participants knew that a writer had been assigned to argue for the particular position advocated in an essay? Here, the situational constraints were far from invisible. So, why didn't the participants discount appropriately and decide that the target person's behavior was perfectly well accounted for by the situational constraints and thus refrain from making any inference about the person at all? The answer is that the cognitive machinery we draw on when using the discounting principle doesn't work that way.

Let's review the logic of the discounting principle, depicted in **Figure 4.9A**. By that logic, we simultaneously weigh what we've seen (or heard or read) about the person's behavior and the context of that behavior to figure out what kind of person we're dealing with—that is, to draw a dispositional inference. What is puzzling about the fundamental attribution error, then, is why we don't give enough weight to the situational information when we know perfectly well (as did the participants in the attitude attribution paradigm) that it is sufficient to produce the observed behavior.

That would indeed be a puzzle if, in fact, people reasoned along the lines depicted in **Figure 4.9A**. But research by Dan Gilbert makes it clear that we don't reason that way at all. Instead, we reason in the manner depicted in **Figure 4.9B**, and by that reasoning, our failure to discount sufficiently for situational influences is not so puzzling after all (Gilbert, 2002). Gilbert has shown that we do not weigh behavioral and situational information simultaneously to figure out how to characterize what the actor is like. Instead, we observe the behavior in question and initially identify what that behavior is and what it means. For example, we see a certain pattern of gaze, a certain constriction of the muscles around the eyes, and a certain upturn of the corners

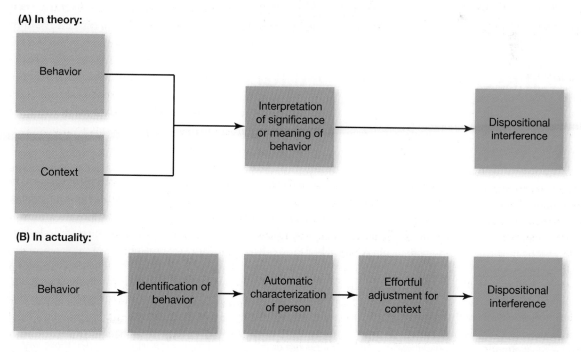

(A) In theory:

Behavior / Context → Interpretation of significance or meaning of behavior → Dispositional interference

(B) In actuality:

Behavior → Identification of behavior → Automatic characterization of person → Effortful adjustment for context → Dispositional interference

FIGURE 4.9 Inferring Dispositions According to the discounting principle, a potential cause is discounted as a possible cause of a particular outcome if other causes might have produced the outcome. (A) In theory, we should simultaneously weigh both the person's behavior and the surrounding context to arrive at an explanation of a behavior. (B) In actuality, we first automatically characterize the person in terms of the behavior and then sometimes make an effortful adjustment for the context to arrive at an explanation of the behavior.

of the mouth, and we must identify whether we're seeing nervousness or bemusement (Trope, 1986). We see one person in the arms of another, and we must decide whether the latter is carrying, helping, or kidnapping the other (Vallacher & Wegner, 1985).

Once we've identified what we've seen, we immediately—and automatically—characterize the person in terms of the behavior observed (Carlston & Skowronski, 1994; Moskowitz, 1993; Newman, 1993; Todorov & Uleman, 2003; Uleman, 1987; Winter & Uleman, 1984). Someone who acts in a hostile manner is seen as hostile regardless of what prompted the hostility; someone who acts in a compassionate manner is seen as compassionate, again, regardless of what may have prompted the compassion. Initially, that is. Then, but only upon reflection, we consciously and deliberately take in what we know about the prevailing situational constraints and adjust our initial dispositional inference if warranted. Thus, the situational information is not weighed simultaneously along with the behavioral information; it is taken into account sequentially, after an initial dispositional inference has been made (see Figure 4.9B).

The primacy of the behavioral information gives it one of its advantages. The situational information is not taken into account on its own terms, but is used to adjust the initial dispositional inference. Such adjustments, unfortunately, tend to be insufficient (see **Box 4.2**), and so the initial characterization of the person is weighed too heavily. Moreover, because the initial characterization of the person happens automatically, it does not require much energy to perform and cannot easily be dampened or eliminated. The adjustment stage, however, requires deliberate effort, attention, and energy to perform and thus can easily be dampened or short-circuited. This suggests that when people are tired, unmotivated, or distracted, they are more likely to commit the fundamental attribution error (or to make a bigger error) because the second stage is shortened or skipped altogether.

BOX 4.2 FOCUS ON COGNITIVE PROCESSES

Weighed Down by Anchors

We often estimate uncertain quantities by tinkering with some value we know is not quite right. For example, we might estimate the number of lives likely to be lost in an act of terrorism by adjusting from the number known to have been lost in the last terrorist act. Or we might estimate the number of layoffs in a looming recession by modifying the number in a previous recession.

Research indicates that when people estimate uncertain quantities, the adjustments they make from these initial "anchor" values tend to be insufficient and their estimates tend to fall short of the true value (Tversky & Kahneman, 1974). Suppose you find yourself a contestant

in the quiz-show experiment described earlier, and you are asked when George Washington was first elected president. Chances are you don't know, but you reason that it has to be after 1776, the year the United States declared its independence from Great Britain—and so you adjust up. The adjustment you would make is unlikely to be sufficient, however, as the estimates people make on average (1780) fall short of the actual year (1789) (Epley & Gilovich, 2001).

You might be thinking that this is a disturbing result because it means that your judgments are at the mercy of, say, a clever salesperson who might get you to seize on one anchor value or another

and, without your awareness, influence your behavior. Such fears are justified. In one marketing study, for example, "end-of-the-aisle" products were listed on sale either as "50 cents each" or "4 cans for $2" in order to anchor people's thoughts about how many they should buy—either 1 or 4, respectively. Sure enough, customers bought 36 percent more cans when the products were advertised as 4 for $2. In another study, a sign in the candy section read either "Snickers Bars—buy them for your freezer" or "Snickers Bars—buy 18 for your freezer." Anchored on 18, those who confronted the latter sign bought 38 percent more (Wansink, Kent, & Hoch, 1998).

Gilbert has conducted a number of ingenious experiments that demonstrate the automatic nature of dispositional inference and the deliberate nature of people's efforts to take situational information into account. In one study, participants were shown a videotape, without the sound, of a young woman engaged in a conversation with another person. The woman appeared anxious throughout: "She bit her nails, twirled her hair, tapped her fingers, and shifted in her chair from cheek to cheek" (Gilbert, 1989, p. 194). Half the participants were told something that could explain her anxious demeanor—namely, that she was responding to a number of anxiety-inducing questions (about her sexual fantasies or personal failings, for example). The other participants were told that she was responding to questions about innocuous topics (world travel or great books, for example). Gilbert predicted that all participants, regardless of what they were told about the content of the discussion, would witness the woman's anxious demeanor and immediately and automatically assume that she was an anxious person. Those told that she was discussing anxiety-producing topics, however, would then deliberately adjust their initial characterization and conclude that maybe she was not such an anxious person after all. Those told that she was discussing a series of bland topics would not make such an adjustment. As **Figure 4.10** indicates, that is just what happened. Those told she was discussing a series of innocuous topics thought she was more dispositionally anxious than those told she was discussing a series of anxiety-producing topics.

So far, this is just a standard attribution experiment. But Gilbert added a wrinkle. He gave another two groups of participants the same information he gave the first two, but he had these groups perform another task simultaneously. Specifically, participants in these latter two groups were asked to memorize a list of words while watching the videotape. Gilbert reasoned that this extra demand on their attention would make them less able to carry out the deliberative stage of the attribution process, in which the initial characterization of the person is adjusted to account for situational constraints. If so, then those who knew that the young woman was discussing anxiety-provoking topics should nevertheless rate her as being just as anxious as those in the innocuous topics condition. As Figure 4.10 indicates, that is just what happened. When participants were busy memorizing a list of words, they did not have the cognitive resources that were needed to adjust their initial impression, and so they rated the woman as just as anxious when they were told she was discussing anxiety-provoking topics as when they were told she was discussing innocuous topics.

But some of you may remain unconvinced. You may object that *of course* the "busy" participants failed to use the situational information (the topics the young woman was discussing) to adjust their initial, overly dispositional impression of her. They may have been so distracted by the need to memorize their list of words that they failed to notice the situational information. Thus, they failed to use the situational information not because they were too busy to do so, but because they were so busy that they didn't notice it was there to use! Gilbert anticipated this objection and incorporated a clever element of his experimental design to overcome it. The words he had his "busy"

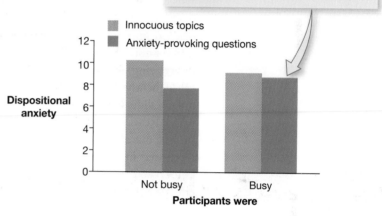

FIGURE 4.10 Adjusting Automatic Characterizations Observers had to judge how generally anxious a person was who appeared anxious while discussing either innocuous or anxiety-provoking topics. (Source: Adapted from Gilbert, 1989.)

participants memorize were the words specifying the very topics the woman was being asked to discuss! These participants, then, could hardly be unaware of the situational influences on the woman's behavior, and yet they were so preoccupied that they failed to use this information.

What Gilbert's work shows us is that the seeds of the fundamental attribution error are sown into the very cognitive machinery we use to determine what someone is like. There are two reasons people have a strong tendency to make overly dispositional attributions. First, information about situational influence is used to adjust an immediate dispositional characterization, and such adjustments, like adjustments of all sorts, tend to be insufficient. Second, the adjustment phase requires energy and attention, so it can be disrupted by anything that tires or distracts. Because our lives are so busy and complicated and we are so often preoccupied with planning our own actions and self-presentations, we frequently lack sufficient resources to do justice to the correction phase of a comprehensive attributional analysis (Geeraert, Yzerbyt, Corneille, & Wigboldus, 2004).

It stands to reason that we would focus initially on the person and only subsequently adjust to account for the situation, because people are compelling stimuli of considerable importance to us. But what about those occasions in which it is the situation that is of greatest importance? What happens, for example, when we see someone react to a new ride at an amusement park, and we want to know whether the ride is scary or not? Do we immediately and automatically characterize the situation (the ride is terrifying) in terms of the behavior we've seen (these people are terrified), and only subsequently correct this initial situational inference in light of what we know about the individuals involved (they're rookies who've never been to a first-rate amusement park)? Research suggests that we do indeed. When people are primarily interested in finding out about the situation in which they observe someone behave (and are less interested in the person engaged in the behavior), the attributional sequence that Gilbert so carefully revealed is reversed. In such cases, people will automatically and effortlessly draw strong inferences about the situation (Krull, 1993; Krull & Dill, 1996; Krull & Erickson, 1995).

The Actor-Observer Difference in Causal Attributions

It may have occurred to you that exactly how oriented we are toward either the person or the situation depends on whether we're engaged in the action ourselves or observing someone else engaged in the action. In the role of "actor," we're often more interested in determining what kind of situation we're dealing with. In the role of "observer," in contrast, we're often interested in determining what kind of person we're dealing with. What's more, given what we've just learned about the attribution process, these different orientations should have predictable effects on the causal attributions made by actors and observers. In particular, actors should be more likely than observers to make situational attributions for their behavior. Indeed, there is considerable evidence for just such a difference (Jones & Nisbett, 1972; Pronin, Lin, & Ross, 2002; Saulnier & Perlman, 1981; Schoeneman & Rubanowitz, 1985; Watson, 1982).

In one of the most straightforward demonstrations of this **actor-observer difference** in attribution, participants were asked to explain why they chose the college major that they did or why their best friends chose the major that they did. When the investigators scored the participants' explanations, they found that participants more often referred to characteristics of the person when explaining someone else's choice than when explaining their own choice, and they referred more often to the specifics of the major when explaining their own choice than when explaining someone else's

actor-observer difference A difference in attribution based on who is making the causal assessment: the actor (who is relatively disposed to make situational attributions) or the observer (who is relatively disposed to make dispositional attributions).

choice. You might attribute your own decision to major in psychology, for instance, to the fact that the material is fascinating, the textbooks beautifully written, and the professors dynamic and accessible. In contrast, you might attribute your friend's decision to major in psychology to "issues" he needs to work out (Nisbett, Caputo, Legant, & Maracek, 1973).

This phenomenon has significant implications for human conflict, both between individuals and between nations. Married couples, for example, often squabble over attributional differences. A husband may cite a late meeting or unusually heavy traffic to explain why an errand did not get done, whereas his wife may be more inclined to argue that he is lazy, inattentive, or "just doesn't care." Similarly, at the national level, the United States is likely to explain the stationing of its troops in so many locations across the globe as a necessary defense against immediate and future threats. Other countries may be more inclined to see it as a manifestation of U.S. "imperialism."

Like the fundamental attribution error, there is no single cause of the actor-observer difference. Several processes give rise to it. First, assumptions about what it is that needs explaining can vary for actors and observers. When asked, "Why did you choose the particular college major that you did?," a person might reasonably interpret the question to mean "Given that you are who you are, why did you choose the particular college major that you did?" The person is taken as a given and therefore need not be referenced as part of the explanation. This is much like Willie Sutton's explanation of why he robbed banks: "Because that's where the money is." He takes it as given that he's a crook and thus interprets the question as one about why he robs *banks* rather than why he's a robber. Notice, in contrast, that when asked about another person ("Why did your roommate choose his or her particular college major?"), the nature of the person cannot be taken as given and is thus "fair game" in offering an explanation (Kahneman & Miller, 1986; McGill, 1989).

Second, the perceptual salience of the actor and the surrounding situation is different for the actor and the observer (Storms, 1973). The actor is typically oriented outward, toward situational opportunities and constraints. Observers, in contrast, are typically focused on the actor and the actor's behavior. Because, as we saw earlier, people tend to make attributions to potential causes that are perceptually salient, it stands to reason that actors will tend to attribute their behavior to the situation, and observers will tend to attribute behavior to the actor.

Third, note that actors and observers differ in the amount and kind of information they have about the actor and the actor's behavior (Andersen & Ross, 1984; Jones & Nisbett, 1972; Prentice, 1990; Pronin, Gilovich, & Ross, 2004). Actors know what their intentions are in behaving a certain way; observers can only guess at those intentions. Actors are also much more likely to know whether a particular action is typical of them or not. An observer may see someone slam a door and conclude that he's an angry person. The actor, in contrast, may know that this is an unprecedented outburst and hence does not warrant such a sweeping conclusion. (In the attribution language used earlier, the actor is in a much better position to know if the behavior is *distinctive* and thus merits a situational rather than a dispositional attribution.)

The Actor-Observer Difference People often explain their own actions in terms of the situation, and the actions of others in terms of the person. This demonstrator hurls a Molotov cocktail after riot police fire tear gas. He would probably see his actions as a response to an untenable situation, while others might see him as an aggressive and criminal hooligan.

LOOKING BACK We have seen that our attributions are subject to predictable errors and biases. We often exhibit a self-serving bias, attributing success to the self and failure to the situation. We exhibit the fundamental attribution error when we attribute behavior to a person's dispositions rather than to the situation, even when there are powerful situational factors operating that we ought to consider.

Actors are more likely than observers to attribute behavior to the situation, whereas observers are more likely than actors to attribute behavior to dispositions of the actor. We now turn to the role of culture in causal attributions and ask whether the same attribution tendencies are exhibited by people from more interdependent cultures.

CULTURE AND THE FUNDAMENTAL ATTRIBUTION ERROR

Can we assume that the fundamental attribution error occurs in all cultures? After all, nearly everyone wishes to live in a just world; other people and their dispositions are everywhere more salient and capture attention more readily than the situation; and all people have the same basic cognitive machinery. Indeed, the error does appear to be widespread. For example, the classic Jones and Harris (1967) finding that people assume that a speech or essay presented by another person represents that person's own opinion on the topic, despite the presence of obvious situational demands, has been demonstrated in many societies, including China (Krull et al., 1996), Korea (Choi & Nisbett, 1998), and Japan (Kitayama & Masuda, 1997). Nevertheless, despite these findings, cultural differences have been found in what people in different cultures pay attention to and in their attributions for certain behaviors and outcomes.

Cultural Differences in Attending to Context

We have suggested that most of the world's people tend to pay more attention to social situations and the people who comprise them than do Westerners. If this is indeed so, we might guess that Westerners would be particularly susceptible to the fundamental attribution error, whereas people from collectivist cultures would be less so. And in fact, the kinds of social factors that are background for North Americans appear to be more salient to people from other cultures (Hedden et al., 2000; Ji, Schwarz, & Nisbett, 2000). In a particularly telling experiment, Takahiko Masuda and his colleagues showed Japanese and American participants cartoon figures having various expressions on their faces (Masuda, Ellsworth, Mesquita, Leu, & van de Veerdonk, 2004; see **Figure 4.11**). The central, target face was always surrounded by smaller, less salient faces, with expressions that were dissimilar to those of the target. For example, the target might appear to be happy, whereas most of the surrounding faces might appear to be sad. The Japanese judgments about the facial expression of the target were more influenced by the surrounding faces than were the judgments of the Americans. A happy face surrounded by sad faces was judged less happy by Japanese participants than by American participants, and a sad face surrounded by happy faces was judged less sad.

Westerners are less likely to pay attention to contexts even of a nonsocial kind. Masuda and Nisbett (2001) showed Japanese and American university students animated cartoons of underwater scenes, asking them afterward what they had seen (see **Figure 4.12**). The first thing the Americans reported was likely to be something about the "focal objects"—the most salient, rapidly moving, brightly colored things in the environment ("I saw three fish, maybe trout, moving off to the left"). The first thing

FIGURE 4.11 Attention to the Social Situation How much do the expressions of the background individuals influence people's impressions of the focal individual? Masuda and his colleagues found that Japanese participants are more influenced by the surrounding faces than are American participants. (Source: Masuda, Ellsworth, Mesquita, Leu, & van de Veerdonk, 2004)

the Japanese tended to report was information about the context ("It looked like a stream, there were some rocks and plants on the bottom"). In all, although Japanese and Americans reported similar amounts of information about the focal objects, the Japanese students reported 60 percent more information about the environment. Moreover, when asked after they had viewed all the scenes whether they had seen particular focal objects before, the Japanese were thrown off if the object wasn't shown in its original surroundings. Whether it was shown in the original surroundings or in novel surroundings made no difference to American students. Thus, for the Japanese, the object was "bound" to the environment in memory, and probably in initial perception as well, but for the Americans, the objects seem to have been detached from their surroundings (Chalfonte & Johnson, 1996).

FIGURE 4.12 Noticing the Context What do you see? Japanese and American participants differ in their answers to this question. Americans are more likely than Japanese participants to make reference to the focal objects (that is, the fish), whereas the Japanese are more likely than the Americans to make reference to the context (that is, the rocks and plants). (Source: Masuda & Nisbett, 2001.)

Asians and Westerners also differ in the degree to which they attend to context even when they are perceiving inanimate, static objects. In a task called the Rod and Frame Test, researchers asked participants to look into a long box, at the end of which was a rod and a frame (Witkin et al., 1954). The rod and frame could be tilted independently of each other, and participants were asked to ignore the frame and make judgments about the verticality of the rod. Chinese participants' judgments about the verticality of the rod were more influenced by the position of the frame (that is, the context) than were the judgments of American participants (Ji, Peng, & Nisbett, 2000). In a particularly elegant demonstration of Western insensitivity to context and a complementary sensitivity to the properties of a focal object, Kitayama, Duffy, Kawamura, and Larsen (2002) asked Japanese and American participants to examine a square with a line drawn at the bottom (see **Figure 4.13**). They then led their participants to another part of the room, showed them a square of a different size, and asked them either to draw a line of the same length as the original or to draw a line having the same length *in relation to* the original square. Americans were better at the absolute judgment, which required ignoring the context, whereas Japanese were better at the relative judgment, which required paying attention to the context.

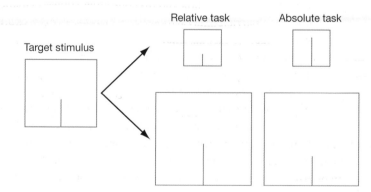

FIGURE 4.13 Sensitivity to Context and the Framed Line Task Participants are shown the target stimulus and then, after a brief interval, are asked to draw a vertical line at the bottom of an empty box. In the relative task, the line must be drawn in the same *proportion* to the box as it was originally. In the absolute task, the new line must be the exact same length as the original line. Japanese participants are better at the relative task and American participants are better at the absolute task. (Source: Kitayama, Duffy, Kawamura, & Larsen 2002.)

Causal Attribution for Independent and Interdependent Peoples

Given the pronounced difference between Asians' and Westerners' attention to context, it should come as no surprise to learn that Asians are more inclined than Westerners to attribute behavior to the situation.

For example, attributions for the outcomes of sports events are not the same in independent cultures as they are in interdependent cultures. Soccer coaches and players in the United States tend to see positive outcomes as the result of the abilities of individual players and the actions of coaches ("We've got a very good keeper in Bo Oshoniyi, who was defensive MVP of the finals last year"). In contrast, the attributions of Hong Kong coaches and players are more likely to refer to the other team and the context ("I guess South China was a bit tired after having played in a quadrangular tournament") (Lee, Hallahan, & Herzog, 1996).

Other work shows that Westerners see dispositions and internal causes where Asians see situations and contexts. Morris and Peng (1994) showed that Americans are more likely than Chinese to see even the behavior of fish as being more dispositionally determined. They showed participants animated cartoons of an individual fish swimming in front of a group of fish. In some scenes, the individual fish scooted off from the approaching group; in other scenes, the fish was joined by the group and they swam off together; in still other scenes, the individual fish joined the group. Participants were asked why these events occurred. Americans tended to see the behavior of the individual fish as internally caused, and Chinese were more likely to see the behavior of the individual fish as externally caused (see also Kashima, Siegal, Tanaka, & Kashima, 1992; Rhee, Uleman, Lee, & Roman, 1995; Shweder & Bourne, 1984).

These differences in causal perception are likely due to differences in cultural outlook that in turn result in differences in what is attended to. As Markus and Kitayama (1991) put it, "If [like Asians] one perceives oneself as embedded within a larger context of which one is an interdependent part, it is likely that other objects or events will be perceived in a similar way." Westerners, in contrast, are more likely to see themselves as independent agents; consequently, they are more inclined to see people, animals, and even objects as behaving in ways that have relatively little to do with context.

It's not just Asians who differ from Westerners in explanatory tendencies. Al-Zahrani and Kaplowitz (1993) found that Saudi Arabian students were more collectivistic in orientation than Americans. We would therefore expect them to be less likely to show the fundamental attribution error in their causal explanations. The researchers gave brief vignettes describing morally positive and negative behaviors to Saudi Arabian students and American students and asked them to indicate the degree to which they thought the behaviors were caused by something internal to the person versus something external. They found that the American attributions were more internal than the Saudi attributions.

There are also differences in attributional tendencies among American subcultures. This has been measured by determining how often people mention traits in their descriptions. Puerto Rican children use fewer traits when describing themselves than do Anglo children (Hart, Lucca-Irizarry, & Damon, 1986) and are less likely to use traits to describe other people's behavior (Newman, 1991). Zarate, Uleman, and Voils (2001) also found that Mexican-Americans and Mexicans were less likely to make trait inferences than were Anglos.

Priming Culture

In today's world of highly mobile populations, many people have spent significant parts of their lives in both independent and interdependent societies. Such people offer

Priming Culture   To prime Western associations and individualistic attributions, investigators might show participants a photo of (A) the U.S. Capitol building or (B) an American cowboy roping a steer. To prime Asian associations and collectivist attributions, the investigators might show participants a photo of (C) a Chinese temple or (D) a Laotian dragon.

psychologists an opportunity to better understand cultural influences on attribution. For example, Hong Kong has been the location for several fruitful cultural studies because the British governed Hong Kong for 100 years. The culture there is substantially Westernized, and children learn English when they are quite young. People in Hong Kong, it turns out, can be encouraged to think in either an interdependent way or an independent way when presented with images that suggest one culture or the other. Hong, Chiu, and Kung (1997) showed some participants the U.S. Capitol building, a cowboy on horseback, and Mickey Mouse. They showed other participants a Chinese dragon, a temple, and men writing Chinese characters using a brush. They also showed a control group of participants neutral pictures of landscapes. Next the investigators showed all participants the animated cartoons of an individual fish swimming in front of a group of other fish, devised by Morris and Peng (1994), and asked them why they thought this was happening. Participants who initially saw the American pictures gave more reasons having to do with motivations of the individual fish and fewer explanations having to do with the other fish or the context than did participants who initially saw the Chinese pictures. Participants who initially saw the neutral pictures gave explanations that were in between those of the other two groups.

Other natural experiments are made possible by the fact that many people living in North America are of Asian descent and feel themselves to be partly Asian and partly Western. In one study, researchers asked Asian-American participants either to recall an experience that made their identity as an American apparent to them or to recall an experience that made their Asian identity salient. They then showed the students a battery of highly abstract cartoon vignettes suggestive of physical movements, such as an object falling to the bottom of a container of liquid, and asked them to rate the extent to which the object's movement was due to dispositional factors (for example, shape, weight) versus contextual factors (for example, gravity, friction). Participants who had had their American identity primed rated causes internal to the objects as more important than did participants who had had their Asian identity primed (Peng & Knowles, 2003; see also Benet-Martinez, Leu, Lee, & Morris, 2002).

Dispositions: Fixed or Flexible?

So do Asians think like "social psychologists," putting great emphasis on situational determinants of behavior, whereas Westerners think like "personality psychologists," putting more emphasis on dispositional determinants? Not quite. It may be more accurate to say that Asians think like both. We European-American social psychologists find that we have no trouble gossiping about other people with our Asian friends. We understand people using the same dimensions of judgment—which are essentially the "Big Five" personality dimensions of extraversion, neuroticism, agreeableness, conscientiousness, and openness to experience. And the evidence shows that these dimensions play almost as much of a role in judging people's personalities, including one's own, for Asians as they do for Westerners (Cheung et al., 2001; McCrae, Costa, & Yik, 1996; Piedmont & Chase, 1997; Yang & Bond, 1990). Norenzayan, Choi, and Nisbett (1999) asked Korean and American college students a number of questions intended to tap their theories about the causes of behavior and found that although Koreans and Americans rated the importance of personality the same, the Koreans reported situations to be more important than did the Americans.

Ara Norenzayan and his colleagues also asked their participants several questions about their beliefs regarding the malleability of personality—whether it is something about them that can't be altered much or whether it is subject to change. The Koreans thought that personalities are more malleable than the Americans did. The belief that personality is malleable, of course, is consistent with the view that behavior is substantially influenced by external factors.

The view that personality is changeable is also consistent with the view—much more characteristic of interdependent peoples than of independent peoples—that abilities are malleable through environmental factors and through effort (Dweck, 1999; Dweck, Chiu, & Hong, 1995; Dweck, Hong, & Chiu, 1993). Americans report placing a greater value on education than Asians do, but American students spend much less time studying than do Asian students (Stevenson & Stigler, 1992). The belief in the value of effort to overcome inadequacy is deeply rooted in the cultures of China, Korea, and Japan. In an experiment that makes this point well, Heine and his colleagues (2001) asked Japanese and Canadian university students to perform a task said to be reflective of their "creativity." They gave false feedback to the participants, telling some they had done well and others that they had done badly. The experimenters then gave the participants the opportunity to continue to work on the task. Canadian students worked more at the task if they had succeeded, savoring their newfound confidence in their creativity. Japanese students, seeing an opportunity for self-improvement, worked more on the task if they had failed. The experiment has a fascinating implication: Westerners will tend to get better on the things they already do well; Easterners seem likely to become Jacks and Jills of all trades.

Thus, the processes of attribution and impression formation are in many ways the same and in many ways quite different across cultures. Asians and other interdependent peoples live in more interconnected social worlds than do Westerners. And probably as a consequence, they are attuned to more of their environment. Embedded in a social web themselves, they are inclined to see the contexts in which other people, and even other animals and objects, operate (see **Box 4.3**). Asians, like Westerners, do tend to make the fundamental attribution error. But they err to a lesser degree, presumably because they are more attuned to situational contexts and are more likely to correct their judgments when the context is highlighted in some way (Choi & Nisbett, 1998).

 We have seen that the fundamental attribution error is made by people in non-Western cultures, but that Westerners are more susceptible to it. People in interdependent cultures pay more attention to social situations and the people within these situations than do Westerners. For individuals reared in both interdependent and independent cultures, it is possible to prime the different ways of perceiving and attributing behavior.

BOX 4.3 **FOCUS ON DIPLOMACY**

One Cause or Many?

An international conflict occurred between China and the United States when a Chinese fighter plane collided with a U.S. surveillance plane in 2001 and the surveillance plane was forced to land on a Chinese island without receiving permission from the ground. The Chinese held captive the crew of the surveillance plane, demanding an apology for the incident from the United States. The Americans refused, asserting that the cause of the accident was the recklessness of the Chinese fighter pilot. Political scientist Peter Hays Gries and social psychologist Kaiping Peng

argued that the conflict was intensified by the two adversaries' very different conceptions of causality (Gries & Peng, 2002). They noted that to the Chinese, the insistence that there was such a thing as *the* cause of the accident was hopelessly limited in its perspective. Relevant to the accident were a host of considerations, including the fact that the United States was, after all, spying on China and there was a history of interaction between the particular surveillance plane and the particular fighter pilot. Given the complexity and ambiguity of causality, the Chinese

believed that the very least the United States could do would be to express its regrets that the incident had occurred. The presumed ambiguity of causality may lie behind Eastern insistence on apology for any action that results in harm to someone else, no matter how unintentionally and indirectly. Ultimately, the "regret" formula was the one that the two countries hit upon to resolve the impasse, but it is not likely that many people on either side understood the role played in the conflict by the differing conceptions of causality that Gries and Peng identified.

BEYOND THE INTERNAL/ EXTERNAL DIMENSION

The question of whether a given action is mainly due to something about the person involved or to the surrounding situational context is an important part of the story of everyday causal analysis. But this person/situation question is not the only one we ask, and it is not the whole story of everyday causal analysis. We often ask ourselves additional questions about people's behavior to arrive at a more nuanced understanding of its meaning and to enable us to make more refined predictions about future behavior. In particular, we're often interested in understanding a person's intentions (Heider, 1958; Jones & Davis, 1965; Malle, 1999).

Think of it this way: We engage in causal analysis to make the world more predictable—to find the "glue" that holds all sorts of varying instances of behavior together. Sometimes that glue is a trait in the person—for example, her kindness explains her long hours at the soup kitchen, her unfailing politeness to everyone in the residence hall, and her willingness to share her notes with others in her class. Other times the glue is in the situation itself—for example, some people walk out of a horror film, some hold on tight to the arms of their seats, and others squeal with delight because the film is so terribly scary. Still another type of glue is provided by knowing someone's intentions—for example, the long hours in the library, the ingratiating behavior toward the professor, and the theft of another student's notes all come together and are rendered sensible by knowing that the individual has a particularly strong desire to get a good grade (Malle, Moses, & Baldwin, 2001; Searle, 1983).

Empirical studies of everyday explanations of behavior attest to the significance people attach to understanding the reasons for a given behavior. Roughly 80 percent of the time, for example, people explain intentional actions with reference to the actor's reasons (Malle, 2001). Reasons for action, of course, are many and varied, but the overwhelming majority of the reasons offered to explain behavior fall into two classes:

desires and beliefs. Why did the senator endorse an amendment banning the burning of the American flag? Because she *wants* to be reelected, and she *believes* she needs to appease her constituents. Why does he put up with his wife's abusive insults? Because he doesn't *want* to be alone, and he *believes* no one else would be interested in him. Beliefs and wants are what give rise to intentional action, and so it stands to reason that when we want to understand the behavior of others, we have to understand what they're seeking and what they believe will allow them (or not allow them) to get it.

 LOOKING BACK We have seen that when we want to understand a person's intentions, the attributional question we are most inclined to ask concerns the *reason* for the person's behavior. Understanding a person's reasons for a particular action, in turn, often requires understanding the person's beliefs and desires.

Summary

From Physical Appearance to Inferences about Personality Traits

- We almost instantaneously make judgments about people's personalities based on their appearance. These judgments tend to focus on whether or not someone is trustworthy and safe to approach and whether someone is dominant. We also tend to think of people who have facial features characteristic of the very young—large eyes, a large head, and a relatively small, rounded chin—as likely to be relatively naive, weak, and incompetent.

From Acts to Dispositions: The Importance of Causal Attribution

- We constantly search for the causes of events, and our attributions affect our behavior. People have chronically different *explanatory styles*. Some people have a pessimistic style, attributing good outcomes to external, unstable, and local causes and bad outcomes to internal, stable, and global causes. This style is associated with poor health, poor performance, and depression.

The Processes of Causal Attribution

- We use the *covariation principle* to make attributions. When we know that a person engages in a given behavior across many situations and that other people tend not to engage in the behavior, we are likely to attribute the behavior to the person. When we know that the person only engages in the behavior in a particular situation and that most people in that situation also engage in the behavior, we tend to attribute the behavior to the situation.

- *Counterfactual thoughts* can powerfully affect attribution. We often perform mental simulations, adding or subtracting elements about the person or the situation and using these simulations to guide our attributions. Joy or pain in response to an event is *amplified* when it is easy to see how things might have turned out differently.

- Our ability to imagine what others would likely do in a given situation allows us to make use of the *discounting* and *augmentation principles*. If situational constraints could plausibly have caused an observed behavior, we discount the role of the person's dispositions. If there were strong forces that would typically inhibit the behavior, we augment its implications and assume that the actor's dispositions were particularly powerful.

Errors and Biases in Attribution

- Our attributions are not always fully rational. We sometimes attribute events to causes that flatter us beyond what the evidence calls for—revealing *self-serving attributions*.

- The *fundamental attribution error* is the tendency to attribute behavior to real or imagined dispositions of the person and to neglect influential aspects of the situation confronting the person. Even when it ought to be obvious that the situation is a powerful influence on behavior, we often attribute behavior to presumed traits, abilities, and motivations.

- One of the reasons we make such erroneous attributions is due to the *just world hypothesis*. We like to think that people get what they deserve and that bad outcomes are produced by bad or incompetent people.

- Another reason for the fundamental attribution error is that people and their behavior tend to be more salient than situations.

- A final reason for the fundamental attribution error is that attribution appears to be a two-step process. People are initially and automatically characterized in terms consistent with their behavior, and this initial characterization is only later adjusted to take account of the impact of prevailing situational forces.

- There are *actor-observer differences* in attributions. In general, actors tend to attribute their behavior much more to situations than do observers. This is partly due to the fact that actors can usually see the situations they confront better than observers can.

Culture and the Fundamental Attribution Error

- There are marked cultural differences in susceptibility to the fundamental attribution error. Interdependent peoples are less likely to make the error than independent peoples, in part because their tendency to pay attention to context encourages them to look to the situation confronting the actor. For bicultural people, it is possible to prime one culture or the other and get very different causal attributions.

Beyond the Internal/External Dimension

- Much of the time, we are concerned with more than whether to attribute behavior to the situation versus the person and are interested in discerning the intentions and reasons that underlie a person's behavior.

Key Terms

actor-observer difference (p. 140)
attribution theory (p. 112)
augmentation principle (p. 122)
causal attribution (p. 115)
consensus (p. 120)
consistency (p. 120)

counterfactual thoughts (p. 124)
covariation principle (p. 120)
discounting principle (p. 122)
distinctiveness (p. 120)
emotional amplification (p. 124)
explanatory style (p. 116)

fundamental attribution error (p. 131)
just world hypothesis (p. 136)
self-serving bias (p. 128)

Further Reading

Gilbert, D. T. (1995). Attribution and interpersonal perception. In A. Tesser (Ed.), *Advanced social psychology* (pp. 99–147). New York: McGraw-Hill. An insightful and enjoyable analysis of how people make attributions for one another's behavior.

Malle, B. F., Moses, L. J., & Baldwin, D. A. (2001). *Intentions and intentionality: Foundations of social cognition.* Cambridge, MA: MIT Press. A comprehensive treatment of the importance of perceived intentions in everyday social understanding.

Roese, N. J., & Olson, J. M. (1995). *What might have been: The social psychology of counterfactual thinking.* Mahwah, NJ: Lawrence Erlbaum Associates. A compendium of some of the most important work on counterfactual thinking.

Ross, L., & Nisbett, R. E. (1991). *The person and the situation: Perspectives of social psychology.* New York: McGraw-Hill. A systematic analysis of situationism and its relation to the broader field of social psychology.

ⓢ Online Study Tools

StudySpace

Go to StudySpace, wwnorton.com/studyspace, to access additional review and enrichment materials, including the following resources for each chapter:

Organize

- Study Plan
- Chapter Outline
- Quiz+ Assessment

Learn

- Ebook
- Chapter Review

- Critical-Thinking Questions
- Visual Quizzes
- Vocabulary Flashcards

Connect

- Apply It! Exercises
- Author Insights Podcasts
- Social Psychology in the News

Social Judgment

EARLY IN THE MORNING ON June 28, 1993, New York State troopers on Long Island's Southern State Parkway noticed a Mazda pickup with no license plates. When they motioned for the driver to pull over, he sped off, leading them on a 25-minute chase that ended when the Mazda slammed into a utility pole. After arresting the driver, the officers noticed a foul odor emanating from under a tarp in the back of the truck. When the tarp was removed, the officers discovered the badly decomposed body of a 22-year-old woman. Subsequent investigation implicated the driver, Joel Rifkin, in the murders of 16 other women, making him the most prolific serial killer in New York State history. Those who knew Rifkin expressed shock at the news. One neighbor told reporters, "When I would come home at 1 or 2 in the morning, if I saw the garage light on, I'd feel safe because I knew Joel was around." A second neighbor said he was "simply a gentle young man." Classmates asserted he was "not the kind of guy who would do something like this."

As this story makes clear, social judgments can have serious consequences. Mistaking a serial killer as someone who's "gentle" and "safe" to be around can be a lethal mistake. More generally, effective action requires sound judgment about the world around us. "How will my professor react if I ask for more time?" "Are they developing nuclear weapons?" "Will my boyfriend be faithful?" "Is it worth it?"

Our discussion of social judgment—and sources of error in judgment—proceeds in five parts. Each focuses on a critical component of social judgment: (1) We first note that judgments are only as effective as the quality of the information on which they are based, and we discuss some of the sources of bias in the information encountered in everyday life. (2) The way information is presented, including the order in which it is presented and how it is framed, can affect the judgments that people make. (3) People don't just passively take in information. They often actively seek it out, and we review evidence of a pervasive bias in people's information-seeking strategies that often distorts their conclusions. (4) Judgments

Errors in Social Judgment Despite being the most prolific serial killer in New York's history, Joel Rifkin's neighbors insisted he was "not the kind of guy who would do something like this" and that he was "a gentle young man."

arise from a complex interaction between information that individuals acquire and stored knowledge accumulated from a lifetime of experience. We thus examine how a person's preexisting knowledge, expectations, and mental habits can influence the construal of new information and thus substantially influence judgment. (5) We end with a discussion of the two mental systems—intuition and reason—that people use in making complex judgments.

WHY STUDY SOCIAL JUDGMENT?

Chapter 4 discusses one particular type of judgment—judgments about the causes of events. Here we examine social judgment more generally, exploring how people arrive at judgments (causal and otherwise) that help them interpret the past, understand the present, and predict the future. The field of social psychology has always been concerned with judgment because social psychology has always been a very cognitively oriented branch of psychology. Indeed, one of the earliest and most fundamental principles of social psychology is the construal principle introduced in Chapter 1: If we want to know how a person will react in a given situation, we must understand how the situation is experienced by that person. Social stimuli rarely influence people's behavior directly; they do so indirectly through the way they are interpreted and construed.

The example that began this chapter does more than testify to the importance of judgment in everyday life. It also highlights the fact that our judgments are not always flawless. We trust some people we shouldn't. We make some investments that turn out to be unwise. Some of our mistakes are harmless, and others have dire consequences, but all of them can help us figure out how to do better next time. They are informative to psychologists as well because they provide particularly helpful clues about how people go about the business of making judgments. They give psychologists hints about the strategies, or rules, people follow to make judgments—both those that turn out to be successful and those that lead to disaster.

The strategy of scrutinizing mistakes has a long tradition in psychology. Perceptual psychologists study illusions to illuminate general principles of perception. Psycholinguists learn about speech production by studying speech errors. Personality psychologists gain insights into healthy functioning by examining different types of psychopathology. Whether rare or common, mistakes often tell a lot about how a system works by showing its limitations. Thus, researchers interested in social judgment have often explored the limitations of everyday judgment.

THE INFORMATION AVAILABLE FOR JUDGMENT

A tennis tournament has 125 contestants. On losing a match, a contestant drops out. The winner must win all the matches she plays. How many matches (involving all players) are needed to complete the tournament? (Answer is on p. 154.)

Although many people find "word problems" like this annoying, they do have one very appealing feature: all the information necessary for the solution is provided, and that fact is known in advance. Such is not always the case for many real-world problems. Often we may not have—or may not know if we have—all the information needed to render an accurate judgment. Furthermore, some of the information that is available may be inaccurate. These limitations place something of a ceiling on the accuracy of the judgments we make. But note that judgments can be perfectly sound, or rational, even if invalid information is used as input—and no matter how unhappy the outcome may be. The standard by which the quality of judgments should be assessed is not how well they turn out, but how sensibly they were made in light of the information available.

Because of the strong link between information quality and judgmental accuracy, it is important to know when information is likely to be accurate and when it is likely to be misleading. We discuss some of the most common sources of distortion next.

Biases in Information Presented Firsthand

Some of the information we have about the world comes to us firsthand, through direct experience. The rest comes to us secondhand, through gossip, news accounts, biographies, textbooks, and so on. In many cases, the information collected firsthand is more accurate because it has the advantage of not having been filtered by someone else, who might slant things in a particular direction. But firsthand experiences can also be deceptive, as when we are inattentive toward, or misconstrue, events that happen before our eyes. Our own experience can also be unrepresentative, as when we judge what the students are like at a given university from the one student we encounter during a tour of the campus or what "the people" are like in a foreign country from the few we encounter at hotels, restaurants, or museums. Finally, some of the firsthand information we acquire is information we extract from other people's behavior. But people's behavior sometimes springs from a desire to create an impression that is not a true reflection of who they really are, and such discrepancies can give rise to predictable errors in judgment.

Answer to tennis tournament problem on p. 153:
The tournament has one winner and 124 losers, each of whom loses once and only once. Thus, there are 124 matches in all. (Don't feel bad if you couldn't solve this problem; the solution wasn't obvious to us at first either.)

Pluralistic Ignorance One common type of situation in which other people's overt behavior can give rise to erroneous conclusions is exemplified by the following familiar scenario (Miller & McFarland, 1991): A professor finishes a discussion of a difficult topic by asking, "Are there any questions?" Numerous students are completely mystified, but no hands are raised. The befuddled students conclude that everyone else understands the material and that they alone are confused.

This is just one example of a phenomenon known as **pluralistic ignorance**. The phenomenon arises whenever people act at variance with their private beliefs because of a concern for the social consequences. The result is that everyone misperceives the group norm. It is embarrassing to admit that you did not understand a lecture when you suspect that everyone else grasped the essential points. However, when everyone follows that logic, an illusion about the nature of social reality is created. People conclude from the illusory group consensus that they are deviant, and this reinforces the difficulty of acting in accordance with what they really believe.

Pluralistic ignorance is particularly common in situations in which "toughness" is valued, leading people to be afraid to show their kinder, gentler impulses. Gang members, for example, have been known privately to confess their objections to brutal initiation procedures and the lack of concern for human life, but they are afraid to say so out of fear of being ridiculed by their peers. The result is that few realize how many of their fellow gang members share their private reservations. Prison guards likewise often think they are alone in their sympathy for inmates because the prevailing norm of being tough deters everyone from revealing whatever sympathetic feelings they have for the prisoners (Kauffman, 1981; Klofas & Toch, 1982).

Another example of pluralistic ignorance that is close to home for many college students involves attitudes toward alcohol consumption. Deborah Prentice and Dale Miller (1993) examined the discrepancy between private attitudes and public norms about alcohol at Princeton University. They thought there might be a discrepancy between the two for the following reasons:

> The alcohol situation at Princeton is exacerbated by the central role of alcohol in many of the university's institutions and traditions. For example, at the eating clubs, the center of social life on campus, alcohol is on tap 24 hours a day, 7 days a week. Princeton reunions boast the second highest level of alcohol consumption for any event in the country after the Indianapolis 500. The social norms for drinking at the university are clear: Students must be comfortable with alcohol use to partake of Princeton social life.
>
> In the face of these strong norms promoting alcohol use, we suspected that students' private attitudes would reveal substantial misgivings about drinking. Within their first few months at college, students are exposed to vivid and irrefutable evidence of the negative consequences of excessive alcohol consumption: They nurse sick roommates, overlook inappropriate behavior and memory losses, and hear about serious injuries and even deaths that result from drinking. They may have negative experiences with alcohol themselves and may notice its effects on their academic performance. This accumulating evidence of the ill effects of alcohol is likely to affect their private attitudes but not the social norm: Indeed, believing that others are still comfortable with alcohol, students will perpetuate that norm by continuing to adopt a nonchalant demeanor that masks their growing concerns. (Prentice & Miller, 1993, pp. 244–245)

To find out if their hunch was correct, Prentice and Miller asked Princeton undergraduates how comfortable they felt about drinking habits at Princeton, as well as how

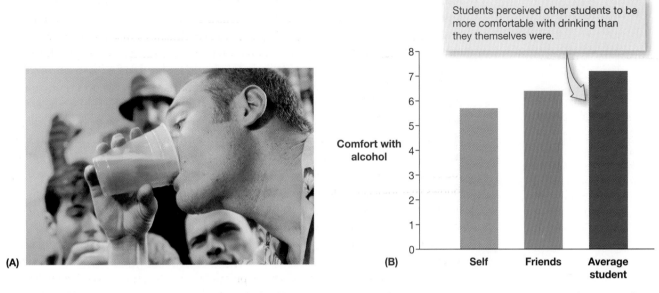

FIGURE 5.1 **Pluralistic Ignorance** (A) University students believe that drinking alcohol is more popular among their peers than it really is. Because of this belief, they censor their own reservations about drinking, thus furthering the illusion that alcohol is so popular. (B) Princeton University students' ratings of their own and other students' comfort with campus drinking habits at Princeton.

comfortable they thought both the *average undergraduate* and their *friends* felt about campus drinking habits. If the students were suffering from pluralistic ignorance on this issue, they would indicate that they were less comfortable with drinking than they supposed most students were. The results, shown in **Figure 5.1**, indicate that that is exactly what happened. Hidden discomfort with alcohol existed side by side with perceived popular support.

What would happen if students were made aware of their misperceptions? Would they drink less? A study by Schroeder and Prentice (1998) indicates that accurate knowledge of peers' opinions does indeed produce less drinking. The researchers had students participate in one of two discussions with their peers about drinking —one focused on pluralistic ignorance and how the false norms about alcohol on campus might have developed, and the other a more traditional, individual-focused discussion about how students might make more responsible decisions about alcohol consumption. Six months later, they found that the students who had participated in the norm-focused discussions reported drinking 40 percent less than those in the individual-based discussions.

Nicole Shelton and Jennifer Richeson (2005) examined a form of pluralistic ignorance on college campuses and elsewhere that has profound implications for how readily people might form friendships and get along with members of different ethnic groups. They predicted that individuals might worry that someone from another ethnic group is unlikely to be interested in talking to them. Initiating conversation would therefore seem risky, something they might want to avoid out of fear of being rejected. As a result, no opening gesture is made and no contact established. But how do people interpret the missed opportunity? When Shelton and Richeson asked students a series of focused questions to probe this issue, they found that the students tended to attribute their own failure to initiate contact to their fear of rejection, but the other person's failure to get things started to a lack of interest in establishing friendships across ethnic lines. Such a conclusion, of course, makes it harder to initiate contact the next time one has an opportunity to do so with someone from that same ethnic group.

Memory Biases Memory was once believed to be a passive registry of information a person had encountered. And it is easy to see why. Many of its most prominent features make it seem like a passive storage device. New information seems to crowd out the old (storage is limited); too much input at one time garbles the information that is retained (things not stored properly initially are hard to find later on); and the clarity and detail of remembered episodes appear to decay gradually over time (storage is leaky). One of the great triumphs of psychological science in the twentieth century was correcting this misconception about memory. We now know beyond any doubt that memory is an active, constructive process in which inferences about "what must have been" guide memories of "what was."

Given that memories are not passively recorded and subsequently retrieved, but instead are actively constructed from general theories about how the world works, we have to be concerned about more than simply forgetting. We need to be concerned about constructing memories of events that never happened (Bartlett, 1932; Loftus, 1979, 2003; Schacter, 2001). Of course, either shortcoming—not remembering enough or "remembering" what never happened—can distort judgments based on information retrieved from memory.

The concern about false memories achieved prominence (in both academic psychology and the broader culture) in the 1980s and '90s with the controversy over "recovered memories." Many people have claimed that they experienced a traumatic event during childhood that they had completely forgotten or repressed, but then recovered much later in life—often during psychotherapy. The most commonly reported recovered memory is one of childhood sexual abuse. In one of the most striking examples, Eileen Franklin accused her father of having molested and murdered her close friend when the two of them were 8 years old. Eileen made the accusation 20 years after her friend's murder, having had no memory of the event before that. The memory came back to her one day while she was playing with her own children. Based almost exclusively on his daughter's testimony, George Franklin was convicted of murder and served six years in prison before his conviction was overturned. (Although not one of the reasons his conviction was overturned, the case against Mr. Franklin was further weakened by

Recovered Memories (A) Eileen Franklin (center) believed that she had repressed and then recovered memories of her father, George Franklin, Sr., molesting and murdering her childhood friend 20 years earlier. (B) Based on his daughter's testimony about her recovered memories, George Franklin was found guilty and imprisoned until new evidence emerged showing that he could not have committed the crime.

DNA evidence showing that he did not commit a second murder his daughter said he committed.)

Often we cannot say whether recovered memories are real or not. If evidence is obtained establishing that one such memory was constructed, that does not imply that all of them were. Likewise, evidence indicating that one such case did in fact occur does not attest to the reality of all of them. Given what is known about the fallibility of human memory, however, it is irresponsible to insist, as some psychotherapists have, that all such accounts are valid.

One reason for caution in accepting claims about vividly remembered events is that even the most vivid memories can be inaccurate—completely made up in some cases, critical details notably altered in others (see **Box 5.1**). Both John Adams and Thomas Jefferson wrote late in their lives that they remembered signing the Declaration of Independence on July 4, but it is a matter of historical record that they did not sign it (nor did anyone else) until August 2. The success of the new nation made July 4 a hallowed day in American history, and so it made sense that Adams and Jefferson would have signed the document that day. And what was sensible became, in their minds, what actually happened.

Another way in which people's beliefs about the way things should be can influence their memories of the way they *were* involve their general theories about stability and change. Most people assume that certain things in life tend to stay largely the same (such as one's political party affiliation or one's IQ) but that others tend to change (such as one's level of wisdom or one's taste in clothes). Such theories of stability and change might distort people's memories when actual events don't fit their theories (Ross, 1989).

One study that examined the impact of such theories on people's memories focused on attitudes about busing to achieve racial integration (Goethals & Reckman, 1973). Massachusetts high school students filled out a questionnaire assessing their attitudes toward numerous political and social issues, including the desirability of busing for purposes of racial integration. Then, 4 to 14 days later, they participated in a group discussion as part of an investigation of high school students' thoughts about controversial issues. The topic was busing. The discussion groups were composed of an experimental confederate and students who were either all opposed to busing or all in favor of it. The confederate was a "ringer" from the same high school who had been armed by the experimenters with forceful arguments in favor of both perspectives. His task was to change the students' opinions, which he did with great success. A questionnaire administered after the discussion indicated that anti-busing students became substantially more pro-busing, and pro-busing students became substantially more anti-busing. Most important, when students were asked to recall what their original attitudes had been, their recollections of their previous attitudes were distorted to fit their new opinions. Those with newly formed anti-busing attitudes recalled having always been anti-busing, and vice versa.

You might object that the students were merely *presenting* themselves as consistent. They may have felt some pressure to appear consistent (nobody wants to come across as wishy-washy), so they knowingly provided incorrect accounts of their past attitudes that were more consistent with their current thoughts on the matter. The experimenters anticipated this objection, and to rule it out, they instructed the students to complete the attitude measures exactly as they had done before and informed them that the accuracy of their memories would be evaluated by comparing their responses to those they had made on the original questionnaire. Despite this strong encouragement for accurate recall, the students' memories were substantially biased in the direction of their current attitudes.

What about the flip side of this phenomenon? Are there times when people have implicit theories of change that lead them to recall changes that have not in fact taken

BOX 5.1 **FOCUS ON DAILY LIFE**

Flashbulb Memories

Flashbulb memories are vivid recollections of the moment someone learned some dramatic, emotionally charged news. For example: "I know exactly where I was and what I was doing when I heard about the 9/11 attacks on the World Trade Center." Such memories were once thought to be unusually accurate (Brown & Kulik, 1977). Though they are no doubt frequently both indelible and correct, subsequent research has shown that they are not always accurate. In one study, people were asked about their memories of the explosion of the space shuttle *Challenger*, both the day after it happened and 2½ years later. Although the respondents described their later memories as vivid, and confi-dently asserted that they were accurate, most of these memories nonetheless had various discrepancies from their earlier memories, and more than a third of the later memories were wildly differ-ent from the originals (Neisser & Harsch, 1992). Consider the recollections of one person in this study who remembered the event as follows at the two different points in time. It's hard to imagine them coming from the same person:

24 HOURS AFTER THE EXPLO-SION: When I first heard about the explosion I was sitting in my fresh-man dorm room with my roommate and we were watching TV. It came on a news flash and we were both totally shocked. I was really upset and I went upstairs to talk to a friend of mine and then I called my parents.

2½ YEARS AFTER THE EXPLO-SION: I was in my religion class and some people walked in and started talking about [it]. I didn't know any details except that it had exploded and the schoolteacher's students had all been watching which I thought was so sad. Then after class I went to my room and watched the TV program talking about it and I got all the details from that. (Reported in Neisser & Harsch, 1992.)

Flashbulb Memories   People have vivid (although not always accurate) memories of where they were and what they were doing when they learned some dramatic news, such as (A) the explosion of the *Challenger* space shuttle, and (B) the collapse of the World Trade Center towers in New York City as a result of the 9/11 terrorist attacks.

place? Conway and Ross (1984) argued that such memory distortions are common among participants in various "self-help" programs, such as diet regimens, speed-reading courses, and self-confidence seminars. Many of these programs have been found to be ineffective (or even harmful), and yet their effectiveness is acclaimed by satisfied participants. What's going on? Conway and Ross argued that people begin such programs with the expectation of success. (Why participate otherwise?) Participants then apply this general theory of improvement to their knowledge of what they are like at the end of the program, and they infer that they must have been really bad off beforehand. In other words, they get what they want out of the program (improvement) by unknowingly revising their assessment of where they stood initially.

To investigate their thesis, Conway and Ross interviewed students who had participated in a college study skills program. As predicted, the students who completed the program thought their initial study skills had been worse than they actually were. This led them to think that their skills had improved (which they hadn't) and to anticipate receiving higher grades (which they didn't). Note, furthermore, that these sorts of theory-driven memory distortions are in all likelihood intensified by a powerful set of rationalization processes we discuss in Chapter 6.

One word of caution before we leave the subject of memory distortions. The research indicating that memory is prone to certain systematic errors does not mean that our memories are hopelessly unreliable. Our memories are undoubtedly much more often right than wrong, and they serve us just fine most of the time. We remember where we parked the car, what we ordered the last time we visited our favorite restaurant, whether we made love last night, and so on. What the research on memory errors shows is that our memories are not recording machines; they are perhaps better thought of as devices for construing the past.

Biases in Information Presented Secondhand

Do you believe that global warming is caused by humans? That Walt Disney was anti-Semitic? That your roommate's father is a good parent? Different people will have different answers to such questions, of course. But their different responses are alike in one important respect: all are based to a large extent on secondhand information. Few of us have any firsthand knowledge of the links between industrialization and climatological data. None of us knows firsthand what Walt Disney thought about Jews. Similarly, for most people, knowledge of their roommate's father is restricted to whatever stories the roommate has told about him.

Because so many of our judgments are based on secondhand information, we must come to grips with the question of how accurate the information we receive from others is likely to be. What are some of the variables that influence the accuracy of secondhand information? What factors reduce the reliability of secondhand information, and when are these factors likely to come into play?

Sharpening and Leveling One source of inaccuracy lies in the need for second-hand accounts to summarize what happened, since listeners are typically not patient enough, nor speakers motivated enough, to provide a full account of everything that happened. In summarizing, important elements are emphasized, which is called **sharpening**; irrelevant details are eliminated, which is called **leveling**. To tell a story that allows a person to see the forest and not just the trees, essential elements are sharpened and extraneous features are leveled.

A notable example comes from the early history of psychology: the story of the classical conditioning of Little Albert. As most introductory psychology textbooks proclaim, a 9-month-old child by the name of Albert once participated in an experiment

flashbulb memories Vivid recollections of the moment one learned some dramatic, emotionally charged news.

"It is all too common for caterpillars to become butterflies and then to maintain that in their youth they had been little butterflies. Maturation makes liars of us all."

—George Vaillant

sharpening Emphasizing important or more interesting elements in telling a story to someone else.

leveling Eliminating or deemphasizing seemingly less important details when telling a story to someone else.

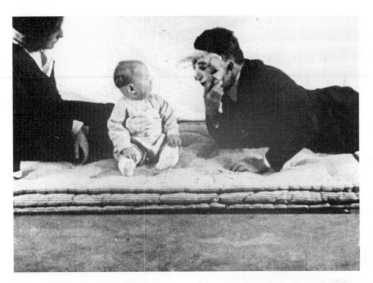

Sharpening and Leveling in Secondhand Accounts "Little Albert" was conditioned to fear white rats, but reports of the details of the experiment have been simplified and distorted to make a more compelling story.

" . . . almost every canonical tale is false in the same way—a less interesting reality converted to a simple story with a message."

—Stephen Jay Gould

in which he was greeted by the frightening sound of a hammer striking a metal bar every time he went near a white rat. Not surprisingly, Albert developed a fear of white rats, a fear that was maintained long after the experimenters stopped striking the metal bar each time he encountered a rat. Albert is also said to have developed a fear of objects that shared some of the features of the white rat, such as a rabbit, cotton balls, and a white beard.

Many of the elements of the customary story about Little Albert are true. Nevertheless, the original research report has been sharpened and leveled to make a simpler, more compelling story about how people develop phobias about seemingly harmless objects and how acquired fears can generalize to other, similar objects. For example, the experimenters also made a loud noise next to Albert's head when he was near the rabbit, thereby calling into question the claim that Albert's fear of the rat "generalized" to the rabbit. Furthermore, when Albert's fear of the rat seemed to diminish after 5 days without hearing the threatening sound, the experimenters decided to "freshen" Albert's reaction by reintroducing the loud noise. These details cloud the central theme of the story, so they have been leveled out of it. In addition, some of the most memorable aspects of the story of Little Albert were simply made up. A number of textbooks, for example, have invented a happy ending—one in which Albert's fear is eliminated through "reconditioning" (Harris, 1979).

Secondhand Impressions of Other People To a social psychologist, a particularly interesting class of judgments based on secondhand information involves judgments about other people. It is not at all uncommon for people to have impressions, sometimes strong impressions, about people they have never met. Many of us think we have a sense of what Tina Fey, Yo-Yo Ma, or Michelle Obama is "really like"—without ever having made their acquaintance. Likewise, we might have strong impressions of our partner's former boyfriend or girlfriend—even when we are lucky enough to have avoided the person entirely.

How might such secondhand impressions differ from those formed firsthand? Stated differently, might secondhand accounts of a person's actions be sharpened and leveled in systematic ways? Perhaps. As we discuss in Chapter 4, behavior tends to be attributed to people more than to situations; so secondhand accounts of another person's actions may tend to be organized around the person rather than the context in which the actions took place. After all, it is the person who is typically the focus of the story (although there are exceptions). Thus, information about the person and the person's actions tends to be sharpened, whereas information about the surrounding context tends to be leveled. (Recall that there is evidence that this is less true for interdependent peoples; see Chapter 4.) The net result of this selective sharpening and leveling is that secondhand impressions of other people may be relatively unaffected by knowledge of how their actions were influenced by extenuating circumstances. Secondhand impressions may therefore tend to be relatively extreme.

Evidence of this phenomenon is provided by experiments in which "first-generation" participants watch a videotape of a person describing a number of autobiographical events. These participants rate the person on a number of trait dimensions and then provide a tape-recorded account of what they have seen. "Second-generation" participants then listen to these first-generation accounts and also make trait ratings. As the analysis of selective sharpening and leveling would suggest, the second-generation participants tend to make more extreme trait ratings than their first-generation counterparts (Gilovich, 1987; Inman, Reichl, & Baron, 1993). These experiments suggest that the processes of sharpening and leveling are ubiquitous. They are invoked even when there is no motivation to provide a slanted account.

Ideological Distortions Of course, the biasing effects of sharpening and leveling are accentuated when there is a motivation to slant the story in a particular direction. Transmitters of information often have an ideological ax to grind, and that leads them to accentuate some elements of a story and suppress others in order to foster certain beliefs or behaviors. Sometimes such motivated distortion is relatively "innocent." The person fervently believes in the message; it is just that certain details that might detract from the core message have been dropped. For example, when prepping Harry Truman for his 1947 speech on the containment of the Soviet Union, Undersecretary of State Dean Acheson remarked that it was necessary to be "clearer than the truth."

"Here it is—the plain, unvarnished truth. Varnish it."

Of course, not all distortions are so innocent. People often knowingly provide highly misleading accounts for the express purpose of misleading. Republicans trumpet all manner of misleading statistics to make the Democrats look bad, and the Democrats do likewise to the Republicans. In areas of intense ethnic strife, such as Kashmir, Congo, Gaza, and Rwanda, all sides wildly exaggerate their own righteousness and shamelessly inflate tales of atrocities committed against them (even though the reality is bad enough).

Distortion in the Media One of the most pervasive sources of distortion in secondhand accounts is the desire to entertain. On a small scale, this happens in the stories we swap with one another. We often exaggerate a tale to make it more interesting. Being trapped in an elevator with 20 people for an hour is more interesting than being trapped with 6 people for 15 minutes. So we round up, generously. Or we make an event more interesting by enhancing our proximity to it. We describe something that happened to someone we barely know as happening to a "friend of mine." We tell the story of an event we only heard about as if we had actually been there.

On a larger scale, the need to entertain distorts the messages people receive through the mass media. One way that print and broadcast media can attract an audience is to report—indeed, overreport—negative, violent, and sensational events. Bad news tends to be more newsworthy than good news, a truism captured in the news world's dictum "If it bleeds, it leads."

The most frequently voiced concern about this bad-news bias is that it distorts people's judgments of the dangers present in everyday life. To be sure, the media provide a distorted view of reality. In the world as seen through the media, 80 percent of all crime is violent; but in the real world, only 20 percent is violent (Center for Media and Public Affairs, 2000; Marsh, 1991; Sheley & Askins, 1981). In addition, news coverage of crime does not correlate with the rise and fall of the crime rate. There is just as much coverage during the best of times as there is during the worst of times (Garofalo, 1981; Windhauser, Seiter, & Winfree, 1991). The world as presented in motion pictures and television dramas is even more violent (Gerbner, Gross, Morgan, & Signorielli, 1980).

Media Distortion and Fear of Victimization   There is a positive correlation between watching television crime shows such as *Law and Order* (shown here) and the belief that the world is a dangerous place.

There is concern that exposure to such a distorted view of reality can lead people to believe they are more at risk of victimization than they really are. To find out whether that might be the case, investigators have conducted surveys in which people are asked how much television they watch and then asked questions about the prevalence of crime (for example, "How likely do you think it is that you or one of your close friends will have their house broken into during the next year?" or "If a child were to play alone in a park each day for a month, what do you think the chances are that he would be the victim of a violent crime?").

Such studies have consistently found a positive correlation between the amount of time spent watching television and the fear of victimization (Doob & MacDonald, 1979; Gerbner et al., 1980). As with all correlational studies, however, this finding by itself is difficult to interpret. Perhaps there is something about the kind of people who watch a lot of television—besides their television habits—that makes them feel so vulnerable. To address this problem, researchers have collected a variety of other measures (income, gender, race, residential location) and examined whether the findings hold up when these other variables are statistically controlled. When this is done, an interesting pattern emerges. The correlation between television-viewing habits and perceived vulnerability is substantially reduced among people living in low-crime neighborhoods, but remains strong among those living in high-crime areas (Doob & MacDonald, 1979; Gerbner et al., 1980). People who live in dangerous areas and do not watch much television feel safer than their neighbors who watch a lot. Thus, the violence depicted on television can make the world appear to be a dangerous place, especially among people for whom the televised images resonate with certain aspects of their environment.

The Asymmetry between Positive and Negative Information   The tendency on the part of the news media to hype bad news raises the more fundamental psychological question of why it's in the media's interest to do so. This translates to the question of why audiences are more interested in, titillated by, or receptive to negative information.

There are doubtless many reasons, one of which implies that even if positive and negative information were presented evenhandedly, they would not have symmetrical effects.

Consider the following situation: You have just delivered a speech in a class on rhetoric. Seven of your classmates compliment you on your presentation; one comments that your introduction lacked punch. If you are like most people, you will find yourself obsessed with the one negative comment, even though it was outnumbered by the complimentary remarks.

This all-too-common reaction is one manifestation of a pervasive human tendency that has implications for our very survival. That is, we may be more attentive to negative information than to positive information because the former may have more implications for our well-being. Some negative events constitute threats to survival, and thus they need to be attended to quickly. Organisms that fail to do so put themselves at risk. To be sure, many positive events, such as eating, also have survival implications, but they are usually not as urgent. A morsel of food not eaten now can be eaten later; a predator that is not avoided now never will be. The net result is that people may be more vigilant for potential threats than for potential benefits (Dijksterhuis & Aarts, 2003; Hansen & Hansen, 1988; Pratto & John, 1991; see also Baumeister, Bratslavsky, Finkenauer, & Vohs, 2001; Forgas, 1992; Rozin & Royzman, 2001).

Positive and Negative Information in the Media The media are more likely to report on negative than on positive information, as the public seems more interested in negative information —perhaps as an evolutionary outgrowth of survival concerns. We saw and heard a great deal in the media about the devastation left by the 2005 tsunami in South Asia, but much less about relief efforts to help the victims, including U.S. marines' distribution of humanitarian aid to victims in Indonesia, as shown in this photo of a tsunami victim thanking a U.S. marine.

We have seen that there are many sources of potential bias in the information available to us—and on which we base our judgments. Even firsthand information can be biased, as, for example, when people behave in ways that do not reflect their true attitudes or when firsthand information must be recalled from our occasionally suspect memories. There are also several sources of error in secondhand information. When people provide us with secondhand accounts of events, they typically sharpen some elements and level others. Communicators also sometimes distort information in the interest of profit or ideology. Finally, perceptual vigilance inclines us to attend more to threatening stimuli than to unthreatening stimuli, which may account for why the media overreport negative, violent, and sensational stories. In the next section, we focus on how our reactions to the information available to us can be powerfully influenced by structural aspects of the way information is presented.

HOW INFORMATION IS PRESENTED

As an example of the power of how information is presented, consider the marketing and advertising of products. In an economy of abundance, companies can easily produce enough to satisfy the needs of society, but they find it useful to stimulate sufficient "need" so that there will be enough demand for what can be readily produced in abundance. By manipulating the messages people receive about various products through marketing, producers hope that consumers' buying impulses will be affected. The key to successful marketing, in turn, is not simply the selection of *what* information to present, but *how* to present it. It is an article of faith among advertisers that the way information is presented has a powerful influence on what people think and do.

We will examine that article of faith, but not in the domain of advertising. Instead, we will examine what social psychologists have discovered about the presentation of information and how it affects judgment more broadly. As we shall see, slight variations in the presentation of information can have profound effects on people's judgments.

Order Effects

How happy are you with your life in general? How many dates have you been on in the past month?

If you are like most people, there may have been some connection, but not a strong one, between your responses to the two questions. After all, there is much more to life than dating. Indeed, when survey respondents were asked these two questions in this order, the correlation between their responses was only .32.

But when another group of respondents was asked the two questions in the opposite order, the correlation between their responses was more than twice as strong—.67. Asking about their recent dating history in the first question made them very aware of how that part of their life was going, which then had a notable effect on how they answered the second question (Strack, Martin, & Schwarz, 1988; see also Haberstroh, Oyserman, Schwarz, Kühnen, & Ji, 2002; Schwarz, Strack, & Mai 1991; Tourangeau, Rasinski, & Bradburn, 1991).

Results such as these provide striking confirmation of something many people grasp intuitively—namely, that the order in which items are presented can have a powerful influence on judgment. That is why we all worry so much about whether we should go on first or last in any kind of performance. Sometimes the information presented first exerts the most influence, a phenomenon known as a **primacy effect**. On other occasions, it is the information presented last that has the most impact, a phenomenon known as a **recency effect**.

Order effects are not limited to public performances and opinion polls, of course, but are pervasive in everyday life. In one study that is particularly germane to social life, Solomon Asch (1946) once asked people to evaluate a hypothetical individual described in the following terms: intelligent, industrious, impulsive, critical, stubborn, and envious. The individual was rated favorably, no doubt because of the influence of the two very positive terms that began the list—intelligent and industrious. A second group read the same trait adjectives in the opposite order and formed a much less favorable impression. Thus, there was a substantial primacy effect. Traits presented at the beginning of the list had more impact than those presented later on. Etiquette books (and your parents) are right: first impressions matter a lot.

Order effects arise for a number of reasons. Some arise because of information-processing limitations. Primacy effects, for example, often result from a tendency to pay great attention to stimuli presented early on, but then to lose focus during the presentation of later items. In Asch's experiment, for example, it is impossible to miss that the person described in the first list is intelligent and industrious, but once an initial positive impression is formed, it is easy to gloss over the person's stubbornness and envy. Recency effects, in contrast, typically result when the last items are easiest to recall. Information remembered obviously receives greater weight than information forgotten, so later items sometimes exert more influence on judgment than information presented earlier.

Other order effects arise because the initial information affects how later information is construed. All of the traits in Asch's experiment have different shades of

primacy effect The disproportionate influence on judgment of information presented first in a body of evidence.

recency effect The disproportionate influence on judgment of information presented last in a body of evidence.

meaning, and how each is construed depends on the information already encountered. Take the word "stubborn." When it follows positive traits, such as "intelligent" and "industrious," one interprets it charitably, as steadfast or determined. In contrast, when it follows "envious," it is seen more negatively, as closed-minded or rigid (Asch & Zuckier, 1984; Biernat, Manis, & Kobrynowicz, 1997; Hamilton & Zanna, 1974; Higgins & Rholes, 1976).

Framing Effects

Order effects like those we have just discussed are a type of **framing effect**. That is, the order in which information is presented can "frame" the way it is processed and understood. Asking survey respondents first about how many dates they have had recently invites them to consider this information when evaluating how happy they are with their lives in general.

Order effects like this are a type of "pure" framing effect. The frame of reference is changed even though the content of the information is exactly the same in the two versions; only the order is different. Consider the (probably apocryphal) story of the monk whose request to smoke while he prayed was met with a disapproving stare by his superior. When he mentioned this to a friend, he was told: "Ask a different question. Ask if you can pray while you smoke." The request is the same in both versions. But there is a subtle difference in the frame of reference. The latter presupposes smoking; the former does not.

framing effect The influence on judgment resulting from the way information is presented, including the order of presentation.

"It's not just compared to the table, damn it. This is a small portion."

Spin Framing Framing effects are not limited to the order in which information is presented. Advertisers, for example, try to induce consumers to frame a buying decision in terms favorable to the product being advertised. They do so by utilizing what might be called spin framing, a less "pure" form of framing that varies the content, not just the order, of what is presented. A company with a competitive edge in quality will introduce information that frames the issue as one of quality. Another company with an edge in price will feature information that frames the issue as one of savings.

Participants in political debates likewise try to frame the discussion by "spinning," or highlighting, some aspects of the relevant information and not others. Thus, we hear advocates of different positions talk of "anti-abortion" versus "the right to life," "terrorists" versus "freedom fighters," "occupying army" versus "peacekeeping forces," "illegal aliens" versus "undocumented workers," even "torture" versus "extreme interrogation." The power of such terms to frame the relevant issues is what led the United States in 1947 to change the name of the *War* Department to the more benign-sounding *Defense* Department.

Politicians (and some polling organizations with a political mission) also engage in spin framing when they conduct opinion polls to gather support for their positions. People are more likely to say they are in favor of repealing a "death" tax than an "inheritance" tax. And asking people whether they are in favor of "tax relief" is almost guaranteed to elicit strong support because the very word "relief" implies that taxes are a bad thing—a burden—that one needs relief from (Lakoff, 2004). Shading survey questions in a particular way has been shown to dramatically influence public opinion on abortion, foreign aid, environmental policy, and a host of other policy issues. Because it is so easy to slant public opinion questions in a particular direction, it is

Spin Framing Is this U.S. soldier in Afghanistan a "liberator" or a member of an "occupying army"? The words used to describe him highlight different information, which affects how people react to him.

important to know who sponsored a particular poll, as well as the exact wording of the questions. Without these details, one would be wise to adopt the same attitude toward polls as that of former Israeli foreign minister Shimon Peres, who treats them "like perfume—nice to smell, dangerous to swallow."

Positive and Negative Framing Nearly everything in life is a mixture of good and bad. Ice cream tastes great, but it has a lot of saturated fat. Loyalty is a virtue, but it can make one blind to another's faults. The mixed nature of most things means that they can be described, or framed, in ways that emphasize the good or the bad, with predictable effects on people's judgments. A piece of meat described as 75 percent lean is considered more appealing than one described as 25 percent fat (Levin & Gaeth, 1988), and students feel much safer using a condom described as having a 90 percent success rate than one described as having a 10 percent failure rate (Linville, Fischer, & Fischhoff, 1993). Note that the exact same information is provided in each frame (pure framing); only the focus is different. Note also that there is no "correct" frame. It is every bit as valid to state that a piece of meat is 75 percent lean as it is to state that it is 25 percent fat.

These sorts of framing effects influence judgments and decisions of the greatest consequence, even among individuals with considerable expertise on the topic. In one study, for example, over 400 physicians were asked whether they would recommend surgery or radiation for patients diagnosed with a certain type of cancer. Some were told that of 100 previous patients who had the surgery, 90 lived through the postoperative period, 68 were still alive after a year, and 34 were still alive after five years. Eighty-two percent of these physicians recommended surgery. Others were given the exact same information, but framed in different language: that 10 died during surgery or the postoperative period, 32 had died by the end of the first year, and 66 had died by the end of five years. Only 56 percent of the physicians given the information in this form recommended surgery (McNeil, Pauker, Sox, & Tversky, 1982).

Because, as we saw earlier, negative information tends to attract more attention and have greater psychological impact than positive information (Baumeister, Bratslavsky, Finkenauer, & Vohs, 2001; Rozin & Royzman, 2001), information framed in negative terms will tend to elicit a stronger response. To some extent, the results just described reflect that. Ten people dying sounds more threatening than 90 out of 100 surviving. More direct support for this idea comes from studies that have examined people's reactions to losses versus unrealized gains (Tversky & Kahneman, 1981). People hate losing things much more than failing to have them in the first place. Consider **Figure 5.2**. If you are like most people, you would probably be willing to pay much more to restore the forest than you would to grow more trees.

We have seen that the way information is presented, including the order in which it is presented, can affect judgment. Primacy effects occur when information presented first has more impact than information presented later, often because the initial information influences the way later information is construed. Recency effects occur when later-presented information has more impact, typically because later information is more accessible to memory than earlier information. We are susceptible to many framing effects in information presentation. Sometimes

(A) Positive framing: How much would you pay to grow more trees?

(B) Negative framing: How much would you pay to restore what has been lost?

FIGURE 5.2 Positive and Negative Framing   How information is framed has a powerful influence on the responses it elicits. Because negative information typically has greater impact, people tend to be more inclined to pay more to restore what was lost (B) than to bring about the same benefit anew (A).

communicators spin information so as to influence our judgment, deliberately changing the frame of reference, but sometimes framing effects are unintended. One of the most powerful framing effects concerns whether an object or outcome is described using positive or negative language. In the next section, we consider what happens when people go beyond the information presented to them and seek out information themselves.

HOW INFORMATION IS SOUGHT OUT

Suppose a friend gives you a bunch of potted plants for your dorm room or apartment, saying, "I'm not sure, but they might need frequent watering. You should check that out." How would you do that? If you are like most people, you would water them often and see how they do. What you would *not* do is give a lot of water to some, very little to the others, and compare the results.

Confirmation Bias

When evaluating a proposition (a plant needs frequent watering; a generous allowance spoils a child; Hispanics place a high value on family life), people usually seek out evidence that would support the proposition more readily, reliably, and vigorously than information that would contradict it. This is known as the **confirmation bias** (Klayman & Ha, 1987; Skov & Sherman, 1986). In one study that examined this

confirmation bias The tendency to test a proposition by searching for evidence that would support it.

tendency, one group of participants was asked to determine whether working out the day before an important tennis match makes a player more likely to win. Another group was asked to determine whether working out the day before a match makes a player more likely to lose. Both groups could examine any of four types of information before coming to a conclusion—the number of players in a sample who worked out the day before and won their match, the number of players who worked out and lost, the number of players who did not work out the day before and won, and the number of players who did not work out and lost. In fact, all four types of information are needed to make a valid determination. (You have to calculate the ratio of the number of winners who worked out the day before the match and the number of winners who did not work out beforehand; then you have to calculate the ratio of the number of losers who worked out the day before the match and the number of losers who did not work out. If the first ratio is higher than the second, then working out the day before increases the chances of winning.)

But participants tended not to seek out all of the necessary information. Instead, as **Figure 5.3** makes clear, participants were especially interested in examining information that could potentially confirm the proposition they were investigating. Those trying to find out whether practicing leads to winning were more interested in the number of players who practiced and won than were those trying to find out whether practicing leads to losing—and vice versa (Crocker, 1982).

This tendency to seek out confirming information can lead to all sorts of false beliefs because we can find supportive evidence for almost anything (Gilovich, 1991; Shermer, 1997). Are people more likely to come to harm when there is a full moon? There will certainly be many months in which hospital ERs are unusually busy during the full moon. Do optimistic people live longer? You can probably think of some very elderly people who are unusually upbeat. But evidence consistent with a proposition is not enough to draw a firm conclusion because there might be even more evidence against it—more days with empty ERs during the full moon; more pessimists living long lives ("grumpy old men"). The danger of the confirmation bias, then, is that if we look mainly for one type of evidence, we are likely to find it. To truly test a proposition, we must seek out the evidence against it as well as the evidence for it.

In the social realm, the tendency for the confirmation bias to distort our judgments is compounded by the fact that the questions we ask of others often unwittingly shape the answers we get, thereby providing illusory support for what we're trying to find out. In a particularly telling study, one group of participants was asked to interview someone and determine whether the target was an extravert; another group was asked to determine whether the target was an introvert (Snyder & Swann, 1978). Participants selected their interview questions from a list provided. Those charged with determining whether the target was an extravert tended to ask questions that focused on sociability ("In what situations are you most talkative?"), whereas those charged with determining whether the target was an introvert tended to ask questions that focused on social withdrawal ("In what situations do you wish you could be more outgoing?"). Of course, if you ask people about when they are most sociable, they pretty much have to answer in ways that will make them seem relatively outgoing, even if they are not. And if you ask about their social reticence, they will almost certainly answer in ways that make them seem relatively introverted—again, even if they are not. In a powerful demonstration of this tendency, the investigators tape-recorded the interview sessions, edited out the questions, and then played the responses to another, uninformed set of participants. These latter participants rated those who had been interviewed by someone testing for extraversion as more outgoing than those who had been interviewed by someone testing for introversion.

FIGURE 5.3 Confirmation Bias The evidence consulted by participants trying to find out whether practicing the day before a tennis match makes a player more likely to win (orange bars) and by participants trying to find out whether practicing the day before makes a player more likely to lose (green bars).

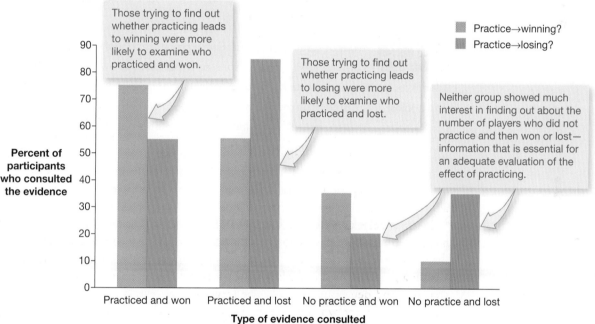

Those trying to find out whether practicing leads to winning were more likely to examine who practiced and won.

Those trying to find out whether practicing leads to losing were more likely to examine who practiced and lost.

Neither group showed much interest in finding out about the number of players who did not practice and then won or lost—information that is essential for an adequate evaluation of the effect of practicing.

■ Practice→winning?
■ Practice→losing?

Percent of participants who consulted the evidence

Type of evidence consulted

Practiced and won   Practiced and lost   No practice and won   No practice and lost

Motivated Confirmation Bias

In the preceding examples—and fairly often in daily life—the individuals who fall prey to the confirmation bias are not *trying* to confirm a particular outcome. They have no stake in it one way or the other; as far as they are concerned, they are simply testing a proposition. Even so, they end up engaging in a biased, and potentially misleading, search for evidence.

This doesn't mean, of course, that people don't sometimes deliberately search for evidence that would confirm their preferences or expectations. They do. Someone who wants a given proposition to be true may energetically (and not disinterestedly) sift through the pertinent evidence in an effort to uncover information that confirms its validity. In such cases, information that supports what one wants to be true is readily accepted, whereas information that contradicts what one would like to believe is subjected to critical scrutiny and often discounted (Dawson, Gilovich, & Regan, 2002; Ditto & Lopez, 1992; Gilovich, 1983, 1991; Kruglanski & Webster, 1996; Kunda, 1990; Pyszczynski & Greenberg, 1987). In one notable examination of this tendency, proponents and opponents of capital punishment read about studies of whether or not the death penalty serves as a deterrent to crime. Some read about state-by-state comparisons purportedly showing that crime rates are not any lower in states with the death penalty than in states without the death penalty, but also about how crime rates within a few states went down as soon as the death penalty was put in place. Other participants read about studies showing the exact opposite: state-by-state comparisons that made the death penalty look effective and before-and-after comparisons that made it look ineffective. Those who favored the death penalty interpreted the evidence, whichever set they were exposed to, as strongly supporting their position. Those opposed to the death penalty saw just the opposite. Both sides jumped on the problems associated with the studies that contradicted their positions, but readily embraced the studies that supported them. Their preferences tainted how they viewed the pertinent evidence (Lord, Ross, & Lepper, 1979).

 We have seen that human judgment is often tainted by two pronounced types of confirmation bias. One type occurs when we look for evidence consistent with propositions or hypotheses we wish to evaluate. To evaluate propositions satisfactorily, however, it is necessary to examine evidence both for it and against it. The other type of confirmation bias occurs when we want a given proposition to be true, and so we seek out evidence that confirms our beliefs or preferences and explain away evidence that contradicts them.

PRIOR KNOWLEDGE AND KNOWLEDGE STRUCTURES

What is being described in the following paragraph?

> The procedure is quite simple. First you arrange things into different groups. Of course, one pile may be sufficient, depending on how much there is to do. If you have to go somewhere else due to lack of facilities, that is the next step; otherwise you are pretty well set. (Bransford & Johnson, 1973, p. 400)

Not so easy to figure out, is it? *What* is arranged into different groups? *What* facilities might be lacking? Most people find it difficult to understand what the paragraph is about. But suppose it had the title "Washing Clothes." Now read the paragraph again. Suddenly it is no longer inscrutable. Each sentence makes perfect sense when construed from the perspective of doing the laundry.

That this paragraph is so easy to understand in the proper context and yet so incomprehensible outside it is a powerful testament to how our stored knowledge—what we already know—helps us properly construe new events. What we know about doing laundry helps us comprehend what it means to "arrange things into different groups" and to "go somewhere else due to lack of facilities." Understanding involves bringing together new information with what we already know. What we know about human nature and about different contexts allows us to determine whether another person's tears are the product of joy or sadness. What we know about norms and customs enables us to decide whether a gesture is hostile or friendly.

Perceiving and understanding the world involves the simultaneous operation of **bottom-up** and **top-down processes**. Bottom-up processes consist of taking in relevant stimuli from the outside world—text on a page, gestures in an interaction, sound patterns at a cocktail party, and so on. At the same time, top-down processes filter and interpret bottom-up stimuli in light of preexisting knowledge and expectations. The meaning of stimuli is not passively recorded; it is actively construed.

Preexisting knowledge is necessary for understanding, and it is surely required for judgment. Indeed, as the laundry example makes clear, judgment and understanding are inextricably linked. They both involve going beyond currently available information and extrapolating from it. Psychologists who study judgment, then, have been interested in how people use their stored knowledge to make a variety of everyday judgments.

One principle that psychologists have discovered is that stored information is not filed away bit by bit. Instead, information is stored in coherent configurations, or **knowledge structures**, in which related information is stored together. Information about Hillary Rodham Clinton, secretary of state, is tightly connected to information about Hillary Rodham Clinton, Wellesley grad, Hillary Rodham Clinton, former First Lady, and Hillary Rodham Clinton, best-selling author. Different theorists have given such knowledge structures different names, such as schemas, scripts, frames, prototypes, or personae (Bartlett, 1932; Markus, 1977; Nisbett & Ross, 1980; Schank & Abelson, 1977; Smith & Zarate, 1990). **Schema** is the most generic of these terms, so we will use it as our primary term to refer to any organized body of prior knowledge (see Chapter 1). Thus, for example, you no doubt have schemas for a fast-food restaurant (chain, so-so food, bright primary colors for decor, limited choices, cheap), a party animal (boisterous, drinks to excess, exuberant but none-too-graceful dancer), and an action film (good guy establishes good guy credentials, bad guy gains the upper hand, good guy triumphs and bad guy perishes in eye-popping pyrotechnical finale).

How Do Schemas Influence Judgment?

The myriad schemas we all possess affect our judgments in many ways: by directing our attention, influencing our construals, and structuring our memories (Brewer & Nakamura, 1984; Hastie, 1981; Taylor & Crocker, 1981). Without schemas, our lives would be a buzzing confusion. On the other hand, as we will see, schemas can sometimes lead us to mischaracterize the world.

Attention Attention is selective. We cannot focus on everything, and the knowledge we bring to a given situation allows us to allocate our attention to the most important elements and to ignore the rest. The extent to which our schemas and expectations guide our attention was powerfully demonstrated by an experiment in which participants watched a videotape of two "teams" of three people each—with the members of one team wearing white shirts and the members of the other team wearing black shirts—passing a basketball back and forth. Each participant was asked to count the number of passes made by the members of one of the teams. Forty-five seconds into the action, a person wearing a gorilla costume strolled into the middle of the action. Although this was about as noticeable a stimulus as one can imagine, only half the participants noticed it! The participants' schemas about what is likely to happen in a game of catch directed their attention so intently to some parts of the videotape that they failed to see a rather dramatic stimulus that they did not expect to see (Simons & Chabris, 1999).

bottom-up processes "Data-driven" mental processing, in which one takes in and forms conclusions on the basis of the stimuli encountered in one's experience.

top-down processes "Theory-driven" mental processing, in which one filters and interprets new information in light of preexisting knowledge and expectations.

knowledge structures Coherent configurations (known as schemas, scripts, frames, prototypes, or personae) in which related information is stored together.

schema A knowledge structure consisting of any organized body of stored information.

FIGURE 5.4 Scientific Method: Selective Attention

Hypothesis: Our expectations guide our attention, making it hard to see what we don't expect.

Research Method:

1 Participants watched a video of one team wearing white shirts and one team wearing black shirts, passing a basketball to each other.

2 The viewers were asked to count the number of times the basketball was passed by members of one of the teams.

3 Forty-five seconds into the action, a person wearing a gorilla costume strolled into the middle of the action.

© 2005, Daniel J. Simons

Results: Half of the participants did not notice the person in the black gorilla costume.

Conclusion: We cannot focus on everything, and the knowledge we bring to bear on a given situation allows us to allocate our attention to what is generally the most important elements and to ignore the rest.

Source: Simon & Chabris (1999).

Inference and Construal Meet Donald, who may seem to you like a contestant in an "Extreme" sports competition. In actuality, Donald is a fictitious person who has been used as a stimulus in numerous experiments on the effect of prior knowledge on social judgment.

> Donald spent a great amount of his time in search of what he liked to call excitement. He had already climbed Mt. McKinley, shot the Colorado rapids in a kayak, driven in a demolition derby, and piloted a jet-powered boat—without knowing very much about boats. He had risked injury, and even death, a number of times. Now he was in search of new excitement. He was thinking, perhaps, he would do some skydiving or maybe cross the Atlantic in a sailboat. By the way he acted one could readily guess that Donald was well aware of his ability to do many things well. Other than business engagements, Donald's contacts with people were rather limited. He felt he didn't really need to rely on anyone. Once Donald made up his mind to do something it was as good as done no matter how long it might take or how difficult the going might be. Only rarely did he change his mind even when it might well have been better if he had. (Higgins, Rholes, & Jones, 1977, p. 145)

In one early study in which Donald was the featured stimulus, students participated in what they thought were two unrelated experiments (Higgins, Rholes, & Jones, 1977). In the first, they were shown a number of trait words projected on a screen as part of a perception experiment. Half of the participants were shown the words *adventurous, self-confident, independent,* and *persistent* embedded in a set of ten traits. The other half were shown the words *reckless, conceited, aloof,* and *stubborn.* After completing the "perception" experiment, the participants moved on to the second, "reading comprehension" study in which they read the short paragraph about Donald and rated him on a number of trait scales. (The paragraph is intentionally ambiguous with respect to whether Donald is an adventurous, appealing sort or a reckless, unappealing person.) The investigators were interested in whether the words the participants encountered in the first experiment, having just been primed (mentally activated) and therefore at the "top of the head," might affect their evaluation of Donald.

The results indicated that this was exactly what happened. Those who had previously been exposed to the words *adventurous, self-confident, independent,* and *persistent* formed more favorable impressions of Donald than did those who had been exposed to the less flattering words. Thus, the trait categories that had recently been primed influenced the kind of inferences the participants made about Donald (Wyer & Srull, 1981).

The broader point, of course, is that information stored in the brain—in this case information that had just been primed—can influence how we construe new information. This is most likely to occur when the stimulus, like many of Donald's actions, is ambiguous (Trope, 1986). When this is the case, we must rely more heavily on top-down processes to compensate for the inadequacies of the information obtained from the bottom up.

Memory Because schemas influence attention, they also influence memory. Indeed, former *New York Times* science writer Daniel Goleman has referred to memory as "attention in the past tense" (Goleman, 1985). It is difficult to remember stimuli to which one has devoted scant attention. The influence of schemas on memory is also important for judgment. After all, many judgments are not made immediately; rather, they are made later on the basis of information retrieved from memory. Schematic influences on memory therefore have a reverberating impact on judgment.

The impact of schemas on memory has been documented in numerous experiments (Fiske & Taylor, 1991; Hastie, 1981; Stangor & McMillan, 1992). In a particularly straightforward study, students were asked to watch a videotape of a husband and wife having dinner together (Cohen, 1981). Half the students were told that the woman in the tape was a librarian; the other half that she was a waitress. The students were later given a quiz that assessed their memory of various features of what they had witnessed. The central question was whether the students' memories were influenced by their stereotypes (or schemas) of librarians and waitresses. They were asked, for example, whether the woman was drinking wine (librarian stereotype) or beer (waitress stereotype) and whether she had received a history book (librarian) or romance novel (waitress) as a gift. The tape had been constructed to contain an equal number of items consistent and inconsistent with each stereotype.

Did thinking that the person was a librarian make it easier to recall librarian-consistent details? It did indeed. Students who thought that the woman was a librarian recalled librarian-consistent information more accurately than librarian-inconsistent information; those who thought she was a waitress recalled waitress-consistent information more accurately than waitress-inconsistent information. Information that fits a preexisting expectation or schema often enjoys an advantage in recall (Carli, 1999; Zadny & Gerard, 1974).

This study shows that schemas might influence memory by affecting the **encoding** of information—how information is filed away in memory—in that schemas might affect what information a person attends to and how that information is initially interpreted. But schemas might also influence the **retrieval** of information, or how information is extracted from a storehouse of knowledge.

encoding Filing information away in memory based on what information is attended to and the initial interpretation of the information.

retrieval The extraction of information from memory.

Because we know that schemas direct attention, we have good reason to believe that they influence encoding. One way to find out whether schemas influence retrieval as well would be to provide people with a schema or expectation *after* they have been exposed to the relevant information, when it obviously cannot influence encoding. Numerous experiments have used this tactic. The typical result is that providing a schema after the relevant information has been encountered does not affect memory as much as providing it beforehand (Bransford & Johnson, 1973; Howard & Rothbart, 1980; Rothbart, Evans, & Fulero, 1979; Wyer, Srull, Gordon, & Hartwick, 1982; Zadny & Gerard, 1974). Nonetheless, occasionally it does have a substantial effect (Anderson & Pichert, 1978; Carli, 1999; Cohen, 1981; Hirt, 1990). Thus, the appropriate conclusion seems to be that schemas influence memory through their effect on both encoding and retrieval, but the effect on encoding is typically much stronger.

How Is New Information Mapped onto Preexisting Schemas?

In the librarian/waitress experiment just described, there is little doubt about which schema participants will apply to the information they encounter in the videotape. The experimenter informs them that the woman is a librarian (or waitress), and they know nothing else about her. It stands to reason, then, that they would view the videotape through the "lens" of the librarian (or waitress) schema. In real life, however, the situation is often more complicated. For instance, one might know that besides being a librarian, the woman is a triathlete, a Republican, and a gourmet cook. Which schema (or combination of schemas) is likely to be thought of, or "activated," and used to evaluate the information presented?

For a schema to guide the interpretation of new information, an association must be made between the schema and the incoming information. But what determines whether a given schema will be associated with incoming information?

Similarity, or Feature Matching The most common determinant of whether a particular schema will be activated and brought to bear in interpreting new information is the degree of similarity, or "fit," between critical features of the schema and the incoming stimulus (Andersen, Glassman, Chen, & Cole, 1995; Higgins & Brendl, 1995). Suppose you are taking a drive through the countryside and you see a rather large, formally dressed group of people assembled on a hill. Whether you apply a wedding or a funeral schema to help you interpret the scene will surely depend on whether they are wearing black or more festive attire, whether a supply of champagne is packed in ice, and so on. The features of the situation tell you what kind of situation it is, and then the relevant schema is applied to assist with further interpretation of what you encounter (Holyoak & Thagard, 1995; Read, 1984, 1987; Spellman & Holyoak, 1992).

In one study that illustrates this feature-matching process, some participants played the Ultimatum Game in an environment laid out with a number of objects associated with business environments—a briefcase, boardroom table, fountain pens. In the Ultimatum Game, one of two participants proposes how a sum of money given by the experimenter should be split between them. The second participant can either accept the proposed split or reject it, in which case neither participant receives anything (Thaler, 1988). Exposure to objects associated with business led participants to infer that the situation called for the type of competitive behavior associated with

"But, seriously . . ."

the business world, leading them to make less generous offers compared to those in a control condition (Kay, Wheeler, Bargh, & Ross, 2004).

Feature matching ensures that the right schema will typically be recruited to encode a given situation. Applying a wedding schema to what is, in reality, a funeral would create too much of a mismatch between the features of the schema and the event—with the result that the wedding schema would soon be abandoned. Remember, perception and judgment are the product of both bottom-up and top-down processes. An activated schema does not always "win out," determining what we see or understand irrespective of what's out there. Still, the process of applying what is stored in the head to newly encountered events leaves open the possibility of occasional misapplication. The wrong schema, in other words, might sometimes be applied to a given situation.

A particularly interesting circumstance that can give rise to schema misapplication is when the schema shares certain irrelevant, superficial features with the stimulus being evaluated, but the schema and stimulus are not well matched on relevant or more important dimensions. This was demonstrated in an experiment that examined the impact of the schemas we have (knowingly or not) regarding U.S. intervention in military conflicts overseas. Specifically, during the last 35 years, the debate about U.S. military intervention has often taken the form of "dueling metaphors." Those who favor intervention argue that we cannot sit by like the Allies did before World War II and let aggression triumph unchecked. "We should have stood up to Hitler" is how it is often put. On the other hand, those who oppose intervention tend to invoke the specter of Vietnam: "We don't want another Vietnam, a quagmire from which the United States had difficulty extricating itself." The implication is that viewing a given conflict through a World War II lens is more likely to lead to intervention than viewing it through a Vietnam schema. Those who supported the 2003 U.S. invasion of Iraq, for example, explicitly mentioned the World War II analogy as an argument for removing Saddam Hussein from power. Those opposed to the looming invasion explicitly mentioned Vietnam as a cautionary analogy.

In a study that investigated whether irrelevant similarities between aspects of a looming crisis and one of these schemas might affect policy recommendations, students in a course on international relations were presented with a hypothetical crisis and asked for their recommendations for how to solve it. The crisis involved a small democratic country that was threatened by its aggressive, totalitarian neighbor.

The threatening country had initially confined its efforts to subversive activity, but now there were reports that it was also amassing troops on the border for a possible invasion. The country being threatened requested assistance from the United States. What to do?

The description of this crisis contained various features that were designed in one version to remind the reader of Vietnam and in another of World War II. For example, the area to the east of the two countries was depicted as a body of water in the Vietnam version in order to suggest the Indochina peninsula, and ethnic minorities who were fleeing the beleaguered country were described as doing so via small boats along the coast (reminiscent of the exodus of the Vietnamese "boat people"). In the World War II version, the people were described as leaving the country via box cars in freight trains (one of the most salient images of human suffering caused by the Nazi regime). All other variations between the two versions were similar in that they had no implications for the best policy to pursue, but they nevertheless triggered strong associations to either World War II or Vietnam. And these associations had a significant impact on the policy recommendations the students made. Despite their irrelevance to the advisability of intervention, the features that triggered the association to World War II prompted participants to recommend stronger U.S. military intervention than did those who read the Vietnam version (Gilovich, 1981).

Expectations   Sometimes we apply a schema because of a preexisting expectation about what we will encounter (Hirt, MacDonald, & Erikson, 1995; Sherman, Mackie, & Driscoll, 1990; Stangor & McMillan, 1992). The expectation activates the schema, and the schema is then readily applied (see **Box 5.2**). If the expectation is warranted, this saves considerable mental energy. For example, applying a "haggling" schema to a given commercial transaction allows us to dismiss the stated price without much thought or anxiety, and it frees us to make a counteroffer. Misapplying

---

BOX 5.2   **FOCUS ON DAILY LIFE**

Self-Fulfilling Prophecies

Expectations often do more than guide how we interpret information. They also affect our behavior, which then influences the very interaction we are observing. Often the result is a self-fulfilling prophecy, whereby our expectations lead us to behave in ways that elicit the very behavior we expect from others. The most famous demonstration of the impact of self-fulfilling prophecies is a study in which elementary school teachers were told that aptitude tests indicated that several of their students could be expected to "bloom" intellectually in the coming year (Rosenthal & Jacobson, 1968). In reality, the students

so described were chosen randomly. Nevertheless, the expectation that certain students would undergo an intellectual growth spurt set in motion a pattern of student-teacher interaction that led those students to score higher on IQ tests administered at the end of the year. People often unknowingly engineer the very behavior they expected all along (Jussim, 1986; Smith, Jussim, & Eccles, 1999).

Self-fulfilling prophecies have generated so much attention that it is important to note that not all prophecies are self-fulfilling. There must be some mechanism that translates a given

expectation into confirmatory action. In the study of teachers' expectations, the mechanism was the teachers' behavior. In particular, the teachers tended to challenge the students they thought were about to "bloom," giving them more material, and more difficult material, to learn. Not all prophecies have that link. Someone might think that you are rich, but it is hard to imagine how that belief would help to make it so. In fact, some prophecies can even be self-negating, such as when a driver believes "nothing bad can happen to me" and therefore drives recklessly (Dawes, 1988).

the haggling schema, on the other hand, can lead to the embarrassment of making a counteroffer when it is not appropriate.

Recent Activation Expectations, as we saw earlier, influence information processing by lowering the threshold for the application of a given schema. The expectation essentially pre-activates, or primes, the schema, and the schema is readily applied at the slightest hint that it is applicable. Schemas can be pre-activated (or partly activated) in other ways as well. Recent activation is one of the most common and important examples. If a schema has been used recently, it tends to be more accessible for reuse (Ford & Kruglanski, 1995; Herr, 1986; Sherman et al., 1990; Srull & Wyer, 1979, 1980; Stapel & Koomen, 2000, 2001; Todorov & Bargh, 2002).

We have already discussed the influence of recent activation in the priming study conducted by Tory Higgins and his colleagues (Higgins et al., 1977). Recall that participants in that study who had previously been exposed to trait adjectives such as *adventurous* formed more favorable impressions of Donald than did those who had been exposed to adjectives such as *reckless* (see p. 173). Of course, schemas can be activated by stimuli other than words. People's judgments and behavior have been shown to be influenced by schemas primed by features of the surrounding environment (Aarts & Dijksterhuis, 2003; Gosling, Ko, Mannarelli, & Morris, 2002; Kay et al., 2004), cultural symbols, such as a country's flag (Ferguson & Hassin, 2007; Hassin, Ferguson, Shidlovsky, & Gross, 2007), the pursuit of a goal (Aarts, Gollwitzer, & Hassin, 2004), a significant other (Shah, 2003), even a passing smell (Holland, Hendricks, & Aarts, 2005).

Consciousness of Activation: Necessary or Not? Carefully conducted interviews with participants at the end of many priming experiments have found that very few (and, in many cases, none) of them suspected that there was any connection between the two parts of the study—the initial priming phase and the subsequent judgment phase. This raises the question of how conscious a person must be of a stimulus for it to effectively prime a given schema. Recent research suggests a clear-cut answer: not at all. A great many studies have shown that stimuli presented outside of conscious awareness can prime a schema sufficiently to influence subsequent information processing (Bargh, 1996; Debner & Jacoby, 1994; Devine, 1989b; Draine & Greenwald, 1998; Ferguson, 2008; Ferguson, Bargh, & Nayak, 2005; Greenwald, Klinger, & Liu, 1989; Klinger, Burton, & Pitts, 2000; Lepore & Brown, 1997; Neuberg, 1988; Shah, 2003).

In one study, researchers showed a set of words to participants on a computer screen so quickly that it was impossible to discern what the words were (Bargh & Pietromonaco, 1982). The researchers asked participants in a control condition to simply guess the identity of each word. They were unable to do so (guessing less than 1 percent of the words correctly), which established that the words were indeed presented too quickly to be consciously perceived. Participants in the other conditions were shown either mainly hostile words (for example, *hate, whip, stab, hostile*) or mainly nonhostile words (for example, *water, long, together, every*). Immediately afterward, the researchers asked them to read a short paragraph about an individual who had committed a number of moderately hostile acts and then to rate that person on a number of trait dimensions. The participants who had previously been exposed to predominantly hostile words rated the target person more negatively than did those exposed to predominantly nonhostile words. They did so, mind you, even though they were not consciously aware of the words to which they had been exposed. Thus, schemas can be primed through prior activation, even when the presentation of the activating stimuli is **subliminal**—that is, below the threshold of conscious awareness.

subliminal Below the threshold of conscious awareness.

We have seen that knowledge structures, or schemas, play a role in judgment. Schemas influence judgment by guiding attention, aiding in the construal of information, and affecting memory at both the encoding and retrieval stages. Schemas are particularly likely to influence the evaluation of current information if they are habitually used or have been recently activated by other information. It is not necessary that the person be aware of the activation of a schema for it to exert its effects. Schemas normally allow us to make judgments quickly and with accurately, but they can also mislead. Next we consider the role of reason, intuition, and heuristic processes in everyday judgment and problem solving.

REASON, INTUITION, AND HEURISTICS

Suppose you were offered a chance to win $10 by drawing, without looking, a red marble from a bowl containing a mixture of red and white marbles. Suppose, further, that you have a choice of two bowls from which you can make your selection: a small bowl with 1 red marble and 9 white marbles or a large bowl containing 9 red marbles and 91 white marbles. Which bowl would you choose?

If you are like most people, you might experience some conflict here. The rational thing to do is to select the small bowl because it offers better odds: 10 percent versus 9 percent. But there are nine potential winning marbles in the large bowl and only one in the other. The greater number of winning marbles gives many people a "gut feeling" that they should select from the large bowl, regardless of the objective odds. Indeed, in one experiment, 61 percent of those who faced this decision chose the larger bowl, the one with the lower odds of winning (Denes-Raj & Epstein, 1994).

These results show that we are often "of two minds" about certain problems. Indeed, a great deal of research suggests that our responses to stimuli are guided by two systems of thought, analogous to intuition and reason (Epstein, 1991; Evans, 2007; Kahneman & Frederick, 2002; Sloman, 2002; Stanovich & West, 2002; Strack & Deutsch, 2004). The intuitive system operates quickly and automatically, is based on associations, and performs many of its operations simultaneously—"in parallel." The rational system is slower and more controlled, is based on rules and deduction, and performs its operations one at a time—"serially."

The rapid, parallel nature of the intuitive system means that it will virtually always produce some output—an "answer" to the prevailing problem. That output will sometimes be overridden by the output of the slower, more deliberate rational system. For instance, if you had to predict the outcome of the next coin flip after witnessing five heads in a row, your intuitive system would quickly tell you that six heads in a row is rare and that you should therefore bet on tails. But then your rational system would remind you of a critical feature of coin flips that you may have learned in a statistics or probability course: the outcomes of consecutive flips are independent, so you should ignore what happened on the earlier flips.

Note that several things can happen with the output of these two systems: (1) They can agree. For example, you might have a good feeling about one job candidate over another, and the former's qualifications might fit your rule to "always go with the person with more experience." (2) As in the coin flip example, they can disagree, and the message from the rational system can override the message from the intuitive system. (3) Finally, the intuitive system can produce a response that "seems right" and do so with such speed that the rational system is never engaged. In that case, you simply go with the flow—that is, with the quick output of the intuitive system.

"I know too well the weakness and uncertainty of human reason to wonder at its different results."

—Thomas Jefferson

We will focus on this last pattern in the balance of the chapter as we discuss Amos Tversky and Daniel Kahneman's work on the heuristics of judgment, work that has had great impact not only in psychology, but also in economics, management, law, medicine, political science, and statistics (Gilovich, Griffin, & Kahneman, 2002; Kahneman, Slovic, & Tversky, 1982; Tversky & Kahneman, 1974). Tversky and Kahneman have argued that there are mental operations that the intuitive system automatically performs—assessments of how easily something comes to mind or of how similar two entities are—that powerfully influence judgment. They refer to these mental operations as **heuristics**—mental "shortcuts" that provide serviceable, but inexact, answers to common problems of judgment.

Tversky and Kahneman draw an analogy between our use of heuristics and our use of perceptual cues. In judging how far away an object is, for example, we can't help but notice how clear it looks, and we use that assessment of clarity to help estimate its distance. All else being equal, the farther away something is, the less distinct it appears. But all else is not always equal, and so an overreliance on clarity can give rise to misperception and illusion. On a clear day, objects appear closer than they really are; on hazy days, they appear farther away. Thus, unless our rational system steps in and says, "Wait. It's hazy out; adjust estimate accordingly," the "clarity heuristic" will be misleading.

Tversky and Kahneman have argued that we are similarly misled in many of our everyday, nonperceptual judgments. Our intuitive system generates an assessment that relates to the task at hand and suggests what may seem like a perfectly acceptable answer to the problem. When this initial intuitive assessment is not modified or overridden by a more considered analysis, important considerations may be ignored, and our judgments may be systematically biased. Let's examine how this works in the context of two of the most general and extensively researched heuristics: the availability heuristic and the representativeness heuristic. We rely on the **availability heuristic** when we judge the frequency or probability of some event by the readiness with which similar events come to mind. We use the **representativeness heuristic** when we try to categorize something by judging how similar it is to our conception of the typical member of the category.

The Availability Heuristic

Which state experiences more tornadoes per year: Nebraska or Kansas? Even though the two states average the same number, you, like most people, may have answered "Kansas." If so, then you were guided by the availability heuristic. For most people, thinking about a tornado in Kansas immediately brings to mind the one that whisked away Dorothy and her little dog Toto in *The Wizard of Oz*.

We can't prevent ourselves from assessing the ease with which examples from Nebraska and Kansas come to mind, and once we've made such assessments, they seem to give us our answer. It is easier to think of a tornado in Kansas (never mind that it was fictional) than one in Nebraska, so we conclude that there are probably more tornadoes in Kansas. The implicit logic seems compelling: If examples can be quickly brought to mind, there must be many of them. Most often, that is true. It's easier to think of male presidents of Fortune 500 companies than female presidents, easier to think of successful Russian novelists than successful Norwegian novelists, and easier to think of instances of German military aggression than Swiss military aggression precisely because there are more male presidents, more successful Russian novelists, and more instances of German military aggression. The availability heuristic, therefore, normally serves us well. The ease with which relevant examples can be brought to

Intuitive Processing and Mistaken Judgment Nicola Calipari, an Italian intelligence officer, was mistakenly shot and killed by a U.S. patrol in Iraq while protecting an Italian journalist whom he had just helped to free from her captors. Their car was speeding along the dangerous road to the Baghdad airport when it approached a temporary checkpoint, and the U.S. patrol, fearing that the car contained insurgents, reacted intuitively and opened fire.

heuristics Intuitive mental operations that allow us to make a variety of judgments quickly and efficiently.

availability heuristic The process whereby judgments of frequency or probability are based on the ease with which pertinent instances are brought to mind.

representativeness heuristic The process whereby judgments of likelihood are based on assessments of similarity between individuals and group prototypes or between cause and effect.

The Availability Heuristic   People often judge the likelihood of an event based on how readily pertinent examples come to mind. (A) While tornadoes are equally common in Kansas and Nebraska, people tend to think that they are more common in Kansas because tornadoes in Kansas come more readily to mind thanks to our familiarity with (B) *The Wizard of Oz,* in which a tornado in Kansas whisks Dorothy and Toto to the land of Oz.

mind (that is, the extent to which they are "available") is indeed a reasonably accurate guide to overall frequency or probability.

But the availability heuristic is not an infallible guide. Certain events may simply be more memorable or retrievable than others, making availability a poor guide to true number or probability. Nebraska has as many tornadoes as Kansas, but none of them are as memorable as the one in *The Wizard of Oz.* In an early demonstration of the availability heuristic, Kahneman and Tversky (1973a) asked people whether there are more words that begin with the letter "r" or more words with "r" in the third position. A large majority thought there are more words that begin with "r," but in fact, there are more words with "r" in the third position. Because words are stored in memory in some rough alphabetical fashion, words that begin with "r" (*rain, rowdy, redemption*) are easier to recall than those with "r" as the third letter (*nerd, harpoon, barrister*). The latter words, although more plentiful, are harder to access.

Disentangling Ease of Retrieval from the Amount of Information Retrieved   As we have seen, the availability heuristic involves judging the frequency of an event, the size of a category, or the probability of an outcome by the *ease* with which relevant instances can be brought to mind (Schwarz & Vaughn, 2002). Note that it is not simply an assessment of the *number* of instances that are retrieved. But how do we know that? After all, not only do people have an easier time thinking of words that begin with "r"; they also can think of many more of them. How do we know that people arrive at their answers by consulting their experience of how easy it is to think of examples rather than by simply comparing the number of examples they are able to generate? It is difficult to distinguish between these two explanations because they are so tightly intertwined. If it is easier to think of examples of one category, we will probably also think of more of them.

An ingenious experiment by Norbert Schwarz and his colleagues managed to untangle the two interpretations (Schwarz et al., 1991). In the guise of gathering material for a relaxation-training program, students were asked to review their lives for experiences relevant to assertiveness. There were four conditions in the experiment. One group was asked to list 6 occasions when they had acted assertively, and another was asked to list 12 such examples. A third group was asked to list 6 occasions when they had acted unassertively, and the final group was asked to list 12 such examples.

TABLE 5.1 The Availability Heuristic

This table shows average ratings of participants' own assertiveness after they were asked to think of 6 or 12 examples of their own assertiveness or unassertiveness.

Number of Examples	Type of Behavior	
	Assertive	Unassertive
6	6.3	5.2
12	5.2	6.2

Source: Schwarz et al. (1991).

The requirement to generate 6 or 12 examples of either behavior was carefully chosen: thinking of 6 examples would be easy for nearly everyone, but thinking of 12 would be extremely difficult.

Notice how this disentangles the *ease* of generating examples and the *number* of examples generated. Those who have to think of 12 examples of either assertiveness or unassertiveness will think of more examples, but they will find it hard to do so. What, then, has a greater effect on judgment? To find out, the investigators asked the participants to rate themselves in terms of how assertive they are. As Kahneman and Tversky would have predicted, the results indicated that it is the ease of generating examples that seems to guide people's judgments (see **Table 5.1**). Those who provided 6 examples of their assertiveness subsequently rated themselves as more assertive than those who provided 12 examples, even though (obviously) the latter thought of more examples. Similarly, those who provided 6 examples of their failure to be assertive subsequently rated themselves as less assertive than those who provided 12 examples. Indeed, the effect of ease of generation was so strong that those who thought of 12 examples of unassertiveness rated themselves as more assertive than those who thought of 12 examples of assertiveness!

Biased Assessments of Risk One area in which the availability heuristic rears its head in everyday life harks back to our earlier discussion of negative information being overreported in the news. As we saw, this has the unfortunate effect of making some people more fearful than might be appropriate. But not all hazards are equally overreported. Some receive more news coverage than others. As a result, if people assess risk by the ease with which they can bring relevant episodes to mind, their assessments should be predictable from how much press attention various hazards receive (Slovic, Fischoff, & Lichtenstein, 1982).

Press attention does indeed affect the availability of information, as the following examples make clear. Do more people die each year by homicide or suicide? As you have surely noticed, homicides receive much more press coverage, and so most people think they are more common. In reality, however, suicides outnumber homicides in the United States by a 3 to 2 margin. Are people more likely to die by accident or disease? Statistics indicate that disease claims over 16 times as many lives as accidents, but because accidents (being more dramatic) receive disproportionate press coverage, most people erroneously consider them to be as lethal as disease. Finally, do more people die each year in fires or drownings? Again, the drama of fires garners disproportionate media attention, so most people think that fires claim more lives than drownings. In reality, there are more drownings each year than deaths by fire.

People typically overestimate the frequency of "dramatic" deaths that claim the lives of many people at once. Deaths due to plane crashes, earthquakes, and tornadoes are

TABLE 5.2 Biased Assessments

This table shows the most notable biases in the perceived commonness of causes of death.

Most Overestimated	Most Underestimated
All accidents	Smallpox vaccination
Motor vehicle accidents	Diabetes
Tornadoes	Lightning
Flood	Stroke
All cancers	Asthma
Fire	Emphysema
Homicide	Tuberculosis

Source: Adapted from Slovic, Fischoff, & Lichtenstein (1982).

good examples. In contrast, people underestimate the commonness of "silent" deaths that quietly claim individual lives, such as deaths resulting from emphysema and strokes. People also underestimate the lethality of maladies they frequently encounter in nonfatal form—deaths from vaccinations, diabetes, and asthma. Because everyone knows healthy asthmatics and healthy diabetics, it is easy to lose sight of the number of lives that have been lost to these afflictions. Lists of the most over- and underestimated hazards are provided in **Table 5.2**, where it can be seen that death from accidents tends to be overestimated and death from disease underestimated.

Biased Estimates of Contributions to Joint Projects Another example of how the availability heuristic can distort everyday judgment involves the dynamics of joint projects. People sometimes work together on a project and then afterward decide who gets the bulk of the credit. You work with someone on a class project and turn in a single paper. Whose name is listed first? You and an acquaintance are hired to write a computer program for a lump-sum payment. How do you split the money?

With the availability heuristic in mind, social psychologist Michael Ross predicted that people would tend to overestimate their own contributions to such projects. After all, because we devote so much energy and attention to our own contributions, they should be more available than the contributions of everyone else. He and Fiore Sicoly conducted several studies that verified this prediction (Ross & Sicoly, 1979). In one study, pairs of individuals who were conversing around campus were asked (separately) how much they thought each had contributed to the conversation. Respondents tended to give themselves more credit than their partners did. In another study, married couples were asked to apportion responsibility for various tasks or outcomes in their everyday life—how much each contributed to keeping the house clean, maintaining the social calendar, starting arguments, and so on. Once again, the respondents tended to give themselves too much credit. In most cases, when the estimates made by the two participants were summed, they exceeded the logically allowable maximum of 100 percent. (Our favorite example concerns a couple asked to estimate their relative contributions to making breakfast. The wife stated that her share was 100 percent on the reasonable grounds that she bought the food, prepared it, set the table, cleared the table, and washed the dishes. The husband estimated his contribution to be 25 percent—because he fed the cat!)

It is important to note that the overestimation of one's own contributions held for negative outcomes (such as starting arguments) as well as positive outcomes (such as taking care of the house). This shows that it is the availability heuristic rather than garden-variety motivational bias that gives rise to this phenomenon. If the effect only held true for positive items, we would be tempted to conclude that it arose from egocentric motivations because people want to see themselves, and have others see them, in the most favorable light.

Availability's Close Cousin: Fluency

Just as examples of some categories are easier to think of than others, some individual stimuli are easier to process than others. Psychologists have a term for this—**fluency**, which refers to the ease or difficulty associated with information processing. A clear image is easy to process, or fluent. An irregular word (for example, imbroglio) is hard to process, or disfluent. The subjective experience of fluency, much like the subjective sense of availability, influences all sorts of judgments we are called on to make (Jacoby & Dallas, 1981; Oppenheimer, 2008). For example, we judge fluent names to be more famous, fluent objects to be better members of the categories to which they belong, and common adages that rhyme to be more valid and truthful than those that don't (Jacoby, Woloshyn, & Kelley, 1989; McGlone & Tofighbakhsh, 2000; Whittlesea & Leboe, 2000). Fluency also influences the perceived difficulty of a task that is being described. When the font (typeface) of a recipe is hard to read, people estimate that the dish would be harder to cook (Song & Schwarz, 2008).

In addition to such direct effects on judgment, fluency appears to influence *how* people process relevant information. In many respects, the feeling of fluency (or disfluency) has the same effect as being in a good (or bad) mood (see Chapter 7). A feeling of disfluency while processing information leads people to take something of a "slow down, be careful" approach to making judgments and decisions. In one study that examined this tendency, participants were given the Cognitive Reflection Task (Frederick, 2005) printed in either a normal, easy-to-process font or a degraded font (**Figure 5.5**). Performing well on the Cognitive Reflection Task requires stifling an immediate gut feeling to get the correct answer to each question. For example: "A bat and ball cost $1.10 in total. The bat costs $1 more than the ball. How much does the

fluency The feeling of ease associated with processing information.

FIGURE 5.5 You Be The Subject: Cognitive Reflection Test

Some subjects were asked to answer the following questions from the Cognitive Reflection Test (Frederick, 2005) presented in a normal, easy to read font. Try it. What are the answers to these two questions?

1 In a lake, there is a patch of lily pads. Every day, the patch doubles in size. If it takes 48 days for the patch to cover the entire lake, how long would it take for the patch to cover half the lake? _____ days

2 If it takes 5 machines 5 minutes to make 5 widgets, how long would it take 100 machines to make 100 widgets? _____ minutes

Other subjects were presented with the questions in a difficult to read font. Try them again.

1 IN A LAKE, THERE IS A PATCH OF LILY PADS. EVERY DAY, THE PATCH DOUBLES IN SIZE. IF IT TAKES 48 DAYS FOR THE PATCH TO COVER THE ENTIRE LAKE, HOW LONG WOULD IT TAKE FOR THE PATCH TO COVER HALF THE LAKE? _____ DAYS

2 IF IT TAKES 5 MACHINES 5 MINUTES TO MAKE 5 WIDGETS, HOW LONG WOULD IT TAKE 100 MACHINES TO MAKE 100 WIDGETS? _____ MINUTES

Conclusion: The effort subjects put into reading the disfluent font carried over to their approach to solving the problems, putting them into a more deliberative mindset. They were therefore more likely to see that it would take 47 days for the lily pads to cover half of the lake and that it would take 5 minutes for the 100 machines to make 100 widgets.

Source: Alter et al. (2007).

ball cost?" You need to think beyond the immediate response of 10 cents to arrive at the correct response of 5 cents ($0.05 + $1.05 = $1.10). The participants in the study answered more questions correctly when the questions were presented in a degraded, and hence disfluent, font (Alter, Oppenheimer, Epley, & Eyre, 2007).

The Representativeness Heuristic

We sometimes find ourselves wondering whether someone is a member of a particular category. Is he gay? Is she Jewish? Is the host a Republican? In making such assessments, we automatically assess the extent to which the person in question *seems* gay, Jewish, or Republican. In so doing, we rely on what Kahneman and Tversky (1972) have dubbed the representativeness heuristic. Assessments of similarity substitute for the assessment of likelihood. "Is this person likely to be Jewish?" becomes "Does this person seem Jewish?" or "Is this person similar to my prototype of a Jew?" The use of the representativeness heuristic thus reflects an implicit assumption that "like goes with like." A member of a given category ought to resemble the category prototype; an effect ought to resemble its cause.

The Representativeness Heuristic Neither (A) Ted Bundy, who was convicted of committing multiple murders of young women, nor (B) Scott Peterson, who was convicted of killing his pregnant wife, fits our prototype of a murderer (because they are clean-cut, educated professionals, which is not part of our prototype). Because of the representativeness heuristic, people are surprised to learn that they were, in fact, the perpetrators.

base-rate information Information about the relative frequency of events or of members of different categories in the population.

The representativeness heuristic is generally useful in making judgments about people and events. Members of certain groups often resemble the group prototype (the prototype must come from somewhere), and effects often resemble their causes. The degree of resemblance between person and group, or between cause and effect, is thus often a helpful guide to group membership and causal status. So assessing whether or not someone is gay by how much he resembles a prototypically gay man is perfectly fine—as far as it goes. The strategy is effective to the extent that there is some validity to the prototype, and the members of the category cluster around the prototype.

But even when the prototype is valid, the representativeness heuristic can create difficulties if we rely on it exclusively. The problem with the representativeness heuristic is that a strong sense of resemblance can blind us to other potentially useful sources of information. One source of useful information, known as **base-rate information**, concerns information you have about relative frequency. How many members of the category in question are there relative to the members of all other categories? The individual in question is more likely to be a Republican if there are a lot of Republicans in the local population. But as we shall see, there are times when a strong sense of representativeness leads people to ignore base-rate likelihood, which could (and should) be put to good use.

The Resemblance between Members and Categories: Base-Rate Neglect In one of the earliest studies of the representativeness heuristic, Kahneman and Tversky (1973b) asked participants to consider the following description of Tom W., which was supposedly written during Tom's senior year in high school by a psychologist who based his assessment on Tom's responses on personality tests. The participants were also told that Tom is now in graduate school.

> Tom W. is of high intelligence, although lacking in true creativity. He has a need for order and clarity and for neat and tidy systems in which every detail

finds its appropriate place. His writing is rather dull and mechanical, occasionally enlivened by somewhat corny puns and by flashes of imagination of the sci-fi type. He has a strong drive for competence. He seems to have little feel and little sympathy for other people and does not enjoy interacting with others. Self-centered, he nonetheless has a deep moral sense. (Kahneman & Tversky, 1973b, p. 238)

One group of participants was asked to rank nine academic disciplines (for example, law, computer science, social work) in terms of how likely it was that Tom chose them as his field of specialization. A second group was asked to rank the nine disciplines in terms of how similar they thought Tom was to the typical student in each discipline. A final group was never shown the description of Tom; these participants merely estimated the percentage of all graduate students in the United States who were enrolled in each of the nine disciplines.

Consider the participants trying to assess the likelihood that Tom would choose each discipline for graduate study. What should they do? They should certainly assess how similar Tom is to the type of person who pursues each field of study—that is, they should consider how representative Tom is of the people in each discipline. But representativeness will not be a perfect guide. Some of the least lawyerly people study law, and some of the least people-oriented individuals pursue social work. Because representativeness is not a perfect guide in this context, any additional useful information should also be considered, such as how many graduate students there are in each field compared to all graduate students—that is, base-rate information. Clearly, Tom W. is more likely to belong to a discipline that has a thousand members on campus than one that has ten. A savvy judgment, then, would somehow combine representativeness with an assessment of the popularity of each field.

What did the participants actually do? **Table 5.3** provides the rankings of the nine disciplines by each of the three groups of participants—those asked to assess likelihood, similarity, and base rate. The first thing to note is that the rankings of the likelihood that Tom chose to *study* each of the disciplines is virtually identical to the rankings of how *similar* Tom is to the students in each discipline. In other

TABLE 5.3 The Representativeness Heuristic

Participants ranked nine academic disciplines either in terms of likelihood that Tom W. chose that graduate field, the perceived similarity between the description of Tom W. and the prototypical student in that field, or number of graduate students enrolled in each field.

Discipline	Likelihood	Similarity	Base Rate
Business administration	3	3	3
Computer science	1	1	8
Engineering	2	2	5
Humanities and education	8	8	1
Law	6	6	6
Library science	5	4	9
Medicine	7	7	7
Physical and life sciences	4	5	4
Social science and social work	9	9	2

Source: Adapted from Kahneman & Tversky (1973b).

words, the participants' responses were based entirely on how much the description of Tom resembled the "typical" student in each field. This is unfortunate, because by basing their responses exclusively on representativeness, the participants failed to consider the other source of useful information—base-rate frequency. As you can see from Table 5.3, the likelihood rankings did not correspond at all to what the participants knew about the overall popularity of each of the fields. Useful information was ignored.

Numerous studies have documented this tendency for people to ignore, or "underutilize," base-rate information when assessing whether someone belongs to a particular category (Ajzen, 1977; Bar-Hillel, 1980; Ginosar & Trope, 1980; Kahneman & Tversky, 1973b; Tversky & Kahneman, 1982). The automatic assessment of the "fit" between the person and the category often blinds us to the usefulness of additional sources of information.

It should be pointed out, however, that although base-rate neglect is often observed, it is not inevitable or universal (Bar-Hillel & Fischhoff, 1981). Certain circumstances encourage the use of base-rate frequency. Two circumstances stand out as having the greatest impact. The first is whether the base-rate information has some causal significance to the task at hand (Ajzen, 1977; Tversky & Kahneman, 1982). For example, if you were given a description of an individual's academic strengths and weaknesses and were asked to predict whether the person passed an exam, you would not be indifferent to the fact that 70 percent of the students who took the exam failed (that is, that the base rate of failure was 70 percent). Note that the base rate has causal significance in this case: the fact that 70 percent of the students failed means the exam was difficult, and the difficulty of the exam is what *causes* a person to fail. People use the base rate in such contexts because its relevance is obvious. When the base rate is not causally relevant, as in the Tom W. experiment, its relevance is less obvious. If twice as many people major in business as in the physical sciences, it would make it *more likely* that Tom W. is a business major, but it would not *cause* him to be a business major. The relevance of the base rate is thus less apparent.

Another way to improve people's use of base-rate information is to change their fundamental approach to the problem. People typically try to assess whether someone belongs to a particular category by taking an "inside" view of the task. Who is this person, and what "type" does the person resemble? Notice that it is the details of the particular case at hand that are the focus of attention. But it is possible to take an "outside" view of the problem. Suppose, for example, that you are asked to predict the undergraduate majors of a large number of students, not just Tom W. The details about each individual might now seem less important, and the significance of other, purely "statistical" considerations, such as base-rate frequency, might become more apparent. In the extreme case, if everyone in a sample of 20 resembled a pre-law student, most people would nevertheless hesitate to guess that all were pre-law students. Indeed, circumstances that encourage an outside perspective have been shown to reduce base-rate neglect and other biases of human judgment (Gigerenzer, 1991; Griffin & Tversky, 1992; Kahneman & Lovallo, 1993; Kahneman & Tversky, 1982b, 1995).

The Planning Fallacy A common pitfall that results from adopting an inside view is the tendency to be unrealistic about how long it takes to complete a project. This tendency, known as the **planning fallacy**, is something of a paradox because people's overly optimistic assessments about their ability to finish a current project exist side by side with their knowledge that the amount of time needed in the past has typically exceeded their original estimates. Students, for example, often confidently assert that they will have all assignments done well in advance of an exam so that they can calmly

planning fallacy The tendency for people to be unrealistically optimistic about how quickly they can complete a project.

The Planning Fallacy   People typically estimate that all sorts of projects, from homework assignments to large-scale public works efforts, will be completed sooner than they actually are—even when they are aware of past efforts that took much longer than originally estimated to complete. (A) It took ten years longer than estimated to complete construction of the Sydney Opera House. (B) The Central Artery/Tunnel Project (the "Big Dig") in Boston was designed to replace an aging, elevated highway with a modern underground expressway. The Big Dig was plagued by unforeseen problems that massively delayed completion of the project.

and thoroughly review the material beforehand. As students well know, however, it is distressingly common for calm review to give way to feverish cramming. Students aren't the only victims of the planning fallacy. None of us is immune. The error is illustrated most dramatically by setbacks in large-scale building projects. When the people of Sydney, Australia, decided in 1957 to build their now iconic opera house, the original estimates were that it would be completed by 1963 and cost $7 million. It opened in 1973 at a cost of $102 million. Similarly, when Montreal was named host of the 1976 summer Olympics, the mayor announced that the entire Olympiad would cost $120 million and that many events would take place in a stadium with a first-of-its-kind retractable roof. The Olympics, of course, went on as planned in 1976, but the stadium did not get its roof until 1989. Moreover, the final cost of the stadium was $120 million, the amount budgeted for the entire Olympics!

To shed light on the planning fallacy, psychologists Roger Buehler, Dale Griffin, and Michael Ross (1994) have conducted a number of studies of people's estimates of completion times. In one study, students in an honors program were asked to predict as accurately as possible when they would turn in their theses. They were also asked to estimate what the completion date would be "if everything went as poorly as it possibly could." Fewer than a third of the students finished by the time they had estimated. More remarkably, fewer than half finished by the time they had estimated under the assumption that "everything went as poorly as it possibly could."

Follow-up experiments laid the blame for people's optimistic forecasts on the tendency to approach the task from an exclusively inside perspective (see **Box 5.3**). In one study, participants were asked to verbalize their thoughts as they were trying to estimate how long a task would take. Nearly all of their thoughts were about various plans and scenarios whereby the project would be finished. Only a precious few dealt with the participants' track record on previous tasks. Thus, the inside perspective (What are the steps by which *this* project will be completed?) crowds out the potentially informative outside perspective (How often do I get such things done on time?). People have personal histories that would be helpful in accurately estimating completion times.

BOX 5.3 **FOCUS ON CULTURE**

Predictions East and West

The philosopher Ludwig Wittgenstein had this to say about the direction of the future, "When we think about the future of the world, we always have in mind its being where it would be if it continued to move as we see it moving now. We do not realize that it moves not in a straight line . . . and that its direction changes constantly."

As it turns out, Wittgenstein was a little too ready to say "we." Whereas Westerners, or at any rate Americans, are indeed inclined to predict that the world will move in whatever direction it now moves, East Asians are likely to expect the world to reverse field. Ji, Nisbett, and Su (2001) point out that there is a tradition in the East that is thousands of years old that emphasizes change. The *Tao* (the Way) envisions the world as existing in one of two states at any given time—*yin* and *yang* (light and dark, male and female, and so on)—which alternate with one another. The fact that the world is in one state is a strong indication that it is about to be in the other state. This preparation for change is indicated by the dark dot

inside the white swirl and the white dot inside the dark swirl of the *Tao* symbol.

Ji and her colleagues reasoned that the tradition of the *Tao* would cause East Asians to judge events as being likely to reverse course rather than to continue moving in their current direction. They tested this in several ways. In one study, they asked participants to read brief stories and predict how they would turn out. For example, participants read about a dating couple and were asked if it was likely they would continue to date. The Americans thought this was likely; the Chinese thought it was less likely. Participants also read about a poor young man and were asked how likely it was that he would become rich. The Americans thought this was not so likely; the Chinese thought it was more likely. In another study, Ji and her colleagues showed various time trends to participants. The graphs were alleged to be recent movements in a variety of indicators that participants would be likely to know nothing about—for example, world economic growth rate and world cancer death rate. Trends were

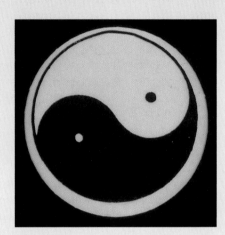

The Tao symbol

shown as either decidedly increasing or decidedly decreasing. American respondents were overwhelmingly likely to predict that the trends would continue—up if they had been up to that point, down if they had been down to that point. Chinese respondents were much more likely than Americans to predict that the trends would reverse course—to move down if they had been going up and to move up if they had been going down.

They just don't use them. When Buehler and his colleagues asked people how often they completed tasks by the time they initially expected, the average response was only a third of the time. We don't want to depress you, but none of us has managed to regularly avoid the planning fallacy when estimating how long it would take to write an article. And don't even ask how long we thought it would take to finish this textbook!

The Resemblance between Cause and Effect The representativeness heuristic also affects people's assessments of cause and effect (Downing, Sternberg, & Ross, 1985; Gilovich & Savitsky, 2002). In particular, people are predisposed to look for and accept causal relationships in which "like" goes with "like." Big effects are thought to have big causes, small effects to have small causes, complicated effects to have complicated causes, and so on. This assumption is often validated by everyday experience. Being hit with a small mallet typically produces a smaller bruise than being hit with a large mallet. Resolving the complicated mess in the Middle East will probably require complex, sustained negotiation, not some simple suggestion that has yet to be made. Large effects often do have large causes, small effects often have small causes, and complicated effects often have complicated causes. But not always. Tiny viruses give rise to devastating diseases like malaria or AIDS; splitting the nucleus of the atom releases an awesome amount of energy. Sometimes small causes create big effects and vice versa. Let's consider some examples of representativeness-based thinking in various walks of life (see **Box 5.4**).

Health and medicine are areas in which the impact of representativeness on causal judgments is particularly striking. Historically, people have often assumed that the symptoms of a disease should resemble either its cause or its cure (or both). In ancient Chinese medicine, people with vision problems were fed ground bat in the mistaken belief that bats had particularly keen vision and that some of this ability might be transferred to the recipient (Deutsch, 1977). Preliterate peoples have been known to feed liver (thought to be the locus of mercy) to the mean-spirited. Others have prescribed the ground-up skull of the red bush monkey for epilepsy; the herky-jerky movements of that animal resemble the violent movements of an epileptic seizure, and so some ingredient of the former is thought to be an effective cure for the latter.

Western medical practice has likewise been guided at times by the representativeness heuristic. For instance, early Western medicine was strongly influenced by what was known as the "doctrine of signatures," or the belief that "every natural substance which possesses any medicinal virtue indicates by an obvious and well-marked external character the disease for which it is a remedy, or the object for which it should be employed" (cited in Nisbett & Ross, 1980, p. 116). Thus, physicians prescribed the lungs of a fox (known for its endurance) for asthmatics and the yellow spice turmeric for jaundice.

The representativeness heuristic continues to influence people's beliefs about bodily states to this day. People think that you should avoid milk if you have a cold and potato chips if you suffer from acne. Why? Because milk seems so representative of phlegm, and the greasiness of potato chips so representative of the oily skin that often accompanies acne. Sometimes this belief that "you are what you eat" is taken to almost magical extremes. In one experiment, college students were asked to make inferences about the attributes of members of (hypothetical) tribes (Nemeroff & Rozin, 1989). One group was told about a tribe that ate wild boar and hunted sea turtles for their shells; a second group was told about a tribe that ate sea turtles and hunted wild boar for their tusks. The students' responses indicated that they assumed that the characteristics of the food would "rub off" on the tribe members. Members of the turtle-eating tribe were considered better swimmers and more generous; those who ate boar were thought to be more aggressive and more likely to have beards. To be sure, people are affected by what they eat—people gain weight by eating lots of fat and can develop an orange tint to the skin by consuming too much carotene. But becoming a better swimmer by eating sea turtles is a bit of a stretch.

The allure of representativeness-based associations may also be responsible for the popularity of various New Age beliefs. Some New Age ideas doubtless have merit, but others are highly dubious. Consider the practice of "rebirthing," in which individuals reenact their own births (often through hypnosis or by immersion in a pool of water) in an effort to correct personality defects caused by having been born in an "unnatural" fashion. Not surprisingly, the defects supposedly caused by particular unnatural births are never established empirically. Instead, the claims arise from their intuitive fit—that is, from the representativeness between each defect and style of birth. One individual who was born breech (that is, feet first) underwent rebirthing to cure his sense that his life was always going in the wrong direction. Another person, born Caesarean, sought the treatment because of a lifelong difficulty in seeing things to completion and relying on others to finish tasks for her. As one author quipped, "God knows what damage forceps might inflict . . . a lifelong neurosis that you're being dragged where you don't want to go?" (Ward, 1994).

BOX 5.4   **FOCUS ON SPORTS**

Hot Hands and Cold Statistics

The belief that effects ought to resemble their causes can be thought of more broadly as the belief that outcomes should resemble the processes that produce them. This belief helps to account for a misconception known as the *clustering illusion*. Consider coin flips. The most salient feature of a coin flip is that it is a 50-50 proposition—there is an equal chance of heads and tails. Thus, following the representativeness heuristic, people expect a sequence of coin flips to consist of roughly 50 percent heads and 50 percent tails. In the long run, they will not be disappointed: the "law of averages" guarantees that with a large number of flips, there will be close to 50 percent heads and 50 percent tails.

In the short term, however, all bets are off. In a short sequence of, say, five or ten flips, it is not at all uncommon to observe a marked departure from a 50-50 split. Random sequences, such as those produced by flipping a coin, tend to be more clustered than people expect. As a result, truly random sequences often do not "look" random. Thus, HTTHTH seems random, whereas HTTTTT does not, although both patterns are equally likely.

This helps explain why gamblers often think they're "on a roll" when playing craps, roulette, and a host of other casino games. Although the nature of the dice and roulette wheel precludes the possibility that a gambler's chances are better during some periods than others, it's easy to see why gamblers might be fooled into thinking they are. "Streaks" of consecutive wins (or losses) are more common than people think and thus appear more meaningful and mysterious than they really are. But the important point is that riding such a streak—having won four, five, or six times in row—means nothing about what is likely to happen next.

There are other walks of life in which people tend to see too much order, meaning, and significance in random sequences. One of the most interesting can be found in the game of basketball. Anyone who has ever played or watched the game of basketball knows that players occasionally get a "hot hand"—they go through periods in which their game is elevated to a higher level, and they feel they "can't miss." Thus, the hot hand represents a belief that success breeds success—that making several shots in a row will make a player feel relaxed and confident, which will make the player more likely to continue to do well in the immediate future.

But this belief just isn't true (Gilovich, Vallone, & Tversky, 1985). As the table here indicates, basketball players—even the stars of the NBA—are not more likely to make a basket after having made their previous shot than after having missed their previous shot. Additional analyses indicate that this is true when their shooting percentages after having made several consecutive shots are compared with their shooting percentages after having missed several consecutive shots. In perhaps the most telling analysis, college basketball players who took 100 shots from a set distance were asked to indicate when they felt hot. It turns out that they did no better than average when they said they were hot.

This does not mean that performance in basketball is "random." It is certainly not random that Pierce, Duncan, and Nowitzki are in the NBA and Gilovich, Keltner, and Nisbett only dream of being there. It is only the *distribution* of hits and misses in a player's performance record that is "random"—and even that is random only in the sense that the outcome of a given shot is unaffected by the outcome of previous shots. There are many nonrandom determinants of whether a player makes a given shot, such as the skill of the player, the spot on the floor from which the shot is taken, and the amount of defensive pressure. But the research on the hot hand demonstrates that the player's recent history of hits and misses actually has no impact. Thus, the belief that basketball shooting is "streakier" than flipping coins is, astonishingly, an illusion.

Probability of a Player Making a Shot Given a Hit or Miss on the Previous Shot*

	P(hit|hit)	P(hit|miss)
Michael Jordan	.56	.53
Magic Johnson	.39	.45
Larry Bird	.49	.38
Isaiah Thomas	.44	.44
Kevin McHale	.53	.61
Dominique Wilkins	.42	.51
K. Abdul Jabbar	.49	.49
Joe Dumars	.41	.47
Vinnie Johnson	.49	.44
Dennis Rodman	.55	.63
Danny Ainge	.44	.43

*Data from 1986–1987 season.
Source: Larkey, Smith, & Kadane (1989).

TABLE 5.4 Representativeness and Astrological Signs

This table shows the personality traits that are supposedly characteristic of people born under 9 of the 12 astrological signs.

Astrological Sign	Personality Characteristics
Aries (the Ram)	Quick tempered; headstrong
Taurus (the Bull)	Plodding; prone to rage
Gemini (the Twins)	Vacillating; split personality
Cancer (the Crab)	Attached to their homes
Leo (the Lion)	Proud; leader
Virgo (the Virgin)	Modest; retiring
Libra (the Scales)	Well balanced; fair
Scorpio (the Scorpion)	Sharp; secretive
Capricorn (the Goat)	Hardworking; down to earth

Source: Huntley, 1990; A. W. Read et al. (1978).

Another area in which representativeness affects causal judgments is in the realm of pseudoscientific belief systems. Consider, for example, the case of astrological signs and representative personality traits. A central tenet of astrology is that an individual's personality is influenced by the astrological sign under which the person was born. The personalities associated with specific astrological signs are listed in **Table 5.4**. Notice the resemblance between the features we associate with each animal namesake and those that supposedly characterize individuals born under each astrological sign. Were you born under the sign of the lion (Leo)? Then you are likely to be a proud, forceful leader. Born under the sign of the ram (Aries)? Then you tend, ram-like, to be headstrong and quick-tempered. Born under the sign of the virgin (Virgo)? Then you are inclined to be modest and retiring.

The personality profiles that supposedly accompany various astrological signs have been shown time and again to have absolutely no validity (Abell, 1981; Schick & Vaughn, 1995; Zusne & Jones, 1982). Why, then, is astrology so popular? Part of the reason is that astrology takes advantage of people's use of the representativeness heuristic. Each of the personality profiles has some superficial appeal because each draws on the intuition that like goes with like. Who is more inclined to be vacillating than a Gemini (a twin)? Who is more likely to be fair and well balanced than a Libra (the scales)?

"Men will cease to commit atrocities only when they cease to believe absurdities."

—Voltaire

The Joint Operation of Availability and Representativeness

The availability and representativeness heuristics sometimes operate in tandem. For example, a judgment that two things belong together—that one is representative of the other—can make an instance in which they do indeed occur together particularly available. The joint effect of these two heuristics can thus create an **illusory correlation** between two variables, or the belief that they are correlated when in fact they are not. A judgment of representativeness leads us to expect an association between the two entities, and this expectation in turn makes instances in which they are paired unusually memorable.

illusory correlation The belief that two variables are correlated when in fact they are not.

"For what it's worth, next week all your stars and planets will be in good aspect for you to launch an invasion of England."

A classic set of experiments by Loren and Jean Chapman illustrates this point nicely (Chapman & Chapman, 1967). The Chapmans were struck by a paradox observed in the practice of clinical psychology. Clinicians often claim that they find various projective personality tests helpful in making clinical diagnoses, but systematic research on these tests has shown many of them to be completely lacking in validity. (Projective tests require people to respond to very unstructured and ambiguous stimuli, such as the famous Rorschach inkblots, and thus "project" their personalities onto what they see.) Why would intelligent, conscientious, and well-trained clinicians believe that such tests can diagnose psychopathologies when they cannot? Why, in other words, do some clinicians perceive an illusory correlation between their clients' pathologies and their responses on such tests?

To find out, the Chapmans first asked numerous clinicians about which specific test responses on the part of their clients were indicative of which specific pathological conditions. Much of their work focused on the Draw-a-Person Test, in which the client simply draws a picture of a person, and the therapist interprets the picture for signs of various psychopathologies. The clinicians reported that they observed numerous connections between particular drawings and specific pathological conditions—drawings and pathologies that seem, intuitively, to belong together. People suffering from paranoia, for example, were thought to be inclined to draw unusually large or small eyes. People insecure about their intelligence were thought to be inclined to draw a large (or small) head.

To investigate these illusory correlations further, the Chapmans gathered a sample of 45 Draw-a-Person pictures—35 drawn by psychotic patients in a nearby hospital and 10 drawn by graduate students in clinical psychology. They then attached a phony statement to each picture that supposedly described the pathological condition of the person who drew it. Some came with the description "is suspicious of other people," others with the description "has had problems of sexual impotence," and so on. The Chapmans were careful to avoid any correlation between the nature of a drawing and the pathological condition attached to each. For example, "is suspicious of other people" appeared just as often on pictures with unremarkable eyes as on pictures with large or small eyes.

These pictures (with accompanying pathological conditions) were then shown to college students who had never heard of the Draw-a-Person Test. Although the study was carefully designed so that there was no connection between the pictures and pathological conditions, the students nonetheless "saw" the same relationships reported earlier by the clinical psychologists. To the students, too, it seemed that prominent eyes were likely to have been drawn by individuals who were suspicious of others. This suggests, of course, that the clinical psychologists were not detecting any real correlations between pathological conditions and responses on the Draw-a-Person Test. Instead, they were "detecting" the same illusory correlations that the undergraduate students were detecting—illusory correlations produced by the joint operation of availability and representativeness. Certain pictures are representative of specific pathologies (for example, prominent eyes and paranoia), and this ensures that instances in which the two are observed together (for example, a paranoid individual drawing a person with large eyes) will be particularly noteworthy and memorable.

In a final study, the Chapmans simply asked students to indicate the extent to which various conditions (suspiciousness, impotence, dependence) "called to mind" different parts of the body (eyes, sexual organs, mouth). Tellingly, their responses matched the correlations reported by the earlier groups of clinicians and students.

The Chapman and Chapman studies and a great many other investigations of intuitive judgment make it clear that the intuitive system produces many errors—some of them far from trivial in their consequences. Is it possible to increase the sway of the rational system at the expense of the intuitive system? The answer is yes, and you are doing it now in your studies at your university. Many of the errors we have discussed can be reduced by training in statistics and research methods (Nisbett, Fong, Lehman, & Cheng, 1987). Moreover, some of the framing effects we discussed earlier can be reduced by training in economics (Larrick, Morgan, & Nisbett, 1990). Such training increases the scope and sophistication of our rational faculties and the likelihood that they will intervene to override or offset a mistake spawned by the intuitive system. So, although our errors may be disconcerting, they can be reduced markedly by training.

We have seen that two mental systems appear to guide our judgments and decisions: one akin to intuition and the other akin to reason. The intuitive system operates quickly and automatically, while the rational system tends to be more deliberate and controlled. These systems can lead to the same judgments; they can lead to opposite judgments; or the intuitive system may produce a satisfying judgment so quickly that the rational system is never engaged. The intuitive system uses heuristics to make its quick assessments, which can sometimes bias judgment. One heuristic is the availability heuristic, which may lead to biased assessments of risk and biased estimates of people's contributions to joint projects. Another heuristic is the representativeness heuristic, which may result in base-rate neglect and mistaken assessments of cause and effect. When these two heuristics operate together, they can lead to an illusory correlation between two variables.

Summary

how? → learn to avoid mistakes

memory = reconstructive

Why Study Social Judgment?

- By focusing on errors in judgment and decision making, we can come to understand how people make judgments and learn to avoid mistakes.

The Information Available for Judgment

- Sometimes our judgments are biased because they are based on misleading information, which can occur even when the information is encountered firsthand.

- One bias that can taint information experienced firsthand is that of *pluralistic ignorance*, which tends to arise when people are reluctant to express their misgivings about a perceived group norm, with their reluctance reinforcing the false norm.

- Although people tend to believe that their memories are the product of recording mechanisms, in actuality they are reconstructions based on general knowledge, abstract theories, and fragments of truly remembered events. The reconstructive nature of memory occasionally gives rise to recollections of events that never occurred.

- *Flashbulb memories* are powerful images of the moment when we learned of some dramatic news, but they too are subject to error, despite the sense of certainty and vividness attached to them.

- Information received secondhand can also be biased, as speakers often do not provide a full account of what happened or may be motivated (because of ideology or the desire to entertain) to stress certain elements at the expense of others.

- When people describe events, they tend to *sharpen* some elements—that is, emphasize points that are salient to them and that they think will interest us—and to *level*, or deemphasize, other elements.

- There is evidence that people who watch local newscasts, with their steady drumbeat of danger and harm, exaggerate the dangers in their lives.

How Information Is Presented

- How information is presented can also affect judgment. For example, the *order* in which information is presented can be quite important. When the information presented first is more influential, we say there is a *primacy effect*, which often results from the initial information affecting the way subsequent information is interpreted. When information presented last is more influential, we say there is a *recency effect*, which usually results from such information being more available in memory.

- Order effects are a type of *framing effect*. Others include the "spinning" of information by varying the language or structure of the information that is presented to produce a desired effect in an audience.

How Information Is Sought Out

- People tend to examine whether certain propositions or possibilities are true by searching for information consistent with the proposition or possibility in question. This *confirmation bias* can lead people to believe things that aren't true because evidence can generally be found in support of even the most questionable propositions.

Prior Knowledge and Knowledge Structures

- *Knowledge structures*, including *schemas*, influence our interpretation of information. Knowledge structures are the *top-down* tools we use to understand the world, as opposed to the *bottom-up* tools of perception and memory.

- Schemas influence what we attend to, guide our inferences and construal of information, and direct our memories to recover what seems relevant.

- The likelihood that a given schema will be applied to incoming information is a function of the degree to which the information matches the critical features of the schema. Unfortunately, sometimes the information available increases the similarity to a schema but not the appropriateness of applying it.

- Other things being equal, the more recently a schema has been "activated," the more likely it is to be applied to new information. It is not necessary that we be consciously aware of a schema to be influenced by it.

Reason, Intuition, and Heuristics

- We seem to have two different systems for processing information: an *intuitive*, automatic one and a *rational*, analytical one. Intuitive responses are based on rapid, associative processes, whereas rational responses are based on slower, rule-based reasoning.

- Intuitive *heuristics*, or mental shortcuts, are useful and seem to provide us with sound judgments most of the time, but several heuristics sometimes lead us into errors of judgment.

- We use the *availability heuristic* when we judge the frequency or probability of some event by the readiness with which relevant instances come to mind. This can encourage us to overestimate how much we have contributed to group projects, and it can lead us to overestimate the risks posed by salient, memorable hazards like earthquakes and homicide and to underestimate the likelihood of silent killers like asthma and stroke.

- The sense of *fluency* that we experience when processing information can influence the judgments we make about the information, with disfluent stimuli leading to more deliberate, reflective judgment.

- We use the *representativeness heuristic* when we try to categorize something by judging how similar it is to our conception of the typical member of the category or when we try to make causal attributions by assessing how similar an effect is to a possible cause. The strategy is fine as far as it goes. The problem is that we often overlook highly relevant considerations such as *base-rate information*—how many members of the category there are in a population.

- The "inside" perspective for making judgments causes us to make errors such as the *planning fallacy*, which could be avoided if the we took an "outside" perspective, attending to our history of finishing similar tasks in a given time.

- When availability and representativeness operate together, they can produce potent *illusory correlations*, which result when we think that two variables are correlated, both because they resemble one another and because the co-occurrence of two similar events is more memorable than the co-occurrence of two dissimilar events.

[handwritten note: top ↓ interpretation → understand; bottom ↑ perception → memory]

Key Terms

availability heuristic (p. 179)

base-rate information (p. 184)

bottom-up processes (p. 171)

confirmation bias (p. 167)

encoding (p. 173)

flashbulb memories (p. 159)

fluency (p. 183)

framing effect (p. 165)

heuristics (p. 179)

illusory correlation (p. 191)

knowledge structures (p. 171)

leveling (p. 159)

planning fallacy (p. 186)

pluralistic ignorance (p. 154)

primacy effect (p. 164)

recency effect (p. 164)

representativeness heuristic (p. 179)

retrieval (p. 173)

schema (p. 171)

sharpening (p. 159)

subliminal (p. 177)

top-down processes (p. 171)

Further Reading

Gilbert, D. (2006). *Stumbling on happiness*. New York: Knopf. Although its main focus is on happiness, this book offers a penetrating and engaging review of how the mind works.

Gilovich, T. (1991). *How we know what isn't so: The fallibility of human judgment in everyday life*. New York: Free Press. A study of how the general principles of human judgment can lead people to hold all sorts of questionable and erroneous beliefs.

Hastie, R., & Dawes, R. (2001). *Rational choice in an uncertain world: The psychology of judgment and decision making*. Thousand Oaks, CA: Sage. An informative overview of scholarship on judgment and decision making.

Tversky, A., & Kahneman, D. (1974). Judgment under uncertainty: Heuristics and biases. *Science, 185*, 1124–1131. A landmark article that helped spark the great upsurge in research on human judgment during the last quarter of the twentieth century—and that continues today.

Online Study Tools

StudySpace

Go to StudySpace, wwnorton.com/studyspace, to access additional review and enrichment materials, including the following resources for each chapter:

Organize

- Study Plan
- Chapter Outline
- Quiz+ Assessment

Learn

- Ebook
- Chapter Review
- Critical-Thinking Questions
- Visual Quizzes
- Vocabulary Flashcards

Connect

- Apply It! Exercises
- Author Insights Podcasts
- Social Psychology in the News

Attitudes, Behavior, and Rationalization

THROUGHOUT THE UNITED STATES' long and painful military involvement in Vietnam—a conflict that split the nation into "hawks" and "doves," consumed the energies of three administrations, and ultimately cost the lives of 58,000 U.S. soldiers—the government put a positive spin on the enterprise. It maintained that there was "light at the end of the tunnel," that Communist North Vietnam would soon be vanquished, that a satisfactory peace agreement would soon be struck, or that the South Vietnamese regime that the United States was supporting would soon be sufficiently strong to conduct its own defense. But despite repeated positive pronouncements of this sort, many government officials had doubts about the U.S. effort in Vietnam and the prospects for success. These doubts often surfaced as key decisions needed to be made, such as whether to increase the number of U.S. soldiers stationed in South Vietnam or whether to initiate a bombing campaign against North Vietnam.

Lyndon Johnson, the U.S. president responsible for the biggest buildup of American troops in Vietnam, employed an interesting tactic to deal with those in his administration who began privately to express such doubts and to waver from the administration's policy on the war (Halberstam, 1969). Johnson would send those with doubts about the war on a "fact-finding" mission to Vietnam, nearly always with a group of reporters in tow. One might think this a rather risky move on Johnson's part because if any of these less-than-staunch supporters expressed their doubts to the press, the administration's policies would be undermined. But Johnson knew they would not express their doubts publicly, preferring to try to influence administration policy from the inside. Unwilling to express their doubts to the public and confronted by criticism of the war effort by reporters, the doubters would be thrust into the position of publicly *defending* administration policy. This public advocacy, Johnson reasoned, would serve to lessen their doubts and help turn the skeptics in his administration into advocates. Known as an unusually

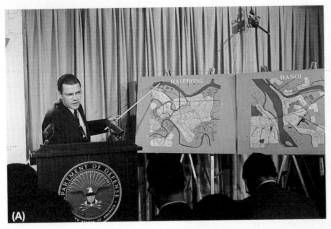

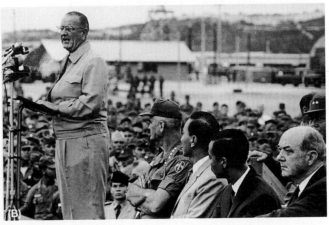

Public Advocacy and Private Acceptance   Despite the continuing problems in fighting the Vietnam War, U.S. president Lyndon Johnson publicly declared that the war was going well and insisted that his advisers and cabinet members also publicly express their support and confidence. (A) Defense Secretary Robert McNamara had reservations about the war that may have been alleviated to a degree by the constant necessity of defending it. Here he is shown briefing the press on U.S. air attacks. (B) To bolster morale, Johnson himself spoke to U.S. troops in South Vietnam, while U.S. general William Westmoreland, South Vietnamese general Nguyen Van Thieu, South Vietnamese premier Nguyen Cao Ky, and U.S. secretary of state Dean Rusk looked on.

cagey politician, Johnson was using some very clever psychology—psychology we will explore in this chapter—to win support for his policy.

Johnson's strategy highlights some important questions about the consistency between attitudes and behavior, especially whether the consistency between the two is the result of attitudes influencing behavior or behavior influencing attitudes. We know that both types of influence exist. Those with strong pro-environment attitudes are more likely to vote Green or Democratic than Republican. Attitudes influence behavior. But we also know that people rationalize, and so behavior influences attitudes as well. Environmentally minded individuals who drive gas-guzzling cars tend to convince themselves that automobile exhaust contributes only a small part to air pollution or global warming—or that they personally don't drive that much anyway.

Behavior Can Influence Attitudes   Although he considers himself an environmentalist, Arnold Schwarzenegger was one of the first to drive a gas-guzzling Hummer and his actions helped promote the car as a civilian vehicle. Driving a Hummer may lead people who are concerned about the environment to rationalize their actions and come to believe that the vehicle is actually not having a negative impact on the environment.

The relative strength of these two effects is worth pondering. Which is stronger: the effect of attitudes on behavior or the effect of behavior on attitudes? It's a question that's difficult to answer, but what *is* clear from decades of research on the topic is that the influence of attitudes on behavior is a bit weaker than most people would suspect and that the influence of behavior on attitudes is much stronger than most would suspect. Thus, Johnson was right: get budding skeptics to publicly endorse the policy and they will be skeptics no more. More generally, give people a slight nudge to get them to behave in a particular way and their attitudes will typically follow.

In this chapter, we'll examine what social psychologists have learned about the consistency between attitudes and behavior. Research shows that attitudes are often a surprisingly poor predictor of behavior, but also specifies the circumstances under which they predict behavior most powerfully. We'll also examine several "consistency theories" that explain why people tend to maintain consistency among their attitudes and between their attitudes and behavior. The research inspired by these theories has shown how powerfully people's behavior influences their attitudes.

PREDICTING BEHAVIOR FROM ATTITUDES

Most academic discussions of how well attitudes predict behavior begin with a remarkable study conducted by Richard LaPiere in the early 1930s (LaPiere, 1934). LaPiere spent two years touring the United States with a young Chinese couple, visiting numerous hotels, auto camps, restaurants, and cafés. Although prejudice and discrimination against Chinese individuals were common at the time, it is reassuring to learn that LaPiere and his traveling companions were denied service by only one of the 250 establishments they visited. Maybe anti-Chinese prejudice wasn't so strong after all.

To find out, LaPiere wrote to all of the establishments they had visited and asked whether their policy was to serve "Orientals." Approximately 90 percent of those who responded said they would not, a response rate that is stunningly inconsistent with what LaPiere actually observed during his earlier tour of the country. This was unfortunate in human terms because it indicated that anti-Chinese prejudice was indeed rather robust. And it was unfortunate from the perspective of psychological science because it suggested that attitudes do not predict behavior very well. To a scientific discipline that had treated attitudes as powerful determinants of people's behavior, this was truly surprising—and rather unsettling—news.

Note that this was not some fluke associated with the particulars of LaPiere's study. Numerous experiments conducted over the next several decades yielded similar results. Indeed, a much-cited review in the 1960s of the existing literature on attitudes and behavior concluded, "The present review provides little evidence to support the postulated existence of stable, underlying attitudes within the individual which influence both his verbal expressions and his actions" (Wicker, 1969, p. 75).

Most people find this result surprising. Why? Why do we think that people's attitudes are strong predictors of their behavior when careful empirical studies reveal that they are not? Part of the reason there is such a rift between perception and reality stems from a sampling problem and something of a failure of logic. Every day, we see plenty of evidence that attitudes and behavior go together. People who picket abortion clinics have attitudes opposed to abortion. People who show up at the local bowling alley have positive attitudes toward the sport. Families with a large litter of kids (usually) have positive attitudes about children. Evidence of a tight connection between attitudes and behavior is all around us. But this evidence only tells us that if people behave in a certain way, they are likely to have a positive attitude toward that behavior. This does not mean, however, that people with a positive attitude toward a given behavior are likely to behave in a manner consistent with their attitude. What is not so salient

Attitudes Do Not Always Predict Behavior This store in Elk City, Idaho, displays a sign declaring "No Earth Firster or Sympathizer Allowed." The store owners may indeed intend to bar environmentalists from the store, but like the owners of the establishments visited by LaPiere, would they fail to live up to their intentions and offer them the same service they offer everyone else?

in everyday life are the numerous instances of people with positive attitudes toward bowling who do not bowl or people with positive attitudes toward kids who do not have children.

There are, after all, many reasons why people may fail to act on their attitudes. And once we delve into all of these reasons, the finding that attitudes so often fail to predict behavior may no longer seem so surprising. Even more important, we may be able to specify *when* attitudes are likely to be highly predictive of behavior and when they are not (Glasman & Albarracin, 2006). So let's consider various reasons why people often act at odds with their underlying attitudes.

Attitudes Sometimes Conflict with Other Powerful Determinants of Behavior

Suppose you were asked to predict the strength of the relationship between (1) people's attitudes toward dieting and (2) actual successful dieting. Would you expect a strong relationship? Certainly not. Although people who like the idea of dieting may cut back on food consumption more than those who don't like the idea, the relationship is unlikely to be strong because cutting back is determined by so many things other than the person's attitude about dieting, including eating habits, individual physiology, and whether a roommate is pigging out or dieting as well. Attitudes toward dieting thus compete with a lot of other determinants of behavior, including attitudes toward other things, such as (in this case) Ben & Jerry's ice cream, Krispy Kreme donuts, and french fries.

What is true about attitudes toward dieting is true about attitudes in general. They all compete with other determinants of behavior. The situationist message of social psychology (and of this book) leads us to expect that attitudes will not always win out over these other determinants, and hence attitudes will not always be so tightly connected to behavior.

One particularly potent determinant of a person's actions that can weaken the relationship between attitudes and behavior is an individual's understanding of the prevailing norms of appropriate behavior. You might relish the idea of talking in animated fashion with the person next to you in the movie theater or lecture hall, but let's hope you refrain from doing so out of the recognition that it just isn't done. Others would disapprove. Similarly, the hotel and restaurant owners in LaPiere's study may have wanted to turn away the Chinese couple but refrained from doing so out of concern about how it would look and the scene it might cause.

Attitudes Are Sometimes Inconsistent

Many people report having a hard time pinning down their attitude toward the actor Russell Crowe. They acknowledge great admiration for his skill as an actor, but they just don't like him. This highlights two important facts about attitudes. First, attitudes may conflict with one another. We might like great acting but dislike arrogance. Second, there are several components of an attitude, and the different components may not always align. In particular, there can be a rift between the affective component (what we feel about Russell Crowe) and the cognitive component (what we think about him). When there is an inconsistency between the affective and cognitive components of an attitude, it's hardly surprising that the attitude may not predict behavior very well. The cognitive component might determine the attitude we express, but the affective component might determine our behavior (or vice versa). The restaurant and hotel owners from LaPiere's study, for example, might have thought it was bad for their business to serve Chinese individuals, but the feelings aroused by a living, breathing Chinese couple may have made it hard to deny them service.

Inconsistency between Affective and Cognitive Components of Attitudes Evidence supports the idea that attitudes tend to be poor predictors of behavior when there is an inconsistency between the affective and cognitive components. In one study, students indicated both their thoughts and feelings about participating in psychology experiments (Norman, 1975). The students were then ranked in terms of how positively they *felt* about participating and how positively they *thought* about participating (for example, whether they thought participating would advance their goals). This permitted each student to be scored for affective-cognitive consistency. Those who ranked high on both thoughts and feelings about participating in psychology experiments were deemed consistent, as were those who ranked low in both. Those who ranked high on one but low on the other were deemed inconsistent. Three weeks later, a different experimenter asked the students if they would participate in a psychology experiment. Those who ranked high on both thoughts and feelings tended to say yes, and those who ranked low on both tended to say no. The behavior of students who were affectively and cognitively consistent, in other words, was predictable. The behavior of the inconsistent students was not. Among these students, neither their thoughts nor their feelings about participating in psychology experiments were very good predictors of whether they actually agreed to participate (Chaiken & Baldwin, 1981).

Introspecting about the Reasons for Our Attitudes The inconsistency we sometimes experience between our thoughts and feelings about something has important implications for what we are likely to get out of introspecting about the reasons we like or dislike it. Consider your attitude toward someone you're attracted to. Why are you attracted to that person? If you put this question to yourself, a number of factors are likely to spring to mind: "He's cute." "She's ambitious." "She's not demanding."

But many times it's not so easy to know exactly why we like someone. It may not be because of specific, readily identifiable attributes; we may simply share some indescribable chemistry. When introspecting, however, we may focus on what is easy to identify, easy to justify, and easy to capture in words—and thus miss the real reasons for our attraction. Timothy Wilson and his colleagues put this idea to empirical test by asking students about the person they were dating. Participants in one group were simply asked for an overall evaluation of their relationship. Those in another group were first asked to list why they felt the way they did and then to give an overall evaluation of their relationship. The researchers then contacted the participants again nearly nine months later and asked about the status of their relationship. The attitudes of participants in the first group were much more accurate predictors of the current status of the relationship than were those of participants who had introspected about their reasons for liking their partners (Wilson, Dunn, Bybee, Hyman, & Rotondo, 1984). Thinking about why we like someone can sometimes lead to confusion about what our true feelings really are.

Wilson has shown that this effect applies far beyond our attitudes toward romantic partners and that introspecting about the reasons for our attitudes about all sorts of

Inconsistent Attitudes There is often a disconnect between attitudes and behavior when a person's attitudes have inconsistent components. Elliot Spitzer, disgraced former governor of New York, had campaigned on the importance of high ethical standards among public officials and vowed to "change the ethics of Albany." He resigned after it was revealed that he was a frequent customer in a high-priced prostitution operation. Was there an inconsistency between what he thought and felt about morality, or did his participation in a prostitution ring not fit his prototype of immoral behavior?

things can undermine how well those attitudes guide our behavior. The cause in all cases is the same: introspection may lead us to focus on the easiest-to-identify reasons for liking or disliking something at the expense of the *real* reasons for our likes and dislikes. When people are induced to think carefully about the reasons they prefer one product over another (as opposed to simply stating a preference), their choices are less likely to correspond to the "true" value of the product as determined by experts (Wilson & Schooler, 1991). Also, when people reflect on their reasons before making a choice (again, as opposed to simply choosing), they are more likely to subsequently regret their choice (Wilson et al., 1993).

Does this mean that introspection is always (or even typically) harmful and that we should dispense with careful analysis and always go with our gut? Not at all. In deciding whether to launch a military campaign, for example, it is imperative that no analytical stone goes unturned and that the reasons for and against the idea are exhaustively considered from all angles. More generally, there are many occasions when the real reasons for our attitude are perfectly easy to identify and articulate, and so introspection will produce no rift between the variables we think are guiding our attitude and those that actually are. The contaminating effect of introspection is limited to those circumstances in which the true source of our attitude is hard to pin down—as when the basis of our attitude is largely affective; in such cases, a cognitive analysis is likely to seize on seemingly plausible but misleading cognitive reasons. When the basis of our attitude is largely cognitive, however, the search for reasons is more likely to yield the real reasons, and introspection is unlikely to diminish the relationship between attitude and behavior (Millar & Tesser, 1986; Wilson & Dunn, 1986). Thus, introspecting about the reasons why you like a certain artist may create a rift between your expressed attitude and your subsequent behavior, but introspecting about why you would prefer one digital camera over another is unlikely to create such a rift.

Attitudes Are Sometimes Based on Secondhand Information

What is your attitude toward Fiji? Speaker of the House Nancy Pelosi? Child actors? Chances are you have attitudes about all three, perhaps even very strong ones. Yet, you've probably never been to Fiji, have never met Speaker Pelosi, and have never been in the presence of a child celebrity. This creates the possibility that your attitude may be a bit off the mark and may not match how you would behave if you actually went to Fiji, met Speaker Pelosi, or were confronted by one of the young cast members of the *Harry Potter* film series. Similarly, the hoteliers and restaurateurs in LaPiere's study may have had precious little exposure to Chinese individuals, and what they imagined "Orientals" were like may not have matched the actual Chinese couple they encountered. Thus, their abstract attitude toward "Orientals" did not predict the behavioral response elicited by this particular Chinese couple.

Numerous experiments have shown that attitudes based on direct (firsthand) experience predict subsequent behavior much better than those derived indirectly (secondhand). In one of the earliest studies, Dennis Regan and Russ Fazio (1977) measured Cornell University students' attitudes about a housing shortage that caused some freshman students to spend the first month or two of the year sleeping on a cot in a dormitory lounge. Some of the students had firsthand experience with the housing crisis because they were the ones forced to sleep on the cots; others had merely heard about the crisis or read about it in the student newspaper. The students expressed their attitudes on such questions as how much they thought the affected students had suffered as a result of the crisis, how concerned they thought the administration was about the shortage, and what priority the administration should assign to solving the crisis. The students were also given an opportunity to act on their attitudes—to sign a petition demanding that the administration take steps to solve the crisis, write a letter that the researchers would take to the administration, and sign up to join a committee to make recommendations about the housing situation.

Clearly, the students who were directly affected by the crisis were more likely to take action, but that was not the focus of the study. Instead, Regan and Fazio were interested in whether the *correlation* between the students' attitudes and their overt behavior was higher among the directly affected students than among the others. It was. Among the directly affected students, those with strong attitudes about the crisis were much more likely to take relevant action than those with less strong opinions. Among students who were not directly affected, this relationship was much weaker.

Additional studies have shown this to be a very reliable effect. Attitudes about participating in psychological research predict actual participation much more strongly among those who have previously taken part in research (Fazio & Zanna, 1978). Attitudes about solving intellectual puzzles predict more strongly who will attempt to solve them among those who have previously tried their hands at such puzzles (Regan & Fazio, 1977). And attitudes about flu shots predict who will get inoculated more strongly among those who have received flu shots in the past (Davidson, Yantis, Norwood, & Montano, 1985). When the attitude we have about some object or event is based on firsthand experience, our attitude turns out to be a rather telling guide to our subsequent actions after all.

The Mismatch between General Attitudes and Specific Targets

Closely related to the previous point is the possibility that our attitude may not match the attitude "target" we confront. Typically, in fact, the attitudes we express are about general classes of things—the environment, pushy people, French cooking, or global trade. But the attitude-relevant behavior that is typically assessed deals with a particular instance of that class—donating to Greenpeace, reacting to a specific pushy individual, ordering *foie gras*, or picketing a meeting of the World Trade Organization. Because of such a vast mismatch between general attitudes and specific instances of real behavior, it is no wonder that attitudes do not always predict behavior particularly well.

Several studies have shown that attitude-behavior consistency is higher when the attitude and behavior are at the same level of specificity. Highly specific attitudes typically do a better job of predicting specific behaviors, and rather general attitudes typically do a better job of predicting how one behaves "in general" across a number of different manifestations of, say, environmentalism, political activism, or xenophobia (Ajzen, 1987).

In one study that illustrates this point nicely, 244 married women were asked a number of questions about their attitudes toward birth control pills (Davidson & Jaccard, 1979). The questions varied from the general (what they thought about birth control) to the specific (what they thought about using birth control *pills* during the next two years). The investigators then waited two years before contacting the respondents again, at which time they asked them whether they had used birth control pills at any point since the initial survey. What the investigators discovered was that the

General Attitudes and Specific Targets A person with a general negative attitude toward global free trade may not demonstrate against the World Trade Organization (WTO). But someone with a more specific antipathy toward the WTO, believing that it plays a particularly important role in undermining enviromental protection and harming the labor movement, is more likely to protest against it, as here in Seattle, Washington.

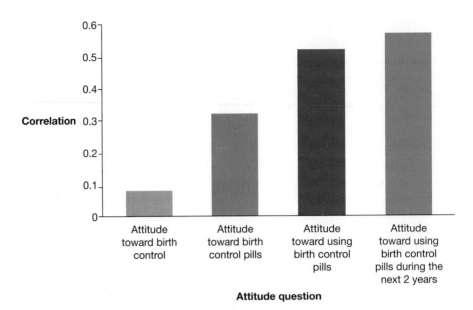

FIGURE 6.1 Attitude Specificity and the Ability of Attitudes to Predict Behavior
The correlation between whether or not a sample of women used birth control pills during a two-year period and their responses to a number of different attitude questions. More positive attitudes are related to increased use. (Source: Davidson & Jaccard, 1979.)

women's general attitudes toward birth control were unrelated to whether they used birth control pills during the period of the study. But their more specific attitudes about using birth control pills in the near future were strongly predictive of whether they actually used them (see **Figure 6.1**).

These findings may also help to explain LaPiere's results. The attitudes expressed by the various merchants LaPiere surveyed were rather general—whether they would serve "Orientals." But the behavior, of course, involved one specific Chinese couple with a specific demeanor and bearing and dressed in a specific fashion. Perhaps the results would have been different if LaPiere had asked the merchants whether they would serve a well-dressed Chinese couple who seemed pleasant and agreeable. If you want to predict a specific behavior accurately, you have to measure people's attitudes toward that specific behavior.

The broader point here is that what we usually think of as attitudes toward different classes of people, places, things, and events are often expressions of our attitude toward a prototype of a given category. But if we encounter a specific situation or person who doesn't fit the prototype, it's likely that our behavior will not reflect our stated attitude. Our general attitude doesn't apply to *that* sort of person. Consider the findings of a study by Charles Lord, Mark Lepper, and Diane Mackie (1984) in which they asked male college students about their attitudes toward gay men. The researchers also elicited from each student his stereotype of the "typical" gay man. Two months later, the students were approached by a different experimenter and asked if they would be willing to show some visiting students around campus. One of the visitors, "John B.," was described in such a way that the participants would think he was gay. For half the participants, the rest of the description of "John B" was crafted to fit their own, individualized stereotype of a male homosexual; for the other half, it was not. What the investigators found was that the students' willingness to show "John B." around campus was strongly predicted by their attitudes toward gay men (those with positive attitudes said they were willing; those with negative attitudes said they were not), but only if "John B." matched their prototype of a gay individual (Lord et al., 1984; see also Lord, Desforges, Ramsey, Trezza, & Lepper, 1991).

"Automatic" Behavior That Bypasses Conscious Attitudes

When most people think of attitudes influencing behavior, they think of a person reflecting on her attitude and then choosing to behave in line with it (or not); the influence of the attitude on behavior is conscious and deliberate. But many times our behavior is more reflexive than reflective, and the surrounding situational context may elicit behavior automatically.

To be sure, sometimes our automatic behavior is consistent with—indeed, caused by—our attitudes. In fact, that's one of the purposes of attitudes: they allow us to respond quickly, without having to do much weighing of pros and cons. We go with our gut feeling. But some types of automatic behavior bypass our attitudes altogether, as when we jump away from something that looks like a snake in the grass. When such actions are elicited directly and mindlessly from the surrounding context, the connection between attitudes and behavior will necessarily be weak. One of the strongest and most influential research trends in social psychology over the past two decades has been uncovering more and more instances in which our behavior is automatically elicited by stimuli present in the environment. Let's consider some noteworthy examples.

In an experiment described as an investigation of "language proficiency," participants were asked to perform a sentence completion task. They were given 30 sets of 5 words each and were asked to form a grammatical English sentence using 4 of the 5 words. For half the participants, embedded within these 150 words were many that are stereotypically associated with the elderly—"gray," "wrinkle," "Florida," "bingo," and so on. This was designed to **prime** (mentally activate) the concept of the elderly among these participants. The remaining participants were exposed to neutral words that are not associated with the elderly, and hence their concept of the elderly was not primed. The experimenter then thanked the participants for their efforts, and the study, from the participants' perspective, was over.

But it had only begun. A second experimenter covertly timed how long it took each participant to walk from the threshold of the laboratory to the elevator down the hall. The investigators had predicted that merely activating the concept of the elderly for some of the participants would make them walk more slowly down the hallway because "slow" is a trait associated with the elderly. Amazingly, it did. Participants who had performed the sentence completion task using numerous words associated with the elderly took 13 percent longer to walk to the elevator (Bargh, Chen, & Burrows, 1996; see also Cesario, Plaks, & Higgins, 2006).

Social psychologists have recently been remarkably successful in demonstrating numerous instances of this sort of automatic behavior. The activation of different mental contents—traits, stereotypes, and goals—often directly elicits behavior dictated by those mental contents without any awareness on the part of the individuals so affected. Activating the traits of rudeness or intelligence, for example, has been shown to make people behave more assertively or to perform better on tests of general knowledge (Bargh, Chen, & Burrows, 1996; Dijksterhuis & van Knippenberg, 1998). Activating the goal of achievement has been shown to lead people to persevere longer at difficult tasks (Bargh, Gollwitzer, Lee-Chai, Barndollar, & Trotschel, 2001). Playing German music has resulted in increased sales of German wine at the expense of French wine, whereas playing French music has resulted in increased sales of French wine—without customers realizing what type of music was being played (North, Hargreaves, & Mckendrick, 1999). In possibly the most remarkable set of demonstrations, Dutch social psychologists Ap Dijksterhuis and Ad van Knippenberg primed students either with a social category associated with intellectual accomplishment (professors) or with a social category not noted for refined habits of mind (soccer hooligans). Those primed

"Civilization advances by extending the number of operations we can perform without thinking about them."

—Alfred North Whitehead

prime To mentally activate a concept and hence make it accessible. (Also used as a noun—a stimulus presented to activate a concept.)

with the professor cues subsequently performed better on a test of general knowledge than those primed with cues associated with soccer hooligans (Dijksterhuis & van Knippenberg, 1998).

More remarkably still, Dijksterhuis, van Knippenberg, and their colleagues demonstrated that activating the category of professor or supermodel led participants to perform in a manner *consistent* with the category, but activating a specific example of the category (for example, Albert Einstein, Claudia Schiffer) led participants to perform in a manner *inconsistent* with the category stereotype. That is, they performed worse on the general-knowledge test when primed with Einstein and better when primed with Claudia Schiffer (Dijksterhuis et al., 1998). These results fit the general tendency for the activation of *categories* to produce behavior in line with the category in question because it affects construal. People think of themselves as more intelligent (and act that way!) when viewing themselves—however implicitly—through the "lens" of a professor than they do when viewing themselves through the lens of a fashion model. The activation of *instances* of a category, in contrast, tends to yield behavior that contrasts with the category in question (Herr, 1986; Schwarz & Bless, 1992; Stapel, Koomen, & van der Plight, 1997; Stapel & Suls, 2007). This is because instances tend to serve as standards of judgment—in this case, Einstein serves as a very high standard (making people feel unintelligent), and Claudia Schiffer serves as a relatively low standard (making people feel smart).

Much of this recent work on the automatic nature of everyday social behavior provides another reason why there is often a limit to how well attitudes predict behavior. Automatic behavior that bypasses our conscious attitudes are, by definition, beyond the influence of our stated attitudes.

Priming Activating general categories like professor or supermodel may lead people to construe themselves along the lines of that category and to act as they think someone in that category would act. Activating a specific instance of that category, however, such as (A) Albert Einstein or (B) Claudia Schiffer, may have the opposite effect, as people may compare themselves to these specific people and feel that they aren't much like them at all.

LOOKING BACK We have seen that attitudes can be surprisingly weak predictors of behavior. This occurs because attitudes sometimes conflict with social norms about appropriate behavior, because general attitudes sometimes do not correspond to the specific action that is required in a given situation, because different attitudes can conflict with one another or the affective and cognitive components of an attitude may not be in sync, and because some behavior is automatic and bypasses conscious thought altogether. In the next section, we will see that behavior often influences attitudes to a marked degree.

PREDICTING ATTITUDES FROM BEHAVIOR

Many young people have chafed at being sent to church, temple, or mosque, often with the complaint, "Why do I have to go? I don't believe any of this stuff." And many of them have been told, "It doesn't matter if you believe it. What's important is that you continue with your studies and your prayers." Some resist to the very end and abandon the endeavor the minute their parents give them permission. But a remarkable number stick with it and eventually find themselves genuinely holding some of the very religious convictions and sentiments they originally resisted. Over time, mere outward behavior can give way to genuine inner conviction.

This illustrates the second part of our story on the connection between attitudes and behavior. We just learned that attitudes can predict behavior, but not as strongly as most people would suspect. That is one part of the story. The second part is how powerfully behavior can influence attitudes. Social psychological research over the past half century has documented time and time again the surprising extent to which people tend to bring their attitudes in line with their actions. This urge reflects the powerful tendency to justify, or rationalize, our behavior and to minimize any inconsistencies between our attitudes and actions.

Cognitive Consistency Theories

Why does our behavior have such a powerful influence on our attitudes? A number of influential theories have been put forward to explain this relationship. As a group, they are referred to as cognitive consistency theories, and they attempt to account for some of the most common sources of rationalization people use to bring their attitudes in line with their actions.

Balance Theory   The earliest social psychological consistency theory was Fritz Heider's **balance theory**. Heider (1946) claimed that people try to maintain balance among their beliefs, cognitions, and sentiments. If your two friends like each other, everything is fine and balanced. But if your two friends detest each other, you've got a problem: you have an imbalanced set of relationships on your hands. According to Heider, you will exert psychological energy to achieve or restore balance in this set of relationships. You may, for example, decide you like one friend less or conclude that their dislike of each other is a misunderstanding based on a relatively trivial issue.

balance theory The theory that people try to maintain balance among their beliefs, cognitions, and sentiments.

In a threesome (or triad), things are balanced if the product of the three sentiments (+ for liking, – for disliking) is positive. If my enemy (–) is disliked by a particular person (–), balance is achieved by my liking that person (+): $(-) \times (-) \times (+) = +$. You'll recognize that advertisers take advantage of this desire for balance. They'll have a beloved celebrity (+) say positive things (+) about a burger establishment or brand of basketball shoe, which puts psychological pressure on you to like that type of burger or shoe: $(+) \times (+) \times (+) = +$.

Balance Theory   People like to maintain balance between what their heroes like and what they like. When LeBron James of the Cleveland Cavaliers endorses the latest sneakers, his fans may be inclined to buy those sneakers to maintain balance between their support for James, the products he likes, and the products that they themselves like.

Support for Heider's balance theory comes from studies that either establish two relationships in a triad and then elicit people's inferences about the third or present various balanced and imbalanced relationships and then examine how well people remember them or how favorably they rate them. People "fill in" unspecified relations by assuming balance, and they remember balanced relationships better and rate them more favorably (Gawronski, Walther, & Blank, 2005; Hummert, Crockett, & Kemper, 1990; Insko, 1984). It would be easier to remember that *American Idol*'s Paula and Randy get along with each other but both have a hard time with Simon than to recall that Paula likes Simon but Randy doesn't. And if you know that the president likes his vice president and likes to watch NBA games, you'll be tempted to conclude that the vice president likes to watch the NBA too.

cognitive dissonance theory The theory that inconsistencies between a person's thoughts, sentiments, and actions create an aversive emotional state (dissonance) that leads to efforts to restore consistency.

Cognitive Dissonance Theory By far the most influential consistency theory, and one of the most influential theories in the history of social psychology, is Leon Festinger's **cognitive dissonance theory** (Festinger, 1957). Like Heider, Festinger argued that people are troubled by inconsistency between their thoughts, sentiments, and actions and that they will expend psychological energy to restore consistency. More specifically, Festinger thought that an aversive emotional state—dissonance—is aroused whenever people experience inconsistency between two cognitions. And because the cognitions can be about their own behavior (for example, "I just failed to live up to my vow"), people are troubled by inconsistency between their cognitions and their behavior as well. This unpleasant emotional state motivates efforts to restore consistency.

What counts as cognitive inconsistency, and how do people get rid of it? According to Festinger, people try to eliminate or reduce inconsistency by changing one or more of the discrepant cognitions to make them more consistent with one another. No controversy there. But his views about what exactly constitutes inconsistency have been modified by the tremendous amount of research that his theory inspired. Festinger argued that we experience inconsistency (and dissonance) whenever the opposite of one cognition follows from the other. If you think Friends of the Earth is a more worthy charity than the American Society for the Prevention of Cruelty to Animals (ASPCA), you'll experience some dissonance if you give your money to the ASPCA instead of Friends of the Earth. As we shall see, this definition of inconsistency doesn't quite work, both because it's vague (it's not always clear what the opposite of a given cognition might be) and because it predicts more dissonance than people actually experience (if you claim you don't like surprises and yet you find yourself delighted by a surprise birthday party, you are unlikely to be troubled by the inconsistency). Although Festinger may have been a bit off the mark in this regard, the overall theory has proved very insightful and productive, and subsequent efforts to specify exactly what constitutes psychological inconsistency have done a great deal to further our understanding of psychological conflict and rationalization.

Leon Festinger Studying how people bring their attitudes in line with their behavior, Leon Festinger developed cognitive dissonance theory.

Experiencing and Reducing Dissonance

To develop some sense of the kinds of inconsistency that people find troubling and to get a flavor for the diverse phenomena that can be explained by the theory of cognitive dissonance, let's take a look at some of the classic experiments on the subject—experiments that have excited generations of students of social psychology.

Decisions and Dissonance Even a moment's reflection tells us that all hard decisions arouse some dissonance. Because the decision is hard, there must be some desirable features of the rejected alternative, some undesirable features of the chosen alternative, or both. These elements are inconsistent with the choice that was made and hence produce dissonance (Brehm, 1956). If you move to Los Angeles from a small town in the Midwest in pursuit of good weather, you'll enjoy the sun, but the dirty air and hours spent in traffic will likely arouse dissonance. According to Festinger, once you've made an irrevocable decision to move to L.A., you'll exert mental effort to reduce this dissonance. You'll rationalize. You'll maintain that the lack of visibility is mainly due to haze, not smog, and you'll tell your friends about how much you'll learn from the audiobooks you'll play on your car stereo during your long commute.

Numerous experiments have documented this tendency for people to rationalize their decisions. In one study, the investigators interviewed bettors at a racetrack, some just before and some just after placing their bets (Knox & Inkster, 1968). The investigators reasoned that the act of placing a bet and making an irrevocable choice of a particular horse would cause the bettors to reduce the dissonance associated with all the negative features of the chosen horse (doesn't do well on a wet track) and all the positive features of the competing horses (the perfect distance for one horse, the best jockey on another). Dissonance reduction should be reflected in greater confidence on the part of those interviewed right *after* placing their bets. That is exactly what the investigators found. Those who were interviewed as they waited in line to place their bets gave their horses, on average, a "fair" chance of winning the race; those who were interviewed after they had placed their bets

and were leaving the ticket window gave their horses, on average, a "good" chance to win. One participant provided some extra commentary that serves as something of a window on the process of dissonance reduction. This participant had been interviewed while waiting in line (before placing his bet), but then, emerging from the ticket window, he approached another member of the research team and said, "Are you working with that other fellow there? Well, I just told him that my horse had a fair chance of winning. Will you have him change that to a good chance? No, by God, make that an excellent chance." Making hard decisions triggers dissonance, which in turn triggers processes of rationalization that make us more comfortable with our choices. Similar findings have been observed in elections: voters express greater confidence in their candidates when they are interviewed after they have voted and

are leaving the polling station than when they are interviewed approaching it (Frenkel & Doob, 1976; Regan & Kilduff, 1988).

Festinger argued that dissonance reduction processes only arise after an irrevocable decision has been made. He maintained, for example, that "there is a clear and undeniable difference between the cognitive processes that occur during the period of making a decision and those that occur after the decision has been made. Reevaluation of alternatives in the direction of favoring the chosen or disfavoring the rejected alternative . . . is a post-decision phenomenon" (Festinger, 1964, p. 30).

The evidence from the betting and election studies seems to support Festinger's contention. But this claim is at odds with other things we know about people. One of humankind's distinguishing characteristics is the ability to anticipate the future. If, in the process of making a decision, we see that there are blemishes associated with what is emerging as our favorite option, why not start the process of rationalization beforehand so that dissonance is minimized or eliminated altogether (Wilson, Wheatley, Kurtz, Dunn, & Gilbert, 2004)?

Indeed, more recent research has established that the same sorts of rationalization and distortion that dissonance experiments have documented after decisions have been made also subconsciously take place *before* they are made. This research has shown that whether choosing restaurants, vacation spots, consumer goods, or

Rationalizing Decisions, Reducing Dissonance After placing a bet at the track, as here at the Kentucky Derby, people are likely to concentrate on the positive features of the horse they bet on and to downplay any negative features. This rationalization process gives them greater confidence in the choice they made.

political candidates, once people develop a slight preference for one option over the others, they distort subsequent information to support their initial preference (Brownstein, 2003; Brownstein, Read, & Simon, 2004; Russo, Medvec, & Meloy, 1996; Russo, Meloy, & Medvec, 1998; Simon, Krawczyk, & Holyoak, 2004; Simon, Pham, Le, & Holyoak, 2001). Thus, the small size of a French restaurant tends to be rated as a plus by those leaning toward French food ("nice and intimate"), but as a minus by those leaning toward Thai food ("we won't be able to talk without everyone overhearing us"). It appears, then, that Festinger was right that decisions evoke dissonance and dissonance reduction, but these processes occur more often and more broadly than he anticipated—they can occur both before and after decisions are made.

Effort Justification The element of dissonance theory that rings most true to many people is the idea that if you pay a high price for something—in dollars, time, or effort—and it turns out to be disappointing, you're likely to experience dissonance. As a result, you're likely to devote mental energy to justifying what you've done. The most salient example of **effort justification** on campus, perhaps, is fraternity hazing. Someone who undergoes a painful or humiliating initiation ritual will have a need to believe it was all worthwhile, and one way to do that is to extol the virtues of being in that particular fraternity. The Greek system, in other words, capitalizes on cognitive dissonance. The same dynamics exist elsewhere, of course. Those who don't have pets often suspect that pet lovers exaggerate the pleasure they get from their animals to offset all the early-morning walking, poop scooping, and furniture wrecking. And those who choose not to have children suspect that homebound, sleep-deprived, overtaxed parents are fooling themselves when they say that nothing in life brings greater pleasure.

The role of dissonance reduction in such situations was explored in an early study in which female undergraduate students signed up for an experiment thinking it involved joining an ongoing discussion group about sex (Aronson & Mills, 1959). When they arrived, however, they were told that not everyone can speak freely and comfortably about such a topic, and so potential participants needed to pass a screening test in order to join the group. Those assigned to a control condition simply read aloud a list of innocuous words to the male experimenter. Those assigned to the mild initiation condition read aloud a list of mildly embarrassing words—for example, "prostitute," "petting," "virgin." Finally, those assigned to the severe initiation group had to read aloud a list of quite obscene words and a passage from a novel describing sexual intercourse.

All participants were then told they had passed their screening test and could join the discussion group. The group was meeting that very day, but because everyone else had been given a reading assignment beforehand, the participants were told that it was best if they just listened in on this session. Then, over headphones in a nearby cubicle, the participants heard a stultifyingly boring discussion of the sex life of invertebrates. Not only was the topic not what the participants had in mind when they signed up for a discussion group about sex, but the members of the discussion group ". . . contradicted themselves and one another, mumbled several non sequiturs, started sentences that they never finished, hemmed, hawed, and in general conducted one of the most worthless and uninteresting discussions imaginable" (Aronson & Mills, 1959, p. 179).

The investigators predicted that the discussion would be boring and disappointing to all the participants but that it would produce dissonance only for those who had undergone a severe initiation to join the group. The cognition "I suffered to get into this group" is inconsistent with the realization that "this group is worthless and boring." One way for the participants in the severe initiation condition to reduce dissonance would be to convince themselves that the group and the discussion were

effort justification The tendency to reduce dissonance by finding reasons for why we have devoted time, effort, or money to something that has turned out to be unpleasant or disappointing.

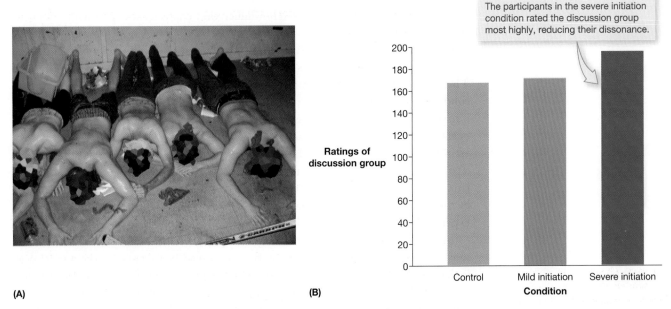

The participants in the severe initiation condition rated the discussion group most highly, reducing their dissonance.

(A)

(B)

FIGURE 6.2 Group Initiation and Liking for the Group (A) Fraternities try to increase how committed their members are to the group by having them undergo difficult and embarrassing initiation rituals, such as that depicted here. (B) This tradition is supported by empirical research. Ratings of a discussion group by participants who experienced no initiation, a mild initiation, or a severe initiation to join the group. (Source: Adapted from Aronson & Mills, 1959.)

not so boring after all. And that's just what they did. When the experimenters asked participants at the end of the study to rate the quality of the discussion on a number of scales, those in the severe initiation condition rated it more favorably than those in the other two conditions (see **Figure 6.2**).

This sort of *sweet lemons rationalization* ("it's really not so bad") is fairly common. Fraternities extract loyalty and commitment from their pledges by making them go through painful initiation rituals. Religious groups require that their members devote a great deal of time and money to their organizations. And certain high-end restaurants may be cementing their reputations as the very best places to dine by charging their customers exorbitant prices.

Induced Compliance and Attitude Change Dissonance theory can also explain what often happens as a result of **induced (forced) compliance**—that is, as a result of inducing individuals to behave in a manner that is inconsistent with their beliefs, attitudes, or values. Most people will feel some discomfort with the mismatch between their behavior and their attitudes. One way to deal with the inconsistency—the easiest and most likely way, given that the behavior cannot be taken back—is for people to change their original attitudes or values. This was the core idea behind Lyndon Johnson's stratagem, described in the opening to this chapter: by having doubters in his administration give press conferences in which they publicly defended the administration's position, the inconsistency between their private doubts and their public comments led them to dispel their doubts.

Numerous experiments have demonstrated how powerfully induced compliance can shift a person's original attitudes. In the very first experiment that demonstrated such an effect, Leon Festinger and Merrill Carlsmith (1959) had participants engage in what can only be described as experimental drudgery for an hour (loading spools on a tray over and over, turning pegs on a pegboard one-quarter turn at a time). Participants in the control condition were sent immediately afterward to see someone

induced (forced) compliance Subtly compelling individuals to behave in a manner that is inconsistent with their beliefs, attitudes, or values, which typically leads to dissonance and to a change in their original attitudes or values in order to reduce their dissonance.

from the psychology department who would interview them about their experience as research volunteers. When asked how much they enjoyed the experiment, they gave quite low ratings. No surprise there.

Participants in two other conditions were told that the experiment was about how people's performance on a task is influenced by their expectations about it beforehand. These participants were led to believe that they were in a control, "no expectation" condition, but that other subjects were told beforehand that the study was either very interesting or boring. Looking rather sheepish, the experimenter explained that the next participant was about to show up and needed to be told that the study was interesting. This was usually done, the experimenter explained, by a confederate posing as a participant. But the confederate was absent, putting the experimenter in a bit of a jam. Would you, the experimenter asked the participant, play the role usually played by the confederate and tell the next participant that the experiment is interesting? The experimenter offered the participant either $1 or $20 for doing so.

In this "play within a play," the true participant thinks he's a confederate. What is most important to the experiment, and what is readily apparent to the participant, is that he has just lied (nearly every participant agreed to the request) and said that a mind-numbingly boring study is interesting. Festinger and Carlsmith argued that this act would produce dissonance for those participants who were given only $1 for the assignment. Their words were inconsistent with their beliefs, and $1 was not enough to justify the lie. Those given $20 could at least tell themselves that yes, they did lie, but they were justified in doing so (and just about anyone else would have lied too) because the pay was good and the lie was of little consequence.

Festinger and Carlsmith predicted that participants in the $1 condition would rationalize their behavior—that is, they would reduce their dissonance—by changing their attitude about the task they had performed. By convincing themselves that the task was not uninteresting after all, their lie would not really be a lie. When later asked by the person from the psychology department to evaluate their experience, these participants would rate the task more favorably. As **Figure 6.3** indicates, that is exactly what they did. Only the participants in the $1 condition rated the activities above the neutral point.

There is a very important lesson here about the best way to influence someone else's attitudes, a lesson that has important implications for child rearing, among other things. If you want to get people to do something (take school seriously, take care of the environment, refrain from using foul language) and you want them to internalize the broader message behind the behavior, then use the smallest amount of incentive or coercion necessary to get them to do it. In other words, don't go overboard with the incentives. If the inducements are too substantial, people will justify their behavior by the inducements (like the $20 condition of Festinger and Carlsmith's study), and they will not need to rationalize their behavior by coming to believe in the broader purpose or philosophy behind it. But if the inducements are just barely sufficient (as in the $1 condition), people's need to rationalize will tend to produce a deep-seated attitude change in line with their behavior. So if you're going to pay your children for doing their homework, be sure you pay them the least amount necessary to get them to do it.

Evidence in support of this idea—and of its potential role in child rearing—comes from experiments using what is known as the "forbidden toy" paradigm (Aronson & Carlsmith, 1963; Freedman, 1965; Lepper, 1973). In one experiment of this type, an experimenter showed nursery school children a set of five toys and asked the children to tell him how much they liked each one. The experimenter then explained that he would have to leave the room for a while, but that he would be back soon. In the meantime, the child was free to play with any of the toys except for the child's second favorite. Half the children were told not to play with the forbidden toy and that the

FIGURE 6.3 Scientific Method: Induced Compliance and Attitude Change

Hypothesis: Participants induced to say something they don't believe with little incentive to do so will come to believe what they say.

Research Method:

1 Participants worked on a series of boring tasks.

2 Participants were then asked to tell another person that the tasks were interesting and enjoyable. Some participants were paid $1 to do so, others, $20. Control participants were not asked to tell the other person that the tasks were interesting.

3 Later, participants reported to someone seemingly unconnected to the experiment how much they enjoyed the task they had worked on.

Results: Ratings by participants in the control, $1, and $20 conditions of how much they enjoyed the (boring) experimental tasks after telling another student they were interesting. Participants in the $1 condition rated the tasks as more enjoyable than those in the control or $20 conditions, who did not differ significantly from one another:

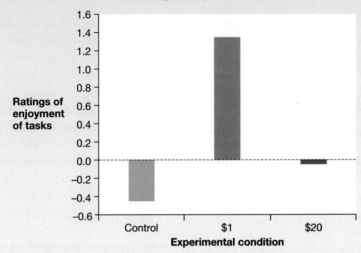

Conclusion: Saying something that we don't believe, and doing so with little justification ($1 instead of $20), produces dissonance. Dissonance is an unpleasant internal state that leads people to change their original attitudes or beliefs.

Source: Festinger & Carlsmith (1959).

---

experimenter would "be annoyed" if they did. This was the *mild threat* condition. In the *severe threat* condition, the children were told that if they played with the forbidden toy, the experimenter "would be very angry" and "would have to take all of my toys and go home and never come back again."

While the experimenter was gone, each child was covertly observed, and none played with the forbidden toy. Aronson and Carlsmith predicted that not playing with the forbidden toy would produce dissonance, but only for the children in the mild threat condition. For them, the desirability of the toy would be inconsistent with their not playing with it, an inconsistency that Aronson and Carlsmith predicted the children would resolve by derogating the toy—by convincing themselves that it wasn't such a great toy after all. Those who received the severe threat should experience no such dissonance because not playing with it was justified by the threat they received. Thus, there was nothing to cause them to derogate the toy. To find out if their predictions were correct, Aronson and Carlsmith had the children reevaluate all five toys when the experimenter returned. As expected, the children in the severe threat condition either did not change their opinion of the forbidden toy or they liked it even more than before (see **Figure 6.4**). In contrast, many of those in the mild threat condition viewed

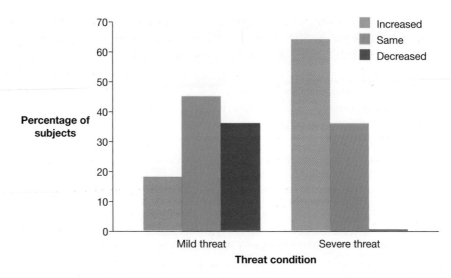

FIGURE 6.4 Derogation of the Forbidden Toy The percentage of children in the mild and severe threat conditions whose opinion of the forbidden toy increased, stayed the same, or decreased. (Source: Aronson & Carlsmith, 1963.)

the toy less favorably. Thus, the threat of severe punishment will keep children from doing something you don't want them to do, but they will still, later on, want to do it. The threat of mild punishment—if it's just enough of a threat to keep them from doing it—can bring about psychological change, such that they will no longer even be tempted to do what you don't want them to do.

When Does Inconsistency Produce Dissonance?

We saw earlier that there is some trouble with Festinger's original statement of when people will experience dissonance. Festinger thought that people would experience dissonance whenever they held two inconsistent cognitions. But what constitutes inconsistency? Is it really inconsistent to refrain from playing with an attractive toy if an authority figure asks you not to? Apparently it is, given the results obtained by Aronson and Carlsmith (and subsequent investigators). But what's so jarringly unpleasant about such inconsistency? There are many things we refrain from doing that we know we would find enjoyable, even when we have no compelling reason (like a severe threat) to refrain from doing them. Which of these are likely to induce dissonance and which are not?

One of the earliest and most significant contributors to our understanding of cognitive dissonance, Eliot Aronson, took this question to heart and offered a solution. A particular inconsistency will arouse dissonance, Aronson argued, if it implicates our core sense of self (Aronson, 1969). People like to think of themselves as rational, morally upright, worthy individuals, and anything that challenges such assessments is likely to arouse dissonance. Thus, expending great effort to join a boring group calls into question our wisdom and rationality; telling another student that a boring task is interesting challenges our integrity. Cognitions and behaviors that are inconsistent with our sense of self are what produce dissonance (Sherman & Gorkin, 1980).

To understand the sorts of cognitions likely to challenge our sense of judgment and personal character, it is useful to think about when *someone else's* actions make us question *that person's* character—or better still, to think of the justifications others could offer that would *prevent* us from questioning the person's judgment or moral fiber. First, we are unlikely to draw negative inferences about others when they can offer an excuse that indicates they could hardly have acted otherwise. If a computer-savvy friend doesn't drop by to help with a pressing computer problem because his boss wouldn't let him off work, we would not be justified in thinking ill of him. He had no choice. Second, we are unlikely to draw negative inferences about others when they offer, not an excuse, but a justification for their actions (see Chapter 4). Justifications carry an implicit acknowledgment that one could have behaved otherwise, but to do so would not have been the best course of action. Thus, we wouldn't think ill of a friend who didn't help with a pressing computer problem because he had to console a distraught roommate. Third, we are likely to judge others harshly in rough proportion to the magnitude of harm they have done. We would (justifiably) think worse of a friend whose failure to help with a computer problem caused us to fail a course as opposed to just being unable to turn in an assignment early. Finally, we are unlikely to judge other people as harshly if the harm they caused was unforeseen. If a friend had no way of knowing how critical his help would have been, we would not feel justified in questioning his character.

This analysis of when we hold other people responsible for their actions provides some insight into when people will hold *themselves* responsible for their actions and thus experience dissonance as a result of those actions. This analysis suggests, in other words, that people ought to experience dissonance whenever they act in ways that are inconsistent with their core values and beliefs and (1) the behavior was freely chosen, (2) the behavior was not sufficiently justified, (3) the behavior had negative consequences, and (4) the negative consequences were foreseeable.

Free Choice The critical role of freedom of choice has been apparent since the very earliest dissonance experiments and has been demonstrated most often and most clearly in the induced-compliance paradigm. In the first demonstration of this kind, students at Duke University were offered either $.50 or $2.50 to write an essay in favor of a state law banning Communists from speaking on college campuses. (This experiment was done in the mid-1960s, and both payments may now seem low; for comparable amounts today, it would be reasonable to multiply these amounts by a factor of 6 to 8.) Because the law was at variance with the U.S. Constitution's guarantee of freedom of speech, nearly all students were opposed to it, and their essays thus conflicted with their true beliefs. For half the participants, their freedom to accept or decline the offer to write such an essay was emphasized. For the other half, it was not. There was no dissonance effect among these latter participants. Indeed, those paid $2.50 later expressed attitudes more in favor of the ban than did those paid $.50 (presumably because writing the essay was associated with the good feelings that

accompany the larger reward). In the free-choice group, however, the standard dissonance effect was obtained: those paid $.50 changed their attitude more than those paid $2.50 (Linder, Cooper, & Jones, 1967).

Insufficient Justification This last experiment, like all of the induced-compliance studies, also demonstrates the importance of insufficient justification in producing dissonance. If a person's behavior is justified by the existing incentives, even behavior that is dramatically in conflict with the person's beliefs and values will not produce dissonance—and the rationalizations that arise to combat it. Those paid $2.50 for writing an essay that was inconsistent with their true beliefs felt no pressure to change their attitudes because their behavior was psychologically justified by the large cash payment. Those paid only $.50 had no such justification and thus felt the full weight of their inconsistency. Thus, it appears that most of us are willing to sell our souls for money, and if the money is good enough, it doesn't even seem necessary to justify the sale.

Negative Consequences If nothing of consequence results from acting at variance with our attitudes and values, it is easy to dismiss it as a trivial matter. This suggests that people will only experience dissonance if their behavior results in harm of some sort. This has been demonstrated in a number of experiments, including one that utilzed the paradigm pioneered by Festinger and Carlsmith (and described earlier). Specifically, participants were induced to tell someone (a confederate) who they thought was about to take part in a boring experiment that it was really very interesting. The participants were provided with either a small or large incentive for doing so. Half the time the confederate seemed convinced that the boring task really was going to be interesting, and half the time the confederate clearly remained unconvinced ("Well, you're entitled to your own opinion, but I don't think that I have ever enjoyed an experiment, and I don't think that I will find this one much fun."). Note that there were no negative consequences when the person appeared unconvinced: no one was deceived. Thus, if negative consequences are necessary for the arousal of cognitive dissonance, the standard dissonance effect should occur only when the person is convinced. That is exactly what was found: the boring task was rated more favorably only by those participants who were offered little incentive to lie to another person and that person appeared to believe the lie (Cooper & Worchel, 1970; Nel, Helmreich, & Aronson, 1969).

Foreseeability We typically do not hold people responsible for harm they have done if the harm was not foreseeable. If a dinner guest who is allergic to peanuts becomes ill after eating an entrée with a mild peanut sauce, we do not hold the host responsible if the guest never informed the host of the allergy. This suggests that it may be the *foreseeable* negative consequences of our actions that generate cognitive dissonance. Negative consequences that are not foreseeable do not threaten our self-image as a moral and decent person, and thus they may not arouse dissonance.

This hypothesis has been verified in experiments in which participants were induced to write an essay in favor of a position they personally disagreed with (for example, that the size of the freshman class at their university should be doubled). If any negative consequences of such an action (for example, the essays are to be shown to a university committee charged with deciding whether to implement the policy) are made known to the participants after the fact, there is no dissonance and hence no attitude change in the direction of the essay they wrote. But if the negative consequences were either foreseen (participants knew beforehand that their letters would be shown to the committee) or foreseeable (participants knew beforehand that their letters *might* be shown to such a committee), the standard dissonance effect was obtained (Cooper, 1971; Goethals, Cooper, & Naficy, 1979).

Self-Affirmation and Dissonance

If dissonance results from challenges or threats to people's sense of themselves as rational, competent, and moral, then it follows that they can ward off dissonance not only by dealing directly with the specific threat itself, but also indirectly by taking stock of their other qualities and core values. Claude Steele and his colleagues have argued that this sort of **self-affirmation** is a common way that people cope with threats to their self-esteem (Cohen, Aronson, & Steele, 2000; Sherman & Cohen, 2002, 2006; Steele, 1988; Steele, Spencer, & Lynch, 1993): "Sure, I might have violated a friend's confidence, but I am very empathetic when other people are having difficulties." "I know I drive an SUV, but no one attends church services more regularly than I do." By bolstering themselves in one area, people can tolerate a bigger hit in another.

self-affirmation Bolstering our identity and self-esteem by taking note of important elements of our identity, such as our important values.

In one of the cleverest demonstrations of the effects of self-affirmation, Steele (1988) asked science majors and business majors at the University of Washington to participate in an experiment using the post-decision dissonance paradigm (see pp. 208–209). In a control condition, both groups showed the usual dissonance effect of finding hidden attractions in the chosen alternative and hidden flaws in the unchosen alternative. But in another condition, the experimenters had the business and science majors put on white lab coats before rendering their final evaluations. Steele predicted that wearing a lab coat would affirm an important identity for the science majors, but not for the business majors. The results supported his predictions. The business majors reduced dissonance just as much as participants in the control condition; the science majors did not. If you feel good about yourself, you don't have to sweat the small stuff like minor decisions.

Is Dissonance Universal?

We have been discussing cognitive dissonance as if it were a cross-culturally universal phenomenon. Is it? There is substantial evidence on the question, yielding a very interesting answer. Heine and Lehman (1997) used the free-choice, self-affirmation paradigm in which all participants were asked to choose between two objects (CDs in this case), but some were first provided self-affirmation in the form of positive feedback on a personality test. Heine and Lehman's participants were Japanese and Canadian, and the researchers wanted to see if the dissonance effect was the same in people from these two different cultures. They found the usual result for the Canadians: participants exhibited a substantial dissonance effect in the control condition, finding previously unnoticed attractions in the chosen CD and previously unnoticed flaws in the unchosen one, but they showed no dissonance effect if they were given positive feedback about their personalities. The Japanese participants, in contrast, were unaffected by the self-affirmation manipulation. More striking still, they showed no dissonance effect in either condition, which led Heine and Lehman to conclude that cognitive dissonance might be a phenomenon unique to Westerners. But Sakai (1981), using an induced-compliance paradigm in which participants were persuaded to do something they didn't want to do, found dissonance effects for Japanese participants—if they were led to think that other students were observing their behavior.

So does this imply that East Asians may experience dissonance in the induced-compliance paradigm but not in the free-choice paradigm? That would be messy. Fortunately, there's another way to reconcile the two sets of results. Throughout this book, we have emphasized that East Asians, along with many other people in the world, are more attuned to other people and their reactions than are Westerners. If East Asians exhibit dissonance effects in the induced-compliance paradigm because they question their actions when others are observing them, then they should also exhibit dissonance effects in the free-choice paradigm if they are led to think about other people's reaction to their choice. And this is indeed the case. Kitayama, Snibbe, Markus, and Suzuki (2004) asked Japanese and Canadian participants to choose between two CDs. In one condition (the standard condition used by investigators for the past 50 years), participants were asked, after ranking a large number of CDs, to choose between two of the middle-ranked CDs. In the other condition, participants were also asked to rank the presumed preferences of the "average college student." In this way, the researchers "primed," or made salient, a "meaningful social other" (see **Box 6.1**). This manipulation made no difference for the Canadians, but it made a great deal of difference for the Japanese. The Japanese showed almost no dissonance effect in the standard condition, but they showed an even larger dissonance effect than the Canadians in the socially primed condition. Hoshino-Browne, Zanna, Spencer, and Zanna (2004) showed a similar effect of social priming when they asked participants to choose a CD either for themselves or for a friend. Euro-Canadians, as well as Asian-Canadians who only weakly identified themselves as Asians, showed much larger dissonance effects when choosing for themselves than when choosing for a friend; but Asian-Canadians who

BOX 6.1 **FOCUS ON CULTURE**

Culture and Priming Effects of "Social" Stimuli in the Free-Choice Paradigm

The priming of social cues has very different effects on Japanese and American participants in free-choice situations. Kitayama, Snibbe, Markus, and Suzuki (2004) asked participants to choose between two CDs. For some participants, hanging right in front of them at eye level was the poster below. The poster was simply a figure from another, unrelated experiment, and the investigators' intention was to see whether the schematic faces in it might prime the concept of other people and hence prompt the Japanese participants to show a strong dissonance effect. That was exactly what was found. In the standard free-choice condition, the Japanese showed no evidence of dissonance reduction, but in the poster condition they did. American participants actually showed slightly less dissonance reduction in the poster condition than in the standard condition.

Impression	Semantic Dimension		
	Activity	Negative Valence	Potency
High			
Low			

Culture and Priming   Note: The critical elements of the poster were the schematic faces. The labels were included simply to make the poster look like part of another, unrelated experiment.

strongly identified themselves as Asians showed much larger dissonance effects when choosing for a friend than when choosing for themselves.

So it appears that post-decision dissonance may indeed be universal, but the conditions that prompt it may be very different for different peoples. For independent Westerners, it may be prompted by a concern about the ability of the self to make an adequate choice that reflects well on one's decisiveness; for Easterners and perhaps other interdependent peoples, it may be prompted by a concern about the ability of the self to make choices that would be approved by others.

 We have seen that behavior can have a powerful impact on our attitudes, largely because people like their attitudes to be consistent with one another and with their behavior. When there is inconsistency among cognitions, values, or actions, dissonance is likely to be aroused. We can reduce dissonance by changing our attitudes to be in line with our behavior. Dissonance is more pronounced when the inconsistency implies that the self is deficient in some way. Therefore, when we can affirm the self somehow, we are less susceptible to dissonance. Finally, different cultures find different circumstances dissonance arousing.

SELF-PERCEPTION THEORY

Like all prominent theories that have been around for a long time, dissonance theory has faced many theoretical challenges and has had to withstand numerous critiques. One critique, however, stands out above all others in its impact: Daryl Bem's self-perception theory (Bem, 1967, 1972). The theory began as an alternative account of all of the dissonance findings, but it has important implications for self-understanding more generally, and it offers novel explanations for many real-life choices and behaviors.

Daryl Bem Bem's self-perception theory offered a new way of understanding ourselves by looking outward.

self-perception theory A theory that people come to know their own attitudes by looking at their behavior and the context in which it occurred and *inferring* what their attitudes must be.

Inferring Attitudes

According to Bem's **self-perception theory**, people come to know their own attitudes not, as we would expect, by "looking inward" and discerning what they think or how they feel about something. Rather, they look outward, at their behavior and the context in which it occurred, and *infer* what their attitudes must be. Self-perception works just like social perception. People come to understand themselves and their attitudes in the same way that they come to understand others and their attitudes.

At first glance, this seems bizarre—as implausible as the old joke about two behaviorists who've just finished having sex: One turns to the other and says, "That was great for you, how was it for me?" The theory feels wrong on a gut level because we're convinced there are times when we "just know" how we feel about something, and we don't need to engage in any process of inference to find out. On closer inspection, however, self-perception theory makes much more sense, in part because Bem concedes that sometimes we can just introspect and "read off" our attitudes. It is only when our prior attitudes are "weak, ambiguous, and uninterpretable," he argues, that "the individual is functionally in the same position as an outside observer." The caveat is helpful. We would all agree with Bem, certainly, that there are times when we figure out how we feel about something by examining our behavior. "I guess I was hungrier than I thought," we might say after downing a second Double Whopper with cheese. The key question, then, is whether the inference process that constitutes the core of self-perception theory applies only to such trivial matters as these or whether such processes are engaged when we grapple with attitudes of substance—for example, about volunteering to fight in Afghanistan or to work in a political campaign or to help underprivileged children.

By offering self-perception theory as an alternative account of the findings obtained in cognitive dissonance experiments, Bem was certainly laying claim to the idea that self-perception processes are responsible for much more than trivial attitudes. His account of the dissonance effects is quite simple. He argues that people in these studies are not troubled by any unpleasant state of arousal like dissonance; they merely engage in a dispassionate inference process. They do not *change* their attitudes in these studies; rather, they infer what their attitudes must be. People value what they have chosen more after having chosen it because they infer that "if I chose this, I must like it." People form tight bonds to groups that have unpleasant initiation rituals because they reason that "if I suffered to get this, I must have felt it was worth it." And people who are offered little incentive to tell someone that a task was interesting come to view the task more favorably because they conclude that "there's no other reason I would say this is interesting if it wasn't, so it really must be."

Evidence of Self-Directed Inference

How can we decide whether participants' responses in dissonance experiments are the product of such dispassionate reasoning? Bem offered two main types of evidence. First, he argued that if these are the processes that participants in those experiments go through—taking note of their behavior and the context in which it occurred to infer their true attitudes—it stands to reason that if we give *anyone* the same information about a participant's behavior and the context in which it occurred, that person should be able to infer the participant's true attitudes. Accordingly, Bem conducted a number of what he called **interpersonal simulations**. In an interpersonal simulation, an "observer-participant" is given a detailed description of one condition of a dissonance experiment, is told how a participant behaved in that situation, and is asked to predict the attitude of the participant on the basis of that behavior. The results of these studies have tended to support the self-perception account: the predictions of the observer-participants tend to mirror the actual responses observed in the original studies. Those told about someone who was paid $1 in the Festinger-Carlsmith experiment, for example, predict that the participant's attitude toward the task would be more favorable than the attitude of someone who had been paid $20. Because these observer-participants, with only their powers of inference to work with, can anticipate the true participants' attitudes, perhaps the true participants themselves are relying solely on *their* powers of inference.

But why do people need to infer their own attitude? Why not simply remember and report it? Bem argues that surprisingly often there is no stored attitude to recall and report. To support this element of self-perception theory, Bem conducted a standard induced-compliance experiment, but with a twist. Participants were either given a choice or no choice to write an essay stating that students should have no control over the courses offered at their university. The participants had indicated earlier in the semester that (not surprisingly) they disagreed with this position. After writing these essays, half the participants were asked to indicate their current attitude on the issue. The standard dissonance effect was obtained: those who freely chose to write these counterattitudinal essays reported being less in favor of student input into the curriculum than those required to write the essays. The other half of the participants, however, were not asked about their current attitudes; instead, they were asked to report what their old attitudes had been earlier in the semester. They knew, furthermore,

"How do I know what I think until I hear what I say?"

—Anon.

infer not Δ

interpersonal simulations Experiments in which an "observer-participant" is given a detailed description of one condition of a dissonance experiment, is told how a participant behaved in that situation, and is asked to predict the attitude of that participant.

that the experimenters had their earlier attitude surveys and could therefore check the accuracy of their responses. Despite this incentive to report their earlier attitudes as accurately as possible, participants' memories were biased by their experience of having written a counterattitudinal essay. Those who had freely chosen to write such essays misrecalled their earlier attitudes, thinking they had been less in favor of student input into the curriculum than they actually had been (Bem & McConnell, 1970).

These memory findings, along with the results of the interpersonal simulations, compel us to take self-perception theory seriously. So, too, do a host of related phenomena (see **Box 6.2**). For example, what's known as the foot-in-the-door compliance technique (see Chapter 8) appears to result from people looking at their behavior (their compliance with a small request) and the context in which it occurred (no strong incentive to do so) and inferring that they must be the type of person who agrees to such requests (which then makes them more likely to agree to subsequent requests). Similarly, people's emotional reactions are often strengthened or weakened when they observe the surrounding context and infer how emotional they must be (see Chapter 7). For example, people who are anxious about their performance on an upcoming task calm down and become more confident if they are led to believe that their symptoms of anxiety are the product of white noise delivered over headphones (Savitsky, Medvec, Charlton, & Gilovich, 1998).

But these results, however supportive of self-perception theory they might be, do not tell us whether the results of the dissonance experiments are really the result of self-perception processes rather than efforts to reduce dissonance. To settle a theoretical dispute like this one, a very different type of experiment is required. We need to identify the conditions under which the two theories make different predictions, experimentally create just those conditions, and observe which prediction is confirmed. That's rather difficult in this case because the two theories make the *same* prediction in nearly all circumstances. This is not surprising, given that self-perception theory was offered specifically to account for all of the phenomena previously explained by the theory of cognitive dissonance.

Testing for Arousal

The one critical difference between the two theories, and hence the necessary focus of any decisive test, is whether people experience arousal in all of the standard dissonance paradigms (for example, the induced-compliance paradigm) and their everyday-life analogues. Dissonance theory posits that the inconsistency between behavior and prior attitudes (or values) produces an unpleasant physiological state that motivates people to reduce the inconsistency. No arousal, no attitude change. Self-perception theory, in contrast, contends that there is no arousal involved: people coolly and rationally infer what their attitudes must be in light of their behavior and the context in which it occurred.

So how do we determine if people are indeed aroused after making difficult choices, exerting great effort for minimal benefit, and behaving in ways at variance with their earlier attitudes? In one clever early test, participants were asked to write an essay in which they argued against the position they truly believed and then were immediately put in a situation that assessed their performance on a simple task and on a difficult task. It has been known for some time that arousal tends to make people perform better on simple tasks and perform worse on difficult tasks (see Chapter 14). Therefore, we should see just this pattern of performance if writing an essay inconsistent with participants' beliefs really does produce arousal. And that is indeed what happened. Compared to those who had just written an essay consistent with their prior attitudes, those who had written a counterattitudinal essay performed better on the easy task

BOX 6.2 **FOCUS ON EDUCATION**

The Overjustification Effect and Superfluous Rewards

If you dropped in on a family dinner in a foreign land and heard a parent tell a child that he had to eat his *pfunst* before he could eat his *pfeffatorst*, you would immediately conclude that the child did not like the *pfunst* but loved *pfeffatorst*. Things that people do to get something else are typically things they do not particularly like. But what happens when the child actually likes *pfunst*? Because the parents are making the child eat *pfunst* in order to have the privilege of eating *pfeffatorst*, the child may conclude that maybe *pfunst* isn't so great after all.

Self-perception theory makes just such a prediction. It maintains that we look at our behavior (I did X) and the context in which it occurs (in order to get Y) to draw conclusions about our underlying attitudes (I don't really like X in and of itself). This tendency to devalue those activities that we perform in order to get something else is known as the *overjustification* effect (Lepper, Greene, & Nisbett, 1973). The justification for performing the activity is overly sufficient: we would do it because it's inherently rewarding (or, more generally, for "intrinsic" reasons), but also because there is an external payoff for doing it

("extrinsic" reasons). Because the extrinsic reasons would be sufficient to produce the behavior, we might discount the intrinsic reasons for performing it and conclude that we don't much like the activity for its own sake.

Particularly intriguing evidence for the overjustification effect comes from a study of children's choice of activities in school. Elementary school children were shown two attractive drawing activities. In one condition, the kids were told they could first do one drawing activity and then the other. In a second condition, they were told they *had to* first do one activity *in order to* get to do the other (in both conditions, the experimenters counterbalanced which activity came first). For several days after this initial drawing session, the experimenters put out both drawing activities during the school's free-play period and covertly observed how long the children played with each. Those kids who earlier had simply drawn first with one and then the other played with both equally often. But those who earlier had done one *in order to* get to the other tended to avoid the former (Lepper, Sagotsky, Dafoe, & Greene, 1982). Their intrinsic

interest in the first drawing activity had been undermined.

The overjustification effect has important implications for how rewards should be used in education and child rearing. It is common practice, for example, to reward children for reading books, getting good grades, or practicing the piano. That's fine if the child wouldn't otherwise read, study, or practice. But if the child has some interest in these activities to begin with, the rewards might put that interest in jeopardy. In one powerful demonstration of this danger, researchers introduced a set of novel math games into the free-play portion of an elementary school curriculum. As **Figure 6.5** indicates, the children initially found them interesting, as indicated by the amount of time the children chose to play with them at the outset of the experiment (baseline phase). Then, for several days afterward, the investigators instituted a "token-economy" program whereby the children could earn points redeemable for prizes by playing with the math games. The more they played with the math games, the more points they earned. The token-economy program was effective in increasing how much

and worse on the difficult task (Waterman, 1969). As dissonance theory predicts, it seems that acting at variance with our true beliefs does indeed generate arousal (Elliot & Devine, 1994; Galinsky, Stone, & Cooper, 2000; Harmon-Jones, 2000; Norton, Monin, Cooper, & Hogg, 2003).

If arousal is indeed generated, it should be possible to influence the impact of that arousal—that is, whether it will lead to attitude change or not—by altering how it is interpreted (Cooper, Zanna, & Taves, 1978; Losch & Cacioppo, 1990). This has been done in experiments using "misattribution" manipulations (see Chapter 7). In one study, participants were given a drug (in reality, a placebo) and told either that it would have no effect, that it would make them feel tense, or that it would make them the children played the games (see the bar in the treatment phase). But what happened when the token-economy program was terminated and the children no longer earned points for playing with the games? Would they still play with them? As the bar on the right in the figure indicates, they did not. Having once received rewards for these activities, the children came to see them as something only done to get a reward, and their original interest was diminished (Greene, Sternberg, & Lepper, 1976).

This doesn't imply that giving out rewards is always a bad thing. People aren't always intrinsically motivated, and when they aren't, rewards are often the best way to get them to do something they would not otherwise do. Rewards can also be administered in ways that minimize their negative impact. For instance, there can be performance-contingent rewards—that is, rewards based on how well someone performs. These have been shown to be less likely to decrease interest in an activity than task-contingent rewards, which are simply based on doing a task or not (Deci & Ryan, 1985; Harackiewicz, Manderlink, & Sansone, 1984; Sansone & Harackiewicz, 2000).

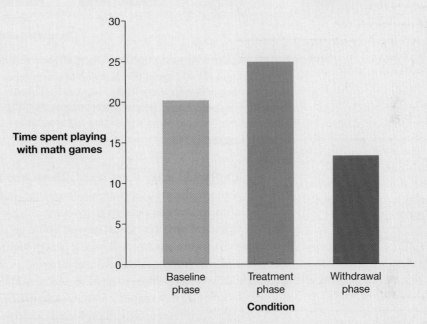

FIGURE 6.5 **The Effects of Superfluous Rewards** The amount of time elementary school children spent playing math games originally (baseline phase), when they received rewards for playing them (treatment phase), and afterward (withdrawal phase). (Source: Greene, Sternberg, & Lepper, 1976.)

feel relaxed (Zanna & Cooper, 1974). The participants then wrote, under free-choice or no-choice conditions, an essay arguing that inflammatory speakers should be barred from college campuses, a position with which they strongly disagreed. The investigators expected to find the standard dissonance effect among participants who were told that the drug would have no effect—greater attitude change in favor of banning inflammatory speakers on the part of those who freely chose to write the essay as opposed to those in the no-choice condition. As the middle bars in **Figure 6.6** show, that is precisely what happened.

But the results from the other conditions are more telling. The investigators predicted that this effect would disappear when participants were told (incorrectly)

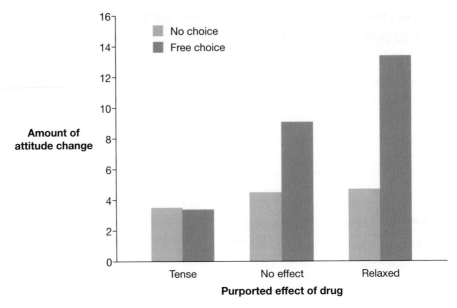

FIGURE 6.6 **Does Arguing against One's Prior Attitude Produce Arousal?** The amount of attitude change in the direction of a previously objectionable proposition on the part of participants who wrote essays—under free-choice and no-choice conditions—in support of the proposition. Before writing these esays, participants were given a pill and told either that it would make them tense, have no effect, or make them relaxed. (Source: Zanna & Cooper, 1974.)

that the drug would make them tense. Those who freely chose to write the essay would experience the arousal state of dissonance, but they would attribute it to the drug and thus feel no compulsion to do something (change their attitude) to get rid of their unpleasant physiological state—it would go away, they were led to believe, as soon as the drug wore off. As the leftmost bars in Figure 6.6 show, that prediction, too, was confirmed. What about the participants who were told that the drug would relax them? Those who freely chose to write the essay would experience arousal, an internal state inconsistent with the experimenter's earlier statement that the drug would make them feel relaxed. The researchers predicted that this would make them think, however implicitly, "I must *really* have done something wrong if I am this upset"—thoughts that should set in motion particularly powerful efforts at dissonance reduction. This prediction was also confirmed. As the rightmost bars in Figure 6.6 reveal, the greatest difference between participants in the free-choice and no-choice conditions—that is, the biggest dissonance effect—was observed among participants who had been told that the drug would make them feel relaxed.

Reconciling the Dissonance and Self-Perception Accounts

The experiment just described speaks volumes about the relative merits of dissonance theory and self-perception theory. It is clear that behavior that is inconsistent with prior attitudes does indeed generate arousal (Croyle & Cooper, 1983; Elkin & Leippe, 1986) and that it is the effort to dispel that arousal that motivates the types of attitude change found in the various dissonance experiments (Harmon-Jones, Brehm, Greenberg, Simon, & Nelson, 1996). In that sense, Festinger was right. Dissonance theory is the proper account of the phenomena observed in these experiments (and their real-world counterparts), not self-perception theory.

But note the irony here: the experiment that most powerfully supports the cognitive dissonance interpretation depends on the very processes of inference that lie at the core of self-perception theory. When participants in that experiment implicitly reasoned, "I'm aroused, but the experimenter told me the drug would make me anxious, so therefore . . .," they were—just as self-perception theory predicts—making inferences about what was going on inside of them. Self-perception theory may not provide an accurate account of what happens when people behave in a way that challenges their sense of self as a moral and rational person, but it does capture some very important aspects of how the mind works.

A consensus has thus emerged among social psychologists that both dissonance reduction processes and self-perception processes occur and influence people's attitudes and broader views of themselves. Dissonance reduction processes are invoked when people act in ways that are inconsistent with preexisting attitudes that are clear-cut and of some importance. Self-perception processes, in contrast, are invoked when behavior "clashes" with attitudes that are relatively vague or of little import (Chaiken & Baldwin, 1981; Fazio, Zanna, & Cooper, 1977).

This revised view makes sense from at least three perspectives. First, and most important, it is consistent with the pertinent empirical tests, such as the studies just described. Second, it is consistent with most people's everyday experience with the rationalizations that are provoked by psychological inconsistency—rationalizations

BOX 6.3   **FOCUS ON DAILY LIFE**

Body over Mind

Recent research has yielded evidence for a rather radical extension of self-perception theory's core thesis that our attitudes are influenced by our actions. It appears that the physical movements we engage in while evaluating stimuli have a significant effect on how favorably those stimuli are evaluated. Thus, engaging in movements that typically accompany positive reactions leads us to evaluate stimuli more favorably, even when the stimuli are not particularly desirable to begin with. The opposite is true of movements that typically accompany negative reactions. In one early demonstration of this effect, Gary Wells and Richard Petty (1980) had students ostensibly test a set of headphones by moving their heads up and down or side to side while listening to music and radio editorials. When later asked about the viewpoints advocated in the editorials, the students indicated that they agreed with them more if they had listened to them while nodding their heads up and down than if they had listened to them while shaking their heads

from side to side. We nod our heads at things we approve of, and this lifelong association leads us to view more favorably those things we encounter while nodding (Epley & Gilovich, 2001; Forster & Strack, 1996).

Similar effects result from other movements associated with positive and negative reactions. Fritz Strack and his colleagues had some students hold a marker with their teeth, which creates a smiling expression (see **Figure 6.7** on the next page and try it!). Others were asked to hold the marker with their lips, creating an expression akin to a frown. While holding the marker in one of these ways, the participants were asked to rate how amused they were by a number of cartoons. As you can probably anticipate, students who held the marker in their teeth (the smilers) thought the cartoons were more amusing than did students in a control condition, and those who held the marker with their lips (the frowners) thought the cartoons were less amusing (Strack, Martin, & Stepper, 1988).

Other researchers have explored the implications of our tendency to push away things we find aversive and pull toward us things we find appealing, as we saw in Chapter 1. Thus, arm extension is associated with negative stimuli and arm flexion is associated with positive stimuli. These bodily movements also have predictable effects on attitudes. In one study, John Cacioppo, Joseph Priester, and Gary Berntson (1993) showed Ohio State University students a series of 24 Chinese ideographs while they were either pressing down on a table (arm extension) or lifting up on a table from underneath (arm flexion). The students evaluated the ideographs presented during arm flexion more favorably (see also Chen & Bargh, 1999). Other studies using this procedure have shown that arm flexion fosters creative insight on various problem-solving tasks (Friedman & Forster, 2000) and makes people more inclined to accept their initial stab at estimating unknown values (Epley & Gilovich, 2004).

FIGURE 6.7 **You Be the Subject: Self-Perception Affected by Movement**

Try putting a pen or pencil between your teeth as shown below:

Try watching a TV show while in the first position; after the first commercial break, switch to the second position.
Was the TV show more or less amusing before or after the commercial break?

Results: Research evidence suggests that the physical movements we engage in while evaluating stimuli can affect how those stimuli are evaluated (see Box 6.3 for further discussion).

that *feel* like they are motivated by a desire to reduce dissonance (Gilbert, Lieberman, Morewedge, & Wilson, 2004; Gilbert, Morewedge, Risen, & Wilson, 2004; Gilbert, Pinel, Wilson, Blumberg, & Wheatley, 1998). When a fabulously wealthy man sees hardworking people living in hovels and barely getting by, he does not coolly observe his behavior (failing to help the poor) and decide, "I must think that the income disparity is justified." Instead, the poverty of others—and his failure to do anything about it—is troubling, and the tension this produces sets in motion the wealthy man's very active attempts to feel better about not doing anything to help ("I've worked hard for my money"; "If they keep working hard, things will get better for them, because in our society, hard work and talent always win out in the end"). Finally, the revised view fits with Bem's original statement of self-perception theory: that it is only when a person's attitudes are "weak, ambiguous, and uninterpretable" that "the individual is functionally in the same position as an outside observer." Bem's only error, then, was to assert that the attitudes being tapped in the various cognitive dissonance experiments were the weak, ambiguous sort that engage self-perception processes rather than the strong, clear-cut, and salient sort that produce dissonance.

But before getting too comfortable with this revised view, it is important to take note of what it leaves out. Although it is true that self-perception processes are engaged primarily when our prior attitudes are weak or unclear, a considerable body of research has made it abundantly clear that a surprising proportion of our attitudes *are* rather weak and ambiguous. Although self-perception processes may less often influence important attitudes than unimportant ones, they nevertheless do at times influence important attitudes—and important subsequent behavior. Self-perception manipulations, for example, have been shown to influence such significant phenomena as whether we are likely to contribute to the public good (Freedman & Fraser, 1966; Uranowitz, 1975), whether we are likely to cheat to reach a goal (Dienstbier & Munter, 1971; Lepper, 1973), the precise emotion we are feeling and how strongly we feel it (Dutton & Aron, 1974; Schachter & Singer, 1962; White & Kight, 1984), our assessment of our own personality traits (Schwarz et al., 1991; Tice, 1993), and whether we truly enjoy an activity we have engaged in our entire life (Lepper & Greene, 1978). Thus, the revised view might make it seem as if self-perception processes are relegated to the trivial fringe of social life. They are not.

In fact, the basic postulates of self-perception theory are consistent with neuroscientific evidence concerning how the mind is structured. There is increasing evidence that the brain is organized into numerous semidiscrete modules, each performing its own specified function. The clearest example of this is language. There appear to be universal aspects of grammar that are shared by everyone in the world (Chomsky, 1975, 1988; see Chapter 1), and the brain regions involved in language use and learning are well known. There is also increasing evidence that at least one brain module functions as something of an interpreter, registering the output of all other modules, including information about our actions, and making sense of them (Gazzaniga, 1985; see **Box 6.3** on p. 225). Particularly intriguing evidence for this proposition comes from research on "split-brain" patients (see **Figure 6.8**), who—unlike the rest of us—do not have a functioning corpus callosum that allows the two cerebral hemispheres to communicate with each other. Imagine, then, that two pictures are presented to the two hemispheres of a split-brain patient: (1) a picture of a snow scene to the nonverbal right hemisphere (by presenting it to the left visual field), and (2) a picture of a bird's claw to the verbal left hemisphere (by presenting it to the right visual field). The patient is then asked to select from an array of pictures the one that fits the stimuli she has just seen. She is told to point with both hands to the picture she has selected.

What happens? Typically, the patient selects two pictures: (1) with the left hand (controlled by the right hemisphere), she might select a picture of a shovel to go

FIGURE 6.8 Interpretation of Behavior by Split-Brain Patients

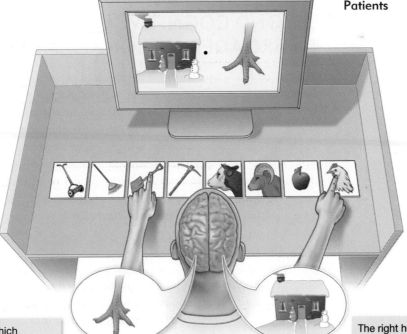

1 A split-brain participant watches as different images flash simultaneously on the left and right. What is presented on the left is seen by the right brain, and what is presented on the right is seen by the left brain.

2 Below the screen is a row of other images.

3 The patient is asked to point, with both hands, to the image they just saw.

The left hemisphere (which controls the right hand) points at a picture of a chicken head. The left hemisphere (which controls language) says that the chicken claw goes with the chicken head.

The right hemisphere points the left hand at a picture of a snow shovel. The left hemisphere, which controls language and therefore must report what the participant is doing, decides that the shovel is used to clean up after chickens. (It does not see the snow-covered house.)

with the snow scene presented to the right hemisphere, and (2) with the right hand (controlled by the left hemisphere), she might select a picture of a chicken head to go with the claw presented to the left hemisphere. Both responses fit the relevant stimulus because the response mode—pointing—is one that is controlled by each hemisphere. But what happens when the patient is asked to explain the choices she has made? Even though the reason for selecting the shovel (by the nonverbal right hemisphere) is not accessible to the verbal "explanation module" in the left hemisphere, the response is typically immediate and involves such answers as, "Oh, that's simple. The chicken claw goes with the chicken, and you need a shovel to clean out the chicken shed" (Gazzaniga, 1985). Such a response fits nicely with the postulates of self-perception theory. Behavior (selecting the two pictures) is observed, and what it must mean is instantly computed by a module in the brain dedicated to sense making or explanation.

 We have seen that self-perception theory maintains that people infer their attitudes from their behavior, thus providing an alternative explanation of why people often change their attitudes when the attitudes conflict with their actions. Experimental evidence, however, has shown that arousal is indeed generated when behavior is not consistent with attitudes and that this arousal does indeed often motivate attitude change. Nevertheless, researchers have reconciled dissonance theory and self-perception theory, showing that dissonance theory best explains attitude change for preexisting clear-cut attitudes, whereas self-perception theory best explains attitude change for less clear-cut attitudes.

BEYOND COGNITIVE CONSISTENCY TO BROADER RATIONALIZATION

The core of dissonance theory is the idea that people find psychological inconsistency uncomfortable and therefore engage in psychological work to lessen the discomfort. There are other tensions, of course, that produce similar types of psychological discomfort and elicit similar efforts at rationalization and justification. Two relatively recent theories have been offered to explain how we respond to two such sources of discomfort. One deals with the discomfort that comes from thinking about the problems associated with the broader social and political system to which we are committed. The other deals with the extreme discomfort—indeed, the terror—that comes with the realization of the inevitability of death.

System Justification Theory

Chapter 3 discusses people's need to think well of themselves, or what some have called ego justification motives (Jost, Banaji, & Nosek, 2004). Chapter 12 discusses people's need to think well of the groups to which they belong, or group justification motives. But beyond the desire to think highly of our own talents, virtues, and habits or to take pride in being, say, a Canadian, a Californian, a Christian, or a Cowboys fan, there is a desire to think highly of the broader political and social systems to which we belong. We are a part of the existing social, cultural, and political order in which we live, and we therefore feel some psychological pressure to see it as fair, just, and desirable (Jost & Banaji, 1994; Jost et al., 2004).

Those who have studied these system justification tendencies have noted that social and political systems do not serve everyone's needs equally. Those who benefit the most from a given system, such as those who are wealthier and occupy more powerful positions in society, have both a psychological and an economic incentive to defend the system. Those who don't benefit from the system (or are even disadvantaged by it) obviously do not have an economic incentive to defend the system, but they do have a psychological incentive to do so. Believing that the world is or should be fair, combined with salient evidence of inequality, can generate a fair amount of ideological dissonance. Extolling the virtues of the prevailing system is typically an easier way of reducing that dissonance than bringing about effective change. Protest is hard; justification is easy.

Common observations that seem to support **system justification theory** are the fact that women often feel that they deserve lower pay than men doing the same work (Jost, 1997; Major, 1994) and the fact that low-income groups in the United States tend not to support more egalitarian economic policies over the status quo (Fong, 2001; Jost, Pelham, Sheldon, & Sullivan, 2003). Some of the most interesting support

for the system justification perspective comes from studies that look at compensatory stereotypes, or beliefs that those who occupy less privileged roles in a society nonetheless derive a number of compensatory benefits: "Low-income people may be poor, but they're happier than the wealthy." "Women may not have much power, but they're nicer, warmer, and more socially connected than men." Exposure to such stereotypes is thought to give ideological support to the status quo, making people more accepting of current gender roles ("In general, relations between men and women are fair"; "The division of labor in families generally operates as it should") and more accepting of the broader sociocultural status quo ("Most policies serve the greater good"; "Everyone has a fair shot

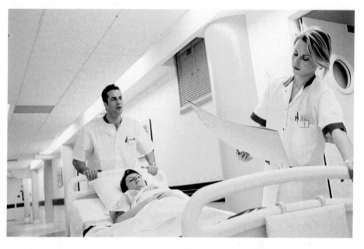

at wealth and happiness"). People are also more supportive of the status quo after they have been exposed to compensatory stereotypes of the poor being happier and more honest than the rich (Jost & Kay, 2005; Kay & Jost, 2003).

System Justification To defend the broader social and political systems to which they belong, economically disadvantaged people often defend their own disadvantage. Female nurses like the one depicted here sometimes admit to feeling that they deserve to make less money than their male counterparts doing the same work.

Terror Management Theory

Humans may be the only organisms that know with certainty that they will die. That's not such a blessing. Indeed, many people find that thinking about the inevitability of their own death—really thinking about it and letting it sink in—brings on a level of anxiety that verges on debilitating. People need to deal with that potentially crippling anxiety in order to get on with life. **Terror management theory (TMT)** specifies the processes people use to do so. The most common way that people deal with the problem is simply to deny it—to maintain that it is only their bodies and this particular earthly existence that will come to an end. Most people the world over believe they will go on living in some form after their lives on earth have ended. But beyond this common form of what has been called "the denial of death" (Becker, 1973), people can derive some solace from believing that although they personally will cease to exist, many of the things they value will live on. For many people, this sort of indirect immortality is achieved by thinking about their role as parent. They won't live on, but their children and grandchildren will. This is probably why men who are reminded of the inevitability of their own death express an interest in having more children (Wisman & Goldenberg, 2005).

TMT emphasizes two other ways that people try to comfort themselves with thoughts of symbolic immortality. One is by thinking of themselves as connected to a broader culture, worldview, and set of valued institutions that will live on after they personally have died. You will certainly die at some point, but many of the things you value most—America; freedom and democracy; Christianity, Buddhism, or Islam; or even your alma mater or favorite sports franchise—will live on long after. To the extent that people are closely connected to such institutions, they symbolically live on along with them. This suggests that people will most vigorously embrace their broader worldview and prevailing culture and institutions when they are reminded of their own inevitable death.

Of course, we can't be said to live on, even symbolically, with a broad cultural institution whose norms and values we haven't adhered to. Our connection to the institutions that live on must be solid and meaningful. This results in the second way that TMT maintains that people strive for immortality: by striving to achieve and maintain high self-esteem. Self-esteem comes from the sense that we have met or exceeded the standards specified by the values, norms, and roles of a given cultural worldview. By meeting those standards, we satisfy the criteria of being meaningfully connected to that worldview, allowing us to feel symbolically immortal.

The way that terror management theorists have tested their ideas—that people will defend their worldviews and strive for self-esteem with particular vigor when they are especially aware of their own mortality—is to subject participants to various mortality salience manipulations. The most common way this has been done is to have participants write out responses to two directives: (1) "Briefly describe the emotions that the thought of your own death arouses in you," and (2) "Jot down, as specifically as you can, what you think will happen to *you* as you physically die." In other studies, the same objective has been accomplished by having participants fill out surveys either in front of a funeral home or at a control location not associated with death or by showing participants pictures of fatal car accidents or control photographs not connected to death.

Consistent with the tenets of TMT, mortality salience manipulations have been shown to make people more hostile to people who criticize their country (Greenberg et al., 1990), more committed to their ingroups and more hostile to outgroups (Dechesne, Greenberg, Arndt, & Schimel, 2000; Greenberg et al., 1990), more punitive towards those who challenge prevailing laws and established procedures (Rosenblatt, Greenberg, Solomon, Pyszczynski, & Lyon, 1989), and more reluctant to use cultural artifacts such as a crucifix or the U.S. flag for a mundane, utilitarian purpose (Greenberg, Simon, Porteus, Pyszczynski, & Solomon, 1995). Making death salient, in other words, makes people want to uphold the values of the institutions with which they are identified that will live on after them.

It isn't difficult to think of potential political implications of terror management concerns. For example, in the run-up to the 2004 U.S. presidential election, survey respondents were asked their opinions about either the Democratic challenger, John Kerry, or the incumbent Republican president, George W. Bush. Some did so after the usual mortality salience manipulation, others after writing about their experience with dental pain. Because Bush, as the incumbent president, was the head of the country and was seen by many as the leader of the fight against Al Queda and other terrorist organizations, the investigators predicted that survey respondents would be more favorable to Bush and less favorable to Kerry after a mortality salience manipulation.

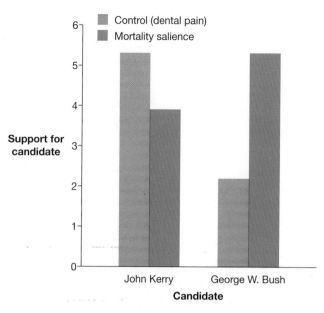

FIGURE 6.9 Mortality Salience and Support for President George W. Bush and Candidate John Kerry during the 2004 U.S. Presidential Election Survey respondents' attitudes toward presidential candidates John Kerry and George W. Bush. Some gave their responses under normal survey conditions; others after mortality salience manipulation.

As **Figure 6.9** indicates, their prediction was confirmed (Landau, Solomon, Greenberg, Cohen, & Pyszczynski, 2004). Convergent support for this idea comes from an analysis of public opinion polls during that election that showed that support for Bush tended to go up whenever the terrorist threat level announced by the Department of Homeland Security went up; presumably, heightened threat warnings made the public's mortality very salient (Willer, 2004).

Terror management concerns are certainly not unique to Americans. Iranian respondents read about statements issued by either a radical ("The U.S. represents the world power that Allah wants us to destroy") or a peaceful Islamist ("One should treat other humans with respect and care, no matter what racial, ethnic, or religious background"). Some did so after a mortality salience manipulation, others after a control procedure. Participants in the mortality salience condition expressed more support of the radical Islamist and martyrdom attacks than those in the control condition (Pyszczynski et al., 2006).

Considerable evidence also supports the TMT contention that awareness of the inevitability of death increases striving for self-esteem (Arndt, Schimel, & Goldenberg, 2003; Kasser & Sheldon, 2000; Taubman-Ben-Ari, Florian, & Mikulincer, 1999). In one particularly telling study, participants in one condition read an essay stating that the consensus scientific opinion regarding reports of near-death experiences—the feeling of leaving and looking down at one's body, of moving down a long, brightly lit tunnel, and so on—is that these experiences are exactly what we would expect, given the makeup of the brain, and that they do not suggest in any way that there might be life after death. Participants in another condition read that the consensus scientific opinion was just the opposite, that reports such as these point to the plausibility of some sort of life after death. All participants then received favorable feedback about themselves from very dubious sources, such as horoscopes and questionable personality tests, and then rated the validity of the feedback they received. Those who read the essay that cast doubt on life after death rated the feedback as more valid than those who read the essay that encouraged belief in an afterlife. In other words, if we can believe that there is life after death, we needn't be so concerned with living on symbolically, and so the need for self-esteem is reduced (Dechesne et al., 2003).

We have seen that people's tendencies to rationalize go beyond their attempts to resolve personal cognitive inconsistencies. People are also motivated to see the broader social and political systems in which they live as fair and just and good. They are also motivated to deal with the anxiety that comes from the knowledge of human mortality, which they often do by bolstering their worldview and their own place in it.

Summary

Predicting Behavior from Attitudes

- It can be surprisingly difficult at times to predict behavior from attitudes because attitudes are sometimes *ambiguous* or *inconsistent*; attitudes sometimes *conflict* with other powerful determinants of behavior; attitudes are sometimes based on *secondhand information* about the object; attitudes (for example, toward the environment) and the attitude targets we actually confront (for example, whether to donate to Greenpeace) may be at different *levels of generality* and may be "about" very different things; and some of our *behavior is automatic* and can bypass our conscious attitudes altogether.

Predicting Attitudes from Behavior ~~consistency~~

- Behavior can have very substantial effects on attitudes. Most of the research showing such effects grew out of *cognitive consistency theories*, which stress how much people value consistency among their various attitudes and between their attitudes and behavior. ~~balance~~

- *Balance theory* was the earliest consistency theory. It specifies that people desire balance among their beliefs and sentiments and thus prefer to hold attitudes that "follow from" other attitudes ("My enemy's enemy is my friend") and prefer to behave in ways that align with their attitudes.

- *Cognitive dissonance theory* is based on the idea that people experience *dissonance*, or discomfort, when attitudes and behavior are inconsistent. People therefore often try to reduce the dissonance they are feeling by bringing their attitudes in line with their behavior.

- People engage in dissonance reduction when making decisions. After making a choice between two objects or courses of action, they find "hidden attractions" in the chosen alternative and previously undetected flaws in the unchosen alternative. This reduces the dissonance aroused by having to give up some desired object or action.

- People engage in *effort justification* when they exert effort toward some goal and the goal turns out to be disappointing. They justify their expenditure of energy by deciding that the goal is truly worthwhile.

- People attempt to reduce dissonance in *induced-compliance* situations—that is, in situations in which other people prompt them to do or say something, with little incentive or coercion, that is contrary to their beliefs. For example, when induced by another person to argue for a position at variance with their true attitudes, people who are undercompensated for doing so feel that they must justify their behavior and typically do so by changing their attitudes to better align with their behavior.

- Dissonance resulting from inconsistency between attitudes and behavior should be felt only when there is *free choice* (or the illusion of it) to engage in the behavior; there is *insufficient justification* for the behavior; the behavior has *negative consequences* either for the self or for another; and the consequences of the behavior were *foreseeable.*

- The negative effects of psychological inconsistency, and the negative effects of threats to self-identity and self-esteem more generally, can be offset or reduced by engaging in self-affirmation—that is, by taking note of and affirming other important elements of our identity, such as our important values.

- Dissonance is apparently universal, but there are cultural differences in the conditions that prompt people to experience it. For example, the Japanese tend to experience postdecision dissonance only when asked to think about how another person would choose.

Self-Perception Theory

- *Self-perception theory* originated as an alternative explanation for the results obtained in dissonance experiments. It is based on the premise that people do not change their attitudes to align with their behavior because they are motivated to justify them; they do so because they observe their behavior and the circumstances in which it occurs and infer, just as an observer might, what their attitudes must be.

- Whereas self-perception may well play a role in generating the effects in some dissonance experiments, the empirical evidence clearly indicates that there is often a motivational component as well. "Mere" self-perception appears to account for attitude change in situations in which attitudes are weak or unclear to begin with, whereas more motivated, dissonance reduction processes are invoked when attitudes are more strongly held to begin with.

Beyond Cognitive Consistency to Broader Rationalization

- According to *system justificaiton theory*, in addition to *ego* and *group* justification motives that stem from the need to think well of themselves and of the groups to which they belong, people are also motivated to justify the broader political and social systems of which they are a part. One way this is done is through stereotypes that play up the advantages of belonging to relatively disadvantaged groups, such as the belief that the poor are happier than the rich and that women get more from being nurturing and developing social connections than they lose from their relative lack of power and influence.

- The knowledge that we are all destined to die can elicit paralyzing anxiety that needs to be managed if we are to get on with our lives. *Terror management theory* maintains that people often cope with this anxiety by striving for symbolic immortality through their offspring and through the institutions and cultural worldviews that live on after their own individual death and by convincing themselves that they are valued members of their cultures who have embodied the values of the prevailing worldview.

Key Terms

balance theory (p. 207)

cognitive dissonance theory (p. 208)

effort justification (p. 210)

induced (forced) compliance (p. 211)

interpersonal simulations (p. 220)

prime (p. 205)

self-affirmation (p. 217)

self-perception theory (p. 219)

system justification theory (p. 229)

terror management theory (p. 229)

Further Reading

Bargh, J. A., Chen, M., & Burrows, L. (1996). Automaticity of social behavior: Direct effects of trait construct and stereotype activation on action. *Journal of Personality and Social Psychology, 71,* 230–244. A "modern classic," this paper reports the results of several experiments that demonstrate that we can behave reflexively in response to cues in the environment.

Festinger, L. (1957). *A theory of cognitive dissonance.* Stanford, CA: Stanford University Press. The original statement of one of the most influential theories in the history of social psychology.

Pyszczynski, T. A., Solomon, S., & Greenberg, J. (2003). *In the wake of 9/11: The psychology of terror.* Washington, DC: American Psychological Association. An application of terror management theory to the events that followed the terrorist attacks on the World Trade Center and the Pentagon.

Wilson, T. D. (2002). *Strangers to ourselves: Discovering the adaptive unconscious.* Cambridge, MA: Harvard University Press. An insightful review of current thinking about the impact of nonconscious processes on human behavior.

⑤ Online Study Tools

StudySpace

Go to StudySpace, wwnorton.com/studyspace, to access additional review and enrichment materials, including the following resources for each chapter:

Organize

- Study Plan
- Chapter Outline
- Quiz+ Assessment

Learn

- Ebook
- Chapter Review

- Critical-Thinking Questions
- Visual Quizzes
- Vocabulary Flashcards

Connect

- Apply It! Exercises
- Author Insights Podcasts
- Social Psychology in the News

Emotion

EADWEARD MUYBRIDGE WAS BORN in England in 1830 and at the age of 22 emigrated to San Francisco, California, where he ran a bookshop with his brother. On July 2, 1860, Muybridge boarded a stagecoach bound for St. Louis, Missouri, where he was to catch a train and then make his way to Europe in search of rare books. In northeastern Texas, the driver of the stagecoach lost control of the horses, and the coach careened down a mountainside and crashed. Muybridge was thrown violently headfirst into a tree, probably damaging his orbitofrontal cortex, a part of the brain often harmed during head trauma. The orbitofrontal cortex is connected to brain regions involved in emotion, including the amygdala (see Chapter 9), and it helps us rely on our emotions to make decisions and act appropriately in different social situations (Rolls, 2000).

Miraculously, Muybridge survived his accident and made the trip to England, where he spent six years recuperating and becoming a photographer. He returned to California in 1866, but he was not the same man. He expressed little interest in friends or in socializing, showed no concern over his dress or hygiene, and expressed little love for his new son. Muybridge's emotional problems were most evident when he became convinced that his wife had had an affair while he was away on assignment, taking photos of Yosemite. Agitated and suspicious, Muybridge took a train to Calistoga in Napa Valley, California, where his wife's suspected paramour, Harry Larkyns, was working on a ranch. Finding Larkyns with a group of friends, Muybridge coolly greeted Larkyns and without a trace of emotion killed him with a bullet to the chest. At his ensuing trial, the jury acquitted Muybridge on the grounds of "justifiable homicide."

The case of Eadweard Muybridge raises a fascinating question: What would our lives be like if we couldn't be guided by our emotions? Many writers in the traditions of Western thought would say that life would be more balanced and reasonable

Eadweard Muybridge   (A) After suffering an accident that may have injured his orbito-frontal cortex, Eadweard Muybridge was prone to emotional outbursts and inappropriate behavior. (B) Muybridge (also known as Helios) was an innovative photographer who took a series of photographs of Yosemite, including this photo of himself perched on a thin rock ledge 2,000 feet above the river below.

(Oatley, 2004). The emotions have long been viewed as disruptive of harmonious social bonds, and many important thinkers have portrayed the emotions as enemies of reason and sound moral judgment. Social psychology has arrived at a different conclusion, maintaining that emotions are vital to our ability to get along with others, as revealed in Muybridge's emotional deficits and social difficulties.

In this chapter, we will seek answers to five enduring questions about emotions: To what extent are emotions universal, and to what extent do they vary across cultures? What is the role of emotions in our social relationships? How do emotions influence our reasoning? To what extent are emotions shaped by our bodily responses? And finally, What is happiness? Before we tackle these questions, let's first define emotion, which is no simple task.

CHARACTERIZING EMOTION

Light is something everyone knows when they see it, but it is exceptionally hard to define. The same is true of the emotions. When you experience cold feet before making a speech, what is that experience like? What happens when a stranger's anonymous kindness moves you to tears? To begin our study of the emotions, we must first consider two questions: How do emotions, such as anger, guilt, or gratitude, differ from other feeling states, such as moods or general feelings of well-being or despair? And what are the components of emotions that differentiate them from one another?

Differentiating Emotions from Other Feelings

People's waking lives are filled with different feelings: moods ("I just feel invincible today"); deep, enduring states that clinicians classify as emotional disorders ("I've been depressed for two months and feel no joy"); and emotions, the focus of this chapter. How do emotions differ from moods and emotional disorders?

First, emotions are *brief*; they last for seconds or minutes, not hours or days as moods and disorders do. Facial expressions of emotion typically last between 1 and 5 seconds (Ekman, 1992). Many of the physiological responses that accompany emotion—sweaty palms, the blush, and goosebumps, for example—last dozens of seconds or minutes. In contrast, the moods that we experience—for example, when we feel irritable or blue—last for hours and even days. Emotional disorders, such as depression, last for weeks or months.

Emotions are also *specific*. We feel emotions about specific people and events. Philosophers call the focus of an emotional experience its "intentional object," and here again there is a difference between emotions and moods and disorders. When you're angry, you have a very clear sense of what you're angry about (for example, the embarrassing story your dad has told about your first date). In contrast, when you're in an irritable mood, it is not so obvious why you feel the way you do, and the intentional object may not be clear (although it might be all too clear to other people!).

Finally, emotions typically help individuals with their *social goals*. Unlike general mood states and disorders, emotions motivate people to act in specific ways that promote important relationships (DeSteno & Salovey, 1996; Frijda & Mesquita, 1994; Keltner & Haidt, 1999; McCullough, Kilpatrick, Emmons, & Larson, 2001; Oatley & Jenkins, 1992; Parrott, 2001; Salovey & Rodin, 1989; Salovey & Rothman, 1991; Tiedens & Leach, 2004). Anger motivates people to redress injustice. Gratitude rewards others for their cooperative actions. Guilt motivates us to make amends when we have harmed other people. Not every episode of emotion, we hasten to note, is beneficial. Some of our anger, for example, may produce maladaptive outcomes (for example, making sarcastic comments to a traffic cop). But in general, emotions motivate goal-directed behavior that typically helps us navigate our social environment. Having defined **emotions** as brief, specific, socially oriented states, let's now consider in greater depth the different components of emotion.

emotions Brief, specific psychological and physiological responses that help humans meet social goals.

The Components of Emotion

One of the complexities in the study of emotion is that emotions involve many components. These include ancient physiological responses shared by all mammals (indeed, that are shared with reptiles; the part of the brain that is the primary seat of the rage and fight-or-flight responses is known as the reptilian brain). At the other end of the complexity continuum, emotions also include more cognitive factors rooted in language (Lang, Greenwald, Bradley, & Hamm, 1993; Levenson, 1999). Emotions arise as a result of **appraisal processes**, which refer to how we evaluate events and objects in our environment according to their relation to our current goals (Lazarus, 1991; Smith & Ellsworth, 1985). The appraisals that trigger different emotions, known as **core-relational themes**, are fairly similar across cultures (Lazarus, 1991; Mauro, Sato, & Tucker, 1992; Mesquita, 2003; Mesquita & Ellsworth, 2001; Mesquita & Frijda, 1992; Scherer, 1997). For example, appraisals of loss trigger sadness in different parts of the world; violations of rights trigger anger; expressions of affection trigger love; and undeserved suffering triggers compassion (Boucher & Brandt, 1981; Rozin et al., 1997).

appraisal processes The ways we evaluate events and objects in our environment according to their relation to our current goals.

core-relational themes Distinct themes, such as danger or offense or fairness, that define the essential meaning for each emotion.

"Nothing's either good or bad but thinking makes it so."

—William Shakespeare, *Hamlet*

In the **primary appraisal stage**, unconscious, fast, and automatic appraisals of whether the even is consistent or inconsistent with the person's goals give rise to general pleasant or unpleasant feelings (Lazarus, 1991; LeDoux, 1993; Mischel & Shoda, 1995; Zajonc, 1980). These more automatic appraisals involve the amygdala and are triggered by stimuli like smiling and angry faces, snakes, pleasant and unpleasant sounds, odors, the relative lightness and darkness of an object, as well as whether its edges are curved or sharp and angular (Dimberg & Öhman, 1996; Murphy & Zajonc, 1993). In the **secondary appraisal stage**, more specific appraisals—for example, regarding who is responsible for the event, whether or not it is consistent with social norms, and how fair it is—transform initial pleasant or unpleasant feelngs into more specific emotions, such as fear, anger, pride, gratitude, or sympathy (Barrett, 2006; Lazarus, 1991; Roseman, 1991; Russell, 2003; Smith & Ellsworth, 1985).

Appraisal processes get emotions going. Once under way, emotions involve many different responses. We express our emotions with facial expressions, voice (Scherer, Johnstone, & Klasmeyer, 2003), posture, physical touch (Hertenstein, 2002), and in language, art, poetry, and music, which give shape to our conscious experience of emotion (Feldman-Barrett, Mesquita, Ochsner, & Gross, 2007; Oatley, 2003; Wilson & Gilbert, 2008). When feeling different emotions, we see our lives and the world through an emotion-tinted lens, selectively perceiving emotion-congruent events in our current environment and recalling emotion-related episodes from the past (Niedenthal, 2008). For example, when feeling intense fear, people are more likely to hear threatening words (for example, "death") in one ear when asked to attend to information presented to the other ear; they are more likely to interpret words with multiple meanings, known as ambiguous homophones ("dye/die"), in terms of their threatening meaning; and they are more likely to recall threatening episodes from the past (Mathews & MadLeod,1994). Emotions involve activation in specific regions of the brain (such as the orbitofrontal cortex and amygdala), physiological responses in the body, and neurotransmitters such as dopamine or oxytocin (Davidson, Pizzagalli, Nitzschke, & Kalin, 2003; Levenson, 2003).

Social psychologists studying emotions are like the proverbial group of blind men asked to describe the elephant when touching different parts of its body. Answers to the questions depend on what component of emotion is being measured. Having a rudimentary knowledge of the emotional landscape, we are ready to tackle our first empirical question: In what ways are emotions universal, and in what ways do they vary across cultures?

 We have seen that the emotional landscape involves different kinds of experiences, including emotions, moods, and disorders. Emotions are brief, specific experiences that help individuals meet social goals. Emotions involve many components. They arise out of primary appraisal processes—quick automatic evaluations of whether a stimulus is good or bad—and more complex secondary appraisal processes—for example, who is responsible or whether the event is fair. Emotions are reflected in different kinds of expressive behavior, in our language, in physiological responses in the brain and body, and in how we think.

UNIVERSALITY AND CULTURAL SPECIFICITY OF EMOTION

As Charles Darwin circumnavigated the globe on the *Beagle*, he encountered many indigenous peoples living as hunter-gatherers. When he and the rest of the crew first encountered the Fuegians of Tierra del Fuego, Chile, the Fuegians greeted them naked with arms flailing wildly. The crew of the *Beagle* was dumbfounded at this emotional expression—except for Darwin. Darwin took this display to be a greeting display of affection and was the first to make friends with the Fuegians by reciprocating their friendly chest slaps. Darwin's experience of this first encounter illustrates the question we answer in this section: To what extent are expressions of emotion universal, and how do they vary across cultures? The Fuegians developed a specific way of expressing affection to strangers—to flail their arms. Underneath this idiosyncratic expression, though, is likely to be some kind of universal display (open-handed gestures of warmth and kindness).

Evolutionary and cultural approaches arrive at different answers to the question of universality and cultural variability of emotional expression. An evolutionary approach assumes that emotions are biologically based adaptations that increase the likelihood that our genes will be passed on to the next generation (Ekman, 1992; Nesse, 1990; Öhman, 1986; Tooby & Cosmides, 1992). This is because, the reasoning

---

BOX 7.1   FOCUS ON NEUROSCIENCE

Felt and False Smiles

Are smiles emotional or not? This seemingly modest question has been the subject of intense debate among emotion researchers. How can the smile be the primary signal of positive emotion, as Ekman (1993) asserts, and at the same time occur during anger, disgust, or grief? Answers to these kinds of questions can be found in *The Mechanism of Human Facial Expression*, published in 1862 by a French physician named Duchenne de Boulogne. In this book, Duchenne detailed the results of his research on stimulating the facial muscles with electrical currents. He identified the actions of two muscles: (1) the *zygomatic major* muscle, which pulls the lip corners upward, and (2) the *orbicularis oculi,* which surrounds the eye and in contracting causes crow's-feet to form, the upper cheek to raise, and a pouch to form under the lower eyelid.

Based on this anatomical distinction, Ekman has coined the term the *Duchenne smile*, which is the smile that involves the action of the *orbicularis oculi* and tends to be associated with the experience of positive emotion. Research has shown that the Duchenne smile differs in many ways from smiles

Different Kinds of Smiles   (A) A polite, non-Duchenne smile, and (B) a Duchenne, or enjoyment, smile, as demonstrated by Paul Ekman.

that do not involve this muscle action. Duchenne smiles tend to last between 1 and 5 seconds, and the lip corners tend to be raised to equal degrees on both sides (Frank, Ekman, & Friesen, 1993). Duchenne smiles tend to be associated with activity in the left anterior portion of the brain, whereas non-Duchenne smiles are associated with activity in the right anterior portion of the brain (Ekman & Davidson, 1993; Ekman,

Davidson, & Friesen, 1990). This is consistent with a rich literature showing that positive emotions are more strongly associated with activation in the left side of the brain (Davidson et al., 2003). Duchenne smiles are associated with pleasure, whereas in some studies, non-Duchenne smiles have been shown to be associated with negative emotion (Hess, Banse, & Kappas, 1995; Keltner & Bonanno, 1997; Ruch, 1995).

goes, emotions such as fear enable adaptive responses to threats to survival, whereas emotions such as love, compassion, and jealousy help form and maintain reproductive relationships just as critical to gene replication (Keltner, 2009). The many components of emotion—facial expression, vocalization, physiological response—enable adaptive responses to the threats to survival and opportunities related to gene replication faced by all humans. By implication, these components of emotion, including facial expression, should be universal.

In contrast, the cultural approach assumes that emotions are strongly influenced by self-construals, values, roles, institutions, and socialization practices and that these vary in different cultures (Ellsworth, 1994; Markus & Kitayama, 1991; Mesquita, 2003; Oatley, 1993). As a result, people in different cultures should express their emotions in much different ways. Whereas evolutionary approaches make strong claims about the universality of emotional expression, cultural approaches predict significant cultural variation. Like many great debates about human nature, both perspectives will prove to be correct. Let's begin our study of emotional expression with Charles Darwin, a founding figure in the field.

Darwin and Emotional Expression

In 1872, Charles Darwin published *The Expression of Emotions in Man and Animals*, a book that he wrote feverishly in four months. In Darwin's time, creationists held that God had given humans special facial muscles that allowed them to express uniquely human sentiments—emotions like love, sympathy, and rapture—that are unknown to "lower" species. The clear implication is that human emotional expression differs dramatically from the emotional expression of other species—a direct challenge to Darwin's theory that humans descended from other primate species.

To counter this thinking, Darwin proposed his **principle of serviceable habits,** which maintains that expressions of human emotion that we observe today derive from habitual patterns of behavior that proved useful in the evolution of our primate and mammalian predecessors. For example, all the observable signs of anger—the furrowed brow and teeth display, the tightened posture and clenched fists, the fierce growl—are vestiges of threat displays and attack behavior observed in our mammalian relatives that were useful in conflicts and aggressive encounters.

Darwin's analysis generated three hypotheses about emotional expression. First is the prediction of universality. Darwin reasoned that because all humans have the same 30 to 40 facial muscles and have used these muscles to communicate similar emotions in the past, people in all cultures should communicate and perceive emotion in a similar fashion. A second prediction concerns the similarity between our emotional expression and that of our primate and mammalian ancestors. Darwin reasoned that because humans share an evolutionary history with other primates and mammals, our emotional expressions should resemble the emotional expressions of other species. In support of this thesis, Darwin drew fascinating parallels between human emotion and the expressions of animals in the London zoo as well as his favorite dogs at home. Finally, Darwin argued that blind individuals, lacking the rich visual input a culture provides in how to display emotion, will still show similar expressions as sighted individuals because the tendency to express emotions in particular ways is encoded in the human nervous system.

The Universality of Facial Expression

Interested in gathering data about the universality of emotional expression, Darwin queried English missionaries living in other cultures about whether they had

principle of serviceable habits Charles Darwin's thesis that emotional expressions are remnants of full-blown behaviors that helped our primate and mammalian predecessors meet important goals in the past.

Signaling Intentions Darwin believed that animals signal their intentions through displays such as (A) this dog signaling his hostile intentions toward another dog and (B) this dog signaling submission to another dog.

observed expressions not seen in Victorian England. The result? They had not. Of course, his question was rather biased and may have encouraged the answer he sought. Nevertheless, Darwin was one of the first scientists to use cross-cultural methods, and approximately 100 years later, his work served as inspiration for an important series of studies carried out by Sylvan Tomkins, Paul Ekman, Wallace Friesen, and Carroll Izard (Ekman, Sorenson, & Friesen, 1969; Izard, 1971; Tomkins, 1962, 1963).

Let's focus on the most notable research in this area, work by Paul Ekman and Wallace Friesen. To test Darwin's universality hypothesis, Ekman and Friesen initially took more than 3,000 photos of people well trained in expression, such as actors, as they portrayed anger, disgust, fear, happiness, sadness, and surprise according to Darwin's descriptions of the muscle configurations. In a first set of studies, they presented photos of these six emotions to people in Japan, Brazil, Argentina, Chile, and the United States. The participant's task was to select from six emotion terms the single term that best matched the feeling the person was showing in each photo. The results? A home run for Darwin. Across these five cultures, accuracy rates were typically between 80 and 90 percent for the six emotions, while chance guessing (randomly selecting one term out of six) would be 16.6 percent (Ekman et al., 1969). The critics, however, were unconvinced. They noted a fundamental flaw in this study: participants in these cultures had all seen Western media, and they may have learned how to identify the expressions via exposure to U.S. actors portraying those emotions. The universality in judging emotion that Ekman and Friesen documented may have been produced only by the media that these cultures share.

Ekman and Friesen now faced a surprisingly difficult challenge: to find a culture that had little or no exposure to Westerners or to Western media. In light of these concerns, Ekman went to Papua New Guinea to study the Fore (pronounced "foray"), a hill tribe living in Stone Age conditions. Ekman lived with the tribe for six months. The Fore who participated in Ekman's study had seen no movies or magazines, did

Charles Darwin   Not only did Charles Darwin formulate the theory of evolution, he also studied emotional expressions in non-human species and humans and sought to document that human emotional expressions have their parallels in other species, and are universal to people of all cultures.

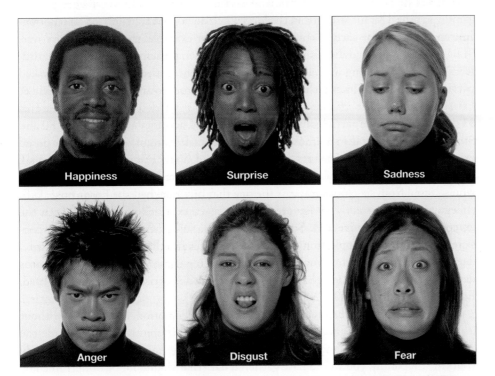

Facial Expressions   Groundbreaking studies by Ekman, Friesen, and Izard identified these six facial expressions as universal.

FIGURE 7.1 **Scientific Method: Universality of Facial Expressions**

Hypothesis: Facial expressions of emotion have been shaped by evolution and are universal.

Research Method:

1. American actors were photographed showing expressions that conveyed emotions such as happiness, sadness disgust, anger, and fear.

2. These photographs were then shown to members of the isolated and preliterate Fore tribe in New Guinea.

3. All participants who saw the photos were asked to pick the emotion story that matched each photograph.

4. Then the procedure was reversed. New Guinea tribesmen were photographed portraying various facial expressions, and American college students were then asked to pick the emotion label that matched each photograph.

Happiness

Disgust

Results: Fore and American participants reliably judged the emotion expressed in the photos at much higher levels of accuracy than expected by chance.

Conclusion: Facial expressions of emotion are universal.

Source: Ekman, Sorenson, & Friesen (1969).

not speak English or Pidgin (a combination of English and a native language), had never lived in Western settlements, and had never worked for Westerners. After gaining approval for his study from the local witch doctor, Ekman devised an emotion-appropriate story for each of the six emotions. For example, the sadness story was: "The person's child had died, and he felt sad." He then presented photos of three different expressions along with a story that matched one of the expressions and asked participants, both adults and children, to match the story to an expression (Ekman & Friesen, 1971). Here chance guessing would have yielded an accuracy rate of 33 percent. The Fore participants, however, achieved accuracy rates between 80 and 90 percent in judging the six emotions. In another task, Ekman videotaped the posed expressions of Fore participants as they imagined being the individual in the six emotion-specific stories and then presented these clips to Western college students, who selected from six emotion terms the one that best matched the Fore's pose. U.S. college students correctly interpreted the posed expressions of the Fore, with the exception of fear (**Figure 7.1**). Subsequent studies in dozens of cultures have consistently found that people from cultures that differ in religion, political structure, development, and self-construals nevertheless agree in how they label the photos depicting anger, disgust, fear, happiness, sadness, and surprise (Ekman, 1984, 1993; Elfenbein & Ambady, 2002, 2003; Izard, 1971, 1994).

This study was a catalyst for the scientific study of emotion, but it is not without its limitations. How might you have done the study differently had you made the arduous trip to the highland hills of Papua New Guinea and conducted the study yourself? Hopefully, you would have gathered data that would not be undermined by the **free-response critique**: in Ekman's study and almost all other judgment studies, researchers provided the terms with which participants labeled the facial expressions.

free-response critique A critique of Ekman and Friesen's emotion studies based on the fact that researchers provided the terms with which participants labeled facial expressions rather than allowing the participants to label the expressions with their own words.

If given the chance to label the faces in their own words (with free responses), perhaps people from different cultures would choose different terms that reflect culture-specific concepts. For example, people from interdependent cultures are more likely to think of positive emotions in terms of socially engaging terms (for example, "harmony") rather than disengaging terms (for example, "pride") (Kitayama, Karasawa, & Mesquita, 2004). If the Fore had been allowed to label the photos with their own words, they might have labeled a smile as "gratitude" rather than "happiness" or label it with some concept that does not map onto Western conceptions of emotion. But in fact, when participants in different cultures are allowed to use their own words to label facial expressions, they do show high degrees of similarity (Haidt & Keltner, 1999; Izard, 1971).

What about Darwin's second claim, that human emotional expressions resemble those of our mammalian relatives, given our shared evolutionary history? This idea has a firm anatomical foundation: our closest primate relatives, chimpanzees, have facial musculatures very similar to our own (Matsumoto, Keltner, Shiota, & O'Sullivan, 2008). This second idea of Darwin's has proved remarkably fruitful in helping researchers understand the origins of different emotional expressions. For example, chimps show threat displays and whimpers that would surprise you in how closely they resemble our own displays of anger and sadness. When affiliating in friendly fashion, nonhuman primates show a teeth-revealing display known as the "fear grimace" that resembles our smile, but when playing and wrestling, they show the "open mouth pant hoot," the predecessor to the human laugh (Preuschoft, 1992).

This interest in the parallels between human and nonhuman display helped reveal the deeper functions of a seemingly most human emotion—embarrassment. Initial studies of people in embarrassing situations (making funny faces, sucking on pacifiers in front of friends) have identified the distinct nonverbal display of embarrassment. When people feel embarrassed, they shift their gaze down, they smile in a compressed, self-conscious way, they often touch their faces, and they move their heads down and typically to the left, exposing their necks (Harris, 2001; Keltner, 1995). What is the meaning of these behaviors? Careful cross-species comparisons revealed that human displays of embarrassment resemble appeasement displays in other mammals (Keltner & Buswell, 1997). Embarrassment signals remorse for

Embarrassment and Appeasement and the Maintenance of Social Bonds
To maintain harmonious social relations, humans may exhibit displays that remind us of appeasement displays in nonhuman species. (A) This little boy would rather be elsewhere, but instead of running away, he averts his gaze from the little girl and exhibits a pained smile of embarrassment. (B) This prairie dog lies on its back and extends its arms and legs toward the other animal in a sign of appeasement.

social transgressions, prompting forgiveness and reconciliation when people violate social norms (Miller, 1992, 1996; Miller & Leary, 1992; Miller & Tangney, 1994; Parrott & Smith, 1991). In one study, participants observed an individual knocking over a supermarket display (Semin & Manstead, 1982). In one condition, he seemed visibly embarrassed; in the other condition, he was unperturbed. Participants had more favorable evaluations of the person who showed embarrassment. This appeasement function of embarrassment explains many everyday social phenomena. When people are just getting to know one another, they often embarrass themselves with self-deprecating stories as a way of demonstrating commitment to the social contract. When defendants first appear in a courtroom, there is often considerable concern about the degree to which they show remorse, a self-conscious emotion related to embarrassment. (Some defendants are better at it than others. The talented actor Mark Wahlberg was a self-admitted delinquent who reports that the best acting he ever did was in juvenile court.)

Let's turn to a final line of research by Jessica Tracy and her colleagues on the expression of pride that brings together Darwin's ideas about universality, cross-species similarities, and the expressions of those without eyesight. Pride is the feeling associated with achievement—with gaining in status through socially valued actions. This emotion is reliably signaled with dominance-related behaviors seen in other mammals: expansive posture, head movements up and back, arm thrusts upward (Tracy & Robins, 2004). When Jessica Tracy and Rick Robins traveled to Burkina Fhasa, in Africa, they found that a remote tribe readily identified displays of pride as being of that emotion (Tracy & Robins, 2007). And in a recent study, Jessica Tracy and David Matsumoto carefully analyzed the emotional expressions of sighted and blind Olympic athletes just after they had either won or lost a judo competition (Tracy & Matsumoto, 2008). Sure enough, after victory, sighted and blind athletes alike threw their arms in the air with chest out as an expression of pride. After losing, both groups of athletes dropped their heads and slumped their shoulders in a display of shame. The atheletes hailed from over 20 different countries, suggesting that these shame and pride displays are universal.

These studies of emotional expression suggest that facial expressions of emotion are universal, that they are similar to the expressions of our mammalian relatives, and that they are seen in blind individuals. All of these findings are quite consistent with Darwin's analysis long ago that human emotion evolved out of the patterns of expressive behavior in our mammalian relatives (Ekman, Friesen, & Ellsworth, 1982a, 1982b; Elfenbein & Ambady, 2002, 2003; Matsumoto et al., 2008; Mesquita & Frijda, 1992). Now let's consider how emotion varies across different cultures.

Cultural Specificity of Emotion

When anthropologists began studying different cultures, it wasn't hard to find examples of cultural variation in emotional expression. For example, the Inuit of Alaska (colloquially referred to as Eskimos) were never observed to express anger (Briggs, 1960), and seventeenth-century Japanese wives of Samurai soldiers would smile upon receiving the news that their husbands had died nobly in battle.

One way to think about how cultures vary in their emotional expression is that cultures develop **emotion accents**—that is, highly stylized, culturally specific ways of expressing particular emotions (Elfenbein & Ambady, 2002). In a study conducted in India and the United States, for example, participants were asked to judge two expressions of embarrassment, shown in **Figure 7.2** along with the rates at which members of the two cultues identified the two expressions as embarrassment (Haidt & Keltner, 1999). As you can see, members of both cultures interpreted the expression on the left

emotion accents Culturally specific ways that individuals from different cultures express particular emotions, such as the tongue bite as an expression of embarrassment in India.

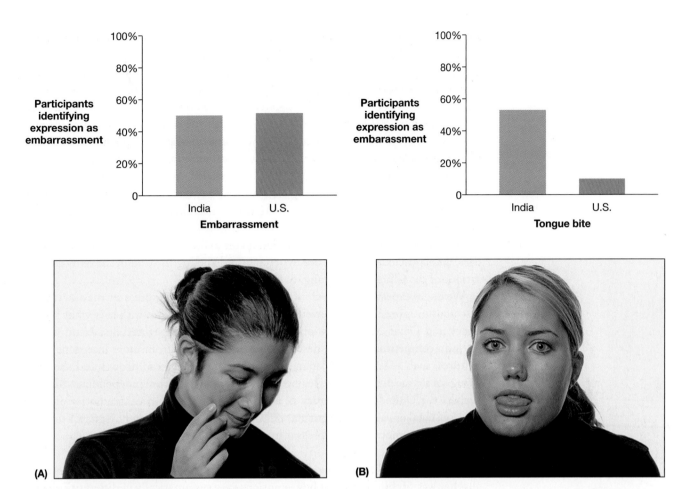

FIGURE 7.2 Universality and Cultural Variation in Emotional Expression People in the United States and India agree in their judgments of a prototypical embarrassment display (A), but only people in India recognize the ritualized tongue bite as a display of embarrassment (B). (Source: Haidt & Keltner, 1999.)

as embarrassment. But Indian participants also readily perceived the tongue bite—an emotion accent in India—as embarrassment, while U.S. college students were bewildered by this display and saw little embarrassment in it.

This kind of research indicates that there is clearly a great deal of cultural variability in how members of different cultures express their emotions. The deeper challenge is to show how cultures vary in emotional expression according to cultural factors, such as particular self-construals or values. Empirical studies have risen to this challenge, documenting several ways that members of different cultures vary in their emotional expression.

Culture and Focal Emotions If you have traveled to another country, you may have come to the conclusion that cultures seem to be defined by particular emotions: Mexico is a proud culture, Tibet a kind one, Japan a modest one. This intuition was shared by early anthropologists, who often described cultures as angry cultures, shame- or guilt-prone cultures, or gentle cultures. In considering these observations, Batja Mesquita has made the important point that cultures vary in which emotions are focal. **Focal emotions** are the more common emotions in the everyday lives of the members of a culture, presumably experienced and expressed with greater frequency and intensity (Mesquita, 2003). For example, for individuals from cultures that value honor, sexual and family insults are highly charged events and trigger higher levels of anger than in members of cultures that do not prioritize honor (Rodrigues, Fischer, &

focal emotions Emotions that are especially common within a particular culture.

Manstead, 2000, 2004). Anger appears to be a more focal emotion in honor-based cultures.

Or consider the expression of self-conscious emotions like embarrassment and shame. Self-conscious emotions express modesty, an appreciation of others' opinions, and a sense of how the self is located within a social collective. These qualities of the self-conscious emotions are consistent with the core concerns in interdependent cultures—to maintain harmony and be mindful of others. We might therefore expect shame or embarrassment to be more focal emotions in more interdependent cultures, and that is what recent studies have revealed. For example, cultures vary in the extent to which they **hypercognize** emotions—that is, in the number of words they use to represent different emotions (Russell, 1991). In Tahiti, for example, there are 46 separate terms that refer to anger. In China, a highly interdependent culture, there are at least 113 words that describe shame and embarrassment, suggesting that these self-conscious emotions are hypercognized and highly focal in the daily conversations of the Chinese (Li, Wang, & Fischer, 2004).

We might expect members of interdependent cultures to express shame and embarrassment in more intense nonverbal behavior displays. Indeed, that is what Jessica Tracy and David Matsumoto observed in their study of sighted and blind Olympic judo competitors that we described earlier. Athletes from more interdependent cultures, such as China and Japan, showed more intense head droops and shoulder shrugs of shame in response to losing than did individuals from independent cultures, such as the United States (Tracy & Matsumoto, 2008). When an emotion fits the self-construal or value of a particular culture, people develop richer languages to communicate the emotion and express it in more intense nonverbal display.

Culture and Ideal Emotions Recently, Jeanne Tsai and her colleagues have offered another way of thinking about how emotions vary systematically in different cultures (Tsai, 2007; Tsai, Knutson, & Fung, 2006). In her affect valuation theory, Tsai reasons that cultures vary in which emotions they value or idealize. Emotions that promote specific cultural values and ideals are valued more and as a result should play a more prominent role in the social lives of individuals.

For example, Tsai and colleagues reason that in the United States excitement is greatly valued. Excitement enables individuals to pursue a cultural ideal of self-expression and achievement. In contrast, in many East Asian cultures greater value is attached to feelings of calmness and contentedness, because these positive emotions more readily enable the individual to fold into harmonious relationships and groups (Kitayama, Karasawa, & Mesquita, 2004; Kitayama, Markus, & Kurokawa, 2000; Kitayama, Mesquita, & Karasawa, 2005; see also Mesquita, 2001; Mesquita & Karasawa, 2002). These differences in which emotions are valued readily translate into striking cultural differences in emotional behavior. You may be surprised to learn that Americans, as compared to East Asians, are more likely to participate in risky recreational practices (for example, mountain biking), are more likely to advertise consumer products with intense smiles of excitement, are more likely to get addicted to excitement-enhancing drugs (cocaine), express preferences for upbeat exciting music rather than soothing slower songs, and their children's books are more likely to feature highly excited protagonists (Tsai, 2007). All of these differences in social practice, Tsai reasons, flow out of the value placed on excitement in America.

One clear prediction about emotional expression is that in Western European cultures, joy and excitement should be more frequently expressed, whereas in East Asian cultures, greater restraint will be placed on the expression of these positive

hypercognize To represent a particular emotion with numerous words and concepts.

emotions. How so? Paul Ekman proposed that cultures vary in their **display rules**, which refer to culturally specific rules that govern how and when and to whom we express emotion (Ekman & Friesen, 1969). People can *de-intensify* their emotional expression—for example, suppressing the urge to laugh at a friend's fumbling on a romantic quest. People can *intensify* their expression—for example, smiling widely upon receiving yet another unfashionable sweater from Grandma. They can *mask* their negative emotion with a polite smile. And they can *neutralize* their expression with a poker-faced demeanor.

Consistent with Tsai's thinking about the different value placed on excitement in the East versus the West, several studies are revealing that people from more interdependent cultures de-intensify their outward expression of excitement. For example, anthropologist Catherine Lutz observed that in the interdependent Ifaluk people, living on a small island in Micronesia, children were actively discouraged from expressing their excitement (Lutz, 1988). In many Asian cultures, it is inappropriate to speak of personal enthusiasms, and in these cultures, people may also de-intensify their expressions of pleasure at personal success. Across dozens of cultures, people from more interdependent cultures report being more likely to suppress positive emotional expression than individuals from independent cultures (Matsumoto et al., 2008; Mesquita & Leu, 2007). People from interdependent cultures are more likely to temper their experience of positive emotion with negative emotions (Schimmack, Oishi, & Diener, 2002). And Tsai herself has found that in responding to emotional stimuli of various kinds, people from independent cultures are more likely to show intense smiles of excitement (Tsai & Levenson, 1997). People from India have been known to refer to Americans as "dogs," with no real offense intended. It's just that Americans are always saying "wow, wow!"

Neutralizing Expressions According to the display rules of poker, this woman masks any feelings about her cards with a neutral poker face.

LOOKING BACK We have seen evidence of the legacy of Charles Darwin: he inspired dozens of studies that found that human emotional expression is universal, is seen in other species, and is evident in the blind. At the same time, it is clear that emotional expression varies across cultures. Cultures have specific emotion accents, such as the tongue bite for embarrassment. Cultures vary in which emotions are focal in their culture, and they express focal emotions more intensely. Cultures vary in which emotions they value, and they regulate emotions that are less valued with specific display rules—that is, the rules governing how and when to express emotions.

EMOTIONS AND SOCIAL RELATIONSHIPS

The sad life of Eadweard Muybridge is a testament to how important emotions are to social relationships. After his accident, his reason was intact, as was his language. But being devoid of emotion, he found it difficult to care, connect, or cooperate. Emotions are at the core of our most important social commitments (Frank, 1988). For example, the expression of gratitude is a building block of friendships (McCullough et al., 2001; Nesse, 1990 Trivers, 1971); our romantic relationships might not ever get off the ground without experiencing sexual desire and romantic love (Buss, 1992; Ellis & Malamuth, 2000; Gonzaga, Keltner, Londahl, & Smith, 2001); and feelings of sympathy and concern are a bedrock of communal relations in which individuals are invested in the welfare of others. In this section, we'll consider how emotions are vital to our relationships with friends, intimate partners, and group members.

Emotions in Friendship and Intimate Relationships

Oxytocin and Trust Economist Paul Zak has argued that trust is the engine of cooperative relationships and the glue of healthy communities and nations (Zak, 2003). Within interpersonal relationships, there are numerous ways to build trust: a firm handshake, a steady tone of voice, friendly eye contact. Or you might just sneak a little oxytocin into the water of a friend.

Oxytocin is a peptide composed of nine amino acids that is produced in the hypothalamus and released into the brain and bloodstream. Receptors for this peptide are found in the olfactory system, limbic-hypothalamic system, brainstem, and regions of the spinal cord that regulate the autonomic nervous system, especially the parasympathetic branch. Oxytocin is involved in uterine contractions, lactation, maternal bonding, and sexual interaction (Carter, 1998). And it may be your key to matrimonial happiness.

Why such a dramatic claim? Because in nonhuman species, oxytocin increases pair-bonding and caregiving behavior. Comparisons between prairie voles, which display pair-bonding, and closely related montane voles, which do not, reveal differences in the location of oxytocin receptors in the brain of each species (Carter, 1998; Insel, Young, & Zuoxin, 1997). Injection of oxytocin into the montane vole promotes preferences for single partners in this otherwise promiscuous rodent (Williams, Insel, Harbaugh, & Carter, 1994).

In humans, new studies are revealing oxytocin to be a source of trust. One of the most dramatic studies involved the trust game (Kosfeld, Heinrichs, Zak, Fishbacher, & Fehr, 2005). In the trust game, participants are given a certain amount of money—say, $10—and asked to give some portion of that money to a stranger. The experimenter then triples the value of that gift, and the stranger then gives some portion of this new sum back to the original participant. Like so many endeavors in life, you have to trust the other person with initial acts of generosity in the hopes of stimulating more mutually beneficial relationships. In one condition, participants inhaled oxytocin prior to playing. In the other condition, they inhaled a saline solution. As you can see in **Figure 7.3**, participants feeling the trust promoted by oxytocin were more than twice as likely to give away the maximal amount of money.

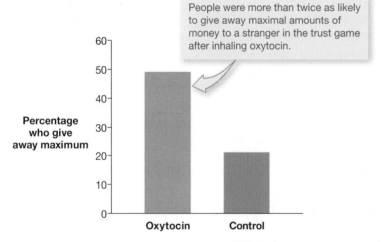

People were more than twice as likely to give away maximal amounts of money to a stranger in the trust game after inhaling oxytocin.

FIGURE 7.3 Effect of Oxytocin on Trust and Genoristy (Source: Kosfeld et al., 2005.)

Which emotions are related to oxytocin? One good candidate is love (Gonzaga, Turner, Keltner, Campos, & Altemus, 2006; Taylor, 2002). To pin this hypothesis down, Gian Gonzaga and his colleagues first explored the nonverbal signals of romantic love and sexual desire in young romantic partners, guided by the ideas of Darwin described earlier. From videotaped conversations between romantic partners, these researchers found that when feeling love, romantic partners displayed brief, coordinated patterns of smiling, mutual gaze, affiliative, open hand gestures, and open posture. When feeling desire, in contrast, they showed a variety of lip-related actions, including puckers, lip licks, wipes, and tongue protrusions (Gonzaga et al., 2001, 2006). And in a second study of women recalling an experience of warmth toward another person, intense displays of love but not desire were associated with greater release of oxytocin into the bloodstream (Gonzaga et al., 2006).

Touch and Closeness To touch, the great artist Michelangelo said, is to give life. What he might have said, had he been a social psychologist, is that touch (the right kind) promotes closeness between friends and intimates. The early ethologists, making observations of social behavior in hunter-gatherer groups in different parts of the world, quickly discovered that touch is central to soothing, flirtation, greeting, play, and proximity maintenance (Eibl-Eibesfeldt, 1989; Henley, 1973). More recent studies have revealed how touch is vital to friendship and intimate relationships.

Touch promotes closeness in four different ways. First of all, touch provides rewards to others; it is as pleasurable as a bright smile or a taste of chocolate. The right kind of touch stimulates specific cells under your skin—the largest organ in your body—that trigger activation in the orbitofrontal cortex, a brain region involved in the representation of rewards (Rolls, 2000). Touch, again the right kind, can also trigger the release of oxytocin (Keltner, 2009).

A second way that touches builds closeness is that it soothes in times of stress. Touch reduces levels of the stress hormone cortisol (Francis & Meaney, 1999). In one study, married women anticipating an electric shock showed decreased threat-related activity in stress-related regions of the brain (for example, the right anterior insula, superior frontal gyrus, and hypothalamus) when holding the hand of a spouse, but not that of a stranger (Coan, Schaefer, & Davidson, 2006).

A third way that touch promotes closeness is that it encourages reciprocity, a foundation of friendships and intimate bonds. Nonhuman primates spend up to 20 percent of their day grooming and systematically share food with other non-kin who have groomed them earlier in the day. In humans, friendly patterns of touch have been found to increase compliance to requests (Willis & Hamm, 1980) and cooperation toward strangers in economic games (Kurzban, 2001).

Finally, touch promotes friendship and intimate relations most directly through the communication of prosocial emotions like compassion and gratitude (Hertenstein, Keltner, App, Bulleit, & Jaskolka, 2006). In a demonstration of this, a toucher and a touchee sat at a table separated by a black curtain, which prevented all communication between the two participants other than touch. The toucher attempted to convey different emotions by making contact with the touchee for 1 second on the forearm. Upon being touched, the touchee, as in the Ekman studies, selected which emotion had been communicated from a list of emotion terms. As you can see in **Figure 7.4**, people in the United States and Spain could reliably communicate prosocial emotions such as love, compassion, and gratitude with brief tactile contact. You may also be interested to know that the Spaniards, a high-touch culture, proved to be better at communicating emotion through touch. This finding fits with studies that suggest that individuals from interdependent cultures are better able to communicate emotion through touch. For example, in one study of friends talking in a café, British friends were observed to touch not once, Americans touched each other twice, and Puerto Ricans touched each other 180 times (Jourard, 1966).

Emotional Mimicry In the aftermath of the terrorist attacks of 2001, anxiety rashes spread through schools in the United States. In these epidemics of anxiety, one girl would be overcome with anxiety and express this in a rash, and the sight of that rash would stimulate rashes in other girls in the classroom and eventually spread through the school. We are an imitative species (Hatfield, Cacioppo, & Rapson, 1994). People imitate the face touches of confederates in an experiment (Chartrand & Bargh, 1999), subliminally presented smiles in photos (Dimberg & Öhman, 1996), the postures of

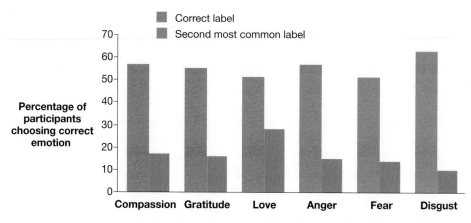

FIGURE 7.4 Communicating Emotion through Touch With a brief touch to the forearm, participants could reliably communicate several different emotions to a stranger. (Source: Hertenstein et al., 2006.)

high-power individuals, and even the postures of sculptures in a museum (Oatley, Keltner, & Jenkins, 2006). We are especially likely to imitate the emotions of others. Simply hearing another person laugh can trigger laughter (Provine, 1992). We blush when we see a friend blushing (Shearn, Bergman, Hill, Abel, & Hinds, 1992).

This kind of emotional mimicry appears to be a central ingredient of friendship. Consider the case of laughter. Jo-Anne Bachorowski has devoted years to unlocking the mysteries of laughter, spending hundreds of hours analyzing the acoustic profiles—the rhythm, pitch, and variability—of different laughs (Bachorowski & Owren, 2001). She has catalogued different kinds of laughs. You may be embarrassed to learn (or feel validated, as the case may be) that men are much more likely than women to produce "grunt" laughs that sound like the noises that emanate from the gorilla compound at the local zoo. And in a remarkable study, she has found that within milliseconds of participating in amusing tasks, the laughs of friends but not strangers begin to mimic each other (Smoski & Bachorowski, 2003).

Does emotional mimicry actually produce increased liking? Cameron Anderson and his colleagues have indeed found this to be the case (Anderson, Keltner, & John, 2003). In one study, new roommates came to the laboratory at the fall and spring of the academic year and at each visit reported their emotional reactions to different evocative stimuli, such as humorous or disturbing film clips. Quite remarkably, the roommates' emotions became increasingly similar (compared to two randomly selected individuals) over the course of the year. This emotional mimicry, furthermore, predicted increased closeness in friendships. Such emotional mimicry establishes similarity between individuals, which, as we describe in Chapter 10, increases closeness and liking.

Some cultures depend on mimicry more than others to establish rapport. Sanchez-Burks, Bartel, and Blount (2009) had employees of a large southwestern firm undergo mock interviews in which they were instructed to do their best to impress the interviewer favorably. Interviewees were either Anglo-Americans or Hispanics. In one condition, the interviewer mimicked the behavior of the interviewee: if the interviewee crossed his leg, the interviewer crossed his leg. In another condition, the interviewer never mimicked the interviewee. A group of observers then rated the interviewees' performance. The no-mimicking condition made no difference to raters' judgments about how impressive the interviewee was. But Hispanics were rated much higher than Anglo-Americans in the condition where the interviewer had established rapport by mimicking the interviewee's behavior.

BOX 7.2 **FOCUS ON CULTURE**

Flirtation and the Five Kinds of Nonverbal Display

Flirting is the pattern of behavior, both verbal and nonverbal, conscious and at times out of awareness, that communicates our attraction to a potential romantic partner.

Givens (1983) and Perper (1985) spent hundreds of hours in singles bars, charting the flirtatious behaviors that predict romantic encounters. They found that in the initial attention-getting phase, men roll their shoulders and engage in exaggerated motions to show off their resource potential, raising their arms to let others admire their well-developed pecs and washboard abs, or ordering a drink in a way that lets others see their flashy Rolex watch. Women smile coyly, preen, flick their hair, and walk with arched back and swaying hips. In the recognition phase, the potential romantic partners lock their gaze upon one another, expressing interest by raised eyebrows, sing-song voices, and laughter. In the touching phase, the

Flirting Can you tell from the woman's nonverbal language what she is trying to convey?

potential romantic partners move close, and they create opportunities to touch with provocative brushes of the arm, pats on the shoulder, or not-so-accidental bumps against one another. Finally, in the keeping-time phase, the potential partners express and assess each other's interest by lining up their actions. When they are interested in one another, their faces and hair touch, their glances and laughter mirror each other, and their shoulders and faces are aligned.

What is the nonverbal language of flirtation, or of other interactions for that matter? Paul Ekman and Wallace Friesen (1969) have organized the rich language of nonverbal behavior, so evident in flirtation, into five categories. The first is *affective displays*, or emotional expressions, which we have seen are universal. The four other categories of nonverbal behavior are more likely to vary across cultures. There are *emblems*, which are nonverbal gestures that directly translate to a word. Well-known emblems in English include the peace sign, the thumbs-up sign, the rubbing of one forefinger with the other to say "shame on you," and, in the late 1960s, the raised, clenched fist for Black Power. Researchers have analyzed over 800 emblems throughout the world, and surely there are many more. It is wise not to assume that emblems have the same meaning in different cultures. For example, the gesture in which you form a circle with your thumb and forefinger means "OK" in the United States, "money" in Japan, "zero" in France, and "let's have sex" in parts of Mediterranean Europe. When accepting an invitation to dinner in Greece, be careful not to make this gesture.

Illustrators are nonverbal behaviors that we use to make our speech vivid, engaging, and easy to visualize. We

Black Power American athletes at the 1968 Olympics in Mexico City raise their fists and display the emblem for Black Power.

rotate our hands in the air and use dramatic fist shakes to indicate the power of our convictions. We raise our eyebrows when uttering important phrases, we nod our head, and we move our torso to show empathy. When Bill Clinton was president, one of his characteristic illustrators was a fist with a partially exposed thumb, which he hoped would signify that he was optimistic and strong.

Regulators are nonverbal expressions we use to coordinate conversation. People look and point at people to whom they want to speak. They look and turn their bodies away from those they wish would stop speaking.

Finally, there are *self-adaptors*, which are the nervous, seemingly random behaviors people engage in when tense, as if to release nervous energy. People touch their noses, twirl their hair, jiggle their legs, and rub their chins. The author Joseph Conrad suggested that people always touch their faces when entering public places. Try the experiment yourself. See how frequently people touch their faces when entering a restaurant or bar. Be sure to include an appropriate baseline of comparison.

Emotion within and between Groups

Emotions and Role Negotiation within Groups One of the central dimensions of an individual's role within a group is that person's status, as discussed in Chapter 11. The benefits of having high status are many, and the costs of negotiating status can be high. Conflicts over who is higher in a group's hierarchy are often violent and deadly in humans and nonhumans alike. As a result, different nonhuman species rely on nonverbal displays to establish hierarchy. Apes pound their chests, frogs croak, stags roar endlessly for hours, chimps flash their fangs, and deer lock up in their horns. These kinds of ritualized displays enable group members to establish who has power and who doesn't in less costly fashion than direct aggressive encounter. Think we're beyond such chest pounding and roaring? Perhaps, but humans do negotiate their places within group hierarchies through emotional displays.

For example, anger is clearly a high-power emotion. It has force and strength behind it. And several studies converge on the notion that expressions of anger lead to gains in power within groups. People attribute elevated status and power to individuals displaying anger (Knutson, 1996). People assume that high-power people respond to difficulties with anger (Tiedens, 2001). High-power negotiators who display anger are more likely to get their way and prompt more subordinate behaviors in their counterparts (Sinaceur & Tiedens, 2006; Van Kleef, De Dreu, Pietroni, & Manstead, 2006). Even more on point, one experiment found that people attributed greater power to leaders, such as Bill Clinton, when they displayed anger as opposed to other emotions (Tiedens, 2001). We are reminded of the trial lawyer's adage that when you have the law on your side you should argue the law, when you have the facts on your side you should argue the facts, and when you have neither on your side you should pound the table!

Is there a low-power emotional counterpart to anger? One possibility is embarrassment. Among the Awlad'Ali, a nomadic tribe living in Egypt, being in the presence of someone more powerful is a source of embarrassment and shame, or *hasham*. In this culture, the experience of *hasham*, as well as its display in the kind of embarrassment-related gaze and modest smiles we described earlier, signals to group members the individual's subordinate status and dependence on others (Abu-Lughod, 1986). The display of *hasham* is a way in which people act out lower-status positions. In experimental research, people who display embarrassment are judged to be of lower status and physically smaller (Ketelaar, 2005). Much as anger signals power within groups, embarrassment signals submissiveness.

Emotion and Group Boundaries When African-American children first attended white schools in the South following the 1954 decision (*Brown v. Board of Education of Topeka*) that made segregation illegal, they were greeted with violent protests from white crowds. What is most astonishing in the films of these historic moments is the emotion—facial expressions of anger, fists thrust into the air, inhuman howls and shrieks of rage. As readily as emotions unite people together, they can divide groups.

In their intergroup emotion theory, Diane Mackie and Eliot Smith argue that group members experience emotions vis-à-vis other groups according to their identification with their own group and their feeling of strength or weakness relative to the outgroup (Mackie, Silver, & Smith, 2004). They have found that anger and contempt are felt toward outgroups when group members feel that their group is stronger than the outgroup and when the members are passionately identified with their own group. By contrast, group members are more likely to feel fear when they feel weak vis-à-vis the outgroup. For example, U.S. citizens were particularly enraged following the 9/11 terrorist attacks when they identified as Americans and felt that America was much stronger than the terrorists.

Emotions divide groups through a second process known as infrahumanization (Cortes, Demoulin, Rodriguez, Rodriguez, & Leyens, 2005). **Infrahumanization** is the tendency for ingroup members to attribute animal-like qualities to outgroup members—that is, to deny them full human standing. Emotions play a critical role in infrahumanization. In many different parts of the world, and relatively independent of group conflict, group members assume that their own group is more likely than outgroup members to experience more complex, sophisticated emotions such as pride or sympathy (Cortes et al., 2005). These more complex emotions involve more uniquely human cognitive capacities—a sense of self, taking others' perspectives—and are especially important in how group members define their own group's identity. By contrast, group members attribute similar levels of more basic emotions, such as anger or disgust, to their own group and different outgroups. Group members attribute less complex emotions to outgroups to elevate their own moral standing and will even punish outgroup members who exhibit secondary emotions because they threaten their ethnocentric views (Vaes, Paladino, Castelli, Leyens, & Giovanazzi, 2003). As you might imagine, infrahumanization can readily feed into violence toward outgroup members.

 We have seen how vital emotions are to social relationships. In the development of friendships and romantic partnerships, oxytocin promotes trust. Touch, a rich medium of emotional communication, promotes closeness through its capacity to reward, to soothe, to encourage reciprocity, and to communicate emotions such as compassion and gratitude. And we have seen that emotional mimicry produces increased closeness. Emotions are powerful forces in group dynamics. Emotions such as anger and embarrassment signal different levels of power and help group members find their place within social hierarchies. Our universal tendency to fail to attribute the more human emotions (pride, compassion, and regret, for example) to outgroups can readily give rise to aggression and violence.

EMOTIONS AND SOCIAL COGNITION

When Eadweard Muybridge regained consciousness after hitting his ahead against the tree, he felt disoriented. Damage to the frontal lobes often results in the inability to rely on current emotions to make sound decisions. A person with frontal lobe damage, for example, will fail to consult feelings of fear and anxiety when facing risky decisions and will often suffer the costs of taking inappropriate risks (Damasio, 1994). And a person with frontal lobe damage will often be unable to access feelings of distress and sympathy when seeing another person suffer, which may produce alarmingly cool behavior toward others in need (Blair, Jones, Clark, & Smith, 1997).

The sad tale of Eadward Muybridge reveals yet another surprising side to our emotions: emotions are guides to important decisions. When you choose a graduate school, or a neighborhood to live in, or a person to marry, your gut feelings are a powerful guide. This thesis has not enjoyed great popularity in Western thought. For centuries, philosophers have argued that emotions are lower or more primitive ways of perceiving the world (Haidt, 2001; Oatley, 2004). Our metaphors of emotion reveal this bias: we speak of emotions as forms of insanity ("I'm mad with love") and disease ("I'm sick with envy") rather than forms of clarity, reason, and health. Twenty-five years of research, however, suggests that emotions generally have principled, systematic effects on cognitive processes and that emotions lead to reasonable judgments of the world (Clore, Gasper, & Garvin, 2001; Clore & Parrott, 1991;

infrahumanization The tendency to attribute animal-like qualities to outgroup members and be reluctant to attribute more complex emotions, such as pride or compassion, to outgroup members.

"Reason is and ought to be the slave of passion."

—David Hume

Forgas, 1995, 2003; Isen, 1987; Lerner & Keltner, 2001; Loewenstein & Lerner, 2003; Rozin, 1996).

Emotions Provide Information for Judgments

Most serious judgments in life are complex. For instance, a thorough answer to a question about how satisfied you are with your life might lead you to think about whether you're meeting your goals of getting prepared for a career, whether your health is good, whether your finances will ever be in order, how serious global warming is, and so on. Given this complexity, Norbert Schwarz and Jerry Clore have argued that we often rely on a simpler assessment that is based on our current feelings, asking ourselves, "How do I currently feel about it?" This account of how emotions influence judgment goes by the name of the **feelings-as-information perspective** (Clore, 1992; Clore & Parrott, 1991; Schwarz, 1990; Schwarz & Clore, 1983). Its basic assumption is that emotions provide us with rapid, reliable information about events and conditions within our current social environment—gut feelings, so to speak—that shape our most important judgments.

In a first test of this feelings-as-information perspective, Schwarz and Clore (1983) studied the potent effects that bright sunny days and gloomy, overcast days have on the emotional lives of people in the Midwest. They telephoned people in Illinois on either a cloudy day or a sunny day. They asked participants, "All things considered, how satisfied or dissatisfied are you with your life as a whole these days?" Participants had to indicate their satisfaction on a 10-point scale, with 10 being "completely satisfied with life." In one condition, researchers simply asked participants about their mood and life satisfaction on that day. The researchers predicted that participants who were called on a sunny day would be happier and would report greater life satisfaction than participants who were called on a gloomy day. In a second condition, before being asked about mood and life satisfaction, other participants were asked, "How's the weather down there?" Schwarz and Clore reasoned that this question would lead those participants to attribute their current mood and life satisfaction to the weather and not to use their feelings in evaluating their life satisfaction (see **Table 7.1**). Finally, at the end of this brief survey, participants indicated how happy they felt at that moment.

When asked only about their mood and life satisfaction, the participants' responses confirmed Schwarz and Clore's hypothesis about how people use their current feelings to make important judgments: people were happier when called on sunny days than when called on overcast, gray days, and they also indicated greater life satisfaction. In contrast, when participants were initially asked about the weather, they tended to discount the relevance of their feelings related to the weather and thus reported equivalent levels of life satisfaction whether it was a sunny day or a gloomy day.

This study set the stage for subsequent experiments that have revealed how people rely on different emotions to make important judgments and decisions. In keeping with Schwarz and Clore's formulation, people in a bad mood are more likley to arrive at negative judgments about consumer products, political figures, and economic policies (Forgas & Moylan, 1987). Several studies, for example, have focused on anger and lend credence to the old notion that when people are angry about something—say, a bad day at work—that emotion is likely to influence all sorts of judgments. Simply recalling an angry event in the past can cause people to rely on that emotion to blame others for current problems and to assume that unfair things will happen to them in the future (DeSteno, Petty, Wegener, & Rucker, 2000; Feigenson, Park, & Salovey, 2001; Keltner, Ellsworth, & Edwards, 1993; Lerner, Goldberg, & Tetlock, 1998; Quigley & Tedeschi, 1996).

feelings-as-information perspective
A theory that since many judgments are too complex for us to thoroughly review all the relevant evidence, we rely on our emotions to provide us with rapid, reliable information about events and conditions within our social environment.

TABLE 7.1 Feelings as Information

People often use their current feelings to make complex social judgments. In a study of the feelings-as-information hypothesis, Schwarz and Clore asked people to indicate how happy they were with life on either an overcast or a sunny day. People reported feeling less happy and less satisfied with life on overcast days, revealing that people use the gloomy feelings of gray days to judge their happiness and life satisfaction. This was not true, however, for people who consciously attributed their feelings to the weather, because these people no longer judged their weather-related feelings to be relevant to their overall happiness and life satisfaction.

	Not attributing feelings to the weather	Attributing feelings to the weather
Happiness		
Sunny	7.43	7.29
Overcast	5.00	7.00
Life Satisfaction		
Sunny	6.57	6.79
Overcast	4.58	6.71

Source: Adapted from Schwarz & Clore (1983).

Still other emotions feed into other judgments. People feeling a state of fear perceive greater risk in their environment, pay more attention to those threats, and offer pessimistic estimates about the bad things that are likely to happen to them in the future (Lerner & Keltner, 2001; Mathews & MacLeod, 1994; Mineka, Rafaeli, & Yovel, 2003). For example, in a national field experiment conducted right after the 9/11 terrorist attacks, people who were induced to feel fear (as opposed to anger) about the attacks perceived greater risks in their environnment, related not just to terrorism but to other matters as well, such as the possibility of a flu epidemic (Lerner & Gonzalez, 2005; Lerner, Gonzalez, Small, & Fischhoff, 2003). Do emotions always guide our judgments? No, according to Joseph Forgas (Forgas, 1995, 2000). Forgas has found that we are most likely to rely on our emotions when we make more complex judgments ("How will global warming influence the American economy 20 years from now?") as opposed to simple judgments ("Is my car's tire flat?") and when we do not have preexisting schemas to guide our judgment.

Emotions Influence Reasoning

Thus far, we have seen that emotions feed into our judgments by acting as guides about how good or bad something is, about how fair things are, and about whether there is risk to worry about. Emotions also influence our reasoning processes, as indicated by research on the **processing style perspective**. Most studies in this tradition have compared the effects of positive and negative moods. These studies suggest that positive moods facilitate use of already existing knowledge structures, such as heuristics and stereotypes, whereas negative moods—in particular, sadness—facilitate more careful attention to situational details (Bless et al., 1996; Bless, Mackie, & Schwarz, 1992; Bless, Schwarz, & Wieland, 1996; Bodenhausen, Kramer, & Süsser, 1994; Fiedler, 2001; Forgas, 1998a, 1998b, 1998c; Lambert, Khan, Lickel, & Fricke, 1997). Moreover, Bodenhausen has found that people induced to experience sadness are less likely to stereotype others than are people feeling anger (Bodenhausen, Sheppard, & Kramer, 1994). Stereotypes are automatic, effort-saving tools for judging others, and

processing style perspective A theory that different emotions lead people to reason in different ways—for example, that positive moods facilitate preexisting heuristics and stereotypes, whereas negative moods facilitate more careful attention to situational details.

people are more likely to use them when experiencing moods and emotions—for example, happiness or anger—that make them less systematic.

Let's take a more in-depth look at a research program interested in how positive emotions influence the creativity and complexity of our reasoning. We tend to assume that positive emotions are sources of simplistic or lazy thinking. Think of a creative genius—a Monet, Woolf, Beethoven, or Darwin—and odds are that you'll imagine their creative acts as having been produced during moments of struggle, tension, somberness, and even despair.

Research by Alice Isen (1987, 1993) suggests that this view of creativity is wrong. She contends that happiness prompts people to think in ways that are flexible and creative. In her studies, Isen induces positive emotion with trivial events. She gives participants little bags of candy. Participants find a dime. They give associations for positive words. They watch an amusing film clip. These subtle ways of making participants feel good produce striking changes in their reasoning. When given one word (for example, "carpet") and asked to generate a related word, people feeling positive emotions generate more novel associations (for example, "fresh" or "texture") than people in a neutral state, who tend to produce more common responses (for example, "rug"). People feeling positive moods categorize objects in more inclusive ways, rating fringe members of categories (for example, "cane" or "purse" as an example of clothing) as better members of that category than people in a neutral state, whose categories tend to be more narrowly defined. These effects of positive emotion have important social consequences. Negotiators in a positive mood are more likely to reach an optimal agreement that incorporates the interests of both sides, because positive moods allow opponents to think flexibly about the positions and interests of the other side (Carnevale & Isen, 1986; Forgas, 1998b).

Amplifying on Isen's findings, Barbara Fredrickson has advanced her **broaden-and-build hypothesis** regarding positive emotions (Fredrickson, 1998, 2001). Fredrickson proposes that positive emotions broaden our thoughts and actions to help us build emotional and intellectual resources such as empathy or the acquisition of knowledge. These increases in intellectual resources, in turn, build our social resources, such as friendships and social networks. Fredrickson and her colleagues have found that when people are led to experience positive emotions (by watching an amusing film clip, for example), they broaden and build in several ways (Fredrickson, 2001; Waugh & Fredrickson, 2006). People feeling positive emotion, for example, rate themselves as more similar to outgroup members, suggesting that they broaden their way of looking at how they resemble people from different groups. Within developing relationships, people feeling positive emotion see greater overlap between their self-concepts and those self-concepts of their friend or romantic partner.

Emotions and Moral Judgment

When advising jurors to render legal judgments, judges in the United States encourage the jurors to put aside their emotions in making important moral judgments about the guilt or innocence of the defendant and about sentence length and punitive damages. This view of emotion is rooted in Western suspicions about the emotions, but according to Jonathan Haidt, it is naive. Haidt claims that emotions are essential guides to our moral decisions (Haidt, 2001). To get a sense of how this is so, read the following scenario, and decide whether you think the action described is right or wrong:

Mark and Julie are brother and sister. They are traveling together in France on a summer vacation from college. One night they are staying alone in a cabin near the

broaden-and-build hypothesis
The hypothesis that positive emotions broaden thought and action repertoires, helping us build social resources.

beach. They decide that it would be interesting and fun if they tried making love. At the very least it would be a new experience for each of them. Julie was already taking birth control pills, but Mark uses a condom, too, just to be safe. They both enjoy making love, but they decide not to do it again. They keep that night as a special secret, which makes them feel even closer to each other.

When asked whether such a situation is wrong, nearly all college students immediately say yes, typically with pronounced disgust (Haidt, 2001). They're in good company. All cultures around the world view incest as immoral (Brown, 1991). When pressed to explain why Julie and Mark's encounter is wrong, people may reason that it is dangerous to inbreed, only to remember that Julie and Mark are using birth control. They may contend that each would be hurt emotionally, but recall that it was clearly specified that Julie and Mark were not harmed in any way by the event. Eventually, when all of their possible reasons have been refuted, people may simply say, "I can't explain why, I just know this is wrong" (**Figure 7.5**).

Haidt argues that moral judgments—judgments of right or wrong, of virtue and character—are often founded on gut feelings (Batson, Engel, & Fridell, 1999; Greene & Haidt, 2002; Haidt, 2003). These gut feelings take the form of specific emotions that guide moral action and judgment. *Self-critical* emotions, such as shame, embarrassment, and guilt, arise when we have violated social norms and moral codes or ideas about virtue and character (Baumeister, Stillwell, & Heatherton, 1994; Higgins, 1987; Keltner & Anderson, 2000; Keltner & Buswell, 1997; Tangney, Miller, Flicker, & Barlow, 1996). Emotions like embarrassment and guilt motivate us to make amends for our inappropriate actions. People who are "shameless," who are less likely to experience emotions like embarrassment and guilt, are actually more likely to engage in violence and criminal behavior (Beer, Heerey, Keltner, Scabini, & Knight, 2003; Blair, Jones, Clark, Smith, 1997; Keltner, Moffitt, & Stouthamer-Loeber, 1995). *Other-praising* emotions, most notably gratitude and "elevation," or awe, signal our approval of others' moral virtues (Haidt, 2003; Keltner & Haidt, 2003; McCullough et al., 2001).

More empirical attention has been given to *harm-related* emotions like sympathy and compassion. These emotions motivate prosocial behavior toward people who suffer or are vulnerable, as discussed in Chapter 13 (Batson & Shaw, 1991; Eisenberg et al., 1989). Sympathy also sways moral judgments in the realm of punishment (Rudolph, Roesch, Greitemeyer, & Weiner, 2004; Weiner, Graham, & Reyna, 1997). People who attribute a criminal defendant's immoral action to contextual causes (for example, an impoverished environment or abusive family background) are more likely to feel sympathy and to recommend less severe forms of punishment that focus on reforming the character of the defendant, whereas people who blame the defendant

---

FIGURE 7.5 You Be the Subject: Emotions and Moral Judgment

Try Jonathan Haidt's demonstration of the role of emotion in moral judgment on a friend.

1 Read the "Mark and Julie" scenario to a friend, and pay close attention to their facial expressions and voices as they listen.

2 Then ask your friend to explain why it is wrong.

3 Refute each argument (as in the text).

Results: In the end, most people who hear this story will say something like they know in their gut that incest is wrong, even though it might not harm anyone. This demonstrates how emotions act as moral intuitions.

and feel anger are more likely to recommend harsher forms of punishment (Lerner et al., 1998; Quigley & Tedeschi, 1996).

The best studied of the moral emotions are *other-condemning* emotions, such as anger and disgust. We feel these emotions in response to others' immoral acts. But empirical studies find that anger and disgust tend to be involved in different moral domains. Unfair violations of rights and freedoms, such as when people are not allowed to speak their mind or given fair access to an opportunity, are more likely to trigger anger than disgust (Rozin, Lowery, Imada, & Haidt, 1999; Vasquez, Keltner, Ebenbach, & Banaszynski, 2001). By contrast, disgust makes people condemn others for being impure in body, mind, or character (Haidt, Koller, & Dias, 1993; Wheatley & Haidt, 2005). For example, people who morally condemn cigarette smoking and meat consumption are particularly likely to find these acts disgusting (Rozin & Singh, 1999). Feelings of disgust but not anger are also a strong determinant of the tendency to condemn homosexuality as immoral (Tapias, Glaser, Wickens, & Keltner, 2006; Van de Ven, Bornholt, & Bailey, 1996).

 We have seen that emotions influence social cognition in powerful ways. People consult their emotions as information in making judgments about life satisfaction, how fair things are, and how much risk is in the environment. Emotions shape how we reason, perhaps most evident in the broaden-and-build hypothesis, which shows that positive emotions lead to broadened, more creative thought patterns, which in turn help build intellectual and social resources. Emotions are also powerful intuitions that feed into our moral judgments, shaping our judgments of punishment and wrongdoing.

EMOTION IN THE MIND AND BODY

William James and Emotion-Specific Physiology

In 1884, William James wrote an influential essay in the journal *Mind* titled "What Is an Emotion?" Most theorists up until that time had argued that the experience of emotion follows the perception of an emotionally exciting stimulus, which causes emotion-related physiology and behavior. James altered this sequence in a now-famous formulation: he argued that an emotionally exciting stimulus generates a physiological response, the perception of which is the experience of emotion. In more specific terms, James argued that each and every emotion, from lust to sympathy to the wonder you might feel upon entering a European cathedral, involves a distinct "bodily reverberation," or what we now know as a response in the **autonomic nervous system** (ANS) (see **Figure 7.6**). The sympathetic branch of the ANS increases heart rate, blood pressure, and cardiac output and shuts down digestive processes to allow the individual to engage in physically demanding actions. The parasympathetic branch helps with restorative processes, reducing heart rate and blood pressure and increasing digestive processes.

James's evidence was largely in the form of thought experiments, such as the following: What would be left of fear, or any emotion, for that matter, if you took away the heart palpitations, muscle tension, feelings of warmth or coldness in the skin, stomach sensations, and other ANS-produced responses from the experience of those emotions? James argued that you would be left with a purely intellectual state. James's thesis raised two questions: (1) to what extent does emotion reside in the body (in

autonomic nervous system (ANS) The glands, organs, and blood vessels throughout the body that are controlled by nerve cells originating in the spinal cord and that regulate the body's internal environment and help the individual deal with emergency situations.

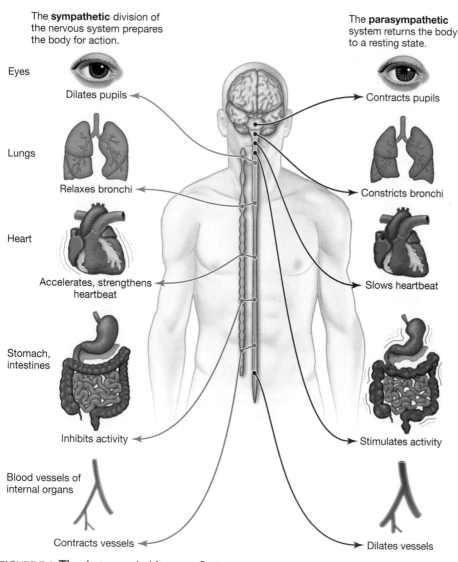

The **sympathetic** division of the nervous system prepares the body for action.

The **parasympathetic** system returns the body to a resting state.

Eyes
Dilates pupils
Contracts pupils

Lungs
Relaxes bronchi
Constricts bronchi

Heart
Accelerates, strengthens heartbeat
Slows heartbeat

Stomach, intestines
Inhibits activity
Stimulates activity

Blood vessels of internal organs
Contracts vessels
Dilates vessels

FIGURE 7.6 **The Autonomic Nervous System**

particular, in the activity of the ANS), and to what extent does emotion originate in the mind as part of our complex interpretation of the social environment, and (2) are there distinct ANS patterns for the different emotions? To answer these questions, we will first discuss an influential two-factor theory that takes a much different approach to emotional experience from that offered by James.

Schachter and Singer's Two-Factor Theory of Emotion

In 1962, Stanley Schachter and Jerome Singer proposed a **two-factor theory of emotion** (Schachter & Singer, 1962; see also Reisenzein, 1983). The theory assumed that there are two components to emotional experience: (1) undifferentiated physiological arousal, and (2) construal of the state of undifferentiated arousal, which determines which emotion will be experienced. In other words, the specific emotion the individual experiences—for example, anger, guilt, or shame—depends largely on the meaning of the situation to which the person attributes the arousal. For example, drinking too much coffee in the morning will make you tense and jittery at lunch. If you've forgotten that the coffee is the source of your tension, you might experience your jitteriness from the coffee as anger toward your roommate who is sleeping in late after keeping

two-factor theory of emotion A theory that there are two components to emotional experience: undifferentiated physiological arousal and a person's construal of that state of undifferentiated arousal.

you up the night before. Or take the situation of picking up your date at her parents' house. You arrive at your date's home, are grilled by her imposing parents, and in this heightened state of arousal and confusion fall madly in love with your date as she descends the stairs. In short, the two-factor theory says that for an emotion to be experienced, the person must both be in a state of general physiological arousal and attribute that arousal to an emotional stimulus.

In the classic study testing the two-factor theory, participants arrived at the laboratory, where the experimenter told them that the experiment concerned the effects of a vitamin compound, Suproxin, on vision. The experimenter then put some participants into a state of arousal; specifically, a medical doctor gave participants a shot, either of epinephrine (adrenaline), which stimulates the sympathetic autonomic nervous system (SANS) and the fight-or-flight response (increased blood pressure, heart rate, and so on), or a placebo saline solution, which should have no reliable effects on SANS activity. Those given a shot of epinephrine experienced arousal and were divided into two groups. Those in the *epinephrine-informed* condition were told the actual effects they would be likely to experience from the epinephrine. They were informed that the shot would likely make their hands shake, their hearts pound, and their faces feel flushed and warm. Those in the *epinephrine-ignorant* condition were not informed of any likely effects of the shot. Thus, some of the participants were physiologically aroused and some were not. For those who were aroused, some were given an explanation of that arousal in nonemotional terms and some were given no explanation.

We now turn to the manipulation of the situation, which, according to Schachter and Singer, should most affect those participants experiencing unexplained arousal. After the doctor had departed, the experimenter returned with a participant, actually a confederate, who allegedly had also received the shot of Suproxin and was to wait with the participant for 20 minutes before the vision tasks were to begin. The experimenter then left, apologizing for the rather disheveled condition of the laboratory. In the *euphoria condition*, the confederate carried out a variety of exhilarating activities. He first crumpled up sheets of paper and attempted jump shots into the trash can. After announcing "I feel like a kid again," he made a paper airplane and launched it into the air. He shot pieces of paper with a rubber-band slingshot, built a tower out of manila folders, and, at the peak of euphoria, began playing with hoola hoops left behind a portable blackboard.

In the *anger condition*, the experimenter asked the confederate and the participant, sitting across a table from each other, to complete the same five-page questionnaire. The confederate first commented on the excessive length of the questionnaire. Then at question 9 ("Do you ever hear bells?"), he blurted out, "Look at question 9. How ridiculous can you get? I hear bells every time I change classes." After questions about his childhood diseases, his father's annual income, and psychiatric symptoms family members had shown, the confederate exploded. When asked how often he had sexual intercourse each week, and "With how many men (other than your father) has your mother had extramarital relationships?" (for which the lowest response category was "4 and under"!), the confederate erupted and stomped out of the lab room.

Schachter and Singer gathered two kinds of measures. They coded the extent to which the participant showed euphoric or angry behaviors like those of the confederate, and they had participants report how angry and happy they felt on a questionnaire administered after the experiment.

According to Schachter and Singer's two-factor theory, participants should feel especially happy when (1) they were physiologically aroused but did not expect to be aroused by the shot and (2) they were then placed in the euphoria condition, which would lead to a positive construal of their arousal. In contrast, participants should feel particularly angry when (1) they were physiologically aroused from the shot of

"We all know that emotions are useless and bad for our peace of mind and our blood pressure."

—B. F. Skinner

epinephrine but did not expect to be aroused by the shot and (2) they were placed in the anger condition, which would provide an anger-related interpretation of their arousal. This turned out to be the case, both in terms of self-ratings of emotional state (happiness versus anger) and in terms of behavioral ratings. A surprise finding, however, was that informed participants, who knew that the shot would produce arousal, were actually less emotional than placebo subjects who received no injection. This suggests a particularly interesting cognitive twist: perhaps the informed subjects "overattributed" their arousal to the drug, discounting any arousal symptoms because they thought they knew how the symptoms had originated.

Schachter and Singer's experiment provided an initial glimpse into the importance of cognition in the experience of emotion. Their theory would later provide impetus for theories of attribution and self-perception. In the field of emotion, the idea that arousal could be misattributed to different causes generated a wave of interesting studies. The **misattribution of arousal** has been pursued in dozens of experiments exploring how arousal from one source (for example, difficulties at work) can be attributed to some other, salient source in the environment (the proverbial dog that the frustrated person kicks). One major finding is that participants who engage in arousing physical exercise have greater emotional responses to stimuli presented a few moments later when they think their arousal has subsided (Zillman, 1988, 1989). Thus, people who are presented with cartoons or erotica after exercising find the cartoons to be funnier and the erotica to be more arousing than do those who have not first engaged in the arousing exercise (Zillman, 1978). Perhaps most dramatically, individuals who complain of insomnia actually fall asleep more quickly when given a pill that was described as a stimulant (Storms & Nisbett, 1970). This allows them to attribute their anxieties produced by daily life to the pill rather than to the actual causes of their insomnia. Relieved, they fall asleep.

misattribution of arousal Attributing arousal produced by one cause (for example, exercise) to another stimulus in the environment.

Facial Expression of Anger
In this photograph, Winston Churchill looks like an angry bulldog, having just had his ever-present cigar taken away from him by the photographer. His eyebrows are drawn together and down, his upper eyelid is raised, his lower lip is pushed up, and his lips are pressed together.

Emotion in the Body: Evidence for ANS Specificity in Emotion

Let's now return to William James's original claim, that each emotion has a distinct ANS pattern. Schachter and Singer asserted that this was not true, and the field largely took this as gospel for the ensuing 20 years. Yet, Paul Ekman noticed something in his studies of facial expression that suggested otherwise. Ekman and Friesen developed an anatomically based system that allows researchers to code facial muscle actions according to how they change the appearance of the face (Ekman & Rosenberg, 1997). To develop this system, Ekman and Friesen spent thousands of hours moving their facial muscles, taking careful notes about how these movements created new creases, wrinkles, dimples, bulges of skin, and changes to the shape of the eyes or lips. In the course of this endeavor, Ekman observed that moving his facial muscles seemed to change how he felt. When he furrowed his brow, his heart rate and blood pressure seemed to increase. This raised an interesting possibility: Might moving facial muscles into emotion configurations produce specific ANS activity?

To answer this question, Robert Levenson, Paul Ekman, and Wallace Friesen (1990) conducted a study using the **directed facial action (DFA) task**. They had participants follow muscle-by-muscle instructions to configure their faces into the expressions of the six basic emotions that Ekman had studied in his cross-cultural studies. For example, for the anger expression, participants were instructed as follows:

1. Pull your eyebrows down and together.
2. Raise your upper eyelid.
3. Push your lower lip up and press your lips together.

directed facial action task A task in which moving emotion-specific facial muscles triggers different autonomic responses.

TABLE 7.2 Facial Expressions of Emotion Generate Emotion-Specific ANS Physiology

To address whether emotions are associated with specific ANS responses, as William James had claimed, Levenson, Ekman, and Friesen had participants move their facial muscles in ways that would express different emotions while the researchers measured changes in ANS physiology. Three findings suggest some specificity for negative emotions: (1) disgust produced lower heart rate than the other negative emotions, (2) both fear and disgust elicited higher skin conductance responses, and (3) anger led to higher finger temperature than fear. Thus, the researchers showed that posing facial expressions associated with different negative emotions activates specific autonomic physiology.

	Anger	Fear	Sadness	Disgust
Heart rate*	5.0	5.5	4.2	0.7
Skin conductance	.41	.58	.43	.52
Finger temperature	.20	−.05	.07	.07

*Heart rate refers to increases in number of heartbeats per minute compared to a baseline.
Source: Adapted from Levenson, Ekman, & Friesen (1990).

Participants held these expressions for 10 seconds, during which time the researchers continually took measures of ANS activity and then compared them to the measures from a neutral baseline.

Let's take a look at the autonomic activation associated with four different negative emotions, presented in **Table 7.2**. When you look closely, you will notice results that support James's physiological specificity hypothesis. First, heart rate is greater for fear, anger, and sadness than for disgust. Second, skin conductance, the measure of sweat activity in the hands, is greater for fear and disgust than for anger and sadness. Third, finger temperature is greater for anger than for fear, suggesting that when someone is angry, blood flows freely to the hands (perhaps to aid in combat), whereas when someone is fearful, blood remains near the chest to support flight-related locomotion. Thus, four different negative emotions have different autonomic profiles (but see Cacioppo, Klein, Berntson, & Hatfield, 1993, for a critique). Subsequent studies have replicated these emotion-specific ANS patterns in elderly adults (those aged 65 and older), although elderly adults show weaker ANS responses (Levenson, Carstensen, Friesen, & Ekman, 1991). Similar emotion-specific ANS activity was also observed in the Minangkabau, a matrilineal Muslim people in West Sumatra, Indonesia, suggesting that these emotion-specific ANS responses may be universal (Levenson, Ekman, Heider, & Friesen, 1992).

Are there other emotion-specific ANS responses? One obvious candidate is the blush, about which Mark Twain once observed: "Humans are the only species who blush, and the only one that needs to." As it turns out, Twain was not entirely correct: some nonhuman primates show reddening in the face as an appeasement gesture (an indication to another primate that one acknowledges its higher status and power; Hauser, 1996). Darwin devoted a chapter to the blush, noting that it is associated with embarrassment, shyness, and shame. Why do we blush? Darwin suggested that the blush is produced when we direct our attention to our appearance. More recently, researchers have pinpointed a more specific cause of the blush: negative, self-focused attention (Leary, Britt, Cutlip, & Templeton, 1992).

What about the autonomic physiology of the blush? In studying self-conscious emotion, researchers were particularly mischievous, setting up situations in which participants were made to think they had broken an experimenter's camera or knocked over a confederate's coke (which spilled into the confederate's backpack) or in which participants were required to suck on pacifiers (Buck & Parke, 1972). A study by Donald Shearn and colleagues may have been the most mortifying (Shearn, Bergman, Hill, Abel, & Hinds, 1990). In the blush condition, participants first sang "The Star Spangled Banner" (not the simplest song to sing with correct pitch) while being videotaped. As if that weren't bad enough, in the second phase of the study, participants watched the videotape of their own rendition of "The Star Spangled Banner" with a group of people. Researchers compared the participants' ANS activity in this condition with that of participants who were about to give a prepared speech, a powerful elicitor of anxiety. Embarrassment involved increased vasodilation and blood flow to the cheeks, the blush. This blush response was not observed in the anxiety condition, suggesting that the blush is unique to self-conscious emotions, such as embarrassment and shame. Here is yet another way in which emotion involves distinct ANS patterning (see also Gross, Fredrickson, & Levenson, 1994; Levenson, 2003; Porges, 1995; Schwartz, Weinberger, & Singer, 1981; Stemmler, 1989, 2003).

LOOKING BACK We have reviewed evidence indicating that emotion resides both in body and mind. Schachter and Singer's two-factor theory and the studies it inspired suggest that once aroused, our emotional experience is shaped by the causes to which we attribute our arousal. At the same time, Levenson and others have conducted studies that have produced evidence for ANS specificity for various emotions, lending credence to James's assertion that different emotions are associated with different physiological responses in the body.

HAPPINESS

It is only fitting that we conclude this chapter by asking a question that has long preoccupied philosophers and laypeople alike: What is happiness? The Declaration of Independence refers to inalienable rights, among which are "life, liberty, and the pursuit of happiness." Various philosophers have considered happiness one of the highest aims of living and a measure for assessing the moral quality of human action and the fairness of economic and political systems.

Over time, the meaning of happiness has changed (McMahin, 2006). In early Greek life, happiness was to be found in ethical behavior, in being temperate, fair, and dutiful. In the Middle Ages, as plagues and wars darkened the times, happiness was thought to be found in the afterlife, in communion with God when the soul was liberated from the passions of earthly life. With the rise of the age of the enlightenment, people sought out happiness in hedonistic experiences or in actions that advanced the happiness of as many people as possible (the idea of the greater good). And we have learned from recent cultural studies that there is great cultural variation in the meaning of happiness. Americans are likely to associate happiness with personal achievement (Yuchida & Kitayama, 2009). As you might have anticipated, happiness in East Asian cultures is more often thought of as an experience to be found in harmonious interactions with others and fulfilling duties (Kitayama, Karasawa, et al., 2004).

What, then, is happiness? What determines if we will experience pleasure? Can we predict what will make us happy? What actually brings us lasting happiness? We will now explore the scientific answers to these questions.

"Embarrassment is not an irrational impulse breaking through socially proscribed behavior but part of this orderly behavior itself."

—Erving Goffman

The Determinants of Pleasure

Pleasure is a core element of many experiences of happiness. But what makes for a pleasurable experience? Barbara Fredrickson (1998) and Daniel Kahneman (1999) have found some surprising answers to this question. In their research, they have had people experience pleasure in different ways. For example, in one study, participants watched pleasurable films, such as a comedy routine or a puppy playing with a flower (Fredrickson & Kahneman, 1993). While participants watched these clips, they rated their second-by-second pleasure using a dial. These second-by-second ratings were then correlated with their ratings of their overall pleasure at the end of the clip. The question of interest was: How do participants' immediate reports of pleasure predict their overall recollections of pleasure?

This study and others like it have documented three determinants of people's overall assessments of pleasure. First, the *peak moment* of pleasure associated with an event—for example, that burst of joy as you eat an ice-cream sundae—strongly predicts how much pleasure you will associate with the event. Second, how you feel at the *end* of the event also strongly predicts your overall reports of pleasure. If you are planning a backpacking trip through Europe or a first date, make sure that last day (or last 5 minutes) is really pleasurable. Finally, and somewhat surprisingly, the length of the pleasurable experience is unrelated to overall reports of pleasure, a bias called **duration neglect**. Whether the neck massage lasts 20 minutes or 60 minutes, whether a first date lasts 1 hour or 10, seems to have little sway over our experience of pleasure. What matters is whether the peak moment and ending are good. The same principle holds for negative experiences. Remembered pain is predicted by peak and end discomfort, not by its duration (Kahneman, 1999).

duration neglect The relative unimportance of the length of an emotional experience, be it pleasurable or unpleasant, in judging the overall experience.

Knowing What Makes Us Happy

Can we reliably predict what will make us happy and what will bring us despair? These kinds of predictions are profoundly important. We burn the midnight oil at work on the assumption that career success will bring lasting joy. We choose graduate schools, careers, vacations, and marriage partners based on the sense that one option will bring more happiness than others. In deciding what career or romantic partner to choose, we may begin with practical questions, but we are very likely to come back to the basic question: What will make us happy? Is the answer simple? Regrettably, it is not as simple as we would like it to be.

In their research on **affective forecasting**, Daniel Gilbert and Timothy Wilson have documented a variety of biases that undermine our attempts to predict what will make us happy (Gilbert, Brown, Pinel, & Wilson, 2000). Take one study that examined the expected and actual impact of breaking up with a romantic partner (Gilbert, Pinel, Wilson, Blumberg, & Wheatley, 1998). People who had not experienced a romantic breakup, called "luckies," reported on their own overall happiness and then predicted how unhappy they would be two months after a romantic breakup. This estimate was compared with the happiness of people who had recently broken up, labeled "leftovers." As seen in **Figure 7.7**, leftovers were just as happy as luckies, but luckies predicted that they would be much less happy two months after a breakup than leftovers actually were. People overestimated how much a romantic breakup would diminish their life satisfaction.

affective forecasting Predicting our future emotions—for example, whether an event will make us happy or angry or sad, and for how long.

A related study looked at the predicted and actual effects of getting tenure (Gilbert et al., 1998). As you may know, professors are evaluated around six years into their job and either given tenure (which means they have a permanent position at the university)

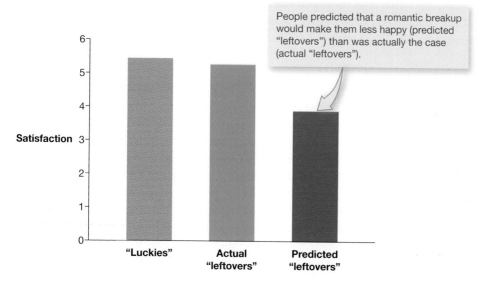

People predicted that a romantic breakup would make them less happy (predicted "leftovers") than was actually the case (actual "leftovers").

FIGURE 7.7 Do We Know What Makes Us Happy? Daniel Gilbert and his colleagues asked whether people are accurate in their judgments of how happy they will be following a romantic breakup. The results were consistent with their claims about biased affective forecasting. (Source: Adapted from Gilbert, Pinel, Wilson, Blumberg, & Wheatley, 1998.)

or sent packing. The tenure process is fraught with anxiety, awakening young professors in cold sweats at all hours of the night, and it is the source of a host of soothing rationalizations and jokes ("Did you hear why Jesus didn't get tenure? He was a great teacher, but he didn't publish much").

As it turns out, many of these tenure-related anxieties and aspirations may be misguided. Professors who did not get tenure were not significantly less happy than those who did. Once again, predictions differed from reality. Young assistant professors predicted a level of happiness after getting tenure that was far above what was actually observed in professors who did get tenure. And assistant professors expected a level of happiness after a denial of tenure that was far below what was actually observed in professors who had been denied tenure.

A variety of biases interfere with our attempts to predict the level of our future happiness. One is **immune neglect** (Gilbert et al., 1998). We are often remarkably resilient in responding to painful setbacks, in large part because of what Gilbert and Wilson call the "psychological immune system," which allows us to rise above the effects of negative experience and trauma. We find the silver lining, the humor, the potential for growth, insight, and positive change in the face of painful setbacks and traumatic experiences, and these "immune-related" processes allow us to return to satisfying lives in the face of negative experiences. The problem in predicting happiness, however, is that we fail to consider these processes when estimating the effects of traumatic events like breakups or failures at work. We assume that we will be devastated by traumatic negative events, but in fact we often respond in resilient fashion. As a consequence, we have difficulties predicting our future happiness.

Another bias is **focalism**: we focus too much on the main elements of significant events, such as the initial despair after learning that we have been denied tenure, neglecting to consider how other aspects of our lives will also shape our satisfaction (Wilson, Wheatley, Meyers, Gilbert, & Axson, 2000). As we move through life, it is common for us to assume that once a particular event happens—for example, once we ace our GREs, get married, or have children—we will be truly happy. What we forget

immune neglect The tendency to underestimate our capacity to be resilient in responding to difficult life events, which leads us to overestimate the extent to which life's difficulties will reduce our personal well-being.

focalism A tendency to focus too much on a central aspect of an event while neglecting to consider the impact of ancillary aspects of the event or the impact of other events.

to consider is that after those exam scores arrive, after our wedding, or after the arrival of our children, many other events—such as problems on our job, conflicts with our spouse, or difficulties with our children—will impinge on our happiness.

The Happy Life

Our final question concerning happiness may be the most important of all: What brings people happiness in their lives? Finding sound answers to this question will not only help you fare better in your marriage and career, it will also help you live longer. Sonja Lyubomirsky, Laura King, and Ed Diener reviewed several hundred studies of the correlates and consequences of happiness (Lyubomirsky, King, & Diener, 2005). Their conclusion is that happiness is good for your marriage. Marriage expert John Gottman has observed that for marriages to fare well, partners need to experience and express five positive emotions for every negative one (Gottman, 1993). Marriages with higher ratios of laughter, gratitude, appreciation, love, and kindness to anger, contempt, and fear are more likely to last. Happiness makes for more creative and better-performing workers, which makes sense in light of the influences of positive emotion on creative thought. Happiness also helps people live longer. One well-known study found that nuns who at age 20 reported greater happiness in personal narratives as they entered the convent were 2½ times less likely to die between the ages of 80 and 90 than nuns who reported being less happy in their narratives (Danner, Snowdon, & Friesen, 2001).

What, then, are the sources of happiness? One way to answer the question is to look at the broad demographic, or cultural, factors, that make for happier individuals. Do you have any intuitions about who is happier: women or men? It turns out that gender matters little in the realm of happiness: women are about as happy as men. The same is true for age: although people become a bit happier as they age, in general age has a weak effect on happiness. So much for midlife crises.

What about money? Here the story is a bit complicated and not what we might expect. In wealthier countries, money has little relationship with life satisfaction. College undergraduates now state that earning a lot of money is the primary reason for going to college. (A whopping 74 percent reported this in one recent survey, up from 24 percent 20 years ago. It remains to be seen whether the recent collapse of the financial industry causes students to rethink their career plans.) But for people who have attended college, more money is not likely to lead to more satisfaction (Myers, 2000b). And some recent research suggests that the pursuit of material gain as a central purpose in life actually makes people less happy (Lyubomirsky, 2006). But money does shape the life satisfaction for people who have little. People from poorer nations are less happy than those in rich nations. This may be because they often suffer from a lack of jobs, poor nutrition, and diseases that are correlated with poverty.

Broader ideological factors matter as well. In surveys of individuals from different countries, people are happier in independent cultures, in cultures where individuals have rights—for example, the right to vote—and in countries where there is more rather than less economic equality (Diener, 2000). These survey studies point to broad forces that enable people to be happy: some degree of economic well-being, equality, freedom, and individual rights.

And finally, as you might have guessed, scientists who study happiness all agree that the most powerful source of happiness is relationships (Lyubomirsky, 2006). All kinds of relationships—romantic relationships, friendships, family connections, neighborhood ties—lift people's spirits. In the 1970s and '80s in the United States, married people were twice as likely to say that they were "very happy" (48 percent) than were unmarried people (24 percent). Moreover, contact with friends consistently correlates strongly with levels of life satisfaction (Myers, 1999). We are social beings, and having strong social bonds brings great satisfaction.

Cultivating Happiness

People devote a great deal of energy to being happier and to trying to make their children, friends, coworkers, and romantic partners happier—and for good reason. The literature we have just reviewed suggests that cultivating happiness makes for healthier families, workplaces, communities, and cultures. Can we choose to live in ways that make us happier? In a recent theoretical paper, Sonja Lyubomirsky, Ken Sheldon, and David Schkade say yes (Lyubomirsky, Sheldon, & Schkade, 2005). In their survey of the literature on the genetic and environmental determinants of happiness, they suggest that about half of the variation among individuals in happiness is due to genetic factors. Studies of identical and fraternal twins, for example, find that identical twins, genetically the same, are about twice as similar in their levels of happiness as fraternal twins. Another 10 percent of the variation in happiness is due to the quality of the current environment—the neighborhood you grow up in; whether your country is at war or not; the rights, freedoms, and opportunities you enjoy. The remaining 40 percent of variation in happiness is shaped by the activities people choose, the patterns of thought that they develop, the ways that they handle stress, and the relationship style they cultivate with others.

So what does social psychology have to say about the freely chosen paths to happiness? One clear piece of wisdom concerns how you handle stressful times. Deeply stressful times—difficulties at work, trying times in a marriage, the loss of a loved one, turbulent times with parents and children—are part of living. And if these kinds of stresses are chronic, they can make you less happy, wear down your immune system, and lead to poor health.

One piece of wisdom we can offer is to create a narrative of your life, during good times and bad. Write about the emotions of life's trials and tribulations. James Pennebaker and his colleagues have conducted dozens of studies in which they have had participants write about the emotions associated with traumas they have experienced (Pennebaker, 1989, 1993; Pennebaker, Hughes, & O'Heeron, 1987; Smyth, 1998). Researchers have used this procedure with people who are bereaved or divorced, who have experienced devastating earthquakes, who are Holocaust survivors, and, more recently, who were directly affected by the 9/11 terrorist attacks. People who write about the most difficult emotions associated with the trauma, compared with people who write in more factual fashion about the same trauma, benefit in myriad ways. They are less likely to visit the doctor, they experience elevated life satisfaction, they show enhanced immune function, they report fewer absentee days at work or school, and they do better in school (Pennebaker, 1993).

Why does putting your emotions into words help? There are several reasons. First, people who give narrative structure to their emotions gain insight into their interior life, which enhances their efforts to deal with their troubles and difficulties (Pennebaker, Mayne, & Francis, 1997). Pennebaker and his colleagues laboriously coded participants' written narratives, and they found that the increased use of insight words, such as "I now see" or "perspective," correlate with increased benefits. Second, putting emotions into words reduces the distress associated with not expressing your emotions. Inhibiting the expression of emotion has been shown to heighten heart rate and blood pressure (Gross, 1998), and we know that chronically heightened blood pressure can produce health problems (Sapolsky, 1994). Expressing emotions should help to bring your blood pressure back to normal. Finally, labeling emotions also identifies what our emotions are due to, thus reducing the extent to which they color our judgments of irrelevant domains (Keltner, Locke, & Audrain, 1993; Wilson & Brekke, 1994; Wilson, Centerbar, & Brekke, 2002; Wilson & Gilbert, 2008). If you know that your frustration is due to a prima donna at work, it is less likely to influence your view of other facets of your life. The message is to keep writing those diaries and poems, even if they never bring you accolades or six-figure book contracts. It even appears that writing about more positive life themes, such as your most important goals, has similar benefits (Emmons, McCullough, & Tsang, 2003; King & Miner, 2000). For example, Laura King and her colleagues had undergraduates write about their best possible selves in the future and then weeks later measured their well-being and health. This act of envisioning a hopeful future centering on a better self increased students' reports of well-being and reduced their reports of problematic health symptoms. And writing about goals and values has been found to improve the academic functioning of minority junior high students (Cohen, Garcia, Apfel, & Master, 2006; Oyserman, Bybee, & Terry, 2006).

A second piece of wisdom is to cultivate the many positive emotions that are so vital to personal well-being and relationships. A life that is rich with positive emotions—amusement, gratitude, love, and contentment—is one of the clearest paths to life satisfaction. You might start your pursuit of happiness with gratitude. For many social theorists, including Adam Smith and Charles Darwin, gratitude is the glue of cooperative communities. The expression of gratitude rewards others for their generous acts.

BOX 7.3   **FOCUS ON POSITIVE PSYCHOLOGY**

Nirvana in Your Brain

Ever since the Buddha found enlightenment meditating under a bo tree 2,500 years ago, billions of people have turned to meditation to find peace and happiness. There are many kinds of meditation practices, but they share certain principles. They encourage you to mindfully slow down your breathing to a healthy, steady rhythm (and slowing down breathing through deep exhalations reduces stress-related cardiovascular arousal). Many meditation practices encourage a mindful attention to different sensations in your body. They likewise encourage nonjudgmental awareness of the stream of thoughts flowing through your mind. And many meditation practices—for example, those popularized by the Dalai Lama—encourage training the mind in loving kindness or compassion. Here the meditator extends feelings of compassion to family members, friends, loved ones, strangers, the self, and ultimately adversaries, to encourage a more compassionate stance toward fellow human beings.

Does meditation work? Neuroscientist Richard Davidson has been seeking a rigorous answer to that question, often packing his brain-recording instruments to the Himalayas. In one line of work he has studied Tibetan monks, who spend upward of 4 or 5 hours a day quietly and devotedly meditating. He scanned the brain of a Tibetan monk—an Olympic athlete at meditation—and found that this individual's resting brain showed levels of activation in the left frontal lobes—regions of the brain involved in positive emotion—to literally be off the charts. In another observation, Davidson blasted the monk with a loud burst of white noise to assess the startle response of the monk. For most mortals, this kind of stimulus activates an ancient and powerful startle response, the strength of which is a good indicator of how stressed out the individual is. The monk didn't even blink.

Okay, you're thinking, whose resting brain state wouldn't shift to the left

if you meditated 4 to 5 hours a day on loving kindness, as Tibetan Buddhists do, if you lived in the Himalayas with little laundry to do and no power struggles with roommates or romantic partners? Fair enough. When Richie and Jon Kabat Zinn and colleagues had software engineers train in the techniques of mindfulness meditation—an accepting awareness of the mind, loving kindness toward others—six weeks later these individuals showed increased activation in the left frontal lobes. They also showed enhanced immune function as evident in the magnitude of the immune response in the skin to a flu shot (Davidson et al., 2003). In similarly motivated work, Barbara Fredrickson and her colleagues have found that practicing mindfulness meditation, with a focus on being mindful of breathing and extending loving kindness to others, boosts happiness several weeks later (Fredrickson et al., 2008).

You learned earlier that we can express gratitude with simple touches to the forearm of others, touches that are likely to stimulate reward regions of the brain. Gratitude is also a way of looking at life that promotes happiness. Sonja Lyubomirsky (2006) had people count five blessings once a week and found that these grateful individuals, compared with an appropriate control, reported higher levels of happiness and health several weeks later. Simply reflecting on the meaningful things that life offers—the pleasures of friendship, an unusually beautiful day, a terrific meal—increased well-being. Reflecting on reasons for being grateful leads to increased happiness and fewer problematic health symptoms measured several weeks later (Emmons et al., 2003).

The same is true of other positive emotions. Forgiving someone increases well-being and promotes reduced stress-related physiology (Lawler et al., 2003). Increasing laughter and play in your relationships makes for more satisfying bonds. Cultivating feelings of contentment and interest make for long-term gains in overall well-being (Fredrickson, 2001). The path to a happy life is through the emotions.

 LOOKING BACK We have seen that our retrospective experiences of pleasure are based on peak and end pleasures, but not on the duration of the pleasurable experience. People have difficulty predicting whether they will be happy in the future, as they are often more resilient than they think, and they also tend to focus on certain aspects of future events while neglecting other aspects that will actually be important in the future. Being happy is good for your relationships, your work life, and your health. Some broad demographic factors (gender, age, income) matter little in shaping our happiness; others (equality, rights, a minimum level of economic well-being) matter a lot. Finally, happiness can be cultivated through narratives of tough times and cultivating positive emotions like gratitude, laughter, and forgiveness.

Summary

Characterizing Emotion

- The experience of emotion is generally *brief*, lasting on the order of seconds or minutes, as opposed to the experience of moods, which often last for hours or days.

- Emotions are generally felt about *specific* people and events, motivating individuals to achieve specific goals, such as redressing injustice or fleeing from a dangerous situation or promoting and *preserving social bonds*.

- Appraisal processes are the construal processes that trigger emotions. In the primary appraisal stage, we evaluate whether ongoing events are congruent with our goals, experiencing positive emotions for goal-congruent events and negative emotions for goal-incongruent events. In the secondary appraisal stage, we determine why we feel as we do and what to do about it, considering different ways of responding and possible future consequences of different responses.

- Emotions involve expressive processes, enabling us to communicate our feelings and reactions through configurations of muscles in the face, as well as through touch, the voice, and art.

- Emotions involve cognitive processes. Language enables us to label our emotions. At the same time, emotion shapes our memories and judgments as well as what we pay attention to.

Universality and Cultural Specificity of Emotion

- There are universal aspects to emotion based on evolutionary factors, not surprising given that emotions enable us to respond quickly and effectively to threats and opportunities related to survival.

- Paul Ekman's studies revealed that people in dramatically different cultures judge expressions of anger, disgust, fear, happiness, sadness, and surprise in highly similar fashion.

- There are cultural differences in when and which emotions are expressed. Some cultures develop specific ways of expressing a particular emotion, known as an emotion accent. Cultures vary in which emotions are focal, or common in everyday experience. Cultures vary in how many words they have in their langue to describe emotion. For example, it appears that the Chinese *hypercognize* self-conscious emotion; they have over 100 words to describe experiences of shame and embarrassment. And cultures vary in which emotions are highly valued, or idealized. For example, in the United States, excitement is a highly valued emotion.

Emotions and Social Relationships

- Emotions are vital to intimate relationships. A chemical known as oxytocin, which circulates through the brain and bloodstream, promotes trust and devotion.
- Touch is a rich medium in which to express emotion. With brief touches we can communicate emotions like love, compassion, and gratitude, which are vital to intimate relationships.
- We often mimic the expressive behaviors and emotions of others, and this process of emotional mimicry brings people closer together.
- Emotions are important to group dynamics as well. The expression of some emotions, like anger, gives people high status within groups, whereas other emotions, such as embarrassment, are part of a person's low-status role in a group.
- Emotions establish group boundaries as well. Group members have been shown to *infrahumanize* the emotions of outgroup members: they attribute basic emotions like anger and disgust to outgroups, but assume that outgroups do not so readily experience the more complex emotions, like embarrassment.

Emotions and Social Cognition

- Emotions influence social cognition in profound ways. The *feelings-as-information perspective* says that emotions provide rapid and reliable information for different judgments when we don't have enough time to evaluate detailed and complex information. Relevant studies have found that momentary emotions influence judgments of life satisfaction and risk.
- The *processing style perspective* says that different emotions lead us to process information in different ways, with positive emotions leading to the use of heuristics and stereotypes and negative emotions leading to more systematic and detailed assessments. The *broaden-and-build hypothesis* holds that positive emotions broaden our thought, even prompting us to see greater similari-

ties with individuals from other groups and build stronger relationships.
- Emotions influence moral judgments of right and wrong in powerful ways. For example, feelings of disgust make us judge impure behaviors (for example, cigarette smoking) as wrong.

Emotion in the Mind and Body

- Emotions involve physiological processes, including changes in the *autonomic nervous system*. The sympathetic autonomic nervous system (SANS) prepares the body for action by increasing heart rate, blood pressure, and cardiac output, among other effects, while the parasympathetic autonomic nervous system (PANS) restores the body's resources by decreasing heart rate and blood pressure, among other effects.
- William James believed that an emotionally exciting stimulus generates a physiological response, the perception of which is the emotion, and that each emotion has a distinct bodily response.
- Stanley Schachter and Jerome Singer proposed a *two-factor theory of emotion* in which the two components are undifferentiated physiological arousal and the construal of the state of undifferentiated arousal. Their studies showed the importance of cognition in the experience of emotion, as participants often made a *misattribution of arousal*.
- Paul Ekman and Wallace Friesen found distinct patterns of facial expression for different emotions. Using the *directed facial action (DFA) task*, Ekman and Friesen, along with Robert Levenson, directed participants to make faces of the sort that would be produced by various emotions. They found that different expressions resulted in different autonomic patterns for anger, disgust, and fear.

Happiness

- Our overall assessments of pleasure seem closely tied to the peak and end of the pleasurable stimulus and, surprisingly, have little to do with its duration. Our ability to predict the sources of happiness turns out to be suspect, in part due to two biases: *immune neglect* and *focalism*.
- Many objective factors, such as gender, age, and money, have surprisingly small effects on our happiness. In contrast, sociocultural factors, such as relationships with friends and family and social equality, have substantial effects on our happiness.
- A new science of happiness says that happiness promotes healthy marriages and helps you live longer.

- About 40 percent of a person's happiness is due to the habits and practices the individual chooses to cultivate. Writing about times of difficulty and stress makes for healthier adjustment, as does cultivating positive emotions like gratitude.

Key Terms

affective forcasting (p. 264)
appraisal processes (p. 237)
autonomic nervous system (ANS) (p. 258)
broaden-and-build hypothesis (p. 256)
core-relational themes (p. 237)
directed facial action (DFA) task (p. 261)
display rules (p. 247)

duration neglect (p. 264)
emotion accents (p. 244)
emotions (p. 237)
feelings-as-information perspective (p. 254)
focal emotions (p. 245)
focalism (p. 265)
free-response critique (p. 242)
hypercognize (p. 246)
immune neglect (p. 265)

infrahumanization (p. 253)
misattribution of arousal (p. 261)
principle of serviceable habits (p. 240)
primary appraisal stage (p. 238)
processing style perspective (p. 255)
secondary appraisal stage (p. 238)
two-factor theory of emotion (p. 259)

Further Reading

Damasio, A. R. (1994). *Descartes' error: Emotion, reason, and the human brain*. New York: Free Press. An excellent summary of how emotions are vital to our most important decisions, and an early neuroscientific approach to those issues.

Darwin, C. (1872/1998). *The expression of emotions in man and animals* (3rd ed.). New York: Oxford University Press. Darwin's classic on the evolution of the expressions of different emotions.

Forgas, J. P. (1995). Mood and judgment: The affect infusion model (AIM). *Psychological Bulletin, 117*(1), 39–66. A classic article detailing how moods and emotions influence different kinds of judgments.

Keltner, D. (2009). *Born to Be Good: The Science of a Meaningful Life*. New York: W. W. Norton & Company. A recent statement about the evolution of positive emotions like love, awe, compassion, and mirth, and their place in evolution.

Lyubomirsky, S. (2007). *The How of Happiness*. New York: The Penguin Press. An uplifting read on what makes us happy, and how.

Oatley, K. (2004). *Emotions: A Brief History*. Malden, MA: Blackwell. A great review of how we have thought about emotions over 2,000 years of western thought.

ⓢ Online Study Tools

StudySpace

Go to StudySpace, wwnorton.com/studyspace, to access additional review and enrichment materials, including the following resources for each chapter:

Organize
- Study Plan
- Chapter Outline
- Quiz+ Assessment

Learn
- Ebook
- Chapter Review
- Critical-Thinking Questions
- Visual Quizzes
- Vocabulary Flashcards

Connect
- Apply It! Exercises
- Author Insights Podcasts
- Social Psychology in the News

PART THREE

Influencing Others

Part Two focused on psychological processes occurring inside the individual—processes that both influence our interactions with others and are influenced by those interactions. Part Three shifts the focus outside the individual to an explicit examination of how we influence one another. In Chapter 8, we discuss how conformity pressures can lead us to think and act alike, even causing us to obey the commands of a malevolent authority. We also explore some of the most effective tactics for getting people to comply with requests. In Chapter 9, we examine social influence more broadly with a review of the research on what makes some persuasive messages, especially those presented through the mass media, more effective than others.

CHAPTER 8

Social Influence

A NUMBER OF YEARS AGO, over 500 experimental social psychologists (your three textbook authors among them) gathered in San Antonio, Texas, for the field's annual conference. Like nearly everyone who visits the city, most of us paid a visit to the area's most prominent tourist attraction, the Alamo.

An eighteenth-century Franciscan mission, the Alamo was the scene of epic bravery in Texas's war for independence from Mexico. Settlers from the United States had formed a provisional government and an army with the intention of separating from Mexico. In 1836, a group of fewer than 200 Texan soldiers were garrisoned at the Alamo when word was received that 4,000 Mexican troops under the command of General Antonio López de Santa Anna were approaching to take back the fort. The commander of the Alamo, Lieutenant Colonel William Travis, offered each soldier the opportunity to leave before the battle began. And he apparently did so in dramatic fashion, using his saber to draw a line in the sand and inviting all who wished to advance the cause of Texas's independence to cross the line and join him in the defense of the Alamo. All of them did, and all of them were killed trying to hold off Santa Anna's forces.

It is a moving story, not only because they all chose to stay and face their deaths, but also because they fought fiercely and heroically, holding off Santa Anna's forces for 12 days, a period of time that historians contend was crucial to Texas's efforts to organize an effective army under the command of Sam Houston. Indeed, six weeks after the taking of the Alamo by the Mexican army, Houston's forces defeated Santa Anna at San Jacinto, and Texas's independence from Mexico was secured. At least one commander is believed to have rallied his troops during the decisive battle with the cry, "Remember the Alamo!"

There is no denying the heroism of those 200 men. They gave (in Lincoln's words about another historic battlefield) their "last full measure of devotion" to the cause. But there is something about experiencing the Alamo in the presence of so many social psychologists—people attuned to the importance of the tiniest situational detail—that made it hard to imagine that the event actually occurred in such a storybook fashion. Given what we know about human behavior, it is unlikely that all 200 individuals enthusiastically crossed the line to join Travis. It is much more likely that the most devoted did so, and then a few more crossed the line so as not to be outdone, and then the others only reluctantly did so, after thinking to themselves, "Oh #@!$%, everyone's staying! What am I going to do?"

One of the great lessons of social psychology is that many seemingly subtle details of a given situation—the possibility of embarrassment, the presence of a few other people, the violation of routines—can have a powerful impact on people's behavior. As a result, the study of social psychology changes forever the way we view human behavior, whether it be the behavior of bona fide heroes, like those who defended the Alamo, or, at the other end of the spectrum, those who become suicide bombers or participate in acts of genocide, such as the Holocaust in Europe or, more recently, the massacres in the Darfur region of Sudan. Nowhere is this lesson more pointedly demonstrated than in the discussion of social influence.

In examining this topic, we will discuss a number of "situationist classics" in social psychology. By that we mean experiments that have become well known—both inside psychology and out in the broader culture—for revealing how seemingly inconsequential elements of a social situation can have surprisingly powerful effects on people's behavior. The results of these experiments have surprised and intrigued generations of students, forcing them to rethink some of their basic assumptions about human nature. We will begin by defining social influence and then discuss the factors that produce conformity to peers, obedience to authorities, and compliance with requests.

Social Influence and the Situation At the Battle of the Alamo in 1836, Texan defenders were all killed trying to prevent the Mexican army from retaking the fort. Each individual's decision to stay and fight to the death likely resulted from his sense of duty and conviction but also from social influence.

WHAT IS SOCIAL INFLUENCE?

Social influence, broadly speaking, refers to the myriad ways that people affect one another. It involves the changes in attitudes, beliefs, feelings, and behavior that result from the comments, actions, or even the mere presence of others. Social influence is a subject to which everyone can relate. Other people routinely attempt to influence us—whether it be a friend's pressure to go out drinking; Madison Avenue's efforts to get us to adopt the latest fashion; a charity's plea for our time or money; or a parent's, politician's, or priest's attempts to shape our moral, political, or religious values. We are also often the agent of social influence, as when we unconsciously smile at someone for actions we like and frown at someone for actions we dislike or when we deliberately try to coax a friend into dating

social influence The myriad ways that people impact one another, including changes in attitudes, beliefs, feelings, and behavior, that result from the comments, actions, or even the mere presence of others.

Janice in order to reduce the competition for Jane. Doing well in the world demands that we know when to yield to the influence attempts of others and when—and how—to resist. It also demands that we exercise some skill in our attempts to influence others.

Social psychologists distinguish among several types of social influence. The one most familiar to the average person is **conformity**, which social psychologists define as changing one's behavior or beliefs in response to some real (or imagined) pressure from others. Pressure to conform can be implicit, as when you decide to toss out your loose-fitting jeans in favor of those with a tighter cut (or vice versa) simply because other people have done so. But conformity pressure can also be explicit, as when members of a peer group pointedly encourage one another to smoke cigarettes, try new drugs, or push the envelope on some new extreme sport. When conformity pressure is explicit, it shades into another type of social influence called **compliance**, which social psychologists define as responding favorably to an explicit request by another person. Compliance attempts can come from people with some power over you, as when your boss or professor asks you to run an errand or babysit her kids, or from peers, as when a classmate asks to borrow your notes. Compliance attempts of the former variety are often not as nuanced and sophisticated as the latter because they don't have to be (think how much easier it would be for your professor to get you to agree to loan her $20 than it would be for the person sitting next to you in the classroom). Finally, another type of social influence, which social psychologists refer to as **obedience**, occurs when the power relationship is unequal and the more powerful person issues a command rather than a request, to which the less powerful person submits.

Is a tendency to go along with others a good thing or a bad thing? In today's Western society, which prizes autonomy and individual initiative, the term *conformity* connotes something bad to most people. If someone called you a conformist, for instance, you probably wouldn't like it. And some types of conformity *are* bad. Going along with a crowd to perpetrate a hurtful prank, to try a dangerous new drug, or to drive a vehicle while intoxicated are good examples. Other types of conformity are neither good nor bad, as when we conform to the norm to wear athletic shorts very short (1970s) or very long (1990s). Still other types are clearly beneficial, both to ourselves (because we don't have to deliberate about every possible action) and to others (because it eliminates potential conflict and makes human interaction so much smoother). Conformity plays a big part, for example, in getting many people to inhibit anger; to pay taxes; to form lines at the theater, museum, and grocery store; and to stick to the right side of the sidewalk or roadway. Would any of us really want to do away with those conformist tendencies? Indeed, evolutionary psychologists and anthropologists have argued that a tendency to conform is generally beneficial. We may be well served by doing what others are doing in the same situation unless we have a good reason not to (Boyd & Richerson, 1985; Henrich & Boyd, 1998).

conformity Changing one's behavior or beliefs in response to explicit or implicit pressure (whether real or imagined) from others.

compliance Responding favorably to an explicit request by another person.

obedience In an unequal power relationship, submitting to the demands of the more powerful person.

CONFORMITY

If you examined a snapshot of a National Basketball Association game in 1980 and compared it with one taken today, two differences would stand out. The players are much more muscular now, perhaps because of increased weight lifting and improved training techniques. But just as striking is a monumental difference in the popularity of tattoos. Almost no players had them in 1980, but now they are hugely popular, with many players sporting a veritable collage of symbols and statements on their skin. This change in the NBA, not surprisingly, mirrors a change in the broader society. Before the late 1980s, tattoos were rarely seen on anyone other than sailors

Conformity Pressures and Fashion Social influence affects what we do and say and how we present ourselves to others. Today, tattoos are common in the National Basketball Association (A), but were rare among previous generations of players (B).

ideomotor action The phenomenon whereby merely thinking about a behavior makes its actual performance more likely.

and prison inmates. Now they can be found on architects, homemakers, even college professors. The surge in the prevalence of tattoos is reflected in the fact that only about 10 percent of Americans over 40 have tattoos, compared to approximately 40 perent of those under 40 (Pew Research Center, 2007).

The sudden rise in the popularity of tattoos is a compelling demonstration of the power of conformity. After all, the millions of people who went to their local tattoo parlor and paid for a permanent image somewhere on their body did not suddenly all sense the virtues of body art on their own. They influenced each other. Doubtless the influence was sometimes purely implicit ("Look at that cool tattoo Lebron James has on his bicep"), and other times it was more explicit ("Check out our sorority letters on my ankle; you should get them too"). The same is true when prison guards abuse inmates (see Chapter 1) or when individuals fail to stop a bully. Sometimes the conformity pressures from the people around them are explicit, and sometimes they are implicit. We will try to understand the forces that elicit this type of social influence by exploring the full range of the implicit-explicit continuum.

Automatic Mimicry

As the cartoon on the next page illustrates, sometimes we mindlessly imitate other people's behavior. It is often said that yawning and laughter are contagious, but a lot of other behavior is as well. Like it or not, we are often subconscious copycats.

This tendency to reflexively mimic the posture, mannerisms, facial expressions, and other actions of those around us has been examined in a number of recent experiments. In one study, undergraduates at New York University took part in two 10-minute sessions in which each of them, along with another participant, was asked to describe various photographs from popular magazines such as *Newsweek* and *Time*. The other participant was, in reality, a confederate of the experimenter, and there was a different confederate in each of the two sessions. The confederate in one session frequently rubbed his or her face, whereas the confederate in the other session continuously shook his or her foot. As the participant and confederate went about their business of describing the various photographs, the participant was surreptitiously videotaped. This allowed the investigators to determine whether participants tended to rub their face in the presence of the face-rubbing confederate and shake their foot in the presence of the foot-shaking confederate. The videotapes, it is important to note, were taken of the participant only—the confederate was not visible on the tape. This ensured that those timing how long each participant rubbed her face or shook her foot were unaffected by knowledge of what the confederate was doing.

As predicted, the participants tended to mimic (conform to) the behavior exhibited by the confederate. They shook their foot more often when in the presence of a foot-shaking confederate and rubbed their face more often when in the presence of a face-rubbing confederate (see **Figure 8.1**). Follow-up studies have shown that this tendency to mimic others is particularly strong among people who have an empathic orientation toward others or who have a need to affiliate with others (Chartrand & Bargh, 1999; Lakin & Chartrand, 2003).

But why do we mindlessly copy others' behavior? There appear to be two reasons. William James (1890) provided the first explanation by proposing his principle of **ideomotor action**, whereby merely thinking about a behavior makes its actual performance more likely. Merely thinking about eating a bowl of gourmet ice cream, for example, makes it more likely that we will actually open the freezer, take out the ice cream, and indulge. And merely thinking that we might type the wrong letter on the computer keyboard makes it more likely that we'll make the mistake we fear (Wegner, 1994; Wegner, Ansfield, & Pilloff, 1998). The principle of ideomotor

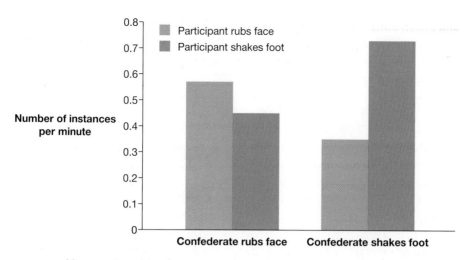

FIGURE 8.1 Unconscious Mimicry Average number of times per minute participants performed an action (face rubbing, foot shaking) while in the presence of someone performing that action or not. (Source: Chartrand & Bargh, 1999.)

action is based on the fact that the brain regions responsible for perception overlap with those responsible for action. Applied to mimicry, this means that when we see others behave in a particular way, the idea of that behavior is brought to mind (consciously or otherwise), making it more likely that we will behave that way ourselves.

The second reason we tend to reflexively mimic others is to prepare for interaction with them, interaction that is likely to go more smoothly if we establish some rapport. Chapter 6 discusses a study in which participants who were led to think about old people acted a bit like old people themselves, taking longer to walk out of the laboratory to the elevator. It's as if the very idea of old people made them mindlessly prepare for being around the elderly by slowing down their own movements. This idea receives support from follow-up studies showing that this tendency to automatically adopt the behavior of members of different social categories only holds for those with a positive attitude toward the group in question—that is, those who might be expected to want to interact with members of the category and have the interaction go well. Individuals with positive attitudes toward the elderly tended to walk more slowly when the category "elderly" was primed, but those with negative attitudes toward the elderly tended to walk faster (Cesario, Plaks, & Higgins, 2006).

It appears, then, that we tend to mimic others as a way of laying the groundwork for smooth, gratifying interaction. And it works! Studies have found that people tend to like those who mimic them more than those who do not (Chartrand & Bargh, 1999). What's more, individuals who have been mimicked tend to engage in more prosocial behavior immediately afterward—such as donating money to a good cause or leaving large tips to the person who mimicked them (van Baaren, Holland, Kawakami, & van Knippenberg, 2004; van Baaren, Holland, Steenaert, & van Knippenberg, 2003). Mimicry seems to be a helpful first step on the road to harmonious interaction and goodwill.

As it happens, cultures differ in how much they expect mimicry in social interactions and in how

"I don't know why. I just suddenly felt like calling."

Ideomotor Action and Conformity   When we see others behave in a particular way, we may unconsciously mimic their postures, facial expressions, and behavior. Before the signing of the 1995 Mideast Peace Accord, Bill Clinton, Israeli Prime Minister Yitzhak Rabin, Egyptian President Hosni Mubarak, and King Hussein of Jordan all adjusted their ties, as Yasser Arafat, who was not wearing a tie, looked on.

much they are thrown off by a failure of interaction partners to mimic them. Sanchez-Burks, Bartel, and Blount (2009) interviewed middle managers in a large corporation. The interview resembled a job interview and participants had a chance to win a large monetary prize if they performed particularly well. In some of the sessions, the interviewer deliberately mirrored the behavior of the interviewee, crossing his legs when the interviewee crossed his or hers, resting his chin on his hand when the interviewer did that, and so on. In some of the interviews, the interviewer was careful to avoid mirroring the interviewee. Some of the interviewees were Anglo-Saxon Americans and some were Hispanic Americans. Because being attuned to the emotions and behavior of others is more characteristic of Hispanic cultures than of Anglo-Saxon cultures, and because Sanchez-Burks and his colleagues believed that such attunement includes sympathetically mirroring the behavior of others, they anticipated that the Hispanic interviewees would do better in the interview when the interviewer mirrored their behavior than when he did not. This is what they found. When the interviewer mirrored the interviewee, the interviewee reported less anxiety and was rated more highly by observers than when the interviewer did not do any mirroring—if the interviewee was Hispanic. For Anglo-Saxon interviewees, it made no difference whether the interviewer mirrored their behavior or not.

Informational Social Influence and Sherif's Conformity Experiment

An early conformity experiment by Muzafer Sherif (1936) dealt with a type of conformity that lies further along the implicit-explicit continuum—conformity that is less automatic and reflexive. Sherif was interested in how groups influence the behavior of individuals by shaping how reality is perceived. He noted that even our most basic perceptions are influenced by frames of reference. In the well-known Müller-Lyer illusion reproduced in **Figure 8.2**, one horizontal line appears longer than the other because of how the lines are "framed" by the two sets of arrows. Sherif designed his experiment to examine the circumstances in which other people serve as a *social* frame of reference.

Sherif's experiment was built around the **autokinetic illusion**, the tendency of a stationary point of light in a completely darkened environment to appear to move. The phenomenon was noted by ancient astronomers and stems from the fact that with complete darkness there are no other stimuli to anchor one's sense of the light's location. Perhaps, Sherif thought, other people would fill the void and serve as a frame of reference against which one's perceptions of the light's movement would be assessed. To begin, Sherif put individual participants in a darkened room, presented them with a stationary point of light on trial after trial, and had them estimate how far it "moved" each time. What he found was that some people thought, on average, that it moved very little on each trial (say, 2 inches), and others thought it moved a good deal more (say, 8 inches).

Sherif's next step was to bring several participants into the room together and have them call out their estimates for each to hear. He found that people's estimates tended to converge over time. Those who individually had thought the light had moved a fair amount soon lowered their estimates; those who individually had thought it had moved very little soon raised theirs (see **Figure 8.3**). Sherif argued that everyone's individual judgments quickly fused into a group norm, and the norm influenced how far the light was seen to move. His interpretation was reinforced by a follow-up experiment that found that when participants were brought back for individual testing up to one year later, their judgments still showed the influence of their group's earlier responses (Rohrer, Baron, Hoffman, & Swander, 1954).

The behavior of Sherif's participants is typically interpreted as the result of **informational social influence**, or the use of other people—their comments and actions—as a source of information about what's likely to be right, proper, or effective (Deutsch & Gerard, 1955). We want to be right, and the opinions of other people are a useful source of information we can draw on to "get it right." Although we shouldn't mindlessly go along with what other people think all the time, we shouldn't simply ignore their opinions either. Indeed, we do so at our peril. The tendency to use others as a source of information is particularly pronounced when we are uncertain of the right answer. We are more likely to conform to others' views about the appropriate macroeconomic policy to follow than about the relative quality of the climate in Buffalo versus Honolulu. New York City residents were doubtless more inclined to follow the behavior of others right after the 9/11 attack on the World Trade Center than they were on a typical autumn day. Note that the task Sherif asked his participants to perform is about as ambiguous as it gets, and so informational social influence is at its peak. The light, in fact, doesn't move it all; it just appears to. And that appearance, being so uncertain and ambiguous, is readily influenced by the expressed judgments of others (see also Baron, Vandello, & Brunsman, 1996; Levine, Higgins, & Choi, 2000; Tesser, Campbell, & Mickler, 1983).

Normative Social Influence and Asch's Conformity Experiment

You may be thinking to yourself, "What's the big deal here? Why *wouldn't* participants conform to one another's judgments? After all, the task was impossible, and

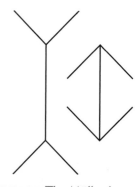

FIGURE 8.2 The Müller-Lyer Illusion In the Müller-Lyer illusion, the framing of the vertical lines by the arrows affects the perception of their lengths, just as social perception is affected by frames of reference. Even though the two vertical lines are exactly the same length, the vertical line on the left appears longer than the vertical line on the right because of its outward-pointing "fins" at the top and bottom, as opposed to the inward-pointing "fins" at the top and bottom of the line on the right.

autokinetic illusion The apparent motion of a stationary point of light in a completely darkened environment.

informational social influence The influence of other people that results from taking their comments or actions as a source of information about what is correct, proper, or effective.

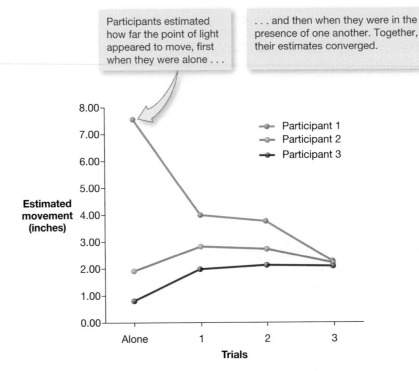

Participants estimated how far the point of light appeared to move, first when they were alone . . .

. . . and then when they were in the presence of one another. Together, their estimates converged.

FIGURE 8.3 Informational Social Influence Sherif's conformity experiment used the autokinetic effect to assess group influence. (Source: Sherif, 1936.)

Solomon Asch A pioneer of conformity research, Asch studied the effect of normative social influence.

no one could have felt confident in his or her own estimates. Why *not* rely on others?" If you were entertaining such thoughts, you were pursuing a line of reasoning advanced by another pioneer of conformity research, Solomon Asch. Asch thought that Sherif's experiment, although informative about a certain type of conformity, did not speak to those situations in which there is a clear conflict between one's own judgment and that of the group. It does not apply, for example, to the experience of knowing that you've consumed too much alcohol to drive safely while being urged to do so by your peers ("Come on. Don't be a wimp, you'll be fine"). Asch predicted that when there is a clear conflict between one's own judgment and the judgments advanced by the group, there will be far less conformity than that observed by Sherif. He was right. But the reduced rate of conformity was not what made his experiment one of the most famous in the history of psychology. What made his study so well known was how often participants *did* conform, even when they thought the group was out of its collective mind.

You may already be familiar with Asch's experiment (Asch, 1956). Eight individuals were gathered together to perform a simple perceptual task—to determine which of three lines was the same length as a target line (see **Figure 8.4**). Each individual called out his judgment publicly, one at a time. The task was sufficiently easy that the experience was uneventful—at first.

On the third trial, however, one individual found that his private judgment was at odds with the expressed opinions of everyone else in the group. That one individual was the one true participant in the experiment; the seven others were confederates instructed by Asch to respond incorrectly. The confederates responded incorrectly on 11 more occasions before the experiment was over, and the question was how often the participant would forsake what he knew to be the correct answer and conform to the incorrect judgment rendered by everyone else. Here there was no ambiguity, as there was in Sherif's experiment; the right answer was clear to participants, as evidenced by

FIGURE 8.4 Scientific Method: Normative Social Influence

Hypothesis: Participants conform to the opinions expressed by the majority even when they know the majority is incorrect.

Research Method:

1 One true participant (the man in the middle) and seven confederates were asked to say which of the three test lines was the same length as the target line.

2 On some trials, the confederates unanimously responded incorrectly, making the true participant doubt his own judgment (he is seen leaning forward to take another look at the lines).

A B C

Test lines   Target line

Results: The true participant conformed to the erroneous majority on a third of the trials.

Conclusion: To avoid the disapproval of the group, many participants conformed to the judgments of the majority rather than express their own judgment.

Source: Asch (1956).

the fact that individuals in a control group who made these judgments by themselves, without any social pressure, almost never made a mistake.

As Asch predicted, there was less conformity in this study than in Sherif's, but the rate of capitulation to the will of the group was still surprisingly high. Three-quarters of the participants conformed to the erroneous majority at least once. Overall, participants conformed on a third of the critical trials. The reason that Asch's experiment has had such impact is not simply that the results are surprising, but that they are disturbing to many people as well. We like to think of people, ourselves especially (Pronin, Berger, & Molouki, 2007), as sticking to what is thought to be right rather than following the herd, and we worry about people abandoning the dictates of their own conscience to follow others into potentially destructive behavior.

As this discussion implies, informational social influence is not thought to be the main source of conformity pressure in Asch's experiment. There is undoubtedly some informational social influence at work here; the erroneous judgments called out by the

BOX 8.1 **FOCUS ON HEALTH**

Bulimia and Social Influence

Why do young women engage in binge eating and then purging by vomiting or using laxatives? The phenomenon is relatively new. Such behavior, known as bulimia, was virtually unheard of until roughly 40 years ago. Does it exist because the fashion industry and media have persuaded women to want to be thinner than it is natural for them to be (see Chapter 10)? Is it because depression and anxiety have increased in recent decades? Is it because body image and self-esteem have worsened?

All of these factors may play a role in the current epidemic of bulimia, but another factor is social influence. Christian Crandall (1988) studied sorority women at a large midwestern university and found that the more bulimic a woman's friends were, the more bulimic she was likely to be. This was not because bulimic women discovered each other and became friends while nonbulimic women sought out peers who preferred to keep their food down. Early in the school year, when women had known each other only for a short while, there was no association between the level of a woman's engagement in bulimic activity and the level of her friends' engagement in such activity. But over the course of the year, women in now-established friendship groups (not *new* groups of friends) came to have similar levels of bulimia.

Crandall studied two different sororities and found two slightly different patterns of influence. In one sorority, women who differed in their level of bulimic activity from the average level in the sorority were less likely to be popular. Crandall inferred from this that there was an "appropriate" or normative level of bulimia in that sorority, and deviations from it *in either direction* were punished by rejection. In the other sorority, more binge eating (up to quite a large amount) was associated with more popularity. In that sorority, Crandall concluded, there was pressure toward considerable binge eating, and those most inclined to binge were rewarded with popularity.

Thinness and Social Influence
These models do whatever they can to maintain their slim bodies.

---

normative social influence The influence of other people that comes from the desire to avoid their disapproval, harsh judgments, and other social sanctions (for example, barbs, ostracism).

majority were for lines that were between ½ and ¾ inch off the correct answer, and some participants may have questioned their own judgment and therefore regarded the confederates' responses as informative. But the primary reason people conformed was to avoid standing out, negatively, in the eyes of everyone else (see **Box 8.1**). Social psychologists refer to this as **normative social influence**, or the desire to avoid the disapproval, harsh judgments, and other social sanctions (barbs, ostracism) that others might deliver (Deutsch & Gerard, 1955). People are often loathe to depart from the norms of society, or at least the norms of those subgroups they care most about, because of a fear of the social consequences (Cialdini, Kallgren, & Reno, 1991). The normative social pressures in Asch's experiment are sufficiently intense that the participants found themselves in a wrenching dilemma: "Should I say what I truly think it is? But what would everyone else think? They all agree, and they all seem so confident. Will they think I'm nuts? Will they interpret my disagreement as a slap in the face? But what kind of person am I if I go along with them? What the #@!$% should I do?"

To get an idea of the intensity of their dilemma, imagine the following scenario. As part of a discussion of Asch's experiment, your social psychology professor shows an overhead of the target line and the three test lines and reports that although the right answer is line B, the confederates all say it's C. As your professor attempts to move on from the basics of Asch's experiment, one student raises his hand firmly and announces with conviction, "But the right answer *is* C!"

What would happen? Doubtless everyone would chuckle, making the charitable assumption that the student was trying to be funny. But if the student insisted that the confederates' answer was correct, the chuckles would turn to awkward, nervous laughter, and everyone would turn toward the professor in an implicit plea to "make this awkward situation go away." On subsequent lectures, most people would avoid sitting by the individual in question, and a buffer of empty seats would surround him. (And, of course, lunch invitations, dating opportunities, and offers to join a fraternity or other social clubs would diminish as well.) *That* is the fate that Asch's participants felt they risked if they departed from the majority's response. It is no great surprise that they so often chose not to take the risk (Janes & Olson, 2000; Kruglanski & Webster, 1991; Levine, 1989; Schachter, 1951). Let's now consider the factors that influence the potency of these conformity pressures.

Factors Affecting Conformity Pressure

Several generations of researchers have examined the characteristics of the group and the characteristics of the task that influence the tendency to conform. We review some of that research here to gain a clearer understanding of when the tendency to conform will be particularly strong and when it will not. Central to our review is the distinction between informational and normative social influence. As we shall see, as either source of influence intensifies, so does the rate of conformity.

Group Size It is surely no surprise to learn that conformity increases as the size of the group increases. Larger groups exert both more normative influence (better to be disliked or shunned by a few than by many) and more informational social influence than smaller groups (all things being equal, a position advanced by many is more likely to be correct than a position advanced by a few). What is more surprising, perhaps, is that the effect of group size levels off pretty quickly (see **Figure 8.5**). Research using Asch's paradigm, for example, has shown an increase in conformity as the size of the group increases, but only to a group size of three or four; after that, the amount of conformity levels off (Campbell & Fairey, 1989; Gerard, Wilhelmy, & Conolley, 1968; Insko, Smith, Alicke, Wade, & Taylor, 1985; Rosenberg, 1961).

This makes sense, of course, from the standpoint of both informational and normative social influence. The larger the number of people who venture a particular opinion, the more likely it has merit. But only to a certain point. After a while, the opinions offered are unlikely to be independent of one another, and thus the responses of additional people do not offer any real information. Also, as the number of people increases, the fear of being judged harshly increases. But here, too, only to a point. There is only so much embarrassment one can feel, and the difference between being viewed as odd, foolish, or difficult by 2 versus 4 people is psychologically much more powerful than the difference between being viewed that way by 6 versus 8 or by 12 versus 14.

Group Unanimity One of the more powerful effects observed in Asch's original studies was what happened when the unanimity of the group was broken. Recall that in the basic paradigm, when all group members but the one true participant reported an incorrect answer, the participant went along and reported the wrong answer a third of the time. That figure dropped to 5 percent when the true participant had an ally—that is, when just one other member of the group deviated from the majority. This effect occurs because the presence of an ally weakens both informational social influence ("Maybe I'm not crazy after all") and normative social influence ("At least

"'The way to get along,' I was told when I entered Congress, 'is to go along.'"

—John F. Kennedy

"It takes a great deal of bravery to stand up to our enemies, but just as much to stand up to our friends."

—Albus Dumbledore, *Harry Potter and the Sorcerer's Stone*

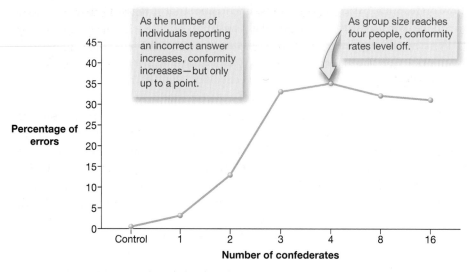

As the number of individuals reporting an incorrect answer increases, conformity increases—but only up to a point.

As group size reaches four people, conformity rates level off.

Percentage of errors

Number of confederates

FIGURE 8.5 The Effect of Group Size on Conformity (Source: Asch, 1951.)

I've got someone to commiserate with"). This effect also suggests a powerful tool for protecting independence of thought and action. If you expect to be pressured to conform and want to remain true to your own beliefs, bring an ally along.

Note that the other individual who breaks the group's unanimity doesn't need to offer the correct answer—just one that departs from the group's answer. Suppose the right answer is the shortest of the three lines, and the majority claims it's the longest. If the fellow dissenter states that it's the middle line, it reduces the rate of conformity, even though the participant's own view hasn't been reinforced. What matters is the break in unanimity. This fact has important free speech implications. It suggests that we might want to tolerate loathsome and patently false statements ("The Holocaust never happened"; "The President is a child molester"; "The World Trade Center attacks were a government hoax") not because there is any value in what is said, but because it liberates *other people* to say things of value. The presence of voices, even bizarre voices, that depart from conventional opinion liberates the body politic to speak out and thus can foster productive political discourse. Conversely, the tendency to consult news sources that agree with us—Web sites and blogs that pitch their news to a narrow and possibly highly biased range of opinions—can create an echo chamber in which all the voices are in agreement. This can leave people with a misplaced confidence in their views.

The liberating effects of having an ally, along with the relationship between group size and conformity discussed earlier, have interesting implications for how juries might best be constructed. What is the optimal size of a jury? In the United States, most juries have 12 members, but that number is not specified in the U.S. Constitution. Other sizes are allowed, and juries of 6 and 8 are used in some states. From a purely pragmatic standpoint, smaller juries would be preferred (they cost less in time and money), provided they are as effective as larger ones. But are they? One important consideration that legal scholars urge us to guard against is the "tyranny of the majority"—of having a near-unanimous majority intimidate a sole individual into swallowing his or her true convictions and caving in to the majority.

On these grounds, the conformity research makes it clear that 12-person juries are to be preferred to smaller ones. Because conformity pressures level off at 4 or 5 members, 12-person juries may be no more "tyrannical" than, say, 6-person juries. And on purely statistical grounds, someone who dissents from the majority is more likely to have an ally—a bracing partner in dissent—in a group of 12 than in a group of 6. Thus, if a fair trial is to include the possibility of a minority viewpoint swaying all other jury members or, more likely, creating a "hung jury" (one that cannot reach unanimity), then fairness is best achieved by a 12-person jury than by a smaller one (Valenti & Downing, 1975).

Expertise and Status Imagine that you were a participant in Asch's experiment and that the other participants who were inexplicably stating what you thought was the wrong answer were all former major-league batting champions. On the assumption that one can't lead the league in hitting without exceptional eyesight, it is likely that you would grant the group considerable authority and go along with their opinion. In contrast, if the rest of the group were all wearing Coke-bottle eyeglasses, it's unlikely you would take their opinions seriously.

As this thought experiment illustrates, the expertise and status of the group members powerfully influence the rate of conformity. Expertise and status often go together, of course, as those with special expertise are granted greater status, and those with high status are often assumed (not always correctly) to have considerable expertise (Koslowsky & Schwarzwald, 2001). To the extent that they are separable, however, expertise primarily affects informational social influence. Experts are more likely to be right, and so their opinions are taken more seriously. Status, in contrast, mainly affects normative social influence. The disapproval of high-status individuals can hurt more than the disapproval of people one cares less about.

The effect of expertise and status has been demonstrated in numerous studies (Cialdini & Trost, 1998; Crano, 1970; Ettinger, Marino, Endler, Geller, & Natziuk, 1971). One of our favorites was one of the earliest, and it used a paradigm that is quite different from Asch's. Torrance (1955) gave the members of navy bombing crews—pilot, navigator, and gunner—a number of reasoning problems, such as this horse-trading problem:

> A man bought a horse for $60 and then sold it for $70. He then repurchased the horse for $80 and then, changing his mind yet again, sold it again for $90. How much money did he make on his series of transactions? (Answer on p. 289)

The crews then had to report one answer for the whole group. Torrance monitored the group's deliberations and found that if the pilot originally came up with the correct solution, the group eventually reported it as their answer 91 percent of the time. If the navigator offered the correct answer, the group reported it 80 percent of the time. But if the lowly gunner offered the correct answer, the group offered it up only 63 percent of the time. The opinions of higher-status individuals thus appear to carry more weight with the group as a whole (Foushee, 1984).

Culture We have emphasized throughout this book that people from interdependent cultures are much more concerned about their relations to others and about fitting into the broader social context than are people from independent cultures. People reared in interdependent cultures are therefore likely to be more susceptible to both informational social influence (the actions and opinions of others are likely to be considered more telling) and normative social influence (the high regard of others is likely to be considered more important). Thus, we might expect people from interdependent cultures to conform more than those from independent cultures.

Evidence supports this contention. In one early test of cross-cultural differences in conformity, Stanley Milgram (1961) conducted experiments using Asch's paradigm in Norway and France. Milgram maintained that Norwegians emphasize

"If there is any principle of the Constitution that more imperatively calls for attachment than any other it is the principle of free thought—not free thought for those who agree with us but freedom for the thought that we hate."

—Oliver Wendell Holmes

Expertise, Status, and Social Influence When the United States was preparing to invade Iraq to unseat Saddam Hussein and secure his putative weapons of mass destruction in March 2003, the U.S. administration sent Secretary of State Colin Powell to speak to the delegates of the United Nations because he had great credibility. Powell presented what he believed were the facts about Iraq's weapons of mass destruction and hoped to convince the delegates of the need to invade Iraq.

group cohesiveness more than the French, and just as he expected, he found that the Norwegian participants conformed more than the French participants.

But why study Norway and France (other than that both are delightful places to visit and conduct research)? In our examination of independent versus interdependent cultures throughout this book, France and Norway have not loomed large in the discussion. What about the greater independent/interdependent divide that exists between a broader sample of the world's regions? A more systematic analysis of the results of experiments using the Asch paradigm in 133 different studies in 17 countries found that conformity does indeed tend to be greater in interdependent countries than in independent countries (Bond & Smith, 1996). The individualism that is highly valued in American and Western European societies has given individuals in those societies a greater willingness to stand apart from the majority. Note also that the willingness to resist the influence of the majority may be increasing. More recent conformity experiments in the United States and Great Britain using Asch's procedure have tended to find lower rates of conformity (Bond & Smith, 1996; Perrin & Spencer, 1981).

Gender To grow up as a boy or girl in a given society is to grow up in a slightly different culture. Societies differ tremendously in how they socialize boys and girls, but all societies sex-type to some degree. Thus, if there are cultural differences in conformity, might we not expect gender differences as well? Perhaps. Women are raised to value interdependence and to nurture important social relationships more than men are, whereas men are raised to value and strive for autonomy and independence more than women are. We might therefore expect women to be more subject to social influence and hence to conform more than men.

But as you will see, people are more likely to conform when they are confused by the events unfolding around them. And if women are taught to attend to relationships, and hence are more likely to be the "experts" on human relationships, their greater sophistication about relationships may give them the confidence necessary to resist the influence of the majority.

The research findings are what you might expect given these two opposing considerations. Reviews of the literature on gender differences in conformity have shown that women tend to conform a bit more than men—but only a bit (Bond & Smith, 1996; Eagly, 1987; Eagly & Carli, 1981; Eagly & Chrvala, 2006). The difference tends to be biggest when the conformity situation is of the face-to-face type like that in Asch's original study. But the difference also seems to be strongly influenced by the specific content of the issue at hand. To illustrate, would you be more likely to conform to other people when they assert that the atomic number of beryllium is 62 or when they assert that the most important ingredient in a good sandwich is horseradish? If you're like most people, you know more about sandwiches than about the periodic table, so you would be more likely to stand your ground on matters related to lunchtime meals. Analyses of the specific contexts in which men and women differ in the tendency to conform reveal just this effect (Sistrunk & McDavid, 1971). Thus, women tend to conform more in stereotypically male domains (for example, on questions about geography or deer hunting), whereas men tend to conform more in stereotypically female domains (for example, on questions about cosmetics or child rearing). It should therefore come as no surprise that, overall, there is a difference in conformity between men and women, but only a small one. Women are socialized to nurture relationships more than men are, so they are more subject to social influence. But their greater comfort with relationships and knowledge about relationships may also give them a more solid foundation from which they can resist social influence attempts.

Difficulty (or Ambiguity) of the Task Comparing the Asch and Sherif experiments highlights the importance of how challenging the task is and hence how difficult it is to arrive at a confident answer. When the judgment at hand is unambiguous and easy to make, informational social influence is virtually eliminated. Only normative social influence is at work, and resistance to the group is stronger (Allen, 1965; Baron et al., 1996). Imagine, for example, that you are visiting a foreign country and you are uncertain about what is called for in a given situation. Would you be decisive and assertive? Certainly not. When the "right" thing to do is unclear, we are particularly inclined to rely on others for guidance.

Anonymity While an easy task eliminates informational social influence, the ability to respond anonymously eliminates normative social influence. When nobody else is aware of our judgment, there is no need to fear the group's disapproval. This highlights an important distinction between the impact of informational and normative social influence. Informational social influence, by influencing how we come to see the issues or stimuli before us, tends to influence **internalization**, or our **private acceptance** of the position advanced by the majority (Kelman, 1958). We don't just ape a particular response, we adopt the group's perspective. We see it their way or tend to assume they've got things right. Normative social influence, in contrast, often has a greater impact on **public compliance** than on private acceptance. To avoid disapproval, we sometimes do or say one thing but continue to believe another.

The Interpretative Context of Disagreement A particularly surprising aspect of Asch's experiment is that the participants conformed to the erroneous judgments of a group of strangers. Why would the participants care so much about what these other people think of them, people whom they have never seen before and likely will never see again? If people conform this much to the questionable judgment of strangers, surely they would conform even more to the judgments of those they know well, care about, and must deal with in the future (Lott & Lott, 1961; Wolf, 1985).

How can we explain this curious feature of Asch's experiment? What is responsible for such high rates of conformity when the social pressures to conform might seem rather weak? The key to resolving this question is to note that participants in Asch's experiment face a double whammy. First, they must confront the fact that everyone else sees things differently than they do. Second, they have no basis for understanding *why* everyone else sees things differently. ("Could I be mistaken? No, it's plain as day. Could they be mistaken? I don't see how because they're not any farther away than I am and it's so clear. Are they any different than I am? No, they don't look different from anyone else.")

Knowing why our opinions are different ("They don't see the lines the way I do because they're wearing distorting glasses") can embolden us to hold our ground because it can lessen both informational and normative social influence. Informational social influence is lessened because the explanation can diminish the group's impact as a source of information ("They're biased"). Normative social influence is lessened because we can assume that those in the majority are aware of why we differ from them. For instance, if we have different views on some burning political issue of the day, those with whom we disagree might think we're biased, selfish, or have different values, but at least they won't think we're

Answer to horse problem on p. 287: $20

internalization (private acceptance) Private acceptance of a proposition, orientation, or ideology.

public compliance Agreeing with someone or advancing a position in public, even if we continue to believe something else in private.

crazy. In Asch's situation, in contrast, the participants faced the reasonable fear that if they departed from everyone else's judgment, their behavior would look truly bizarre and everyone would think they were nuts.

Lee Ross and his colleagues sought to examine this interpretation of Asch's experiment by replicating his results in one condition but adding another condition in which participants *could* explain to themselves why their own judgments differed from those of the majority (Ross, Bierbrauer, & Hoffman, 1976). The participants in this study were asked to judge not the length of lines but the duration of tones. First one tone was played and then another, and the participant's task was to state which was longer in duration. Participants earned points for each correct response, according to the payoff matrix depicted in the left-hand portion of the table in **Figure 8.6**. The matrix shows that participants were to receive 10 points for each correct response (saying "1" when it really was 1, and saying "2" when it really was 2) and nothing for an incorrect response.

But in another, "big-payoff" condition of the experiment, participants learned that the other three participants (who in reality were confederates of the experimenters) would be operating under a different payoff scheme, depicted in the right-hand portion of the table. The experiment unfolded just like Asch's: most trials were uneventful, with the confederates calling out what the true participant knew to be the correct answer. No problem. But on a select number of trials, the confederates all called out "2" when the true participant knew it was 1. How to respond?

Note that in the condition that replicates Asch's experiment—the one in which the basic payoff matrix is in effect for everyone—the participant has no explanation for why everyone else is responding incorrectly. Baffled, these participants ought to conform at roughly the same level observed in Asch's study. But those in the "big-payoff" condition do have an explanation: everyone else is being seduced by the possibility of a big 100-point payoff and is calling out "2" as something of a long shot. This understanding ought to embolden participants and reduce how much they conformed.

As Figure 8.13 illustrates, that is exactly what happened. Participants in the Asch-like condition called out the incorrect response (that is, they conformed) much more often than those in the big-payoff condition—and much more often than those in a control condition, who called out their responses when they were alone (a condition included to verify that the correct response really was easy for participants to discern).

The lesson here is that it is difficult to act independently when we don't know what to make of things. It is hard to be assertive when we are puzzled by what is going on. It is easier to stand our ground, in other words, when we have a clear understanding of what might be causing others to make erroneous judgments. This lesson will also prove crucial to understanding our next topic, obedience. Before we get to that, however, we must take note of the fact that small minorities sometimes sway the opinion of entire societies, so let's examine when and how minority viewpoints have their greatest impact.

The Influence of Minority Opinion on the Majority

There was a time in the United States when people owned slaves, when women were not allowed to vote, and when children worked long hours for scandalously low pay in unhealthy conditions. But small groups of abolitionists, suffragettes, and child welfare advocates saw things more clearly than their peers and worked tirelessly to change public opinion about each of these issues. And they succeeded. The views of the broader public were changed in each case, and important legislation was passed. Minority opinion became the opinion of the majority.

Examples such as these remind us that although conformity pressures can be powerful, majority opinion does not always prevail. Not only can conformity pressure

"Give me a firm place to stand and I will move the world."

—Archimedes of Syracuse

FIGURE 8.6 Scientific Method: Interpretive Context and Conformity

Hypothesis: People conform less when they have an explanation for why others are responding differently.

Research Method:

1 A participant, among a group of three confederates of the experimenter, listened as first one tone was played and then another, and the participant was asked to state which one was longer in duration.

2 In the "Asch-like" condition of the experiment, participants earned points for each correct response, according to the payoff matrix below. Participants were to receive 10 points for each correct response (saying "1" when it really was 1, saying "2" when it really was 2) and nothing for an incorrect response.

3 In an alternative, "big-payoff" condition of the experiment, the true contestant learned that the three confederates would be operating under a different payoff scheme, below, in which there is a chance of a big 100-point payoff when "2" is called out.

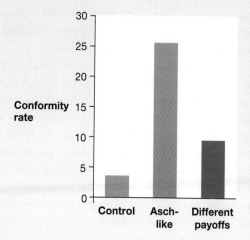

Basic matrix

P's response

True answer	1	2
1	10	0
2	0	10

Alternative matrix

P's response

	1	2
1	10	0
2	0	100

4 On most trials, the confederates called out what the true participant knew to be the correct answer. But on a select number of trials, the confederates all called out "2" when the true participant knew it was 1.

Results: For those participants in the "Asch-like" condition, there was no explanation for why everyone else was responding incorrectly. They tended to conform with the confederates much more often than participants in the "big-payoff" condition, who had an explanation for the confederates' divergent responses.

Conclusion: It is easier to stand your ground when you have a clear understanding of why others are responding differently.

Source: Ross, Bierbrauer, & Hoffman (1976).

be resisted, but minority voices can be heard sufficiently clearly that the prevailing majority opinion can be changed. How do minority opinions come to influence the majority? Are the sources of influence the same as those that majorities bring to bear on minorities?

In the first experimental examination of these questions, Serge Moscovici and his colleagues had participants in a group setting call out whether a color was green or blue (Moscovici, Lage, & Naffrechoux, 1969). The border between blue and green, of course, is not always clear, but the critical stimuli shown to the participants were ones that the participants, when tested alone, nearly always thought were blue. The

Minority Influence on the Majority Minority opinions can exert social influence on the prevailing majority opinion through consistent and clear messages that persuade the majority to systematically examine and reevaluate its opinions. (A) British suffragette Emmaline Pankhurst presented her views in favor of women's right to vote to an American crowd in 1918. (B) Rosa Parks refused to give up her seat at the front of a bus in Montgomery, Alabama, in December 1955. Her actions resulted in a citywide bus boycott that eventually led the U.S. Supreme Court to declare that segregation was illegal on the city bus system.

experimenter showed participants these stimuli in the presence of a minority of respondents (confederates of the experimenter) who responded "green," and recorded how the true participants responded.

When the minority responded with "green" consistently, the true participants responded likewise 8 percent of the time. When the minority varied their responses randomly between "green" and "blue," the participants did so only 1 percent of the time, about the same as when they responded alone. But that was not the only effect the minority had. When the participants thought the experiment was over, the experimenter introduced them to a second experimenter who, they were told, was also interested in color vision. This second experimenter showed participants a series of blue-green colors and noted where each participant, individually, thought blue left off and green began. What Moscovici and his colleagues found was that participants who had earlier been exposed to a consistent minority now identified more of these stimuli as green—their sense of the border between blue and green had shifted. Thus, the consistent minority opinion had both a direct effect on participants' responses in the public setting and a "latent" effect on their subsequent, private judgments.

Further investigation of minority influence in paradigms like Moscovici's has shown that minorities have their effect primarily through informational social influence (Moscovici, 1985; Nemeth, 1986; Wood, Lundgren, Ouellette, Busceme, & Blackstone, 1994). People in the majority are typically not terribly concerned about the social costs of stating their opinion out loud—they have the majority on their side, and normative social influence is minimized. But they might wonder why the minority keeps stating its divergent opinion. This can lead them to consider the stimulus more carefully, leading to a level of scrutiny and systematic thought that can lead to a genuine change in attitude or belief. Thus, majorities typically elicit more conformity, but it is often of the public compliance sort. In contrast, minorities typically influence fewer people, but the nature of the influence is often deeper, resulting in true private acceptance (Maass & Clark, 1983).

We have seen that conformity can occur in response to implicit or explicit social pressures and can be the result of automatic mimicry, informational social influence, or normative social influence. We have seen that group size is important for normative influence, but it appears to reach maximum effect at around four people. Unanimity also is crucial in conformity, and a single ally can help an individual hold out against the group. We have seen that people from more interdependent cultures conform more than people from more independent cultures and that women conform slightly more than men. More difficult tasks create more conformity, and plausible explanations for why others might hold views different from our own tend to reduce conformity. Conformity pressures notwithstanding, minorities often do have an influence, primarily through informational social influence. We next consider the consequences of a particular type of conformity—obedience to the orders of a person in authority.

OBEDIENCE TO AUTHORITY

The study of when and why people obey the commands of someone in authority has been dominated by the one set of social psychological experiments more famous than Asch's—those of Stanley Milgram. Milgram's experiments constitute what is arguably the most widely known research program in all of psychology. Milgram's experiments are sufficiently well known, in fact, that "they have become part of our society's shared intellectual legacy—that small body of historical incidents, biblical parables, and classic literature that serious thinkers feel free to draw on when they debate about human nature or contemplate human history" (Ross, 1988).

The Setup of the Milgram Experiments

Milgram's research on obedience began as an investigation of conformity. He was intrigued by Asch's findings but wondered about their limitations in much the same way that Asch had wondered about the limitations of Sherif's findings. Recall that Asch thought it only natural that people would readily conform to others' responses when they didn't have a firm opinion themselves. But what would happen, he wondered, if there was a clear conflict between the individual's personal convictions and the responses of the group? Asch found considerable conformity even then, which surprised him. Milgram's findings surprised Milgram even more.

Milgram was interested in whether the kind of conformity pressures observed in Asch's paradigm were sufficiently powerful to lead people to do something far more significant than report an incorrect line length. He wondered what would happen if he asked participants to deliver electric shock whenever a subject performing a task (in reality the experimenter's confederate) responded incorrectly. Would participants conform here, when doing so involved hurting another human being?

This is an interesting question, but Milgram never pursued it. The reason is that he first needed to obtain data from a control group to see how willing participants would be to deliver electric shock in the absence of any conformity pressure (Evans, 1980).

Stanley Milgram Using a "shock generator" that looked real but was actually just a prop, Milgram studied whether participants would continue to obey instructions and shock a learner even after believing that the learner was in grave distress as a result of the shocks.

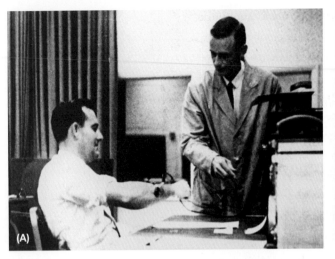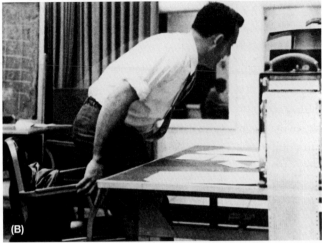

The Milgram Experiment Participants were led to believe that the shock generator had 30 levels of shock, ranging from "slight shock" to "danger: severe shock" to "XXX." (A) The participant was given a sample shock of 45 volts (this was the only real shock in the experiment). (B) The participant stood up to ask the experimenter if he could stop the experiment when he thought that the learner had passed out from the shocks.

And that is where he received his experimental surprise, one that changed his research program entirely. A surprising large percentage of his participants were willing to do something they thought was hurting another human being even when there was no group of other participants leading the way.

We described Milgram's basic procedure (his intended control group) in Chapter 1, so we will describe it only briefly here before turning our attention to a number of important variations. Responding to an ad in a New Haven newspaper, participants in Milgram's study reported for an experiment on learning. A "random" draw was rigged so that the participants always became the "teacher" and the confederate always became the "learner." The teacher's job was to administer electric shock every time the learner—a genial, middle-aged man who was strapped into a chair with his arm on a shock delivery apparatus—made a mistake and reported the wrong word from a list of word pairs presented at the beginning of the study (for example, glove/book, grill/detergent, anvil/pope). Teachers were briefly strapped to the chair themselves and given a 45-volt shock so that they would know that the shocks were painful. The teacher then started off delivering 15 volts after the learner's first mistake and increased the shock in 15-volt increments after each subsequent mistake. As the mistakes accumulated, participants found themselves required to deliver 255, 300, 330— all the way up to 450—volts of electricity. (In reality, no electric shock was actually delivered.) If a participant expressed reservations or tried to terminate the experiment, the experimenter would respond with a carefully scripted set of responses—"Please continue," "The experiment requires that you continue," "It is absolutely essential that you continue," "You have no other choice, you must go on."

The great surprise in these studies was that people continued to obey the experimenter's orders and to shock the confederate. In the remote-feedback condition, in which the learner was in an adjoining room and could not be heard except when he vigorously pounded on the wall after a shock of 300 volts, 66 percent of the participants continued the learning experiment and delivered the maximum shock of 450 volts. In the voice-feedback condition, the participants could hear a series of increasingly desperate pleas by the learner—including screaming that he had a heart condition—until finally, and ominously, he became silent. Despite these cues that the learner was suffering, 62.5 percent of the participants delivered the maximum shock (Milgram, 1965, 1974).

Opposing Forces

Milgram's participants found themselves in an agonizing conflict, caught between two opposing sets of forces. On the one hand were the forces compelling them to complete the experiment and to continue delivering shock (Reeder, Monroe, & Pryor, 2008). Among these was a sense of "fair play"—they had agreed to serve as participants, they had already received payment for having done so, and they felt that they now had to fulfill their part of the bargain. Some participants were also likely motivated by the reason they had agreed to be participants in the first place—to advance science and the understanding of human behavior. Another important motivating factor was normative social influence—in this case, the desire to avoid the disapproval of the experimenter or of anyone else associated with the experiment whom they imagined they might encounter on their way out. Closely related to this concern was the very human desire to avoid "making a scene" and not upsetting others (Goffman, 1966; Miller, 1996).

On the other hand, there were several powerful forces compelling the participants to want to terminate the experiment. Foremost among these was the moral imperative to stop the suffering of the learner. This may have reflected a concrete desire not to see this particular individual hurt as well as a more abstract injunction against hurting others (and the implication of what the abandonment of this abstract principle would say about the kind of people they were). Some participants were also probably concerned about what would happen if something went wrong. "What if he dies or is permanently injured?" "Will there be a lawsuit?" Still others may have wondered about the prospect of having to walk out with the learner after everything was over and the embarrassment (even retaliation) it might bring. And how could the participants be sure that the roles wouldn't be reversed? At the moment, they occupied the teacher role, but could they be certain that there wouldn't be a new round in which *they* were strapped into the shock machine?

"Tuning in" the Learner By specifying the opposing forces acting on participants, we can gain an understanding of why they responded the way they did and why the whole experience was so stressful. We can also gain some insight into how the rate of obedience might be altered by modifying the strength of these opposing forces (Blass, 2000, 2004; Miller, 1986). This is exactly what Milgram did in a comprehensive series of studies. First, he tried to increase the forces that compel people to terminate the experiment. These were all triggered by an awareness of the learner's suffering, so Milgram attempted to increase these forces by increasing the prominence of the learner. He called this "tuning in the learner." (Participants spontaneously tried to do the opposite—that

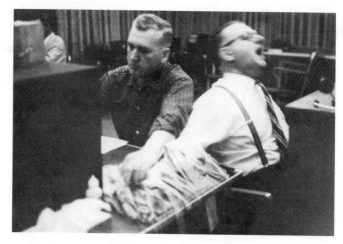

Tuning in the Learner In a "touch-proximity" condition, participants were required to force the learner's hand onto the shock plate, which reduced the participants' obedience rates.

is, deal with their own discomfort by tuning *out* the learner, sometimes literally turning away from him in their chair.) In the remote-feedback condition, the learner could neither be seen nor heard (except for one episode of vigorous pounding). In the voice-feedback condition, the learner still could not be seen, but he and his vigorous protests could be heard very clearly, which made the teacher constantly aware of him.

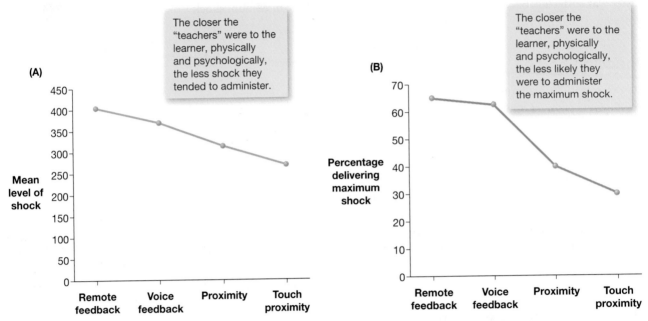

(A)

The closer the "teachers" were to the learner, physically and psychologically, the less shock they tended to administer.

Mean level of shock

450
400
350
300
250
200
150
100
50
0

Remote feedback · Voice feedback · Proximity · Touch proximity

(B)

The closer the "teachers" were to the learner, physically and psychologically, the less likely they were to administer the maximum shock.

Percentage delivering maximum shock

70
60
50
40
30
20
10
0

Remote feedback · Voice feedback · Proximity · Touch proximity

FIGURE 8.7 Tuning in the Learner The effect of experimental manipulations that make the learner more and more salient on (A) the mean level of shock participants delivered and (B) the percentage of participants who delivered the maximum amount of shock. (Source: Milgram, 1965.)

In a proximity condition, the learner received his shock in the same room in which the participant delivered it, from only 1.5 feet away. Finally, in the touch-proximity condition, the participant was required to force the learner's hand onto the shock plate (using a sheet of insulation so that the participant would not also be shocked). **Figure 8.7** shows the effect of these manipulations. As the learner became more and more present and "real," it became more and more difficult for the teachers to deliver the shocks, and obedience rates diminished.

One lesson to be drawn from this is chilling. The more removed we are from others, the easier it is to hurt them. And the technology that societies have developed to inflict harm allows individuals to inflict it from a great distance. Combat is often no longer hand to hand. Lethal weapons systems can be activated by a mere push of a button, guiding a predator drone to a target or firing a missile from an underground silo a continent away. The remoteness of the victims in such cases makes the harm done to them abstract, so the emotional brakes on aggression are lessened dramatically.

Tuning out the Victim When missiles are fired from a ship at sea, the victims of the target cannot be seen, which makes the harm more abstract. Orders to fire such weapons are not likely to be questioned.

"Tuning out" the Experimenter Another way to influence obedience in Milgram's paradigm is to strengthen or weaken the "signal" coming from the experimenter and thus strengthen or weaken the forces acting on participants to complete the experiment. Milgram conducted a number of variations on this theme as well. In the standard version of the study, the experimenter was present in the same room, right next to the participant. In an experimenter-absent condition, the experimenter gave the initial instructions alongside the participant but then left the room and issued his orders over the telephone. In so doing, the power of the experimenter was diminished by removing him physically from the scene.

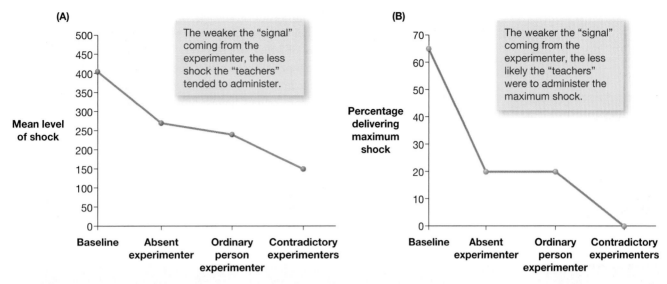

FIGURE 8.8 Tuning out the Experimenter The effect of experimental manipulations that make the experimenter less and less salient on (A) mean level of shock participants delivered and (B) the percentage of participants who delivered the maximum amount of shock. (Source: Milgram, 1965.)

Another way to alter the experimenter's power is to alter his authority. In one version, for example, an "ordinary person" (ostensibly another participant, but in reality a confederate) was the one who delivered the orders to increase the shock level each time the learner made a mistake. In still another version, there were two experimenters who initially instructed the participant to shock the victim. At one point, however, one of the two experimenters announced that he found the proceedings objectionable and argued with the other experimenter, who continued to urge the participant to complete the experiment.

Figure 8.8 shows the results of these manipulations. As the experimenter became less of an authority in the participant's mind, it became easier for the participant to defy the experimenter, and so the rate of obedience declined. Note that this series of experimental variations had a more pronounced effect than the earlier series (compare Figures 8.7 and 8.8). This tells us that making it *easier* for participants to disobey can be more effective than increasing their *desire* to disobey. As we shall see, this provides an important clue to understanding the surprising levels of obedience observed in Milgram's experiments.

Would You Have Obeyed?

As we mentioned in Chapter 1, no one anticipated such widespread obedience. A group of psychiatrists predicted that fewer than 1 percent of all participants—a pathological fringe—would continue until they delivered the maximum amount of shock. This failure of prediction is matched by an equally noteworthy failure of after-the-fact insight: almost no one believes, even after hearing the basic results and all the experimental variations, that he or she would deliver very high levels of shock. Thus, although the variations give us some understanding of when and why people engage in such surprising behavior, they do not give us a fully satisfying explanation of this phenomenon. As one social psychologist put it, they do not pass a critical "empathy test" (Ross, 1988). They do not lead us to empathize fully with the obedient participants and take seriously the possibility that *we* would also obey to the end—as most participants did. A truly satisfying explanation might not convince us that we would *surely* do so, but it should at least convince us that we *might* act that way.

Are there elements of Milgram's studies, and any explanations based on them, that *do* satisfy the empathy test? There are, and we present them here, along with a discussion of the real-world relevance of Milgram's research. Milgram's work is often taken to speak to the question of how people sometimes obey the directives of malevolent government officials and engage in sadistic, demeaning torture, such as that observed at Abu Ghraib, or commit hideous crimes against humanity, such as those witnessed during the Holocaust in Nazi Germany, in the "ethnic cleansing" in Bosnia, or in the tribal massacres in Rwanda. Explanations of such incomprehensible cruelties vary along an "exceptionalist-normalist" continuum. The exceptionalist thesis is that such crimes are perpetrated only by "exceptional" people—that is, exceptionally sadistic, desperate, or ethnocentric people. Many Germans were virulent anti-Semites. The Serbs had long-standing hatred and resentment against the Bosnians. The Rwandan Hutus had a score to settle with the Tutsi. The normalist thesis, in contrast, is that the capacity

BOX 8.2 FOCUS ON TODAY

Would Milgram Get the Same Results Now?

If you conducted Milgram's experiments today, would you get the same results? Some argue that today's more intense media coverage of such events as the abuses at Abu Ghraib prison or the suppression of dissent before the 2003 invasion of Iraq might make people less trusting of authority and hence less likely to obey instructions to shock another individual. Perhaps. But it is difficult to find out because ethical concerns make it impossible to replicate Milgram's experiments today. All psychological research must now be approved by an "institutional review board" whose job it is to make sure that any proposed program of research will not cause undue stress to the participants or harm them in any way. Few if any review boards would approve a replication of Milgram's experiments.

But Jerry Burger of Santa Clara University did the next best thing, conducting a near-replication of Milgram's basic experiments that tells us a lot about whether there has been any change since Milgram's time in obedience to authority (Burger, 2009). Burger noted that there was a critical moment in the

proceedings when disobedience was most likely—just after the participant had (supposedly) delivered 150 volts of electricity and the learner protested and demanded to be released ("That's all. Get me out of here. I told you I had heart trouble. My heart's starting to bother me now. Get me out of here, please ... I refuse to go on. Let me out."). It is something of a now-or-never moment: four out of five participants who don't stop at this point never stop at all.

Burger saw an opportunity. It is clearly unethical to put people through the stress of deciding between disobeying the experimenter or administering 300 or 400 volts of electricity (and making some participants confront the fact that they are the type of person who would do such a thing). But the procedure is not so stressful—and hence ethically more acceptable—up to the 150-volt level. After all, until that point the learner hasn't protested and the voltage, it is assumed, can't be that bad or the experimenter wouldn't approve it. Burger therefore sought and received permission from Santa Clara's review board to replicate Milgram's basic experiment up

to that point only. What percentage of the participants chose to go on after this critical juncture, and how does it compare to what Milgram observed?

Burger also took several steps to safeguard the welfare of his participants. First, individuals who had responded to newspaper ads or flyers and were interested in participating were asked over the phone whether they ever had a psychiatric disorder, were currently in psychotherapy or taking medication for anxiety or depression, or had ever experienced any serious trauma, such as child abuse, domestic violence, or combat. Anyone who answered yes to any of these questions was not allowed to participate. Second, those who passed this initial screening were told they would receive $50 for two 45-minute sessions. In the first session, participants filled out a number of psychological scales, such as the Beck Depression Inventory, and then were interviewed by a licensed clinical psychologist. If the psychologist detected any sign in the participants' questionnaire responses or in their face-to-face interviews that they might not be up to the challenge of being in for such destructive obedience lies in all of us and given the right circumstances can be perpetrated by almost anyone. Milgram's research, of course, is typically taken to support the normalist position. Milgram himself certainly took this position. When asked by Morley Safer on the CBS show *60 Minutes* whether he thought something like the Holocaust could happen in the United States, Milgram offered this opinion:

> I would say, on the basis of having observed a thousand people in the experiment and having my own intuition shaped and informed by these experiments, that if a system of death camps were set up in the United States of the sort we had seen in Nazi Germany, one would be able to find sufficient personnel for those camps in any medium-sized American town. (Quoted in Blass, 1999, p. 955)

Let's take a closer look.

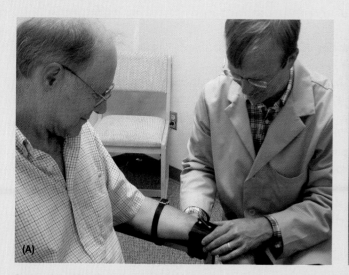 

Revisiting Milgram In Jerry Burger's partial replication of the Milgram experiments, participants faced the same conflict over whether to administer increasing levels of shock (up to 165 volts) to the "learner" or to call a halt to his suffering by refusing to continue.

the study, they were paid their $50 right then and excluded from the second session.

Those who made it past both screenings were run through a replication of the voice-feedback condition of Milgram's experiment. The results were essentially the same as those obtained by Milgram himself. In Burger's study, 70 percent of the participants were willing to administer the next level of shock (165 volts) after hearing the learner's protest. This compares with 82 percent of Milgram's participants, not a statistically significant difference. Men and women were equally likely to continue past the critical 150-volt level, and whether or not participants obeyed the experimenter was unrelated to how they scored on personality scales measuring empathy or their desire to control events in their lives. Today, people seem to react to pressure to obey the same way they did almost 50 years ago.

They Tried but Failed One of the reasons people think they would never behave the way the average participant in Milgram's experiments behaved is that they misunderstand exactly how the average participant acted (Ross, 1988). People conjure up images of participants blithely going along with the experimenter's commands, increasing the shock level from trial to trial, being relatively inattentive to the learner's situation. Indeed, Milgram's experiments have often been described as demonstrations of "blind" obedience.

But that's not what happened. Participants did not mindlessly obey. Nearly all tried to disobey in one form or another. Nearly everyone called the experimenter's attention to the learner's suffering in an implicit plea to stop the proceedings. Many stated explicitly that they refused to continue (but nonetheless went on with the experiment). Some got out of their chair in defiance, only to sit back down moments later. The participants tried to disobey, but they just weren't particularly good at it. As Lee Ross (1988) put it, "the Milgram experiments have less to say about 'destructive obedience' than about ineffective and indecisive *dis*obedience."

This distinction is critical in giving all of us the sense, however reluctant, that yes, perhaps we would have delivered about as much shock as the average participant. We know that we wouldn't *intend* to be obedient, and we wouldn't ignore the learner's suffering. But most of us have had the experience of having good intentions but being unable to translate those intentions into effective action. We've *wanted* to speak up more forcefully and effectively against racist or sexist remarks, but we were too slow to respond or the words didn't come out right. Or we've *wanted* to reach out to those who are ignored at social gatherings, but we got distracted by all that was going on and our own social needs. Most of us can relate to being good-hearted but ineffective, but not to being uncaring.

A chilling parallel to the behavior of Milgram's participants can be found in the behavior of some (we emphasize *some*) of the German soldiers called on to execute Polish Jews during World War II (Browning, 1992). Members of German Reserve Police Battalion 101, for example, were mostly individuals who hoped to avoid the inevitable violence of the war by volunteering for police duty in the German city of Hamburg. After the invasion of Poland, however, they were removed from Hamburg and made to serve as military police in occupied Poland. Most of what they were called on to do was innocuous, routine police work. But on July 13, 1942, they were roused from their barracks before dawn and taken to the outskirts of the village of Jozefow, where they were given their gruesome orders—to round up all the Jewish men, women, and children from the village, send all able-bodied young men to a work camp, and shoot the rest.

Most were shocked by their orders and found them abhorrent. Many resisted. But their resistance, like that of Milgram's participants, was feeble. Some occupied themselves with petty errands or moved to the back of the battalion, hoping they wouldn't be called on to take part. Others took part in the roundup, but then refrained from shooting if no one was watching. Still others fired but missed intentionally. What they *didn't* do was assertively state that they wouldn't participate, that what they were being asked to do was wrong. They tried to find an easy way to disobey, but there was no easy way.

In the case of Milgram's experiments, the difficulty that participants experienced in trying to halt the proceedings was partly due to the fact that the experimenter was not playing by the normal rules of social life. The participants offered *reasons* why the experiments should be stopped, but the experimenter largely ignored those reasons, coming back with minimally responsive statements such as "The experiment requires that you continue." Participants could be forgiven for being a bit confused and uncertain about how to act. And as we saw in the discussion of conformity, people are unlikely to act decisively when they do not have a solid grasp of the events transpiring around them. What are we to do when charged with administering electric shock in order to "teach" someone who is no longer trying to learn anything, at the insistence of an authority figure who seems unconcerned about the learner's predicament? How are we to respond when events have stopped making sense?

This has important implications for those real-world instances of destructive obedience with which we should be most concerned. Many of the most hideous episodes of genocide, for example, have occurred right after large-scale social upheaval. With reliable norms of appropriate behavior absent, the confidence required for decisive action to stop such atrocities is hard to come by. The abuses at Abu Ghraib prison in Iraq took place in a country whose social institutions had been torn down by a military invasion and involved individuals far from their home country, performing duties that many of them had never before performed. Those who would want to stop such actions—and would rein them in under normal circumstances—may be unusually uncertain and indecisive about how to do so.

Release from Responsibility Participants' ineffectiveness in stopping the experiment meant that they were trapped in a situation of terrible conflict and stress. They knew that what was happening shouldn't continue, and yet they were unable to bring it to an end. They were therefore desperate for anything that would reduce their stress. Fortunately for the participants (but unfortunately for the learner had he really been receiving electric shock), the experimenter provided something to reduce their stress by taking responsibility for what was happening. When participants asked, as many did, "Who is responsible for what happens here?," the experimenter responded, "I am responsible." Participants seized on this as a justification for their actions, and the stress they were experiencing was, to a significant degree, reduced.

This, too, should make us consider the possibility that we might, after all, have delivered quite a bit of electric shock ourselves. We have all been in stressful, confusing situations in which we wanted the stress and confusion to end. "All of my friends are making me uncomfortable by savagely teasing that guy in our English class, and they'll think I'm a jerk if I speak out." "Everyone's popping those pills as if they weren't harmful, and they'll think I'm a wimp if I don't too." It is always tempting in such

Legitimacy of Experiment To see how participants would react if the experiment were not conducted at Yale and the authority seemed less legitimate, Milgram had the participants report to "Research Associates of Bridgeport," located above a storefront in downtown Bridgeport and inside a seedy office. Obedience rates declined somewhat but remained high even under these conditions.

situations to grab at anything that would make the dilemma "go away." "Maybe the guy in our class really does deserve it, and I'm being too sensitive." "Maybe the pills really are harmless, and I'm blowing things out of proportion."

Of course, the cover, or "out," that the experimenter provided in Milgram's experiments only worked because the person taking responsibility was perceived to be a legitimate authority. People wouldn't allow just anyone to take responsibility and then assume that everything was okay. If you were approached by a strange character on campus who said, "Quick, help me set fire to the psychology building. I'll take full responsibility," we trust that you would refrain from pitching in. In Milgram's experiments, however, participants believed they could legitimately transfer responsibility to the experimenter. He was a representative of science, a respected field, and in nearly all variations of Milgram's paradigm, he was affiliated with Yale University, a respected institution (although obedience was still high in a condition in which the experimenter operated out of a storefront in downtown Bridgeport). These facts made it easier for participants to reduce their own stress over what was happening by assuming the experimenter knew better and was ultimately responsible for what happened.

The cover provided by authorities perceived to be legitimate has implications for some of the worst acts of destructive obedience in history. In Nazi Germany, in Rwanda, and at Abu Ghraib, the demands to obey have been issued by authority figures who either explicitly assumed responsibility or whose position supported an assumption of responsibility. And the claim of responsibility has nearly always been legitimized by some overarching ideology. Whether it be nationalism, religious ideology, or ethnic identity, all appeals to such organized aggression have been draped in a legitimizing ideology that seeks to transform otherwise hideous actions into what is seen as morally appropriate behavior (Staub, 1989; Zajonc, 2002).

Step-by-Step Involvement It also seems more plausible that we ourselves might have acted like the average participant when we recognize that participants did not deliver 450 volts of electricity out of the blue. We hear "450 volts" and think to ourselves, "No way would I do that." And we wouldn't—not right off the bat. But that is not what Milgram's participants were asked to do.

Recall that each participant first had to administer only 15 volts to the learner. Who wouldn't do that? That's feedback, not punishment. Then 30 volts. No problem there either. Then 45, 60, 75—each step is a small one. Once we've started down this path (and who wouldn't start?), it's hard to get off, and we slide down a slippery slope that leads to more shock. Indeed, the increments are so small that if a certain level of shock seems "too much," why wouldn't the previous level have been too much as well (Gilbert, 1981)?

Recognizing the importance of the step-by-step nature of participants' obedience also helps us pass the "empathy test." Most of us have had the experience of gradually getting in over our heads in this fashion. We may tell a very innocuous "white" lie— one that sets in motion a cascade of events that requires more and more deception. (Sitcoms could barely exist if not for this element of human behavior.) Or we may "dig in our heels" over a small matter in a dispute—which leads to more recalcitrance and the inability to ever make an appropriate concession. Our behavior often creates its own momentum, and it is hard to know in advance where it will lead. Milgram's participants can certainly be forgiven for not foreseeing how everything would unfold. Would we have seen it any more clearly?

The parallels between this element of Milgram's procedure and what happened in Nazi Germany are striking. German citizens were not asked, out of the blue, to

BOX 8.3   **FOCUS ON HISTORY**

Step-by-Step to Genocide

Anti-Jewish laws and policies of the German government before and during World War II. Note the gradual nature of anti-Jewish statutes and policies.

1. April 1, 1933

Boycott of Jewish businesses is declared.

2. April 7, 1933

Law for the Restoration of the Professional Civil Service authorizes the dismissal of non-Aryan (especially those with Jewish parents or grandparents) civil servants (except for those who had held that status since 8/1/14, who had fought at the front for Germany in World War I, or whose father or son had been killed in action in World War I).

3. September 22, 1933

Reestablishment of Reich Chamber of Culture leads to the removal of non-Aryans from organizations and enterprises related to literature, the press, broadcasting, music, and art.

4. September 15, 1935

Reich Citizenship Law defines citizens of the Reich as only those who are of German or kindred blood.

5. September 16, 1935

Law for the Protection of German Blood and German Honor forbids marriage between Jews and nationals of German or kindred blood and declares marriages conducted in defiance of this law void, and forbids relations outside of marriage between Jews and nationals of German or kindred blood, forbids Jews from employing in their household female nationals of German or kindred blood who are under age 45.

6. November 16, 1936

Jews are prohibited from obtaining passports or traveling abroad, except in special cases.

7. April 1938

Jews are forced to register with the government all property valued at 5,000 marks or more.

8. July 25, 1938

Fourth Decree of the Reich Citizenship Law terminates the licenses of Jewish physicians as of September 30, 1938.

9. September 27, 1938

Fifth Decree of the Reich Citizenship Law allows Jewish legal advisers to attend professionally only to the legal affairs of Jews.

10. October 5, 1938

Jewish passports and ration cards are marked with a J.

11. January 1, 1939

All Jews are required to carry a special ID card.

12. July 1940

Purchases by Jews are restricted to certain hours and stores; telephones are taken away from Jews.

13. September 19, 1941

Jews are forced to display the Jewish badge prominently on their clothing and with few exceptions are not allowed to use public transportation.

14. October 14, 1941

Massive deportation of German Jews to concentration camps begins.

15. October 23, 1941

Jewish emigration is prohibited.

16. January 20, 1942 (The Wansee Conference)

Nazi leaders decide that 11 million Jews (every Jew in Europe) are to be killed.

---

assist with or condone the deportation of Jews, Gypsies, homosexuals, and communists to the death camps. Instead, the rights of these groups were gradually stripped away. First, certain business practices were restricted, then travel constraints were imposed, then citizenship was narrowed, and only after some time were people loaded into boxcars and sent to the death camps (see **Box 8.3**). The Nazis would doubtless have had a much harder time had they started with the last step. Their own citizens would likely have been less cooperative; their victims would probably have resisted more actively. It is telling in this regard that the most vigorous defiance of the Nazis' genocide plans tended to take place not in Germany, but in the countries Germany overran. There are many reasons for this, of course, but one of them may well be that the pace of Germany's implementation of the "final solution" was much more rapid in the conquered countries than in Germany itself.

"It is easier to resist at the beginning than at the end."

—Leonardo da Vinci

LOOKING BACK We have tried to shed light on the mystery of people's willingness to obey leaders who demand immoral behavior. We focused on several elements of the situation that make obedience easier to understand: a person's attempts to disobey are often blocked; responsibility for what happens is frequently taken by the person in authority; and once the obedience begins, there is typically no obvious point at which to stop. But when the circumstances lead the individual to be "tuned in" to the victim, obedience is substantially reduced. When the circumstances lead the individual to "tune out" the person in authority, obedience is also greatly reduced. In Milgram's experiments, the person making the demands was always an authority. What happens when we are asked to do something by someone who is not in a position of authority? To answer this question, we turn to our next topic, compliance.

COMPLIANCE

Milgram's research teaches us how common it is for people to obey the insistent commands of someone who occupies a position of authority—and why they so commonly do so. But attempts to influence behavior often come from people without any special authority or status. Charities urge us to give money. Con men try to induce us to go along with their schemes. Salespeople want us to buy their products. And friends ask us for favors. If you want to get someone to do something and you have no power over the person and no special status to trumpet and only your wits to help you, what approach should you take? Conversely, if you're worried about being taken advantage of by those who have their own (and not your) best interests at heart, what techniques should you watch out for? Social psychologists have studied different strategies for eliciting compliance, and their research gives us some clues about how (and how effectively) these strategies work.

Compliance attempts come in roughly two types: those directed at the mind and those directed at the heart. People can be led to do things because they come to see that there are good reasons for doing so or because their feelings guide them to do so. Of course, the heart and mind are not so neatly separable, and many compliance attempts represent a blend of the two approaches. If we want to do something, for example, we work hard to find sufficient reason for doing it (see Chapter 6). Similarly, if our head tells us about the wisdom of a particular course of action, our heart often follows. Still, it is useful for understanding the techniques of compliance to recognize that some are primarily reason based and others primarily emotion based.

Reason-Based Approaches

When someone does something for us, we usually feel compelled to do something for that person in return. Indeed, all societies that have ever been studied possess a powerful **norm of reciprocity**, according to which people should benefit those who benefit them (Fiske, 1991b; Gouldner, 1960). This norm also exists in many bird and mammal species. For example, when one monkey removes parasites from another's back, the latter typically returns the favor, which helps to cement the social bond between the two.

When someone does us a favor, it creates an obligation to agree to any reasonable request he or she might make in turn. To fail to respond is to violate a powerful social norm and run the risk of social sanction (Cotterell, Eisenberger, & Speicher, 1992). Indeed, the English vocabulary is rich in derogatory terms for those who do not uphold

norm of reciprocity A norm dictating that people should provide benefits to those who benefit them.

their end of the norm of reciprocity: *sponge, moocher, deadbeat, ingrate, parasite, bloodsucker, leech.* If you do a favor for someone, that person is likely to look favorably on a reasonable request you subsequently make because of the fear of being seen as a sponge, moocher, and so on. Perhaps that is why restaurant customers often leave larger tips when they are given a piece of candy by the waitstaff (Strohmetz, Rind, Fisher, & Lynn, 2002).

The influence of the norm of reciprocity in eliciting compliance was demonstrated with great clarity in a simple experiment in which two individuals were asked to rate a number of paintings, ostensibly as part of an experiment on aesthetics (Regan, 1971; see also Whatley, Webster, Smith, & Rhodes, 1999). One of the individuals was a real participant; the other was a confederate of the experimenter. In one condition, the confederate returned from a break in the procedure with two sodas and proceeded to offer one to the participant. "I asked (the experimenter) if I could get myself a Coke, and he said it was OK, so I bought one for you, too." In another condition, the confederate returned empty-handed. Afterward, during another pause in the experiment, the confederate asked the participant for a favor. He explained that he was selling raffle tickets for which the prize was a new car and that he stood to win a $50 prize if he sold the most raffle tickets. He then proceeded to ask if the participant was willing to buy any raffle tickets, which cost 25 cents apiece: "Any would help, the more the better." (To make sure all participants had the means to purchase some tickets, they had already been paid—in quarters!—for their participation in the study.)

In a testament to the power of the norm of reciprocity, participants who were earlier given a Coke by the confederate bought twice as many raffle tickets as those who were not given a Coke (or were given a Coke by the experimenter, to control for the possibility that simply receiving a Coke may have put participants in a good mood and that it was that, and not the compulsion to reciprocate, that had increased compliance). Thus, doing a favor for someone creates an uninvited debt that the recipient is obligated to repay. Solicitors often try to take advantage of this pressure by preceding their request with a small gift. Insurance agents give out calendars or return-address labels. Pollsters who want you to complete a survey send it along with a dollar. Cult members offer a flower before giving their pitch. Our hearts sink when we see these gifts coming, and we often go to great lengths to avoid them—and the obligations they bring.

The Reciprocal Concessions, or the Door-in-the-Face Technique Robert Cialdini, social psychology's most innovative contributor to the literature on compliance, has explored a novel application of the norm of reciprocity. The inspiration for his decision to conduct research on the technique is best introduced in his own words:

> I was walking down the street when I was approached by an eleven- or twelve-year-old boy. He introduced himself and said that he was selling tickets to the annual Boy Scouts circus to be held on the upcoming Saturday night. He asked if I wished to buy any at five dollars apiece. Since one of the last places I wanted to spend Saturday evening was with the Boy Scouts, I declined. "Well,"

Reciprocity and Compliance
The norm of reciprocity leads people to want to comply with a request from someone who has done them a favor. This candidate hands out daffodils at the market when she is campaigning for office, which may lead people to want to reciprocate the favor by voting for her in the election.

"All contacts among men rest on the schema of giving and returning the equivalent."

—G. Simmel

"There is no duty more indispensable than that of returning a kindness."

—Cicero

he said, "if you don't want to buy any tickets, how about buying some of our big chocolate bars? They're only a dollar each." I bought a couple and, right away, realized that something noteworthy had happened. I knew that to be the case because: (a) I do not like chocolate bars; (b) I do like dollars; (c) I was standing there with two of his chocolate bars; and (d) he was walking away with two of my dollars. (Cialdini, 1984, p. 47)

Cialdini's experience with the Boy Scout led him to articulate a general compliance technique whereby people are led to feel compelled to respond to a concession with one of their own (Cialdini et al., 1975; O'Keefe & Hale, 1998, 2001; Reeves, Baker, Boyd, & Cialdini, 1991). First, you ask someone for a very large favor that he or she will certainly refuse, and then you follow that request with one for a more modest favor that you are really interested in receiving. The idea is that the drop in the size of the request will be seen as a concession, a concession that the target of the request must match to honor the norm of reciprocity. The most available concession is to comply with the second request. Another way of looking at this **reciprocal concessions technique** is that the first favor is so large and unreasonable that it is inevitably refused, slamming the door in the face of that request but then keeping it open just a crack for the subsequent, smaller request. The combination of a large request followed immediately by a smaller request is hence also known as the **door-in-the-face technique**.

Cialdini demonstrated the power of this reciprocal concessions, or door-in-the-face, technique in a field study in which students were approached on the Arizona State University campus by members of Cialdini's research team posing as representatives of the "County Youth Counseling Program" and asked if they would be willing to chaperone a group of juvenile delinquents on a day trip to the zoo. Not surprisingly, the overwhelming majority, 83 percent, refused. But the experience—and the response rate—was much different for another group of students who had first encountered a much larger request. They were first asked whether they would be willing to counsel juvenile delinquents for 2 hours a week for a minimum of the next two years. All of them refused, at which point they were asked about chaperoning the trip to the zoo. Now 50 percent of the students agreed to chaperone—triple the rate of the other group (Cialdini et al., 1975). A series of carefully crafted follow-up studies revealed that it was the pressure to respond to what was perceived as a concession that was responsible for the dramatic increase in compliance. For example, this technique does not work when the two requests are made by different individuals. In that case, the second, smaller request is not seen as a concession, and hence it does not create the same obligation.

Do you want to put this technique to good use in your own life? Then consider an experiment in which professors were asked if they would be willing to meet for "15 to 20 minutes" to discuss a topic of interest to a student. When faced with this request by itself, 57 percent agreed. But 78 percent agreed to the request when it was preceded by another request—to spend "2 hours a week for the rest of the semester" with the student (Harari, Mohr, & Hosey, 1980).

The That's-Not-All Technique Another technique that uses the norm of reciprocity in a similar way, the **that's-not-all technique**, may be more familiar to you. Suppose you're at an electronics store and have asked about a widescreen plasma TV you've been wanting. You're told it costs $1,999 and comes with a three-year warranty. After a moment in which you say nothing, the salesperson says, "And that's not all; it also comes with a free DVD player!" This add-on can strike people as something of a gift from the store or the salesperson, creating some pressure to reciprocate. If so, this pressure can result in increased sales.

door-in-the-face technique (reciprocal concessions technique) Asking someone for a very large favor that he or she will certainly refuse and then following that request with one for a more modest favor (which tends to be seen as a concession that the target will feel compelled to honor).

that's-not-all technique Adding something to an original offer, which is likely to create some pressure to reciprocate.

Jerry Burger has demonstrated the effectiveness of this technique. At an arts fair on the Santa Clara University campus, half of the individuals who approached the booth of the Psychology Club bake sale were told that one cupcake and two medium-sized cookies cost a total of 75 cents. The other half of the participants were initially told that each cupcake cost 75 cents, and then, before they responded whether they wanted one or not, they were told that the price included two medium-sized cookies. Seventy-three percent of the participants in the latter, "that's-not-all" condition purchased the snacks, compared to only 40 percent in the control "all-at-once" condition (Burger, 1986; Burger, Reed, DeCesare, Rauner, & Rozolis, 1999; Pollock, Smith, Knowles, & Bruce, 1998).

The Foot-in-the-Door Technique All of us perform certain actions because they are consistent with our self-image. Environmentalists take the time to recycle (even when sorely tempted to toss a bottle or can into the trash) because that's part of what it means to be an environmentalist. Skiers rise early to tackle fresh snow (even when they really want to sleep in) because that's what real skiing enthusiasts do. This suggests that if requests can be crafted to appeal to a person's self-image, the likelihood of compliance can be increased.

One way to do this is to employ what's known as the **foot-in-the-door technique**. It complements the door-in-the-face technique because it starts with a small request to which everyone complies (which allows the person making the request to get a foot in the door) and then follows up with a larger request involving the real behavior of interest. The idea is that the initial agreement to the small request will lead to a change in the individual's self-image as someone who does this sort of thing or who contributes to such causes. The person then has a reason for agreeing to the subsequent, larger request: "It's just who I am."

In the first systematic examination of the foot-in-the-door technique, the investigators knocked on doors in a California neighborhood and asked homeowners whether they would be willing to have a large billboard sign bearing the slogan "Drive Carefully" installed on their lawn for one week (Freedman & Fraser, 1966). One group of residents was shown a picture of the sign and how large and unattractive it was, and so it is not surprising that only 17 percent agreed to the request. Another group of residents had first been asked two weeks earlier to comply with a much smaller request—to display in a window of their home a 3-inch-square sign bearing the words "Be a safe driver." Virtually all of them agreed to do so. When they were later asked to display the billboard on their lawn, a staggering 76 percent of them agreed to do so. To examine the breadth of this effect, the investigators ran another condition in which the first request was of a very different sort (signing a petition) than the second and involved a very different issue (keeping California beautiful). Even with these differences in the two requests, asking the first led nearly half the respondents to agree to the second, larger request. Perhaps we should be even more careful than we already are about agreeing to the requests that others make of us. Performing the most trivial favors can set us up to give in to much more substantial requests (Burger, 1999; Burger & Guadagno, 2003; Schwartzwald, Bizman, & Raz, 1983).

You may have noticed the similarity between the foot-in-the-door technique and the step-by-step nature of the requests made by Milgram in his study of obedience. In both studies, eliciting compliance to a small and unobjectionable action (signing a petition, administering 30 volts of electricity) paves the way to much

foot-in-the-door technique A compliance technique in which one makes an initial small request to which nearly everyone complies, followed by a larger request involving the real behavior of interest.

Foot-in-the-Door Technique After the beauty consultant succeeds in getting the potential customer to agree to sit down for the application of makeup, it may be easier for her to get the customer to agree to a second request to purchase some cosmetics.

more serious behavior. The similarity between the two experiments also shows that taking away a reason for *not* doing something can be as powerful as providing a reason for doing it. Having administered, say, 160 volts of electricity takes away a reason for refusing to administer 175 volts. After all, what's so different about the two levels of shock? And consenting to an earlier request like displaying a small sign takes away a reason for refusing to put up a much larger sign ("No thanks, I don't do that sort of thing.").

Another technique that works in precisely this way involves legitimizing the tiniest imaginable contribution. Charities might solicit money, for example, by ending their request with the words "even a penny would help." Such a request invalidates the thought that "I can't really afford to give." Furthermore, once the decision to give is made, there are a host of reasons why most people would be reluctant to make a truly small donation. Indeed, research on the effectiveness of this technique shows that such "even a penny" appeals substantially increase the percentage of individuals who donate, but do not lower the amount that is typically given (Brockner, Guzzi, Kane, Levine, & Shaplen, 1984; Cialdini & Schroeder, 1976; Reeves, Macolini, & Martin, 1987; Weyant, 1984). The net result is that such appeals increase overall charitable giving.

Emotion-Based Approaches

Cognitive, or reason-based, appeals can be effective in obtaining compliance, but so can affective, or emotion-based, approaches.

Positive Mood Suppose you want to ask your dad for a new computer, a new amplifier for your guitar, or simply to borrow the family car for a road trip. When would you ask? When he's just come home from work in a foul mood, cursing his boss and his suffocating job? Or after he's just landed a promotion and a big raise? It doesn't take an advanced degree in psychology to know that it's better to ask when he's in a good mood. When people are in a good mood, they feel expansive, charitable, and affirmative, and they are therefore more likely to agree to such requests. Even little children know to ask someone for a favor when that person is in a good mood.

The wisdom of this approach has been verified in countless experiments. In one study, participants received a telephone call from someone who claimed to have spent her last dime on this very ("misdialed") call and who asked if the participant would dial the intended number and relay a message (Isen, Clark, & Schwartz, 1976). In one condition, no more than 20 minutes before receiving the call, participants had been given a free sample of stationery to put them in a positive mood. In another condition, participants did not receive a free sample before receiving the call. When the request was made of individuals who had not earlier been given the free sample, only 10 percent complied. But the compliance rate shot up dramatically among participants who received the request a few minutes after having been given the gift (see **Figure 8.9**), and then it declined gradually the longer the delay between the gift and the request.

Feeling good clearly makes people more likely to agree to requests and, more generally, to help others. This has been shown in experiments that have lifted participants' moods by telling them they did well on a test, having them think happy thoughts, giving them cookies, or playing cheerful music and then confronted them with requests to make change, donate to charity, help with experiments, give blood, and tutor students (Carlson, Charlin, & Miller, 1988; Isen, 1999). Positive moods tend to increase compliance for two main reasons. First, our mood colors how we interpret events. Requests for favors are more likely to be perceived as less intrusive and less threatening when we are in a good mood. Giving others the benefit of the doubt, we may look on someone who asks to borrow our notes not as an irresponsible or lazy individual who doesn't deserve to be

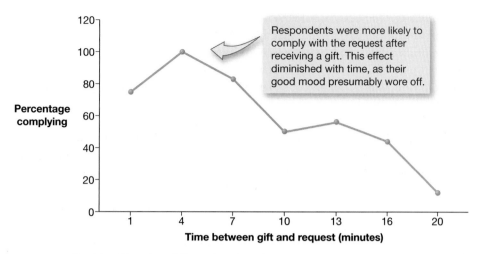

Respondents were more likely to comply with the request after receiving a gift. This effect diminished with time, as their good mood presumably wore off.

Time between gift and request (minutes)

Percentage complying

FIGURE 8.9 Positive Mood and Compliance Percentage of respondents who agreed to help a stranger by making a telephone call and relaying a message 1 to 20 minutes after receiving a small gift. (Source: Isen, Clark, & Schwartz, 1976.)

bailed out, but as a victim of circumstance who could get back on track with a little assistance (Carlson, Charlin, & Miller, 1988; Forgas, 1998a, 1998b; Forgas & Bower, 1987).

Another reason a good mood increases compliance involves what is known as mood maintenance. Pardon the tautology, but it feels good to feel good, and we typically want the feeling to last as long as possible (Clark & Isen, 1982; Wegener & Petty, 1994). And one way to sustain a good mood is to do something for another person (Dunn, Aknin, & Norton, 2008). Or stated differently, one way to wreck a good mood is to turn down a request and invite all sorts of self-recrimination ("What kind of heartless person am I?") that pollutes and erodes a positive mental state. Several studies implicate mood maintenance as an important component of the impact of a positive mood on compliance. In one study, participants were first either given cookies (which put them in a good mood) or not given cookies. They were then asked (by someone other than the person who provided the cookies) if they would be willing to assist with an experiment by serving as a confederate. Half the participants were told the job of confederate would involve *helping* the "true" participant in the experiment; the other half were told it would involve *hindering* the participant. Having received a cookie (and being in a good mood) increased the compliance rate when the task involved helping the participant, but not when it involved hindering the participant (Isen & Levin, 1972). Helping another person promotes feeling good; hurting someone does not.

Negative Mood If a good mood increases compliance, we might expect a bad mood to decrease it. It can, but even the slightest introspection reveals that certain types of bad moods are likely to *increase* compliance, not decrease it. And people know this and use it to their advantage. Suppose, for example, that your boyfriend or girlfriend was being excessively flirtatious with someone (alas, not you, or it wouldn't be excessive), and you point out the offense. Would that be a good time to ask your partner

Positive Mood and Requests When people are in a good mood, they are more likely to agree to requests. People at this charity ball in Monaco are dancing and having a good time and are therefore more likely to donate money to the Princess Grace Foundation.

for something? You bet it would! When people feel guilty, they are often motivated to do what they can to get rid of that awful feeling. So one type of bad mood at least, that associated with feeling guilty, should enhance compliance.

Social psychologists have demonstrated a strong, positive association between guilt and compliance in numerous experiments in which participants have been led to feel guilty by being induced to lie, break a camera, knock over stacks of carefully arranged index cards, or injure an adorable laboratory rat (Carlsmith & Gross, 1969; Darlington & Macker, 1966; O'Keefe & Figgé, 1997; J. Regan, 1971; D. T. Regan, Williams, & Sparling, 1972). In a particularly clever test of the effect of guilt on compliance, researchers asked Catholics to donate to the March of Dimes either when they were on their way into church for confession or on their way out. The presumption was that those on their way in were rehearsing their sins and thus feeling guilty; those on their way out had expiated their sins and hence were no longer plagued by guilt. As the investigators predicted, those solicited on the way in gave more money than those solicited on the way out (Harris, Benson, & Hall, 1975).

The desire for expiation is only one reason that guilt is likely to increase compliance, however, and the other reasons make it clear that other negative emotions can lead to increased compliance as well. This was suggested by the results of an experiment in which participants were recruited to assist in a supposed study of growth and development (J. Regan, 1971). The study was described as having already been running for six weeks, and the participant's task was to monitor a voltage meter (located to the participant's left) to make sure the stimulation delivered to a 2-month-old albino rat (located to the participant's right) "stayed at the predetermined mild level." Meanwhile, the experimenter was stationed in an adjoining room, ostensibly to measure the rat's pulse, but from where the participant's every move could be surreptitiously monitored. As the experiment got under way, all participants performed their assigned task—for a while. But because the voltage meter registered the same 109 to 110 volts moment by monotonous moment, pretty soon all participants turned their

Negative State Relief Oskar Schindler saved the lives of 1,200 Polish Jews during the Holocaust. Initially driven by the desire for easy profits, he took over a Jewish factory, which he ran with cheap Jewish labor. Perhaps in a desire for negative state relief or from sheer humanitarianism, he used the millions he made from the cheap labor to bribe officials in order to save the Jews who were slated for death. He is pictured here in Tel Aviv with some of those he saved and their descendants.

attention to the rat itself. When they did, the experimenter delivered an intense shock through the floor of the rat's cage, causing the rat to jump and squeal in pain and the voltage meter to shoot up from 110 to 140 volts. The experimenter then called out from the adjoining room, "Something's wrong . . . his pulse is wild . . . [with a tone of frustration] Six weeks!" The experimenter then proceeded to terminate the experiment and sent the participant to the department secretary to receive the promised payment. While at the secretary's office, the participant received an appeal to donate to a charitable cause.

The unsettling experience with the rat, of course, was designed to make participants feel guilty (because their inattentiveness to the assigned task apparently caused the rat to receive too much shock and thus jeopardized the experiment). It also permitted an examination of whether their guilt would increase the amount they gave to the charitable cause. It did. Participants who thought their actions had led to the fiasco donated nearly three times as much money as participants who went through the procedure uneventfully, with nothing bad happening to the rat. Once again, guilt increased compliance.

But another condition of the experiment yielded a telling result. Participants in this condition also witnessed the rat jump and squeal, but at a random moment, not right after they had turned their attention away from their assigned task. And they heard the experimenter yell from the adjoining room, "There has been a short circuit in here. . . . This isn't your fault at all." These participants, then, had no reason to feel guilty over what had happened, and yet they ended up donating just as much as the guilty participants. Apparently, *witnessing* harm is enough to enhance the impulse to "do good"; one needn't be the cause of the harm. Thus, simply feeling upset, or even sad, can lead to an increase in people's willingness to comply with requests.

These results suggest that one reason that bad moods tend to increase compliance is that we don't want to feel bad, and so we jump at the opportunity to do something to brighten our mood. Doing something for someone else, especially when it's done for a good cause, is one way to make us feel better. We help others, in other words, largely to help ourselves. This has come to be known as the **negative state relief hypothesis** (Cialdini, Darby, & Vincent, 1973; Cialdini & Fultz, 1990; Cialdini et al., 1987).

negative state relief hypothesis The idea that people engage in certain actions, such as agreeing to a request, in order to relieve negative feelings and to feel better about themselves.

Support for the negative state relief hypothesis comes from experiments like the following (Cialdini et al., 1973). Participants were greeted individually and told that the study was part of the experimenter's undergraduate research methods course and would be conducted in the office of a graduate student who had offered it for use. In one condition, the experimenter gestured for the participant to have a seat at a table. Things were arranged so that when the participant sat down as instructed, three boxes of computer cards crashed to the floor (computer cards are relics of the days when computers could not accept data typed on a keyboard). The experimenter then exclaimed, "Oh no! I think it's the data from Tom's master's thesis. . . . They seem to be hopelessly mixed up. I guess we should clean up the mess as best we can and go on with the experiment." The experimenter then left the room, ostensibly to get materials needed for the study. While the experimenter was away, a second experimenter appeared and explained:

> She [the first experimenter] said it would be alright if I asked her subjects to help me out with my class project. I'm interested in surveying undergraduate study habits, and I need some people who would be willing to call students on the phone and administer a 10-minute interview concerning their study habits. I can't give you any experimental credit for doing this, but I would appreciate your help. Would you make some interview calls for me? Any number of calls up to 15 would help. (Cialdini et al., p. 507)

The spilling of the computer cards, of course, was choreographed to make the participant feel guilty, and the request to make phone calls was the means to assess whether their guilt increased their compliance. It did. As **Figure 8.10** indicates, guilty participants volunteered to make an average of 4.4 calls, compared to an average of 2.8 on the part of control participants who hadn't previously spilled the boxes of cards. But here's the telling part. Participants in two additional conditions had an experience between the time they knocked over the computer cards and the time the second experimenter made her request, and this experience was designed to rid them of the negative state they were experiencing. One group of participants was given an unexpected sum of money for completing an innocuous task; participants in the other group were lavishly praised for their performance on an innocuous task. The investigators reasoned that if it is the specific emotion of guilt that motivates people to comply, the compliance rate among these two groups should be just like that in the "guilty" condition. After all, these participants may be in a better mood overall, but they are

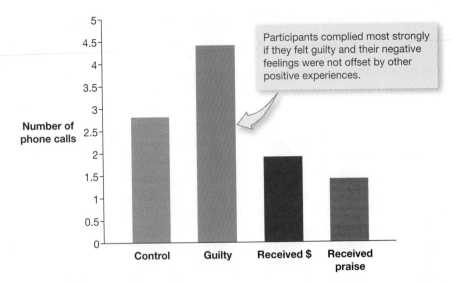

FIGURE 8.10 Test of the Negative State Relief Hypothesis Number of phone calls participants agreed to make, depending on experimental condition. (Source: Cialdini, Darby, & Vincent, 1973.)

every bit as guilty as they were before their unexpected, mood-lifting experience. In contrast, if it is the simple desire to get rid of a bad mood that increases compliance, the compliance rate among these two groups should be just like that in the control group. They no longer feel bad, so they no longer need to seek out a means to lift their mood.

As Figure 8.10 illustrates, the results strongly support the negative state relief hypothesis. Participants in these two conditions offered to make significantly fewer phone calls than did participants who were made to feel guilty but who did not enjoy a mood-lifting experience. It appears that the primary reason that people are motivated to comply with requests when they are in a bad mood is to get into a better frame of mind.

Does this mean that all there is to the link between bad moods and increased compliance is the desire for negative state relief? Almost certainly not. Although the desire to improve our mood may be the most consistent and powerful motive at play, there are other considerations as well. Even if we desire relief from guilt, sadness, and embarrassment equally, the behaviors we are willing to engage in to achieve that relief may be different for some of these emotions. Guilt and sadness can both lead to withdrawal—which can interfere with compliance—but the circumstances that elicit withdrawal are likely to be very different for the two states. When sad, you might be reluctant to be around those who are happy; when feeling guilty, you might want to avoid anyone or anything that reminds you of your transgression. And another type of bad mood, that produced by anger, is likely to be another story entirely. People sometimes revel in their anger and hence, at least for a time, may be less interested in seeking relief from it. So, although all sorts of bad moods increase compliance because doing someone a favor promises relief from a negative state, the precise profile of the relationship between mood and compliance is likely to be different for different types of bad moods. Historically, social psychologists who have studied compliance have focused on the effects of the rather pronounced difference between being in a good mood or being in a bad mood. But research that distinguishes between the different varieties of good and bad moods is proving to be informative in related areas of social psychology, and the field of compliance awaits the results of similar, more fine-grained investigations (Lerner, Gonzalez, Small, & Fischhoff, 2003; Lerner, Small, & Loewenstein, 2004; Tiedens & Linton, 2001).

BOX 8.4 **FOCUS ON POSITIVE PSYCHOLOGY**

Resisting Social Influence

"I'd rather be a free man in my grave
Than living as a puppet or a slave."

—Reggae legend Jimmy Cliff

People don't always conform, comply, and obey. They sometimes engage in heartening, even heroic, acts of independence—refusing to go along with misguided peers, declining to kowtow to a corrupt boss, or blowing the whistle on unethical business practices. What enables people to hold their ground, obey their conscience, and resist the influence attempts of others?

One thing to note is that the pressure to give in to others can be offset by the tendency for people to resist attempts to restrict their freedom to act or think as they wish. According to **reactance theory**, people experience an unpleasant state of arousal when they believe their freedoms are threatened, and they often act to reduce this unpleasant arousal by reasserting their prerogatives (Brehm, 1956). If your parents tell you that you cannot dye your hair, is your desire to have it dyed diminished or increased? Reactance theory predicts that the moment you feel your freedom is being taken away, it becomes more precious, and your desire to maintain it is increased.

But once motivated to resist, what factors might increase your ability to stand firm? One important variable is practice. We saw in Milgram's experiments that many participants wanted to disobey and even tried to do so, but they weren't very good at it. Maybe if they had been trained to disobey when the situation called for it, they would have done a better job. The bumper sticker "Question Authority" may be effective in this regard. By frequently questioning authority, we become better at doing so, making it easier and easier with each opportunity. There is evidence that the Christians who tried to save Jews during the Holocaust tended to be peo-

ple who had a history of helping others, either as part of their job or as volunteers. Those who did the most to help, in other words, often did not have any higher regard for their Jewish neighbors than did those who did little: they were simply more practiced in reaching out and providing aid.

Another way to increase the ability to resist social influence is to have an ally. We saw in Asch's experiments that just having one additional person depart from the majority was sufficient to produce a drastic reduction in conformity. If you know in advance that your friend, your employee, or your child is likely to be subject to intense social pressure, make sure he or she is with a friend or colleague. The presence of one other person dramatically reduces normative social influence.

We also saw in Milgram's experiments that the stepwise nature of the procedure likely played an important role in the surprising levels of obedience observed in those studies. This suggests that we all need to be wary of potentially slippery slopes. We would be well served to look ahead and ask ourselves, "If I'm going along with this because it's just one . . . [drink, fib, concession], will I be in a better position to resist once I've given in to this first step, or will I be in a worse position?" It's often easiest to resist influence from the start, rather than giving in and hoping to put a halt to things later on. As the Catholic Church teaches, "Avoid the near occasion of sin."

We saw in our discussion of compliance that many influence attempts are based on appeals to emotion. A particularly effective strategy for dealing with these types of appeals is simply to put off a response—to delay. If there is a "first law" of emotional experience, it is that emotional states fade. What is felt strongly now is likely to be felt less strongly later. Therefore,

the compulsion to give in because one is caught up in a particular emotion can be diminished by simply waiting to respond. The advice "Better sleep on it" is wise, because an initial emotional compulsion is likely to dissipate, so the question of whether to comply with a request can then be evaluated on the merits of the idea, not on the basis of an intense emotional state.

Resisting Social Influence The women pictured on this cover of Time magazine all refused to go along with those who were knowingly covering up wrongdoing. Cynthia Cooper (left) was a vice president of the internal audit department of WorldCom who discovered an accounting fraud and confronted the company's controller with her findings. Coleen Rowley (center) was an FBI agent who told her superiors prior to 9/11 that the flight training of known suspects may have constituted a terrorist threat. Sherron Watkins (right) was a vice president of corporate development at Enron who identified fraud at the company and wrote a letter to her boss detailing her suspicions rather than pretending that nothing was wrong.

LOOKING BACK We have seen that reason-based approaches induce compliance by providing good reasons for people to comply with a request. One of these reasons is the norm of reciprocity, by which people feel compelled to benefit those who have benefited them. In the door-in-the-face, or reciprocal concessions technique, people who have refused a large request are induced to then agree to a smaller request. In the that's-not-all technique, people are induced to buy an expensive product because a gift has been added to the deal. In the foot-in-the-door technique, people comply with a small request and then are induced to grant a larger request. Emotion-based approaches also can lead to compliance. People who are in a positive mood are more likely to comply with a request in order to maintain their good mood. On the other hand, according to the negative state relief hypothesis, people who feel guilty or sad are also likely to comply with a request in order to feel better. With all these ways to be influenced, it is comforting to know that there are some tested ways of avoiding social influence (see **Box 8.4**).

Summary

Conformity
Compliance
Obedience

What Is Social Influence?

- There are three types of social influence. *Conformity* involves a change in a person's attitudes or behavior in response to (often implicit) pressure from others. *Compliance* involves going along with explicit requests made by others. Finally, *obedience* involves giving in to the commands of an authority.

Conformity

- There are three sources of conformity. Sometimes conformity is mindless and automatic, elicited by the very perception of someone else's behavior. Other times, people conform because of *informational social influence*—that is, they view the actions of others as informative about what is best to do. Still other times people conform because of *normative social influence*—that is, out of concern for the social consequences of their actions.

- Several characteristics of the group affect conformity pressure. The larger the *group size*, the greater its influence—but only up to a size of about four people. *Unanimous groups* are far more effective than those with even a single other dissenter. Moreover, the greater the *expertise* and *status* of group members, the greater their influence.

- Culture and gender affect conformity. People from more interdependent cultures are more likely to conform than people from independent cultures. Women are somewhat more likely to conform than men. But both men and women conform more in domains in which they are less knowledgeable.

- Several task factors affect conformity pressure. The more *difficult* and *ambiguous* the task, as with the autokinetic experiment, the greater the conformity. When people's responses are *anonymous*, they are less affected by others' responses. Finally, when people have *satisfying explanations* of others' judgments, they are less affected by others' responses.

- The direction of influence is not always from the majority to the minority. Sometimes *minority influence* can be substantial, especially when it is a consistent minority.

Obedience to Authority

- The study of obedience has been dominated by the experiments of Stanley Milgram, who documented that most people go along with seemingly harmful commands of an authority.

- Participants in obedience experiments are caught in a conflict between two opposing forces: *normative social influence* and *moral imperatives*. The balance between these forces shifts toward the former when participants tune out the learner and tune in the experimenter.

- Although Milgram's results strike nearly everyone as wildly counterintuitive, they can be rendered less surprising by considering the *stepwise nature* of his commands, the (mostly ineffective) *attempts to terminate* the experiment made by most participants, and the ability of participants to place the onus of *responsibility* on the experimenter, not themselves.

Compliance

- Compliance with the requests of others may be elicited through both *reason-based techniques* and *emotion-based techniques*.
- Powerful reason-based approaches include invoking the *norm of reciprocity* by, for example, doing a favor for someone or making a concession (the *door-in-the-face technique*) or using the *foot-in-the-door process* by first getting someone to agree to a small request before making the more substantial request that is really wanted.
- Powerful emotion-based approaches include getting the targeted person in a good mood, which is likely to increase compliance because of *mood maintenance* and because of the influence of the good mood on how the request is interpreted.
- Compliance may also result from a desire for *negative state relief,* as an act of compliance may reduce guilt or sadness.

Key Terms

autokinetic illusion (p. 281)
compliance (p. 277)
conformity (p. 277)
door-in-the-face technique (reciprocal concessions technique) (p. 306)
foot-in-the-door technique (p. 307)
ideomotor action (p. 278)

informational social influence (p. 281)
internalization (private acceptance) (p. 289)
negative state relief hypothesis (p. 311)
normative social influence (p. 284)
norm of reciprocity (p. 304)

obedience (p. 277)
public compliance (p. 289)
reactance theory (p. 312)
social influence (p. 276)
that's-not-all technique (p. 306)

Further Reading

Blass, T. (2004). *The man who shocked the world: The life and legacy of Stanley Milgram.* New York: Basic Books. A comprehensive and informative summary of the most famous experiments in the history of psychology.

Cialdini, R. B. (2000). *Influence: Science and practice* (4th ed.). Boston: Allyn & Bacon. A very engagingly written treatment of many of the most common and effective compliance techniques and an analysis of how and why they work.

Gladwell, M. (2000). *The tipping point: How little things can make a big difference.* Boston: Little, Brown. Best-selling treatment of how social trends develop and change.

Thaler, R. H., & Sunstein, C. R. (2008). *Nudge: Improving decisions about health, wealth, and happiness.* New Haven: Yale University Press. An analysis of how psychological knowledge of compliance and decision making can be used to craft more effective social policies.

ⓢ Online Study Tools

StudySpace

Go to StudySpace, wwnorton.com/studyspace, to access additional review and enrichment materials, including the following resources for each chapter:

Organize
- Study Plan
- Chapter Outline
- Quiz+ Assessment

Learn
- Ebook
- Chapter Review

- Critical-Thinking Questions
- Visual Quizzes
- Vocabulary Flashcards

Connect
- Apply It! Exercises
- Author Insights Podcasts
- Social Psychology in the News

Persuasion

IN 1964, THE SURGEON GENERAL RELEASED its Report on Smoking and Health. This report detailed a scientifically established relationship between smoking tobacco and lung cancer. Since that time, we have witnessed one of the great persuasion battles of our time. The U.S. government has spent billions of dollars on public service announcements in print, on television and radio, and on the Internet portraying the perils of smoking. And the tobacco industry has countered, spending billions of dollars extolling the pleasures of smoking. This battle over smoking has been expensive and passionate and continues to this day. Meanwhile, millions of lives have been lost, and millions of people have begun or continued to smoke.

The public service ads that try to persuade people to stop smoking are graphic, powerful, and backed by highly credible, prestigious, and expert sources from the medical profession and the government. These ads have made people aware of the high risks of smoking, including the facts that one out of every three cancer-related deaths is related to smoking, that smoking causes between 400,000 and 500,000 premature deaths each year in the United States, that smoking increases the chances of early impotence in men, and that women who smoke are four times as likely to have serious side effects from birth control pills and to suffer from fertility problems. The results of these public service ads have been remarkable. In the 1950s, about half of all Americans smoked. Today, just a little over 30 percent of Americans smoke.

But what about that remaining 30 percent who continue to smoke, despite being fully aware of the significant health risks of doing so? The $3 billion that the tobacco industry spends each year on advertising is no doubt partially responsible for the large number of people who still smoke. One especially effective campaign promoting smoking was the "Joe Camel" campaign in which Joe Camel, a cartoon mascot of Camel cigarettes, appeared on billboards, in magazines, and on promotional items, such as T-shirts. Soon after the start of the campaign, Camel's market share among underage smokers rose from 0.5 to 32.8 percent! Another successful

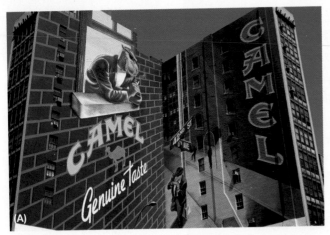

Advertising and Smoking   (A) In 1985, the R. J. Reynolds Company introduced an advertising campaign for Camel cigarettes that featured the "cool" cartoon character Joe Camel. The ads appealed to children and led to a huge increase in the sales of cigarettes to children and teenagers. The Federal Trade Commission successfully sued R. J. Reynolds for targeting children and forced the company to end the Joe Camel campaign. (B) Public service ads were created to persuade people to stop smoking. This Cancer Country ad parodies the Marlboro cigarette ads in which cowboys are smoking cigarettes and looking rugged and manly and instead stresses the connection between smoking and cancer.

"The object of oratory alone is not truth, but persuasion."

—Thomas Babington Macaulay

"The receptive ability of the masses is very limited, their understanding small; on the other hand, they have a great power of forgetting. This being so, all effective propaganda must be confined to a very few points which must be brought out in the form of slogans until the very last man is enabled to comprehend what is meant by any slogan. If this principle is sacrificed by the desire to be many sided, it will dissipate the effectual working of the propaganda, for the people will be unable to digest or retain the material that is offered them."

—Adolf Hitler

campaign increased sales of Virginia Slims cigarettes. Their slogan, "You've come a long way, baby," targeted women and linked smoking Virginia Slims cigarettes to women's quest for success, independence, and thinness. After the introduction of the Virginia Slims campaign, smoking by 12-year-old girls more than doubled.

This story about the battle over smoking, about the millions of people who have kicked the habit as well as the large numbers of people who continue to smoke, reveals the two overarching themes of this chapter: our susceptibility to persuasion and our resistance to it. People can be remarkably susceptible to persuasion. Charismatic leaders like Nelson Mandela, Martin Luther King Jr., or Mohandas (Mahatma) Gandhi can stir the masses to bring about radical social change in the absence of significant institutional power or money. Approximately one in ten young adults who spend a weekend retreat with the Moonies—that is, followers of the Reverend Sun Myung Moon and his Unification Church, which many think of as a religious cult—will become a full-fledged member, often abandoning family and friends forever (Galanter, 1989). An underdog in the 2008 presidential election—Barack Obama—transformed into his party's frontrunner, a record fund-raiser, and the eventual president because of the power of his message, the strong, positive impression he made on voters, and a campaign that spread virally through the Internet and throughout communities.

At the same time, people can also be remarkably resistant to persuasion. It is estimated that only 1 percent of prisoners of war in the Korean War altered their political beliefs, even though they were tortured and indoctrinated in the most extreme ways (Zimbardo & Leippe, 1991). And many well-financed and skillfully designed campaigns to encourage people to practice safe sex often fail, as do antidrug programs, as we shall see (Aronson, Fried, & Stone, 1991). People can be stubbornly resistant to changing their minds, even when it affects their health or their economic well-being.

We will organize this chapter around a fascinating tension: Why is it that in response to attempts at persuasion, from political indoctrination to door-to-door religious proselytizing, people sometimes change their minds, whereas other times they do not? What are the mechanics of attitude change? How do persuasive messages change people's attitudes, often in lasting and significant ways? And how do people resist attitude change? Moreover, what does this resistance to persuasion reveal about people's attitudes and convictions? But before we consider why attitudes change and why they do not, we first need to consider what attitudes are, how they are measured, and why people have them in the first place.

THE BASICS OF ATTITUDES

What exactly is an attitude? In the most general sense, an **attitude** is an evaluation of an object in a positive or negative fashion. Let's break this definition down a bit more. Most theorists assume that attitudes include three different elements: affect, cognitions, and behavior (Breckler, 1984; Eagly & Chaiken, 1998; Zimbardo & Leippe, 1991). And how do we measure attitudes? As you will see, we can measure attitudes by several means. But first let's examine the three components.

attitude An evaluation of an object in a positive or negative fashion that includes the three elements of affect, cognitions, and behavior.

The Three Components of Attitudes

At their core, attitudes involve *affect*—that is, emotional reactions to the object (Breckler, 1984; Zanna & Rempel, 1988). Attitudes have to do with how much we like or dislike an object, be it a politician, a landscape, the latest athletic shoe, laundry detergent, or ourselves. In fact, almost all objects trigger some degree of positive or negative emotion, and this is the affective component of attitudes (Bargh, Chaiken, Raymond, & Hymes, 1996; Cacioppo & Berntson, 1994; Fazio, Jackson, Dunton, & Williams, 1995; Fazio, Sanbonmatsu, Powell, & Kardes, 1986). Several lines of research suggest that our negative attitudes may be more potent than our positive ones (see **Box 9.1**).

Attitudes also involve *cognitions*. These include knowledge about the object, as well as beliefs, ideas, memories, and images. Your attitude toward a beloved sports team includes esoteric knowledge about the team's strengths and weaknesses and its players' statistics, but it also includes memories of the team's exhilarating wins and heartbreaking losses.

Finally, attitudes are associated with specific *behaviors* (Fishbein & Ajzen, 1975). When our attitudes are primed—that is, brought to mind, even unconsciously—we are more likely to act in ways consistent with the attitude (Bargh, Chen, & Burrows, 1996). Recent studies in neuroscience even suggest that our attitudes activate a region in the brain—the motor cortex—that supports specific actions (Preston & de Waal, 2002). You see a young child crying or a delicious-looking hot fudge sundae, and your mind prepares your body for action. Thus, attitudes are associated with specific intentions and actions.

This analysis of attitudes will help us understand issues that we will turn to shortly. For example, how might you change another person's attitudes? It's clear that there are several dimensions to our attitudes, implying that there may be several ways to bring about a change. Prompting someone to behave in a particular way can do the trick. Providing compelling information can also lead to attitude change, as can changing

BOX 9.1 **FOCUS ON NEUROSCIENCE**

Is the Bad Stronger than the Good?

At the very core of our attitudes is a positive or negative response to an attitude object, whether it's an old friend's voice, a roommate's messy pile of dishes, or the smell of freshly cut grass. Pioneering research by neuroscientist Joseph LeDoux has found that one part of the brain—the amygdala—is central to the initial affective evaluation that lies at the core of our attitudes (LeDoux, 1989, 1993, 1996). This almond-shaped region of the brain receives sensory information about a stimulus from the thalamus and then provides information about the positive or negative valence, or value, of the object. This evaluation occurs, remarkably, before the mind has categorized the object. Thus, before we even know what an object is, we have a gut feeling about it. Moreover, when scientists recorded individual neurons in the amygdala, they discovered that it was particularly sensitive to emotional stimuli—for example, faces. When the amygdala is damaged, various animals no longer have appropriate evaluations of objects: they eat feces, attempt to copulate with members of other species, and show no fear of threatening stimuli such as snakes or dominant animals. (In Chapter 7, we consider further implications of this important research, describing how our minds are designed to form very rapid, even unconscious preferences.)

LeDoux's research raises another interesting question: Are our initial positive and negative evaluations of stimuli comparable? Reviews by Shelley Taylor (1991), Paul Rozin and Edward Royzman

(2001), Roy Baumeister and his colleagues (Baumeister, Bratslavsky, Finkenauer, & Vohs, 2001), and John Cacioppo and Wendy Gardner (1999) provide a seemingly conclusive, perhaps unsettling answer: negative evaluations are stronger than positive evaluations. It would certainly make evolutionary sense for an organism to be more vigilant and responsive to pain than to pleasure, to danger than to safety. Without such a bias, the chances of survival would seem to be diminished.

Consider a few generalizations that support the conclusion that the bad is stronger than the good. Negative stimuli, such as frightening sounds or noxious smells, bring about more rapid and stronger physiological responses than positive stimuli, such as delicious tastes. Losing $10 seems more painful than gaining $10 is pleasurable. Negative trauma, such as the death of a loved one or sexual abuse, can change the individual for a lifetime; there don't appear to be equivalent effects from positive events. Or consider Paul Rozin's ideas about contamination. Brief contact with a cockroach will spoil a delicious meal (the negative stimulus contaminates, indeed overwhelms, the positive stimulus). The inverse—making a pile of cockroaches delicious by touching it with your favorite

food—is unimaginable (Rozin & Royzman, 2001).

In important work directly addressing the claim that our negative evaluations are more potent than our positive evaluations, Tiffany Ito, John Cacioppo, and their colleagues presented participants with positively valenced pictures—for example, photographs of pizza or of a

Contamination A cockroach on food spoils a delicious meal.

bowl of chocolate ice cream—and negatively valenced slides—for example, photographs of a mutilated face or of a dead cat (Ito, Larsen, Smith, & Cacioppo, 1998). They carefully recorded participants' electrocortical activity on the scalp and studied one region of the brain known to be involved in the evaluative response to stimuli. In several studies like this, they discovered a clear negativity bias in evaluation: the negative stimuli generated greater brain activity than the positive or neutral stimuli. It seems, alas, that the bad is indeed stronger than the good.

the emotion the person feels in the presence of the attitude object. These ideas will inspire our discussion about the most effective routes to attitude change.

Our analysis reveals just as readily why it can be so hard to change another person's attitudes. To do so requires overcoming a tangle of emotions, thoughts, and behaviors, both past and present. It's not always easy. But before moving to a discussion of attitude change, let's consider how we measure attitudes.

Measuring Attitudes

Attitude questionnaires may be the most widely used methodology in social psychology. Researchers routinely ask how participants feel about members of other groups, their romantic partners, themselves, the president, and so on. The simple approach to measuring attitudes is to have participants rate an attitude object on a **Likert scale**, named after Rensis Likert, its inventor. The Likert scale lists a set of possible answers, with anchors on each extreme—for example, 1 = never, 7 = always. To determine your attitudes toward the use of cell phones while driving, you might be asked to respond on a 1 to 7 scale, with 1 being the least favorable answer ("it's never acceptable") and 7 being the opposite anchor ("it's always acceptable"). You've probably responded to many of these kinds of queries yourself. Yet, when it comes to the study of complex attitudes—for example, your attitude toward gay marriage or your state senator— researchers have had to develop more sophisticated techniques.

To understand why, answer the following questions: How much do you value freedom? How strongly do you feel about the reduction in discrimination? How important to you is a less polluted environment? If an investigator asked these questions of a random selection of individuals—especially a random selection of university students—odds are that most would provide strong positive responses. But surely people must vary in their real attitudes toward these issues. How, then, do we capture people's real attitudes if traditional Likert scales sometimes fail to differentiate people with stronger and weaker attitudes?

One approach, developed by Russell Fazio, is to measure the *accessibility* of the attitude—that is, the degree to which the attitude is ready to become active in the individual's mind, guiding thought and behavior (Fazio, 1995; Fazio & Williams, 1986). Fazio and his colleagues measure the accessibility of attitudes by simply assessing the time it takes the individual to respond to the attitude question, which is known as a **response latency**. A person who takes 750 milliseconds to respond affirmatively to the question, "Do you approve how the president is handling the war in Afghanistan?" would presumably possess stronger attitudes in this realm than the individual who takes several seconds. This, indeed, is what Fazio and colleagues have found. For example, in a study conducted five months before Ronald Reagan and Walter Mondale squared off in the 1984 presidential election, Fazio and Williams (1986) measured how long it took participants to answer how good a president the opposing candidates would make. The time it took participants to respond to this question was a strong predictor of who they felt won the first debate between the two candidates, and more importantly, it predicted the candidate they voted for six months later. Attitude accessibility, then, is one way to refine our measurement of strong, meaningful attitudes.

A second approach to assessing attitude strength is to determine the *centrality* of the attitude to the individual's belief system (Krosnick & Petty, 1995). To assess centrality, researchers measure a variety of attitudes within a domain and calculate the extent to which a particular attitude is linked to the other attitudes. For example, in a study of social and political attitudes, a researcher might ask you your attitudes toward abortion, stem cell research, offshore drilling, gay marriage, sex education in high school, cutting carbon emissions, a clean environment, drug legalization, taxation, and subsidizing the automobile industry. To the extent that an attitude is really important to you, it should be highly correlated with your attitudes

Likert scale A numerical scale used to assess people's attitudes that includes a set of possible answers and that has anchors on each extreme.

response latency The time it takes an individual to respond to a stimulus such as an attitude question.

toward other issues. For example, if cutting carbon emissions is a defining social issue for you, as it is for many, then your attitude toward cutting carbon emissions is likely to strongly correlate with your attitutde toward the automobile industry or offshore drilling.

There are several other ways of measuring attitudes that do not rely on explicit self-reports. In Chapter 12, where we explore stereotypes and prejudice, we discuss a measure known as the implicit association task, which captures people's more implicit attitudes toward different objects (Greenwald, McGhee, & Schwartz, 1988). Researchers can rely on nonverbal measures of attitudes, assessing, for example, people's smiling behavior or degree of physical closeness as indices of positive attitudes toward others. Researchers are increasingly turning to physiological measures to capture people's attitudes. In Box 9.1, you saw how patterns of brain activity recorded from the surface of the scalp reveal the strength of an individual's attitudes. Later you will learn that fear is a core component of conservative political attitudes. This would suggest that fear-related physiological responses—for example, increased heart rate or sweaty palms—might capture more conservative political attitudes. And indeed, that is what one recent study found (Oxley et al., 2008). Participants who endorsed more conservative beliefs supporting military spending, warrantless searches, and opposition to immigration showed stronger skin conductance responses when shown threatening images of spiders or weapons.

 We have seen that attitudes have several elements—affect, cognitions, and behaviors—and we have delved briefly into how to measure attitudes. But why do people have attitudes in the first place?

FUNCTIONS OF ATTITUDES

What purposes do attitudes serve? One answer is that they guide behavior—a valid assumption, although attitudes guide behavior less powerfully than most people suspect (see Chapter 6). Researchers have, however, highlighted four other functions of attitudes (Eagly & Chaiken, 1998; Pratkanis, Breckler, & Greenwald, 1989). As we discuss these different functions, we will cast our net broadly, reviewing research that attests to the importance of attitudes in topics as wide-ranging as food preferences and the fear of death.

The Utilitarian Function of Attitudes

utilitarian function An attitudinal function that serves to alert us to rewarding objects and situations we should approach and costly or punishing objects or situations we should avoid.

Attitudes serve what has been called a **utilitarian function**—that is, they alert us to rewarding objects we should approach and to costly or punishing objects we should avoid. When you become aware of an attitude you hold—say, toward the smell of popcorn or the sight of your new boss—you are by definition aware of positive and negative information about the attitude object.

In numerous studies, researchers have shown that attitudes toward fairly neutral objects can be modified by pairing that object with a stimulus that generates a strong positive or negative reaction (Petty & Wegener, 1998). People's attitudes toward political slogans, consumer products, persuasive messages, and other people can be changed when paired with emotionally arousing stimuli such as pleasing odors, electric shock, harsh sounds, or pleasant pictures (Gresham & Shimp, 1985; Janis, Kaye, & Kirschner, 1965; Razran, 1940; Staats & Staats, 1958; Zanna, Kiesler, & Pilkonis, 1970). In these instances, the attitude toward one object becomes associated with a new object—a principle that advertisers have long exploited. Ads that use animals, babies, or sexually alluring young women and men are more likely to sell products than those that use less intrinsically rewarding objects, like cartoons or historical figures (Pratkanis & Aronson, 2000).

Food preferences also illustrate the utilitarian function of attitudes. Here our dietary likes and dislikes help us to eat foods that are beneficial to survival and to avoid foods that are potentially dangerous. The typical human has 10,000 taste buds devoted to sweet, sour, salty, and bitter tastes. Each taste bud has receptor cells with 50 short hairlike structures that, when stimulated by food particles, send a signal to parts of the brain that convert that electrochemical signal to our experience of taste. The preference for sweet foods—no doubt one of our strongest positive attitudes—helps us identify foods of nutritional value, such as foods that provide vitamin C, which humans, unlike many mammals, do not synthesize in their body.

Many foods also contain bitter-tasting, pungent-smelling toxins, which are often released by plants when threatened by a predator (for example, the proverbial onion that releases toxins when it is cut). When you eat a turnip or cabbage, you are getting a sublethal dose of these toxins. Our strong distaste, or dislike, for bitter foods helps us avoid these toxins (Profet, 1992; Rozin & Kalat, 1971). Interestingly, women are particularly sensitive to bitter tastes and pungent smells during the first trimester of pregnancy. They often experience this sometimes overwhelming negative attitude toward tastes and smells as the nausea of pregnancy sickness, which prevents them from eating these foods and thus protects the fetus from being exposed to dangerous toxins at a particularly vulnerable stage of development (Profet, 1992).

Or consider how attitudes toward different kinds of natural settings may serve utilitarian functions. Evolutionary psychologists have made interesting claims about why we prefer certain landscapes over others (Orians & Heerwagen, 1992). They assert that people prefer landscapes that have water, lush trees and bushes, semi-open space, ground cover, and distant views to the horizon. These kinds of environments offered our ancestors reliable sources of water, opportunities for hunting animals and gathering food, shelter, and the means to detect and hide from predators. We have positive attitudes toward these kinds of environments today, the argument goes, because of the evolutionary advantages these attitudes conferred on those who possessed and acted on them.

The Ego-Defensive Function of Attitudes

In addition to signaling rewards and threats, attitudes also serve an **ego-defensive function**, protecting us from being aware of unpleasant facts or emotions. We develop certain attitudes, this reasoning holds, to maintain cherished beliefs about ourselves

Attitudes and Associations
Our attitudes alert us to rewarding objects—or threatening or neutral ones. A positive attitude toward a beautiful woman may help sell a car if an association is created between the woman and the car. Here an attractive model poses next to a sports car, thereby pairing the emotionally arousing stimulus of the beautiful woman with the car.

"It's broccoli, dear."
"I say it's spinach, and I say the hell with it."

ego-defensive function An attitudinal function that enables us to maintain cherished beliefs about ourselves by protecting us from awareness of our negative attributes and impulses or from facts that contradict our cherished beliefs or desires.

terror management theory A theory that to ward off the anxiety we feel when contemplating our own demise, we cling to cultural worldviews and strongly held values out of a belief that by doing so part of us will survive death.

or our world. One way that we protect our valued beliefs is addressed in **terror management theory** (see Chapter 6). This account holds that our fear of dying leads us to adopt death-denying attitudes—for example, the adoption of religious beliefs, more positive evaluations of our own group, greater patriotism, increased religious conviction, greater conformity to cultural standards, and a greater inclination to punish moral transgressors. Death is one of life's few certainties and a source of many of our strongest attitudes and deepest values.

John Jost and his colleagues have made a similar argument about the core of political conservatism, that this political ideology is a form of motivated or ego-defensive cognition that helps people ward off certain anxieties (Jost, Glaser, Kruglanski, & Sulloway, 2003). Summarizing dozens of empirical studies spanning several decades and different cultures, these researchers identify two core values to political conservatism. The first is resistance to change. Conservatives express greater qualms about change of any kind, whether it take the form of political revolution, changes in social conventions or sexual identities, or even artistic change or scientific advance. A second core dimension of conservatism is the endorsement of inequality. Societies bring about inequalities in resources and opportunities (although they vary in the degree of inequality). Conservatives are more willing to accept these inequalities.

So where do these two core values of conservatism come from? According to Jost and colleagues, these core values are attempts to manage fear and uncertainty. With respect to fear, conservatives consistently show higher levels of fear: they judge the world to be a more dangerous place, react more quickly to danger-related words, and even are more prone to nightmares. With respect to uncertainty, conservatives show less interest in new technnological innovations, unfamiliar music, changes in job requirements—all things that require some tolerance of uncertainty. To ward off fear and uncertainty, conservatives gravitate to beliefs that envision a structured and orderly world, which gives rise to their core values—resistance to change and tolerance of inequality.

Survival and Preferred Landscapes Some evolutionary psychologists claim that people have evolved a preference for landscapes that have water, semi-open space, ground cover, and distant views to the horizon because these environments provided survival advantages to our ancestors. This view of the Husch Vineyards in California shows such preferred characteristics.

The Value-Expressive Function of Attitudes

value-expressive function An attitudinal function whereby attitudes help us express our most cherished values—usually in groups in which they can be supported and reinforced.

reference groups Groups whose opinions matter to us and that affect our opinions and beliefs.

We can also think about political conservatism in terms of a third function of attitudes, the **value-expressive function**, by which attitudes help us express our most cherished values, usually in groups where they can be supported and reinforced. If you were to predict which first-year students at your college would join various groups on your campus—the Korean Christian group, the Young Republicans, the Students for Diversity, Take Back the Night, and so on—surely those students' social attitudes would be a big help in making predictions. The same is true of which Facebook sites you visit and which Twitters you receive. We join groups, in part, to express our attitudes. These groups are known as our **reference groups**—that is, groups whose opinions matter to us and that affect our opinions and beliefs.

The value-expressive function of attitudes accounts for a variety of phenomena. For example, children in the United States express an early allegiance to the Democratic or Republican Party, in part to express the values of a very important group, the family (Niemi & Jennings, 1991). People who are committed to having low prejudice are more

Value Expression and Reference Groups We express our values through our membership in reference groups in which we can freely espouse our attitudes with like-minded others. (A) At a gay wedding in Tel Aviv, Israel, individuals express their support of gay marriage. (B) Here the Shades of Praise gospel choir performs in New Orleans, relying on one of the oldest ways to express convictions collectively—singing.

likely to associate with groups that promote those attitudes, and they feel guilt and shame when their actions contradict their attitudes toward minority groups (Devine, Monteith, Zuwerink, & Elliot, 1991; Devine, Plant, Amodio, Harmon-Jones, & Vance, 2002; Plant & Devine, 1998). Our commitment to the idea that people in the groups we join share our attitudes can even lead to certain forms of bias: within political groups, people tend to overestimate the similarity between their own attitudes and the attitudes of their leaders (Judd, Kenny, & Krosnick, 1983).

Theodore Newcomb's study of student attitudes at Bennington College richly illustrates the value-expressive function of attitudes (Newcomb, 1958). Newcomb studied all 600 students who attended Bennington, an isolated, experimental liberal arts college in pastoral Vermont—brand new at the time of Newcomb's study in the mid-1930s. The school was left-leaning in its politics, and it was run by charismatic, liberal professors. The students, on the other hand, were largely from upper-class, Protestant, Republican families. The question is: Would the students' conservative background or the liberal context in which they were immersed for several years prevail in shaping their political attitudes?

As it turns out, the experience at Bennington College shaped the students' political attitudes profoundly and in a lasting fashion (which may, in part, account for your parents' ambivalence about your departure to college!). In a four-year period, most students' political conservatism changed dramatically. This attitude change played out in their voting preferences, as you can see in **Figure 9.1**. First-year students were much more likely to prefer the Republican candidate; fourth-year students the Democratic or radical left-wing candidate. And in a follow-up study of 129 students about 25 years later, 60 percent of these former students voted for the more liberal presidential candidate, John F. Kennedy, in his election against Richard Nixon, suggesting that the changes these women underwent during college stayed with them throughout their lives.

Other findings attest to the value-expressive function of holding liberal attitudes at Bennington College. Most notably, liberal students tended to garner greater respect from their Bennington peers and to be better integrated into college groups than the conservative students. The conservative students, in contrast, were less likely to be leaders in the eyes of their peers, and they felt more alienated at the college and were

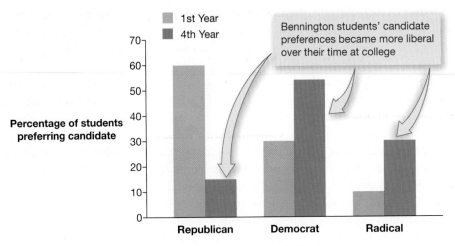

FIGURE 9.1 **The Value-Expressive Function of Attitudes**   (Source: Newcomb, 1958.)

likely to spend more time at home. Whether students became liberals or remained conservatives, their attitudes reflected a deep value-expressive function.

The Knowledge Function of Attitudes

knowledge function An attitudinal function whereby attitudes help organize our understanding of the world, guiding how we attend to, store, and retrieve information.

A fourth function of attitudes is the **knowledge function**, by which attitudes help organize our understanding of the world. Our attitudes guide what we attend to and remember, making us more efficient, and on occasion more biased, social perceivers of the complex social situations we find ourselves in. Most typically, we pay attention to and recall information that is consistent with our preexisting attitudes (Eagly & Chaiken, 1998).

For example, in one study by Lepper, Ross, Vallone, and Keavney (unpublished data), supporters of Jimmy Carter and Ronald Reagan, as well as undecided voters, watched a videotape of a debate between the two candidates during the 1980 presidential campaign. Members of these three groups answered a simple question: Who won the debate? As you can see in **Figure 9.2**, students' preexisting attitudes led

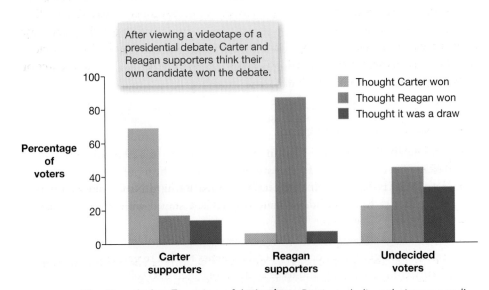

FIGURE 9.2 **The Knowledge Function of Attitudes**   Partisans believe their own candidates prevail in debates, even when viewing the same video. (Source: Lepper, Ross, Vallone & Keavney, unpublished data.)

partisans to much different conclusions about who emerged victorious. Carter supporters thought Carter had won. Reagan supporters were more strongly convinced that Reagan had won. And the undecided voters were intermediate, although more of them concluded that Reagan had prevailed.

This theme, that our attitudes lead us to seek out and selectively attend to information that bolsters our preexisting attitudes, is a robust one in social psychology and one we return to in other chapters. Our attitudes toward ourselves lead us to selectively recall past experiences that are consistent with those self-evaluations (Greenwald, 1980; Markus, 1977; see Chapter 3). Prejudicial attitudes toward different outgroups lead us to selectively interpret the actions of members of those groups in ways that are consistent with our prejudices (Hamilton & Trolier, 1986; see Chapter 12). We like physically attractive individuals, and we interpret their actions more favorably (Dion, Berscheid, & Walster, 1972; see Chapter 10).

Clearly, there is a bit of irony at work here. Our attitudes are built on our experiences and our acquisition of knowledge. Yet, eventually our attitudes become entrenched, and they bias us toward inferring that new information supports our attitudes. In the service of efficiency, our attitudes can sometimes sacrifice open-minded inquiry.

 We have seen that our attitudes serve four functions that are vital to our daily living. They help us identify rewards and threats. They help us avoid unpleasant realities about life and who we are. They are part of why we belong to different groups. And they are powerful guides to our construal of the social world. Changing them, we shall now see, is no trivial matter. The question of how to do so has led social psychologists to study persuasion.

PERSUASION AND ATTITUDE CHANGE

There is overwhelming consensus within the scientific community that we humans are causing the surface of the earth to warm and that this global warming will likely yield catastrophic events—frequent hurricanes that dwarf Katrina (the scourge of New Orleans), the rising of sea levels (which could put vast parts of coastal states like Florida under water and eliminate many tropical islands), the melting of the polar caps, rampant wildfires, and the disappearance of thousands of species. It is also quite clear that there are many things we can do to cut our carbon emissions, a primary source of global warming. Here are just a few:

- We can drive our cars less and rely more on bikes or public transportation.
- We can fly less on vacations.
- We can cut red meat from our diet (you'd be surprised how much that can help).
- We can use energy-efficient light bulbs, toilets, heating systems, and solar panels, all things that right now cost more than the conventional options but that yield many benefits in the long run.
- We can turn off computers and lights when not in use.
- We can buy local produce or grow our own food (this can help reduce carbon emissions because trucking isn't required to deliver the food).

Now imagine that you were charged with the task of producing a public service campaign to persuade people to adopt these habits. This would not be as difficult as changing people's sexual practices to curb AIDS, as has been attempted in African countries. Still, there are plenty of barriers to changing attitudes and behaviors related to cutting carbon emissions. People would have to change old habits (like driving their cars), give up strong preferences (those mouth-watering double cheeseburgers), and adjust their daily routine, taking a bit of extra time out of their day to take public transport or shop at the farmer's market. So what kind of green campaign would you design? The literature we are about to review suggests that there are no simple, one-solution-fits-all, means of persuasion. In fact, there are multiple routes to persuasion, and success depends on whom we are trying to persuade.

A Two-Process Approach to Persuasion

Two important theoretical models were developed in the 1980s to explain how people change their attitudes in response to persuasive messages. The two models, Shelly Chaiken's **heuristic-systematic model** of persuasion (Chaiken, 1980; Chaiken, Liberman, & Eagly, 1989) and Richard Petty and John Cacioppo's **elaboration likelihood model (ELM)** of persuasion (Petty & Cacioppo, 1979, 1984, 1986) were developed independently and employ different vocabularies. But in their essentials they are quite similar (see **Figure 9.3**). For the sake of convenience, our discussion is organized around the elaboration likelihood model.

The ELM starts from the assumption that there are two routes to persuasion. Through the **central route** (known as the **systematic route** in Chaiken's model), people think carefully and deliberately about the content of the message. They attend to the logic and cogency (how convincing the argument is) of the arguments contained in the message, as well as to the evidence and principles that are cited, and they retrieve relevant experiences, memories, and images. All of this elaborate thinking can lead the individual to change an attitude or not, based on a sifting of the arguments and the evidence.

Through the **peripheral route** (known as the **heuristic route** in Chaiken's model), people primarily attend to superficial aspects of the message that are tangential to its substance. Here the individual might consider how long the message is or how expert the communicator seems. Using the peripheral route, the individual relies on relatively

heuristic-systematic model A model of persuasion that maintains that there are two different routes of persuasion: the systematic route and the heuristic route.

elaboration likelihood model (ELM) A model of persuasion that maintains that there are two different routes of persuasion: the central route and the peripheral route.

central (systematic) route A persuasive route wherein people think carefully and deliberately about the content of a message, attending to its logic, cogency, and arguments, as well as to related evidence and principles.

peripheral (heuristic) route A persuasive route wherein people attend to relatively simple, superficial cues related to the message, such as the length of the message or the expertise or attractiveness of the communicator.

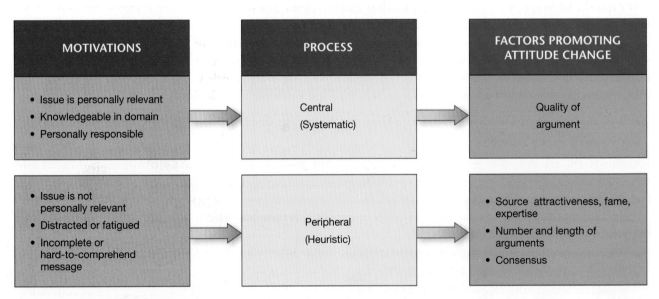

FIGURE 9.3 A Two-Process Approach to Persuasion According to Petty and Cacioppo's elaboration likelihood model, there are two routes to persuasion: a central route and a peripheral route, which are engaged by different motivations and which promote attitude change by different factors. Chaiken's model refers to these two processes as the systematic and heuristic routes.

simple, sometimes implicit communication heuristics, or rules of thumb, to justify attitude change. Thus, the person might change an attitude toward red meat because "a lot of people seem to be saying you shouldn't eat it" or "because there are a lot of arguments against it." Or peripheral cues might change the individual's basic emotional reaction to the attitude object (**Figure 9.4**). An attractive communicator, for example, might make the receiver feel more positively toward the attitude object—not eating red meat—simply by eliciting general feelings of liking or attraction.

What determines whether we will go through the central or peripheral route in responding to a persuasive message? One factor is our *motivation* to devote time and energy to a message. When the message has personal consequences for us, for example, we are more likely to go through the central route. A second factor is our *ability* to process the message in depth. When the message is clear and we have time, we are able to process it deeply. When we have little motivation and little ability to process the message, we instead attend to the peripheral cues associated with the message—for example, the appearance and credentials of the communicator.

In more concrete terms, three factors make the central route to persuasion more likely: (1) the *personal relevance* of the message—that is, whether it bears on our goals, concerns, and well-being; (2) our *knowledge* about the issue—the more we know, the more likely we are to scrutinize the message with care and thoughtfulness; and (3) whether the message makes us feel *responsible* for some action or outcome—for example, when we have to explain the message to others. In contrast, peripheral processing is triggered by factors that (1) reduce our motivation or (2) interfere with our ability to attend to the message carefully (Eagly & Chaiken, 1993; Petty & Cacioppo, 1986; Petty & Wegener, 1998). Thus, when people are distracted—for example, if they are carrying out some other task—they will be more likely to attend primarily to the peripheral cues of the message. This is also true of people who are tired, who are in an uncomfortable posture, or who are given messages that are incomplete or hard to comprehend (Kiesler & Mathog, 1968; Petty & Wegener, 1998).

To test the ELM approach to persuasion, researchers typically first generate strong and weak arguments related to an issue. They then present these strong and weak arguments as part of a message. They also vary the potency of various peripheral cues associated with the message, such as the number of arguments offered or the communicator's fame. Finally, they typically vary some factor, such as the personal relevance of the issue, to manipulate the likelihood that the individual will process the message centrally or peripherally. If participants process the message via the central route to persuasion, they should be influenced mainly by the strong and not the weak arguments. The strength of the arguments should be less important for individuals who are attending only to the peripheral cues of the message, however, as these participants should be more affected by such things as the number of arguments and the attractiveness of the communicator.

Consider one study that varied the strength of the arguments, the relevance of the issue, and a peripheral cue, the source expertise. In this study, participants either read eight weak arguments in support of a comprehensive exam to be implemented at their school or they read eight strong arguments (Petty, Cacioppo, & Goldman, 1981). Personal relevance was manipulated by notifying the participants that this exam would be initiated either the following year, which would mean the participants would have to take the exam, or in ten years, after the students' graduation (presumably!). Finally, source expertise was varied: half of the participants were told the arguments

FIGURE 9.4 You Be the Subject: Central and Peripheral Persuasion Tactics

Go to www.thegreenguide.com

List the central persuasion tactics: the strength, cogency, and clarity of the evidence.

_____

_____

_____

_____

_____

List the peripheral persuasion tactics: the attractiveness and credibility of the source, and the number of arguments and supporters cited.

_____

_____

_____

_____

_____

Results: You probably gravitated to areas of the site that are more in keeping with your preferences and expertise. In areas of the site more relevant to you (perhaps a section on travel), you likely cared more about arguments and evidence or central persuasion tactics. In areas less relevant to you (perhaps the section on gardening), you may have been more influenced by peripheral tactics, such as the beauty of the imagery.

"Of the modes of persuasion furnished by the spoken word there are three kinds. The first kind depends on the personal character of the speaker; the second on putting the audience into a certain frame of mind; the third on the proof, provided by the words of the speech itself."

—Aristotle

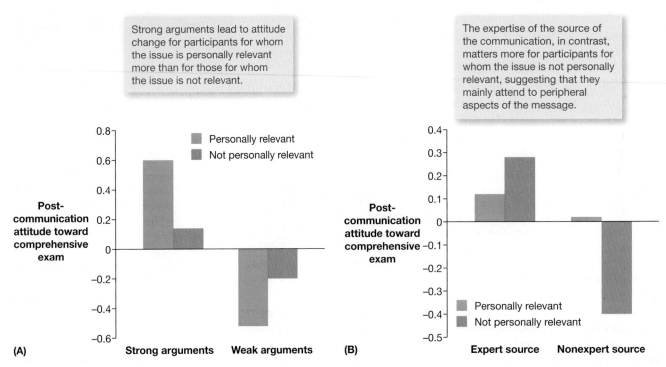

Strong arguments lead to attitude change for participants for whom the issue is personally relevant more than for those for whom the issue is not relevant.

The expertise of the source of the communication, in contrast, matters more for participants for whom the issue is not personally relevant, suggesting that they mainly attend to peripheral aspects of the message.

FIGURE 9.5 Central or Peripheral Route to Persuasion Attitude change can be brought about by strong arguments when people are motivated and by the expertise of the communicator when people aren't motivated. (Source: Adapted from Petty & Cacioppo, 1986, p. 154.)

were generated by a local high school class, and half were told that the arguments were generated by the "Carnegie Commission on Higher Education" chaired by a Princeton University professor.

Take a close look at **Figure 9.5**. You can see that when the message was not relevant to the students—that is, when the exam was to be implemented ten years later—the expertise of the source mattered but the strength of the argument did not. The participants with scant motivation to attend to the message gave little thought to the quality of the arguments, but they were moved by whether the arguments were produced by a high school class or a professorial committee. The results differed for participants who would have to take the exam, for whom the message was clearly relevant. They were more persuaded by strong than by weak arguments, but they were not influenced by whether the communicator was an expert or not.

The routes to persuasion, then, are twofold. Some messages persuade by prompting us to thoughtfully integrate new arguments and evidence into our belief systems, thus prompting change. Other messages persuade with more superficial cues—the beauty or charm of the communicator, for example—or even with subliminal cues (see **Box 9.2**). If you're interested in more enduring attitude change, however, your best bet is to convince people through the central route. With the central route, people attend to the message more carefully, and its effects are more pronounced. The central compared to the peripheral route of persuasion is thought to bring about attitude change that is more enduring, more resistant to persuasion, and more predictive of behavior (Eagly & Chaiken, 1993; Mackie, 1987; Petty, Haugtvedt, & Smith, 1995).

The Who, What, and Whom of Persuasion

Now that you have a better sense of how persuasive messages work, let's look at some more specific investigations of how—and how well—persuasion works. Many of these

BOX 9.2 **FOCUS ON MODERN LIFE**

A Subliminal Route to Persuasion?

In 1990, the rock band Judas Priest was tried for contributing to the suicide deaths of Ray Belknap and James Vance. Prosecutors alleged that the men had been led down the path to suicide by the subliminal message "Do it" that the band had embedded into one of its songs. Can subliminal messages have such powerful effects? Might subliminal messages be a third, implicit or unconscious route to persuasion?

You will see numerous times in this book that subliminally presented stimuli can activate certain concepts and even shape people's everyday thoughts, feelings, and actions (Dijksterhuis, Aarts, & Smith, 2005). Consider a pair of laboratory experiments that suggest that subliminal persuasion attempts may be effective. In one, pictures of a target person were shown to participants immediately after a subliminal presentation of either a pleasant image (for example, a child playing with a doll) or an unpleasant one (for example, a bloody shark). When later asked to evaluate the target person, those for whom the target was paired with positive subliminal images provided more favorable evaluations than those exposed to negative images (Krosnick, Betz, Jussim, & Lynn, 1992). In a study that directly examined the impact of subliminal messages on behavior, participants were told not to drink anything for 3 hours before arriving at the experiment (Strahan, Spencer, & Zanna, 2002). Upon arrival, half the participants were allowed to quench their thirst and half were kept thirsty. Participants were then subliminally primed, some with words related to thirst ("thirst," "dry") and some with neutral words ("pirate," "won"). They were then allowed to drink as much as they wanted of each of two beverages. Thirsty participants who were primed with thirst-related words drank significantly more than thirsty participants

primed with neutral words. A follow-up study using the same procedure found that subliminal messages can even influence a person's *choice* of beverage. Specifically, the two beverages that participants were offered were described as sports drinks, with one labeled Super-Quencher and the other Power-Pro. When asked at the end of the experiment how many discount coupons for the two drinks they would like, thirsty participants who were exposed to thirst-related subliminal messages requested 24 percent more of the Super-Quencher coupons than thirsty participants exposed to neutral subliminal messages.

Should we be alarmed that advertisers, political campaign managers, or rock bands might try to alter our behavior by bombarding us with messages we can't see and hence can't defend ourselves against? Not so fast. There are a number of important differences between the outside world and the laboratory environment that make it less likely that these effects could be obtained in daily life. The focus of the persuasion attempt in these studies is typically something about which one has no firm opinion, such as a new sports drink. It's one thing to shift people's attitudes and behavior with respect to neutral stimuli; it's another thing entirely to shift people's

attitudes and behavior with respect to more familiar, psychologically significant stimuli—for example, to get Republicans to vote for a Democratic candidate or to induce Coke drinkers to switch to Pepsi. In addition, the subliminal message in the laboratory is presented right before the target attitude or behavior is assessed, and the individual encounters no competing messages in the interim. That's rarely, if ever, the case in the real world. A subliminal command to "Drink Coke" could conceivably motivate people to leave their seats to get a drink, but once in the lobby, with advertisements for all sorts of merchandise screaming at them, they might be as likely to drink Pepsi as Coke or even to order a candy bar instead of a beverage.

In fact, there has never been a demonstration, nor is there any reason to believe that there ever would be, of subliminal stimuli inducing people to do something that they are opposed to doing. There is no reason to believe that being subliminally primed with the words "Do it" would lead anyone not already comfortable with the idea of suicide to kill himself. Nor is there any reason to believe that Democrats can be subliminally induced to vote Republican, Apple enthusiasts to buy a Dell, or clean-cut adolescents to join a cult.

Subliminal Advertising   In a television ad run by the Republicans during the 2000 presidential election, the word "RATS" was quickly flashed on the screen in a subliminal attack on Al Gore, the Democratic candidate, and his Medicare plan.

studies were inspired by an influential approach to attitude change developed by Carl Hovland and his colleagues at Yale University starting in the 1940s and '50s (Hovland, Janis, & Kelley, 1953). Their Yale School approach, which was stimulated by their work on mass communication for the army during World War II, broke down the persuasive message into three components: (1) the *who*, or source, of the message, (2) the *what*, or content, of the message, and (3) the *whom*, or target of the message.

Source Characteristics Perhaps more than ever, the rich, the famous, and the good looking are spokespeople for social causes. David de Rothschild, a scion of the famous Rothschild family, is a dashing, globe-trotting, wealthy, 6-foot 4-inch spokesman for the environmentalist movement. He has built a boat entirely out of recycled plastic bottles—the *Plastiki*—to sail 11,000 miles from San Francisco to Austrailia to draw attention to the problem of waste in our seas and the need to recycle. What are the effects of having such striking spokespeople for different causes? These kinds of questions concern *who* delivers the message, or what we'll call source characteristics. **Source characteristics are independent of the actual content of the message, and they can be powerful peripheral means for changing people's attitudes.**

One important source characteristic is the *attractiveness* of the communicator. The lead singer of U2, Bono, has emerged as the best-known spokesperson for the plight of African nations, just edging out Angelina Jolie. Glamorous movie stars regularly appear in public service announcements—for example, urging teens to read, stay in school, or avoid drugs and cigarettes. The beautiful and talented singer Shakira Mebarak Ripoll, of Barranquilla, Colombia, has organized a mass movement to introduce early childhood education to Latin America. From one perspective, these campaigns make no sense, for beauty (or celebrity) has no logical connection to the trustworthiness of an opinion about a consumer product or risky behavior. Here the ELM helps. Attractive communicators promote attitude change through the peripheral route of persuasion. We like and trust physically attractive people (see Chapter 10), and for good or ill we are more likely to endorse the attitudes they communicate.

Social psychological research shows that attractive communicators are more persuasive than less attractive communicators (Petty & Cacioppo, 1986). More attractive communicators are particularly persuasive to people for whom the message is not important and who have little knowledge in the domain, circumstances that make people more likely to attend to the message's peripheral cues (Chaiken, 1980; Petty, Cacioppo, & Schumann, 1983; Wood & Kallgren, 1988).

A second influential source characteristic is the *credibility* of the communicator. Credibility refers to the combination of expertise and trustworthiness of the communicator. Advertisers try to use credibility to their advantage. Ads for toothpaste and aspirin cite the testimonials from medical professionals who endorse the product. Actors who play doctors on television and who have no obvious knowledge about medicine have even been brought in to endorse health-related products. ("I'm not a real doctor, but I play one on TV.") Is this an effective tactic? What would the ELM predict? As we hope you anticipated, such communicators produce more attitude change

source characteristics Characteristics of the person who delivers the message, including the person's attractiveness, credibility, and expertise.

Credibility and Persuasion
If people believe that a communicator is sincere, knowledgeable, and trustworthy, they will be more likely to believe the message. Martin Luther King Jr., is pictured here at the Lincoln Memorial during the March on Washington in August 1963 as he is about to give his "I Have a Dream" speech. His actions in the months leading up to the rally, as well as his strong and poetic words and dramatic presentation, contributed to his credibility and ability to persuade.

in circumstances that promote the peripheral route to persuasion—namely, when the individual is less motivated and has reduced ability to attend to the message. Thus, communicators perceived to be high in credibility produce more persuasion when the topic is of little personal relevance to the target or when the target is distracted, since such a target would not be paying much attention to the message itself (Kiesler & Mathog, 1968; Petty, Cacioppo, & Goldman, 1981; Rhine & Severance, 1970).

What about all the noncredible communicators who crowd the airwaves these days—the crackpots maintaining that the Holocaust never happened, that AIDS is not caused by sexual contact, or that global warming is a hoax? Do these messages fall on deaf ears? An early study by Hovland and Weiss (1951) suggests otherwise. In this study, participants first rated the likelihood that a nuclear submarine would be built in the near future (at the time they did not exist). Five days later, participants read an essay about the imminence of nuclear submarines, written either by the highly credible physicist Robert Oppenheimer, the "father of the atomic bomb," or by a noncredible journalist who worked for *Pravda*, the propaganda newspaper of the former Soviet Union. As we might expect, the Oppenheimer essay led to greater attitude change than the essay by the less credible *Pravda* writer, even though the content of the essay was exactly the same.

Much more surprising, however, was that four weeks later, the participants who had read the essay by the *Pravda* writer, although unmoved initially, actually shifted their attitudes toward the position he advocated. This latter effect came to be known as the **sleeper effect**—that is, messages from unreliable sources exert little influence initially but over time have the potential to shift people's attitudes. Careful research by Anthony Pratkanis, Tony Greenwald, and their colleagues has identified how the sleeper effect works. It seems that over time, people dissociate the source of the message from the message itself. You hear some loose cannon on talk radio arguing forcibly against the evidence for global warming. Initially, you discount his message because of his lack of credibility. But over time, the message has the chance to influence your views because you dissociate the source of the message from its content. Importantly, when cues that discount the noncredible source *precede* the message—for example, when the trustworthiness of the communicator is called into question at the get-go—the sleeper effect does not occur (Pratkanis, Greenwald, Leippe, & Baumgardner, 1988). In this case, people develop a negative reaction to the ensuing message and counterargue against it, thus reducing its impact.

Message Characteristics Ever since Aristotle, philosophers have sought to elucidate the principles of persuasive messages, taught today in courses on rhetoric and marketing. What are the **message characteristics** that make a communication persuasive? By now you should anticipate what the ELM might say: that it depends on the audience's motivation and ability to process the message.

As we saw in Figure 9.3, *high-quality messages* are more persuasive in general and are especially so for people who find the message relevant, who have knowledge in the domain, and who feel responsible for the issue. What, then, makes for high-quality messages? In general, higher-quality messages convey the desirable yet novel consequences of taking action in response to the message (Burnstein & Vinokur, 1973); they often appeal to core values of the audience (Cacioppo, Petty, & Sidera, 1982); and they are straightforward, clear, and logical (Chaiken & Eagly, 1976; Leippe & Elkin, 1987).

In general, you will produce more attitude change if you make your conclusions explicit (Hovland, Lumsdaine, & Sheffield, 1949) and if you explicitly refute the opposition, thereby giving the receiver of the message material with which to counterargue against subsequent opposing messages (Hass & Linder, 1972; Petty & Wegener, 1998). And you will be more persuasive if you argue against your own self-interest.

"Every time a message seems to grab us, and we think, 'I just might try it,' we are at the nexus of choice and persuasion that is advertising."

—Andrew Hacker

sleeper effect An effect that occurs when messages from unreliable sources initially exert little influence but later cause individuals' attitudes to shift.

message characteristics Aspects of the message itself, including the quality of the evidence and the explicitness of its conclusions.

Arguing against Self-Interest   Patrick Reynolds, the grandson and heir of the late R. J. Reynolds (founder of the R. J. Reynolds Tobacco Company, the second-largest tobacco company in the United States and manufacturer of such brands as Camel, Kool, Winston, and Salem cigarettes), is shown speaking to students about the dangers of smoking. He watched his father and older brother both die of emphysema and lung cancer brought on by cigarette smoking and decided to devote his life to antismoking advocacy. His antismoking speeches and support for a smoke-free society have high credibility given his family history and the fact that his arguments, if effective, would have the effect of reducing his inheritance.

identifiable victim effect   The tendency to be more moved by the plight of a single, vivid individual than by a more abstract aggregate of individuals.

For example, Walster, Aronson, and Abrahams (1966) found that a message delivered by a prison inmate advocating longer prison sentences was more persuasive than a message in which the same prisoner argued for shorter sentences. When someone argues in a direction contrary to obvious self-interest, the source of the message is perceived to be more sincere.

What about the truth of persuasive messages? (See **Box 9.3**.) Do facts stand a chance when pitted against vivid but improbable statements? Research by Hamill, Wilson, and Nisbett (1980) suggests that *vivid information* embedded in a personal narrative with emotional appeal can be more persuasive than statistical facts that are objectively more informative. In their study, the researchers first assessed participants' attitudes toward welfare. In one condition, participants read a vivid, gripping story about a woman who was a lifetime welfare recipient. This mirrored a story Ronald Reagan told to great effect about a "welfare queen," a lifetime recipient of welfare who exploited the system to enjoy a life of comfort and leisure. In another condition, participants were given facts about welfare: that the average stay was two years and that only 10 percent of welfare recipients received welfare for four years or more. In a third condition, participants were given both the vivid narrative and the facts. In this condition, it should have been clear that the case they read about was quite atypical of welfare recipients in general. Which message do you think would lead to more attitude change: the vivid but unrepresentative story or the plain facts? You no doubt are anticipating our punch line: students were much more likely to change their attitudes after hearing the vivid story—even when they also had the cold statistics. The facts did little to alter their attitudes.

Vivid images abound in the media, and apparently to great effect. Messages warning of global warming depict baby polar bears floating perilously on melting blocks of ice in the sea. The nightly news highlights the single murder, kidnapping, or fire in its local coverage. (If it bleeds, it leads.) More generally, a common phenomenon that speaks to the power of vivid images is the **identifiable victim effect**. Vivid, flesh-and-blood victims are often more powerful sources of persuasion than abstract statistics (Collins, Taylor, Wood, & Thompson, 1988; Shedler & Manis, 1986; Taylor & Thompson, 1982). For example, Ryan White contracted HIV at age 13 and struggled nobly with the disease until succumbing some six years later. Following his death, the U.S. Congress passed the Ryan White Care Act, which funds the largest set of services for people living with AIDS in the country. It is clear that Ryan's moving, noble six-year struggle with AIDS did more to shift people's attitudes about the disease than any amount of statistics or medical argument.

What does fear do for persuasive communications? Let's return to our hypothetical question about running a carbon emissions reduction campaign. Should you scare the daylights out of people with images of refugees, food shortages, wildfires, and flooded coastal areas? The ELM offers somewhat competing notions regarding fear and persuasion. On the one hand, intense fear could disrupt the careful, thoughtful processing of the message, thus reducing the chances of persuasion. On the other hand, the right kind of fear might heighten the participant's motivation to attend to the message, thus increasing the likelihood of attitude change.

What does the evidence say? In general, it is advisable to make ad campaigns frightening and also to provide information about how to act on that fear (Boster &

BOX 9.3   **FOCUS ON POP CULTURE**

Lie to Me

The popular television show *Lie to Me* is based on the research of social psychologist Paul Ekman, who did the early studies of the universality of facial expression. Lying, of course, is one of the most challenging acts of persuasion: to get someone to believe the opposite of what you actually believe. Ekman, Bella DePaulo, and others have discovered certain clues to discern whether someone is lying or telling the truth. When people lie, they are more likely to show speech hesitations, face touches, micro-expressions of negative emotion, leg jiggles, speech dysfluencies (when two words get mixed up and form new words), sudden rises in the pitch of the voice, and increased eye contact (DePaulo, Lanier, & Davis, 1983; Ekman, O'Sullivan, Friesen, & Scherer, 1991; Mehrabian & Williams, 1969; Riggio & Friedman, 1983).

How good are we at catching liars? It turns out that we are surprisingly inept at this important task. Ekman and his colleagues have presented videotapes of people lying and telling the truth to thousands of people (Ekman & O'Sullivan, 1991). The simple task these participants had was to indicate whether each person was lying or telling the truth. Whereas chance guessing would yield accuracy rates of 50 percent, people on average were correct only 57 percent of the time. This same research yielded interesting answers about who's particularly good at catching liars. What's your guess? Contrary to what you might expect, those sages of knowing the human character—judges, clinicians, and psychological scientists—proved no better than the average person. The one group that shone in their ability to catch liars was secret service agents, because they get a sound training in the social psychology of lying we have just reviewed and that has produced this popular TV show.

Mongeau, 1984). In a study that first lent support to this recommendation, Howard Leventhal and his colleagues tried to change the smoking habits of participants in one of three ways. Some participants were shown a graphic film of the effects of lung cancer, which included footage of a lung operation in which the blackened lung of a smoker was removed. Other participants were given a pamphlet with suggestions about how to quit smoking. A third group was shown the film and given the pamphlet (Leventhal, Watts, & Pagano, 1967). Participants who saw the scary film reduced their smoking more than did those who just read the pamphlet (and thus would not have had their motivation to quit increased by a fear induction). Fear by itself can be persuasive. But participants who both saw the film and read the pamphlet decreased their smoking the most, as you can see in **Figure 9.6**, which presents participants' self-reports of their daily smoking behavior one month after the intervention. In general, persuasive messages that provide information that can be acted on can be highly effective (Leventhal, 1970; Leventhal et al., 1967; Robberson & Rogers, 1988). On the other hand, it is possible to frighten people so much that they will choose to deny the danger rather than act to combat it, especially if there is no clear recommendation about how to deal with the threat (Becker & Josephs, 1988; Job, 1988; Rogers & Mewborn, 1976).

Vividness and fear aren't the only things that matter in a persuasive message. How a message is targeted to a particular cultural group also matters. Thus, a substantial difference exists in the sort of message content we find in the media of independent and interdependent societies. Marketing experts Sang-pil Han and Sharon Shavitt analyzed the advertisements in American and Korean news magazines and women's magazines (Han & Shavitt, 1994). They found that the American ads emphasized benefits to the individual ("Make your way through the crowd" or "Alive with pleasure"), whereas Korean ads focused on benefits to collectives ("We have a way of bringing people closer together" or "Ringing out the news of business friendships that really work"). Han and Shavitt also conducted experiments in which they manipulated

The Identifiable Victim Effect
Here a mourner touches a photo of Laci Peterson, who was killed by her husband. Her tragic death made her a highly identifiable victim, and likely shaped people's attitudes about crime.

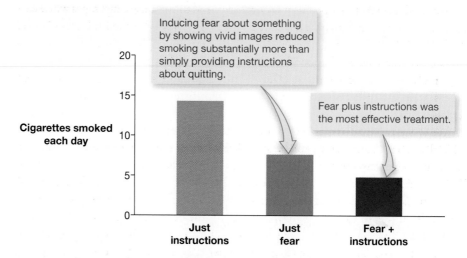

FIGURE 9.6 Fear and Persuasive Messages Moderate levels of fear lead to attitude change. (Source: Leventhal, Watts, & Pagano, 1967.)

the content of advertisements and measured their effectiveness. They found that the individual-oriented ads were more effective with American participants and that the collective-oriented ads were more effective with Korean participants.

Receiver Characteristics Communication by its very nature always involves both a communicator and someone who receives the message. We have seen throughout this section that the receiver, or target, matters. Consistent with the ELM, receivers who are more personally involved, knowledgeable, and responsible respond to messages quite differently than those who are less motivated. More generally, are certain people more vulnerable, or amenable, to persuasion? As you will see, **receiver characteristics** such as personality, mood, and age can matter, often in surprising and significant ways.

One facet of personality that influences the likelihood of attitude change is called the *need for cognition* (Cacioppo, Petty, Feinstein, & Jarvis, 1996). This refers to the degree to which people like to think deeply about things. People high in the need for cognition like to think, to puzzle, to ponder, and to consider multiple perspectives on issues. This is the kind of person who passes her time on the subway reading *Scientific American* or completing complex puzzles. People low in the need for cognition don't find thought and contemplation to be that much fun. How does the need for cognition influence persuasion? As you might imagine, people with a high need for cognition are more persuaded by high-quality arguments and are relatively unmoved by peripheral cues of persuasion (Cacioppo, Petty, & Morris, 1983; Haugtvedt & Petty, 1992).

A second important audience characteristic is *mood*. People who are good at communication go to great lengths to create a particular mood in their audience. Ronald Reagan, known as "the great communicator," was famous for his disarming, infectious humor during his speeches and press conferences. (Our favorite Reagan story concerns his appearance before a university audience that was giving him the silent treatment because he cut state funding for colleges. After walking past ranks of silent protesters, Reagan turned, put a finger to his mouth, and said, "Shhh.") Hitler staged enormous rallies for his most important speeches, surrounded by bold Nazi banners, awesome displays of military strength, and thousands of supporters signaling in unison. His intent was to stir the emotions of his audience to make them more receptive to his ideas.

receiver characteristics Characteristics of the person who receives the message, including age, mood, personality, and motivation to attend to the message.

Early studies found that people who were exposed to persuasive messages while eating or listening to beautiful music were more likely to change their attitudes (McGuire, 1985). Work by Duane Wegener and Richard Petty strongly suggests that persuasion is more likely when the mood of the message matches the mood of the receiver. Thus, more pessimistic, counterattitudinal messages tend to prompt greater message processing in sad or depressed people, whereas uplifting, optimistic, pro-attitudinal messages prompt greater message processing in happy people (Bless et al., 1996; Mackie & Worth, 1989; Wegener & Petty, 1994; Wegener, Petty, & Smith, 1995).

Finally, what about the *age* of the audience? As you might have guessed, younger people are more susceptible to persuasive messages than are adults or the elderly (Sears, 1986). This finding has great real-world significance. For example, one of the main sources of Ronald Reagan's political success was the overwhelming support he received from the 18 to 25 age-group, the very same demographic group that would back Barack Obama in overwhelming numbers 28 years later. This young age-group—many of you—is quite malleable in their political allegiances. Very recently, the party identification of your age-group has shifted dramatically toward the Democrats, signaling perhaps a generation of liberal dominance in politics.

Another real-world application of the age effect in persuasion has to do with relying on children as witnesses in legal cases. To what extent should we take seriously the testimony of young children—for example, in child abuse cases—if their attitudes can be so readily altered by motivated attorneys and misleading questions (Loftus, 1993, 2003)? A final problem concerns the extent of advertising directed at young children. Given that advertising, and the media more generally, can shape

> "The death of a single Russian soldier is a tragedy. The death of a million soldiers is a statistic."
>
> —Joseph Stalin

(A)

(B)

Message Characteristics and Targeting Messages may differ based on the times and culture. Messages are often targeted to collective concerns in interdependent societies and to individual concerns in independent societies. Similarly, messages may vary at different times in the same society. (A) During World War II, U.S. army posters stressed collective concerns. (B) In recent times army recruitment posters highlight individual characteristics service cultivates, such as individual strength.

Persuasion and Mood   The mood of an audience can affect whether a message will lead to attitude change. (A) In Germany in the 1930s, Adolf Hitler staged rallies like this one of Hitler Youth to create a mood of strength and unity that would encourage people to support his ideas. (B) In 2008, Barack Obama's campaign trail included record-sized crowds, whose euphoria was part of his historic victory.

people's attitudes and does so more for the young than for the old, perhaps we should worry about the immense amount of advertising that is directed at children aged 16 and younger.

David Sears has drawn on this link between age and susceptibility to persuasion as part of a broader commentary on the persuasion literature (Sears, 1986). Most studies of attitude change involve participants who are students in their first couple of years in college. These individuals are at a developmental stage that is very dynamic, as we saw in the Bennington College study, and they are particularly prone to attitude change. And as people age, their attitudes become less malleable. Sears poses a thorny question: Does the literature on attitude change that we have reviewed generalize to other age-groups? It is likely, he concludes, that the persuasion literature overestimates the extent to which our attitudes can be changed by would-be persuaders. In the final section of this chapter, we will elaborate on this theme and consider instances in which people resist attitude change.

Let's now return to your campaign to change people's everyday habits to reduce carbon emissions. How might the literature on persuasion help you? Perhaps the most important lesson is to tailor your message according to whether the audience is likely to go through the central or peripheral route to persuasion. Certain people are likely to go through the central route. These are individuals for whom global warming is personally relevant, who know quite a bit about the crisis, who feel a sense of personal responsibility about it, and who have a high need for cognition. For people like this, there is no substitute for high-quality messages, ones that are logical and clear, that make subtle rather than heavy-handed recommendations, and that appeal to clear consequences and values.

For many other people, and in many contexts, the peripheral route to persuasion is likely to be a better bet. This is likely to be true for younger audiences, for those who know less about global warming, and for people who don't think that global warming is relevant to their lives. For these people, the peripheral route is likely to be more effective. Here you might resort to attractive environmentalists (Leonardo DiCaprio), highly credible ones (Nobel prize–winning scientists), and messages that have the weight of various communication heuristics working in your favor.

LOOKING BACK We have seen how the elaboration likelihood model spells out two ways of processing persuasive messages. In the central route to processing, it is primarily the quality of the arguments that is attended to. In the peripheral route, such factors as the sheer number of arguments and communicator attractiveness are likely to be more important. Messages tend to be more effective if they are clearly laid out, if they refute opposing messages, and if they are vivid. Recipients of a message who have a high need for cognition are more likely to process messages through the central route. Moreover, recipients who are in a good mood are more persuadable than those who are not, and younger people are more persuadable than older people. We will now consider how these and other factors are used by the media in their attempts to persuade us.

THE MEDIA AND PERSUASION

The mass communication media make up a $200-billion-a-year industry. Each year the average American watches 1,550 hours of television, or about 3 to 4 hours a day, listens to almost 1,200 hours of radio, and spends about 180 hours reading newspapers. Each day the average American sees about 100 ads on television and is exposed to another 100 to 300 ads in newsprint and on the radio (Pratkanis & Aronson, 2000). The new social media—the Internet, Facebook, iPhones, and Twitter—no doubt increase the amount of media that the average American experiences. All told, half of Americans' waking hours are spent in contact with the media, which significantly exceeds the time they spend in face-to-face social interaction with friends and family.

Given our media-saturated lives, it's easy to imagine that almost all of our attitudes are shaped by mass communication. Decisions to buy a Dell or an Apple laptop or the Levi or Gap jeans could be guided by commercials recently seen on TV or heard on the radio. Which candidate we choose in the voting booth could be guided by recent political ads. Many conspiracy theories capitalize on this notion: according to these accounts, daily life is controlled by all-pervasive media organizations, owned and operated by a hidden and nefarious elite. Is there anything to such theories?

In what is known as the **third-person effect**, most people assume that "other people" are more prone to being influenced by persuasive campaigns than they themselves are—that others do not share their powers of rational analysis and restraint (Duck & Mullin, 1995; Hoorens & Ruiter, 1996; Perloff, 1993; Vallone, Ross & Lepper, 1985). In one study of the third-person effect, participants judged the likely impact of three media presentations on themselves and on other respondents (Innes & Zeitz, 1988). For all three presentations—a political ad campaign, a story about levels of violence portrayed in the media, and a campaign designed to deter people from associating with individuals who drink and drive—participants rated others as more likely to be influenced than themselves.

So how powerful are the media in actually shaping our attitudes? Documenting the effects of the media on people's attitudes is no simple task. Researchers have done some experiments, but more typically they have relied on survey methodologies in which people report which programs and ads they have seen. Retrospective self-reports, however, are notoriously fallible. If participants say they have seen some ad, or say they have not, how can we be sure? How can we be certain that viewers saw the ad under the same conditions? And once again, what about self-selection effects? For

third-person effect The assumption by most people that "other people" are more prone to being influenced by persuasive messages (such as those in media campaigns) than they themselves are.

example, highly motivated citizens are more likely to tune in to political ads than are less motivated citizens (Iyengar, 2004). Any effect of the ad campaign is confounded by these differences in political motivation.

Notwithstanding these difficulties, many studies attest to the power of the media, and in different parts of this book we consider some of these studies. In Chapter 13, for example, we show that violence in the media and video games does indeed make people more aggressive. But the effects of the media are not always as robust as you might imagine. Let's study a few examples of how the media sometimes produce surprisingly little attitude change. This review will serve as a platform for considering how people resist persuasive attempts.

The Surprisingly Weak Effects of the Media

William McGuire reviewed the evidence regarding the effects of intensive media campaigns on fairly specific behaviors and found remarkably small, sometimes nonexistent, effects (McGuire, 1985, 1986). His conclusions have for the most part stood the test of time. People are often quite independent-minded in the face of the media glut. Let's look at three specific cases in which the media have had surprisingly weak or nonexistent effects.

Consumer Advertising First, what about consumer advertising? Advertising in the United States is a multibillion-dollar industry. Do the captivating Nike or Abercrombie and Fitch commercials make you go out and buy their products? McGuire claims they don't. When we look carefully at the correlation between the ad budget of a product and its market share—that is, the proportion of consumers who buy a product—we find a very weak or nonsignificant correlation. Even when such effects do occur, they are usually short-lived, typically lasting less than one year (Bird, 2002; Landes & Rosenfield, 1994). How much a company spends on a product may have little direct effect on whether people buy it or not. Ads do have other effects, however, that may indirectly influence purchasing behavior. Ads have been shown to increase product loyalty, product awareness, and warm or excited feelings about the product, all of which may in turn influence purchasing behavior (McGuire, 1986).

Political Advertising What about political ads? As elections draw near, our TVs become filled with dramatic and, at times, controversial political ads. Here numerous studies by political scientists have challenged conventional wisdom: most studies document no significant correlation between the amount a candidate spends on an election and success in the election (Jacobson, 1978; Levitt, 1994). While a study of the 1976 Democratic presidential primaries did find a correlation between a candidate's expenditures and the number of votes obtained, this was only true during the early stages of the campaign. Other variables, such as the candidate's previous success, were more important in predicting the candidate's ultimate success (Grush, 1980). Turning to the effects of political ads, relevant studies indicate that they have very small effects on voting behavior (Kaid, 1981). They mainly influence late-deciding voters, and they are as likely to influence voters against as for the advertised candidate. Work by Ansolabehere and Iyengar (1995) suggests that certain kinds of ads, most notably negative ads that aggressively critique the opponent, may turn potential voters off from voting. As support for this claim, they note the historical rise in negative ads and the drop in voter turnout in presidential elections. In 1960, voter turnout for the presidential election was 62 percent; by 1988, it had slipped to 50 percent (although it did rise to 57 percent in the 2008 election). In a careful study of the 1992 Senate campaigns, Ansolabehere and Iyengar divided campaigns into negative ones, defined by attack

(A)

(B)

Political Advertising In presidential elections, billions of dollars are spent in advertising. (A) The Obama-Biden ticket focused on change and was wildly successful on the Internet. (B) The McCain-Palin ticket emphasized leadership and experience, attempting to capitalize on McCain's long record of service.

advertisements, and positive ones, defined by ads offering reasons to vote for a given candidate. The positive Senate campaigns averaged a higher voter turnout (57 percent) than the negative campaigns (49.7 percent).

Public Service Announcements Public service announcements (PSAs) are inserted into television breaks and urge the public to follow beneficial health or social practices. They provide compelling arguments against taking drugs or smoking cigarettes or engaging in unsafe sex. Other PSAs encourage parents to read to their children, to play with them, and to praise them. Do these have much effect on later behavior? Again, the answer appears to be no (Tyler, 1984). Careful studies have found that well-designed, heavily exposed campaigns against drug abuse, for example, have had little impact on children's knowledge about the dangers of drugs or, more importantly, their drug-taking behavior (Schanie & Sundel, 1978). This includes the D.A.R.E. campaign that you may have participated in as a junior high school student. D.A.R.E. is an extremely expensive and widely used program to discourage drug use. A recent longitudinal study, however, found that children who participated in the D.A.R.E. program in sixth grade did not use drugs more or less, either initially, immediately after the program, or ten years later, than appropriately matched comparison children who did not participate in D.A.R.E. (Lynam et al., 1999).

Though standard mass communication efforts often have little impact, some novel methods of persuasion have proved effective. For example, when adolescents are taught by the use of scenarios how to turn away requests for unprotected sex, reports of unprotected sex and rates of sexually transmitted diseases (STDs) go down (Jemmott, Jemmott, & Fong, 1998; Jemmott, Jemmott, Braverman, & Fong, 2005). In Chapter 15, we discuss the sometimes enormous impact of the "entertainment education" format of telenovelas begun by a Mexican TV executive and now found throughout the world.

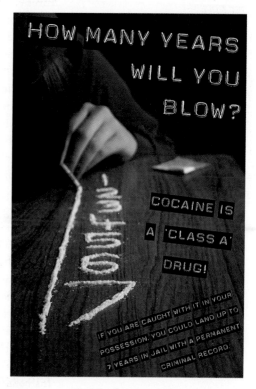

Public Service Ads Public service ads try to persuade people to avoid drugs or alcohol or cigarettes or unsafe sex and to instead engage in healthy and productive behaviors. This anti-drug ad was part of a campaign to encourage kids to choose not to take drugs.

The Media and Conceptions of Social Reality

How do we respond to McGuire's claim of low media impact? One angle is to argue that McGuire has focused on the wrong type of influence. Perhaps it is unrealistic to expect specific ads to affect specific behaviors. Our behaviors, after all—whether we buy the BlackBerry or iPhone, whether we engage in safe sex or not—are determined by a complex combination of different forces. It seems unlikely that out of the white noise of the competing messages from the media that bombard us each day, one message in particular would prompt us to take specific action.

Another response is to argue that the media have an even more unsettling influence: they shape our very conception of social reality. Specific advertisements may not lead us to buy specific products, but they might lead us to have an unlimited desire for shopping, or a conviction that personal happiness is to be found in materialistic pursuits. Political ads may not lead us to vote for a particular candidate, but they may lead us to conclude that the country is going downhill (Eibach, Libby, & Gilovich, 2003).

Political scientist Shanto Iyengar refers to this effect of the media as **agenda control**: the media shapes what you think is important and true. For example, the prominence of issues in the news media—fear of crime or concern about traffic congestion or worry about the condition of the economy—is correlated with the public's perception that those issues are important (Dearing & Rogers, 1996; Iyengar & Kinder, 1987). In one experiment, viewers saw a series of newscasts. In one condition, they saw three stories dealing with U.S. dependence on foreign energy sources; in another, six such stories; and in a final condition, no stories like this. When exposed to no news about dependence on foreign energy, 24 percent of the viewers cited energy as one of the three most important problems facing the country. This percentage rose to 50 percent for the participants who saw three stories on the subject and 65 percent for the participants who saw six stories (Iyengar & Kinder, 1987). So a politician in office should hope that news reports focus on things that are going well at the time, and a politician who wishes to defeat the incumbent should hope that the media focus on things that are not going well (see **Box 9.4**). Many believe that one of the main reasons for Barack Obama's success was that he, and not Hillary Clinton or subsequently John McCain, became the voice for change—a central interest in a nation in the midst of an emerging economic recession and an unpopular war.

George Gerbner and his colleagues have shown that the media shape our broader conceptions of social reality (Gerbner, Gross, Morgan, & Signorielli, 1986). These researchers have laboriously coded the content of television programs, and they have found that the world depicted on TV scarcely resembles social reality. On prime-time programs, for example, males outnumber females by a factor of 3 to 1. Ethnic minorities, young children, and the elderly are substantially underrepresented. Many jobs, such as those in the service industry or the blue-collar world, are likewise underrepresented. Crime is wildly more prevalent per unit of time on prime-time television than in the average U.S. citizen's real life.

In careful assessments of the television-viewing habits of individuals, Gerbner and his colleagues have documented that heavy television viewers—namely, those who watch 5 hours or more per day—construe social reality much like the reality they view on television. Heavy television viewers tend to endorse more racially prejudiced attitudes. They assume that women have more limited abilities than men. They overestimate the prevalence of violent crime and assume that the world is quite dangerous and sinister. And they overestimate the number of physicians and lawyers in the population. Of course, you should be worried about the possibility of self-selection effects producing these results. Perhaps more prejudiced, cynical, and ignorant people watch more television in the first place and it is these individual differences that produce the

agenda control Efforts of the media to select certain events and topics to emphasize, thereby shaping which issues and events we think are important.

BOX 9.4   **FOCUS ON THE MEDIA**

The Hostile Media Phenomenon

On July 23, 2008, with the presidential race heating up and the gap between John McCain and Barack Obama narrowing, John McCain sat down to talk with Fox News's Sean Hannity. Along with a discussion of the war in Iraq, the central topic they covered was media bias. Their claim was that the media were treating Barack Obama uncritically, in biased fashion, reacting to him as if he were a rock star rather than looking critically at his political agenda. This allegation of media bias was in part political ploy, but also a tendency long observed in politicians and citizens alike. President George W. Bush liked to refer to the media as "the filter," expressing the conviction that the mainstream media have reported on his presidency through a biased political lens that reflected badly on his views and agenda. Richard Nixon felt that the media were run by an elite Jewish clique. The thesis that the media are ideologically biased regularly produces best sellers that appeal to liberals and conservatives alike. An entire organization, Fairness and Accuracy in Reporting (FAIR; www.fair.org), is devoted to documenting bias in the media (for example, showing that conservatives are more likely to appear as experts on news shows like *Nightline*).

Research by Robert Vallone, Lee Ross, and Mark Lepper (1985) suggests that we tend to believe that the media are biased against our preferred causes. These researchers reason that the hostile media phenomenon stems from the conviction that most people feel that they see the world in a reasonable, objective fashion. By implication, individuals who have differing opinions—or in the case of the media who attempt to present both sides of an issue—must be biased. This basic tendency to perceive the media as hostile is a regularity in the political theater of presidential politics and a common feature of our perception of the media. For example, in one telephone survey conducted 3 days before the 1980 presidential election, among Jimmy Carter supporters who felt that the media had favored one candidate in its coverage, 83 percent thought that it favored Reagan. In contrast, for Reagan supporters who felt the media had been biased, 96 percent felt that the media had favored Carter.

---

aforementioned results and not television viewing. Nevertheless, Gerbner and his colleagues advance a provocative thesis: pervasive media exposure may very well determine our most basic assumptions about the world we live in, about the groups that make up our society, about how we derive satisfaction and well-being, and about human nature.

 We have seen that media persuasion effects—at any rate, advertising effects—are weaker than we might assume, even though most people believe that the media are quite effective, at least for other people! It seems that the greatest effects of the media involve influencing our conceptions of reality and exerting agenda control—that is, making us feel that some issues are particularly important. In the next section, we examine some of the reasons that people might be less susceptible to persuasion and thus better able to resist it than we might assume.

RESISTANCE TO PERSUASION

Although the media may have their biggest effects indirectly in shaping our most basic assumptions about social reality, we must still explain why they do not have more powerful direct effects. If McGuire is right that media effects are generally small and even nonexistent, how can we explain why this is so? As we will now see, part of the answer lies in the fact that many of the important principles of social psychology—the power of our perceptual biases, of preexisting commitments, and of prior knowledge—serve as sources of independent thought and significant forces of resistance in the face of persuasive attempts.

Attentional Biases and Resistance

When the office of the surgeon general issued its 1964 report linking smoking to lung cancer, it would seem to have provided incontrovertible evidence requiring smokers and nonsmokers alike to shift their attitudes toward smoking. The report, after all, represented the carefully weighed opinion and near-unanimous consensus of the scientific community. And yet, after the release of the report, 40 percent of smokers found the report flawed compared with 10 percent of nonsmokers. We would like to think that we can absorb data and information in relatively unbiased fashion (Pronin, Gilovich, & Ross, 2004) and that if we learned that a habit was dangerous to our health, we would alter our attitudes toward that habit accordingly. But as we have seen, our minds sometimes go about their business very differently, responding selectively to information in a way that maintains our original attitudes.

Let's break this assertion down a bit. First, several studies indicate that people are inclined to *attend selectively* to information that confirms their original attitudes (Eagly & Chaiken, 1998; Sweeney & Gruber, 1984). That is, we tune in to information that reinforces our attitudes, and we tune out information that contradicts them. In one illustrative study, students who either supported the legalization of marijuana or opposed it listened to a message that advocated legalization (Kleinhesselink & Edwards, 1975). The message contained 14 arguments: 7 that were strong and difficult to refute (and clearly appealing to the pro-marijuana students) and 7 that were silly and easy to refute (and very attractive to the anti-legalization students). The stu-

dents heard the message over earphones accompanied by a continual static buzz. To combat this problem, students were allowed to press a button to eliminate the buzz for 5 seconds. This allowed the researchers to determine the information to which the students preferred to attend—arguments that were consistent with their attitudes or that opposed their position.

As you might have anticipated, the pro-legalization students pushed the button more often when the speaker was delivering the strong arguments in favor of legalization—wanting to hear the information that would reinforce their preexisting attitudes. The anti-legalization students, in contrast, were more likely to push the button while the speaker offered up the easy-to-refute arguments in favor of legalization, the very information that would reinforce their position. In a similar study, students who were asked to write essays about federal funding for abortion or the use of nuclear energy tended to select as reference material for their essays magazine articles that supported their opinion (McPherson, 1983). We suspect that during the last presidential election, you yourself were much more inclined to read newspapers, blogs, and Web sites that supported your candidate and avoid those that supported the opposition.

Not only do we selectively attend to and seek out information that supports our attitudes, we also *selectively evaluate* the information we take in. Specifically, we are prone to look favorably upon information that supports our attitudes and critically upon information that contradicts our attitudes. For example, in one study, Ziva Kunda (1990) had female and male students read a story presented as a *New York*

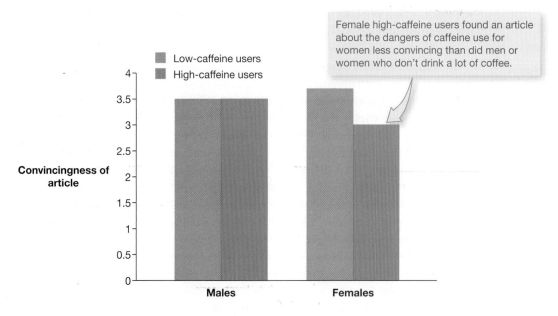

FIGURE 9.7 Selective Evaluation People who are personally motivated will derogate information that challenges cherished beliefs. (Source: Kunda, 1990.)

Times article that detailed how caffeine consumption in females is associated with an increased risk of fibrocystic disease. Half of the participants were high-caffeine users—fans of lattes, cappuccinos, and on hot days diet Coke or Mountain Dew. The other half of the participants were low-caffeine users. The article, of course, should be most threatening to the female high-caffeine users and thus be greeted with the greatest skepticism by that group. As you can see in **Figure 9.7**, this proved to be the case. Independent of caffeine use, the male participants found the article fairly convincing, as did the females who used little caffeine. It was the high-caffeine-using females who were less convinced by and more critical of the article.

Kunda's study raises an interesting question: How do partisans of an issue respond to the mixed scientific evidence that so often characterizes complex social problems? Is capital punishment an effective deterrent to murder? Will tax cuts targeted to the rich produce "trickle-down" benefits to all? Do generous welfare benefits discourage significant segments of society from joining the workforce? One possible result—the one that as citizens we would hope for—is that mixed evidence would lead partisans to a more moderate position. In this scenario, partisans consider the facts in support of their own position and that of the other side, and they integrate this information into a more balanced, moderate position if that is what the facts call for. An alternative view, the belief polarization hypothesis, holds that people will dismiss evidence that contradicts their initial views, and derive support from evidence that is consistent with their views.

To test this hypothesis, Lord, Ross, and Lepper (1979) had death penalty opponents and proponents read two different studies that examined the deterrent effects of capital punishment. One study suggested that the death penalty had a deterrent effect, reducing murder rates in the states in which it was implemented. The other study suggested that murder rates were actually higher in states with capital punishment. As in Kunda's study of caffeine consumers, both sides found the study that supported their views to be the more rigorously conducted. And both sides were highly critical of the design and details of the study that contradicted their position. As a result of reading the two studies, the two sides' differences were actually *greater* at the end of the study. Thus, when we encounter mixed evidence on an issue of importance to us, we often become even more firmly entrenched in our attitudes. It is no wonder that we are resistant to so many persuasive communications.

In related research, Peter Ditto and colleagues have shown that people are more critical of evidence that violates cherished beliefs about their personal health (Ditto & Lopez, 1992). Patients who receive diagnoses indicating that they are unhealthy are more likely to downplay the seriousness of the diagnosis and the validity of the test that produced the diagnosis (Ditto, Jemmott, & Darley, 1988). In a clever extension of this work, Ditto and Lopez (1992) gave undergraduates a test of a fictitious medical condition called "TAA deficiency" that was supposedly associated with pancreatic disorders later in life. The test was simple: to put saliva on a piece of yellow paper and observe whether it would change color in the next 20 seconds. In the deficiency condition, participants were told that if the paper remained the same color (yellow), they had the medical condition; in the no-deficiency condition, participants were told that if the paper changed to a dark green, they had the medical condition. The paper remained yellow throughout the study. Clearly, participants in the deficiency condition would be motivated to see the paper change color, and they should be disturbed by the evidence with which they were confronted—that the paper remained yellow. And indeed, these participants took almost 30 seconds longer than participants who received more favorable evidence to decide that their test was finished. Given our tendency to selectively attend to and evaluate incoming messages in ways that confirm our preexisting attitudes, it is no wonder, then, how difficult it can be for the media to produce attitude change. Most messages, it would seem, are preaching to the choir.

Previous Commitments and Resistance

Many persuasive messages fail because they cannot overcome the target's previous commitments. For example, recent empirical research is revealing that our political allegiances are often passed from parent to child and seem to be part of our DNA (see **Box 9.5**). Such allegiances rooted in our upbringing and family background may be deeply intertwined with our social identity (McGuire, 1985). Political ads that try to convince potential voters to shift their political allegiances must, in effect, convince voters to abandon these deep commitments—not a likely outcome. Similarly, antidrug campaigns are designed to reduce the drug-taking behavior of individuals who may be engaging in a habitual act that is embedded in a way of life and a community of friends.

There is also evidence that public commitments make people resistant to attitude change (it also makes people resistant to conformity; see Asch's line judgment studies in Chapter 8). In some studies, participants are asked to make public statements regarding their attitudes (Kiesler, 1971; Pallak, Mueller, Dollar, & Pallak, 1972). When participants make public commitments to their attitudes—as people do every day when they discuss politics and social issues with their friends—they are more resistant to subsequent counterattitudinal messages than are control participants.

Why might public commitments increase our resistance to persuasive communications? The most obvious reason is that it is hard to back down from a public commitment, even when evidence is presented against the position we took. Another reason is not so obvious: public commitments engage us in more extended thought about a particular issue, which tends to produce more extreme, entrenched attitudes. This is supported by Abraham Tesser's **thought polarization hypothesis**. To test his hypothesis, Tesser measured participants' attitudes toward social issues, such as legalizing prostitution (Tesser & Conlee, 1975). He then had the participants think for a few moments about the issue. When they stated their attitudes toward the same

thought polarization hypothesis The hypothesis that more extended thought about a particular issue tends to produce more extreme, entrenched attitudes.

BOX 9.5 **FOCUS ON BIOLOGY**

The Genetic Basis of Attitudes

One of the deepest sources of our commitment to important attitudes, and our resistance to persuasive messages, is our genes. Work by Abraham Tesser (1993), of the University of Georgia, suggests that our attitudes are in part inherited. To support this claim, Tesser examined the attitudes of monozygotic (identical) twins, who share 100 percent of their genes, and the attitudes of dizygotic (fraternal) twins, who share 50 percent of their genes. For most attitudes surveyed, there was a greater similarity in the attitudes of identical twins versus fraternal twins. This was true, for example,

for attitudes about the death penalty, jazz, censorship, divorce, and socialism. Moreover, researchers found that the more-heritable attitudes were also more accessible, less susceptible to persuasion, and more predictive of feelings of attraction to a stranger who shared those attitudes. Of course, there is no gene for attitudes toward censorship or socialism; the hereditary transmission must be via some other element of temperament, such as a fear of novelty (which might make you dislike jazz but be more tolerant of censorship), impulsivity, or a preference for risk taking.

More recent research by James Fowler and his collaborators has found that genes account not only for politically relevant attitudes, as Tesser documented, but political participation (Fowler, Baker, & Dawes, 2008). More specifically, they found that identical twins were more likely to resemble each other than were fraternal twins in sharing party affiliations and in their likelihood of voting in an election in Los Angeles. No wonder it's often hard to shift people's political attitudes and voting preferences; this would appear to require that you change a basic part of who we are.

issue a second time, they routinely gave stronger ratings: opponents and proponents polarized. The repeated expression of attitudes has led to more extreme attitudes in a variety of domains, including attitudes toward people, artwork, fashions, and football strategies (Downing, Judd, & Brauer, 1992; Judd, Drake, Downing, & Krosnick, 1991; Tesser, Martin, & Mendolia, 1995). A caveat is in order here, however. Increased thought about an attitude object can lead to more moderate attitudes for people who have previously had little motivation to think about the issue or little preexisting knowledge about the issue (Judd & Lusk, 1984).

Knowledge and Resistance

In our review of the ELM approach to attitude change, we saw that prior knowledge makes people scrutinize messages much more carefully. People with a great deal of knowledge are more resistant to persuasion. Such people have more beliefs, emotions, and habits tied up with their attitudes, which should make their attitudes more resistant to change. This intuition has been borne out in the experimental literature (Haugtvedt & Petty, 1992; Krosnick, 1988; Lydon, Zanna, & Ross, 1988; Zuwerink & Devine, 1996). For example, in a study of attitudes toward environmental preservation, Wendy Wood (1982) divided students into two groups: those who were pro-preservation and knew a lot about the issue and those who were pro-preservation but less knowledgeable about the subject. In a second session, she exposed these two groups of students to a message opposed to environmental preservation. The students with a great deal of knowledge about the environment moved only a little in their attitudes, and they counterargued a great deal in response to the message, relying on what they already knew and strongly believed about the issue. The less knowledgeable students, however, shifted their attitudes in the direction of the anti-preservation message, for they had less knowledge to rely on to counterargue against the message.

Attitude Inoculation

Thus far, we have examined how people's belief systems—their biases, commitments, and preexisting knowledge—make them resistant to attitude change. This is due to the more general tendency to selectively attend to, and favorably evaluate, evidence that supports preexisting attitudes. There are also techniques that can be used to further these tendencies to resist persuasion—or to instill them in people with less commitment, knowledge, and confidence in their opinions.

William McGuire has developed such a technique that finds inspiration in a rather unusual source: the inoculations we receive against viruses. When we receive an inoculation, we are exposed to a weak dose of the virus. Exposure to this small dose of the virus stimulates our immune system, which then is prepared to defend against exposure to larger doses of the virus. McGuire believed that resistance to persuasion could be encouraged in a similar fashion, by **attitude inoculation**—small attacks

attitude inoculation Small attacks on our beliefs that engage our attitudes, prior commitments, and knowledge structures, enabling us to counteract a subsequent larger attack and be resistant to persuasion.

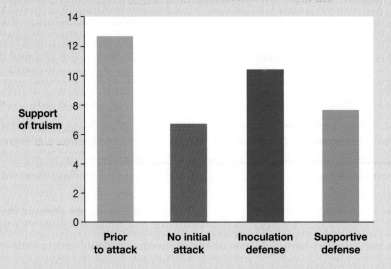

FIGURE 9.8 Scientific Method: Attitude Inoculation

Hypothesis: Defending small attacks on core attitudes makes people resistant to persuasion.

Research Method:

1 Researchers assessed the participant's endorsements of different cultural truisms.

2 Participants were then exposed to a small attack on their belief in the truism.

3 In some conditions, the researchers asked the participants to refute that attack by offering arguments against it; this was the attitude inoculation. In other conditions, the researchers asked the participants to consider arguments in support of the truism.

4 Between one hour and seven days later, the researchers asked the participants to read a three-paragraph-long, full scale attack on the truism.

Results: Prior to the atacks participants strongly endorsed the truism. The subsequent, forceful attack did indeed reduce the belief in the truism for those people who faced no initial attack (the second column). But having earlier refuted a mild attack against the truism led people to substantially resist the subsequent stronger attack (third column). Furthermore, counterarguing against the initial attack was clearly more effective than generating arguments that supported the truism (fourth column).

Conclusion: Attitude inoculation, in which people use preexisting attitudes, commitments, and knowledge to come up with counterarguments, makes people more resistant to attitude change.

Source: McGuire & Papageorgis (1961).

on our beliefs that would engage our attitudes, prior commitments, and knowledge structures and thereby counteract the larger attack (McGuire & Papageorgis, 1961).

In studies that attest to the efficacy of attitude inoculation, McGuire first assessed participants' endorsements of different cultural truisms, such as "It's a good idea to brush your teeth after every meal if at all possible" or "The effects of penicillin have been, almost without exception, of great benefit to mankind" (McGuire & Papageorgis, 1961). More than 75 percent of the participants checked 15 on a 15-point scale to indicate their agreement with truisms like these.

Now comes the intervention. McGuire and Papageorgis exposed participants to a small attack on their belief in the truism. For example, in the tooth-brushing example, the participants might read, "Too frequent brushing tends to damage the gums and expose the vulnerable parts of the teeth to decay." In some conditions, the researchers asked the participants to refute that attack by offering arguments against it; this was the attitude inoculation. In other conditions, the researchers asked the participants to consider arguments in support of the truism. Then, some time between 1 hour and 7 days later, the researchers asked the participants to read a three-paragraph-long, full-scale attack on the truism.

In **Figure 9.8**, we present data that attest to the immunizing effectiveness of attitude inoculation. As you can see in the first column, prior to the attack, participants strongly endorsed the truism. The subsequent, forceful attack did indeed reduce the belief in the truism for those people who faced no initial attack (the second column). But having earlier refuted a mild attack against the truism led people to substantially resist the subsequent stronger attack (the third column). Furthermore, counterarguing against the initial attack was clearly more effective than generating arguments that supported the truism (the fourth column).

Think how useful attitude inoculation might be. For example, in smoking prevention programs, adolescents might be presented with pro-smoking arguments likely to be advanced by peers and advertisements (for example, "Smoking is about freedom and maturity") and then encouraged to counterargue against these pressures—a clear example of attitude inoculation.

LOOKING BACK We have seen that media efforts and attempts by others to change people's attitudes are not as effective as we would believe. People often selectively attend to and evaluate information that confirms their original attitudes and beliefs, and they ignore or criticize information that disconfirms them. We have also seen that preexisting commitments to political ideologies or values increases resistance to counterattitudinal messages and persuasion. Finally, we have shown how attitude inoculation, or small attacks on our beliefs, can make us resistant to attitude change, as the small attacks give us the chance to muster arguments that we can use when faced with stronger attacks on our beliefs and attitudes.

Summary

dispositions

The Basics of Attitudes

- *Attitudes* are dispositions to evaluate objects in a negative or positive light. Attitudes include three different elements: *affective evaluations* (emotions), *cognitions* (thoughts and knowledge), and *action tendencies* (behaviors).

- Attitudes can be measured with self-report *Likert scales*, with response latencies that capture *attitude accessibility* (the degree to which the attitude is ready to become active in an individual's mind), and with attitude linkage measures that gauge *attitude centrality* (the extent to which an attitude is correlated to attitudes about other issues).

Functions of Attitudes

- Attitudes serve several functions. They serve an *utilitarian function*, signaling rewards and punishments. They serve an *ego-defensive function*, protecting people from undesirable beliefs and emotions—for example, the recognition that their lives will inevitably end. They serve a *value-expressive function,* reflecting values that people want others, especially their *reference groups,* to acknowledge. And attitudes serve a *knowledge function*, organizing how people construe the social world and guiding how people attend to, store, and retrieve information.

Persuasion and Attitude Change

- Both the *heuristic-systematic model* of persuasion and the *elaboration likelihood model* of persuasion hypothesize that there are two routes to persuasion. Factors that determine which route is used include motivation, or how important the message is to the person, and ability to process the message.

- When using the *central (systematic) route* to persuasion, people attend carefully to the message, and they consider relevant evidence and underlying logic in detail. People are especially likely to go through this route when the message is relevant to them, when they have knowledge in the domain, and when the message evokes a sense of personal responsibility. When going through the central route, people are more persuaded by high-quality messages.

- In the *peripheral (heuristic) route to persuasion* people attend to superficial aspects of the message. They use this route when they have little motivation or time or ability to attend to its deeper meaning. In this route, people are persuaded by source characteristics, such as

attractiveness and credibility of the communicator, and message characteristics, such as how many arguments there are and whether the conclusions are explicit.

- The elements of the persuasive process can be broken into three components: the *source* of the message, the *content* of the message, and the *target* of the message.

- A noncredible source is unlikely to induce immediate attitude change, but with time, a *sleeper effect* may occur. This is when attitude change occurs after time has passed and the message has become dissociated from its source.

- Vivid communications, including images of *identifiable victims,* are usually more effective than more pallid ones, and fear-evoking communications that provide fear-reducing courses of action produce more attitude change than either nonfear-evoking communications or fear-evoking communications that do not provide fear-reducing courses of action.

- Message content often varies in independent and interdependent societies, with ads in independent cultures emphasizing the individual and ads in interdependent societies emphasizing the collective.

- The target, or audience, of a message also affects whether a particular message is effective and whether attitude change occurs. Audience, or *receiver*, characteristics include the need for cognition (that is, how deeply people like to think about issues), mood, and age.

The Media and Persuasion

- According to the *third-person effect*, most people believe that other people are more likely to be influenced by the media than they are. But in fact, the media have surprisingly weak effects on most people. This is true in the case of consumer advertising (which rarely leads to long-lived effects), political advertising (which has small effects on most voters and mainly affects late-deciding voters), and public service announcements (which are unlikely to have a lasting impact on behavior unless they are also accompanied by specific suggestions and practice in avoiding negative behaviors).

- The media are most effective in *agenda control*—that is, in shaping what people think about. They do so through the number of stories and discussions they present on various issues, like terrorism, moral values, war, the environment, or the economy, and therefore are likely to be present in people's minds.

Resistance to Persuasion

- People can be resistant to persuasion because of pre-existing biases, commitments, and knowledge. People selectively attend to and evaluate information in accordance with their original attitudes, tuning in information that supports their preexisting attitudes and beliefs and tuning out information that contradicts them.

- Public commitment to a position helps people to resist persuasion. Just thinking about an attitude object can produce *thought polarization*, or movement toward extreme views that can be hard for a communicator to alter.

- People with more knowledge are more resistant to persuasion because they are able to counterargue against messages that take an opposite position to what they know and believe.

- Resistance to persuasion can be encouraged through *attitude inoculation*, exposing a person to weak arguments against his or her position and allowing the person to generate arguments against it.

Key Terms

agenda control (p. 342)

attitude (p. 319)

attitude inoculation (p. 348)

central route (p. 328)

ego-defensive function (p. 323)

elaboration likelihood model (ELM) (p. 328)

heuristic route (p. 328)

heuristic-systematic model (p. 328)

identifiable victim effect (p. 334)

knowledge function (p. 326)

Likert scale (p. 321)

message characteristics (p. 333)

peripheral route (p. 328)

receiver characteristics (p. 336)

reference groups (p. 324)

response latency (p. 321)

sleeper effect (p. 333)

source characteristics (p. 332)

systematic route (p. 328)

terror management theory (p. 324)

third-person effect (p. 339)

thought polarization hypothesis (p. 346)

utilitarian function (p. 322)

value-expressive function (p. 324)

Further Reading and Films

Eagly, A. H., & Chaiken, S. (1993). *The psychology of attitudes*. Fort Worth, TX: Harcourt Brace & Company. An excellent overview of the literature on attitudes.

Orwell, G. (1990). *1984*. New York: Signet (originally published in 1945). A superb consideration of propaganda by a great novelist and essayist.

Pratkanis, A. R., & Aronson, E. (2000). *Age of propaganda*. New York: Freeman. A terrific broad overview of the empirical science of the media and propaganda.

Reifenstahl, L. (1934). *Triumph of the will*. An unnerving documentary of the Nazi Party rally at Nuremberg in 1934, showing Adolf Hitler's persuasive power as an orator as he whips a large number of people into an emotional state.

Zimbardo, P. G., & Leippe, M. R. (1991). *The psychology of attitude change and social influence*. New York: McGraw-Hill. An excellent and engaging treatment of attitudes and persuasion.

ⓢ Online Study Tools

StudySpace

Go to StudySpace, wwnorton.com/studyspace, to access additional review and enrichment materials, including the following resources for each chapter:

Organize

- Study Plan
- Chapter Outline
- Quiz+ Assessment

Learn

- Ebook
- Chapter Review

- Critical-Thinking Questions
- Visual Quizzes
- Vocabulary Flashcards

Connect

- Apply It! Exercises
- Author Insights Podcasts
- Social Psychology in the News

Social Relations

I n Part Four, we examine our broader connections to others and, in so doing, our fundamental sociality. Chapter 10 proceeds from the (happy) observation that our connections to others are not always externally imposed. We have some choice over with whom we spend our time, and so in this chapter we investigate some of the most important determinants of why we are more attracted to some people than to others. Chapter 11 takes the investigation a step further. We form relationships with those to whom we are attracted—and, alas, often with those to whom we aren't. In this chapter, we explore many of the different types of human relationships and a number of variables that determine whether or not they go well. Chapter 12 deals with the interaction between different groups and the friction that often accompanies those interactions. We focus on the faulty thinking that gives rise to stereotypes of dubious validity and how those stereotypes go hand in hand with

prejudicial feelings and discriminatory behavior. In Chapter 13, we examine another of the low points of human interaction, exploring the determinants of aggression and our impulses to hurt others. But we also explore some of the highest elements of the human experience, examining our altruistic sentiments and our impulses to help others, as well as our tendencies to cooperate with one another for mutual benefit. Chapter 14 examines group life—how groups can influence performance and alter decisions and how certain types of behavior emerge only in groups. We conclude, in Chapter 15, with a focused discussion of the practical, or applied, implications of the knowledge gained through social psychological investigation. In particular, we discuss how the field of social psychology can enhance people's physical and mental health, how it can help people get more out of their financial resources, and how it can improve our schools' efforts to educate our children.

Attraction

IF YOU FOLLOW U.S. POLITICS CLOSELY, like to listen to the talking heads on TV news shows, or tune in every four years to presidential election coverage, you have probably seen Mary Matalin and James Carville—possibly more often than you'd like. Matalin is a very outspoken TV personality who was a chief strategist for the campaigns of both Presidents Bush (George H. W. and George W.), has served as an aide to Vice President Dick Cheney, and is currently chief editor of *Threshold Editions*, a division of Simon & Schuster devoted to the publication of conservative literature. James Carville, equally outspoken, could hardly be more different politically. He rose to prominence as the "ragin' Cajun" for his spirited efforts as lead strategist for Bill Clinton's successful presidential campaign in 1992, has worked for Labor Party politicians in Israel and the United Kingdom and for the Liberal Party in Canada, and was a prominent supporter of Hillary Clinton in her unsuccessful bid for president in 2008.

You might think that if they were ever in the same room, Matalin and Carville would immediately start battling, going at it hammer and tongs. But in fact, they have been married since 1993 and have two children. Huh? One can only wonder what their dinner conversations are like. Can two people with such different political orientations truly be in love? Are they secretly more in tune politically than their public personas would suggest?

The marriage of James Carville and Mary Matalin speaks to the mysterious nature of interpersonal attraction. It is sometimes hard to figure out why two people are drawn to each other and get along so well. Sometimes it's even hard to figure out why we ourselves are attracted to certain people. Although we typically know whether or not we like someone, we are often at a loss to explain why. To be sure, we know that we like people who are nice to us, make us laugh, share our values, and so on. But these obvious influences notwithstanding, it is also abundantly clear that sometimes we are drawn to some people and repulsed by others

Interpersonal Attraction
Mary Matalin, a long-time Republican political consultant, and James Carville, a long-time Democratic political consultant. Despite their marked differences in political affiliation, they were attracted to each other and eventually got married. Their mutual attraction was surprising to many observers because of a wide-spread—and generally valid—conviction that people tend to like those who are similar to themselves on important dimensions such as political philosophy.

"I do not like thee, Dr. Fell.
The reason why I cannot tell.
But this I know, and know full well, I do not like thee, Dr. Fell."

—Mother Goose Nursery Rhyme

for reasons we can't explain.. "We just hit it off." "He rubs me the wrong way." "We share a certain chemistry."

The goal of this chapter is to unravel these mysteries. What are the most powerful determinants of whether you will like someone? What is the underlying basis of good or bad "chemistry"? We'll examine what makes people like one another in all sorts of contexts, but with an emphasis on romantic attraction. As you will see, many of the influences on whom we choose as friends also influence whom we choose as romantic partners.

We will consider the effects of three particularly potent determinants of attraction—proximity, similarity, and physical attractiveness. We will then examine efforts to integrate these different determinants into one overarching theory.

STUDYING ATTRACTION

Interpersonal attraction exists between acquaintances, coworkers, friends, teammates, lovers, and countless others. It can be based on sexual arousal, intellectual stimulation, or respect for another's actions or beliefs. Attraction to others can also be conscious or nonconscious, based on well-thought-out beliefs or automatic "gut feelings." Because these ideas are already known to most people, some have argued that there is little to gain by studying attraction. We already know the important stuff, they claim, and scientific investigation is unlikely to take us much further.

Others, meanwhile, essentially make the *opposite* argument—that the causes of attraction, far from being widely known, are unlikely to yield to empirical investigation. Indeed, some have argued that a satisfying analysis of interpersonal attraction not only cannot be achieved, but *should not* be attempted. Doing so would rob us of some of the appeal of this delightful aspect of human experience. As Keats put it, "Do not all charms fly at the mere touch of cold philosophy?" Or consider the comments of former Wisconsin senator William Proxmire, a longtime critic of government funding of basic research in the behavioral sciences: "If scientists could understand, weigh, measure, and calculate love, there'd be a lot less of it going on. I love the mystery" (Stewart, 1988, pp. 56–61). In Proxmire's view, more knowledge would bring less enjoyment.

Although ambiguity and uncertainty can indeed sometimes enhance the appeal of something or someone (Norton, Frost, & Ariely, 2007; Wilson, Centerbar, Kermer, & Gilbert, 2005), surely we can dismiss Proxmire's anti-intellectual stance. When we learn more about something, we usually appreciate it more, not less. Knowing that a rainbow is the result of light refracted through droplets of water does not render it less beautiful. Knowing that all living things have been sculpted by evolution does not diminish the wonder of existence. In both cases, a deeper understanding results in a richer, not a diminished, experience.

So there is no reason to believe that psychologists should refrain from unraveling the mysteries of interpersonal attraction. But can they do so successfully? Have those who have worked in this area discovered any "secrets" of liking and loving that most people do not already know? You be the judge. At the end of this chapter, you can decide for yourself whether you understand the underpinnings of attraction better than you did before. We think you'll find that the scientific study of interpersonal attraction has indeed yielded a few surprises. It has implicated certain variables that few people would suspect play any role at all in who likes whom. More often, however, the relevant research has shown that our intuitions in this area are pretty good. Many of the variables that the average person would expect to influence our affections do indeed have an effect—but sometimes a much more powerful effect than almost anyone would guess. The surprises, in other words, lie not only in the discovery of new and unanticipated causes of attraction, but in demonstrations of how powerful certain "unsurprising" causes can be.

PROXIMITY

Something that *has* to influence whether people become friends or lovers is simple physical proximity, also called **propinquity**. You cannot come to like someone you never encounter (although not all encounters need to be face-to-face). This is particularly easy to illustrate in a college environment. Who are your best friends on campus? Are they the people who were on your hall freshman year? Are they the ones you encountered often in the same classes? Are they your peers on the track team, drama club, or debate society? The most enduring friendships are forged between people whose paths cross frequently. Out of numerous chance encounters comes a sense of comfort and familiarity that often gives rise to something deeper and long lasting.

propinquity Physical proximity.

Studies of Proximity and Attraction

A number of studies have demonstrated the effects of proximity on who becomes friends and romantic partners. Remember that these studies are important not so much because they demonstrate that a relationship between proximity and attraction exists (most people would guess that anyway), but because they demonstrate how *strong* the relationship is. As one person put it, "Cherished notions about romantic love notwithstanding, the chances are about 50-50 that the 'one and only' lives within walking distance" (Eckland, 1968).

One study of proximity was conducted in the 1940s in a married student housing project at MIT known as Westgate West (Festinger, Schachter, & Back, 1950). The project had been built to house American servicemen (and their families) who had returned from World War II and wished to begin or resume their college education with financial assistance provided by the GI bill. The housing project consisted of 17 ten-unit apartment buildings that were isolated from other residential areas of the city. The incoming students were randomly assigned to their residences, and few of them knew one another beforehand. Friendships were sure to develop among many of the residents, and the question was how much of an impact proximity would have on who befriended whom.

To find out, the investigators conducted a **sociometric survey.** They asked each resident to name the three people they saw socially most often in the entire housing project. The effect of proximity was striking: two-thirds of those listed as friends lived in the same building as the respondent, even though those in the same building represented only 5 percent of the residents of Westgate West. More striking still was the pattern of friendships *within* each building. **Figure 10.1** shows the layout of the Westgate West apartment houses. Note that the physical distance between apartments was quite small—19 feet between the doorways of adjacent apartments and 89 feet between those at the ends of each corridor. Nevertheless, even within such a confined space, greater proximity led to more friendships. Forty-one percent of those living in adjacent apartments listed one another as friends, compared to only 10 percent of those living at opposite ends of the corridor.

"Despite the fact that a person can pick and choose from a vast number of people to make friends with, such things as the placement of a stoop or the direction of a street often have more to do with determining who is friends with whom."

—William Whyte,
The Organization Man

sociometric survey A survey that attempts to measure the interpersonal relationships in a group of people.

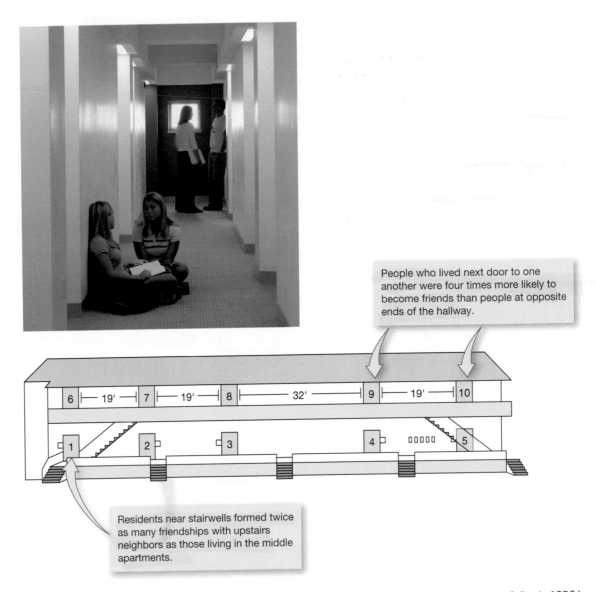

People who lived next door to one another were four times more likely to become friends than people at opposite ends of the hallway.

Residents near stairwells formed twice as many friendships with upstairs neighbors as those living in the middle apartments.

FIGURE 10.1 **Proximity**   Diagram of an MIT apartment complex. (Source: Festinger, Schachter, & Back, 1950.)

functional distance An architectural layout's tendency to encourage or inhibit certain activities, like contact between people.

Proximity presumably leads to friendship because it facilitates chance encounters. If so, then pure physical distance should matter less than what might be called **functional distance**, the tendency of an architectural layout to encourage contact between certain people and discourage it between others. The MIT study shows just how important functional distance is. As Figure 10.1 indicates, the stairs are positioned such that upstairs residents will encounter the occupants of apartments 1 and 5 much more often than the occupants of the middle apartments. And in fact, the residents of apartments 1 and 5 formed twice as many friendships with their upstairs neighbors as did those living in the middle apartments. Note also that the residents of apartments 1 and 6 and apartments 2 and 7 are equally distant from one another physically. They reside directly above one another. But the stairs that pass the door of apartment 1 make it and apartment 6 vastly closer from a functional perspective. Are the residents of apartments 1 and 6 more likely to become friends than the residents of apartments 2 and 7? Absolutely. The residents of apartments 1 and 6 were 2½ times more likely to become friends than were the residents of apartments 2 and 7. Thus, it is functional distance more than physical distance that is decisive. Proximity promotes friendship because it (literally) brings people together.

The effect of proximity on friendship formation was also nicely demonstrated in an investigation of the social organization of the Training Academy of the Maryland State Police (Segal, 1974). The aspiring police officers were assigned alphabetically to their dormitory rooms and classroom seats. Thus, Cadet Aronson should have found himself cheek by jowl with future officer Asch, as should Cadets Zajonc and Zimbardo. Did these frequent encounters lead to friendship? They did indeed, and **Figure 10.2** shows how strongly. Both axes of Figure 10.2 represent the alphabetical position of each of the 45 trainees (from, say, Aronson to Zimbardo). Each point in the diagram thus represents the alphabetical position of those people named as friends (the horizontal axis) by trainees with a particular alphabetical position themselves (the vertical axis). Notice that nearly all of the points lie close to the diagonal line. This means that Aronson and Asch tended to become friends with each other, and not with Zajonc and Zimbardo.

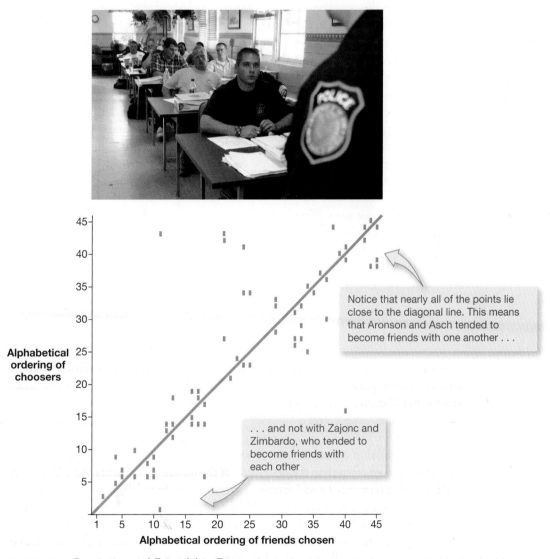

FIGURE 10.2 Proximity and Friendship Formation Friendship choices among trainees at the Maryland State Police Training Academy. Numbers across the bottom indicate place in alphabetical ordering of friends chosen. Numbers along the left margin indicate place in the alphabetical ordering of the choosers. (Source: Segal, 1974.)

Once again, simple physical proximity was found to exert a much more powerful effect than one would imagine on who befriends whom by encouraging some contacts and discouraging others. This effect, mind you, was obtained in a situation in which *all* of the 45 trainees lived and studied together. It was not as if the Aronsons and Zimbardos were assigned to different campuses. Minor differences in proximity produced profound effects on patterns of friendship. The correlation between the alphabetical position of each person and the average alphabetical position of those people he named as friends was .9.

But are any cautions in order? You may be wondering about the diversity of the populations examined in both the MIT and Police Academy studies. Perhaps proximity has a powerful effect on friendship formation in homogeneous groups, but not in diversified groups in which it must "compete" with other determinants of who befriends whom—such as similarity of age, race, ethnicity, or religion. Indeed, the populations in both studies were notably lacking in diversity (all of the trainees in the Police Academy, for example, were young males, and all but one were white).

In fact, in studies involving more diverse populations, the biggest effects of proximity on friendship formation have been found between people of *different* races, ages, or social classes. One study, for example, examined the patterns of friendships in a Manhattan housing project in which half the residents were black, one-third were white, and the rest were Puerto Rican (Nahemow & Lawton, 1975). Each ethnic group contained people of all ages. Both proximity and similarity had strong effects on who befriended whom. Eighty-eight percent of those designated as a "best friend" lived in the same building as the respondent, and nearly half lived on the same floor. Interestingly, the effect of proximity was particularly pronounced in friendships that developed *across* age and racial groups. Seventy percent of the friendships between people of different ages and races involved people who lived on the same floor as one another, compared to only 40 percent of the same-age and same-race friendships. It appears that people are willing to look beyond the immediate environment to find friends of their own age and race; their friendships with people of a different age or race, on the other hand, tended to be those that fell in their laps.

Explanations of Proximity Effects

So it appears that proximity has a surprisingly large effect on acquaintanceship and friendship. Why is this effect so much greater than we might have expected? There are three main reasons why proximity leads to friendship. One is availability, or simple contact. Another is our tendency to be nice to those with whom we expect to have frequent encounters. A third is the comfort created by repeated exposure to a person.

Availability and Proximity You need to make contact with another person if you are to become friends, and proximity makes contact more likely. Of course, the same is true for people you *dislike*: proximity can bring about the kind of unpleasant encounters with others that drive you nuts. Indeed, there is evidence that the people we dislike the most tend to live nearby as well (see **Box 10.1**).

But proximity does not simply make friendship *possible*; it also *encourages* it. Proximity brings about the kind of "passive contacts" between people from which friendships grow—the first "hello" in the hallway; the first discussion of the weather near the mailbox. Without these encounters, friendships fail to develop, and without proximity, these encounters often fail to occur.

The Effect of Anticipating Interaction We tend to give people we expect to interact with the benefit of the doubt. Simply knowing that we will interact with someone makes

BOX 10.1 **FOCUS ON DAILY LIFE**

Liking, Disliking, and Proximity

Whom do you dislike the most on campus? Is it your neighbor next door or the person downstairs who blasts the stereo whenever you try to study, the bass notes shaking the very desk at which you try to work? Is it the person who leaves discarded dental floss, half-eaten pizza slices, and soiled laundry in the hallway, bathroom, or lobby? What about the person who always seems to commandeer the adjacent table in the dining hall, so that his or her grating voice, bombastic boasts, and offensive jokes are impossible to ignore?

It seems that we most dislike those who do the most to annoy us. It also seems that it is typically easier to be annoyed by someone who is close at hand. This has been empirically demonstrated by Ebbe B. Ebbesen and his colleagues (Ebbesen, Kjos, & Konecni, 1976). Ebbesen thought that not only do our friends tend to come

from those who live close to us, but our enemies do as well. Only those nearby can readily spoil our environment and thereby earn our wrath.

Ebbesen asked residents of a large suburban condominium complex in Southern California to list the three people in the complex they liked the most and the three people they disliked the most. Proximity was related to both. Sixty-three percent of those named as "most liked" lived in the same cluster within the complex as the respondent. The effect was even stronger for those named as "most disliked," as 73 percent were from the same cluster. Furthermore, the average distance between the respondents and those they named as most liked was 236 feet, but the average distance between the respondents and those they most disliked was 151 feet.

The effects of proximity on liking and disliking stem in part from a common mechanism. Proximity provides the opportunity for both. But beyond that, the causes of each are different. Proximity promotes liking by facilitating the frequency of pleasing encounters; it engenders disliking by allowing a person's environment to be spoiled by others. This was confirmed when the respondents were asked why they liked and disliked the people they did. The most common reason they gave for liking someone was a characteristic of the person named; the most common reason for disliking someone was something he or she did to ruin the local environment.

That disliking is even more tightly connected to proximity should not be surprising. After all, we can always travel to find friends, but who would do so to find enemies?

us like that person more. In one demonstration of this effect, women at the University of Minnesota were given information about the personalities of two other students—one who would later join them in a discussion of student dating habits and the other with whom they would have no future contact (Darley & Berscheid, 1967). The two personality profiles were made equivalent through **counterbalancing**. Half the participants were told they would meet one student (say, student A rather than student B); the other half were told they would meet the other student (student B rather than student A). Thus, on average, the person with whom the participants expected to interact was, objectively speaking, no more or less appealing than the person they would not meet. Nevertheless, participants liked the person they expected to meet significantly more.

This initial positive stance toward others is likely to create a positive cycle in which the favorable expectations of each partner are reinforced by the positive behavior of the other. The powerful effects of proximity on friendship are one result. Because we know we must occasionally interact with those next door or down the hall, we make an effort to have our initial encounters go well. As a result, most initial interactions are rewarding and help advance friendships. This was demonstrated in a simple but telling experiment in which previously unacquainted participants arrived in threes. Person A and person C each had a get-acquainted conversation with person B. A and C never interacted, although they did witness each other's interaction with B. Afterward, everyone rated how much they liked everyone else, and the consistent result was that A and C liked one another the least (Insko & Wilson, 1977). Interactions tend to be rewarding.

counterbalancing A methodological procedure used to ensure that any extraneous variable (for example, a stimulus person's name) that might influence the dependent measure (for example, liking) is distributed equally across experimental conditions (so that, for example, specific names are used often equally in all conditions of the experiment).

The Mere Exposure Effect Robert Zajonc has offered what is arguably the simplest, most basic explanation of why proximity, and the frequent contact that comes with proximity, leads to liking. Zajonc contends that the "mere repeated exposure of the individual to a stimulus is a sufficient condition for the enhancement of his [or her] attitude toward it" (Zajonc, 1968, p. 1). In other words, the more you are exposed to something, the more you tend to like it—the **mere exposure effect**. Things that you already like become more likable; things you find hard to tolerate become a bit more tolerable. This may strike you as implausible. After all, what about all those pop tunes that seem to become more irritating each time they are played on the radio? Or what about the wisdom captured in such sayings as "Familiarity breeds contempt" and "Absence makes the heart grow fonder?" Zajonc's claim does not seem to square with intuition.

Upon reflection, however, the claim is less perverse than it first appears. It's a good bet that you can recall hating a song that played all the time on the radio when you were younger, only to discover—quite reluctantly—some nostalgic virtue in it when you now hear it from time to time on some "golden oldies" retrospective. Familiarity seems to breed not contempt but liking.

Researchers have collected a massive amount of empirical support for the claim that mere repeated exposure facilitates liking (Bornstein, 1989; Moreland & Beach, 1992; Zajonc, 1968). Some of the most striking (albeit less convincing) evidence is correlational. For instance, there is a remarkable correlation between the frequency with which people are exposed to various items in a given domain and how much they like those items. As one example, people report that they like those flowers that are mentioned frequently in our language more than those that are mentioned less frequently. Lilies and violets are liked more than geraniums and hyacinths, and they appear roughly six times as often in written texts. The same is true of people's preferences for trees, fruits, and vegetables. People like pines more than birches, apples more than grapefruits, and broccoli more than leeks, and in each case, the former appears roughly six times as often in print. Moving beyond things that grow in the ground, the same relationship is found among countries of the world and U.S. cities. Americans prefer the frequently encountered Venezuela to the less frequently encountered Honduras, and the commonly mentioned Chicago to the less commonly mentioned Omaha.

Zajonc would like to argue that all of these relationships exist partly because the more often people are exposed to something, whether it be a fruit, vegetable, or U.S. city, the more they tend to like it. He readily acknowledges, however, that it could just as easily be the opposite. Rather than liking roses because they are often written about, people might write about them because they like them. In certain domains, however, this alternative explanation is less compelling. For example, there is a strong correlation between people's preference for various letters in the English alphabet and how often they appear in the language (Alluisi & Adams, 1962). It is hard to imagine that there are so many e's or r's in the English language because people like those letters. It's more plausible that people like them because they are exposed to them so often. Each of us also tends to be disproportionately exposed to the letters in our own names, and so it is no surprise that we tend to be disproportionately fond of them, although there are other explanations of this "letter-name" effect as well—for example, that we like them because they're "ours" (Hoorens, Nuttin, Herman, & Pavakanun, 1990; Nuttin, 1987; Pelham, Mirenberg, & Jones, 2002).

Ultimately, of course, the true test of this or any other hypothesis is how well it fares in experimental tests. To set up one such test, Zajonc (1968) created a stimulus set of Turkish words that were utterly unfamiliar to his participants—for example, *kadirga, afworbu,* and *lokanta*. Different words within this set were then shown to his participants 0, 1, 2, 5, 10, or 25 times. Afterward, the participants were asked to

---

mere exposure effect The finding that repeated exposure to a stimulus (for example, an object or person) leads to greater liking of the stimulus.

The Influence of Mere Exposure on Liking   It may seem hard to believe, but many now-revered landmarks elicited anything but reverence initially. (A) When the Eiffel Tower was completed in Paris, France, in 1889, to commemorate the French Revolution's centennial, a group of artists and intellectuals, including Alexandre Dumas, Guy de Maupassant, and Emile Zola, signed a petition calling it "useless and monstrous" and "a disgraceful column of bolts." (B) San Francisco's TransAmerica building likewise elicited negative reactions initially, with noted *San Francisco Chronicle* columnist Herb Caen angrily suggesting knitting a giant tea cozy to cover the spire.

indicate the extent to which they thought each word referred to something good or bad. The more times participants saw a given word, the more they assumed it referred to something good. Zajonc has replicated this experiment with Chinese pictographs (symbols used in Chinese writing) and college yearbook photos as stimuli (in the latter case, subjects judged how much they thought they would like the person). The mere exposure effect was obtained each time.

A critic might suggest another interpretation of these results, however. Note that the context in which the experiment took place was rather pleasant. The surroundings were agreeable, the atmosphere congenial, and the experimenters endeavored to make the participants feel relaxed. Perhaps the positive feelings induced by this atmosphere "rubbed off" on the stimuli that were presented, leaving participants with a favorable impression of those that were presented most often. Thus, perhaps it was not mere exposure that produced the results, but repeated positive associations.

To test this interpretation, Zajonc and his colleagues conducted an experiment in which the stimuli were associated with a pleasant context for half the participants and an unpleasant context for the other half (Saegert, Swap, & Zajonc, 1973). If the same effects could be obtained under both conditions, then the researchers could rule out the possibility that they are due to a link between the stimuli and an earlier positive context.

Female undergraduates from the University of Michigan arrived in groups of six for a study of the "psychophysics of taste" and were led to individual cubicles and given their instructions. The purpose of the experiment was ostensibly to study their "perception of the tastes of substances that differ from each other in specific ways and which you will taste in different orders." Each cubicle contained a different substance, which participants were to rate in terms of taste. Participants were sent back and forth between cubicles according to a carefully arranged schedule to make their ratings. The

FIGURE 10.3 You Be the Subject: The Mere Exposure Effect

Which image do you prefer, the one on the left or the one on the right?

Results: People prefer true photos of others, but mirror-image photos of themselves. (The one on the right is the true image.)

Explanation: People see themselves when they look in the mirror, which means that they are familiar with a reverse image of themselves—and this is the image they generally prefer. They see others, however, as they truly are and usually prefer this true image to a mirror image.

schedule was crafted such that each participant occupied the same cubicle as another participant, with no conversation allowed, either 10, 5, 2, 1, or 0 times. The six participants were thus "merely exposed" to one another a different number of times, without the manipulation of exposure being a salient feature of the experiment. In addition, for half the participants the substances being tasted were pleasant (three flavors of Kool-Aid) and for the other half unpleasant (weak solutions of vinegar, quinine, and citric acid).

After the taste tests were completed, the participants were asked to indicate how likable they thought each of their fellow participants was. The results were clear-cut: whether encountered while tasting pleasant or unpleasant stimuli, those who were encountered most often were the most liked. It appears that *mere* repeated exposure is sufficient to increase liking.

Two other experiments on the mere exposure effect are particularly noteworthy. The first rests on the observation that the image each of us has of our own face is not the same as the image our friends have of us. Because we typically see ourselves in the mirror, the image we have of ourselves is a mirror image, whereas our friends typically see our "true" image. Thus, if simple exposure induces liking, we should prefer our mirror image, and our friends should prefer our true image. And when an experiment showing participants mirror-image and true-image photographs was conducted, that was exactly what happened (Mita, Dermer, & Knight, 1977) (see **Figure 10.3**).

Perhaps the most intriguing test of the mere exposure effect was done with albino rats (Cross, Halcomb, & Matter, 1967). One group of rats was raised for the first 52 days of life in an environment in which selections of Mozart's music were played for 12 hours each day (specifically, *The Magic Flute*, Symphony nos. 40 and 41, and the Violin Concerto no. 5). A second group was exposed to an analogous schedule of music by Schoenberg (specifically, *Pierrot Lunaire, A Survivor from Warsaw, Verklarte Nachte, Kol Nidre*, and Chamber Symphony nos. 1 and 2). The rats were then placed individually in a test cage that was rigged so that the rat's presence on one side of the cage would trip a switch that caused previously unheard selections of Mozart to be played, whereas the rat's presence on the other side would generate new selections of Schoenberg. The rats were thus able to "vote with their feet" and express a preference for the quintessentially classical music of Mozart or the modern, atonal compositions of Schoenberg. The results support the mere exposure effect: rats raised on a musical diet of Mozart moved significantly more often to the side of the cage that led to Mozart being played, whereas those raised on a diet of Schoenberg moved to the side that led to Schoenberg's music being played (see **Figure 10.4**). (In case you're wondering, rats in a control condition with no initial exposure to music later exhibited a preference for Mozart.)

But *why* does mere repeated exposure lead to liking? There appear to be two explanations. First, people find it easier to perceive and cognitively process familiar stimuli—the processing of familiar stimuli is more "fluent." And because people find the experience of **fluency** inherently pleasurable (see Box 10.4 later in this chapter),

fluency The experience of ease associated with perceiving and thinking.

FIGURE 10.4 Scientific Method: Mere Exposure and Musical Preferences

Hypothesis: Exposure leads to liking.

Research Method:

1 One group of rats was raised for the first 52 days of life in an environment in which Mozart was played for 12 hours each day (specifically, *The Magic Flute*, Symphonies 40 and 41, and the Violin Concerto No. 5).

2 A second group of rats was exposed to an analogous schedule of atonal music by Schoenberg.(specifically, *Pierrot Lunaire, A Survivor form Warsaw, Verklärte Nacht, Kol Nidre*, and Chamber Symphonies 1 and 2).

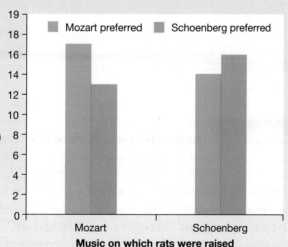

3 The rats were then placed individually in a test cage that was rigged so that the rat's presence on one side of the cage would trip a switch that caused previously unheard selections of Mozat to be played, whereas the rat's presence on the other side would generate new selections of Schoenberg.

Results: Rats raised on a musical diet of Mozart moved significantly more often to the side of the cage that led to Mozart being played, whereas those raised on a diet of Schoenberg moved more often to the side that led to Schoenberg's music being played.

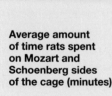

Average amount of time rats spent on Mozart and Schoenberg sides of the cage (minutes)

Legend: Mozart preferred / Schoenberg preferred

Mozart (raised): Mozart preferred ≈ 17, Schoenberg preferred ≈ 13
Schoenberg (raised): Mozart preferred ≈ 14, Schoenberg preferred ≈ 16

Music on which rats were raised

The height of the bars represents the average number of minutes the rats who had earlier been exposed to either Mozart or Schoenberg chose to inhabit a side of their cage that led to Mozart or Schoenberg being played.

Conclusion: Exposure leads to liking. Being exposed to Mozart led to a preference for Mozart's music. Being exposed to Schoenberg led to a preference for Schoenberg's music.

Source: H.A. Cross, Halcomb, & Matter (1967).

those positive feelings make the stimuli more appealing (Reber, Schwarz, & Winkielman, 2004; Winkielman & Cacioppo, 2001).

Robert Zajonc offered a second interpretation that draws on some of the most fundamental psychological processes, those involved in classical conditioning. Recall from your introductory psychology class Pavlov's famous dogs, who would salivate (an unconditioned response) when presented with food (an unconditioned stimulus). When a bell (the conditioned stimulus) was repeatedly presented along with the food, the dogs soon began to salivate (the conditioned response) merely upon hearing the bell. The dogs, in other words, learned to associate the bell with the food and hence responded to the bell in some of the same ways they responded to the food. In the case of repeated exposure, the stimulus is likewise paired with something very rewarding—the *absence* of any negative consequence. We therefore learn to associate the stimulus with the absence of anything negative, and a comfortable, pleasant attachment to the stimulus is formed. Mere repeated exposure thus leads to attraction because it is reinforcing. More broadly, this conditioning process helps organisms to distinguish stimuli that are "safe" from those that are not and to develop tendencies to approach the former and avoid the latter (Zajonc, 2001).

The sheer weight of Zajonc's analysis and all of the correlational and experimental evidence marshaled to support it lead to one irresistible conclusion: the more often people are exposed to something, the more they tend to like it. This mere exposure effect is surely one of the most important elements of successful advertising. The warm, comfortable feeling about a product to which we have been frequently exposed is undoubtedly part of what leads us to reach for one brand rather than another on the supermarket shelf—or to vote for one political candidate over another.

 We have seen that proximity is a potent determinant of who ends up being friends, lovers, and spouses. Proximity not only enables such relationships; it encourages them. Proximity to others means that we tend to encounter them more, and the more we encounter people, the more we tend, through mere exposure, to like them. Also, when people know they will interact frequently with one another, they often assume the best of one another and typically do their best to make sure their interactions go smoothly. Another factor that tends to make interactions go smoothly—and that likewise facilitates attraction—is similarity, a subject we turn to next.

SIMILARITY

We began this chapter by discussing James Carville and Mary Matalin, who are married to each other despite being on opposite ends of the political spectrum. Carville works mainly for Democratic politicians, and Matalin provides assistance to Republican candidates and officeholders. Many people wonder how these two can get along, a reaction that nicely illustrates a second important determinant of attraction—similarity. People tend to like other people who are similar to themselves (Berscheid & Reis, 1998; Byrne, 1961; Byrne, Clore, & Smeaton, 1986; Caspi & Herbener, 1990; Locke & Horowitz, 1990; Ptacek & Dodge, 1995; Rosenblatt & Greenberg, 1988). And everyone knows this. After all, "Birds of a feather flock together." Not that friends agree about everything, of course. If Carville and Matalin didn't root for the same baseball team or couldn't agree about the best musical groups of the 1990s, no one would be puzzled. But disagreement among friends and lovers on core political values is rather mystifying. It is hard to fathom how two people with such different political views could be drawn to each other. Perhaps Carville and Matalin share similar beliefs about other things that matter greatly to them but that are not clear to others.

Studies of Similarity and Attraction

An early demonstration of the importance of similarity in attraction comes from a study that, coincidentally, also testifies to the importance of the variable we just discussed—proximity. In his 1956 classic *The Organization Man*, William Whyte presented data on various social gatherings that took place in the Chicago suburb of Park Forest (Whyte, 1956). **Figure 10.5** is a modified version of one of his charts. Color coding indicates that the residents of particular houses participated in the social event described in the legend. Note the importance of proximity. Those invited to the surprise baby shower all lived next to or across the street from one another, as did those attending the Valentine's Day costume party, the picnic at the forest preserve, and the two New Year's Eve parties. Note also, however, that there are exceptions to the rule of proximity. People with shared interests sometimes went beyond their immediate neighborhood to find one another and establish an interaction. This was true, for example, of those in the gourmet society and those in the Saturday night bridge group. Similarity of interests, like proximity, can lead to interaction and to liking.

The impact of similarity on attraction has been demonstrated in many ways. Couples who intend to marry are quite similar to each other on an extremely wide

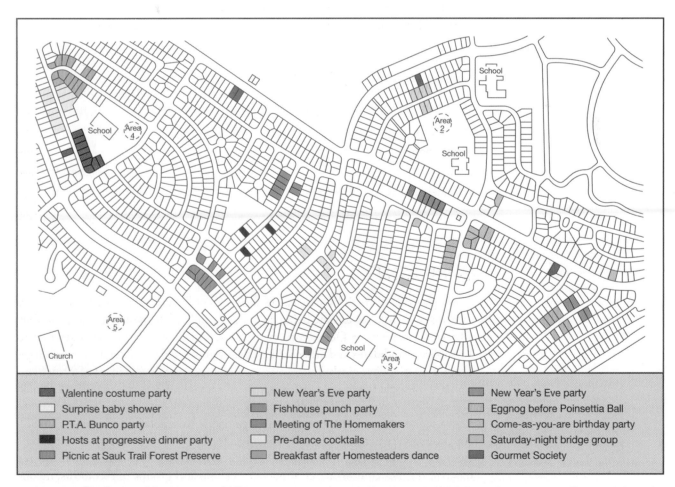

FIGURE 10.5 Similarity of Interests and Liking Layout of shared activities in the Park Forest housing tract. (Source: Adapted from Whyte, 1956.)

range of characteristics. In one study, the members of 1,000 engaged couples—850 of whom eventually married—were asked to provide information about themselves on 88 characteristics (Burgess & Wallin, 1953). The average similarity of the couples was then compared with the similarity of random "couples" created by pairing individual members of one couple with individual members of another couple. This analysis revealed that members of engaged couples were significantly more similar to one another than members of random couples on 66 of the 88 characteristics. Furthermore, for none of the characteristics were the members of engaged couples more *dissimilar* than the randomly created "couples." The similarity of engaged couples was strongest for demographic characteristics (such as social class and religion) and physical characteristics (such as health and physical attractiveness; see **Box 10.2**) and was less strong—but still present—for personality characteristics (such as leadership and sensitivity). Subsequent research that has focused on personality per se has also

---

BOX 10.2 **FOCUS ON DAILY LIFE**

Do Couples Look More Alike over Time?

Many people claim that not only do the two people in a couple tend to look like each other, but they look more alike the longer they have been together. There are many reasons why this might be so. People who live together may adopt similar styles of dress and grooming. They doubtless have similar diets, which may make them look more alike over time. They obviously live in the same region of the country, and because of climatic factors, they may acquire the same suntan and the same number of wrinkles.

Perhaps most interesting from a psychological perspective, couples also experience many of the same emotions. The death of a child devastates both parents; winning the lottery brings elation to both. More generally, a downbeat household is typically one in which both members are unhappy; an upbeat household is one in which both are happy. Eventually, a lifetime of experiencing the same emotions may have similar effects on the face and physical bearing of each member of the couple. As someone once said, "After age 40, we all have the faces we deserve." A happy lifetime tends to produce "crow's feet" around the eyes; an unhappy one tends to leave creases around the outside of the mouth. Thus,

people who live together and experience the same emotions may converge in facial appearance.

Is there truth to this idea? Robert Zajonc and his colleagues have collected evidence indicating that there is indeed (Zajonc, Adelmann, Murphy, & Niedenthal, 1987). They enlisted the help of 12 married couples to see whether they came to look more alike over time. The members of each couple were 50 to 60 years old, and they provided both current photos of themselves and photos

Physical Similarity Over time, the members of a couple tend to look like each other, perhaps because of initial physical similarities, but also because of shared diet, living conditions, and emotional experiences.

taken during their first year of marriage, approximately 25 years earlier. The photos were cropped and reproduced so that extraneous identifying information, such as style of dress and type of film, was eliminated. Judges who were unaware of who was married to whom were then asked to assess how much each of the men resembled each of the women (for both the current and older photos).

To check for the possibility that older people as a whole are simply more alike, Zajonc and his colleagues established a set of control couples by pairing members of different couples with one another and then assessing the similarity of these "random" couples. Contrary to the notion that older people are generally more homogeneous in appearance, there was no tendency for these random couples to converge in appearance over time. This set them apart from the actual couples, who looked significantly more alike roughly 25 years into their marriages than they did as newlyweds. Thus, not only do we seek mates who are similar to ourselves, we become even more similar in appearance over time. Not only do birds of a feather flock together—but being in the same flock can make the feathers still harder to distinguish.

shown that married couples exhibit considerable similarity in the behaviors indicative of such core personality characteristics as extraversion and genuineness (Buss, 1984). Interestingly (and analogous to what we saw with proximity), interracial and interethnic couples tend to be more similar to each other in terms of their personality traits than couples of the same race and ethnicity. It is as if people compensate for dissimilarity on one dimension by seeking out greater similarity on others (Rushton & Bons, 2005).

A second type of evidence that supports the link between similarity and attraction comes from studies in which individuals are thrown together for an extended period of time. In one study, Theodore Newcomb recruited male University of Michigan transfer students to live for a year, rent free, in a large house in exchange for filling out questionnaires a few hours each week (Newcomb, 1956, 1961). Newcomb made sure that none of the students knew one another beforehand. Among the questionnaires they filled out were several that asked them to indicate how much they liked each of their housemates. To an increasing degree over the course of the 15-week study, as students got to know one another better and better, the students' liking of one another was predictable from how similar they were. Interestingly, although this was true of similarity in values and attitudes, it was *most* true in terms of shared opinions about the other house members. Bob and Dennis were more likely to hit it off if both detested Rick than if they differed in their evaluations of Rick's merits (see also Griffitt & Veitch, 1974).

The third type of evidence that supports the proposition that people are attracted to those who are similar to themselves comes from the "bogus stranger" paradigm (Byrne, 1961; Byrne et al., 1986; Byrne, Griffitt, & Stefaniak, 1967; Byrne & Nelson, 1965; Griffitt & Veitch, 1971; Tan & Singh, 1995). In these experiments, participants are given the responses to attitude or personality questionnaires supposedly filled out by someone else. In reality, the responses are constructed by the experimenter to create a given level of similarity to the participants' own responses—which, to avoid suspicion, are typically assessed much earlier in a classroom setting. The experiment is described as a study of "the accuracy of interpersonal judgments based on limited information." After reading the responses of the bogus stranger, the participants rate the bogus stranger on a number of dimensions, including how likely it is that they would like the person in question. In study after study of this type, the more similar the stranger is to the participant, the more the participant likes him or her.

But Don't Opposites Attract?

Although most people accept the idea that similarity fosters attraction, they also endorse the opposite theory of **complementarity**—that opposites attract. The idea is that individuals with divergent characteristics should complement each other nicely and thus get along well. Children are taught the role of complementarity through the Mother Goose nursery rhyme of Jack Sprat: "Jack Sprat could eat no fat. His wife could eat no lean. And so between them both you see, they licked the platter clean."

It does seem that a dependent person might profit from being with someone who is nurturing or that a person who is quiet might get along with someone who likes to talk. The yin and yang of two divergent personalities ought to create a successful unity.

But is there any evidence to support this complementarity hypothesis? The first thing to note is that complementarity, if it exists, is surely more limited in scope than the widespread impact of similarity on attraction. Unlike similarity, for example, there is no reason to expect that complementarity of attitudes, beliefs, or physical characteristics will lead to attraction. People with different attitudes or beliefs tend to quarrel over them, and people with different physical attributes often come from

complementarity The tendency for people to seek out others with characteristics that are different from and that complement their own.

different geographical regions (and thus have to overcome a lack of proximity and the absence of a shared culture).

Complementarity, if it exists at all, is probably limited to personality traits—and not all personality traits at that. The hypothesis really makes sense only for those traits for which one person's needs can be met by the other (Levinger, 1964). Someone who is dependent can have his or her needs taken care of by a partner who is nurturing. But someone who is a hard worker probably won't want to be with someone who is lazy; and someone who values honesty is not likely to associate with a habitual liar. Thus, we might reasonably expect to find complementarity in such traits as dependence-nurturance or introversion-extraversion, but not in such traits as honesty, optimism, or conscientiousness.

What about this restricted set of personality characteristics? Is there any evidence for complementarity among them? Although a few studies have been offered in support of the complementarity hypothesis (Wagner, 1975; Winch, 1955; Winch, Ktanes, & Ktanes, 1954, 1955), many of them have been criticized on methodological grounds (Katz, Glucksberg, & Krauss, 1960), and there are many more studies that have failed to provide evidence for the hypothesis (Antill, 1983; Boyden, Carroll, & Maier, 1984; Levinger, Senn, & Jorgensen, 1970; Meyer & Pepper, 1977; Neimeyer & Mitchell, 1988).

Thus, similarity appears to be the rule, and complementarity the exception. And that should not be surprising. For one thing, complementarity conflicts with (and thus is masked by) the more powerful effect of similarity on attraction. And to the extent that complementarity exists, it exists sporadically. Even when two people seem to represent a perfect example of complementarity, they are likely to complement each other on only one or two features of their personalities. All of their other characteristics are likely to be similar or unrelated. Such a couple would thus embody considerable evidence of similarity and only a little support for complementarity.

Why Does Similarity Promote Attraction?

Interactions with people who share our beliefs, values, and personal characteristics tend to be rewarding, which tends to increase our attraction toward them. All told, similarity leads to attraction for at least four reasons.

Similar Others Validate Our Beliefs and Orientations People who share our beliefs validate our beliefs. People who endorse our values reinforce our values. In short, it is often a pleasure to interact with similar others because they reinforce rather than challenge our beliefs, outlooks, ideologies, and personal strivings. This is perhaps easiest to appreciate by considering our interactions with people who do *not* share our beliefs and attitudes. If you've ever had a contentious political discussion, you know that interacting with someone who challenges our beliefs and assumptions can be unsettling, and this often makes us dislike the person associated with such unsettling feelings. An experiment in which people's physiological reactions were monitored by a polygraph machine makes this point nicely (Clore & Gormly, 1974). The participants were confronted by a confederate who either agreed or disagreed with their attitudes. Not surprisingly, the participants tended to like the confederate who agreed with their views more than the confederate who disagreed with them. More important, the amount of arousal the participants experienced while listening to the confederate predicted the strength of their affective reactions. The more aroused they were while hearing the confederate agree with them, the more they liked the confederate; the more aroused they were while hearing the confederate disagree with them, the more they disliked the confederate. Validation is comforting, and it can make us like those who provide it; contradiction is unpleasant, and it can make us dislike those who force it upon us.

Similarity Facilitates Smooth Interactions

Interactions with similar others are often rewarding because they tend to go smoothly. Two people who share a religious faith, for example, often find common ground when they watch a movie, listen to the news, or take a vacation together. Two atheists tend to do likewise. But if the believer and the atheist are paired, their views will often clash, putting their enjoyment of the movie, news, or vacation at risk. Those who share similar views, beliefs, and orientations are able to interact with less conflict.

"We are so in synch. I was just about to ask *you* for a divorce."

One study contrasted an attitude's overall importance with its importance in interactions (Davis, 1981). The logic was as follows. Some of your beliefs and attitudes, such as your view of human nature or political orientation, are extremely important to you. Other characteristics, such as your food preferences or taste in music, are often less important but may have more impact on your day-to-day interactions with another person. Similarity on which characteristics is more important in whether you like someone? Are you more likely to be drawn to someone with whom you share qualities that come into play in everyday interaction or to someone with whom you share more important characteristics that don't come into play much in social interactions?

To answer this question, the researchers asked participants how much they liked people who agreed or disagreed with them on various attitudes. They also rated each attitude for both overall importance and importance in day-to-day interaction. The results showed that similarity of attitudes relevant to everyday interaction had more influence on the participants' sentiments than similarity of attitudes of overall importance. Thus, similarity fosters attraction in part because it encourages smooth interaction.

We Expect Similar Others to Like Us

Someone who is similar to us on many dimensions can be counted on to see the world the way we do, including that part of the world that is most important to us—ourselves. There surely are few psychological phenomena more basic than our tendency to like people who like us (Condon & Crano, 1988; Curtis & Miller, 1986; Kenny & LaVoie, 1982; Kenny & Nasby, 1980). Part of the reason we like similar others, then, stems from our basic narcissism.

Similar Others Have Qualities We Like

We tend to think that most of our beliefs and attitudes have merit. We think of them as reasoned positions derived from careful review of relevant information. In short, we tend to think that most of our beliefs, values, tastes, and habits are the "right" ones to have. To a certain extent, we also think that most of our personality characteristics are the appropriate ones to have. Although we may admit that we have a few personal foibles, we nonetheless strive to be the best that we can be on those characteristics we deem most important.

The logical consequence of such an orientation is that we tend to think that people who are similar to ourselves have the right qualities, just as we do. Or, stated another way, if we believe that our views and characteristics are largely the product of reason, then someone who disagrees with us will strike us as "unreasonable" (Pronin, Gilovich, & Ross, 2004). Similar others should thus be favored over dissimilar others. After all, who wouldn't prefer a reasonable person to an unreasonable one?

 We have seen that, all else being equal, people are more inclined to like those who are similar to themselves than people who are dissimilar to themselves. Similar others validate our beliefs and values; they have qualities we like, and our interactions with them tend to be less marred by conflict. So birds of a feather do flock together. Having established the importance of proximity and similarity on attraction, we now turn to physical attractiveness.

PHYSICAL ATTRACTIVENESS

It is hardly surprising to learn that one of the most powerful determinants of interpersonal attraction is physical attractiveness—whether another person is "good looking." After all, who receives the most attention at parties, at the health club, or in the checkout line at the supermarket? Attractive people have an advantage in winning other people's attention and affection. This advantage is certainly more important initially than later on in a relationship, but it rarely disappears altogether. And even if it did, its initial effect would still be considerable. As your parents may have told you, you never get a second chance to make a first impression.

Empirical research indicates that a person's looks play an even more important role in interpersonal attraction than intuition might suggest. Physical features also exert a powerful influence on attraction surprisingly early in life and in a surprising number of different domains.

Before reviewing these potentially distressing findings, however, it is worthwhile to consider (and keep in mind) some important caveats that offer hope to those of us (that is, most of us) who don't have movie-star looks. First, although there are certain constellations of features that are deemed attractive by most people, there is considerable variability in what individual people find attractive. The prospect of requited love is by no means limited to those regarded as physically attractive by most people. Second, although people are predisposed to like those who are physically attractive, the reverse is also true. We tend to find people we like more attractive than those we don't like (Kniffin & Wilson, 2004). More heartening still, perhaps, is that happy couples tend to idealize one another's physical attractiveness—that is, they perceive each other as physically attractive even if they are not seen that way by others (Murray & Holmes, 1997; Murray, Holmes, & Griffin, 1996). Finally, although some people are considered good looking throughout their lives, physical attractiveness is less stable than most of us think (Zebrowitz, 1997; Zebrowitz, Olson, & Hoffman, 1993). People who are unattractive in their teens sometimes bloom in young adulthood, while the looks of the kings and queens of the high school prom may fade. In a long life, most of us have our moments in the sun and in the shade.

Impact of Physical Attractiveness

What have social psychologists discovered about the impact of physical attractiveness in everyday life? The most frequently documented finding—and possibly the least surprising—is that attractive individuals are much more popular with members of the opposite sex than are their less attractive counterparts. This has been shown in studies

"There are many more obscure, miserable, and impoverished geniuses in the world than underappreciated beauties."

—Jerry Adler, *Newsweek*

in which indices of popularity, such as dating frequency and friendship ratings, are correlated with physical attractiveness (Berscheid, Dion, Walster, & Walster, 1971; Curran & Lippold, 1975; Feingold, 1984; Reis, Nezlek, & Wheeler, 1980); in investigations in which blind dates are later asked how attracted they are to their partners (Brislin & Lewis, 1968; Curran & Lippold, 1975; Walster, Aronson, Abrahams, & Rottman, 1966); and in studies of video dating services in which participants indicate how attracted they are to individuals shown on videotape (Riggio & Woll, 1984; Woll, 1986). In all of these situations, attractive individuals are sought out more than their less attractive peers.

But attractive individuals benefit in other areas as well. For those interested in good grades, note that an essay supposedly written by an attractive author is typically evaluated more favorably than one attributed to an unattractive author (Anderson & Nida, 1978; Cash & Trimer, 1984; Landy & Sigall, 1974; Maruyama & Miller, 1980). For those interested in money, studies have shown that each 1-point increase (on a 5-point scale) in physical attractiveness is worth approximately $2,000 in additional annual salary (closer to $3,500 in inflation-adjusted dollars; Frieze, Olson, & Russell, 1991; Hamermesh & Biddle, 1994; Roszell, Kennedy, & Grabb, 1989; see also Cash & Kilcullen, 1985). For those worried about receiving help in an hour of need, consider that men are more likely to come to the aid of an injured female if she is good looking (West & Brown, 1975). For those tempted to commit a crime, note that attractive defendants are often given a break by jurors (Efran, 1974); and when convicted, attractive criminals receive lighter sentences by judges (Stewart, 1980). In one study, for example, participants recommended prison sentences that were 86 percent longer for unattractive defendants than for attractive defendants (Sigall & Ostrove, 1975). Crime may not pay, but the wages are clearly better for those who are good looking.

The Halo Effect Attractive individuals also benefit from a **halo effect**, the common belief—accurate or not—that attractive individuals possess a host of positive qualities beyond their physical appearance. Thus, people may endeavor to date, mate, and affiliate with the physically attractive, not only because of their looks, but also because of numerous other attributes attractive people are thought to have. In experiments in which people were asked to make inferences about individuals depicted in photographs, good-looking men and women were judged to be happier, more intelligent, and more popular and to have more desirable personalities, higher incomes, and more professional success (Bar-Tal & Saxe, 1976; Dion, Berscheid, & Walster, 1972; Eagly, Ashmore, Makhijani, & Longo, 1991; Feingold, 1992b; Jackson, Hunter, & Hodge, 1995; Moore, Graziano, & Millar, 1987). The only consistently negative inferences about them are that they are immodest and less likely to be good parents (Bar-Tal & Saxe, 1976; Dion et al., 1972; Wheeler & Kim, 1997). Attractive women are sometimes also seen as vain and materialistic (Cash & Duncan, 1984; Dermer & Theil, 1975; Podratz, Halverson, & Dipboye, 2004).

The halo effect appears to vary in predictable ways across different cultures. In independent cultures such as the United States, physically attractive individuals are assumed to be more dominant and assertive than their less attractive counterparts. In interdependent cultures such as Korea, attractive individuals are thought to be more generous, sensitive, and empathic than unattractive individuals. But in both independent and interdependent cultures, attractive individuals are thought to be

"Beauty is life's E-Z Pass."

halo effect The common belief—accurate or not—that attractive individuals possess a host of positive qualities beyond their physical appearance.

smarter, better adjusted, and more sociable than less attractive individuals (Wheeler & Kim, 1997).

Is there any validity to these beliefs? Given the preferential treatment that physically attractive people often receive, it would be surprising if there were not some impact on their development. Indeed, there is evidence that physically attractive individuals do have more winning personalities. The effects are not large, but they are present on the very personality dimensions one might expect. Physically attractive people are not above average in intelligence, for example (Sparacino & Hansell, 1979). Nonetheless, they do seem to be somewhat happier, less stressed, and more satisfied with their lives, and they perceive themselves as having greater control over what happens to them (Diener, Wolsic, & Fujita, 1995; Umberson & Hughes, 1987).

Some of the personality correlates of physical attractiveness were revealed in an experiment in which participants had 5-minute telephone conversations with members of the opposite sex. The experimenters rated all participants for physical attractiveness. Because the conversations took place over the phone, however, the participants themselves did not know what the person they were talking to looked like. Nevertheless, when the participants rated their partners afterward on a number of personality dimensions, those who had been deemed attractive by the experimenters were rated as more likable and socially skilled than their less attractive counterparts (Goldman & Lewis, 1977). A lifetime of easier, rewarding social encounters appears to instill in attractive individuals the confidence and social skills that bring about still more rewarding interactions in the future (Langlois et al., 2000; Reis et al., 1982).

But what happens when the attractiveness of the conversation partner is known? Because much of the population is so taken with physical beauty and because those who are physically attractive are thought to possess a host of other desirable characteristics, people may make a greater effort when dealing with someone who is good looking. They may listen better and be more responsive, more energetic, and more willing to express agreement with an attractive person. The net result is that attractive people may be given an advantage that makes it easier to come across as socially skilled—even when that is not the case. The physical attractiveness stereotype may give rise to a **self-fulfilling prophecy**—a tendency for people to act in ways that bring about the very thing they expect to happen (see Chapters 5 and 12). People who believe that an attractive person possesses certain desirable characteristics may act in ways that elicit those very characteristics.

This was demonstrated in a clever experiment in which undergraduate men were asked to have a get-acquainted conversation with an undergraduate woman over the phone. Each of the male participants was given a photograph supposedly taken of his conversation partner. In reality, the photos were chosen to be quite attractive for half the participants and unattractive for the others (their actual conversation partners, of course, represented the full range of attractiveness). The conversations were tape-recorded, and when just the woman's comments—and *only* the women's comments—were played to *other* participants who were not shown the woman's photo and thus had no preconceptions about her appearance, a rather stunning result emerged. They rated the woman who had talked to someone who thought she was attractive as warmer and more socially poised than the woman who had talked to someone who thought she was unattractive (Snyder, Tanke, & Berscheid, 1977). Once again, the deck is stacked in favor of the physically attractive: people talk to them in ways that bring out their warmth and confidence, thereby confirming the stereotype that they are socially skilled.

Early Effects of Physical Attractiveness Perhaps the most remarkable aspect of the impact of physical attractiveness is how early in life it has an effect. Attractive

self-fulfilling prophecy The tendency for people to act in ways that bring about the very thing they expect to happen.

infants receive more affectionate and playful attention from their mothers than do less attractive infants, and this occurs even before leaving the hospital in which they were born (Langlois, Ritter, Casey, & Sawin, 1995). Their good fortune continues in nursery school, where they are more popular with their peers than are unattractive children (Dion, 1973; Dion & Berscheid, 1974). Furthermore, nursery school and elementary school teachers tend to assume that attractive pupils are more intelligent and better behaved than their less attractive classmates (Adams, 1978; Adams & Crane, 1980; Clifford & Walster, 1973; Martinek, 1981). Even more disturbing are the findings of an experiment in which college students were given a written report that described a transgression committed by a 7-year-old child. Attached to the report was a photograph of the child. Half the time the child was attractive, and half the time the child was unattractive. When asked to evaluate the episode, those who thought the transgression was committed by an attractive child viewed it as less serious. They also thought that the attractive child was less likely to act out in the future, and they considered that child to be more honest and pleasant (Dion, 1972). What could be less fair?

Studies such as these demonstrate that even very young children are the object of discrimination based on physical appearance. Research has also shown that children—infants, in fact!—are the perpetrators of such discrimination as well. In these experiments, infants as young as 3 months were shown slides of two human faces side by side. One of the faces was previously judged by adults as attractive and the other as unattractive. The slides were typically shown to the infant for 10 seconds, and the amount of time the infant spent looking at each one was recorded by someone who was unaware of which slide, the one on the left or right, was the attractive one. (The infant's eye movements were videotaped, and the scoring was done from the videotape so that the stimulus slides were beyond the judge's field of vision.) Looking time was interpreted as an index of the infant's preference. In several studies, infants showed a clear preference for attractive over unattractive faces (Langlois et al., 1987; Langlois, Ritter, Roggman, & Vaughn, 1991; Samuels & Ewy, 1985; Slater et al., 1998). This was true even though the attractive and unattractive faces were not extreme (the attractive faces were not the *most* attractive faces the investigators could find, nor were the unattractive faces the least attractive), and the preference held true for male faces, female faces, and even faces of other infants (Langlois et al., 1991). Thus, the prejudice in favor of physically attractive people is exhibited extremely early in life and may even be present at birth. Moreover, by the end of the first year, when infants' behavioral repertoires are more advanced, they are more inclined to play contentedly with an adult stranger if the adult is attractive than if the adult is unattractive. The infants, for example, turned or moved away from an unattractive stranger more than three times as often as they did from an attractive stranger (Langlois, Roggman, & Rieser-Danner, 1990).

Early Effects of Physical Attractiveness Physical attractiveness brings benefits early in life. Attractive children receive more affectionate attention from their parents and are assumed by their teachers to be more intelligent and better behaved.

Gender and the Impact of Physical Attractiveness Physical attractiveness affects men and women differently. One glance at the newsstand, even by a visitor from Mars, would reveal that attractive women's faces and bodies predominate in the visual media. In short, the world tends to focus on and evaluate women's attractiveness more than men's.

It should come as no surprise, then, that attractiveness is more important in determining women's life outcomes than men's. Obesity, for example, negatively affects women's social mobility, but not men's. Overweight girls are less likely to be accepted to college than their average or thin peers (Wooley & Wooley, 1980). Women deemed unattractive at work experience more negative outcomes than men (Bar-Tal & Saxe, 1976). And physical attractiveness matters more in terms of popularity, dating prospects, and even marriage opportunities for women than for men (Margolin & White, 1987). Simply growing up with fluoridated water, which improves the look and quality of one's teeth, is associated with a 4 percent average increase in a woman's annual earnings in adulthood, but has no effect on a man's earnings (Glied & Neidell, 2008).

So beauty can translate into power for women. It functions as a kind of currency that women can use in obtaining financial and social resources. Barbara Fredrickson and Tomi-Ann Roberts (1997) have argued that these kinds of external rewards encourage women's preoccupation with their own attractiveness, even coaxing them to adopt a kind of outsider's point of view on their physical selves. What Freud called women's "vanity" may be more appropriately viewed as a survival tactic in a world that so heavily emphasizes women's physical attractiveness.

Why Does Physical Attractiveness Have Such Impact?

Having established the importance of physical appearance in attraction, we now turn to the important question of why. Why is physical attractiveness so important in everyday social life? There are at least three reasons.

Immediacy A person's physical appearance often trumps other characteristics, such as intelligence, ambition, moral character, and personality, because it is so visible—and visible so *immediately*. It affects our immediate, "gut" reaction to someone we meet for the first time. A person's keen intelligence and strong moral fiber can be demonstrated, but it usually takes time. Beauty is manifest right away. We might think that intelligence ought to matter more than beauty in our interactions with others. But let anyone who thinks so "show up at a trendy restaurant like Indochine at 9:30 on a Friday night and try to get a table on the strength of his IQ" (Adler, 1994). Perhaps this is why a sperm bank established to sell the genes of Nobel Prize winners was a complete flop: would-be parents opted for beauty over brains virtually every time (Nobel gene biz bombs, 1985).

Prestige Imagine that you are attending your high school reunion accompanied by your current boyfriend or girlfriend, whom you met in college. How much do you care about your boyfriend's or girlfriend's appearance?

Now imagine that you are returning to your high school for a sentimental visit. You will be visiting after hours when no one—certainly none of your old high school friends—is likely to be around. Again, your boyfriend or girlfriend agrees to go with you. Now how much do you care about your partner's appearance?

Most people will confess to being more concerned about their partner's appearance at the reunion than during the clandestine visit. A partner's looks often matter more in public than in private. To be sure, good looks are valued in and of themselves, with no thought of what effect they may have on others. A person "consumes" the good looks of his or her partner through such direct effects as aesthetic appreciation and sexual excitement. But in addition, there are substantial indirect effects of having an attractive partner: other people may evaluate you more highly because you are able to attract such a desired "commodity." Knowing this can increase the motivation to seek out a physically attractive boyfriend or girlfriend.

Experimental research bears this out. In one study, each participant entered a waiting room and was seated across from two other students, one male and one female, who were confederates of the experimenter (Sigall & Landy, 1973). The man was described as a fellow participant in an experiment on perception, and he was made up to look completely average in appearance. The appearance of the woman was varied across experimental conditions. To half the participants, she came across as physically attractive: her clothes and makeup were chosen to accentuate her natural good looks. To the other half of the participants, she came across as unattractive: she "wore an unbecoming wig, no makeup, and unflattering clothes" (Sigall & Landy, 1973, p. 219). In addition, half the time she was described as the girlfriend of the male confederate, and half the time she was introduced as someone waiting to see another professor.

After this brief introductory scene, the participant was led to a separate cubicle and asked to give his or her first impressions of the other "participant" as part of an experiment on the perception of people. As predicted, participants' impressions of the male confederate were influenced by whether or not he was thought to be the boyfriend of an attractive or unattractive woman. Participants thought the confederate was more likable, friendly, and confident when his "girlfriend" was attractive than when she was unattractive. The attractiveness of the female confederate had no such effect when she was thought to be merely waiting to see someone else.

Subsequent research has reinforced this general finding while simultaneously qualifying it in predictable ways (Bar-Tal & Saxe, 1976; Hebl & Mannix, 2003). For instance, the effect is much stronger for impressions of males than for impressions of females in heterosexual relationships: being with an attractive woman boosts a man's image more than being with an attractive man boosts a woman's image. Perhaps this is why most of the famous "mismatches" involve a stunning woman with an accomplished, but less attractive man—Beyoncé and Jay-Z, Angelina Jolie and (before Brad) Billy Bob Thornton, and almost all heavy-metal rockers and their groupies. Note, futhermore, that the effect of having a physically attractive partner is somewhat nuanced: being with an attractive woman boosts a man's presumed intelligence, income, and occupational status more than his presumed personality, popularity, or happiness.

Biology Before we can discuss the third reason so many people are drawn to those who are physically attractive, we must consider what it is that people find attractive. What do people who are considered attractive look like? What features set them apart from everyone else?

It might seem that there could be no answer to this question. After all, doesn't it depend on who is doing the judging—on one's unique preferences as well as the more general tastes of the culture or historical era to which one belongs? In short, doesn't the assessment of what is attractive vary enormously from person to person, culture to culture, and era to era?

To be sure, there is considerable variation from person to person as to specific preferences (Beck, Ward-Hull, & McLear, 1976; Wiggins, Wiggins, & Conger, 1968). Some are attracted to blond men with Nordic features; others are drawn to those with a more Mediterranean look. Some prefer sultry women; others opt for a more "pixieish" type. There is also substantial variation in preferences between cultures and subcultures and across historical periods, particularly in terms of preferences for different skin colors, body weights, amount of body hair, and various ornamentation practices, such as nose rings, teeth filing, and hairstyles (Darwin, 1871; Fallon, 1990; Ford & Beach, 1951; Hebl & Heatherton, 1997; see **Box 10.3**).

But such variation across people, cultures, and historical periods does not mean that all determinants of physical attractiveness are arbitrary or subject to the whims of fashion. In fact, there is reason to believe that there *have* to be some features of the human face and body that have universal appeal. For one thing, there is widespread agreement among Western judges as to who is and who is not attractive (Cross & Cross, 1971; Iliffe, 1960; Langlois et al., 2000). Individuals may not always be able to

BOX 10.3 **FOCUS ON HEALTH**

The Flight to Thinness

Anyone who has seen the paintings of Renoir or Rubens is aware of how times have changed when it comes to the ideal weight for women. This has received a great deal of media attention in recent years because much of the world, the United States in particular, is obsessed with thinness. And it's an unhealthy obsession at that, having been blamed for the alarming increase in such eating disorders as bulimia and anorexia nervosa in young women (Brumberg, 1997). Society's current preference for thin women is something of an anomaly, given the historical preference for heavier physiques. To be sure, heaviness was not always viewed as negatively as it is now. Just consider this claim by the eighteenth-century French gourmand Brillat-Savarin: "To acquire a perfect degree of plumpness . . . is the life study of every woman in the world" (Shapin, 2006).

The modern trend toward thinness has been documented in a number of ways. Researchers examined photographs of women appearing in *Vogue* and *Ladies' Home Journal* over the course of the twentieth century, computing the relative size of the women's busts and waists. The bust-to-waist ratio declined markedly across this time span, indicating a turning away from a more voluptuous standard of female beauty (Silverstein, Perdue, Peterson, & Kelly, 1986). Analyses of *Playboy* center-folds and Miss America contestants over

the latter half of the twentieth century have revealed a similar trend toward slenderness (Garner, Garfinkel, Schwartz, & Thompson, 1980; Wiseman, Gray, Mosimann, & Ahrens, 1992). This trend is captured more vividly, perhaps, by the reaction of one of today's recognized beauties, model Elizabeth Hurley, at an exhibition of the clothes worn by a sex symbol of another era: "I've always thought Marilyn Monroe looked fabulous, but I'd kill myself if I was that fat" (*Allure* magazine, January 2000).

Recent cross-cultural findings may help to make sense both of the historical norm and the current deviation. Judith Anderson and her colleagues examined the preferred female body type in 54 cultures and found a relationship between these preferences and the reliability of the food supply in each culture (Anderson, Crawford, Nadeau, & Lindberg, 1992). What they found was that in cultures with a relatively uncertain food supply, moderate to heavyset women were considered more desirable. But in cultures with very reliable supplies of food, a relatively thin body type was generally preferred. And it is hard to imagine a culture with a more stable food supply and a more pronounced infatuation with slender bodies than that of the contemporary United States.

And get this! What Anderson found cross-culturally over long time periods has also been found among individuals

over much shorter time periods. Leif Nelson and Evan Morrison asked male students who were entering a cafeteria (and were presumably hungry) to indicate what body weight they "personally consider ideal in a member of the opposite sex." The hungry participants entering the cafeteria expressed a preference for a significantly heavier female body type than did the sated participants leaving the cafeteria (Nelson & Morrison, 2005).

The current obsession with thinness also appears to be characterized by some unfortunate misperceptions. In one telling study, male and female undergraduates were shown a series of nine drawings of body types ranging from very thin to very heavy (Fallon & Rozin, 1985). The participants were asked to identify the body types along that continuum that represented: (1) their own current body type, (2) the body type they would most want to have, (3) the body type they thought would be most attractive to the opposite sex, and (4) the body type of the opposite sex that they personally found most attractive (this time, of course, on a set of line drawings of the opposite sex). The male students, on average, thought that their current body type was precisely as heavy as the ideal body type. Moreover, they also believed that their body type was most attractive to female University of Pennsylvania students (although in actuality the women preferred a more slender male physique than the men anticipated).

---

articulate *why* they find someone physically attractive, but they do tend to agree with one another. What was true for former Supreme Court justice Potter Stewart with respect to pornography appears to be true for physical attractiveness: We may not be able to define it, but we "know it when we see it."

There is also widespread agreement among people from different cultures and subcultures as to who is generally considered attractive (Cunningham, Roberts, Barbee, Druen, & Wu, 1995; Langlois et al., 2000; Rhodes et al., 2001). Asians, blacks, and whites, for example, share roughly the same opinions of which Asian, black, and white faces they find attractive (Bernstein, Lin, & McClellan, 1982; Maret, 1983;

Preferred Body Types   In the United States today, most women wish to be thin, but for centuries there was a preference for women with a heavier body type and more curves, as shown in the paintings of Peter Paul Rubens in the early seventeenth century and Auguste Renoir in the early twentieth century. (A) Rubens's *Venus before a Mirror* (1614–1615). (B) Renoir's *Blond Bather* (1919). The trend toward ever-thinner figures continues in recent times and can be seen in these images of a sex symbol from the 1950s and 60s, (C) Marilyn Monroe, and today, (D) Keira Knightley.

The results were quite different for the female students. The women judged themselves to be considerably heavier than their own ideal and considerably heavier than what they thought would be most attractive to men. Perhaps the most disturbing finding is that the women in this study thought that what was most attractive to men was a body type considerably more slender than what the men actually preferred. An unfortunate pair of "thought bubbles" spring immediately to mind: a women standing next to a man worrying that "I'd feel more comfortable around him if only I lost a few pounds," while the man is simultaneously thinking, "She looks great, but she would look even better if she'd gain a few pounds."

But why would women think that men are more attracted to slender physiques than they actually are? Most explanations center on the mass media, which confront women with images of rail-thin supermodels, actresses, and newscasters. There is doubtless considerable truth to this claim, but it begs an additional question: Why would the media perpetuate an image of an ideal body type that neither men nor women truly think is ideal? One explanation places the blame on the fashion industry. Designers want their clothes to take center stage, not the models who wear them, and a curvaceous figure more often than not "spoils the line." Stated differently, many clothes look better (or at least top fashion designers believe they look better) on lanky women. The net result is the current madness in which society is quite literally making itself sick (through excessive dieting, anorexia, or bulimia) in the service of the narrow interests of the fashion industry.

Maret & Harling, 1985; Perrett, May, & Yoshikawa, 1994; Thakerar & Iwawaki, 1979). Moreover, as we discussed earlier, infants prefer to look at faces that adults consider attractive more than at faces that adults consider unattractive. Thus, before receiving much exposure to cultural conceptions of beauty, infants possess some (possibly innate) notion of what constitutes physical attractiveness (Langlois et al., 1987; Langlois et al., 1991; Samuels & Ewy, 1985).

But what is the basis of this widespread agreement among infants and adults, both within and across different cultures? What features characterize the physically attractive? Most attempts to address this question have been guided by biological, or

reproductive fitness The capacity to
get one's genes passed on to subsequent generations.

evolutionary, theorizing. The central idea is that we have evolved to have a preference, or "taste," for people possessing physical features that signify health or, more generally, **reproductive fitness**. Reproductive fitness refers to the capacity to get one's genes passed on to subsequent generations. By mating with reproductively fit individuals, people maximize the chances of their own genes being passed on. They increase the chances, in other words, for their genes' long-term evolutionary survival.

Consider a person from our deep evolutionary past who had a powerful, inherited attraction to individuals with features characteristic of ill health—say, unusually blotchy skin or skeletal features badly out of proportion. Mating with someone with such afflictions may be—from a narrow, biological perspective only—a losing proposition. The ill health that may underlie such physical symptoms may prevent a woman from carrying a fetus to term or render a man unable to provide much assistance to the child and mother. Furthermore, if these afflictions are genetic, they may be passed on to any offspring who do survive, which may place them at risk of failing to make it to reproductive age. Either way, a strong sexual attraction to individuals with signs of ill health puts one at risk of an evolutionary dead end. People with such passions are likely to leave relatively few offspring in subsequent generations, and so there are few people around today who have such passions.

Universal Agreement on Attractiveness Most people in all cultures and subcultures would find the facial features of the women in this Miss World contest to be attractive, whether they are Asian, black, or white.

It may strike you as odd that such a fundamentally cognitive product—a *judgment* about whether a person is attractive—could be inherited and shaped by evolution. It may make sense that biological traits like height, brain size, and hair color are inherited, but it may seem implausible that psychological assessments and inclinations might have similar biological roots. It may also seem like a rather strange thesis because you are doubtless unaware of assessing someone's reproductive fitness when deciding (quite quickly and automatically) whether you find that person attractive.

Such reservations, although understandable, can be put to rest. Numerous tastes are inherited. For example, there is nothing inherently pleasing about sugar or salt. Their good taste resides not in their chemical structures, but in our senses. Sugar and salt taste good to us because of the taste receptors that evolution has bequeathed to us. Earlier organisms that lacked these receptors did not seek out the most advantageous foods, and so they did not do as well in the evolutionary struggle for survival.

Note also that our appetite for nutritious food is anything but deliberate. We do not seek out sugar, salt, or fat because we think they are healthy for us. In fact, we often try to *avoid* such foods because we think they are *un*healthy. (They are considered unhealthy mainly because they contribute to "old-age" diseases like cancer and arteriosclerosis that typically occur after peak reproductive age. The critical point here is that *getting* to reproductive age might be enhanced by consuming such foods, even though life beyond peak reproductive age may be diminished by their consumption.) Nonetheless, the benefits to survival that these foods provide have given us the cravings that we have, and it is these cravings—not their evolutionary significance—that drive our behavior.

If evolution has given us a taste for sugar and salt, what features of the human face and body has it made us find attractive? Following the evolutionary thesis, we should be attracted to people with features that signify reproductive fitness and not to people with features that might indicate disease or reproductive problems. Thus, we might expect people to steer clear of facial features that are too unusual—for example, eyes placed so close together that the person looks like a cyclops, or so far apart that the person looks like an extraterrestrial. At the extremes, such features could be a reflection of genetic problems or an indication that something has gone wrong during early development—both of which could make the person's offspring poor evolutionary prospects.

There is evidence that people do indeed find unusual facial features unattractive and that they are drawn to "average" faces (see **Figure 10.6**). Through either photographic or computer technology, we can make a composite face out of any number of individual faces (Galton, 1878; Langlois & Roggman, 1990). Such composite (or average) faces of both men and women are typically considered more attractive than the average individual face in the set of faces from which they were constructed, and this effect is stronger the more individual faces are put into the composite. To a significant extent, then, the more average, or typical, a face is, the more attractive it is. (Perhaps, then, we should not be envious of those who are physically attractive because, after all, they are "just average"!) Notice that this preference for average faces connects to the common intuition that there are fewer "types" of attractive people than unattractive people. Those near the average will, as Tolstoy said of happy families, tend to be largely the same, but there are many ways to depart from average.

This does not mean that averageness is all there is to attractiveness. Far from it. It just means that averageness is an important component of perceived facial beauty. Beyond overall facial configuration, you no doubt can think of many people who are attractive precisely *because* of something extreme about them. The "bee sting" lips of supermodels depart from the norm, and people with strikingly colored eyes are thought to be especially attractive by most people.

> "Happy families are all alike; every unhappy family is unhappy in its own way."
>
> —Leo Tolstoy, *Anna Karenina*

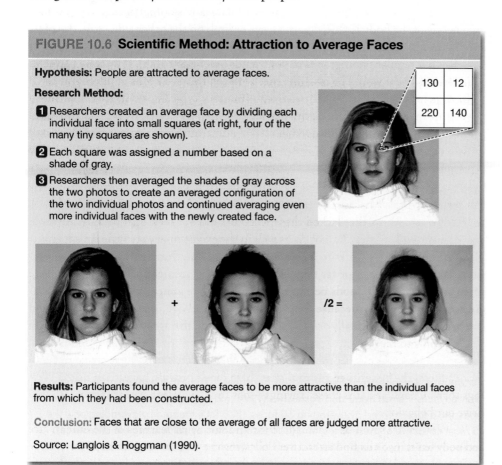

FIGURE 10.6 Scientific Method: Attraction to Average Faces

Hypothesis: People are attracted to average faces.

Research Method:

1. Researchers created an average face by dividing each individual face into small squares (at right, four of the many tiny squares are shown).

2. Each square was assigned a number based on a shade of gray.

3. Researchers then averaged the shades of gray across the two photos to create an averaged configuration of the two individual photos and continued averaging even more individual faces with the newly created face.

130	12
220	140

+ /2 =

Results: Participants found the average faces to be more attractive than the individual faces from which they had been constructed.

Conclusion: Faces that are close to the average of all faces are judged more attractive.

Source: Langlois & Roggman (1990).

Preferred Facial Features
(A) Queen Nefertiti, of prebiblical times, was considered physically attractive in her time—and in ours. Her clear skin, widely spaced and large eyes, small nose and chin, full lips, and high eyebrows are features deemed attractive in all eras. (B) These same features can be found in many people considered very attractive today, such as Angelina Jolie.

Indeed, there is evidence that averageness is not the be-all and end-all of attractiveness. A study using composite faces made this point using three types of composites: (1) an *average* composite that was constructed by averaging all the faces from a pool of 60 photographs, (2) an *attractive* composite formed by averaging only the photographs of the 15 faces previously judged to be most attractive, and (3) an *attractive + 50 percent* composite that was created by calculating the point-by-point differences between the average and attractive composites and then exaggerating these differences by 50 percent (Perrett et al., 1994) (**Figure 10.7**).

If averageness were all there was to attractiveness, then the average composite should be the most attractive because it was created by averaging a greater number of faces. In addition, any composite that is exaggerated away from the average should be perceived as less attractive than an average face. Yet neither of these results was obtained. Instead, the attractive composite was considered by both British and Japanese judges to be significantly more attractive than the average composite, and the attractive +50 percent composite was judged to be even more attractive than the simple composite (average) face. Both the attractive and attractive +50 percent composite faces had higher cheekbones and larger eyes than the purely average composite.

Another feature of the face and body that might signal physical health and therefore play an important role in judgments of physical attractiveness is bilateral symmetry. Humans and most other animals tend to be bilaterally symmetrical: an eye or limb on one side of the body is paired with an eye or limb on the other side. Still, few of us are perfectly symmetrical. That is why we tend to prefer mirror-image photographs of ourselves but regular photographs of our friends (see Figure 10.5). If we were perfectly symmetrical, there would be no difference between the two kinds of photographs.

Biologists believe that departures from symmetry typically result from injuries to the organism in utero (before birth), particularly injuries caused by exposure to parasites. This has been empirically documented in numerous animal species (Hubschman

FIGURE 10.7 Attraction to Exaggerated Features To further explore attraction to average faces, Perrett, May, and Yoshikawa (1994) made three different kinds of composite faces: (A) a face created by averaging 60 faces, (B) a face created by averaging only the 15 most attractive of these faces, and (C) a face created by calculating the differences between the first two composites and then exaggerating these differences by 50 percent. Participants found the exaggerated faces to be the most attractive.

& Stack, 1992; Moller, 1992b; Polak, 1993). Moreover, the degree of body asymmetry in human infants has been shown to be correlated with the number of infectious diseases experienced by the mother during pregnancy (Livshits & Kobyliansky, 1991). Because parasitic infections during development lead to departures from perfect symmetry, bilateral symmetry serves as a signal of an organism's ability to resist disease. Indeed, bilaterally symmetrical adults tend to have fewer respiratory and intestinal infections than their less symmetrical peers (Thornhill & Gangestad, 2005). Therefore, according to evolutionary theory, individuals who are bilaterally symmetrical should be sought out by potential mates. Disease resistance is obviously an advantageous trait, and so organisms that possess it should be in demand.

And they are. Bilaterally symmetrical individuals have been shown to have an advantage in sexual competition in a variety of animal species (Manning & Hartley, 1991; Markow & Ricker, 1992; Moller, 1992a). More to the point, this also appears to be true for humans. Facial attractiveness is correlated with the degree of bilateral symmetry (Scheib, Gangestad, & Thornhill, 1999; Thornhill & Gangestad, 1993).

Thus, two features that signal health and reproductive fitness—averageness and bilateral symmetry—are important determinants of perceived attractiveness (see **Box 10.4**). Each of these effects, by the way, exists independently of the other: averageness affects attractiveness ratings when symmetry is statistically controlled, and vice versa. This is important to establish because a face that is "average" in configuration will also be highly symmetrical. These findings testify to the value of a biological approach to attraction, one that examines the reproductive significance of features that contribute to attractiveness.

Sex Differences in Mate Preferences and Perceived Attractiveness

Do men and women differ in what they consider attractive in someone of the opposite sex? Many people believe that they do, and the differences have been ascribed to both evolution and cultural upbringing. Because the evolutionary interpretation has proved to be so controversial and has received so much attention in the popular press, we will discuss it at length. The controversy surrounds the claims that there are inherited, biologically based differences between men and women in how much physical attractiveness matters in selecting a mate, as well as biologically based differences in what is considered the most desirable age in a partner. We begin our discussion of this perspective with a presentation of the core ideas laid out by evolutionary psychologists and some of the evidence they offer to advance their claims. We then provide an extensive critique of this evolutionary approach and the evidence so frequently cited to support it, a critique that, among other things, involves a consideration of an alternative, sociocultural perspective.

Investment in Offspring The core idea, once again, is that evolution has instilled in everyone—males and females—certain desires that provide reproductive advantage. Evolutionary psychologists also claim that evolution favors fundamentally different preferences in women and men. The basis of these predicted differences lies mainly in the differences between men and women in the amount they typically *invest in their offspring*. Women tend to invest much more, a difference in investment that starts even before the child's conception. Men contribute infinitesimally small sperm, which contain little more than genetic material for the potential zygote; women provide a much larger ovum, which contains both genetic material and nutrients the zygote needs in the initial stages of life. Because of this difference, ova are much more "expensive" to produce, and so the average woman will produce only 200 to 250 mature ova in her

BOX 10.4　**FOCUS ON POSITIVE PSYCHOLOGY**

The Basis of Beauty

What makes the Golden Gate Bridge so aesthetically pleasing? Why do mathematicians describe certain proofs as "beautiful"? And why are pandas and harp seals considered more adorable than mollusks and vultures? Thinkers throughout the ages have pondered and argued about the nature of aesthetic beauty. Those who have taken the *objectivist* view, the ancient Greeks especially, argue that beauty is inherent in the properties of objects that produce pleasant sensations in the perceiver. Their goal has been to try to identify the stimulus features that have such effects—balance, proportion, symmetry, contrast, the Golden ratio. All of these and others have been put forward as important elements of beauty. Other scholars, those who subscribe to the *subjectivist* view, argue that "beauty is in the eye of the beholder" and therefore the search for general laws of beauty is futile.

Psychologists have recently offered a different view, one that attributes aesthetic pleasure to perceptual and cognitive fluency (Reber, Schwarz, & Winkielman, 2004). Fluency refers to the ease with which information can be processed. Some objects are more easily identified than others (perceptual fluency), and some are more easily interpreted, defined, and related to one's existing semantic knowledge (cognitive fluency). The core idea is that the more fluently one can process an object, the more positive one's aesthetic experience. An important part of this argument is that people experience pleasure when processing fluent stimuli. Electromyography (EMG) recordings of people's faces reveal more activation of the zygomaticus major (the "smiling muscle") when they are exposed to fluent stimuli rather than disfluent stimuli (Winkielman & Cacioppo, 2001). And another critical part of the argument is that all of the features that objectivists

regard as inherently pleasing—symmetry, contrast, and so on—tend to increase perceptual fluency.

Symmetrical patterns are processed efficiently and, as we have seen, symmetrical faces are considered particularly good looking—as are symmetrical structures like the Eiffel Tower, the Chrysler Building, and the Golden Gate Bridge. Objects characterized by high figure-ground contrast can be recognized especially quickly, and studies have found that laboratory stimuli with high contrast are judged especially attractive—as are flowers, goldfinches, and the photographs of Ansel Adams (Reber, Winkielman, & Schwarz, 1998). In addition to the impact of these classic aesthetic features, this perspective maintains that anything that increases the fluent processing of an object ought to increase its aesthetic appeal. Previous exposure to a stimulus makes it easier to process, and as we have seen, mere repeated exposure leads to greater liking. Prototypical members of a category are processed fluently, and as we have seen, people find "average" faces attractive—as well as average automobiles, birds, and fish (Halberstadt & Rhodes, 2000, 2003).

But how does this explain people's aesthetic appreciation of complicated stimuli, such as Beethoven's 9th symphony, the Bilbao Museum, or the ceiling of the Sistine Chapel? Simple stimuli are surely processed more fluently than complex stimuli, but the simplest things are not always the most pleasing. True enough. What seems to

be particularly appealing is "simplicity in complexity." People seem to like those things that are processed more easily than one might expect given their overall complexity. Processing a simple image fluently is often unsatisfying; but a complex image or sound pattern that is made accessible by some underlying structure often yields the greatest sensation of aesthetic pleasure. This also explains why experts in a given domain—music, architecture, painting—often have more elaborate aesthetic tastes than novices. Their expertise allows them to process complex material more fluently.

This fluency perspective on aesthetic beauty thus occupies a middle ground between the objectivist and subjectivist views. Beauty is indeed in the eye of the beholder, but not in the sense that it is completely arbitrary and variable from person to person. Rather, beauty lies in the processing experience of the beholder, experience that is strongly determined by how objective stimulus properties influence perceptual and cognitive fluency.

Positive Psychology Symmetrical stimuli are easy to process (i.e., they're fluent) and, like fluent stimuli in general, tend to be experienced as aesthetically pleasing. The symmetry of the Golden Gate Bridge may be one reason it is regarded as one of the most beautiful bridges in the world.

lifetime, compared to the millions of sperm the average man produces each *day*. After conception, of course, in utero development takes place entirely within the woman, taxing her physiologically and preventing her from conceiving another child for at least nine months (during which time her male partner is free—biologically—to conceive a large army). After the child is born, an extended period of nursing further taxes the woman and drastically reduces her fertility, thus lengthening the period during which no additional offspring can typically be produced. The burden of bringing a child into the world is not equally shared.

But how do differences between men and women in parental investment lead to systematic differences in what is considered attractive in a potential mate? Biologists have observed throughout the animal kingdom that the sex that invests the most in the offspring is almost always more "selective" in choosing a mate than the sex that invests less. Because males typically invest less than females, they must compete more vigorously among themselves for access to "choosy" females. As a result of their direct competition with one another (**intrasex competition**), evolution has favored those with greater size. That is why males are bigger than females in so many species. (Females tend to be larger than males in those species—such as the hyena—in which it is the *male* that invests more heavily in the offspring.) Part of this competition is the quest for females' attention and affection (**intersex attraction**). This is why it is typically the male who is the louder, gaudier member of the species—he tends to have the more colorful plumage, the more elaborate mating dance, the more intricate song. (Note, of course, that humans are something of an exception in this regard. Although in some societies men have been the more extensively adorned sex, in many they have not—including those most likely to spring to your mind.)

Thus, one of the most straightforward predictions from evolutionary psychology is that women ought to be more selective in their choice of mates, or, stated the other way, men should be more indiscriminate than women. This hypothesis conforms to both the historical record and to everyday observation: in virtually all societies in which this has been systematically studied, the average man appears ready to jump into bed much more quickly and with a much wider range of potential partners than the average female. (Note that the world's oldest profession, prostitution, is one in which it is nearly always a man making the payment.) A number of studies make this point empirically, with the most ambitious being a cross-cultural study with over 16,000 participants from societies all over the globe. Men and women in this study were asked: "Ideally, how many different sexual partners would you like to have" over different time intervals, ranging from one month to the rest of their lives. Across every time interval and in all regions of the world, men expressed a desire for a greater number of sexual partners (Schmitt, 2003).

If women are indeed more discriminating than men, what do women find attractive in a potential mate? And although men may be less discriminating, what do they find attractive in a mate? Evolutionary psychologists contend that the difference between men and women in parental investment should give rise to different criteria for what each considers desirable. Consider the situation for men. If they are to reproduce successfully, they need to find mates who are fertile. Those who seek out mates who are less fertile tend to leave fewer offspring; the genes of men with such a predilection would have been less likely to make it to the present day. But how does one spot a fertile woman? There are no direct cues, of course. Nevertheless, because women experience a relatively narrow window of lifetime fertility (the much-discussed "biological clock"), there is at least one reasonably good indirect cue—youth. Past a certain age, women are no longer capable of reproducing, and so men (who, like women, have evolved to pursue their reproductive interests), should be drawn to youth and the cues associated with youth—smooth skin, lustrous hair, full lips, and a figure in which the waist is

intrasex competition Direct competition between two or more males or two or more females for access to members of the opposite sex.

intersex attraction The interest in and attraction toward a member of the opposite sex.

parental investment

much narrower than the hips (Singh, 1993). Being attracted to women who possess such characteristics, the argument goes, should increase the chances of mating with a woman who is fertile, and therefore it should increase the likelihood of getting one's genes represented in subsequent generations.

The key reproductive facts confronting women are much different. A man's biological clock is set to a much more leisurely pace; although the quality of a man's sperm tends to decline in older age, men typically continue to be fertile throughout life. Thus, there is no evolutionary pressure for women to develop an equally strong attraction to men with youthful characteristics. Instead, given the demands of nine months of gestation and years of breast-feeding, a critical task confronting women in our ancestral past was to acquire a mate who had resources and who could be counted on to invest them in their children. According to evolutionary psychologists, then, women should be attracted to men who either possess material resources or possess characteristics associated with acquiring them in our ancestral past—physical strength, industriousness, and social status.

Taken together, these considerations have led evolutionary psychologists to predict that men ought to be more interested than women in finding mates who are physically attractive and who have a youthful appearance. In contrast, women should be more interested than men in finding mates who can and will provide material resources. Former Colorado congresswoman Pat Schroeder expressed this hypothesized sex difference memorably by noting that a middle-aged congresswoman does not appear to exert the same animal magnetism on the opposite sex that a middle-aged congressman does (Wright, 1995). You no doubt have noticed just such a pattern of apparent preferences in everyday life. It is not uncommon on college campuses, or anywhere else, for men to date women who are younger than they are. Women date younger men less often, and when they do, it is often with a little extra deliberation ("Is this okay?") and a little extra explanation to others ("He's very mature for his age.").

This asymmetry in what is desired in a mate has been examined systematically in studies of personal ads in the United States, Canada, and India (Harrison & Saeed, 1977; Kenrick & Keefe, 1992; Rajecki, Bledsoe, & Rasmussen, 1991). What has been found is an overwhelming tendency for men to seek youth and beauty and to offer material resources, but for women to seek resources and accomplishment and to offer youth and beauty. The result is so reliable—and so unsurprising—that even rather elliptical references to the phenomenon (like the cartoon on p. 373) can be counted on to elicit knowing reactions (for more extensive evidence, see Feingold, 1990, 1992a).

This hypothesis has also been tested cross-culturally in a study involving over 10,000 participants from 37 different cultures (Buss, 1989, 1994a). Among those surveyed were respondents from the West (Germany, the Netherlands, Israel, and Brazil), from industrialized regions in non-Western countries (Shanghai, China, and Tehran, Iran), and from more rural societies (the Gujarati Indians and South African Zulus). It is noteworthy (and heartening) that when asked what they desire in a mate, both men and women in *all* cultures rated kindness and intelligence more highly than either physical attractiveness or earning potential. Nevertheless, just as evolutionary psychologists would predict, men in nearly every culture rated physical attractiveness as more desirable in a mate than women did (see **Figure 10.8A**). And in *every* culture, men preferred marriage partners who were younger than they were (see **Figure 10.8B**). The magnitude of the preferred age difference varied from less than a year in Finland to over seven years in Zambia (the mean difference was 2.7 years). At the same time, women consistently preferred partners who were older than they were. They also consistently assigned greater importance than men did to various indices of a potential mate's ability to provide material resources, such as having "good financial prospects," "social status," and "ambition-industriousness" (see **Figure 10.8C**).

"It is a truth universally acknowledged, that a single man in possession of a good fortune, must be in want of a wife."

—Jane Austen, *Pride and Prejudice*

Sex Differences in Mate Preferences Evolutionary psychologists contend that issues of reproductive fitness lead men to prefer young, beautiful women who are likely to produce healthy offspring, and women to prefer men with material resources and power who will be good providers. Larry King and his wife, Shawn Southwick-King, epitomize these differences in mate preferences.

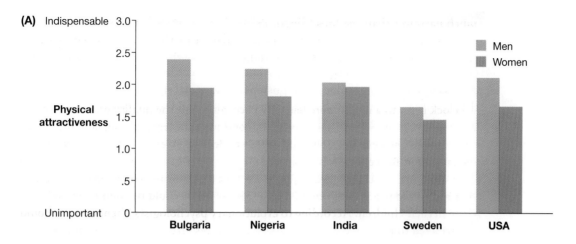

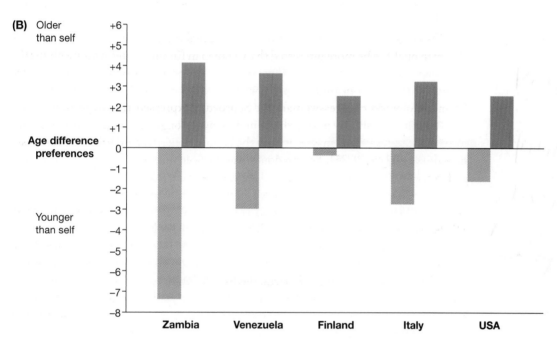

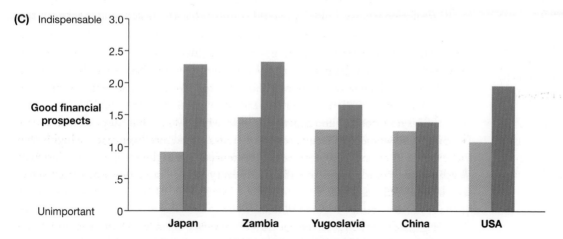

FIGURE 10.8 Differences in Male and Female Mating Preferences The bars show representative findings from a cross-cultural survey of mating preferences. (The importance of physical attractiveness and good financial prospects was rated on a 4-point scale ranging from "indispensable" to "unimportant." Age difference preferences are simply the respondents' average preferred age difference between self and spouse.) (Source: Buss, 1989.)

"The mind is not sex-typed."

—Margaret Mead

"Friendly young busty brunette seeks financially secure gentleman."

"White male, 50, looking for female to be spoiled and pampered in palatial home. Please be 21–34 and have extremely sexy figure."

"Blond bombshell 5'7" slender grad student seeking friend/companion/lover. You must be confident, financially secure, mature, and willing to please."

—Personal ads from *The Village Voice*

Critique of Evolutionary Theorizing on Sex Differences in Attraction We doubt that the empirical evidence we have presented on sex differences in attraction comes as much of a surprise. One cannot fail to notice that, for better or worse, men tend (and we emphasize *tend*) to value youth and appearance in a mate more than women do, and women tend to value accomplishment and social status more than men do. Is this, then, a triumph of evolutionary theorizing? Should we judge the theory on the basis of how well it fits with data such as these?

This is not an easy question. Consistency with the available data is certainly one criterion by which theories are judged. Yet, nearly all of these predictions could have been made by the average person on the basis of everyday observation—without reference to evolution and reproductive fitness. Furthermore, nearly all of these results can be explained without reference to reproductive fitness or any inherited male-female differences. For example, the tendency for women in all known cultures to be attracted to men bearing status and material resources might very well be the result of a flexible, nonbiological adaptation to an environment in which women in all cultures find themselves. Because men everywhere have, on average, greater physical size and strength and do not suffer from the handicaps of pregnancy and nursing, men may have disproportionate control over material resources in virtually all cultures. Being economically vulnerable, women might quite rationally be more concerned with material needs than men are (Eagly & Wood, 1999; Wood & Eagly, 2002).

One implication of this difference in material resources is that in societies where the two sexes have relatively equal power, the greater female emphasis on finding a mate with status and economic resources should be lessened. In a reanalysis of the cross-cultural data collected by evolutionary psychologists, Wood and Eagly (2002) found just this pattern. The greater the gender equality in a society (as indicated by United Nations data on income differential, the proportion of women in the national legislature, and so on), the less importance women placed on earning capacity in a potential mate. Gender equality did not affect how much importance men placed on women's attractiveness, however. Yet, Eagly and Wood point out that it is widely believed that attractive women have better social skills than unattractive women (Eagly et al., 1991). Thus, it may be that men are seeking potential mates with presumably better social skills and commensurately better child-raising skills.

If the most frequently cited evidence in support of the evolutionary approach to sex differences in attraction can be so easily questioned, why buy into the approach at all? Evolutionary psychologists would counter that the best way to deal with this problem is the way it is always handled in science—by examining what happens across a range of conditions in an effort to obtain a nuanced pattern of results that no other theory can accommodate. Thus, broad evolutionary theorizing is bolstered by research that examines the characteristics of different species that inhabit different social and physical environments. For example, female primates vary in promiscuity, from the rather monogamous gibbon to the philandering chimpanzee. As it happens, the size of male testes across all primates is highly correlated with the extent of female promiscuity in the different species. Males in species with promiscuous females have large testes (chimps, for example), whereas those in species with "trustworthy" females have smaller testes (gibbons, for example). This pattern fits, and thus supports, broad evolutionary ideas. If a male's sexual partner has mated with someone else, the male increases his reproductive chances by also mating with her shortly thereafter and depositing as much sperm as possible to win out over the deposit left by his rival (Harcourt, Harvey, Larson & Short, 1980; Short, 1979).

Or consider those species, such as the Panamanian poison-arrow frog, in which it is the *male* who invests more in the offspring. Does the typical pattern of behavioral sex differences found so widely in the animal kingdom reverse in such species? Absolutely. The females in these species are typically larger than their male counterparts, and they compete with one another more fiercely for the favors of the relatively choosy males (Trivers, 1985). Once again, the broader evolutionary theory is strengthened by the exception that "proves" (that is, tests) the rule.

To examine what happens across a broad range of conditions was, of course, precisely the point of the ambitious cross-cultural studies described earlier (Buss, 1989; Schmitt, 2003). The guiding logic has surface appeal: if the predicted sex differences show up in culture after culture, it is unlikely that they are the result of socialization practices (which, for many practices and institutions, vary so widely from culture to culture). But as we have just discussed, it is not clear how rigorous this logic is. The uniformity across cultures may be the indirect result of relatively simple differences between men and women in size and strength, and in gestation and lactation, that ultimately result in certain behavioral patterns—not the direct result of genetically inherited behavioral tendencies. In the end, cross-cultural studies like the ones described here cannot overcome the problems they were designed to address. Ultimately, they never overcome the problem of resting on a sample size of one—the human species.

A second problem with the evolutionary account of sex differences in human mating behavior is that not all of the most celebrated findings can, in fact, be rigorously derived from evolutionary theory. Consider the prediction that men should value a potential mate's physical attractiveness more than women do. Unlike the prediction that men should emphasize youth more than women do (which is a straightforward derivation from male and female differences in length of lifetime fertility), this prediction is, if anything, *easier* to derive from everyday observation than from the theory of evolution. Stripped of its relationship with youth, physical attractiveness is simply not much of a cue to fertility. There may be some correlation between physical attractiveness and fertility—certain gross physical pathologies may lead to reduced fertility. But shouldn't a tendency to avoid mating with such a person be at least as important to females as to males? After all, females have historically mated with fewer partners than men have, so being tethered to an infertile partner is reproductively more catastrophic for women.

What, then, would count as truly unambiguous support for the evolutionary framework? The answer is simple: any empirical result that would not be discovered without the guidance of evolutionary theory and that all other accounts would have difficulty explaining. As it turns out, there are some findings that fit the bill. Recall our earlier discussion of bilateral symmetry and its relationship to physical attractiveness. Symmetrical individuals are sought out, the argument goes, because symmetry is a sign of "good genes," and combining a sexual partner's good genes with our own increases the chances that our own genes will survive and be passed on in future generations. This logic has led investigators to propose that symmetry ought to be especially preferred in potential mates when the probability of conception is relatively high (the only time, after all, when issues of genetic transmission are relevant). Thus, in one study, women who were at various phases of their menstrual cycles were asked (we're not kidding) to sniff a number of T-shirts that had earlier been worn by a group of men who varied in their degree of bilateral symmetry. As the investigators anticipated, the T-shirts of the symmetrical men were judged to have a better aroma than those of less symmetrical men—but only by those women who were close to the ovulation phase of their menstrual cycle (Gangestad & Thornhill, 1998; Thornhill & Gangestad, 1999; Thornhill et al., 2003). It is highly unlikely that anyone, without the help of evolutionary theory, would ever have predicted or sought to test such a relationship.

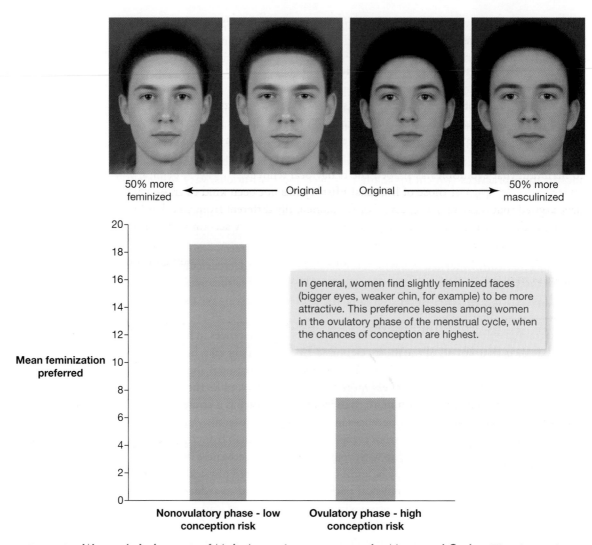

50% more feminized ← Original   Original → 50% more masculinized

In general, women find slightly feminized faces (bigger eyes, weaker chin, for example) to be more attractive. This preference lessens among women in the ovulatory phase of the menstrual cycle, when the chances of conception are highest.

Mean feminization preferred

Nonovulatory phase - low conception risk

Ovulatory phase - high conception risk

FIGURE 10.9 Women's Judgments of Male Attractiveness across the Menstrual Cycle The photos depict faces that have been altered to be 50 percent more feminized (left) from the original photo and 50 percent more masculinized (right). Women were asked to select the one face they thought was most attractive from a set of five such faces that varied from 50 percent masculinized to 50 percent feminized. The graph shows that the women tended to select somewhat feminized faces overall, but the mean degree of feminization of the selected face was less for women who were at a stage in their cycle when pregnancy was especially likely.

It has also been argued that the "strong jaw" of a particularly masculine-looking male face is also a sign of good genes. So, do women actually find such masculinized faces attractive? Not typically (see **Figure 10.9**). In general, women rate slightly *feminized* faces as most attractive (Perrett et al., 1998). But when women are ovulating and the chances of conception are highest, their preferences tend to shift toward more masculinized faces (Penton-Voak et al., 1999). This pattern, too, is one that would have been hard to anticipate without the guidance of the evolutionary perspective. Additional studies along these lines have shown that women during the ovulatory phase of their menstrual cycle can more quickly recognize male faces as male (but not female faces as female) than during other times of the month, would prefer to have a "fling" with a man with a lower, more masculine voice (Puts, 2005), and prefer men who pursue more confident, assertive, and competitive tactics of self-presentation (Gangestad, Simpson, Cousins, Garvar-Apgar, & Christensen, 2004; Macrae, Alnwick, Milne, & Schloerscheidt, 2002).

To our minds, studies such as these, which assess changes in judgments of attractiveness across biologically meaningful conditions, provide the strongest support for the evolutionary approach to human attraction. They take us far beyond simple empirical demonstrations of male and female differences that most people have already observed in their daily lives. Meanwhile, it is important to bear in mind that the broader theory of evolution is unsurpassed in its ability to explain many of the complicated behavioral patterns observed throughout the animal kingdom. Biological accounts of human behavior will always spark controversy, and we should remain skeptical of glib, overreaching accounts (Bem, 1993). Nonetheless, it would be hard to maintain that evolution has shaped the behavioral tendencies of every plant and animal on earth but not those of humans! History has not been kind to those who have argued that humans are "special," or fundamentally different from all other life on earth. Therefore, rather than simply dismissing evolutionary accounts of human behavior (sex differences included), we need to examine such accounts critically and modify them when necessary, thereby contributing to a fuller understanding of the origins of human behavior.

 We have seen that one of the most powerful determinants of interpersonal attraction is physical attractiveness. Physically attractive individuals are more popular with the opposite sex than are less attractive people, are evaluated more positively than less attractive people, and tend to have somewhat better social skills than less attractive individuals. The effects of physical attractiveness arise as early as infancy, are especially important for women's life outcomes, and appear to be based in part on biological predispositions, as certain elements of physical attractiveness may indicate reproductive fitness.

THEORETICAL INTEGRATION

Thus far, we have examined three important causes of interpersonal attraction—proximity, similarity, and physical attractiveness. That each of these variables is related to attraction is not in itself surprising. Most of you have observed for yourselves that people often want to befriend physically attractive others who share their values and live nearby. The lessons to be learned—the *surprise*, if you will—is how *much* of an impact each of these variables has. This is perhaps particularly true of proximity: people are typically horrified at the thought that even their most cherished relationships could be so powerfully influenced by something that is often beyond their control.

For knowledge of interpersonal attraction to advance, however, social psychologists must do more than expand everyday intuitions about the causes of attraction. They must also integrate these determinants into a coherent conceptual framework or theory.

The Reward Theory of Interpersonal Attraction

One of the most widely accepted theories of interpersonal attraction has the virtue of simplicity: people tend to like those who provide them with rewards. The rewards don't have to be tangible, they don't have to be immediate, and they don't have to come from direct interaction. But according to this reward framework, we tend to like those who make us feel good (Clore & Byrne, 1974; Lott & Lott, 1974).

"We always do believe in praise of ourselves. Even when we know it is not disinterested, we think it is deserved."

—David Lodge, *Thinks*

"Love is often nothing but a favorable exchange between two people who get the most of what they can expect, considering their value on the . . . market."

—Erich Fromm

Here is a test: Think of all your friends, and ask yourself whether reward theory helps explain your liking for them. Some of the rewards are easy to identify. Your friendship with one person, for example, may give you access to a clique to which you would otherwise not belong. You may like another person because she is hilarious and you have fun when you are around her. For many of your friends, however, the rewards may be more indirect and less obvious. Indeed, the very best friends are those whose rewards may be the most indirect of all: they are the ones who make you feel good about yourself when you are around them.

The reward theory of attraction certainly fits with the three influences we have discussed in this chapter. Being with physically attractive people can bring rewards by pleasing our senses or by boosting our status in the eyes of others. Being with people similar to ourselves is rewarding because they validate our views, they can be counted on to like us, and interactions with them tend to go smoothly. Evolutionary accounts of heterosexual attraction likewise fit this theory: we tend to be attracted to those who seem likely to increase our reproductive fitness and thus bring about the ultimate reward of passing our genes on to future generations. The evolutionary perspective is a specific variant of the reward perspective.

Reward theory doesn't apply as well to the impact of proximity on attraction, but even here there is a connection. Because we know we will often encounter those who live nearby, we make sure to be on our best behavior as we approach each encounter with them. As a consequence, the interactions tend to go well, and we walk away pleased (and therefore rewarded by the other person).

The reward framework also helps in identifying other potential influences on interpersonal attraction. Indeed, the reward perspective can provide a basis for answering that most practical of questions: What can you do to get others to like you? From what we have discussed thus far, it would seem wise to get an apartment near the mailbox, steer clear of off-the-wall opinions, and wash your hair regularly. The reward perspective goes further. If you want people to like you, reward them. Make other people feel good about themselves when they are around you. This is reminiscent of the advice given by Dale Carnegie in his phenomenally popular book *How to Win Friends and Influence People*: To win friends, "Dole out praise lavishly."

It might seem that such a strategy would backfire. People surely see through most efforts at ingratiation and resent the attempt to influence them. Wealthy individuals, for example, are surely alert to the existence of "gold diggers" who feign affection in an effort to get them to part with their money. But there probably wouldn't even be the term *gold digger* if a considerable number were not successful in their quest. This suggests that ingratiation may be more effective than perhaps it "should" be. Flattery may get you pretty far after all (Jones, 1964; Vonk, 2002).

The reward theory of interpersonal attraction is not without its critics. For example, studies have shown that we are not always most enamored of those who reward us the most. Someone who consistently sings our praises is not always liked more than someone who is initially less positive and then comes around to see our virtues (Aronson & Linder, 1965; Mettee, Taylor, & Friedman, 1973; but see also Berscheid, Brothen, & Graziano, 1976). This finding does not fit with a straightforward derivation of the reward framework because the person who liked us from the beginning has provided us with more rewards and therefore should earn more of our affection.

But such findings are not really at variance with reward theory if we adopt a broader perspective on rewards. The person who is initially cool to us but then warms up, for example, might very well provide us with the most rewards because we experience the additional pleasure of getting such a person to come around to our side. In addition, it can be more gratifying to earn the affections of someone who is discerning than of someone who doles out praise indiscriminately.

The Social Exchange Theory of Interpersonal Attraction

The reward theory of interpersonal attraction is really just one variant of a broader theory that views much of human interaction as social exchange (Kelley & Thibault, 1978; Rusbult, 1983). **Social exchange theory** starts with the assumption that people are motivated to maximize their own feelings of satisfaction. People seek out rewards in their interactions with others, and they are willing to pay certain costs to obtain them. Typically, people desire interactions or relationships in which the rewards exceed the costs. Such interactions yield a net gain. If rewarding interactions are not available, however, an individual is likely to seek out those interactions in which the costs exceed the rewards by the smallest amount. More generally, social exchange theories maintain that people tend to pursue those interactions that yield the most favorable difference between rewards and costs. (Note, however, that too large a discrepancy between rewards and costs can sometimes be aversive. Indeed, **equity theory** maintains that people are also motivated to pursue fairness, or equity, in which rewards and costs are shared equally among individuals.)

Although it can be a bit jarring to view our interactions with others in such harsh "economic" terms, the central notion that people are mindful of costs and benefits has been stressed by many observers of the human condition. This notion has been expressed by individuals as different as the seventeenth-century French writer François de La Rochefoucauld ("Friendship is a scheme for the mutual exchange of personal advantages and favors") and the twentieth-century American economist Thomas Schelling ("Aside from everything else that it is, marriage in this country is a voluntary contractual arrangement between people who are free to shop around"). The notion of "shopping around" is key to the social exchange perspective: people are seen by social exchange theorists as shopping around for the interactions that yield the most favorable trade-offs of costs and benefits.

"Will he ever be able to produce revenue again?"

social exchange theory A theory based on the fact that there are costs and rewards in all relationships and that how people feel about a relationship depends on their assessments of its costs and rewards and the costs and rewards available to them in other relationships.

equity theory A theory that maintains that people are motivated to pursue fairness, or equity, in their relationships, with rewards and costs shared roughly equally among individuals.

We have seen that the reward theory of interpersonal attraction maintains that people tend to like those who provide them with rewards, including immediate and deferred rewards, tangible and intangible rewards. Social exchange thoery maintains that people are motivated to maximize their own satisfaction and generally desire interactions in which rewards exceed costs, whereas equity theory maintains that people seek equity, or equally shared rewards and costs. When applied to the subject of interpersonal attraction, the social exchange perspective implies that people will be most attracted to those who provide the most rewards at the least cost. But because costs and benefits are exchanged in the context of a relationship that unfolds over time, the role of exchange in attraction is really just one facet of the broader issue of the role of exchange in relationships, a topic discussed further in Chapter 11.

"A proposal of marriage in our society tends to be a way in which a man sums up his social attributes and suggests to a woman that hers are not so much better as to preclude a merger or a partnership in these matters."

—Erving Goffman

Summary

Proximity

- A major determinant of who we end up being attracted to is *proximity*, or sheer closeness of contact with potential targets of attraction. To a remarkable extent, the people we know and like and even love are those whom we come in contact with most frequently in neighborhoods, on the job, and in recreational settings.

- Three reasons for the power of proximity are: sheer *availability*: we have to come in contact with others to have a chance to know and like them; *anticipation of interaction*: we tend to put our best foot forward for those we know we will see again; and the *mere exposure effect*: simply encountering a person or object, even under negative circumstances, makes us like the target more.

Similarity

- A second major source of attraction is *similarity*. Engaged couples are more similar to each other than are randomly paired men and women. Studies using the *bogus stranger* paradigm invariably find that people like individuals who resemble them more than individuals who do not. There is scant evidence that "opposites attract."

- Four reasons for the effect of similarity on attraction are: similar others validate our beliefs and values; similarity facilitates smooth interactions; we expect similar others to like us (which is rewarding); and similar others have qualities we like.

Physical Attractiveness

- *Physical attractiveness* is another major source of attraction. Physically attractive people are much more popular with the opposite sex. Attractive people are given higher grades for their work. People who are physically attractive earn more money in the workplace, and they even receive lower sentences for crimes. In short, they benefit from a *halo effect* in that they are believed to have many positive qualities that go beyond their physical appearance.

- Attractiveness has an impact even in infancy and childhood: attractive infants receive more attention from their mothers, and attractive children are believed to be more intelligent by their teachers. People think a transgression by a child is less serious if the child is attractive. Moreover, even 3-month-olds will look longer at an attractive face than at an unattractive one.

- *Gender* is an important variable when it comes to attractiveness, with physical appearance affecting the lives of women more than the lives of men. Women deemed unattractive at work suffer worse outcomes than men who are considered unattractive.

- Physical attractiveness has such impact because: it has immediacy—you see it before any other virtues or faults; the attractiveness of our friends and partner affects our prestige; and biology plays a role—that is, we are wired to appreciate some kinds of physical appearance more than others.

- Evolutionary psychologists argue that our biology prompts an attraction to features that signify *reproductive fitness*—that is, the capacity to perpetuate our genes in future generations if we were to mate and have children with a person who possesses those features. These include physical characteristics that signal vitality, fertility, and likely reproductive success.

- Evolutionary psychologists also claim that there are biologically based differences between men and women in the importance placed on attractiveness and in the determinants of attractiveness.

- In species in which parental investment is greater for the female, the males must compete vigorously among themselves (*intrasex competition*) for access to choosy females. The males also must compete for the females' attention (*intersex attraction*) and so are typically the louder and gaudier of the species.

- In humans, say evolutionary psychologists, differential parental investment on the part of men and women leads women to prefer fewer sexual partners than men. It leads men to prefer women whose physical appearance gives the impression that they will be fertile—for example, features such as smooth skin and a waist that is narrow in relation to hips. Women are attracted to men who can be expected to provide for them and for their children—men who are strong, industrious, and have social status.

- Though much evidence from the animal kingdom and from the study of humans supports the hypotheses of evolutionary psychologists, most of the human findings can be explained without resorting to an evolutionary explanation. The strongest support for the evolutionary approach to attractiveness in humans comes from studies showing that women increase their preference for attractive (or at least symmetrical) and masculine men during the ovulatory phase of their menstrual cycles, when they have a higher probability of conceiving.

Theoretical Integration

- The notion of *reward* can explain most of the reasons we like people—we tend to like those who provide us with the greatest rewards (broadly construed).

- Another way to understand attraction is in terms of *social exchange*. This theory holds that people pursue those interactions that provide the most favorable difference between rewards and costs.

Key Terms

complementarity (p. 369)
counterbalancing (p. 361)
equity theory (p. 393)
fluency (p. 365)
functional distance (p. 358)

halo effect (p. 373)
intersex attraction (p. 385)
intrasex competition (p. 385)
mere exposure effect (p. 362)
propinquity (p. 357)

reproductive fitness (p. 380)
self-fulfilling prophecy (p. 374)
social exchange theory (p. 393)
sociometric survey (p. 357)

Further Reading

Etcoff, N. L. (1999). *Survival of the prettiest: The science of beauty.* New York: Doubleday. An application of evolutionary theory to understanding what we consider beautiful and why.

Fredrickson, B. L., & Roberts, T. (1997). Objectification theory: Toward understanding women's lived experiences and mental health risks. *Psychology of Women Quarterly, 21,* 173–206. An analysis of the broad-based effects on women of the great emphasis placed on their physical attractiveness.

Miller, G. (2000). *The mating mind: How sexual choice shaped the evolution of human nature.* New York: Doubleday. A very readable and scholarly treatment of how sexual selection has influenced human nature.

Regan, P. C., & Berscheid, E. (1999). *Lust: What we know about human sexual desire.* Thousand Oaks, CA: Sage. A review of theory and research on human sexual desire and its personal, interpersonal, and societal implications.

Ⓢ Online Study Tools

StudySpace

Go to StudySpace, wwnorton.com/studyspace, to access additional review and enrichment materials, including the following resources for each chapter:

Organize
- Study Plan
- Chapter Outline
- Quiz+ Assessment

Learn
- Ebook
- Chapter Review
- Critical-Thinking Questions
- Visual Quizzes
- Vocabulary Flashcards

Connect
- Apply It! Exercises
- Author Insights Podcasts
- Social Psychology in the News

CHAPTER 11

Relationships

ON A CHILLY JANUARY MORNING IN 1800, a filthy, naked, 12-year-old boy, scampering around on all fours, was spotted digging for potatoes in the fields of the French village of Saint Sernin. He had survived for years on his own in the forest scavenging for acorns and hunting small animals. The owner of the field captured the wild-eyed boy and took him home.

The boy, soon to be named Victor, had many difficulties living inside the owner's house. He prowled restlessly on all fours and refused to wear clothes. He defecated in public without shame and rejected all food except acorns and potatoes. His communication was restricted to grunts, howls, and bursts of wild laughter. He was unresponsive to human language, but would turn quickly at the sounds of nuts being cracked. He showed no interest in humans, except fear, and never smiled, cried, or met the gaze of other people.

Eventually, Jean Itard, a 26-year-old doctor from the Paris Deaf-Mute Institute, took Victor, known as the "Wild Boy of Aveyron," into his custody and devoted five years to teaching Victor language and human ways. Victor could learn only a few words, but he did learn to wear clothes, sleep in beds, eat at a table, and take baths. He came to feel real affection for Jean Itard, but he never learned much in the way of human decorum. At a dinner party at a wealthy socialite's home, where Dr. Itard hoped to show off Victor's progress, Victor wolfed down his food, stuffed desserts into his pockets, stripped to his underwear, and leaped through the trees like a monkey. Victor eventually died in his 40s, house trained but wild, fearful, and virtually mute (Itard, 1801/1962).

There are over 35 documented cases of feral (wild) children like Victor, who grew up in the wild on their own. They have long provoked the human imagination, for they reveal an answer to an age-old question: What is human nature stripped of the influences of society and civilization? Without parents or other adults to raise them, cut off from human family, friends, and groups, such children do not develop

Feral Children and Social Deficits Victor, the Wild Boy of Aveyron, was a feral child who grew up alone in the woods, without human contact, until he was about 12 years old. Although he eventually learned to wear clothes, to eat at a table, and to say some words, he was never comfortable in highly socialized settings, he never developed complex language skills, and he did not develop strong attachments with people. His lack of early relationships with other humans affected his social functioning for his entire life.

language, morals, or manners; they remain largely unresponsive to other people; they show no sexual interest in the opposite sex; and they lack self-awareness. Their lives highlight the core theme of this chapter—that relationships are central to human functioning. In fact, relationships help create human nature.

In contrast to the impoverished bonds between Victor and other humans were the strong bonds forged between six young German-Jewish Holocaust survivors whose parents had died in gas chambers. When they were between the ages of 6 and 12 months, these children had all been sent to Terezin, a concentration camp in Czechoslovakia. While they were cared for in the camp by fellow inmates, they did not develop relationships with their caregivers, since these adults were likely to disappear quickly from their lives. They did, however, form strong attachments to each other. After the war, the children were taken to England, and they continued to maintain the strong bonds they had forged with each other, fearing separation, clinging to each other, and helping each other to adjust to their new circumstances (Freud & Dann, 1951). These children learned to speak, learned manners and morals, and eventually learned to forge well-adjusted relations with adults. The relationships that they had with each other saved them from the fate of Victor and other feral children like him.

What, then, does social psychology have to say about relationships? This chapter moves beyond the topic of attraction, discussed in Chapter 10, to the study of more enduring relationships—with parents, friends, romantic partners, and those we need to interact with in hierarchies. We start by characterizing what relationships are and then consider how central they are to our functioning. We review evidence for the claim that humans have a basic need for relationships and that social rejection is a horrible fate to endure. We then turn to a theory—attachment theory—that seeks answers to a difficult question: What are the origins of our patterns of relating to others? We will discover that our early attachment style, established in our relations with our parents, lays an important foundation for our romantic relations and personal successes and difficulties later in life. We then examine the different ways of relating to others. We discuss communal, family-like relationships and exchange, equity-based relationships. Then we continue with a discussion of power and hierarchical relationships, focusing on who rises in power (you'll be surprised, we suspect, by the answer) and why power can make people act in such foolish and often socially inappropriate fashion. We conclude with a discussion of perhaps the most mysterious and compelling relationship, the romantic bond. We will consider the causes of divorce and marital dissatisfaction, as well as what makes for fulfilling romantic relations.

CHARACTERIZING RELATIONSHIPS

In this chapter we discuss **interpersonal relationships**, attachments in which bonds of family or friendship or love or respect or hierarchy tie together two or more individuals over an extended period of time. Relationships are generally characterized by an interdependence in which the individuals think about, influence, and engage in joint activities or have joint memories of shared experiences.

Within social psychology, the study of relationships is relatively recent (Duck, 1997; Hartup & Stevens, 1997). The problems in studying relationships are different from those that we encounter elsewhere in the book (Bradbury & Karney, 1993; Finkel & Eastwick, 2008; Gonzalez & Griffin, 1997; Karney & Bradbury, 1995). Many of the studies we will review in this chapter are not true experiments with random assignment of participants to different conditions. Instead, these studies rely on longitudinal methods to look at the dynamics of relationships that have already formed over time, attempting to understand, for example, what factors early in a relationship make for happier or more problematic bonds. This kind of research faces a challenging methodological problem called *self-selection*, which occurs whenever investigators do not have control over assignment of participants to the conditions that are to be compared. When participants "select" their own condition, we can never know in what ways—other than the particular condition they are in—they may differ from other participants. In the case of Victor and other feral children, it seems reasonable to assume that their profound isolation led them to develop in abnormal ways. Yet, we have to ask ourselves, why exactly were these children abandoned by their parents? Were they strange, unusually difficult and fussy, or unresponsive to others? Were their parents themselves unbalanced and antisocial to begin with?

We would reach very different conclusions, depending on the answers to these questions. Lacking the ability to perform an actual experiment—randomly assigning some children to a "grow up alone" condition—we cannot know for sure if we are seeing the effects of severe social deprivation or some other set of factors. As it happens, Harry Harlow (1959) performed a classic series of experiments with baby rhesus monkeys that give us reason to think that the evidence about feral children means exactly what it seems to—that they suffer from the severe effects of social deprivation. Some monkeys were raised without contact with other rhesus monkeys but with access to two "mother surrogates"—props vaguely resembling monkeys. One was a wire contraption that gave the infant food; the other was covered with terry cloth. The monkeys spent most of their time clinging to the terry-cloth mother, and when they were frightened, they rushed to the terry-cloth mother for comfort (**Figure 11.1**).

Much like feral children, monkeys raised in isolation were in no way normal when they reached adolescence. As adolescents, they were highly fearful, could not interact with their peers, and engaged in inappropriate sexual behaviors—for example, attacking potential mates or failing to display typical sexual positions during copulation.

It is not just monkeys and people who require social interaction to be fully functioning members of their species. A natural experiment with elephants makes a similar point. A natural experiment involves an accidentally produced set of conditions (rather than conditions created by an experimenter) that largely avoids self-selection problems. Elephants in some areas of Africa have been slaughtered for the ivory in their tusks, leaving young elephants to grow up on their own, much like the wild boy of Aveyron or Harlow's rhesus monkeys. These adolescent elephants prove to be quite antisocial and aggressive, not only toward their own species but toward others as well, killing rhinoceroses for sport, for example. African gamekeepers have solved the problem of the wild elephants by importing adult elephants to show them how to be elephants. Elephants, like humans, require relationships to become proper members of their species.

FIGURE 11.1 Scientific Method: Harlow's Monkeys and Their "Mothers"

Hypothesis: Infant monkeys will form an attachment to a surrogate mother that provides warmth and comfort rather than one that provides nutrients.

Research Method: Infant rhesus monkeys were put in a cage with two different "mothers":

1 One was made of cloth and looked like a monkey, but could not give milk.

2 The other was made of wire, but could give milk.

Results: The monkeys clung to the cloth mother and went to it for comfort in times of threat. The monkeys approached the wire mother only when hungry.

Conclusion: Infant monkeys will prefer and form an attachment to a surrogate mother that provides warmth and comfort over a wire surrogate mother that provides nutrients.

Source: Harlow (1959).

THE IMPORTANCE OF RELATIONSHIPS

Many people from Western cultures define themselves from an independent (individualistic) perspective, focusing on how they are different and separate from others. Many Westerners seek to find out who they really are in solitary rites of passage—for example, while backpacking in the woods or hitchhiking across Europe. While these practices are no doubt appealing, they ignore a deeper truth: human nature is profoundly social, and who we really are is found in our social relationships. Humans have what appears to be a biological need to belong in relationships. Not surprisingly, rejection is often an unimaginably painful fate, often worse than physical pain. Our sense of self, which for many—particularly those from independent backgrounds—seems autonomous and separate from others, is in fact continually shaped by our past relationships.

"We are all in this together, by ourselves."

—Lily Tomlin

The Need to Belong

It is self-evident that humans have biologically based needs for food, oxygen, warmth, and safety. Without nutritional intake, air, or water, we die. Roy Baumeister and Mark Leary claim that the same is true for relationships: we have a need to be embedded in healthy relationships, sharing bonds with family members, romantic partners, friends, and fellow group members (Baumeister & Leary, 1995). This was certainly apparent in the studies of feral children and Harlow's monkeys. What kind of evidence would

The Need to Belong   There is an evolutionary basis for the need to belong. (A) Not only do elephant parents feed and protect young elephants, but they teach them appropriate social behavior that enables them to live in groups. If the young elephants grow up without adults, they are likely to become antisocial and aggressive and have difficulty living in groups. (B) Primates have a need to belong, as evidenced in this photo showing a friendship between a female (left) and male olive baboon. They groom each other frequently, rest together, and enhance each other's reproductive fitness.

[handwritten margin notes: evolutionary basis / universal / guide social cognition / satiable / suffer profound negative consequences]

convince you that we have a biological need to belong? For Baumeister and Leary, five kinds of arguments and evidence make the case.

First, there should be an *evolutionary basis* for our relationships (Simpson & Kenrick, 1998). Here there is a great deal of consensus that relationships help individuals and offspring survive, thus contributing to the increased likelihood of the replication of the individual's genes. Long-term romantic bonds evolved, to a large extent, to facilitate reproduction and to raise human offspring, who are especially vulnerable and dependent for many years (Diamond, 2003; Ellis, 1992; Ellis & Malamuth, 2000; Emlen, 1997; Fisher, 1992; Hrdy, 1999). Parent-offspring attachments ensure that infants and children have sufficient protection to survive until they can function independently (Bowlby,1982; Buss, 1994b; Daly, Salmon, & Wilson, 1997). Friendships evolved as a means for nonkin to cooperate and to avoid the costs and perils of competition and aggression (Dunn & Herrera, 1997; Fehr, 1996; Palombit, Seyfarth, & Cheney, 1997; Smuts, 1985; Trivers, 1971).

Second, if relationships have an evolutionary basis and there is a basic need to belong, then they should also be *universal*. We should see similar kinds of dynamics between romantic partners, parents and children, siblings, friends, and group members in different cultures around the world. In different cultures, for example, women assign greater weight to a potential mate's resources than men do, whereas men more heavily value the beauty of a potential mate than women do, although there is considerable cultural variation in what resources are of value and who is considered beautiful (see Chapter 10). Early ethologists who studied hunter-gatherer groups in their natural environments documented patterns of social behavior—the caregiving between mother and child, the wrestling of siblings, the flirtations of young people who are courting, the affection between romantic partners, the dominance displays between adolescent males—that appear to be quite universal (Eibl-Eibesfeldt, 1989). Elsewhere in this chapter, we will consider universality and cultural variation in relationships.

Third, if the need to belong is the product of millions of years of evolution, it should *guide social cognition*, just as hunger momentarily heightens our sensitivity to the odors and sights that promise food. Social psychologists have been quite active

"No more fiendish punishment could be devised, were such a thing physically possible, than that one should be turned loose in society and remain absolutely unnoticed by all the members thereof."

—William James

in assessing this thesis (Baldwin, 1992; Karney & Coombs, 2000; Reis & Downey, 1999). Relationships serve as important categories for how we process and store social information (Fiske, 1991b; Sedikides, Olsen, & Reis, 1993). Witness a complicated scene in a city buzzing with activity and you are likely to organize your understanding of that scene in terms of the relationships of the people involved—likely friends, couples, work colleagues, and so on. Our attributions of social behavior are shaped by our relationships: as people become close to us, we tend to make similar attributions for their behaviors as we do for our own (Fincham & Bradbury, 1993). Relationships guide social thought.

Fourth, the need to belong should be *satiable*. Thus, in specific relationships, the need to belong should motivate thoughts and behaviors, much as thirst and hunger do, until the need is satisfied. Consider one kind of relationship that is important to us all—friendship. In Western European cultures, college students tend to restrict their meaningful interactions to, on average, about six friends (Wheeler & Nezlek, 1977). It seems that we satisfy our need for friendship with a limited number of close friends, and once that is satisfied, we no longer seek it in others. But if the need to belong is no longer satisfied in existing relationships, people will seek to satisfy that need in other relationships. Observational studies in prisons, for example, find that prisoners suffer great anguish at the loss of contact with their family. As a result, they often form substitute families based on kinship-like ties with other prisoners (Burkhart, 1973).

Finally, if the need to belong is chronically unmet, as we saw with feral children and Harlow's monkeys, the individual should *suffer profound negative consequences*. Here the evidence strongly shows that relationships are vital to our physical and mental well-being (see also Chapter 7 and Chapter 15). Consider the following findings. Mortality rates are higher for divorced, unmarried, and widowed individuals (Lynch, 1979). Admissions to hospitals for psychological problems are 3 to 23 times higher for divorced than for married individuals, depending on the study and nature of the psychological problems in question (Bloom, White, & Asher, 1979). Suicide rates are higher for single and divorced individuals (Rothberg & Jones, 1987). So, too, are crime rates (Baumeister & Leary, 1995). More generally, having a lot of support from others strengthens our cardiovascular, immune, and endocrine systems, a theme we develop in our treatment of health in the final chapter of this book (Oxman & Hull, 1997; Uchino, Cacioppo, & Kiecolt-Glaser, 1996).

It would seem, then, that humans have a basic need to belong, to connect, to be embedded in a rich network of relationships. Relationships have an evolutionary

Universality of Relationships   (A, B) Siblings in different cultures all play, support, and fight with each other, although the specific kinds of play, support, and conflict may vary according to the culture. (C) Parents in different cultures show similar kinds of attachment behaviors, including patterns of touch and eye contact.

basis—they are a universal part of human nature. They motivate thoughts and behaviors until satisfied, and without them, we suffer both physically and psychologically.

The Costs of Social Rejection

Terry Anderson was the chief Middle East correspondent for the Associated Press in 1985. On March 16, 1985, he was kidnapped in Lebanon by members of the terrorist group Hezbollah and held in captivity for 7½ years—longer than any hostage in American history. Much of the time he spent in a small, dark cell in solitary confinement. Initially, he experienced the range of emotions you might expect in such a situation—intense longing for his fiancé and family; panic; fleeting bursts of hope. But gradually something more profound happened. He lost his mind.

"Ezra, I'm not inviting you to my birthday party, because our relationship is no longer satisfying to my needs."

He hallucinated. Sapped of his energy, he would sleep much of the day or lie motionless in a catatonic state. He was prone to violent outbursts. He beat his head against the wall of his cell. Reflecting on his own experience of solitary confinement, John McCain said that it "crushes your spirit and weakens your resistance more effectively than any other form of mistreatment."

How does solitary confinement crush the spirit? Geoff MacDonald and Mark Leary have recently offered an answer to this question in their theorizing about social exclusion, or what we will call social rejection (MacDonald & Leary, 2005). In human evolution, MacDonald and Leary reason, being socially rejected from the group was akin to a death warrant, given our profound dependence on others for food, shelter, defense, and affection. Given the many evolutionary advantages to being integrated into groups, social rejection came to activate a threat defense system, which involves stress-related cardiovascular arousal; the release of the stress hormone cortisol; defensive aggressive tendencies, such as striking out to defend ourselves; and feelings of distress and pain. Early in primate evolution, this threat defense system was attuned to cues of physical aggression, such as the predator's attack, and it enabled our predecessors to fare well in aggressive encounters. As humans evolved into the most social of primates, social cues—hearing someone gossip about you, seeing an acquaintance's sneer or contemptuous eye roll, hearing a superior's critical tone of voice—acquired the power to trigger this threat defense system and its associated action tendencies and feelings.

In our mammalian relatives, social rejection does indeed jeopardize the chances of survival and reproduction. For example, baboon infants of socially connected mothers are more likely to survive than the infants of more isolated baboon mothers (Silk, Alberts, & Altmann, 2003). Rhesus macaques who show little interest in social contact are less likely to survive (Kling, Lancaster, & Benitone, 1970). Adolescent coyotes who fail at rough-and-tumble play with their peers (for example, they bite too aggressively) are ostracized and live shorter lives (Bekoff & Pierce, 2009).

In humans, dozens of studies reveal how chronic social rejection, such as solitary confinement, can be the worst form of torture. First, social rejection stimulates feelings of pain. For example, people who feel rejected report higher levels of chronic physical pain, physical ailments, and even greater pain during childbirth

(MacDonald & Leary, 2005). To study experimentally the painful consequences of rejection, Kip Williams has developed the ball-tossing paradigm, which may remind you of the politics of playing four square on your grammar school playground many years ago. In this paradigm, one participant plays a ball toss game with two confederates, tossing a ball around like old friends. At a predetermined point in the experiment, the two confederates stop throwing the ball to the participant and only throw the ball to each other for 5 painful minutes. Sure enough, being the rejected participant in this game triggers feelings of distress, shame, and self doubt and submissive, slouched posture (Williams, 2007). In a neuroimaging study conducted by Kip Williams, Naomi Eisenberger, and Matthew Lieberman (Eisenberger, Lieberman, & Williams, 2003), a participant played the ball-tossing game online with two other virtual participants (whose behavior was actually programmed by the experimenters). When the participant experienced this virtual form of rejection, fMRI images revealed that a region of the brain that processes physically painful stimuli, known as the anterior cingulate, lit up. So social rejection activates the same regions of the brain involved in processing physical pain. Williams has even found that many people would prefer physical pain (being hit) to the social pain of being excluded (Williams, 2007).

Other studies find that the pain of social rejection undermines our ability to think. You yourself may have had experiences similar to this—for example, you're not invited to the party all your friends are going to, and you find it hard to concentrate on your term paper. The thinking of Roy Baumeister and colleagues on this is that social rejection activates older regions of the brain involved in threat detection, which takes resources away from regions of the brain involved in higher-order reasoning, and in the heat of rejection intellectual performance declines (Baumeister, Twenge, & Nuss, 2002). In their research, participants who were told, based on a personality questionnaire, that they would have a lonely future (social rejection) as compared to control participants, performed worse on an IQ test and portions of the Graduate Record Exam. These findings have profound implications for academic achievement. Clearly, forms of rejection—threats from teachers or peers or even society at large, for example—jeopardize children's ability to excel academically (see Chapter 12).

And there's a wealth of evidence that feeling socially rejected triggers aggression. People who report a chronic sense of rejection are more likley to act aggressively in their romantic relationships, as we shall see later in this chapter. People who physically abuse their romantic partners systematicaly report feeling rejected (Dutton, 2002). And in important experimental work, Jean Twenge and her colleagues have found that individuals who were led to imagine a lonely, socially rejected future, compared to appropriate controls, were more likley to administer unpleasant noise blasts to strangers, individuals who had nothing to do with the participant's sense of social rejection (Twenge, Baumeister, Tice, & Stucke, 2001). Putting these findings together, MacDonald and Leary have argued that social rejection is a root cause of the school shootings that are tragically all too common these days in the United States and other countries, such as Scotland and Germany (Leary, Kowalksi, Smith, & Phillips, 2003). Social rejection is a health concern as significant as any today.

 We have seen that relationships are essential to our social adjustment. Our need to belong in relationships is an evolved, universal motive that shapes our thoughts and actions. If not satisfied, it can have highly negative consequences for our well-being. Social rejection triggers feelings of intense distress, disrupts cognitive functioning, and can lead to aggression.

"Sticks in a bundle are unbreakable."

—Kenyan proverb

THE ORIGINS OF HOW WE RELATE TO OTHERS

You may be wondering about your own relationships. Do you have a consistent way of relating to your friends, family, and romantic partners? If so, what are the origins of this style of relating to others? What does it have to do with your early experience with your parents? These are fundamental questions that have motivated the influential theory of human attachment.

Attachment Theory

Attachment theory was first advanced by John Bowlby, a seminal theorist in the study of relationships and one of the early advocates of evolutionary accounts of human behavior (Bowlby, 1969/1982; Hazan & Shaver, 1994; Mikulincer & Shaver, 2003; Simpson & Rholes, 1998). The central thesis of Bowlby's theory is that our early attachments with our parents and other caregivers shape our relationships for the remainder of our lives.

Unlike many mammals, human infants are born with few survival skills. In fact, they are the most vulnerable offspring on the face of the earth, requiring several years to reach some degree of independence. They cannot flee predators, find food or feed themselves, or locate shelter. They survive, Bowlby reasons, by forming intensely close attachments to parents or parental figures. Evolution has given infants a variety of traits that promote parent-offspring attachments, including the heart-warming smiles, laughs and coos, and baby-faced features that evoke love and devotion (Berry & McArthur, 1986; McArthur & Baron, 1983). These features, including large head and large eyes, also evoke attachment for other mammals toward their offspring. In fact, their babies pull at our own heartstrings. Likewise, evolution has led to a variety of parental traits that promote attachment—most notably, strong feelings of parental

attachment theory A theory about how our early attachments with our parents shape our relationships for the remainder of our lives.

"The person tends to assimilate a new person with whom he may form a bond, such as a spouse, or child, or employer, or therapist, to an existing model (either of one or other parent or of self), and often to continue to do so despite repeated evidence that the model is inappropriate."

—John Bowlby

Traits That Evoke Attachment Evolution has led infants to have traits that evoke attachment, so that primary caregivers, most typically parents, will feed, shelter, and protect them until they are able to do so themselves. Thus, the chimp, kitten, and seal pup have such features as large eyes, which evoke positive emotion and attachment—even from members of other species, such as humans. Similar features in human infants, as well as smiles and coos, also promote attachment of parents to infants and make the adults want to protect the infants from harm.

love and protective instincts toward their infants (Fehr, 1994; Fehr & Russell, 1991; Hazan & Shaver, 1987, 1994; Hrdy, 1999).

Early in development, children rely on their parents for a sense of security, which allows them to explore the environment and to learn. A child's confidence in the secure base that the parents provide derives in part from the parents' availability and responsiveness to the child's ever-shifting emotions. This is evident in the literature on depressed mothers. Depressed mothers are less responsive to their children's actions, and their children in turn tend to feel less secure and more anxious (Field, 1995). Of course, there are alternative accounts of this finding. Researchers have learned that depression and anxiety are partially inherited and tend to be found together. In light of this, it is possible that depressed mothers are transmitting to their children genes that predispose them to depression and anxiety, rather than producing anxiety through their own behavior.

As children form attachments to parents, they develop working models of how relationships function (Baldwin, Keelan, Fehr, Enns, & Koh-Rangarajoo, 1996; Collins & Read, 1994; Pietromonaco & Feldman-Barrett, 2000). These models are based on children's experiences with how available their parents are and the extent to which their parents provide a sense of security. A **working model of relationships**, then, is the individual's beliefs about another's availability, warmth, and ability to provide security. These working models, Bowlby claimed, originate early in life and shape our relationships from "cradle to grave."

Inspired by Bowlby's theorizing, Mary Ainsworth classified the attachment patterns of infants according to how the children responded to separations and reunions with their caregivers, both in the laboratory and in the home (Ainsworth, 1993; Ainsworth, Blehar, Waters, & Wall, 1978). Using an experimental procedure that came to be known as the **strange situation**, Ainsworth had the infants and their caregivers enter an unfamiliar room containing a large number of interesting toys. As the infant explored the room and began to play with some of the toys, a stranger walked in. The stranger remained in the room, and the caregiver quietly left. Returning after 3 minutes, the caregiver greeted and comforted the infant if he or she was upset. The separation typically caused infants to be distressed. Infants whose caregivers responded quickly and reliably to their distress cries, as assessed by outside observers, were typically securely attached. Such infants were comfortable in moving away from their caregivers to explore a novel environment—with the occasional glance back at the caregiver to make sure that things were okay. These children felt safe even though they weren't in contact with their caregiver. Caregivers who were not so reliable in their responses

working model of relationships A conceptual model of relationships with our current partners—including their availability, warmth, and ability to provide security—as derived from our childhood experience with how available and warm our parents were.

strange situation An experimental situation designed to assess an infant's attachment to the caregiver. An infant's reactions are observed after her caregiver has left her alone in an unfamiliar room with a stranger and then when the caregiver returns to the room (the reunion).

The Strange Situation Mary Ainsworth set up an experimental situation in which she was able to measure infants' attachment to their caregiver. (A) A mother and child would enter an unfamiliar room with many interesting toys. The infant would explore the room and play with the toys. In the meantime, a stranger would enter the room and then the mother would leave. (B) When the mother returned to the room, she would pick up the infant and comfort him if he was upset that she had left the room. (C) The mother would then put the infant down, and the infant would be free to return to playing with the toys or might react by crying and protesting the separation.

to their infants—sometimes intruding on the child's activities and sometimes rejecting the child—tended to have infants who showed anxious attachment; these infants were likely to cry or show anger when placed in novel environments and were less comforted by contact with their caregiver when it occurred. Caregivers who rejected their infants frequently tended to produce children with avoidant attachment. In a strange situation, the avoidant child might not seek out the caregiver and might even reject attention when it was offered.

Attachment Styles

To classify adults' attachment styles, researchers have developed different self-report measures (for example, Bartholomew & Horowitz, 1991; Brennan, Clark, & Shaver, 1998; Hazan & Shaver, 1987). One such approach is presented in **Table 11.1**. Read each of the three paragraphs and decide which one best describes your feelings toward close others in your life. In classifying the attachment patterns of infants and adults, researchers have concentrated on three specific styles. Individuals with a **secure attachment style** feel secure in relationships; they are comfortable with intimacy and want to be close to others during times of threat and uncertainty. Individuals with an **avoidant attachment style** feel insecure in relationships; they exhibit compulsive self-reliance, prefer distance from others, and during times of threat and uncertainty are dismissive and detached. Individuals with an **anxious attachment style** also feel insecure in relationships, but they respond differently than avoidant individuals. Anxious individuals compulsively seek closeness, express continual worries about relationships, and during times of threat and uncertainty make excessive attempts to get closer to others. Such anxious individuals are often the proverbial high-maintenance romantic partners that some of your friends might bemoan.

secure attachment style An attachment style characterized by feelings of security in relationships. Individuals with this style are comfortable with intimacy and want to be close to others during times of threat and uncertainty.

avoidant attachment style An attachment style characterized by feelings of insecurity in relationships. Individuals with this style exhibit compulsive self-reliance, prefer distance from others, and are dismissive and detached during times of threat and uncertainty.

anxious attachment style An attachment style characterized by feelings of insecurity in relationships. Individuals with this style compulsively seek closeness, express continual worries about relationships, and excessively try to get closer to others during times of threat and uncertainty.

TABLE 11.1 Measuring Attachment Styles

Researchers present participants with paragraphs like those below to assess their attachment styles. In this method, participants are asked to select the paragraph that best describes how they relate to other people.

Attachment Style	Description
Secure Style	I find it relatively easy to get close to others and am comfortable depending on them and having them depend on me. I don't often worry about being abandoned or about someone getting too close.
Avoidant Style	I am somewhat uncomfortable being close. I find it difficult to trust completely, difficult to allow myself to depend on anyone. I am nervous when anyone gets close, and often, romantic partners want me to be more intimate than I feel comfortable being.
Anxious Style	I find that others are reluctant to get as close as I would like. I often worry that my partner doesn't really love me or won't stay with me. I want to merge completely with another person, and this desire sometimes scares people away.

Source: Adapted from Hazan & Shaver (1987).

BOX 11.1 **FOCUS ON CULTURE**

Building an Independent Baby in the Bedroom

If you are a white, middle-class North American, odds are you slept by yourself in your own bedroom from infancy on. And that probably seems perfectly normal to you. Normal, maybe; common, definitely not. There are few cultures in the world where such a sleeping arrangement is customary. In an article entitled "Who Sleeps with Whom Revisited," Shweder, Jensen, and Goldstein (1995) describe the sleeping arrangements of people in many of the world's cultures. The sleeping arrangements predict fairly well how independent and individualistic a given culture is. In Japan, most children sleep with their parents until they are adolescents. In the non-Western, nonindustrial world, it is virtually unheard of for a very young child not to sleep with his or her parents, and such a practice would be regarded as a form of child abuse. Even in the United States, 55 percent of African-American children less than 1 year of age sleep with a parent every night, and 25 percent of African-American children 1 to 5 years old sleep with a parent. In a white, predominantly blue-collar community in Appalachian Kentucky, 71 percent of children between the ages of 2 months and 2 years were found to sleep with their parents, as well as 47 percent of children between 2 and 4 years of age.

This study reveals the extent to which interdependent and independent self-construals permeate social behavior. In more interdependent cultures, young children are much more likely to sleep side by side with their parents than in independent cultures. While we can only speculate about the effects these patterns of sleep have on attachment patterns, we might expect secure attachments in the independent cultures to be defined by greater independence and autonomy than secure patterns in interdependent cultures.

A central claim of attachment theory is that these attachment styles are stable across life; that is, the attachments you form early in life shape how you relate as an adult to your romantic partners, your children, and your friends. Evidence supports this provocative thesis. Individuals classified as secure, avoidant, or anxious at age 1 tend to be similarly classified in early adulthood (Fraley & Spieker, 2003; see **Box 11.1**). A four-year longitudinal study of adults found that 70 percent of adults reported the same attachment style across all four years of the study (Kirkpatrick & Hazan, 1994). Secure individuals were particularly likely to remain secure (83.3 percent remained secure across the four years). But it is important to note that this study also reveals that some people change over time in their attachment style (Baldwin & Fehr, 1995; Baldwin et al., 1996).

Important early life events are also associated with later attachment styles. Brennan and Shaver (1993) found that anxious individuals were more likely to have experienced parents who divorced, the death of a parent, or abuse during childhood. In a 40-year longitudinal study of women who graduated from Mills College in Oakland, California, in 1960, Klohnen and Bera (1998) found that women who classified themselves as avoidant at age 52 had also reported greater conflict in the home 30 years earlier at age 21.

Attachment styles exert important influences on people's behavior within intimate relationships (Collins & Feeney, 2000; Feeney & Collins, 2001; Rholes, Simpson, & Orina, 1999; Simpson, Ickes, & Grich, 1999; Simpson, Rholes, & Phillips, 1996). In one imaginative study, Chris Fraley and Phil Shaver (1998) surreptitiously observed romantic partners as they said good-bye in airports. Afterward, they had the romantic partners fill out attachment questionnaires. Avoidant partners sought less physical contact and engaged in fewer embraces and less hand-holding as they departed from one another. Anxious individuals, on the other hand, expressed greater fear and sadness.

In self-report studies, secure individuals were more likely to report that their partners and friends were more forthcoming in offering support than did anxious and avoidant individuals (Florian, Mikulincer, & Bucholtz, 1995). Secure individuals also tended to interpret their partners' negative behavior—for example, criticism or insensitivity—in a more positive fashion than did either anxious or avoidant individuals (Collins, 1996).

In light of the these findings, you might expect that a secure attachment style would predict more positive life outcomes. And indeed, you would be right (for example, Cooper, Shaver, & Collins, 1998). Compared to those with different attachment styles, secure individuals report the greatest relationship satisfaction (Shaver & Brennan, 1992). In the four-year longitudinal study we described earlier, secure individuals were less likely to have experienced a romantic breakup (25.6 percent) over the four-year period under study than avoidant individuals (52.2 percent) or anxious individuals (43.6 percent). In the Mills College study, secure individuals were more likely to be married at age 52 than were avoidant individuals (82 percent versus 50 percent) and to report fewer marital tensions. Moreover, several studies have uncovered more general life problems associated with an anxious attachment style (Mikulincer & Shaver, 2003). Anxiously attached individuals are more likely to interpret life events in pessimistic, threatening fashion, which increases the chances of depression. They are also more likely to suffer from eating disorders, maladaptive drinking, and substance abuse, in part to reduce their distress and anxiety.

"O.K., step away from the laptop and hold up your end of the conversation."

Finally, experimental evidence indicates that when people are made to think about secure attachments when they are in threatening situations, this opens them up to be more trusting in relationships in general. You can prime secure attachment processes through the power of thought. Mario Mikulincer, of Bar-Ilan University, in Israel, and his colleagues have presented participants with words related to secure attachments—for example, "hug" and "love." These security-related words, even when presented below the participants' awareness, led the participants to be less prejudicial toward outgroups after feeling threatened (Mikulincer & Florian, 2000) and to be more altruistic toward others (Mikulincer, Gillath, & Shaver, 2002).

Anxious Attachment Attachment styles influence how people behave with intimate others. Avoidant partners are likely to avoid physical contact and leave each other quickly. Clearly, that is not the case with this couple. A better bet is that they both enjoy more secure attachment styles, comfortable in closeness and contact.

The story we have told here about attachment applies mostly to modern Western cultures (Morelli & Rothbaum, 2008). In cultures that place less value on autonomy, there may be much less fearless exploration of the environment by infants who are left in a room without their mothers, and the reunion with the mother may be much more turbulent. This should not be taken to imply that such children are insecurely attached. It should be taken to mean instead that they are being socialized to be interdependent with others, especially with family members.

Relationships and the Sense of Self

Attachment theory is an account of how your sense of others originates in the early patterns of your relationships with your parents. Susan Andersen and Serena Chen have offered a fascinating account of the very process by which our relationships shape our sense of self, fittingly called **relational self theory** (Andersen & Chen, 2002). They argue that an important part of the self-concept is the **relational self**, which refers to the beliefs, feelings, and expectations about ourselves that derive from our relationships with significant others in our lives. The relational selves that derive from our relationships with our parents, our romantic partners, our friends, and authority figures may well be different. When we encounter someone who reminds us of a significant other, a specific relational self is activated, along with associated feelings, beliefs, and self-evaluations, which then shape our interactions with that new individual, often outside of our awareness. For example, your mother may have always been critical of your efforts and accomplishments. Around her, your relational self would be defined by a sense of inadequacy and feelings of shame. When you encounter someone who reminds you of your mother—say, a supervisor at work or a traffic court judge—these beliefs, feelings, and interaction patterns will likely be transferred to that person and will shape the content of the new relationship.

To document how past relationships shape our current beliefs, feelings, and interactions, Andersen and her colleagues developed the following experimental technique. In a pretest session, participants first write down 14 descriptive sentences about a positive significant other—namely, someone they like and feel close to—and a negative significant other—namely, someone they don't like and want to avoid. Most typically, participants write about parents and, secondarily, siblings and friends. Two weeks later, participants engage in a study of acquaintanceship with another participant, who actually does not exist, but is purported to be in another room. Participants are given a description of this other person that either resembles the participant's own positive or negative significant other or, in a control condition, the positive or negative significant other of another participant. To what extent do our relationships with significant others transfer to new people who resemble that person? A great deal, as we will see.

First of all, interacting with someone who resembles a significant other alters our working self-concept—that is, how we think about ourselves in the current moment. In one study, after describing a significant other, participants wrote down 20 sentences that described what they were like with that person (Hinkley & Andersen, 1996). Two weeks later, participants were exposed to descriptions of a new person who resembled their significant other or someone else's, and they then wrote 14 statements describing themselves. Participants exposed to a new person reminiscent of their significant other were more likely to describe themselves in terms that resembled what they are like with that significant other than were participants in the control condition. For example, if a participant listed traits like "silly" and "irreverent" when describing what she was like with her father, these traits were more likely to appear in her self-description two weeks later after simply encountering someone who reminded her of her father. Thus, encountering people who remind us of significant others alters how we think about ourselves in the current situation, often at an automatic level, shaping the more immediate, accessible thoughts we have about ourselves.

Encountering people who remind us of significant others also shapes our emotional lives (Baldwin, 1994; Baldwin & Holmes, 1987; Collins & Read, 1994). To examine this claim, Andersen and her colleagues assessed participants' facial expressions as

relational self theory A theory that examines how prior relationships shape our current beliefs, feelings, and interactions vis-à-vis people who remind us of significant others from our past.

relational self The beliefs, feelings, and expectations that we have about ourselves that derive from our relationships with significant others in our lives.

Relational Self Theory and Transference Phenomena
Sometimes a new person resembles a significant other from our past, which affects how we react to him or her. When George W. Bush met Vladimir Putin for the first time, he reported that he looked into Putin's eyes and saw he could trust him. Is it possible that Bush saw in Putin a reminder of some person who was generally seen as threatening but was personally reasonable in his dealings with Bush?

they were exposed to information about a new person who resembled either a positive or a negative significant other (Andersen, Reznik, & Manzella, 1996). Those participants who read about someone who resembled a positive significant other as compared to a negative significant other expressed more positive emotion as judged by their facial expressions, and they liked the new person more. In a similar vein, Mark Baldwin and colleagues found that graduate students at the University of Michigan felt less confident about their research ideas after being subliminally primed with a photograph of a powerful authority figure in their department, Robert Zajonc, looking stern and disapproving (Baldwin, Carrell, & Lopez, 1990). Our significant others profoundly shape how we feel about ourselves and our most significant endeavors.

gut feelings

These findings reveal to what degree significant others influence our current emotions. They may also account for the gut feelings we have about other people—that is, when we simply feel good or bad about someone for no explicable reason. Perhaps the new person resembles someone significant in our lives, good or bad, and we transfer our feelings about our significant other onto the new person. Our leaders are not immune to these transference phenomena. President Harry S. Truman is said to have trusted Joseph Stalin at first because, although Truman knew him to be a wicked man in many respects, he reminded Truman of "Boss Pendergast" of the Missouri

---

FIGURE 11.2 Scientific Method: The Relational Self and Interactions with Others

Hypothesis: Interactions with people who remind us of positive significant others increase our positive emotion.

Research Method:

1 Participants first wrote about a positive or negative significant other. They then interacted with someone who reminded them of a positive or negative significant other in their own lives, or someone else's significant other.

2 The researchers then coded those interactions for the amount of positive emotion shown by the new interaction partner.

Results: The new interaction partner expressed more positive emotion toward the participant when he or she reminded the participant of a positive significant other in the participant's own life.

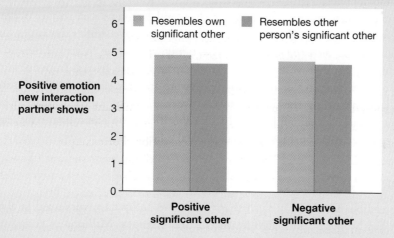

Conclusion: New interaction partners are more likely to express positive emotion toward us when they remind us of positive significant others.

Source: Anderson, Reznik, & Manzella (1996).

Democratic machine—a man who was thoroughly corrupt but always aboveboard in his dealings with Truman.

The relational self not only activates specific self-beliefs and emotions; it also shapes our current interactions. In one illustrative study, participants, whom we'll call perceivers, interacted with another participant, whom we'll call the target (Berk & Andersen, 2000). In the usual fashion, the experimenter manipulated whether the target resembled a positive or negative significant other of the perceiver. Participants liked a new person who resembled a positive significant other more than a person who resembled a negative significant other or other people's significant others, and the well-liked new person was more likely to show positive emotion toward the participant, as you can see in **Figure 11.2**. The process seems to be: (1) the target reminds me of good old X, (2) I therefore like the target, (3) so I express positive affect toward the target, and (4) as a consequence, the target expresses positive affect toward me.

Clearly, one message from this research on the relational self is that we should try to surround ourselves with people who remind us of positive individuals in our lives. We should also be wary of our immediate, gut dislikes of people, for those reactions may have more to do with previous relationships than with the new person in our life. The broader lesson is that our relationships with significant others can shape our emotions, our self-evaluations, and our behavior in new relationships.

 We have seen that our way of relating to our intimate others has origins in our early bonds with our parents. This attachment exerts considerable effects on our current relationships, on how we act toward others and appraise events within our relationships, and on our personal well-being. The more secure our attachment style, the healthier our relationships and lives tend to be. Our sense of self, or relational self, shifts according to whether the people around us remind us of positive or negative significant others.

DIFFERENT WAYS OF RELATING TO OTHERS

Thus far, we have seen that relationships are essential to our well-being and that our early attachments to significant others lay a foundation for how we eventually relate to others as adults, how we think of ourselves, and even how well we fare in life. You may be wondering, though, whether all relationships have similar dynamics, similar emotions and patterns of interaction. Certainly, we behave in very different ways, depending on whether we are with a new romantic partner, friends from our ultimate frisbee team, a minister or rabbi, or supervisors at work (Fiske, 1992; Moskowitz, 1994). Understanding the distinctions between different kinds of relationships is the task of this section, and we will focus specifically on communal relationships, exchange-based relationships, and hierarchical relationships.

Communal and Exchange Relationships

The incredible economic growth that China and India have witnessed in the past decade has brought about significant cultural changes. Millions of young people have left their villages, boarded trains, and moved to the large cities that have mushroomed in these new economic superpowers. A quiet village life of friends and family has been replaced by one of long work hours and urban living. How might we think about these changes in psychological terms? Margaret Clark and Judson Mills have an answer, and it is based on their notion that there are two fundamentally different types of relationships—communal relationships and exchange relationships—that arise in different contexts and are governed by different norms (Clark, 1992; Clark and Mills, 1979, 1993).

Communal relationships tend to be long-term bonds in which the individuals feel a special responsibility for one another. Communal relationships are based on a sense of sameness and family-like sharing of common identity (Fiske, 1992). People in communal relationships, such as close friends, come to resemble one another in the timing of their laughter and their specific emotional experiences. In communal relationships, individuals give and receive according to the principle of need—that is, according to who has the most pressing need at any given moment in time. Clear examples of communal relationships are relations between family members and between close friends—the kinds of relationships that are the social fabric of communal life in small villages. Children who take care of their elderly parents do so simply because their parents need help, not because they expect a benefit in return (although those who anticipate a sizable inheritance may do so more diligently than those who do not!).

Exchange relationships, by contrast, tend to be short-term, trading-based relationships in which individuals feel no responsibility toward one another. In exchange relationships, giving and receiving are governed by concerns about equity (that you get what you put into the relationship) and reciprocity (that what you give is returned in kind). Examples of exchange relationships include interactions between strangers, new acquaintances, a student working for a professor, or workers working for an employer in a factory or an organization.

Clark and Mills have relied on two different methods to show how communal and exchange relationships differ. In one method, they compare the behavior of friends (who are more likely to have a communal relationship) with the behavior of mere acquaintances (who are more likely to approach one another with an exchange orientation). With the other method, they experimentally manipulate the communal versus exchange status of the relationship by varying the motives of the individuals in their experiments. In the communal condition, participants hear about another participant in the study (the target person), who is described as a new transfer student who has signed up for the experiment in the hope of meeting people. This is designed to make the participants want a communal relationship with the target person. In the exchange condition, participants are told that the target person has been at the university for two years and signed up for the experiment because it was a convenient time for her husband to pick her up afterward. This is designed to encourage the participants to keep things on an exchange basis with the target person.

Using these two methods, Clark and Mills have documented that communal and exchange relationships operate according to much different principles. In communal relationships, people are more likely to keep track of each other's needs. Thus, in one study, one participant completed a task in which she formed four-letter words out of letters

communal relationships Relationships in which the individuals feel a special responsibility for one another and give and receive according to the principle of need; such relationships are often long-term.

exchange relationships Relationships in which the individuals feel little responsibility toward one another and in which giving and receiving are governed by concerns about equity and reciprocity; such relationships are often short-term.

"O.K., who else has experienced the best-friend relationship as inadequate?"

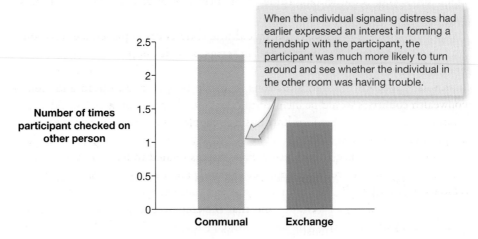

When the individual signaling distress had earlier expressed an interest in forming a friendship with the participant, the participant was much more likely to turn around and see whether the individual in the other room was having trouble.

FIGURE 11.3 Sensitivity to Others' Needs in Exchange and Communal Relationships Participants completed a word formation task with another individual (the experimenter's accomplice) who was in another room and who signaled difficulties with the task by turning on a red light that flashed behind the back of the real participant. (Source: Clark, Mills, & Powell, 1986.)

provided by the experimenter while another participant (actually an accomplice of the experimenter) worked on a similar but more difficult task in an adjacent room (Clark, Mills, & Powell, 1986). When the task was too difficult for the participant (the accomplice) next door, she was to signal her need for help to the real participant by turning on a red light, which the participant needed to turn around to see. As you can see in **Figure 11.3**, participants in the communal condition (interacting with someone who had expressed an interest in meeting people) turned around to check in on the other "participant" almost twice as often as participants in the exchange condition (interacting with someone who had not expressed an interest in friendship). If you're in need, you're best served by having friends around, a theme further discussed in Chapter 13.

In exchange relationships, people are concerned about their own and the other person's contributions to any joint effort and how to reward those inputs accordingly. This would make sense if people in exchange relationships were concerned with equity; they would want to make sure that their inputs corresponded to the outputs they received. Since individuals in communal relationships are governed by considerations of need, they should be less concerned with whether their own and their partner's respective contributions are similar. In a test of this hypothesis, Clark and Mills told their participants that they would take part in a visual-search task, in which they and another participant (the accomplice) would search a large matrix of numbers for specified sequences and circle them. They would receive a reward based on the number of sequences they each circled. After the experimental manipulation designed to activate communal or exchange orientations (in which the accomplice did or did not express an interest in meeting someone new), researchers gave the participant the matrix with several numbers circled by the other "participant" in the other room. The dependent measure of interest was whether the real participant would choose a pen having the same color ink or one having a different color to circle numbers. As expected, in the exchange condition, participants were much more likely than those in the communal condition to choose a different color ink, to ensure that their unique contribution would be known and rewarded (Clark, 1984; Clark, Mills, & Powell, 1986). Communally oriented participants, by contrast, were less concerned about being sure that their efforts were rewarded according to the principle of equity (that their inputs matched the rewards they got).

Clark and Mills' work sheds light on cultural differences in patterns of relationships. First, societies differ a great deal in terms of which approach they prefer in general. People in East Asian and Latin American societies are inclined to take a communal approach to many situations in which people in European and Commonwealth countries would be inclined to take an exchange approach. Consider the question, raised in Chapter 1, of how businesspeople would treat an employee who had put in 15 good years of service but over the past year had fallen down on the job and showed little chance of recovering. East Asians tended to feel that there was a company obligation to treat the employee as family and to keep him on the payroll. Western businesspeople were more likely to feel that the relationship was a purely contractual, or exchange-based, one and that the employee should be let go. There are differences among Western nations, however, with people from Catholic countries more likely to take a communal stance than people from Protestant countries. Indeed, even within the United States, Catholics are more likely to take a communal stance in relationship matters than are Protestants (Sanchez-Burks, 2002, 2004; Sanchez-Burks, Nisbett, & Ybarra, 2000).

Power and Hierarchical Relationships

In writing about power in the 1930s, with the threat of Nazism looming large, the English philosopher Bertrand Russell stated: "The fundamental concept in social science is Power, in the same sense that Energy is the fundamental concept in physics. . . . The laws of social dynamics are laws which can only be stated in terms of power." What Russell was claiming is that all relationships are shaped by concerns over power—who is in control and who is not. At the office and in the board meeting, power is at play as colleagues jockey for status. In the family, adolescents and parents clash over their different values. Even young siblings spend a good deal of their time in struggles over power, ultimately finding separate niches to develop in distinct ways (see Chapter 3).

In a culture that values egalitarianism, as in the United States or Canada, Bertrand Russell's view that all relationships are governed by power dynamics may seem a gross exaggeration. Yet the recent study of power is revealing power to be more important to relationships than Americans and Canadians would like to believe. Starting as early as age 2, people arrange themselves into social hierarchies, with some individuals occupying higher positions than others. Within a day or so, young adults within groups agree about who has high status and who has low status (Anderson, John, Keltner, & Kring, 2001). Power struggles are evident even in romantic relationships and the parent-child relationship (Bugental & Lewis, 1999). Power, indeed, is a basic force in human relationships.

If you scrutinize social relationships carefully, you quickly realize how pervasive the effects of power are. Power influences the way we speak: low-power individuals generally speak politely, making requests indirectly or by asking vague questions, whereas high-power individuals generally speak forcefully and directly, asking pointed questions and issuing commands (Brown & Levinson, 1987). Power influences how we look at each other (Dovidio, Brown, Heltman, Ellyson, & Keating, 1988; Dovidio, Ellyson, Keating, Heltman, & Brown, 1988): high-power individuals look at listeners when speaking and are looked at when speaking, whereas low-power individuals look away when speaking but look at others when listening (Ellyson & Dovidio, 1985). Power even shapes the way we dress. For example, it

"The fundamental concept in social science is Power, in the same sense that Energy is the fundamental concept in physics. . . . The laws of social dynamics are laws which can only be stated in terms of power."

—Bertrand Russell

"You see what power is— holding someone else's fear in your hand and showing it to them!"

—Amy Tan

is common practice for more senior medical doctors to wear longer white lab coats than more junior doctors.

So far, we have characterized power in general terms, but now we need to deal with three fundamental questions concerning power and hierarchical relations: What is power? Where does it come from? And how does power influence behavior?

What Is Power? **Power** is typically defined as the ability to control our own outcomes and those of others and the freedom to act (S. Fiske, 1993; Kelley & Thibaut, 1978). Power is related to status, authority, and dominance, but it is not synonymous with them. **Status** is the outcome of an evaluation of attributes that produces differences in respect and prominence, which in part determines an individual's power within a group (French & Raven, 1959; Kemper, 1991). But it is possible to have power without status (for example, the corrupt politician) and status without relative power (for example, a religious leader in a slow-moving line at the Department of Motor Vehicles). **Authority** is power that derives from institutionalized roles or arrangements (Weber, 1947). Nonetheless, power can exist in the absence of formal roles (for example, within social groups). **Dominance** is behavior that has the acquisition or demonstration of power as its goal. Yet, power can be attained without performing acts of dominance (as in the case of leaders who attain their positions through their cooperative and fair-minded style).

Where Does Power Come From? How do people attain their positions within social hierarchies? This question may be of interest to you, particularly in light of the many advantages that people in the upper echelons enjoy. For example, as you rise in rank in terms of socioeconomic status (SES)—that is, your level of education and wealth—you are less likely to suffer from depression and anxiety, and you are more likely to enjoy improved health and a greater life expectancy (Adler et al., 1994; Williams & Collins, 1995). As it turns out, the sources of power vary, which is why you might feel powerful in certain contexts and relatively weak in others.

At the interpersonal level, power within a group can originate from five different sources (French & Raven, 1959). Power can derive from *authority*, based on the roles within the group. This is true in formal hierarchies, such as the workplace, as well as in informal hierarchies, such as family structures in cultures that have historically given older siblings elevated power vis-à-vis younger siblings (Sulloway, 1996). Power can derive from *expertise*, based on knowledge. A medical doctor wields power over her patients because of her specialized knowledge and experience. Power can derive from *coercion*, based on the ability to use force and aggression. Power can stem from the ability to provide *rewards* to others. This helps explain why members of elevated socioeconomic status often wield power over those of lower socioeconomic status (Domhoff, 1998). It explains why majority group members are generally more powerful than minority group members (Brewer, 1979; Ng, 1980). And it explains why ethnic and gender background matter in terms of the power of white men over black men and the power of men over women (Sidanius, 1993). Finally, power derives from the ability to serve as a role model, which is known as *reference power*. This is likely to contribute to the power that resident assistants generally have over the students they oversee in college dormitories.

What kinds of individuals rise in social hierarchies independent of their authority or expertise or reference power or ability to provide resources and rewards to others. What's your intuition here? Who tends to rise in rank? Is it survival of the fittest? The strongest? The most cunning? The influential Italian philosopher Niccolò Machiavelli certainly had his own hypotheses. His thesis was that the acquisition and maintenance

power The ability to control our own outcomes and those of others; the freedom to act.

status The outcome of an evaluation of attributes that produces differences in respect and prominence, which in part determines an individual's power within a group.

authority Power that derives from institutionalized roles or arrangements.

dominance Behavior that has the acquisition or demonstration of power as its goal.

Power and Intimidation High-power individuals often feel less constrained by social rules about appropriate behavior than do low-power individuals. Lyndon Johnson approaches Senator Theodore Green more closely than is socially acceptable, touches his arm, and leans in close to his face as he seeks to intimidate him into voting the way Johnson wants him to.

of power is founded on the pursuit of Machiavellian strategies—to be deceptive, to ruthlessly pit competitors against one another to establish one's own power, and to lead by fear and manipulation rather than affection and honesty (Machiavelli, 1532/2003).

It turns out that this Machiavellian line of reasoning is dead wrong. It also flies in the face of recent evolutionary analyses of power, which hold that as the social intelligence of hominids expanded, group members developed the increasing capacity to form alliances (for example, Boehm, 1999; Keltner, van Kleef, Chen, & Kraus, 2008; de Waal, 1986). The ability for subordinates to form alliances radically shifted the dynamics of how to gain and maintain power: alpha males and females could no longer simply use physical strength to overpower subordinates; instead, they needed to build strong bonds with other group members to maintain their positions of elevated rank amid shifting alliances of subordinates. Power became more a matter of social engagement—creating rapport, resolving conflicts, building cooperative bonds—than brute force.

Consistent with this line of thinking, it is the chimpanzees and bonobos who build strong alliances, negotiate conflicts between subordinates, and maintain just allocations of resources who acquire and maintain elevated positions of rank in primate hierarchies (de Waal, 1986). A similar story emerges in studies of human hierarchies. For example, in a study of how children sort themselves into hierarchies at a summer camp, Savin-Williams (1977) found that it was the more socially dynamic, outgoing children who rose to positions of leadership. In a study of a fraternity, it was the more dynamic, playful members who were found to have elevated peer-rated power within the fraternity (Keltner, Young, Heerey, Oemig, & Monarch, 1998). In studies of hierarchies in dorms and social groups on college campuses, it is the highly extraverted individuals, who are socially engaged and relationship builders, who quickly gain respect and status from their peers (Anderson, Keltner, John, & Kring, 2001). And in the workplace, highly extraverted individuals tend to acquire positions of leadership (Judge, Bono, Ilies, & Gerhardt, 2002), with emotionally intelligent individuals— those who can read the moods and needs of others—making more effective managers (Côté & Miners, 2006). Thus, the evidence seems pretty clear. Power goes to the most socially engaged, cooperative, and emotionally intelligent, not the most Machiavellian.

How Does Power Influence Behavior? The findings that we have just reviewed— that people who are socially engaged, extraverted, and emotionally intelligent rise in

BOX 11.2 **FOCUS ON BUSINESS**

Power, Profligacy, and Accountability

In 2001 and 2002, Enron, the energy-trading company based in Houston, Texas, collapsed in spectacular fashion. Once one of the most lauded companies in the world, it proceeded to lose billions of dollars in stockholders' assets and had to lay off thousands of workers, in large part due to fraudulent accounting practices. Most emblematic of the Enron managers who exhibited corruption, greed, and immorality was Jeffrey Skilling.

Fresh from earning an MBA from Harvard University, Skilling was hired at Enron and saw himself as the company visionary, specializing in creating energy markets. He was aggressive, brash, and out of control. He would shout profanities at financial analysts who questioned his proposals. He took his favorite employees on outrageous vacations—in one, he and his friends trashed expensive SUVs in the Australian outback. He frequented Enron parties with strippers and eventually divorced his wife to marry his secretary, whom he quickly promoted to a new job with an annual salary of $600,000. He had difficulties with alcohol. Eventually, it was his reckless, deceptive business practices that fueled the Enron demise.

One way to understand the Enron collapse is to think about the context that gave rise to its reckless culture and often illegal investment style. It is a lesson about the perils of unchecked power. This story fits what we have learned about the disinhibiting effects of power. Another approach is to think about how people who actively seek out, desire, and express their power might be more likely to act in such out-of-control fashion. This was the tack taken by David Winter and his colleagues. They investigated the correlates of the need for power, which was measured from people's interpretations of the ambiguous social situations portrayed in Thematic Apperception Test scenes (Winter, 1973, 1988; Winter & Barenbaum, 1985). They found that college students who need a lot of power are more likely to hold offices in their dorms, fraternities, and university organizations; they are more likely to seek high-power careers—for example, in the law; and they are more likely to engage in profligate, disinhibited behaviors reminiscent of Jeffrey Skilling's reckless actions. They are more likely to gamble, drink, and seek one-night stands.

Winter and his colleagues also documented an important factor that constrains the disinhibiting effects of power: accountability. Accountability refers to the condition in which one individual feels responsible to others. When individuals who have a high need for power experience accountability-enhancing life events—for example, having children—they are less likely to engage in profligate behaviors like gambling or drinking.

---

social hierarchies—may have left you scratching your head. Much of human history, it would seem, is defined by astonishing abuses of power. What about the horrifying genocides perpetrated by despotic leaders—the likes of Hitler, Stalin, Mao tse-tung, Pol-Pot, and Saddam Hussein? What about the impulsive actions of so many leaders—President Kennedy's Bay of Pigs invasion, Bill Clinton's reputation-ruining affair with intern Monica Lewinsky? What about the sometimes outrageous excesses of Hollywood stars and executives alike (see **Box 11.2**)? This impulsive, even immoral side to power is reflected in time-honored sayings: "Power corrupts." "Money [a source of power] is the root of all evil." And it begs for a social psychological explanation.

approach/inhibition theory A theory that states that higher-power individuals are inclined to go after their goals and make quick judgments, whereas low-power individuals are more likely to constrain their behavior and attend to others carefully.

A recent theoretical formulation known as the **approach/inhibition theory** of power offers one account of how power influences behavior in this fashion (Keltner, Gruenfeld, & Anderson, 2003; Keltner et al., 2008). As you have learned, elevated power is defined by the sense of control, the freedom to do whatever you wish, and the lack of social constraint. As a consequence, the theory goes, when you experience elevated power, you should be less concerned about the evaluations of others and more inclined to engage in approach-related behavior to satisfy your goals and desires (for example, Guinote, 2007). In contrast, reduced power is associated with increased threat from others, punishment, and social constraint. As a result, experiencing reduced power should make you more vigilant and careful in social judgment and more inhibited in social behavior. Experiences of elevated power, in effect, give the green light to the unbridled pursuit of our goals and desires.

This approach/inhibition theory of power translates into two hypotheses. The first concerns the influence of power on how people perceive other individuals. High-power individuals, inclined to go after their own goals, should be a little less systematic and careful in how they judge other people (Brauer, Chambres, Niedenthal, & Chatard-Pannetier, 2004; S. Fiske, 1993; Vescio, Snyder, & Butz, 2003). In keeping with this hypothesis, high-power individuals are more likely to thoughtlessly stereotype others, rather than carefully attending to individuating information (S. Fiske, 1993; Goodwin, Gubin, Fiske, & Yzerbyt, 2000; Neuberg & Fiske, 1987; see also Vescio, Snyder, & Butz, 2003).

Members of powerful groups have an increased tendency to stereotype as well. Sidanius and Pratto have found that **social dominance orientation**—the desire to see one's own group dominate other groups—is more strongly endorsed by individuals associated with more powerful groups (Pratto, 1996; Sidanius, 1993). These include men as compared with women, European-Americans as compared with African-Americans, and individuals in hierarchy-enhancing careers (for example, the police) as compared with hierarchy-attenuating careers (for example, social workers). Measures of social dominance, in turn, correlate with increased stereotyping and prejudice. Just being a member of a more powerful group, it would seem, inclines a person to stereotype others.

Predisposed to rely on stereotypes, high-power individuals should judge others' attitudes and emotions in less accurate fashion. A study of the attitudes and judgments of more powerful, tenured college professors and their less powerful, untenured colleagues confirmed this prediction (Keltner & Robinson, 1996, 1997). The high-power professors judged the attitudes of the less powerful, untenured colleagues less accurately than did the low-power professors. In a similar vein, power differences may account for the tendency of males to be slightly less accurate than females in judging expressive behavior (Henley & LaFrance, 1984; LaFrance, Henley, Hall, & Halberstadt, 1997; but see also Hall, 1984). Power may even be at work in the striking finding that younger siblings, who experience reduced power vis-à-vis older siblings, outperform their older siblings on theory-of-mind tasks, which assess the ability to construe correctly the intentions and beliefs of others (Jenkins & Asington, 1996; Perner, Ruffman, & Leekam, 1994; see Chapter 1).

Perhaps the most dramatic demonstration of the extent to which power reduces the ability to accurately perceive others has been provided by Joseph Magee and his colleagues (Magee, Galinsky, Inesi, & Gruenfeld, 2006). These investigators first induced people to feel powerful or to feel powerless by having them recall a time when they exerted control over another person or when they were controlled by someone else. Participants then performed a simple perspective-taking task: they were asked to draw an "E" on their forehead so that someone across from them could read it. What this requires is that the participant take the perspective of the other person and draw the "E" in reverse. As you can see in **Figure 11.4**, participants feeling the surges of power were much less likely to spontaneously draw the "E" in a way that took the other person's perspective. Power reduces the ability to empathize.

These power-related influences on social perception have unfortunate consequences. Theresa Vescio and her colleagues, for example, have found that powerful men who stereotyped female employees by focusing exclusively on their weaknesses devoted few resources to those employees (Vescio, Gervais, Snyder, & Hoover, 2005), evaluated female employees more negatively in a masculine context, and anticipated less success for the female employees relative to others (Vescio, Snyder, & Butz, 2003). In a similar vein, the experience of power leads high-prejudice whites to focus to

social dominance orientation The desire to see one's own group dominate other groups.

"Power is the ultimate aphrodisiac."

—Henry Kissinger

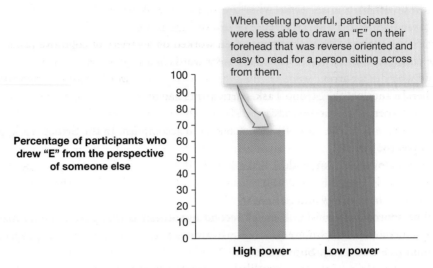

When feeling powerful, participants were less able to draw an "E" on their forehead that was reverse oriented and easy to read for a person sitting across from them.

Percentage of participants who drew "E" from the perspective of someone else

FIGURE 11.4 Power and Empathy Failures Power diminishes our capacity to take the perspective of others. (Source: Magee, Galinsky, Inesi, & Gruenfeld, 2006.)

a greater extent on the weaknesses of black employees relative to other employees (Vescio et al., 2006). (For an exercise on observing power differences, see **Figure 11.5**)

Are there costs to the heightened vigilance that low-power people demonstrate as they carefully attend to others? Indeed there are. The experience of reduced power makes people less flexible in their thought and less able to shift their attention to meet different demands of the task at hand (Smith & Trope, 2006). For example, in a series of studies, Pamela Smith and her colleagues induced people to feel elevated power

---

FIGURE 11.5 You Be the Subject: Power Differences

Make careful observations in a situation where there are power differences. For example, it might be in a dorm room where there are higher- and lower-status friends. Or it could be on a class project, where one person acts as leader. Or it might be at work.

Look for postural cues (expanded chest, arms akimbo, slumping shoulders), hesitations during speech, eye contact (how much the person looks away while speaking, a sign of low power), and who interrupts whom.

Note the markers of high power:

_____
_____
_____

Note the markers of low power:

_____
_____
_____

Results: If you looked carefully, you might have noticed classic signs of power. Certain behaviors are more likely to lead to gains in status in social groups, such as bringing people together, telling jokes, and proposing activities and collective behaviors. Other kinds of actions are more typical of people who feel they have a lot of power: interrupting, being impulsive, and having an inability to understand others. And still other behaviors are typical of people who feel they have little power: displaying inhibited postures, fearful expressions, and hesitations in speech.

or low power by priming them with low- or high-power words ("obey," "dominate") or having them recall an experience of low or high power (Smith, Jostmann, Galinsky, & van Dijk, 2008). Participants then worked on a variety of cognitive tasks. In one task, participants were flashed different words in a sequence and asked to determine whether a current word on the screen matched the word presented two trials earlier. In another, the Stroop Task, participants had to read the color name of a word ("Red") when it was presented in a different color (for example, in blue ink). These tasks require cognitive flexibility and control to accomplish. In the Stroop Task, for example, the participant must ignore the color of the ink when reading the word. As predicted, low-power individuals proved less effective in performing these cognitive tasks. The vigilant and narrowed focus of reduced power diminishes the individual's ability to think flexibly and creatively.

The approach/inhibition theory's second hypothesis is that power should make people behave in disinhibited (less constrained) and at times more inappropriate fashion (see Box 11.2). Support for this hypothesis is found in numerous studies. High-power individuals are more likely to touch others and approach them closely physically (Goffman, 1967; Henley, 1977; Heslin & Boss, 1980). People given power in an experiment are more likely to feel attraction to a random stranger (Bargh, Raymond, Pryor, & Strack, 1995), to turn off an annoying fan in the room where the experiment is being conducted (Galinsky, Gruenfeld, & Magee, 2003), and to flirt in overly direct ways (Rudman & Borgida, 1995).

In contrast, low-power individuals show inhibition of a wide variety of behaviors (for example, Guinote, Judd, & Brauer, 2002). Individuals with little power often constrict their posture (Ellyson & Dovidio, 1985), inhibit their speech (Holtgraves & Lasky, 1999; Hosman, 1989) and facial expressions (Keltner et al., 1998), and clam up and withdraw in group interactions (Moreland & Levine, 1989).

Perhaps most unsettling are studies showing that elevated power makes antisocial behavior more likely. For example, high-power individuals are more likely to violate politeness-related communication norms: they are more likely to interrupt, speak out of turn, and act rudely at work (DePaulo & Friedman, 1998; Pearson & Porath, 1999). Now consider a study in which two low-power fraternity members and two high-power members were brought to the laboratory and asked to tease each other by making up nicknames and telling amusing stories about one another (see **Figure 11.6**). Teasing is a way that group members socialize one another and teach each other the ropes about how to behave and a way that friends pass the time. And in this study, high-power fraternity members teased low-power targets in more aggressive and humiliating fashion, whereas low-power fraternity members were quite restrained in how they teased their high-power brothers (Keltner et al., 1998). Across a wide variety of contexts—school playgrounds, hospital settings, the workplace—high-power individuals are more likely to tease in hostile fashion (Keltner, Capps, Kring, Young, & Heerey, 2001).

Power disinhibits more harmful forms of aggression as well, leading to violent behavior against low-power individuals. For example, power asymmetries predict the increased likelihood of sexual harassment (Studd, 1996). The prevalence of rape rises with the cultural acceptance of male dominance and the subordination of females (Reeves-Sanday, 1997). The incidence of hate crimes against minority groups (that is, nonwhites) rises in direct relation to the numerical advantage (power) whites enjoy in a particular neighborhood vis-à-vis the minority members (Green, Wong, & Strolovitch, 1996).

We have not portrayed power in a flattering light. High-power individuals tend to act in overly direct, impulsive, and even aggressive fashion. This may help shed light

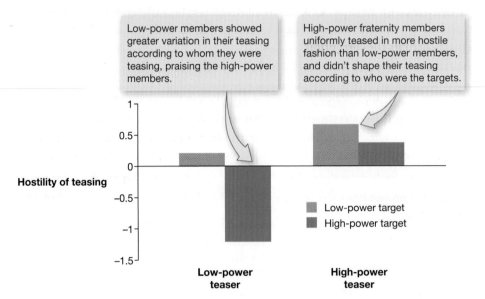

Low-power members showed greater variation in their teasing according to whom they were teasing, praising the high-power members.

High-power fraternity members uniformly teased in more hostile fashion than low-power members, and didn't shape their teasing according to who were the targets.

Hostility of teasing

■ Low-power target
■ High-power target

Low-power teaser   High-power teaser

FIGURE 11.6 An Approach/Inhibition Theory of Power and the Dynamics of Teasing   The approach/inhibition theory of power holds that high-power individuals are more impulsive in their behavior, whereas low-power individuals are more likely to inhibit their behavior and shift it according to social context. In this study, high- and low-power fraternity members teased each other in groups of four by making up nicknames about each other. (Source: Keltner, Young, Heerey, Oemig, & Monarch, 1998.)

on certain disturbing trends in society—the child abuse perpetrated by some Catholic priests, the excessive bonuses of CEOs while the company is going down the tubes. Such tendencies are all the more alarming when we consider the scrutiny to which people in power are subject and the influence they have over our lives.

What are we to do? Research suggests that we should be careful about who gains power, for power seems to allow individuals to express their true inclinations, both good and bad. If the person is inclined toward malevolent or competitive behavior, power will increase the likelihood of such behavior. If, on the other hand, the person is more good-natured, power will amplify the expression of those tendencies. In a study that nicely illustrates this claim, Serena Chen and her colleagues identified and preselected participants who were either more self-interested and exchange oriented or more compassionate and communal oriented (Chen, Lee-Chai, & Bargh, 2001). Each participant was then randomly assigned to a high-power or low-power position in a clever, subtle manner: high-power individuals were seated in a snazzy leather professorial chair during the experiment; low-power individuals were seated in a plain chair typical of psychology experiments. Participants were then asked to volunteer to complete a packet of questionnaires with the help of another participant, who was late. Consistent with the idea that power amplifies the expression of preexisting tendencies, the communal-oriented participants with high power took on the lion's share of filling out the questionnaires. In contrast, the exchange-oriented

"I'm not a machine, Deborah, I can't just turn my greed on and off."

participants with high power acted in more self-serving fashion, leaving more of the task for the other participant. The effects of power, then, depend on who is in power. Power corrupts the corruptible.

 We have considered the dynamics of three different kinds of relationships. In communal relationships, generally of long duration, people are concerned with each other's needs and are likely to help each other. Exchange relationships are governed by concerns over equity and are of short duration. We have also studied the dynamics of power relationships, looking at who gains power within social groups (the more socially engaged) and what power does to those individuals once they have it (it makes them less careful in social thought and more impulsive in social behavior).

ROMANTIC RELATIONSHIPS

Each year, 2.3 million couples wed in the United States (and roughly 90 percent of all North Americans marry). The typical cost of a wedding is about $20,000, which exceeds the life savings of the average American. Guest lists are negotiated, dresses fitted, invitations embossed and mailed, appetizers and music selected. What follows is a surreal day of rapturous emotion. The modern wedding ceremony is one of the most elaborate, expensive rituals in human history.

What brings two romantic partners together and leads them to the altar? It turns out that the reasons for marrying have varied dramatically across cultures and time (Coontz, 2005). In hunter-gatherer cultures, parents "married off" their children to members of other nearby tribes. This had the effect, whether intended or not, of ensuring more cooperative trading relationships between groups. For much of Western European history, marriages were arranged, again by parents, to consolidate ties with other families and to ensure that property and wealth stayed within families. And

Marriage across Cultures   Wedding ceremonies vary in the specifics but are practiced throughout different cultures. Here we see ceremonies in (A) Lapland, Scandinavia; (B) Gondar, Ethiopia; and (C) Shanghai, China.

triangular theory of love A theory that states that there are three major components of love—passion, intimacy, and commitment—which can be combined in different ways.

today, it is all about love. According to Robert Sternberg's **triangular theory of love**, young lovers stand at the altar, ready for one of life's great journeys, because of three magical elements: passion, intimacy, and commitment (Sternberg, 1986).

Early in the relationship, romantic partners experience intense, at times all-consuming feelings of passion, or sexual arousal, for each other. These feelings of passion are responsive to specific physical cues: beautiful skin, full lips, and warm, glistening eyes; physical signs of strength in men and youth and fecundity in women (Miller, 2000). These feelings of passion are registered in specific metaphors: the young lovers feel knocked off their feet, hungry for each other, mad with desire (Lakoff & Johnson, 1980). These metaphors speak to the singlemindedness and loss of control characteristic of early passion. These feelings of passion are registered in specific patterns of touch, cuddling, and sexual behavior and fluctuate for women with rising levels of certain sex hormones—estrogen in particular. They peak for both partners as the woman approaches ovulation (Konner, 2003). And importantly, this early passion is felt uniquely for a preferred romantic partner. Eli Finkel and colleagues have pioneered the speed-dating approach to the study of early desire (Finkel & Eastwick, 2008). In this imaginative research, a dozen or so young women and a dozen or so young men arrive at the lab and engage in a series of rapid-fire, 2-minute get-acquainted conversations with all the other members of the opposite sex. After each of these supercharged interactions, the participants rate their sexual desire and felt chemistry for one another. Finkel and colleagues have found that when one individual feels unique desire and chemistry for another, those feelings are reciprocated (Eastwick, Finkel, Mochon, & Ariely, 2007). Just as importantly, those speed daters who felt chemistry for many other people actually generated little desire or chemistry in their dating partners. Early passion needs to lock in on one person to set the stage for more enduring relationships. And apparently, people can detect whether interest is targeted or promiscuous.

Suvey studies indicate that with increasing time together, this kind of passion diminishes and a second element of the romantic relationship emerges—a deep sense of intimacy (Acevedo & Aron, 2009; Sprecher & Regan, 1998). The couple will feel comfort and security in the sense of being close, of knowing each other, of feeling their identities merge. As part of increasing intimacy, romantic partners will include their partner's perspectives, experiences, and characteristics into their own self-concept (Aron & Aron, 1997; Aron, Aron, & Allen, 1989; Aron & Fraley, 1999). In one relevant study, married couples first rated 90 trait adjectives for how accurately they described themselves and their spouse (Aron, Aron, Tudor, & Nelson, 1991). After a brief distracter task, participants viewed each trait on a computer screen and were asked to indicate as quickly as possible whether the trait was "like me" or "not like me." As you can see in **Figure 11.7**, participants were faster in identifying traits on which they were similar to their spouse and slower to ascribe traits to themselves that their partner did not also possess. Within increasing intimacy, it is as if the two partners become one.

Long-term relations are nothing without high levels of the dreaded "C" word—commitment—the third element of enduring love in Sternberg's theory (Frank, 1988; Gonzaga, Keltner, Londahl, & Smith, 2001). As their intimacy deepens, partners develop a sense of commitment to each other. A long-term commitment entails many sacrifices—the foregoing of other flirtations, relationships, and reproductive opportunities; the commitment of resources to each other; the pragmatic demands of coordinating two sets of interests, values, friends, career aspirations, and recreational and social preferences.

So let's go back to that wedding day. There our newlyweds stand, no doubt filled with consummate love and buoyed by visions of picket fences and barbecues, children

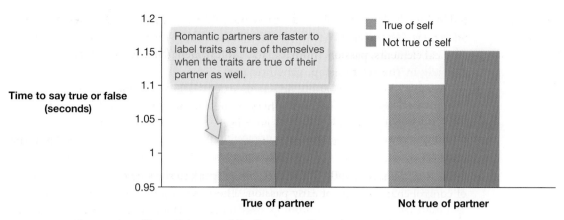

Romantic partners are faster to label traits as true of themselves when the traits are true of their partner as well.

FIGURE 11.7 Construing Close Others as We Construe Ourselves When we fall in love, do our identities merge with our romantic partners? As one way to answer this question, the Arons and their colleagues had romantic partners label traits as true or not true of the self. Some traits were also true of their partner; others were not. (Source: Adapted from Aron, Aron, Tudor, & Nelson, 1991.)

and grandchildren, family celebrations, soccer games, and going off into the sunset of life together. Regrettably, approximately 47 percent of those individuals who stand at the altar will become disillusioned, dissatisfied, and divorce, often within a year or two of their wedding day (Berscheid & Reis, 1998; Bradbury, 1998; Fincham, 2003; Hill & Peplau, 1998; Myers, 2000a). What determines which way a marriage will go—toward dissatisfaction and divorce or contentedness and happiness? What are the predictors of unhappy romantic relationships? And what makes for more satisfying romantic relationships? These questions are the focus of this last section of the chapter.

An Investment Model of Romantic Satisfaction

One useful way to understand why some long-term romantic relationships survive and others don't is provided by Caryl Rusbult in her **investment model of interpersonal relationships** (Rusbult, 1980, 1983). A flowchart of the investment model is presented in **Figure 11.8**. Once partners are in a long-term romantic bond, three ingredients make them more committed to each other: rewards, few alternative partners, and investments in the relationship. The first and most obvious determinant of enduring

investment model of interpersonal relationships A model of interpersonal relationships that maintains that three things make partners more committed to each other: rewards, few alternative partners, and investments in the relationship.

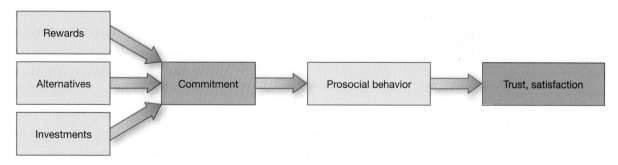

FIGURE 11.8 Rusbult's Investment Model of Romantic Commitment According to Rusbult's model, three factors determine how committed romantic partners are: how many rewards they derive from the relationship, the available romantic alternatives, and how much they have invested in the relationship. More committed partners, in turn, are more likely to engage in prosocial behavior, like forgiveness, and are more likely to feel trust and satisfaction in the bond.

commitment is *rewards*. Time after time, in questionnaires that ask romantic partners to rate the rewards they receive from their relationship as well as what they give, one of the strongest determinants of romantic satisfaction in long-term relationships is how much they get out of the relationship (Cate, Lloyd, Henton, & Larson, 1982). In fact, John Gottman, a leading marriage researcher, has argued that for long-term romantic relationships not to succumb to divorce, the rewarding positive experiences must outweigh the negative ones by a factor of 5 to 1 (Gottman, 1993).

Simple rewards, however, are not enough. Whether or not there are *alternative partners* also is a strong contributor to the enduring commitment a partner feels. The fewer alternatives a romantic partner has, the more committed, and the more likely the partner will remain in the relationship. For example, in questionnaire studies, romantic partners who report few alternative partners are less likely to break up later on (White & Booth, 1991). A person may stick with a relationship that is not terribly satisfying if it is the only game in town. In contrast, people sometimes leave gratifying relationships in pursuit of others that appear to be even more promising. (Think of the multiple marriages of the gorgeous movie star or the wealthy entrepreneur.)

The third determinant of commitment is the one that gives it its name: the *investments* that the couple has put into the relationship. Satisfaction and possible alternative partners aside, a person is more likely to remain in a relationship if he or she has invested heavily in it in the past. Investments can be direct, such as the time, effort,

---

TABLE 11.2 Measuring the Elements of the Commitment Model of Romantic Relationships

To assess how strong the bonds between romantic partners are, researchers ask the partners to respond to statements that reveal possible alternative romantic partners, investment in the relationship, commitment to the relationship, and satisfaction with the relationship.

Element of Model	Sample Item
Alternatives	"All things considered, how attractive are the people other than your partner with whom you could become involved?"
Rewards	"Are there special activities associated with your relationship that you would in some sense lose or that would be more difficult to obtain if the relationship were to end (for example, shared friends, child rearing, recreational activities, job)?"
Investments	"Have you devoted your time and effort and money to buying and improving the home you share, cultivating friendships, rearing children, or building a business together, which would be lost or damaged if the relationship were to end?"
Commitment	"For how much longer do you want your relationship to last?"
Satisfaction	"All things considered, to what degree do you feel satisfied with your relationship?"

Source: Adapted from Rusbult (1980).

BOX 11.3 **FOCUS ON DAILY LIFE**

Investment and the Return of the Battered Woman

One of the most telling studies of the predictive power of the investment model is one in which it was used to predict whether women who had sought shelter from abusive husbands would return to them (Rusbult & Martz, 1995). Some of the women returned to their husbands right away (defined as within three months), some only after an extended period (between three months and a year), and some never returned. Rusbult was interested in whether the investments these women had made in their relationships and the quality of the alternatives that were available to them would predict whether they would reconcile with their husbands. (Satisfaction level was anticipated to have little impact in this case, because, given the severity of the abuse these women had experienced, there was unlikely to be much satisfaction left for any of them.) As part of the standard admissions procedure in a battered women's shelter, the women were asked a number of questions that could serve as measures of investments (for example, duration of relationship, number of children) and alternatives (for example, independent income source, transportation available). Consistent with the investment model, measures of each of these constructs were related to whether and when the women returned to their abusive husbands. Women who were heavily invested in their relationship and who had limited opportunities for alternative arrangements were most likely to return.

caring, and love given to the relationship. Or they can be indirect, such as the shared memories, mutual friends, and shared possessions that are part of the relationship.

Empirical tests of Rusbult's investment model have typically had romantic partners report on the three determinants of their commitment (rewards, alternative partners, and investments), their level of commitment, and how satisfied they are in their relationship (see **Table 11.2**) every six months or so for a couple of years (Berg & McQuinn, 1986; Rusbult, 1983; Simpson, 1987). In this research, each of the three determinants of commitment—rewards, alternative possibilities, and investments—each predicts a couple's decision to stay or leave (see **Box 11.3**). And other studies find that more committed partners enjoy more satisfying and stable bonds. When asked to describe their relationship, the more-committed partners are more likely to use plural pronouns ("we") and are more likely to represent their own identity and that of their partner as overlapping (Agnew, Van Lange, Rusbult, & Langston, 1998). If you hear a new romantic interest of yours ask "What are we doing this weekend?" or "When will we apply to graduate school?," it's safe to assume that he or she feels committed to you. Commitment promotes a sense of merged identity.

Highly committed partners were found to be more likely to engage in prosocial behaviors, like self-sacrifice and accommodation, rather than retaliation, in the face of demands on the part of their partner (Wieselquist, Rusbult, Agnew, & Foster, 1999). For example, a more-committed married partner, in adjusting to the demands of a first child, would be more likely to adjust his or her personal life, sacrificing regular exercise at the gym, poker night with the boys, or two movies a week, so that the family thrives.

The research that Rusbult's model has inspired reveals the core elements of long-term commitment that predict gratifying and meaningful marriages: rewards, few alternative partners, and investments. This investment model provides a broad framework for understanding studies concerning the demise of romantic relationships and the dynamics that enable romantic partnerships to thrive. In these studies, researchers must do longitudinal research, as Rusbult has done, studying romantic partners for several years. Early in the study, they identify the process of interest—criticism or forgiveness, for example—and ascertain whether the early presence of that behavior, holding constant many other things, such as how satisfied the couple is to begin with, predicts how satisfied the relationship is years later. This new science of romantic relationships has revealed several clues to finding happiness in long-term romantic bonds.

Marital Dissatisfaction

Marriages are proving to be quite difficult these days. Approximately one-half of first marriages now end in separation or divorce (Martin & Bumpass, 1989; Myers, 2000a). Marital partners' self-reports indicate that marriages are less satisfying today than they were 30 years ago (Glenn, 1991; Myers, 2000a). Marital conflict stimulates adrenal and pituitary stress responses, which are known to cause cardiac problems and inhibit immune responses (Kiecolt-Glaser, Malarkey, Cacioppo, & Glaser, 1994). And now we are learning that there is a legacy of unhappy marriages. Children of divorced parents can experience greater personal and academic difficulties, both during childhood and later in adulthood (Amato & Keith, 1991;Wallerstein, Lewis, & Blakeslee, 2000). As we saw in the section on attachment, early divorce of parents is associated with an anxious attachment style in the child—a style that is associated with romantic and personal difficulties.

"I hope when I grow up I'll have an amicable divorce."

Given that romantic dissastisfaction is so widespread and has such far-reaching effects, learning what predicts romantic dissatisfaction and divorce is an important enterprise. Understanding what these factors are will help us get our romantic relationships right so that they are less likely to end in the loosening of romantic bonds and in divorce.

Neuroticism, Socioeconomic Status, and Age as Predictors of Dissatisfaction and Divorce One way to understand unhappy romantic bonds is to ask whether certain kinds of people or certain circumstances make marital dissatisfaction or divorce more likely. Does the kind of person you marry matter? What about their class background or age? To answer these questions, researchers relate measures of the partners' satisfaction (see Table 11.2) to measures of personality and background.

What we have learned is this. First, personality matters. Neurotic people, who tend to be anxious, tense, emotionally volatile, and plaintive, have less happy romantic relationships and are more likely to divorce (Karney & Bradbury, 1997; Karney, Bradbury, Fincham, & Sullivan, 1994; Kurdek, 1993). Highly neurotic individuals are more likely to experience negative emotion, to experience health problems (Watson & Pennebaker, 1989), and to react strongly to interpersonal conflict (Bolger & Schilling, 1991). All of these tendencies, within the framework of Rusbult's investment model, are likely to reduce the day-to-day rewards of the union and reduce partners' satisfaction and likelihood of staying together. For similar reasons, people who are highly sensitive to rejection have greater difficulties in intimate relationships (Downey & Feldman, 1996; Downey, Freitas, Michaelis, & Khouri, 1998; see also Murray, Holmes, MacDonald, & Ellsworth, 1998). Moreover, romantic partners and friends who are sensitive to rejection respond with greater hostility when feeling rejected by intimate others (Ayduk, Downey, Testa, Yen, & Shoda, 1999; Downey, Feldman, & Ayduk, 2000). And relationships in which both partners are sensitive to rejection are more likely to end sooner (Downey, Freitas, et al., 1998).

Certain demographic factors also predict problems in romantic relationships. Most notably, individuals from lower socioeconomic backgrounds are more likely to divorce (Williams & Collins, 1995). Socioeconomic status (SES) refers to the combination of your family's educational background, wealth, and occupational prestige. Being from a lower socioeconomic background is more likely to introduce into the relationship financial difficulties and the burdens of finding gratifying and stable work, which are some of the primary reasons why marriages break up (Berscheid & Reis, 1998). And quite obviously, not having economic resources is likely to diminish certain rewards in the couples' life—the ease with which they can go out to a nice dinner or enjoy a vacation, the kinds of opportunities and experiences they can readily provide to their children.

Finally, people who marry at younger ages are more likely to divorce. There are several possible explanations of this finding. It may be that younger people are not as effective at being partners in long-term romantic relations. Or people who marry young may not be as effective at choosing the right romantic partners. (It might be worth noting that although some species of penguins eventually "get married" to a lifetime partner, even the ones that do are quite fickle when young, bouncing from one relationship to another with abandon!)

The Four Horsemen of the Apocalypse Thus far, we have learned that certain people—those who are neurotic, from lower SES backgrounds, and young when married—have the odds stacked against them when they start their married life. As romantic partnerships mature, they are founded on conversations and emotional exchanges about parenting, children, finances, intimacy, and patterns of communication. Are there telltale signs in these patterns of communication that indicate that a couple will be headed for divorce or that a couple will remain happy together for the rest of their lives? To answer this question, John Gottman and Robert Levenson have pioneered the **interaction dynamics approach** to studying marriages, which identifies the specific emotions and patterns of communication that predict disatisfaction and divorce in both gay and heterosexual relationships (Levenson & Gottman, 1983; Gottman & Levenson, 1992).

Gottman and Levenson have studied married partners engaged in intense conversations, which are videotaped in the laboratory and then studied carefully for clues to romantic dissatisfaction. In a conflict discussion task, partners talk for 15 minutes about an issue that they both recognize is a source of intense conflict in their relationship, and they try their best to resolve it. For example, partners might talk about unsatisfying sex, the mountain of debt they are facing, the husband's inability to get better-paying work, or their child's difficulties in high school. Gottman and Levenson then code the interactions for anger, criticism, defensiveness, stonewalling, contempt, sadness, and fear, as well as several positive behaviors, including affection, enthusiasm, interest, and humor.

In one long-term study, starting in 1983 and continuing to this day, Gottman and Levenson have followed the marriages of 79 couples from Bloomington, Indiana. Based on their observations, they have identified "the Four Horsemen of the Apocalypse"—that is, the negative behaviors that are most harmful to relationships. One is *criticism*. A robust finding in the marriage literature is that, just as we would expect, more-critical partners who continually carp and find fault with their partners have less satisfying marriages.

interaction dynamics approach A methodological approach to the study of the behaviors and conversations of couples, with a focus on both negative behaviors (such as anger, criticism, defensiveness, contempt, sadness, and fear) and positive behaviors (such as affection, enthusiasm, interest, and humor).

The next two predictors of dissatisfaction and divorce are *defensiveness* and *stone-walling* (resisting dealing with problems). When romantic partners are unable to talk openly and freely about their difficulties without being defensive—refusing to consider the possibility that something they are doing might contribute to the conflict—they are in trouble. This is especially true of men. To the extent that the male partner stonewalls, withdraws, denies, and rejects the issues the female partner brings up, there is great dissatisfaction in the relationship. In contrast, the more partners disclose to each other, the more they tend to like each other (Collins & Miller, 1994).

Finally, there is one emotion that is particularly toxic to romantic bonds, and that is *contempt*. Contempt is the emotion felt when one person looks down on another. It has to do with rejection and feelings of superiority. You might feel contempt when you hear a person bragging to a group of friends and you know that what he is saying isn't true. In Gottman and Levenson's work, a wife's expression of contempt is especially predictive of dissatisfaction and divorce. In **Figure 11.9**, we present the frequency that contempt was observed for couples who eventually divorced and for those who did not (Gottman & Levenson, 1999). The couples who eventually divorced expressed more than twice as much contempt as the couples who stayed together.

It should be noted that the Gottman and Levenson studies are susceptible to a version of the self-selection problem we referred to at the outset of this chapter: Do married couples get divorced because they express contempt and other unpleasant emotions, or do they express these emotions because their relationship is on rocky

FIGURE 11.9 Scientific Method: Contempt and Marital Dissatisfaction

Hypothesis: Contempt and feelings of superiority harm intimate relationships.

Research Method:

1. Researchers coded facial expressions of contempt from a 15-minute conversation between married partners.

2. They then related the number of contempt expressions to the likelihood that the couple would eventually divorce or stay together.

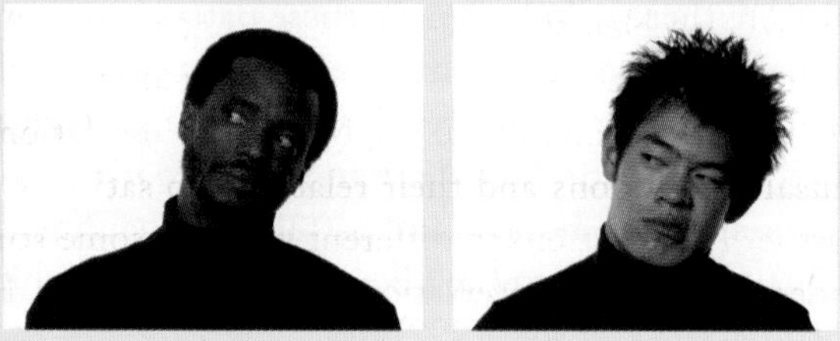

Results: Married partners who expressed more contempt were more likely to be divorced 14 years later than married partners who expressed less contempt.

Frequency of contempt expressions shown in a 15-minute conversation

Wife
Husband

Still together   Divorced

Conclusion: Contempt and derisive feelings toward your romantic partner are toxic for the relationship.

Source: Gottman & Levenson (1999).

ground? If the former is the case, then the lesson is very clear: be pleasant or face the consequences. If the latter is the case, then there isn't much of a lesson at all—just the sad recognition that when things are going badly in a relationship, the partners are going to express unpleasant affect. Two additional findings by Gottman and Levenson, however, suggest that negative affect may in fact make a direct contribution to relationship stability.

In the study of 79 couples from Indiana, Gottman and Levenson used measures of the four toxic behaviors (criticism, defensiveness, stonewalling, and contempt) to predict who would stay together and who would be divorced 14 years later. Quite remarkably, they could predict who would stay married and who would divorce with 93 percent accuracy based on these four measures gathered from a 15-minute conversation (Gottman & Levenson, 2000). This finding suggests, though it does not prove, that affect plays a role in the breakup.

For the couples who eventually divorced, it was possible to predict which couples would do so earlier and which couples would stay in the marriage somewhat longer. For early-divorcing couples, who were divorced on average 7.4 years after they were married, negative affect—for example, contempt and anger—was especially predictive of the demise of the marriage. For later-divorcing couples, who divorced on average 13.9 years after they were married, it was the absence of positive emotions like humor and interest that predicted the end of their bond.

Dangerous Attributions So far, we have seen that divorce and dissatisfaction are more likely to befall romantic partners from certain backgrounds and romantic partners who are especially prone to criticize, to be defensive and stonewall, and to express certain kinds of negative emotion. Clearly, in Rusbult's terms, these relationships are tilted toward a relationship lacking in rewards and rife with costs and conflicts. In light of a central theme of this book, we would also expect certain construal tendencies to be problematic in maintaining romantic bonds. One robust construal tendency associated with dissatisfaction and dissolution is *blame*. In a review of 23 studies, Bradbury and Fincham (1990) looked at the relationship between romantic partners' causal attributions and their relationship satisfaction. The researchers studied the partners' attributions in different ways. In some studies, partners' attributions were coded from their conversations with one another. For example, a participant might spontaneously attribute a partner's rudeness at a gathering with work colleagues either to situational factors—the noise and drunkenness of the crowd—or to dispositional factors—the partner's characteristic boorishness and arrogance. In other studies that were reviewed, romantic partners were asked to make attributions for hypothetical things their partners might do. In still other studies, partners made attributions for the most negative and the most positive event that had occurred that day in their relationship.

What is clear from these studies is that dissatisfied, distressed couples make attributions that cast their partner and their relationship in a negative light (Karney & Bradbury, 2000; McNulty & Karney, 2001). Distressed couples attribute rewarding, positive events in their relationships to unstable causes that are specific, unintended, and selfish. For example, a distressed partner might interpret a partner's unexpected gift of flowers as the result of some whim, particular to that day, which would no doubt be followed by some selfish request. Happier couples tend to attribute the same unexpected gift of flowers to stable causes that are general, intended, and selfless. A satisfied romantic partner would thus attribute the gift of flowers to the partner's enduring kindness. In terms of negative events in the relationship, we see a complementary pattern of results. Happier partners attribute negative events—the forgotten anniversary or sarcastic comment—to specific and unintended causes, whereas distressed partners attribute the same kinds of negative events to stable and global causes and see their partners as blameworthy and selfish.

Creating Stronger Romantic Bonds

So far, we have painted a bleak picture, focusing on the demise of romantic relationships. Let's now turn to the kinds of things you can do to build more healthy romantic bonds. The literature we have just reviewed provides some clues. You might be wise to marry when a bit older; to avoid highly anxious, rejection-sensitive, neurotic individuals when choosing a partner; to minimize the criticism, defensiveness, stonewalling, and contempt in your interactions; and to try to interpret your partner's actions in a praiseworthy fashion. There is also a more positive side to romantic relationships—rewards, in Rusbult's investment model—that can be cultivated as well.

Capitalize on the Good If there is a lesson to be learned from the work of Gottman and Levenson, it is that our conversations with our partners say a lot about the course our marriage will take. Are there signs of healthier conversations that enable more satisfying intimate bonds? Shelly Gable and her colleagues think so and argue that it is particularly important to capitalize on what is good in your partner's life (Gable, Gonzaga, & Strachman, 2006; Gable, Reis, Impett, & Asher, 2004).

What Gable and colleagues mean is to share what is good in your life with your partner (and vice versa)—to spread the good news, so to speak. In more specific terms, there are four ways that couples can capitalize on each other's positive experiences. *Active constructive* responses are evident when one partner responds to the good news of the other partner with engaged enthusiasm. For example, at the news of a partner's forthcoming art show, the actively constructive partner might ask questions about what pieces to show and whom to invite—questions that reveal an active engagement in this positive development in the partner's life. *Passive constructive* responses, by contrast, are still supportive but not actively so; they are quieter, less engaged, and less vocal. Here the partner in our example might simply say "that's great" at the news of the partner's art show and move on to a new topic. Then there is the dark side to how partners respond to each other's good news: *active destructive* responses involve direct criticisms or undermining of the positive event (here the partner might raise doubts about where the art show is being held or whether it will sell any pieces); and *passive destructive* responses are defined by a disinterest or nonchalance.

In initial research on these different kinds of capitalization, Gable and colleagues found that individuals who received active, constructive capitalization from their significant others reported greater relationship satisfaction (Gable et al., 2004). And in more recent work in keeping with Gottman and Levenson's interaction dynamics approach, Gable and colleagues had romantic partners talk about a recent positive event and then coded the partner's response into one of the four capitalization categories we just described (Gable et al., 2006). And indeed, partners who responded to their partner's positive event in an active constructive fashion reported being in more satisfying, committed relationships two months later, whereas those who responded with active destructive fashion were less satisfied.

Be Playful Courtship and the early phases of a relationship involve unprecedented levels of fun: late-night dancing, candlelit exchanges of poetry, weekend getaways, summer trips, and other exhilarating activities. The later stages of a relationship, especially when children are involved, become oriented around diaper changing, bottle cleaning, sibling conflict, paying bills, helping children with fevers and math problems, and chauffeuring to soccer practice and piano lessons. It's not surprising that having children, while bringing many joys, typically leads to a drop in romantic satisfaction (Myers, 2000a). In fact, married partners typically only return to their previous level of satisfaction once the children leave home. (This reminds us of an exhange between a priest, a rabbi, and a minister on when life begins. The priest says at conception, the rabbi says at birth, and the minister says when the dog dies and the last child goes away to college.)

One obvious recommendation, then, is to buck this trend and engage in playful, novel, and exhilarating activities throughout the relationship. Correlational studies lend credence to this endorsement of keeping play alive in the romantic partnership. For example, more happily married couples often possess many playful nicknames for each other, which they use to joke around and banter as they carry out their family duties of cooking dinner or doing housework (Baxter, 1984). When negotiating a conflict, more satisfied couples were found to more readily playfully tease one another during the conflict instead of directly criticizing (Keltner et al., 1998). Humor and laughter—the right kind, of course—can de-escalate intense conflicts to more peaceful exchanges (Gottman, 1993).

Art Aron and his colleagues have actually done experimental work that attests to the benefits of a bit of exhilarating silliness in a marriage (Aron, Norman, Aron, McKenna, & Heyman, 2000). In their study, spouses who had been married for several years engaged in one of two tasks. In the novel, playfully arousing condition, partners were tied together at the knees and wrists with velcro straps, and they were required to move a soft ball positioned between their heads across a long mat. This unusual activity, a great hit at the summer picnic, was a source of amusement. In the other condition, each partner had to push a ball on his or her own to the middle of the mat with a stick. Just as much physical exercise was involved, but not as much mirth or humor with the partner. Spouses reported significantly higher marital satisfaction after engaging in the novel, amusing task, both compared with participants in the other condition and compared with an earlier assessed baseline. The moral: Stay playful, and keep trying new and pleasurable things.

Care and Forgive We have learned that it is important to increase the rewards of a relationship—capitalize on the good things in life and look for opportunities of levity, play, and novelty. This all sounds pretty good. But what are we to do about the

Keys to Good Relationships (A) Shared laughter and play are vital to healthy relationships. Open communication and disclosure during conflicts is more helpful than stonewalling (B).

conflicts and problems that are inherent to intimate life: difficulties at work, debilitating struggles with adolescent children, health problems, financial difficulties, and, in 15 to 20 percent of all marriages, infidelity. Although these types of problems may be relatively infrequent in romantic relationships, their occurrence can be disastrous. An affair can ruin a marriage. The frustrations brought about by a partner's foibles and flaws can become unbearable. To love, in the words of Woody Allen, is to suffer. And recent research has found ways to make the best of that suffering.

One way is to care, to cultivate compassionate love for your partner. Lisa Neff and Ben Karney define compassionate love as a positive regard for the partner and, importantly, an honest recognition and appreciation of the partner's foibles and weaknesses (Neff & Karney, 2009). In their longitudinal research of married partners, they have assessed the partners' compassionate love for each other by measuring the extent to which they love their partner, even for their quirks and difficult traits. They have found that partners' reports of compassionate love for one another predict more supportive behavior in a 10-minute conversation about a relationship difficulty and the reduced likelihood of divorce during the first four years of marriage.

A second tip is to forgive. Forgiveness involves a shift in feeling toward someone who has done you harm, away from ideas about revenge and avoidance toward a more positive understanding of the humanity of the person who engaged in the harmful act (McCullough, Worthington, & Rachal, 1997). Forgiveness does not involve a mindless glossing over or avoidance of the harm a partner has done; instead it involves recognizing that to err is human, that mistakes are part of relationships. So in romantic relationships, is to forgive indeed divine, as the old saying goes? That appears to be the case. In different longitudinal studies of forgiveness, Michael McCullough and his colleagues have studied how forgiveness influences the level of satisfaction in romantic partnerships and families (Hoyt, Fincham, McCullough, Maio, & Davila, 2005). In this work, they measured three dimensions related to forgiveness: the urge for revenge, the desire to avoid the partner (both the opposite of forgiveness), and a more compassionate view of the partner's mistake. And what they found is that forgiveness promotes relationship satisfaction. For example, in one 9-week long longitudinal study, McCullough and colleagues followed students who had suffered a recent transgression in a relationship (Tsang, McCullough, & Fincham, 2006). The participants reported classic kinds of harm: being cheated on, insulted, rejected, left out of a social activity. Sure enough, partners who managed to forgive their partner earlier in the relationship reported greater closeness and commitment to their partner weeks later (see also, Finkel, Rusbult, Kumashiro, & Hannon, 2002).

Illusions and Idealization in Romantic Relationships   To increase the rewards of a romantic relationship, we have offered time-honored wisdom now bolstered by science: capitalize on the good, be playful, care and forgive (and sacrifice for the good of the relationship (see **Box 11.4**). If you've cultivated these positive relationship patterns, you're probably ready for the last piece of advice we can offer: see your partner through the rosy lens of illusion and flattery.

One of the most striking qualities of love is its delirious irrationality. We describe love as sickness, madness, or fever. We call the person we love a deity, a treasure, a person of unimaginable beauty and virtue. Perhaps this irrationality has some benefit for the relationship. In terms of Rusbult's investment model, to the extent that we idealize our partner, we are likely to feel that his or her actions are all the more rewarding and that there are no comparable alternative partners. The end result of our irrational constructions is enhanced commitment.

Sandra Murray and her colleagues have collected compelling evidence that suggests that the idealization of romantic partners is an important ingredient in satisfying

BOX 11.4 **FOCUS ON POSITIVE PSYCHOLOGY**

The Good Sacrifice

Relationships require sacrifices. Undergraduates report sacrificing for their partners in innumerable ways: spending time with their partner's friends or family, not getting their way in a particular leisure activity, doing errands (even laundry!) for the partner, avoiding other romantic flirtations, even helping edit term papers (Impett, Gable, & Peplau, 2005; Impett, Strachman, Finkel, & Gable, 2008).

These kinds of sacrifices can derail a relationship. Or, when construed in the right light, they can be a source of meaningful commitment (investment, in Rusbult's terms) and even gratification (see Chapter 13). The key, according to Emily Impett and her colleagues, is how you construe the sacrifice. One mind-set is to think about how your sacrifice brings you closer to your partner, or serves approach motives. Here you might decide to spend less time surfing the net because it gives you more time for goofing around and relaxing with your partner; the personal sacrifice yields greater closeness with your partner. Another mind-set is to think about how your sacrifice keeps your partner from getting stressed or tense. Impett and colleagues call these reasons for sacrificing—to reduce stress and conflict —avoidance motives. Here you might spend less time surfing the net to avoid frustrating your partner, to avoid the conflicts that usually ensue from this habit.

In one study lasting several weeks, romantic partners filled out daily surveys of their sacrifices, their approach- and avoidance-related motives for their sacrifices, and their personal well-being and relationship quality. And the clear verdict is that relationships are better off when partners feel they are sacrificing for approach motives. On days when partners sacrificed for approach motives (to get closer), they reported more positive emotions, greater personal well-being, and higher relationship quality. One month later, these couples were more likely to have stayed together. By contrast, partners who sacrificed to avoid negative outcomes reported more negative emotion and lower relationship satisfaction on that day and one month later were more likely to have broken up, regardless of how committed or satisfied they were with the relationship at the start of the study.

---

intimate bonds (Murray & Holmes, 1993, 1997; Murray, Holmes, Dolderman, & Griffin, 2000; Neff & Karney, 2002). In one study, married couples and dating partners rated themselves and their partner on 21 traits related to virtues (for example, understanding, patient), desirable attributes within romantic relationships (for example, easygoing, witty), and faults (for example, complaining, distant) (Murray, Holmes, & Griffin, 1996). Murray and her colleagues also gathered measures of the romantic partners' relationship satisfaction. They then compared the participants' ratings of their partner's virtues and faults to their ratings of their satisfaction in the relationship.

What do you think would predict satisfaction in the relationship: knowing the truth about your partner's virtues, faults, and traits or idealizing your partner? Idealization was captured in the tendency for participants to overestimate their partner's virtues and underestimate their faults when compared with the partner's own self-ratings. Two findings suggest that Blake's poem about the beneficial blindness of love stands the test of time. Individuals who idealized their romantic partners were more satisfied in their relationship. Individuals also reported greater relationship satisfaction when they themselves were idealized by their partners.

In other studies, Murray and Holmes (1999) have examined how people idealize their romantic partners. In one study, people were asked to write about their partner's greatest fault. Satisfied partners engaged in two forms of idealization, as coded from the descriptions of their partner's greatest fault. First, they saw virtue in their partner's faults. For example, an individual might write that his or her partner was melancholy, but that melancholy gave the partner a depth of character that was incomparably rewarding. Second, satisfied partners were more likely to offer "yes, but" refutations of the fault. For example, a satisfied partner might write that her husband did not like

"Love to faults is always blind,

Always is to joy inclined,

Lawless, winged, and unconfined,

And breaks all chains from every mind."

—William Blake

BOX 11.5 **FOCUS ON NEUROSCIENCE**

This Is Your Brain in Love

As the work of Murray and colleagues suggests, the mind does amazing things when in love, turning faults into charming idiosyncracies. What does your brain do during love? Recently, neuroscientists and relationship researchers have joined forces to answer this question, and their answers are both intuitive and surprising. In these studies, fMRI images of the brain's pattern of activation are gathered while a person looks at a picture of a romantic partner or is in the throes of feeling intense love (Fisher, Aron, & Brown, 2006). What is not suprising is that these neuroimaging methods reveal that romantic love

is associated with activation in reward regions of the brain (the ventral striatum)—regions rich with oxytocin and dopamine receptors. Oxytocin promotes trust and love (see Chapter 7). And dopamine promotes approach-related behavior. Love-related activation in these regions of the brain are sensible in light of what we know about the experience of love. What may surprise you, though, is that romantic love also deactivates our friend the amygdala, a region of the brain associated with the perception of threat (again, see Chapter 7). It would appear that in the throes of love, the brain disables your ability to see

what is threatening or dangerous about the new love. This finding may help your parents understand why you might fall in love with someone who does not quite live up to their ethical standards. Your brain simply isn't reacting to potential signs of risk in your new love—the fondness for motorcycles, the tattoos, the disregard for conventional society. These neuroscience findings also help shed light on what the brain might be doing as you turn your partner's faults and flaws (which in others might activate the amygdala) into pleasing virtues, as Murray and colleagues found.

to hold down a steady job, but at least that gave him more time to help out at home (see a possible neuroscientific explanation of this in **Box 11.5**).

Hawkins, Carrere, and Gottman (2002) suggest that more satisfied couples also idealize their partner's emotions. In this study, 96 couples from the Seattle, Washington, area completed the conflict discussion task that we described earlier. They then returned to the lab and viewed their interaction on videotape, using a rating dial to provide continuous ratings of how much positive and negative affect their partner expressed during the interaction. These self-report measures were compared with judges' ratings of the partner's positive behavior (humor, affection) and negative behavior (anger, contempt). More-satisfied romantic partners overestimated how much positive affect their partner was showing compared with judges' ratings, and they underestimated their partners' negative emotion. Several other studies have shown that happier couples interpret their spontaneous interactions in a more positive light than do outside observers (Robinson & Price, 1980).

Love and Marriage in Other Cultures (Most of Them, in Fact) To a degree that is hard for modern Westerners to comprehend, some of our generalizations about love and marriage do not apply to most of the world's cultures, nor even to most Western cultures until relatively modern times. Though romantic love seems to be experienced in almost every culture (Fisher, 1992), it has generally not been regarded as a prerequisite to marriage (Dion & Dion, 1993). The more typical pattern is a marriage arranged by the parents. A young man's parents and a young woman's parents come to an agreement about the suitability of the pair for each other, and the marriage transaction is announced to their children. We mean "transaction" even in an economic sense: often a dowry is required from the prospective bride's parents or, somewhat less often, the groom's parents pay a "bride price." This is still true today in much of South, East, and Southeast Asia and in much of Africa.

Love, even if not in the romantic sense, frequently follows marriage, and many cultures have an expression for this— "Loves comes in the pillow." In other words, the "postromantic" feelings of companionability, affection, and commitment are expected to follow rather than precede marriage. You might be surprised to learn that some historians believe that the idea that romantic love should precede marriage is relatively recent, emerging only in the past 500 years or so. Prior to that, and for a long time after that in their countries of origin, arranged marriage was the tradition.

You should avoid the ethnocentric assumption that arranged marriages are inferior. Arranged marriages avoid some of the pitfalls of marrying for romantic love, including mismatches between the couple's socioeconomic status and religion—two factors associated with relatively high rates of divorce. They also make it more likely that in-laws will regard one another with respect—a stance perhaps less likely when the in-laws are dragged together for reasons having nothing to do with mutual regard. The lack of expectation that there should be romantic love makes it less likely that it's inevitable fading will be a source of disappointment and discontent. Though we are aware of no comparisons about divorce statistics, it certainly is clear that the divorce rate is not markedly higher in cultures that practice arranged marriage.

LOOKING BACK We have seen that romantic relationships are a human universal, essential to our well-being, but in today's world a difficult enterprise. One way to understand the complexities of marriage is to study what predicts marital dissatisfaction and dissolution, and here we have learned that personality and demographic factors can predict unhappiness in marriage, as can toxic behaviors like criticism, defensiveness, stonewalling, contempt, and blame. There is also a positive side to long-term romantic bonds to cultivate, and here the science of relationships is yielding important insights: partnerships make it when the individuals capitalize on the good, choose to be playful, care, sacrifice (for the right reasons), forgive, and see their partner in a flattering fashion.

Summary

Characterizing Relationships

- Relationships occur when individuals depend on one another to help in meeting life's demands.

The Importance of Relationships

- There is a biologically based *need to belong,* evident in the evolutionary benefits and universality of different relationships and in the negative consequences that accompany the absence of relationships, as shown by the deficits in feral children.

- Social rejection activates a threat defense system and is associated with experiences of pain, defensive aggressive behavior, and the neural activation associated with actual pain. There may be no greater form of pain than social rejection.

The Origins of How We Relate to Others

- John Bowlby's *attachment theory* holds that early in development, children rely on their parents for a sense of security. Some children are luckier than others in these formative relationships. People having a *secure attachment style* are comfortable with intimacy and wish to be close to other people when they are stressed. People having an *avoidant attachment style* feel insecure in relationships and distance themselves from others. People who have an *anxious attachment style* are also insecure in relationships but respond to this insecurity by compulsively seeking closeness and by obsessing about the quality of their relations with others.

- Researchers have discovered that attachment styles are quite stable over the life span. Secure, anxious, and avoidant individuals live quite different lives, enjoying different levels of relationship satisfaction (securely attached individuals are the most satisfied and the least likely to break up) and suffering different kinds of difficulties (anxiously attached individuals are particularly prone to psychological problems).

- Relationships shape the sense of self and how social events are remembered and explained. People have certain *relational selves*, or beliefs, feelings, and expectations that derive from their relationships with particular other people. When one of these is activated by a particular person, the person is seen in the light of the relevant relational self.

Different Ways of Relating to Others

- Clark and Mills have contrasted *communal relationships* over the long term with *exchange relationships* of short duration that are governed by concerns of equity.

- Power is based in the sense of control and the freedom to act. It derives from interpersonal sources, such as a person's position of authority or expertise, as well as individual factors, in particular the ability to engage with others socially and build strong alliances. As an account of how power can lead to excesses and abuses, the *approach/inhibition theory* of power holds that elevated power makes people look at things in more simplistic fashion and act in more disinhibited ways.

Romantic Relationships

- The most mysterious and compelling relationship is the romantic bond. Romantic relationships are an important part of our social life, and they are important to our satisfaction with our lives and even our physical health. According to the triangular theory of love, romantic love is founded on passion, intimacy, and commitment.

- A useful approach to understanding the long-term course of romantic bonds is the investment model of relationships. According to this model, happy romantic relations are affected by *commitment*, which is a function of *rewards* in the relationship, *alternatives* to the relationship, and *investments* in the relationhip.

- Longitudinal research has identified several factors that predict romantic problems. Divorce and marital dissatisfaction are often caused by *marrying young, criticism, defensiveness, stonewalling, contempt,* and *blame*.

- Similar research has uncovered certain secrets to satisfied romantic relationships. Happy couples *capitalize* on the good events in their lives, have *fun, care, sacrifice,* and *forgive*, and they have more *positive illusions* about their partners.

- Many cultures do not link romantic love and marriage. Indeed, in many cultures, marriages are arranged by a couple's parents. Love—and not necessarily the romantic kind—is expected to follow marriage.

Key Terms

anxious attachment style (p. 407)
approach/inhibition theory (p. 418)
attachment theory (p. 405)
authority (p. 416)
avoidant attachment style (p. 407)
communal relationships (p. 413)
dominance (p. 416)
exchange relationships (p. 413)

interaction dynamics approach
(p. 429)
interpersonal relationships (p. 398)
investment model of interpersonal
relationships (p. 425)
power (p. 416)
relational self (p. 410)
relational self theory (p. 410)

secure attachment style (p. 407)
social dominance orientation
(p. 419)
status (p. 416)
strange situation (p. 406)
triangular theory of love (p. 424)
working model of relationships
(p. 406)

Further Reading

Bowlby, J. (1969/1982). *Attachment and loss.* Vol. 1. *Attachment* (2nd ed.). New York: Basic Books. A definitive theoretical statement about the evolution of different attachment processes.

Gottman, J. (1993). *Why marriages succeed or fail.* New York: Simon & Schuster. Includes great tips for happy marriages.

Keltner, D., Gruenfeld, D., & Anderson, C. A. (2003). Power, approach, and inhibition, *Psychological Review,* 110, 265–284. A good treatment of how power influences thought processes, emotion, and social behavior.

Mikulincer, M., & Shaver, P. R. (2003). The attachment behavioral system in adulthood: Activation, psychodynamics, and interpersonal processes. In M. P. Zanna (Ed.), *Advances in experimental social psychology* (Vol. 35, pp. 53–152). New York: Academic Press. This review brings together all that has been learned about human attachment in recent scientific studies.

Online Study Tools

StudySpace

Go to StudySpace, wwnorton.com/studyspace, to access additional review and enrichment materials, including the following resources for each chapter:

Organize

- Study Plan
- Chapter Outline
- Quiz+ Assessment

Learn

- Ebook
- Chapter Review
- Critical-Thinking Questions
- Visual Quizzes
- Vocabulary Flashcards

Connect

- Apply It! Exercises
- Author Insights Podcasts
- Social Psychology in the News

I AM GAY

AND THIS IS WHERE I PLAY

We have always been a part of this community.

Gay and straight, we play ball together, and see each other at the barbershop and church. It's time to treat us with the love we deserve.

CHAPTER 12

Stereotyping, Prejudice, and Discrimination

CRISTOBAL COLÓN, KNOWN TO MOST of us as Christopher Columbus, was no doubt in an exceptionally good mood on the morning of October 12, 1492, when he went ashore in the Bahamas on Guanahani Island, which he promptly renamed San Salvador. It had been 11 weeks since he set sail from Spain in his effort to find a western route to Japan, China, and the East Indies. Although he began his voyage with confidence (based—oddly—as much on a prophecy from the book of Isaiah as on sound knowledge of geography), he could not be certain his plan had merit. But now, after having spotted land, the glory he sought was ensured, as was his appointment as viceroy and governor-general of all territories he might discover—an appointment that would be passed on to his heirs in perpetuity.

It is understandable, then, that Colón was rather expansive in his journal that day. His good mood was reflected in his description of the inhabitants of San Salvador (Columbus, 1492/1990):

> They swam out to the ships' boats where we were and brought parrots and balls of cotton thread and spears and many other things, and they bartered with us for other things which we gave them, like glass beads and hawks' bells. In fact they took and gave everything they had with good will. . . . They were well built, with handsome bodies and fine features. Their hair is thick, almost like a horse's tail. . . . They do not carry arms and do not know of them because I showed them some swords and they grasped them by the blade and cut themselves. . . . They are all fairly tall, good looking and well proportioned.
>
> They ought to make good slaves.

Colón's journal on that day captures a great deal of the material in this chapter—stereotyping, prejudice, and discrimination. He was well on his way toward developing a (rather favorable) stereotype of those he encountered, characterizing the

Stereotyping Outgroups
Upon landing on an island in the Bahamas, Christopher Columbus was greeted by the natives and offered gifts of welcome, as shown in this German engraving. Yet, Columbus was prejudiced against the indigenous people because they differed from Europeans, and he stereotyped them as a group that would make good slaves.

islanders as a whole on the basis of those individuals he happened to meet that day. Nevertheless, he was immediately prejudiced against the islanders, whose appearance and customs differed from those of his own people. And he felt no need to treat them as he would treat his crew or other Europeans, as his chilling statement "They ought to make good slaves" makes clear.

It is tempting to dismiss Colón's reactions as outdated. It would be nice to think that people are more enlightened today. In some ways, they are. Slavery still exists but no longer as a sanctioned, state-sponsored enterprise. Genocide also still exists, but now perpetrators must (sometimes) answer to an international tribunal. Moreover, the world is now more truly multicultural than it has ever been, with members of different races, ethnicities, and religions living and working alongside one another more peacefully and productively than ever before. And of course, the United States has just recently elected its first African-American president, a triumph that nearly all of the pioneers of the civil rights movement said they never thought would happen in their lifetime.

Despite such progress, however, it is abundantly clear that the human tendencies to stereotype, harbor prejudice, and engage in discrimination are still with us. We only have to note the awful events in Darfur, Rwanda, Bosnia, and Somalia or acknowledge the intractable conflicts in the Middle East, Kashmir, and Sri Lanka to recognize that intergroup enmity and conflict continue to be a distressingly common element of the human condition. Nor can we feel smug that such problems are confined to these other, more troubled parts of the world. We only have to recall the all-too-common videotapes of police officers brutalizing a member of a minority group or the countless occasions in which minorities are passed over by cab drivers and potential employers or pulled over by the police for no cause to realize that stereotyping, prejudice, and discrimination prevail in the Unites States, too. They are part of the fabric of everyday life the world over.

The continued existence of ethnic, religious, and racial animosity challenges us to understand the underlying causes of intergroup tension. Where do stereotypes, prejudice, and discrimination come from? Why do they persist? What can be done to eliminate or reduce their impact?

Any serious attempt to address these questions must begin with the recognition that there is unlikely to ever be a single, comprehensive theory of stereotyping, prejudice, or discrimination. The causes of each are many and varied, and any satisfactory account of these phenomena must incorporate numerous elements. Our discussion will therefore focus on several different perspectives that shed light on these issues.

These different perspectives should not be seen as competing accounts, but as complementary elements of a more complete analysis. We will first consider the *economic perspective*, which identifies the roots of much intergroup hostility in the competing interests that set many groups apart from one another. Next we will examine the *motivational perspective*, which emphasizes the psychological needs and wishes that lead to intergroup conflict. We will then turn to the *cognitive perspective*, which traces the origin of stereotyping to the same cognitive processes that allow us to categorize, say, items of furniture into distinct classes of chairs, couches, and tables. As part of this perspective, we will examine the frequent conflict between people's consciously held beliefs and values and their quick, unelaborated reactions to members of specific racial, ethnic, occupational, or other demographic groups. Note that these three perspectives are exactly that—perspectives, not sharply defined categories. Sometimes the same phenomenon or the same empirical finding can rightfully be considered an example of both an economic influence and a motivational influence. Nevertheless, despite the sometimes fuzzy boundaries between them, the distinctions are useful for the purpose of organizing and thinking clearly about the various causes of stereotyping, prejudice, and discrimination.

We will then examine some of the psychological effects on the victims of stereotyping, prejudice, and discrimination before closing with a discussion of how intergroup antipathy and conflict can be lessened.

CHARACTERIZING INTERGROUP BIAS

Do you believe that Asians are industrious, that Italians are temperamental, that Muslims are fanatical, or that Californians are "laid back"? Such beliefs are **stereotypes**—beliefs that certain attributes are characteristic of members of particular groups. They can be positive or negative, true or false; and whether valid or not, they are a way of categorizing people. Stereotyping involves thinking about a person not as an individual, but as a member of a group, and bringing to bear what (you think) you know about the group onto your expectations about the individual.

Some stereotypes have at least some truth to them. Consider the old joke that heaven is a place where you have an American house, a German car, French food, British police, an Italian lover, and everything is run by the Swiss. Hell, on the other hand, is a place where you have a Japanese house, a French car, British food, German police, a Swiss lover, and everything is run by the Italians. American housing is indeed superior to that found in Japan, and towns are rarely abuzz with talk about how hard it is to get reservations at a new British restaurant. Some stereotypes are accurate. On the other hand, is there any reason to be especially wary of German police? There certainly was during the 1930s and 1940s, but has German law enforcement been particularly likely to encroach on civil liberties since then? Maybe, maybe not. Are Italian lovers to be preferred to Swiss? You make the call.

But stereotypes about German police work or British cooking or Italian lovers (again, whether valid or not) are not what concerns social psychologists (Judd & Park, 1993). Most of the concern with stereotyping has focused on those thought to be the

stereotypes Beliefs that certain attributes are characteristic of members of particular groups.

prejudice A negative attitude or affective response toward a certain group and its individual members.

discrimination Unfair treatment of members of a particular group based on their membership in that group.

most questionable and those most likely to give rise to the most pernicious forms of prejudice and discrimination.

Prejudice refers to an attitudinal and affective response toward a certain group and its individual members. Negative attitudes have received the most attention, but it's also possible to be positively prejudiced toward a particular group. Prejudice involves *prejudging* others because they belong to a specific category. **Discrimination** refers to negative or harmful behavior directed toward members of particular groups. It involves unfair treatment of others—treatment based not on their character or abilities but on their membership in a group.

Roughly speaking, stereotyping, prejudice, and discrimination refer to the belief, attitudinal, and behavioral components, respectively, of negative intergroup relations.

Stereotyping, prejudice, and discrimination often go together. People are more inclined to injure those they hold in low regard. But the components of intergroup bias need not be in sync. A person can discriminate without prejudice, for example. Jewish parents sometimes say they don't want their children to marry outside the faith, not because they have a low opinion of other groups, but because they are concerned about assimilation and its implications for the future of Judaism. Members of nearly all ethnic groups have harbored similar sentiments out of the same concern about preserving a cultural identity or way of life. Sometimes, of course, statements that "I have nothing against them, but . . ." are merely cover-ups of underlying bigotry. At other times, they are sincere (Lowery, Unzueta, Knowles, & Goff, 2006).

It is also possible to be prejudiced and yet not discriminate. This is particularly likely when the culture frowns on discrimination. Civil rights laws in the United States are specifically designed to uncouple prejudiced attitudes and discriminatory actions. The threat of punishment is intended to keep people's discriminatory impulses in check.

Stereotyping, Prejudice, and Discrimination Stereotyping, prejudice, and discrimination often go together. (A) Stereotypes of African Americans as more likely to break the law can be combined with anti-black sentiment to lead to discrimination, such as a tendency for police officers to be more likely to pull over African-American drivers. (B) Sterotypes linking Islam with extremism can lead to negative reactions toward Muslims.

Modern Racism

Throughout much of the world, the norms about how different groups of people are to be viewed and treated have changed. In Western countries in particular, it is not legally acceptable to engage in many forms of discrimination that were common half a century ago, nor is it socially acceptable to express the sorts of prejudices and stereotypes that were common until relatively recently. This change has created conflict in many people between what they really think and feel and what they think they *should* think and feel (or what they believe it's prudent to say or do publicly). For many, it has also created a conflict between competing beliefs and values (for example, a belief in equal treatment versus a desire to make up for past injustice through affirmative action) or between competing abstract beliefs and gut-level reactions (for example, a belief that we ought to feel the same toward members of all groups versus some hard-to-shake resistance to that belief). These sorts of conflicts have inspired social psychologists to develop new theoretical accounts to explain this modern, more constrained or ambivalent sort of prejudice.

This theoretical shift is particularly noteworthy with respect to accounts of race relations in the United States. Some have argued that old-fashioned racism has largely disappeared in the United States but has been supplanted by a subtler, more modern counterpart (Kinder & Sears, 1981; McConahay, 1986; Sears, 1988; Sears & Henry, 2005; Sears & Kinder, 1985; see Haddock, Zanna, & Esses, 1993, and Swim, Aiken,

Hall, & Hunter, 1995, for similar accounts of homophobia and sexism, respectively). In one example of this theoretical shift, **modern racism** (sometimes called **symbolic racism**) is identified as a rejection of explicitly racist beliefs (for example, that there are genetic differences between racial groups in intelligence) while maintaining an enduring suspicion and animosity toward African-Americans. The animosity is fueled in part by a worry that blacks are undermining cherished principles of justice and equality (McConahay & Hough, 1976), self-reliance (considered to be undermined by affirmative action policies), and "family values" (considered to be undermined by a disproportionate number of black welfare recipients, unwed mothers, and violent criminals). Whether these worries are valid or not, they fuel modern racism.

Gaertner and Dovidio (1986; Dovidio & Gaertner, 2004) have offered a similar account, maintaining that many Americans hold strong egalitarian values that lead them to reject prejudice and discrimination. Yet, many white Americans harbor unacknowledged negative feelings and attitudes toward minority groups that stem from ingroup favoritism and a desire to defend the status quo (Sidanius & Pratto, 1999). Whether these individuals will act in a prejudiced or discriminatory manner will very much depend on the details of the situation. If the situation offers no justification or "disguise" for discriminatory action, their responses will conform to their egalitarian values. But if a suitable rationalization is readily available, the modern racist's prejudices will emerge.

In an early experimental test of this idea, participants were in a position to aid a white or black individual in need of medical assistance (Gaertner & Dovidio, 1977; see also Dovidio, Smith, Donella, & Gaertner, 1997; Saucier, Miller, & Doucet, 2005). If the participants thought they were the only one who could help, they came to the aid of the black victim somewhat more often (94 percent of the time) than they did for the white victim (81 percent). But when they thought that other people were present and their inaction could be justified on nonracial grounds ("I thought somebody else with more expertise would intervene"), they helped the black victim much less often than the white victim (38 percent versus 75 percent). In situations such as this, the prejudice or discrimination is "masked," and the individual remains comfortably unaware of being racist. Thus, modern racism only shows itself in subtle ways. This sort of racist would never join the Ku Klux Klan, but might consistently give black passersby a wider berth. Such a person might never utter a racist word, but might also never support any social policy designed to aid black Americans.

Or consider a study in which white participants evaluated black and white applicants to college (Hodson, Dovidio, & Gaertner, 2002). Participants who scored high on the Attitudes toward Blacks Scale (were prejudiced toward blacks) and participants who scored low (were not prejudiced toward blacks) rated white and black applicants the same when the applicants excelled on all pertinent dimensions or were below par on all dimensions. But when the applicants excelled on certain dimensions and were below average on others, the ratings of prejudiced and unprejudiced participants diverged: the prejudiced participants rated the black applicants less favorably than did the unprejudiced participants. In these latter cases, prejudiced participants' discriminatory responses could be defended as nondiscriminatory—that is, they could be hidden—by claiming that the dimensions on which the black applicants fell short were more important than those on which they excelled. Note that the desire to appear unprejudiced is sometimes sufficiently strong—when, say, the audience might be particularly disapproving—that the *opposite* result is observed: bias directed at the ingroup. In one study, white participants who read about black applicants who were strong on some dimensions and weak on others rated them *more* favorably than they rated comparable white applicants by judiciously choosing which dimensions of

modern racism (symbolic racism) Prejudice directed at other racial groups that exists alongside rejection of explicitly racist beliefs.

accomplishment should receive more weight (Norton, Vandello, & Darley, 2004; see also Harber, 1998).

Benevolent Racism and Sexism

Statements like "Some of my best friends are _____" (fill in the blank) or "I'm not sexist, I love women!" illustrate a common conviction that stereotypes must be negative to be harmful. In fact, however, many of our "isms" (racism, sexism, ageism) are ambivalent, containing both negative and positive features. Someone might believe, for example, that Asians are colder and more rigid than whites—and at the same time believe they are more intellectually gifted. Similarly, someone might believe that women are less competent and intelligent than men—and at the same time believe they are warmer and have better social skills.

In their work on ambivalent sexism, Peter Glick and Susan Fiske (2001a, 2001b) have interviewed 15,000 men and women in 19 nations and found that benevolent sexism (a subjectively favorable, chivalrous ideology that offers protection and affection to women who embrace conventional roles) often coexists with hostile sexism (antipathy toward women who are viewed as usurping men's power). Is benevolent sexism a problem? Glick and Fiske argue that such partly positive stereotypes aren't necessarily benign. Ambivalent sexist or racist attitudes may be particularly resistant to change. The favorable features of such belief structures enable the stereotype holder to deny any prejudice. Think of the trucker who romanticizes women so much he decorates his mudflaps with their likeness. Also, when we idealize only certain members of outgroups—those who meet our positive expectations (for example, the athletically talented black person, the happy housewife, or the *Playboy* centerfold)—we are likely to disparage those who don't fulfill that positive stereotype (Lau, Kay, & Spencer, 2008). By rewarding women for conforming to a patriarchal status quo, or blacks, Hispanics, or Asians for conforming to a racist status quo, benevolent sexism and racism inhibit equality. In other words, those who hold ambivalent attitudes tend to act positively toward members of outgroups only if they fulfill their idealized image of what such people should be like. Those who deviate tend to be treated with hostility.

Measuring Implicit Attitudes

The conflict between what is felt inside and what is publicly stated, between competing beliefs and values, and between consciously held convictions and less-than-conscious emotional reactions has inspired social psychologists to develop new methods of assessing people's stereotypes and prejudices (Wittenbrink & Schwarz, 2007). Surveys of people's attitudes toward certain groups cannot always be trusted because respondents may not think it's acceptable to express what they really feel or because what people report verbally is only a part of their stance toward members of other groups. Given that so many forms of prejudice are ambivalent, uncertain, or hidden—even from the self—they are not likely to be revealed through self-report (Crandall & Eshleman, 2003). Social psychologists have therefore developed a number of indirect measures, two of which we discuss here.

The Implicit Association Test (IAT) Anthony Greenwald and Mazarin Banaji (1995) have pioneered a technique called the **Implicit Association Test** (IAT) for revealing subtle, nonconscious prejudices, even on the part of those who advocate universal equality and high regard for all groups. The technique works like this: a series of words and/or pictures are presented on a computer screen, and the respondent is told to press a key with the left hand if the picture or word conforms to one rule and

Implicit Association Test (IAT) A technique for revealing nonconscious prejudices toward particular groups.

FIGURE 12.1 You Be the Subject: An Implicit Association Test (IAT)

First, as you read each word in the column below, tap your left index finger if it is either a female name or a "weak" word, and your right index finger if it is either a male name or a "strong" word.

Martha
Vigorous
Jason
Small
David
Powerful
Karen
Delicate
Gloria
Feather
Tony
Mighty
Matthew
Wispy
Rachel
Robust
Amy
Fine
George
Flower
Betsy
Stout
Charlene
Iron

Then repeat the procedure, but now as you read each word, tap your left index finger if it is either a female name or a "strong" word, and your right index finger if it is either a male name or a "weak" word.

Did you find yourself tapping faster as you read the words the first time or the second?

to press another key with the right hand if it conforms to another rule. You can try a noncomputerized version in **Figure 12.1**. As you read through the list of words, tap the index finger on your left hand for either a female name or a word you would describe as "weak" and tap the index finger on your right hand for either a male name or a word you would describe as "strong." Try it.

Now read through the list again, this time tapping the index finger on your left hand for either a female name or a strong word, and the index finger on your right hand for either a male name or a weak word. Do you notice any difference in how fast you can do this? Your authors swear they are not sexist, and yet we find ourselves tapping faster in the first block than the second.

Such is the logic of the IAT. Greenwald and Banaji argued that respondents would react faster when they were to press one key for members of a particular group and words stereotypically associated with that group than when they were to press the same key for members of that group and words that contradict the stereotype associated with that group. It's easy to respond quickly when the category members and the attributes associated with the group are "lined up" and are to be signaled with the same hand, not "mixed up" and to be signaled with different hands. The same general procedure is used to assess implicit prejudice, but now participants are first asked to press one key for both positive words and either photos or the names of people in one group, and another key for both negative words and people in another group. People prejudiced against old people, for example, should be faster to press the appropriate key when the same key is used for old faces and negative words (because old people are viewed negatively) and slower when the same key is used for old faces and positive words. Participants then repeat the procedure with the pairings of the two groups and positive/negative words switched. A nonconscious prejudice toward old people would be captured by the difference between the average time it takes to respond to young faces/positive words and the average time it takes to respond to young faces/negative words. You can see whether you hold any implicit stereotypes or prejudice toward a variety of different groups by taking some of the IATs at: https://implicit.harvard.edu/implicit/research/

Well over a million people have taken the Web version of the IAT. Among other results, researchers have found that both young and older individuals show a pronounced prejudice in favor of the young over the old, and about two-thirds of white respondents show a strong or moderate prejudice for white over black (Nosek, Banaji, & Greenwald, 2002). Interestingly, about half of all black respondents also show some prejudice in favor of white faces (see the Southern Poverty Law Center Web site).

An important question, however, is whether a person's responses on the IAT are predictive of behavior that is more significant than pressing computer keys (Amodio & Devine, 2006; Brendl, Markman, & Messner, 2001; Karpinski & Hilton, 2001). There is considerable evidence that they are indeed (Lane, Banaji, Nosek, & Greenwald, 2007; Rudman & Ashmore, 2007). In one study, participants in a brain-imaging machine were shown pictures of black and white faces. The participants' earlier IAT responses were significantly correlated with heightened neural activity in the amygdala (a brain center associated with emotional learning and evaluation; see Chapter 7) in response to the black faces. Their scores on a more traditional, conscious measure of prejudice, the Modern Racism Scale, were not correlated with this difference in neural activity, suggesting that the IAT assessed an important component of their attitudes that participants were unable or unwilling to articulate (Phelps et al., 2000). In another study, participants first interacted with a white experimenter, took the IAT, and then interacted with a black experimenter. Their IAT scores, it turns out, were predictive of the discrepancy between how much they spoke to the white versus the black experimenter, how often they smiled at the white versus the black experimenter, and the number of speech errors and hesitations they exhibited when interacting with the white versus the black experimenter (McConnell & Leibold, 2001). Subtle and largely unconscious prejudices toward members of different groups can therefore be uncovered with this paradigm.

Priming and Implicit Prejudice Social psychologists have also measured prejudices that individuals might not know they have, or that they may wish to deny, by using a number of **priming** (mental activation) procedures. The logic of these procedures is simple: If I show you the word "butter" and then ask you to tell me, as quickly as you can, whether a subsequent string of letters is a word, you'll recognize that "bread" is a word more quickly than you'll recognize that "car" is a word because of your preexisting association between bread and butter. Similarly, if you associate nuns with virtue and charity, you are likely to respond quickly to positive terms ("good," "benevolent," "trustworthy") after seeing a picture of a nun. But if you have negative associations to nuns as, say, strict, rigid, or cold, you are likely to respond more quickly to negative terms ("mean," "unhappy," "unbending") after seeing a picture of a nun. An implicit measure of prejudice can thus be derived by comparing a person's average reaction time to positive and negative words preceded by faces of members of the target category (compared to "control" trials in which positive and negative words are preceded by faces of noncategory members). As we will see later in this chapter, numerous studies using these priming methods have shown that people often have subtle prejudices against various target groups that they would steadfastly deny having (Banaji, Hardin, & Rothman, 1993; Bessenoff & Sherman, 2000; Dijksterhuis, Aarts, Bargh, & van Knippenberg, 2000; Dovidio, Kawakami, & Gaertner, 2002; Fazio & Hilden,

priming A procedure used to increase the accessibility of a concept or schema (for example, a stereotype).

2001). And there is no reason to assume that people are lying when they deny such prejudices. As we have seen repeatedly, people simply do not have conscious access to many of their attitudes and beliefs; that's why we call them "implicit." We may have particular difficulty accessing implicit attitudes and beliefs that we consciously feel are inappropriate or reprehensible.

 We have seen that in much of today's Western world, prejudice and discrimination are frowned upon. This has led to an explicit rejection of prejudiced attitudes that nonetheless is sometimes accompanied by subtle and often nonconscious discriminatory behavior. The schism between what people consciously maintain and how they sometimes feel or act has led to the development of various indirect measures of attitudes toward different groups. These include priming procedures and the Implicit Association Test, which measure the degree to which different groups trigger positive or negative associations. Next we will consider some of the underlying causes of prejudice and discrimination, beginning with economic factors.

THE ECONOMIC PERSPECTIVE

We can understand the economic approach to prejudice and discrimination through the story of Cain and Abel, the biblical account of the world's first murder, one inspired by rivalry. The Bible says, "And the Lord had regard for Abel and his offering [a lamb] but for Cain and his offering [fruit] he had no regard. So Cain was very angry." Cain presumably felt jealous that his brother had the Lord's attention and affection and he did not. So he "rose up against his brother Abel and killed him." The battle for a limited resource—in this case, the Lord's good favor—led Cain to try to win the competition by eliminating his rival. Cain is not unique in that regard. Like most biblical characters, Cain's impulses represent those of all humankind. Ethically, people tend not to shine when engaged in competition over scarce resources.

The economic view of prejudice and discrimination makes the same claim about groups. Groups develop prejudices about one another and discriminate against one another when they compete for material resources. Religious groups, racial groups, and cultural groups all have the capacity, like Cain, to protect and promote their own interests by lashing out at those they perceive to be threatening them.

Realistic Group Conflict Theory

One version of the economic perspective has been dubbed **realistic group conflict theory** because it acknowledges that groups sometimes confront real conflict over what are essentially economic issues (LeVine & Campbell, 1972). According to this theory, prejudice and discrimination often arise from competition over limited resources. The theory predicts, correctly, that prejudice and discrimination should increase under conditions of economic difficulty. When there is less to go around or when people are afraid of losing what they have, competition intensifies. The theory also predicts that prejudice and discrimination should be strongest among groups that stand to lose the most from another group's economic advance. For example, people in the working class in the United States exhibited the most antiblack prejudice in the wake of the civil rights movement (Simpson & Yinger, 1985; Vanneman & Pettigrew, 1972). Working-class jobs were most at risk once millions of black Americans were allowed

realistic group conflict theory A theory that group conflict, prejudice, and discrimination are likely to arise over competition between groups for limited resources.

to compete more freely for entry-level manufacturing jobs in companies from which they had previously been excluded.

Realistic group conflict theory also specifies some of the ways that conflict between groups is likely to be played out. First of all, a pronounced **ethnocentrism** develops— that is, the other group is vilified and one's own group is glorified. Anyone who has ever played pickup basketball knows this phenomenon well. An opponent whose antics seem intolerable instantly seems more likable once that person becomes a teammate. More generally, people in the outgroup are often thought of in stereotyped ways and are treated in a manner normally forbidden by one's moral code. At the same time, loyalty to the ingroup intensifies. A "circle the wagons" mentality develops. For example, in the wake of the 9/11 attacks on the World Trade Center, many people reported that different racial groups in the United States seemed to pull together more than they had beforehand. In an experimental investigation of this tendency, telling white students that the attacks were directed at all Americans, regardless of race and class, served to reduce prejudice toward African-Americans (Dovidio et al., 2004).

Many of these elements of ethnocentrism that are brought about by intergroup competition, and the parallel "we" feelings directed toward the ingroup, were examined in one of social psychology's classic experiments, one that took place at a summer camp for boys.

The Robbers Cave Experiment

In 1954, Muzafer Sherif and his colleagues carried out a very ambitious experiment far from the confines of the psychology laboratory (Sherif, Harvey, White, Hood, & Sherif, 1961). Twenty-two fifth-grade boys were taken to Robbers Cave State Park, in southeastern Oklahoma (so named because the outlaws Belle Star and Jesse James were thought to have hidden there). The boys had signed up for a 2½-week summer camp experience that, unbeknownst to them, was also a study of intergroup relations. The research team spent over 300 hours screening boys from the Oklahoma City area to find 22 who were "average" in nearly every respect: none had had problems in school, all were from intact, middle-class families, and there were no notable ethnic group differences among them. The boys, none of whom knew each other beforehand, were divided into two groups of 11 and taken to separate areas of the park.

Competition and Intergroup Conflict   In the first phase of the experiment, the two groups independently engaged in activities designed to foster group unity (for example, pitching tents, preparing meals) and contented themselves with common camp activities such as playing baseball, swimming, and putting on skits. Neither group even knew of the other's existence. Considerable cohesion developed within each group, and each chose to give itself a name—the Eagles and the Rattlers. A consistent hierarchical structure also emerged within each group, with "effective initiators"—the boys who made suggestions that the others accepted—being rated most popular.

In the second phase, the Eagles and Rattlers were brought together for a tournament. The boys were told that each member of the winning team would receive a medal and a highly coveted pocket knife (a type of reward that researchers would be unlikely to hand out to adolescent boys today!). Members of the losing team would get nothing. The tournament lasted five days and consisted of such activities as baseball, touch football, tug-of-war, cabin inspections, and a treasure hunt. The competitive nature of the tournament was designed to encourage each group to see the other as an impediment to the fulfillment of its own goals and hence as a foe. And that is exactly what happened.

ethnocentrism Glorifying one's own group while vilifying other groups.

"Without knowledge of the roots of hostility we cannot hope to employ our intelligence effectively in controlling its destructiveness."

—Gordon Allport

The Robbers Cave Experiment Muzafer Sherif divided ten-year-old boys into two groups to observe how the groups would relate to each other. (A) During an early phase of the study when the two groups competed for prizes, they reacted hostilely toward each other. (B) When a truck carrying supplies broke down, however, they worked together to get it moving. (C) The boys in the two groups set aside their difference and became friends after accomplishing the superordinate goal.

From the very first competitive encounter, and with steadily increasing frequency throughout the tournament, the two groups hurled insults at each other, calling those in the other group "bums," "cowards," "stinkers," and so on. Although such terms may be tame by today's trash-talking standards, they are clearly not terms of endearment, and they differ markedly from how the boys referred to members of their own group, which were primarily self-glorifying and congratulatory comments about fellow group members. The expression of intergroup hostility, moreover, was not limited to words. The Eagles captured and burned the Rattlers' flag, which of course brought about a retaliatory theft of the Eagles' flag. Food fights broke out in the dining area, raids were conducted on each other's cabins, and numerous challenges to engage in physical fights were issued.

It is particularly interesting to note how the internal dynamics of the two groups changed as they became locked into this competitive struggle. Boys who were either athletically gifted or who advocated a more aggressive stance toward the outgroup tended to gain in popularity. The initial leader of the Eagles, for example, had neither of these characteristics, and he was essentially deposed by someone who was more athletic and more of a firebrand.

In addition to diligently recording episodes of hostility, the investigators conducted a number of more tightly controlled assessments of the degree to which the boys tended to look favorably on members of their own group while derogating members of the other group. In one assessment, the investigators scattered a large quantity of beans around a field and asked the two groups to pick up as many as they could in a 1-minute period. The group collecting the most would receive $5. When the contest was over, but before the winner was announced, an image of each boy's collection of beans was briefly projected on a wall, and everyone was asked to estimate the number of beans that the boy had collected. In reality, the same quantity of beans (35) was always shown, but this was impossible to discern because of the brief duration of the projection and the large quantity of beans shown. The boys' estimates revealed clear ingroup favoritism: each group estimated that boys who were members of *their* group had collected more beans than boys who were members of the other group.

Reducing Intergroup Conflict through Superordinate Goals The third and final part of the experiment is in many respects the most important. It was devoted to assessing ways to reduce the conflict between the two groups. First, on seven occasions over the next two days, the two groups were simply brought together in various noncompetitive settings to ascertain whether their hostility would dissipate. It did not. Simple contact between the two groups just led to more name-calling, jeering, food fights, and insults.

Given that simple noncompetitive contact did not reduce intergroup friction, the investigators contrived to confront the boys with a number of crises that could only be resolved through the cooperative efforts of both groups. For example, the water supply to the camp was disrupted, and the entire length of pipe from the reservoir to the campgrounds had to be inspected to find the source of the problem—a task made much more manageable if all the boys in both groups were assigned to inspect a given segment of the line. Also, a truck carrying supplies for a campout at a distant area of the park mysteriously "broke down." How to get it running again? The investigators had left a large section of rope near the truck in the hope that the boys might try to pull the truck to get it started. One of the boys said, "Let's get our tug-of-war rope and have a tug-of-war against the truck." They did so, with members of both groups intermingled throughout the length of rope and pulling it together.

Relations between the two groups quickly showed the effects of these **superordinate goals**—that is, goals that could not be achieved by either group alone but could be accomplished by both working together. Name-calling abruptly dropped off, and friendships between members of the two groups developed. When the study was completed and it was time to return to Oklahoma City, the boys insisted that everyone return on the same bus rather than on the separate buses by which they had arrived. In fact, a rather touching incident took place during the trip home. When the bus pulled over at a roadside diner, the group that had won $5 in the bean collection contest—the Rattlers—decided to spend their money on malted milks for everyone, Eagles included. The hostility produced by five days of competition was erased by the joint pursuit of common goals, resulting in a happy ending.

The Robbers Cave experiment offers several important lessons. One is that neither differences in background, nor differences in appearance, nor prior histories of conflict are necessary for intergroup hostility to develop. All that is required is that two groups enter into competition for goals that only one can achieve. Another lesson is that competition against "outsiders" often increases group cohesion. Note that this is often used by political demagogues who invoke the specter of outside enemies to try to stamp out dissension or to distract attention from problems or conflict within the group itself. The final lesson points to how intergroup conflict can be diminished. If we want to reduce the hostility that exists between certain groups, we should think of ways to get them to work together to fulfill common goals. Simply putting adversaries together "to get to know one another better" is usually not enough (Bettencourt, Brewer, Croak, & Miller, 1992; Brewer & Miller, 1988; Stephan & Stephan, 1996; Wilder, 1986). It is the pursuit of superordinate goals that keeps everyone's eyes on the prize and away from meddlesome subgroup distinctions.

Evaluating the Economic Perspective

The economic perspective "works" in the sense that it fits nicely with what we see around us as the successes and failures of intergroup relations. Consider race and ethnic relations in the United States and the effort to build harmonious relations between groups with long histories of conflict and suspicion. Where have efforts toward integration been most successful? Many analysts cite the integration of blacks, Hispanics, Native Americans, and whites in the military (as well as many white subgroups that have not always looked on one another favorably, such as Irish, Italians, Slavs, Jews, and Catholics). The success of integration in the military makes perfect sense in light of the lessons learned from the Robbers Cave experiment. Different

superordinate goals Goals that transcend the interests of one individual group and that can be achieved more readily by two or more groups working together.

ethnic and religious groups in the military are in the equivalent of phase 3 of the Robbers Cave experiment. Their whole purpose is to be ready to defend the United States against a common outside enemy. They must therefore engage in cooperative, interdependent action to accomplish shared goals—precisely the set of circumstances that brought about healthy intergroup functioning in the Robbers Cave experiment. In such circumstances, the group or category to which a person belongs recedes in importance, and what he or she can contribute to the joint effort becomes more prominent (Gaertner, Mann, Dovidio, Murrell, & Pomare, 1990; Gaertner, Murrell, & Dovidio, 1989; Miller & Brewer, 1986). Group members stand out as individuals, not as representatives of a particular subgroup.

What implications does this have for race and ethnic relations on college campuses? For many students, minorities and majority alike, their college years are the first time they have had close and sustained contact with members of other ethnic groups. How well does it work? The first thing to note is that the conditions of intergroup contact are not as favorable in the classroom as they are on the battlefield. Although students will assist their close friends to help them achieve higher grades, rarely do students feel a strong cooperative bond with their classmates in general. Few students ask themselves, "Is there anything I can do to increase the mean grade of everyone else in the class?" Rather, the common reliance on curved grading encourages a highly competitive struggle of all against all in which another student's triumph is seen as a threat to one's own grade.

This implies that the integration effort on college campuses may be less successful than it has been in the military. This may indeed be the case. Students, faculty, and administrators on countless college campuses are discussing what, if anything, ought to be done about the tendency for students of different races or ethnic origins to inhabit entirely different niches in the university. Many students segregate themselves almost exclusively with other members of their own race or ethnic group in their choice of residence, dining hall, and even fields of study. To be sure, many students—perhaps most—of many ethnic groups do mix on college campuses, and the effort to integrate college campuses on the whole has been a great success. We have no wish to claim otherwise. What we do wish to suggest, however, is that the integration effort at the university may have lagged behind that in the military—a result that a close look at the Robbers Cave experiment would lead us to expect (see **Box 12.1**).

Integration of the Military
Successful integration of blacks and whites has occurred in the U.S. military forces, where soldiers cooperate to accomplish the shared goal of defending the nation.

LOOKING BACK We have seen that prejudice can arise from realistic conflict between groups over scarce resources. The Robbers Cave experiment serves as an instructive model of this sort of conflict, showing how otherwise friendly boys could turn into enemies when placed in groups competing for limited resources. The enmity between the groups evaporated when they had to cooperate to achieve superordinate goals of value to both groups, a result with considerable implications for managing potentially troublesome intergroup relations around the globe. We will now consider other sources of intergroup hostility.

BOX 12.1   FOCUS ON EDUCATION

The "Jigsaw" Classroom

If the competitive atmosphere of most classrooms exacerbates racial tensions in integrated schools, what would happen if the classroom were made less competitive? Might a more cooperative learning environment improve academic performance and race relations in integrated settings?

Social psychologist Elliot Aronson developed a cooperative learning procedure to find out. When the public school system in Austin, Texas, was integrated in 1971, the transition was not smooth. A disturbing number of physical confrontations took place between black, Hispanic, and white children, and the atmosphere in the classrooms was not what proponents of integration had hoped it would be. Aronson was invited by the superintendent of schools to do something to improve matters. Mindful of the lessons of the Robbers Cave experiment, Aronson wanted to institute procedures that would unite students in the common goal of mastering a body of material, rather than competing for the highest grades and the attention of the teacher. What he and his colleagues came up with was something called the "jigsaw" classroom (Aronson, Stephan, Sikes, Blaney, & Snapp, 1978; Aronson & Thibodeau, 1992).

In the jigsaw classroom, students are divided into small groups of roughly six students each. Every effort is made to balance the groups in terms of ethnicity, gender, ability level, leadership, and so on. The material on a given topic is then divided into six parts, and each student is required to master one part (and only one part) and to teach it to the others. For a lesson on Bill Clinton, for example, one student might be responsible for his early years, another for his governorship of Arkansas, a third for the Monica Lewinsky and other scandals, a fourth for his foreign policy accomplishments as president, a fifth for his domestic accomplishments, and a sixth for his post–White House years. By dividing the material in this way, no student can learn the entire lesson without help from peers. Each student's material must, like the pieces of a jigsaw puzzle, fit together with all the others for everyone in the group to learn the whole lesson.

Each student's dependence on the others in the group dampens the usual competitive atmosphere and encourages the students to work cooperatively toward a common goal. To the extent that the groups are ethnically heterogeneous, members of different ethnic groups gain the experience of working productively with one another as individuals rather than as representatives of particular ethnic groups. Variants of the jigsaw classroom have been found to improve academic performance as well as to reduce prejudice (Slavin, 1995). This is probably true at least in part because students typically learn material best when they are equipped to teach it.

The effectiveness of the jigsaw classroom has been assessed in field experiments that compare students in classrooms that use the jigsaw procedure with those in classrooms that teach the same material in the usual fashion. These studies have typically found that students in the jigsaw classrooms like school more and develop more positive attitudes toward different ethnic groups than do students in traditional classrooms.

The lessons learned from the Robbers Cave experiment, that intergroup hostility can be diminished by cooperative activity directed at a superordinate goal, have profound practical significance. A simple classroom procedure derived from these lessons—one that can be used in conjunction with traditional, more individualistic classroom exercises—can both boost academic performance and facilitate positive ethnic relations.

THE MOTIVATIONAL PERSPECTIVE

Intergroup hostility, it turns out, can develop even in the absence of competition. This was apparent in the Robbers Cave experiment itself, as there were signs of increased ingroup solidarity when the two groups first learned of each others' existence—*before* they were engaged in, or even knew about, the organized competition. Midway through phase 1 of the experiment, when the two groups were still being kept apart, they were allowed to get within earshot of one another. The mere fact that another group existed made each set of boys take their group membership much more seriously. Both groups quickly became territorial, referring to the baseball field as *"our* diamond" rather than "the diamond" and a favorite swimming spot as *"our* swimming hole." The Eagles, who beforehand had not found it necessary to have a group name, quickly settled on the name Eagles once they learned that there was another group of boys in the park. Furthermore, when the two groups learned about each other's existence, both wanted to "run them off" and "challenge them."

Since all of this took place before any competition had been arranged, it indicates that intergroup hostility can develop because of the mere fact that another group exists. The existance of group boundaries among any collection of individuals, then, can be sufficient to initiate group discrimination.

The Minimal Group Paradigm

People's readiness to adopt an "us/them" mentality has been extensively documented in experiments employing the **minimal group paradigm** pioneered by Henri Tajfel (Tajfel, Billig, Bundy, & Flament, 1971; Tajfel & Billig, 1974; see also Ashburn-Nardo, Voils, & Monteith, 2001; Brewer, 1979). This is an experimental setup in which researchers create groups based on arbitrary and seemingly meaningless criteria and then examine how the members of these "minimal groups" are inclined to behave toward one another. The participants first perform a rather trivial task and are then divided into two groups, ostensibly on the basis of their responses. In one type of task, for example, participants estimate the number of dots projected on a screen. Some participants are told they belong to a group of "overestimators," and others are told they belong to a group of "underestimators." In reality, the participants are randomly assigned to the groups, and they only learn about the group to which they themselves belong—they never learn who else is in their group or who is in the other group. Thus, what it means to be part of a "group" is boiled down to the bare minimum.

In the second part of the experiment, the participants are taken individually to different cubicles and asked to assign points redeemable for money to successive pairs of their fellow participants. They do not know the identity of those to whom they are awarding points; they only know their "code number" and group membership. Participants are asked to assign points to, say, "Number 4 of the overestimator group" and "Number 2 of the underestimator group." Some of the options participants can choose provide relatively equal outcomes for members of both groups but with slightly more for the member of the outgroup; some choices offer to maximize what the ingroup member can receive but still result in more points for the members of the outgroup; and some maximize the relative ingroup advantage over the outgroup but don't provide much in the way of absolute reward for members of the ingroup.

Numerous experiments have shown that a majority of participants are interested more in maximizing the *relative* gain for members of their ingroup than in maximizing the absolute gain for their ingroup. A moment's reflection reveals just how extraordinary this is. The participants do not know who the ingroup and outgroup members are; the choices are never for themselves; and, of course, the ostensible basis for establishing the two groups is utterly trivial. Yet, they still exhibit a tendency to favor their minimal ingroup! Moreover, they are willing to do so at a cost to the ingroup, which gets less than it would if the focus were on absolute gain rather than "beating" the other group. That ingroup favoritism emerges in this context is testimony to how easily we slip into thinking in terms of "us" versus "them" (Brewer & Brown, 1998). And if history has taught us anything, it is that the us/them distinction, once formed, can have enormous—and enormously *unfortunate*—implications.

minimal group paradigm An experimental paradigm in which researchers create groups based on arbitrary and seemingly meaningless criteria and then examine how the members of these "minimal groups" are inclined to behave toward one another.

Social Identity Theory

An astute reader might now be thinking, "Yes, yes, I understand the pervasiveness and tenacity of ingroup favoritism, but what does it have to do with the *motivational* perspective on prejudice? Might it not reflect a purely cognitive tendency to divide the world into categories of 'us' and 'them'? Just as all children quickly learn to distinguish the self from all others, might we not all learn to distinguish 'my side' from the 'other side'?"

Good point. Much of the psychology behind ingroup favoritism might very well reflect cognitive influences. The us/them distinction may be one of the basic cuts we make in dividing up and organizing the world. Still, the ingroup favoritism observed in the minimal group situation cannot be the product of cognition alone. People's cognitive processes might lead them to make the us/them distinction, but cognitive processes alone cannot lead to one group being favored over the other. For that we need a motivational theory—a theory to explain why, once the us/them distinction is made, "we" are treated better than "they." Some divisions into "we" and "they" have material or economic implications, and those implications are often motivation enough to treat ingroup members better than outgroup members. But not all motivations are economic, and note that there are no economic implications riding on the ingroup/outgroup partition in the minimal group paradigm. To explain that sort of ingroup favoritism, a much broader motivational theory is needed.

The most widely recognized theory that attempts to explain the ubiquity of ingroup favortism, even when the ingroups and outgroups do not differ in any significant way, is Henri Tajfel and John Turner's **social identity theory** (Tajfel & Turner, 1979). The theory rests on the undeniable fact that our self-concept and self-esteem derive not only from our personal identity and accomplishments, but also from the status and accomplishments of the various groups to which we belong. Being "an American" is an element of the self-concept of most Americans, and with it comes the pride associated with, say, the Bill of Rights, U.S. economic and military muscle, and the accomplishments of American scientists, industrialists, and athletes. With it, too, comes the shame associated with American slavery and the treatment of Native Americans. Similarly, being a gang member, a professor, a film buff, or a surfer means that our identity and esteem are intimately tied up with the triumphs and tribulations of our fellow gang members, academics, film buffs, and surfers.

Boosting the Status of the Ingroup Because our self-esteem is based in part on the status of the various groups to which we belong, we might be tempted to do what we can to boost the status and fortunes of these groups and their members. Therein lies a powerful cause of ingroup favoritism. By giving advantage to fellow members of an

> "Cruelty and intolerance to those who do not belong to it are natural to every religion."
>
> —Sigmund Freud

social identity theory A theory that a person's self-concept and self-esteem not only derive from personal identity and accomplishments, but from the status and accomplishments of the various groups to which the person belongs.

Social Identity Theory People derive their sense of identity not only from their individual accomplishments but also from those of the groups to which they belong. (A) These delegates at the Republican National Convention identify with the Republican Party. (B) These children sitting on a fence at a ranch identify with cowboys.

ingroup, we boost the group's standing and thereby potentially elevate our own self-esteem. Thus, feeling better about the group leads us to feel better about ourselves. Evidence in support of this thesis comes from studies that have assessed participants' self-esteem after they have had an opportunity to exhibit ingroup favoritism in the minimal group situation. As expected, those who had been allowed to engage in intergroup discrimination had higher self-esteem than those who had not been given the opportunity to discriminate (Lemyre & Smith, 1985; Oakes & Turner, 1980). Other research has shown that people who take particularly strong pride in their group affiliations are more prone to ingroup favoritism when placed in a minimal group situation (Crocker & Luhtanen, 1990). And people who are highly identified with a particular group react to criticism of the group as if it were criticism of the self (McCoy & Major, 2003).

Basking in Reflected Glory Social identity theory also receives support from the everyday observation that people go to great lengths to announce their affiliation with a certain group when that group is doing well. Sports fans, for example, often chant "We're number 1!" after a team victory. But what does "We're number 1" mean? It is a rare fan indeed who throws a block, sets a screen, or does anything other than heckle referees and opposing players. Yet, countless fans want to be connected to the effort when the outcome is a victory. Not so after a loss. As one person put it, "Victory finds a hundred fathers but defeat is an orphan" (Ciano, 1945, p. 521).

Robert Cialdini called this tendency to identify with a winning team **basking in reflected glory**. He investigated the tendency by recording how often students wore their school sweatshirts and T-shirts to class after their football team had just won or lost a game. As expected, students wore the school colors significantly more often following victory than after defeat. Cialdini and his colleagues also tabulated students' use of first-person ("We won") and third-person ("They lost") pronouns following victory and defeat. The inclusive "we" was used significantly more often after a win, and the more restrictive "they" was used more often after a loss (Cialdini et al., 1976). As social identity theory predicts, the triumphs and failings of the groups with which we affiliate impact our self esteem—even when the group is simply a favorite sports team (Hirt, Zillman, Erikson, & Kennedy, 1992). This gives us an incentive to identify with such groups when they do well, but to distance ourselves from them when they lose.

> **basking in reflected glory** The tendency to take pride in the accomplishments of those with whom we are in some way associated (even if it is only weakly), as when fans identify with a winning team.

Basking in Reflected Glory
Sports fans identify with their team and feel happiness when the team wins and dejection when it loses. To connect themselves to the team, fans often wear team jerseys to the game—and to class or work the next day if the team wins.

Derogating Outgroups to Bolster Self-Esteem To bask in reflected glory is to use ingroup identity to bolster self-esteem. But what about derogating outgroups? Does that boost self-esteem? Does tearing down another group make people feel better about their own group—and hence themselves? Several studies have documented how stereotyping and prejudice can boost or maintain self-esteem in this way. In one study, half of the participants had their self-esteem threatened by being told they had just performed poorly on an intelligence test; the other half were told they had done well (Fein & Spencer, 1997). The participants then watched a videotaped interview of a job applicant. The content of the videotape made it clear to half of the (non-Jewish) participants that the applicant was Jewish, but not to the other half. When later asked

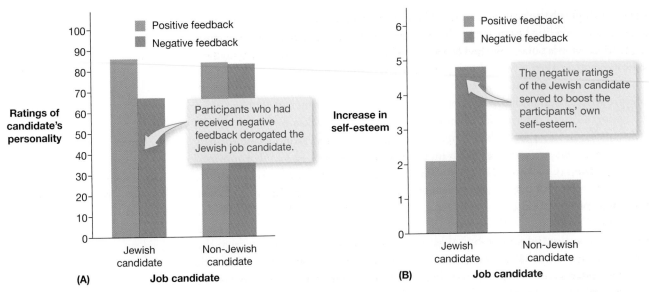

FIGURE 12.2 Bolstering Self-Esteem Average ratings of a job candidate's personality and the increase in raters' self-esteem, depending on whether or not the candidate was Jewish and whether the rater had earlier received positive or negative feedback. (Source: Fein & Spencer, 1997.)

to rate the job applicant, those who thought she was Jewish rated her more negatively than did those who were not told she was Jewish, but only if they had earlier been told they had performed poorly on the intelligence test (see **Figure 12.2A**). In addition, the participants who had had their self-esteem threatened and had "taken it out" on the Jewish applicant experienced an increase in their self-esteem from the beginning of the experiment to the end (see **Figure 12.2B**). Stereotyping and derogating members of outgroups, it appears, serve to bolster self-esteem.

A rather stunning demonstration of this tendency was reported by Lisa Sinclair and Ziva Kunda (1999). In their study, participants were either praised or criticized by a white or black doctor. Sinclair and Kunda predicted that the participants would be motivated to cling to the praise they received but to challenge the criticism—and that they would use the race of their evaluator to help them do so. In particular, they thought that individuals who received praise from a black doctor would tend to think of him more as a doctor (a prestigious occupation) than as a black man, whereas those who were criticized by a black doctor would tend to think of him more as a black man than as a doctor.

To test their predictions, Sinclair and Kunda had their participants perform a lexical decision task right after receiving their feedback from the doctor. That is, the researchers flashed a series of words and nonwords on a computer screen and asked the participants to indicate, as fast as they could, whether each string of letters was a word. Some of the words were associated with the medical profession (for example, "hospital," "prescription") and some were associated with common stereotypes of blacks (for example, "rap," "jazz"). Sinclair and Kunda reasoned that if the participants were thinking of their evaluator primarily as a doctor, they would recognize the medical words faster; if they were thinking of their evaluator primarily as a black man, they would recognize the words associated with the black stereotype faster.

Figure 12.3 shows that that is exactly what happened. Participants were particularly fast at recognizing words associated with the black stereotype when they had been criticized by the black doctor, and particularly slow to recognize those words when praised by the black doctor (see **Figure 12.3A**). When he criticized them, in other words, participants saw him as a black man, but not when he praised them (or not so readily). The pattern was reversed for how long it took participants to recognize the medical words (see **Figure 12.3B**). Participants were particularly fast at recognizing medical words when they had been praised by the black doctor, and particularly slow to do so when criticized by the black doctor.

Frustration-Aggression Theory

Anyone who has ever been stuck in traffic en route to an important meeting is familiar with one of the most consistent and powerful laws of psychology, a law captured in **frustration-aggression theory**. Simply put, frustration leads to aggression. The probability of blaring the horn or swearing at a nearby motorist is much higher when the smooth transit to one's destination is blocked. This idea has been incorporated into a another motivational account of prejudice and discrimination, one that holds that people are particularly likely to vilify outgroups under conditions that foster frustration and anger. The theory predicts that frustrating times will be marked by increased aggression. Note that the theory is a good illustration of the sometimes blurry line between economic and motivational accounts of stereotyping and prejudice. If the source of frustration is the very group to which prejudice and discrimination are directed, frustration-aggression theory is both an economic and a motivational account. But sometimes the source of frustration is not the targeted group—it can be an overheated room (Miller & Bugelski, 1948) or recalling an earlier experience that elicited anger (DeSteno, Dasgupta, Bartlett, & Cajdric, 2004). In these cases, the motivation is not economic competition, and the two accounts diverge.

frustration-aggression theory The theory that frustration leads to aggression.

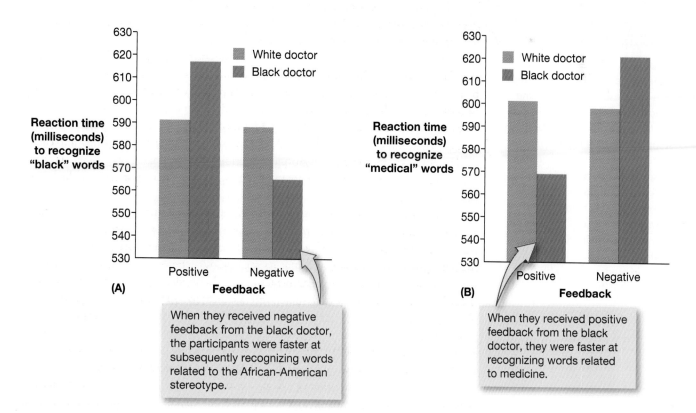

FIGURE 12.3 Self-Esteem and Racial Prejudice   Participants were either praised or criticized by a white or black doctor. Reaction times to "black" words and "medical" words after criticism or praise by white doctors were virtually the same. But this was not true for reaction times after criticism or praise by black doctors. (Source: Sinclair & Kunda, 1999.)

From Generalized to Targeted Aggression By itself, the link between frustration and aggression cannot explain the origins of prejudice and discrimination because frustration leads to *generalized* aggression. As we all know from experience, we sometimes lash out at the ones we love. So the link between frustration and aggression doesn't explain why hard times should lead to aggression targeted at specific groups.

Another fact from everyday experience provides the rest of the explanation. Often we cannot lash out at the true source of our frustration without getting into further difficulty, so we *displace* our aggression onto a safer target. The person who is denied a raise at work takes it out on the kids at home. Thus, frustration-aggression theory predicts that hardship will generate malevolence directed at minority groups, who, by virtue of being outnumbered and in a weaker position, constitute particularly safe and vulnerable targets. The classic example is anti-Semitism. Throughout history, Jews have been welcomed and accepted into numerous societies that, when times got tough, suddenly targeted Jews as scapegoats and directed their anger at the Jewish community.

In one of the most frequently cited studies of frustration and displaced aggression, Carl Hovland and Robert Sears (1940) examined the relationship between the price of cotton and the number of lynchings of blacks in the South between 1882 and 1930. Cotton was enormously important to the Southern economy during this period, and so it was assumed that times were good and frustrations low when the price was high, and times were tough and frustrations high when the price was low. Sure enough, Hovland and Sears observed a strong negative correlation between the price of cotton in a given year and the number of lynchings that took place that year. Lean times saw numerous lynchings; good times, relatively few.

Displaced Aggression Four white police officers were charged with using excessive force in the racially motivated beating of Rodney King, a black man, after they stopped him for a traffic violation. After the officers were acquitted in April 1992 by an all-white jury, the black community erupted in violence. Unable to lash out at the police or the jury, however, they took out their anger and frustration by rioting and looting stores in predominantly black neighborhoods.

A reanalysis of Hovland and Sears's data that used more modern statistical techniques in some ways provides even stronger support for the frustration-aggression account (Hepworth & West, 1988). The investigators found the same negative correlation reported previously, but unlike Hovland and Sears, they also found a similar—though weaker—negative correlation between economic conditions in the South and the number of lynchings of *whites*. This fits with the frustration-aggression account because frustration increases generalized aggression. But the fact that the relationship is stronger for blacks than for whites is also consistent with the idea that frustration leads to aggression that tends to be displaced toward relatively powerless groups. Indeed, without this element of displacement, the frustration-aggression account is not really a theory of discrimination at all, just a theory of unguided aggression.

Evaluating the Motivational Perspective

The strength of the motivational perspective is that it builds on two undeniably important elements of the human condition. First, people readily draw the us/them distinction, and the various groups to which they belong are intimately connected to the motive to enhance self-esteem. Second, people tend to react to frustration with aggression, and often direct their aggression at the "safest" and least powerful targets. Social psychologist Roger Brown once likened conflict between groups to "a sturdy three-legged stool" because it rests on the pervasive and enduring human tendencies to stereotype, to glorify the ingroup, and to form societies in which there are unequal distributions of resources (Brown, 1986, p. 533). Both the motivational and economic perspectives have shown us how readily we will reward our own and penalize outsiders—leg number 2. Both perspectives also speak to how an unequal distribution of resources can sow the seeds of intergroup hostility—leg number 3. To examine leg number 1 of Brown's stool—stereotyping—we will need to turn to the cognitive perspective.

 We have seen that people are inclined to favor ingroups over outgroups—even when the basis of group membership is trivial—in part because people identify with their groups and feel good about themselves when they feel good about their groups. Threats to self-esteem also result in the denigration of outgroup members. A variant of frustration-aggression theory tells us that frustration is more likely to result in aggression toward the relatively powerless. In the next section, we will examine the nature of stereotyping and the potential role it plays in prejudice and discrimination.

THE COGNITIVE PERSPECTIVE

From the cognitive perspective, stereotyping is inevitable. It stems from the ubiquity and necessity of categorization. We categorize nearly everything, both natural (bodies of water—creek, stream, river) and artificial (cars—sports car, sedan, SUV). Even color, which arises from continuous variation in electromagnetic wavelength, is perceived as distinct categories.

All of this categorizing has a purpose: it simplifies the task of taking in and processing the incredible volume of stimuli that confronts us. The person who is thought to have given us the term *stereotype*, the American journalist Walter Lippmann, stated that "the real environment is altogether too big, too complex, and too fleeting, for direct acquaintance. We are not equipped to deal with so much subtlety, so much variety, so many permutations and combinations. . . . We have to reconstruct it on a simpler model before we can manage with it" (Lippmann, 1922, p. 16). Stereotypes provide us with those simpler models that allow us to deal with the "great blooming, buzzing confusion of reality" (Lippmann, 1922, p. 96). More generally, according to the cognitive perspective, stereotypes are a natural result of the way our brains are wired to store and process information.

Stereotypes and Conservation of Mental Reserves

According to the cognitive perspective, stereotypes are useful cognitive categories that allow us to process information efficiently (Macrae & Bodenhausen, 2000). If so, we should be particularly inclined to use them when we are overloaded, tired, or mentally taxed in some way—that is, when we are in need of a shortcut. Several experiments have demonstrated exactly that (Kim & Baron, 1988; Macrae, Hewstone, & Griffiths, 1993; Pratto & Bargh, 1991; Stangor & Duan, 1991; Wigboldus, Sherman, Franzese, & van Knippenberg, 2004). In one intriguing demonstration, students were shown to be more likely to invoke stereotypes when tested at the low point of their circadian rhythm. "Morning people" were more likely to invoke a common stereotype and conclude, for example, that a person charged with cheating on an exam was guilty if he was an athlete—but only when they were tested at night. "Night people" were more likely to conclude that a person charged with dealing drugs was guilty if he was black—but only when they were tested in the morning (Bodenhausen, 1990). Thus, people are most likely to fall back on mindless stereotypes when they lack mental energy.

If the use of stereotypes conserves intellectual energy, then encoding information in terms of relevant stereotypes should furnish extra cognitive resources that can be applied to other tasks. Resources not used on one task can be applied to another. In one test of this idea, students were asked to perform two tasks simultaneously. One required them to form an impression of a (hypothetical) person described by a number of trait terms presented on a computer screen (for example, "rebellious," "dangerous," "aggressive"). The other task involved monitoring a tape-recorded lecture on the economy and geography of Indonesia. For half of the students, the presentation of the trait terms was accompanied by an applicable stereotype (for example, skinhead); for the remaining students, the trait terms were presented alone. The key questions were whether the applicable stereotype would facilitate the students' later recall of the trait terms they had seen and, more important, whether it would also release extra cognitive resources that could be devoted to the lecture on Indonesia. To find out, the students were given a brief quiz on the contents of the lecture ("What is Indonesia's official religion?" "Jakarta is found on which coast of Java?").

As the experimenters anticipated, the use of stereotypes eased the students' burden in the first task and thereby facilitated their performance on the second (see **Figure 12.4**). Students who were provided with a stereotype not only remembered the relevant trait information better, they also performed better on the surprise multiple-choice test on Indonesia (Macrae, Milne, & Bodenhausen, 1994).

Construal Processes and Biased Assessments

The use of stereotypes conserves cognitive resources. That is their up side. But as is often the case, the benefit comes at a cost. What is gained in efficiency is paid for by

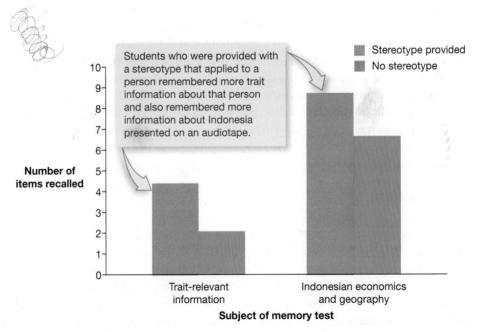

FIGURE 12.4 **Stereotypes and Conservation of Cognitive Resources** Do stereotypes facilitate recall of stereotype-consistent information and conserve cognitive resources that can be used to aid performance on an additional task? Apparently so. (Source: Macrae, Milne, & Bodenhausen, 1994.)

occasional inaccuracy and error. In particular, not all category members are well captured by the stereotype. Invoking the stereotype may save time and effort, but it can lead to mistaken impressions and unfair judgments about individuals. In addition, biased information processing can help explain why even stereotypes completely lacking in validity nevertheless develop and endure. If we suspect—because of what we've been told, or the implications of a joke we heard, or a hard-to-interpret performance difference—that a particular group of people might differ from the mainstream in some way, it is shockingly easy to construe pertinent information in such a way that our suspicion is confirmed, solidified, and elaborated.

"Why is it we never focus on the things that unite us, like falafel?"

The cognitive perspective on stereotyping does more than point out the obvious fact that stereotypes can distort our perceptions of others. Cognitively oriented social psychologists also seek to identify the precise construal processes that give rise to such distortions. What kind of faulty reasoning processes give rise to inaccurate stereotypes? How, in other words, might a well-meaning person, lacking any malice, nonetheless come to hold the kind of troublesome and inaccurate convictions that are at the heart of the most worisome stereotypes? How might such beliefs arise from cognitive processing alone? To answer these questions, we must consider the kinds of construal processes that are invoked once individuals are perceived as belonging to different groups.

Accentuation of Ingroup Similarity and Outgroup Difference There is an apocryphal story about a man who owned a farm near the Russian-Polish border. European history being what it is, the farm had gone back and forth under the rule of each country numerous times. Indeed, with the establishment of the most recent boundaries, the farmer was uncertain whether he lived in Poland or Russia. To settle the issue, the farmer saved up to have a proper survey conducted and his national identity established. The surveyor worked long and hard making the most careful measurements. When he had finished, the farmer could scarcely contain his anticipation: "Well, do I live in Russia or Poland?" The surveyor replied that although remarkably near the border, the entire farm was located in Poland. "Good," the farmer stated, "I don't think I could take those harsh Russian winters."

The point of the story, of course, is that although an arbitrary national border cannot affect the weather at a fixed location, arbitrary categorical boundaries can have significant effects on the human mind. Although few people would make an error like the one depicted in this story, research has shown that merely dividing a continuous distribution into two groups leads people to see less variability within each group and more variability between the two. In one early experiment, participants were shown a series of lines, with adjacent lines in the series varying from one another in length by a constant amount (Tajfel & Wilkes, 1963). When the series was split in half to create two groups, the participants tended to underestimate the differences between adjacent lines within each group and to overestimate the difference between the adjacent lines that formed the intergroup border. In more social tests of this idea, participants are divided into two "minimal" groups. They then fill out an attitude questionnaire twice—once to record their own attitudes and once to record how they think another ingroup or outgroup member might respond. Participants consistently assume that their beliefs are more similar to those of another ingroup member than to those of an outgroup member—even when group membership is arbitrary (Allen & Wilder, 1979; Wilder, 1984).

What is remarkable here is *not* that people assume more similarity between members within a group than across groups. That only makes sense. After all, why categorize members into groups in the first place if the members of each group are not, on average, more similar to one another than they are to the members of the other group? What *is* remarkable, and potentially troubling, is that people make such assumptions even when the groups are formed arbitrarily or when they are formed on the basis of a dimension (for example, skin color) that may have no bearing on the particular attitude or behavior under consideration. In these circumstances, the pure act of categorization distorts our judgment.

The Outgroup Homogeneity Effect Think of a group to which you do not belong: Islamic fundamentalists, stamp collectors, heroin addicts, Winnebago owners. It is tempting to think of such groups as a unitary "they." We tend to call to mind an image of such groups in which all members think alike, act alike, even look alike. What this indicates is that the tendency to assume within-group similarity is much stronger for outgroups than for ingroups. *They* all think, act, and look alike. *We* don't. This is the **outgroup homogeneity effect**.

outgroup homogeneity effect The tendency to assume that within-group similarity is much stronger for outgroups than for ingroups.

One study examined the outgroup homogeneity effect by showing Princeton and Rutgers students a videotape of other students making a decision, such as whether to listen to rock or classical music or whether to wait alone or with other participants during a break in an experiment. Half of the Princeton and Rutgers students were told that the students shown on the tape were from Princeton; half were told they were from Rutgers. After watching the tape, the participants estimated the percentage of students at the same university who would make the same choices as those they had seen on the tape. The results indicated that the participants assumed more similarity among outgroup members than among ingroup members. Princeton students who thought they had witnessed the behavior of a Rutgers student were willing to generalize that behavior to other Rutgers students. In contrast, Princeton students who thought they had witnessed the behavior of a *Princeton* student were less willing to generalize. The opposite was true for Rutgers students. People see more variability of habit and opinion among members of the ingroup than they do among members of the outgroup (Quattrone & Jones, 1980; see also Linville, 1982; Linville, Fischer, & Salovey, 1989; Ostrom & Sedikides, 1992; Park & Judd, 1990; Park & Rothbart, 1982; Read & Urada, 2003).

Overcoming the Outgroup Homogeneity Effect We often think of outgroups as having members who all think, dress, and act alike. We might expect that all Hasidic bands would be alike, but we would soon realize that this Hasidic reggae band differs from other Hasidic bands, as well as from mainstream bands, and that individual differences also exist within the band. We see lead singer Matisyahu dressed in traditional Hasidic garb, while the other members of his band are not.

It is easy to understand why this might be so. For one thing, we typically have much more contact with fellow members of an ingroup than with members of an outgroup, giving us greater opportunity to encounter evidence of divergent opinions and discrepant habits among ingroup members. Indeed, sometimes all we know about outgroup members is what their stereotypical characteristics are reputed to be. But differences in the number of interactions make up only half the story. The nature of the interactions we have with ingroup and outgroup members is likely to be different as well. Because we share the same group membership, we do not treat an ingroup member as a representative of a group. It is the person's idiosyncratic likes, dislikes, talents, and shortcomings that are front and center in the interaction. Not so with outgroup members. We often treat an outgroup member as a representative of a group, with the person's unique characteristics often receding to the background.

Biased Information Processing As we have just seen, people are more likely to assume that an individual action is typical of a group if the group is not their own. But regardless of the group under consideration, people do not generalize equally from everything they see. Some acts (an epileptic seizure, for example) discourage generalization no matter who the actor is; other acts (rudeness, for example) invite it. In general, people are more likely to extrapolate from behaviors they already suspect may be typical of an individual's fellow group members. Stereotypes can therefore be self-reinforcing. Actions that are consistent with an existing stereotype are noticed, deemed significant, and remembered, whereas those at variance with the stereotype may be ignored, dismissed, or quickly forgotten (Bodenhausen, 1988; Kunda & Thagard, 1996; von Hippel, Sekaquaptewa, & Vargas, 1995).

Stereotypes also influence how the details of events are interpreted. In one striking demonstration of this effect (Duncan, 1976; see also Dunning & Sherman, 1997; Kunda & Sherman-Williams, 1993; Plant, Kling, & Smith, 2004; Sagar & Schofield, 1980), white participants watched a videotape of a heated discussion between two men and were asked, periodically, to code the behavior they were watching into one of several categories (for example, "gives information," "playing around," "aggressive behavior"). At one point in the video, one of the individuals shoved the other. For half the participants, it was a black man doing the shoving; for the other half, it was a white man. The race of the person made a difference in how the action was seen. When perpetrated by a white man, the incident tended to be coded as more benign (as "playing around," for example). When perpetrated by a black man, it was coded as a more serious action (as "aggressive behavior," for example).

The results of this study are remarkable because the shove was presented in front of the participants' eyes. The influence of stereotypes is likely to be even greater when the episode is presented to people secondhand and is therefore more amenable to differential construal. In one study, for example, participants listened to a play-by-play account of a college basketball game and were told to focus on the exploits of one player in particular, Mark Flick. Half the participants saw a photo of Mark that made it clear he was African-American, and half saw a photo that made it clear he was white. When participants rated Mark's performance during the game, their assessments reflected commonly held stereotypes about black and white basketball players. Those who thought Mark was African-American rated him as more athletic and as having played better; those who thought he was white rated him as having exhibited greater hustle and as having played a more savvy game (Stone, Perry, & Darley, 1997).

Studies such as these make it clear that people do not evaluate information evenhandedly. Instead, information that is consistent with a group stereotype typically has more impact than information that is inconsistent with it.

Self-Fulfilling Prophecies Sometimes our stereotypical beliefs can further this tendency by creating a **self-fulfilling prophecy**—that is, we act toward members of certain groups in ways that encourage the very behavior we expect. Thinking that members of a particular group are hostile, we may act toward them in a guarded manner, thereby eliciting a coldness that we see as proof of their hostility (Shelton & Richeson, 2005). A teacher who thinks that members of a particular group lack intellectual ability may fail to offer them adequate instruction, increasing the chances that they will indeed fall behind their classmates. As Robert Merton, who coined the term *self-fulfilling prophecy*, once said, "The specious validity of the self-fulfilling prophecy perpetuates a reign of error. For the prophet will

"Stereotypic beliefs about women's roles, for example, may enable one to see correctly that a woman in a dark room is threading a needle rather than tying a fishing lure, but they may also cause one to mistakenly assume that her goal is embroidery rather than cardiac surgery."

—Dan Gilbert

self-fulfilling prophecy Acting in a way that tends to produce the very behavior we expected in the first place, as when we act toward members of certain groups in ways that encourage the very behavior we expect from them.

cite the actual course of events as proof that he was right from the very beginning" (Merton, 1957, p. 423).

The role of self-fulfilling prophecies in the maintenance of stereotypes was powerfully illustrated in an experiment in which white Princeton students interviewed both black and white men pretending to be job applicants (Word, Zanna, & Cooper, 1974). The interviews were monitored, and it was discovered that the students (the white interviewers) unwittingly treated black and white applicants differently. When the applicant was black, the interviewer tended to sit farther away, to hem and haw throughout the session, and to terminate the proceedings earlier than when the applicant was white. This is not the type of environment to inspire self-possession and smooth interview performance.

Sure enough, the second phase of the experiment showed just how difficult it had been for the black applicants. Interviewers were trained to treat *new* applicants, all of whom were white, the way that either the white or the black applicants had been treated earlier. These interviews were tape-recorded and later rated by independent judges. Those applicants who had been interviewed in the way the black applicants had been interviewed earlier were evaluated more negatively than those who had been interviewed the way the white applicants had been interviewed. In other words, the white interviewers' negative stereotypes of blacks were confirmed by placing black applicants at a disadvantage. Analogous results have been obtained in interview studies of homosexual job applicants (Hebl, Foster, Mannix, & Dovidio, 2002).

Distinctiveness and Illusory Correlations Although the cognitive perspective emphasizes the role of pure cognition in the formation and maintenance of stereotypes, it is not always clear where impartial information processing leaves off and passions, motives, and self-interest begin. We do not wish to suggest that all of the biases we have just reviewed are solely the product of flaws in our cognitive machinery. Some doubtless reflect motivational influences as well. Participants in the interview study just described, for example, may have felt uncomfortable interviewing someone of a different race, and it may have been their discomfort, not any expectations they had about the applicant, that led them to act in ways that made things difficult for the job applicant.

But there is at least one type of stereotyping bias that does arise from cognitive processes alone. People sometimes "see" correlations (relationships) between events, characteristics, or categories that are not actually related, a phenomenon referred to as **illusory correlation** (Fiedler, 2000; Fiedler & Freytag 2004; Garcia-Marques & Hamilton, 1996; Hamilton & Sherman, 1989; Hamilton, Stroessner, & Mackie, 1993; Klauer & Meiser, 2000; Shavitt, Sanbonmatsu, Smittipatana, & Posavac, 1999; Stangor & Lange, 1994). Some illusory correlations result simply from the way we process anomalous events.

Distinctive events capture attention. We would notice if a classmate were to attend a lecture wearing a clown outfit or nothing at all. Because we attend more closely to distinctive events, we are also likely to remember them better, with the result that they may become overrepresented in our memory. This has important implications for the kinds of stereotypes that are commonly associated with minority groups. By definition, minority groups are distinctive to most members of the majority, and so minority group members stand out. Note also that negative behaviors—robbing, assaulting, murdering—are (fortunately) much less common than positive behaviors—lawn mowing, saying thank you, obeying traffic signs—and so negative behaviors are distinctive as well. This means that negative behavior on the part of members of minority groups is doubly distinctive and doubly memorable. And because negative behavior by the majority or positive behavior by the minority is not as memorable, negative actions by the minority

"Oppression has no logic—just a self-fulfilling prophecy, justified by a self-perpetuating system."

—Gloria Steinem

illusory correlation An erroneous belief about a connection between events, characteristics, or categories that are not in fact related.

are likely to seem more common than they really are. Minority groups are therefore often thought to be responsible for more problematic behavior than they actually engage in.

An experiment by David Hamilton and Robert Gifford (1976) demonstrates the impact of **paired distinctiveness**—the pairing of two distinctive events that stand out even more because they co-occur. Participants were shown a series of 39 slides, each of which described a positive or negative action initiated by a member of "group A" or "group B." ("John, a member of group A, visited a sick friend in the hospital." "Bill, a member of group B, always talks about himself and his problems.") The groups were completely mythical, and so any judgments made about them could not be the result of any preexisting knowledge or experience on the part of the participants. Two-thirds of the actions were attributed to group A, making A the majority group. Most of the actions attributed to each group were positive, and this was equally true of both groups: 9 of 13, or 69 percent, of the actions attributed to group B were positive, as were 18 of 26, or 69 percent, of the actions attributed to group A. There was thus no correlation between group membership and the likelihood of positive or negative behavior.

After viewing the entire series of slides, the participants were shown just the behaviors they had seen earlier—that is, with no names or groups attached—and were asked to indicate the group membership of the person who had performed each one. They were also asked to rate the members of the two groups on a variety of trait scales. Both measures indicated that the participants had formed a distinctiveness-based illusory correlation. They overestimated how often a negative behavior was performed by a member of group B (the smaller group), and they underestimated how often such a behavior was performed by a member of group A (the larger group) (see **Figure 12.5 left**). As a result, they also rated members of the larger group more favorably (see **Figure 12.5 right**).

paired distinctiveness The pairing of two distinctive events that stand out even more because they co-occur.

FIGURE 12.5 Scientific Method: Distinctiveness and Illusory Correlation

Hypothesis: Two distinctive events stand out, are better remembered, and leave even more of an impression because they co-occur.

Research Method:

❶ Participants were shown a series of slides, each of which described a positive or negative action initiated by a member of group A or group B.

❷ Two-thirds of the actions were attributed to group A, making A the majority group. Most of the actions attributed to each group were positive (equally true of both groups).

Results: Members of the minority group were thought to be disproportionately responsible for the negative behaviors.

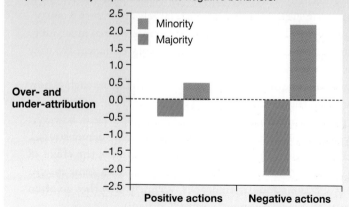

Over- and under-attribution

Members of the minority group were rated more highly on negative traits and less highly on positive traits than members of the majority group.

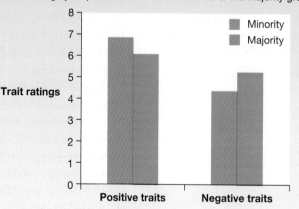

Trait ratings

Conclusion: Jointly distinctive events (minority status and rare behavior) stand out and form the basis of illusory correlations.

Source: Hamilton & Gifford (1976).

To show that it was paired distinctiveness, rather than something about negative behavior, that produced their results, Hamilton and Gifford showed that an illusory correlation was also obtained when it was positive behaviors that were less common. Under these circumstances, participants overestimated how often a *positive* behavior was associated with the smaller group.

In thinking about generalizing Hamilton and Gifford's results to the types of rich, consequential, and firmly-held stereotypes seen in the everyday world, we need to keep two important points in mind. The first is that their results are particularly impressive because they were obtained in a barren context that excluded elements that might encourage illusory correlations in everyday life. In particular, when members of different ethnic groups come together, they are often acutely aware of one another's ethnicity. And when you are especially aware of a person's ethnicity and that person proceeds to do something unusual, ethnicity is often the first thing you think of in trying to account for the action. If you have seen few Polynesians in your life, for instance, but you see a Polynesian curse out the bank teller who is serving your line, you will be sorely tempted to conclude that something about being Polynesian was at least partly responsible for the incident. ("I guess that's just the way they are.") Of course, if the same action were to be displayed by a member of your own ethnic group, you would be unlikely to consider the person's ethnicity as a possible explanation (Risen, Gilovich, & Dunning, 2007).

But one feature of Hamilton and Gifford's work does not fit real-world stereotyping so well. Their analysis predicts that people should be prone to develop illusory correlations between any two variables that are jointly distinctive. But that does not happen. Being left-handed and being a vegetarian are both relatively rare, but our culture has no stereotype of southpaws being particularly averse to eating meat. Nor are Latinos thought to be particularly likely to be gay, or Asians thought to be particularly likely to snowboard. Thus, although Hamilton and Gifford's provocative analysis captures something real and important about some illusory correlations, it overpredicts. Where their analysis falls short, then, is in specifying *which* jointly distinctive pairings are likely to form the core of commonly held stereotypes, and which are not.

Paired Distinctiveness Eating a tremendous number of hot dogs is unusual, which might make a non-Japanese observer who witnessed this Japanese man's triumph in a hot dog eating contest wonder whether the Japanese are particularly fond of hot dogs.

Explaining Away Exceptions

It is a rare stereotype that escapes occasional disconfirmation. Groups known for their intellectual talents nonetheless include a few dolts. Those renowned for their athletic abilities are sure to include a klutz or two. Evidence contradicting a stereotype is almost certain to be encountered, even if the stereotype is largely accurate. Of course, if the stereotype is invalid, evidence of disconfirmation is encountered that much more often. What happens when people encounter such contradictory evidence? Do they abandon their stereotypes or hold them less confidently?

How people respond to stereotype disconfirmation varies with factors such as how emotionally involved they are in the stereotype, whether they hold the stereotype in isolation or belong to a group that preaches it, and so on. One thing is clear, however: people do not give up their stereotypes easily. As numerous studies have demonstrated, people evaluate disconfirming evidence in a variety of ways that have the effect of dampening its impact. An understanding of these processes provides some insight into one of the most vexing questions about stereotypes—namely, why they so often persist in the face of evidence that would seem to contradict them.

The first thing to note is that no stereotype contains an expectation of perfectly invariant behavior. Groups thought to be dishonest, lazy, or carefree are thought to be dishonest, lazy, or carefree *on average*, or more dishonest, lazy, or carefree than other groups. It is not expected that all of their members behave in those ways all the time. This allows people to remain unmoved by apparent disconfirmations of their stereotypes because anyone who acts at variance with the stereotype is simply walled off into a category of "exceptions." Psychologists refer to this as **subtyping** (Richards & Hewstone, 2001; Weber & Crocker, 1983). Sexists who believe that women are passive and dependent and should stay home to raise children are likely to subcategorize assertive, independent women who choose not to have children as "militant" or "strident" feminists, thereby leaving their stereotype of women largely intact. Similarly, racists who maintain that blacks are not fit to excel outside of sports and entertainment are unlikely to be much troubled by the likes of, say, Barack Obama ("He's half white") or Condoleeza Rice ("Her father was a guidance counselor"). To the racist mind, they are merely the "exceptions that prove the rule." (Incidentally, if you've ever wondered how an exception can prove a rule—it can't. The expression uses the word *prove* in its secondary meaning: "to test.")

This echoes the more general truth that evidence that supports a stereotype is treated differently from evidence that refutes it. Supportive evidence tends to be accepted at face value, whereas contradictory evidence is often critically analyzed and discounted. One way we do this is by attributing behavior consistent with a stereotype to the dispositions of the people involved and attributing inconsistent behavior to external causes (Crocker, Hannah, & Weber, 1983; Deaux & Emswiller, 1974; Kulik, 1983; Swim & Sanna, 1996; Taylor & Jaggi, 1974). An anti-Semite who believes that Jews are "cheap" is likely to dismiss a Jew's acts of philanthropy as due to a desire for social acceptance, but to attribute any pursuit of self-interest as a reflection of some "true" Jewish character. Thus, episodes consistent with a stereotype reinforce its perceived validity; those that are inconsistent with it are deemed insignificant (Pettigrew, 1979).

Another way that we differentially process supportive and contradictory information is by varying how abstractly we encode the actions of people from different groups. Almost any action can be construed at different levels of abstraction (Vallacher & Wegner, 1987). If you see someone lifting an individual who has fallen, you could describe the action as exactly that— an act of lifting. Alternatively, you could say that the person was "helping" the fallen individual. More broadly still, you might see the person as

Explaining Away Exceptions
People who hold negative stereotypes of ethnic groups sometimes dismiss examples of individuals who don't conform to the stereotype as exceptions or members of relatively rare subtypes.

"helpful" or "altruistic." These different levels of abstraction carry different connotations. The more concrete the description, the less it says about the individual involved. Nearly anyone can lift, but not everyone is altruistic. Thus, if people's evaluations are guided by their preexisting stereotypes, we might expect them to describe actions that are consistent with a stereotype in broad terms (thus reinforcing the stereotype), but to describe actions that are inconsistent with it in concrete terms (thus averting a potential challenge to the stereotype). Stereotypes may insulate themselves from disconfirmation, in other words, by influencing the level at which relevant actions are encoded (von Hippel, Sekaquaptewa, & Vargas, 1995).

This prediction was tested in a study that took place during the annual *palio* competition in Ferrara, Italy (Maass, Salvi, Arcuri, & Semin, 1989). The *palio* are horse-racing competitions that have taken place in various Italian towns since the thirteenth century (with a brief interruption during the time of the Black Plague). The races pit different teams, or *contrade*, against one another and take place in the context of an

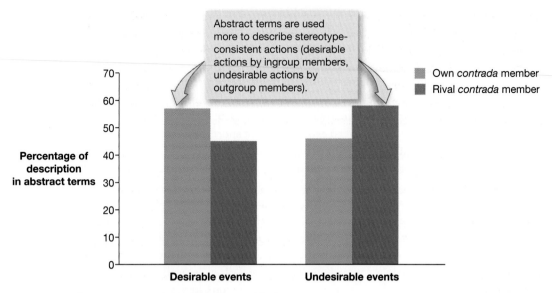

FIGURE 12.6 **Stereotypes and the Encoding of Behavior**   Events that are consistent with preexisting stereotypes are encoded at a broader, and therefore more meaningful, level of abstraction than events that are inconsistent with preexisting stereotypes. The figure depicts the percentage of abstract versus concrete terms used to describe desirable and undesirable actions by members of the ingroup and outgroup. Abstract terms consist of state verbs or trait terms (for example, *hates, hateful*), and concrete terms consist of descriptive and interpretative action verbs (for example, *hits, hurts*). (Source: Maass, Salvi, Arcuri, & Semin, 1989.)

elaborate festival in which supporters of each *contrada* root for their team. In the weeks leading up to the *palio*, feelings of intergroup competition run high.

Before one such *palio* competition, the supporters of two *contrade*, San Giorgio and San Giacomo, were recruited to participate in an experiment. Each participant was shown a number of sketches depicting a member of their own *contrada* or of the rival *contrada* engaged in an action. The *contrada* membership of the person depicted was established simply by having the color of the protagonist's shirt match that of one *contrada* or another. Some of the sketches portrayed desirable actions (for example, helping someone), and some portrayed undesirable actions (for example, littering). After inspecting each sketch, the participants were asked to describe what it depicted, and their responses were scored for level of abstraction.

The results revealed a clear bias (see **Figure 12.6**). Actions consistent with a participant's preexisting orientation (that is, positive actions by a member of one's own *contrada*; negative actions by a member of the rival *contrada*) were described at a more abstract level than actions at variance with a participant's preexisting orientation (that is, negative actions by a member of one's own *contrada*; positive actions by a member of the rival *contrada*). This asymmetry feeds the tendency to perceive the ingroup in a favorable light. Concretely encoding events that violate one's preferences or expectations renders them less consequential; abstractly encoding those that fit one's stereotypes lends them greater import. "Cheating" someone is more significant than "taking" something from them, "helping" someone is more significant than "lifting" them, and "showing concern" about someone is more significant than "visiting" them.

Automatic and Controlled Processing

Some of the cognitive processes that give rise to stereotyping and prejudice are rather deliberate, elaborate, and "mindful"—that is to say, conscious. This is likely to be the case, for example, when people observe a member of a stigmatized group behave in a counterstereotypical fashion and quickly invent a subcategory of, say, "white-collar" Hispanics or "environmental" lawyers that preserves their preexisting stereotype (Devine & Baker, 1991; Kunda & Oleson, 1995; Weber & Crocker, 1983). Other cognitive processes, in contrast, give rise to stereotyping and prejudice rapidly and automatically, without much conscious attention and elaboration. This is likely to be the case for distinctiveness-based illusory correlations and the outgroup homogeneity effect.

In the past 20 years, researchers have explored the interplay between automatic and controlled processes and how together they give rise to the way people react to members of different groups (Bodenhausen, Macrae, & Sherman, 1999; Devine & Monteith, 1999; Fazio & Olson, 2003; Sherman et al., 2008; Wittenbrink, 2004). This research has shown that our reactions to different groups of people are to a surprising degree guided by quick and automatic mental processes that we can override, but not eliminate. This research has also highlighted the common rift that exists between our immediate, reflexive reactions to outgroup members and our more reflective responses.

Patricia Devine (1989b) examined the joint operation of automatic and controlled processes by investigating the schism that exists for many people between their knowledge of racial stereotypes and their own personal beliefs and attitudes toward those same groups. More specifically, Devine sought to demonstrate that what separates prejudiced and nonprejudiced people is not their knowledge of derogatory stereotypes, but whether or not they resist the stereotypes. To do so, she relied on the distinction between **automatic processes**, which we do not consciously control (like the use of binocular disparity to judge distance), and **controlled processes**, which, as the name suggests, we direct more consciously. The activation of stereotypes is typically an automatic process; thus, stereotypes can be triggered even if we don't want them to be. Even a nonprejudiced person will, under the right circumstances, access an association between Muslims and fanaticism, blacks and criminality, and WASPs and emotional repression, because those associations—valid or not—are present in our culture. Whereas a bigot will endorse or employ such stereotypes, a nonprejudiced person will employ more controlled cognitive processes to suppress them—or at least try to.

To test these ideas, Devine selected groups of high- and low-prejudiced participants on the basis of their scores on the Modern Racism Scale (McConahay, Hardee, & Batts, 1981). To show that these two groups do not differ in their automatic processing of stereotypical information, she presented to each participant a set of words, one at a time, so briefly that they could not be consciously identified. She showed some of the participants neutral words ("number," "plant," "remember") and other participants words stereotypically associated with blacks ("welfare," "jazz," "busing"). Devine hypothesized that although the stereotypical words were presented too briefly to be consciously recognized, they would nonetheless prime the participants' stereotypes of blacks. To find out if this indeed happened, she next presented the participants with a written description of an individual who acted in an ambiguously hostile manner (to highlight a trait—hostility—characteristic of the African-American stereotype). In one incident, for example, the target individual refused to pay his rent until his apartment was repaired. Was he being needlessly belligerent or appropriately assertive? The results indicated that he was seen as more hostile—and more negative overall—by participants who had earlier been primed by words designed to activate their stereotypes of blacks (words, it is important to note, that were not otherwise connected to the concept of hostility). Most important, this was equally true of prejudiced and nonprejudiced participants. Because the stimulus words unconsciously activated their stereotypes, the nonprejudiced participants

automatic processes Processes that occur outside of our awareness, without conscious control.

controlled processes Processes that occur with conscious direction and deliberate thought.

were "caught off guard" and were unable to suppress the automatic processing of stereotypical information.

To demonstrate that prejudiced and nonprejudiced individuals differ primarily in their *controlled* cognitive processes, Devine next asked her participants to list characteristics of black Americans. As predicted, the two groups differed substantially in the output of this consciously controlled procedure: prejudiced participants listed many more pejorative characteristics stereotypically associated with blacks than did nonprejudiced participants. Thus, even though both prejudiced and nonprejudiced individuals have stored in their minds the same negative stereotypes of black Americans (as shown in the first part of Devine's study), prejudiced individuals believe them and are willing to voice these beliefs, whereas nonprejudiced individuals reject them.

Subsequent investigations have qualified one element of Devine's research: automatic negative stereotypes associated with members of various stigmatized groups appear to be more easily activated among prejudiced individuals than among nonprejudiced individuals (Fazio, Jackson, Dunton, & Williams, 1995; Lepore & Brown, 1997; Wittenbrink, Judd, & Park, 1997). Nevertheless, even among nonprejudiced individuals, there is often a rift between the beliefs and sentiments elicited by automatic processes and those elicited by more controlled processes. This was shown in an interesting way by a study that examined the areas of the brain that were activated when white participants were shown pictures of black faces and white faces (Cunningham et al., 2004; see also Lieberman, Hariri, Jarcho, Eisenberger, & Bookheimer, 2005). The key manipulation in this study was the amount of time participants were exposed to the black and white faces. When shown the faces for only 30 milliseconds, the participants exhibited greater activation in the amygdala (which registers emotional response) after exposure to black faces than after exposure to white faces. Furthermore, the amount of amygdala activation was related to participants' implicit prejudice as measured by the IAT. But when the faces were shown for 525 milliseconds, there was no difference in amygdala activation when exposed to black versus white faces, suggesting that these participants—all of whom had expressed a strong desire to avoid prejudice—initially had an automatic response to black versus white faces that they then tried to control. Indeed, at 525 milliseconds, black faces caused more activity in the prefrontal cortex—an area of the brain associated with cognitive and behavioral regulation—than did white faces.

The implications of the rift between people's automatic and controlled reactions to members of a different racial group were further investigated by Dovidio, Kawakami, and Gaertner (2002). The researchers first used a priming procedure like that described on p. 448 to assess white participants' implicit prejudice toward blacks and also measured their explicit attitudes with the Attitudes toward Blacks Scale (Brigham, 1993). They then had the participants engage in two 3-minute conversations, one with a white student and one with a black student. They videotaped and later scored these conversations, once with the sound removed and once with all channels included, for the amount of friendliness exhibited by the participant.

Dovidio and colleagues predicted that the explicit measure of prejudice would predict ratings of the participants' friendliness made from the full videotape because those ratings would be primarily determined by what participants said, and people can readily control what they say. But they expected that the implicit measure of prejudice would predict participants' nonverbal friendliness—that is, the ratings of participants' friendliness made from the video channel only—because nonverbal behavior is harder to control. And that is just what they found. Participants' scores on the Attitudes toward Blacks Scale predicted how differentially friendly they were to the white and black students as assessed from the full videotape. These scores were also related to how differentially friendly the participants themselves thought they were. But it was their scores on the implicit measure of prejudice (their reaction times) that predicted how differentially friendly they were to the white and black students as assessed from the video-only ratings. These scores were also related to how friendly their *conversation partners* thought they had been. Explicit measures of prejudice, it seems, can predict controlled behavior, but implicit measures may do a better job of predicting automatic behavior (see also Fazio et al., 1995).

The results of another study of people's automatic reactions to members of stigmatized groups are rather disturbing. Payne (2001) had participants decide as quickly as possible whether an object depicted in a photo was a handgun or a hand tool (for example, pliers). Each photograph was immediately preceded by a picture of either an African-American or a white face. Payne found that the (white) participants were faster to identify a weapon as a weapon when it was preceded by an African-American face and faster to identify a hand tool as a hand tool when it was preceded by a white face (see also Payne, Lambert, & Jacoby, 2002; see **Figure 12.7**).

Is this pattern the result of automatic prejudice toward African-Americans on the part of white participants? That is, is the recognition of handguns facilitated by African-American faces because both handguns and African-Americans are evaluated negatively by white participants? Or is this effect due to automatic stereotyping? That is, is the facilitation caused by a stereotypical association between handguns and African-Americans that exerts its effect even among nonprejudiced individuals?

The good news (limited good news, we admit, but good news nonetheless) is that it appears to be the latter. Charles Judd, Irene Blair, and Kristine Chapleau (2004)

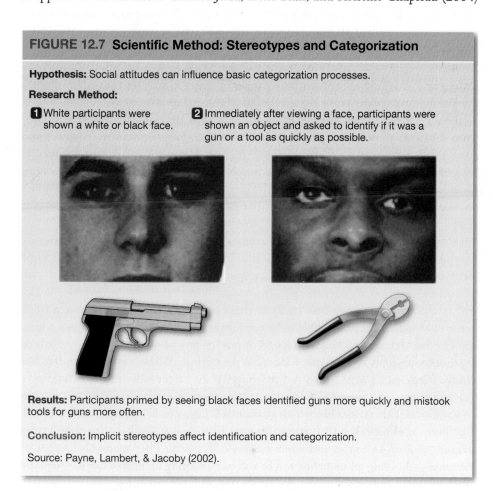

FIGURE 12.7 Scientific Method: Stereotypes and Categorization

Hypothesis: Social attitudes can influence basic categorization processes.

Research Method:

1 White participants were shown a white or black face.

2 Immediately after viewing a face, participants were shown an object and asked to identify if it was a gun or a tool as quickly as possible.

Results: Participants primed by seeing black faces identified guns more quickly and mistook tools for guns more often.

Conclusion: Implicit stereotypes affect identification and categorization.

Source: Payne, Lambert, & Jacoby (2002).

BOX 12.2 **FOCUS ON THE LAW**

Stereotypical Facial Features and the Death Penalty

The election of Barack Obama as the 44th president of the United States highlights the often ambiguous nature of race. Although the child of a white mother and black father, he is almost always referred to as the first African-American president, not the first biracial president. This is no doubt a legacy of the "one-drop rule": historically, individuals were considered black if they had any trace of black ancestry at all. This astandard was used in various Southern states to back the notorious Jim Crow laws that enforced racial segregation and restricted the rights of blacks. But now that society has moved beyond the one-drop rule,

we are left with the difficult issue of "who counts" as black, white, Asian, Hispanic, and so on. Indeed, many biologists question whether racial categories make any sense at all—that is, whether race really exists (Bamshad & Olson, 2003).

If people impose discrete racial categories on continuous variation in genetic features, it stands to reason that race-based judgments about others—prejudices and stereotypes—should reflect this variation. They do. African-American faces with more stereotypically African features (darker skin, fuller lips, more flared nostrils) elicit prejudiced reactions more readily than faces with

less stereotypical features (Livingston & Brewer, 2002). Furthermore, both black and white individuals with more stereotypically African features are assumed to have traits associated with common stereotypes of African-Americans (Blair, Judd, Sadler, & Jenkins, 2002). In the most consequential manifestation of this tendency, Jennifer Eberhardt and her colleagues found that black individuals with stereotypically African features who were accused of capital crimes were more likely to end up on death row than similarly accused blacks with less stereotypically African features (Eberhardt, Davies, Purdie-Vaughns, & Johnson, 2006).

replicated Payne's experiment with four types of target stimuli that varied in whether they were viewed positively or negatively and whether they were stereotypically associated with African-Americans. Specifically, the stimuli associated with African-Americans consisted of pictures of handguns (negative) and sports equipment (positive), and the stimuli not associated with African-Americans consisted of pictures of insects (negative) and fruit (positive). Judd and his colleagues found that African-American faces facilitated the recognition of both positive and negative stereotypical items (handguns and sports equipment), but not the nonstereotypical items (insects and fruits), regardless of whether they were positive or negative.

A similar conclusion emerges from studies with even more chilling implications for the everyday lives of African-Americans. This research was inspired by the tragic death of Amadou Diallo, a black African immigrant who in 1999 was riddled with 19 bullets by police officers who said afterward that they thought, incorrectly, that he was reaching for a gun (see **Box 12.2**). In these studies, participants watched a video game in which, at unpredictable moments, a target individual—sometimes white, sometimes African-American—popped up out of nowhere holding either a gun or some other object (Correll, Park, Judd, & Wittenbrink, 2002; Correll, Urland, & Ito, 2006). Participants were instructed to "shoot" if the target individual was holding a gun and to press a different response key if he was not. Participants were instructed to respond as quickly as possible, which guaranteed there would be occasional mistakes. The pattern of mistakes is shown in **Figure 12.8**, and it is clear that participants treated African-American and white targets differently. They made both types of mistakes—shooting an unarmed target and not shooting an armed target—equally often when the target individual was white. But for African-American targets, they were much more likely to make the mistake of shooting if the target was unarmed than failing to shoot if the target was armed. The same effect, it is important to note, was obtained in a follow-up experiment with African-American participants.

Evaluating the Cognitive Perspective

Critics of the cognitive perspective have said that although the approach has made some strides in advancing our knowledge of intergroup conflict, the recent emphasis on reaction-time methods and brief, reflexive phenomena may cause us to lose sight of the causes of the truly disturbing manifestations of prejudice and discrimination that are all-too-common elements of real-world experience. Indeed, when ethnic groups in Africa, the Middle East, Indonesia, and elsewhere are bent on subjugating or exterminating one another, and when police officers in countries the world over brutalize minorities with alarming frequency, reaction-time assessments of subtle prejudices can seem rather removed from the heart of the matter. Critics have also noted that many of the effects documented in this literature are very short-lived. Seeing a person who belongs to a particular ethnic group may automatically activate our stereotypical associations to that group, but the activation is typically brief. One team of investigators reported that they could find no trace of stereotype activation after a mere 10 minutes of interaction with a member of a minority group (Kunda, Davies, Adams, & Spencer, 2002).

As important as it is to keep these concerns in mind, it's also important to note that a great deal of damage can be done on the basis of people's initial, quick responses, as the shooting studies we just reviewed make so abundantly clear. It is surely no consolation to Amadou Diallo's family to know that the cognitive operations that made the police officers think Diallo was reaching for a gun rather than a wallet would shortly have been overridden by more level-headed processes. It's also important to note that however brief these initial, automatic processes might be, they can get the ball rolling in an unfortunate direction. They can be the seeds from which deeper sorts of prejudice and discrimination are sown.

Automatic Reactions and Stereotyping White police officers in New York City attempted to question Amadou Diallo, a black West African immigrant who had gone outside his apartment building to get some air and who seemed to fit the description of the serial rapist they were looking for. Diallo ran up the steps of his building and then reached inside his jacket for what police believed was a gun but was actually his wallet. Reacting out of fear that Diallo was about to start firing a weapon, the four police officers fired 41 shots, striking the innocent Diallo 19 times and killing him.

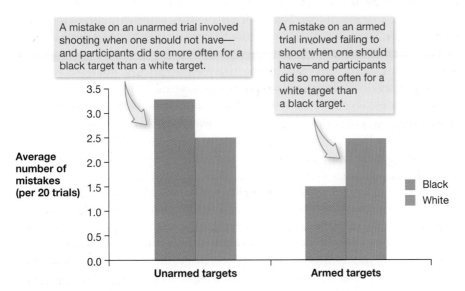

A mistake on an unarmed trial involved shooting when one should not have—and participants did so more often for a black target than a white target.

A mistake on an armed trial involved failing to shoot when one should have—and participants did so more often for a white target than a black target.

Average number of mistakes (per 20 trials)

Black
White

Unarmed targets   Armed targets

FIGURE 12.8 Automatic Stereotyping Participants were shown images of an armed or unarmed individual that appeared suddenly on a computer screen. They were told to respond as quickly as possible by pressing one button to "shoot" an armed individual and another button if the individual was unarmed. (Source: Correll, Park, Judd, & Wittenbrink, 2002.)

It is the cognitive perspective, furthermore, that has done the most to make it clear that we all tend to stereotype and that we all have the capacity to harbor troubling prejudices—prejudices we are often unaware we have. Subjecting yourself to implicit measures of prejudice like the IAT (see Figure 12.3) can yield undeniable evidence that you have certain negative associations to particular groups that you'd rather not have. That knowledge can be the first step toward overcoming prejudice, and it has been the insights of social psychologists working from the cognitive perspective that give us that knowledge.

 We have seen that stereotypes help us to make sense of the world and to process information efficiently, freeing us to use cognitive resources for other work. But they can also cause us to make many errors, such as seeing outgroup members as more homogeneous than they actually are. They can also lead to self-fulfilling prophecies, in which our expectations of what a group of people is like lead us to behave in ways that elicit behavior consistent with our expectations. This can make stereotypes resistant to disconfirmation, as does the tendency to explain away information that violates a stereotype and the tendency to subcategorize those who don't fit the stereotype. Stereotypes can result from both automatic and controlled processing. Even people who do not express prejudicial views may reflexively respond to individuals on the basis of stereotypes and prejudices of which they are unaware. We next consider some of the consequences of knowing that other people hold stereotypes about your group.

BEING A MEMBER OF A STIGMATIZED GROUP

So far, we have been concerned with the perpetrators of prejudice (who, it should be abundantly clear by now, can include all of us). What about the victims of prejudice? They, of course, pay an obvious and unfair price in terms of numerous indicators of material and psychological well-being—health, wealth, employment prospects, and longevity among them. But members of stereotyped or stigmatized groups are also typically aware of the stereotypes that others hold about them, and this awareness also can have negative effects on them (Crocker, Major, & Steele, 1998; Herek, 1998; Jones et al., 1984; Pinel, 1999; Shelton, Richeson, & Salvatore, 2005). Social psychologists have focused on two burdens that come with knowing that others may be prejudiced against one's group: attributional ambiguity and stereotype threat.

Attributional Ambiguity

As discussed in Chapter 4, people want to know the causes of events around them in order to achieve a sense that they live in an ordered, predictable world. But this sense is threatened for members of stigmatized groups because they cannot tell whether many of their experiences have the same origins as those of everyone else or whether they are the result of prejudice. "Did my officemate get the promotion instead of me because I'm so overweight?" "Would the state trooper have pulled me over if I were white?" "Did I get that fellowship because I'm Latino?"

These sorts of questions may be particularly vexing with respect to negative outcomes, but they are also disconcerting in the context of positive outcomes. When someone has to wonder whether an accomplishment is the product of an affirmative action policy, it can be difficult to completely "own" it and reap the full measure of pride it would ordinarily afford.

In one study that examined this sort of attributional predicament, African-American and white students received flattering or unflattering feedback from a white student in an adjacent room (Crocker, Voelkl, Testa, & Major, 1991). Half the participants were led to believe that this other student could see them through a one-way mirror, and half were led to believe they could not be seen (because a blind covered the mirror). Whether or not they could be seen had no effect on how white students reacted to the feedback. But it did affect how black students reacted. When black students thought the other person could not see them—and therefore didn't know their race—their self-esteem went down from the unflattering feedback and was boosted by the positive feedback. When they thought the other person could see them, in contrast, their self-esteem was not injured by the bad news, nor was it enhanced by the good news. Thus, this study indicates that members of stigmatized groups quite literally live in a less certain world, not knowing whether to attribute positive feedback to their own skill or to others' condescension and not knowing whether to attribute negative feedback to their own error or to others' prejudice.

Stereotype Threat

An extensive program of research initiated by Claude Steele and his colleagues speaks dramatically to a second difficulty confronting members of stigmatized groups (Steele, 1997; Steele, Spencer, & Aronson, 2002). In particular, this research has shown that the performance of members of stigmatized groups can be impaired by **stereotype threat**—the fear that they will confirm the stereotypes that others have regarding some salient group of which they are a member. In one study, Steven Spencer, Claude Steele, and Diane Quinn (1999) looked at the effect on women's math test scores of making salient the stereotype that women do not perform well in mathematics. In one condition, participants were told there was no gender difference on a particular test they were about to take. Other participants were told that there was a gender difference in favor of men. As can be seen in **Figure 12.9**, men and

stereotype threat The fear that we will confirm the stereotypes that others have regarding some salient group of which we are a member.

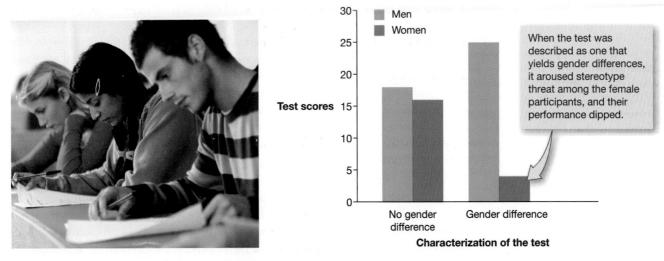

FIGURE 12.9 **Stereotype Threat and Performance**   Math test performance by men and women when the test was described as one that yields gender differences (and hence aroused stereotype threat among women) or was described as one that does not yield gender differences. (Source: Spencer, Steele, & Quinn, 1999.)

women performed equivalently when told there was no gender difference on the test, but women performed worse than men when they were told that there was a gender difference.

It's not necessary to be so blatant in the manipulation of stereotype threat for it to have an effect. Michael Inzlicht and Talia Ben-Zeev (2000) had university women take a math test either in the company of two other women or in the company of two men. Those who took the test with other women got 70 percent of the problems right on average. Those who took the test with men got 55 percent right on average.

Claude Steele and Joshua Aronson (1995) examined the sensitivity to stereotype threat on the part of African-American students. Playing on the stereotype that questions blacks' intellectual ability, they gave black and white Stanford University students a difficult verbal test taken from the Graduate Record Exam. Half of the students were led to believe that the test was capable of measuring their intellectual ability, and half were told that the investigators were in the early stages of trying to develop the test and that nothing could be learned about intellectual ability from their scores. This manipulation had no effect on the performance of white students. African-American students did as well as white students when they thought it was the test that was being tested, but they performed much worse than white students when they thought their intellectual ability was being tested. Moreover, a blatant manipulation was not required to produce a significant effect on the performance of African-Americans. It was enough simply to have them indicate their race at the top of the page to cause their performance to be worse than in a control condition in which they did not indicate their race (Steele & Aronson, 1995).

It seems that no one is safe from stereotype threat. Joshua Aronson and his colleagues (1999) showed that the math performance of white males deteriorated when they were reminded of Asian proficiency in math. And in a particularly clever experiment, Jeff Stone and his colleagues had college students perform a laboratory golf task that was described as a measure of "natural athletic ability," "sports intelligence," or "sports psychology" (Stone, Lynch, Sjomeling, & Darley, 1999). White and black students performed equally well in the "sports psychology" condition. But black students performed significantly worse when it was described as a test of "sports intelligence," and white students performed worse when it was described as a test of "natural athletic ability."

How does stereotype threat undermine performance? It appears that there is more than one pathway from concern about confirming a negative stereotype to impaired performance. Stereotype threat leads to increased arousal, which can directly interfere with performance on complex tasks (Ben-Zeev, Fein, & Inzlicht, 2005) and serve as a source of distraction that interferes with concentration on the task at hand (Cheryan & Bodenhausen, 2000). Furthermore, knowing that one's group is "suspect" in the eyes of others tends to elicit negative thinking (Cadinu, Maass, Rosabianca, & Kiesner, 2005), which can both directly undermine performance and lead individuals to "play it safe" by being more obsessed with avoiding failure than reaching for success (Seibt & Forster, 2004).

Although everyone is vulnerable by dint of group membership to some type of stereotype threat, Steele (1997) maintains that the vulnerability of African-Americans has particular potential for damage. Stereotype threat can result in poorer overall academic performance, which undermines confidence, rendering the individual still more susceptible to stereotype threat. This vicious cycle can result in "disidentification" from academic pursuits, as students who feel the threat most acutely opt out of academics altogether and identify other areas in which to invest their talent and energy and from which to derive their self-esteem.

We have seen how victims of stereotyping can suffer attributional ambiguity, not knowing whether performance feedback is genuine or based on their group membership. We also saw how they can suffer from stereotype threat, performing worse because they are afraid of affirming some stereotype that exists about their group.

REDUCING STEREOTYPES, PREJUDICE, AND DISCRIMINATION

We began this chapter by discussing the progress that has been made in intergroup relations in the United States and across much of the globe—and how much further we must go to achieve true equality of opportunity for all Americans and for all citizens of the world. What has contributed to the improved relations we have witnessed thus far, and what principles can we draw on to advance further?

The factors that have brought about improved relations between gays and straights, blacks and whites, Latinos and Anglos, and numerous other groups are many and varied and include specific legal interventions, broad economic developments, and seemingly incidental sociological trends. One factor that is both cause and conse-

quence of these developments is the increased day-to-day interaction between members of different groups. When people interact frequently, it becomes easier to see one another more as individuals and less as representatives of particular groups. As Barack Obama put it in his inaugural address, "As the world grows smaller, our common humanity shall reveal itself."

But simple contact between broad cross sections of different groups is not the be-all and end-all of harmonious relations, and some types of contact are more helpful than others. Numerous studies were conducted to assess the effect of the Supreme Court's desegregation decision in *Brown v. the Board of Education of Topeka* on race relations in U.S. schools. The initial studies did not provide strong support for what came to

Reducing Prejudice Advocates of the "contact hypothesis" maintain that greater familiarity with members of stigmatized groups can reduce prejudice directed toward those groups, particularly when the increased contact takes place under certain favorable conditions.

be known as the "contact hypothesis"—the straightforward idea that bringing together students of different races and ethnicities would reduce prejudice and discrimination. One review of the relevant literature found that in a majority of the studies that looked at the effect of integration on interracial attitudes, an *increase* in prejudice was observed (Stephan, 1986).

This was not an encouraging finding, to be sure, but in many ways it is not surprising either. After all, simply bringing the Rattlers and Eagles together did not reduce the animosity between the two groups at Robbers Cave. Contact between different groups is likely to be more positive and more productive if certain conditions are met. First, the different groups need to have equal status. If one group feels superior and the other resentful, it is unlikely that harmonious, productive interactions will be the norm. Second, as we saw in the Robbers Cave study, productive intergroup interactions are facilitated if the different groups have a shared goal that requires their cooperative interaction. Third, broader social norms should be supportive of intergroup contact. If kids of different races, religions, and ethnicities go to school with one another but their parents send them begrudgingly and rarely miss an opportunity to speak ill of the "other" children, the students themselves are unlikely to reach out across group boundaries. Finally, the contact should encourage one-on-one interactions between members of the different groups. Doing so puts each person's identity as an individual in the foreground and downplays a person's group membership. An analysis of numerous studies on the effect of desegregation, involving tens of thousands of students in over 25 different nations, found that when most of these conditions are met, contact between members of different groups does indeed tend to be effective in reducing prejudice (Pettigrew & Tropp, 2000, 2006). To put this into a context that should be particularly easy for college students to appreciate, university students who are assigned roommates of a different race report reduced anxiety about cross-race interactions and register a significant improvement on implicit measures of attitudes toward the other group (Shook & Fazio, 2008).

Note, though, that even if increased intergroup contact were entirely effective in eliminating prejudice, even if the level of intergroup hostility were reset to zero, the ideas discussed in this chapter make it clear that new prejudices and animosities might soon arise. What we have seen is that there are powerful elements of human nature that encourage stereotyping, prejudice, and discrimination—forces that require constant attention if relations between different groups are to remain harmonious. Resources are finite, and realistic conflict over who should get them guarantees that there will always be conflict between groups (the economic perspective). Also, people need to feel valued and have a sense of self-worth, a sense that stems in part from the groups to which they belong. Thus, even when conflict over scarce resources is diminished, these motivational concerns can sour intergroup relations (the motivational perspective). And what psychologists have learned about how the mind works makes it clear that people categorize and make inferences in a way that sharpens distinctions between groups and can serve to exacerbate intergroup conflict (the cognitive perspective).

Thus, the capacity to stereotype, harbor prejudice, and act in a discriminatory fashion is present in all of us, and the responsibility for reducing intergroup hostility and conflict lies with each of us as well. Intergroup harmony requires constant attention. We must all do our part as citizens to make sure, at a societal level, that civil rights laws are honored and enforced, that media depictions of different groups are not biased, and that different groups are given more opportunities to work together to achieve common goals rather than compete against one another for scarce resources. Moreover, on an individual level, we must all do our part to overcome our fear that members of other groups don't really want to interact with us (Shelton & Richeson, 2005) and engage with them anyway, to reach out and interact with members of other groups as individuals so that group boundaries begin to lose their significance, and to slowly accumulate the kinds of positive interactions that can replace troublesome associations we inherit from slanted media depictions with the more positive associations that come from person-to-person, equal-status contact.

 We have seen that contact between members of different groups can go a long way toward reducing group stereotypes and intergroup hostility. Intergroup contact is particularly likely to be beneficial when members of different groups interact as equals, work together to try to accomplish common goals, come together on a one-on-one basis, and have their interaction supported by broader societal norms.

Summary

Characterizing Intergroup Bias

- *Stereotypes* are generalizations about groups that are often applied to individual group members. *Prejudice* involves a negative attitude and emotional response to members of a group. *Discrimination* involves negative behavior toward an individual because of the person's membership in a group.

- Blatant, explicit racism in much of the world is now relatively rare. But subtle *modern racism* is more widespread, whereby people may hold overtly egalitarian attitudes and values while at the same time unconsciously having negative attitudes and exhibiting more subtle forms of prejudice toward members of certain groups.

- *Benevolent racism and sexism* consist of attitudes the individual thinks of as favorable toward a group but that have the effect of supporting traditional, subservient roles for members of oppressed groups.

- In recent years, there have been successful efforts to measure people's nonconscious attitudes with "implicit" measures. One of these is the *Implicit Association Test*, which compares reaction times when grouping outgroup pictures (or words) and positive items together versus outgroup pictures (or words) and negative items together. Another implicit measure involves *priming* with a picture of a member of some group. If the prime increases the time it takes to recognize subsequently presented positive words and decreases the time it takes to recognize subsequently presented negative words, this is an indication of prejudice toward the group.

- Three different approaches to prejudice and discrimination are the economic perspective, the motivational perspective, and the cognitive perspective.

The Economic Perspective

- One version of the *economic perspective* on prejudice and discrimination is *realistic group conflict theory*, which reflects the fact that groups are sometimes in competition for scarce resources and that this can lead to prejudice and discrimination. The classic Robbers Cave experiment put two groups of boys in competition at a camp. Soon the groups were expressing open hostility toward each other. When the groups were brought together in noncompetitive situations where they had to cooperate to achieve *superordinate goals*—that is, goals that could only be achieved when the two groups worked together—the hostility dissipated.

The Motivational Perspective

- The *motivational perspective* on prejudice and discrimination reflects the sad fact that sometimes poor relations between groups occur simply because there *are* two groups and a we/they opposition results. This occurs even in the *minimal group paradigm*, where people find out they are members of one of two groups that have been defined in a trivial and arbitrary way. They will favor members of their own group over members of the other group, even when it actually costs their group something to "beat" the opposition.

- *Social identity theory* attempts to explain ingroup favoritism, maintaining that self-esteem is derived in part from group membership and group success.

- *Frustration-aggression theory* accounts for some of the most dangerous behavior toward outgroups. When people are frustrated in their attempt to reach some goal—for example, the goal of economic prosperity—they often lash out at less powerful individuals or groups. Challenges to a person's self-esteem can have similar effects, and experiments have shown that people express more antagonism toward outgroup members when they have suffered a blow to their self-esteem.

The Cognitive Perspective

- The *cognitive perspective* on prejudice and discrimination focuses on stereotypes, which are a form of categorization. People rely on them all the time, but especially when they are tired or overloaded.

- Several construal processes lead to inaccurate stereotypes. Because we know our own groups best, we tend to assume that outgroups are more *homogeneous* than ours are, leading to the *outgroup homogeneity effect*. We also often engage in *biased information processing*, seeing those aspects of other groups that confirm our stereotypes and failing to see facts that are inconsistent with them. Moreover, we often unknowingly create *self-fulfilling prophecies*—acting toward people in such a way as to bring about the very behavior we expect of them.

- Distinctive groups (because they are in the minority) are often associated with distinctive (because they are rare) behaviors. This sort of *paired distinctiveness* results in our attributing illusory properties to such groups, creating illusory correlations.

- Encountering contradictory evidence about groups may not change our ideas about them because we treat the evidence as if it were merely an exception that proves the rule. We tend to code favorable evidence about ingroup members at high levels of generality and the same sort of evidence about outgroup members at low levels of generality. The converse is true for unfavorable evidence. Moreover, behavior consistent with a stereotype is often attributed to the dispositions of the group members, whereas behavior that is inconsistent with a stereotype is often attributed to the situation.

- We sometimes respond to outgroup members reflexively, relying on *automatic processes* wherein prejudice is unleashed outside of our awareness. Sometimes these automatic reactions can be corrected by conscious, *controlled processes*.

Being a Member of a Stigmatized Group

- Members of stigmatized groups suffer not just from prejudice and discrimination but also from *attributional*

ambiguity. They have to ask whether others' negative or positive behavior toward them is due to prejudice or to some factor having nothing to do with their group membership.

- The performance of members of stigmatized groups can be impaired by *stereotype threat*—the fear that they will confirm the stereotypes that others have regarding some salient group of which they are a member.

Reducing Stereotypes, Prejudice, and Discrimination

- Contact between members of different groups can lessen intergroup animosity, especially if the contact involves one-on-one interactions between individuals of equal status, if it encourages the cooperative pursuit of superordinate goals, and if it is supported by the prevailing norms in each group.

Key Terms

automatic processes (p. 471)
basking in reflected glory (p. 457)
controlled processes (p. 471)
discrimination (p. 444)
ethnocentrism (p. 450)
frustration-aggression theory (p. 459)
illusory correlation (p. 466)

Implicit Association Test (IAT) (p. 446)
minimal group paradigm (p. 455)
modern racism (symbolic racism) (p. 445)
outgroup homogeneity effect (p. 464)
paired distinctiveness (p. 467)
prejudice (p. 444)

priming (p. 448)
realistic group conflict theory (p. 449)
self-fulfilling prophecy (p. 465)
social identity theory (p. 456)
stereotypes (p. 443)
stereotype threat (p. 477)
subtyping (p. 469)
superordinate goals (p. 452)

Further Reading

Allport, G. (1954). *The nature of prejudice.* Reading, MA: Addison-Wesley. A classic treatment of prejudice, with a particular emphasis on racial prejudice in the U.S.

Herek, G. M. (1998). *Stigma and sexual orientation: Understanding prejudice against lesbians, gay men, and bisexuals.* Thousand Oaks, CA: Sage Publications. A social psychological look at prejudice and discrimination directed at sexual minorities.

Obama, B. (1995). *Dreams from my father: A story of race and inheritance.* New York: Random House. Best-selling memoir of America's first African-American president.

Sidanius, J., & Pratto, F. (1999). *Social dominance: An intergroup theory of social hierarchy and oppression.* New York: Cambridge University Press. A broad and rich theoretical analysis of the social psychology of power and intergroup conflict.

of complex situations can give rise to violence in some cases and to charitable action in others. We will also turn to recent studies of evolution and of culture to understand how aggression and altruism are universal tendencies and how these tendencies can vary by geographical region, gender, and kinship ties. Finally, we will ask how cooperative relations emerge and what facilitates them.

AGGRESSION

In terms of the sheer number of people killed by their fellow human beings, the last century was the most violent in history. Rwanda and Darfur were just two of several large-scale genocides. How can we account for such wanton acts of destruction? Why, after so many years of civilization, are we still killing one another in such alarming numbers? To address these questions, we will examine various situational, cultural, and evolutionary determinants of aggression, and we will explore how construal processes make aggression more or less likely.

Explanations for why aggression occurs vary according to whether it is hostile or instrumental aggression. **Hostile aggression** refers to behavior motivated by feelings of anger and hostility and whose primary aim is to harm another, either physically or psychologically. Clearly, much of the genocide in Rwanda emerged for purely hostile reasons: Hutus seeking revenge upon Tutsis out of anger about past hostilities. **Instrumental aggression**, in contrast, refers to behavior that is intended to harm another in the service of motives other than pure hostility. People harm others, for example, to gain status, to attract attention, to acquire wealth, and to advance political and ideological causes. Some of the genocide in Rwanda was in the pursuit of political purposes: the Hutu were seeking to displace the more powerful Tutsis. Many acts of aggression involve a mix of hostile and instrumental motives. A football player who intentionally harms another might do so out of aggressive emotion (hostile aggression) or for a variety of instrumental reasons—for example, to foster a fearless reputation, to help his team win, or to make the kind of plays that secure a place on the team or that earn a lucrative contract.

hostile aggression Behavior intended to harm another, either physically or psychologically, and motivated by feelings of anger and hostility.

instrumental aggression Behavior intended to harm another in the service of motives other than pure hostility (for example, to attract attention, to acquire wealth, or to advance political and ideological causes).

Situational Determinants of Aggression

What is striking about the massacres of Rwanda and Darfur is how quickly peaceful, stable relations between groups can turn to aggression. Clearly, situational factors can give rise to violence. In Darfur, for example, drought, desertification, the loss of farming lands, and overpopulation produced a level of desperation that contributed to the genocide. Social psychologists have long been interested in the kinds of situational factors that give rise to aggression. One such factor—heat—most certainly was at play in the massacres at Rwanda and Darfur.

Heat The first line of Spike Lee's movie *Do the Right Thing* comes from a radio newscaster who says, "It's hot out there, folks." It's early in the morning, and the main characters, clad in T-shirts and shorts, are already uncomfortable and sweating profusely. By the end of the day, tensions between African-Americans and Italian-Americans escalate, and a race riot ensues.

People have long believed that moods and actions are closely tied to the weather. Perhaps the most widely assumed connection is between heat and aggression. We

"I pray thee good Mercutio,
let's retire;
The day is hot, the Capulets
abroad.
And, if we meet, we shall not
'scape a brawl,
For now, these hot days, is the
mad blood stirring."

—Shakespeare, *Romeo and Juliet*

Heat and Violence   People are more likely to become aggressive when the temperatures are especially high. Communities have organized to combat the influences of heat on aggression by building skate parks and creating basketball leagues to allow young men to play more during the hot summer months and reduce aggressive behavior.

think of angry people as "boiling over," "steamed," and "hot under the collar." This is in part due to what anger does to the body: it literally raises the temperature of the hands. The connection between anger and heat may also have to do with what the ambient temperature does to people's emotions and actions.

Are people more aggressive when it's hot? As early as the nineteenth century, social theorists observed that violent crime rates were higher in southern France and southern Italy, where the temperatures are hotter, than in northern France and northern Italy. Of course, other factors—such as levels of unemployment, per capita income, ethnic composition, or average age—might also have produced these regional differences in aggression.

Craig Anderson has provided evidence that higher than normal temperatures are associated with increased aggression (Anderson, 1987, 1989). First, there are higher rates of violent crimes in hotter regions. Anderson examined the crime rates of 260 cities throughout the United States. For each city, he identified the number of days in which the temperature exceeded 90 degrees Fahrenheit. The number of hot days (above 90 degrees) was a strong predictor of elevated violent crime rates but not nonviolent crime rates. This was true even when Anderson controlled for the city's level of unemployment, per capita income, and average age of its citizens (Anderson, 1987).

People are also more violent during hot months, such as July and August, than during cooler months, like January and February (the one exception is December, when violent crime rates also rise—so much for holiday cheer). In **Figure 13.1**, for example, you can see that murder and rape rise during the summer months. Moreover, in one of the cleverest of the "heat" studies, it was found that major league baseball pitchers are more likely to hit batters as the weather gets hotter and hotter (Reifman, Larrick, & Fein, 1991). This is not due to reduced competence; neither wild pitches nor bases on balls go up with the temperature (see also Kenrick & MacFarlane, 1984).

What is it about high temperatures that might make people more aggressive? One possible explanation involves attributional processes. According to the misattribution perspective, people are aroused by the heat, but they are largely unaware of their arousal. When they encounter circumstances that prompt anger—say, a frustrating driver or an irritating romantic partner—they attribute their arousal to that person, and this misattributed arousal gives rise to amplified feelings of anger and aggression. Another possibility is that heat triggers basic unpleasant feelings of anger, which increase the chances of all kinds of aggressive behavior. Later we will consider this explanation in greater detail.

Media Violence   One of the lessons of the tragedy in Rwanda is the power of the media in inciting violence. The frenzy toward genocide in Rwanda was stirred by a manifesto known as the "Hutu Ten Commandments," published in a widely read newspaper, the *Kangura*, and spread like wildfires by local radio stations. The "Hutu Ten Commandments" warned of the dangers of the Tutsis, insisting that Tutsi women were secret agents bent on Hutu demise, that Hutu men who married or employed Tutsi women were traitors, and that Hutus who did business with a Tutsi were enemies of the Hutu people. The media spread rumors and fears about the Tutsis that in many ways instigated the Rwandan genocide. This document may have played the same role in the slaughter of Tutsis that the "Protocols of Zion," alleging ritual murder of Christian babies by Jews, played in the Holocaust.

The Western media is saturated with images of aggression. The average American child watches 3 to 4 hours of television a day, and many of the programs children watch are violent. Prime-time television programs on average have about five to six violent acts per hour, and about 90 percent of the programs that children watch portray at least some violence (Gerbner, Gross, Morgan, & Signorielli, 1986). By the age of 12, the average viewer of American television has seen about 100,000 acts of violence, from car crashes on reality police shows to murders and beatings on weekly crime or courtroom dramas to dead bodies on the nightly news. Some estimates are that the average high school graduate in America has seen 13,000 killings on TV, not to mention those seen in the movies and in video games.

Does the violence portrayed in the media make people more aggressive? Every year, concerned citizens urge the entertainment industry to curtail its depiction of violence. Journalists routinely decry the violence on television and in the movies. Are these movements founded on an empirically established link between violent media and aggressive behavior?

Several strands of evidence suggest that people who campaign against media violence are correct in their basic assumption—that exposure to media violence increases aggressive behavior. Let's start with copycat violence—that is, the imitation of specific violent acts depicted in the media (see **Box 13.1**). In March 1981, John Hinckley Jr. attempted to assassinate President Ronald Reagan, shooting him in the chest and, by many accounts, severely impairing Reagan's ability to lead the country in the months afterward. What investigators soon discovered was unnerving evidence about the nature of copycat violence. Hinckley had seen Martin Scorsese's movie *Taxi Driver*, which starred Robert DeNiro as a violent sociopath who attempts to kill a politician to win the love of a young prostitute played by Jodie Foster. In Hinckley's own hotel

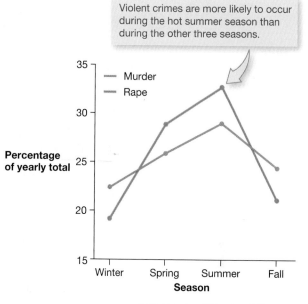

FIGURE 13.1 **Effects of Season on Violent Behavior**   Do the hot months of summer make people more aggressive? Various studies of aggressive behaviors throughout different months of the year indicate that they do. (Source: Adapted from Anderson, 1989, p. 82.)

BOX 13.1 **FOCUS ON THE MEDIA**

Copycat Violence

David Phillips (1986) has marshaled evidence that indicates that one type of copycat violence, namely suicide—which is the ultimate form of violence against the self—is a very real phenomenon. In a first study, Phillips identified 35 suicides reported in the U.S. media from 1947 to 1968 and asked whether suicide rates rose in the following months. He compared the suicide rates of those months with the rates observed during the same months the year prior to each suicide, as well as during the same months the year after. This allowed him to control for the effects of weather and season on aggressive behavior (which, as we have seen, are significant).

In 26 of the 35 widely reported suicides, the suicide rate rose substantially more in the month following the suicide than in the two comparison months. For example, Marilyn Monroe's widely publicized overdose in August 1962 was followed by a 12 percent increase in suicides in the United States and a 10 percent increase in Great Britain. Phillips also observed a strong positive correlation between the amount of media coverage the suicide received and the increase in the suicide rate. That is, the greater the amount of newspaper space devoted to a suicide, the greater the increase in copycat suicides. And more detailed analyses suggested that people were not engaging in copycat suicides out of grief; people even imitated the suicides of despised individuals—for example, the suicide of a leader of the Ku Klux Klan.

You might be wondering about the effect of a number of variables that Phillips could not measure. For example, were particularly depressive or aggressive people—that is, those more inclined initially to harm self or others—most likely to imitate the publicized acts of violence and commit suicide? Phillips's data do not allow us to tell. But even if people who were depressed or aggressive were more likely to commit copycat suicide, this would not undermine Phillips's claim about imitative suicide; it would just indicate that the effect is particularly pronounced among certain segments of the population.

room, there was a letter addressed to Jodie Foster, in which he declared that he was going to kill President Reagan for her.

How prevalent is copycat violence? We know the answer for media violence, not only for the short term, but over much of the life span as well. The work of people like Rowell Huesmann and Leonard Eron and their colleagues in many different countries has led to a clear verdict on the question of whether early exposure to media violence leads to aggressive behavior later in life. Consider one study in which Eron and Huesmann assessed the television viewing habits of 211 boys in Columbia County, in upstate New York, from childhood to adulthood (Huesmann, Moise-Titus, Podolski, & Eron, 2003). They wanted to know if a boy's preference for watching violent TV at age 8 would predict how much criminal activity he would engage in by age 30. One potential problem with this study is that perhaps aggressive boys at age 8 like to watch violent TV, committing violent acts later. If so, any relationship between violent TV watched at age 8 and subsequent aggression could be attributed to the aggressiveness of the boy and not to watching violent TV. To account for this, Huesmann and Eron controlled for how aggressive the child was at age 8 to look at the "pure" relations between violent TV watched at age 8 and subsequent aggressive behavior. As you can see in **Figure 13.2**, watching a lot of violent TV at age 8 was associated with substantially more serious criminal activity by age 30.

The conclusions that Huesmann and Eron have drawn from this research have been reinforced by the results of laboratory studies on the effects of exposure to media violence on aggression immediately afterward (Anderson, Berkowitz, et al., 2003; Geen, 1998). In these studies, participants typically view aggressive films and then are given an opportunity to act in an aggressive fashion—for example, by shocking a confrontational confederate (for review, see Berkowitz, 1993). The results of these studies

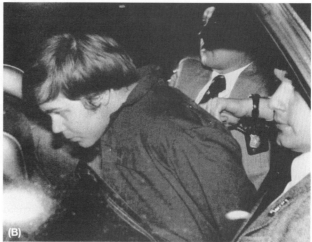

Copycat Violence Violence in the media sometimes is imitated in real life, as demonstrated in the attempted assassination of President Ronald Reagan in imitation of an attempted assassination of a politician in the film *Taxi Driver*. (A) Robert De Niro played the would-be assassin in the film. (B) John Hinckley Jr. attempted to assassinate the president after seeing the film.

indicate that watching aggressive films does indeed make people more aggressive. For example, one study showed that watching aggressive films compared with control films made juvenile delinquents staying at a minimum-security penal institution more aggressive (Leyens, Camino, Parke, & Berkowitz, 1975). And in another study, male college students behaved more aggressively toward a female when they were angered and exposed to violent media imagery (Donnerstein, 1980; Donnerstein & Berkowitz, 1981). Exposure to violent pornography increases the endorsement of aggression against women (Allen et al., 1995).

By controlling the specific kinds of violent media participants view, these experimental studies have uncovered the sorts of media violence that are most likely to lead to aggression. People tend to be more aggressive, for example, after seeing films in which they identify with the perpetrator of the violent act (Leyens & Picus, 1973). People are also more likely to be aggressive after watching violent films that portray justified violence—that is, violence perpetrated against "bad people" (Berkowitz, 1965). When participants are led to direct their attention away from the aggressive content of the violent film—for example, by focusing on the aesthetic features of the film—they are less likely to be aggressive (Leyens, Cisneros, & Hossay, 1976).

Violent Video Games The new technologies—Web sites, YouTube, and video games—have introduced new opportunities to be exposed to aggressive imagery. For example, about 85 percent of American teens play video games regularly (Anderson & Bushman, 2001). Among 8- to 13-year-old boys, the average is more than 7.5 hours per week (Roberts, Foehr, Rideout, & Brodie, 1999). And as with anything, there are the extremes—the video game addicts. Two percent of college-age males in America play video games 20 hours or more a week.

Two such aficionados of video games were Eric Harris and Dylan Klebold. They played violent video games habitually, their favorite being the game Doom. Harris himself created a custom version of Doom in which two shooters, armed with extra weapons and unlimited ammunition, would gun down an array of helpless victims

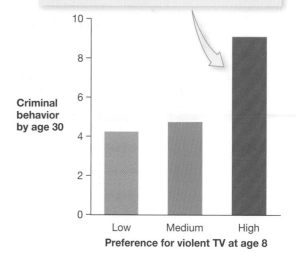

Men who liked to watch violent TV at age 8, holding constant for how aggressive they were at that age, were more likely to commit serious criminal acts at age 30 than were men who had had little or moderate liking for violent TV at age 8.

FIGURE 13.2 Preference for Media Violence and Aggressiveness The *y*-axis scale for criminal behavior reflects two measures: number of criminal convictions and seriousness of each crime. (Source: Huesmann, 1986.)

Video Games and the Columbine Massacre   (A) An image from a violent video game. The correlation between playing violent video games and aggressive thoughts and behavior documented in the laboratory may play out in real life. (B) Eric Harris and Dylan Klebold spent hours playing the violent video game *Doom*, in which two shooters gun down helpless victims. Some observers have speculated that this may have contributed to their decision to plant bombs and shoot their classmates at Columbine High School in Littleton, Colorado. Here, cameras in the school cafeteria on April 20, 1999, showed them armed with guns and getting ready to shoot their fellow students, who were huddled beneath the tables. They killed 12 students and 1 teacher before killing themselves.

who could not fight back. A short time later, on April 20, 1999, their actions mirrored their video game world. Harris and Klebold planted bombs and took several guns and massive amounts of ammunition to their school, Columbine High School, in Littleton, Colorado, where they killed 12 of their classmates and 1 teacher, as well as injuring another 23 students, before killing themselves.

Are video games the cause of this kind of violence? Certainly not the only cause, and many in the video game industry vehemently argue that there is *no* relationship between playing video games and violence. In a May 12, 2000, interview on CNN, Doug Lowenstein, president of the Interactive Digital Software Association, stated, "There is absolutely no evidence, none, that playing a violent video game leads to aggressive behavior." Yet, research by Craig Anderson and Brad Bushman and their colleagues indicates otherwise and suggests that we have reason to worry about the prevalence of video games in youth culture today (Anderson & Bushman, 2001; Anderson & Dill, 2000).

In one study, 43 undergraduate women and men with an average amount of experience playing video games were randomly assigned to play one of two video games. Some played Mortal Kombat, a video game in which the player chooses to be one character and attempts to kill six other characters. The more killings and the more violent the deaths, the more points the participant wins. Others played PGA Tournament Golf, a video game in which they completed 18 holes of simulated golf, choosing appropriate clubs and shots best suited to the simulated wind conditions, sand traps, and trees. All participants then played a competitive game with a confederate. When participants lost, they were punished by the confederate with a burst of white noise. When participants won, they punished the confederate with a burst of white noise. The finding: Participants who had played Mortal Kombat gave longer and more intense bursts of white noise to their competitor than those who had played the golf game.

In a review of 35 studies like the one just described, Anderson and Bushman documented five disturbing effects of playing violent video games (Anderson & Bushman, 2001). Playing violent video games increases aggressive behavior; reduces prosocial behavior, like helping or altruism; increases aggressive thoughts; increases aggressive emotions; and increases blood pressure and heart rate, physiological responses associated with fighting and fleeing. These effects were observed in children and adult women as well as in men.

Construal Processes and Aggression

Thus far, we have seen that several situational factors—excessive heat, media violence, and violent video games—make people more aggressive. In fact, powerful situational factors, such as being raised in a violent family, are necessary for individuals genetically predisposed to aggression to actually act in violent fashion (see **Box 13.2**). Of course, as we emphasize throughout this book, situations do nothing by themselves. Rather, their influences are channeled through construal processes. Consider another situational factor that influences levels of aggression—income inequality. Martin Daly, Margot Wilson, and Shawn Vasdev (2001) have observed that homicide rates at every population level—from neighborhoods to nations—rise as degrees of inequality rise. They believe that this happens because inequality throws males into competition for economic resources and females—two sources of conflict that often lie behind murder and other crimes. Some people respond to the inequality around them with feelings of anger and aggressive behavior. Others, by contrast, respond with a sense of resignation or despair. Understanding how people construe specific situational factors such as heat, violent imagery in the media, or inequality reveals more specifically when and why people become aggressive. In this section, we zero in on how specific construal processes—in particular, those prompted by unpleasant feelings of anger—increase aggressive behavior.

BOX 13.2 FOCUS ON GENES AND ENVIRONMENT

Nature or Nurture? It's Both

Many biological factors predispose people to act in aggressive fashion (White, 1997; Yudko, Blanchard, Henne, & Blanchard, 1997). For example, testosterone, a male sex hormone, tends to be associated with higher levels of aggression: delinquents were shown to have higher levels than college students (Banks & Dabbs, 1996), and members of rowdier fraternities had higher levels than members of more responsible fraternities (Dabbs, 2000).

Important research by Avshalom Capi and Terrie Moffitt and their colleagues has found that aggression might best be thought of as the interaction between situational factors and genetically based individual differences

(Caspi et al., 2002). In this study, Caspi, Moffitt, and colleagues tested for the two forms of the monoamine oxidase A (MAOA) gene. Monoamine oxidase is an enzyme that metabolizes different neurotransmitters in the brain and allows for smooth communication between neurons. Humans and non-humans with a defective MAOA gene have been shown to be more violent. Caspi and colleagues identified men with this defective gene and those without it. In terms of situational factors, they also identified men who had or had not been mistreated by their parents as children—one of the most potent precursors of violence in adulthood. Overall, the defective MAOA gene alone did

not have an effect on whether the boys committed violent crimes (rape, assault, robbery) by the age of 26. Boys who had the defective gene *and* who were mistreated as children, however, were three times as likely to have been convicted of a violent crime by age 26 as the boys who had the defective gene but who had not been mistreated. Although those with the gene for low MAOA activity who had also suffered mistreatment were only 12 percent of the population of boys in the cohort, they were responsible for 44 percent of the cohort's convictions for violent crime. Some 85 percent of the boys with the low MAOA gene who were severely mistreated developed some form of antisocial behavior.

frustration The internal state that accompanies the thwarting of an attempt to achieve some goal.

The Frustration-Aggression Hypothesis In the late 1930s and 1940s, Neal Miller and John Dollard offered a simple account of aggression that was based largely on laboratory studies of rats (Dollard, Doob, Miller, Mowrer, & Sears, 1939; Miller, 1941). Miller and Dollard argued that *the* determinant of aggression is **frustration**, the thwarting of an individual's attempts to achieve some goal. Individuals act in aggressive fashion, this perspective holds, when they feel thwarted in their attempt to reach some goal, and all frustrations lead to aggression—or at any rate, the desire to commit it.

What kinds of specific construals give rise to aggression? Miller and Dollard proposed that aggression increases in direct proportion to: (1) the amount of satisfaction the person anticipates before a goal is blocked, (2) the more completely the person is prevented from achieving the goal, (3) the more frequently the person is blocked from achieving the goal, and (4) the closer the individual believes he or she is to achieving the goal (Miller, 1941). In a study that illustrates some of these principles (and may remind you of your own experience with aggression), a confederate cut in front of individuals waiting patiently in line to see a movie. In one condition, the target was twelfth in line; in the second condition, the target was second in line, about to purchase a ticket and therefore close to 2 hours of anticipated pleasure. As predicted by the frustration-aggression hypothesis, the target who was second in line was much more aggressive in response to the confederate who cut in line than the person who was twelfth in line (Harris, 1974).

Critiques of the Frustration-Aggression Hypothesis The frustration-aggression hypothesis is an important first step toward understanding the construal processes that give rise to aggression. When an individual feels blocked in the pursuit of a goal, aggression is more likely. As compelling as this account may be, closer examination reveals several problems with this line of thinking (Berkowitz, 1993). One criticism has called into question the hypothesis that all aggressive behaviors follow from frustration, or the perceived thwarting of goal-directed activity. Consider again the relationship between heat and aggression. How does heat block an individual's goals? Other findings also suggest that aggression follows stimuli that do not directly block goal-directed behavior. When animals are shocked, for example, they often aggress against others in their vicinity (Berkowitz, 1993). When people are exposed to extreme levels of pollution, they are also more likely to act aggressively (Rotton & Frey, 1985). And some forms of instrumental aggression, such as bullying, are not the direct product of the blocking of goals (Olweus, 1979, 1980). For example, bullies often act aggressively against weaker peers out of an interest in getting attention, raising their status, or showing off. In each of these cases, the stimulus that produces aggression has nothing to do with blocking an individual's goals.

A second problem with the frustration-aggression hypothesis is that frustration does not necessarily lead to aggression, as assumed in this account. Frustration can lead to other responses. The best example here comes from the literature on **learned helplessness**, the passive and depressive responses some people show when their goals are blocked and they believe that they have no control over their outcomes (Seligman, 1975). In a series of frequently cited studies, dogs were shocked and prevented from escaping. After repeated exposure to this uncontrollable, negative stimulus, the dogs did not show aggression; instead, they collapsed into a pitiable state of helplessness and resignation.

learned helplessness Passive and depressed responses that individuals show when their goals are blocked and they feel that they have no control over their outcomes.

A Neo-Associationistic Account of Aggression The two critiques of the frustration-aggression hypothesis highlight how important construal processes are to the initiation of aggressive behavior. It is not just having our goals blocked that leads to aggression; it is how we interpret the events that seem to have caused it. To take one example, acts that we construe as having been intentionally harmful are more likely to make us aggressive than acts seen to be accidental that produce equivalent harm (Worchel, 1974). Observations such as these set the stage for Leonard Berkowitz's neo-associationistic account of aggression, which suggests that unpleasnt feelings of anger associated with different aversive stimuli are what give rise to aggression.

Berkowitz (1989) has argued that any aversive event can elicit an aggressive response—pain, hunger, fatigue, humiliation, anxiety, insults, you name it. For example, in one of his studies, participants led to experience pain by having to hold their arms raised horizontally for several minutes offered harsher, more hostile assessments of their mothers and romantic partners than did control subjects (Berkowitz & Troccoli, 1990). The critical determinant is whether the event produces unpleasant feelings of anger. As we explain in Chapter 7, anger is associated with thoughts about blame, fight-or-flight physiology, and feelings of injustice and revenge. Once activated, these thoughts, feelings, and physiological reactions make intentional harm against another—aggression—more likely (see **Figure 13.3**). To return to our heat example, sometimes extreme heat does not trigger anger (for example, it might prompt relaxation), and in these instances, it will not lead to aggressive behavior. Other times, however, extreme heat does trigger feelings of anger, and it is at this time that heat makes people act aggressively. The crucial thing, then, is whether or not the stimulus triggers unleasant feelings of anger (see **Figure 13.4**). This line of thinking would help illuminate when different features of the situation—heat, pollution, or what we consider next, weapons—lead to violence and when they do not.

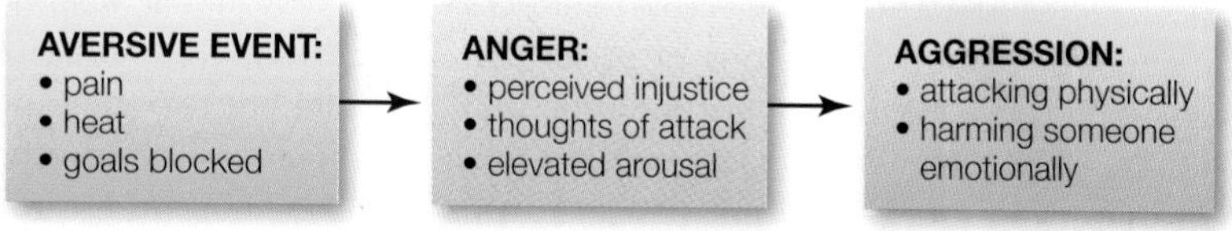

AVERSIVE EVENT:	ANGER:	AGGRESSION:
• pain	• perceived injustice	• attacking physically
• heat	• thoughts of attack	• harming someone
• goals blocked	• elevated arousal	emotionally

FIGURE 13.3 The Neo-Associationistic Account of Aggression This theory holds that aggression occurs following aversive events that make people angry. (Source: Adapted from Berkowitz, 1989.)

Weapons and Violence We live in an era in which weapons are everywhere. Worldwide, there are over 638 million guns in the hands of nonmilitary citizens (United Nations, 2002). In the United States alone, there are over 200 million guns in private hands. Gun control is one of the most divisive political issues in the United States today. Opponents of gun control see the possession of firearms as a constitutionally guaranteed right to bear arms. Advocates of gun control believe that restricting the purchase and use of guns would reduce the incidence of lethal aggression.

Berkowitz has gathered data that might be used by advocates of gun control. According to Berkowitz, guns serve as a powerful cue that primes anger-related construals, making aggression more likely (see **Box 13.3**). To test his hypothesis, Berkowitz had male participants engage in an experiment with a male confederate on "the effects of physiological stress upon work" (Berkowitz & LePage, 1967). The participant and a confederate worked on a series of problems, and they took turns "evaluating each

FIGURE 13.4 You Be the Subject: Neo-Associationistic Account of Aggression

As per the Berkowitz & Troccoli study (1990), have a friend hold out his arm for 6 minutes (under the ruse that this is a measure of physical strength).

About 4 minutes into the demonstration, ask your friend how he is getting along with his parents, or how well school is going or how much he likes his professors.

Results: The person with the arm out should be biased to provide more negative, even hostile answers, compared to someone not experiencing pain.

Explanation: Incidental pain can make people more aggressive.

BOX 13.3 **FOCUS ON SPORTS**

The Effect of Uniform Color on Aggression

The tendency to act more aggressively when a weapon is nearby reinforces one of the core lessons of social psychology—the situationist message that seemingly small changes in the environment can have a substantial impact on behavior. It also raises the question of whether there are other environmental cues that might foster or inhibit aggression. Thus, the clothes people wear may exert an impact on how they behave, including whether or not they behave aggressively. Might the menacing black shirts worn by Hitler's S.S. (*Schutzstaffel*) have made it easier for them to brutalize the populace of conquered lands?

Support for such a possibility comes from research on the effect of uniform color on aggressiveness in professional sports (Frank & Gilovich, 1988). The investigators began by examining the penalty records of all teams in professional football (the NFL) and ice hockey (the NHL) from 1970 to 1985. As shown in the accompanying figure, the black-uniformed teams consistently ranked near the top in penalties every year. As pronounced as this tendency might be, however, it cannot tell us whether wearing black actually causes players to be more aggressive. There are two other possibilities. First, because of some rather negative stereotypes involving the color black (for example, cinematic villains typically dress in black), players in black uniforms may look more malevolent even if they play no differently than players on other teams. Thus, players in black uniforms may be more likely than others to be penalized for marginal infractions. Second, the finding may simply be a selection effect; that is, the management of certain teams may believe that aggressiveness pays off in victories and so recruit particularly aggressive players and, incidentally, give them black uniforms to foster an image.

The latter interpretation can be ruled out. By a convenient twist of fate, several teams switched uniforms from non-black to black during the period under investigation, and all experienced a corresponding increase in penalties. One team, the NHL's Pittsburgh Penguins, changed uniform colors in the middle of a season, meaning the switch was not accompanied by any changes in players, coaches, or front-office personnel. Nevertheless, the Penguins averaged 8 penalty minutes in the blue uniforms they wore before the switch and 12 penalty minutes in the black uniforms they wore after—a 50 percent increase.

Follow-up laboratory experiments have obtained support both for perceptions of aggressiveness and actual aggressiveness of players in black (**Figure 13.5**). Thus, the tendency for black-uniformed teams to accrue so many penalties appears to be the joint effect of a bias on the part of the referees and a tendency for players wearing black to act more aggressively (Frank & Gilovich, 1988).

But does wearing black always make people more aggressive? Probably not. The effect seems to be limited to contexts that are already associated with confrontation and aggression. Thus, the black clothing worn by Catholic clerics and Hasidic Jews may not make them any more aggressive, but the black shirts worn by Hitler's S.S. might very well have contributed to their brutality.

other's performance." They did so by delivering between one and ten shocks—with the instruction to deliver more shocks for performances that most needed improvement.

The researchers had the participants work on the problems first. Unknown to the participants, the confederate delivered shocks based on whether the participants had been assigned to a neutral or anger condition (not based on their actual performance). The confederate shocked those assigned to the neutral condition one time and those assigned to the anger condition seven times. The participant then watched the confederate work on the problems and gave his evaluation of the confederate's performance in the form of shocks under one of three conditions. In a "no object" condition, there were no objects near the shock machine. In a "neutral object" condition, there were badminton rackets and shuttlecocks near the shock machine. In a "gun" condition, there was a revolver and a shotgun sitting near the shock machine—rather unusual experimental props, to say the least! According to the neo-associationistic account of aggression, participants who were angry and primed to think aggressive thoughts by the presence of the guns should be particularly aggressive toward the confederate. As you can see in **Figure 13.6**, that is what Berkowitz found.

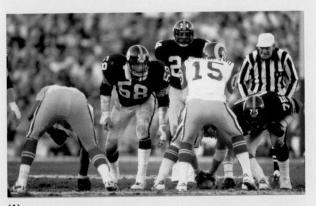

(A)

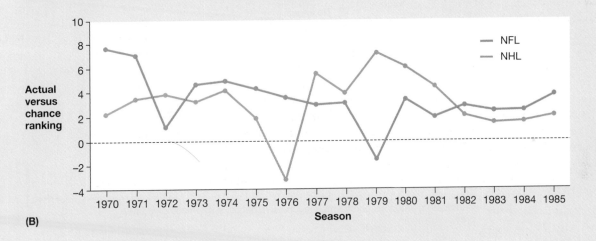

FIGURE 13.5 Uniform Color and Aggression
(A) The Pittsburgh Steelers, wearing black uniforms, were known for their aggressive play. (B) Penalty records of black-uniformed teams in the NFL and NHL from 1970 to 1985 (note that the hockey season always stretches across two calendar years; thus, "1985" corresponds to the 1985–1986 season). Points on the graph represent the difference between the average ranking of the black-uniformed teams and the average to be expected on the basis of chance alone (represented by the dotted horizontal line at 0). (Source: Adapted from Frank & Gilovich, 1988.)

(B)

It's critical to note that the aggression-priming effect of the guns was observed only in the condition in which subjects were made angry; the guns had no effect if participants were not angry (see also Frodi, 1975; Turner & Leyens, 1992). That is, guns make people aggressive when they combine with or elicit anger-related construals, as Berkowitz reasoned. In further corroboration of this point, Bartholow, Anderson, and colleagues found that hunters do not become more aggressive when presented with images of guns, because they construe guns as sources of recreation rather than violence (Bartholow, Anderson, Carnagey, & Benjamin, 2005).

Culture and Aggression

Anthropologists have long noted dramatic cultural variation in levels of aggression. People in certain cultures have been observed to be kind, peaceful, and cooperative. Alaskan Inuits, for example, have been described as rarely expressing anger or aggression and remarkably kind in their actions with others. People in other cultures have been portrayed as violent, belligerent, and aggressive. Among the Yanomamo,

FIGURE 13.6 **Scientific Method: Priming of Anger-Related Aggression**

Hypothesis: Aggression is most likely when anger is combined with hostile objects or images perceived in the environment.

Research Method:

1 A male participant and a confederate worked on a series of problems and took turns evaluating each other's performance by delivering between one and ten shocks, with the participant believing that more shocks are delivered for performances that most needed improvement.

2 Participants unwittingly assigned to the "neutral" condition were shocked by the confederate once, whereas participants unwittingly assigned to the "anger" condition were shocked several times.

3 The participant then watched the confederate work on the problems and gave his evaluation of the confederate's performance in the form of shocks. In a "no object" condition, there were no objects near the shock machine. In a "neutral object" condition, there were badminton rackets and shuttlecocks near the shock machine. In a "gun" condition, there was a revolver and a shotgun sitting near the shock machine.

Results: Participants who were angered by shocks they received from a confederate were more likely to retaliate with shocks when there were violent weapons as opposed to harmless objects near the shock machine.

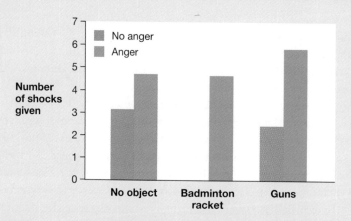

Conclusion: Weapons primed more aggressive behavior when combined with preexisting anger.

Source: Berkowitz & LePage (1967).

aggression is encouraged in children, intratribal fighting with spears and knives is a weekly source of injury and death, and rape and war are considered an intrinsic part of human nature (Chagnon, 1997).

The challenge for social psychologists, of course, is to bring cultural variations in aggression into the laboratory and find explanations for them. The cultural perspective on aggression holds that there are certain values, as well as habitual ways of construing the self and others, that make members of one culture more aggressive and violent than others, or more prone to specific kinds of aggression. Let's look at two distinct lines of research that illustrate the cultural approach to aggression.

culture of honor A culture that is defined by its members' strong concerns about their own and others' reputations, leading to sensitivity to slights and insults and a willingness to use violence to avenge any perceived wrong or insult.

The Culture of Honor Richard Nisbett and Dov Cohen have explored regional differences in violence in the United States (Cohen & Nisbett, 1997; Cohen, Nisbett, Bowdle, & Schwarz, 1996; Nisbett, 1993; Nisbett & Cohen, 1996). Nisbett and Cohen argue that in the South, many people are part of a **culture of honor**, concerned about their reputation for toughness, machismo, and the willingness and ability to avenge a wrong or insult. These concerns give rise to firm rules of politeness and other

Culture and Aggression   There are cultural as well as individual differences in the expression of aggression. (A) The Alaskan Inuits rarely express anger or aggression. (B) The Yanomamo encourage aggression in their children and are known for their violent raids against their enemies.

means by which people recognize the honor of others, thus lending stability to social relations and reducing the risk of violence. The downside of the concern with honor is that it makes people particularly sensitive to slights and insults and makes them feel obligated to respond with violence to protect or reestablish their honor.

In Chapter 2, we reviewed several lines of evidence using an array of different methods that indicate that Southerners are more likely to respond with aggression than Northerners when their honor is slighted (Nisbett & Cohen, 1996). In archival research, Nisbett and his colleagues found that murders in the context of a felony were about equally common in the North, South, and Southwest, but that honor-related homicides were far more common in the South and Southwest than in the North (see **Figure 13.7**). To examine participants' sensitivity to slights and insults, Cohen and his

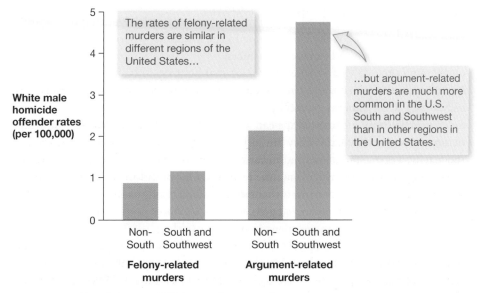

FIGURE 13.7 The Culture of Honor and Homicide   The rates point to a sensitivity to slights and insults that characterizes a culture of honor in the South and Southwest. (Source: Nisbett & Cohen, 1996, p. 21; based on data from Fox & Pierce, 1987.)

colleagues exposed Southerners and Northerners to an insult that arose in the context of a laboratory study. Insulted students from Southern states showed more anger in their facial expressions than did students from the North (Cohen et al., 1996), they showed higher levels of testosterone and cortisol, they shook another person's hand more firmly, and they refused to move out of the way of an imposing confederate walking toward them in a narrow hallway. And in a field experiment, Cohen and Nisbett (1997) found that potential Southern employers actually expressed a good deal of warmth toward a potential job applicant who confessed to having been convicted of manslaughter after defending his honor.

What are the deeper origins of this culture-related variation in aggression? Why is honor-related homicide more common in the South? Could it just be the higher temperatures there? It's not likely, because honor-related homicides are more common in the relatively cool mountain regions of the South than in the relatively hot lowlands. Could it be the brutal history of slavery? Again, it's not likely, and for the same geographical reason. Homicide is more common in the highlands, where slavery was relatively uncommon, than in the lowlands, where slavery was ubiquitous.

Instead, Nisbett and Cohen (1996) argue that the culture of honor in the South is a variant of an ethos found worldwide among people who earn their living by herding animals. Herders are susceptible to losing their entire wealth in an instant if someone steals their cows, pigs, or sheep. Farmers, in contrast, are susceptible to no such rapid and catastrophic loss—at least not at the hands of another person. The vulnerability of the herder means that he has to develop a tough exterior and make it clear that he is willing to take a stand against the slightest threat, even an insult or a joke at his expense. This difference fits the pattern of violence in the United States because the North was founded primarily by farmers from England, Germany, and the Netherlands, whereas the South was founded primarily by Scottish and Irish settlers—Celtic peoples who had herded, rather than farmed, since prehistoric times. Thus, the people in the Southern highlands, where the herding culture continued to be a major economic activity until quite recently, were more likely to be violent than those in the lowlands, where settlers had taken advantage of the rich soil to become farmers.

Rape-Prone Cultures Rape, the coercive forcing of sex by one person (overwhelmingly male) upon another (typically female), is one of the most disturbing acts of violence. The consequences of rape can be cataclysmic, deep, and lasting. Many rape victims are scarred for years. They can suffer posttraumatic stress, generalized anxiety, and fearfulness in open places and toward strange men. Many suffer eating disorders and develop problems in their romantic relations. One of the greatest tragedies in the genocides in Rwanda and Darfur is that rape is systematically used by the perpetrators of the genocide against women and girls.

What makes rape more prevalent in one culture than another? And how would you tackle this question empirically? Peggy Reeves Sanday (1981, 1997) relied on archival records to address the cultural determinants of rape. She read descriptions provided by historians and anthropologists about 156 cultures dating back to 1750 BC and continuing to the 1960s. She looked carefully for references to rape in these accounts and identified what she called **rape-prone cultures**. She defined such cultures according to whether they used rape as (1) an act of war against enemy women,

rape-prone cultures Cultures in which rape tends to be used as an act of war against enemy women, as a ritual act, and as a threat against women so that they will remain subservient to men.

BOX 13.4 **FOCUS ON THE ENVIRONMENT**

Green Neighborhoods Make for More Peaceful Citizens

The current environmentalist movement was inspired by several philosophers known as the transcendentalists, which included Henry David Thoreau and Ralph Waldo Emerson. These writers found great calm and peace in being out in the woods and cultivated a reverential attitude toward nature. Their writings inspired a young naturalist, John Muir, whose experiences as a young man in the Sierras led him to found the Sierra Club and argue on behalf of state and national parks, which he helped create.

Frances Kuo is a social psychologist who is in effect part of the environmentalist movement. In her research she has asked whether being in more natural environments makes for more calm, less aggressive citizens (Kuo, 2001). In one study, she compared the self-reported levels of violence of two comparable groups of citizens living in housing projects in Chicago: one of the groups lived in a housing project with nice parks and lawns nearby; the other lived in a housing project with no greenery, surrounded by barren asphault. Sure enough, those citizens in the green urban areas reported less aggression in their neighborhood and performed better on a test that assessed the ability to concentrate. Green spaces calm people's minds, enabling them to handle the frustrations of daily living better.

(2) a ritual act—for example, as part of a wedding ceremony or of an adolescent male's rite of passage to adulthood, and (3) a threat against women so that they would remain subservient to the men.

Of the 156 cultures Sanday studied, 47 percent were classified as rape free, 18 percent as rape prone, and 35 percent as rape present, where rape occurs but not as a ritual, threat, or act of war. You should be skeptical of these percentages, of course. They are based largely on anthropologists' observations, and rape is one of the most difficult acts to observe and is a taboo subject in many cultures. It would not be surprising if these figures underestimated the prevalence of rape proneness across cultures.

Putting these concerns aside, let's look at what Sanday found. One question she addressed is the following: What sexual attitudes predict the prevalence of rape across the 156 cultures? We might theorize that in more sexually repressed cultures, individuals would resort to rape to gratify their sexual desire. But she did not find that to be so. She assessed the extent of each culture's sexual repressiveness according to the prevalence of postpartum (the period shortly after the birth of a child) taboos and premarital sex taboos. The prevalence of rape in each culture was unrelated to these sexually restrictive beliefs or practices.

What about the general level of violence in the culture? If rape at its core is an act of violence, then it should be more prevalent in more aggressive, violent cultures. This would fit with Berkowitz's account of aggression; that is, members of highly aggressive, hostile cultures, where anger-related ideas are in the air, so to speak, should be more prone to act in aggressive ways, including being prone to rape. This indeed proved to be the case. Rape-prone cultures were more likely to have high levels of violence, a history of frequent warfare, and an emphasis on machismo and male toughness.

Finally, many scholars have treated rape as an act of dominance, a means of subordinating women, relegating them to lower-status positions. This suggests that rape may be more prevalent in cultures in which women have lower status. This, too, proved to be true. Women in rape-prone cultures were less likely to participate in education and political decision making than were women in rape-free cultures. Women in rape-free cultures were more empowered and likely to be granted equal status with men.

Consider the Mbuti Pygmies as an illustration of these findings (Turnbull, 1965). In this (reportedly) nearly rape-free society, there is minimal interpersonal violence and fighting. Great prestige is attached to the raising of children, and women's contribution to society is valued. Women and men assume different duties, but they have equal standing. And women and men participate equally in political decision making.

Evolution and Aggression

Evolution for many connotes a violent struggle for survival and the opportunity to reproduce. And indeed, evolutionary theorists have offered new insights into the origins of aggression. Here we will focus on violence between step-relations and violence between husbands and wives.

Throughout the world, literature is full of tales of wicked stepparents who abuse their children. In the animal kingdom, "step-relations" seem similarly prone to violence. To take one example, when male lions acquire a new mate, they routinely kill all of the cubs from prior relations. Evolutionary psychologists Margo Wilson and Martin Daly suggest that these propensities in our mammalian forebears have left their trace in human nature as well (Daly & Wilson, 1996; Wilson, Daly, & Weghorst, 1980).

Natural selection, Daly and Wilson reason, has rewarded those parents who devote resources to their own offspring. All the behaviors related to parental care—from filial love to breast-feeding—assist the survival of our own offspring, thereby increasing our **inclusive fitness**—that is, our own survival plus that of individuals carrying our genes. Parental care, however, is costly, as any parent of a newborn will tell you, requiring time, effort, and the commitment of resources. In evolutionary terms, these expenditures are offset by the gains enjoyed by having offspring—namely, the survival of our genes. Stepparents, on the other hand, incur the same costs with no enhancement of their inclusive fitness, since they do not share genes with their stepchildren.

Survey research consistently finds that relations between stepparents and stepchildren tend to be more distant and conflict laden and less committed and satisfying than

inclusive fitness The evolutionary tendency to look out for ourselves, our offspring, and our close relatives together with their offspring so that our genes will survive.

Violence against Stepchildren   Literature and fairy tales in particular abound with tales of stepchildren treated badly by their stepmothers, as illustrated in (A) Cinderella, who becomes the scullery maid for her stepmother and stepsisters, and (B) Hansel and Gretel, who are sent out to die in the forest at the urging of their stepmother.

relations between parents and their genetic offspring (Hobart, 1991). The archival evidence is even more ominous. Daly and Wilson (1996) found that in the United States, children who are less than 2 years of age are 100 times more likely to suffer lethal abuse at the hands of stepparents than at the hands of genetic parents, and in Canada, they are 70 times more likely to suffer lethal abuse from stepparents than from genetic parents. These findings hold, it is important to note, even when researchers control for a variety of likely contributing causes, such as poverty, youth of the mother, duration of coresidency, number of children in the house, or reporting biases. In a study of a South American foraging people, 43 percent of children raised by a mother and stepfather died before their 15th birthday, more than twice the rate of death (19 percent) of children raised by two genetic parents. (This does not imply that the stepchildren were killed; but at the very least, they were more likely to have been denied resources—for example, food and physical care—that were made available to genetic offspring.)

A second kind of aggression that is informed by evolutionary ideas is the violence that men perpetrate against romantic partners over concerns of infidelity. The reasoning goes as follows. In a monogamous union, the genetic interests of women and men merge. They both devote resources to their offspring. Infidelity, however, affects women and men differently. Women know when the child is theirs; it came from their womb. With men, there is always some uncertainty. Hence the saying "Mamma's baby, papa's maybe." Thus, the husband risks investing resources in an offspring that is not his—which is why the maternal grandparents go to such great pains to assert that a newborn looks so much like the father (Daly & Wilson, 1982)! He also is likely to forego other reproductive opportunities. As a result, we would expect sexual infidelity to be more likely to trigger distress and aggression in men against women than vice versa (Wilson & Daly, 1996). That indeed proves to be the case. For example, Wilson and Daly found that in nearly four out of five spousal homicides in Canada, it is the husband who is the killer. They also found that lethal violence against wives in Australia, Canada, and the United States is two to five times higher when the couple are separated than when they are together (see **Figure 13.8**). When they are separated, the reasoning goes, the wife has more

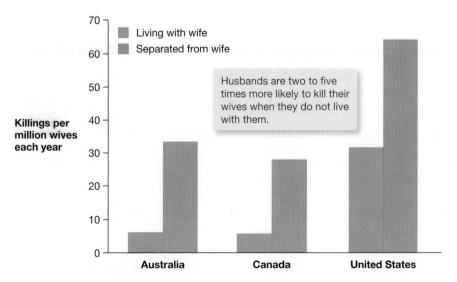

FIGURE 13.8 Concerns about Infidelity and Violence According to Wilson and Daly, the increase in killings is due to the husband's overpowering jealousy about the possibility that his wife might have children with another man. (Source: Adapted from Wilson & Daly, 1996.)

opportunities to reproduce with other men—an unbearable prospect to her mate. (Wilson, Johnson, & Daly, 1995).

Gender and Aggression

When we hear about school shootings or think about teen violence or when we read about the genocides and rape of Rwanda and Darfur, it almost goes without saying that these acts of aggression are committed by young men. Physical aggression is, in fact, from early childhood to old age, the most marked and stubborn gender difference in behavior. Ninety-nine percent of all people arrested for rape, 88 percent of all arrested for murder, 92 percent arrested for robbery, and 87 percent arrested for aggravated assault are men (Kimmel, 2004). Men are also overwhelmingly the victims of violence.

Women, of course, are also aggressive, but in different ways. New research is exploring the "relational aggression" in which girls and women are said to excel—through the use of gossip, alliance formation, and exclusion (Dodge & Schwartz, 1997). Many female readers will remember with a wince the vicious ways girls can behave toward one another in middle school, speaking behind people's backs, tarnishing reputations, and the like. Obviously, this kind of aggression can be extremely hurtful emotionally. It does appear that while young men are more prone to acts of physical aggression—many of which we have profiled in this chapter—young women are more prone to acts of emotional aggression.

These striking gender differences in overall levels of aggression (men far surpass the women) have been considered by evolutionary and cultural theorists alike, and this provides a fitting conclusion to our discussion of aggression.

Let's first consider an evolutionary approach to the tendency for men to engage in more aggressive behavior, in particular that which relies on physical violence. Evolutionists reason that during the period of evolutionary adaptation in early human history, men were hunters and protectors and almost exclusively the ones to engage in violent, intertribal warfare. Women, by contrast, were much more likely to be caretakers of infants and children. This basic division of labor in our evolutionary past helps illuminate why males are so much more aggressive today. They were the ones who developed greater upper body strength, greater muscle mass, and a greater predilection to aggressive behavior because certain demands of survival—finding sources of meat, defense against attacks—required this. Women, as caretakers, developed greater abilities to empathize and care—forces that inhibit aggressive behavior and produce greater altruistic behavior, as we detail in the next section.

Evolutionists also reason that the ability for men to mate generally depended on their status within the social hierarchy (Daly & Wilson, 1988). High-status men were much more successful than low-status men in terms of their reproductive success, or number of offspring. Thus, some men had offsrping with many women, whereas some men had no offspring. By contrast, reproductively healthy women who wanted to pass on their genes were, almost without exception, able to do so. This basic difference in reproductive patterns required men to evolve strategies—one being violence—to outcompete other males to gain access to mates. This in part accounts for a large portion of violence seen around the world: men are 20 times as likely to kill other men as women are to kill other women (Daly & Wilson, 1988).

Cultural theorists counter by arguing that men are socialized into different roles that differentially prioritize physical aggression. Parents, teachers, media sources, and social institutions systematically, and often unwittingly, cultivate more aggressive tendencies in men. Consider, for example, how young boys are treated from the first moments of life. In short, they are expected to be more aggressive. When parents are presented with a video of an infant looking startled, if the infant is described as a boy, the parents say the infant is angry. If the same infant is described as a girl, the parents say the infant is fearful (Condry & Condry, 1976). Mothers talk more about emotions with their daughters than with their sons, which may cultivate greater empathy in women (Fivush, 1991). The one exception to this parenting trend is anger, which mothers are more likely to mention in labeling the emotions of their sons. In effect, from very early in life, anger and aggressive reactions are made more salient to young boys than to young girls. Given that we have learned that anger is a primary determinant of aggression, this socialization process might account for at least some of the gender differences in aggression we have considered here.

We have seen that several situational factors—heat, violent television, violent video games, and inequality—can make people more aggressive. We have also seen that construal processes matter. In particular, when we blame others for their actions and experience unpleasant feelings of anger, we are more likely to act in an aggressive fashion. We have also discussed how aggression may vary from one society to another, exploring how people who adhere to a culture of honor are more prone to certain kinds of violence and how violent cultures that do not give women equality and power are more prone to rape. We have looked at evolutionary accounts of aggression, which provide compelling explanations of the elevated violence perpetrated against stepchildren and romantic partners. We also engaged evolutionary and cultural approaches as to why men are more aggressive than women.

ALTRUISM

During the genocide of Rwanda, Paul Rusesabagina, a Hutu, was the acting manager of the Mille Collines, the most prestigious hotel in the capital city of Kigali. As the massacres unfolded, he hid over a thousand people (both Tutsis and moderate Hutus) at the hotel. Each day, the Hutu *interahamwe* would arrive and demand to take some of the Tutsis away. Rusesabagina would plead desperately and ply them with beer and money to prevent further massacres. Around the clock he frantically called and faxed influential contacts, appealing for their help. Often risking his own life and those of his children and wife, he argued time and time again for the survival of his guests.

Rusesabagina's actions are clear examples of **altruism**—unselfish behavior that benefits others without regard to consequences for the self. When do we act altruistically, and when not? There would appear to be feelings of compassion and altruistic inclinations that act as forces leading us to behave in ways that benefit others who are suffering, often at a cost to ourselves. At the same time, we don't always act on these prosocial feelings; there are numerous forces inhibiting altruistic action—basic tendencies toward self-preservation or fear of embarrassment (say, misinterpreting a mundane situation as an emergency). With this approach in mind, let's look at the determinants of altruism, beginning with studies that address whether there is such a pure other-oriented kind of altruism at all.

altruism Unselfish behavior that benefits others without regard to consequences for the self.

Altruism in Rwanda Paul Rusesabagina, acting manager of the Mille Collines Hotel in Kigali, Rwanda, saved over a thousand people from massacre by sheltering them at the hotel, bribing the *interahamwe,* and appealing to influential contacts.

Empathic Concern: A Case of Pure Altruism?

During the Los Angeles riots of 1992, Reginald Denny, a white truck driver, was being beaten severely by four black youths. Several black residents who lived near the area saw the beating live on television and rushed to the scene to save Denny's life, risking their own lives in the process. What motivates this kind of action?

In an important line of research, Daniel Batson has made a persuasive case for a selfless, other-oriented state that motivates altruistic behavior like that displayed by Paul Rusesabagina and Reginald Denny's saviors (Batson & Shaw, 1991). Batson begins by proposing that there are several motives that are likely to be in play in producing altruistic action. Two of these motives are at base selfish (egoistic); a third is more purely oriented toward unselfishly benefiting another person.

The first selfish motive is the **social rewards** motive. Those motivated by social rewards help others to order to elevate how they are esteemed by others (Campbell, 1975; Nowak & Sigmund, 1998; Nowak, Page, & Sigmund, 2000). The second selfish motive for helping is the **experienced distress** motive. People are motivated to help others in need to reduce their *own* distress (Cialdini & Fultz, 1990; Cialdini & Kenrick, 1976). The most direct way to alleviate their own distress is to reduce the distress of the other person, and helping behavior is one way to accomplish that aim.

Finally, there is **empathic concern**, the feeling people experience when identifying with the person in need, accompanied by the intention to enhance the other person's welfare. When we encounter another person in need or distress, we often imagine what their experience is like. From the first moments of life, we respond to others' distress with our own distress. For example, in one study, 1-day-old infants heard a tape recording of either their own crying, the crying of another 1-day-old, or the crying of an 11-month-old (Martin & Clark, 1982). One-day-olds actually cried the most in response to the cries of distress of another 1-day-old. We are wired to feel distress when witnessing others in need. As we grow older, when we take the other's perspective, we feel an empathic state of concern for that person, imagining how it would feel to suffer, and we are motivated to have that person's needs addressed, to enhance that person's welfare, even at our own expense. This experience of empathic concern produces a selfless, or other-oriented altruism.

Now comes the tricky part. How can we demonstrate that behavior can be motivated by empathic concern? Batson and his colleagues have taken an imaginative approach to this question in experiments in which participants are exposed to another person in distress. The experiments are set up so that egoistic motives—to reduce personal distress or gain social rewards—would lead to little helping behavior. At the same time, the participant is led to empathize with the person in need. If an empathic concern produces helping, even in the face of egoistic opportunities to avoid it, we can confidently infer that there is an empathy-based form of helping that is not selfishly motivated. Let's see how this empirical strategy plays out in two studies.

The first study pitted the selfish motive of reducing personal distress against the motive of empathic concern by allowing participants to escape their aversive arousal by simply leaving the experiment. The researchers anticipated that if they still helped, it must be due to empathic concern (Batson, O'Quin, Fultz, Vanderplas, & Isen, 1983). Participants were told that they would interact with another participant of the same sex. The other participant was to complete several trials of a digit recall task and to receive a shock after each mistake. In the easy-escape condition, the participant was only required to watch the confederate receive two of the ten shocks, and the participant was then free to leave the experiment while the confederate finished the study. In this condition, if participants were guided primarily by the egoistic motive to reduce personal distress, there should be relatively little helping behavior, for the participant could simply leave. In the difficult-to-escape condition, the participant was told it would be necessary to watch the other person take all ten shocks.

After the first two trials, the confederate, made to look a little pale, asked for a glass of water, mentioned feelings of discomfort, and recounted a traumatic shock

social rewards Benefits like praise, positive attention, tangible rewards, honors, and gratitude that may be gained from helping others.

experienced distress A motive for helping those in distress that may arise from a need to reduce our *own* distress.

empathic concern Identifying with another person—feeling and understanding what that person is experiencing—accompanied by the intention to help the person in need.

Extraordinary Altruism
Wesley Autrey, pictured here with his daughter, jumped on the New York subway tracks to save a fallen man in the face of an oncoming train.

Compassion by Strangers Sometimes even strangers will respond to an individual's distress and offer aid without thought of rewards or danger. (A) During the riots in Los Angeles in 1992, Reginald Denny was pulled from his truck and severely beaten. (B) Upon seeing the incident on television, Bobby Green (pictured here) and several other local residents rushed to the scene to rescue him.

experience from childhood. At this time, the participant provided self-reports of distress-related emotions (for example, feeling upset, worried, perturbed) and empathic concern (for example, feeling sympathetic, compassionate, tender). Batson and his colleagues used the self-reports to divide participants into those who were feeling egoistic distress and those who were feeling empathic concern. In the next phase of the experiment, the experimenter turned to the participant to ask whether he or she would sit in for the confederate, taking some of this person's shocks. If there is such a thing as altruism based on empathic concern, Batson and colleagues reasoned, then they should see substantial levels of altruism (agreeing to sit in for the confederate) on the part of participants who felt empathic concern for the confederate, even when they could simply leave the experiment and escape their empathic distress. That is just what Batson and his colleagues observed. Those participants who mostly felt distress and could escape the situation took few shocks on behalf of the confederate. Those participants who felt empathic concern, on the other hand, volunteered to take more shocks, even when they could simply leave the study.

For those still skeptical of a pure altruism based on empathic concern, you might have a few concerns about this study. First of all, empathic concern was not manipulated; instead, Batson and his colleagues identified empathic participants according to their self-reports. Perhaps there was a selection bias in this study—namely, the high-empathy participants might just be more helpful in general for reasons other than a selfless response to the confederate in need. Second, the experimenter knew of the participants' actions, so a social rewards account of this study cannot be ruled out. Perhaps participants who took more shocks on behalf of the confederate hoped to impress the experimenter or wanted to avoid embarrassing themselves by leaving a

Empathy among Newborns When newborns hear another newborn cry, they feel the distress of the other baby and will also begin to cry, as seen in this photo of newborns in a hospital nursery.

person in obvious need. It would be much more telling to document substantial rates of helping when volunteering to do so is completely anonymous. That notion motivated Batson's next study.

In this study, female participants engaged in an impression formation task while seated at separate cubicles (Fultz, Batson, Fortenbach, McCarthy, & Varney, 1986). The communicator (a confederate), supposedly a student named Janet Arnold, wrote two notes to the participant, expressing supposedly honest information about herself. The task of the listener (the actual participant) was to form as accurate an impression of the communicator as possible. This time empathic concern was manipulated. In the low-empathy condition, the participant was told to be as objective as possible when reading the notes, to concentrate on the facts at hand. In the high-empathy condi-

tion, the participant was told to imagine as vividly as possible how the communicator—the other person—felt. In the first note to the participant, Janet confessed to feeling out of place at her new home at the university. In the second note, Janet expressed a strong need for a friend, and she rather forthrightly asked the participant if she'd like to pal around a bit. At the end of the second note, the participant was told that Janet had finished and left the study. At this point, the experimenter gave the participant a form that described another "long-term relationship study" and asked whether the participant would like to spend time with the other communicator, our lonely Janet Arnold. In the low-social-evaluation condition, Janet's notes were delivered in sealed envelopes and not read or known by the experimenter. Similarly, the participant indicated how much time she would spend with Janet on a form that she enclosed in a sealed envelope that would be sent to the professor conducting the study (who was never to meet the participant). Neither the experimenter nor Janet would know of the participant's response. In the high-social-evaluation condition, things were much different. The experimenter and the participant read Janet's notes, and Janet and the experimenter were privy to the participant's indication of how much time she would spend with Janet. The critical dependent measure was the number of hours the participant volunteered to spend with Janet. As you can see in **Figure 13.9**, participants feeling empathic concern for Janet volunteered to spend more time with her, even when no one would know of their action.

Let's review one final study that is especially helpful in assessing whether there is some kind of selfless state, as Batson supposes, that motivates altruistic behavior. Particularly strong evidence for such a motive would be to show that empathic concern has a distinct physiological signature that predicts whether or not a person will act altruistically. Nancy Eisenberg and her colleagues have conducted such a study (Eisenberg et al., 1989). In this experiment, participants, either second graders, fifth graders, or college students, watched a videotape of a woman and her children who had recently been in an accident. Her children were forced to miss school while they recovered from their injuries in the hospital. As the participants watched this moving videotape, their facial expressions were recorded on videotape and continuous measures of heart rate were taken. After watching the videotape, the participants were given the opportunity to help by taking homework to the recovering children during their recess (and thus sacrificing their playtime, which was highly valued by the younger participants). What Eisenberg and her colleagues found was that children and college

FIGURE 13.9 **Scientific Method: Empathy and Altruism**

Hypothesis: Empathy promotes altruistic behavior.

Research Method:

1 Female participants were seated at separate cubicles and asked to engage in an impression formation task. The communicator (a confederate), supposedly a student named Janet Arnold, wrote two notes to the participant, expressing supposedly honest information about herself. The task of the listener (the actual participant) was to form as accurate an impression of the communicator as possible.

2 In the low-empathy condition, the participant was told to be as objective as possible when reading the notes, to concentrate on the facts at hand.

3 In the high-empathy condition, the participant was told to imagine as vividly as possible how the communicator—the other person—felt.

4 Then the experimenter gave the participant a form that described another long-term relationship study and asked whether the participant would like to spend time with the other communicator, our lonely Janet Arnold.

5 In the low-social-evaluation condition, Janet's notes were delivered in sealed envelopes and not read or known by the experimenter. Similarily, the participant indicated how much time she would spend with Janet on a form that she enclosed in a sealed envelope.

6 In the high-social-evaluation condition, the experimenter and the participant read Janet's notes, and Janet and the experimenter were privy to the participant's indication of how much time she would spend with Janet.

Results: Participants who were encouraged to feel empathy for another student, Janet, who reported feeling lonely, volunteered to spend more time with her, even in the low-social-evaluation condition, where their volunteering was anonymous.

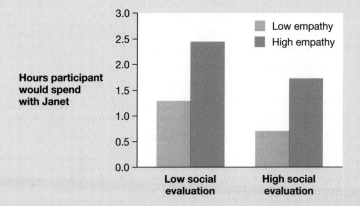

Conclusion: Even in anonymous conditions where no social reward can be gained, empathy promotes altruistic behavior.

Source: Fultz, Batson, Fortenbach, McCarthy, & Varney (1986).

students alike who felt sympathy and concern in response to the accident victims—or empathic concern, in Batson's terms—showed oblique eyebrows, a concerned gaze, and heart rate deceleration—a physiological response that is the opposite of fight-or-flight physiology. They were also more likely to help. In contrast, those participants who reported distress while watching the videotape showed a painful wince in the face and heart rate acceleration, and they were less likely to help. Not only does empathic concern produce more helping behavior than distress, but it appears to do so in part through a different physiological response.

Empathic concern also appears to be a primary determinant of other prosocial acts. For example, Allen Omoto and Mark Snyder have studied volunteerism, which they define as nonmonetary assistance that people provide to other people, strangers, in need, with no expectation of receiving any compensation (Omoto & Snyder, 1995; Penner, Dovidio, Piliavin, & Schroeder, 2005). In the United States, it is estimated that over 61 million people, close to 30 percent of the population, volunteer at least once during the year, providing companionship to the elderly, helping mentor troubled children, or assisting the sick and dying (Omoto, Malsch, & Barraza, 2009). As with altruism, volunteerism has many motives, including a desire for social rewards and a desire to reduce personal distress. But Omoto and colleagues have found that self-reports of feelings of empathic concern predict the likelihood that an individual will engage in different forms of volunteerism (Omoto et al., 2009).

As we leave this section, you may wonder what cultivates empathic concern in people. What produces the Paul Rusesbaginas of the world or the good-hearted citizens who sacrifice to volunteer for others? One answer comes from the remarkable work of the Oliners (Oliner & Oliner, 1988). They interviewed over 100 rescuers from World War II, individuals who risked their lives to save Jews during the Nazi Holocaust (Sam Oliner himself was saved by such a person in Poland as a young boy). In the course of these interviews, rescuers reported that altruism and compassion were highly valued in their homes—a frequent topic of dinnertime conversation and in the books they read. They were aspirations that the parents expressed and passed down to their children. Empathic concern is a powerful force for good in human societies and can be readily cultivated.

Situational Determinants of Altruism

Thus far, we have learned that there is a state—empathic concern—that motivates altruistic action and volunteerism. Clearly, we don't always act on such empathic concern. This is no more tellingly revealed than the horrifying tragedy that befell Kitty Genovese. In the early morning hours of March 13, 1964, Winston Moseley stalked Kitty Genovese as she walked home in Queens, New York. He tackled her in front of a bookstore near her apartment and stabbed her in the chest. As she screamed for help, lights went on and several windows opened in the surrounding apartments. From his seventh-floor window, one neighbor yelled, "Let that girl alone!"

Moseley left the woman, only to return a short while later. He stalked his screaming victim to a stairwell in her apartment house, stabbed her eight more times, and sexually assaulted her. New York police received their first call about the incident at 3:50 a.m., 30 minutes after the cries of distress first awakened neighbors. By the time they arrived, Kitty Genovese was beyond help.

Thirty-eight of the neighbors admitted to having heard her screams. Clearly, they must have felt the pangs of empathic concern. However, no one intervened aside from the neighbor who yelled from afar. Not a single person called the police. Instead, investigators heard explanations such as "I was tired"; "We thought it was a lover's quarrel"; "We were afraid." One couple simply watched the assault from behind curtains in their dimly lit apartment.

The Kitty Genovese incident shocked the American public. Like the Milgram studies of obedience to authority (see Chapters 1 and 6), the Kitty Genovese incident also raises fundamental questions about what we are like as a species. Are we really that callous to the suffering of others? The findings that we have reviewed on empathic concern, altruism, and volunteerism suggest not. The Kitty Genovese incident moved several social psychologists to attempt to understand the processes that inhibit altruistic action and cause people to fail to intervene during emergencies.

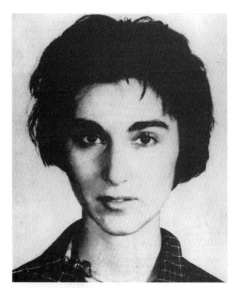

Failure to Intervene in an Emergency Kitty Genovese was a young woman who was stalked and killed in Queens in front of her apartment as her neighbors watched from their windows and failed to intervene.

No research better reveals the powerful situational determinants of altruism than a classic study by John Darley and Daniel Batson from 1973 (discussed briefly in Chapter 1). Their study was modeled on the timeless tale of the Good Samaritan, which talks about different reactions to a man who has been robbed, stripped, and left in a ditch. In the Bible story, a busy priest first walks by. Despite being a religious leader and ostensibly concerned with those in need, he fails to stop and help the man. Next a Levite, another religious functionary, arrives and also avoids the man. Finally, a resident of Samaria, a member of a group that followed different religious customs and was despised by mainstream society, sees the half-dead man. The Samaritan stops, helps the man, takes him to an inn, and provides money for clothes and food, which restores the victim's strength.

Darley and Batson's study, which was inspired by the Good Samaritan parable, makes for an even better story than the classic tale itself. The lesson is that subtle situational factors, such as whether or not you are late, powerfully determine whether you will help someone in need.

Darley and Batson (1973) asked students attending Princeton Theological Seminary to give a talk to undergraduate students on another part of the Princeton campus. In one condition, the seminary students were told that the topic of the talk would be the jobs that seminary students typically can find upon graduating. In a second condition, they were to give a talk on the tale of the Good Samaritan. The experimenter then gave them a map of the Princeton campus and showed them the building in which they were to give their talk. In one condition, the no hurry condition, participants were told they had plenty of time to get to the designated room. In a moderate hurry condition, it was clear that the seminary students would have to hustle a bit to be on time. In the high hurry condition, the seminarians were told that they were already a bit late for the students waiting to hear their words of wisdom.

As the seminarians crossed the Princeton campus, their path led them past a man (actually a confederate) who was slumped over and groaning in a passageway. When the seminary students got within earshot, he complained that he was having trouble breathing. The man was visibly and audibly in distress. The question was: What proportion of seminary students in the various conditions would stop to help the man?

The topic of the talk had no statistically significant effect on the seminary students, though the tendency was for those who were to talk about the Good Samaritan to be more likely to help than those who thought they were to talk about jobs. The big effect was produced by the most subtle of variables: whether or not the students were late. Seminary students who were not in a hurry were more than six times as likely to stop and attend to the suffering man than were the seminary students who were in a hurry to give a talk. Only 10 percent of the students who were in a hurry stopped to help (see Figure 1.1 in Chapter 1).

Like so many of the classic studies in social psychology, this one offers lasting lessons about how powerful situations can be. Being late made it unlikely that the very people we would expect to exhibit altruism—students studying to be spiritual leaders—would do so. We don't like to discover that we are so susceptible to such minor situational factors. The study itself has many compelling features: the use of seminary students as participants, the naturalistic setting, the assessment of real behavior as the dependent measure. Let's now look at other kinds of situational factors that affect the likelihood of altruistic behavior.

Audience Effects One extremely important factor influencing helping is whether other people are present. Researchers who have studied **bystander intervention**—that is, how likely it is for people to intervene in an emergency—have found that people are less likely to help when other people are around (Latané & Nida, 1981). In part,

bystander intervention Helping a victim of an emergency by those who have observed what is happening. Bystander intervention is generally reduced as the number of observers increases, as each individual feels that someone else will probably help.

the presence of other bystanders at emergencies reduces the likelihood of helping due to a **diffusion of responsibility**. Knowing that others have seen the emergency, each individual is likely to assume that others will intervene, and thus each feels less responsibility for helping the victim. The witnesses of the Kitty Genovese murder may have seen other apartment dwellers' lights go on, or they may have seen others in the windows, and they may have assumed that others would help. The end result is a disturbing lack of action.

Consider one of the best known of the studies of audience constraints on helping, a study by John Darley and Bibb Latané inspired by the Kitty Genovese tragedy (Darley & Latané, 1968). College students sat in separate cubicles discussing the problems associated with living in an urban environment. They engaged in this conversation over an intercom system, which allowed only one participant to talk at a time. In one condition, participants were led to believe that their discussion group consisted of two people (the participant and the future victim). In another condition, the conversation was among three people (the participant, the future victim, and another person). And in a final condition, the audience was the largest: the conversation apparently involved six people (the participant, the future victim, and four other people). A confederate (one of the authors of this book, as it happens) played the role of the victim.

In the first round of comments, the future victim described his difficulties adjusting to urban life and mentioned that he had problems with seizures from time to time, especially when under stress. After the first round of comments, the victim took his second turn. As he did so, he became increasingly loud and incoherent; he choked and gasped. Before falling silent, he uttered the following words:

> If someone could help me out it would it would er er s-s-sure be sure be good . . . because er there er er a cause I er I uh I've got a a one of the er sei-er-er things coming on and and and I could really er use some help so if somebody would er give me a little h-help uh er-er-er-er-er c-could somebody er er help er uh uh uh (choking sounds) . . . I'm gonna die er er I'm gonna die er help er er seizure er (chokes, then quiet). (Darley & Latané, 1968, p. 379)

The question, of course, was whether the other students would leave their cubicles to help the victim, who was presumably suffering from a potentially lethal epileptic seizure.

The presence of others had a strong effect on helping rates. Eighty-five percent of the participants who were in the two-person condition, and hence the only witness of the victim's seizure, left their cubicles to help. In contrast, 62 percent of the participants who were in the three-person condition and 31 percent of the participants in the six-person condition attempted to help the victim (see **Box 13.5**). The presence of other people, at least of strangers, strongly inhibits helping behavior (Latané & Nida, 1981).

Several different types of studies have pursued this question of whether we are less likely to help when other people are around or when we are alone (for review, see Latané & Nida, 1981). In some studies, people witnessed a victim who was in danger or in pain. For example, participants might witness a person who had passed out in a subway. In other studies, participants might witness a staged theft in a liquor store or on the beach. Across these kinds of studies, 75 percent of people helped when they were alone compared to 53 percent who helped when they were in the presence of others.

Victim Characteristics Needless to say, altruism is not blind. One powerful determinant of helping is whether there is anything about the victim that suggests it might be costly to render assistance. In one study, carried out on a subway train in Philadelphia, a victim (actually a confederate) staggered across the car, collapsed to the

BOX 13.5 **FOCUS ON DAILY LIFE**

Likelihood of Being Helped

A given bystander is less likely to help in an emergency situation if there are other bystanders around. But what are the chances of your receiving help from *any* of the bystanders? When there are more bystanders, there are more people who might help. Consider the "seizure" study described in the text. When participants thought they were alone, they helped 85 percent of the time. When they thought there was one other person who might help, they intervened 62 percent of the time. If there really had

been two bystanders, each of whom had a 62 percent chance of intervening, the victim would have received help 86 percent of the time—virtually identical to the rate of receiving help with one bystander (probability of receiving help = $1 - .38^2 = .86$). When participants thought there were four other people who might render assistance, they intervened 31 percent of the time. Again, had there really been five bystanders, each of whom had a 31 percent chance of intervening, the victim

would have received help 85 percent of the time (probability of receiving help = $1 - .69^5 = .85$)! Does this mean that it doesn't matter whether there are many or few people around? Not so fast. These studies have also measured how quickly people come to the aid of someone in distress, and they have consistently found that single bystanders act more quickly than the *quickest* person to react in a group of bystanders. And when you're in an emergency situation, a lack of speed can kill.

---

floor, and then stared up at the ceiling (Piliavin & Piliavin, 1972). In one condition, a trickle of blood was seen to flow from the victim's chin. In the other condition, there was no blood on the victim. The researchers believed that bystanders would find it more costly to help the bleeding victim, who would likely expose the helper to greater trauma and might require greater medical care. The influence of such anticipated costs was reflected in the results of this study. The victim was less likely to get help when he was bleeding (65 percent of the time) than when he had no blood trickling from his mouth (95 percent of the time). Even though the bleeding victim's need was more apparent, the likely costs of helping inhibited altruistic intervention.

More enduring characteristics of the victim also powerfully influence rates of helping. People are more likely to help similar others (Dovidio, 1984; Dovidio & Gaertner, 1981), including those from their own racial or ethnic group (Latané & Nida, 1981). The effect of similarity is seen in other species as well. Several nonhuman primates will give up the opportunity to eat, and will partially starve themselves, if their action will terminate a shock that is being administered to a member of their own species— something they will not do for members of other species (Preston & de Waal, 2002). Moreover, interpersonal attraction, which is enhanced by similarity (see Chapter 10), is also likely to increase helping behavior.

When harm to the victim is clear and the need is unambiguous, helping is more likely (Clark & Word, 1972; Gaertner & Dovidio, 1977). Researchers have studied altruistic intervention where a person in need either screams or remains silent. Bystanders help victims who scream and make their needs known between 75 and 100 percent of the time compared to helping silent victims between 25 and 40 percent of the time.

The gender of the victim also matters. In general, women tend to receive more help than men (Latané & Nida, 1981). But this varies according to the appearance of the female confederate. More attractive and femininely dressed women tend to receive more help from passersby (Piliavin & Unger, 1985). We can readily think of several explanations for this. Women in feminine attire fit the gender stereotype that women are more dependent and helpless and thus may be seen to be in greater need of help.

And male passersby may view their intervention as a foot in the door for a possible romantic involvement with the attractive woman in need.

As we have discussed the findings pertaining to the situational determinants of helping, we hope you have been putting yourself in the participant's position. What would go through your mind if you encountered a person slumped over in a hallway while on your way to a talk or if you witnessed someone passing out on the subway? What is it about being late, or hearing unambiguous cries of distress, or being in the presence of others that influences our predilection to help? We now turn to an integrative answer to these questions, which focuses on the construal processes that influence whether we help or not.

Construal Processes and Altruism

In their theorizing about the determinants of bystander intervention, Latané and Darley (1969) have highlighted how construal processes make helping more or less likely. Many instances of distress are surprisingly ambiguous. A loud apparent dispute between a man and a woman overheard on the street might be careening toward violence and require intervention. Or perhaps it's a nonthreatening lovers' spat. A large group of adolescent boys may be mercilessly pummeling a smaller boy. Or perhaps they're just playfully wrestling.

Given the ambiguity of many emergencies, helping requires first that the potential helper perceive that a person is suffering and that there is a need for intervention. The details of the victim's behavior contribute to the inference that help is needed. When a victim's distress is not salient, the victim is less likely to receive help. As we have seen, when people in need vocalize their distress with loud cries, they are much more likely to be helped (Clark & Word, 1972; Schroeder, Penner, Dovidio, & Piliavin, 1995). In a similar vein, another study found that people are more likely to help when they are aware of the events leading up to the victim's distress (Piliavin, Piliavin, & Broll, 1976). When the situation is vivid and dramatic, the bystander is more likely to notice what is happening and to understand what is going on. In one condition, participants saw another person, a confederate, faint and slowly regain consciousness. In the less vivid condition, the participant only saw the aftermath of the incident—a confederate just regaining consciousness. Participants were much more likely to come to the individual's aid (89 percent versus 13 percent) when they saw the entire drama unfold, which led them to understand the full nature of the problem.

Pluralistic Ignorance
Bystanders may do nothing if they are not sure what is happening and don't see anyone else responding. Here, this crowd of children may collectively arrive at the conclusion that the boys are just playing when bullying may be taking place given the ambiguous responses of other kids.

The surrounding social context also plays an important role in determining whether bystanders conclude that assistance is called for. A form of pluralistic ignorance occurs when people are uncertain about what is happening and assume that nothing is wrong because no one else is responding or appears concerned. When everyone in some potentially dangerous situation is behaving as if nothing is amiss, there will be a tendency for people to mistake each other's calm demeanor as a sign that no emergency is actually taking place (Latané & Darley, 1968). There are strong norms that we maintain a cool, calm, and collected demeanor in public, especially during emergencies. It is somewhat embarrassing, after all, to be the one who loses composure when no danger actually exists. During emergencies we can collectively lead one another to the inference, shaped by our calm demeanor, that there is in fact no serious problem, no person in need.

In one study that examined the role of pluralistic ignorance in bystander intervention, researchers asked participants to fill out a stack of questionnaires in a laboratory room (Latané & Darley, 1968). The participants did so in one of three conditions: alone, in a room with two passive confederates exhibiting the calm demeanor that was intended to produce pluralistic ignorance, or with two other real participants. As participants in these three conditions filled out their questionnaires, a rather strange and unnerving thing happened that, you would think, would serve as a fairly clear signal of likely danger: smoke started to filter into the room underneath a door, filling the laboratory room.

When participants were alone and they had no input from other participants as to what was happening, they were quite likely to take action. Seventy-five percent of the participants in this condition left the room and reported the smoke to the experimenter (we have to wonder what the other 25 percent of the participants were thinking!). In the two other conditions, pluralistic ignorance took hold, and participants were less likely to assume that an emergency was occurring. With three real participants, only 38 percent of the participants left to report the smoke.

"I said, 'I'm not on duty! I just came back to get my flip-flops.'"

And quite remarkably, with two passive confederates showing no signs of concern, only 10 percent of the participants reported the smoke to the experimenter. Apparently, people prefer the risk of physical danger to the prospect of embarrassing themselves in front of strangers. Anecdotal evidence from this study suggests that participants construed the smoke much differently in the three conditions. Participants who did not report the smoke to the experimenter consistently told the experimenter that they did not feel it was dangerous. One participant ventured the hypothesis that it was truth gas! The students who did report the smoke construed it much differently, as a sign of imminent danger.

Bystanders are less likely to fall prey to pluralistic ignorance when they can clearly see someone else's expressions of concern. This hypothesis was tested in an interesting study in which participants were led through a construction-filled hallway to a lab (Darley, Teger, & Lewis, 1973). As they walked to the lab, they passed several stacks of wooden frames used in construction and a workman who seemed to be doing repairs. Once in the lab room, they began the ostensible task of the experiment—they were to do their best drawing of a model horse. Darley and his colleagues varied the degree to which participants would be able to see others' nonverbal expressions, those reliable signals of concern about a possible emergency. In the control condition, the participant was alone. In another condition, two participants were seated facing each other as they drew the model horse. With this alignment, they would see each other's immediate, spontaneous expressions of emotion when the emergency occurred. In a final condition, participants were seated back-to-back. Here they had no visual access to each other's immediate reactions.

As the participants labored over their drawings, they suddenly heard a loud crash and the workman crying out in obvious pain, "Oh, my leg!" The results of this study clearly indicate that seeing others' spontaneous emotional expressions reduces the effects of pluralistic ignorance. Ninety percent of the participants who were alone left the room to help the workman. Eighty percent of the participants who were seated face-to-face did so. Only 20 percent of the participants who were seated back-to-back left to help. Not having others' reactions to help interpret the incident, these participants collectively assumed that nothing was wrong.

So how do you improve the chances of getting help when you need it? According to John Darley, who studied the factors affecting bystander intervention for more than a decade, there are two things you can do that are likely to be effective: (1) make your need clear—"I've twisted my ankle and I can't walk; I need help"—and (2) select a specific person—"You there, can you help me?" By doing so, you overcome the two biggest obstacles to intervention: you prevent people from concluding there is no real emergency (thereby eliminating the effect of pluralistic ignorance), and you prevent them from thinking that someone else will help (thereby overcoming diffusion of responsibility).

Culture and Altruism

In our review of research on aggression, we asked whether regional culture affects the amount and kind of aggression and violence common to different geographical regions. Indeed, it did. Let's now ask a comparable question about altruism. Are people more helpful in different parts of the country? Do you think you'd be more likely to be helped by a stranger in the country or the city? Imagine that your car breaks down on a street late at night. Where do you think you'd be more likely to receive help: in a large metropolis or in a small rural town?

Interestingly, survey research indicates that people in rural areas actually report higher levels of empathic concern (for example, Smith, 2009). Does that translate to different levels of altruistic behavior? To investigate this question, researchers have systematically examined helping rates in rural and urban environments. Nancy Steblay (1987) reviewed 35 different studies that permitted comparisons of helping rates in rural and urban environments. She looked at the helping rates in communities of different sizes, ranging from fewer than 1,000 to more than 1 million. In all, 17 different kinds of helping behaviors were created experimentally, typically in naturalistic settings. Researchers examined whether people would grant simple requests (for example, give the time of day), whether they would intervene to stop a crime, and whether they would help people in need (for example, an injured pedestrian).

Steblay's analysis showed that strangers are significantly more likely to be helped in rural communities than in urban areas. The effect of population size was particularly pronounced in towns with populations between 1,000 and 50,000. Thus, you're much more likely to be helped in a town of 1,000 than of 5,000, in a town of 5,000 than of 10,000, and so on. Once the population rises above 50,000, however, there is little effect of increasing population. To get a better picture of these results, consider the specific findings presented in **Figure 13.10**. As you can see, people are more likely to engage in a variety of helping behaviors—for example, correcting an overpayment, helping a lost child, giving a donation—in rural environments.

Let's dissect this finding a bit. One question you might ask is whether it's the context a person is currently in that matters or the context in which the person was brought up. For example, if you were brought up in a small rural town but currently live in a big city, which is more likely to influence whether you will engage in helping behavior? Is it the current situation or your background and upbringing? As it turns out, it's the current situation. In analyzing these 35 studies, Steblay found that the participant's current context, rural or urban, was a much stronger predictor of helping behavior than the person's rural or urban background. This is another nod to the power of the current situation. And incidentally, it is a finding that makes it less likely

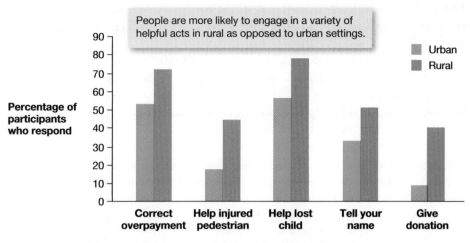

FIGURE 13.10 **Helping in Rural versus Urban Environments**   (Source: Steblay, 1987.)

that the rural-urban differences are merely due to self-selection as opposed to a real difference between rural and urban environments.

What accounts for this rural-urban difference in helping rates? Researchers have offered three explanations. Stanley Milgram (1970) attributed it to stimulus overload. The amount of stimulation in modern urban environments is so great that you cannot attend to all of it. There are simply too many inputs, and so you shut down a bit and are less likely to attend to the needs of others and less likely to act altruistically. This means that the ordinary ways you notice and interpret emergencies are interfered with, inhibiting your impulses to help. As you walk down a city street, for example, the traffic, the construction, the swarms of people are, in combination, too much to take in fully. You narrow your focus, both attentionally and in terms of what circumstances you recognize as having a claim on your thoughts, feelings, and actions. This limits your responsiveness to people in need. A second explanation might be labeled the diversity hypothesis. Earlier we noted that people are more likely to help others who are similar to themselves. Urban areas, of course, are made up of more diverse populations. Thus, on average, you're more likely to encounter someone similar to yourself in a rural environment than in an urban environment. This may contribute to the observed urban-rural difference in helping rates. Finally, there are likely to be

Helping in the Country   People living in rural settings (A) are more likely to help others than people in the city (B), as shown here in the different responses to people in need.

BOX 13.6 **FOCUS ON POSITIVE PSYCHOLOGY**

Spending Money on Others Brings Greater Happiness Than Spending on the Self

We work hard to earn money to gratify personal desires. Right? When Elizabeth Dunn and her colleagues surveyed several hundred college students, they found that to be the pervasive belief (Dunn, Aknin, & Norton, 2008). When they conducted a nationally representative survey of 632 Americans, they found that spending on personal matters (bills, gifts for the self) outpaced more prosocial forms of spending (gifts to others and charity) by a factor of 10 ($1,713.91 annually versus $145.96 annually). The trouble is, these researchers also documented that more prosocial forms of spending bring greater boosts of happiness than self-focused spending. In one survey, they found that personal spending did not correlate with happiness, whereas prosocial spending did, independent of income. In a second study, six weeks after receiving a bonus, prosocial spending, again in the form of gifts to others and to charity, predicted rises in happiness, whereas personal spending did not. Finally, Dunn and colleagues conducted a telling experiment. Forty-six participants first rated their overall happiness in the morning. They then received an envelope with a sum of money in it and were instructed either to spend it on a bill or gift to the self by 5 p.m. of that day or spend it on a gift to someone else or a charitable donation by 5 p.m. Participants were called after 5 p.m. to report on their happiness, and these reports may unsettle economists. The people who spent the money on someone else reported increased happiness from the morning, whereas the people who indulged their own desires with the money did not. It pays to be generous.

more people around to help in urban areas than in more rural environments, and so a diffusion of responsibility may discourage people from helping in urban areas.

Evolution and Altruism

Few behaviors are more problematic to explain from an evolutionary perspective than altruism. Natural selection, you'll recall, favors behaviors that increase the likelihood of survival and reproduction. Altruistic behavior, by its very nature, is costly; it devotes precious resources to others that could be used for ourselves or our genetic relatives. The costs of altruism can include the ultimate sacrifice. Consider the fates of four college-aged friends who took a day off from their jobs at a summer camp in upstate New York to relax at a swimming hole formed from waterfalls. Walking down a steep path to get there, one of them slipped and fell into a whirlpool. When he was sucked down under the raging, foamy water, each of his three friends was moved by altruistic concerns and, in succession, jumped into the river to save the others. They all died. Individuals guided by unbounded altruism would not have fared well in evolutionary history.

How, then, have evolutionary theorists accounted for altruistic behavior, which surely exists? Two evolutionary explanations have been offered: kin selection and reciprocity.

kin selection The tendency for natural selection to favor behaviors that increase the chances of survival of genetic relatives.

Kin Selection One evolutionary explanation for altruism is based on the concept of **kin selection**, which refers to the tendency for natural selection to favor behaviors that increase the chances of survival of genetic relatives (Hamilton, 1964). This derives from an individual's inclusive fitness, which, as we have noted, is an evolutionary tendency for people to look out for themselves, their offspring, and their close relatives together with *their* offspring, ensuring that their genes survive. Thus, from the perspective of kin selection, people should be more likely to help those who share more of their genes, helping siblings more than first cousins, first cousins more than second cousins, and so on. Much altruism, therefore, is not really selfless, for it is designed to help individuals who share the helper's own genes. By helping relatives survive, people help their own genes survive so that they can be passed on to future generations.

A first prediction guided by the kin selection thesis is that we should have a highly developed capacity to recognize kin. This would help us determine whom to help and whom to ignore. Indeed, there is evidence that at least some nonhuman animals reared apart can recognize their kin through specific visual cues and smells (Rushton, Russell, & Wells, 1984). And human mothers can recognize their new babies from photographs, even when they have had very little contact with the baby (Porter, Cernoch, & Balogh, 1984), and from smells left by the baby on T-shirts (Porter, Cernoch, & McLaughlin, 1983). (To our knowledge, there is no evidence that fathers are equally capable of identifying their own offspring. If there were, the possibility of cuckoldry would likely not be the enormous concern that it is.)

The more obvious prediction from kin selection theory is that we should direct more of our helping behavior toward kin than toward nonkin. There is support for this hypothesis. Take two cases in the animal world. Mockingbirds have been observed to be more likely to feed hungry, closely related nestlings that are not their own but that are more closely related than other hungry nestlings (Curry, 1988). Ground squirrels, when sensing that a predatory coyote or weasel is in the vicinity, will be more likely to emit an alarm call, which puts themselves in danger by alerting the predator as to where they are, in order to warn a genetic relative or a squirrel with which they have lived than to warn unrelated squirrels or squirrels from other areas (Sherman, 1985).

In humans, genetic relatedness seems to influence helping as well. Across numerous cultures, people report receiving more help from close kin than from more distal relatives or nonrelatives (Essock-Vitale & McGuire, 1985). When hypothetical situations are described to them, people report being more willing to help closely related individuals (especially those young enough to still have children) than more distantly related individuals or strangers (Burnstein, Crandall, & Kitayama, 1994). In a study of kidney donors, donors were about three times as likely to engage in this altruistic act for a relative (73 percent) than for nonrelatives (27 percent) (Borgida, Conner, & Manteufel, 1992). In a puzzle task that required cooperation, identical twins, who share all their genes, were found to cooperate about twice as often (94 percent) than fraternal twins (46 percent), who share only half of their genes (Segal, 1984; see also Burnstein, 2005). A recent neuroimaging study found that young mothers responded with activation in the orbitofrontal cortex—a region of the brain involved in prosocial emotion and approach behavior—to pictures of their own young babies but not to pictures of other equally cute babies (Nitschke et al., 2004).

Reciprocity Genetic relatedness, then, is a powerful determinant of our helping behavior. But what about helping nonkin? We often go to great lengths to help our friends. We give them money, let them sleep at our apartments and eat out of our refrigerators, help them move, and so on. And sometimes we put our lives on the line to help them, as we saw in the story of the friends who died trying to save their friend from drowning. Even more compelling, perhaps, is the frequency with which we help total strangers. People will dive into icy waters to save strangers, give money anonymously to charities, and engage in all sorts of more ordinary, less costly behaviors, such as taking the time to help someone cross a street. Such actions can be accounted for in part by reciprocity and cooperation, which form the basis of the second major evolutionary explanation for altruism.

"A chicken is only an egg's way of making another egg."

—Samuel Butler, *Life and Habit*

"An organism is a gene's way of making another gene."

—Richard Dawkins

BOX 13.7 **FOCUS ON NEUROSCIENCE**

The Cooperative Brain

Cooperation is vital to human survival, but it is an inherently fragile arrangement. When we cooperate, we risk being exploited by others. Often, the rewards of cooperation are to be enjoyed much later—for example, when we cooperate with work colleagues on a long-term project. James Rilling and his colleagues have found that the brain may be wired in such a fashion to enable cooperation in the face of these kinds of uncertainties (Rilling et al., 2002). They have shown that during acts of cooperation, our brains fire as if we are receiving rewards. In their study, they had 36 women play the prisoner's dilemma game over the Internet with another player. They used fMRI technology to scan the brains of these women when they cooperated with the stranger—which was their most common choice. They found that reward-related regions of the brain (the nucleus accumbens, ventral caudate, and ventromedial/orbitofrontal cortex) lit up when the women cooperated. These regions of the brain are rich in dopamine receptors and are activated by different rewards, such as sweet tastes, pleasant smells, pictures of tropical vacations, and pleasing touches. Cooperation, apparently, is inherently rewarding.

reciprocal altruism The tendency to help others with the expectation that they are likely to help us in return at some future time.

In traditional, preliterate societies, individuals living in groups were best able to survive when they cooperated with each other. To explain how cooperation evolved, evolutionary theorists most commonly invoke the concept of **reciprocal altruism**, or the tendency to help other individuals with the expectation that they will likely help in return at some other time (Trivers, 1971). Cooperation among nonkin provides many benefits that increase the chances of survival and reproduction for both parties. Reciprocal altruism reduces the likelihood of dangerous conflict, helps overcome the problems arising from scarce resources, and offers a basis for individuals to form alliances and constrain more dominant individuals (Preston & de Waal, 2002).

There is select evidence for the mutual helping that is at the core of the reciprocal altruism thesis. Vampire bats need blood meals to survive and may starve to death if they do not have a blood meal after 60 hours. Researchers have found that satiated bats will regurgitate blood to feed bats that have given to them in the past, but will not make a donation to a bat that has not been a donor itself (Wilkinson, 1990). In his observations of chimpanzees and bonobos, Frans de Waal (1996) has found that primates are disposed to share food with other primates who share with them, trade looking after each other's offspring, and systematically groom other primates who have groomed them earlier. Reciprocity is a rule of primate social behavior.

Riciprocal Altruism Vampire bats will regurgitate blood to feed starving bats that have given blood to them in the past, but they will not give blood to bats that have not helped them in the past.

In humans, reciprocity is a most powerful principle, and the impulse to return favors appears to be a human universal (Gouldner, 1960). Consider the following experiment. Researchers mailed Christmas cards to numerous complete strangers. About 20 percent reciprocated by sending their own Christmas cards back to the senders, whom they had never met (Kunz & Woolcott, 1976). Either the participants had too few friends to accommodate the stacks of Christmas cards they bought, or they felt compelled by the norm of reciprocity to respond with a Christmas card to the sender. Once primed, reciprocity also generalizes to other people: participants who receive favors from a confederate are more helpful to others in an ensuing interaction (Berkowitz & Daniels, 1964). Thus, altruistic behavior directed toward nonkin appears to follow rules related to reciprocity and is an important part of the social contract.

Reciprocal Grooming among Mammals Reciprocity helps promote group living and reduce aggression, as evidenced by grooming in (A) macaques, and (B) lionesses.

We have examined altruism, unselfish behavior that benefits others. We have seen that altruism can be in the service of selfish motives, such as reducing experienced distress or gaining social rewards, but that some acts of altruism are based on a more selfless state of empathic concern. We have shown how there are powerful situational determinants of whether people help others or not. We have considered how the presence of other bystanders may lead to a diffusion of responsibility in which everyone assumes someone else will help. We have discussed how characteristics of the victim also affect whether people will help, with people being more likely to help similar others. Moreover, we have discussed how construal processes influence helping, showing how pluralistic ignorance leads people to be less likely to help. We have seen how culture can affect helping, with people in rural settings being more likely to help than people in urban settings. And we have also discussed two evolutionary concepts that explain patterns of altruism: kin selection and reciprocity.

COOPERATION

We began this chapter with dispiriting news—reports of the massive amounts of violence that the world has witnessed in the past 100 years in the form of wars and genocides. There is a different lens on our current times, however, one offered by Harvard psychologist Steve Pinker (Pinker, 2007). Pinker argues that, in fact, today we are enjoying one of the most cooperative, humane periods in the history of humanity. The data that he draws on to make this claim are broad in scope. For example, people are dramatically less likely to die in today's wars as opposed to those in the past. Murder rates have also fallen precipitously in every European culture that has been analyzed. Consider that in fifteenth-century England, the murder rate was 24 of 100,000 people; in 1960 England, it was 0.6 per 100,000. Torture of the horrifying kind seen at Abu Ghraib is increasingly rare; several hundred years ago, such torture was the norm for how prisoners of war were treated.

How do we explain such broad cultural shifts in violence and the more humane treatment of our foes? One explanation is that the world has become substantially

Cooperation During World War I, there were instances of cooperation between enemy soldiers, as during this informal Christmas truce in 1914, when soldiers from both sides emerged from their trenches and fraternized in no-man's-land, as shown in this lithograph published in 1915.

more interconnected, our interests are more intertwined with the interests of people from other communities, states, and nations. Globalization has made businesses multinational. Solutions to global warming will require treaties that involve many countries. Many college campuses draw students from all over the world. People communicate with others in distant lands over the Internet, on Facebook, and on Twitter. People are much more likely to marry and form friendships with people from different backgrounds. This expanding interdependence has given rise to greater cooperation between nations, states, and communities (Wright, 2000). Cooperation, Pinker argues, has short-circuited more aggressive tendencies and given rise to greater prosocial behavior.

The tendency for humans to cooperate is part of our evolutionary heritage. From archaeological studies of the bones of animals our hominid predecessors killed for food, we know that those early humans hunted in cooperative groups (Mithen, 1996). The profound vulnerability of our offspring—born prematurely to accommodate their enormous brains—required cooperative child care, with both parents sharing the burdens of raising such dependent offspring (Konner, 2003). To cooperate is to be human. The core principles that account for this rise in cooperation are revealed with the use of an experimental paradigm known as the prisoner's dilemma game (also see Chapter 1).

The Prisoner's Dilemma Game

Imagine being in an experiment in which you are ushered into a small cubicle by the experimenter, who informs you that there is another participant (whom you will never meet) in a cubicle nearby. What is required of each of you is to make a simple decision: you must independently choose to "cooperate" with each other (do what will benefit both of you) or "defect" (do what will disproportionately benefit yourself). You will be paid for your participation, and your compensation will depend on the choices you make. If both of you cooperate, you will each receive $5. If both of you defect, you will each get $2. If one cooperates and the other defects, the defector will receive $8, and the cooperator will not receive anything. The experimenter says that you will be paid as soon as each of you makes your choice, and reiterates that you and the other subject will never meet. What do you do?

From the perspective of maximizing your own self-interested outcomes, the best, or "rational," thing to do is to defect. Whatever your partner does, you make more money by defecting than by cooperating. To see this, consult the summary of payoffs presented in **Figure 13.11**. If your partner cooperates, you receive $8 by defecting but only $5 by cooperating. If your partner defects, you receive $2 by defecting and nothing by cooperating. Defection thus "dominates" cooperation. So why not defect?

Here's the catch: the payoffs are the same for both players, and so if both reason this way and choose to defect, they receive only $2 rather than the $5 that would be theirs through mutual cooperation. The "best" choice for each individual (defection) is a terrible choice from the standpoint of the two subjects as a whole.

Countless individuals have participated in over 2,000 experiments of just this type, involving what is known as the prisoner's dilemma game. The name derives from a problem in game theory: Two suspects are arrested and held in separate cells on suspicion that they have committed a crime. They are both guilty, but there is no evidence, and they cannot be convicted unless they confess. If neither confesses, neither of them can be convicted. Thus, it is in the best interests of both to cooperate by not confessing. But if one of them cooperates (not confessing to the crime) and the other defects (confessing to the crime), the defector will get a light sentence (say, one year) and the cooperator will get a heavy sentence (say, ten years). If both defect and confess the crime, both will get heavy sentences that are lightened a bit (say, eight years) because of their admission of guilt.

On the surface, the prisoner's dilemma game seems to hold little promise for teaching us anything significant about real human interaction. Unlike many real-world situations, there isn't a range of cooperative to competitive behaviors from which to choose; there are only two—cooperate or defect. In addition, participants are not allowed to discuss the choices beforehand, and they are never permitted to explain or justify them afterward. It all seems too limited, too artificial, to tell us anything significant about real-world cooperation and competition.

Looks may be deceiving, however. As simple as the prisoner's dilemma might seem, it nevertheless captures the essential features of many significant real-world situations (Dawes, 1980; Schelling, 1978). Consider a real-world analogue: India and Pakistan have been engaged in an arms race for decades. Like nearly all such struggles, the contest is ultimately futile because its structure is that of the prisoner's dilemma. Each country must decide whether to spend more on armaments or to stop spending money on more arms and enjoy a significant economic "peace dividend," as the United States did following the breakup of the Soviet Union. Regardless of what the other does, it is "better" to acquire more arms. (If India freezes its acquisition of weapons, Pakistan can achieve an edge by spending more. If India builds up its arsenal, Pakistan has to spend more to avoid vulnerability.) Nonetheless, because the new weapons systems developed by one side are quickly matched by the other, the net effect is waste. The two countries pay dearly for a military balance that was attainable for less expense. The thousands of studies using the prisoner's dilemma game provide some excellent insights regarding conflict and cooperation, illuminating why people or groups or countries would be likely to defect or cooperate and suggesting what might be done.

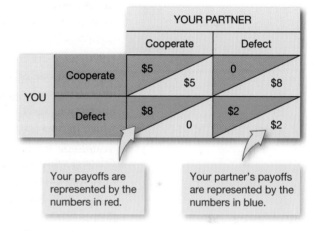

FIGURE 13.11 **Payoff Matrix for Prisoner's Dilemma Game**

One of the most striking things about human relations is how quickly competitive relationships can become cooperative (and vice versa). In World War II, the mortal enemies of the United States were the Germans and Japanese. Shortly after the end of the war, they became strong allies. The relations between the Hutus and Tutsis in Rwanda have oscillated between genocidally aggressive and more collaborative. About half of those romantic partners who choose to marry begin in euphoric states of cooperation and sacrifice and end as adversaries.

In the remainder of this chapter, we'll explore the various factors leading to cooperation.

Developing Cooperative Relationships Here a Tutsi woman in Rwanda coexists peacefully with a Hutu man who had killed people close to her.

Situational Determinants of Cooperation

Are you choosing to work with people with more competitive values or more cooperative ones? Are you playing basketball with more competitive types or more cooperative individuals more interested in a good game than in coming out on top? Are you in a romantic relationship with someone who is interested in winning arguments—who views love as war, as the old saying goes—or someone who sees relationships as a matter of mutual benefits and collaboration? An important study by Kelley and Stahelski (1970) suggests that the cooperative or competitive outcomes in your relationships depend on one of the most important features of the situation—the people you're interacting with. This study found that competitive people create more competitive interactions and thus come to construe their counterparts as also being competitive—which in turn justifies their own competitive behavior.

More specifically, upon arriving at the laboratory, participants were shown the prisoner's dilemma game and its payoff matrix. Was the goal to beat the other person or to maximize mutual gain? Some participants made it clear that they thought that competition was the goal; others indicated that they thought cooperation was the goal. The experimenters paired off cooperators with cooperators, cooperators with competitors, and competitors with competitors and had the participants play a number of rounds of the game. After a certain number of trials, the players had to judge whether their partners were competitors or cooperators, as originally assessed prior to the prisoner's dilemma game.

What happened with these various combinations? A revealing tale emerged about how competition begets increased competition. First, the competitors made everyone, including the cooperators, more competitive. Wouldn't you be competitive if your partner consistently defected on you, enjoying high rewards at your expense? Second, whereas cooperators were pretty accurate in their judgments of whether they were interacting with a cooperator or a competitor, competitors were not. Competitive participants, who made others more competitive, mistakenly assumed that everyone was competitive! This study provides insight into how readily competition can spread. It evokes escalating competitive responses in others and prompts perceptions that justify competition. The competitive apple spoils the barrel when, as in the prisoner's dilemma game, competition lowers the outcomes obtained by all.

Construal Processes and Cooperation

Construal factors matter enormously in shaping interactions toward more cooperative or competitive outcomes, as you might imagine. If someone yells at us in traffic, we sometimes take it out on an undeserving store clerk. Having just seen a film biography of Mother Teresa, we may be temporarily more inclined to act kindly toward others. Certainly, construal factors were at play in the study we just described: competitors viewed their partners through a competitive lens and created more competitive interactions.

In a compelling demonstration of the power of construal in shaping levels of cooperation, Steve Neuberg (1988) had male undergraduates participate in a standard prisoner's dilemma experiment. Before doing so, however, the participants were subliminally "primed" with one of two different sets of stimulus words, ostensibly as part of another experiment. For one group, Neuberg flashed 22 hostile words (for example, "competitive," "hostile," "unfriendly") for 60 milliseconds—too fast for anyone to "see" them and consciously register what they were, but also long enough, research has shown, for them to leave a subconscious impression. He showed another group a list of neutral words (for example, "house," "looked," "always") for an equally brief period. The question was whether exposure to the hostile words would lead participants to think "it's a dog-eat-dog world out there" in which every person has to look out for his own interests because no one else will.

Exposure to the hostile words did affect the actions of the participants. Eighty-four percent of the participants exposed to the hostile words defected on a majority of the trials in the subsequent prisoner's dilemma game; only 55 percent of the participants exposed to the neutral words did so. This study gives reason for concern about the kinds of stimuli to which people are commonly exposed. The ideas in the air—the competitive and aggressive images we see in the media, in video games, in films—are likely to foster a more competitive society.

Based on the results of Neuberg's study, it might seem that the way we explicitly label different situations might influence levels of competition and cooperation. If we think of international crises as buildups to war, diplomatic solutions may become less likely. When lawyers treat divorce settlements as adversarial and as opportunities to get their client the best outcome at the expense of the estranged spouse, entrenched bitterness seems inevitable.

In a striking demonstration of the power of labels, Liberman, Samuels, and Ross (2002) conducted a study with students at Stanford University in which they labeled the prisoner's dilemma game in one of two ways. Half of the participants were told they were going to play the Wall Street game; the others were told it was the community game. Everything else about the experiment was the same for the two groups. What might seem to be a trivial change of labels had a dramatic effect on the participants' behavior. Those playing the community game cooperated on the opening round twice as often as those playing the Wall Street game. Moreover, these initial differences were maintained throughout the subsequent rounds of the experiment. The Wall Street label doubtless made the participants adopt a perspective in which maximizing their own profits was paramount. In contrast, the community label no doubt conjured up a different set of images and motives that increased the appeal of maximizing the participants' joint outcomes.

Culture and Cooperation

Given how labels and construals shape levels of cooperation, you might expect cultural factors to likewise influence the tendency to cooperate or compete. Consider the influence of a relatively specific subculture on cooperation—the discipline you choose to study in college and eventually apply in your own career. One of the most popular majors on campus is economics. Economic theory assumes that people are rational actors who always act in self-interested fashion, attempting to maximize their own gains. This sounds bad to many people, but following eighteenth-century philosopher Adam Smith, economists have assumed that individuals and society are best served if individuals are allowed to selfishly pursue their own ends. The storekeeper and restaurateur will succeed to the extent that they serve their patrons well, simultaneously improving the lot of their customers and doing well themselves by charging as much as a competitive market will allow.

Does training in the discipline of economics encourage people to act in more competitive fashion? The results of several studies indicate that it does (Carter & Irons, 1991; Frank, Gilovich, & Regan, 1993b; Marwell & Ames, 1981). In one study, Cornell undergraduates who were majoring in economics and in a variety of other disciplines participated in a single-trial prisoner's dilemma game in which great pains were taken to ensure that each person's response would remain anonymous (Frank, Gilovich, & Regan, 1993b). Seventy-two percent of the economics majors defected on their partners, whereas only 47 percent of those majoring in other disciplines defected. In a random sample of over 1,000 professors in 23 different disciplines, participants were asked how much money they gave annually to public television, the United Way, and other charitable causes. The economists were twice as likely as the members of all the other academic disciplines to "free ride" on the contributions of their fellow citizens—that is, to give nothing at all to charity while presumably enjoying services such as public television to the same extent as everyone else. The subculture in which people are immersed appears to have a powerful influence on their inclination to cooperate with others or look after themselves.

Let's broaden out and consider the prevalence and determinants of cooperation in different cultures around the world. Joseph Henrich and his colleagues recruited individuals from 15 differerent small societies to play the ultimatum game, which is a close relative of the prisoner's dilemma game (Henrich et al., 2001). In the ultimatum game, an *allocator* is given a certain amount of money (say, $10) and told to keep a certain amount and allocate the rest to a second participant, a *responder*. The responder is then given the choice to either accept or reject the allocator's offer. If rejection is the choice, neither player receives anything. In effect, in the ultimatum game the allocator reveals on average how much he or she is willing to share with a stranger. The participants in this important study were foragers, slash-and-burn farmers, nomadic herding groups, and individuals in settled, agriculturalist societies in Africa, South America, and Indonesia. What they were allowed to offer an anonymous stranger differed—in some cultures it was money, in others a cherished good, such as tobacco.

A first finding of note concerns how cooperative humans are in much different cultures. A rational, self-interested economist would likely argue that the sensible offer of the allocator is something like 10 percent of the good ($1 if the allocator has been given $10). In this way, the material wealth of both allocator and responder would be advanced. In contrast, Henrich and colleagues observed a pattern of results that would trouble Adam Smith. In the 15 different cultures, allocators on average offered 39 percent of the good to anonymous strangers. (In more recent research across different cultures, 71 percent of the allocators offered the responder between 40 and 50 percent of the money; Fehr & Schmidt, 1999.)

Henrich and colleagues then looked closely at the 15 cultures to ascertain what cultural factors predict the likelihood of cooperative generosity in the ultimatum game. One factor stood out—the degree to which individuals in a culture needed to collaborate with others to gather resources to survive. The more the members of a culture depended on one another to gather food and survive, the more they offered to a stranger as allocators in the ultimatum game. For example, the Machiguenga

"... every individual, therefore, endeavors as much as he can ... to employ his capital in the support of domestic industry, and so to direct that industry that its produce may be of greatest value; every individual necessarily labours to render the annual revenue of the society as great as he can. He ... neither intends to promote the public interest, nor knows how much he is promoting it. By ... directing that industry in such a manner as its produce may be of greatest value, he intends only his own gain, and he is in this, as in many other cases, led by an invisible hand to promote an end which was no part of his intention."

—Adam Smith (1776)

Cooperation in Different Cultures   (A) The Machiguenga of Peru collaborate little with other outside their family and gave little in the ultimatum game. (B) The Lamerala of Indonesia collaborate extensively in fishing, and gave a lot.

people of Peru rarely collaborate with members outside of their family to produce food. Their average allocation in the ultimatum game was 26 percent of the resource. The Lamerala of Indonesia, by contrast, fish in highly collaborative groups of individuals from different families. Cooperation is essential to their livelihood and subsistence. Their average gift in the ultimatum game was 58 percent. Interdependence increases our cooperation and generosity.

Evolution and Cooperation: Tit for Tat

In *The Evolution of Cooperation*, Robert Axelrod (1984) asks the following question: How might cooperation emerge in competitive environments governed by the ruthless pursuit of self-interest? In the context of human evolution, how might nonkin begin to act on behalf of advancing the welfare of others?

Axelrod assumed that cooperation was part of our evolutionary heritage, given its universality and its emergence in even the most unlikely of social contexts. For example, in the trenches of World War I, British and French soldiers were separated from their enemies, the Germans, by a few hundred yards of no-man's-land (Axelrod, 1984). Brutal assaults by one side were typically met with equally fierce resistance by the other. And yet, even here cooperation frequently emerged, allowing soldiers to eat meals peacefully, to enjoy long periods of nonconfrontation, and even to fraternize with one another. The two sides would fly special flags, make verbal agreements, and fire symbolic yet misguided shots, all to signal and maintain peaceful cooperation in between episodes of attack in which each side was bent on the extermination of the other.

The principles that help illuminate the evolutionary origins of cooperation are found in a study by Robert Axelrod that, although simple in design, yields rather profound lessons. Axelrod, a seminal figure in the prisoner's dilemma game tradition, ran a tournament in which players—academics, prize-winning mathematicians, computer hackers, and common folk—were invited to submit computer programs that specified what choice to make on a certain round of the prisoner's dilemma game, given what had happened on previous rounds (Axelrod, 1984). In Axelrod's first tournament, 14 different strategies were submitted. Each strategy played 200 rounds of the prisoner's dilemma game with each other strategy. The points were tallied, and an overall winner was declared. The winner? It was a so-called "tit-for-tat" strategy, which was submitted by Anatol Rapaport.

tit-for-tat strategy A strategy in which the individual's first move is cooperative and thereafter the individual mimics the other person's behavior, whether cooperative or competitive.

The **tit-for-tat strategy** is disarmingly simple: It cooperates on the first round with every opponent and then reciprocates whatever the opponent did on the previous round. An opponent's cooperation was rewarded with immediate cooperation; defection was punished with immediate defection. In other words, start out cooperatively, and reciprocate your partner's previous move. Axelrod held a second tournament that attracted the submission of 62 strategies. All of the entrants knew the results of the first round, namely that the tit-for-tat strategy had won. In the second tournament, the tit-for-tat strategy again prevailed. It is important to note that the tit-for-tat strategy did not win every round when pitted against different strategies. Instead, it did better overall against the diversity of strategies. What makes the tit-for-tat strategy special, and why might it be relevant to your own life?

Axelrod contends that the tit-for-tat strategy is based on a set of principles that we would all be well advised to follow. As we form friendships, deal with the occasional difficult personality at work, negotiate with bosses, persevere in long-term romantic bonds, and raise children, the tit-for-tat strategy might be a good framework by which to abide. Five factors make it an especially compelling strategy. First, it is *cooperative*, and thus it encourages mutually supportive action toward a shared goal. Second, it is *not envious*. A partner using this strategy can do extremely well without resorting to competitive behavior. Third, it is *not exploitable*—that is, it is not blindly prosocial. If you defect on the tit-for-tat, it will defect on you. Fourth, the tit-for-tat *forgives*—that is, it is willing to cooperate at the first cooperative action of its partner, even after long runs of defection and competition. Finally, the tit-for-tat is *easy to read*—that is, it should not take long for others to know that the tit-for-tat strategy is being played.

As Axelrod put it, "Its niceness prevents it from getting into unnecessary trouble. Its retaliation discourages the other side from persisting whenever defection is tried. Its forgiveness helps restore mutual cooperation. And its clarity makes it intelligible to the other player, thereby eliciting long-term cooperation" (Axelrod, 1984, p. 54). Being nice, stalwart, forgiving, and clear—not a bad set of principles to live by.

 We have seen that cooperation is part of our evolutionary heritage. The prisoner's dilemma game models the many situations in everyday life in which defection is the best solution for each individual but cooperation benefits the two as a whole. Situational factors, such as the kind of person you are interacting with, influence levels of cooperation and competition. So, too, do construal processes: people can be primed to cooperate or defect. Studies of different cultures find that cooperation is a human universal and that the degree of interdependence promotes increased cooperation. The tit-for-tat strategy involves initial cooperation and then reciprocation of whatever your opponent has done in the previous round. It is a useful strategy to follow, as it encourages cooperation and does not blindly permit an opponent to take advantage.

Summary

Aggression

- *Hostile aggression* is motivated by anger and hostility, with the primary aim of harming others, either physically or psychologically. *Instrumental aggression* is behavior intended to achieve some goal that just happens to require aggression.

- *Media violence* has been shown to cause violence and aggression in real life. When a media-publicized suicide occurs, copycat suicides follow. Longitudinal studies show that children who watch lots of violence on TV commit more serious crimes as adults than children who watch less violence. Watching violence on TV also causes more violent behavior in the short run. Violent video games also increase the likelihood of violence.

- *Heat* affects levels of violence. There are higher rates of violent crime in hotter cities and more violence during hot months than during cool months.

- According to the *frustration-aggression hypothesis*, aggression results from thwarted goal-directed behavior, and thwarted goal-directed behavior results in aggression.

- Construal processes affect both anger and aggression. Acts that seem to be intentional are more likely to cause aggression than identical acts that do not seem intentional.

- People in many parts of the world, including many people in the U.S. South, adhere to a *culture of honor*, meaning that they are inclined to respond to insults and actions that convey malicious intentions with violence or threats of violence. Such cultures can be found wherever there is a history of herding, with its greater attendant risks of losing all wealth.

- Rape-prone cultures have high levels of violence in general and use rape as a weapon in battle. They also use rape as a ritual act and as a threat to keep women subservient to men. Relatively rape-free cultures tend to grant women equal status.

- Evolutionary theory provides a useful perspective on *family violence*. Stepchildren are more subject to abuse than genetic offspring who can carry on the genetic line. Men, who have more to gain by eliminating romantic rivals, are vastly more likely to kill other men than women are to kill other women.

- Violent and aggressive acts are more likely to be committed by men than by women. Women are likely to be aggressive in different ways than men, using relational violence such as gossip and ostracism to hurt others emotionally.

Altruism

- People help others out of selfish motives, including to reduce their felt distress and to gain social rewards, such as praise, attention, or gratitude.

- A form of pure, undiluted altruism is based on *empathic concern*—the feeling of concern for another person after observing and being moved by that person's needs. Experimenters have found clever ways to distinguish between people who help for empathic and nonempathic reasons. Those who help for egoistic distress avoidance reasons actually show different physiological patterns than those who help for empathic reasons.

- Empathic concern also motivates volunteerism, actions people take to enhance the welfare of others (for example, tending to the sick or dying when there is no expectation of compensation).

- Situational determinants of altruism can be far stronger than our intuitions tell us they should be. Being late reduced the likelihood of a seminary student's helping a victim from 60 percent to 10 percent.

- Whether someone offers help to a victim or not (*bystander intervention*) also depends greatly on the number of people who observe some incident. The presence of others leads to a *diffusion of responsibility*, in which no one individual takes responsibility for helping the victim.

- *Pluralistic ignorance* occurs when people are uncertain about what is happening and do nothing, often out of fear of embarrassment in case nothing is really wrong. Their reaction reinforces everyone's erroneous conclusion that the events are innocuous.

- *Victim characteristics* that increase the likelihood of being helped include whether the victim is similar to the target, whether the victim screams and makes known the situation, and whether the victim is female.

- People who live in rural settings are more likely to help others than people who live in urban settings.

- Evolutionary approaches to altruism lead initially to a puzzle as to why it would exist at all. From the standpoint of evolution, all our actions should serve to increase the likelihood of survival and reproduction. The *kin selection* hypothesis explains, however, that people will help others to preserve the genes of close kin so as to benefit their own gene pool.

- Another kind of helping behavior, *reciprocal altruism*, also arises out of selfish motives. The reciprocity motive entails that people grant others favors or help others in the belief that those whom they have helped will at some future time grant them favors of similar value.

Cooperation

- Cooperation is part of our evolutionary heritage, and it emerges in almost all societies.

- The prisoner's dilemma game is used to study cooperation. It tempts participants to maximize their own outcomes at the expense of another person by defecting. This strategy backfires if the other person also defects. The optimum outcome is for both to settle for something less than the maximum by cooperating.

- Interacting with more cooperative types of individuals leads to higher rates of cooperation.

- Being primed with cooperative concepts leads to increased cooperation.

- Cooperation is widespread in different cultures, in particular in those whose members are dependent on each other to gather resources.

- The tit-for-tat strategy in the prisoner's dilemma game is a reciprocal strategy that is cooperative, nonenvious, nonexploitable, forgiving, and easy to read. This strategy helps maximize outcomes in potentially competitive situations that occur in real life.

Key Terms

altruism (p. 505)
bystander intervention (p. 511)
culture of honor (p. 498)
diffusion of responsibility (p. 512)
empathic concern (p. 506)

experienced distress (p. 506)
frustration (p. 494)
hostile aggression (p. 487)
inclusive fitness (p. 502)
instrumental aggression (p. 487)

kin selection (p. 518)
learned helplessness (p. 494)
rape-prone cultures (p. 500)
reciprocal altruism (p. 520)
social rewards (p. 506)
tit-for-tat strategy (p. 528)

Further Reading

Batson, C. D. (1991). *The altruism question: Toward a social-psychological answer.* Hillsdale, NJ: Lawrence Erlbaum. An outstanding review of the evidence regarding the different motives of altruism.

Berkowitz, L. (1993). *Aggression.* New York: McGraw-Hill. A comprehensive overview of the social psychological study of aggression.

Nisbett, R. E., & Cohen, D. (1996). *Culture of honor: The psychology of violence in the South.* Boulder, CO: Westview Press. This book summarizes one of our author's work on the culture of honor.

Schroeder, D. A., Penner, L. A., Dovidio, J. F., & Piliavin, J. A. (1995). *The psychology of helping and altruism.* New York: McGraw-Hill. An excellent review of the vast 30 years of literature on altruism.

Sober, E., & Wilson, D. S. (1998). *Unto others: The evolution and psychology of unselfish behavior.* Cambridge, MA: Harvard University Press. A philosopher and evolutionary theorist combine talents to consider how altruism could have emerged in evolution.

ⓢ Online Study Tools

StudySpace

Go to StudySpace, wwnorton.com/studyspace, to access additional review and enrichment materials, including the following resources for each chapter:

Organize

- Study Plan
- Chapter Outline
- Quiz+ Assessment

Learn

- Ebook
- Chapter Review
- Critical-Thinking Questions
- Visual Quizzes
- Vocabulary Flashcards

Connect

- Apply It! Exercises
- Author Insights Podcasts
- Social Psychology in the News

100% Jamaican
even if you're not ting

Groups

JOHN MCCAIN, LONG-TIME SENATOR from Arizona and the Republican nominee for president in 2008, was a 31-year-old navy pilot when, on October 26, 1967, he took off for his 23rd bombing run over North Vietnam. His target was a power plant located on the edge of a small lake in the center of Hanoi, the capital of North Vietnam. Diving at 550 miles per hour, his radar detection alarm sounded, indicating that a surface-to-air-missile was locked onto his plane and rapidly approaching. He waited just long enough to release his bombs before beginning evasive maneuvers. It was too late. The missile blew off his right wing, and his jet plummeted to earth.

As he ejected from his aircraft, he struck part of the plane, breaking both arms and one leg. He landed in the middle of the lake near his target and was immediately set upon by an angry mob. Dragging him from the lake, they broke his shoulder with a rifle butt and stabbed him with a bayonet in his ankle and groin. Before the mob could finish with him, a Vietnamese army truck arrived, and soldiers took him to the infamous "Hanoi Hilton," where a great many American prisoners spent the duration of the war.

During his captivity, McCain was savagely beaten, sometimes for refusing to divulge information, other times for refusing an offer of early release because he was the son of Admiral Jack McCain, commander of U.S. forces in the Pacific. (The soldiers' code of conduct stipulates that prisoners of war should be released in the order in which they were captured.) Before his ordeal was over, McCain spent five and a half years as a prisoner of war, two in solitary confinement.

In interviews, McCain has consistently maintained that despite his severe injuries, despite all the beatings, despite imprisonment in "a filthy room, about 20 feet by 20 feet, lousy with mosquitoes and rats," the hardest part of his ordeal was the experience of solitary confinement—being cut off from his fellow human beings. "What part of my time as a POW was more difficult, physical mistreatment or

Group Bonds (A) John McCain (lower right) and other U.S. Navy pilots during the Vietnam War. (B) In October 1967 during a bombing raid over North Vietnam, McCain was shot down and taken prisoner by the enemy. He remained a prisoner of war for five and a half years, during which time he suffered great hardship, including prolonged social isolation.

solitary confinement? It was without question being held captive in solitary confinement . . . taking this interaction away is a tremendous torture to the spirit" (McCain, 1999, 2003).

The importance of companionship and of living in groups is taken as a given in social psychology. With this in mind, our focus in this chapter is life in groups and the ways people are influenced by the presence and actions of those around them. We examine how the presence of others influences our performance on tasks, how groups sometimes morph into unruly mobs, and how and why group decisions sometimes differ from those made by individuals.

THE NATURE AND PURPOSE OF GROUP LIVING

McCain's experience, and his reaction to it, speaks to the fundamentally social nature of human beings. Humans are creatures who live in groups. We might ask *why* humans live in groups, or, to put the question more broadly, why all large primates (except the orangutan) live in groups. The answer, surely, is that group life offers large primates some not-well-understood advantages in the struggle for survival. The advantages are not well understood because both solitary and group lifestyles have been successfully pursued by different mammal species. Wolves live in groups but bears do not, and neither appear any worse off for the particular lifestyle they have pursued.

Still, it is generally maintained that life with others offered our human ancestors protection from predators, efficiency in food acquisition, assistance with child rearing, and defense against human aggressors—benefits that we are less equipped to do without than are, say, bears or orangutans. It is also generally maintained that these benefits are so crucial to survival that we have a psychological need to be with others and belong to groups (Baumeister & Leary, 1995; Correll & Park, 2005). When isolated from others, people typically experience great stress and become extremely upset. Hermits frequently succumb to acedia—becoming listless and alienated and eventually unresponsive to stimuli. McCain's experience reflects the difficulty of being kept in solitary confinement. Many who are kept socially isolated for a sufficiently long time lose their minds. And young humans, even those old enough to have the skills necessary to provide for themselves, have great difficulty surviving without being in a group. The same is true of young gorillas and chimps.

Before examining how groups influence individual performance, reactions, and decisions, we should first consider the question: What, exactly, is a group? This is not an easy question, as there are so many different types of groups, and the different types don't always share many features. The members of a baseball team are clearly a group, but are the members of a large lecture course a group? Most people would say that the individuals riding together in an elevator are not a group. But suppose the elevator breaks down, and those inside must figure out how to escape or summon help? Most would say that the individuals in the elevator now seem more like a real group. But why?

Capturing these intuitions, Cartwright and Zander maintained that a group is "a collection of individuals who have relations to one another that make them interdependent to some significant degree" (Cartwright & Zander, 1968, p. 46). Thus, the people in the functioning elevator do not make up a group because they are not very interdependent. But once the elevator breaks down and they must decide on joint action (or whether to take joint action), they become interdependent and hence more of a group. Note that interdependence varies along a continuum; therefore, so should whether or not a collection of people constitutes a group (McGrath, 1984). And to most people this seems right. The members of a family are more of a "real" group than are participants in a seminar, and they in turn are more of a group than are students in a large lecture course. By this reasoning, a nation's citizens make up something of a group, but they are less of a group than are the members of a tribe or band, who interact with one another more frequently and are more directly dependent on one another.

Now let's examine the psychological impact of different types of groups that vary along this continuum. First, we'll consider the impact of other people—be they strangers or members of a tight-knit group—on how well we perform. Then we'll examine how and why we sometimes act more impulsively when we get "lost" in a crowd. Finally, we'll examine how the decisions made by groups—typically intact, highly cohesive groups—differ from those made by individuals.

> "No man is an island, entire of itself; every man is a piece of the continent, a part of the main."
>
> — John Donne

SOCIAL FACILITATION

What effect does the presence of other people have on human performance? That is, does the presence of others typically help or hinder performance, or does it exert no effect at all? To address this question, let's consider it in more personal and vivid terms. Suppose you are off by yourself trying to perfect a skill—practicing the piano, developing a topspin lob for your tennis game, or working through the intricacies of conjugating Latin verbs. You feel you are making progress when along comes someone else who takes a seat nearby and proceeds to observe—a perfect stranger, your mother, or even, say, Oprah Winfrey or George Clooney. What does this other person's presence do to your performance? Does it provide you with the energy and focus necessary to bring your performance to new heights? Or do you become so nervous and distracted that your performance suffers?

Initial Research

Norman Triplett was the first person to experimentally examine this question. Triplett was something of a bicycling enthusiast (or "wheelman" as they were known at the time). After reviewing speed records put out by the Racing Board of the League of American Wheelmen, Triplett noticed that the fastest times were recorded when cyclists competed directly against one another on the same track at the same time. Much slower speed records were obtained when cyclists raced alone against the clock. Thus, Triplett believed that the presence of others tended to facilitate human performance.

Triplett realized, however, that the cycling records were not the best test of his hypothesis. For one thing, different cyclists performed in the different events: one cyclist might race only against the clock, another only against another cyclist. Thus, the superior times recorded under direct competition might not be due to the competition itself, but to something about the kind of people who chose to compete against one another rather than against the clock (the self-selection problem we discuss in Chapter 2). Also, cyclists competing against one another might benefit from reduced wind resistance by taking turns "drafting" just behind one another.

To overcome such problems, Triplett (1898) conducted what is widely regarded as social psychology's first experiment. He invited a group of 40 children to his laboratory and had them reel in fishing lines as fast as they could. Each child did so on six trials with rest periods in between. On three trials the child was alone, and on three trials there was another child alongside doing the same thing. What Triplett found under these more controlled conditions matched what he had seen in his analysis of cycling times. The children tended to reel in fishing lines faster when in the presence of another child engaged in the same activity. The presence of others appeared to facilitate human performance. Research on this subject thus came to be known as **social facilitation** research.

A number of subsequent experiments reinforced Triplett's findings and extended them in two important ways. First, the same effects were obtained when the others present were not doing the same thing (that is, not "coacting"), but were merely present as an audience of passive observers (Gates, 1924; Travis, 1925). Second, the same effect was also observed in a vast number of animal species, indicating that the phenomenon is really quite general and fundamental. For example, animals as diverse as dogs, fish, armadillos, opossums, and frogs have been shown to eat more when in the presence of other members of the same species than when alone (Boice, Quanty, & Williams, 1974; Platt & James, 1966; Platt, Yaksh, & Darby, 1967; Ross & Ross, 1949; Uematsu, 1970). It has also been shown that ants dig more earth (Chen, 1937), fruit flies do more preening (Connolly, 1968), and centipedes run faster through mazes (Hosey, Wood, Thompson, & Druck, 1985) when together than when alone. For both humans and other animals, then, much of the research on this topic indicates that the presence of others facilitates performance.

Unfortunately, not all of the relevant findings conform to this pattern. Numerous exceptions emerged soon after Triplett's original findings. Floyd Allport (1920), for example, asked students at Harvard and Radcliffe to refute philosophical arguments as best they could in a 5-minute period. The students provided higher-quality refutations when working alone than when working in the presence of another student. The presence of others has also been shown to inhibit performance on arithmetic problems,

Social Facilitation and Competition Performance is typically enhanced in the presence of others when the activity is well learned. Here Lance Armstrong is energized by the presence and cheering of the spectators as he competes in the 2004 Tour de France.

social facilitation Initially a term for enhanced performance in the presence of others; now a broader term for the effect—positive or negative—of the presence of others on performance.

"The bodily presence of another rider is a stimulus to the racer in arousing the competitive instinct; that another can thus be the means of releasing or freeing nervous energy for him that he cannot of himself release."

—Norman Triplett

memory tasks, and maze learning (Dashiell, 1930; Pessin, 1933; Pessin & Husband, 1933). And the presence of other members of the same species has also been found to sometimes inhibit the performance of animals (Allee & Masure, 1936; Shelley, 1965; Strobel, 1972).

Resolving the Contradictions

Putting all of these findings together, it seemed for a time that the best answer to the question "What is the effect of the presence of others on performance?" was that it sometimes helps and sometimes hurts. That is not a terribly satisfying answer, of course. It is as helpful as a political pundit saying that the Republicans will gain a majority in the next election, . . . but then again they might not. You would certainly ask for more from any political forecaster and you can legitimately ask for more from those who study the effects of the presence of others on performance.

Zajonc's Theory Fortunately, a more satisfying understanding was eventually obtained. After a period of about 25 years, during which those in the field largely became discouraged by the lack of progress on this topic and moved on to other issues, social psychologist Robert Zajonc proposed an unusually elegant theory to account for all of the divergent findings on this topic. Zajonc (1965) argued that the presence of others, indeed the *mere* presence of others, tends to facilitate performance on simple or well-learned tasks, but to hinder performance on difficult or novel tasks. Even more important, Zajonc's theory explained *why* the presence of others has these effects.

Zajonc's theory has three components. First, the mere presence of others makes a person more aroused. (More generally, the mere presence of another member of the same species tends to arouse any organism, but we will focus on people for now.) People are dynamic and unpredictable stimuli, capable of doing almost anything at any time. We thus need to be alert, or aroused, in their presence in order to be able to react to what they might do.

Robert B. Zajonc

dominant response In a hierarchy of responses, the response you are most likely to make.

Second, arousal tends to make a person more "rigid," in the sense that the person becomes even more inclined to do what he or she is already inclined to do. In the language Zajonc used, arousal makes a person more likely to make a **dominant response** (see **Box 14.1**). Think of it this way: In any situation, there are a variety of responses you can make, and these responses can be arranged in a hierarchy according to their likelihood of occurrence. Whatever you are most inclined to do in that situation is at the top of the hierarchy and is thus the "dominant response." Suppose, for example, that you are typing a memo, and you wish to type the letter "d." You would most likely do so correctly by pressing down on the middle finger of your left hand. As we all know from experience, however, we sometimes make mistakes, and our mistakes are not random. If you don't press the correct key, you are likely to press the "s" key next to it or the "c" just below. All possible responses can be ordered in a hierarchy according to the likelihood that you will make them. When aroused, Zajonc argued, people are even more inclined to make the response that is at the top of their hierarchy.

The third component of Zajonc's theory links the increase in dominant response tendencies to the facilitation of simple tasks and the inhibition of complex tasks. For easy or well-learned tasks, the dominant response is the correct response. Indeed, that is tantamount to what it means for a task to be easy or well learned. Your reflexive response is the correct response. Thus, the presence of other people, by facilitating your dominant response, facilitates the correct response and improves performance. In contrast, for difficult or novel tasks, the dominant response is unlikely to be the correct response. Again, that is what it means for a task to be difficult or novel. Your reflexive

BOX 14.1 **FOCUS ON DAILY LIFE**

Social Facilitation of Prejudice

One aspect of the social facilitation of dominant response tendencies is surprising. It is generally believed that prejudiced individuals are less likely to show their prejudice in most public settings. To do so is to risk others' disapproval. But if some forms of prejudice represent dominant response tendencies, they might nevertheless sometimes be facilitated in the presence of others—even when those others disapprove of prejudice. In one study that examined this idea, students were seated in front of a computer and shown, very briefly, pairs of images—a black or white face followed by a picture of a gun or a hand tool. The students were asked to respond as quickly as possible as to whether the second image was a gun or a tool (see Chapter 12). If they didn't respond within a half second, they were informed that they did not respond quickly enough. This procedure was repeated over and over, and the experimenters recorded, as a measure of prejudice, the number of mistakes participants made. In particular, they were interested in how often a hand tool was mistakenly identified as a gun when it was preceded by a black face compared to when it was preceded by a white face.

Some participants did this task alone, not expecting to have to interact with anyone in the experiment. Others did the task expecting to share their responses with others after they were finished. What the investigators found was that participants made 13 percent more errors (calling a tool a gun if it was preceded by a black face) when they expected to interact with others than when they did not (Lambert et al., 2003). To be sure, this result can be explained without reference to social facilitation (perhaps expecting to compare their results with others later on simply distracted participants and therefore made it harder for them to control their prejudices). But it is consistent with the social facilitation account, and the investigators were inspired to conduct the research by previous work on social facilitation.

response is not the correct response. Thus, the presence of others facilitates an *incorrect* response and hinders performance. This is shown schematically in **Figure 14.1**.

Testing the Theory   Zajonc's theory brought much-needed clarity to this field by providing a remarkably accurate summary of the diverse findings that existed at the time. Like any theory, however, Zajonc's formulation needed to be subjected to more stringent tests. The existing findings did not offer a sufficiently rigorous test; after all, the theory was based on the existing findings and therefore *had* to be consistent with them. Thus, since its publication, Zajonc's theory has been tested in a variety of ways on numerous occasions, and it has held up extremely well.

Let's explore one of these tests in detail. Although certain superficial features of the experiment may seem silly (for one thing, cockroaches, not humans, were the participants), it provides an effective way of examining the theory. Zajonc and his colleagues placed cockroaches in the start box of one of two mazes and then shone a light at the start box (Zajonc, Heingartner, & Herman, 1969). Because cockroaches find light aversive, they typically flee from it and head toward a dark area—in this case, the goal box. In the simple maze (a "runway"), getting to the darkened chamber was easy. The cockroach only needed do what it does instinctively: run directly away from the light (its dominant response). In contrast, getting to the darkened chamber in the complex maze was something of a challenge. The cockroach had to do more than follow its instincts and flee from the light; it had to execute a turn. Note that two features of this setup were especially important. First, Zajonc didn't have to guess at what the dominant response might be. Because cockroaches invariably run from light, it is clear that that is their dominant response. Second, it was possible to construct two different conditions, one in which the dominant response led to the goal (the simple maze) and one in which it did not (the complex maze).

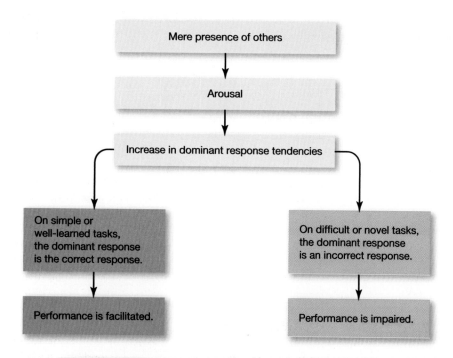

FIGURE 14.1 Zajonc's Model of Social Facilitation The presence of others (indeed, their mere presence) increases arousal and facilitates dominant response tendencies. This facilitates performance on easy or well-learned tasks, but hinders performance on difficult or novel tasks.

Zajonc had his cockroaches run one of these two mazes either alone or with another cockroach. He predicted that cockroaches running the simple maze would get to the goal box more quickly when together than when alone, but that those running the complex maze together would take longer to reach the chamber. Indeed, that is exactly what happened: the presence of another cockroach facilitated performance on the simple maze, but hindered performance on the complex maze (**Figure 14.2**).

Finally, to show that it is the *mere* presence of another cockroach that has these effects—as opposed to competition or some other more complex factor than the presence of conspecifics (others of the same species)—Zajonc added a condition in which the cockroach ran the maze not with another cockroach running alongside, but with other cockroaches merely present as a passive "audience." To accomplish this, Zajonc built a set of Plexiglas boxes, or "grandstands," that flanked the two mazes and filled them with observer cockroaches. Here, too, he predicted that the presence of the observing cockroaches would facilitate performance on the simple maze, but inhibit performance on the complex maze. And indeed, as Figure 14.5 indicates, the results were exactly as predicted. The presence of a passive audience helped performance on the simple task but interfered with performance on the difficult task.

Now, having validated Zajonc's theory in experiments such as this, we can apply it to the real world by making more precise predictions than we could before about what ought to happen in everyday life (Ben-Zeev, Fein, & Inzlicht, 2005; Thomas, Skitka, Christen, & Jurgena, 2002). An experiment conducted

Why cockroaches give lousy surprise parties.

FIGURE 14.2 Scientific Method: Social Facilitation on Simple and Complex Tasks

Hypothesis: The presence of other members of the same species—even for cockroaches—will facilitate performance on an easy task and hinder performance on a difficult task.

Research Method:

1 Researchers placed cockroaches in the start box of two mazes and shone a light that caused the cockroaches to head toward a dark area (the goal box).

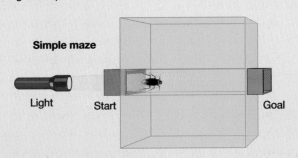

Simple maze

Light   Start   Goal

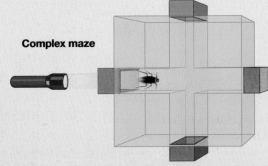

Complex maze

In the **simple maze**, the cockroach need only follow its dominant response and run directly away from the light to get to the goal.

In the **complex maze**, the cockroach's dominant response does not easily lead it to the goal. The cockroach must execute a turn.

2 The cockroaches ran one of these two mazes either alone, with another cockroach, or with an audience of cockroaches behind a transparent wall.

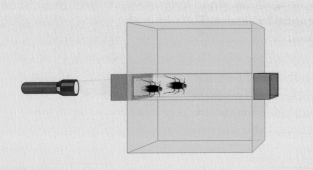

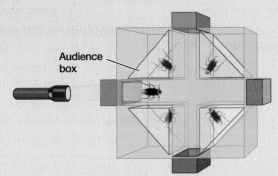

Audience box

Results: The cockroaches take less time to run simple mazes when they are in the presence of others but more time to run complex mazes with others present.

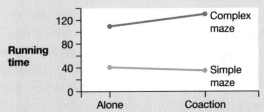

Running time

Average time (in seconds) taken by cockroaches to negotiate simple or complex mazes when alone or alongside another cockroach.

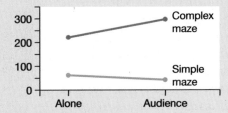

Average time to negotiate simple or complex mazes when alone or in the presence of an audience.

Conclusion: Social facilitation effects can be observed widely in the animal kingdom. For cockroaches, as for humans, the presence of others increases dominant response tendencies, leading to better performance on easy tasks and worse performance on difficult tasks.

Source: Zajonc, Heingartner, & Herman (1969).

in a university pool hall is a particularly informative example of such a real-world extension (Michaels, Blommel, Brocato, Linkous, & Rowe, 1982). Students playing recreational pool were unobtrusively observed and deemed skilled or unskilled based on their performance. Zajonc's theory, again, predicted that the presence of an audience would make the skilled players perform better (for them, the task is easy or well learned) but make the unskilled players perform worse (for them, the task is difficult or novel). To test this prediction, the experimenters walked up to the pool tables and watched. As expected, the good players did even better than before, and the poor players did even worse.

Mere Presence or Evaluation Apprehension?

Zajonc's theory remains to this day the most compelling and widely accepted account of social facilitation. Few theorists question Zajonc's contention that the presence of others increases arousal, and virtually no one disputes the claim that the presence of others tends to facilitate performance on easy tasks and to hinder performance on difficult tasks (Geen, 1989; Guerin, 1993; Sanna, 1992; Thomas et al., 2002). There is one element of Zajonc's theory, however, that is disputed—whether it is the *mere* presence of other people that increases arousal. When most people reflect on why they would be aroused in the presence of others, it is not the mere presence of others that seems decisive. Instead, it seems to be a matter of **evaluation apprehension**—a concern about looking bad in the eyes of others, about being evaluated—that is important (Blascovich, Mendes, Hunter, & Salomon, 1999; Cottrell, Wack, Sekerak, & Rittle, 1968; Seta & Seta, 1992).

evaluation apprehension A concern about how we appear in the eyes of others—that is, about being evaluated.

Testing for Evaluation Apprehension A number of social psychologists have argued that evaluation apprehension is the critical element underlying social facilitation. To evaluate this contention experimentally, there must be three conditions: one with the subject performing alone, one with the subject performing in front of an evaluative audience, and one with the subject performing in front of an audience that cannot evaluate the subject's performance. In one such experiment, the investigators cleverly built "from scratch" a response hierarchy in their participants so that they would know exactly what the dominant and subordinate responses were (Cottrell et al., 1968). The participants were given a list of ten nonsense words, such as "nansoma," "paritaf," or "zabulon." The participants were asked to pronounce two of the ten words once, two words twice, two words 5 times, two words 10 times, and two words 25 times. They were thus much more familiar with some of the words than with others. After this initial training phase of the experiment, the test phase began. Now the participants were told that these same words would be flashed on a screen very briefly (some so briefly they might not be visible), and their task would be to identify each word as it was shown. If they could not identify a word, they should guess. Unbeknownst to the participants, none of the target words was actually shown, and they were reduced to guessing on every trial (this task is thus known as a "pseudorecognition" test).

The participants performed this task either (1) alone, (2) in the presence of two fellow students who watched the proceedings attentively, or (3) in the presence of blindfolded "observers." The blindfolds in the latter, "mere presence" condition were supposedly to prepare the blindfolded individuals for an experiment in perception, but in reality they were to make it clear to the participants that these individuals could not evaluate them. The researchers were interested in how often the participants guessed a "dominant" word (those they had pronounced 25 times) and how this varied across the three conditions. The results, shown in **Figure 14.3**, highlight the importance of evaluation apprehension. Individuals performing in front of an evaluative audience made more dominant responses than those performing alone; those performing in front of a blindfolded audience did not. Thus, the audience that could not evaluate what was going on had no effect on performance. This experiment seems to demonstrate conclusively that it is the concern about others as a source of evaluation, not

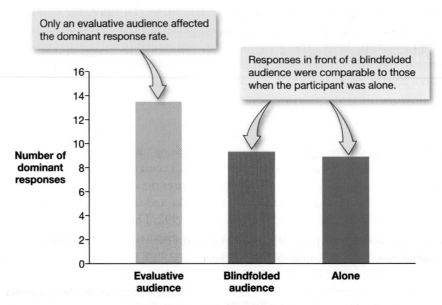

FIGURE 14.3 **Evaluation Apprehension and Social Facilitation** Average number of dominant responses made by participants who were responding alone, next to a blindfolded audience (who therefore couldn't monitor or evaluate their performance), or next to an attentive audience (who could evaluate their performance). (Source: Cottrell, Wack, Sekerak, & Rittle, 1968.)

their mere presence, that is responsible for social facilitation. But maybe there is less to this demonstration than meets the eye.

Testing for Mere Presence As you've just seen, three conditions are necessary to distinguish between the mere presence and evaluation apprehension accounts of social facilitation: an alone condition, a condition with another person merely present, and a condition with a potentially evaluative person present. The previous experiment appears to have met these three conditions, but appearances can be deceiving. Although participants in the alone condition were alone in an objective sense (no one else was physically present), they may not have been psychologically alone. After all, they were in an experiment, one in which they were asked to perform a strange task. It seems likely they would feel apprehensive about performing and about the prospect of their performance being surreptitiously recorded (which it was!). Thus, the alone condition used in this study may not have been a "true" alone condition. Participants may have felt the presence of the experimenter even when the experimenter was not physically present.

Note that this would artificially raise the dominant response rate in the alone condition, so that it would not be significantly different from the mere presence condition. Of course, this still leaves a substantial difference between the mere presence and evaluation conditions (see Figure 14.3), but that is not a problem for Zajonc's theory. His theory states that the mere presence of another person is *sufficient* to induce arousal. It is not inconsistent with the possibility that arousal could be increased still further by factors such as evaluation apprehension. To adequately test Zajonc's theory, then, it is essential to create a condition in which participants feel truly alone.

An ingenious experiment by Hazel Markus (1978) managed to create a true alone condition. When participants arrived individually for the experiment, they were told to go into an adjoining room to wait for the other participants to arrive. While there, they were to put on the necessary attire for the experiment. In particular, they were asked to (1) take off their own shoes, (2) put on a pair of lab socks over their own socks, (3) put on a pair of oversized lab shoes, and (4) put on a similarly oversized lab coat. The participants did all this and waited, in vain, for the "other participants" to arrive. In reality, there were no other participants. After 10 minutes, the experimenter reappeared and stated that the other participants were apparently not coming, and the experiment would have to be scratched. The participants were then instructed to change back into their own clothes.

Unbeknownst to the participants, all of this changing of clothes was surreptitiously observed and timed through a one-way mirror. Markus was interested in how quickly participants could perform the novel tasks of putting on and taking off the unfamiliar lab coat, socks, and shoes, as well as how quickly they could perform the well-learned tasks of taking off and putting on their own, very familiar, shoes. Participants did this either alone, with another person watching attentively, or in the mere presence of a repairman working on a piece of apparatus with his back to the participant.

Notice how the alone condition in this experiment improves on those used in previous studies. Not only is the subject physically alone, but there is no reason to worry about being observed or evaluated. From the participant's perspective, the experiment has yet to begin. He or she is *not doing anything*, and therefore there is no cause for evaluation apprehension. The subject is both physically and psychologically alone.

Even though the participants did not think they were "performing," Zajonc's theory predicts that they should change their own clothes faster and the novel clothes more slowly when in the mere presence of another person. As shown in **Table 14.1**, that is exactly what happened. Participants took off and put on their own shoes more quickly, and the experimenter's shoes, socks, and coat more slowly, when in the presence of another person—even when the other person had his back turned and was unable to observe. Thus, when a true alone condition is included, an effect of the *mere* presence of another person can be observed. Note again that the effects were stronger for an attentive audience than for a merely present audience, but that is not a problem for the theory. It just means that evaluation apprehension can add to a person's arousal and thus compound the effect of mere presence. Overall, these results strongly support Zajonc's theory.

Current Perspectives

On the basis of Markus's experiment and similar investigations (Platania & Moran, 2001; Rajecki, Ickes, Corcoran, & Lenerz, 1977; Schmitt, Gilovich, Goore, & Joseph,

TABLE 14.1 Social Facilitation and the Effect of an Audience

The amount of time, in seconds, participants took to change each item of clothing varied based on whether they were changing their own clothing or novel, lab clothing and whether they were alone or in the presence of another person who was ignoring them (merely present) or evaluating them (attentive audience).

	Alone	Merely Present Audience	Attentive Audience
Well-learned tasks (own shoes)	16.5	13.5	11.7
Novel tasks (lab shoes, socks, and coat)	28.8	32.7	33.9

Source: Markus (1978).

1986), it seems safe to say that the mere presence of others is sufficient to increase arousal and thus facilitate performance on well-learned tasks and inhibit performance on novel tasks. At the same time, there continues to be an interesting and healthy debate about *why* the mere presence of others has such effects. Some social psychologists have argued, in fact, that it is not the mere presence of another person that has these effects, but something that always accompanies the awareness of the mere presence of another. They have put forward a **distraction-conflict theory** of social facilitation based on the idea that being aware of another person's presence creates a conflict between attending to that person and attending to the task at hand. They believe that it is this attentional conflict that is arousing, and that it is *this* arousal that underlies the standard social facilitation effects (Baron, 1986; Baron, Moore, & Sanders, 1978; Groff, Baron, & Moore, 1983; Huguet, Galvaing, Monteil, & Dumas, 1999; Sanders, 1981). Thus far, not enough supportive data have been collected to settle the issue in favor of either this account or Zajonc's formulation (Guerin, 1993). But intriguingly, researchers have shown that nonsocial distractions (for example, being required to perform two tasks simultaneously) can generate effects just like the standard social facilitation effects (Sanders & Baron, 1975).

One hundred years of research on social facilitation has also made it clear that people are complex stimuli and that their presence can have a variety of effects that often overlay the more basic mere presence effects we have focused on here. As we have seen, people are often very concerned about making a good impression, and this evaluation apprehension can intensify arousal and lead to more pronounced social facilitation effects. There are occasions, however, in which the presence of others can mask the typical social facilitation effects. If those who are present belittle effort and devalue accomplishment, then performance will be inhibited even on simple tasks. In many work settings, for example, there are powerful norms against working too hard, and "rate busters" are made to feel the wrath of the group, with output suffering on even the simplest tasks (Homans, 1965). Similarly, African-American students sometimes put out less effort—and hence don't perform as well—in the presence of other African-Americans in order to avoid "acting white" (Ogbu, 1991; Ogbu & Davis, 2003). And consider Erving Goffman's rather charming example of adolescent boys riding a carousel. When others are present, the boys engage in a variety of behaviors designed to convey "role distance," or disinterest in the carousel (Goffman, 1961). If such a desire to maintain role distance were to emerge in a performance setting, it would surely impede output, regardless of how energizing the presence of others might be.

Perhaps the most common pattern of responses that runs counter to the social facilitation effects we have discussed is what social psychologists call **social loafing**, or the tendency to exert less effort when working on a group task in which individual contributions cannot be monitored (Hoeksema-van Orden, Gaillard, & Buunk, 1998; Karau & Williams, 1995; Latané, Williams, & Harkins, 1979; Plaks & Higgins, 2000; Sanna, 1992; Shepperd, 1995; Shepperd & Taylor, 1999; Williams, Harkins, & Latané, 1981). If you and your friends have to move a couch up a flight of stairs, for example, you might be tempted to "coast" a bit and hope that the more vigorous efforts of your friends will get the job done. In these situations, people often loaf because their contributions are not seen as crucial to the success of the effort and because their individual contributions—and hence they themselves—cannot be assessed.

Practical Applications

The basic pattern of facilitation of simple tasks and inhibition of complex tasks is reliable enough to warrant some practical advice. Of greatest relevance to student life, perhaps, is the obvious recommendation for how to study. Study alone. When the material is unfamiliar and must be committed to memory, it is best to do so without the arousal and distraction brought on by the presence of others. Study groups may be helpful for reviewing or for dividing up and summarizing vast amounts of material, and groups can be invaluable when some members have information or approaches that the others do not, but the hard work of absorbing and integrating new ideas should be done alone. Then, once the material is assimilated, sitting cheek by jowl with the other students in the examination room should aid performance.

Another potentially important practical application involves the way work spaces might be designed. If the tasks to be accomplished are simple or repetitive (and the workforce is highly motivated), then the setting should be designed so that people are in contact with one another. Such a design reaps the benefits of social facilitation of simple tasks. If the tasks to be performed are challenging and ever-changing, however, then it may be wise to give everyone the luxury of privacy. Such a design avoids the costs of social inhibition of performance on complex tasks.

Dominant Responses and Social Facilitation People tend to do better on well-learned tasks but worse on difficult or poorly mastered tasks in the presence of others. Presumably, the children who know the material well will do better on these standardized tests in the presence of other test takers because their dominant responses will be the correct responses. But children who don't know the material well will be more likely to give incorrect answers in the presence of others.

LOOKING BACK We have seen how even the most minimal group situation—the mere presence of a single other person—can influence performance. The presence of others is arousing, and arousal accentuates a person's existing performance tendencies. Easy tasks are made easier, and difficult tasks are made more difficult. The presence of a great many people, of course, is typically even more arousing and can affect our behavior beyond its influence on performance. We therefore turn to the impact of large groups of people—crowds—on social behavior and to the question of why crowds sometimes turn into mobs.

DEINDIVIDUATION AND THE PSYCHOLOGY OF MOBS

Consider the following very similar reactions to two very different events in San Francisco. The first involves the tragic circumstances surrounding the murders of Mayor George Moscone and Supervisor Harvey Milk in 1978. In early November of that year, Milk's political rival Dan White resigned his seat on the Board of Supervisors, citing the difficulty of raising a family on a supervisor's meager salary. Shortly afterwards, White had a change of heart and informed Mayor Moscone that he wanted to reclaim his seat. Moscone refused, and on November 27 he was prepared to name a successor to White. That day, however, White entered City Hall with a .38-caliber revolver, tracked down the mayor in his office, and shot him four times at point-blank range. White then left the mayor's office through a back door. Reloading his revolver in the hallway, he walked across the building to the supervisors' offices. There he found Milk, San Francisco's first openly gay supervisor, and killed him with a fusillade of five shots. White then fled City Hall, but turned himself in to police a little over an hour later.

The Psychology of Mobs (A) Upon learning of the killing of Harvey Milk and George Moscone by Dan White, a mob of demonstrators gathered to mourn their passing. (B) When Dan White was given a light sentence in his trial for their murder, demonstrators again took to the streets, rioting and setting cars on fire in protest of what they saw as a travesty of justice.

In a rather swift trial, White's lawyers argued that he was minimally responsible for his deeds because of the severe depression he was experiencing as a result of financial pressures and his decision to resign his seat on the Board of Supervisors. His lawyers claimed that his depression led him to subsist on a junk-food diet, which further "diminished his capacity" to distinguish right from wrong and to understand the implications of his actions. These tactics were ridiculed in the press as the now-infamous "Twinkie defense." Ridiculous or not, it was effective. Instead of the first-degree murder conviction that prosecutors sought, White was found guilty of the lesser charge of voluntary manslaughter. Rather than the death penalty or life imprisonment, White faced a maximum sentence of eight years. With good behavior, he would be eligible for parole in less than five years. (White ended up serving a little over five years, but 22 months after his release from prison, he committed suicide.)

The verdict was anathema to members of San Francisco's gay community. Many thought the verdict would have been more severe if a supervisor other than Harvey Milk had been slain. The evening of the verdict, gay activists organized a peaceful protest march, but events quickly got out of hand. It began with several demonstrators smashing the glass windows and doors of City Hall. Over the pleas of rally organizers urging calm, the crowd began to chant, "Kill Dan White! Get Dan White!" Vandalism and violence soon intensified. When police moved in to quell the disturbance, a battle ensued. The demonstrators threw rocks and bottles at police, set fire to numerous police cars, and looted nearby stores. In the end, 12 police cars were gutted by fire, 20 police officers were injured, and 70 demonstrators needed medical attention. Eight people were arrested.

As unfortunate and destructive as the rioting was, it nevertheless strikes most people as understandable—it fits with the average person's conception of human nature. The rioters were lashing out against a system that the protesters thought had failed. When frustrated, people aggress.

Now consider the striking similarity to events that erupted in the same city three years later in response to a much less understandable cause. The stimulus, believe it or not, was the San Francisco 49ers' *victory* over the Cincinnati Bengals in Super Bowl XVI, a victory that earned the city its first professional championship in any sport.

Within minutes of the game's conclusion, giddy fans poured out of homes and bars and into the streets to celebrate. Initially, it was all harmless, celebratory stuff—horns blared, beer was chugged, champagne was sprayed. As the evening wore on, however, events took a more sinister turn, eventually echoing what had transpired in the aftermath of the Dan White verdict. Bonfires were started in an intersection and atop a car. When police tried to restore order, they were met with a barrage of stones, bricks, and bottles. Before the streets were cleared, 8 police officers and 100 others were treated for injuries and 70 arrests were made.

Emergent Properties of Groups

These two events in San Francisco's history, as well as a great many similar events around the world, challenge us to come to grips with the question of how large groups of people are sometimes transformed into unruly mobs. How is it that peaceful gatherings can spin out of control and become violent? How is it that when immersed in a crowd, law-abiding citizens engage in acts of destruction they would never commit alone? How can we understand, in other words, the psychology of "the mob"?

Social psychologists have addressed this question in the context of examining the **emergent properties of groups,** or those behaviors that only surface ("emerge") when people are in groups. People do things in groups that they would never do alone. Indeed, we often hear people say that the group has "a mind of its own." As a result, the behavior of large groups of people is more than the sum of the behavioral propensities of its individual members.

emergent properties of groups
Those behaviors that only surface ("emerge") when people are in groups.

A simple thought experiment may be helpful. Imagine you have won a contest in which first prize is a free ticket to a U2 concert at your local arena. Being something of a U2 fan, you do not hesitate to attend. What sort of behavior do you observe or engage in at the concert? Chances are you and the rest of the crowd are quite boisterous. There is dancing in the aisles, "air guitar" imitations of The Edge, and frequent shouts of "Bono!" or "With or Without You."

Now contrast that experience with winning a slightly different contest. In this case, first prize entitles you to your own *personal* U2 concert. The band comes to your school and gives a concert just for you in the biggest amphitheater on campus. How do you behave? No doubt you would still have an enjoyable time, but we suspect you would not dance much, your talent at air guitar would not be displayed, and you wouldn't scream out requested songs with the same gusto. We do things in group settings that we do not do alone.

It should be noted at the outset that the psychology of the mob and other emergent properties are extremely difficult to study—much more difficult, certainly, than studying the effect of the presence of others on human performance. Indeed, the previous topic, social facilitation, is almost ideally suited for experimental investigation. First, people are more than willing to perform in laboratory settings, and they are motivated to do well. Second, it is easy to create a performance setting in the laboratory in which an audience is either present or absent, providing ready manipulation of the independent variable. Finally, there are countless objective measures of the quality and quantity of human performance, taking care of the dependent variable as well.

Emergent Properties of Groups Some behaviors only surface when people are part of a group and submerge their individual identities into the group. The people in this flash mob converged at this store after receiving e-mails telling them the time and place at which to gather. Their screams and raised arms reflect the fact that they are in a group—behavior that would be highly unlikely if each were there alone.

Studying the impulsive and often destructive behavior of the mob presents more of a challenge. People are on their best behavior when they enter a scientific laboratory, so it's difficult to create a laboratory situation in which they will "act out." Also, there are ethical constraints against putting people in situations in which aggressiveness and acts of destruction are likely. The psychology of the mob is thus difficult to re-create in a laboratory. Therefore, as we shall see, some of the most informative research on the subject takes place out in the world and not in the laboratory.

Deindividuation and the Group Mind

One of the first people to offer an extensive analysis of the psychology of the mob was not an experimental social psychologist, but a French sociologist, Gustav LeBon (1895). LeBon thought that people tended to lose their higher mental faculties of reason and deliberation when they were in large groups: "By the mere fact that he forms part of an organised crowd, a man descends several rungs in the ladder of civilization" (p. 52). For LeBon, this descent stems from the collection of individual, rational minds giving way to a less reflective "group mind."

Social psychologists have expanded on LeBon's ideas by examining how the thought patterns of individuals change when they come together in large groups and how these changes make them more susceptible to group influence. What general orientation to the world do people typically maintain when they are alone, and how does that orientation change when they are in a group? How does a collection of individual minds evolve into a group mind? A number of social psychologists have cited the importance of a sense of **deindividuation**—that is, the loss of individual identity accompanied by diminished self-regulation—that comes over people when they are in a large group (Diener, 1980; Festinger, Pepitone, & Newcomb, 1952; Prentice-Dunn & Rogers, 1989; Singer, Brush, & Lublin, 1965; Zimbardo, 1970). Most of the time, we feel individuated—that is, we feel individually identifiable by others, we consider ourselves individually responsible for our actions, and we are concerned with the propriety and future consequences of our behavior. When in large crowds, however, we sometimes feel deindividuated—that is, we feel "lost in the crowd," caught up in what is happening in the moment, with responsibility for our actions diffused.

Deindividuation and Rioting
When people are in a group and angry, they may let go of self-control and give in to impulses to wreak havoc. Normally law-abiding citizens merge into this crowd and break windows and smash cars with little thought to personal responsibility or the law.

deindividuation The reduced sense of individual identity accompanied by diminished self-regulation that comes over people when they are in a large group.

A Model of Deindividuation Philip Zimbardo (1970) proposed a theoretical model of deindividuation that specifies how certain conditions create the kind of psychological state that promotes the impulsive and often destructive behaviors observed in mobs (see **Figure 14.4**). Perhaps the most important of these conditions are the anonymity that individuals enjoy by blending in with a large group and the diffusion of responsibility that occurs when there are many people to share the blame. (It is often easier to mete out a stiff penalty to an individual than to everyone in a large group.) These conditions, along with the arousal, heightened activity, and sensory overload that often accompany immersion in a large group, lead to the internal state of deindividuation. The deindividuated state is characterized by diminished self-observation and self-evaluation and a lessened concern with how others evaluate us.

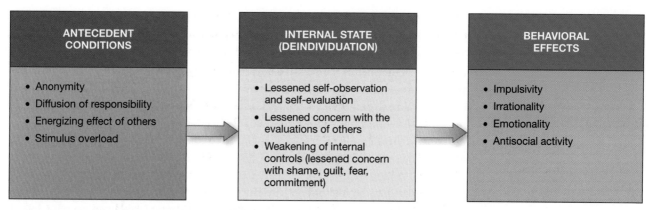

ANTECEDENT CONDITIONS	INTERNAL STATE (DEINDIVIDUATION)	BEHAVIORAL EFFECTS
• Anonymity • Diffusion of responsibility • Energizing effect of others • Stimulus overload	• Lessened self-observation and self-evaluation • Lessened concern with the evaluations of others • Weakening of internal controls (lessened concern with shame, guilt, fear, commitment)	• Impulsivity • Irrationality • Emotionality • Antisocial activity

FIGURE 14 .4 A Theoretical Model of Deindividuation   Certain antecedent conditions lead to an internal state of deindividuation, which in turn leads to behavioral effects that in other situations would be kept under control. (Source: Zimbardo, 1970.)

Thus, a deindividuated person is less aware of the self, more focused on others and the immediate environment, and hence more responsive to behavioral cues—for good or for bad. Being in a deindividuated state lowers the threshold for exhibiting actions that are typically inhibited. People are more likely to engage in a host of impulsive behaviors, both because there is more of a "push" to do so (because of increased arousal and many impulsive others to imitate) and because the constraints that usually "pull" them back from such actions are weakened (because of a lessened sense of evaluation and responsibility).

What emerges is the kind of impulsive, irrational, emotional, and occasionally destructive behavior that we think of as characteristic of mobs. This kind of behavior often creates its own momentum and is less responsive to stimuli that might otherwise bring it under control, making it difficult to terminate. Thus, Zimbardo's model of deindividuation is not an account of mob violence per se. Instead, it is a theoretical analysis of crowd-induced *impulsive* behavior—behavior that because of its very impulsivity often turns violent (Spivey & Prentice-Dunn, 1990).

One element that is not explicitly spelled out in the model but that is a very important part of the thinking behind it is that people often find the impulsivity that accompanies deindividuation to be liberating. Zimbardo argues that people go through much of their lives in a straitjacket of cognitive control. Living under such constraints can be tiresome and stifling, and so people sometimes yearn to break free of the straitjacket and act in a more spontaneous, impulsive fashion. In support of this idea, Zimbardo notes that virtually all societies try to safely channel the expression of this need by scheduled occasions in which people are encouraged to "let loose." We see this in harvest rites in agrarian cultures, carnivals in religious societies, galas and festivals throughout history, and, perhaps, in the mosh pits and use of intoxicants at modern rock concerts.

Deindividuation and Impulsive Behavior   During carnivals and festivals, people tend to "let loose" and relax their usual control over their behavior. A woman unleashes her inhibitions during a Mardi Gras parade in New Orleans.

Testing the Model   It is probably safe to say that this model sounds plausible to most readers. It also fits media accounts of events that have transpired in various riots and other episodes of mass antisocial actions. The key question, then, is how well the model stands up to systematic empirical test. Our intuitive sense of what is plausible is not an infallible guide to what is actually true, and media accounts cannot always be accepted at face value.

As we said earlier, most of the best empirical work on this subject has taken place not in the laboratory, but in the real world (for exceptions, see Lea, Spears, & de Groot, 2001; Postmes & Spears, 1998). Note also that this work involves very few controlled experiments (neither in the real world nor in a laboratory setting). Instead, most of the work involves the examination of archives—data originally gathered with no thought to its relevance to deindividuation. These records are used to search for predicted correlations between the various antecedent conditions and resultant behaviors.

Because these empirical tests are not controlled experiments, they do not "control for," or rule out, various alternative interpretations of the results. Indeed, we trust that many readers will be able to think of other explanations having nothing to do with deindividuation for some of the empirical results we report here. Nevertheless, it is important to ask whether a given alternative interpretation can account for *all* of the relevant findings. One result may be flawed in one way and thus be open to a particular alternative interpretation, while a second result may be flawed in a very different way that takes care of the first objection. If each finding requires a *different* alternative explanation, but all fit the model of deindividuation, we have reason to prefer the deindividuation account.

Suicide Baiting Imagine that you are on your way to class when you notice a disturbance up ahead. When you get closer, you find that everyone, with necks craned, is looking up at one of the top floors of a high-rise dormitory. It appears that a student, clearly upset, is halfway out an open window and is threatening to jump. What do you do?

Most of you would no doubt think about what you could do to stop the poor soul from jumping or whom you might summon for help. But not everyone responds that way. Hard as it may be to believe, people occasionally engage in suicide baiting, urging the individual to jump. Is suicide baiting more likely when there are a great many individuals gathered below and they form a mob? Are people more likely to engage in suicide baiting when they are deindividuated?

To answer these questions, researchers examined 15 years of newspaper accounts of suicidal jumps and averted jumps (Mann, 1981). They found 21 instances of attempted suicide, with suicide baiting occurring in 10 of them. They then analyzed the data to determine whether two variables associated with deindividuation, the cover of darkness and the presence of a large group of onlookers, were present when suicide baiting occurred and absent when it did not occur. As shown in **Figure 14.5**, both variables were indeed associated with suicide baiting. Suicide baiting was more than twice as likely when the crowd size exceeded 300. Also, suicide baiting was more than four times as likely if the episode took place after 6 p.m. As people feel more anonymous, either by being lost in a large crowd or under the cloak of darkness, they are more inclined to taunt and egg on a potential suicide.

Although it is possible to question some of the details of these analyses (for example, why were the cutoffs set at 300 people and 6 p.m.?) and to suggest alternative interpretations (the larger the group, the more likely it is to contain a psychopath who starts the taunting), the data are nevertheless consistent with the idea that variables that lead to deindividuation also lead to antisocial behavior.

The Conduct of War Wars have always been a part of what English novelist and scientist C. P. Snow calls the "long and gloomy history of man." The conduct of warfare, however, has varied enormously from culture to culture and epoch to epoch. Warfare practices vary in their ferocity, for example. At the "high" end of the ferocity scale, we find head-hunting, ritualistic torture, and the systematic slaughter of civilian noncombatants. At the very low end would be what Tom Wolfe (1979) has described as "single-combat" warfare: the David

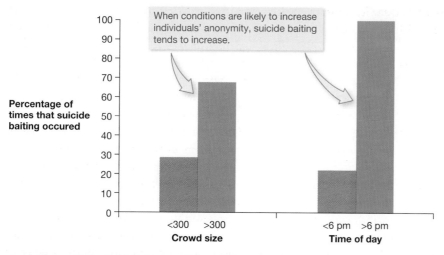

When conditions are likely to increase individuals' anonymity, suicide baiting tends to increase.

Percentage of times that suicide baiting occured

FIGURE 14.5 Deindividuation and Suicide Baiting (Source: Adapted from Mann, 1981.)

and Goliath battles in which the warring parties select a single warrior to do battle with each other. The losing side pays a price in territory or some other form of wealth, but less damage is done to both groups.

Is the brutality of warfare related to deindividuation? The theory predicts that it should be. It should be easier for people to "let go" of the usual prohibitions against barbarity when they feel anonymous and unaccountable for their actions. To determine whether such a relationship exists, the warfare practices of 23 non-Western cultures were investigated (Watson, 1973). Each culture was examined for whether its warriors were deindividuated before battle (that is, whether they wore masks or war paint) and for how aggressively they waged war (that is, did they torture the enemy, did they fight to the death in all battles?). As predicted, there was a strong correlation between deindividuation and aggressiveness in warfare. Among those cultures in which warriors changed their appearance before battle, 80 percent were deemed particularly aggressive; among those cultures in which warriors did not change their appearance, only 13 percent were deemed especially aggressive. When warriors are disguised in battle, they fight more ferociously (see **Box 14.2**).

Warfare and Deindividuation
Warriors in tribes that deindividuate themselves before battle by wearing war paint and war masks tend to engage in more brutal warfare practices.

Halloween Mayhem To American readers, one of the most familiar occasions for uninhibited and impulsive behavior is Halloween night. The destructive acts that are perpetrated on that holiday range from mild episodes of egg throwing to much more serious hooliganism. One group of social psychologists decided to take advantage of the Halloween atmosphere to conduct an ambitious test of the role of deindividuation in antisocial behavior (Diener, Fraser, Beaman, & Kelem, 1976). They set up research stations in 27 homes throughout the city of Seattle and monitored the behavior of over 1,000 trick-or-treaters. At each participating house, the children were told they could take one piece of candy from a large bowl sitting on a table in the entrance to the house. Next to the bowl of candy was a bowl filled with coins. To assess antisocial behavior, the experimenter excused herself from the scene and covertly monitored the children's actions. Would the children take just their allotted single piece of candy, or would they take more—perhaps even some coins?

BOX 14.2 **FOCUS ON HISTORY**

Celts and Warfare

The ancient Romans were terrified of the Gauls, who fought savagely and with little thought to self-preservation. Depending on your point of view, Gallic fighters were either extremely individuated or extremely deindividuated: They fought naked! The Romans eventually succeeded in pushing them to the far corners of the empire, where they became Bretons, Welsh, Irish, and Scots and in modern times have been known as Celts. The Scots painted their faces blue in battle for many centuries (which you may have seen in the film *Braveheart*), and they were regarded as ferocious fighters. Their descendants, the so-called Scotch Irish (some Scot-

tish, some Irish, and some Scots who had settled in Northern Ireland), were the main settlers of Appalachia and the U.S. South. Body paint was no longer required for them to maintain their reputations as fearsome fighters, first against the Native Americans and then in the Civil War, when they out-generaled and out-soldiered the North. The tradition has continued into the twenty-first century. Southerners are heavily overrepresented in the U.S. military.

Fierce Scotsmen A statue of Scottish leader William Wallace, whose life is depicted in the film *Braveheart*.

The investigators examined the influence of two variables connected to deindividuation. First, the children arrived individually or in groups, and the investigators expected that those in groups would feel more anonymous and therefore be more likely to transgress. Second, the experimenter purposely "individuated" a random sample of children arriving both alone and in groups. In particular, the experimenter asked each child his or her name and address and then repeated this information aloud for emphasis. Individuating the children—that is, identifying them by name so they would no longer feel anonymous—was predicted to inhibit any temptation to transgress.

As can be seen in **Figure 14.6**, both variables had the anticipated effect. The children who arrived in groups were much more likely to transgress than those who were alone, regardless of whether they were anonymous or not. Children who were anonymous were much more likely to transgress than those who were individuated, regardless of whether they were alone or in groups. Putting these two findings together, the children in anonymous groups were the most likely to transgress.

Summary of the Evidence The strength of each of the studies mentioned thus far lies in the "realness" and significance of the dependent variables—suicide baiting, warfare practices, and stealing. Unfortunately, with but one exception, all of the results are correlational findings, so we cannot be sure of the direction of causality. The one exception is the Halloween study. Part of the study was correlational: some participants showed up alone, and others arrived in groups. Perhaps being in a group does indeed cause a person to feel deindividuated and therefore to be more likely to act out, but perhaps it is just that rowdier people prefer to trick-or-treat with others. The other half of the study, however, is a true experiment and does not suffer from this self-selection problem. Children were randomly assigned to the anonymous and individuated conditions, so we can be sure that *on average* the two groups consisted of the same type of children. The tendency of anonymous children to act out can

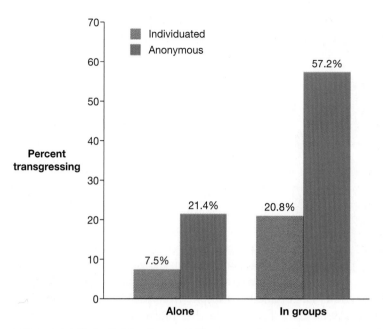

FIGURE 14.6 Deindividuation and Transgression The percentage of trick-or-treaters who transgressed was affected by whether they had been asked to give their name (individuated condition) or not (anonymous condition) and whether they were alone or in a group.

therefore confidently be attributed to anonymity per se and not to the kind of children who seek out anonymity.

Self-Awareness and Individuation

If "losing ourselves" in a crowd and becoming deindividuated makes us more likely to behave impulsively, it stands to reason that being especially self-conscious would have the opposite effect. Anything that focuses attention on the self, such as being in front of a camera, seeing ourselves in a mirror, or wearing a name tag, may lead to **individuation** and make us particularly inclined to act carefully and in accordance with our sense of propriety. This is just what **self-awareness theory** predicts. When people focus their attention inward on themselves, they become concerned with self-evaluation and how their current behavior conforms to their internal standards and values (Duval & Wicklund, 1972).

Studies of Self-Awareness Numerous experiments have shown that people do indeed act in ways that are more consistent with their enduring attitudes and values when they have been made self-conscious by being placed in front of a mirror or an attentive audience (Beaman, Klentz, Diener, & Svanum, 1979; Carver, 1974; Carver & Scheier, 1981; Duval & Lalwani, 1999; Froming, Walker, & Lopyan, 1982; Gibbons, 1978; Scheier, Fenigstein, & Buss, 1974). In one study, college students were asked to solve a series of anagrams and told to stop when a bell sounded. In a control condition, nearly three-quarters of them fudged a bit by continuing to work beyond the bell. But in a condition in which participants were made self-aware by working in front of a mirror, fewer than 10 percent cheated (Diener & Wallbom, 1976). Although most students *say* that cheating is a bad thing, it appears to take a bit of self-awareness to get them to act on that belief. Note that because being in a state of self-awareness is the flip side of feeling deindividuated, all of these experiments that support self-awareness theory also provide indirect support for the model of deindividuation.

individuation An enhanced sense of individual identity produced by focusing attention on the self, which generally leads people to act carefully and deliberately and in accordance with their sense of propriety and values.

self-awareness theory A theory that maintains that when people focus their attention inward on themselves, they become concerned with self-evaluation and how their current behavior conforms to their internal standards and values.

Individuation and Self-Awareness Anything that focuses attention on the self and individual identity is likely to lead to heightened concern with self-control and propriety. Name tags on these people at a business conference lead to individuation and, most likely, restrained behavior.

spotlight effect People's conviction that other people are attending to them—to their appearance and behavior—more than is actually the case.

Self-Consciousness and the Spotlight Effect The negative relationship between self-consciousness and deindividuation raises the question of how self-conscious people typically are in the normal course of events. There are pronounced individual differences, of course, in the degree to which people are focused on themselves and the degree to which they believe others are focused on them as well (Fenigstein, Scheier, & Buss, 1975). But there is also reason to believe that the typical level of self-consciousness, at least when other people are around, is fairly high. This was implied by our earlier discussion of institutionalized rituals such as carnivals, galas, and festivals that encourage deindividuation. People participate in such events so they can "let go" and get a respite from their usual self-conscious state. Roy Baumeister (1991) takes this a step further and argues that such disparate actions as binge eating, drinking to excess, masochistic behavior, and even suicide are ways of escaping self-consciousness and not attending to the self.

The evidence is clear that drinking alcohol can have precisely these effects (Hull, Levenson, Young, & Sher, 1983; Hull & Young, 1983; Hull, Young, & Jouriles, 1986). In one telling study, college students who were given gin and tonics or just tonic water were asked to give an extemporaneous speech. Those who had consumed alcohol delivered speeches with significantly fewer first-person pronouns—"I," "me," or "myself" (Hull et al., 1983). Thus, when people say they "lose themselves to the bottle," they mean it. It is noteworthy in this regard that recovering alcoholics who score high on measures of self-consciousness are nearly twice as likely to relapse as those who score low (Hull, Young, & Jouriles, 1986). The escape from self-consciousness that alcohol provides these individuals appears to be too appealing for them to live without.

Further evidence that people typically have a high level of self-consciousness comes from research on the **spotlight effect**—that is, people's conviction that other people are attending to them—to their appearance and behavior—more than is actually the case (**Figure 14.7**). People who make an insightful comment in a group discussion, for example, believe that others will notice their comment and remember it better than others actually do. Skiers who ski near the chairlifts are convinced that the people riding the lifts are carefully scrutinizing their form. Yet, when riding the lifts

---

FIGURE 14.7 You Be the Subject: Spotlight Effect

Imagine that you go to a dinner party and discover that everyone else brought a gift for the host except you.

1 Rate how harshly you would be judged by the host for this omission:

Totally fine 0 1 2 3 4 5 6 7 8 9 10 **Unforgivable**

2 Rate how harshly you would judge a guest who failed to bring a gift.

Totally fine 0 1 2 3 4 5 6 7 8 9 10 **Unforgivable**

Which ratings are lower?

Result: Did you assign a higher number for rating #1 than rating #2? Most people do, in part because people are prone to the spotlight effect, thinking that their own actions (the social blunder in this case) stand out more than they actually do.

themselves, they claim to only occasionally scrutinize anyone else. And people who suffer an embarrassing mishap, such as triggering an alarm in a public building or falling down while entering a lecture hall, think they will be judged more harshly by others than is actually the case (Epley, Savitsky, & Gilovich, 2002; Fortune & Newby-Clark, 2008; Gilovich, Kruger, & Medvec, 2002; Gilovich, Medvec, & Savitsky, 2000; Savitsky, Epley, & Gilovich, 2001).

In one of the clearest demonstrations of the spotlight effect, participants who arrived (individually) for an experiment were asked to put on a T-shirt sporting a picture of the pop singer Barry Manilow. Despite obvious signs of displeasure, everyone did so. They then reported to another room down the hall where, upon entering, they found a group of fellow students filling out questionnaires. After leaving the room moments later, the participants were asked to estimate the percentage of those other students who would be able to recall the person pictured on the T-shirt. As predicted, the participants overestimated how much they had stood out in their new shirt. They estimated that roughly half of the other students would be able to identify that it was Barry Manilow pictured on their shirt, when in fact only about a quarter were able to do so (Gilovich et al., 2000).

 We have seen that social psychologists have examined the relationship between self-consciousness and behavior from two directions. Research on deindividuation has shown that the diminished sense of self-awareness that sometimes occurs when we are immersed in large groups makes us get "caught up" in ongoing events and encourages impulsive—and sometimes destructive—actions. Research on self-awareness and the spotlight effect has shown how carefully we typically monitor our own behavior with an eye toward what others might think and how our awareness of self encourages us to act with a greater sense of propriety. A concern with what others might think about us also plays a role when we come together with others to make group decisions, the topic to which we now turn.

GROUP DECISION MAKING

When people come together in groups, one of the most important things they do is make decisions. Groups that cannot decide what to do or how to act do not function well. They wallow, bicker, and often split apart. It should come as no surprise, then, that social psychologists have spent considerable energy studying how—and how well—groups make decisions (Hinsz, Tindale, & Vollrath, 1997; Kerr, MacCoun, & Kramer, 1996; Laughlin, Hatch, Silver, & Boh, 2006; Levine & Moreland, 1990, 1998; Sommers, 2006).

Much of this research on group decision making was guided by the assumption that decisions made by groups are typically better than those made by individuals. Many heads are better than one. And indeed, when groups and individuals are presented with problems for which there is a precise, factual answer (such as the horse-trading problem discussed in Chapter 8), groups are more likely to arrive at the solution than the average individual (Laughlin, 1988; Laughlin & Ellis, 1986).

Yet, there are many contexts in which group decisions are no better than those rendered by individuals. The key to understanding such contexts is to recognize that although arriving at a best possible solution to a problem may be the *group's* most important goal, it may not be the most important goal for any of the individual group members. Individuals may be more concerned with how they will be judged by everyone else, how they can avoid hurting someone's feelings, how they can dodge responsibility if things go wrong, and so on. In fact, you've probably witnessed this kind of thing in the classroom: although question-and-answer sessions are meant for answering student questions and clarifying the course material, many of those who speak up craft their questions as much to show off as to obtain information. Similarly, when people get together to make group decisions, a number of predictable social psychological processes unfold that can subvert the stated goal of arriving at the best possible choice.

> When people "come together ... they may surpass, collectively and as a body, the quality of the few best. ... When there are many who contribute to the process of deliberation, each can bring his share of goodness and moral prudence."
>
> —Aristotle

Groupthink

Among peer groups and in informal settings in which social harmony is all-important and the costs of rendering an incorrect decision are not so great, it is hardly surprising that defective decision making sometimes results from group pressures to reach a unanimous decision. But what about those contexts in which life and death are literally at stake and the incentives to "get it right" are high? In those contexts, surely people wouldn't go along with faulty reasoning merely to preserve group harmony or to avoid embarrassment, would they? Yes, they would—and they do.

Irving Janis carefully analyzed a number of decisions made at the very highest levels of government and found evidence of just this sort of calamitous group decision making (Janis, 1972, 1982; see also Esser, 1998). Here are a few of the "fiascos" Janis looked at:

- The Kennedy administration's attempt to foster the overthrow of Fidel Castro's regime by depositing a group of CIA-trained Cuban refugees on the beaches of Cuba's Bay of Pigs but failing to provide air cover. (The refugees were captured in short order, thus humiliating the United States internationally, both for its role in trying to undermine a sovereign nation and for initially denying its involvement in the affair.)
- The Johnson administration's decision to increase the number of U.S. soldiers fighting in Vietnam. (This policy failed to advance U.S. objectives in the region and substantially increased the number of lives lost.)
- The conclusion by the U.S. naval high command that there was no need to take extra precautions at Pearl Harbor in response to warnings of an imminent attack by the Japanese. (This had severe repercussions on December 7, 1941, the "day of infamy," when U.S. ships at the Pearl Harbor naval base were destroyed in a surprise attack by the Japanese.)

groupthink A kind of faulty thinking on the part of highly cohesive groups in which the critical scrutiny that should be devoted to the issues at hand is subverted by social pressures to reach consensus.

Janis argues that these calamitous decisions were made because of **groupthink**, a kind of faulty thinking on the part of highly cohesive groups in which the critical scrutiny that should be devoted to the issues at hand is subverted by social pressures to reach consensus. Other investigators have made the same claim about other disasters, such as the ill-fated launches of the space shuttles *Challenger* and *Columbia* (Esser & Lindoerfer, 1989; Glanz & Schwartz, 2003; see **Box 14.3**).

Symptoms and Sources of Groupthink According to Janis, groupthink is a sort of psychological diminishment characterized by a shallow examination of information, a narrow consideration of alternatives, and a sense of invulnerability and moral superiority (see **Figure 14.8**). In his words, "Groupthink refers to a deterioration of mental efficiency, reality testing, and moral judgment that results from ingroup pressures" (Janis, 1972, p. 9). Victims of groupthink, often under the direction of a strong leader, ignore or reject alternative viewpoints, discourage others from coming forward with other ideas and assessments, and end up believing in the wisdom and moral

BOX 14.3   **FOCUS ON GOVERNMENT**

Groupthink in the Bush Administration

Groupthink seems to have played a role in the miscalculations that plagued the Bush administration's decision to invade Iraq in 2003. A report by the U.S. Senate Intelligence Committee identified groupthink as one factor that led the Bush administration to err so badly in its claim that Iraq possessed weapons of mass destruction (WMD). Specifically, the report concluded that many of the groups involved in assessing the threat posed by Iraq "demonstrated several aspects of groupthink: examining few alternatives, selective gathering of information, pressure to conform

within the group or withhold criticism, and collective rationalization" (Select Committee on Intelligence, 2004). The committee also found fault with administration analysts for failing to put in place common safeguards against groupthink. They stated that "the presumption that Iraq had active WMD programs was so strong that formalized . . . mechanisms established to challenge assumptions and 'groupthink,' such as . . . 'devil's advocacy,' and other types of alternative or competitive analysis, were not utilized."

Unfortunately, this tendency on the

part of policy-making groups to seek support for existing views rather than subject them to critical scrutiny is not confined to this particular administration or to the deliberations about whether to invade Iraq. It is sufficiently common that the U.S. military has its own name for the phenomenon— "incestuous amplification," which is defined by *Jane's Defense Weekly* as "a condition in warfare where one only listens to those who are already in lock-step agreement, reinforcing set beliefs and creating a situation ripe for miscalculation."

correctness of their proposed solutions. Thus, the very source of a group's potentially superior decision making—the airing of divergent opinions and the presentation of varied facts and perspectives—never comes into play.

It is clear from the historical record that social psychological forces have had a hand in numerous instances of faulty decision making—faulty decision making with the

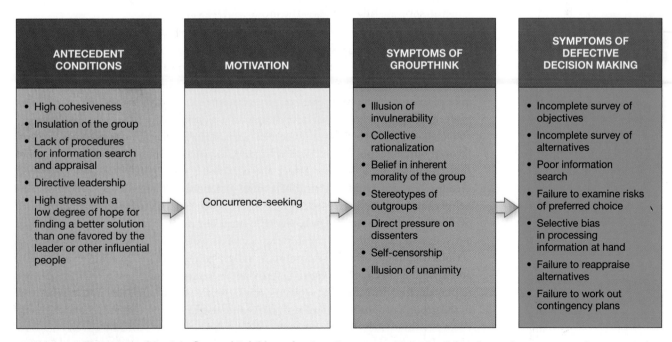

FIGURE 14.8 Elements of Janis's Groupthink Hypothesis   Certain conditions lead decision-making groups to be excessively concerned with seeking consensus, which detracts from a full, rational analysis of the existing problem. (Source: Adapted from Janis & Mann, 1977, p. 132.)

most disastrous consequences. What is less clear, however, is whether these psychological processes cluster together to produce a recognizable condition of groupthink (Choi & Kim, 1999; Henningsen, Henningsen, Eden, & Cruz, 2006; Turner & Pratkanis, 1998). Do such conditions as cohesiveness, insularity, and high stress tend to occur together, or are they separate variables that tend to inhibit effective decision making? And are the various sources and symptoms of groupthink *essential* ingredients of this sort of faulty decision making? Is group cohesiveness, for example, a necessary element of groupthink? Questions such as these have not been adequately resolved, and the evidence gathered to test Janis's thesis has been mixed at best (Aldag & Fuller, 1993; Longley & Pruitt, 1980; McCauley, 1989; Tetlock, Peterson, McGuire, Chang, & Feld, 1992). Nonetheless, his observations have been useful in identifying social factors that can lead to calamitous decisions, as well as factors that can improve group decision making.

For example, strong, directive leaders who make their preferences known sometimes intimidate even the most accomplished group members and stifle vigorous discussion (McCauley, 1998). Also, just as Janis contends, there are times when the issue that must be decided is so stressful that groups seek the reassurance and comfort of premature or illusory consensus. And both strong leaders and the drive to find consensus breed **self-censorship**, or the decision to withhold information or opinions. Janis reeports that Arthur Schlesinger, a member of President Kennedy's inner circle during the Bay of Pigs deliberations, was ever afterward haunted "for having kept so silent during those crucial discussions in the Cabinet Room . . . I can only explain my failure to do more than raise a few timid questions by reporting that one's impulse to blow the whistle on this nonsense was simply undone by the circumstances of the discussion" (Janis, 1982, p. 39). Some of the participants in that fiasco have written that the pressures to agree with the unsound plan were so great because the group was a newly created one and the participants were reluctant to step on one another's toes. People did not want to risk their own prestige by putting that of others on the line. In contrast, by the time they came together to deliberate over subsequent crises, they had been around the block with one another and were more willing to offer and accept criticism without worrying so much about threatening their relationship with the group.

self-censorship The tendency to withhold information or opinions in group discussions.

Preventing Groupthink Even though the theory may be less than precise, Janis's suggestions for how to improve group deliberations (or, in his terms, to prevent groupthink) have considerable merit. Freer, more vigorous discussion is likely to take place, for example, if the leader refrains from making his or her opinions or preferences known at the beginning. Just as scientists make sure that their data are collected and coded by "blind" observers who are in the dark about the investigator's favored outcome, policymakers are wise to install analogous procedures to ensure that the boss's views do not affect the comments and opinions of everyone else. Groups can also avoid the kind of tunnel vision and illusory consensus (the false belief that everyone agrees) that Janis describes by making sure the group is not cut off from outside input. Individuals who have not been privy to the early stages of a discussion can provide a fresh perspective as well as put the brakes on any rash actions that might otherwise develop. Finally, a similar safeguard against rash action and unsound argumentation can be provided by designating one person in the group to play devil's advocate—to be given every incentive to name any and all weaknesses in the group's proposed plan of action. Again, just as scientists are taught to evaluate their pet theories by trying to find their weakest elements and by specifying how alternative theories could explain the very same data, policymakers would be wise to install procedures that encourage the identification of every plan's Achilles' heel.

In addition to his analysis of foreign policy fiascos, Janis also examined a number of highly successful decisions—for example, the Marshall Plan to rebuild Europe after World War II and the Kennedy administration's handling of the Cuban missile crisis—and claimed that the deliberations leading to these decisions were not marked by symptoms of groupthink.

In the case of the Cuban missile crisis, Janis reviewed the historical record of the crisis and discovered how John Kennedy and his advisers sought to avoid another fiasco after the Bay of Pigs incident early in his administration. Severely embarrassed by that event, both by the woeful outcome and the shoddy decision processes it revealed, Kennedy took steps to ensure that all policies would be evaluated more thoroughly from then on. When faced with a wrenching decision as to what to do about Soviet missiles in Cuba, for example, Kennedy took a number of steps that could have been crafted by Irving Janis himself. Kennedy frequently excused himself from the group so as not to constrain the discussion. He also brought in outside experts to critique his advisers' analysis and tentative plans, and he appointed specific individuals (his brother, Robert Kennedy, and Theodore Sorensen) to act as devil's advocates. These safeguards seem to have paid off, as the negotiations that kept Soviet missiles out of Cuba were one of the enduring highlights of the tragically short Kennedy administration.

Preventing Groupthink John F. Kennedy's cabinet met during the Cuban missile crisis to try to resolve the impasse with the Soviets over Soviet missiles in Cuba. They took steps to avoid groupthink by encouraging vigorous debate and making recommendations based on unbiased analysis.

Janis's investigation of disastrous group decision making and of successful group decision making led him to be convinced about the need to carefully deliberate and to avoid self-censorship. His message is clear: Fall victim to groupthink and open the door to disaster; avoid groupthink and the likelihood of a satisfactory decision increases substantially.

Groupthink in Other Cultures Groupthink is a problem that can look different in non-Western cultures. The drive toward harmony is greater, for example, in East Asian cultures such as Japan than in Western cultures such as the United States (Nisbett, 2003). Groupthink in places like Japan can be so great, in fact, that even at scientific meetings there is rarely true debate or any other exchange that might appear confrontational or cause anyone to "lose face." Japanese scientists who are familiar with Western norms of scientific discourse believe that their science suffers as a consequence of not giving ideas a public airing. In fact, there is evidence that Japanese science is underperforming, given the amount of money spent on scientific research in that country (French, 2001). Still, Japanese corporations are in general highly effective, and in some industries they are the most competitive in the world. How is this possible if open and free debate does not take place? Japanese managers have meetings at which policy issues are discussed, but they may only appear on the surface to be like Western meetings. Nothing is really debated; instead, participants simply nod their approval of the proposal that is brought to them. This sounds like a recipe for disaster, but it turns out that managers typically discuss matters with everyone individually before the meeting to find out their views. The frank exchange goes on prior to the meeting, consensus is achieved as a result of these individual encounters, and the larger meeting is then little more than a rubber stamp. Although this procedure of one-on-one discussion and consensus finding may be different from procedures to improve group decision making in Western organizations, it appears to be helpful in preventing groupthink.

Group Decisions: Risky or Conservative?

Implicit in all the concern over avoiding groupthink is the suspicion that groups are often too rash—that decisions made by groups are often riskier and less thoroughly thought out than those made by individuals. But popular culture tends to hold precisely the opposite belief—namely, that groups abhor risk and tend to adopt middle-of-the-road solutions. Thus, in the United States at least, we tend to celebrate the swashbuckling CEO or politician who breaks free of institutional inertia and "takes chances" and "gets things done." So which is it? Do groups tend to make riskier or more risk-averse decisions than individuals? What type of error do we invite—risky or conservative—when we turn over a difficult decision to a group?

An MIT graduate student by the name of James Stoner put this very question to the test in 1961 by having participants make decisions about various choice dilemmas. That is, they had to render advice to a set of hypothetical individuals considering various risky courses of action. In one scenario, for example, an engineer had to decide whether to stay in his current job, which paid a moderate salary, or take a position with a new firm in which, if successful, he could earn a great deal more money. Should he stick with the security of his current firm or take a gamble on the new job? Here is the dilemma in full:

> Mr. A., an electrical engineer who is married and has one child, has been working for a large electronics corporation since graduating from college five years ago. He is assured of a lifetime job with a modest, though adequate, salary, and liberal pension benefits upon retirement. On the other hand, it is very unlikely that his salary will increase much before he retires. While attending a convention, Mr. A. is offered a job with a small, newly founded company that has a highly uncertain future. The new job would pay more to start and would offer the possibility of a share in the ownership if the company survived the competition of the larger firms. (Adapted from Stoner, 1961)
>
> Imagine that you are advising Mr. A. Listed below are several probabilities or odds of the new company's proving financially sound.
>
> Please check the lowest probability that you would consider acceptable to make it worthwhile for Mr. A to take the new job.
>
> ___ The chances are 1 in 10 that the company will prove financially sound.
> ___ The chances are 3 in 10 that the company will prove financially sound.
> ___ The chances are 5 in 10 that the company will prove financially sound.
> ___ The chances are 7 in 10 that the company will prove financially sound.
> ___ The chances are 9 in 10 that the company will prove financially sound.
> ___ Place a check here if you think Mr. A should not take the new job no matter what the probabilities.

As you can see, participants were asked to give their advice by specifying the likelihood of success that would be necessary for the engineer to decide to take the job with the new company. If the new company was sure to succeed, clearly the engineer should take it because it would pay more money; if it was sure to fail, the engineer should stay put. Participants had to decide what the new firm's chances had to be to make the switch worthwhile.

Stoner's participants rendered such decisions for 12 different choice dilemmas. First they did so individually, and then they met with other participants to discuss each dilemma and arrive at a consensus answer. Stoner then compared the consensus, or group, odds with the average odds specified by each individual. He expected the group to insist on higher odds of success (that is, to make a more conservative recommendation) than the average odds specified individually by each group member. What he found was just the opposite. The groups tended to recommend riskier courses of action than did the individual group members. Stoner, and many after him, concluded that groups tend to make riskier decisions than individuals, a pattern that came to be known as the **risky shift** (Stoner, 1961; Wallach, Kogan, & Bem, 1962). And the group members weren't just feigning boldness to appear courageous to everyone else. When participants were subsequently asked to render new *individual* decisions, the group discussion had left its mark. These later individual recommendations tended to be riskier than what these same individuals had recommended originally.

risky shift The tendency for groups to make riskier decisions than individuals would.

But as with the findings on social facilitation, the initial, clear picture as to whether groups make riskier decisions than individuals soon became murky. Several follow-ups to Stoner's work found decisions made by groups that were more cautious or "risk averse" than those made by individuals. Groups sometimes insist on greater odds of success, in other words, before they are willing to recommend a risky course of action. Indeed, such a result was even found on two of Stoner's 12 original choice dilemmas. But the notion that groups sometimes make riskier decisions than individuals and sometimes make less risky decisions is hardly satisfying. Can't social psychologists tell us *when* groups tend to be risky and *when* they

"It's agreed, then, that we move forward on the philodendron."

tend to be more cautious? Have they been able to discern some higher-order clarity to the mixed pattern of results as they did for the mixed results from experiments on social facilitation?

The key to discovering whether there is any higher-order clarity is to examine, in detail, the kind of issues that tend to elicit conservative group decisions and the kind that tend to induce risky decisions. We've already seen an example of an issue for which group discussion tends to make everyone riskier. Now consider a choice dilemma for which group discussion tends to make everyone more cautious:

> *Mr. C., a married man with a 7-year-old son, can provide his family with all the necessities of life, but few of the luxuries. Mr. C.'s mother recently died, leaving his son (that is, her grandson) a small inheritance she had accumulated by scrimping and saving, making regular donations to a savings account at her local bank. Mr. C. would like to invest his son's inheritance in the stock market. He is thinking about investing in a group of "blue-chip" stocks and bonds that should earn a 6 percent return on investment with reasonable certainty. However, he recently received a reliable tip about a new biotech company that has excited all the venture capitalists. If things go as well as predicted, he could more than quadruple his son's investment in the company within the first year; if things do not go well, however, he could lose the money and join the long list of those who have been burned by investing in high-tech start-ups. (Adapted from Stoner, 1961)*

How does this example differ from the earlier one? Many people report that their first reaction to the two scenarios is very different. In the first, stay-or-switch-jobs dilemma, they find themselves thinking, "Go for it. Don't be stuck in a dead-end job all your life; you'll regret it later." In contrast, when reading the second scenario, they find themselves thinking, "Not so fast! You shouldn't put your son's (and his grandmother's) legacy at risk."

Group Polarization

Researchers hypothesized that what group discussion does is make people more inclined to go in the direction in which they are already predisposed to go. If the issue is one that prompts most people to be inclined toward risk, talking it over with other members of a group may make everyone even more risk seeking. If the issue is one that prompts most people to be reluctant to take a chance, talking it over may make everyone even more conservative. And that's just what the research literature has shown. There is no overall risky shift; groups do not always make riskier choices than individuals. Rather, there is a **group polarization** effect; that is, group decisions tend to be more *extreme* than those made by individuals. Whatever way the majority of the individuals are leaning, group discussion tends to make them lean further in that direction (Moscovici & Zavalloni, 1969; Myers & Bishop, 1971; Zuber, Crott, & Werner, 1992).

If that is so, it implies that the same result should hold true even when groups discuss issues other than "choice dilemmas"—issues that have nothing to do with risk. And it does. In one study, for example, French students expressed their opinions about General Charles DeGaulle and about Americans, first individually and then again after having discussed them in groups. The results? Their initially positive sentiments toward DeGaulle became even more positive, and their initially negative sentiments toward Americans became even more negative (Moscovici & Zavalloni, 1969). It appears that we are more likely to hear the term *ugly American* from a group of foreigners than from a collection of individual foreigners.

But why does group discussion lead to more extreme inclinations on the part of group members? Why don't the individuals in the group simply conform to the group average, with the result that group discussion does not tend to move the group in one direction or the other? Subsequent research indicates that two causes work in concert to produce group polarization. One involves the force of the nature of the information brought up during group discussion; the other involves the tendency of people to try to claim the "right" position in the distribution of opinions within the group. Let's consider each explanation in turn.

The "Persuasive Arguments" Account

When trying to decide whether to pursue a risky or conservative course of action, people consider the different arguments in favor of each course. It stands to reason that on those dilemmas for which people are predisposed to take chances, they can think of more and better arguments in favor of risk. On those dilemmas for which people are predisposed to play it safe, they can think of more and better arguments that favor caution. But any one person is unlikely to think of *all* the arguments in favor of one alternative or the other. Thus, when the issue is discussed by the group, each person is likely to be exposed to new arguments. This expanded pool of arguments, in turn, is likely to be skewed in favor of risk when the issue is one for which people are already predisposed toward risk (otherwise, where would the initial inclination come from?) and likely to be skewed in favor of caution when the issue is one for which people are already predisposed to play it safe (otherwise—well, you get the picture).

The net result, then, is that group discussion tends to expose the average person to even more arguments in favor of the position that the average person was already inclined to take. This only serves to strengthen those initial inclinations, and group polarization is the inevitable result. This suggests that personal, face-to-face discussion is not necessary to produce group polarization. All that should be required is exposure to the pool of arguments that true group discussion tends to elicit. Several studies have tested this idea by having participants read the arguments of other group members in private so that they are exposed to the arguments without knowing who in the group might have advanced them. In support of the persuasive arguments interpretation, these studies have tended to show that this is sufficient to produce group polarization (Burnstein & Vinokur, 1973; Burnstein, Vinokur, & Trope, 1973; Clark, Crockett, & Archer, 1971).

The "Social Comparison" Interpretation Although exposure to the full pool of arguments is sufficient to induce group polarization, that's not all there is to this effect. There are other social psychological processes at work that give rise to the same outcome. Foremost among them is the very human tendency to compare ourselves with everyone else. We all want to know how we stack up against others. "Am I as smart as most people here?" "Does everyone else drive a better car than I do?" "Am I getting as much out of life as the average Joe?"

Leon Festinger developed his highly influential **social comparison theory** to account for the ubiquity of such comparisons. Festinger (1954) argued that people use objective means to evaluate themselves and comprehend their world whenever objective means are available. The way we determine if we have the ability to dunk a basketball is simply to give it a try. But for many questions—"Am I a wimp?" "Am I a kind person?"—there is no objective standard, and so we must compare how we stand in relation to others (Is everyone else backing down too? Are others kinder than I am?). An extensive body of research inspired by Festinger's theory has shown that such comparisons are extremely common, are often automatic (Blanton & Stapel, 2008; Mussweiler, 2003), and have important consequences (Stapel & Blanton, 2004; Suls & Wheeler, 2000; Wood, 1989).

For our present purposes, however, consider how these comparisons might lead to group polarization. When considering an issue for which people are inclined to take risks (a career choice early in life), it is likely that most people will tend to think that they are more tolerant of risk than the average person. In this case, riskiness is valued, and people like to think of themselves as having more than an average amount of a valued trait. When considering an issue for which people are inclined to be cautious (investing money that belongs to a beloved relative), however, it is likely, for the same reason, that most people will think they are more risk averse than the average person. People tend to think, in other words, that they are farther out on the correct side of the opinion distribution on most issues.

But what happens when they discuss an issue with others who are inclined to make the same choice and are also inclined to think of themselves as farther out on the correct side of the opinion distribution? Many will find, inevitably, that they do not occupy as desirable a location on the opinion distribution as they thought. This leads to an attempt on the part of some individuals to reclaim the "right" position. The group as a whole, then, becomes a bit riskier on those issues for which a somewhat risky approach initially seemed warranted, and a bit more conservative on those issues for which a somewhat cautious approach seemed warranted. In other words, the desire to be a bit different from others, but in the right direction—that is, to be "better" than others—leads quite predictably to the group polarization effect.

The way to test this interpretation, of course, is to do just the opposite of what was done to test the persuasive arguments account. There it was necessary to expose people to a pool of arguments without conveying any information about the positions endorsed by everyone else. Here it is necessary to expose people to everyone else's positions without conveying the content of any of the arguments for or against one position or

social comparison theory A theory that maintains that when there isn't an objective standard of evaluation or comprehension, people evaluate their opinions and abilities by comparing themselves to others.

another. And as predicted, when people are told only about others' positions and not the basis of those positions, the group polarization effect is observed (Teger & Pruitt, 1967). Interestingly, the group polarization effect in this experiment was weaker than usual, which is also just what one should expect if both the persuasive arguments and social comparison interpretations are valid and contribute to the effect.

Valuing Risk There is one more piece of the puzzle to be explained. Social psychologists have provided perfectly satisfactory accounts of why group discussion tends to intensify group members' initial leanings. But why do group members tend to lean so often in the risky direction? Recall that in Stoner's original investigation, a shift toward greater risk was observed on 10 of the 12 scenarios, a predisposition toward risk that has been replicated in countless subsequent studies. Why?

The logic of both the persuasive arguments and social comparison interpretations leads to the inescapable inference that people—at least the American college students who have made up the bulk of the participants in these studies—must typically value risk taking over caution. This would explain why arguments in favor of a relatively risky course of action resonate so effectively with the participants in these studies (the persuasive arguments account) and why people try to stake out the risky end of the opinion distribution (the social comparison account). It is not hard to show that this is the case. When participants read descriptions of people, some of whom come across as risk takers and others who do not, they assume that the risk takers possess a variety of favorable traits such as intelligence, confidence, and creativity as well (Jellison & Riskind, 1970). Also, when participants are asked to specify the level of risk with which they are comfortable in a given situation, the level of risk with which the average person is comfortable, and the level of risk with which the person they *most admire* is comfortable, the latter is assumed to be comfortable with the greatest risk (Levinger & Schneider, 1969). Clearly, risk is valued.

The high value placed on risk, by U.S. participants at least, is typically attributed to the broader culture in which they live. The hard-edged capitalism that is such an integral feature of U.S. life requires an active encouragement of risk and a willingness to take on the possibility of failure. (Note that two-thirds of all new businesses in the United States go under within a year.) Thus, we celebrate the stories of people like J. C. Penney, who went bankrupt twice before making his fortune, or Ted Turner, who bet the ranch on his vision of a global, 24-hour television news service (CNN). Some have even argued (in what we consider to be a very shaky contention) that the American love affair with risk is part of our biological makeup. Because America is a nation of immigrants, the argument goes, we inherited the genes of those who took a chance on life in the New World—a gamble that was not taken by those who had a cautious outlook (Farley, 1986).

Regardless of why Americans place a high value on derring-do, it implies that a shift toward greater riskiness after group discussion should occur more often among U.S. participants than among participants in other cultures that do not value risk as highly. And that is indeed the case. In studies conducted in Uganda and Liberia, the recommendations made by participants in response to the Choice Dilemma Questionnaire scenarios tended to be more cautious than those made by U.S. participants. In addition, the recommendations made by participants in these two African countries tended not to become more risky—as they did among U.S. participants—after group discussion (Carlson & Davis, 1971; Gologor, 1977).

Polarization in Modern Life

How do the phenomena we've just discussed affect group decision making on controversial issues in modern life? What would a group of university administrators concerned about declining support for affirmative action think about affirmative action policies after a group discussion? How would those alarmed about the rise of radical Islam feel about the proper policies to combat Islamic terrorism after they had had a chance to talk things over with others in their group?

Note that these issues are unlike those typically studied in the research literature on group polarization. They are not the sort for which people generally lean in the same direction. They are, after all, contentious public policy questions, which means there are strong advocates for all sides on each issue. The movement toward the extremes that we saw in the group polarization literature depends on there being a general direction in which most people lean—toward riskiness on one issue, caution on another; pro–Charles DeGaulle on one hand, anti-American on the other. It might seem, then, that there is no basis for predicting what effect discussion might have on the group members' attitudes about public policy disputes.

But here appearances are deceiving. Although the issues under discussion are indeed subject to contentious debate, the people most likely to meet in a group to discuss them are those who share the same general perspective, concerns, and preferences. Thus, they would be homogeneous groups, and they would tend to lean in the same direction on the issues. Thus, the lessons of group polarization would indeed apply. When homogeneous groups come together, their discussions are likely to lead to even stronger attitudes than the ones the group members came in with (Schulz-Hardt, Frey, Luthgens, & Moscovici, 2000).

Is this a problem? At the very least, group homogeneity robs the group of one of its greatest potential strengths—the give and take of *different* perspectives and sources of information that allow the best course of action to be discerned (Surowieki, 2004). Heterogeneous groups tend to outperform homogeneous groups when it comes to making the most effective decisions. (Note, however, that this effect is not as strong as we might suppose, in part because of a tendency for group members to talk about information they *share*—information that is often easier to talk about and that leads to more congenial discussion—rather than information unique to one person or another; Kelly & Karau, 1999; Postmes, Spears, & Cihangir, 2001; Stasser, 1999; Stasser & Titus, 1985). This effect was anticipated by the founding fathers of the United States, who spoke passionately about the evils of opinion homogeneity and took steps (the much-praised "checks and balances") to guard against the tyranny of the majority. Their view, strongly validated by subsequent social psychological research, was that deliberative bodies function best when they provide for the airing of competing views.

To the modern mind, group polarization may be particularly troubling because of the possibility that contemporary life may encourage dialogue primarily among like-minded individuals. At one level, society is more heterogeneous and multicultural than it has ever been, and there are more varied voices to be heard in public debate. But at the same time, it has become easier and easier to screen our inputs to hear only those voices we want to hear. For our nightly news, we can choose from the cacophony of niche programming (geared toward those with conservative views or liberal views), selecting those programs offering the opinions we already hold. Rather than reading a metropolitan newspaper serving the diverse interests of a broad community, we can avail ourselves of the Internet, where we can carefully tailor our media input—the information and opinions we receive—to fit our preexisting preferences. And rather than coming together to discuss the issues of the day with a broad spectrum of the general public, we can sit at home and discuss them with a set of like-minded individuals who contribute to the same blog or are all signed up to the same Internet chat group (McKenna & Bargh, 1998).

This would be problem enough if such a restricted range of inputs served only to reinforce our preexisting beliefs. But the literature on group polarization makes it clear that more than this happens. Group discussion among like-minded individuals

"The differences of opinion, and the jarrings of parties ... promote deliberation and circumspection; and serve to check the excesses of the majority."

—Alexander Hamilton, *The Federalist*

doesn't just reinforce existing opinion; it makes it more extreme. Thus, modern communication technologies such as the Internet may incubate extremism. The various hate groups that make extensive use of Internet communication were certainly not created by the Internet. Nevertheless, this mode of communication, and the group polarization it fosters, might very well feed their extremist views.

 We have seen how groupthink can lead to defective decision making, as people in highly cohesive groups may censor their reservations, ignore or reject alternative viewpoints, and succumb to ingroup pressures. To avoid this, the group should encourage the airing of all viewpoints, the leader should refrain from stating his or her opinions at the outset, and someone should be designated to play devil's advocate. We have also seen how group decision making can lead to group polarization, in which group decisions tend to be more extreme than those made by individuals because of the force of persuasive arguments and social comparison. To avoid the growing polarization in the modern world and to promote well-reasoned decisions, it is important to have a dialogue among diverse groups of people to air a full range of opinions.

Summary

The Nature and Purpose of Group Living

- Human beings, like all large primates except the orangutan, are group-living animals who influence and must get along with others.

Social Facilitation

- The presence of other people sometimes facilitates human performance and sometimes hinders it, but in predictable ways. Research on *social facilitation* has shown that the presence of others is arousing, and that arousal increases people's tendencies to do what they are already predisposed to do. On easy tasks, people are predisposed to respond correctly, and so increasing this tendency facilitates performance. On novel or difficult tasks, people are not predisposed to respond correctly, and so arousal hinders performance by making it more likely that they will respond incorrectly.

- A number of clever experiments have indicated that it is the *mere presence* of others that leads to social facilitation effects, although other factors, including *evaluation apprehension*, can intensify them. Moreover, *distraction-conflict theory* explains social facilitation by noting that awareness of another person can distract an individual and create a conflict between attending to the other person and to the task at hand, a conflict that is itself arousing.

- *Social loafing* is the tendency to exert less effort on a group task when individual contributions cannot be monitored.

Deindividuation and the Psychology of Mobs

- There is a tendency for large groups of people to sometimes transform into unruly mobs. This may happen because the anonymity and diffusion of responsibility that are often felt in large groups can lead to a mental state of *deindividuation* in which people are less concerned with the future, with normal societal constraints on behavior, and with the consequences of their actions.

- The deindividuated state of "getting lost in the crowd" stands in marked contrast to how people normally feel, which is quite individually identifiable. *Self-awareness theory* maintains that focusing attention on the self leads people to a state of *individuation*, marked by careful deliberation and concern with how well their actions conform to their internal moral standards.

- Most people overestimate how much they personally stand out and are identifiable to others, a phenomenon known as the *spotlight effect*.

Group Decision Making

- *Groupthink* is the tendency for members of cohesive groups to deal with the stress of making highly consequential decisions by pursuing consensus more vigorously than a critical analysis of all available information. Groupthink has been implicated in the faulty decision making that has led to a number of policy fiascos.

- Group decision making is affected by how cohesive a group is, how directive its leader is, and ingroup pressures that can lead to the rejection of alternative viewpoints and *self-censorship*, the tendency for people to refrain from expressing their true feelings or reservations in the face of apparent group consensus.

- Exchanging views with fellow group members can lead to more extreme decisions and make people more extreme in their attitudes. The *risky shift* refers to those cases in which groups make riskier decisions than individuals.

- Group discussion tends to create *group polarization*: initial leanings in a risky direction tend to be made more risky by group discussion, and initial leanings in a conservative direction tend to be made more conservative.

- Group polarization is created in part because group discussion exposes members to a greater number of *persuasive arguments* in favor of the consensus opinion than they would have thought of themselves. It is also pro-

duced through *social comparison*, whereby people compare their opinions and arguments with those of others when there are no objective standards of evaluation.

- People from cultures that place a high value on risk are more likely to make risky decisions after group discussion than people from cultures that do not value risk as highly.

- Polarization is a particularly common outcome in homogeneous groups, something that may be a particular problem in the modern world, as people are likely to read newspapers and watch news programs that fit their preexisting views. This polarization may be further reinforced through communication on the Internet, which makes it increasingly easy for people to find like-minded others and to exchange information solely with those who share their opinions.

Key Terms

deindividuation (p. 548)
distraction-conflict theory (p. 544)
dominant response (p. 537)
emergent properties of groups (p. 547)

evaluation apprehension (p. 541)
group polarization (p. 562)
groupthink (p. 556)
individuation (p. 553)
risky shift (p. 561)
self-awareness theory (p. 553)

self-censorship (p. 558)
social comparison theory (p. 563)
social facilitation (p. 536)
social loafing (p. 544)
spotlight effect (p. 554)

Further Reading

Janis, I. L. (1983). *Groupthink: Psychological studies of policy decisions and fiascoes.* Boston: Houghton-Mifflin. The classic formulation of the theory of Groupthink, with supportive evidence.

Hackman, R. (in press). Group performance. In S. T. Fiske & D. T. Gilbert (Eds.), *The Handbook of social psychology* (5th ed.). Hoboken, NJ: Wiley. A state of the art, comprehensive review of social psychological influences on performance in groups.

Sunstein, C. R. (2003). *Why societies need dissent.* Cambridge, MA: Harvard University Press. An important application of social psychological research on group polarization to the free exchange of ideas and opinion formation in the modern world.

Surowieki, J. (200). *The wisdom of crowds.* New York: Random House. Best-selling account of how and why the aggregate of many independent opinions can be tremendously accurate.

⑤ Online Study Tools

StudySpace

Go to StudySpace, wwnorton.com/studyspace, to access additional review and enrichment materials, including the following resources for each chapter:

Organize
- Study Plan
- Chapter Outline
- Quiz+ Assessment

Learn
- Ebook
- Chapter Review

- Critical-Thinking Questions
- Visual Quizzes
- Vocabulary Flashcards

Connect
- Apply It! Exercises
- Author Insights Podcasts
- Social Psychology in the News

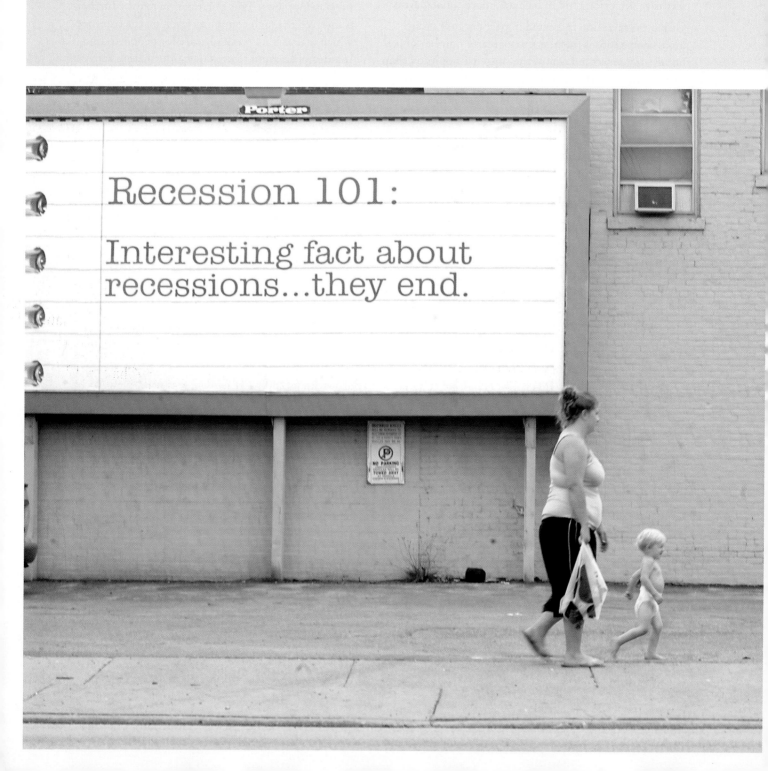

CHAPTER 15

Healthy, Wealthy, and Wise: Social Psychology Applied

IN THE EARLY 1940S, the United States and its allies found itself at war with Japan and Germany. The war machines of both countries were formidable, and American lives were being lost at a horrendous rate. The propaganda machines of Japan and Germany were also formidable, attempting to sap the will of Allied soldiers to fight. One of the most famous propaganda figures of the time was Axis Sally, a woman from Portland, Maine, who had gone to Germany to study music but became enamored of Nazi Germany and stayed on through the war. She played American songs to attract an audience of U.S. soldiers and tried to undermine morale with antisemitic rhetoric and attacks on the character and motives of President Roosevelt. Her stock in trade was trying to convince the Allied soldiers that while they were fighting for a losing cause in Europe, their wives and girlfriends were being unfaithful. Equally famous was Tokyo Rose (actually about a dozen female English-speaking broadcasters), whose broadcasts reached Allied sailors and marines listening near the Japanese mainland. The intent of the Tokyo Rose broadcasts was to damage morale. They named individual units and sometimes even individual soldiers and promised, often accurately, that deadly attacks were imminent.

The U.S. government recognized that a counter-propaganda effort was essential and made films for both the military and the civilian population called *Why We Fight*. The War Department hired Nathan Maccoby, Carl Hovland, Irving Janis, and many other psychologists to evaluate the effectiveness of those films. The psychologists found that the films were forgotten in a matter of weeks and that the effect on attitudes and opinions was even weaker. Carl Hovland began a program of research on effective communication for the military, which he brought to Yale as the Program of Research on Communication and Attitude Change. The Yale program conducted more than 50 experiments with speeches, face-to-face communication, and illustrated lectures to find out what kinds of communication,

Axis Sally and Tokyo Rose   A photo of Millard Gillars, a.k.a. Axis Sally (A), and one of the women who played Tokyo Rose (B). Their broadcasts aimed at American soldiers in World War II were designed to weaken the soldiers' morale.

what kinds of communicators, and what kinds of audiences had the biggest effect on attitudes. The program was one of pure research—that is, the investigators had no intrinsic interest in convincing anyone of anything; they simply wanted to find out what were effective communication strategies.

You can read more about this program in Chapter 8. What is clear, however, is that a great deal was learned about effective communication. This knowledge has been put to work by governments, by corporations, and by universities and other institutions with the goal of changing opinions. This applied work is often assessed as to its effectiveness, with the results being fed back into general theories about persuasion and attitude change. Those theories have had a major impact on the nature of persuasive communication of all kinds—from advertisements to political campaigning to government health announcements.

We have structured this book with the inextricable linkage of basic and applied research very much in mind. We have discussed important principles and research in social psychology without separating theory from practice, or basic issues from applied. As we discussed the core ideas in the field, we trust that you have noticed all sorts of applied implications we have laid out. And hopefully you thought about a number of potential practical applications yourselves.

We could have left it at that. But to leave no room for doubt that the field of social psychology can be a tremendous source of good in the world, we have decided to end with a chapter specifically devoted to applied ideas. We first discuss research in the field of health psychology, research that provides a number of very helpful guides for how to live in a way that promotes physical health, psychological flourishing, and longevity. We then discuss research from the field of behavioral economics, a hybrid of the two disciplines of psychology and economics, that can help you make better decisions when you spend, save, and invest. Finally, we discuss applications of social psychology to education.

HEALTHY: SOCIAL PSYCHOLOGICAL INFLUENCES ON MENTAL AND PHYSICAL HEALTH

Marie Antoinette was a notorious queen of France during the late eighteenth century. Fond of gambling, fine clothes, behind-the-scenes political maneuvers, and extramarital affairs, she was a favorite target of the revolutionaries when they overthrew the monarchy during the French Revolution. Legend has it that after her capture, during the night that she awaited her execution by guillotine, Marie Antoinette's hair turned white.

Marie Antoinette

We now know that it is physiologically impossible for hair to turn white during the course of a day. But stress—in Marie Antoinette's case caused by her imminent demise, her husband's execution, and the political upheaval she helped bring about—can damage our bodies. For example, physicians now estimate that about 1 to 2 percent of the cases in which people present with the symptoms of a heart attack actually reflect a syndrome known as apical ballooning syndrome (ABS). This condition arises when stress hormones such as epinephrine flood the left ventricle of the heart, causing it to balloon to dangerous levels. ABS is often triggered by extreme emotional stress—the death of a child, the loss of a spouse, or exposure to warfare and extreme violence. In 1 percent of the cases, ABS can prove fatal.

To understand what makes for healthy lives, we will return to the central concepts of our field. We will look at how evolution has crafted the stress response, which in the short run enables us to handle immediate pressures, but when chronically active can lead to myriad health problems. We will look at how one kind of culture—social class—influences our health, with people from lower-class backgrounds suffering more frequently from almost every kind of health problem. We will consider how one dimension of situations—the richness of our social connections—improves our health. And we will see that specific construal processes—perceptions of control and optimism—make for healthier lives.

Evolution and Health: Short-Term and Chronic Stress

As Marie Antoinette neared her day of execution, she must have experienced incredible levels of stress. She wouldn't have used the term *stress*, or its French equivalent, for this term we so commonly use today was coined only in the past century. But stress must have colored her every waking thought.

Psychological stress results from the sense that our challenges and demands surpass our current capacities, resources, and energies (Lazarus, 1966; Sapolsky, 1994). Not all challenges or demands trigger stress equally, though. A review of over 200 stress studies reveals that it is the challenges that threaten our social identity and our connection to others that are particularly likely to trigger stress (Dickerson & Kemeny, 2004). In our modern lives, the demands that we face often exceed our capacities. As a result, stress can arise in almost any situation: pressures at work, the loss of a loved one, economic hardship, conflicts with family members, trying times in a marriage.

psychological stress The sense that your challenges and demands surpass your current capacities, resources, and energies.

Even positive events in life can be surprisingly stressful: graduations, new jobs, planning a wedding, the early stages of marriage. And young children, while introducing incomparable joys, place new demands on us and create unexpected stress. In any of these circumstances, we may feel that we don't have the energy or skill to effectively handle the demands of life; as a result, we feel stress.

Insights into how stress harms our physical health are found in the study of a region of the body known as the hypothalamic-pituitary-adrenal (HPA) axis and the stress-related hormone *cortisol* (see **Figure 15.1**). Stressful events activate the amygdala, a region of the brain that processes information related to threat (see Chapters 7 and 9). The amygdala stimulates the paraventricular nucleus of the hypothalamus, which sends electrochemical signals to the anterior pituitary, which produces adrenocorticotropin hormone (ACTH). ACTH stimulates the adrenal glands (near our kidneys) to release the stress hormone cortisol into our bloodstream.

Cortisol has many effects on the body. Most notably, cortisol increases heart rate and blood pressure, distributing blood to appropriate muscle groups involved in fight-or-flight behavior. Our hands sweat—a process that some think evolved to facilitate grasping. Cortisol suppresses the activity of our immune system, keeping precious resources available for metabolically demanding fight-or-flight behavior. It is even involved in forming flashbulb, stress-related memories in the hippocampus, helping us form enduring memories about the serious sources of danger in our environment. (As we discuss in Chapter 5, however, not all flashbulb memories are accurate.)

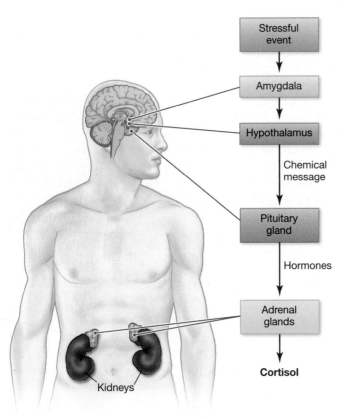

FIGURE 15.1 The Hypothalamic Pituitary Adrenal (HPA) Axis

rumination The tendency to think about some stressful event over and over again.

In the short run, activation of the HPA axis and the accompanying increase in cortisol in our bloodstream help us respond to immediate threats to our survival. During early hominid evolution, this stress response enabled our ancestors to detect an approaching predator or an enraged rival and respond quickly with appropriate action. Today, this same stress response helps us power through lecture notes to study for an exam, avoid danger, or stay up until the wee hours of the morning taking care of a sick friend or child. It should come as no surprise that race car drivers, parachute jumpers, and students taking exams have all been found to have elevated levels of cortisol (Coriell & Adler, 2001).

Our troubles begin when we experience chronic stress, frequently the result of **rumination**, the tendency to think about some stressful event over and over again (Nolen-Hoeksema, 1987). When we ruminate, we take a specific event, and by thinking of all its deep causes and extensive ramifications, turn that specific event into an enduring, general source of stress that touches on all facets of our lives. Say your boss offers some criticism about how to sharpen up a proposal you have been working on. If you were to ruminate about it, you would take the specific event—the criticism about the project—and elaborate upon how that event reflects more general problems you have at work, how you're never living up to expectations, how you'll let your parents down yet again. People who ruminate about a negative event experience prolonged stress compared to people who distract themselves from the event (Lyubomirsky & Nolen-Hoeksema, 1995; Morrow & Nolen-Hoeksema, 1990). Through rumination,

BOX 15.1 **FOCUS ON DAILY LIFE**

How to Stop Ruminating

One thing you're probably ruminating about right now is how to stop ruminating and avoid the toxic effects of chronic stress. Susan Nolen-Hoeksema, the leading scholar in the study of rumination, offers several tips for reducing your tendency to ruminate (Nolen-Hoeksema, 2003). Here are a few. First, *break loose* from your pattern of rumination; turn your attention away from those ruminative thoughts. Nolen-Hoeksema has documented how engaging in distracting activities during stressful periods—doing the crossword puzzle, knitting, reading a novel, or working on that suduko problem—quiets the ruminative mind and calms you during stressful times. A second strategy is the *stop* strategy. Here Nolen-Hoeksema recommends that you simply say "Stop" to yourself, even shout it, when you find yourself ruminating. Shift your attention to other matters in your life rather than what you are ruminating about: think of the things you need to do to get ready for grad school, where you might travel in the upcoming years, or friends you need to contact. And finally, Nolen-Hoeksema recommends that if you are a dyed-in-the-wool ruminator, simply set aside 30 minutes of ruminating time each day, ideally when you're feeling pretty calm. Knowing that you will have time each day to ruminate reduces the likelihood that you'll be overcome unexpectedly by rumination at random times during the day. Ethan Kross and his colleagues have shown that even for that deliberate period of rumination, it is helpful to engage in **self-distancing**, focusing on your feelings from the perspective of a detached observer (Kross, Ayduk, & Mischel, 2005). Revisiting a situation not from the perspective you initially had, but from the standpoint of a real or imagined observer of the situation, allows you to reflect over stressful thoughts and feelings without becoming overwhelmed by negative affect and arousal (Ayduk & Kross, 2008; Kross & Ayduk, 2008).

our specific stresses become chronic ones: a marital spat begins to feel like the fast road to divorce; a dip in the economy feels like a prolonged depression; a transient health problem feels like a verdict of deteriorating health.

And chronic stress can kill. We now know that chronic stress can lead to ulcers, heart disease, cancer, and even cell death in the hippocampus and consequent memory loss, in part because chronically high levels of cortisol damage different cells and organs in the body (Sapolsky, 1994). Feeling chronically stressed makes you more vulnerable to the common cold (Cohen et al., 2008). Chronic stress can even prematurely age parts of your cells. Elissa Epel and her colleagues found that premenopausal women who reported elevated levels of stress showed shortened telomeres, parts of cells that shorten with age (Epel et al., 2004). The telomeres of the most stressed out women in this study had prematurely aged by ten years.

The message from the literature on stress and cortisol couldn't be clearer. Evolution has equipped us with an immediate stress response, associated with elevated HPA activation and cortisol release, which enables adaptive responses to pressing problems in our lives. However, short-term stresses can sometimes become chronic stressors, triggering chronically high levels of cortisol that damage our health. Ruminating over stressful or negative events can have precisely that effect. Now let's consider one kind of culture—social class—that influences the degree of chronic stress an individual must endure and health outcomes of just about every kind.

self-distancing The ability to focus on one's feelings from the perspective of a detached observer.

Culture and Health: Class, Stress, and Health Outcomes

In a celebrated but perhaps apocryphal exchange, F. Scott Fitzgerald told Ernest Hemingway that "the rich are different from you and me." Hemingway retorted, "Yes, they have more money." Hemingway could have added that the rich also lead healthier and longer lives.

Social scientists think of wealth in terms of class, or what is often called socioeconomic status (SES). We often refer to social class with categories like "working class" or "upper class." Social scientists measure social class in terms of three variables: our family wealth and income, our educational achievement (and that of our parents), and the prestige of our work (and that of our parents) (Oakes & Rossi, 2003; Snibbe & Markus, 2005).

Social class is an important cultural dimension of our identity. People of different social class backgrounds tend to prefer different kinds of music: those from a lower-SES background prefer music that highlights the struggles of life, as in many country and western songs and rap; upper-class individuals prefer music that celebrates individual freedoms, often the case in alternative rock (Snibbe & Markus, 2005). People from different social class backgrounds tend to explain personal and societal events in different ways: people from lower-class backgrounds tend to explain personal events, such as how well they did in a job interview, and political events, such as the recent economic downturn, according to the current situation or broader context. Upper middle-class individuals attribute the same events to dispositional causes (Kraus, Piff, & Keltner, in press).

What does social class have to do with your physical health? A great deal, it turns out. Dozens of recent studies have looked at the association between an individual's social class and indicators of physical health. Just about every health problem is more prevalent in lower-SES individuals (see Adler et al., 1994; Coriell & Adler, 2001). Lower-SES newborns are more likely to have a low birth weight—a major predictor of later health problems. Lower-SES children are more likely to suffer from asthma, diabetes, and obesity, again all early predictors of other health problems later in life. In adulthood, lower-SES individuals are more likely to suffer from high blood pressure, cardiovascular disease, diabetes, respiratory illness, and poor metabolic functioning related to blood glucose levels and to subjectively experience poor health in terms of symptoms ranging from stomach upset to headaches and bad backs (Adler et al., 1994; Lehman, Taylor, Kiefe, & Seeman, 2005; Gallo, Bogart, Vranceanu, & Matthews, 2005; Singh-Manoux, Adler, & Marmot, 2003).

Class, Neighborhood, and Stress How would you explain these class-based differences in physical health? We hope that your first inclination would be a situationist one and to think about how the physical environments of lower-SES individuals might give rise to health-impairing chronic stress. Situations matter, and so do physical environments. Live close to someone, and you're more likely to become friends with that person (see Chapter 10). Generous acts are more common in rural settings than in urban settings (see Chapter 13). And it is clear that people from lower- and upper-SES backgrounds inhabit much different social and physical environments (see Coriell & Adler, 2001).

People living in poorer neighborhoods are more often exposed to air and water pollution, pesticides, and hazardous wastes. These kinds of toxins harm the nervous system directly, and they can also boost levels of stress. Lower-SES neighborhoods have fewer recreational spaces and parks. This means that lower-SES individuals have fewer opportunities to exercise, to be outdoors, to relax, to calm down, and to get out and about. It is well known that physical exercise reduces stress and increases physical health (Lyubomirsky, 2007). Lacking basketball courts, play structures, and picnic areas, lower-SES individuals are less likely to enjoy the stress-reducing potential of parks and recreation. Lower-SES neighborhoods also have a higher incidence of violent

Low and High SES Neighborhoods Lower-SES neighborhoods (A) have fewer green spaces and play structures than higher-SES neighborhoods (B), which allow for more stress-reducing play and relaxation.

crime, and individuals living in these neighborhoods experience more pervasive feelings of threat (Macintyre, Maciver, & Solomon, 1993). And lower-SES neighborhoods tend to have fewer health food stores and health care centers, all of which enable a healthier life.

Class, Rank, and Health Another explanation of the class-health connection has to do with rank, or power (Adler et al., 1994). Lower-SES individuals enjoy fewer resources and more limited access to opportunities, and these play an important role in defining a person's rank in society. Scientists have learned that having subordinate status, in human and nonhuman groups alike, leads to chronic feelings of threat and stress and accompanying activation of the HPA axis and elevated cortisol. For example, Robert Sapolsky has found that the subordinate baboons experience chronically higher levels of cortisol, as well as a variety of health problems, including increased chances of cardiovascular disease and lower reproductive success (Sapolsky, 1982, 1994).

Social class, then, may influence physical health through perceptions of rank or relative status. Lower-SES individuals may construe their lives in terms of occupying positions of subordinate status, and it may be this construal that damages physical health. To capture this idea, scientists have begun to measure construals of rank with what is known as the ladder measure. See **Figure 15.2**. Think of the ladder as representing where people stand in the United States. At the top of the ladder are the people who are the best off: those who have the most money, the most education, and the most respected jobs. At the bottom are the people who are the worst off who have the least money, least education, and the least respected jobs or no job. The higher up you are on this ladder, the closer you are to the people at the very top and the lower you are, the closer you are to the people at the very bottom. Where would you place yourself on this ladder?

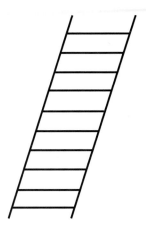

FIGURE 15.2 The Ladder Measure Place a large "X" on the rung where you think you stand.

What's interesting about this measure is that it is based on subjective construal: a fairly wealthy individual living among Fortune 500 CEOs, for example, could indicate a lower rank on this scale. And that would have important health outcomes: with each jump up the ladder of the class hierarchy, you are likely to enjoy better health outcomes. For example, in a study of employees of the British Civil Service, individuals in the lowest-ranked positions (for example, janitors) were three times as likely to die over a ten-year period as the highest-ranked administrators (Marmot, Shipley, & Rose, 1984). The experience of subordinate rank is toxic for our health (and the feeling of being empowered is good for it).

Nancy Adler and her colleagues have found that with each move up the class hierarchy, people are less likely than people just below them on the socioeconomic ladder to die as infants and are less vulnerable to coronary heart disease, lung cancer, bronchitis, respiratory disease, asthma, arthritis, cervical cancer, and neurological disorders (Adler et al., 1994). The experience of subordinate rank, even for people who have a good deal in life (that is, those in the middle or upper middle classes), leads to the chronic activation of the HPA axis and health problems.

Situational Factors and Health: The Benefits of Social Connection

We are a species that has evolved to connect with other people and to enjoy many kinds of relationships. And when we connect, we fare better in terms of health. In Chapter 7, we saw that prosocial touch calms the HPA axis and the stress response. And in Chapter 13, we saw that providing care for elderly individuals can add several years to the caregivers' lives.

To look more explicitly at the relationship between social connection and health, researchers measure the strength of our social support using scales like the one in **Table 15.1**. This scale captures the extent to which we can count on friends and family for support and care. With measures like these, researchers have documented that social connections are vital to our physical health.

Consider some more specific findings. In one study in Alameda County, California, people who had fewer meaningful connections to others were 1.9 to 3.1 times more

---

TABLE 15.1 Measure of Social Support

1. There is a special person who is around when I am in need.
2. There is a special person with whom I can share my joys and sorrows.
3. My family really tries to help me.
4. I get the emotional help and support I need from my family.
5. I have a special person who is a real source of comfort for me.
6. My friends really try to help me.
7. I can count on my friends when things go wrong.
8. I can talk about my problems with my family.
9. I have friends with whom I can share my joys and sorrows.
10. There is a special person in my life who cares about my feelings.
11. My family is willing to help me make decisions.
12. I can talk about my problems with my friends.

Source: From Zimet, Dalhem, Zimet, & Farley (1988).

BOX 15.2 **FOCUS ON POSITIVE PSYCHOLOGY**

Tips for Reducing Stress

One thing is clear from the literature on SES and health: economic hardship is hard on our health. This is certainly a theme more of us are likely to be thinking about during these difficult economic times. What can be done? In her book *The How of Happiness*, Sonja Lyubomirsky summarizes the vast literature on stress and offers some simple recommendations, none of which cost much money but all of which yield great health benefits (Lyubomirsky, 2007).

1. *Focus on an adaptive coping approach to your stresses.* Devise specific strategies about how you'll respond to your stresses one step at a time, with very concrete actions. If you're stressed out about how to get into graduate school, write down the specific actions you need to take to get ready to apply—volunteering in a lab, doing extracurricular activities, forming relationships with different professors, preparing for the GREs.

2. *Exercise (the more, the better).* People seek the "runner's high" not only by jogging, but through many kinds of exercise—dance, pick-up basketball, hiking in the mountains, the lunchtime walk with a friend, cross-country skiing. Almost any kind of exercise tends to lower stress levels.

3. *Cultivate positive emotions.* Several studies suggest that the more we cultivate positive emotions, the less stress we experience. People who experience the many positive emotions we discuss in this book—gratitude, love, contentment, awe—have been found to have lower mortality rates (Moskowitz & Epel, 2008). When feeling stressed out, take a moment to write down something for which you're grateful. If the thing stressing you out is something someone has done to harm you, try to forgive. Go out and see a comedy. Or just take a break and have an outing with friends. All of these experiences bring you different kinds of positive emotion, which, as you learned in our discussion of the tend-and-befriend approach, reduce our stress.

4. *Meditate.* There are many kinds of meditation: focusing on the breath, focusing on different sensations in the body, cultivating a kind approach to other people, being mindful, or aware, of everyday actions such as eating or walking. There is an ever-expanding scientific literature showing that meditation reduces levels of cortisol and stress.

likely to have died nine years later (Berkman & Syme, 1979). People who report that they have strong ties to others live longer (Berkman, 1995; Coriell & Adler, 2001). And Janice Kiecolt-Glaser and her colleagues have found that people who report being lonely show higher levels of cortisol, suggesting that strong social connections calm the HPA axis (Kiecolt-Glaser & Glaser, 1995).

Of course, these correlational studies raise questions about causation. It could be, as we are arguing here, that strong relationships promote physical health. Or it could be that physically healthy people are more likely to enter into psychologically healthy relationships. And of course, both theses are plausible.

Several experiments indicate that physiological stress is calmed by being in the presence of supportive others. In one study, for example, women had to perform stressful, challenging tasks either in the presence of a friend or alone. Those with a friend showed less of a stress-related cardiovascular response to the challenging tasks (Kamarck, Manuch, & Jennings, 1990). In another study, people were required to give a public speech with very little time to prepare, which no doubt caused rattled nerves and elevated cortisol. Those who gave the speech with a supportive person in the audience, compared to those who did not have such an admiring fan in the audience, showed lower blood pressure during the course of the speech (Lepore, Allen, & Evans, 1993). And in still other work, participants had to give a speech about why they would be a good choice for an administrative job on the UCLA campus while two audience members looked on, expressionless, offering few signs of enthusiasm and a great deal of skepticism (Taylor et al., 2008). Before and after the speech, participants' cortisol levels were measured. Participants who reported having strong connections with others and a sense of autonomy and healthy esteem showed less intense cortisol responses to the stressful speech.

Perhaps the most dramatic evidence of the health benefits of social connection came from an influential study by David Spiegel and his colleagues (Spiegel, Bloom, Kraemer, & Gottheil, 1989). Spiegel was interested in whether a sense of social connection would enable more favorable responses to breast cancer. Participants in this study were randomly assigned to one of two conditions. In one condition, participants engaged in weekly sessions of emotionally supportive group therapy with other breast cancer patients; in a second condition, participants were assigned to a nonintervention control group. As you can see in **Figure 15.3**, those in the group therapy condition survived 18 months longer (37 months) than women in the nonintervention control group (19 months).

These findings support our thesis that social connections make for healthier responses to stress and better health overall. To integrate these findings, Shelley Taylor and her colleagues have offered an influential account of the benefits of a "tend-and-befriend" approach to stress (Taylor et al., 2000). Taylor argues that when we tend to others' needs, physiological processes are engaged that calm down our stress-related HPA axis activation, thus paving the way for better health. A central

FIGURE 15.3 Scientific Method: Health Benefits of Social Connection

Hypothesis: Social connections enable more favorable responses to surviving breast cancer.

Research Method:

1 Participants were randomly assigned to one of two conditions. In one condition, participants engaged in weekly sessions of emotionally supportive group therapy with other breast cancer patients.

2 In a second condition, participants were assigned to a nonintervention control group.

Results: Those in the group therapy condition survived 18 months longer (37 months) than women in a nonintervention control group (19 months).

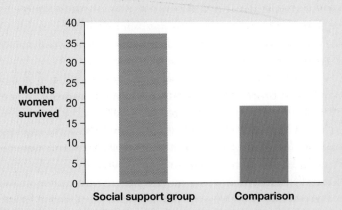

Conclusion: Breast cancer patients survive longer thanks to social support.

Source: Spiegel, Bloom, Kraemer, & Gottheil (1989).

player in this tend-and-befriend branch of the nervous system is oxytocin. Oxytocin floats through your brain and bloodstream and fosters feelings of trust, love, and devotion (see Chapter 7). In nonhuman species from rats to primates, oxytocin increases attachment-related behavior and reduces levels of stress-related cortisol. When we give, care, and connect, Taylor reasons, we activate oxytocin and this attachment system, and one of the benefits is the soothing of stress-related HPA axis activity. One of the most important clues to a healthy life, then, is to stay connected.

Construal and Health: The Benefits of Perceived Control and Optimism

In the early 1980s, Shelley Taylor began a study of how people live with serious disease (see, for example, Taylor, 1983). In one of her studies, Taylor interviewed women who were being treated for breast cancer. One out of seven women in the United States and Canada suffer from breast cancer during the course of their lives. While the survival rates are improving every year, the psychological concomitants of breast cancer are complex. Upon being diagnosed, women often feel anxiety, fear, shame, and even hostility—just the kinds of emotions that trigger the HPA axis and cortisol release and perhaps worsen the course of the disease.

In studying these interviews, Taylor found that women diagnosed with breast cancer did not passively accept their condition. Instead, they actively constructed narratives about this new dimension to their identities. For example, many women found reasons to be grateful in surprising kinds of social comparisons. Women who were diagnosed with breast cancer later in life felt grateful it hadn't happened to them as young women, early in their raising of their children and their careers; they were appreciative of having had the chance to live a full life without cancer. Younger women, by contrast, were grateful that they weren't older when they received their diagnosis, for they felt they had the physical robustness to respond to the disease. These findings suggest that people construe their experiences with diseases in much different ways.

One construal process that seems to benefit health is cultivating a sense of control. This refers to our sense of mastery, autonomy, and efficacy in influencing important life outcomes (Shapiro, Schwartz, & Astin, 1996). In Taylor's study of breast cancer patients, perceived control proved to be a source of good health. Taylor found that over two-thirds of the women with breast cancer reported a sense of control over the disease. The cancer patients assumed that through diet, exercise, or positive beliefs, they could control the course of their disease. (People suffering from other conditions—HIV/AIDS and coronary problems, for example—similarly reveal the belief that they have control over the progression of their disease.) And the more the breast cancer patient reported a sense of control over her breast cancer, the better the response to the disease she enjoyed as assessed by her physician (Taylor, Wood, & Lichtman, 1983). More generally, people who report a more pronounced sense of control enjoy better health outcomes (Cohen & Herbert, 1996). Diseases and other health problems threaten our basic beliefs about the control we enjoy over our bodies and lives; this sense of lack of control is stressful in its own right and activates the HPA axis and cortisol. Cultivating beliefs in control can counter these kinds of stresses and promote better health.

These findings raise an intriguing possibility: Might introducing the sense of control into the lives of people whose health is on the decline improve physical health? That was the question that motivated a striking study by Ellen Langer and Judith Rodin (1976) of elderly individuals in a nursing home. As people age into their later years, they often experience a pronounced loss of control in many realms: the loss of eyesight and physical coordination and strength makes simple physical tasks more challenging; the loss of memory can make for more difficult social interactions. These age-related trends are only amplified, many believe, by the conditions of nursing homes. Once in the nursing home, people can lose even more control—over their schedules, their meals, and their social activities.

So Langer and Rodin did something ingenious. They decided to explore the effects of increasing the sense of control in a nursing home in Connecticut. The participants were all healthy, ambulatory 65- to 90-year-olds living in the home. On one floor, individuals were brought together and led in a discussion by a young male staff member about personal responsibility and about the various ways they had control in the home, ranging from planning their free time to voicing complaints to the staff. They then were each given a small plant and asked to take care of it. In a second condition, on a neighboring floor, participants were told about all the things in the home available to them, but no mention of their control was made. They, too, were each given a plant, but were told that the nurses would water and care for the plants.

Prior to these discussions and again three weeks later, Langer and Rodin gathered several measures of how well the elderly residents were faring (**Figure 15.4**). Sure enough, participants on the floor that emphasized personal control showed greater increases in happiness compared to those on the neighboring floor. They were more likely to attend a free movie. They were ten times as likely to participate in a game proposed by the staff. And as rated by the nurses, nearly four times as many of the participants with the uplifted sense of control were judged to have improved in their overall functioning. Cultivating a sense of control appears to quiet the emotions that activate the HPA axis.

A second construal that has emerged as quite important in health is optimism (see Chapter 4). Highly optimistic people have positive expectations about the future. They are likely to endorse the item "In uncertain times, I usually expect the best" and

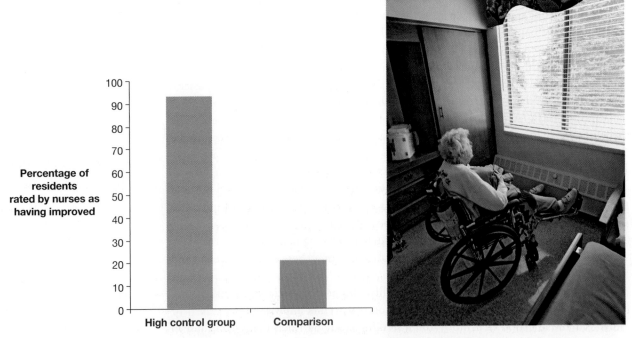

Percentage of residents rated by nurses as having improved

100
90
80
70
60
50
40
30
20
10
0

High control group   Comparison

FIGURE 15.4 Personal Control and Happiness   This older woman appears to be experiencing little control in her nursing home.

disagree with the item "If something can go wrong for me, it will." And people who report higher levels of optimism report greater happiness and well-being—and they enjoy better health outcomes. For example, Charles Carver and Michael Scheier have found that individuals who report higher levels of optimism respond with greater robustness and recover more quickly to coronary artery bypass surgery and breast cancer. Self-reports of pessimism have been found to predict a more rapid aging of the immune system (Wolkowitz, Tillie, Blackburn, & Epel, 2009). In George Valliant's longitudinal study of men who graduated from Harvard in 1945, those individuals who reported higher levels of optimism at age 21 reported higher levels of physical health 35 years later (Peterson, Seligman, & Valliant, 1988).

Taylor and colleagues have argued that beliefs in control and optimism benefit health in several ways. With an increased sense of control, people are likely to respond to stress with less HPA reactivity. Moreover, people with a heightened sense of control and a sense of optimism are likely to engage in better health practices. For example, in one study, optimistic HIV patients showed better health habits (Taylor et al., 1992). These patients are more likely to build up good networks of social support, and they are more likely to engage in better health-related behaviors, all of which improve their health.

 We have seen that evolution has designed the hypothalamic-pituitary-adrenal (HPA) axis, which releases cortisol into the bloodstream to enable fight-or-flight behavior. In the short term, activation of this system helps us respond to emergencies. When chronically active, however, stress and elevated cortisol produce all sorts of health problems. Social class affects physical health: people from lower-SES backgrounds suffer greater incidences of almost every health problem, in part because of the environments they live in and in part from the experience of subordinate rank. Situations filled with supportive relationships foster robust health, in part by activating a "tend-and-befriend" response that counters the toxic effects of stress and cortisol. Two patterns of construal—a sense of control and optimism—are also important to our health.

WEALTHY: BEHAVIORAL ECONOMICS AND PERSONAL FINANCE

On October 10, 2007, the Dow Jones industrial average, a widely cited index of the U.S. stock market and the health of the U.S. economy, stood at $14,164. People with heavy investments in the stock market were flush. Exactly one year later, however, the Dow closed at $8,579, wiping out 40 percent of the retirement savings and college funds of a great many families. Six months later, the Dow closed at $6,547, less than half of what it was at its peak. Unemployment at the beginning of this period was 4.6 percent; a year and a half later, it was twice as high. What happened?

Nothing. That is, there was no great calamity that diminished the productivity of U.S. firms or the country's ability to produce goods and services. No hurricane wiped out our refining capacity. No new war was started. Oil-exporting countries did not boycott the United States. As Franklin Delano Roosevelt famously said with equal truth about an earlier economic depression, "We are stricken by no plague of locusts."

What happened was the accumulation of human error in millions upon millions of economic transactions. People borrowed money against their homes and, since they

"Money is better than poverty, if only for financial reasons."

— Woody Allen

The Stock Market Collapse In the fall of 2008, housing and stock markets throughout the world experienced steep declines, sending the United States and much of the world into the worst economic downturn since the Great Depression.

still owned the house and had more money in their pockets, concluded that they were wealthier than they actually were. Banks approved mortgages to people with very shaky finances and then sold the mortgages on a secondary market to buyers who didn't fully know what they were getting. "Irrational exuberance" (Greenspan, 1996; Shiller, 2000) convinced people that housing and stock prices could only go up and so they had to "get in the game," with borrowed money if necessary.

But housing and stock prices don't only go up. And when they went down, just a bit at first, people and institutions that had borrowed heavily couldn't meet their obligations. If they couldn't borrow even more money, they had to sell. The selling reduced the prices of what they owned, further weakening their balance sheets, which produced more selling. And so on. The housing market sank, pulling down large segments of the banking system and the construction industry, which reverberated into every area of the economy.

According to standard economic thinking, this sort of cascade of human error shouldn't—indeed, couldn't—happen. The field of traditional economics is based on two fundamental assumptions: that people are rational and that people are selfish. Economists assume, in other words, that people can accurately assess how much pleasure or pain they would derive from different outcomes, that they can estimate how likely those different outcomes are with as much accuracy as the available information permits, and that they pursue courses of action that are most likely to advance their self-interests. The behavior of financial markets and the actions of individuals as they work, spend, save, and invest are viewed through the filter of these two assumptions.

Psychologists know better. It is certainly true that people are often rational and can be counted on to pursue their self-interests reasonably well most of the time. But as discussed in Chapter 5, human judgment is often distorted by predictable biases. And as discussed in Chapter 13, people are (thankfully) concerned about more than their own self-interest. Understanding when and why people are likely to violate these twin assumptions of economics is essential if we are to truly understand human economic behavior. Beginning in the 1980s, a group of psychologists and economists became concerned that standard economic theory didn't recognize or address important shortcomings in individual judgment and decision making, shortcomings that could combine to influence the performance of the economy as a whole. They created a new field, typically referred to as **behavioral economics**, that was dedicated to taking insights from psychology about how the mind works and applying them to create more realistic and accurate models of economic behavior. Behavioral economics started out as something of a renegade area within economics and only gradually won over adherents. With the severe recession in the fall of 2008, however, it has reached a much wider audience and won much greater acceptance.

In this section, we will review some of the most important ideas from the field of behavioral economics as we consider some of the ways that people make questionable decisions as they spend, shop, save, and invest. And we'll end the section with some very specific advice about how you should start, *right now*, to think about your money and how to handle it.

behavioral economics A discipline that uses insights from psychology to create realistic and accurate models of economic behavior.

Irrationality in Financial Markets

If people were entirely rational, their buy and sell decisions would not be influenced by factors that have no bearing on the intrinsic value of what they are buying and selling. But such decisions *are* swayed by extraneous factors. We see this when people try to lift themselves out of a bad mood by going shopping, only to end up buying things they regret. But maybe, you might say, this is entirely rational if it succeeds in lifting their moods. Who's to say a better mood is not worth the price of spending "too much" and experiencing later regret? Maybe a strategy whereby "when the going gets tough, the tough go shopping" is entirely rational.

But what if people's moods influence their presumably more sober and consequential investment decisions or influence entire markets? It would be harder to defend the rationality of those outcomes. And it turns out that even the most consequential financial transactions *are* influenced by such things as transitory, irrelevant mood states. An analysis of stock market performance in 26 countries over a 15-year period found that the amount of sunshine on a given day is positively correlated with market performance. The market tends to go up more often on sunny days and down more often on gloomy days, a result that the investigators argue was due to investors attributing their good spirits to positive economic circumstances rather than the true source—sunshine (Hirshleifer & Shumway, 2003; Kamstra, Kramer, & Levi, 2003). Another study found that stock exchanges in different countries tend to decline when their soccer teams are eliminated from important tournaments, such as the World Cup, and that similar dips occur in countries following losses in other sports (cricket, rugby, basketball) popular in those countries (Edmans, Garcia, & Norli, 2007). It's hard to argue that *that* is rational.

It's also hard to maintain that it was rational for investors to bid up the stock of Computer Literacy Inc. by 33 percent in a single day simply because it changed its name to the edgier, more hip-sounding fatbrain.com. (Zweig, 2007). The irrationality of stock movements (or at least the irrationality of *initial* stock movements) was further demonstrated in a study that examined the relationship between the name of a company newly listed on the stock exchange and its performance (Alter & Oppenheimer, 2006). Stocks in companies with easy-to-pronounce names (for example, Belden Inc., Accenture Ltd.) performed better the day after and one week after they were listed than companies with hard-to-pronounce names (for example, Magyar Tavkozlesi Rt., Inspat International NV). Those who initially got taken in by the sound of a stock's name later paid a price for doing so, as the price of easy-to-pronounce

"People who think money can't buy happiness don't know where to shop."

— Dolly Parton

stocks were not higher six months later. Eventually, the performance of the company—it's profitability, not its name—carried the day.

Loss Aversion

Suppose that ten years ago, your grandparents bought you 1,000 shares of stock in ABC corporation at $25 a share and 1,000 shares of XYZ corporation at $75 dollars a share. Suppose further that the stock of both companies is now selling for $50 a share. This means (lucky you!) that you own $50,000 of stock in each company.

Now suppose you want to pay off your $25,000 student loan by selling some of your stock. You can only sell shares in one of the companies. Which would you sell, half your shares in ABC or half your shares in XYZ? Amazingly, the evidence suggests that most people would rather sell their stock in the company that had gone up in price (ABC, from $25 to $50) than the stock in the company that had gone down (XYZ, from $75 to $50). People are more inclined to sell their winners, in other words, than their losers. Why on earth would they do that?

The culprit appears to be the psychological phenomenon known as **loss aversion**, or the tendency for a loss of a given magnitude (for example, losing $100) to have more psychological impact than an equivalent gain (winning $100). Note that loss aversion is a particular instance of the broader phenomenon discussed in Chapters 5 and 8 of bad things hurting more than equivalent good things feel good. Finding or winning $100 feels great, but not to the same degree that losing $100 feels bad. This means that people are likely to go to great lengths to avoid taking a loss—or go to great lengths to create the *illusion* that they haven't taken a loss. So, if you sell shares of the stock that has gone up in price, you're realizing a gain. That feels good. But if you sell shares of the stock that has gone down in price, you're sustaining a loss. And that feels terrible. So people are willing to take a risk to avoid that feeling—the risk being that the losing stock will decline even more in value. (Note, by the way, that there are tax advantages of selling stocks that have declined in value rather than those that have gone up: the amount of the loss, up to a certain amount, can be deducted from your income.)

Although the example we outlined might seem fanciful, people treat their real-life investments just this way. Terrance Odean (1998) studied the buy and sell decisions made by over 10,000 individuals who traded stocks with a discount brokerage firm. What he found was that investors were more likely to sell shares of the stocks that had gone up in price than the stocks that had gone down. And they paid a price for their loss aversion. Over the next year, the stocks they sold (their winners) outperformed those they held onto (their losers) by 3.4 percent. If you take that 3.4 percent annual difference and compound it over a lifetime, it can make the difference between being very rich and not.

Loss Aversion and Framing The principle of construal discussed throughout this book embodies the idea that it is possible to interpret the same stimulus in different ways—and that doing so has a profound impact on people's behavior. When it comes to economic transactions, it is possible for the same outcome to be construed as a loss or gain, depending on how it is framed. For instance, many years ago it was illegal for commercial establishments to charge two different prices for their products—a higher price for a credit card transaction and a lower price for those who paid cash. But because companies pay a fee to the credit card institution (a fee they pass on to the customer in the form of higher prices), a single-price system could be considered unfair to those who pay cash. Cash customers end up subsidizing the credit transactions of others. As a result, Congress agreed to change the laws to permit a two-tiered pricing system. Credit card companies lobbied vigorously to control how the two-tiered

loss aversion The tendency for a loss of a given magnitude to have more psychological impact than an equivalent gain.

system would be labeled. They preferred that it be called a "cash discount" rather than a "credit card surcharge." They wisely reasoned that people would be less inclined to use their credit cards if they had to pay a surcharge to do so. Paying a surcharge is experienced as a direct cost, or loss, whereas declining a cash discount is experienced as a foregone *gain*. Because losses have greater psychological impact than gains, the credit card companies have a huge financial stake in having the price difference labeled as a cash discount.

A few years ago, one of your textbook authors conducted a survey for a large life insurance company in which half the respondents were asked whether they could comfortably save 20 percent of their income. Only half of them said they could. Another group was asked whether they could comfortably live on 80 percent of their income. Nearly 80 percent of them said they could. Of course, saving 20 percent means living on 80 percent, so rationally there should be no difference between the two groups. But saving 20 percent is experienced as a loss of current spending resources, whereas living on 80 percent makes that missing 20 percent feel more like a foregone gain. The loss frame makes it seem more onerous than the gain frame.

The asymmetry in people's reactions to outright losses versus foregone gains makes it easier for the government to pay for programs by granting tax breaks rather than by making cash payments. Paying for something (for example, a tax to pay for public housing) is experienced as a cost, or a loss. Granting a tax break (for example, to companies that invest in public housing) is experienced as a foregone gain—tax revenue that would have been collected, but is not. This may help explain why populist reformers have made little headway in attacking "corporate welfare." Much of the voting public is easily riled by welfare to the poor because it involves direct payments from the government. It is a construed as a loss. It is harder to get the public as upset over corporate welfare because it typically comes in the form of tax deductions rather than direct payments. It is thus construed as a foregone gain.

How outcomes are framed has a particularly strong effect on whether people are likely to make risky or conservative financial decisions. Consider the following example, adapted from Tversky and Kahneman (1986):

> *You are first given $300 and then you must choose between:*
> *a sure gain of $100 or*
> *a 50 percent chance to gain $200 and a 50 percent chance to gain nothing*

Nearly three-quarters of those who are presented with this problem say they would take the sure $100. They don't want to gamble; they are risk averse. But now consider the following, only slightly different, problem:

> *You are first given $500 and then you must choose between:*
> *a sure loss of $100 or*
> *a 50 percent chance to lose nothing and a 50 percent chance to lose $200*

In this case, nearly two-thirds say they would take the gamble. They are risk seeking. This is really quite interesting because if you look closely at both pairs of options, you'll notice that they are objectively identical. In each problem, you must choose between having a final outcome of $400 for sure or a 50 percent chance of $500 and a 50 percent chance of $300. But one version forces you to think of the choice as between two possible gains and the other as between two possible losses. When choosing between possible gains, most people prefer the sure thing over a risky chance of a bigger prize. This **risk aversion** when it comes to gains is due to what economists call "diminishing marginal utility"—that is, each additional dollar you receive yields less utility the more dollars you already own. So, in this case, a gain of $100 is experienced as more than half as valuable as a gain of $200, so why gamble to get $200? Because

"Wealth is the slave of a wise man. The master of a fool."

— Seneca

risk aversion The reluctance to pursue an uncertain option with an average payoff that equals or exceeds the payoff attainable by another, certain option.

BOX 15.3 **FOCUS ON NEUROSCIENCE**

The Intensity of Possible Losses

Consider another study of loss aversion and framing, also by Tversky and Kahneman (1981). One group of participants was asked to imagine that the United States is preparing for the outbreak of a rare disease expected to kill 600 people. Two alternative programs to combat the disease have been proposed:

   If program A is adopted, 200 people will be saved.

   If program B is adopted, there is a one-third probability that 600 people will be saved and a two-thirds probability that no one will be saved.

Among these participants, 72 percent preferred program A, the "safe" option. Saving 200 "for sure" is more appealing than trying to save all 600 lives at the risk of saving none.

   Another group of participants was given the same introduction as before, but with the following options:

   If program C is adopted, 400 people will die.

   If program D is adopted, there is a one-third probability that nobody will die and a two-thirds probability that 600 people will die.

Of these participants, 78 percent preferred program D, the risky option. A one-third probability that no one will die is preferable to the certain death of 400 people. Note, however, that program A in the first version is identical to program C in the second version (200 people saved is equivalent to 400 people who die). Similarly, program B is identical to program D (a one-third probability that 600 people will be saved is equivalent to a one-third probability that nobody will die).

   Chances are you found yourself thinking that you would make the same choice as the majority in each case. The first one, in fact, probably seemed like a no-brainer. If you can save 200 lives, better do it. End of story. In fact, when people in a brain scanner (fMRI machine) are choosing this option, their pattern of brain activation shows just how easy the choice is. When considering the sure gain, there is very little activation along the intraparietal sulcus, a region associated with imagining hypothetical events and their outcomes (top left of **Figure 15.5**). But when these participants consider the risky gain—trying to save all 600 lives at the risk of saving no one—the activity in the intraparietal sulcus is intense (top right of Figure 15.5). Most of us make the easy choice, the one less fraught with uncertainty and agitation.

   But look what happens when thinking about losses. As the bottom of Figure 15.5 indicates, there is considerable activation along the intraparietal sulcus when thinking about the smaller, certain loss or the larger, uncertain loss. Here the decision is more difficult and more stressful. We don't want to accept 400 deaths, but we also don't want to risk having 600 people die. For most people, the decision is resolved, and made easier, by seizing on the fact that a chance that no one will die feels better than the certainty that most of them will die.

   What we see in the brain activation patterns is the neural foundation of both loss aversion (greater activity when considering losses rather than gains) and framing (outcomes described as gains yield a very different pattern of activation than identical outcomes described as losses).

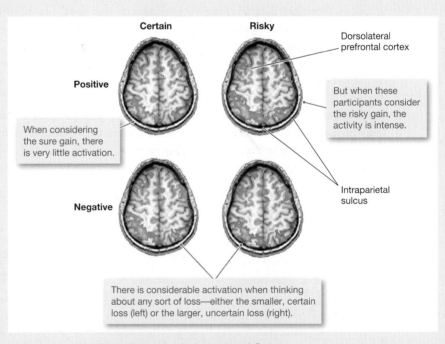

FIGURE 15.5 Activity along the Intraparietal Sulcus

Certain   Risky

Dorsolateral prefrontal cortex

Positive

When considering the sure gain, there is very little activation.

But when these participants consider the risky gain, the activity is intense.

Negative

Intraparietal sulcus

There is considerable activation when thinking about any sort of loss—either the smaller, certain loss (left) or the larger, uncertain loss (right).

diminishing marginal utility works for losses as well, people tend to be **risk seeking** when it comes to choosing between a sure loss of $100 and a risky chance to lose nothing or lose $200. A loss of $100 is more than half as painful as a loss of $200, so why not gamble to (possibly) avoid a loss altogether?

risk seeking The opposite of risk aversion; the tendency to forgo a certain outcome in favor of a risky option with an equal or more negative average payoff.

Loss Aversion and the Sunk Cost Fallacy Imagine that you paid $800 six months in advance for airfare and lodging for a beach vacation with some of your friends over spring break. Over those six months, however, you've had a falling out with two of your "friends" and you find it unpleasant to be around them. As the time to leave draws near, you're also not feeling well and you are at risk of falling catastrophically behind in your course work. Would you still go on the trip, or would you stay home, get well, and take care of your course work?

Now imagine that everything is the same except that you won the airfare and lodging in a raffle. Would you still go on the trip?

Most people say that they would be much more likely to take the trip if they had paid for it than if they had won it in a raffle. This is the **sunk cost fallacy**, a reluctance to "waste" money that leads people to look backward rather than forward when making decisions. In this case, whether or not the vacation was free or was paid for makes no difference in whether it will be rewarding to go. If you paid for the vacation, you're not getting the money back whether you go or not. The key question, in both cases, is whether your overall welfare, or utility, will be advanced more by staying home or going. Rationally, historical costs should not factor into a decision. They're already paid. Only the future costs and benefits of different options should be weighed when deciding between them.

sunk cost fallacy A reluctance to "waste" money that leads people to continue with an endeavor, whether it serves their future interests or not, because they've already invested money, effort, or time in it.

As this example illustrates, however, we are not always entirely rational. Most people pay a great deal of attention to historical costs. The sunk cost fallacy is very alluring. Consider a study in which people interested in a season-ticket subscription to the Ohio University Theater were randomly assigned to one of three groups. One group paid the regular ticket price ($15); another group was given a $2 discount on each ticket; and a third group received a $7 discount on each ticket. The investigators kept track of how often people in each of these three groups actually attended the theater after paying for all of their tickets up front. What they found was that those who paid the most (regular ticket price) attended more often than those who paid a bit less ($2 discount), who in turn attended more often than those who paid even less ($7 discount) (Arkes & Blumer, 1985). The more people paid for their tickets, the greater their sunk costs, and the more importance they attached to seeing the plays.

To really drive home how irrational and yet how human the sunk cost fallacy is, the same investigators presented people with the following hypothetical scenario:

On your way home you buy a TV dinner on sale for $3 at the local grocery store. A few hours later you decide it is time for dinner, so you get ready to put the TV dinner in the oven. Then you get an idea. You call up your friend to ask if he would like to come over for a quick TV dinner and then watch a good movie on TV. Your friend says sure. You go out to buy a second TV dinner. However, all the on-sale TV dinners are gone. You therefore have to spend $5 (the regular price) for the TV dinner identical to the one you just bought for $3. You go home and put both dinners in the oven. When the two dinners are fully cooked, you get a phone call. Your friend is ill and cannot come. You are not hungry enough to eat both dinners. You cannot freeze one. You must eat one and discard, the other. Which one do you eat?

Not surprisingly, most participants expressed no preference. After all, everything is the same regardless of which one you eat—you'll have paid $8 and eaten one TV dinner. But a very substantial minority said they would eat the $5 dinner. Almost no one said they would eat the $3 dinner. Because we honor sunk costs, throwing out the $5 dinner seems more wasteful than throwing out (the same) $3 dinner—even when, rationally, it is not.

Now that you have read about the sunk cost error, will you be less likely to make it? Yes. Richard Larrick and his colleagues taught University of Michigan students about the sunk cost fallacy using materials pretty much like what you just read (Larrick, Morgan, & Nisbett, 1990). Two weeks later, they presented participants with dilemmas that would show whether they would make the sunk cost mistake. The dilemmas were quite different in form from those they had read about in their training material. Nevertheless, those who had had the training were substantially less likely to make the error in responding to the dilemmas than those who had not read the materials.

Mental Accounting

We asked you earlier to imagine taking a trip during spring break. Imagine that it was to the Bahamas, where there is casino gambling. You've allotted yourself $100 to gamble and you sit down to play blackjack. How careful would you be with your bets?

Now suppose that luck is with you and soon you're ahead $100. You take your original $100 stake and put it in your pocket and you are now going to limit yourself to playing with just the $100 you've won. How careful would you now be with your bets?

Many people report that they would be more conservative initially when they were betting with their own money, but that they would bet more boldly with the "house money." This highlights another principle in behavioral economics known as **mental accounting**, or the tendency to treat money differently depending on how it was acquired and to what mental category it is attached. Note that the $100 a person earns at the casino is truly "their" money and should be treated every bit as seriously as the rest of their money. But when they think of it as "house money," it becomes much easier to treat frivolously. Easy come, easy go. (By the way, the casino never treats the money it receives from you as "patron's money"; it's theirs the second you lose it.)

The influence of mental accounting can also be seen in a thought experiment adapted from one of the founders of behavioral economics, economist Richard Thaler (1980): Imagine that you've bought a $200 ticket to see a play, a sporting event, or a rock concert. As you approach the entrance, you realize that you've lost your ticket. You can, however, fork over another $200 and get another ticket. Would you do so?

Many people report that they would not, on the grounds that $400 is too much to see a play, a sporting event, or a concert. But now imagine a slightly different scenario. You have reserved a ticket and will pay the $200 when you arrive. As you approach the entrance, however, you notice that you've lost $200 somewhere in the parking lot. You still have enough money to buy your ticket to the event. Would you do so?

In this case, most people say, "Of course. I want to see the event, it's worth $200 to me, and I have the money." Thus, we see different responses to the slightly different scenarios. But note that they don't differ in any meaningful way. In both cases, the decision you face is the same: you're $200 poorer than you were a moment ago, and you have to decide whether it's worth it to pay $200 to attend—and you have the money to do so. Rationally, then, people should make the same choice in the two circumstances. But that's not what most people do. In one version, the lost $200 is mentally "charged" to the cost of the event, making it seem too steep at $400. In the other case, the lost $200 is mentally charged to some other "accident" or "general expenses" account, keeping the psychological cost of the ticket the same as it was originally—$200.

It can be shown that if we want to make the best use of our money, we should integrate all of our assets and liabilities into one overall account. (We won't trouble

mental accounting The tendency to treat money differently depending on how it was acquired and to what mental category it is attached.

you with how it can be shown; for that you can take a microeconomics course.) But we nevertheless set up different mental accounts all the time, with rather peculiar—and important—implications for how we spend and invest the money we receive. For example, an economist at the Bank of Israel examined the economic behavior of a group of Israelis who were receiving regular payments from the German government as restitution for war crimes during World War II (Landsberger, 1966). Some of them received relatively large payments; others received relatively modest payments (depending on their family's earlier situation in Nazi Germany). What he found was a striking example of mental accounting. Those who received the biggest sums treated the money very seriously, spending relatively little and saving a lot. On average, they spent 23 cents of every dollar they received. Those who received smaller sums treated the money less seriously, spending a lot and saving little. In fact, these individuals spent $2 for every dollar they received in restitution money! Because the sums weren't large, these individuals "put" the money into some sort of "slush fund" or "everyday expense" account and spent it as quickly as spending opportunities arose. Those who received the larger payments "put" the money into a more serious "asset " or "savings" account, making them reluctant to use it for more frivolous purposes.

This mistake comes in many guises. A friend of one of the authors was constantly getting parking tickets. She justified this expense by saying that she didn't eat out at lunchtime, so she had a little nest egg to spend to avoid the trouble of rushing out to the parking meter in the middle of work.

Consider the implications of this sort of mental accounting for national economic policy. On a couple of occasions in the last decade, the federal government has tried to stimulate the economy by giving people tax rebates. In 2001, the government gave out $38 billion dollars to taxpayers in the form of rebates of $300 to $600; in 2008, the government gave out rebates of $600 to $1,200. The rationale behind the rebate programs is that people will spend more if they have more money to spend. Although the rationale has to be true at some level, it seems that it is not as true as government officials hope. Neither the 2001 or 2008 rebate program was as successful as policy makers expected, and the culprit seems to have been mental accounting. By describing the money given out to taxpayers as "rebates," recipients were encouraged to think of it as their own money being returned to them. They thus treated it very seriously and put quite a bit of it in the bank. Given what we know of mental accounting, the government would have been better off labeling the payments "tax bonuses."

Such a simple change in wording has been shown to influence spending rather dramatically. In one study conducted at Harvard University, participants who showed up for an experiment were given, unexpectedly, a $50 check. They were told that it was from the investigator's research budget, which was financed by tuition dollars. This allowed the investigators to describe the money to some participants as a "rebate." Others were told it was a "bonus." When the participants were contacted a week later and asked what they had done with the money, those who received a rebate reported spending less than half as much of it ($9.55) as those who received a bonus ($22.04). The same effect was observed in a follow-up experiment in which participants could purchase items from a "Harvard lab store" on their way out. As you can see in **Figure 15.6**, those who received their money as a rebate spent substantially less of it than those who received their money as a bonus (Epley, Mak, & Idson, 2006).

Thus, the terminology we use to describe our money leads us to assign it to more serious or less serious mental accounts, with pronounced effects on whether we spend it. As one of the authors of these studies put it, "Getting a rebate is more like being reimbursed for travel expenses than like getting a year-end bonus. Reimbursements send people on trips to the bank. Bonuses send people on trips to the Bahamas" (Epley, 2008).

"The only way not to think about money is to have a great deal of it."

— Edith Wharton

Hypothesis: People think of their money as belonging to different "mental accounts," and spend it differently if it is given to them as a "bonus" versus a "rebate."

Research Method:

1 Participants who showed up for an experiment were given, unexpectedly, a $50 check.

2 They were either told that the money was a "rebate" or a "bonus."

3 Participants were then told they could purchase items from a "Harvard lab store" on their way out.

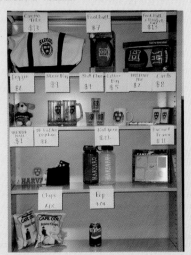

Results: Those who received their money as a rebate spent substantially less than those who received their money as a bonus.

Conclusion: Mental accounting matters. People treat bonus money less seriously than rebate money.

Source: Epley, Mak, & Idson (2006).

Decision Paralysis

Suppose you go to the grocery store to buy a pint of gourmet ice cream. Would you rather shop at a store that offers 45 flavors from five different vendors or a store with 18 flavors from two different vendors? It's a no-brainer, right? It's better to have more options so you can maximize your chances of getting *exactly* what you want. To economists, certainly, it is always better to have more options.

But psychologically, it's another story. Making decisions is hard, and we aren't equipped to deal with an abundance of choices all the time. With so many options from which to choose, we can find ourselves suffering from decision paralysis, unable to decide which option we should select. Consider a study conducted in an upscale grocery store in Menlo Park, California. Catering to the local elite, the store offers its customers over 300 types of jams, 250 different mustards, and 75 varieties of olive oil. The store permitted two social psychologists, Sheena Iyengar and Mark Lepper, the opportunity to set up a tasting booth where they set out a selection of jams. They rotated the selection every hour, so that half the time there were 6 jams on display and half the time there were 24 on display. Shoppers who stopped by the booth were given

The Effect of a Large or Small Choice Set   To examine the effect of the number of choices available on whether customers would end up making a purchase, Iyengar and Lepper (2000) put out on display tables samples of 6 (A) or 24 (B) different jams. The bar-code labels attached to each jam allowed them to assess whether customers were more likely to buy if they had examined a set of 6 jams or a set of 24 jams.

a coupon for $1 off any jam purchased in the store. Iyengar and Lepper were interested in whether shoppers would be stymied by the 24 jams on display, unable to decide what to buy and hence less likely to make a purchase. The coupons shoppers were given had a bar code that allowed the investigators to keep track of whether anyone who ended up purchasing a jar of jam had visited the booth when it had 6 or 24 items on display. What they found was that although many more people visited the booth when it displayed the large assortment of jams, ten times as many customers actually bought a jar when they examined the smaller assortment (Iyengar & Lepper, 2000). Having a large assortment looks good and draws a lot of customers. But it makes deciding hard—so hard, in fact, that many people never decide at all.

But failing to make a decision, of course, is still a decision—often a costly one. To see how costly, consider the decision faced by new employees who must choose whether and how to participate in their company's retirement plan. In today's world, most of these decisions involve the question of which 401K plan is best. In these plans, part of the employee's salary is invested in a stock, bond, or money market fund, often with the employer matching, dollar-for-dollar, what the employee contributes up to a certain amount (say, 5 percent of the employee's salary). For example, if you make $50,000 you might have $5,000 taken out of your paychecks over the year and invested in one of your company's 401K funds, with your employer kicking in an additional $2,500. Because of the employer match, it doesn't make economic sense not to participate. Failing to participate leaves "money on the table."

But nowadays, employees have a bewildering array of different funds in which to invest. Picking a fund, or the right mix of funds, can be daunting. Many people become overwhelmed, telling themselves, "I'll decide later." But many never do, depriving themselves of the "free money" that comes with the employer's match and severely hurting their long-term financial profile. The scope of the problem can be seen in **Figure 15.7**, which depicts the percentage of employees in different firms who enroll in their company's 401K plans as a function of how many plans the company offers (Sethi-Iyengar, Huberman, & Jiang, 2004). As you can see, the more plans that are offered, the harder the choice becomes—so hard, in fact, that many people avoid making it, at considerable cost to their financial future. Sometimes having more options is not such a good thing.

To drive the point home, we leave you with one final example, one a bit more relevant to life on a college campus. Amos Tversky and Eldar Shafir (1992) offered students $5 to complete a lengthy questionnaire. Some were given five days to complete

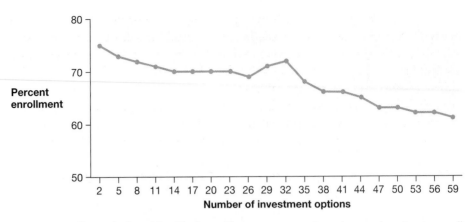

FIGURE 15.7 Overwhelmed by Choice The percentage of employees choosing to enroll in their company's 401K retirement savings plans as a function of the number of different investment funds from which the employee could choose. (Source: Adapted from Sethi-Iyengar, Huberman, & Jiang, 2004.)

it, others were given three weeks, and a third group wasn't given a deadline. Of those who were given only five days to complete the questionnaire, 60 percent turned it in on time versus 42 percent of those who were given three weeks. And only 25 percent of those who weren't given a deadline ever turned it in at all. Does this ring a bell? If so, you might consider asking your professors to give you tight deadlines for all assignments. It seems that the more time we have to complete a task, the less pressure we feel to get started, so we often fail to get started at all.

Getting Started on Your Own Financial Planning

Now that we have considered how various features of the human mind can lead us to make less than ideal decisions when we shop, save, and invest, what can we do about it? What should you keep in mind as you plan your own financial future? What can you do now to make it more likely that you will be financially secure later in life? We briefly describe five simple ideas—call them the Five Pillars—that will improve anyone's financial prospects, regardless of their current economic situation.

Start Early The key to having sufficient savings later in life is to start saving as soon as possible. The earlier you invest, the more the miracle of compound interest works in your favor. Belsky and Gilovich (1999) illustrate this idea with the following example:

> Meet Jill and John, 21-year-old twins who just graduated from college. Jill, immediately upon entering the workforce, began contributing $50 a month to a stock mutual fund and continued to do so for the next eight years, until she got married and found more pressing uses for her money. John, who married his college sweetheart immediately upon graduating and soon after started a family, didn't start investing until he was 29. Still, he, too, contributed $50 a month to the same stock fund, but he continued doing so for 37 years until he retired at age 65. All told, John invested $22,200, while Jill contributed just $4,800. At age 65, which of the two siblings had the most money, assuming they earned an average of 10 percent a year? (p. 121)

The amazing result is that Jill, who invested just $4,800, ends up with more money ($256,650) than her brother John ($217,830), even though he invested over four times as much. If you get a late start on saving, it's hard to catch up. Let the math (compound interest) work for you, not against you.

Diversify You have lived through two of the biggest boom-and-bust events in U.S. economic history—the stock market dive in 2001 and the collapse of the real estate market in 2008. Both episodes point to the difficulty of knowing when a particular class of investments is likely to do well or poorly, making you richer or poorer. But different assets—stocks, bonds, real estate, currency, even precious metals like gold—tend not to rise or fall in sync, and so owning something in each class is a good way to protect your savings. A diversified portfolio of investments is less likely to suffer a wrenching decline even during historic busts like those of 2001 and 2008.

Invest in Mutual Funds Of course, you probably don't have the financial resources to be able to buy a diverse group of stocks or an assortment of bonds, let alone property. But you don't have to. You can start by buying small pieces of each of these assets by purchasing shares in mutual funds. Mutual funds pool your money with that of other investors to buy stocks in a broad range of companies. Because the range of different companies can be quite broad, a mutual fund provides quite a bit of diversification on its own. You can also purchase mutual funds that invest in bonds or in combinations of different assets to further diversify your investments.

Different funds charge investors different fees for investing your money, and you should look for those with very low fees. Predicting market performance—which most mutual fund managers must do—is very difficult, and fund managers who do well one year often fail to do so the next. Therefore, paying the high fees that are often charged by "hot" funds with celebrity fund managers are typically not worth the extra expense. "Index" funds don't try to outfox the market; instead, they merely invest in a broad portfolio of stocks that mirror the market as a whole. Because they are not managed so actively, they typically have the lowest fees and hence represent particularly good investments.

Set Up a Payroll Deduction Plan Once you get a job and start receiving a regular paycheck, you should enroll in a payroll deduction plan that takes some of your wages and invests them, without your seeing the money first, into a savings account, or a stock, bond, or money market mutual fund. This is much better than trying to do the saving and investing yourself. If you get your paycheck and then try to put some of it away for savings, the amount you save will feel like a loss of income. If it's automatically invested before you see your paycheck, the investment feels instead like a foregone gain. And as we discussed earlier, foregone gains are easier to deal with than outright losses. If your employer is willing to match your payroll deductions with an additional payment by the company, you should take the maximum allowable deduction. To do otherwise is to leave money on the table.

Pay Off Credit Card Debt Many people have money in a savings account but don't use it to pay off the balance on their credit cards. It might sound reasonable ("I need some money stashed away for emergencies"), but it's not. People earn very low interest on their savings (typically less than 2 percent as we write this) but pay very hefty interest on their unpaid credit card balance (usually over 16 percent). The difference between the two rates is money going out the door—from you to the credit card companies. If you don't pay off your credit cards, you're fighting the power of compound interest when you want it working for you. By all means you should be saving money, but not at the expense of having to absorb the punishing interest charges on an unpaid credit card balance. If this makes you nervous, note that those same credit card companies that want you to keep a balance on your card will be perfectly happy to lend you money should an emergency arise. And once you pay off your credit card, *then* you can start to put away money for emergencies.

We have seen that people do not always make financial decisions in the fully rational manner specified by traditional economic theory. Instead, people's judgments and decisions about money are subject, as in other domains, to predictable errors and biases. People's choices are powerfully influenced by how different alternatives are framed, and their sensitivity to losses makes them more willing to take risks when outcomes are framed as potential losses rather than potential gains. People are also vulnerable to the sunk cost fallacy and to the effects of mental accounting—treating money differently depending on how it was acquired or how it is construed. A consideration of these different biases leads to some straightforward lessons about everyday financial decision making: start the habit of saving early, diversify investments (as through mutual funds), enroll in payroll deduction savings plans, and don't carry a balance on credit cards.

WISE: SOCIAL PSYCHOLOGY AND EDUCATION

Overheard in Palo Alto: One European American high school senior to another, upon hearing of her super-high SAT scores. "Good grief, Jessica, those scores are positively Asian."

Asian-American students undeniably have very impressive achievements in the academic realm. And Asian students regularly outperform American students in math and science. Why do you suppose this is? What would you do to get European-American and African-American students to perform at Asian levels? Or do you think that such a thing is highly unlikely or impossible?

Social psychologists have begun to see if their findings can improve educational outcomes, especially for minority students, who often perform at less than their capacity for reasons having to do with some of the factors discussed in this book. Social psychology has long provided excellent tools for improving critical thinking—and these can be sharpened by educational interventions that are remarkably brief but effective.

Intelligence: Thing or Process?

Beliefs about personal control affect more than health and well-being. They also affect educational outcomes. Carol Dweck and her colleagues (Dweck & Leggett, 1988) have shown that different people have very different views about the nature of intelligence. Some people believe that intelligence is a malleable quality that can be improved with effort. Dweck and her colleagues call this an *incrementalist* **theory of intelligence**. Other people think that intelligence is a fixed, predetermined "thing" that people have to one degree or another and that there is not much they can do to change it. Dweck and colleagues call this an *entity* **theory of intelligence**. As compared to entity theorists, incremental theorists work more toward goals that will increase their ability and spend less effort trying to document their ability. Incremental theorists believe that they can increase their ability, and they attribute failure to lack of effort (Henderson & Dweck, 1990). Entity theorists are less confident that what they do will make them any smarter and are inclined to feel that there is little they can do about failure because they just don't have what it takes.

Henderson and Dweck (1990) found that students entering junior high school who were incrementalists ended up getting better grades than students who were entity theorists. Moreover, this was true regardless of prior academic achievement: whether the students had a history of good or poor grades in elementary school, they got better

incrementalist theory of intelligence The belief that intelligence is something you get by dint of working.

entity theory of intelligence The belief that intelligence is something you're born with and can't change.

grades in junior high if they believed that their ability was under their control. In another study, Henderson and Dweck found that students who were about equal in their math performance at the beginning of junior high progressively increased their math grades over the course of two years in high school if they were incrementalists but tended not to improve their grades if they were entity theorists (Blackwell, Trzesniewski, & Dweck, 2007).

People who believe that intelligence isn't malleable tend to blame their intellectual ability when they fail, whereas people who think that intelligence is malleable are more likely to blame a failure to work hard enough or to think that the task at hand was just extremely difficult. It should be clear which attitude is more likely to result in an increase in intellectual skills, not to mention self-esteem.

People who believe that intelligence isn't malleable tend to choose tasks that give them opportunities to gain positive views of their intellectual ability and avoid getting negative views—but which provide no opportunity to learn something new. People who believe that intelligence is malleable tend to choose tasks that provide an opportunity to increase their ability, even at the risk of exposing their ignorance and subjecting themselves to negative judgments about their intellectual competence.

But who is right—the entity theorist or the incrementalist? Neither. Or rather, both. If you hold to the entity theory, you're not likely to increase as much in intellectual skills. So you're right: you don't believe that your ability is under your control, so in fact it doesn't increase as much, and your genes exert a greater influence on your ability than they would if you believed otherwise. On the other hand, if you're an incrementalist, you're also right: you believe that your ability is under your control and you act accordingly, thereby building on your genetic strengths and increasing your ability (Nisbett, 2009).

Culture and Achievement

Many people harbor the suspicion that Asians—especially Chinese, Japanese, and Koreans and their Asian-American counterparts—are intrinsically smarter than people of European culture. Something about their genes leads to intellectual superiority.

In fact, however, there is no good evidence that people of Asian heritage have a genetic advantage over Americans of Western origin. And cross-cultural comparisons of Asians with Westerners find no evidence that Asians have higher IQs, though admittedly it can be difficult to compare IQs across different cultures and languages (Flynn, 1991; Nisbett, 2009). A comparison of the IQs of children about to begin first grade in Minneapolis, in Sendai (in Japan), and in Taipei (in Taiwan) found that the American children had higher IQs than either group of Asian children (Stevenson et al., 1990). From what we know about the socialization practices of Asians and Americans, this should not be surprising: Asians focus on social and emotional growth during the early years, and Americans are more likely to focus on teaching intellectual skills (Stevenson et al., 1990). By fifth grade, the IQ differences were gone, but the Asian children were light-years ahead of the Americans in math—partly a result of better teaching of math and longer school years in the Asian countries (Stevenson & Stigler, 1992), but also a result of the Asian children working harder at math (Stevenson & Lee, 1996). In fact, Japanese students study many more hours a week than Americans.

The best evidence we have on the IQ differences between Asian-Americans and European-Americans comes from a massive study of the high school seniors of the class of 1966. Almost all of these students were Americans, though some were first-generation Americans. The IQs of the Asian-Americans were trivially lower than those of the European-Americans, not surprising given that many of them came

BOX 15.4 **FOCUS ON CULTURE**

Confucius and Theories about Ability

"If there is no dark and dogged will, there will be no shining accomplishment; if there is no dull and determined effort, there will be no brilliant achievement."

—Chinese saying

That Asian-Americans whose forebears came from the "Confucian cultures" of China, Japan, and Korea would achieve at levels higher than would be predicted given their ability scores could be expected based on ancient theories about talent. Confucius—the founding father of modern East Asian cultures—was quite clear that although some of our ability is, as he said, a gift from heaven, most of it is due to hard work. For 2,000 years, it was possible for a young person

Confucius

to go from being a poor peasant to being the highest magistrate in China by dint of study and hard work. In no other country until modern times has that been true. As we would expect, East Asians and Americans who spring from that region are devout incrementalists: they believe, much more than European-Americans, that intellectual achievement is mostly a matter of hard work (Chen & Stevenson, 1995; Choi, Nisbett, & Norenzayan, 1999; Heine et al., 2001; Holloway, 1988; Stevenson et al., 1990). When Japanese and Canadians were told that they had either succeeded or failed on a task that presumably measured creativity, the Canadians worked longer on a similar task if they had succeeded on the first one and the Japanese worked longer if they had failed (Heine et al., 2001). If at first you don't succeed. . . .

from homes where English was not the native language. However, their SAT scores were substantially higher. SAT scores, of course, are partly a reflection of the kinds of skills measured by IQ tests (themselves reflecting both genetic and environmental factors) and motivational factors that result in a capacity for hard work. Even more striking, when those students were adults, fully 55 percent of the Chinese-Americans, the largest group of the Asian-Americans, ended up in professional, technical, or managerial positions. Only a third of European-Americans ended up in those jobs. The Asian-Americans capitalized on their ability to a far greater extent than did the European-Americans.

(In case you're wondering, African-Americans and Hispanics have lower IQs and lower academic achievement than either Asian-Americans or European-Americans. There are numerous social reasons for these differences, many of which we cover in this book. Most of these factors are in flux, however, and in recent years the IQ and achievement gaps have begun to lessen substantially; Nisbett, 2009.)

Blocking Stereotype Threat in the Classroom

Claude Steele and Joshua Aronson demonstrated that women and minorities often perform more poorly on ability tests because they are afraid of confirming stereotypes about the abilities of their group (see Chapter 12). With Catherine Good and Michael Inzlicht, Aronson decided to see what would happen if poor minority students could be convinced that their abilities were under their control. They performed an intervention with poor Hispanic students in Texas (Good, Aronson, & Inzlicht, 2003). All students in the study were assigned college student mentors. Control group mentors gave the students cautionary information about drugs and encouraged their students to avoid taking them. Experimental group mentors told their charges that intelligence was changeable and under their control to a substantial extent and taught them how the brain can make new connections throughout life. Students were shown a Web page that reinforced the mentor's message. For students in the experimental group, this Web site showed animated pictures of the brain, including pictures of neurons and dendrites, along with explanations of how the brain forms new connections when novel problems are being solved. The mentors also helped the students design their own Web page, using their own words and pictures, that reinforced the message of the malleability of intelligence.

The experimental intervention had a very big effect. On a statewide academic achievement test, the boys exposed to the intervention scored much higher in math than those not exposed to the intervention. For the girls, who tend to have worries about whether their gender makes them less talented in math, the difference was even greater. For reading skills, both boys and girls exposed to the intervention did substantially better than students in the control group.

Dweck and her colleagues (Blackwell et al., 2007) performed a similar intervention with poor African-American and Latino seventh-grade students in New York City. Like the Texas students, the New York students in the experimental group were given convincing demonstrations of the changes in knowledge and intelligence that are produced by work and study. Junior high is a difficult time for many students, but seems to be particularly so for disadvantaged minority children. Control students in the study performed worse and worse in math as junior high went on. But the decline was arrested for students who received the intervention. They had held entity beliefs about intelligence and thought they were doomed to poor performance because they were incorrigibly unintelligent. Simply being made to believe that their intelligence was under their control had an impact on their academic performance.

Daphna Oyserman and her coworkers carried out a quite different intervention with poor African-American junior high students in Detroit (Oyserman, Bybee, & Terry, 2006). They asked the students to think about what kind of future they wanted to have, what difficulties they would likely have along the way, how they could deal with those difficulties, and which of their friends would be most helpful in dealing with the difficulties. Oyserman and colleagues supplemented these sessions by having students work in small groups on how to deal with everyday problems, with social difficulties, with academic problems, and with the process of getting to high school graduation. The intervention had a modest effect on grade point average and on standardized tests and a very big effect on the likelihood of being held back a grade in school.

A study by Geoffrey Cohen and his colleagues showed that simply having minority students write about their most important values at the beginning of middle school substantially improved their grades over the subsequent years (Cohen, Garcia, Apfel, & Master, 2006). The students were enrolled in a mostly middle-class integrated suburban school. As is frequently the case in such schools, the African-American students in the past had had significantly lower grades than the white students. The African-American students were well aware of this, and the social psychologists who did the study assumed that they were subject to the worries prompted by stereotype threat (see Chapter 12). The social psychologists reasoned that if the students were encouraged to think about their most important values, this experience of self-affirmation in the school context would produce a sense of efficacy and belongingness.

"Education is not filling a bucket but lighting a fire."

— William B. Yeats

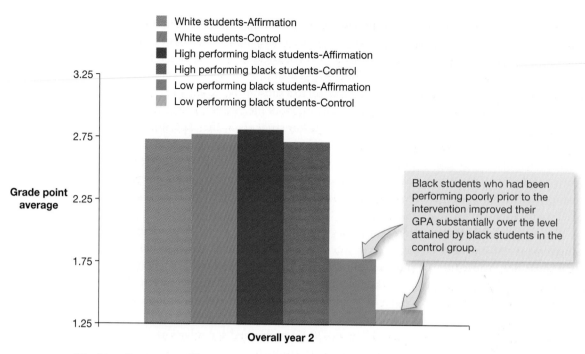

Legend:
- White students-Affirmation
- White students-Control
- High performing black students-Affirmation
- High performing black students-Control
- Low performing black students-Affirmation
- Low performing black students-Control

Grade point average (y-axis): 1.25, 1.75, 2.25, 2.75, 3.25

Overall year 2

Black students who had been performing poorly prior to the intervention improved their GPA substantially over the level attained by black students in the control group.

FIGURE 15.8 **Blocking Stereotype Threat** Mean GPA scores in core courses the year after some students experienced an affirmation intervention (by being asked to write out their most important values). Black students were split into low and high performing groups, reflecting their relative standing within their class. (Source: Cohen, Garcia, Purdie-Vaughns, Apfel, & Brzustoski, 2009.)

In fact, black students who were exposed to the affirmation intervention performed better over the term than black students in the control group (**Figure 15.8**). In the course in which the intervention took place, the students in the affirmation condition reduced the achievement gap with white students by 40 percent, and the likelihood of getting a D or worse was reduced by half. Cohen and colleagues (Cohen et al., 2009) followed the students over the next two years and found that the effects of the intervention were fully sustained. Interestingly, the intervention had no effect on black students who had performed well before entering middle school and were presumably sufficiently confident that the affirmation manipulation was unnecessary. Nor did the affirmation manipulation have any effect on white students, whether previously high performing or not.

Pygmalion in the Classroom

The idea that one person can transform another—even create an extraordinary person from ordinary raw material—has been a theme of literature going back to Greek mythology: a sculptor named Pygmalion made a statue so beautiful that he fell in love with it and with the help of the goddess Venus brought it to life. The most recent version of the myth is the musical *My Fair Lady*, about an eccentric English phonetics professor who coaches a flower girl in manners and accent, helping her pass for a lady in British high society.

In 1968, Robert Rosenthal and Lenore Jacobson (1968) published a study—which they called "Pygmalion in the Classroom"—that created an uproar in the fields of both psychology and education. All students in a particular school were given an IQ test. Allegedly on the basis of the test, Rosenthal and Jacobson told the teachers at the beginning of the school year that some of their students were "late bloomers"—that is, they were expected to show substantial IQ growth over the course of the school year. About 20 percent of the children in each classroom were designated—ostensibly on the basis of the test, but in fact by random assignment—as being such late bloomers. The investigators reported that there were substantial IQ gains over the course of the year for the designated late bloomers. The gains for young children were shockingly high—15 points for first graders and 10 points for second graders. This seemed to indicate that teachers' expectations for children operated as a powerful self-fulfilling prophecy: if the teacher believed that the child was going to gain in intelligence, the teacher behaved in such a way toward the child as to ensure that such gains would occur. Unnervingly, the children in the control group who showed achievement gains that the teacher did not expect of them were rated by the teacher as less interesting, less affectionate, and not as well adjusted. Education critics argued that the results showed that teacher bias, presumably in favor of white middle-class children, was a significant reason that these children performed better in school and scored higher IQs. Conversely, the scores of African-American, Hispanic, and lower-SES children were being pulled down because of teachers' negative expectations for them.

The furor over the Rosenthal and Jacobson experiment persists to this day, with claims ranging from outright accusations of fraud to allegations that the results were an underestimate of what goes on in the classroom all the time. Lee Jussim and Kent Harber (2005) reviewed the almost 400 (!) studies conducted in the first 35 years after the initial report. First, the extremely large effects found by Rosenthal and Jacobson proved to be exceptional; subsequent investigators almost never found the huge effects that they did. Second, it's clear (when expectations are manipulated) that sometimes teacher expectations affect children's IQ and academic performance. (If you don't manipulate, a correlation between the teacher's expectation and children's performance could be due to accuracy on the teacher's part. Children who are believed to be—and are—more talented do better in school.) Third, teacher expectation effects are rarely very strong: about 3 IQ points is as large as is generally obtained, and often the effects of teacher expectations are literally zero. Fourth, teacher expectation effects occur only if expectations are manipulated early in the school year—within the first two weeks. Fifth, teacher expectation effects are greater for first- and second-grade children than for other children. Sixth, and most important, teacher expectation effects can be genuinely large for low-achieving, lower-SES children and for African-American children (Jussim, Eccles, & Madon, 1996). So a modified version of the original claims appears to be correct: if teachers believe that their lower-achieving, lower-SES students and their African-American students can do well intellectually, this can enhance their performance.

Social Fears and Academic Achievement

Cohen, together with Gregory Walton, found a way to improve academic performance for minority students in college (Walton & Cohen, 2007). Most beginning students worry about social acceptance and fitting in on campus, but for minority students this can be particularly worrisome. If they fail to make friends, because there are typically not that many minority students on campus and because they may feel ill at ease with majority students, they may begin to wonder if they belong on campus. It's common for minority students' motivation to flag and for their GPAs to suffer as they go through school.

Walton and Cohen reasoned that lagging performance could be nipped in the bud if minority students knew that worries about social acceptance are common for all students, regardless of ethnicity, and that things would likely improve in the future (Walton & Cohen, 2007). The researchers performed a modest intervention with black students at a prestigious private university. They invited black and white freshmen to participate in a psychology study at the end of their freshman year. The intent of the experimenters was to convince an intervention group that worries about social acceptance were common for students of all ethnicities but tended to vanish as time went on and they made more friends. The experimenters expected that this would help black students realize that the best way to understand their social difficulties was not in terms of their race ("I guess my kind of people don't really belong at this kind of place") but as part of the student experience that is common to everyone ("I guess everybody has these kinds of problems"). The researchers believed that recognition of their common problem—and its likely solution—would help to keep the students from worrying about belonging and help them focus on academic achievement.

To drive the point home, Walton and Cohen had students in the intervention group write an essay about the likelihood of improvement in their social situation in the future and deliver a speech in front of a video camera, which they were told would be shown to new students at the school "so that they know what college will be like." This standard dissonance manipulation for the students—getting them to say publicly something that was actually somewhat different from their own views—was intended to enhance the persuasive communications they had received.

Walton and Cohen measured behavior related to academic achievement over the next week, as well as students' GPAs the subsequent semester. The intervention had a big positive effect on blacks but not on whites. In the period after the intervention, blacks reported studying more, making more contacts with professors, and attending more review sessions and study group meetings. The subsequent term, grades of the blacks in the intervention group reflected these behaviors: their grades were much higher than those of blacks in the control group.

Teaching with Telenovelas

Which reality television show involving young people traveling around the countryside features such contests as how to repulse the advances of someone of the opposite sex? And in which states does the show air? We're guessing you couldn't come up with answers. It's *Haath Se Haath Milaa* (*Hand in Hand Together*), and it airs in the states of Rajasthan, Haryana, Delhi, Uttar Pradesh, and Uttaranchal (India). It's designed to alert young people to the risks of HIV/AIDS, which exists in epidemic proportions in India. The young people, by the way, travel in separate his-and-hers buses. The program is part of a worldwide network of TV shows collectively called "**entertainment-education.**"

entertainment-education Media presentations that are meant to both entertain and persuade people to act in their own (or in society's) best interests.

Albert Bandura is a learning theorist—a scientist who studies how animals and humans learn connections between events and learn which events signal impending rewards, and which signal impending punishments. He was one of the first such scientists to approach the question of how people learn appropriate and effective social behavior (for example, Bandura, 1973). A fundamental principle of his theory is that people learn what to approach and what to avoid simply by watching relevant others. They observe other people's behavior and its consequences and adopt those behaviors that seem to be successful and avoid those that are punished. The people who are considered relevant to the individual are *role models* for that individual.

A Mexican television producer named Miguel Sabido read about Bandura's principles of social learning and decided to create television programs that would educate people about effective and rewarding social behaviors and persuade them to avoid dangerous and unproductive behavior. He produced the original entertainment-education telenovelas in the 1970s and 1980s.

These telenovelas (what we would be inclined to call soap operas) present three types of characters: positive role models, negative role models, and "doubters," those who fall in between (Singhal, Rogers, & Brown, 1993). There are typically four positive role models complemented by four negative role models. There is always a character who approves of the value being promoted (and one who disapproves), one who promotes the value (and one who doesn't), one who exercises the value (and one who doesn't), and one who validates the value (and one who doesn't). There are also three doubters. One of the doubters accepts the value about a third of the way through the series, one about two-thirds of the way through, and one never accepts the value. This latter person usually dies some painful death! In general, those who accept the value are immediately rewarded, and those who don't are punished. Additionally, epilogues are inserted throughout the series, where some famous individual speaks to the audience in order to reinforce the value. Sabido wrote year-long stories that centered around the value. The television programs clearly have an effect on behavior, although much of the early evidence has to be catego-

Teaching with Telenovelas
Actors running through a scene on the set of the Mexican telenovela, *Heridas de Amor* (*Words of Love*).

rized as anecdotal. The anecdotes and the statistics we cite come from Bandura's own account of the success of the programs (Bandura, 2004). One early telenovela by Sabido urged viewers to enroll in a literacy program. The day after it appeared, about 25,000 people descended on the distribution center in downtown Mexico City to obtain their reading materials. The result was a monumental traffic jam in the city. The name of the series was *Ven Comigo* (*Come with Me*), and in the year it aired, enrollment in literacy classes went up tenfold—from about 90,000 to about 900,000. Another drama, *Acompaname* (*Accompany Me*), emphasized family planning. Those who viewed the program were more inclined to think that having fewer children was likely to have social, economic, and psychological benefits. There was a 32 percent increase in new contraceptive users, and national sales of contraceptives went up markedly.

Sabido's telenovelas have been widely imitated. An Indian drama inspired by Sabido's work promoted female rights and family planning. Amazingly, enrollment of girls in elementary schools rose from 10 percent to 38 percent during the year the show was broadcast. A family planning telenovela in Kenya (Westoff & Rodriguez, 1995) found that contraception practices changed for people across the spectrum of social classes. A program designed to combat the spread of HIV in Tanzania (Vaughn, Rogers, Singhal, & Swalehe, 2000) spanned four years. For the first two years, the radio soap opera was not broadcast in a particular region in Tanzania in order to provide a comparison group. The soap opera was found to reduce the number of sexual partners and increase condom use in the parts of Tanzania where the program was shown. The mediating factors that seemed to be crucial in producing behavior change were increased self-efficacy, increased communication about HIV, and increased risk awareness. Interviews with viewers of the program made it clear that they identified with the characters in the soap opera and tried to emulate them, consistent with social learning theory expectations.

Statistics, Social Science Methodology, and Critical Thinking

Consider the following problems.

1. David is a high school senior choosing between two colleges. He has friends at both. His friends at college A like it a lot on social and academic grounds. His friends at college B are not so satisfied, being generally unenthusiastic about the college. He visits both of the colleges for a day and meets some students at college A who are not very interesting and a professor who gives him a curt brushoff. He meets several students at college B who are lively and intelligent, and a couple of professors take a personal interest in him. Which college do you think he should go to? Why?
2. Medical research has established that drinking a moderate amount of alcohol is associated with reduced likelihood of getting cancer or heart disease. Assume you are a teetotaler on economic and moral grounds. Should you start modest tippling?

If you answered for question 1 that David should go to college B because he has to choose for himself (not let his friends choose for him), you are in good company with most undergraduates. We hope, however, that you considered the possibility that although David's samples of the two colleges were based on his own personal experience, the samples were not very large, and the experiences he could expect to have at the two colleges might be very different from his one-day sample. His friends, while they are not David, to be sure, at least have the advantage of having very much larger samples of the two schools. This ought to give David, and you, pause. Moreover, people may have put more energy into ensuring that David got a biased sample of events at college B than at college A. This might be the case, for example, if a friend at college B was particularly eager to get David to go there and arranged things so that he would be favorably impressed.

If you answered for question 2, as we suspect you did, that it might be best to keep your wallet in your pocket and your foot off the bar rail, then you recognized that correlation does not establish causation. Indeed, after decades of hearing from researchers that alcohol in moderation is a disease preventive, some scientists are now saying that the association between moderate drinking and health may be a self-selection effect. People who drink a lot may be damaging their health. People who don't drink at all may avoid it because of poor health or because their income discourages them from drinking (and you already know from this chapter that income is shockingly correlated with health).

Why is social psychology relevant to these statistical and methodological analyses of everyday life events? Because all these principles are taught in social psychology courses and exercised all the time in doing social psychological research. Taking statistics courses and science courses that emphasize research principles are a good start toward being able to be a good critic of research and a good analyst of everyday life situations for which such principles are relevant. But taking a course like this one has made you much more capable of recognizing flawed data in many scientific fields and more able to apply statistical and methodological principles in everyday life.

Darrin Lehman and Richard Nisbett studied the effects of four years in college for students majoring in the humanities, the natural sciences, the social sciences, and psychology. Students majoring in psychology and the social sciences showed a 65 percent improvement in their ability to reason using appropriate statistical and methodological principles like the ones just discussed. Students in the humanities and natural sciences improved by only about 25 percent. (Lest you think few advantages in reasoning come from the study of the humanities and the natural sciences, however, we point out that students in those fields improved by 65 percent in various kinds of logical reasoning, and students in psychology and the social sciences improved not at all.)

Two years of graduate-level training in psychology has a huge impact on people's ability to apply statistical and methodological principles to everyday life—but only if the area of psychology the student specializes in deals with ordinary human behavior (Lehman, Lempert, & Nisbett, 1988). This includes the fields of social psychology, developmental psychology, personality psychology, and developmental psychology. It does not include the fields of biopsychology, cognitive psychology, or cognitive

---

BOX 15.5 FOCUS ON DAILY LIFE

How to Tutor: The Five Cs

At Stanford University, where he teaches, social psychologist Mark Lepper studied college student tutors of elementary school students who were having trouble in math. He made an intriguing discovery. Some tutors had big—and fast—impacts on their pupils. Others had no effect. He then went to work to see what the difference was between the effective and the ineffective tutors. Which behaviors below do you think would be helpful, and which unhelpful?

1. When you start to see a student make even a minor mistake, stop her immediately so as to avoid stamping in the incorrect behavior.

2. If the student makes a mistake, carefully state the rule that the student needs to know to successfully solve the problem.

3. Keep the problems simple so as to avoid damaging self-esteem.

4. Praise the student often for doing work well.

5. Don't get emotionally involved with the student's difficulties, since this could create a dependent stance on the part of the student.

Actually, all of these approaches are unhelpful and are avoided by effective tutors. They violate one or another of the strategies that characterize the successful tutor. Lepper and his colleagues offer Five Cs for effective tutoring (Lepper & Woolverton, 2001; Lepper, Woolverton, Mumme, & Gurtner, 1993):

Foster a sense of *control* in the student, making the student feel that she has command of the material.

Challenge the student—but at a level of difficulty that is within the student's capability.

Instill *confidence* in the student by maximizing success (expressing confidence in the student, assuring the student that the problem she just solved was a difficult one) and by minimizing failure (providing excuses for mistakes and emphasizing the part of the problem the student got right).

Foster *curiosity* through Socratic methods (asking leading questions) and by linking the problem to other problems the student has seen that appear on the surface to be different.

Contextualize by placing the problem in a real-world context or in a context from a movie or TV show.

Expert tutors have a number of strategies that set them apart. They don't bother to correct minor errors like forgetting to put down a plus sign. They try to head the student off at the pass when she is about to make a mistake and attempt to prevent it from occurring. Or sometimes they let the student make the mistake when they think it can provide a valuable learning experience. They never dumb down the material for the sake of self-esteem, but instead change the way they present it. Most of what good tutors do is ask questions. They ask leading questions. They ask students to explain their reasoning. They are actually less likely to give *positive* feedback than are less effective tutors, because, Lepper theorizes, this makes the tutoring session feel too evaluative. And finally, expert tutors are always nurturing and empathic.

neuroscience, despite the fact that students in those fields get a lot of training in statistics and methodology. Students of chemistry and law gain absolutely nothing along those lines.

Is it necessary to major in the behavioral sciences to be able to use statistical and methodological principles for understanding everyday life events? No. Research by social psychologists shows that statistical and methodological principles, as well as economic concepts such as the cost-benefit principle, can be taught in very brief sessions (Fong, Krantz, & Nisbett, 1986; Larrick et al., 1990; Larrick, Nisbett, & Morgan, 1993; Nisbett, Fong, Lehman, & Cheng, 1987). In fact, we're confident that you have already had your economic behavior changed in at least one respect by reading this chapter. Richard Larrick and his colleagues taught participants about the sunk cost fallacy in a session lasting only a few minutes (Larrick et al., 1990). Several weeks later, they phoned the participants in the guise of pollsters conducting an "opinion survey." The survey presented various personal and institutional dilemmas that involved undertaking something undesirable that had already been paid for. The trained participants were much more likely to recognize that such behavior was actually uneconomical. When the underlying principles are presented in abstract form, people can be shown how to apply them to everyday life events. People can readily generalize from such sessions to a wide range of situations and scientific claims.

 We have seen that people who have incremental theories of ability elect to work on problems that challenge them because they believe they can grow even if they perform poorly. People who are entity theorists avoid situations where they might be forced to discover that they lack talent. Members of cultures (such as East Asian) that hold predominantly incrementalist views capitalize on their abilities more than do members of cultures that harbor beliefs that are more in line with entity theory. The intellectual performance of minority students and women can be improved by simple interventions that minimize stereotype threat and help them to believe that their own efforts can increase their intelligence. Education-entertainment such as telenovelas can have a big impact on people's behavior, successfully getting them to engage in safe behaviors that are likely to promote well-being. The social sciences teach thinking skills, relying on statistical, methodological, and economic principles that are crucial for understanding both scientific research that is presented in the media and important everyday life problems.

Summary

Healthy: Social Psychological Influences on Mental and Physical Health

- Evolution has provided us with the hypothalamic-pituitary-adrenal (HPA) axis, which produces the stress hormone cortisol. Constant release of cortisol results in chronic stress, which can be alleviated if you avoid rumination, or thinking about some stressful event over and over again.

- Lower-SES individuals have much worse health than higher-SES individuals, in part because they are subjected to more stress. But even subjectively lower status, such as being a subordinate executive, results in more stress-related illnesses.

- People with more meaningful connections to others are healthier. Having a sympathetic person with you when you are undergoing stress significantly reduces the physiological and psychological indicators of stress. Having a sense of control over your fate also reduces stress and yields health benefits.

Wealthy: Behavioral Economics and Personal Finance

- Behavioral economics is the result of efforts by psychologists and economists to create a microeconomic theory that takes into account people's occasional irrationality when making choices. Examples of irrationality can be found in the tendency of the stock market to go up on sunny days and down on cloudy days and to go up in countries whose national soccer team wins (and down when it loses).

- People respond very differently when making decisions about potential gains and potential losses. They are risk averse for possible gains and risk seeking for possible losses. Framing of choices as losses versus gains therefore makes for irrational—or at any rate, inconsistent—patterns of choice.

- People are susceptible to the sunk cost fallacy. They are inclined to consume something (for example, go to a play or a sporting event) even when it no longer has positive value to them in order to be "economical" and not "waste" the money already paid for the item.

- People keep separate mental accounts when they would be better off having a single account for all of their assets.

- Too many choices results in decision paralysis. The more things you have to choose from, the less likely you are to choose anything.

- Some simple rules about money will have a big impact on your wealth: save early and often, diversify, invest in mutual funds rather than specific stocks or bonds, bind yourself to the mast by setting up a payroll deduction plan, and for heaven's sake, avoid paying the huge interest on credit card balances.

Wise: Social Psychology and Education

- People who believe that intelligence is a thing (entity) are less likely to learn new things by taking on challenges and are likely to attribute small failures to lack of ability. People who believe that intelligence can be changed are incrementalists who take on challenges and attribute failure to task difficulty or failure to work hard. East Asians constitute one large group who tend to be incrementalists and who thereby gain the benefit of hard work and improved ability.

- When minority group members are persuaded that their ability is under their control, they perform at higher levels. The same is true when they are asked to think about their goals in life and how to achieve them. Social fears can hold minority group members back from immersing themselves in the academic enterprise.

- Entertainment-education, based on Albert Bandura's social learning theory, can have a big impact on the likelihood that people will avoid risky behavior and pursue beneficial goals.

- Statistics and social science methodology, including especially social psychology, increase people's critical thinking skills, making them more likely to spot the errors in reported scientific studies and more likely to avoid errors of judgment in their own lives.

Key Terms

behavioral economics (p. 583)
entertainment-education (p. 600)
entity theory of intelligence (p. 594)
incrementalist theory of intelligence (p. 594)

loss aversion (p. 584)
mental accounting (p. 588)
psychological stress (p. 571)
risk aversion (p. 585)
risk seeking (p. 587)

rumination (p. 572)
self-distancing (p. 573)
sunk cost fallacy (p. 587)

Further Reading

Belsky, G., & Gilovich, T. (2010). *Why smart people make big money mistakes*. New York: Simon & Schuster. An accessible guide to the field of behavioral economics and how findings in that hybrid of psychology and economics can help the average person make better financial decisions.

Hacking, I. (1975). *The emergence of probability: A philosophical study of early ideas about probability, induction and statistical inference*. New York: Cambridge University Press. This one's not for sissies. It's a difficult but absolutely fascinating history of the concept of probability from ancient times to the present. You'll be surprised to learn that our ancestors operated with only the most rudimentary of the probabilistic concepts that are part of everyone's mental toolkit today.

Sapolsky, R. M. (1994). *Why zebras don't get ulcers*. New York: Freeman. Sapolsky details the workings of stress-related physiology, explaining how chronic stress damages different branches of our nervous system. The book also includes several useful tips for managing stress.

Zweig, J. (2007). *Your money and your brain*. New York: Simon & Schuster. An entertaining review of what goes on in the brain when people make financial decisions and why so many financial decisions turn out badly.

(S) Online Study Tools

StudySpace

Go to StudySpace, wwnorton.com/studyspace, to access additional review and enrichment materials, including the following resources for each chapter:

Organize

- Study Plan
- Chapter Outline
- Quiz+ Assessment

Learn

- Ebook
- Chapter Review
- Critical-Thinking Questions
- Visual Quizzes
- Vocabulary Flashcards

Connect

- Apply It! Exercises
- Author Insights Podcasts
- Social Psychology in the News

Glossary

A

actor-observer difference A difference in attribution based on who is making the causal assessment: the actor (who is relatively disposed to make situational attributions) or the observer (who is relatively disposed to make dispositional attributions).

actual self The self we truly believe ourselves to be.

affective forecasting Predicting our future emotions—for example, whether an event will make us happy or angry or sad, and for how long.

agenda control Efforts of the media to select certain events and topics to emphasize, thereby shaping which issues and events we think are important.

altruism Unselfish behavior that benefits others without regard to consequences for the self.

anxious attachment style An attachment style characterized by feelings of insecurity in relationships. Individuals with this style compulsively seek closeness, express continual worries about relationships, and excessively try to get closer to others during times of threat and uncertainty.

applied science Science concerned with solving some real-world problem of importance.

appraisal processes The ways we evaluate events and objects in our environment according to their relation to our current goals.

approach/inhibition theory A theory that states that higher-power individuals are inclined to go after their goals and make quick judgments, whereas low-power individuals are more likely to constrain their behavior and attend to others carefully.

attachment theory A theory about how our early attachments with our parents shape our relationships for the remainder of our lives.

attitude An evaluation of an object in a positive or negative fashion that includes the three elements of affect, cognitions, and behavior.

attitude inoculation Small attacks on our beliefs that engage our attitudes, prior commitments, and knowledge structures, enabling us to counteract a subsequent larger attack and be resistant to persuasion.

attribution Linking a cause to an instance of behavior—our own or someone else's.

attribution theory An umbrella term used to describe the set of theoretical accounts of how people assign causes to the events around them and the effects that people's causal assessments have.

augmentation principle The idea that we should assign greater weight to a particular cause of behavior if there are other causes present that normally would produce the opposite outcome.

authority Power that derives from institutionalized roles or arrangements.

autokinetic illusion The apparent motion of a stationary point of light in a completely darkened environment.

automatic processes Processes that occur outside of our awareness, without conscious control.

autonomic nervous system (ANS) The glands, organs, muscles, and blood vessels throughout the body that are controlled by nerve cells originating in the spinal cord and that regulate the body's internal environment and help the individual deal with emergency situations.

availability heuristic The process whereby judgments of frequency or probability are based on the ease with which pertinent instances are brought to mind.

avoidant attachment style An attachment style characterized by feelings of insecurity in relationships. Individuals with this style exhibit compulsive self-reliance, prefer distance from others, and are dismissive and detached during times of threat and uncertainty.

B

balance theory The theory that people try to maintain balance among their beliefs, cognitions, and sentiments.

base-rate information Information about the relative frequency of events or of members of different categories in the population.

basic science Science concerned with trying to understand some phenomenon in its own right, with a view toward using that understanding to build valid theories about the nature of some aspect of the world.

basking in reflected glory The tendency to take pride in the accomplishments of those with whom we are in some way associated (even if it is only weakly), as when fans identify with a winning team.

behavioral economics A discipline that uses insights from psychology to create realistic and accurate models of economic behavior.

bottom-up processes "Data-driven" mental processing, in which one takes in and forms conclusions on the basis of the stimuli encountered in one's experience.

broaden-and-build hypothesis The hypothesis that positive emotions broaden thought and action repertoires, helping us build social resources.

bystander intervention Helping a victim of an emergency by those who have observed what is happening. Bystander intervention is generally reduced as the number of observers increases, as each individual feels that someone else will probably help.

C

causal attribution Linking an instance of behavior to a cause, whether the behavior is our own or someone else's.

central (systematic) route A persuasive route wherein people think carefully and deliberately about the content of a message, attending to its logic, cogency, and arguments, as well as to related evidence and principles.

channel factors Certain situational circumstances that appear unimportant on the surface but that can have great consequences for behavior, either facilitating or blocking it or guiding behavior in a particular direction.

cognitive dissonance theory The theory that inconsistencies between a person's thoughts, sentiments, and actions create an aversive emotional state (dissonance) that leads to efforts to restore consistency.

collective self-beliefs Our identity and beliefs as they relate to the social categories to which we belong.

communal relationships Relationships in which the individuals feel a special responsibility for one another and give and receive according to the principle of need; such relationships are often long-term.

complementarity The tendency for people to seek out others with characteristics that are different from and that complement their own.

compliance Responding favorably to an explicit request by another person.

confirmation bias The tendency to test a proposition by searching for evidence that would support it.

conformity Changing one's behavior or beliefs in response to explicit or implicit (whether real or imagined) pressure from others.

consensus Refers to what most people would do in a given situation—that is, whether most people would behave the same way or few or no other people would behave that way.

consistency Refers to what an individual does in a given situation on different occasions—that is, whether next time under the same circumstances, the person would behave the same or differently.

construal Interpretation and inference about the stimuli or situations we confront.

contingencies of self-worth An account of self-esteem maintaining that self-esteem is contingent on successes and failures in domains on which a person has based his or her self-worth.

control condition A condition comparable to the experimental condition in every way except that it lacks the one ingredient hypothesized to produce the expected effect on the dependent variable.

controlled processes Processes that occur with conscious direction and deliberate thought.

core-relational themes Distinct themes, such as danger or offense or fairness, that define the essential meaning for each emotion.

correlational research Research in which there is not random assignment to different situations, or conditions, and from which psychologists can just see whether or not there is a relationship between the variables.

counterbalancing A methodological procedure used to ensure that any extraneous variable (for example, a stimulus person's name) that might influence the dependent measure (for example, liking) is distributed equally across experimental conditions (so that, for example, specific names are used often equally in all conditions of the experiment).

counterfactual thoughts Thoughts of what might have, could have, or should have happened "if only" something had been done differently.

covariation principle The idea that we should attribute behavior to potential causes that co-occur with the behavior.

culture of honor A culture that is defined by its members' strong concerns about their own and others' reputations, leading to sensitivity to slights and insults and a willingness to use violence to avenge any perceived wrong or insult.

D

debriefing In preliminary versions of an experiment, asking participants straightforwardly if they had understood the instructions, found the setup to be reasonable, and so forth. In later versions, debriefings are used to educate participants about the questions being studied.

deception research Research in which the participants are misled about the purpose of the research or the meaning of something that is done to them.

deindividuation The reduced sense of individual identity accompanied by diminished self-regulation that comes over people when they are in a large group.

dependent variable In experimental research, the variable that is measured (as opposed to manipulated) and that is hypothesized to be affected by manipulation of the independent variable.

diffusion of responsibility A reduction of a sense of urgency to help someone involved in an emergency or dangerous situation under the assumption that others who are also observing the situation will help.

directed facial action task A task in which moving emotion-specific facial muscles triggers different autonomic responses.

discounting principle The idea that we should assign reduced weight to a particular cause of behavior if there are other plausible causes that might have produced it.

discrimination Unfair treatment of members of a particular group based on their membership in that group.

display rules Culturally specific rules that govern how and when and to whom we express emotion.

dispositions Internal factors, such as beliefs, values, personality traits, or abilities, that guide a person's behavior.

distinctiveness Refers to what an individual does in different situations—that is, whether the behavior is unique to a particular situation or occurs in all situations.

distinctiveness hypothesis The hypothesis that we identify what makes us unique in each particular context, and we highlight that in our self-definition.

distraction-conflict theory A theory based on the idea that being aware of another person's presence creates a conflict between attending to that person and attending to the task at hand, and that it is this attentional conflict that is arousing and that produces social facilitation effects.

diversification A principle that maintains that siblings develop into quite different people so that they can peacefully occupy different niches within the family environment.

dizygotic (fraternal) twins Twins who originate from two different eggs fertilized by different sperm cells; like ordinary siblings, they share on average half of their genes.

dominance Behavior that has the acquisition or demonstration of power as its goal.

dominant response In a hierarchy of responses, the response you are most likely to make.

door-in-the-face technique (reciprocal concessions technique) Asking someone for a very large favor that he or she will certainly refuse and then following that request with a more modest favor (which tends to be seen as a concession that the target will feel compelled to honor).

duration neglect The relative unimportance of the length of an emotional experience, be it pleasurable or unpleasant, in judging the overall experience.

E

effort justification The tendency to reduce dissonance by finding reasons for why we have devoted time, effort, or money to something that has turned out to be unpleasant or disappointing.

ego-defensive function An attitudinal function that enables us to maintain cherished beliefs about ourselves by protecting us from awareness of our negative attributes and impulses or from facts that contradict our cherished beliefs or desires.

ego depletion A state produced by acts of self-control, where we don't have the energy or resources to engage in further acts of self-control.

elaboration likelihood model (ELM) A model of persuasion that maintains that there are two different routes of persuasion: the central route and the peripheral route.

emergent properties of groups Those behaviors that only surface ("emerge") when people are in groups.

emotion accents Culturally specific ways that individuals from different cultures express particular emotions, such as the tongue bite as an expression of embarrassment in India.

emotional amplification A ratcheting up of an emotional reaction to an event that is proportional to how easy it is to imagine the event not happening.

emotions Brief, specific psychological and physiological responses that help humans meet social goals.

empathic concern Identifying with another person—feeling and understanding what that person is experiencing—accompanied by the intention to help the person in need.

encoding Filing information away in memory based on what information is attended to and the initial interpretation of information.

entertainment-education Media presentations that are meant to both entertain and persuade people to act in their own (or in society's) best interests.

entity theory of intelligence The belief that intelligence is something you're born with and can't change.

equity theory A theory that maintains that people are motivated to pursue fairness, or equity, in their relationships, with rewards and costs shared roughly equally among individuals.

ethnocentrism Glorifying one's own group while vilifying other groups.

evaluation apprehension A concern about how we appear in the eyes of others—that is, about being evaluated.

exchange relationships Relationships in which the individuals feel little responsibility toward one another and in which giving and receiving are governed by concerns about equity and reciprocity; such relationships are often short-term.

experienced distress A motive for helping those in distress that may arise from a need to reduce our *own* distress.

experimental research In social psychology, research in which people are randomly assigned to different conditions, or situations, and from which it is possible to make very strong inferences about how these different conditions affect people's behavior.

explanatory style A person's habitual way of explaining events, typically assessed along three dimensions: internal/external, stable/unstable, and global/specific.

external validity An experimental setup that closely resembles real-life situations so that results can safely be generalized to such situations.

F

face Who we want others to think we are.

feelings-as-information perspective A theory that since many judgments are too complex for us to thoroughly review all the relevant evidence, we rely on our emotions to provide us with rapid, reliable information about events and conditions within our social environment.

field experiment An experiment set up in the real world, usually with participants who are not aware that they are in a study of any kind.

five-factor model Five personality traits (openness, conscientiousness, extraversion, agreeableness, and neuroticism) that psychologists believe are the basic building blocks of personality.

flashbulb memories Vivid recollections of the moment one learned some dramatic, emotionally charged news.

fluency The feeling of ease associated with processing information.

focal emotions Emotions that are particularly common within a particular culture.

focalism A tendency to focus too much on a central aspect of an event while neglecting to consider the impact of ancillary aspects of the event or the impact of other events.

foot-in-the-door technique A compliance technique in which one makes an initial small request to which nearly everyone complies, followed by a larger request involving the real behavior of interest.

framing effect The influence on judgment resulting from the way information is presented, including the order of presentation.

free-response critique A critique of Ekman and Friesen's emotion studies based on the fact that researchers provided the terms with which participants labeled facial expressions rather than allowing the participants to label the expressions with their own words.

frustration The internal state that accompanies the thwarting of an attempt to achieve some goal.

frustration-aggression theory The theory that frustration leads to aggression.

functional distance An architectural layout's tendency to encourage or inhibit certain activities, like contact between people.

fundamental attribution error The tendency to believe that a behavior is due to a person's disposition, even when there are situational forces present that are sufficient to explain the behavior.

G

Gestalt psychology Based on the German word, *Gestalt*, meaning "form" or "figure," this approach stresses the fact that objects are perceived not by means of some automatic registering device but by active, usually unconscious, interpretation of what the object represents as a whole.

group polarization The tendency for group decisions to be more extreme than those made by individuals. Whatever way the individuals are leaning, group discussion tends to make them lean further in that direction.

groupthink A kind of faulty thinking on the part of highly cohesive groups in which the critical scrutiny that should be devoted to the issues at hand is subverted by social pressures to reach consensus.

H

halo effect The common belief—accurate or not—that attractive individuals possess a host of positive qualities beyond their physical appearance.

heritability The degree to which traits or physical characteristics are determined by genes and hence inherited from parents.

heuristics Intuitive mental operations that allow us to make a variety of judgments quickly and efficiently.

heuristic-systematic model A model of persuasion that maintains that there are two different routes of persuasion: the systematic route and the heuristic route.

hindsight bias People's tendency to be overconfident about whether they could have predicted a given outcome.

hostile aggression Behavior intended to harm another, either physically or psychologically, and motivated by feelings of anger and hostility.

hypercognize To represent a particular emotion with numerous words and concepts.

I

ideal self The self that embodies the wishes and aspirations we and other people maintain about us.

identifiable victim effect The tendency to be more moved by the plight of a single, vivid individual than by a more abstract aggregate of individuals.

identity cues Customary facial expressions, posture, gait, clothes, haircuts, and body decorations, which signal to others important facets of our identity and, by implication, how we are to be treated and construed by others.

ideomotor action The phenomenon whereby merely thinking about a behavior makes its actual performance more likely.

illusory correlation The belief that two variables are correlated when in fact they are not.

immune neglect The tendency to underestimate our capacity to be resilient in responding to difficult life events, which leads us to overestimate the extent to which life's difficulties will reduce our personal well-being.

Implicit Association Test (IAT) A technique for revealing nonconscious prejudices toward particular groups.

impression management Attempting to control the beliefs other people have of us.

inclusive fitness The evolutionary tendency to look out for ourselves, our offspring, and our close relatives together with their offspring so that our genes will survive.

incrementalist theory of intelligence The belief that intelligence is something you get by dint of working.

independent (individualistic) cultures Cultures in which people tend to think of themselves as distinct social entities, tied to each other by voluntary bonds of affection and organizational memberships but essentially separate from other people and having attributes that exist in the absence of any connection to others.

independent variable In experimental research, the variable that is manipulated and that is hypothesized to be the cause of a particular outcome.

individuation An enhanced sense of individual identity produced by focusing attention on the self, which generally leads people to act carefully and deliberately and in accordance with their sense of propriety and values.

induced (forced) compliance Subtly compelling individuals to behave in a manner that is inconsistent with their beliefs, attitudes, or values, which typically leads to dissonance and to a change in their original attitudes or values in order to reduce their dissonance.

informational social influence The influence of other people that results from taking their comments or actions as a source of information about what is correct, proper, or effective.

informed consent Participants' willingness to participate in a procedure or research study after learning all relevant aspects about the procedure or study.

infrahumanization The tendency to attribute animal-like qualities to outgroup members and be reluctant to attribute more complex emotions, such as pride or compassion, to outgroup members.

institutional review board (IRB) A university committee that examines research proposals and makes judgments about the ethical appropriateness of the research.

instrumental aggression Behavior intended to harm another in the service of motives other than pure hostility (for example, to attract attention, to acquire wealth, or to advance political and ideological causes).

interaction dynamics approach A methodological approach to the study of the behaviors and conversations of couples, with a focus on both negative behaviors (such as anger, criticism, defensiveness, contempt, sadness, and fear) and positive behaviors (such as affection, enthusiasm, interest, and humor).

interdependent (collectivistic) cultures Cultures in which people tend to define themselves as part of a collective, inextricably tied to others in their group and having relatively little individual freedom or personal control over their lives but not necessarily wanting or needing these things.

internal validity In experimental research, confidence that it is the manipulated variable only that could have produced the results.

Internalization (private acceptance) Private acceptance of a proposition, orientation, or ideology.

interpersonal relationships Attachments in which bonds of family or friendship or love or respect or hierarchy tie together two or more individuals over an extended period of time.

interpersonal simulations Experiments in which an "observer-participant" is given a detailed description of one condition of a dissonance experiment, is told how a participant behaved in that situation, and is asked to predict the attitude of that participant.

intersex attraction The interest in and attraction toward a member of the opposite sex.

interventions Efforts to change people's behavior.

intrasex competition Direct competition between two or more males or two or more females for access to members of the opposite sex.

investment model of interpersonal relationships A model of interpersonal relationships that maintains that three things make partners more committed to each other: rewards, few alternative partners, and investments in the relationship.

J

just world hypothesis The belief that people get what they deserve in life and deserve what they get.

K

kin selection The tendency for natural selection to favor behaviors that increase the chances of survival of genetic relatives.

knowledge function An attitudinal function whereby attitudes help organize our understanding of the world, guiding how we attend to, store, and retrieve information.

knowledge structures Coherent configurations (known as schemas, scripts, frames, prototypes, or personae) in which related information is stored together.

L

learned helplessness Passive and depressed responses that individuals show when their goals are blocked and they feel that they have no control over their outcomes.

leveling Eliminating or deemphasizing seemingly less important details when telling a story to someone else.

Likert scale A numerical scale used to assess people's attitudes that includes a set of possible answers and that has anchors on each extreme.

longitudinal study A study conducted over a long period of time with the same population, which is periodically assessed regarding a particular behavior.

loss aversion The tendency for a loss of a given magnitude to have more psychological impact than an equivalent gain.

M

measurement validity The correlation between some measure and some outcome that the measure is supposed to predict.

mental accounting The tendency to treat money differently depending on how it was acquired and to what mental category it is attached.

mere exposure effect The finding that repeated exposure to a stimulus (for example, an object or person) leads to greater liking of the stimulus.

message characteristics Aspects of the message itself, including the quality of the evidence and the explicitness of its conclusions.

minimal group paradigm An experimental paradigm in which researchers create groups based on arbitrary and seemingly meaningless criteria and then examine how the members of these "minimal groups" are inclined to behave toward one another.

misattribution of arousal Attributing arousal produced by one cause (for example, exercise) to another stimulus in the environment.

modern racism (symbolic racism) Prejudice directed at other racial groups that exists alongside rejection of explicitly racist beliefs.

monozygotic (identical) twins Twins who originate from a single fertilized egg that splits into two exact replicas that then develop into two genetically identical individuals.

N

natural experiments Naturally occurring events or phenomena having somewhat different conditions that can be compared with almost as much rigor as in experiments where the investigator manipulates the conditions.

natural selection An evolutionary process that molds animals and plants such that traits that enhance the probability of survival and reproduction are passed on to subsequent generations.

naturalistic fallacy The claim that the way things *are* is the way they *should* be.

negative state relief hypothesis The idea that people engage in certain actions, such as agreeing to a request, in order to relieve negative feelings and to feel better about themselves.

norm of reciprocity A norm dictating that people should provide benefits to those who benefit them.

normative social influence The influence of other people that comes from the desire to avoid their disapproval, harsh judgments, and other social sanctions (for example, barbs, ostracism).

O

obedience In an unequal power relationship, submitting to the demands of the more powerful person.

off-record communication Indirect and ambiguous communication that allows us to hint at ideas and meanings that are not explicit in the words we utter.

on-record communication The statements we make that we intend to be taken literally.

ought self The self that is concerned with the duties, obligations, and external demands we feel we are compelled to honor.

outgroup homogeneity effect The tendency to assume that within-group similarity is much stronger for outgroups than for ingroups.

P

paired distinctiveness The pairing of two distinctive events that stand out even more because they co-occur.

parental investment The evolutionary principle that costs and benefits are associated with reproduction and the nurturing of offspring. Because these costs and benefits are different for males and females, one sex will normally value and invest more in each child than will the other sex.

peripheral (heuristic) route A persuasive route wherein people attend to relatively simple, superficial cues related to the message, such as the length of the message or the expertise or attractiveness of the communicator.

personal beliefs Beliefs about our own personality traits, abilities, attributes, preferences, tastes, and talents.

planning fallacy The tendency for people to be unrealistically optimistic about how quickly they can complete a project.

pluralistic ignorance Misperception of a group norm that results from observing people who are acting at variance with their private beliefs out of a concern for the social consequences—behavior that reinforces the erroneous group norm.

possible selves Hypothetical selves we aspire to be in the future.

power The ability to control our own outcomes and those of others; the freedom to act.

prejudice A negative attitude or affective response toward a certain group and its individual members.

prevention focus A sensitivity to negative outcomes often motivated by a desire to live up to our ought self and to avoid the guilt or anxiety that results when we fail to live up to our sense of what we ought to do.

primacy effect The disproportionate influence on judgment of information presented first in a body of evidence.

primary appraisal stage An initial, automatic positive or negative evaluation of ongoing events based on whether they are congruent or incongruent with our goals.

prime To mentally activate a concept and hence make it accessible. Also used as a noun—a stimulus presented to activate a concept.

priming A procedure used to increase the accessibility of a concept or schema (for example, a stereotype).

principle of serviceable habits Charles Darwin's thesis that emotional expressions are remnants of full-blown behaviors that helped our primate and mammalian predecessors meet important goals in the past.

prisoner's dilemma A situation involving payoffs to two people in which trust and cooperation lead to higher joint payoffs than mistrust and defection. The game gets its name from the dilemma that would confront two criminals who were involved in a crime together and are being held and questioned separately. Each must decide whether to "cooperate" and stick with a prearranged alibi or "defect" and confess to the crime in the hope of lenient treatment.

private self-consciousness Our awareness of our interior lives—our private thoughts, feelings, and sensations.

processing style perspective A theory that different emotions lead people to reason in different ways—for example, that positive moods facilitate preexisting heuristics and stereotypes, whereas negative moods facilitate more careful attention to situational details.

promotion focus A sensitivity to positive outcomes, approach-related behavior, and cheerful emotions that result if we are living up to our ideals and aspirations.

propinquity Physical proximity.

psychological stress The sense that your challenges and demands surpass your current capacities, resources, and energies.

public compliance Agreeing with someone or advancing a position in public, even if we continue to believe something else in private.

public self-consciousness Our awareness of what other people think about us—our public identity.

R

random assignment Assigning participants in experimental research to different groups randomly, such that they are as likely to be assigned to one condition as to another.

rape-prone cultures Cultures in which rape tends to be used as an act of war against enemy women, as a ritual act, and as a threat against women so that they will remain subservient to men.

reactance theory The idea that people reassert their prerogatives in response to the unpleasant state of arousal they experience when they believe their freedoms are threatened.

realistic group conflict theory A theory that group conflict, prejudice, and discrimination are likely to arise over competition between groups for limited resources.

receiver characteristics Characteristics of the person who receives the message, including age, mood, personality, and motivation to attend to the message.

recency effect The disproportionate influence on judgment of information presented last in a body of evidence.

reciprocal altruism The tendency to help others with the expectation that they are likely to help us in return at some future time.

reference groups Groups whose opinions matter to us and that affect our opinions and beliefs.

relational self The beliefs, feelings, and expectations that we have about ourselves that derive from our relationships with significant others in our lives.

relational self-beliefs Beliefs about our identities in specific relationships.

relational self theory A theory that examines how prior relationships shape our current beliefs, feelings, and interactions vis-à-vis people who remind us of significant others from our past.

reliability The degree to which the particular way we measure a given variable is likely to yield consistent results.

representativeness heuristic The process whereby judgments of likelihood are based on assessments of similarity between individuals and group prototypes or between cause and effect.

reproductive fitness The capacity to get one's genes passed on to subsequent generations.

response latency The time it takes an individual to respond to a stimulus such as an attitude question.

retrieval The extraction of information from memory.

risk aversion The reluctance to pursue an uncertain option with an average payoff that exceeds the payoff attainable by another, certain option.

risk seeking The opposite of risk aversion; the tendency to forgo a certain outcome in favor of a risky option with an equal or more negative average payoff.

risky shift The tendency for groups to make riskier decisions than individuals would.

rumination The tendency to think about some stressful event over and over again.

S

schemas Generalized knowledge about the physical and social world and how to behave in particular situations and with different kinds of people. A knowledge structure consisting of any organized body of stored information.

secondary appraisal stage A subsequent evaluation in which we determine why we feel the way we do about an event, possible ways of responding to the event, and future consequences of different courses of action.

secure attachment style An attachment style characterized by feelings of security in relationships. Individuals with this style are comfortable with intimacy and want to be close to others during times of threat and uncertainty.

self-affirmation Bolstering our identity and self-esteem by taking note of important elements of our identity, such as our important values.

self-awareness theory A theory that maintains that when people focus their attention inward on themselves, they become concerned with self-evaluation and how their current behavior conforms to their internal standards and values.

self-censorship The tendency to withhold information or opinions in group discussions.

self-complexity The tendency to define the self in terms of many domains and attributes.

self-discrepancy theory A theory that appropriate behavior is motivated by cultural and moral standards regarding the ideal self and the ought self. Violations of those standards produce emotions such as guilt and shame.

self-distancing The ability to focus on one's feelings from the perspective of a detached observer.

self-esteem The positive or negative overall evaluation that we have of ourselves.

self-evaluation maintenance model A model that maintains that we are motivated to view ourselves in a favorable light and that we do so through two processes: reflection and social comparison.

self-fulfilling prophecy Acting in a way that tends to produce the very behavior we expected in the first place, as when we act toward members of certain groups in ways that encourage the very behavior we expect from them.

self-handicapping The tendency to engage in self-defeating behaviors in order to prevent others from drawing unwanted attributions about the self as a result of poor performance.

self-image bias The tendency to judge other people's personalities according to their similarity or dissimilarity to our own personality.

self-monitoring The tendency for people to monitor their behavior in such a way that it fits the demands of the current situation.

self-perception theory A theory that people come to know their own attitudes by looking at their behavior and the context in which it occurred and *inferring* what their attitudes must be.

self-presentation Presenting who we would like others to believe we are.

self-reference effect The tendency to elaborate on and recall information that is integrated into our self-knowledge.

self-schemas Knowledge-based summaries of our feelings and actions and how we understand others' views about the self.

self-selection A problem that arises when the participant, rather than the investigator, selects his or her level on each variable, bringing with this value unknown other properties that make causal interpretation of a relationship difficult.

self-serving bias The tendency to attribute failure and other bad events to external circumstances, but to attribute success and other good events to oneself.

self-verification theory A theory that holds that we strive for stable, accurate beliefs about the self because such beliefs give us a sense of coherence.

sharpening Emphasizing important or more interesting elements in telling a story to someone else.

sleeper effect An effect that occurs when messages from unreliable sources initially exert little influence but later cause individuals' attitudes to shift.

social comparison theory The hypothesis that when there isn't an objective standard of evaluation or comprehension, we compare ourselves to other people in order to evaluate our opinions, abilities, and internal states.

social dominance orientation The desire to see one's own group dominate other groups.

social exchange theory A theory based on the fact that there are costs and rewards in all relationships and that how people feel about a relationship depends on their assessments of its costs and rewards and the costs and rewards available to them in other relationships.

social facilitation Initially a term for enhanced performance in the presence of others; now a broader term for the effect—positive or negative—of the presence of others on performance.

social identity theory A theory that a person's self-concept and self-esteem not only derive from personal identity and accomplishments, but from the status and accomplishments of the various groups to which the person belongs.

social influence The myriad ways that people impact one another, including changes in attitudes, beliefs, feelings, and behavior, that result from the comments, actions, or even the mere presence of others.

social loafing The tendency to exert less effort when working on a group task in which individual contributions cannot be monitored.

social psychology The scientific study of the feelings, thoughts, and behaviors of individuals in social situations.

social rewards Benefits like praise, positive attention, tangible rewards, honors, and gratitude that may be gained from helping others.

social self-beliefs Beliefs about the roles, duties, and obligations we assume in groups.

sociometer hypothesis A hypothesis that maintains that self-esteem is an internal, subjective index or marker of the extent to which we are included or looked on favorably by others.

sociometric survey A survey that attempts to measure the interpersonal relationships in a group of people.

source characteristics Characteristics of the person who delivers the message, including the person's attractiveness, credibility, and expertise.

spotlight effect People's conviction that other people are attending to them—to their appearance and behavior—more than is actually the case.

state self-esteem The dynamic, changeable self-evaluations that are experienced as momentary feelings about the self.

statistical significance A measure of the probability that a given result could have occurred by chance.

status The outcome of an evaluation of attributes that produces differences in respect and prominence, which in part determines an individual's power within a group.

stereotype threat The fear that we will confirm the stereotypes that others have regarding some salient group of which we are a member.

stereotypes Schemas that we have for people of various kinds that can be applied to judgments about people and decisions about how to interact with them. Beliefs that certain attributes are characteristic of members of particular groups.

strange situation An experimental situation designed to assess an infant's attachment to the caregiver. An infant's reactions are observed after her caregiver has left her alone in an unfamiliar room with a stranger and then when the caregiver returns to the room (the reunion).

subliminal Below the threshold of conscious awareness.

subtyping Explaining away exceptions to a given stereotype by creating a subcategory of the stereotyped group that can be expected to differ from the group as a whole.

sunk cost fallacy A reluctance to "waste" money that leads people to continue with an endeavor, whether it serves their future interests or not, because they've already invested money, effort, or time in it.

superordinate goals Goals that transcend the interests of one individual group and that can be achieved more readily by two or more groups working together.

system justification theory The theory that people are motivated to see the existing political and social status quo as desirable, fair, good, and legitimate.

T

terror management theory (TMT) A theory that people deal with the potentially paralyzing anxiety that comes with the knowledge of the inevitability of death by striving for symbolic immortality through the preservation of a valued worldview and the conviction that one has lived up to its values and prescriptions.

that's-not-all technique Adding something to an original offer, which is likely to create some pressure to reciprocate.

theory of mind The understanding that other people have beliefs and desires.

third-person effect The assumption by most people that "other people" are more prone to being influenced by persuasive messages (such as those in media campaigns) than they themselves are.

thought polarization hypothesis The hypothesis that more extended thought about a particular issue tends to produce more extreme, entrenched attitudes.

tit-for-tat strategy A strategy in which the individual's first move is cooperative and thereafter the individual mimics the other person's behavior, whether cooperative or competitive.

top-down processes "Theory-driven" mental processing, in which one filters and interprets new information in light of preexisting knowledge and expectations.

trait self-esteem The enduring level of confidence and regard that people have for their defining abilities and characteristics across time.

traits Consistent ways that people think, feel, and act across classes of situations.

triangular theory of love A theory that states that there are three major components of love—intimacy, passion, and commitment—which can be combined in different ways.

two-factor theory of emotion A theory that there are two components to emotional experience: undifferentiated physiological arousal and a person's construal of that state of undifferentiated arousal.

U

utilitarian function An attitudinal function that serves to alert us to rewarding objects and situations we should approach and costly or punishing objects or situations we should avoid.

V

value-expressive function An attitudinal function whereby attitudes help us express our most cherished values—usually in groups in which they can be supported and reinforced.

W

working model of relationships A conceptual model of relationships with our current partners—including their availability, warmth, and ability to provide security—as derived from our childhood experience with how available and warm our parents were.

References

Aarts, H., & Dijksterhuis, A. (2003). The silence of the library: Environment, situational norm, and social behavior. *Journal of Personality and Social Psychology, 84,* 18–28.

Aarts, H., Gollwitzer, P. M., & Hassin, R. R. (2004). Goal contagion: Perceiving is for pursuing. *Journal of Personality and Social Psychology, 87,* 23–37.

Abell, G. O. (1981). Astrology. In G. O. Abell & B. Singer (Eds.), *Science and the paranormal: Probing the existence of supernatural.* New York: Charles Scribner's Sons.

Abrams, D., Viki, G. T., Masser, B., & Bohner, G. (2003). Perceptions of stranger and acquaintance rape: The role of benevolent and hostile sexism in victim blame and rape proclivity. *Journal of Personality and Social Psychology, 84,* 111–125.

Abramson, L. Y., Metalsky, G. I., & Alloy, L. B. (1989). Hopelessness depression: A theory-based subtype of depression. *Psychological Review, 96,* 358–372.

Abu-Lughod, L. (1986). *Veiled sentiments.* Berkeley, CA: University of California Press.

Acevedo, B. P., & Aron, A. (2009). Does a long-term relationship kill romantic love? *Review of General Psychology, 13,* 59–65.

Adams, G. R. (1978). Racial membership and physical attractiveness effects on teachers' expectations. *Child Study Journal, 8,* 29–41.

Adams, G. R., & Crane, P. (1980). An assessment of parents' and teachers' expectations of preschool children's social preference for attractive or unattractive children and adults. *Child Development, 51,* 224–231.

Adler, J. (1994, November 7). Beyond the bell curve. *Newsweek,* 56.

Adler, N. E., Boyce, T., Chesney, M. A., Cohen, S., Folkman, S., Kahn, R. L., et al. (1994). Socioeconomic status and health: The challenge of the gradient. *American Psychologist, 49,* 15–24.

Agnew, C. R., Van Lange, P. A. M., Rusbult, C. E., & Langston, C. A. (1998). Cognitive interdependence: Commitment and the mental representation of close relationships. *Journal of Personality and Social Psychology, 74,* 939–954.

Ainsworth, M. D. S. (1993). Attachment as related to mother-infant interaction. *Advances in Infancy Research, 8,* 1–50.

Ainsworth, M. D. S., Blehar, M., Waters, E., & Wall, S. (1978). *Patterns of attachment.* Hilldale, NJ: Erlbaum.

Ajzen, I. (1977). Intuitive theories of events and the effects of base-rate information on prediction. *Journal of Personality and Social Psychology, 35,* 303–314.

Ajzen, I. (1987). Attitudes, traits, and actions: Dispositional prediction of behavior in personality and social psychology. In L. Berkowitz (Ed.), *Advances in experimental social psychology* (Vol. 20, pp. 1–63). San Diego, CA: Academic Press.

Aldag, R. J., & Fuller, S. R. (1993). Beyond fiasco: A reappraisal of the groupthink phenomenon and a new model of group decision processes. *Psychological Bulletin, 113,* 533–552.

Alicke, M.D., & Govorun, O. (2005). The better-than-average effect. In M. D. Alicke, D. A. Dunning, & J. I. Krueger (Eds.), *The Self in Social Judgment* (pp. 85–106). New York: Psychology Press.

Allee, W. C., & Masure, R. H. (1936). A comparison of maze behavior in paired and isolated shell-parakeets (*Melopsittacus undulatus Shaw*) in a two-alley problem box. *Journal of Comparative Psychology, 3,* 159–182.

Allen, M., Emmers-Sommer, T. M., Gebhardt, L., Giery, M. (1995). Pornography and rape myth acceptance. *Journal of Communication, 45,* 5–26.

Allen, V. L. (1965). Situational factors in conformity. In L. Berkowitz (Ed.), *Advances in experimental social psychology* (Vol. 2, pp. 133–175). New York: Academic Press.

Allen, V. L., & Wilder, D. A. (1979). Group categorization and attribution of belief similarity. *Small Group Behavior, 10,* 73–80.

Allport, F. H. (1920). The influence of the group upon association and thought. *Journal of Experimental Psychology, 3,* 159–182.

Alluisi, E. A., & Adams, O. S. (1962). Predicting letter preferences: Aesthetics and filtering in man. *Perceptual and Motor Skills, 14,* 123–131.

Alter, A. L., & Oppenheimer, D. M. (2006). Predicting stock price fluctuations using processing fluency. *Proceedings of the National Academy of Sciences, 103,* 9369–9372.

Alter, A. L., Oppenheimer, D. M., Epley, N., & Eyre, R. N. (2007). Overcoming intuition: Metacognitive difficulty activates analytic reasoning. *Journal of Experimental Psychology: General, 136,* 569–576.

Al-Zahrani, S. S. A., & Kaplowitz, S. A. (1993). Attributional biases in individualistic and collectivistic cultures: A comparison of Americans with Saudis. *Social Psychology Quarterly, 56,* 223–233.

Amato, P. R., & Keith, B. (1991). Parental divorce and well-being of children. *Psychological Bulletin, 110,* 26–46.

Ambady, N., Hallahan, M., & Rosenthal, R. (1995). On judging and being judged in zero-acquaintance situations. *Journal of Personality and Social Psychology, 69,* 518–529.

Ambady, N., & Rosenthal, R. (1993). Half a minute: Predicting teacher evaluations from thin slices of nonverbal behavior and physical attractiveness. *Journal of Personality and Social Psychology, 64,* 431–441.

Amodio, D. M., & Devine, P. G. (2006). Stereotyping and evaluation in implicit race bias: Evidence for independent constructs and unique effects on behavior. *Journal of Personality and Social Psychology, 91,* 652–661.

Andersen, S. M., & Chen, S. (2002). The relational self: An interpersonal social-cognitive theory. *Psychological Review, 109,* 619–645.

Andersen, S. M., Glassman, N. S., Chen, S., & Cole, S. W. (1995). Transference in social perception: The role of chronic accessibility in significant-other representations. *Journal of Personality and Social Psychology, 69,* 41–57.

Andersen, S. M., Reznik, I., & Manzella, L. M. (1996). Eliciting facial affect, motivation, and expectancies in transference: Significant-other representations in social relations. *Journal of Personality and Social Psychology, 71,* 1108–1129.

Andersen, S. M., & Ross, L. (1984). Self knowledge and social influence I: The impact of cognitive/affective and behavioral data. *Journal of Personality and Social Psychology, 46,* 280–293.

Anderson, C. A. (1987). Temperature and aggression: Effects on quarterly, yearly, and city rates of violent and nonviolent crime. *Journal of Personality and Social Psychology, 52,* 1161–1173.

Anderson, C. A. (1989). Temperature and aggression: Ubiquitous effects of heat on occurrences of human violence. *Psychological Bulletin, 106,* 74–96.

Anderson, C. A. (1991). How people think about causes: Examination of the typical phenomenal organization of attributions for success and failure. *Social Cognition, 9,* 295–329.

Anderson, C. A., Berkowitz, L., Donnerstein, E., Huesmann, L. R., Johnson, J., Linz, D., et al. (2003). The influence of media violence on youth. *Psychological Science in the Public Interest, 4,* 81–110.

Anderson, C. A., & Bushman, B. J. (2001). Effects of violent video games on aggressive behavior, aggressive cognition, aggressive affect, physiological arousal, and prosocial behavior: A meta-analytic review of the scientific literature. *Psychological Science, 12,* 353–359.

Anderson, C. A., & Deuser, W. E. (1993). The primacy of control in causal thinking and attributional style: An attributional functionalism perspective. In G. Weary, F. Gleicher, & K. L. Marsh (Eds.), *Control motivation and social cognition* (pp. 94–121). New York: Springer-Verlag.

Anderson, C. A., & Dill, K. E. (2000). Video games and aggressive thoughts, feelings, and behavior in the laboratory and in life. *Journal of Personality and Social Psychology, 78,* 772–790.

Anderson, C., John, O. P., Keltner, D., & Kring, A. (2001). Social status in naturalistic face-to-face groups: Effects of personality and physical attractiveness in men and women. *Journal of Personality and Social Psychology, 81,* 1108–1129.

Anderson, C., Keltner, D., & John, O. P. (2003). Emotional convergence between people over time. *Journal of Personality and Social Psychology, 84,* 1054–1068.

Anderson, C. A., Krull, D. S., & Weiner, B. (1996). Explanations: Processes and consequences. In E. T. Higgins & A. W. Kruglanski (Eds.), *Social psychology: Handbook of basic principles* (pp. 271–296). New York: Guilford Press.

Anderson, J. L., Crawford, C. B., Nadeau, J., & Lindberg, T. (1992). Was the duchess of Windsor right? A cross-cultural review of the socioecology of ideals of female body shape. *Ethology and Sociobiology, 13,* 197–227.

Anderson, R., & Nida, S. A. (1978). Effect of physical attractiveness on opposite- and same-sex evaluations. *Journal of Personality, 46,* 401–413.

Anderson, R. C., & Pichert, J. W. (1978). Recall of previously unrecallable information following a shift in perspective. *Journal of Verbal Learning and Verbal Behavior, 17,* 1–12.

Ansolabehere, S., & Iyengar, S. (1995). *Going negative: How political ads shrink and polarize the electorate.* New York: Free Press.

Antill, J. K. (1983). Sex role complementarity versus similarity in married couples. *Journal of Personality and Social Psychology, 45,* 145–155.

Arden, R., Gottfredson, L. S., Miller, G., & Pierce, A. (2008). Intelligence and semen quality are positively correlated [Electronic Version]. *Intelligence.* Retrieved December 8, 2008, from 10.1016/j.intell.2008.11.001

Argyle, M. (1999). Causes and correlates of happiness. In D. Kahneman, E. Diener, & N. Schwarz (Eds.), *Well-being. The foundations of hedonic psychology* (pp. 353–373). New York: Russell Sage.

Arkes, H., & Blumer, C. (1985). The psychology of sunk cost. *Organizational Behavior and Human Decision Processes, 35,* 124–140.

Arkin, R. M., & Baumgardner, A. H. (1985). Basic issues in attribution theory and research. In J. H. Harvey & G. Weary (Eds.), *Self handicapping* (pp. 169–202). New York: Academic Press.

Arkin, R. M., & Maruyama, G. M. (1979). Attribution, affect and college exam performance. *Journal of Educational Psychology, 71,* 85–93.

Arndt, J., Schimel, J., & Goldenberg, J. L. (2003). Death can be good for your health: Fitness intentions as a proximal and distal defense against mortality salience. *Journal of Applied Social Psychology, 33,* 1726–1746.

Aron, A., & Aron, E. N. (1997). Self-expansion motivation and including the other in self. In S. Duck (Ed.), *Handbook of personal relationships: Theory, research, and interventions* (2nd ed., pp. 251–270). Chichester, England: Wiley.

Aron, A., Aron, E. N., & Allen, J. (1989). *The motivation for unrequited love: A self-expansion perspective.* Paper presented at the International Conference on Personal Relationships, Iowa City, IA.

Aron, A., Aron, E. N., Tudor, M., & Nelson, G. (1991). Close relationships as including other in self. *Journal of Personality and Social Psychology, 60,* 241–253.

Aron, A., & Fraley, B. (1999). Relationship closeness as including other in the self: Cognitive underpinnings and measures. *Social Cognition 17,* 140–160.

Aron, A., Norman, C. C., Aron, E. N., McKenna, C., & Heyman, R. E. (2000). Couples' shared participation in novel and arousing activities and experienced relationship quality. *Journal of Personality and Social Psychology, 78,* 273–284.

Aronson, E. (1969). The theory of cognitive dissonance: A current perspective. In L. Berkowitz (Ed.), *Advances in experimental social psychology* (Vol. 4, pp. 1–34). New York: Academic Press.

Aronson, E., & Carlsmith, J. M. (1963). Effect of severity of threat in the devaluation of forbidden behavior. *Journal of Abnormal and Social Psychology, 66,* 584–588.

Aronson, E., Ellsworth, P. C., Carlsmith, J. M., & Gonzalez, M. H. (1990). *Methods of research in social psychology* (2nd ed.). New York: McGraw-Hill.

Aronson, E., Fried, C., & Stone, J. (1991). Overcoming denial and increasing the intention to use condoms through the induction of hypocrisy. *American Journal of Public Health, 81,* 1636–1638.

Aronson, E., & Linder, D. (1965). Gain and loss of esteem as determinants of interpersonal attractiveness. *Journal of Experimental Social Psychology, 1,* 156–171.

Aronson, E., & Mills, J. (1959). The effect of severity of initiation on liking for a group. *Journal of Abnormal and Social Psychology, 59,* 177–181.

Aronson, E., Stephan, C., Sikes, J., Blaney, N., & Snapp, M. (1978). *The jigsaw classroom.* Beverly Hills, CA: Sage.

Aronson, E., & Thibodeau, R. (1992). The jigsaw classroom: A cooperative strategy for reducing prejudice. In J. Lynch, C. Modgil, & S. Modgil (Eds.), *Cultural diversity in the schools* (pp. 110–118). London: Falmer Press.

Aronson, J., Fried, C. B., & Good, C. (2002). Reducing stereotype threat and boosting academic achievement of African-American students: The role of conceptions of intelligence. *Journal of Experimental Social Psychology, 38,* 113–125.

Aronson, J. M., Lustina, M. J., Good, C., Keough, K., Steele, C. M., & Brown, J. (1999). When white men can't do math: Necessary and sufficient factors in stereotype threat. *Journal of Experimental Social Psychology, 35,* 29–46.

Asch, S. E. (1940). Studies in the principles of judgments and attitudes: II. Determination of judgments by group and by ego standards. *Journal of Social Psychology, 12,* 584–588.

Asch, S. E. (1946). Forming impressions on personality. *Journal of Abnormal and Social Psychology, 41,* 258–290.

Asch, S. (1951). Effects of group pressure upon the modification and distortion of judgments. In G. Guetzkow (Ed.), *Groups, leadership, and men* (pp. 177–190). Pittsburgh, PA: Carnegie Press.

Asch, S. (1952). *Social psychology.* Englewood Cliffs, NJ: Prentice-Hall.

Asch, S. (1956). Studies of independence and conformity: A minority of one against a unanimous majority. *Psychological Monographs, 70* (Whole No. 416).

Asch, S. E., & Zuckier, H. (1984). Thinking about person. *Journal of Personality and Social Psychology, 46,* 1230–1240.

Ashburn-Nardo, L., Voils, C. I., & Monteith, M. J. (2001). Implicit associations as the seeds of intergroup bias: How easily do they take root? *Journal of Personality and Social Psychology, 81,* 789–799.

Aspinwall, L. G., & Brunhart, S. M. (1996). Distinguishing optimism from denial: Optimistic beliefs predict attention to health threats. *Personality and Social Psychology Bulletin, 22,* 993–1003.

Aspinwall, L. G., & Taylor, S. E. (1993). Effects of social comparison direction, threat and self-esteem on affect, evaluation and expected success. *Journal of Personality and Social Psychology, 64,* 708–722.

Avis, J., & Harris, P. L. (1991). Belief-desire reasoning among Baka children: Evidence for a universal conception of mind. *Child Development, 62,* 460–467.

Axelrod, R. (1984). *The evolution of cooperation.* New York: Basic Books.

Ayduk, O., Downey, G., Testa, A., Yen, Y., & Shoda, Y. (1999). Does rejection elicit hostility in high rejection sensitive women? *Social Cognition, 17,* 245–271.

Ayduk, O., & Kross, E. (2008). Enhancing the pace of recovery: Self-distanced analysis of negative experiences reduces blood pressure reactivity. *Psychological Science, 19,* 229–231.

Bachorowski, J. A., & Owren, M. J. (2001). Not all laughs are alike: Voiced but not unvoiced laughter readily elicits positive affect. *Psychological Science, 12,* 252–257.

Bain, L. L., Wilson, T., & Chaikind, E. (1989). Participant perceptions of exercise programs for overweight women. *Research Quarterly for Exercise and Sport, 60,* 134–143.

Baldwin, M. W. (1992). Relational schemas and the processing of social information. *Psychological Bulletin, 112,* 461–484.

Baldwin, M. W. (1994). Primed relational schemas as a source of self-evaluative reactions. *Journal of Social and Clinical Psychology, 13,* 380–403.

Baldwin, M. W., Carrell, S., & Lopez, D. F. (1990). Priming relationship schemas: My advisor and the Pope are watching me from the back of my mind. *Journal of Experimental Psychology, 26,* 435–454.

Baldwin, M. W., & Fehr, B. (1995). On the instability of attachment style ratings. *Personal Relationships, 2,* 247–261.

Baldwin, M. W., & Holmes, J. G. (1987). Salient private audiences and awareness of the self. *Journal of Personality and Social Psychology, 53,* 1087–1098.

Baldwin, M. W., Keelan, J. P. R., Fehr, B., Enns, V., & Koh-Rangarajoo, E. (1996). Social-cognitive conceptualizations of attachment working models: Availability and accessibility effects. *Journal of Personality and Social Psychology, 71,* 94–109.

Bamshad, M. J., & Olson, S. E. (2003, December). Does race exist? *Scientific American,* 78–85.

Banaji, M., Hardin, C. C., & Rothman, A. J. (1993). Implicit stereotyping in person judgement. *Journal of Personality and Social Psychology, 65,* 272–281.

Banaji, M. R., & Steele, C. M. (1989). Alcohol and self-evaluation: Is a social cognitive approach beneficial? *Social Cognition, 7,* 139–153.

Bandura, A. (1973). *Social learning theory.* Englewood Cliffs, NJ: Prentice Hall.

Bandura, A. (2004). Social cognitive theory for personal and social change by enabling media. In M. J. Singhal, E. M. Cody, E. M. Rogers, & M. Sabido (Eds.), *Entertainment education and social change: History, research and practice* (pp. 75–96). Mahwah, NJ: Erlbaum.

Banks, T., & Dabbs, J. M., Jr. (1996). Salivary testosterone and cortisol in delinquents and violent urban culture. *Journal of Social Psychology, 136,* 49–56.

Bargh, J. A. (1996). Automaticity in social psychology. In E. T. Higgins & A. W. Kruglanski (Eds.), *Social psychology: Handbook of basic principles* (Vol. 1, pp. 1–40). New York: Guilford Press.

Bargh, J. A., Chaiken, S., Raymond, P., & Hymes, C. (1996). The automatic evaluation effect: Unconditional automatic activation with a pronunciation task. *Journal of Experimental Social Psychology, 31,* 104–128.

Bargh, J. A., Chen, M., & Burrows, L. (1996). Automaticity of social behavior: Direct effects of trait construct and stereotype activation on action. *Journal of Personality and Social Psychology, 1,* 1–40.

Bargh, J. A., Gollwitzer, P. M., Lee-Chai, A., Barndollar, K., & Trotschel, R. (2001). The automated will: Nonconscious activation and pursuit of behavioral goals. *Journal of Personality and Social Psychology, 81,* 1014–1027.

Bargh, J. A., & Pietromonaco, P. (1982). Automatic information processing and social perception: The influence of trait information presented outside of conscious awareness on impression formation. *Journal of Personality and Social Psychology, 43,* 437–449.

Bargh, J. A., Raymond, P., Pryor, J. B., & Strack, F. (1995). Attractiveness of the underling: An automatic power-sex association and its consequences for sexual harassment and aggression. *Journal of Personality and Social Psychology, 68(5),* 768–781.

Bar-Hillel, M. (1980). The base-rate fallacy in probability judgments. *Acta Psychologica, 44,* 211–233.

Bar-Hillel, M., & Fischhoff, B. (1981). When do base-rates affect predictions? *Journal of Personality and Social Psychology, 41,* 671–680.

Baron, R. S. (1986). Distraction-conflict theory: Progress and problems. In L. Berkowitz (Ed.), *Advances in experimental social psychology* (Vol. 19, pp. 1–40). New York: Academic Press.

Baron, R. S., Moore, D., & Sanders, G. S. (1978). Distraction as a source of drive in social facilitation research. *Journal of Personality and Social Psychology, 36,* 816–824.

Baron, R. S., Vandello, J. A., & Brunsman, B. (1996). The forgotten variable in conformity research: Impact of task importance on social influence. *Journal of Personality and Social Psychology, 71,* 915–927.

Barrett, L. F. (2006). Are emotions natural kinds? *Perspectives on Psychological Science, 1,* 28–58.

Barrett, L. F., Mesquita, B., Ochsner, K. N., & Gross, J. J. (2007). The experience of emotion. *Annual Review of Psychology, 58,* 373–403.

Bar-Tal, D., & Saxe, L. (1976). Perceptions of similarly and dissimilarly attractive couples and individuals. *Journal of Personality and Social Psychology, 33,* 772–781.

Bartholomew, K., & Horowitz, L. M. (1991). Attachment styles among young adults: A test for a four-category model. *Journal of Personality and Social Psychology, 61,* 226–244.

Bartholow, B. D., Anderson, C. A., Carnagey, N. L., & Benjamin, A. J. (2005). Interactive effects of life experience and situational cues on aggression: The weapons priming effect in hunters and non-hunters. *Journal of Experimental Social Psychology, 41,* 48–60.

Bartlett, F. A. (1932). *Remembering: A study in experimental psychology.* Cambridge, England: Cambridge University Press.

Batson, C. D., Engel, C. L., & Fridell, S. R. (1999). Value judgments: Testing the somatic-marker hypothesis using false physiological feedback. *Personality and Social Psychology Bulletin, 25,* 1021–1032.

Batson, C. D., O'Quin, K., Fultz, J., Vanderplas, M., & Isen, A. (1983). Self-reported distress and empathy and egoistic versus altruistic motivation for helping. *Journal of Personality and Social Psychology, 45,* 706–718.

Batson, C. D., & Shaw, L. L. (1991). Evidence for altruism: Toward a pluralism of prosocial motives. *Psychological Inquiry, 2,* 107–122.

Baumeister, R. F. (1982). A self-presentational view of social interaction. *Psychological Bulletin, 91,* 3–26.

Baumeister, R. F. (1987). How the self became a problem: A psychological review of historical research. *Journal of Personality and Social Psychology, 52,* 163–176.

Baumeister, R. F. (1991). *Escaping the self: Alcoholism, spirituality, masochism, and other flights from the burden of selfhood.* New York: Basic Books.

Baumeister, R. F., Bratslavsky, E., Finkenauer, C., & Vohs, K. D. (2001). Bad is stronger than good. *Review of General Psychology, 5,* 323–370.

Baumeister, R. F., Bratslavsky, E., Muraven, M., & Tice, D. M. (1998). Ego depletion: Is the active self a limited resource? *Journal of Personality and Social Psychology, 74,* 1252–1265.

Baumeister, R. F., & Leary, M. R. (1995). The need to belong: Desire for interpersonal attachments as a fundamental human motivation. *Psychological Bulletin, 117,* 497–529.

Baumeister, R. F., Smart, L., & Boden, J. M. (1996). Relation of threatened egotism to violence and aggression: The dark side to high self-esteem. *Psychological Review, 103,* 5–33.

Baumeister, R. F., Stillwell, A. M., & Heatherton, T. F. (1994). Guilt: An interpersonal approach. *Psychological Bulletin, 115,* 243–267.

Baumeister, R. F., Twenge, J. M., & Nuss, C. (2002). Effects of social exclusion on cognitive processes: Anticipated aloneness reduces intelligent thought. *Journal of Personality and Social Psychology, 83,* 817–827.

Baumeister, R. F., Vohs, K. D., & Tice, D. M. (2007). The strength model of self-control. *Current Directions in Psychological Science, 16,* 396–403.

Baxter, L. A. (1984). Forms and functions of intimate play in personal relationships. *Human Communication Research, 18,* 336–363.

Beaman, A. L., Klentz, B., Diener, E., & Svanum, S. (1979). Self-awareness and transgression in children: Two field studies. *Journal of Personality and Social Psychology, 37,* 1835–1946.

Beck, S. P., Ward-Hull, C. I., & McLear, P. M. (1976). Variables related to women's somatic preferences of the male and female body. *Journal of Personality and Social Psychology, 34,* 1200–1210.

Becker, E. (1973). *The denial of death.* New York: Simon & Schuster.

Becker, M. H., & Josephs, J. G. (1988). Aids and behavioral change to reduce risk: A review. *American Journal of Public Health, 78,* 394–410.

Beckman, L. (1970). Effects of students' performance on teachers' and observers' attributions of causality. *Journal of Educational Psychology, 61,* 76–82.

Beer, J., Heerey, E. A., Keltner, D., Scabini, D, & Knight, R. (2003). The regulatory function of self-conscious emotion: Insights from patients with orbitofrontal damage. *Journal of Personality and Social Psychology, 85,* 594–604.

Bekoff, M., & Pierce, J. (2009). *Wild justice: The oral lives of animals.* Chicago: University of Chicago Press.

Bell, S. T., Kuriloff, P. J., & Lottes, I. (1994). Understanding attributions of blame in stranger-rape and date-rape situations: An examination of gender, race, identification, and students' social perceptions of rape victims. *Journal of Applied Social Psychology, 24,* 1719–1734.

Belsky, G., & Gilovich, T. (1999). *Why smart people make big money mistakes, and how to correct them.* New York: Simon & Schuster.

Bem, D. J. (1967). Self-perception: An alternative interpretation of cognitive dissonance phenomena. *Psychological Review, 74,* 183–200.

Bem, D. J. (1972). Self-perception theory. In L. Berkowitz (Ed.), *Advances in experimental social psychology* (Vol. 6, pp. 1–62). New York: Academic Press.

Bem, D. J., & McConnell, H. K. (1970). Testing the self-perception explanation of dissonance phenomena: On the salience of pre-manipulation attitudes. *Journal of Personality and Social Psychology, 14,* 23–31.

Bem, S. L. (1993). *The lenses of gender: Transforming the debate on sexual inequality.* New Haven, CT: Yale University Press.

Benet-Martinez, V., Leu, J., Lee, F., & Morris, M. W. (2002). Negotiating biculturalism: Cultural frame switching in biculturals with oppositional versus compatible cultural identities. *Journal of Cross-Cultural Psychology, 33,* 492–516.

Ben-Zeev, T., Fein, S., & Inzlicht, M. (2005). Arousal and stereotype threat. *Journal of Experimental Social Psychology, 41,* 174–181.

Berg, J. H., & McQuinn, R. D. (1986). Attraction and exchange in continuing and noncontinuing dating relationships. *Journal of Personality and Social Psychology, 50,* 942–952.

Berglas, S., & Jones, E. E. (1978). Drug choice as a self-handicapping strategy in response to non-contingent success. *Journal of Personality and Social Psychology, 36,* 405–417.

Berk, M. S., & Andersen, S. M. (2000). The impact of past relationships on interpersonal behavior: Behavioral confirmation in the social-cognitive process of transference. *Journal of Personality and Social Psychology, 79,* 546–562.

Berkman, L. F. (1995). The role of social relations in health promotion. *Psychosomatic Medicine, 57,* 245–254.

Berkman, L. F., & Syme, S. L. (1979). Social networks, host resistance, and mortality: A nine year follow-up study of Alameda County residents. *American Journal of Epidemiology, 100,* 186–204.

Berkowitz, L. (1965). Some aspects of observed aggression. *Journal of Personality and Social Psychology, 2,* 359–369.

Berkowitz, L. (1989). The frustration-aggression hypothesis: An examination and reformulation. *Psychological Bulletin, 106,* 59–73.

Berkowitz, L. (1993). *Aggression.* New York: McGraw-Hill.

Berkowitz, L., & Daniels, L. R. (1964). Affecting the salience of the social responsibility norm: Effect of past help on the responses to dependency relationships. *Journal of Abnormal and Social Psychology, 68,* 275–281.

Berkowitz, L., & LePage, A. (1967). Weapons as aggression-eliciting stimuli. *Journal of Personality and Social Psychology, 7,* 202–207.

Berkowitz, L., & Troccoli, B. T. (1990). Feelings, direction of attention, and expressed evaluation of others. *Cognition and Emotion, 4,* 305–325.

Bernieri, F. J., Zuckerman, M., Koestner, R., & Rosenthal, R. (1994). Measuring person perception accuracy: Another look at self-other agreement. *Personality and Social Psychology Bulletin, 20,* 367–378.

Bernstein, I. H., Lin, T., & McClellan, P. (1982). Cross- vs. within-racial judgments of attractiveness. *Perception and Psychophysics, 32,* 495–503.

Berry, D. S. (1991). Accuracy in social perception: Contributions of facial and vocal information. *Journal of Personality and Social Psychology, 61,* 298–307.

Berry, D. S., & Brownlow, S. (1989). Were the physiognomists right? Personality correlates of facial babyishness. *Personality and Social Psychology Bulletin, 15,* 266–279.

Berry, D. S., & McArthur, L. Z. (1986). Perceiving character in faces: The impact of age-related craniofacial changes in social perception. *Psychological Bulletin, 100,* 3–18.

Berry, D. S., & Zebrowitz-McArthur, L. (1986). Perceiving character in faces: The impact of age-related craniofacial changes in social perception. *Psychological Bulletin, 100,* 3–18.

Berscheid, E., Brothen, T., & Graziano, W. (1976). Gain-loss theory and the "law of infidelity": Mr. Doting versus the admiring stranger. *Journal of Personality and Social Psychology, 33,* 709–718.

Berscheid, E., Dion, K., Walster, E., & Walster, G. W. (1971). Physical attractiveness and dating choice: A test of the matching hypothesis. *Journal of Experimental Social Psychology, 7,* 173–189.

Berscheid, E., & Reis, H. T. (1998). Attraction and close relationships. In D. T. Gilbert, S. T. Fiske, & G. Lindzey (Eds.), *The handbook of social psychology* (4th ed., Vol. 2, pp. 193–281). New York: McGraw-Hill.

Bessenoff, G. R., & Sherman, J. W. (2000). Automatic and controlled components of prejudice toward fat people: Evaluation versus stereotype activation. *Social Cognition, 18,* 329–353.

Bettencourt, B. A., Brewer, M. B., Croak, M. R., & Miller, N. (1992). Cooperation and the reduction of intergroup bias: The role of reward structure and social orientation. *Journal of Experimental Psychology, 28,* 301–319.

Biernat, M., Manis, M., & Kobrynowicz, D. (1997). Simultaneous assimilation and contrast effects in judgments of self and others. *Journal of Personality and Social Psychology, 73,* 254–269.

Bird, K. (2002). Advertise or die: Advertising and market share dynamics revisited. *Applied Economic Letters, 9,* 763–767.

Blackwell, L. S., Dweck, C. S., & Trzesniewski, K. (2004). *Implicit theories of intelligence predict achievement across an adolescent transition: A longitudinal study and an intervention.* Unpublished manuscript, Columbia University.

Blackwell, L., Trzesniewski, K., & Dweck, C. S. (2007). Implicit theories of intelligence predict achievement across an adolescent transition: A longitudinal study and an intervention. *Child Development, 78,* 246–263.

Blair, I. V., Judd, C. M., & Fallman, J. L. (2004). The automaticity of race and Afrocentric facial features in social judgments. *Journal of Personality and Social Psychology, 87,* 763–778.

Blair, I. V., Judd, C., Sadler, M. S., & Jenkins, C. (2002). The role of Afrocentric features in person perception: Judging by features and categories. *Journal of Personality and Social Psychology, 83,* 5–25.

Blair, R. J. R., Jones, R. L., Clark, R., and Smith, M. (1997). The psychopathic individual: A lack of responsiveness to distress cues? *Psychophysiology, 34*(2), 192–198.

Blanton, H., Pelham, B. W., De Hart, T., & Kuyper, H. (1999). When better-than-others compare upward: Choice of comparison and comparative evaluation as independent predictors of academic performance. *Journal of Personality and Social Psychology, 76,* 420–430.

Blanton, H., & Stapel, D. A (2008). Unconscious and spontaneous and . . . complex: The three selves model of social comparison assimilation and contrast. *Journal of Personality and Social Psychology, 94,* 1018–1032.

Blascovich, J., Mendes, W. B., Hunter, S. B., & Salomon, K. (1999). Social "facilitation" as challenge and threat. *Journal of Personality and Social Psychology, 77,* 68–77.

Blass, T. (1999). The Milgram paradigm after 35 years: Some things we now know about obedience to authority. *Journal of Applied Social Psychology, 29,* 955–978.

Blass, T. (2000). *Obedience to authority: Current perspectives on the Milgram paradigm.* Mahwah, NJ: Erlbaum.

Blass, T. (2004). *The man who shocked the world: The life and legacy of Stanley Milgram.* New York: Basic Books.

Bless, H., Clore, G. L., Schwarz, N., Golisano, V., Rabe, C., & Wölk, M. (1996). Mood and the use of scripts: Does a happy mood really lead to mindlessness? *Journal of Personality and Social Psychology, 71*(4), 665–679.

Bless, H., Mackie, D. M., & Schwarz, N. (1992). Mood effects on attitude judgments: Independent effects of mood before and after message elaboration. *Journal of Personality and Social Psychology, 63*(4), 585–595.

Bless, H., Schwarz, N., & Wieland, R. (1996). Mood and the impact of category membership and individuating information. *European Journal of Social Psychology, 26,* 935–959.

Block, J., & Robins, R. W. (1993). A longitudinal study of consistency and change in self-esteem from early adolescence to early adulthood. *Child Development, 64,* 909–923.

Bloom, B. L., White, S. W., & Asher, S. J. (1979). Marital disruption as a stressful life event. In G. Levinger & O. C. Moles (Eds.), *Divorce and separation: Context, causes, and consequences* (pp. 184–200). New York: Basic Books.

Bochner, S. (1994). Cross-cultural differences in the self-concept. *Journal of Cross-Cultural Psychology, 25,* 273–283.

Bodenhausen, G. V. (1988). Stereotypic biases in social decision making and memory: Testing process models of stereotype use. *Journal of Personality and Social Psychology, 55,* 726–737.

Bodenhausen, G. V. (1990). Stereotypes as judgmental heuristics: Evidence of circadian variations in discrimination. *Psychological Science, 1,* 319–322.

Bodenhausen, G. V., Kramer, G. P., & Süsser, K. (1994). Happiness and stereotypic thinking in social judgment. *Journal of Personality and Social Psychology, 66,* 621–632.

Bodenhausen, G. V., Macrae, C. N., & Sherman, J. W. (1999). On the dialectics of discrimination: Dual processes in social stereotyping. In S. Chaiken & Y. Trope (Eds.), *Dual process theories in social psychology* (pp. 271–290). New York: Guilford Press.

Bodenhausen, G., Sheppard, L., & Kramer, G. (1994). Negative affect and social judgment: The different impact of anger and sadness. *European Journal of Social Psychology, 24*, 45–62.

Boehm, C. (1999). *Hierarchy in the forest: The evolution of egalitarian behavior.* Cambridge, MA: Harvard University Press.

Boice, R., Quanty, C. B., & Williams, R. C. (1974). Competition and possible dominance in turtles, toads, and frogs. *Journal of Comparative and Physiological Psychology, 86*, 1116–1131.

Bolger, N., & Schilling, E. A. (1991). Personality and the problems of everyday life: The role of neuroticism in exposure and reactivity to daily stressors. *Journal of Personality, 59*, 355–386.

Bond, M. H., & Cheung, T. (1983). College students' spontaneous self-concept. *Journal of Cross-Cultural Psychology, 14*, 154–171.

Bond, R., & Smith, P. B. (1996). Culture and conformity: A meta-analysis of studies using Asch's line judgment task. *Psychological Bulletin, 119*, 111–137.

Borgida, E., Conner, C., & Manteufel, L. (1992). Understanding living kidney donations: A behavioral decision-making perspective. In S. Spacapan & S. Oskamp (Eds.), *Helping and being helped.* Newbury Park, CA: Sage.

Bornstein, R. F. (1989). Exposure and affect: Overview and meta-analysis of research, 1968–1987. *Psychological Bulletin, 106*, 265–289.

Boster, F. J., & Mongeau, P. (1984). Fear-arousing persuasive messages. In R. N. Bostrom (Ed.), *Communication yearbook* (Vol. 8, pp. 330–375). Beverly Hills, CA: Sage.

Boucher, J. D., & Brandt, M. E. (1981). Judgment of emotion: American and Malay antecedents. *Journal of Cross-Cultural Psychology, 12*, 272–283.

Bowlby, J. (1982). *Attachment and loss* (2nd ed., Vol. 1). New York: Basic Books.

Boyd, R., & Richardson, P. J. (1985). Frequency-dependent bias and the evolution of cooperation. In R. Boyd & P. J. Richardson (Eds.), *Culture and the evolutionary process* (pp. 204–240). Chicago: University of Chicago Press.

Boyden, T., Carroll, J. S., & Maier, R. A. (1984). Similarity and attraction in homosexual males: The effects of age and masculinity-femininity. *Sex Roles, 10*, 939–948.

Bradbury, T. N. (1998). *The developmental course of marital dysfunction.* New York: Cambridge University Press.

Bradbury, T. N., & Fincham, F. D. (1990). Attributions in marriage: Review and critique. *Psychological Bulletin, 107*, 3–33.

Bradbury, T. N., & Karney, B. R. (1993). Longitudinal study of marital interaction and dysfunction. *Clinical Psychology Review, 13*, 15–27.

Bradfield, A., & Wells, G. L. (2005). Not the same old hindsight bias: Outcome information distorts a broad range of retrospective judgments. *Memory and Cognition, 33*, 120–130.

Bransford, J. D., & Johnson, M. K. (1973). Considerations of some problems of comprehension. In W. G. Chase (Ed.), *Visual information processing* (pp. 383–438). New York: Academic Press.

Brauer, M., Chambres, P., Niedenthal, P. M., & Chatard-Pannetier, A. (2004). The relationship between expertise and evaluative extremity: The moderating role of experts' task characteristics. *Journal of Personality and Social Psychology, 86*, 5–18.

Breckler, S. J. (1984). Empirical validation of affect, behavior, and cognition as distinct components of attitude. *Journal of Personality and Social Psychology, 47*, 1191–1205.

Brehm, J. W. (1956). Post-decision changes in desirability of alternatives. *Journal of Abnormal and Social Psychology, 52*, 384–389.

Brendl, C. M., Higgins, E. T., & Lemm, K. M. (1995). Sensitivity to varying gains and losses: The role of self-discrepancies and event framing. *Journal of Personality and Social Psychology, 69*, 1028–1051.

Brendl, C. M., Markman, A. B., & Messner, C. (2001). How do indirect measures of evaluation work? Evaluating the inference of prejudice in the implicit association test. *Journal of Personality and Social Psychology, 81*, 760–773.

Brennan, K. A., Clark, C. L., & Shaver, P. R. (1998). Self-report measurement of adult attachment: An integrative overview. In J. A. Simpson & W. S. Rholes (Eds.), *Attachment theory and close relationships* (pp. 46–76). New York: Guilford Press.

Brennan, K. A., & Shaver, P. R. (1993). Attachment styles and parental divorce. *Journal of Divorce and Remarriage, 21*, 161–175.

Brewer, M. B. (1979). In-group bias in the minimal intergroup situation: A cognitive-motivational analysis. *Psychological Bulletin, 86*, 307–324.

Brewer, M. B. (1988). A dual process model of impression formation. In T. K. Srull & R. S. Wyer (Eds.), *Advances in social cognition.* Hillsdale, NJ: Erlbaum.

Brewer, M. B., & Brown, R. J. (1998). Intergroup relations. In D. T. Gilbert, S. T. Fiske, & G. Lindzey (Eds.), *The handbook of social psychology* (4th ed., Vol. 2, pp. 554–594). New York: McGraw-Hill.

Brewer, M. B., & Gardner, W. (1996). Who is the "we"? Levels of collective identity and self-representations. *Journal of Personality and Social Psychology, 71*, 83–93.

Brewer, M. B., & Miller, N. (1988). Contact and cooperation: When do they work? In P. Katz & D. Taylor (Eds.), *Eliminating racism: Profiles in controversy* (pp. 315–326). New York: Plenum Press.

Brewer, M. B., & Nakamura, G. V. (1984). The nature and functions of schemas. In R. S. Wyer & T. K. Srull (Eds.), *The handbook of social cognition* (Vol. 1). Hillsdale, NJ: Erlbaum.

Briggs, J. L. (1960). *Never in anger: Portrait of an Eskimo family.* Cambridge, MA: Harvard University Press.

Brigham, J. C. (1993). College students' racial attitudes. *Journal of Applied Social Psychology, 23*, 1933–1967.

Brislin, R. W., & Lewis, S. A. (1968). Dating and physical attractiveness: Replication. *Psychological Reports, 22*, 976.

Brockner, J. (1979). The effects of self-esteem, success-failure, and self-consciousness on task performance. *Journal of Personality and Social Psychology, 37*, 1732–1741.

Brockner, J., Guzzi, B., Kane, J., Levine, E., & Shaplen, K. (1984). Organizational fundraising: Further evidence on the effects of legitimizing small donations. *Journal of Consumer Research, 11*, 611–614.

Brown, D. E. (1991). *Human universals.* New York: McGraw-Hill.

Brown, J. D. (1998). *The self.* New York: McGraw-Hill.

Brown, J. D., & Dutton, K. A. (1995). The thrill of victory, the complexity of defeat: Self-esteem and people's emotional reactions to success and failure. *Journal of Personality and Social Psychology, 68*, 712–722.

Brown, P., & Levinson, S. C. (1987). *Politeness: Some universals in language usage.* Cambridge, England: Cambridge University Press.

Brown, R. (1986). *Social psychology* (2nd ed.). New York: Free Press.

Brown, R., & Kulik, J. (1977). Flashbulb memories. *Cognition, 5*, 73–99.

Browning, C. R. (1992). *Ordinary men: Reserve police battalion 101 and the final solution in Poland.* New York: Aaron Asher.

Brownstein, A. L. (2003). Biased predecision processing. *Psychological Bulletin, 129,* 545–568.

Brownstein, A., Read, S. J., & Simon, D. (2004). Bias at the race-track: Effects of individual expertise and task importance on predecision reevaluation of alternatives. *Personality and Social Psychology Bulletin, 57,* 904–915.

Brumberg, J. J. (1997). *The body project: An intimate history of American girls.* New York: Random House.

Buck, R. W., & Parke, R. D. (1972). Behavioral and physiological response to the presence of a friendly or neutral person in two types of stressful situations. *Journal of Personality and Social Psychology, 24,* 143–153.

Buehler, R., Griffin, D., & Ross, M. (1994). Exploring the "planning fallacy": Why people underestimate their task completion times. *Journal of Personality and Social Psychology, 67,* 366–381.

Bugental, D. B., & Lewis, J. C. (1999). The paradoxical misuse of power by those who see themselves as powerless: How does it happen? *Journal of Social Issues, 55,* 51–64.

Burger, J. M. (1981). Motivational biases in the attribution of responsibility for an accident: A meta-analysis of the defensive-attribution hypothesis. *Psychological Bulletin, 90,* 496–512.

Burger, J. M. (1986). Increasing compliance by improving the deal: The that's-not-all technique. *Journal of Personality and Social Psychology, 51,* 277–283.

Burger, J. M. (1999). The foot-in-the-door compliance procedure: A multiple process analysis and review. *Personality and Social Psychology Review, 3,* 303–325.

Burger, J. M. (2009). Replicating Milgram: Would people still obey today? *American Psychologist, 64,* 1–11.

Burger, J. M., & Guadagno, R. E. (2003). Self-concept clarity and the foot-in-the-door procedure. *Basic and Applied Social Psychology, 25,* 79–86.

Burger, J. M., Reed, M., DeCesare, K., Rauner, S., & Rozolis, J. (1999). The effects of initial request size on compliance: More about the that's-not-all technique. *Basic and Applied Social Psychology, 21,* 243–249.

Burgess, E. W., & Wallin, P. (1953). *Engagement and marriage.* Philadelphia: Lippincott.

Burkhart, K. (1973). *Women in prison.* Garden City, NY: Doubleday.

Burnstein, E. (2005). Kin altruism: The morality of biological systems. In D. M. Buss (Ed.), *The handbook of evolutionary psychology* (pp. 528–551). New York: Wiley.

Burnstein, E., Crandall, C., & Kitayama, S. (1994). Some neo-Darwinian decision rules for altruism: Weighing cues for inclusive fitness as a function of the biological importance of the decision. *Journal of Personality and Social Psychology, 67,* 773–789.

Burnstein, E., & Vinokur, A. (1973). Testing two classes of theories about group induced shifts in individual choice. *Journal of Experimental Social Psychology, 9,* 123–137.

Burnstein, E., Vinokur, A., & Trope, Y. (1973). Interpersonal comparison versus persuasive argumentation: A more direct test of alternative explanations for group-induced shifts in individual choice. *Journal of Experimental Social Psychology, 9,* 236–245.

Buss, D. M. (1984). Toward a psychology of person-environment (PE) correlation: The role of spouse selection. *Journal of Personality and Social Psychology, 47,* 361–377.

Buss, D. M. (1989). Sex differences in human mate preference: Evolutionary hypothesis tested in 37 cultures. *Behavioral and Brain Sciences, 12,* 1–49.

Buss, D. (1992). Mate preference mechanisms: Consequences for partner choice and intrasexual competition. In J. H. Barkow, L. Cosmides, & J. Tooby (Eds.), *The adapted mind* (pp. 267–288). New York: Oxford University Press.

Buss, D. M. (1994a). *The evolution of desire: Strategies of human mating.* New York: Basic Books.

Buss, D. M. (1994b). The strategies of human mating. *American Scientist, 82,* 238–249.

Byrne, D. (1961). Interpersonal attraction and attitude similarity. *Journal of Abnormal and Social Psychology, 62,* 713–715.

Byrne, D., Clore, G. L., & Smeaton, G. (1986). The attraction hypothesis: Do similar attitudes predict anything? *Journal of Personality and Social Psychology, 51,* 1167–1170.

Byrne, D., Griffitt, W., & Stefaniak, D. (1967). Attraction and similarity of personality characteristics. *Journal of Personality and Social Psychology, 5,* 82–90.

Byrne, D., & Nelson, D. (1965). Attraction as a linear function of proportion of positive reinforcements. *Journal of Abnormal and Social Psychology, 1,* 659–663.

Cacioppo, J. T., & Berntson, G. G. (1994). Relationship between attitudes and evaluative space: A critical review with emphasis on the separability of positive and negative substrates. *Psychological Bulletin, 115,* 401–423.

Cacioppo, J. T., & Gardner, W. L. (1999). Emotion. *Annual Review of Psychology, 50,* 191–214.

Cacioppo, J. T., Klein, D. J., Berntson, G. G., & Hatfield, E. T. (1993). The psychophysiology of emotion. In M. Lewis & J. M. Haviland (Eds.), *Handbook of emotions* (pp. 119–142). New York: Guilford Press.

Cacioppo, J. T., Petty, R. E., Feinstein, J., & Jarvis, B. (1996). Individual differences in cognitive motivation: The life and times of people varying in need for cognition. *Psychological Bulletin, 119,* 197–253.

Cacioppo, J. T., Petty, R. E., & Morris, K. J. (1983). Effects of need for cognition on message evaluation, recall, and persuasion. *Journal of Personality and Social Psychology, 45,* 805–818.

Cacioppo, J. T., Petty, R. E., & Sidera, J. (1982). The effects of salient self-schema on the evaluation of proattitudinal editorials: Top-down versus bottom-up message processing. *Journal of Experimental Social Psychology, 18,* 324–338.

Cacioppo, J. T., Priester, J. R., & Berntson, G. G. (1993). Rudimentary determinants of attitude. II. Arm flexion and extension have differential effects on attitudes. *Journal of Personality and Social Psychology, 65,* 5–17.

Cadinu, M., Maass, A., Rosabianca, A., & Kiesner, J. (2005). Why do women underperform under stereotype threat? Evidence for the role of negative thinking. *Psychological Science, 16,* 572–578.

Campbell, D. T. (1975). On the conflicts between biological and social evolution and between psychology and moral tradition. *American Psychologist, 30,* 1103–1126.

Campbell, J. D., & Fairey, P. J. (1989). Informational and normative routes to conformity: The effect of faction size as a function of norm extremity and attention to the stimulus. *Journal of Personality and Social Psychology, 57,* 457–468.

Carli, L. L. (1999). Cognitive reconstruction, hindsight, and reactions to victims and perpetrators. *Personality and Social Psychology Bulletin, 25,* 966–979.

Carlsmith, J. M., & Gross, A. E. (1969). Some effects of guilt on compliance. *Journal of Personality and Social Psychology, 11,* 232–239.

Carlson, J. A., & Davis, C. M. (1971). Cultural values and the risky shift: A cross-cultural test in Uganda and the United States. *Journal of Personality and Social Psychology, 20*, 236–245.

Carlson, M., Charlin, V., & Miller, N. (1988). Positive mood and helping behavior: A test of six hypotheses. *Journal of Personality and Social Psychology, 55*, 211–229.

Carlston, D. E., & Skowronski, J. J. (1994). Savings in the relearning of trait information as evidence for spontaneous inference generation. *Journal of Personality and Social Psychology, 66*, 840–880.

Carnevale, P. J., & Isen, A. M. (1986). The influence of positive affect and visual access on the discovery of integrative solutions in bilateral negotiation. *Organizational Behavior and Human Decision Processes, 37*, 1–13.

Carter, C. S. (1998). Neuroendocrine perspectives on social attachment and love. *Psychoneuroendocrinology, 23*(8), 779–818.

Carter, J., & Irons, M. (1991). Are economists different, and if so, why? *Journal of Economic Perspectives, 5*, 171–177.

Cartwright, D., & Zander, A. (1968). *Group dynamics: Research and theory.* New York: Harper & Row.

Carver, C. S. (1974). Facilitation of physical aggression through objective self-awareness. *Journal of Experimental Social Psychology, 10*, 365–370.

Carver, C. S., DeGregorio, E., & Gillis, R. (1980). Ego-defensive attribution among two categories of observers. *Personality and Social Psychology Bulletin, 6*, 4–50.

Carver, C. S., & Scheier, M. F. (1981). The self-attention-induced feedback loop and social facilitation. *Journal of Experimental Social Psychology, 17*, 545–568.

Carver, C. S., & Scheier, M. F. (1982). Control theory: A useful conceptual framework for personality-social, clinical, and health psychology. *Psychological Bulletin, 92*, 111–135.

Cash, T. F., & Duncan, N. C. (1984). Physical attractiveness stereotyping among black American college students. *Journal of Social Psychology, 122*, 71–77.

Cash, T. F., & Kilcullen, R. N. (1985). The eye of the beholder: Susceptibility to sexism and beautyism in the evaluation of managerial applicants. *Journal of Applied Social Psychology, 15*, 591–605.

Cash, T. F., & Trimer, C. A. (1984). Sexism and beautyism in women's evaluations of peer performance. *Sex Roles, 10*, 87–98.

Caspi, A., Elder, G. H., Jr., & Bem, D. J. (1987). Moving against the world: Life-course patterns of explosive children. *Developmental Psychology, 23*(2), 308–313.

Caspi, A., Elder, G. H., Jr., & Bem, D. J. (1988). Moving away from the world: Life-course patterns of shy children. *Developmental Psychology, 24*, 824–831.

Caspi, A., & Herbener, E.S. (1990). Continuity and change: Assortative marriage and the consistency of personality in adulthood. *Journal of Personality and Social Psychology, 58*, 250–258.

Caspi, A., McClay, J., Moffitt, T. E., Mill, J., Martin, J., Craig, I. W., et al. (2002). Role of genotype in the cycle of violence in maltreated children. *Science, 297*, 851–854.

Caspi, A., & Roberts, B. W. (2001). Personality development across the life course: The argument for change and continuity. *Psychological Inquiry, 12*, 49–66.

Cate, R. M., Lloyd, S. A., Henton, J. M., & Larson, J. H. (1982). Fairness and reward level as predictors of relationship satisfaction. *Social Psychology Quarterly, 45*, 177–181.

Center for Media and Public Affairs. (July-August 2000). The media at the millennium: The networks' top topics, trends, and joke targets of the 1990s. *Media Monitor, 14*, 1–6.

Cesario, J., Plaks, J. E., & Higgins, E. T. (2006). Automatic social behavior as motivated preparation to interact. *Journal of Personality and Social Psychology, 90*, 893–910.

Chagnon, N. (1997). *Yanamamo.* New York: Harcourt, Brace, Jovanovich.

Chaiken, S. (1980). Heuristic versus systematic information processing in the use of source versus message cues in persuasion. *Journal of Personality and Social Psychology, 39*, 752–766.

Chaiken, S., & Baldwin, M. W. (1981). Affective-cognitive consistency and the effect of salient behavioral information on the self-perception of attitudes. *Journal of Personality and Social Psychology, 41*, 1–12.

Chaiken, S., & Eagly, A. H. (1976). Communication modality as a determinant of persuasion: The role of communicator salience. *Journal of Personality and Social Psychology, 45*, 241–256.

Chaiken, S., Liberman, A., & Eagly, A. H. (1989). Heuristic and systematic processing within and beyond the persuasion context. In J. S. Uleman & J. A. Bargh (Eds.), *Unintended thought* (pp. 212–252). New York: Guilford Press.

Chalfonte, B. L., & Johnson, M. K. (1996). Feature memory and binding in young and older adults. *Memory and Cognition, 24*, 403–416.

Chapman, L. J., & Chapman, J. (1967). Genesis of popular but erroneous diagnostic observations. *Journal of Abnormal Psychology, 72*, 193–204.

Chartrand, T. L., & Bargh, J. A. (1999). The chameleon effect: The perception-behavior link and social interaction. *Journal of Personality and Social Psychology, 76*, 893–910.

Chen, C., Boucher, H., & Tapias, M. P. (2006). The relational self revealed: Integrative conceptualization and implications for interpersonal life. *Psychological Bulletin, 132*(2), 151–179.

Chen, C., & Stevenson, H. W. (1995). Motivation and mathematics achievement: A comparative study of Asian-American, Caucasian-American and East Asian high school students. *Child Development, 66*, 1215–1234.

Chen, M., & Bargh, J. A. (1999). Consequences of automatic evaluation: Immediate behavioral predispositions to approach or avoid the stimulus. *Personality and Social Psychology Bulletin, 25*, 215–224.

Chen, S., Lee-Chai, A. Y., & Bargh, J. A. (2001). Relationship orientation as moderator of the effects of social power. *Journal of Personality and Social Psychology, 80*, 183–187.

Chen, S. C. (1937). Social modification of the activity of ants in nest-building. *Physiological Zoology, 10*, 420–436.

Cheng, P. W., & Novick, L.R. (1990). A probabilistic contrast model of causal induction. *Journal of Personality and Social Psychology, 58*, 545–567.

Cheryan, S., & Bodenhausen, G. V. (2000). When positive stereotypes threaten intellectual performance: The psychological hazards of "model minority" status. *Psychological Review, 11*, 399–402.

Cheung, F. M., Leung, K., Zhang, J. X., Sun, H. F., Gan, Y. Q., Song, W. Z., & Dong, X. (2001). Indigenous Chinese personality constructs: Is the five-factor model complete? *Journal of Cross-Cultural Psychology, 32*, 407–433.

Choi, I., & Nisbett, R. E. (1998). Situational salience and cultural differences in the correspondence bias and in the actor-observer bias. *Personality and Social Psychology Bulletin, 24*, 949–960.

Choi, I., Nisbett, R. E., & Norenzayan, A. (1999). Causal attribution across cultures: Variation and universality. *Psychological Bulletin, 125*, 47–63.

Choi, J. N., & Kim, M. U. (1999). The organizational application of groupthink and its limitations in organizations. *Journal of Applied Psychology, 84,* 297–306.

Chomsky, N. (1975). *Reflections on language.* New York: Pantheon.

Chomsky, N. (1988). *Language and problems of knowledge: The Managua lectures.* Cambridge, MA: MIT Press.

Chua, H., Leu, J., & Nisbett, R. E. (2005). Culture and the diverging views of social events. *Personality and Social Psychology Bulletin, 31,* 925–934.

Cialdini, R. B. (1984). *Influence: How and why people agree to things.* New York: Quill.

Cialdini, R. B., Borden, R. J., Thorne, A., Walker, M. R., Freeman, S., & Sloan, L. R. (1976). Basking in reflected glory: Three (football) field studies. *Journal of Personality and Social Psychology, 34,* 366–375.

Cialdini, R. B., Darby, B. L., & Vincent, J. E. (1973). Transgression and altruism: A case for hedonism. *Journal of Experimental Social Psychology, 9,* 502–516.

Cialdini, R. B., & Fultz, J. (1990). Interpreting the negative mood-helping literature via "mega" analysis: A contrarian view. *Psychological Bulletin, 107,* 210–214.

Cialdini, R. B., Kallgren, C. A., & Reno, R. R. (1991). A focus theory of normative conduct: A theoretical refinement and reevaluation of the role of norms in human behavior. In M. P. Zanna (Ed.), *Advances in experimental social psychology* (Vol. 24, pp. 201–234). San Diego, CA: Academic Press.

Cialdini, R. B., & Kenrick, D. T. (1976). Altruism as hedonism: A social development perspective on the relationship of negative mood state and helping. *Journal of Personality and Social Psychology, 34,* 907–914.

Cialdini, R. B., Schaller, M., Houlihan, D., Arps, K., Fultz, J., & Beaman, A. L. (1987). Empathy-based helping: Is it selflessly or selfishly motivated? *Journal of Personality and Social Psychology, 52,* 749–758.

Cialdini, R. B., & Schroeder, D. A. (1976). Increasing compliance by legitimizing paltry contributions: When even a penny helps. *Journal of Personality and Social Psychology, 34,* 599–604.

Cialdini, R. B., & Trost, M. R. (1998). Social influence: Social norms, conformity, and compliance. In D. T. Gilbert, S. T. Fiske, & G. Lindzey (Eds.), *The handbook of social psychology* (4th ed., Vol. 2, pp. 151–192). New York: McGraw-Hill.

Cialdini, R. B., Vincent, J. E., Lewis, S. K., Catalan, J., Wheeler, D., & Darby, B. L. (1975). Reciprocal concessions procedure for inducing compliance: The door-in-the-face technique. *Journal of Personality and Social Psychology, 31,* 206–215.

Ciano, G. (1945). *The Ciano diaries.* Garden City, NY: Doubleday.

Clancy, S. M., & Dollinger, S. J. (1993). Photographic depictions of the self: Gender and age differences in social connectedness. *Sex Roles, 15,* 145–158.

Clark, H. H. (1996). *Using language.* Cambridge: Cambridge University Press.

Clark, M., & Isen, A. M. (1982). Toward understanding the relationship between feeling states and social behavior. In A. H. Hastorf & A. M. Isen (Eds.), *Cognitive Social Psychology* (pp. 73–108). New York: Elsevier.

Clark, M. S. (1984). Record keeping in two types of relationships. *Journal of Personality and Social Psychology, 47,* 549–557.

Clark, M. S. (1992). Research on communal and exchange relationships viewed from a functionalist perspective. In D. A. Owens & M. Wagner (Eds.), *Progress in modern psychology: The legacy of American functionalism* (pp. 241–258). Westport, CT: Praeger.

Clark, M. S., & Mills, J. (1979). Interpersonal attraction in exchange and communal relationships. *Journal of Personality and Social Psychology, 37,* 12–24.

Clark, M. S., & Mills, J. (1993). The difference between communal and exchange relationships: What is and is not. *Personality and Social Psychology Bulletin, 19,* 684–691.

Clark, M. S., Mills, J., & Powell, M. C. (1986). Keeping track of needs in communal and exchange relationships. *Journal of Personality and Social Psychology, 51,* 333–338.

Clark, R., Crockett, W., & Archer, R. (1971). Risk-as-value hypothesis: The relationship between perception of self, others, and the risky shift. *Journal of Personality and Social Psychology, 20,* 425–429.

Clark, R. D. I., & Word, L. E. (1972). Why don't bystanders help? Because of ambiguity? *Journal of Personality and Social Psychology, 24,* 392–400.

Clifford, M. M., & Walster, E. (1973). The effect of physical attractiveness on teacher expectations. *Sociology of Education, 46,* 248–258.

Clore, G. L. (1992). Cognitive phenomenology: Feelings and the construction of judgment. In L. L. Martin & A. Tesser (Eds.), *The construction of social judgments* (pp. 133–163). Hilllsdale, NJ: Erlbaum.

Clore, G. L., & Byrne, D. (1974). A reinforcement-effect model of attraction. In T. L. Huston (Ed.), *Foundations of interpersonal attraction* (pp. 143–170). New York: Academic Press.

Clore, G. L., Gasper, K., & Garvin, E. (2001). Affect as information. In J. P. Forgas (Ed.), *Handbook of affect and social cognition* (pp. 121–144). Mahwah, NJ: Erlbaum.

Clore, G. L., & Gormly, J. B. (1974). Knowing, feeling, and liking: A psychophysical study of attraction. *Journal of Research in Personality, 8,* 218–230.

Clore, G. L., & Parrott, W. G. (1991). Moods and their vicissitudes: The informational properties of affective thoughts and feelings. In J. Forgas (Ed.), *Emotion and social judgments* (pp. 107–123). Elmsford, NY: Pergamon Press.

Coan, J. A., Schaefer, H. S., & Davidson, R. J. (2006). Lending a hand: Social regulation of the neural response to threat. *Psychological Science, 17,* 1032–1039.

Cohen, C. E. (1981). Person categories and social perception: Testing some boundaries of the processing effects of prior knowledge. *Journal of Personality and Social Psychology, 40,* 441–452.

Cohen, D., & Gunz, A. (2002). *As seen by the other…: The self from the "outside in" and the "inside out" in the memories and emotional perceptions of Easterners and Westerners.* Unpublished manuscript, University of Waterloo.

Cohen, D., & Nisbett, R. E. (1997). Field experiments examining the culture of honor: The role of institutions in perpetuating norms about violence. *Personality and Social Psychology Bulletin, 23,* 1188–1199.

Cohen, D., Nisbett, R. E., Bowdle, B., & Schwarz, N. (1996). Insult, aggression, and the Southern culture of honor: An "experimental ethnography." *Journal of Personality and Social Psychology, 70,* 945–960.

Cohen, G., Aronson, J., & Steele, C. M. (2000). When beliefs yield to evidence: Reducing biased evaluation by affirming the self. *Personality and Social Psychology Bulletin, 26,* 1151–1164.

Cohen, G. L., Garcia, J., Apfel, N., & Master, A. (2006). Reducing the racial achievement gap: A social-psychological intervention. *Science, 313*, 1307–1310.

Cohen, G. L., Garcia, J., Purdie-Vaughns, V., Apfel, N., & Brzustoski, P. (2009). Recursive processes in self-affirmation: Intervening to close the minority achievement gap. *Science, 324*, 400–403.

Cohen, S., Alper, C. M., Doyle, W. J., Adler, N., Treanor, J. J., & Turner, R. B. (2008). Objective and subjective socioeconomic status and susceptibility to the common cold. *Health Psychology, 27*(2), 268–274.

Cohen, S., & Herbert, T. B. (1996). Health psychology: Psychological factors and physical disease from the perspective of human psychoneuroimmunology. *Annual Review of Psychology, 47*, 113–142.

Collins, N. L. (1996). Working models of attachment: Implications for explanation, emotion, and behavior. *Journal of Personality and Social Psychology, 71*, 810–832.

Collins, N. L., & Feeney, B. C. (2000). A safe haven: An attachment theory perspective on support seeking and caregiving in intimate relationships. *Journal of Personality and Social Psychology, 78*, 1053–1073.

Collins, N. L., & Miller, L. C. (1994). Self-disclosure and liking: A meta-analytic review. *Psychological Bulletin, 116*, 457–475.

Collins, N. L., & Read, S. J. (1994). Cognitive representations of attachment: The structure and function of working models. In K. Bartholomew & D. Perlman (Eds.), *Attachment processes in adulthood: Advances in personal relationships* (Vol. 5, pp. 53–90). London: Kingsley.

Collins, R. L., Taylor, S. E., Wood, J. V., & Thompson, S. C. (1988). The vividness effect: Elusive or illusory? *Journal of Experimental Social Psychology, 24*, 1–18.

Columbus, C. (1492/1990). *Journal of the first voyage*. Warmister, England: Aris and Phillips Ltd.

Colvin, C. R., & Block, J. (1994). Do positive illusions foster mental health? An examination of the Taylor and Brown formulation. *Psychological Bulletin, 116*, 3–20.

Colvin, C. R., Block, J., & Funder, D. C. (1995). Overly positive self-evaluations and personality: Negative implications for mental health. *Journal of Personality and Social Psychology, 68*, 1152–1162.

Condon, J. W., & Crano, W. D. (1988). Inferred evaluation and the relation between attitude and interpersonal attraction. *Journal of Personality and Social Psychology, 54*, 789–797.

Connolly, K. (1968). The social facilitation of preening behavior of Drosophila melanogaster. *Animal Behavior, 16*, 385–391.

Conway, L. G., & Schaller, M. (2002). On the verifiability of evolutionary psychological theories. *Personality and Social Psychology, 6*, 152–166.

Conway, M., & Ross, M. (1984). Getting what you want by revising what you had. *Journal of Personality and Social Psychology, 47*, 738–748.

Cooley, C. H. (1902). *Human nature and the social order*. New York: Charles Scribner's Sons.

Coontz, S. (2005). *Marriage, a History*. New York: Viking Press.

Cooper, J. (1971). Personal responsibility and dissonance: The role and foreseen consequences. *Journal of Personality and Social Psychology, 18*, 354–363.

Cooper, J., & Worchel, S. (1970). Role of undesired consequences in arousing cognitive dissonance. *Journal of Personality and Social Psychology, 16*, 199–206.

Cooper, J., Zanna, M. P., & Taves, T. A. (1978). Arousal as a necessary condition for attitude change following induced compliance. *Journal of Personality and Social Psychology, 36*, 1101–1106.

Cooper, M. L., Shaver, P., & Collins, N. L. (1998). Attachment styles, emotion regulation, and adjustment in adolescence. *Journal of Personality and Social Psychology, 74*, 1380–1397.

Coriell, M., & Adler, N. E. (2001). Social ordering and health. In B.S. McEwen (volume editor) and H. M. Goodman (section editor). *Handbook of physiology. Section 7: the endocrine system*, pp. 533–546. New York: American Physiological Society and Oxford University Press.

Correll, J., & Park, B. (2005). A model of the ingroup as a social resource. *Personality and Social Psychology Review, 9*, 341–359.

Correll, J., Park, B., Judd, C. M., & Wittenbrink, B. (2002). The police officer's dilemma: Using ethnicity to disambiguate potentially threatening individuals. *Journal of Personality and Social Psychology, 83*, 1314–1329.

Correll, J., Urland, G. R., & Ito, T. A. (2006). Event-related potentials and the decision to shoot: The role of threat perception and cognitive control. *Journal of Experimental Social Psychology, 42*, 120–128.

Cortes, B. P., Demoulin, S., Rodriguez, R. T., Rodriguez, A. P., & Leyens, J. P. (2005). Infrahumanization or familiarity? Attribution of uniquely human emotions to the self, the ingroup, and the outgroup. *Personality and Social Psychology Bulletin, 32*(2), 243–253.

Costa, P. T., & McCrae, R. R. (1995). Domains and facets: Hierarchical personality assessment using the Revised NEO Personality Inventory. *Journal of Personality Assessment, 64*, 21–50.

Cota, A. A., & Dion, K. L. (1986). Salience of gender and sex composition of ad hoc groups: An experimental test of the distinctiveness theory. *Journal of Personality and Social Psychology, 50*, 770–776.

Côté, S., & Miners, C. T. H. (2006). Emotional intelligence, cognitive intelligence, and job performance. *Administrative Science Quarterly, 51*, 1–28.

Cotterell, N., Eisenberger, R., & Speicher, H. (1992). Inhibiting effects of reciprocation wariness on interpersonal relationships. *Journal of Personality and Social Psychology, 62*, 658–668.

Cottrell, N. B., Wack, D. L., Sekerak, G. J., & Rittle, R. H. (1968). Social facilitation of dominant responses by the presence of an audience and the mere presence of others. *Journal of Personality and Social Psychology, 9*, 245–250.

Cousins, S. D. (1989). Culture and self-perception in Japan and the United States. *Journal of Personality and Social Psychology, 56*, 124–131.

Crandall, C. S. (1988). Social contagion of binge eating. *Journal of Personality and Social Psychology, 55*, 588–598.

Crandall, C. S., & Eshleman, A. (2003). A justification-suppression model of the expression and experience of prejudice. *Psychological Bulletin, 129*, 414–446.

Crandall, V. C., Katkovsky, W., & Crandall, V. J. (1965). Children's beliefs in their own control of reinforcements in intellectual-academic achievement situations. *Child Development. 36*, 91–109.

Crano, W. D. (1970). Effects of sex, response order, and expertise in conformity: A dispositional approach. *Sociometry, 33*, 239–252.

Crocker, J. (1982). Biased questions in judgment of covariation studies. *Personality and Social Psychology Bulletin, 8*, 214–220.

Crocker, J., Hannah, D. B., & Weber, R. (1983). Person memory and causal attributions. *Journal of Personality and Social Psychology, 44*, 55–66.

Crocker, J., & Luhtanen, R. (1990). Collective self-esteem and ingroup bias. *Journal of Personality and Social Psychology, 58*, 60–67.

Crocker, J., Luhtanen, R. K., Cooper, M. L., & Bouvrette, A. (2003). Contingencies of self-worth in college students: Theory and measurement. *Journal of Personality and Social Psychology, 85*, 894–908.

Crocker, J., Major, B., & Steele, C. (1998). Social stigma. In D. T. Gilbert, S. T. Fiske, & G. Lindzey (Eds.), *The handbook of social psychology* (4th ed., Vol. 2, pp. 504–553). New York: McGraw-Hill.

Crocker, J., & Park, L. E. (2003). Seeking self-esteem: Construction, maintenance, and protection of self-worth. In M. R. Leary & J. P. Tangney (Eds.), *Handbook of self and identity* (pp. 291–313). New York: Guilford Press.

Crocker, J., & Park, L. E. (2004). The costly pursuit of self-esteem. *Psychological Bulletin, 130,* 392–414.

Crocker, J., Sommers, S. R., & Luhtanen, R. K. (2002). Hopes dashed and dreams fulfilled: Contingencies of self-worth and graduate school admissions. *Personality and Social Psychology Bulletin, 28,* 1275–1286.

Crocker, J., Voelkl, K., Testa, M., & Major, B. (1991). Social stigma: The affective consequences of attributional ambiguity. *Journal of Personality and Social Psychology, 60,* 218–228.

Crocker, J., & Wolfe, C. T. (2001). Contingencies of self-worth. *Psychological Review, 108,* 593–623.

Cross, H. A., Halcomb, C. G., & Matter, W. W. (1967). Imprinting or exposure learning in rats given early auditory stimulation. *Psychonomic Science, 7,* 233–234.

Cross, J. F., & Cross, J. (1971). Age, sex, race, and the perception of facial beauty. *Developmental Psychology, 5,* 433–459.

Cross, S. E., & Madson, L. (1997). Models of the self: Self-construals and gender. *Psychological Bulletin, 122,* 5–37.

Cross, S., & Markus, H. (1991). Possible selves across the life span. *Human Development, 34,* 230–255.

Croyle, R. T., & Cooper, J. (1983). Dissonance arousal: Physiological evidence. *Journal of Personality and Social Psychology, 45,* 782–791.

Cunningham, M. R., Roberts, A. R., Barbee, A. P., Druen, P. B., & Wu, C. (1995). "Their ideas of beauty are, on the whole, the same as ours": Consistency and variability in the cross-cultural perception of female physical attractiveness. *Journal of Personality and Social Psychology, 68,* 261–279.

Cunningham, W. A., Johnson, M. K., Raye, C. L., Gatenby, J. C., Gore, J. C., & Banaji, M. R. (2004). Separable neural components in the processing of black and white faces. *Psychological Science, 15,* 806–813.

Curran, J. P., & Lippold, S. (1975). The effects of physical attractiveness and attitude similarity on attraction in dating dyads. *Journal of Personality, 43,* 528–539.

Curry, R. L. (1988). Influence of kinship on helping behavior in Galapagos mockingbirds. *Behavioral Ecology and Sociobiology, 38,* 181–192.

Curtis, R., & Miller, K. (1986). Believing another likes or dislikes you: Behaviors making the beliefs come true. *Journal of Personality and Social Psychology, 51,* 284–290.

Cutrona, C. E. (1982). Transition to college: Loneliness and the process of social adjustment. In L. A. Peplau & D. Perlman (Eds.), *Loneliness: A sourcebook of current theory, research, and therapy* (pp. 291–309). New York: Wiley.

Dabbs, J. M., Jr. (2000). *Heroes, rogues and lovers.* New York: McGraw-Hill.

Daly, M., Salmon, C., & Wilson, M. (1997). The conceptual hole in psychological studies of social cognition and close relationships. In J. A. Simpson & D. T. Kenrick (Eds.), *Evolutionary social psychology* (pp. 265–296). Hillsdale, NJ: Erlbaum.

Daly, M., & Wilson, M. I. (1982). Whom are newborn babies said to resemble? *Ethology and Sociobiology, 3,* 69–78.

Daly, M., & Wilson, M. (1988). *Homicide.* New York: De Gruyter.

Daly, M., & Wilson, M. I. (1996). Violence against stepchildren. *Current Directions in Psychological Science, 5,* 77–81.

Daly, M., Wilson, M., & Vasdev, S. (2001). Income inequality and homicide rates in Canada and the United States. *Canadian Journal of Criminology,* 219–236.

Damasio, A. R. (1994). *Descartes' error: Emotion, reason, and the human brain.* New York: Free Press.

Danner, D., Snowdon, D., & Friesen, W. (2001). Positive emotions in early life and longevity: Findings from the nun study. *Journal of Personality and Social Psychology, 80,* 804–813.

Darley, J. M., & Batson, C. D. (1973). From Jerusalem to Jericho: A study of situational and dispositional variables in helping behavior. *Journal of Personality and Social Psychology, 27,* 100–119.

Darley, J. M., & Berscheid, E. (1967). Increased liking as a result of the anticipation of personal contact. *Human Relations, 20,* 29–40.

Darley, J. M., & Latané, B. (1968). Bystander intervention in emergencies: Diffusion of responsibility. *Journal of Personality and Social Psychology, 8,* 377–383.

Darley, J. M., Teger, A. I., & Lewis, L. D. (1973). Do groups always inhibit individuals' responses to potential emergencies? *Journal of Personality and Social Psychology, 26,* 395–399.

Darlington, R. B., & Macker, C. E. (1966). Displacement of guilt-produced altruistic behavior. *Journal of Personality and Social Psychology, 4,* 442–443.

Darwin, C. (1871). *The descent of man, and selection in relation to sex.* London: John Murray.

Darwin, C. (1872/1998). *The expression of emotions in man and animals* (3rd ed.). New York: Oxford University Press.

Dashiell, J. F. (1930). An experimental analysis of some group effects. *Journal of Abnormal and Social Psychology, 25,* 190–199.

Davidson, A. R., & Jaccard, J. J. (1979). Variables that moderate the attitude-behavior relation: Results of a longitudinal survey. *Journal of Personality and Social Psychology, 37,* 1364–1376.

Davidson, A. R., Yantis, S., Norwood, M., & Montano, D. E. (1985). Amount of information about the attitude object and attitude-behavior consistency. *Journal of Personality and Social Psychology, 49,* 1184–1198.

Davidson, R. J., Kabat-Zinn, J., Schumacher, J., Rosenkranz, M., Muller, D., Santorelli, S.F., et al. (2003). Alterations in brain and immune function produced by mindfulness meditation. *Psychosomatic Medicine, 65,* 564–570.

Davidson, R. J., Pizzagalli, D., Nitzschke, J. B., & Kalin, N. H. (2003). Parsing the subcomponents of emotion and disorders: Perspectives from affective neuroscience. In R. J. Davidson, K. Scherer, & H. H. Goldsmith (Eds.), *Handbook of affective science* (pp. 8–24). New York: Oxford University Press.

Davis, D. (1981). Implications for interaction versus effectance as mediators of the similarity-attraction relationship. *Journal of Experimental Social Psychology, 17,* 96–116.

Davis, M. H. (1980). A multidimensional approach to individual differences in empathy. *JSAS Catalog of Selected Documents in Psychology, 10,* 85.

Davis, M. H., & Franzoi, S. L. (1991). Stability and change in adolescent self-consciousness and empathy. *Journal of Research in Personality, 25,* 70–87.

Davis, M. H., & Stephan, W. G. (1980). Attributions for exam performance. *Journal of Applied Social Psychology, 10,* 235–248.

Dawes, R. M. (1980). Social dilemmas. *Annual Review of Psychology, 31,* 169–193.

Dawes, R. M. (1988). *Rational choice in an uncertain world.* San Diego, CA: Harcourt, Brace, Jovanovich.

Dawson, E., Gilovich, T., & Regan, D. T. (2002). Motivated reasoning and performance on the Wason selection task. *Personality and Social Psychology Bulletin, 28*, 1379–1387.

Dearing, J. W., & Rogers, E. M. (1996). *Agenda-setting.* Thousand Oaks, CA: Sage.

Deaux, K., & Emswiller, T. (1974). Explanations of successful performance on sex-linked tasks: What is skill for the male is luck for the female. *Journal of Personality and Social Psychology, 29*, 80–85.

Deaux, K., Reid, A., Mizrahi, K., & Ethier, K. A. (1995). Parameters of social identity. *Journal of Personality and Social Psychology, 68*, 280–291.

Debner, J. A., & Jacoby, L. L. (1994). Unconscious perception: Attention, awareness, and control. *Journal of Experimental Psychology: Learning, Memory and Cognition, 20*, 304–317.

Dechesne, M., Greenberg, J., Arndt, J., & Schimel, J. (2000). Terror management and sports fan affiliation: The effects of mortality salience on fan identification and optimism. *European Journal of Social Psychology, 30*, 813–835.

Dechesne, M., Pyszczynski, T., Arndt, J., Ransom, S., Sheldon, K. M., van Knippenberg, A., et al. (2003). Literal and symbolic immortality: The effect of evidence of literal immortality on self-esteem striving in response to mortality salience. *Journal of Personality and Social Psychology, 84*, 722–737.

Deci, E. L., & Ryan, R. M. (1985). *Intrinsic motivation and self-determination in human behavior.* New York: Plenum Press.

Denes-Raj, V., & Epstein, S. (1994). Conflict between intuitive and rational processing: When people behave against their better judgment. *Journal of Personality and Social Psychology, 66*, 819–829.

DePaulo, B. M., & Friedman, H. S. (1998). Nonverbal communication. In D. T. Gilbert, S. T. Fiske, & G. Lindzey (Eds.), *Handbook of social psychology* (4th ed., Vol. 2, pp. 3–40). New York: McGraw-Hill.

DePaulo, B. M., Lanier, K., & Davis, T. (1983). Detecting the deceit of the motivated liar. *Journal of Personality and Social Psychology, 43*, 1096–1103.

Deppe, R. K., & Harackiewicz, J. M. (1996). Self-handicapping and intrinsic motivation: Buffering intrinsic motivation from the threat of failure. *Journal of Personality and Social Psychology, 70*, 868–876.

DePue, R. A. (1995). Neurobiological factors in personality and depression. *European Journal of Personality, 9*, 413–439.

Dermer, M., & Theil, D. (1975). When beauty may fail. *Journal of Personality and Social Psychology, 31*, 1168–1177.

DeSteno, D., Dasgupta, N., Bartlett, M. Y., & Cajdric, A. (2004). Prejudice from thin air: The effect of emotion on automatic intergroup attitudes. *Psychological Science, 15*, 319–324.

DeSteno, D., Petty, R., Wegener, D., & Rucker, D. (2000). Beyond valence in the perception of likelihood: The role of emotion specificity. *Journal of Personality and Social Psychology, 78*, 397–416.

DeSteno, D. A., & Salovey, P. (1996). Jealousy and the characteristics of one's rival: A self-evaluation maintenance perspective. *Personality and Social Psychology, 22*, 920–932.

Deutsch, M., & Gerard, H. B. (1955). A study of normative and informational social influence upon individual judgment. *Journal of Abnormal and Social Psychology, 51*, 629–636.

Deutsch, R. M. (1977). *The new nuts among the berries: How nutrition nonsense captured America.* Palo Alto, CA: Ball Publishing.

Devine, P. G. (1989a). Automatic and controlled processes in prejudice: The roles of stereotypes and personal beliefs. In A. R. Pratkanis, S. J. Breckler, & A. G. Greenwald (Eds.), *Attitude structure and function.* Hillsdale, NJ: Erlbaum.

Devine, P. G. (1989b). Stereotypes and prejudice: Their automatic and controlled components. *Journal of Personality and Social Psychology, 56*, 5–18.

Devine, P. G., & Baker, S. M. (1991). Measurement of racial stereotype subtyping. *Personality and Social Psychology Bulletin, 17*, 44–50.

Devine, P. G., & Monteith, M. J. (1999). Automaticity and control in stereotyping. In S. Chaiken & Y. Trope (Eds.), *Dual process theories in social psychology* (pp. 339–360). New York: Guilford Press.

Devine, P. G., Monteith, M. J., Zuwerink, J. R., & Elliot, A. J. (1991). Prejudice with and without compunction. *Journal of Personality and Social Psychology, 60*, 817–830.

Devine, P. G., Plant, E. A., Amodio, D. M., Harmon-Jones, E., & Vance, S. L. (2002). Exploring the relationship between implicit and explicit prejudice: The role of motivations to respond without prejudice. *Journal of Personality and Social Psychology, 82*, 835–848.

de Waal, F. B. M. (1986). The integration of dominance and social bonding in primates. *Quarterly Review of Biology, 61*, 459–479.

de Waal, F. B. M. (1996). *Good natured: The origins of right and wrong in humans and other animals.* Cambridge, MA: Harvard University Press.

Dhawan, N., Roseman, I. J., Naidu, R. K., Thapa, K., & Rettek, S. I. (1995). Self-concepts across two cultures: India and the United States. *Journal of Cross-Cultural Psychology, 26*, 606–621.

Diamond, L. M. (2003). What does sexual orientation orient? A biobehavioral model distinguishing romantic love and sexual desire. *Psychological Review, 110*, 173–192.

Dickerson, S. S. & Kemeny, M. E. (2004). Acute stressors and cortisol responses: A theoretical integration and synthesis of laboratory research. *Psychological Bulletin, 130*, 355–391.

Diener, E. (1980). Deindividuation: The absence of self-awareness and self-regulation in group members. In P. Paulus (Ed.), *The psychology of group influence* (pp. 209–242). Hillsdale, NJ: Erlbaum.

Diener, E. (2000). Subjective well-being: The science of happiness, and some policy implications. *American Psychologist, 55*, 34–43.

Diener, E., Fraser, S. C., Beaman, A. L., & Kelem, R. T. (1976). Effects of deindividuation variables on stealing among Halloween trick-or-treaters. *Journal of Personality and Social Psychology, 33*, 178–183.

Diener, E., & Wallbom, M. (1976). Effects of self-awareness on antinormative behavior. *Journal of Research in Personality, 10*, 107–111.

Diener, E., Wolsic, B., & Fujita, F. (1995). Physical attractiveness and subjective well-being. *Journal of Personality and Social Psychology, 69*, 207–213.

Dienstbier, R. A., & Munter, P. O. (1971). Cheating as a function of the labeling of natural arousal. *Journal of Personality and Social Psychology, 17*, 208–213.

Dijksterhuis, A., & Aarts, H. (2003). On wildebeests and humans: The preferential detection of negative stimuli. *Psychological Science, 14*, 14–18.

Dijksterhuis, A., Aarts, H., Bargh, J. A., & van Knippenberg, A. (2000). On the relation between associative strength and automatic behavior. *Journal of Experimental Social Psychology, 36*, 531–544.

Dijksterhuis, A., Aarts, H., & Smith, P. K. (2005). The power of the subliminal: On subliminal persuasion and other potential applications. In R. R. Hassin, J. S. Uleman, & J. A. Bargh (Eds.), *The new unconscious.* New York: Oxford University Press.

Dijksterhuis, A., Spears, R., Postmes, T., Stapel, D. A., Koomen, W., van Knippenberg, A., et al. (1998). Seeing one thing and doing another: Contrast effects in automatic behavior. *Journal of Personality and Social Psychology, 75,* 862–871.

Dijksterhuis, A., & van Knippenberg, A. (1998). The relation between perception and behavior, or how to win a game of Trivial Pursuit. *Journal of Personality and Social Psychology, 74,* 865–877.

Dimberg, U., & Öhman, A. (1996). Behold the wrath: Psychophysiological responses to facial stimuli. *Motivation and Emotion, 20,* 149–182.

Dion, K. K. (1972). Physical attractiveness and evaluation of children's transgressions. *Journal of Personality and Social Psychology, 24,* 207–213.

Dion, K. K. (1973). Young children's stereotyping of facial attractiveness. *Developmental Psychology, 9,* 183–188.

Dion, K. K., & Berscheid, E. (1974). Physical attractiveness and peer perception among children. *Sociometry, 37,* 1–12.

Dion, K. K., Berscheid, E., & Walster, E. (1972). What is a beautiful good? *Journal of Personality and Social Psychology, 24,* 285–290.

Dion, K. K., & Dion, K. L. (1993). Individualistic and collectivistic perspectives on gender and the cultural context of love and intimacy. *Journal of Social Issues, 49,* 53–69.

Ditto, P. H., Jemmott, J. B., & Darley, J. M. (1988). Appraising the threat of illness: A mental representational approach. *Health Psychology, 7,* 183–200.

Ditto, P. H., & Lopez, D. F. (1992). Motivated skepticism: Use of differential decision criteria for preferred and nonpreferred conclusions. *Journal of Personality and Social Psychology, 63,* 568–584.

Dodge, K. A., & Schwartz, D. (1997). Social information mechanisms in aggressive behavior. In D. M. Stoff & J. Breiling (Eds.), *Handbook of antisocial behavior* (pp. 171–180). New York: Wiley.

Dollard, J., Doob, L. W., Miller, N. E., Mowrer, H. H., & Sears, R. R. (1939). *Frustration and aggression.* New Haven: Yale University Press.

Domhoff, G. W. (1998). *Who rules America?* Mountain View, CA: Mayfield Publishing.

Donnellan, M. B., Trzesniewski, K. H., Robins, R. W., Moffitt, T. E., & Caspi, A. (2005). Low self-esteem is related to aggression, antisocial behavior, and delinquency. *Psychological Science, 16,* 328–335.

Donnerstein, E. (1980). Aggressive erotica and violence against women. *Journal of Personality and Social Psychology, 39,* 269–277.

Donnerstein, E., & Berkowitz, L. (1981). Victim reactions in aggressive erotic films as a factor in violence against women. *Journal of Personality and Social Psychology, 41,* 710–724.

Doob, A. N., & MacDonald, G. E. (1979). Television and fear of victimization: Is the relationship causal? *Journal of Personality and Social Psychology, 37,* 170–179.

Dovidio, J. F. (1984). Helping behavior and altruism: An empirical and conceptual overview. In L. Berkowitz (Ed.), *Advances in experimental social psychology* (pp. 361–427). New York: Academic Press.

Dovidio, J. F., Brown, C. E., Heltman, K., Ellyson, S. L., & Keating, C. F. (1988). Power displays between women and men in discussions of gender-linked tasks: A multichannel study. *Journal of Personality and Social Psychology, 55,* 580–587.

Dovidio, J. F., Ellyson, S. L., Keating, C. F., Heltman, K., & Brown, C. E. (1988). The relationship of social power to visual displays of dominance between men and women. *Journal of Personality and Social Psychology, 54,* 233–242.

Dovidio, J. F., & Gaertner, S. L. (1981). The effects of race, status, ability on helping behavior. *Social Psychology Quarterly, 44,* 192–203.

Dovidio, J. F., & Gaertner, S. L. (2004). Aversive racism. In M. P. Zanna (Ed.), *Advances in experimental social psychology* (Vol. 36, pp. 1–52). San Diego, CA: Elsevier.

Dovidio, J. F., Kawakami, K., & Gaertner, S. L. (2002). Implicit and explicit prejudice and interracial interaction. *Journal of Personality and Social Psychology, 82,* 62–68.

Dovidio, J. F., Smith, J. K. Donella, A. G., & Gaertner, S. L. (1997). Racial attitudes and the death penalty. *Journal of Applied Social Psychology, 27,* 1468–1487.

Dovidio, J. F., ten Vergert, M., Stewart, T. L. Gaertner, S. L., Johnson, J. D., Esses, V. M., et al. (2004). Perspective and prejudice: Antecedents and mediating mechanisms. *Personality and Social Psychology Bulletin, 30,* 1537–1549.

Downey, G., & Feldman, S. (1996). Implications of rejection sensitivity for intimate relationships. *Journal of Personality and Social Psychology, 70,* 1327–1343.

Downey, G., Feldman, S., & Ayduk, O. (2000). Rejection sensitivity and male violence in romantic relationships. *Personal Relationships, 7,* 45–61.

Downey, G., Freitas, A. L., Michaelis, B., & Khouri, H. (1998). The self-fulfilling prophecy in close relationships: Rejection sensitivity and rejection by romantic partners. *Journal of Personality and Social Psychology, 75,* 545–560.

Downing, C. J., Sternberg, R. J., & Ross, B. H. (1985). Multicausal inference: Evaluation of evidence in causally complex situations. *Journal of Experimental Psychology: General, 114,* 239–263.

Downing, J. W., Judd, C. M., & Brauer, M. (1992). Effects of repeated expression of attitudes on attitude extremity. *Journal of Personality and Social Psychology, 63,* 17–29.

Draine, S. C., & Greenwald, A. G. (1998). Replicable unconscious semantic priming. *Journal of Experimental Psychology: General, 127,* 286–303.

Duck, J. M., & Mullin, B. (1995). The perceived impact of the mass media: Reconsidering the third-person effect. *European Journal of Social Psychology, 25,* 77–93.

Duck, S. (1997). *Handbook of personal relationships: Theory, research, and interventions* (2nd ed.). Chichester, England: Wiley.

Duncan, B. L. (1976). Differential social perception and attribution on intergroup violence: Testing the lower limits of stereotyping of blacks. *Journal of Personality and Social Psychology, 34,* 590–598.

Dunn, E. W., Aknin, L., & Norton, M. I. (2008). Spending money on others promotes happiness. *Science, 319,* 1687–1688.

Dunn, J., & Herrera, C. (1997). Conflict resolution with friends, siblings and mothers: A developmental perspective. *Aggressive Behavior, 23,* 343–357.

Dunn, J., & Munn, P. (1985). Becoming a family member: Family conflict and the development of social understanding in the second year. *Child Development, 56,* 480–492.

Dunning, D., & Cohen, G. L. (1992). Egocentric definitions of traits and abilities in social judgment. *Journal of Personality and Social Psychology, 63,* 341–355.

Dunning, D., Meyerowitz, J. A., & Holzberg, A. (1989). Ambiguity and self-evaluation: The role of idiosyncratic trait definitions in self-serving assessments of ability. *Journal of Personality and Social Psychology, 57,* 1082–1090.

Dunning, D., Perie, M., & Story, A. L. (1991). Self-serving prototypes of social categories. *Journal of Personality and Social Psychology, 61,* 957–968.

Dunning, D., & Sherman, D. A. (1997). Stereotypes and tacit inference. *Journal of Personality and Social Psychology, 73,* 459–471.

Dutton, D. G. (2002). The neurobiology of abandonment homicide. *Aggression and Violent Behavior, 7,* 407–421.

Dutton, D. G., & Aron, A. P. (1974). Some evidence for heightened sexual attraction under conditions of high anxiety. *Journal of Personality and Social Psychology, 30,* 510–517.

Duval, T. S., & Lalwani, N. (1999). Objective self-awareness and causal attributions for self-standard discrepancies: Changing self or changing standards of correctness. *Personality and Social Psychology Bulletin, 25,* 1220–1229.

Duval, T. S., & Wicklund, R. A. (1972). *A theory of objective self-awareness.* New York: Academic Press.

Dweck, C. S. (1975). The role of expectations and attributions in the alleviation of learned helplessness. *Journal of Personality and Social Psychology, 31,* 674–685.

Dweck, C. S. (1999). *Self-theories: Their role in motivation, personality and development.* Philadelphia: Taylor and Francis/Psychology Press.

Dweck, C. S., Chiu, C., & Hong, Y. (1995). Implicit theories and their role in judgments and reactions: A world from two perspectives. *Psychological Inquiry, 6,* 267–285.

Dweck, C. S., Davidson, W., Nelson, S., & Enna, B. (1978). Sex differences in learned helplessness: (II) The contingencies of evaluative feedback in the classroom and (III) An experimental analysis. *Developmental Psychology, 14,* 268–276.

Dweck, C. S., Hong, Y.Y., & Chiu, C.Y. (1993). Implicit theories and individual differences in the likelihood and meaning of dispositional inference. *Personality and Social Psychology Bulletin, 19,* 644–656.

Dweck, C. S., & Leggett, E. L. (1988). A social-cognitive approach to motivation and personality. *Psychological Review, 95,* 256–273.

Dweck, C. S., & Reppucci, N. D. (1973). Learned helplessness and reinforcement responsibility in children. *Journal of Personality and Social Psychology, 25,* 109–116.

Eagly, A. H. (1987). *Sex differences in social behavior: A social-role interpretation.* Hillsdale, NJ: Erlbaum.

Eagly, A. H., Ashmore, R. D., Makhijani, M. G., & Longo, L. C. (1991). What is beautiful is good, but … : A meta-analytic review of research on the physical attractiveness stereotype. *Psychological Bulletin, 110,* 109–128.

Eagly, A. H., & Carli, L. L. (1981). Sex of researchers and sex-typed communications as determinants of sex differences in influenceability: A meta-analysis of social influence studies. *Psychological Bulletin, 110,* 109–128.

Eagly, A. H., & Chaiken, S. (1993). *The psychology of attitudes.* Fort Worth, TX: Harcourt Brace.

Eagly, A. H., & Chaiken, S. (1998). Attitude structure and function. In D. T. Gilbert, S. T. Fiske, & G. Lindzey (Eds.), *Handbook of social psychology* (4th ed., Vol. 1, pp. 269–322). New York: McGraw-Hill.

Eagly, A. H., & Chrvala, C. (2006). Sex differences in conformity: Status and gender role interpretations. *Psychology of Women Quarterly, 10,* 203–220.

Eagly, A. H., & Wood, W. (1999). The origins of sex differences in human behavior: Evolved dispositions vs. social roles. *American Psychologist, 54,* 408–423.

Eastwick, P. W., Finkel, E. J., Mochon, D., & Ariely, D. (2007). Selective versus unselective romantic desire: Not all reciprocity is created equal. *Psychological Science, 18,* 317–319.

Ebbesen, E. B., Kjos, G. L., & Konecni, V. (1976). Spatial ecology: Its effects on the choice of friends and enemies. *Journal of Experimental Social Psychology, 12,* 505–518.

Eberhardt, J. L., Davies, P. G., Purdie-Vaughns, V. J., & Johnson, S. L. (2006). Looking deathworthy: Perceived stereotypicality of black defendants predicts capital sentencing outcomes. *Psychological Science, 17,* 383–386.

Eckland, B. (1968). Theories of mate selection. *Social Biology, 15,* 71–84.

Edmans, A., Garcia, D., & Norli, O. (2007). Sports sentiment and stock returns. *Journal of Finance, 62,* 1967–1998.

Efran, M. G. (1974). The effect of physical appearance on judgments of guilt, interpersonal attractiveness, and severity of recommended punishment in a simulated jury task. *Journal of Research in Personality, 8,* 45–54.

Eibach, R. P., Libby, L. K., & Gilovich, T. (2003). When change in the self is mistaken for change in the world. *Journal of Personality and Social Psychology, 84,* 917–931.

Eibl-Eibesfeldt, I. (1989). *Human ethology.* New York: Aldine de Gruyter Press.

Eisenberg, N., Fabes, R. A., Miller, P. A., Fultz, J., Shell, R., Mathy, R. M., et al. (1989). Relation of sympathy and distress to prosocial behavior: A multimethod study. *Journal of Personality and Social Psychology, 57,* 55–66.

Eisenberg, N., & Lennon, R. (1983). Sex differences in empathy and related capacities. *Psychological Bulletin, 94,* 100–131.

Eisenberger, N. I., Lieberman, M. D., & Williams, K. D. (2003). Does rejection hurt? An fMRI study of social exclusion. *Science, 302,* 290–292.

Ekman, P. (1984). Expression and the nature of emotion. In K. Scherer & P. Ekman (Eds.), *Approaches to emotion.* Hillsdale, NJ: Erlbaum.

Ekman, P. (1992). An argument for basic emotions. *Cognition and Emotion, 6,* 169–200.

Ekman, P. (1993). Facial expression and emotion. *American Psychologist, 48,* 384–392.

Ekman, P., & Davidson, R. J. (1993). Voluntary smiling changes regional brain activity. *Psychological Science, 4,* 342–345.

Ekman, P., Davidson, R. J., & Friesen, W. V. (1990). The Duchenne smile: Emotional expression and brain physiology II. *Journal of Personality and Social Psychology, 58,* 342–353.

Ekman, P., & Friesen, W. V. (1969). The repertoire of nonverbal behavior: Categories, origins, usage, and coding. *Semiotica, 1,* 49–98.

Ekman, P., & Friesen, W. V. (1971). Constants across cultures in the face and emotion. *Journal of Personality and Social Psychology, 17,* 124–129.

Ekman, P., Friesen, W. V., & Ellsworth, P. C. (1982a). *Emotion in the human face.* Cambridge, England: Cambridge University Press.

Ekman, P., Friesen, W. V., & Ellsworth, P. C. (1982b). What are the similarities and differences in facial behavior across cultures? In P. Ekman (Ed.), *Emotion in the human face.* Cambridge, England: Cambridge University Press.

Ekman, P., & O'Sullivan, M. (1991). Who can catch a liar? *American Psychologist, 46,* 913–920.

Ekman, P., O'Sullivan, M., Friesen, W. V., & Scherer, K. R. (1991). Face, voice and body in detecting deception. *Journal of Nonverbal Behavior, 15,* 125–135.

Ekman, P., & Rosenberg, E. L. (1997). *What the face reveals.* New York: Oxford University Press.

Ekman, P., Sorenson, E. R., & Friesen, W. V. (1969). Pan cultural elements in facial displays of emotions. *Science, 164,* 86–88.

Elfenbein, H. A., & Ambady, N. (2002). On the universality and cultural specificity of emotion recognition: A meta-analysis. *Psychological Bulletin, 128,* 203–235.

Elfenbein, H. A., & Ambady, N. (2003). Universals and cultural differences in recognizing emotions. *Current Directions in Psychological Science, 12,* 159–164.

Elkin, R. A., & Leippe, M. R. (1986). Physiological arousal, dissonance, and attitude change: Evidence for a dissonance-arousal link and a "don't remind me" effect. *Journal of Personality and Social Psychology, 51,* 55–65.

Elliot, A. J., & Devine, P. G. (1994). On the motivational nature of cognitive dissonance: Dissonance as psychological discomfort. *Journal of Personality and Social Psychology, 67,* 382–394.

Ellis, B. (1992). The evolution of sexual attraction: Evaluative mechanisms in women. In J. H. Barkow, L. Cosmides, & J. Tooby (Eds.), *The adapted mind* (pp. 267–288). New York: Oxford University Press.

Ellis, B. J., & Malamuth, N. M. (2000). Love and anger in romantic relationships: A discrete systems model. *Journal of Personality, 68,* 525–556.

Ellsworth, P. C. (1994). Sense, culture and sensibility. In S. Kitayama & H. R. Markus (Eds.), *Emotion and culture.* Washington, DC: American Psychological Association.

Ellyson, S. L., & Dovidio, J. F. (Eds.). (1985). *Power, dominance, and nonverbal behavior.* New York: Springer-Verlag.

Emlen, S. T. (1997). The evolutionary study of human family systems. *Social Science Information, 36,* 563–589.

Emmons, R. A., McCullough, M. E., & Tsang, J. (2003). Counting blessings versus burdens: An experimental investigation of gratitude and subjective well-being in daily life. *Journal of Personality and Social Psychology, 84,* 377–389.

Epel, E., Epel E. S., Blackburn, E. H., Lin, J., Dhabhar, F. S., Adler, N. E., et al. (2004). Accelerated telomere shortening in response to life stress. *Proceedings of the National Academy of Sciences. 101,* 17312–17315.

Epley, N. (2008, January 31). Rebate psychology. *New York Times,* p. A27.

Epley, N., & Gilovich, T. (2001). Putting adjustment back in the anchoring and adjustment heuristic: Divergent processing of self-generated and experimenter-provided anchors. *Psychological Science, 12,* 391–396.

Epley, N., & Gilovich, T. (2004). Are adjustments insufficient? *Personality and Social Psychology Bulletin, 30,* 447–460.

Epley, N., Mak, D., & Idson, L. (2006). Bonus or rebate?: The impact of income framing on spending and saving. *Journal of Behavioral Decision Making, 19,* 213–227.

Epley, N., Savitsky, K., & Gilovich, T. (2002). Empathy neglect: Reconciling the spotlight effect and the correspondence bias. *Journal of Personality and Social Psychology, 83,* 300–312.

Epstein, S. (1991). Cognitive-experiential self-theory: An integrative theory of personality. In R. Curtis (Ed.), *The self with others: Convergences in psychoanalytic, social, and personality psychology* (pp. 111–137). New York: Guilford Press.

Esser, J. K. (1998). Alive and well after 25 years: A review of groupthink research. *Organizational Behavior and Human Decision Processes, 73,* 116–141.

Esser, J. K., & Lindoerfer, J. S. (1989). Groupthink and the space shuttle *Challenger* accident: Toward a quantitative case analysis. *Journal of Behavioral Decision Making, 2,* 167–177.

Essock-Vitale, S. M., & McGuire, M. T. (1985). Women's lives viewed from an evolutionary perspective II. Patterns of helping. *Ethology and Sociobiology, 6,* 155–173.

Ettinger, R. F., Marino, C. J., Endler, N. S., Geller, S. H., & Natziuk, T. (1971). Effects of agreement and correctness on relative competence and conformity. *Journal of Personality and Social Psychology, 19,* 204–212.

Evans, J. St. B.T. (2007). *Hypothetical thinking: Dual processes in reasoning and judgment.* New York: Psychology Press.

Evans, R. (1980). *The making of social psychology.* New York: Gardner Press.

Eysenck, H. J. (1987). Arousal and personality: The origins of a theory. In J. Strelau & H. J. Eysenck (Eds.), *Personality dimensions and arousal* (pp. 1–13). New York: Plenum Press.

Fallon, A. (1990). Culture in the mirror: Sociocultural determinants of body image. In T. F. Cash & T. Pruzinsky (Eds.), *Body images: Development, deviance, and change* (pp. 80–109). New York: Guilford Press.

Fallon, A. E., & Rozin, P. (1985). Sex differences in perceptions of desirable body shape. *Journal of Abnormal Psychology, 94,* 102–105.

Farber, P. D., Khavari, K. A., & Douglass, F. M., IV. (1980). A factor analytic study of reasons for drinking: Empirical validation of positive and negative reinforcement dimensions. *Journal of Consulting and Clinical Psychology, 48,* 780–781.

Farley, F. (1986, May). The big T in personality. *Psychology Today,* pp. 44–52.

Fazio, R. H. (1995). Attitudes as object-evaluation associations: Determinants, consequences, and correlates of attitude accessibility. In R. E. Petty & J. A. Krosnick (Eds.), *Attitude strength: Antecedents and consequences* (pp. 247–282). Mahway, NJ: Erlbaum.

Fazio, R. H., & Hilden, L. E. (2001). Emotional reactions to a seemingly prejudiced response: The role of automatically-activated racial attitudes and motivation to control prejudiced reactions. *Personality and Social Psychology Bulletin, 27,* 538–549.

Fazio, R. H., Jackson, J. R., Dunton, B. C., & Williams, C. J. (1995). Variability in automatic activation as an unobtrusive measure of racial attitudes: A bona fide pipeline? *Journal of Personality and Social Psychology, 69,* 1013–1027.

Fazio, R. H., & Olson, M. A. (2003). Implicit measures in social cognition research: Their meaning and use. *Annual Review of Psychology, 54,* 297–327.

Fazio, R. H., Sanbonmatsu, D. M., Powell, M. C., & Kardes, F. R. (1986). On the automatic activation of attitudes. *Journal of Personality and Social Psychology, 50,* 229–238.

Fazio, R. H., & Williams, C. J. (1986). Attitude accessibility as a moderator of the attitude-perception and attitude-behavior relations: An investigation of the 1984 presidential election. *Journal of Personality and Social Psychology, 51,* 505–514.

Fazio, R. H., & Zanna, M. P. (1978). Attitudinal qualities relating to the strength of the attitude-behavior relationship. *Journal of Experimental Social Psychology, 14,* 398–408.

Fazio, R. H., Zanna, M., & Cooper, J. (1977). Dissonance and self-perception theory: An integrative view of each theory's proper domain of application. *Journal of Experimental Social Psychology, 13,* 464–479.

Feeney, B. C., & Collins, N. L. (2001). Predictors of caregiving in adult intimate relationships: An attachment theoretical perspective. *Journal of Personality and Social Psychology, 80,* 972–994.

Fehr, B. (1994). Prototype based assessment of laypeoples' views of love. *Personal Relationships, 1,* 309–331.

Fehr, B. (1996). *Friendship processes.* Thousand Oaks, CA: Sage.

Fehr, B., & Russell, J. A. (1991). The concept of love viewed from a prototype perspective. *Journal of Personality & Social Psychology, 60,* 425–438.

Fehr, E., & Schmidt, K. M. (1999). A theory of fairness, competition, and cooperation. *Quarterly Journal of Economics, 114,* 817–868.

Feigenson, N., Park, J., & Salovey, P. (2001). The role of emotions in comparative negligence judgments. *Journal of Applied Social Psychology, 31,* 576–603.

Fein, S., & Spencer, S. (1997). Prejudice as a self-esteem maintenance: Affirming the self through derogating others. *Journal of Personality and Social Psychology, 73,* 31–44.

Feingold, A. (1984). Correlates of physical attractiveness among college students. *Journal of Social Psychology, 122,* 139–140.

Feingold, A. (1990). Gender differences in effects of physical attractiveness on romantic attraction: A comparison across five research paradigms. *Journal of Personality and Social Psychology, 59,* 981–993.

Feingold, A. (1992a). Gender differences in mate selection preferences: A test of the parental investment model. *Psychological Bulletin, 112,* 125–139.

Feingold, A. (1992b). Good looking people are not what we think. *Psychological Bulletin, 111,* 304–341.

Fenigstein, A. (1984). Self-consciousness and the overperception of self as target. *Journal of Personality and Social Psychology, 47,* 860–870.

Fenigstein, A., Scheier, M. F., & Buss, A. H. (1975). Public and private self-consciousness: Assessment and theory. *Journal of Consulting and Clinical Psychology, 43,* 522–527.

Ferguson, M. J. (2008). On becoming ready to pursue a goal you don't know you have: Effects of nonconscious goals on evaluative readiness. *Journal of Personality and Social Psychology, 95,* 1268–1294.

Ferguson, M. J., Bargh, J. A., & Nayak, D. (2005). After-affects: How automatic evaluations influence the interpretation of subsequent, unrelated stimuli. *Journal of Experimental Social Psychology, 41,* 182–191.

Ferguson, M. J., & Hassin, R. R. (2007). On the automatic association between America and aggression in news-watchers. *Personality and Social Psychology Bulletin, 33,* 1632–1647.

Festinger, L. (1954). A theory of social comparison processes. *Human Relations, 7,* 117–140.

Festinger, L. (1957). *A theory of cognitive dissonance.* Stanford, CA: Stanford University Press.

Festinger, L. (1964). *Conflict, decision, and dissonance.* Stanford, CA: Stanford University Press.

Festinger, L., & Carlsmith, J. M. (1959). Cognitive consequences of forced compliance. *Journal of Abnormal and Social Psychology, 47,* 382–389.

Festinger, L., Pepitone, A., & Newcomb, T. (1952). Some consequences of deindividuation in a group. *Journal of Abnormal and Social Psychology, 47,* 382–389.

Festinger, L., Schachter, S., & Back, K. (1950). *Social pressures in informal groups.* Stanford, CA: Stanford University Press.

Fiedler, K. (2000). Illusory correlations: A simple associative algorithm provides a convergent account of seemingly divergent paradigms. *Review of General Psychology, 4,* 25–58.

Fiedler, K. (2001). Affective states trigger processes of assimilation and accommodation. In L. L. Martin & G. L. Clore (Eds.), *Theories of mood and cognition: A user's guidebook.* Mahwah, NJ: Erlbaum.

Fiedler, K., & Freytag, P. (2004). Pseudocontingencies. *Journal of Personality and Social Psychology, 87,* 453–467.

Fiedler, K., Walther, E., & Nickel, S. (1999). Covariation-based attribution: On the ability to assess multiple covariations of an effect. *Personality and Social Psychology Bulletin, 25,* 607–622.

Field, T. (1995). Infants of depressed mothers. *Infant Behavior and Development, 18,* 1–13.

Finch, C. (1975). *The art of Walt Disney.* New York: Abrams.

Fincham, F. D. (1985). Attribution processes in distressed and non-distressed couples: 2. Responsibility for marital problems. *Journal of Abnormal Psychology, 94,* 183–190.

Fincham, F. D. (2003). Marital conflict: Correlates, structure, and context. *Current Directions in Psychological Science, 12,* 23–27.

Fincham, F. D., & Bradbury, T. N. (1993). Marital satisfaction, depression, and attributions: A longitudinal analysis. *Journal of Personality and Social Psychology, 64,* 442–452.

Fincham, F. D., Bradbury, T. N., Arias, I., Byrne, C. A., & Karney, B. R. (1997). Marital violence, marital distress, and attributions. *Journal of Family Psychology, 11,* 367–372.

Finkel, E. J., & Eastwick, P. W. (2008). Speed-dating. *Current Directions in Psychological Science, 17,* 193–197.

Finkel, E. J., Rusbult, C. E., Kumashiro, M., & Hannon, P. A. (2002). Dealing with betrayal in close relationships: Does commitment promote forgiveness? *Journal of Personality and Social Psychology, 82,* 956–974.

Fischhoff, B., Gonzalez, R., Lerner, J. S., & Small, D. A. (2005). Evolving judgments of terror risks: Foresight, hindsight, and emotion. *Journal of Applied Social Psychology, 23,* 124–139.

Fishbein, M., & Ajzen, I. (1975). *Belief, attitude, intention, and behavior: An introduction to theory and research.* Reading, MA: Addison-Wesley.

Fisher, H. (1992). *Anatomy of love.* New York: Fawcett Columbine.

Fisher, H. E., Aron, A.., & Brown, L. L. (2006). Romantic love: A mammalian brain system for mate choice. *Philosophical Transactions of the Royal British Society, 361,* 2173–2186.

Fiske, A. P. (1991a). *Cultural relativity of selfish individualism: Anthropological evidence that humans are inherently sociable.* Beverly Hills: Sage.

Fiske, A. P. (1991b). *Structures of social life: The four elementary forms of human relations.* New York: Free Press.

Fiske, A. P. (1992). The four elementary forms of sociality: Framework for a unified theory of social relations. *Psychological Review, 99,* 689–723.

Fiske, A. P., Kitayama, S., Markus, H. R., & Nisbett, R. E. (1998). The cultural matrix of social psychology. In D. T. Gilbert, S. T. Fiske, & G. Lindzey (Eds.), *Handbook of social psychology* (4th ed., pp. 915–981). New York: McGraw-Hill.

Fiske, S. T. (1993). Controlling other people: The impact of power on stereotyping. *American Psychologist, 48(6),* 621–628.

Fiske, S. T., & Taylor, S. E. (1991). *Social cognition.* New York: McGraw-Hill.

Fivush, R. (1989). Exploring sex differences in the emotional content of mother-child conversations about the past. *Sex Roles, 20,* 675–691.

Fivush, R. (1991). Gender and emotion in mother-child conversations about the past. *Journal of Narrative and Life History, 1,* 325–341.

Fivush, R. (1992). Gender differences in parent-child conversations about past emotions. *Sex Roles, 27,* 683–698.

Fleming, J. H., & Darley, J. M. (1989). Perceiving choice and constraint: The effects of contextual and behavioral cues on attitude attribution. *Journal of Personality and Social Psychology, 56,* 27–40.

Florian, V., Mikulincer, M., & Bucholtz, I. (1995). Effects of adult attachment style on the perception and search for social support. *Journal of Psychology, 126,* 665–676.

Flynn, J. R. (1991). *Asian Americans: Achievement beyond IQ.* Hillsdale, NJ: Erlbaum.

Fong, C. (2001). Social preferences, self-interest, and the demand for redistribution. *Journal of Public Economics, 82,* 225–246.

Fong, G. T., Krantz, D. H., & Nisbett, R. E. (1986). The effects of statistical training on thinking about everyday problems. *Cognitive Psychology, 18*, 253-292.

Ford, C. S., & Beach, F. A. (1951). *Patterns of sexual behavior.* New York: Harper & Row.

Ford, T. E., & Kruglanski, A. (1995). Effects of epistemic motivations on the use of momentarily accessible constructs in social judgment. *Personality and Social Psychology Bulletin, 21*, 950–962.

Forgas, J. P. (1992). Mood and the perception of unusual people: Affective asymmetry in memory and social judgments. *European Journal of Social Psychology, 22*, 531–547.

Forgas, J. P. (1995). Mood and judgment: The affect infusion model (AIM). *Psychological Bulletin, 117*(1), 39–66.

Forgas, J. P. (1998a). Asking nicely? Mood effects on responding to more or less polite requests. *Personality and Social Psychology Bulletin, 24*, 173–185.

Forgas, J. P. (1998b). On being happy and mistaken: Mood effects on the fundamental attribution error. *Journal of Personality and Social Psychology, 75*(2), 318–331.

Forgas, J. P. (1998c). On feeling good and getting your way: Mood effects on negotiation strategies and outcomes. *Journal of Personality and Social Psychology, 74*, 565–574.

Forgas, J. P. (Ed.). (2000). *Feeling and thinking: The role of affect in social cognition.* New York: Cambridge University Press.

Forgas, J. P. (2003). Affective influences on attitudes and judgments. In R. J. Davidson, K. R. Scherer, & H. H. Goldsmith (Eds.), *Handbook of affective sciences* (pp. 596–618). New York: Oxford University Press.

Forgas, J. P., & Bower, G. H. (1987). Mood effects on person perception judgments. *Journal of Personality and Social Psychology, 53*, 53–60.

Forgas, J. P., & Moylan, S. (1987). After the movies: The effect of mood on social judgments. *Personality and Social Psychology Bulletin, 13*, 465–477.

Forster, J., & Strack, F. (1996). Influence of overt head movements on memory for valenced words: A case of conceptual-motor compatibility. *Journal of Personality and Social Psychology, 71*, 421–430.

Forsterling, F. (1985). Attributional retraining: A review. *Psychological Bulletin, 98*, 495–512.

Forsterling, F. (1989). Models of covariation and attribution: How do they relate to the analogy of analysis of variance? *Journal of Personality and Social Psychology, 57*, 615–625.

Fortune, J. L., & Newby-Clark, I. R. (2008). My friend is embarrassing me: Exploring the guilty by association effect. *Journal of Personality and Social Psychology, 95*, 1440–1449.

Foushee, M. C. (1984). Dyads and triads at 35,000 feet. *American Psychologist, 39*, 885–893.

Fowler, J., Baker, L. A., & Dawes, C. T. (2008). Genetic variation in political participation. *American Political Science Review, 102*, 233–248.

Fox, J. A., & Pierce, G. L. (1987). *Supplementary homicide reports 1976–1986 (machine-readable data file).* Ann Arbor, Michigan.

Fraley, R. C., & Shaver, P. R. (1998). Airport separations: A naturalistic study of adult attachment dynamics in separating couples. *Journal of Personality and Social Psychology, 75*, 1198–1212.

Fraley, R. C., & Spieker, S. J. (2003). Are infant attachment patterns continuously or categorically distributed? A taxometric analysis of strange situation behavior. *Developmental Psychology, 34*, 387–404.

Francis, D., & Meaney, M. J. (1999). Maternal care and the development of stress responses. *Development, 9*, 128–134.

Frank, M. G., Ekman, P., & Friesen, W. V. (1993). Behavioral markers and recognizability of the smile of enjoyment. *Journal of Personality and Social Psychology, 64*, 83–93.

Frank, M. G., & Gilovich, T. (1988). The dark side of self and social perception: Black uniforms and aggression in professional sports. *Journal of Personality and Social Psychology, 54*, 74–85.

Frank, R. H. (1988). *Passions within reason.* New York: Norton.

Frank, R. H., Gilovich, T., & Regan, D. T. (1993). Does studying economics inhibit cooperation? *Journal of Economic Perspectives, 7*, 159–171.

Frederick, S. (2005). Cognitive reflection and decision making. *Journal of Economic Perspectives, 19*, 24–42.

Fredrickson, B. L. (1998). What good are positive emotions? *Review of General Psychology, 2*, 300–319.

Fredrickson, B. L. (2001). The role of positive emotions in positive psychology: The broaden-and-build theory of positive emotions. *American Psychologist, 56*, 218–226.

Fredrickson, B. L., Cohn, M. A., Coffey, K. A., Pek, J., & Finkel, S. M. (2008). Open hearts build lives: Positive emotions, induced through loving-kindness meditation, build consequential personal resources. *Journal of Personality and Social Psychology, 95*, 1045–1062.

Fredrickson, B. L., & Kahneman, D. (1993). Duration neglect in retrospective evaluations of affective episodes. *Journal of Personality and Social Psychology, 65*, 45–55.

Fredrickson, B. L., & Roberts, T. (1997). Objectification theory: Toward understanding women's lived experiences and mental health risks. *Psychology of Women Quarterly, 21*, 173–206.

Freedman, J. L. (1965). Long-term behavioral effects of cognitive dissonance. *Journal of Experimental Social Psychology, 1*, 145–155.

Freedman, J. L., & Fraser, S. C. (1966). Compliance without pressure: The foot-in-the-door-technique. *Journal of Personality and Social Psychology, 4*, 195–203.

French, H. W. (2001, August 7). Hypothesis: A scientific gap. Conclusion: Japanese custom. *New York Times*, p. A1.

French, J., & Raven, B. (1959). The bases of social power. In D. Cartwright (Ed.), *Studies of social power* (pp. 150–167). Ann Arbor, MI: Institute for Social Research.

Frenkel, O. J., & Doob, A. N. (1976). Post-decision dissonance at the polling booth. *Canadian Journal of Behavioral Science, 8*, 347–350.

Freud, A., & Dann, S. (1951). An experiment in group upbringing. *Psychoanalytic Study of the Child, 6*, 127–168.

Friedman, R. S., & Forster, J. (2000). The effects of approach and avoidance motor actions on the elements of creative thought. *Journal of Personality and Social Psychology, 79*, 477–492.

Frieze, I. H., Olson, J. E., & Russell, J. (1991). Attractiveness and income for men and women in management. *Journal of Applied Social Psychology, 21*, 1039–1057.

Frijda, N. H., & Mesquita, B. (1994). The social roles and functions of emotions. In S. Kitayama & H. Markus (Eds.), *Emotion and culture: Empirical studies of mutual influence* (pp. 51–87). Washington, DC: American Psychological Association.

Frodi, A. (1975). The effect of exposure to weapons on aggressive behavior from a cross-cultural perspective. *International Journal of Psychology, 10*, 283–292.

Froming, W. J., Walker, G. R., & Lopyan, K. J. (1982). Public and private self-awareness: When personal attitudes conflict with societal expectations. *Journal of Experimental Social Psychology, 18*, 476–487.

Fultz, J., Batson, C. D., Fortenbach, V. A., McCarthy, P. M., & Varney, L. (1986). Social evaluation and the empathy-altruism hypothesis. *Journal of Personality and Social Psychology, 50,* 761–769.

Gable, S. L., Gonzaga, G., & Strachman, A. (2006). Will you be there for me when things go right? Social support for positive events. *Journal of Personality and Social Psychology, 91,* 904–917.

Gable, S. L., Reis, H. T., Impett, E. A., & Asher, E. R. (2004). What do you do when things go right? The intrapersonal and interpersonal benefits of sharing positive events. *Journal of Personality and Social Psychology, 87,* 228–245.

Gaertner, S. L., & Dovidio, J. F. (1977). The subtlety of white racism, arousal, and helping behavior. *Journal of Personality and Social Psychology, 35,* 691–707.

Gaertner, S. L., & Dovidio, J. F. (1986). The aversive form of racism. In J. F. Dovidio & S. L. Gaertner (Eds.), *Prejudice, discrimination, and racism* (pp. 61–89). Orlando, FL: Academic Press.

Gaertner, S. L., Mann, J., Dovidio, J. F., Murrell, A., & Pomare, M. (1990). How does cooperation reduce intergroup bias? *Journal of Personality and Social Psychology, 59,* 692–704.

Gaertner, S. L., Murrell, A., & Dovidio, J. F. (1989). Reducing intergroup bias: The benefits of recategorization. *Journal of Personality and Social Psychology, 57,* 239–249.

Galanter, H. (1989). *Cults: Faith, healing, and coercion.* New York: Oxford University Press.

Galinsky, A. D., Gruenfeld, D. H., & Magee, J. C. (2003). From power to action. *Journal of Personality and Social Psychology, 85,* 453–466.

Galinsky, A. D., Stone, J., & Cooper, J. (2000). The reinstatement of dissonance and psychological discomfort following failed affirmations. *European Journal of Social Psychology, 30,* 123–147.

Gallo, L. C., Bogart, L. M., Vranceanu, A., & Matthews, K. A. (2005). Socioeconomic status, resources, psychological experiences, and emotional responses: A test of the reserve capacity model. *Journal of Personality and Social Psychology, 88*(2), 386–399.

Galton, F. (1878). Composite portraits. *Journal of the Anthropological Institute of Great Britain and Ireland, 8,* 132–142.

Gangestad, S. W., Simpson, J. A., Cousins, A. J., Garver-Apgar, C. E., & Christensen, P. N. (2004). Women's preferences for male behavioral displays change across the menstrual cycle. *Psychological Science, 15,* 203–207.

Gangestad, S. W., & Snyder, M. (2000). Self-monitoring: Appraisal and reappraisal. *Psychological Bulletin, 126,* 530–555.

Gangestad, S. W., & Thornhill, R. (1998). Menstrual cycle variation in women's preference for the scent of symmetrical men. *Proceedings of the Royal Society of London B, 265,* 727–733.

Garcia-Marques, L., & Hamilton, D. L. (1996). Resolving the apparent discrepancy between the incongruency effect and the expectancy-based illusory correlation effect: The TRAP mode. *Journal of Personality and Social Psychology, 71,* 845–860.

Gardner, W. L., Gabriel, S., & Lee, A. Y. (1999). "I" value freedom, but "we" value relationships: Self-construal priming mirrors cultural differences in judgment. *Psychological Science, 10,* 321–326.

Garner, D. M., Garfinkel, P. E., Schwartz, D., & Thompson, M. (1980). Cultural expectations of thinness in women. *Psychological Reports, 47,* 483–491.

Garofalo, J. (1981). Crime and the mass media: A selective review of research. *Journal of Research in Crime and Delinquency, 18,* 319–350.

Gates, G. S. (1924). The effects of an audience upon performance. *Journal of Abnormal and Social Psychology, 18,* 334–342.

Gawronski, B. (2003). Implicational schemata and the correspondence bias: On the diagnostic value of situationally constrained behavior. *Journal of Personality and Social Psychology, 84,* 1154–1171.

Gawronski, B., Walther, E., & Blank, H. (2005). Cognitive consistency and the formation of interpersonal attitudes: Cognitive balance affects the encoding of social information. *Journal of Experimental Social Psychology, 41,* 618–626.

Gazzaniga, M. S. (1985). *The social brain.* New York: Basic Books.

Gazzaniga, M. S., & Heatherton, T. F. (2003). *Psychological science: Mind, brain, and behavior.* New York: Norton.

Geen , R. G. (1989). Alternative conceptions of social facilitation. In P. B. Paulus (Ed.), *Psychology of group influence* (2nd ed., pp. 15–51). Hillsdale, NJ: Erlbaum.

Geen , R. G. (1998). Aggression and antisocial behavior. In D. T. Gilbert, S. T. Fiske, & G. Lindzey (Eds.), *The handbook of social psychology* (4th ed., Vol. 2, pp. 317–356). New York: McGraw-Hill.

Geeraert, N. Y., Yzerbyt, V. Y., Corneille, O., & Wigboldus, D. (2004). The return of dispositionalism: On the linguistic consequences of dispositional suppression. *Journal of Experimental Social Psychology, 40,* 264–272.

Georgeson, J. C., Harris, M., Milich, R., & Young, J. (1999). "Just teasing ...": Personality effects on perception and life narratives of childhood teasing. *Personality and Social Psychology Bulletin, 10,* 1254–1267.

Gerard, H. B., Wilhelmy, R. A., & Conolley, E. S. (1968). Conformity and group size. *Journal of Personality and Social Psychology, 8,* 79–82.

Gerbner, G., Gross, L., Morgan, M., & Signorielli, N. (1980). The "mainstreaming" of America: Violence profile no. 11. *Journal of Communication, 30,* 10–29.

Gerbner, G., Gross, L., Morgan, M., & Signorielli, N. (1986). Living with television: The dynamics of the cultivation process. In J. Bryant & D. Zillman (Eds.), *Perspectives on media effects* (pp. 17–40). Hillsdale, NJ: Erlbaum.

Gibbons, F. X. (1978). Sexual standards and reactions to pornography: Enhancing behavioral consistency through self-focused attention. *Journal of Personality and Social Psychology, 36,* 976–987.

Gigerenzer, G. (1991). How to make cognitive illusions disappear: Beyond "Heuristics and biases." In W. Stroche & M. Hewstone (Eds.), *European review of social psychology* (Vol. 2, pp. 83–115). Chichester, England: Wiley.

Gilbert, D. T. (1989). Thinking lightly about others: Automatic components of the social inference process. In J. S. Uleman & J. A. Bargh (Eds.), *Unintended thought.* New York: Guilford Press.

Gilbert, D. T. (2002). Inferential correction. In T. Gilovich, D. W. Griffin, & D. Kahneman (Eds.), *Heuristics and biases: The psychology of intuitive judgment.* New York: Cambridge University Press.

Gilbert, D. T., Brown, R. P., Pinel, E. E., & Wilson, T. D. (2000). The illusion of external agency. *Journal of Personality and Social Psychology, 79,* 690–700.

Gilbert, D. T., & Jones, E. E. (1986). Perceiver-induced constraint: Interpretations of self-generated reality. *Journal of Personality and Social Psychology, 50,* 269–280.

Gilbert, D. T., Lieberman, M. D., Morewedge, C. K., & Wilson, T. D. (2004). The peculiar longevity of things not so bad. *Psychological Science, 15,* 14–19.

Gilbert, D. T., & Malone, P. S. (1995). The correspondence bias. *Psychological Bulletin, 117,* 21–38.

Gilbert, D. T., Morewedge, C. K., Risen, J. L., & Wilson, T. D. (2004). Looking forward to looking backward: The misprediction of regret. *Psychological Science, 15,* 346–350.

Gilbert, D. T., Pinel, E. C., Wilson, T. D., Blumberg, S. J., & Wheatley, T. (1998). Immune neglect: A source of durability bias in affective forecasting. *Journal of Personality and Social Psychology, 75*, 617–638.

Gilbert, S. J. (1981). Another look at the Milgram obedience studies: The role of the gradated series of shocks. *Personality and Social Psychology Bulletin, 4*, 690–695.

Gilmour, T. M., & Reid, D. W. (1979). Locus of control and causal attribution for positive and negative outcomes on university examinations. *Journal of Research in Personality, 13*, 154–160.

Gilovich, T. (1981). Seeing the past in the present: The effect of associations to familiar events on judgments and decisions. *Journal of Personality and Social Psychology, 40*, 797–808.

Gilovich, T. (1983). Biased evaluation and persistence in gambling. *Journal of Personality and Social Psychology, 44*, 1110–1126.

Gilovich, T. (1987). Secondhand information and social judgment. *Journal of Experimental Social Psychology, 23*, 59–74.

Gilovich, T. (1991). *How we know what isn't so: The fallibility of human reason in everyday life*. New York: Free Press.

Gilovich, T., Griffin, D. W., & Kahneman, D. (Eds.). (2002). *Heuristics and biases: The psychology of intuitive judgment*. New York: Cambridge University Press.

Gilovich, T., Kruger, J., & Medvec, V. H. (2002). The spotlight effect revisited: Overestimating the manifest variability in our actions and appearance. *Journal of Experimental Social Psychology, 38*, 93–99.

Gilovich, T., Medvec, V. H., & Savitsky, K. (2000). The spotlight effect in social judgment: An egocentric bias in estimates of the salience of one's own actions and appearance. *Journal of Personality and Social Psychology, 79*, 211–222.

Gilovich, T., & Savitsky, K. (2002). Like goes with like: The role of representativeness in erroneous and pseudo-scientific beliefs. In T. Gilovich, D. W. Griffin, & D. Kahneman (Eds.), *Heuristics and biases: The psychology of intuitive judgment* (pp. 617–624). New York: Cambridge University Press.

Gilovich, T., Vallone, R., & Tversky, A. (1985). The hot hand in basketball: On the misperception of random sequences. *Cognitive Personality, 17*, 295–314.

Ginosar, Z., & Trope, Y. (1980). The effects of base rates and individuating information on judgments about another person. *Journal of Experimental Social Psychology, 16*, 228–242.

Givens, D. B. (1983). *Love signals: How to attract a mate*. New York: Crown.

Glanz, J., & Schwartz, J. (2003, September 26). Dogged engineer's effort to assess shuttle damage. *New York Times*, p. A1.

Glasman, L. R., & Albarracin, D. (2006). Forming attitudes that predict future behavior: A meta-analysis of the attitude-behavior relation. *Psychological Bulletin, 132*, 778–822.

Gleitman, H., Fridlund, A. J., & Reisberg, D. (2004). *Psychology* (6th ed.). New York: Norton.

Glenn, N. D. (1991). The recent trend in marital success in the United States. *Journal of Marriage and the Family, 53*, 261–270.

Glick, P., & Fiske, S. T. (2001a). Ambivalent sexism. In M. P. Zanna (Ed.), *Advances in experimental social psychology* (Vol. 33, pp. 115–188). Thousand Oaks, CA: Academic Press.

Glick, P., & Fiske, S. T. (2001b). An ambivalent alliance: Hostile and benevolent sexism as complementary justifications of gender inequality. *American Psychologist, 56*, 109–118.

Glied, S., & Neidell, M. (2008). The economic value of teeth. National Bureau of Economic Research Working Paper 13879.

Goethals, G. R., Cooper, J., & Naficy, A. (1979). Role of foreseen, foreseeable, and unforeseeable behavioral consequences in the arousal of cognitive dissonance. *Journal of Personality and Social Psychology, 37*, 1179–1185.

Goethals, G. R., & Reckman, R. F. (1973). The perception of consistency in attitudes. *Journal of Experimental Social Psychology, 9*, 491–501.

Goffman, E. (1959). *The presentation of self in everyday life*. Garden City, NY: Doubleday.

Goffman, E. (1961). *Encounters: Two studies in the sociology of interaction*. New York: Penguin.

Goffman, E. (1966). *Behavior in public places*. New York: Free Press.

Goffman, E. (1967). *Interaction ritual: Essays on face-to-face behavior*. New York: Doubleday.

Goldman, W., & Lewis, P. (1977). Beautiful is good: Evidence that the physically attractive are more socially skillful. *Journal of Experimental Social Psychology, 13*, 125–130.

Goleman, D. (1985). *Vital lies, simple truths: The psychology of self-deception*. New York: Simon & Schuster.

Gollwitzer, P. M., Fujita, K., & Oettingen, G. (2004). Planning and the implementation of goals. In R. F. Baumeister & K. D. Vohs (Eds.), *Handbook of self-regulation: Research, theory and applications* (pp. 211–228). New York: Guilford Press.

Gologor, E. (1977). Group polarization in a non-risk taking culture. *Journal of Cross-Cultural Psychology, 8*, 331–346.

Gonzaga, G. C., Keltner, D., Londahl, E. A., & Smith, M. (2001). Love and the commitment problem in romantic relations and friendship. *Journal of Personality and Social Psychology, 81*, 247–262.

Gonzaga, G. C., Turner, R. A., Keltner, D., Campos, B., & Altemus, M. (2006). Romantic love and sexual desire in close bonds. *Emotion, 6*, 163–179.

Gonzalez, C., Dana, J., Koshino, H., & Just, M. (2005). The framing effect and risky decisions: Examining cognitive functions with fMRI. *Journal of Economic Psychology, 26*, 1–20.

Gonzalez, R., & Griffin, D. (1997). On the statistics of interdependence: Treating dyadic data with respect. In S. Duck (Ed.), *Handbook of personal relationships: Theory, research, and interventions* (2nd ed., pp. 271–302). Chichester, England: Wiley.

Good, C., Aronson, J., & Inzlicht, M. (2003). Improving adolescents' standardized test performance: An intervention to reduce the effects of stereotype threat. *Applied Developmental Psychology, 24*, 645–662.

Goodwin, S. A., Gubin, A., Fiske, S. T., & Yzerbyt, V. Y. (2000). Power can bias impression processes: Stereotyping subordinates by default and by design. *Group Processes and Intergroup Relations, 3*, 227–256.

Gosling, S. D., Ko, S. J., Mannarelli, T., & Morris, M. E. (2002). A room with a cue: Judgments of personality based on offices and bedrooms. *Journal of Personality and Social Psychology, 82*, 379–398.

Gosling, S. D., Kwan, V. S. Y., & John, O. P. (2003). A dog's got personality: A cross-species comparative approach to evaluating personality judgments. *Journal of Personality and Social Psychology, 85*, 1161–1169.

Gottman, J. M. (1993). *Why marriages succeed or fail*. New York: Simon & Schuster.

Gottman, J. M., & Levenson, R. W. (1992). Marital processes predictive of later dissolution: Behavior, physiology, and health. *Journal of Personality and Social Psychology, 63*, 221–233.

Gottman, J. M., & Levenson, R. W. (1999). Rebound from marital conflict and divorce prediction. *Family Processes, 38,* 287–292.

Gottman, J. M., & Levenson, R. W. (2000). The timing of divorce: Predicting when a couple will divorce over a 14–year period. *Journal of Marriage and the Family, 62,* 737–745.

Gould, S. J. (1982). A biological homage to Mickey Mouse. In *The panda's thumb: More reflections on natural history.* New York: Norton.

Gouldner, A. W. (1960). The norm of reciprocity: A preliminary statement. *American Sociological Review, 25,* 161–178.

Gourevitch, P. (1998). *We wish to inform you that tomorrow we will be killed with our families.* New York: Picador Press.

Grammer, K. (1990). Strangers meet: Laughter and nonverbal signs of interest in opposite-sex encounters. *Journal of Nonverbal Behavior, 14,* 209–236.

Green, D. P., Wong, J., & Strolovitch, D. (1996). *The effects of demographic change on hate crime.* New Haven: Institution for Social and Policy Studies, Yale University.

Greenberg, J., Pyszczynski, T., & Solomon, S. (1982). The self-serving attributional bias: Beyond self-presentation. *Journal of Experimental Social Psychology, 18,* 56–67.

Greenberg, J., Pyszczynski, T., Solomon, S., Rosenblatt, A., Veeder, M., Kirkland, S., et al. (1990). Evidence for terror management theory II: The effects of mortality salience on reactions to those who threaten or bolster the cultural worldview. *Journal of Personality and Social Psychology, 58,* 308–318.

Greenberg, J., Simon, L., Porteus, J., Pyszczynski, T., & Solomon, S. (1995). Evidence of a terror management function of cultural icons: The effects of mortality salience on the inappropriate use of cherished cultural symbols. *Personality and Social Psychology Bulletin, 21,* 1221–1228.

Greene, D., Sternberg, B., & Lepper, M. R. (1976). Overjustification in a token economy. *Journal of Personality and Social Psychology, 34,* 1219–1234.

Greene, J. D., & Haidt, J. (2002). How (and where) does moral judgment work? *Trends in Cognitive Sciences, 6,* 517–523.

Greenspan, A. (1996). The challenge of central banking in a democratic society. Speech given to the American Enterprise Institute, December 5.

Greenwald, A. G. (1980). The totalitarian ego: Fabrication and revision of personal history. *American Psychologist, 35,* 603–618.

Greenwald, A. G., & Banaji, M. R. (1995). Implicit social cognition: Attitudes, self-esteem, and stereotypes. *Psychological Review, 102,* 4–27.

Greenwald, A. G., Klinger, M. R., & Liu, T. J. (1989). Unconscious processing of dichotically masked words. *Memory and Cognition, 17,* 35–47.

Greenwald, A. G., McGhee, D. E., & Schwartz, D. L. K. (1998). Measuring individual differences in implicit cognition: The Implicit Association Test. *Journal of Personality and Social Psychology, 74,* 1464–1480.

Gresham, L. G., & Shimp, T. A. (1985). Attitude toward advertisement and brand attitude: A classical conditioning perspective. *Journal of Advertising, 14,* 10–17.

Grice, H. P. (1975). *Logic and conversation.* New York: Academic Press.

Gries, P. H., & Peng, K. (2002). Culture clash? Apologies East and West. *Journal of Contemporary China, 11,* 173–178.

Griffin, D., & Tversky, A. (1992). The weighing of evidence and the determinants of confidence. *Cognitive Psychology, 24,* 411–435.

Griffitt, W., & Veitch, R. (1971). Hot and crowded: Influences of population density and temperature on interpersonal affective behavior. *Journal of Personality and Social Psychology, 17,* 92–98.

Griffitt, W., & Veitch, R. (1974). Preacquaintance attitude similarity and attraction revisited: Ten days in a fall-out shelter. *Sociometry, 37,* 163–173.

Groff, B. D., Baron, R. S., & Moore, D. L. (1983). Distraction, attentional conflict, and drivelike behavior. *Journal of Experimental Social Psychology, 19,* 359–380.

Gross, J. J. (1998). Antecedent-and-response-focused emotion regulation: Divergent consequences for experience, expression, and physiology. *Journal of Personality and Social Psychology, 74,* 224–237.

Gross, J. J., Fredrickson, B. L., & Levenson, R. W. (1994). The psychophysiology of crying. *Psychophysiology, 31,* 460–468.

Grush, J. E. (1980). Impact of candidate expenditures, regionality, and prior outcomes on the 1976 presidential primaries. *Journal of Personality and Social Psychology, 38,* 337–347.

Guerin, B. (1993). *Social facilitation.* New York: Cambridge University Press.

Guilbault, R. L., Bryant, F. B., Brockway, J. H., & Posavac, E. J. (2004). A meta-analysis of research on hindsight bias. *Basic and Applied Social Psychology, 26,* 103–117.

Guinote, A. (2007). Power and goal pursuit. *Personality and Social Psychology Bulletin, 33(8),* 1076–1087.

Guinote, A., Judd, C. M., & Brauer, M. (2002). Effects of power on perceived and objective group variability: Evidence that more powerful groups are more powerful. *Journal of Personality and Social Psychology, 82,* 708–721.

Haberstroh, S., Oyserman, D., Schwarz, N., Kühnen, U., & Ji, L.-J. (2002). Is the interdependent self more sensitive to question context than the independent self? Self-construal and the observation of conversational norms. *Journal of Experimental Social Psychology, 38,* 323–329.

Haddock, G., Zanna, M. P., & Esses, V. M. (1993). Assessing the structure of prejudicial attitudes: The case of attitudes toward homosexuals. *Journal of Personality and Social Psychology, 65,* 1105–1118.

Haidt, J. (2001). The emotional dog and its rational tail: A social intuitionist approach to moral judgment. *Psychological Review, 108,* 814–834.

Haidt, J. (2003). The moral emotions. In R. J. Davidson, K. R. Scherer, & H. H. Goldsmith (Eds.), *Handbook of affective sciences* (pp. 852–870). New York: Oxford University Press.

Haidt, J., & Keltner, D. (1999). Culture and facial expression: Open ended methods find more faces and a gradient of universality. *Cognition and Emotion, 13,* 225–266.

Haidt, J., Koller, S. H., & Dias, M. G. (1993). Affect, culture, and morality, or Is it wrong to eat your dog? *Journal of Personality and Social Psychology, 65,* 613–628.

Halberstadt, J. B., & Rhodes, G. (2000). The attractiveness of non-face averages: Implications for an evolutionary explanation of the attractiveness of average faces. *Psychological Science, 11,* 285–289.

Halberstadt, J. B., & Rhodes, G. (2003). It's not just average faces that are attractive: Computer-manipulated averageness makes birds, fish, and automobiles attractive. *Psychonomic Bulletin and Review, 10,* 149–156.

Halberstam, D. (1969). *The best and the brightest.* New York: Random House.

Hall, J. A. (1984). *Nonverbal gender differences: Accuracy of communication and expressive style.* Baltimore: Johns Hopkins University Press.

Hamermesh, D., & Biddle, J. (1994). Beauty and the labor market. *American Economic Review, 84*, 1174–1194.

Hamill, R., Wilson, T. D., & Nisbett, R. E. (1980). Insensitivity to sample bias: Generalizing from atypical cases. *Journal of Personality and Social Psychology, 39*, 578–589.

Hamilton, D. L., & Gifford, R. K. (1976). Illusory correlation in interpersonal perception: A cognitive basis of stereotypic judgments. *Journal of Experimental Social Psychology, 12*, 392–407.

Hamilton, D. L., & Sherman, S. J. (1989). Illusory correlations: Implications for stereotype theory and research. In D. Bar-Tal, C. F. Graumann, A. W. Kruglanski, & W. Stroebe (Eds.), *Stereotypes and prejudice: Changing conceptions* (pp. 59–82). New York: Springer-Verlag.

Hamilton, D. L., Stroessner, S., & Mackie, D. M. (1993). The influence of affect on stereotyping: The case of illusory correlations. In D. M. Mackie & D. L. Hamilton (Eds.), *Affect, cognition, and stereotyping: Interactive processes in group perception* (pp. 39–61). San Diego, CA: Academic Press.

Hamilton, D. L., & Trolier, T. K. (1986). Stereotypes and stereotyping: An overview of the cognitive approach. In J. F. Dovidio & S. L. Gaertner (Eds.), *Prejudice, discrimination and racism* (pp. 127–163). Orlando, FL: Academic Press.

Hamilton, D. L., & Zanna, M. P. (1974). Context effects in impression formation: Changes in connotative meaning. *Journal of Personality and Social Psychology, 29*, 649–654.

Hamilton, W. D. (1964). The genetical evolution of social behavior. *Journal of Theoretical Biology, 7*, 1–52.

Hampden-Turner, C., & Trompenaars, A. (1993). *The seven cultures of capitalism: Value systems for creating wealth in the United States, Japan, Germany, France, Britain, Sweden, and the Netherlands.* New York: Doubleday.

Han, S., & Shavitt, S. (1994). Persuasion and culture: Advertising appeals in individualistic and collectivistic societies. *Journal of Experimental Social Psychology, 30*, 326–350.

Haney, C., Banks, C., & Zimbardo, P. G. (1973). Interpersonal dynamics in a simulated prison. *International Journal of Criminology and Penology, 1*, 69–97.

Hanna, J. (1989, September 25). Sexual abandon: The condom is unpopular on the campus. *Macleans*, p. 48.

Hansen, C. H., & Hansen, R. D. (1988). Finding the face in a crowd: An anger superiority effect. *Journal of Personality and Social Psychology, 54*, 917–924.

Harackiewicz, J. M., Manderlink, G., & Sansone, C. (1984). Rewarding pinball wizardry: Effects of evaluation and cue value on intrinsic interest. *Journal of Personality and Social Psychology, 47*, 287–300.

Harari, H., Mohr, D., & Hosey, K. (1980). Faculty helpfulness to students: A comparison of compliance techniques. *Personality and Social Psychology Bulletin, 6*, 373–377.

Harber, K. (1998). Feedback to minorities: Evidence of a positive bias. *Journal of Personality and Social Psychology, 74*, 622–628.

Harcourt, A. H., Harvey, P. H., Larson, S. G., & Short, R. V. (1980). Testis weight, body weight and breeding system in primates. *Nature, 293*, 55–57.

Hare, R. D. (1993). *Without conscience: The disturbing world of the psychopaths among us.* New York: Simon & Schuster/Pocket.

Harlow, H. F. (1959). Love in infant monkeys. *Scientific American, 200*, 68–86.

Harmon-Jones, E. (2000). Cognitive dissonance and experienced negative affect: Evidence that dissonance increases experienced negative affect even in the absence of aversive consequences. *Personality and Social Psychology Bulletin, 26*, 1490–1501.

Harmon-Jones, E., Brehm, J. W., Greenberg, J., Simon, L., & Nelson, D. E. (1996). Evidence that the production of aversive consequences is not necessary to create cognitive dissonance. *Journal of Personality and Social Psychology, 70*, 5–16.

Harris, B. (1979). Whatever happened to little Albert? *American Psychologist, 34*, 151–160.

Harris, C. R. (2001). Cardiovascular responses of embarrassment and effects of emotional suppression in a social setting. *Journal of Personality and Social Psychology, 81*, 886–897.

Harris, M. B. (1974). Mediators between frustration and aggression in a field experiment. *Journal of Experimental Social Psychology, 10*, 561–571.

Harris, R. J., Benson, S. M., & Hall, C. L. (1975). The effects of confession on altruism. *Journal of Social Psychology, 96*, 187–192.

Harrison, A. A., & Saeed, L. (1977). Let's make a deal: An analysis of revelations and stipulations in lonely hearts advertisements. *Journal of Personality and Social Psychology, 35*, 257–264.

Hart, D., Lucca-Irizarry, N., & Damon, W. (1986). The development of self-understanding in Puerto Rico and the United States. *Journal of Early Adolescence, 6*, 293–304.

Hartup, W. W., & Stevens, N. (1997). Friendships and adaptation in the life course. *Psychological Bulletin, 121*, 355–370.

Hass, R. G., & Linder, D. E. (1972). Counterargument availability and the effects of message structure on persuasion. *Journal of Personality and Social Psychology, 23*, 219–233.

Hassin, R. R., Ferguson, M. J., Shidlovsky, D., & Gross, T. (2007). Waved by invisible flags: The effects of subliminal exposure to flags on political thought and behavior. *Proceedings of the National Academy of Sciences, 104*, 19757–19761.

Hastie, R. (1981). Schematic principles in human memory. In E. T. Higgins, C. P. Herman, & M. P. Zanna (Eds.), *Social cognition: The Ontario Symposium* (Vol. 1, pp. 39–88). Hillsdale, NJ: Erlbaum.

Hatfield, E., Cacioppo, J. T., & Rapson, R. L. (1994). *Emotional contagion.* New York: Cambridge University Press.

Haugtvedt, C. P., & Petty, R. E. (1992). Personality and persuasion: Need for cognition moderates the persistence and resistance of attitude changes. *Journal of Personality and Social Psychology, 63*, 308–319.

Hauser, C. (2004, May 6). Many Iraqis are skeptical of Bush TV appeal. *New York Times*, p. 13.

Hauser, M. D. (1996). *The evolution of communication.* Cambridge, MA: MIT Press.

Hawkins, M. W., Carrere, S., & Gottman, J. M. (2002). Marital sentiment override: Does it influence couples' perceptions? *Journal of Marriage and the Family, 64*, 193–201.

Hazan, C., & Shaver, P. (1987). Romantic love conceptualized as an attachment process. *Journal of Personality and Social Psychology, 52*, 511–524.

Hazan, C., & Shaver, P. (1994). Attachment as an organizational framework for research on close relationships. *Psychological Inquiry, 5*, 1–22.

Heatherton, T. F., Macrae, C. N., & Kelley, W. M. (2004). What the social brain sciences can tell us about the self. *Current Directions in Psychological Science, 13*, 190–193.

Heatherton, T. F., & Polivy, J. (1991). Development and validation of a scale for measuring state self-esteem. *Journal of Personality and Social Psychology, 60*, 895–910.

Heatherton, T. F., Wyland, C. L., McCrae, C. N., Demos, K. E., Denny, B. T., & Keley, W. M. (2006). Medial prefrontal activity differentiates self from close others. *Social Cognitive Affective Neuroscience, 1,* 18–25.

Hebl, M. R., Foster, J. B., Mannix, L. M., & Dovidio, J. F. (2002). Formal and interpersonal discrimination: A field study of bias toward homosexual applicants. *Personality and Social Psychology Bulletin, 28,* 815–825.

Hebl, M., & Heatherton, T. F. (1997). The stigma of obesity in women: The difference is black and white. *Personality and Social Psychology Bulletin, 24,* 417–426.

Hebl, M., & Mannix, L. (2003). The weight of obesity in evaluating others: A mere proximity effect. *Personality and Social Psychology Bulletin, 29,* 28–38.

Hedden, T., Ji, L., Jing, Q., Jiao, S., Yao, C., Nisbett, R. E., et al. (2000). *Culture and age differences in recognition memory for social dimensions.* Paper presented at the Cognitive Aging Conference, Atlanta.

Heider, F. (1946). Attitudes and cognitive organization. *Journal of Psychology, 21,* 107–112.

Heider, F. (1958). *The psychology of interpersonal relations.* New York: Wiley.

Heine, S. J. (2005). Constructing good selves in Japan and North America. In *Culture and social behavior: The tenth Ontario Symposium* (pp. 115–143). Hillsdale, NJ: Erlbaum.

Heine, S. J., Kitayama, S., Lehman, D. R., Takata, T., Ide, E., Leung, C., & Matsumoto, H. (2001). Divergent consequences of success and failure in Japan and North America: An investigation of self-improving motivations and malleable selves. *Journal of Personality and Social Psychology, 81,* 599–615.

Heine, S. J., & Lehman, D. R. (1995). Cultural variation in unrealistic optimism: Does the West feel more invulnerable than the East? *Journal of Personality and Social Psychology, 68,* 595–607.

Heine, S. J., & Lehman, D. R. (1997). Culture, dissonance, and self-affirmation. *Personality and Social Psychology Bulletin, 23,* 389–400.

Heine, S. J., & Lehman, D. R. (2003). Move the body, change the self: Acculturative effects on the self-concept. In M. Schaller & C. S. Crandall (Eds.), *Psychological foundations of culture* (pp. 305–331). Mahwah, NJ: Erlbaum.

Heine, S. J., Lehman, D. R., Markus, H. R., & Kitayama, S. (1999). Is there a universal need for positive self-regard? *Psychological Review, 106,* 766–794.

Helgeson, V. S., & Mickelson, K. D. (1995). Motives for social comparison. *Personality and Social Psychology Bulletin, 21,* 1200–1209.

Henderson, V. L., & Dweck, C. S. (1990). Achievement and motivation in adolescence: A new model and data. In S. Feldman & G. Elliott (Eds.), *At the threshold: The developing adolescent.* Cambridge, MA: Harvard University Press.

Henley, N. (1977). *Body politics: Power, sex, and nonverbal communication.* Englewood Cliffs, NJ: Prentice-Hall.

Henley, N. M. (1973). Status and sex: Some touching observations. *Bulletin of the Psychonomic Society, 2,* 91–93.

Henley, N. M., & LaFrance, M. (1984). Gender as culture: Difference and dominance in nonverbal behavior. In A. Wolfgang (Ed.), *Nonverbal behavior: Perspectives, applications, intercultural insights.* Lewiston, NY: C. J. Hogrefe.

Henningsen, D. D., Henningsen, M. L. M., Eden, J., & Cruz, M. G. (2006). Examining the symptoms of groupthink and retrospective sensemaking. *Small Group Research, 37,* 36–64.

Henrich, J., & Boyd, R. (1998). The evolution of conformist transmission and the emergence of between-group differences. *Evolution and Human Behavior, 19,* 215–242.

Henrich, J., Boyd, R., Bowles, S., Camerer, C., Gintis, H., McElreath, R., et al. (2001). In search of *Homo economicus*: Experiments in 15 small-scale societies. *American Economic Review, 91*(2), 73–79.

Henrich, J., Heine, S. J., & Norenzayan, A. (2009). *The weirdest people in the world.* Vancouver: University of British Columbia.

Hepworth, J. T., & West, S. G. (1988). Lynchings and the economy: A time-series reanalysis of Hovland and Sears (1940). *Journal of Personality and Social Psychology, 55,* 239–247.

Herek, G. M. (1998). *Stigma and sexual orientation: Understanding prejudice against lesbians, gay men, and bisexuals.* Thousand Oaks, CA: Sage.

Herr, P. M. (1986). Consequences of priming: Judgment and behavior. *Journal of Personality and Social Psychology, 51,* 1106–1115.

Hertenstein, M. J. (2002). Touch: Its communicative functions in infancy. *Human Development, 45,* 70–94..

Hertenstein, M. J., Keltner, D., App, B., Bulleit, B. A., & Jaskolka, A. R. (2006). Touch communicates distinct emotions. *Emotion, 6,* 528–533.

Heslin, R., & Boss, D. (1980). Nonverbal intimacy in airport arrival and departure. *Personality and Social Psychology Bulletin, 6,* 248–252.

Hess, U., Banse, R., & Kappas, A. (1995). The intensity of facial expression is determined by underlying affective states and social situations. *Journal of Personality and Social Psychology, 69,* 280–288.

Hewstone, M., & Jaspers, J. (1983). A re-examination of the roles of consensus, consistency, & distinctiveness: Kelley's cube revisited. *British Journal of Social Psychology, 22,* 41–50.

Hewstone, M., & Jaspers, J. (1987). Covariation and causal attribution: A logical model of the intuitive analysis of variance. *Journal of Personality and Social Psychology, 53,* 663–672.

Higgins, E. T. (1987). Self discrepancy: A theory relating self and affect. *Psychological Review, 94,* 319–340.

Higgins, E. T. (1999). Promotion and prevention as motivational duality: Implications for evaluative processes. In S. Chaiken & Y. Trope (Eds.), *Dual-process theories in social psychology.* New York: Guilford Press.

Higgins, E. T., & Brendl, M. (1995). Accessibility and applicability: Some "activation rules" influencing judgment. *Journal of Experimental Social Psychology, 31,* 218–243.

Higgins, E. T., & Rholes, W. S. (1976). Impression formation and role fulfillment: A "holistic reference" approach. *Journal of Experimental Social Psychology, 12,* 422–435.

Higgins, E. T., Rholes, W. S., & Jones, C. R. (1977). Category accessibility and impression formation. *Journal of Experimental Social Psychology, 13,* 141–154.

Higgins, E. T., Shah, J., & Friedman, R. (1997). Emotional responses to goal attainment: Strength of regulatory focus as a moderator. *Journal of Personality and Social Psychology, 72,* 515–525.

Hill, C. T., & Peplau, L. A. (1998). Premarital predictors of relationship outcomes: A 15-year follow-up of the Boston Couples Study. In T. N. Bradbury (Ed.), *The developmental course of marital dysfunction.* New York: Cambridge University Press.

Hilton, D. J., & Slugoski, B. R. (1986). Knowledge-based causal attribution: The abnormal conditions focus model. *Psychological Review, 93,* 75–88.

Hilton, D. J., Smith, R. H., & Kim, S. H. (1995). Process of causal explanation and dispositional attribution. *Journal of Personality and Social Psychology, 68,* 377–387.

Hinkley, K., & Andersen, S. M. (1996). The working self-concept in transference: Significant-other activation and self change. *Journal of Personality and Social Psychology, 71,* 1279–1295.

Hinsz, V. B., Tindale, R. S., & Vollrath, D. A. (1997). The emerging conceptualization of groups as information processors. *Psychological Bulletin, 121,* 43–64.

Hirshleifer, D, & Shumway, T. (2003). Good day sunshine: Stock returns and the weather. *Journal of Finance, 58*(3), 1009–1032.

Hirt, E. R. (1990). Do I see only what I expect? Evidence for an expectancy-guided retrieval model. *Journal of Personality and Social Psychology, 58,* 937–951.

Hirt, E. R., MacDonald, H. E., & Erikson, G. A. (1995). How do I remember thee? The role of encoding set and delay in reconstructive memory processes. *Journal of Experimental Social Psychology, 31,* 379–409.

Hirt, E. R., McCrea, S. M., & Kimble, C. E. (2000). Public self-focus and sex differences in behavioral self-handicapping: Does increasing self-threat still make it just a man's game? *Personality and Social Psychology Bulletin, 26,* 1131–1141.

Hirt, E. R., Zillman, D., Erickson, G. A., & Kennedy, C. (1992). Costs and benefits of allegiance: Changes in fans' self-ascribed competencies after team victory versus defeat. *Journal of Personality and Social Psychology, 63,* 724–738.

Hobart, C. (1991). Conflict in remarriages. *Journal of Divorce and Remarriage, 15,* 69–86.

Hoch, S. J. (1985). Counterfactual reasoning and accuracy in predicting personal events. *Journal of Experimental Psychology: Learning, Memory and Cognition, 11,* 719–731.

Hodson, G., Dovidio, J. F., & Gaertner, S. L. (2002). Processes in racial discrimination: Differential weighting of conflicting information. *Personality and Social Psychology Bulletin, 28,* 460–471.

Hoeksema-van Orden, C. Y. D., Gaillard, A. W. K., & Buunk, B. P. (1998). Social loafing under fatigue. *Journal of Personality and Social Psychology, 75,* 1179–1190.

Hofstede, G. (1980). *Culture's consequences: International differences in work-related values.* Beverly Hills, CA: Sage.

Holland, R. W., Hendricks, M., & Aarts, H. (2005). Smells like clean spirit: Nonconscious effects of scent on cognition and behavior. *Psychological Science, 16,* 689–693.

Holloway, S. (1988). Concepts of ability and effort in Japan and the United States. *Review of Educational Research, 58,* 327–345.

Holtgraves, T., & Lasky, B. (1999). Linguistic power and persuasion. *Journal of Language and Social Psychology, 18,* 196–205.

Holyoak, K. J., & Thagard, P. (1995). *Mental leaps: Analogy in creative thought.* Cambridge, MA: MIT Press.

Homans, G. C. (1965). Group factors in worker productivity. In H. Proshansky & L. Seidenberg (Eds.), *Basic studies in social psychology.* New York: Holt.

Hong, Y., Chiu, C., & Kung, T. (1997). Bringing culture out in front: Effects of cultural meaning system activation on social cognition. In K. Leung, U. Kim, S. Yamaguchi, & Y. Kashima (Eds.), *Progress in Asian social psychology* (Vol. 1, pp. 135–146). Singapore: Wiley.

Hoorens, V., & Ruiter, S. (1996). The optimal impact phenomenon: Beyond the third person effect. *European Journal of Social Psychology, 26,* 599–610.

Hoorens, V., Nuttin, J. M, Herman, I. E., & Pavakanun, U. (1990). Mastery pleasure versus mere ownership: A quasi-experimental cross-cultural and cross-alphabetical test of the name letter effect. *European Journal of Social Psychology, 20,* 181–205.

Hosey, G. R., Wood, M., Thompson, R. J., & Druck, P. L. (1985). Social facilitation in a non-social animal, the centipede Lithobius forficatus. *Behavioral Processes, 10,* 123–130.

Hoshino-Browne, E., Zanna, A. S., Spencer, S. J., & Zanna, M. P. (2004). Investigating attitudes cross-culturally: A case of cognitive dissonance among East Asians and North Americans. In G. Haddock & G. R. Maio (Eds.), *Contemporary perspectives on the psychology of attitudes* (pp. 375–397). East Sussex, England: Psychology Press.

Hosman, L. A. (1989). The evaluative consequences of hedges, hesitations, and intensifiers: Powerful and powerless speech styles. *Human Communication Research, 15,* 383–406.

Hovland, C. I., Janis, I. L., & Kelley, H. H. (1953). *Communication and persuasion: Psychological studies of opinion change.* New Haven, CT: Yale University Press.

Hovland, C. J., Lumsdaine, A. A., & Sheffield, F. D. (1949). *Experiments on mass communication.* Princeton, NJ: Princeton University Press.

Hovland, C. J., & Sears, R. R. (1940). Minor studies in aggression: VI. Correlation of lynchings with economic indices. *Journal of Abnormal and Social Psychology, 9,* 301–310.

Hovland, C. J., & Weiss, W. (1951). The influence of source credibility on communication effectiveness. *Public Opinion Quarterly, 15,* 635–660.

Howard, J. W., & Rothbart, M. (1980). Social categorization and memory for ingroup and outgroup behavior. *Journal of Personality and Social Psychology, 38,* 301–310.

Hoyt, W. T., Fincham, F. D., McCullough, M. E., Maio, G., & Davila, J. (2005). Responses to interpersonal transgressions in families: Forgivingness, forgivability, and relationship-specific effects. *Journal of Personality and Social Psychology, 89,* 375–394.

Hrdy, S. B. (1999). *Mother nature: A history of mothers, infants, and natural selection.* New York: Pantheon.

Hsu, F. L. K. (1953). *Americans and Chinese: Two ways of life.* New York: Schuman.

Hubschman, J. H., & Stack, M. A. (1992). Parasite-induced changes in chironomus decorus (*Diperta: Chironomidae*). *Journal of Parasitology, 78,* 872–875.

Huesmann, L. R. (1986). Psychological processes promoting the relations between exposure to media violence and aggressive behavior by the viewer. *Journal of Social Issues, 42,* 125–139.

Huesmann, L. R., Moise-Titus, J., Podolski, C.-L., & Eron, L. D. (2003). Longitudinal relations between children's exposure to TV violence and their aggressive and violent behavior in young adulthood: 1977–1992. *Developmental Psychology, 39,* 201–221.

Huguet, P., Galvaing, M. P., Monteil, J. M., & Dumas, F. (1999). Social presence effects in the Stroop task: Further evidence for an attentional view of social facilitation. *Journal of Personality and Social Psychology, 77,* 1011–1025.

Hull, J. G., Levenson, R. W., Young, R. D., & Sher, K. J. (1983). Self-awareness reducing effects of alcohol consumption. *Journal of Personality and Social Psychology, 44,* 461–473.

Hull, J. G., & Young, R. D. (1983). Self-consciousness, self-esteem, and success-failure as determinants of alcohol consumption in male social drinkers. *Journal of Personality and Social Psychology, 44,* 1097–1109.

Hull, J. G., Young, R. D., & Jouriles, E. (1986). Applications of the self-awareness model of alcohol consumption: Predicting patterns of use and abuse. *Journal of Personality and Social Psychology, 51,* 790–796.

Hummert, M. L., Crockett, W. H., & Kemper, S. (1990). Processing mechanisms underlying use of the balance schema. *Journal of Personality and Social Psychology, 58,* 5–21.

Huntley, J. (1990). *The elements of astrology.* Shaftesbury, Dorset, England: Element Books Unlimited.

Ickes, W., Robertson, E., Tooke, W., & Teng, G. (1986). Naturalistic social cognition: Methodology, assessment, and validation. *Journal of Personality and Social Psychology, 51,* 66–82.

Iliffe, A. H. (1960). A study of preferences in feminine beauty. *British Journal of Psychology, 51,* 267–273.

Impett, E. A., Strachman, A., Finkel, E., & Gable, S. L. (2008). Maintaining sexual desire in intimate relationships: The importance of approach goals. *Journal of Personality and Social Psychology, 94,* 808–823.

Impett, E., Gable, S. L., & Peplau, L. A. (2005). Giving up and giving in: The costs and benefits of daily sacrifice in intimate relationships. *Journal of Personality and Social Psychology, 89,* 327–344.

Inman, M. L., Reichl, A. J., & Baron, R. S. (1993). Do we tell less than we know or hear less than we are told? Exploring the teller-listener extremity effect. *Journal of Experimental Social Psychology, 29,* 528–550.

Innes, J. M., & Zeitz, H. (1988). The public's view of the impact of the mass media: A test of the "third person" effect. *European Journal of Social Psychology, 18,* 457–463.

Insel, T. R., Young, L., & Zuoxin, W. (1997). Molecular aspects of monogamy. In C. S. Carter & I. I. Lederhendler (Eds.), *Annals of the New York Academy of Sciences* (Vol. 807, pp. 302–316). New York: New York Academy of Sciences.

Insko, C. A. (1984). Balance theory, the Jordan paradigm, and the Wiest tetrahedron. In L. Berkowitz (Ed.), *Advances in experimental social psychology* (Vol. 18, pp. 89–140). San Diego, CA: Academic Press.

Insko, C. A., Smith, R. H., Alicke, M. D., Wade, J., & Taylor, S. (1985). Conformity and group size: The concern with being right and the concern with being liked. *Personality and Social Psychology Bulletin, 11,* 41–50.

Insko, C. A., & Wilson, M. (1977). Interpersonal attraction as a function of social interaction. *Journal of Personality and Social Psychology, 35,* 903–911.

Inzlicht, M., & Ben-Zeev, T. (2000). A threatening intellectual environment: Why females are susceptible to experiencing problem-solving deficits in the presences of males. *Psychological Science, 11,* 365–371.

Ip, G. W. M., & Bond, M. H. (1995). Culture, values, and the spontaneous self-concept. *Asian Journal of Psychology, 1,* 29–35.

Isen, A. M. (1987). Positive affect, cognitive processes, and social behavior. In L. Berkowitz (Ed.), *Advances in experimental social psychology* (pp. 203–253). New York: Academic Press.

Isen, A. M. (1993). Positive affect and decision making. In M. Lewis & J. M. Haviland-Jones (Eds.), *Handbook of emotions* (pp. 261–278). New York: Guilford Press.

Isen, A. M. (1999). Positive affect. In T. Dalgleish & M. J. Power (Eds.), *Handbook of cognition and emotion* (pp. 521–539). Chichester, England: Wiley.

Isen, A. M., Clark, M., & Schwartz, M. F. (1976). Duration of the effect of good mood on helping: Footprints on the sands of time. *Journal of Personality and Social Psychology, 34,* 385–393.

Isen, A. M., & Levin, P. F. (1972). Effect of feeling good on helping: Cookies and kindness. *Journal of Personality and Social Psychology, 21,* 384–388.

Itard, J. M. G. (1801/1962). *The wild boy of Aveyron* (G. Humphrey & M. Humphrey, Trans.). New York: Appleton-Century-Crofts.

Ito, T. A., Larsen, J. T., Smith, N. K., & Cacioppo, J. T. (1998). Negative information weighs more heavily on the brain: The negativity bias in evaluative categorizations. *Journal of Personality and Social Psychology, 75,* 887–900.

Iyengar, S. (2004). Engineering consent: The renaissance of mass communications research in politics. In J. T. Jost, M. R. Banaji, & D. Prentice (Eds.), *Perspectives in social psychology: The yin and the yang of scientific progress: Perspectives on the social psychology of thought systems.* Washington, DC: APA Press.

Iyengar, S., & Kinder, D. (1987). *News that matters: Television and American opinion.* Chicago: University of Chicago Press.

Iyengar, S. S., & Lepper, M. R. (2000). When choice is demotivating: Can one desire too much of a good thing? *Journal of Personality and Social Psychology, 79,* 995–1006.

Izard, C. E. (1971). *The face of emotion.* New York: Appleton-Century-Crofts.

Izard, C. E. (1994). Innate and universal facial expressions: Evidence from developmental and cross-cultural research. *Psychological Bulletin, 115,* 288–299.

Jackson, L. A., Hunter, J. E., & Hodge, C. N. (1995). Physical attractiveness and intellectual competence: A meta-analytic review. *Social Psychology Quarterly, 58,* 108–122.

Jacobson, G. C. (1978). The effects of campaign spending in house elections. *American Political Science Review, 72,* 469–1191.

Jacoby, L. L., Woloshyn, V., & Kelley, C. (1989). Becoming famous without being recognized: Unconscious influences of memory produced by dividing attention. *Journal of Experimental Psychology: General, 118,* 115–125.

James, W. (1884). What is an emotion? *Mind, 9,* 188–205.

James, W. (1890). *Principles of psychology.* New York: Holt.

James, W. (1892/1948). *Psychology.* Cleveland: World Publishing Company.

Janes, L. M., & Olson, J. M. (2000). Jeer pressure: The behavioral effects of observing ridicule of others. *Personality and Social Psychology Bulletin, 26,* 474–485.

Janis, I. L. (1972). *Victims of groupthink.* Boston: Houghton Mifflin.

Janis, I. L. (1982). *Groupthink: Psychological studies of policy decisions and fiascos* (2nd ed.). Boston: Houghton Mifflin.

Janis, I. L., Kaye, D., & Kirschner, P. (1965). Facilitating effects of eating while reading on responsiveness to persuasive communications. *Journal of Personality and Social Psychology, 1,* 181–186.

Janis, I. L., & Mann, L. (1977). *Decision making.* New York: Free Press.

Jeffery, R. W. (1996). Does weight cycling present a health risk? *American Journal of Clinical Nutrition, 63,* 452S–455S.

Jellison, J. M., & Riskind, J. (1970). A social comparison of abilities interpretation of risk-taking behavior. *Journal of Personality and Social Psychology, 15,* 375–390.

Jemmott, J. B. I., Jemmott, L. S., Braverman, P. K., & Fong, G. T. (2005). HIV/STD risk reduction interventions for African American and Latino adolescent girls at an inner-city adolescent medicine clinic: A randomized controlled trial. *Archives of Pediatrics and Adolescent Medicine, 159,* 440–449.

Jemmott, J. B., III, Jemmott, L. S., & Fong, G. T. (1998). Abstinence and safer sex: A randomized controlled trial of HIV sexual risk-reduction interventions for young African American adolescents. *Journal of the American Medical Association, 279,* 1529–1536.

Jenkins, J. M., & Asington, J. W. (1996). Cognitive factors and family structure associated with theory of mind in young children. *Developmental Psychology, 32,* 70–78.

Ji, L. J., Nisbett, R. E., & Su, Y. (2001). Culture, change, and prediction. *Psychological Science, 12,* 450–456.

Ji, L., Peng, K., & Nisbett, R. E. (2000). Culture, control, and perception of relationships in the environment. *Journal of Personality and Social Psychology, 78,* 943–955.

Ji, L., Schwarz, N., & Nisbett, R. E. (2000). Culture, autobiographical memory, and social comparison: Measurement issues in cross-cultural studies. *Personality and Social Psychology Bulletin, 26,* 585–593.

Job, R. F. S. (1988). Effective and ineffective use of fear in health promotion campaigns. *American Journal of Public Health, 78,* 163–167.

John, O. P. (1990). The "big five" factor taxonomy: Dimensions of personality in the natural language and in questionnaires. In L. A. Pervin (Ed.), *Handbook of personality: Theory and research* (pp. 66–100). New York: Guilford Press.

John, O. P., Naumann, L., & Soto, C. J. (2008). Paradigm shift to the integrative Big Five trait taxonomy: Discovery, measurement, and conceptual issues. In O. P. John, R. W. Robins, & L.A. Pervin (Eds.), *Handbook of personality: Theory and research* (3rd ed., pp. 114–158). New York: Guilford Press.

John, O. P., & Robins, R. W. (1994). Accuracy and bias in self-perception: Individual differences in self-enhancement and the role of narcissism. *Journal of Personality & Social Psychology, 66*(1), 206–219.

John, O. P., & Srivastava, S. (1999). The big five trait taxonomy: History, measurement, and theoretical perspectives. In L. A. Pervin & O. P. John (Eds.), *Handbook of personality: Theory and research* (2nd ed., pp. 102–138). New York: Guilford Press.

Johnson, J. T. (1986). The knowledge of what might have been: Affective and attributional consequences of near outcomes. *Personality and Social Psychology Bulletin, 12,* 51–62.

Jones, C., & Aronson, E. (1973). Attribution of fault to a rape victim as a function of the respectability of the victim. *Journal of Personality and Social Psychology, 26,* 415–419.

Jones, E. E. (1964). *Ingratiation.* New York: Appleton-Century-Crofts.

Jones, E. E., & Davis, K. E. (1965). From acts to dispositions: The attribution process in person perception. In L. Berkowitz (Ed.), *Advances in experimental social psychology* (Vol. 2, pp. 219–266). New York: Academic Press.

Jones, E. E., Davis, K. E., & Gergen, K. J. (1961). Role playing variations and their informational value for person perception. *Journal of Abnormal and Social Psychology, 63,* 302–310.

Jones, E. E., Farina, A., Hastorf, A. H., Markus, H., Miller, D. T., & Scott, R. A. (1984). *Social stigma: The psychology of marked relationships.* New York: Freeman.

Jones, E. E., & Harris, V. A. (1967). The attribution of attitudes. *Journal of Experimental Social Psychology, 3,* 1–24.

Jones, E. E., & Nisbett, R. E. (1972). The actor and the observer: Divergent perceptions of the causes of behavior. In E. E. Jones, D. E. Kanouse, H. H. Kelley, R. E. Nisbett, S. Valins, & B. Weiner (Eds.), *Attribution: Perceiving the causes of behavior.* Morristown, NJ: General Learning Press.

Jost, J. T. (1997). An experimental replication of the depressed entitlement effect among women. *Psychology of Women Quarterly, 21,* 387–393.

Jost, J. T., & Banaji, M. R. (1994). The role of stereotyping in system justification and the production of false consciousness. *British Journal of Social Psychology, 33,* 1–27.

Jost, J. T., Banaji, M. R., & Nosek, B. A. (2004). A decade of system justification theory: Accumulated evidence of conscious and unconscious bolstering of the status quo. *Political Psychology, 25,* 881–919.

Jost, J. T., Glaser, J., Kruglanski, A. W., & Sulloway, F. (2003). Political conservatism as motivated social cognition. *Psychological Bulletin, 129,* 339–375.

Jost, J. T., & Kay, A. C. (2005). Exposure to benevolent sexism and complementary gender stereotypes: Consequences for specific and diffuse forms of system justification. *Journal of Personality and Social Psychology, 88,* 498–509.

Jost, J. T., Pelham, B. W., Sheldon, O., & Sullivan, B. N. (2003). Social inequality and the reduction of ideological dissonance on behalf of the system: Evidence of enhanced system justification among the disadvantaged. *European Journal of Social Psychology, 33,* 13–36.

Jourard, S. M. (1966). An exploratory study of body accessibility. *British Journal of Social and Clinical Psychology, 5,* 221–231.

Judd, C. M., Blair, I. V., & Chapleau, K. M. (2004). Automatic stereotypes vs. automatic prejudice: Sorting out the possibilities in the Payne (2001) weapon paradigm. *Journal of Experimental Social Psychology, 40,* 75–81.

Judd, C. M., Drake, R. A., Downing, J. W., & Krosnick, J. A. (1991). Some dynamic properties of attitude structures: Context induced responses facilitation and polarization. *Journal of Personality and Social Psychology, 60,* 193–202.

Judd, C. M., Kenny, D. A., & Krosnick, J. A. (1983). Judging the positions of political candidates: Models of assimilation and contrast. *Journal of Personality and Social Psychology, 46,* 1193–1207.

Judd, C. M., & Lusk, C. M. (1984). Knowledge structures and evaluative judgments: Effects of structural variables on judgment extremity. *Journal of Personality and Social Psychology, 46,* 1193–1207.

Judd, C. M., & Park, B. (1993a). Definition and assessment of accuracy of social stereotypes. *Psychological Review, 100,* 109–128.

Judd, C. M., & Park, B. (1993b). The assessment of accuracy of social stereotypes. *Psychological Review, 100,* 109–128.

Judge, T. A., Bono, J. E., Ilies, R., & Gerhardt, M. W. (2002). Personality and leadership: A qualitative and quantitative review. *Journal of Applied Psychology, 87,* 765–780.

Jussim, L. (1986). Self-fulfilling prophecies: A theoretical and integrative review. *Psychological Review, 93,* 429–445.

Jussim, L., Eccles, J., & Madon, S. J. (1996). Social perception, social stereotypes, and teacher expectations: Accuracy and the quest for the powerful self-fulfilling prophecy. *Advances in Experimental Social Psychology, 29,* 281–388.

Jussim, L., & Harber, K. (2005). Teacher expectations and self-fulfilling prophecies: Knowns and unknowns, resolved and unresolved controversies. *Personality and social psychology review, 9,* 131–155.

Kagan, J. (1989). Temperamental contributions to social behavior. *American Psychologist, 44,* 668–674.

Kahneman, D. (1999). Objective happiness. In D. Kahneman, E. Diener, & N. Schwarz (Eds.), *Hedonic psychology.* New York: Cambridge University Press.

Kahneman, D., & Frederick, S. (2002). Representativeness revisited: Attribute substitution in intuitive judgment. In T. Gilovich, D. W. Griffin, & D. Kahneman (Eds.), *Heuristics and biases: The psychology of intuitive judgment* (pp. 49–81). New York: Cambridge University Press.

Kahneman, D., & Lovallo, D. (1993). Timid choices and bold forecasts: A cognitive perspective on risk taking. *Management Science, 39,* 17–31.

Kahneman, D., & Miller, D. T. (1986). Norm theory: Comparing reality to its alternatives. *Psychological Review, 93,* 136–153.

Kahneman, D., Slovic, P., & Tversky, A. (1982). *Judgment under uncertainty: Heuristics and biases.* New York: Cambridge University Press.

Kahneman, D., & Tversky, A. (1972). Subjective probability: A judgment of representativeness. *Cognitive Psychology, 3,* 430–454.

Kahneman, D., & Tversky, A. (1973a). Availability: A heuristic for judging frequency and probability. *Cognitive Psychology, 4,* 207–232.

Kahneman, D., & Tversky, A. (1973b). On the psychology of prediction. *Psychological Review, 80,* 237–251.

Kahneman, D., & Tversky, A. (1982a). The simulation heuristic. In D. Kahneman, P. Slovic, & A. Tversky (Eds.), *Judgment under certainty: Heuristics and biases* (pp. 201–208). New York: Cambridge University Press.

Kahneman, D., & Tversky, A. (1982b). Variants of uncertainty. *Cognition, 11,* 143–157.

Kahneman, D., & Tversky, A. (1995). On the reality of cognitive illusions. *Psychological Review, 103,* 582–591.

Kaid, L. L. (1981). Political advertising. In D. D. Nimmo & K. R. Sanders (Eds.), *Handbook of political communication.* Beverly Hills, CA: Sage.

Kamarack, T. W., Manuch, S., & Jennings, J. R. (1990). Social support reduces cardiovascular reactivity to psychological challenge: A laboratory model. *Psychosomatic Medicine, 52,* 42–58.

Kamstra, M. J., Kramer, L. A., & Levi, M. D. (2003). Winter blues: Seasonal affective disorder (SAD) and stock market returns. American Economic Review, 93, 324–343.

Karau, S. J., & Williams, K. D. (1995). Social loafing: Research findings, implications, and future directions. *Current Directions in Psychological Science, 4,* 134–140.

Karney, B. R., & Bradbury, T. N. (1995). The longitudinal course of marital quality and stability:.A review of theory, method, and research. *Psychological Bulletin, 118,* 3–34.

Karney, B. R., & Bradbury, T. N. (1997). Neuroticism, marital interaction, and the trajectory of marital satisfaction. *Journal of Personality and Social Psychology, 72,* 1075–1092.

Karney, B. R., & Bradbury, T. N. (2000). Attributions in marriage: State or trait? A growth curve analysis. *Journal of Personality and Social Psychology, 78,* 295–309.

Karney, B. R., Bradbury, T. N., Fincham, F. D., & Sullivan, K. T. (1994). The role of negative affectivity in the association between attributions and marital satisfaction. *Journal of Personality and Social Psychology, 66,* 413–424.

Karney, B. R., & Coombs, R. H. (2000). Memory bias in long-term relationships: Consistency or improvement? *Personality and Social Psychology Bulletin, 26,* 959–970.

Karpinski, A., & Hilton, J. L. (2001). Attitudes and the Implicit Association Test. *Journal of Personality and Social Psychology, 81,* 774–788.

Kashima, Y., Siegal, M., Tanaka, K., & Kashima, E. S. (1992). Do people believe behaviours are consistent with attitudes? Towards a cultural psychology of attribution processes. *British Journal of Social Psychology, 37,* 111–124.

Kashima, Y., Yamaguchi, S., Kim, U., Choi, S.-C., Gelfand, M. J., & Yuki, M. (1995). Culture, gender, and self: A perspective from individualism-collectivism research. *Journal of Personality and Social Psychology, 69,* 925–937.

Kasser, T., & Sheldon, K. M. (2000). Of wealth and death: Materialism, mortality salience, and consumption behavior. *Psychological Science, 11,* 348–351.

Katz, I., Glucksberg, S., & Krauss, R. (1960). Need satisfaction and Edwards PPS scores in married couples. *Journal of Consulting Psychology, 24,* 205–208.

Kauffman, K. (1981). Prison officer attitudes and perceptions of attitudes. *Journal of Research in Crime Delinquency, 18,* 272–294.

Kay, A. C., & Jost, J. T. (2003). Complementary justice: Effects of "poor but happy" and "poor but honest" stereotype exemplars on system justification and implicit activation of the justice motive. *Journal of Personality and Social Psychology, 85,* 823–837.

Kay, A. C., Wheeler, S. C., Bargh, J. A., & Ross, L. (2004). Material priming: The influence of mundane physical objects on situation construal and competitive behavioral choice. *Organizational Behavior and Human Decision Processes, 95,* 83–96.

Kelley, H. H. (1967). Attribution theory in social psychology. In D. Levine (Ed.), *Nebraska Symposium on Motivation* (Vol. 15, pp. 192–238). Lincoln: University of Nebraska Press.

Kelley, H. H. (1973). The processes of causal attribution. *American Psychologist, 28,* 107–128.

Kelley, H. H., & Stahelski, A. J. (1970). The social interaction basis of cooperators' and competitors' beliefs about others. *Journal of Personality and Social Psychology, 16,* 66–91.

Kelley, H. H., & Thibaut, J. W. (1978). *Interpersonal relations: A theory of interdependence.* New York: Wiley.

Kelly, J. R., & Karau, S. J. (1999). Group decision making: The effects of initial preference and time pressure. *Personality and Social Psychology Bulletin, 25,* 1342–1354.

Kelman, H. C. (1958). Compliance, identification, and internalization: Three processes of attitude change. *Journal of Conflict Resolution, 2,* 51–60.

Keltner, D. (1995). The signs of appeasement: Evidence for the distinct displays of embarrassment, amusement, and shame. *Journal of Personality and Social Psychology, 68,* 441–454.

Keltner, D. (2009). Born to be good: The science of a meaningful life. New York: Norton.

Keltner, D., & Anderson, C. (2000). Saving face for Darwin: Functions and uses of embarrassment. *Current Directions in Psychological Science, 9,* 187–191.

Keltner, D., & Bonanno, G. A. (1997). A study of laughter and dissociation: The distinct correlates of laughter and smiling during bereavement. *Journal of Personality and Social Psychology, 73,* 687–702.

Keltner, D., & Buswell, B. N. (1997). Embarrassment: Its distinct form and appeasement functions. *Psychological Bulletin, 122,* 250–270.

Keltner, D., Capps, L. M., Kring, A. M., Young, R. C., & Heerey, E. A. (2001). Just teasing: A conceptual analysis and empirical review. *Psychological Bulletin, 127,* 229–248.

Keltner, D., Ellsworth, P. C., & Edwards, K. (1993). Beyond simple pessimism: Effects of sadness and anger on social perception. *Journal of Personality and Social Psychology, 64,* 740–752.

Keltner, D., Gruenfeld, D. H., & Anderson, C. A. (2003). Power, approach, and inhibition. *Psychological Review, 110,* 265–284.

Keltner, D., & Haidt, J. (1999). Social functions of emotions at four levels of analysis. *Cognition and Emotion, 13,* 505–521.

Keltner, D., & Haidt, J. (2003). Approaching awe, a moral, spiritual, and aesthetic emotion. *Cognition and Emotion, 17,* 297–314.

Keltner, D., Locke, K. D., & Audrain, P. C. (1993). The influence of attributions on the relevance of negative feelings to personal satisfaction. *Personality and Social Psychology Bulletin, 19,* 21–29.

Keltner, D., Moffitt, T., & Stouthhamer-Loeber, M. (1995). Facial expressions of emotion and psychopathology in adolescent boys. *Journal of Abnormal Psychology, 104,* 644–652.

Keltner, D., & Robinson, R. J. (1996). Extremism, power, and the imagined basis of social conflict. *Current Directions in Psychological Science, 5,* 101–105.

Keltner, D., & Robinson, R. J. (1997). Defending the status quo: Power and bias in social conflict. *Personality and Social Psychology Bulletin, 23*(10), 1066–1077.

Keltner, D., Van Kleef, G. A., Chen, S., & Kraus, M. W. (2008). A reciprocal influence model of social power: Emerging principles and lines of inquiry. *Advances in Experimental Social Psychology, 40,* 151–192.

Keltner, D., Young, R. C., Heerey, E. A., Oemig, C., & Monarch, N. D. (1998). Teasing in hierarchial and intimate relations. *Journal of Personality and Social Psychology, 75,* 1231–1247.

Kemper, T. D. (1991). Predicting emotions from social relations. *Social Psychology Quarterly, 54,* 330–342.

Kenny, D. A., & LaVoie, L. (1982). Reciprocity of interpersonal attraction: A confirmed hypothesis. *Social Psychology Quarterly, 45,* 54–58.

Kenny, D. A., & Nasby, W. (1980). Splitting the reciprocity correlation. *Journal of Personality and Social Psychology, 38,* 249–256.

Kenrick, D. T., & Keefe, R. C. (1992). Age preferences in mates reflect sex differences in reproductive strategies. *Behavioral and Brain Sciences, 15,* 75–133.

Kenrick, D. T., & MacFarlane, S. W. (1984). Ambient temperature and horn-honking: A field study of the heat/aggression relationship. *Environment and Behavior, 18,* 179–191.

Kenyatta, J. (1938). *Facing Mt. Kenya.* Nairobi, Kenya: Heinemann.

Kerr, N. L., MacCoun, R. J., & Kramer, G. P. (1996). Bias in judgment: Comparing individuals and groups. *Psychological Review, 103,* 687–719.

Ketelaar, T. (2005). Emotions and economic decision-making: The role of moral sentiments in experimental economics. In D. De Cremer, K. Murnighan, &. M. Zeelenberg, (Eds.), *Social psychology and experimental economics.* Mahwah, NJ: Erlbaum.

Kiecolt-Glaser, J. K., & Glaser, R. (1995). Psychoneuroimmunology and health consequences: Data and shared mechanisms. *Psychosomatic medicine, 57,* 269– 274.

Kiecolt-Glaser, J. K., Malarkey, W. B., Cacioppo, J. T., & Glaser, R. (1994). Stressful personal relationships: Immune and endocrine function. In R. Glaser & Kiecolt-Glaser (Eds.), *Handbook of human stress and immunity* (pp. 321–339). San Diego, CA: Academic Press.

Kiesler, S. B. (1971). *The psychology of commitment: Experiments linking behavior to belief.* New York: Academic Press.

Kiesler, S. B., & Mathog, R. (1968). The distraction hypothesis in attitude change. *Psychological Reports, 23,* 1123–1133.

Kihlstrom, J. F., & Cantor, N. (1984). Mental representations of the self. In L. Berkowitz (Ed.), *Advances in experimental social psychology* (Vol. 17, pp. 1–47). New York: Academic Press.

Kim, H., & Baron, R. S. (1988). Exercise and illusory correlation: Does arousal heighten stereotypic processes? *Journal of Experimental Social Psychology, 24,* 366–380.

Kim, H., & Markus, H. R. (1999). Deviance or uniqueness, harmony or conformity?: A cultural analysis. *Journal of Personality and Social Psychology, 77,* 785–800.

Kimmel, M. S. (2004). *The gendered society* (2nd ed.). New York: Oxford University Press.

Kinder, D. R., & Sears, D. O. (1981). Prejudice and politics: Symbolic racism versus racial threats to the good life. *Journal of Personality and Social Psychology, 40,* 414–431.

King, L. A., & Miner, K. N. (2000). Writing about the perceived benefits of traumatic events: Implications for physical health. *Personality and Social Psychology Bulletin, 26,* 220–230.

Kirkpatrick, L. A., & Hazan, C. (1994). Attachment styles and close relationships: A four-year prospective study. *Personal Relationships, 1,* 123–142.

Kitayama, S., & Masuda, T. (1997). Shaiaiteki ninshiki no bunkateki baikai model: taiousei bias no bunkashinrigakuteki kentou. (Cultural psychology of social inference: The correspondence bias in Japan.) In K. Kashiwagi, S. Kitayama, & H. Azuma (Eds.), *Bunkashinrigaku: riron to jisho. (Cultural psychology: Theory and evidence).* Tokyo: University of Tokyo Press.

Kitayama, S., Duffy, S., Kawamura, T., & Larsen, J. T. (2002). Perceiving an object in its context in different cultures: A cultural look at the New Look. *Psychological Science, 14,* 201–206.

Kitayama, S., Karasawa, M., & Mesquita, B. (2004). Collective and personal processes in regulating emotions: Emotion and self in Japan and the United States. In P. Philipot & R. S. Feldman (Eds.), *The regulation of emotion* (pp. 251–273). Hillsdale, NJ: Erlbaum.

Kitayama, S., Markus, H. R., & Kurokawa, M. (2000). Culture, emotion, and well-being: Good feelings in Japan and the United States. *Cognition and Emotion, 14,* 93–124.

Kitayama, S., Markus, H. R., Matsumoto, H., & Norasakkunkit, V. (1997). Individual and collective processes in the construction of the self: Self-enhancement in the United States and self-depreciation in Japan. *Journal of Personality and Social Psychology, 72,* 1245–1267.

Kitayama, S., Mesquita, B., & Karasawa, M. (2005). *Culture and emotional experience: Socially engaging and disengaging emotions in Japan and the United States.* Unpublished manuscript.

Kitayama, S., Snibbe, A. C., Markus, H. R., & Suzuki, T. (2004). Is there any "free" choice? Self and dissonance in two cultures. *Psychological Science, 15,* 527–533.

Klauer, K. C., & Meiser, T. (2000). A source-monitoring analysis of illsory correlations. *Personality and Social Psychology Bulletin, 26,* 1074–1093.

Klayman, J., & Ha, Y. (1987). Confirmation, disconfirmation, and information in hypothesis testing. *Psychological Review, 94,* 211–228.

Klein, S. B., & Kihlstrom, J. F. (1986). Elaboration, organization, and the self-reference effect in memory. *Journal of Experimental Psychology: General, 115,* 26–38.

Klein, S. B., & Loftus, J. (1988). The nature of self-referent encoding: The contributions of elaborative and organizational processes. *Journal of Personality and Social Psychology, 55,* 5–11.

Klein, W. M., & Kunda, Z. (1992). Motivated person perception: Constructing justifications for desired beliefs. *Journal of Experimental Social Psychology, 28,* 145–168.

Kleinhesselink, R. R., & Edwards, R. E. (1975). Seeking and avoiding belief-discrepant information as a function of its perceived refutability. *Journal of Personality and Social Psychology, 31,* 787–790.

Kling, A., Lancaster, J., & Benitone, J. (1970). Amygdalectomy in the free ranging vervet (*Ceropithicus aethiops*). *Journal of Psychiatric Research, 7,* 191–199.

Klinger, M. R., Burton, P. C., & Pitts, G. S. (2000). Mechanisms of unconscious priming I: Response competition, not spreading activation. *Journal of Experimental Psychology: Learning, Memory, and Cognition, 26,* 441–455.

Klofas, J., & Toch, H. (1982). The guard subculture myth. *Journal of Research in Crime Delinquency, 19,* 238–254.

Klohnen, E. C., & Bera, S. J. (1998). Behavioral and experiential patterns of avoidantly and securely attached women across adulthood: A 30–year longitudinal perspective. *Journal of Personality and Social Psychology, 74,* 211–223.

Kniffin, K. M., & Wilson, D. S. (2004). The effect of nonphysical traits on the perception of physical attractiveness: Three naturalistic studies. *Evolution and Human Behavior, 25,* 88–101.

Knox, R. E., & Inkster, J. A. (1968). Postdecision dissonance at posttime. *Journal of Personality and Social Psychology, 8,* 319–323.

Knutson, B. (1996). Facial expressions of emotion influence interpersonal trait inferences. *Journal of Nonverbal Behavior, 20,* 165–182.

Konner, M. (2003). *The tangled wing. Biological constraints on the human spirit,* New York: Holt.

Kosfeld, M., Heinrichs, M., Zak, P. J., Fishbacher, U., & Fehr, E. (2005). Oxytocin increases trust in humans. *Nature, 435,* 673–676.

Koslowsky, M., & Schwarzwald, J. (2001). The power interaction model: Theory, methodology, and empirical applications. In A. Y. Lee-Chai & J. A. Bargh (Eds.), *The use and abuse of power: Multiple perspectives on the causes of corruption* (pp. 195–214). Philadelphia: Psychology Press.

Kraus, M., Piff, P., & Keltner, D. (in press). Social class and social explanation. *Journal of Personality and Social Psychology.*

Krosnick, J. A. (1988). The role of attitude importance in social evaluation: A study of policy preferences, presidential candidate evaluations, and voting behavior. *Journal of Personality and Social Psychology, 55,* 196–210.

Krosnick, J. A., Betz, A. L., Jussim, L. J., & Lynn, A. R. (1992). Subliminal conditioning of attitudes. *Personality and Social Psychology Bulletin, 18,* 152–162.

Krosnick, J. A., & Petty, R. E. (1995). Attitude strength: An overview. In R. E. Petty & J. A. Krosnick (Eds.), *Attitude strength: Antecedents and consequences* (pp. 1–24). Mahwah, NJ: Erlbaum.

Kross, E., & Ayduk, O. (2008). Facilitating adaptive emotional analysis: Distinguishing distanced-analysis of depressive experiences from immersed-analysis and distraction. *Personality and Social Psychology Bulletin, 34,* 924–938.

Kross, E., Ayduk, O., & Mischel, W. (2005). When asking "why" does not hurt: Distinguishing rumination from reflective processing of negative emotions. *Psychological Science, 16,* 709–715.

Kruger, J., & Burrus, J. (2004). Egocentrism and focalism in unrealistic optimism (and pessimism). *Journal of Experimental Social Psychology, 40(3),* 332–340.

Kruger, J., Wirtz, D., & Miller, D. (2005). Counterfactual thinking and the first instinct fallacy. *Journal of Personality and Social Psychology, 88,* 725–735.

Kruglanski, A. W., & Mayseless, O. (1990). Classic and current social comparison research: Expanding the perspective. *Psychological Bulletin, 108(2),* 195–208.

Kruglanski, A. W., & Webster, D. M. (1991). Group members' reactions to opinion deviates and conformists at varying degrees of proximity to decision deadline and of environmental noise. *Journal of Personality and Social Psychology, 61,* 212–225.

Kruglanski, A. W., & Webster, D. M. (1996). Motivated closing of the mind: "Seizing" and "freezing." *Psychological Review, 103,* 263–283.

Krull, D. S. (1993). Does the grist change the mill? The effect of the perceiver's inferential goal on the process of social inference. *Personality and Social Psychology Bulletin, 19,* 340–348.

Krull, D. S., & Dill, J. C. (1996). On thinking first and responding fast: Flexibility in social inference processes. *Personality and Social Psychology Bulletin, 22,* 949–959.

Krull, D. S., & Erickson, D. J. (1995). Inferential hopscotch: How people draw social inferences from behavior. *Current Directions in Psychological Science, 4,* 35–38.

Krull, D. S., Loy, M., Lin, J., Wang, C.-F., Chen, S., & Zhao, X. (1996). *The fundamental attribution error: Correspondence bias in independent and interdependent cultures.* Paper presented at the 13th Congress of the International Association for Cross-Cultural Psychology, Montreal, Quebec, Canada.

Kuhlmeier, V., Wynn, K., & Bloom, P. (2003). Attribution of dispositional states by 12-month-olds. *Psychological Science, 5,* 402–408.

Kuhn, M. H., & McPartland, T. S. (1954). An empirical investigation of self-attitudes. *American Sociological Review, 19,* 68–76.

Kühnen, U., & Oyserman, D. (2002). *Thinking about the self influences thinking in general: Cognitive consequences of salient self-concept.* Ann Arbor: University of Michigan.

Kulik, J. A. (1983). Confirmatory attribution and the perpetuation of social beliefs. *Journal of Personality and Social Psychology, 44,* 1171–1181.

Kunda, Z. (1990). The case for motivated reasoning. *Psychological Bulletin, 108,* 480–496.

Kunda, Z., Davies, P. G., Adams, B., & Spencer, S. J. (2002). The dynamic time course of stereotype activation: Activation, dissipation, and resurrection. *Journal of Personality and Social Psychology, 82,* 283–299.

Kunda, Z., & Oleson, K. C. (1995). Maintaining stereotypes in the face of disconfirmation: Constructing grounds for subtyping deviants. *Journal of Personality and Social Psychology, 68,* 565–579.

Kunda, Z., & Sherman-Williams, B. (1993). Stereotypes and the construal of individuating information. *Personality and Social Psychology Bulletin, 19,* 90–99.

Kunda, Z., & Thagard, P. (1996). Forming impressions from stereotypes, traits, and behaviors: A parallel-constraint-satisfaction theory. *Psychological Review, 103,* 646–657.

Kunz, P. R., & Woolcott, M. (1976). Seasons greetings: From my status to yours. *Social Research, 5,* 269–278.

Kurdek, L. A. (1993). Predicting marital dissolution: A 5 year prospective longitudinal study of newlywed couples. *Journal of Personality and Social Psychology, 64,* 221–242.

Kurzban, R. (2001). The social psychophysics of cooperation: Nonverbal communication in a public goods game. *Journal of Nonverbal Behavior, 25,* 241–259.

LaFrance, M., Henley, N. M., Hall, J. A., & Halberstadt, A. G. (1997). Nonverbal behavior: Are women's superior skills caused by their oppression? In M. R. Walsh (Ed.), *Women, men and gender: Ongoing debates.* New Haven: Yale University Press.

Lakin, J. L., & Chartrand, T. L. (2003). Using nonconscious behavioral mimicry to create affiliation and rapport. *Psychological Science, 14,* 334–339.

Lakoff, G. (2004). *Don't think of an elephant: Know your values and frame the debate.* White River Junction, VT: Chelsea Green Publishing.

Lakoff, G., & Johnson, M. (1980). *Metaphors we live by.* Chicago: University of Chicago Press.

Lambert, A. J., Burroughs, T., & Nguyen, T. (1999). Perceptions of risk and the buffering hypothesis: The role of just world beliefs and right-wing authoritarianism. *Personality and Social Psychology Bulletin, 25,* 643–656.

Lambert, A. J., Khan, S. R., Lickel, B. A., & Fricke, K. (1997). Mood and the correction of positive versus negative stereotypes. *Journal of Personality and Social Psychology, 72,* 1002–1016.

Lambert, A. J., Payne, B. K., Jacoby, L. L., Shaffer, L. M., Chasteen, A. L., & Khan, S. R. (2003). Stereotypes as dominant responses: On the "social facilitation" of prejudice in anticipated public contexts. *Journal of Personality and Social Psychology, 84,* 277–295.

Landau, M. J., Solomon, S., Greenberg, J., Cohen, F., & Pyszczynski, T. (2004). Deliver us from evil: The effects of mortality salience and reminders of 9/11 on support for President George W. Bush. *Personality and Social Psychology Bulletin, 30,* 1136–1150.

Landes, E. M., & Rosenfield, A. M. (1994). Durability of advertising revisited. *Journal of Industrial Economics, 43,* 263–277.

Landsberger, M. (1966). Windfall income and consumption: Comment. *American Economic Review, 56,* 534–540.

Landy, D., & Sigall, H. (1974). Beauty is talent: Task evaluation as a function of the performer's physical attractiveness. *Journal of Personality and Social Psychology, 29,* 299–304.

Lane, K. A., Banaji, M. R., Nosek, B. A., & Greenwald, A. G. (2007). Understanding and using the Implicit Association Test: IV: Procedures and validity. In B. Wittenbrink & N. Schwarz (Eds.), *Implicit measures of attitudes: Procedures and controversies* (pp. 59–102). New York: Guilford Press.

Lang, P. J., Greenwald, M. K., Bradley, M. M., & Hamm, A. O. (1993). Looking at pictures: Affective, facial, visceral, and behavioral reactions. *Psychophysiology, 30,* 261–273.

Langer, E. (1975). The illusion of control. *Journal of Personality and Social Psychology, 32,* 311–328.

Langer, E. J., & Rodin, J. (1976). The effects of choice and enhanced personal responsibility for the aged: A field experiment in an institutional setting. *Journal of Personality and Social Psychology, 34,* 191–198.

Langlois, J. H., Kalakanis, L., Rubenstein, A. J., Larson, A., Hallam, M., & Smoot, M. (2000). Maxims or myths of beauty? A meta-analytic review and theoretical review. *Psychological Bulletin, 126,* 390–423.

Langlois, J. H., Ritter, J. M., Casey, R. J., & Sawin, D. B. (1995). Infant attractiveness predicts maternal behaviors and attitudes. *Developmental Psychology, 31,* 464–472.

Langlois, J. H., Ritter, J. M., Roggman, L. A., & Vaughn, L. S. (1991). Facial diversity and infant preferences for attractive faces. *Developmental Psychology, 27,* 79–84.

Langlois, J. H., & Roggman, L. A. (1990). Attractive faces are only average. *Psychological Science, 1,* 115–121.

Langlois, J. H., Roggman, L. A., Casey, R. J., Ritter, J. M., Rieser-Danner, L. A., & Jenkins, V. Y. (1987). Infant preferences for attractive faces: Rudiments of a stereotype. *Developmental Psychology, 23,* 363–369.

Langlois, J. H., Roggman, L. A., & Rieser-Danner, L. A. (1990). Infants' differential social responses to attractive and unattractive faces. *Developmental Psychology, 26,* 153–159.

LaPiere, R. T. (1934). Attitudes versus actions. *Social Forces, 13,* 230–237.

Larkey, P. D., Smith, R. A., & Kadane, J. B. (1989). It's okay to believe in the hot hand. *Chance, 2,* 22–30.

Larrick, R. P., Morgan, J. N., & Nisbett, R. E. (1990). Teaching the use of cost-benefit reasoning in everyday life. *Psychological Science, 1,* 362–370.

Larrick, R. P., Nisbett, R. E., & Morgan, J. N. (1993). Who uses the cost-benefit rules of choice? Implications for the normative status of microeconomic theory. *Organizational Behavior and Human Decision Processes, 56,* 331–347.

Lassiter, G. D., Geers, A. L., Munhall, P. J., Ploutz-Snyder, R. J., & Breitenbecher, D. L. (2002). Illusory causation: Why it occurs. *Psychological Science, 13,* 299–305.

Latané, B., & Darley, J. M. (1968). Group inhibition of bystander intervention in emergencies. *Journal of Personality and Social Psychology, 10,* 215–221.

Latané, B., & Darley, J. M. (1969). Bystander "apathy." *American Scientist, 57,* 218–250.

Latané, B., & Nida, S. (1981). Ten years of research on group size and helping. *Psychological Bulletin, 89,* 308–324.

Latané, B., Williams, K., & Harkins, S. (1979). Many hands make the work light: The causes and consequences of social loafing. *Journal of Personality and Social Psychology, 37,* 822–832.

Lau, G., Kay, A. C., & Spencer, S. J. (2008). Loving those who justify inequality: The effects of system threat on attraction to women who embody benevolent sexist ideals. *Psychological Science, 19*(1), 20–21.

Lau, R. R., & Russell, D. (1980). Attributions in the sports pages: A field test of some current hypotheses about attribution research. *Journal of Personality and Social Psychology, 39,* 29–38.

Laughlin, P. R. (1988). Collective induction: Group performance, social combination processes, and mutual majority and minority influence. *Journal of Personality and Social Psychology, 54,* 254–267.

Laughlin, P. R., & Ellis, A. L. (1986). Demonstrability and social combination processes on mathematical intellective tasks. *Journal of Experimental Social Psychology, 22,* 177–189.

Laughlin, P. R., Hatch, E. C., Silver, J. S., & Boh, L. (2006). Groups perform better than the best individuals on letters-to-numbers problems: Effects of group size. *Journal of Personality and Social Psychology, 90,* 644–651.

Lawler, K. A., Younger, J. W., Piferi, R. L., Billington, E., Jobe, R., Edmondson, K., et al. (2003). A change of heart: Cardiovascular correlates of forgiveness in response to interpersonal conflict. *Journal of Behavioral Medicine, 26,* 373–393.

Lazarus, R. S. (1966). *Psychological stress and the coping process.* New York: McGraw-Hill.

Lazarus, R. S. (1991). *Emotion and adaptation.* New York: Oxford University Press.

Lea, M., Spears, R., & de Groot, D. (2001). Knowing me, knowing you: Anonymity effects on social identity processes within groups. *Personality and Social Psychology Bulletin, 27,* 526–537.

Leary, M. R., Britt, T. W., Cutlip, W. D. I., & Templeton, J. L. (1992). Social blushing. *Psychological Bulletin, 112,* 446–460.

Leary, M. R., & Jones, J. L. (1993). The social psychology of tanning and sunscreen use: Self-presentational motives as a predictor of health risk. *Journal of Applied Social Psychology, 23,* 1390–1406.

Leary, M. R., & Kowalski, R. M. (1990). Impression management: A literature review and two-component model. *Psychological Bulletin, 107,* 34–47.

Leary, M. R., Kowalski, R. M., Smith, L., & Phillips, S. (2003). Teasing, rejection, and violence: Case studies of the school shootings. *Aggressive Behavior, 29,* 202–214.

Leary, M. R., Tambor, E. S., Terdal, S. K., & Downs, D. L. (1995). Self-esteem as an interpersonal monitor: The sociometer hypothesis. *Journal of Personality and Social Psychology, 68,* 518–530.

Leary, M. R., Tchividjian, L. R., & Kraxberger, B. E. (1994). Self-presentation can be hazardous to your health: Impression management and health risk. *Health Psychology, 13,* 451–470.

LeBon, G. (1895). *The crowd.* London: Unwin.

LeDoux, J. E. (1989). Cognitive-emotional interactions in the brain. *Cognition and Emotion, 3,* 267–289.

LeDoux, J. E. (1993). Emotional networks in the brain. In M. Lewis & J. M. Haviland (Eds.), *Handbook of emotions* (pp. 109–118). New York: Guilford Press.

LeDoux, J. E. (1996). *The emotional brain.* New York: Simon & Schuster.

Lee, F., Hallahan, M., & Herzog, T. (1996). Explaining real life events: How culture and domain shape attributions. *Personality and Social Psychology Bulletin, 22,* 732–741.

Lehman, B. J., Taylor, S. E., Kiefe, C. I., & Seeman, T. E. (2005). Relation of childhood socioeconomic status and family environment to adult metabolic functioning in the CARDIA study. *Psychosomatic Medicine, 67,* 846–854.

Lehman, D. R., Lempert, R. O., & Nisbett, R. E. (1988). The effects of graduate training on reasoning: Formal discipline and thinking about everyday life events. *American Psychologist, 43,* 431–443.

Leippe, M. R., & Elkin, R. A. (1987). When motives clash: Issue involvement and response involvement as determinants of persuasion. *Journal of Personality and Social Psychology, 52,* 269–278.

Lemyre, L., & Smith, P. M. (1985). Intergroup discrimination and self-esteem in the minimal group paradigm. *Journal of Personality and Social Psychology, 49,* 660–670.

Lepore, L., & Brown, R. (1997). Category and stereotype activation: Is prejudice inevitable? *Journal of Personality and Social Psychology, 72,* 275–287.

Lepore, S. J., Allen, K. M., & Evans, G. W. (1993). Social support lowers cardiovascular reactivity to an acute stressor. *Psychosomatic medicine, 55,* 518–524.

Lepper, M. R. (1973). Dissonance, self-perception, and honesty in children. *Journal of Personality and Social Psychology, 23,* 65–74.

Lepper, M. R., & Greene, D. (1978). *The hidden costs of reward.* Hillsdale, NJ: Erlbaum.

Lepper, M. R., Greene, D., & Nisbett, R. E. (1973). Undermining children's intrinsic interest with extrinsic reward: A test of the overjustification hypothesis. *Journal of Personality and Social Psychology, 28,* 129–137.

Lepper, M. R., Ross, L., Vallone, R., & Keavney, M. (unpublished data). Biased perceptions of victory and media hostility in network coverage of presidential debates.

Lepper, M. R., Sagotsky, G., Dafoe, J., & Greene, D. (1982). Consequences of superfluous social constraints: Effect on young children's social inferences and subsequent intrinsic interest. *Journal of Personality and Social Psychology, 42,* 51–65.

Lepper, M. R., & Woolverton, M. (2001). The wisdom of practice: Lessons learned from the study of highly effective tutors. In J. Aronson (Ed.), *Improving academic achievement: Contributions of social psychology.* Orlando, FL: Academic Press.

Lepper, M. R., Woolverton, M., Mumme, D. L., & Gurtner, J.-L. (1993). Motivational techniques of expert human tutors: Lessons for the design of computer-based tutors. In S. P. Lajoie & S. J. Derry (Eds.), *Computers as cognitive tools.* Hillsdale, NJ: Erlbaum.

Lerner, J. S., Goldberg, J. H., & Tetlock, P. E. (1998). Sober second thoughts: The effects of accountability, anger, and

authoritarianism on attributions of responsibility. *Personality and Social Psychology Bulletin, 24,* 563–574.

Lerner, J. S., & Gonzalez, R. M. (2005). Forecasting one's future based on fleeting subjective experiences. *Personality and Social Psychology Bulletin, 31(4),* 454–466.

Lerner, J. S., Gonzalez, R. M., Small, D. A., & Fischhoff, B. (2003). Effects of fear and anger on perceived risks of terrorism: A national field experiment. *Psychological Science, 14(2),* 144–150.

Lerner, J. S., & Keltner, D. (2001). Fear, anger, and risk. *Journal of Personality and Social Psychology, 81,* 146–159.

Lerner, J. S., Small, D. A., & Loewenstein, G. (2004). Heart strings and purse strings: Carryover effects of emotions on economic decisions. *Psychological Science, 15,* 337–341.

Lerner, M. J. (1980). *The belief in a just world: A fundamental delusion.* New York: Plenum Press.

Lerner, M. J., & Miller, D. T. (1978). Just world research and the attribution process: Looking back and ahead. *Psychological Bulletin, 85,* 1030–1051.

Lerner, M. J., & Simmons, C. H. (1966). Observer's reactions to the "innocent victim": Compassion or rejection? *Journal of Personality and Social Psychology, 4,* 203–210.

Leslie, A. (2000). "Theory of mind" as a mechanism of selective attention. In M. S. Gazzaniga (Ed.), *The new cognitive neurosciences* (pp. 1235–1247). Cambridge, MA: MIT Press.

Levenson, R. W. (1999). The intrapersonal functions of emotion. *Cognition and Emotion, 13,* 481–504.

Levenson, R. W. (2003). Autonomic specificity and emotion. In R. J. Davidson, K. R. Scherer, & H. H. Goldsmith (Eds.), *Handbook of affective sciences* (pp. 212–224). New York: Oxford University Press.

Levenson, R. W., Carstensen, L. L., Friesen, W. V., & Ekman, P. (1991). Emotion, physiology, and expression in old age. *Psychology and Aging, 6(1),* 28–35.

Levenson, R. W., Ekman, P., & Friesen, W. V. (1990). Voluntary facial action generates emotion-specific autonomic nervous system activity. *Psychophysiology, 27 (4),* 363–384.

Levenson, R. W., Ekman, P., Heider, K., & Friesen, W. V. (1992). Emotion and autonomic nervous system activity in the Minangkabau of West Sumatra. *Journal of Personality and Social Psychology, 62 (6),* 972–988.

Levenson, R. W., & Gottman, J. M. (1983). Marital interaction: Physiological linkage and affective exchange. *Journal of Personality and Social Psychology, 45,* 587–597.

Leventhal, H. (Ed.). (1970). *Findings and theory in the study of fear communications.* New York: Academic Press.

Leventhal, H., Singer, R. P., & Jones, S. H. (1965). The effects of fear and specificity of recommendation upon attitudes and behavior. *Journal of Personality and Social Psychology, 2,* 20–29.

Leventhal, H., Watts, J. C., & Pagano, F. (1967). Effects of fear and instructions on how to cope with danger. *Journal of Personality and Social Psychology, 6,* 313–321.

Levin, I. P., & Gaeth, G. J. (1988). Framing of attribute information before and after consuming the product. *Journal of Consumer Research, 15,* 374–378.

Levine, J. M. (1989). Reaction to opinion deviance in small groups. In P. B. Paulus (Ed.), *Psychology of group influence* (2nd ed, pp. 187–231). Hillsdale, NJ: Erlbaum.

Levine, J. M., Higgins, E. T., & Choi, H. S. (2000). Development of strategic norms in groups. *Organizational Behavior and Human Decision Processes, 82,* 88–101.

Levine, J. M., & Moreland, R. L. (1990). Progress in small group research. *Annual Review of Psychology, 41*, 585–634.

Levine, J. M., & Moreland, R. L. (1998). Small groups. In D. T. Gilbert, S. T. Fiske, & G. Lindzey (Eds.), *The handbook of social psychology* (4th ed., Vol. 2, pp. 415–469). New York: McGraw-Hill.

LeVine, R. A., & Campbell, D. T. (1972). *Ethnocentrism.* New York: Wiley.

Levinger, G. (1964). Note on need complementarity in marriage. *Psychological Bulletin, 61*, 153–157.

Levinger, G., & Schneider, D. J. (1969). Test of the "risk as a value" hypothesis. *Journal of Personality and Social Psychology, 11*, 165–169.

Levinger, G., Senn, D. J., & Jorgensen, B. W. (1970). Progress toward permanence in courtship: A test of the Kerckhoff-Davis hypothesis. *Sociometry, 33*, 427–433.

Levitt, S. D. (1994). Using repeat challengers to estimate the effect of campaign spending on election outcomes in the U.S. House. *Journal of Political Economy, 102*, 777–798.

Lewicki, P. W. (1983). Self-image bias in person perception. *Journal of Personality and Social Psychology, 45*, 384–393.

Lewin, K. (1935). The conflict between Aristotelian and Galilean modes of thought in contemporary psychology. *Journal of General Psychology, 5*, 141–177.

Lewin, K. (1952). Group decision and social change. In G. E. Swanson, T. M. Newcomb, & E. L. Hartley (Eds.), *Readings in social psychology.* New York: Holt.

Leyens, J. P., Camino, L., Parke, R. D., & Berkowitz, L. (1975). Effects of movie violence on aggression in a field setting as a function of group dominance and cohesion. *Journal of Personality and Social Psychology, 32*, 346–360.

Leyens, J. P., Cisneros, T., & Hossay, J. F. (1976). Decentration as a means of reducing aggression after exposure to violent stimuli. *European Journal of Social Psychology, 6*, 459–473.

Leyens, J. P., & Picus, S. (1973). Identification with the winner of a fight and name mediation: Their differential effects upon subsequent aggressive behavior. *British Journal of Social and Clinical Psychology, 12*, 374–377.

Li, J., Wang, L., & Fischer, K. W. (2004). The organization of Chinese shame concepts. *Cognition and Emotion, 18*(6), 767–797.

Liberman, V., Samuels, S. M., & Ross, L. (2002). The name of the game: Predictive power of reputations vs. situational labels in determining Prisoner's Dilemma game moves. *Personality and Social Psychology Bulletin, 30*, 1175–1185.

Lichtenstein, S., Fischhoff, B., & Phillips, L. D. (1982). Calibration of probabilities: The state of the art to 1980. In D. Kahneman, P. Slovic, & A. Tversky (Eds.), *Judgment under uncertainty: Heuristics and biases.* New York: Cambridge University Press.

Lieberman, M. D., Hariri, A., Jarcho, J. M., Eisenberger, N. I., & Bookheimer, S. Y. (2005). An fMRI investigation of race-related amygdala activity in African-American and Caucasian-American individuals. *Nature Neuroscience, 8*, 720–722.

Linder, D. E., Cooper, J., & Jones, E. E. (1967). Decision freedom as a determinant of the role of incentive magnitude in attitude change. *Journal of Personality and Social Psychology, 6*, 245–254.

Linville, P. W. (1982). The complexity-extremity effect and age-based stereotyping. *Journal of Personality and Social Psychology, 42*, 193–211.

Linville, P. W. (1987). Self-complexity as a cognitive bugger against stress-related illness and depression. *Journal of Personality and Social Psychology, 52*, 663–676.

Linville, P. W., Fischer, G. W., & Fischhoff, B. (1993). AIDS risk perceptions and decision biases. In J. B. Pryor and G. D. Reeder (Eds.), *The social psychology of HIV infection* (pp. 5–38). Hillsdale, NJ: Erlbaum.

Linville, P. W., Fischer, G. W., & Salovey, P. (1989). Perceived distributions of the characteristics of in-group and out-group members: Empirical evidence and a computer simulation. *Journal of Personality and Social Psychology, 57*, 165–188.

Lipkus, I. M., Dalbert, C., & Siegler, I. C. (1996). The importance of distinguishing the belief in a just world for self versus for others: Implications for psychological well-being. *Personality and Social Psychology Bulletin, 22*, 666–677.

Lippmann, W. (1922). *Public opinion.* New York: Harcourt Brace.

Livingston, R. W., & Brewer, M. B. (2002). What are we really priming? Cue-based versus category-based processing of facial stimuli. *Journal of Personality and Social Psychology, 82*, 5–18.

Livshits, G., & Kobyliansky, E. (1991). Fluctuating asymmetry as a possible measure of developmental homeostasis in humans: A review. *Human Biology, 63*, 441–466.

Locke, K. D., & Horowitz, L. M. (1990). Satisfaction in interpersonal interactions as a function of similarity in level of dysphoria. *Journal of Personality and Social Psychology, 58*, 823–831.

Lockwood, P. (2002). Could it happen to you? Predicting the impact of downward social comparisons on the self. *Journal of Personality and Social Psychology, 82*, 343–358.

Loehlin, J. C. (1992). *Genes and environment in personality development.* Newbury Park, CA: Sage.

Loewenstein, G., & Lerner, J. S. (2003). The role of affect in decision making. In R. J. Davidson, K. R. Scherer, & H. H. Goldsmith (Eds.), *Handbook of affective sciences* (pp. 619–642). New York: Oxford University Press.

Loftus, E. F. (1979). *Eyewitness testimony.* Cambridge, MA: Harvard University Press.

Loftus, E. F. (1993). The reality of repressed memories. *American Psychologist, 48*, 518–537.

Loftus, E. F. (2003). The dangers of memory. In R. J. Sternberg (Ed.), *Psychologists defying the crowd: Stories of those who battled the establishment and won* (pp. 105–117). Washington, DC: American Psychological Association.

Longley, J., & Pruitt, D. G. (1980). Groupthink: A critique of Janis' theory. In L. Wheeler (Ed.), *Review of personality and social psychology.* Beverly Hills, CA: Sage.

Lord, C. G., Desforges, D. M., Ramsey, S. L., Trezza, G. R., & Lepper, M. R. (1991). Typicality effects in attitude-behavior consistency: Effects of category discrimination and category knowledge. *Journal of Experimental Social Psychology, 27*, 550–575.

Lord, C. G., Lepper, M. R., & Mackie, D. (1984). Attitude prototypes as determinants of attitude-behavior consistency. *Journal of Personality and Social Psychology, 46*, 1254–1266.

Lord, C., Ross, L., & Lepper, M. (1979). Biased assimilation and attitude polarization: The effects of prior theories on subsequently considered evidence. *Journal of Personality and Social Psychology, 37*, 2098–2109.

Lord, C. G., Scott, K. O, Pugh, M. A., & Desforges, D. M. (1997). Leakage beliefs and the correspondence bias. *Personality and Social Psychology Bulletin, 23*, 824–836.

Lorenz, K. (1971/1950). Part and parcel in animal and human societies. In *Studies in animal and human behaviour* (Vol. 2, pp. 115–195). Cambridge, MA: Harvard University Press.

Losch, M. E., & Cacioppo, J. T. (1990). Cognitive dissonance may enhance sympathetic tonus, but attitudes are changed to reduce negative affect rather than arousal. *Journal of Experimental Social Psychology, 26,* 289–304.

Lott, A. J., & Lott, B. E. (1961). Group cohesiveness, communication level, and conformity. *Journal of Abnormal and Social Psychology, 62,* 408–412.

Lott, A. J., & Lott, B. E. (1974). The role of reward in formation of positive interpersonal attitudes. In T. L. Huston (Ed.), *Foundations of interpersonal attraction* (pp. 171–189). New York: Academic Press.

Lowery, B. S., Unzueta, M. M., Knowles, E. D., & Goff, P. A. (2006). Concern for the ingroup and opposition to affirmative action. *Journal of Personality and Social Psychology, 90,* 961–974.

Lutz, C. A. (1988). *Unnatural emotions: Everyday sentiments on a Micronesian atoll and their challenge to Western theory.* Chicago: University of Chicago Press.

Lydon, J., Zanna, M. P., & Ross, M. (1988). Bolstering attitudes by autobiographical recall: Attitude persistence and selective memory. *Personality and Social Psychology Bulletin, 14,* 78–86.

Lynam, D. R., Milich, R., Zimmerman, R., Novak, S. P., Logan, T. K., Martin, C. E., et al. (1999). Project DARE: No effects at 10-year follow-up. *Journal of Consulting and Clinical Psychology, 67,* 590–593.

Lynch, J. J. (1979). *The broken heart: The medical consequences of loneliness.* New York: Basic Books.

Lyubomirsky, S. (2007). *The how of happiness.* New York: The Penguin Press.

Lyubomirsky, S., King, L., & Diener, E. (2005). The benefits of frequent positive affect: Does happiness lead to success? *Psychological Bulletin, 131,* 803–855.

Lyubomirsky, S., & Nolen-Hoeksema, S. (1995). Effects of self-focused rumination on negative thinking and interpersonal problem solving. *Journal of Personality and Social Psychology, 69,* 176–190.

Lyubomirsky, S., Sheldon, K. M., & Schkade, D. (2005). Pursuing happiness: The architecture of sustainable change. *Review of General Psychology, 9,* 111–131.

Ma, V., & Schoeneman, T. J. (1997). Individualism versus collectivism: A comparison of Kenyan and American self-concepts. *Basic and Applied Social Psychology, 19,* 261–273.

Maass, A., & Clark, R. D. III. (1983). Internalization versus compliance: Different processes underlying minority influence and conformity. *European Journal of Social Psychology, 13,* 197–215.

Maass, A., Salvi, D., Arcuri, L., & Semin, G. (1989). Language use in intergroup contexts: The linguistic intergroup bias. *Journal of Personality and Social Psychology, 57,* 981–993.

Maccoby, E. E. (1990). Gender and relationships: A developmental account. *American Psychologist, 45,* 513–520.

Maccoby, E. E., & Jacklin, C. N. (1974). *The psychology of sex differences.* Stanford: Stanford University Press.

MacCoun, R. (1993). Blaming others to a fault. *Chance, 6,* 31–33.

MacDonald, G,. & Leary, M. R. (2005). Why does social exclusion hurt? The relationship between social and physical pain. *Psychological Bulletin, 131*(2), 202–223.

Machiavelli, N. (1532/2003). *The prince,* trans. G. Bull. New York: Penguin Classics.

Macintyre, S., Maciver, S., & Solomon, A. (1993). Area, class, and health: Should we be focusing on places or people? *Journal of Social Policy, 22,* 213–234.

Mackie, D. M. (1987). Systematic and nonsystematic processing of majority and minority persuasive communications. *Journal of Personality and Social Psychology, 53,* 41–52.

Mackie, D. M., Silver, L. A., & Smith, E. R. (2004). Intergroup emotions: Emotion as an intergroup phenomenon. In L. Z. Tiedens & C. W. Leach (Eds.), *The social life of emotions* (pp. 227–246). New York: Cambridge University Press.

Mackie, D. M., & Worth, L. T. (1989). Cognitive deficits and the mediation of positive affect in persuasion. *Journal of Personality and Social Psychology, 57,* 27–40.

Macrae, C. N., Alnwick, K. A., Milne, A. B., & Schloerscheidt, A. M. (2002). Person perception across the menstrual cycle: Hormonal influences on social-cognitive functioning. *Psychological Science, 13,* 532–536.

Macrae, C. N., & Bodenhausen, G. V. (2000). Social cognition: Thinking categorically about others. *Annual Review of Psychology, 51,* 93–120.

Macrae, C. N., Hewstone, M., & Griffiths, R. J. (1993). Processing load and memory for stereotype-based information. *European Journal of Social Psychology, 23,* 77–87.

Macrae, C. N., Milne, A. B., & Bodenhausen, G. V. (1994). Stereotypes as energy-saving devices: A peek inside the cognitive toolbox. *Journal of Personality and Social Psychology, 66,* 37–47.

Macrae, C. N., Stangor, C., & Milne, A. B. (1994). Activating social stereotypes: A functional analysis. *Journal of Experimental Social Psychology, 30,* 370–389.

Magee, J. C., Galinsky, A. D., Inesi, M. E., & Gruenfeld, D. H. (2006). Power and perspectives not taken. *Psychological Science, 17*(12), 1068–1074.

Major, B. (1994). From social inequality to personal entitlement: The role of social comparisons, legitimacy appraisals, and group membership. *Advances in Experimental Social Psychology, 26,* 293–355.

Malle, B. F. (1999). How people explain behavior: A new theoretical framework. *Personality and Social Psychology Review, 3,* 23–48.

Malle, B. F. (2001). Folk explanations of intentional actions. In B. F. Malle, L. J. Moses, & D. A. Baldwin (Eds.), *Intentions and intentionality: Foundations of social cognition.* Cambridge, MA: MIT Press.

Malle, B. F., Moses, L. J., & Baldwin, D. A. (2001). *Intentions and intentionality: Foundations of social cognition.* Cambridge, MA: MIT Press.

Mann, L. (1981). The baiting crowd in episodes of threatened suicide. *Journal of Personality and Social Psychology, 41,* 703–709.

Manning, J. T., & Hartley, M. A. (1991). Symmetry and ornamentation are correlated in the peacock's train. *Animal Behavior, 42,* 1020–1021.

Maret, S. M. (1983). Attractiveness ratings of photographs of blacks by Cruzans and Americans. *The Journal of Psychology, 115,* 113–116.

Maret, S. M., & Harling, G. A. (1985). Cross cultural perceptions of physical attractiveness: Ratings of photos of whites by Cruzans and Americans. *Perceptual and Motor Skills, 60,* 163–166.

Margolin, L., & White, L. (1987). The continuing role of physical attractiveness in marriage. *Journal of Marriage and the Family, 49,* 21–27.

Markow, T. A., & Ricker, J. P. (1992). Male size, developmental stability and mating success in natural populations on three Drosophilia species. *Heredity, 69,* 122–127.

Markus, H. (1977). Self-schemata and processing information about the self. *Journal of Personality and Social Psychology, 35,* 63–78.

Markus, H. (1978). The effect of mere presence on social facilitation. An unobtrusive test. *Journal of Experimental Social Psychology, 14,* 389–397.

Markus, H. R., & Kitayama, S. (1991). Culture and the self: Implications for cognition, emotion, and motivation. *Psychological Review, 98,* 224–253.

Markus, H., & Nurius, P. S. (1986). Possible selves. *American Psychologist, 41,* 954–969.

Marmot, M. G., Shipley, S., & Rose, G. (1984). Inequalities in death—specific explanations of a general pattern. *Lancet, 1,* 1003–1006.

Marsh, H. L. (1991). A comparative analysis of crime coverage in newspapers in the United States and other countries from 1960–1989: A review of the literature. *Journal of Criminal Justice, 19,* 67–79.

Marsh, H. W., & Parker, J. W. (1984). Determinants of student self-concept: Is it better to be a relatively large fish in a small pond even if you don't learn to swim as well? *Journal of Personality and Social Psychology, 47,* 213–231.

Martin, G. G., & Clark, R. D. I. (1982). Distress crying in infants: Species and peer specificity. *Developmental Psychology, 18,* 3–9.

Martin, T., & Bumpass, L. (1989). Recent trends in marital disruption. *Demography, 26,* 37–52.

Martinek, T. J. (1981). Physical attractiveness: Effects on teacher expectations and dyadic interactions in elementary age children. *Journal of Sports Psychology, 3,* 196–205.

Maruyama, G., & Miller, N. (1980). Physical attractiveness, race, and essay evaluation. *Personality and Social Psychology Bulletin, 6,* 384–390.

Marwell, G., & Ames, R. (1981). Economists free ride, does anyone else?: Experiments on the provision of public goods, IV. *Journal of Public Economics, 15,* 295–310.

Masuda, T., Ellsworth, P. C., Mesquita, B., Leu, J., & van de Veerdonk, E. (2004). *A face in the crowd or a crowd in the face: Japanese and American perceptions of others' emotions.* Unpublished manuscript, Hokkaido University.

Masuda, T., & Nisbett, R. E. (2001). Attending holistically vs. analytically: Comparing the context sensitivity of Japanese and Americans. *Journal of Personality and Social Psychology, 81,* 922–934.

Mathews, A., & MacLeod, C. (1994). Cognitive approaches to emotion and emotional disorders. *Annual Review of Psychology, 45,* 25–50.

Matsumoto, D., Keltner, D., Shiota, M. N., O'Sullivan, M., & Frank, M. (2008). Facial expressions of emotion. In M. Lewis, J. M. Haviland-Jones, & L. F. Barrett (Eds.), *Handbook of emotions* (pp. 211–234). New York: Guilford Press.

Matsumoto, D., & Willingham, B. (2006). The thrill of victory and the agony of defeat: Spontaneous expressions of medal winners of the 2004 Athens Olympic games. *Journal of Personality and Social Psychology, 91,* 568–581.

Mauro, R., Sato, K., & Tucker, J. (1992). The role of appraisal in human emotions: A cross-cultural study. *Journal of Personality and Social Psychology, 62,* 301–317.

McAdams, D. P. (2008). Personal narratives and the life story. In O. P. John, R. Robins, & L. Pervin (Eds.), *Handbook of personality: Theories and research* (3rd ed., pp. 242–262). New York: Guilford Press.

McArthur, L. Z. (1972). The how and what of why: Some determinants and consequences of causal attribution. *Journal of Personality and Social Psychology, 13,* 733–742.

McArthur, L. Z., & Baron, R. M. (1983). Toward an ecological theory of social perception. *Psychological Review, 90,* 215–238.

McArthur, L. Z., & Post, D. L. (1977). Figural emphasis and person perception. *Journal of Experimental Social Psychology, 13,* 520–533.

McCain, J. (1999). *The faith of my fathers.* New York: Random House.

McCain, J. (2003). *Personal communication.*

McCauley, C. (1989). The nature of social influence in groupthink: Compliance and internalization. *Journal of Personality and Social Psychology, 57,* 250–260.

McCauley, C. (1998). Group dynamics in Janis's theory of groupthink: Backward and forward. *Organizational Behavior and Human Decision Processes, 73,* 142–162.

McConahay, J. B. (1986). Modern racism, ambivalence, and the modern racism scale. In J. F. Dovidio & S. L. Gaertner (Eds.), *Prejudice, discrimination, and racism* (pp. 91–126). Orlando, FL: Academic Press.

McConahay, J. B., Hardee, B. B., & Batts, V. (1981). Has racism declined in America? It depends upon who is asking and what is asked. *Journal of Conflict Resolution, 25,* 563–579.

McConahay, J. B., & Hough, J. C. J. (1976). Symbolic racism. *Journal of Social Issues, 32,* 23–45.

McConnell, A. R., & Leibold, J. M. (2001). Relations among the implicit association test, discriminatory behavior, and explicit measures of racial attitudes. *Journal of Experimental Social Psychology, 37,* 435–442.

McCoy, S. K., & Major, B. (2003). Group identification moderates emotional responses to perceived prejudice. *Personality and Social Psychology Bulletin, 29,* 1005–1017.

McCrae, R. R., Costa, P. T., & Yik, M. S. M. (1996). Universal aspects of Chinese personality structure. In M. H. Bond (Ed.), *The handbook of Chinese psychology* (pp. 189–207). Hong Kong: Oxford University Press.

McCullough, M. C., Kilpatrick, S. D., Emmons, R. A., & Larson, D. B. (2001). Is gratitude a moral affect? *Psychological Bulletin, 127,* 249–266.

McCullough, M. E., Worthington Jr., E. L., & Rachal, K. C. (1997). Interpersonal forgiveness in close relationships. *Journal of Personality and Social Psychology, 73,* 321–336.

McGill, A. L. (1989). Context effects in judgements of causation. *Journal of Personality and Social Psychology, 57,* 189–200.

McGlone, M. S., & Tofighbakhsh, J. (2000). Birds of a feather flock conjointly(?): Rhyme as reason in aphorisms. *Psychological Science, 11,* 424–428.

McGrath, J. (1984). *Groups: Interaction and performance.* Englewood Cliffs, NJ: Prentice-Hall.

McGuire, W. J. (1985). Attitudes and attitude change. In G. Lindzey & E. Aronson (Eds.), *Handbook of social psychology* (3rd ed., Vol. 2, pp. 233–346). New York: Random House.

McGuire, W. J. (1986). The myth of massive media impact: Savagings and salvagings. *Public Communication and Behavior, 1,* 173–257.

McGuire, W. J., & Padawer-Singer, A. (1978). Trait salience in the spontaneous self-concept. *Journal of Personality and Social Psychology, 33,* 743–754.

McGuire, W. J., & Papageorgis, D. (1961). The relative efficacy of various types of prior belief-defense in producing immunity against persuasion. *Journal of Abnormal and Social Psychology, 62,* 327–337.

McKenna, K. Y. A., & Bargh, J. A. (1998). Coming out in the age of the Internet: Identity demarginalization through virtual group participation. *Journal of Personality and Social Psychology, 75,* 681–694.

McMahin, D. M. (2006). *Happiness: A history.* New York: Grove Press

McNeil, B. J., Pauker, S. G., Sox, H. C., & Tversky, A. (1982). On the elicitation of preferences for alternative therapies. *New England Journal of Medicine, 306,* 1259–1262.

McNulty, J. K., & Karney, B. R. (2001). Attributions in marriage: Integrating specific and global evaluations of a relationship. *Personality and Social Psychology Bulletin, 27,* 943–955.

McPherson, K. (1983). Opinion-related information seeking: Personal and situational variables. *Personality and Social Psychology Bulletin, 9,* 116–124.

Mead, G. H. (1934). *Mind, self, and society.* Chicago: University of Chicago Press.

Medcoff, J. W. (1990). PEAT: An integrative model of attribution processes. In M. P. Zanna (Ed.), *Advances in experimental social psychology* (Vol. 23, pp. 111–209). New York: Academic Press.

Medvec, V. H., Madey, S. F., & Gilovich, T. (1995). When less is more: Counterfactual thinking and satisfaction among Olympic medalists. *Journal of Personality and Social Psychology, 69,* 603–610.

Mehrabian, A., & Williams, M. (1969). Nonverbal concomitants of perceived and intended persuasiveness. *Journal of Personality and Social Psychology, 13,* 37–58.

Merton, R. (1957). *Social theory and social structure.* Glencoe, IL: Free Press.

Mesquita, B. (2001). Emotions in collectivist and individualist contexts. *Journal of Personality and Social Psychology, 80,* 68–74.

Mesquita, B. (2003). Emotions as dynamic cultural phenomena. In R. J. Davidson, K. R. Scherer, & H. H. Goldsmith (Eds.), *Handbook of affective sciences* (pp. 871–890). New York: Oxford University Press.

Mesquita, B., & Ellsworth, P. C. (2001). The role of culture in appraisal. In K. R. Scherer & A. Schorr (Eds.), *Appraisal processes in emotion. Theory, methods, research.* New York: Oxford University Press.

Mesquita, B., & Frijda, N. H. (1992). Cultural variations in emotions: A review. *Psychological Bulletin, 112,* 179–204.

Mesquita, B., & Karasawa, M. (2002). Different emotional lives. *Cognition and Emotion, 16,* 127–141.

Mesquita, B., & Leu, J. (2007). The cultural psychology of emotion. In S. Kitayama & D. Cohen (Eds.), *The handbook of cultural psychology* (pp. 734–759). New York: Guilford Press.

Mettee, D., Taylor, S. E., & Friedman, H. (1973). Affect conversion and the gain-loss effect. *Sociometry, 36,* 505–519.

Meyer, J. P., & Pepper, S. (1977). Need compatibility and marital adjustment in young married couples. *Journal of Personality and Social Psychology, 35,* 331–342.

Michaels, J. W., Blommel, J. M., Brocato, R. M., Linkous, R. A., & Rowe, J. S. (1982). Social facilitation and inhibition in a natural setting. *Replications in Social Psychology, 2,* 21–24.

Mikulincer, M., & Florian, V. (2000). Exploring individual differences in reactions to mortality salience: Does attachment style regulate terror management mechanisms? *Journal of Personality and Social Psychology, 79,* 260–273.

Mikulincer, M., Gillath, O., & Shaver, P. R. (2002). Activation of the attachment system in adulthood: Threat-related primes increase the accessibility of mental representations of attachment figures. *Journal of Personality and Social Psychology, 83,* 881–895.

Mikulincer, M., & Shaver, P. R. (2003). The attachment behavioral system in adulthood: Activation, psychodynamics, and interpersonal processes. In M. P. Zanna (Ed.), *Advances in experimental social psychology* (Vol. 35, pp. 53–152). New York: Academic Press.

Milgram, S. (1961). Nationality and conformity. *Scientific American, 205,* 45–51.

Milgram, S. (1963). Behavioral study of obedience. *Journal of Abnormal and Social Psychology, 67,* 371–378.

Milgram, S. (1965). Some conditions of obedience and disobedience to authority. *Human Relations, 18,* 57–75.

Milgram, S. (1970). The experience of living in cities. *Science, 167,* 1461–1468.

Milgram, S. (1974). *Obedience to authority: An experimental view.* New York: Harper & Row.

Millar, M., & Tesser, A. (1986). Effects of affective and cognitive focus on the attitude-behavior relation. *Journal of Personality and Social Psychology, 51,* 270–276.

Miller, A. G. (1986). *The obedience experiments: A case study of controversy in social science.* New York: Praeger.

Miller, A. G., Ashton, W., & Mishal, M. (1990). Beliefs concerning the features of constrained behavior: A basis for the fundamental attribution error. *Journal of Personality and Social Psychology, 59,* 635–650.

Miller, A. G., Jones, E. E., & Hinkle, S. (1981). A robust attribution error in the personality domain. *Journal of Experimental Social Psychology, 17,* 587–600.

Miller, D. T. (1976). Ego involvement and attributions for success and failure. *Journal of Personality and Social Psychology, 34,* 901–906.

Miller, D. T., & McFarland, C. (1986). Counterfactual thinking and victim compensation: A test of norm theory. *Personality and Social Psychology Bulletin, 12,* 513–519.

Miller, D. T., & McFarland, C. (1991). When social comparison goes awry: The case of pluralistic ignorance. In J. M. Suls & T. A. Wills (Eds.), *Social comparison: Contemporary theory and research* (pp. 287–313). Hillsdale, NJ: Erlbaum.

Miller, D. T., & Taylor, B. R. (1995). Counterfactual thought, regret, and superstition: How to avoid kicking yourself. In N. J. Roese & J. M. Olson (Eds.), *What might have been: The social psychology of counterfactual thinking.* Mahwah, NJ: Erlbaum.

Miller, G. (2000). *The mating mind: How sexual choice shaped the evolution of human nature.* New York: Anchor Books.

Miller, N., & Brewer, M. B. (1986). Categorization effects on ingroup and outgroup perception. In J. F. Dovidio & S. L. Gaertner (Eds.), *Prejudice, discrimination, and racism* (pp. 209–230). Orlando, FL: Academic Press.

Miller, N. E. (1941). The frustration-aggression hypothesis. *Psychological Review, 48,* 337–342.

Miller, N. E., & Bugelski, R. (1948). Minor studies of aggression: II. The influence of frustrations imposed by the in-group on attitudes expressed toward out-groups. *Journal of Psychology, 25,* 437–442.

Miller, P. J. E., & Rempel, J. K. (2004). Trust and partner-enhancing attributions in close relationships. *Personality and Social Psychology Bulletin, 30,* 695–705.

Miller, R. S. (1992). The nature and severity of self-reported embarrassing circumstances. *Personality and Social Psychology Bulletin, 18,* 190–198.

Miller, R. S. (1996). *Embarrassment: Poise and peril in everyday life.* New York: Guilford Press.

Miller, R. S., & Leary, M. R. (1992). Social sources and interactive functions of embarrassment. In M. Clark (Ed.), *Emotion and social behavior.* Newbury Park, CA: Sage.

Miller, R. S., & Tangney, J. P. (1994). Differentiating embarrassment from shame. *Journal of Social and Clinical Psychology, 13,* 273–287.

Mineka, S., Rafaeli, E., & Yovel, I. (2003). Cognitive biases in emotional disorders: Information processing and social-cognitive perspectives. In R. J. Davidson, K. R. Scherer, & H. H. Goldsmith (Eds.), *Handbook of affective sciences* (pp. 976–1009). New York: Oxford University Press.

Mischel, W. (2004). Toward an integrated science of the person. *Annual Reviews of Psychology, 55,* 1–22.

Mischel, W., & Shoda, Y. (1995). A cognitive-affective system theory of personality: Reconceptualizing situations, dispositions, dynamics, and invariance in personality structures. *Psychological Review, 102,* 246–268.

Mischel, W., Shoda, Y., & Mendoza-Denton, R. (2002). Situation-behavioral profiles as a locus of consistency in personality. *Current Directions in Psychological Science, 11,* 50–54.

Mita, T. H., Dermer, M., & Knight, J. (1977). Reversed facial images and the mere-exposure hypothesis. *Journal of Personality and Social Psychology, 35,* 597–601.

Mithen, S. (1996). *The prehistory of the mind: The cognitive origins of art and science.* London: Thames and Hudson.

Moller, A. P. (1992a). Female swallow preference for symmetrical male sexual ornaments. *Nature, 357,* 238–240.

Moller, A. P. (1992b). Parasites differentially increase the degree of fluctuating asymmetry in secondary sexual characteristics. *Journal of Evolutionary Biology, 5,* 691–699.

Monteith, M. J. (1996). Contemporary forms of prejudice-related conflict: In search of a nutshell. *Personality and Social Psychology Bulletin, 22,* 461–473.

Monteith, M. J., Ashburn-Nardo, L., Voils, C. I., & Czopp, A. M. (2002). Putting the brakes on prejudice: On the development and operation of cues for control. *Journal of Personality and Social Psychology, 83,* 1029–1050.

Monteith, M. J., & Voils, C. I. (1998). Proneness to prejudiced responses: Toward understanding the authenticity of self-reported discrepancies. *Journal of Personality and Social Psychology, 75,* 901–916.

Mook, D. G. (1983). In defense of external validity. *American Psychologist, 38,* 379–387.

Moore, J. S., Graziano, W. G., & Millar, M. G. (1987). Physical attractiveness, sex role orientation, and the evaluation of adults and children. *Personality and Social Psychology Bulletin, 13,* 95–102.

Moore, M. M. (1985). Nonverbal courtship patterns in women: Context and consequences. *Ethology and Sociobiology, 6,* 237–247.

Moreland, R. L., & Beach, S. R. (1992). Exposure effects in the classroom: The development of affinity among students. *Journal of Experimental Social Psychology, 28,* 255–276.

Moreland, R. L., & Levine, J. M. (1989). Newcomers and oldtimers in small groups. In P. Paulus (Ed.), *Psychology of group influence* (2nd ed., pp. 143–186). Hillsdale, NJ: Erlbaum.

Morelli, G. A., & Rothbaum, F. (2007). Situating the child in context: Attachment relationships and self-regulation in different cultures. In *Handbook of Cultural Psychology* (pp. 500–527). New York: Guilford Press.

Morris, M. W., & Peng, K. (1994). Culture and cause: American and Chinese attributions for social and physical events. *Journal of Personality and Social Psychology, 67,* 949–971.

Morrow, J., & Nolen-Hoeksema, S. (1990). Effects of responses to depression on the remediation of depressive affect. *Journal of Personality and Social Psychology, 58,* 519–527.

Moscovici, S. (1985). Social influence and conformity. In G. Lindzey & E. Aronson (Eds.), *The handbook of social psychology* (3rd ed., Vol. 2, pp. 347–412). New York: Random House.

Moscovici, S., Lage, E., & Naffrechoux, M. (1969). Influences of a consistent minority on the responses of a majority in a color perception task. *Sociometry, 32,* 365–380.

Moscovici, S., & Zavalloni, M. (1969). The group as a polarizer of attitudes. *Journal of Personality and Social Psychology, 12,* 125–135.

Moskowitz, D. S. (1994). Cross-situational generality and the interpersonal circumplex. *Journal of Personality and Social Psychology, 66,* 921–933.

Moskowitz, G. B. (1993). Individual differences in social categorization: The influence of personal need for structure on spontaneous trait inferences. *Journal of Personality and Social Psychology, 65,* 132–142.

Mullen, B., & Riordan, C. A. (1988). Self-serving attributions for performance in naturalistic settings: A meta-analytic review. *Journal of Applied Social Psychology, 18,* 3–22.

Munro, D. (1985). Introduction. In D. Munro (Ed.), *Individualism and holism: Studies in Confucian and Taoist values* (pp. 1–34). Ann Arbor: Center for Chinese Studies, University of Michigan.

Muraven, M. R., & Baumeister, R. F. (2000). Self-regulation and depletion of limited resources: Does self-control resemble a muscle? *Psychological Bulletin, 126,* 247–259.

Murphy, S. T., & Zajonc, R. B. (1993). Affect, cognition, and awareness: Affective priming with optimal and suboptimal stimulus exposures. *Journal of Personality and Social Psychology, 64,* 723–739.

Murray, S. L., & Holmes, J. G. (1993). Seeing virtues in faults: Negativity and the transformation of interpersonal narratives in close relationships. *Journal of Personality and Social Psychology, 65,* 707–723.

Murray, S. L., & Holmes, J. G. (1997). A leap of faith? Positive illusions in romantic relationships. *Personality and Social Psychology Bulletin, 23,* 586–604.

Murray, S. L., & Holmes, J. G. (1999). The (mental) ties that bind: Cognitive structures that predict relationship resilience. *Journal of Personality and Social Psychology, 77,* 1228–1244.

Murray, S. L., Holmes, J. G., Dolderman, D., & Griffin, D. W. (2000). What the motivated mind sees: Comparing friends' perspectives to married partners' views of each other. *Journal of Experimental Social Psychology, 36,* 600–620.

Murray, S. L., Holmes, J. G., & Griffin, D. W. (1996). The benefits of positive illusions: Idealization and the construction of satisfaction in close relationships. *Journal of Personality and Social Psychology, 70,* 79–98.

Murray, S. L., Holmes, J. G., MacDonald, G., & Ellsworth, P. C. (1998). Through the looking glass darkly? When self-doubts turn into relationship insecurities. *Journal of Personality and Social Psychology, 75,* 1459–1480.

Mussweiler, T. (2003). Comparison processes in social judgment: Mechanisms and consequences. *Psychological Review, 110,* 472–489.

Mwaniki, M. K. (1973). *The relationship between self-concept and academic achievement in Kenyan pupils.* Unpublished doctoral dissertation, Stanford University, California.

Myers, D. G. (1999). Close relationships and quality of life. In K. Kahneman, E. Diener, & N. Schwarz (Eds.), *Well-being: The foundations of hedonic psychology* (pp. 374–391). New York: Russell Sage Foundation.

Myers, D. G. (2000a). *The American paradox.* New Haven: Yale University Press.

Myers, D. G. (2000b). The funds, friends, and faith of happy people. *American Psychologist, 55,* 56–67.

Myers, D. G., & Bishop, G. D. (1971). Enhancement of dominant attitudes in group discussion. *Journal of Personality and Social Psychology, 20,* 386–391.

Nahemow, L., & Lawton, M. P. (1975). Similarity and propinquity in friendship formation. *Journal of Personality and Social Psychology, 32,* 205–213.

Neff, L. A., & Karney, B. R. (2002). Judgments of a relationship partner: Specific accuracy but global enhancement. *Journal of Personality, 70,* 1079–1112.

Neff, L. A., & Karney, B. R. (2009). Compassionate love in early marriage. In B. Fehr, S. Sprecher, & L. G. Underwood (Eds.), *The science of compassionate love.* Malden, MA: Wiley-Blackwell.

Neimeyer, R. A., & Mitchell, K. A. (1988). Similarity and attraction: A longitudinal study. *Journal of Social and Personal Relationships, 5,* 131–148.

Neisser, U., & Harsch, N. (1992). Phantom flashbulbs: False recollections of hearing the news about *Challenger*. In E. Winograd & U. Neisser (Eds.), *Affect and accuracy in recall: Studies of "flashbulb" memories* (pp. 9–13). New York: Cambridge University Press.

Nel, E., Helmreich, R., & Aronson, E. (1969). Opinion change in the advocate as a function of the persuasibility of his audience: A clarification on the meaning of dissonance. *Journal of Personality and Social Psychology, 12,* 117–124.

Nelson, L. D., & Morrison, E. L. (2005). Judgments of food and finances influence preferences for potential partners. *Psychological Science, 16,* 167–173.

Nemeroff, C., & Rozin, P. (1989). "You are what you eat": Applying the demand-free "impressions" technique to an unacknowledged belief. *Ethos, 17,* 50–69.

Nemeth, C. (1986). Differential contributions of majority and minority influence. *Psychological Review, 93,* 23–32.

Nesse, R. (1990). Evolutionary explanations of emotions. *Human Nature, 1,* 261–289.

Neuberg, S. L. (1988). Behavioral implications of information presented outside of conscious awareness: The effect of subliminal presentation of trait information on behavior in the Prisoner's Dilemma game. *Social Cognition, 6,* 207–230.

Neuberg, S. L., & Fiske, S. T. (1987). Motivational influences on impression formation: Outcome dependency, accuracy-driven attention, and individuating processes. *Journal of Personality and Social Psychology, 53,* 431–444.

Newcomb, T. M. (1956). The prediction of interpersonal attraction. *American Psychologist, 1,* 575–586.

Newcomb, T. M. (1958). Attitude development as a function of reference groups. In E. E. Maccoby, T. M. Newcomb, & E. L. Hartley (Eds.), *Readings in social psychology* (3rd ed.). New York: Holt, Rinehart and Winston.

Newcomb, T. M. (1961). *The acquaintance process.* New York: Holt, Rinehart and Winston.

Newman, L. S. (1991). Why are traits inferred spontaneously? A developmental approach. *Social Cognition, 9,* 221–253.

Newman, L. S. (1993). How individualists interpret behavior: Idiocentrism and spontaneous trait inference. *Social Cognition, 11,* 243–269.

Ng, S. H. (1980). *The social psychology of power.* San Diego, CA: Academic Press.

Niedenthal, P. M. (2008). Emotion concepts. In M. Lewis, J. M. Haviland-Jones, & L. F. Barrett (Eds.), *Handbook of emotions* (pp. 587–600). New York: Guilford Press.

Niemi, R. G., & Jennings, M. K. (1991). Issues and inheritance in the formation of party identification. *American Journal of Political Science, 35,* 970–988.

Nisbett, R. E. (1993). Violence and U.S. regional culture. *American Psychologist, 48,* 441–449.

Nisbett, R. E. (2003). *The geography of thought: Why we think the way we do.* New York: Free Press.

Nisbett, R. E. (2009). *Intelligence and how to get it: Why schools and cultures count.* New York: Norton.

Nisbett, R. E., Caputo, C., Legant, P., & Maracek, J. (1973). Behavior as seen by the actor and as seen by the observer. *Journal of Personality and Social Psychology, 27,* 154–164.

Nisbett, R. E., & Cohen, D. (1996). *Culture of honor: The psychology of violence in the South.* Boulder: Westview Press.

Nisbett, R. E., Fong, G. T., Lehman, D. R., & Cheng, P. W. (1987). Teaching reasoning. *Science, 238,* 625–631.

Nisbett, R. E., & Ross, L. (1980). *Human inference: Strategies and shortcomings of social judgment.* Englewood Cliffs, NJ: Prentice-Hall.

Nisbett, R. E., & Wilson, T. D. (1977). Telling more than we can know: Verbal reports on mental processes. *Psychological Review, 84,* 231–259.

Nitschke, J. B., Nelson, E. E., Rosch, B. D., Fox, A. S., Oakes, T. R., & Davidson, R. J. (2004). Orbitofrontal cortex tracks positive mood in mothers viewing pictures of their newborn infants. *NeuroImage, 21,* 583–592.

Nobel gene biz bombs—moms opt for lookers. (1985, October 20). *Chicago Sun-Times.*

Nolen-Hoeksema, S. (1987). Sex differences in unipolar depression: Evidence and theory. *Psychological Bulletin, 101,* 259–282.

Nolen-Hoeksema, S. (2003). *Women who think too much.* New York: Holt.

Norenzayan, A., Choi, I., & Nisbett, R. E. (1999). Eastern and Western perceptions of causality for social behavior: Lay theories about personalities and social situations. In D. Prentice & D. Miller (Eds.), *Cultural divides: Understanding and overcoming group conflict* (pp. 239–272). New York: Russell Sage Foundation.

Norenzayan, A., & Heine, S. J. (2004). *Psychological universals: What are they and how can we know?* Vancouver: University of British Columbia.

Norman, R. (1975). Affective-cognitive consistency, attitudes, conformity, and behavior. *Journal of Personality and Social Psychology, 32,* 83–91.

North, A. C., Hargreaves, D. J., and McKendrick, J. (1999). The influence of in-store music on wine selections. *Journal of Applied Psychology, 84,* 271–276.

Norton, M. I., Frost, J. H., & Ariely, D. (2007). Less is more: The lure of ambiguity, or why familiarity breeds contempt. *Journal of Personality and Social Psychology, 92,* 97–105.

Norton, M. I., Monin, B., Cooper, J., & Hogg, M. (2003). Vicarious dissonance: Attitude change from the inconsistency of others. *Journal of Personality and Social Psychology, 85,* 47–62.

Norton, M. I., Vandello, J. A., & Darley, J. M. (2004). Casuistry and social category bias. *Journal of Personality and Social Psychology, 87,* 817–831.

Nosek, B. A., Banaji, M. R., & Greenwald, A. G. (2002). Harvesting implicit group attitudes and beliefs from demonstration web site. *Group Dynamics: Theory, Research, and Practice, 6,* 101–115.

Nowak, M. A., Page, K. M., & Sigmund, K. (2000). Fairness versus reason in the ultimatum game. *Science, 289,* 1773–1775.

Nowak, M. A., & Sigmund, K. (1998). Evolution of indirect reciprocity by image scoring. *Nature, 393*, 573–576.

Nuttin, J. M. (1987). Affective consequences of mere ownership: The name letter effect in 12 European languages. *European Journal of Social Psychology, 17*, 381–402.

Oakes, J. M., & Rossi, R. H. (2003). The measurement of SES in health research: Current practice and steps toward a new approach. *Social Science and Medicine, 56*, 769–784.

Oakes, P. J., & Turner, J. C. (1980). Social categorization and intergroup behavior: Does minimal intergroup discrimination make social identity more positive? *European Journal of Social Psychology, 10*, 295–301.

Oatley, K. (1993). Social construction in emotion. In M. Lewis & J. Haviland (Eds.), *Handbook of emotions* (pp. 342–352). New York: Guilford Press.

Oatley, K. (2004). *Emotions: A brief history.* Malden, MA: Blackwell.

Oatley, K., & Jenkins, J. M. (1992). Human emotions: Function and dysfunction. *Annual Review of Psychology, 43*, 55–85.

Oatley, K., Keltner, D., & Jenkins, J. (2006). *Understanding emotions* (2nd ed.) Malden, MA: Blackwell.

Ochsner, K. N., & Lieberman, M. D. (2001). The emergence of social cognitive neuroscience. *American Psychologist, 56*, 717–734.

Odean, T. (1998). Are investors reluctant to realize their losses? *Journal of Finance, 53*, 1775–1798.

Ogbu, J. U. (1991). Low performance as an adaptation: The case of Blacks in Stockton California. In M. A. Gibson & J. U. Ogbu (Eds.), *Minority status and schooling* (pp. 249–285). New York: Grand.

Ogbu, J. U., & Davis, A. (2003). *Black American students in an affluent suburb: A study of academic disengagement.* Mahwah, NJ: Erlbaum.

Öhman, A. (1986). Face the beast and fear the face: Animal and social fears as prototypes for evolutionary analysis of emotions. *Psychophysiology, 23*, 123–145.

O'Keefe, D. J., & Figgé, M. (1997). A guilt-based explanation of the door-in-the-face influence strategy. *Human Communication Research, 24*, 64–81.

O'Keefe, D. J., & Hale, S. L. (1998). The door-in-the-face influence strategy: A random-effects meta-analytic review. In M. E. Roloff (Ed.), *Communication yearbook* (Vol. 21, pp. 1–33). Thousand Oaks, CA: Sage.

O'Keefe, D. J., & Hale, S. L. (2001). An odds-ratio-based meta-analysis of research on the door-in-the-face influence strategy. *Communication Reports, 14*, 31–38.

Oliner, S, & Oliner, P. (1988). *The altruistic personality.* New York: The Free Press.

Olweus, D. (1979). Stability of aggressive reaction patterns in males: A review. *Psychological Bulletin, 86*, 852–875.

Olweus, D. (1980). Familial and temperamental determinants of aggressive behavior in adolescent boys: A causal analysis. *Developmental Psychology, 16*, 644–660.

Omoto, A. M., Malsch, A. M., & Barraza, J. A. (2009). Compassionate acts: Motivations for and correlates of volunteerism among older adults. In B. Fehr, S. Sprecher, & L. G. Underwood (Eds.), *The science of compassionate love: Theory, research, and applications* (pp. 257–282). Malden, MA: Wiley-Blackwell.

Omoto, A. M., & Snyder, M. (1995). Sustained helping without obligation: Motivation, longevity of service, and perceived attitude change among AIDS volunteers. *Journal of Personality and Social Psychology, 68*, 671–686.

Orians, G. H., & Heerwagen, J. H. (1992). Evolved responses to landscapes. In J. H. Barlow, L. Cosmides, & J. Tooby (Eds.), *The adapted mind* (pp. 555–580). New York: Oxford University Press.

Ostrom, T. M., & Sedikides, C. (1992). Out-group homogeneity effects in natural and minimal groups. *Psychological Bulletin, 112*, 536–552.

Oveis, C., Cohen, A., Gruber, J., Shiota, M. N., Haidt, J., & Keltner, D. (2009). Resting respiratory sinus arrhythmia is associated with tonic positive emotionality. *Emotion, 9*, 265–270.

Oxley, D. R., Smith, K. B., Alford, J. R., Hibbing, M. V., Miller, J. L., Scalora, M., et al. (2008). Political attitudes vary with physiological traits. *Science, 321*(5896), 1667–1670.

Oxman, T. E., & Hull, J. G. (1997). Social support, depression, and activities of daily living in older heart surgery patients. *Journal of Gerontology: Psychological Sciences, 52*, 1–14.

Oyserman, D., Bybee, D., & Terry, K. (2006). Possible selves and academic outcomes: How and when possible selves impel action. *Journal of Personality and Social Psychology, 91*, 188–204.

Pallak, M. S., Mueller, M., Dollar, K., & Pallak, J. (1972). Effects of commitment on responsiveness to an extreme consonant communication. *Journal of Personality and Social Psychology, 23*, 429–436.

Palombit, R., Seyfarth, R. M., & Cheney, D. L. (1997). The adaptive value of "friendships" to female baboons: Experimental and observational evidence. *Animal Behavior, 54*, 599–614.

Park, B., & Judd, C. M. (1990). Measures and models of perceived group variability. *Journal of Personality and Social Psychology, 59*, 173–191.

Park, B., & Rothbart, M. (1982). Perception of out-group homogeneity and levels of social categorization: Memory for the subordinate attributes of in-group and out-group members. *Journal of Personality and Social Psychology, 42*, 1051–1068.

Parrott, W. G. (2001). Implications of dysfunctional emotions for understanding how emotions function. *Review of General Psychology, 5*, 180–186.

Parrott, W. G., & Smith, S. F. (1991). Embarrassment: Actual vs. typical cases, classical vs. prototypical representations. *Cognition and Emotion, 5*, 467–488.

Paulhus, D. L. (1998). Interpersonal adaptiveness of trait self-enhancement: A mixed blessing? *Journal of Personality and Social Psychology, 74*, 1197–1208.

Payne, B. K. (2001). Prejudice and perception: The role of automatic and controlled processes in misperceiving a weapon. *Journal of Personality and Social Psychology, 81*, 181–192.

Payne, B. K., Lambert, A. J., & Jacoby, L. L. (2002). Best laid plans: Effect of goals on accessibility bias and cognitive control in race-based misperceptions of weapons. *Journal of Experimental Social Psychology, 38*, 384–396.

Pearson, C. M., & Porath, C. L. (1999). *Workplace incivility: The target's eye view.* Paper presented at the Annual Meeting of the Academy of Management, Chicago.

Pelham, B. W., Mirenberg, M. C., & Jones, J. K. (2002). Why Susie sells seashells by the seashore: Implicit egotism and major life decisions. *Journal of Personality and Social Psychology, 82*, 469–487.

Peng, K., & Knowles, E. (2003). Culture, ethnicity and the attribution of physical causality. *Personality and Social Psychology Bulletin, 29*, 1272–1284.

Pennebaker, J. W. (1989). Confession, inhibition, and disease. In L. Berkowitz (Ed.), *Advances in experimental social psychology* (Vol. 22, pp. 211–244). New York: Academic Press.

Pennebaker, J. W. (1993). Putting stress into words: Health, linguistic and therapeutic implications. *Behavioral Research and Therapy, 31,* 539–548.

Pennebaker, J. W., Hughes, C. F., & O'Heeron, R. C. (1987). The psychophysiology of confession: Linking inhibitory and psychosomatic processes. *Journal of Personality and Social Psychology, 52,* 781–793.

Pennebaker, J. W., Mayne, T. J., & Francis, M. (1997). Linguistic predictors of adaptive bereavement. *Journal of Personality and Social Psychology, 72,* 863–871.

Pennebaker, J. W., & Roberts, T. A. (1992). Toward a his and hers theory of emotion: Gender differences in visceral perception. *Journal of Social and Clinical Psychology, 11,* 199–212.

Penner, L. A., Dovidio, J. F., Piliavin, J. A., & Schroeder, D. A. (2005). Prosocial behavior: Multi-level perspectives. *Annual Review of Psychology, 56,* 365–392.

Penton-Voak, I. S., Perrett, D. I., Castles, D. L., Kobayashi, T., Burt, D. M., Murray, L. K., et al. (1999). Menstrual cycle alters face preference. *Nature, 399,* 741–742.

Penton-Voak, I. S., Pound, N., Little, A. C., & Perrett, D. I. (2006). Personality judgments from natural and composite facial images: More evidence for a "kernel of truth" in social perception. *Social Cognition, 24,* 607–640.

Perloff, R. M. (1993). Third-person effect research 1983–1992: A review and synthesis. *International Journal of Public Opinion Research, 5,* 167–184.

Perner, J., Frith, U., Leslie, A. M., & Leekam, S. R. (1989). Exploration of the autistic child's theory of mind: Knowledge, belief and communication. *Child Development, 60,* 689–700.

Perner, J., Leekam, S. R., & Wimmer, H. (1987). Three-year olds' difficulty with false belief: The case for a conceptual deficit. *British Journal of Developmental Psychology, 5,* 125–137.

Perner, J., Ruffman, T., & Leekam, S. R. (1994). Theory of mind is contagious: You catch it from your sibs. *Child Development, 65,* 1228–1238.

Perper, T. (1985). *Sex signals: The biology of love.* Philadelphia: ISI Press.

Perrett, D. I., Lee, K., Penton-Voak, I., Burt, D. M., Rowland, D., Yoshikawa, S., et al. (1998). Sexual dimorphism and facial attractiveness. *Nature, 394,* 884–886.

Perrett, D. I., May, K. A., & Yoshikawa, S. (1994). Facial shape and judgments of female attractiveness. *Nature, 368,* 239–242.

Perrin, S., & Spencer, C. (1981). Independence of conformity in the Asch experiment as a reflection of cultural or situational factors. *British Journal of Social Psychology, 20,* 205–209.

Pessin, J. (1933). The comparative effects of social and mechanical stimulation on memorizing. *American Journal of Psychology, 45,* 263–270.

Pessin, J., & Husband, R. W. (1933). Effect of social stimulation on human maze learning. *Journal of Abnormal and Social Psychology, 28,* 148–154.

Peterson, C. (2000). The future of optimism. *American Psychologist, 55,* 44–55.

Peterson, C., & Barrett, L. C. (1987). Explanatory style and academic performance among university freshmen. *Journal of Personality and Social Psychology, 53,* 603–607.

Peterson, C., Maier, S., & Seligman, M. E. P. (1993). *Learned helplessness.* New York: Oxford University Press.

Peterson, C., Seligman, M. E. P., & Vaillant, G. E. (1988). Pessimistic explanatory style is a risk factor for physical illness: A thirty-five-year longitudinal study. *Journal of Personality and Social Psychology, 55,* 23–27.

Pettigrew, T. (1979). The ultimate attribution error: Extending Allport's cognitive analysis to prejudice. *Personality and Social Psychology Bulletin, 5,* 461–476.

Pettigrew, T. F., & Tropp, L. R. (2000). Does intergroup contact reduce prejudice? Recent meta-analytic findings. In S. Oskamp (Ed.), *Reducing prejudice and discrimination: The Claremont symposium on applied social psychology* (pp. 93–114). Mahwah, NJ: Erlbaum.

Pettigrew, T. F., & Tropp, L. R. (2006). A meta-analytic test of intergroup contact theory. *Journal of Personality and Social Psychology, 90,* 751–783.

Petty, R. E., & Cacioppo, J. T. (1979). Issue involvement can increase or decrease persuasion by enhancing message-relevant cognitive responses. *Journal of Personality and Social Psychology, 37,* 1915–1926.

Petty, R. E., & Cacioppo, J. T. (1984). The effects of involvement on responses to argument quantity and quality: Central and peripheral routes to persuasion. *Journal of Personality and Social Psychology, 46,* 69–81.

Petty, R. E., & Cacioppo, J. T. (1986). The elaboration likelihood model of persuasion. In L. Berkowitz (Ed.), *Advances in experimental social psychology* (Vol. 19, pp. 123–205). New York: Academic Press.

Petty, R. E., Cacioppo, J. T., & Goldman, R. (1981). Personal involvement as a determinant of argument-based persuasion. *Journal of Personality and Social Psychology, 41,* 847–855.

Petty, R. E., Cacioppo, J. T., & Schumann, D. W. (1983). Central and peripheral routes to advertising effectiveness: The moderating role of involvement. *Journal of Consumer Research, 10,* 135–146.

Petty, R. E., Haugtvedt, C. P., & Smith, S. M. (1995). Elaboration as a determinant of attitude strength. In R. E. Petty & J. A. Krosnick (Eds.), *Attitude strength: Antecedents and consequences* (pp. 93–130). Mahwah, NJ: Erlbaum.

Petty, R. E., & Wegener, D. (1998). Attitude change: Multiple roles for persuasion variables. In D. T. Gilbert, S. T. Fiske, & G. Lindzey (Eds.), *Handbook of social psychology* (4th ed., pp. 323–390). New York: McGraw-Hill.

Pew Research Center. (2007, January 9). How young people view their lives, futures, and politics: A portrait of "generation next."

Phelps, E. A., O'Connor, K. J., Cunningham, W. A., Funayama, E. S., Gatenby, J. C., Gore, J. C., et al. (2000). Performance on indirect measure of race evaluation predicts amygdala activation. *Journal of Cognitive Neuroscience, 12,* 729–738.

Phillips, D. P. (1986). Natural experiments on the effects of mass media violence on fatal aggression: Strengths and weakness of a new approach. In L. Berkowitz (Ed.), *Advances in experimental social psychology* (Vol. 19, pp. 207–250). Orlando, FL: Academic Press.

Piedmont, R. L., & Chase, J. H. (1997). Cross-cultural generality of the five-factor model of personality: Development and validation of the NEO-PI-R for Koreans. *Journal of Cross-Cultural Psychology, 28,* 131–155.

Pietromonaco, P. R., & Feldman-Barrett, L. (2000). Internal working models: What do we know about knowing the self in relation to others? *Review of General Psychology, 4,* 155–175.

Piliavin, J. A., & Piliavin, I. M. (1972). The effects of blood on reactions to a victim. *Journal of Personality and Social Psychology, 23,* 253–261.

Piliavin, J. A., Piliavin, I. M., & Broll, L. (1976). Time of arousal at an emergency and likelihood of helping. *Personality and Social Psychology Bulletin, 2,* 273–276.

Piliavin, J. A., & Unger, R. K. (1985). The helpful but helpless female: Myth or reality? In V. O'Leary, R. K. Unger, & B. S. Wallston (Eds.), *Women, gender and social psychology* (pp. 149–186). Hillsdale, NJ: Erlbaum.

Pinel, E. (1999). Stigma consciousness: The psychological legacy of social stereotypes. *Journal of Personality and Social Psychology, 76,* 114–128.

Pinker, S. (1994). *The language instinct.* New York: HarperCollins.

Pinker, S. (2002). *The blank slate: The modern denial of human nature.* New York: Viking.

Pinker, S. (2007). A history of violence [Electronic Version]. *The New Republic Online.* Retrieved March 16, 2009.

Plaks, J. E., & Higgins, E. T. (2000). Pragmatic use of stereotyping in teamwork: Social loafing and compensation as a function inferred partner-situation fit. *Journal of Personality and Social Psychology, 79,* 962–974.

Plant, E. A., & Devine, P. G. (1998). Internal and external motivation to respond without prejudice. *Journal of Personality and Social Psychology, 75,* 811–832.

Plant, E. A., Kling, K. C., & Smith, G. L. (2004). The influence of gender and social role on the interpretation of facial expressions. *Sex Roles, 51,* 187–196.

Platania, J., & Moran, G. P. (2001). Social facilitation as a function of the mere presence of others. *Journal of Social Psychology, 141,* 190–197.

Platt, J. J., & James, W. T. (1966). Social facilitation of eating behavior in young opossums: I. Group vs. solitary feeding. *Psychonomic Science, 6,* 421–422.

Platt, J. J., Yaksh, T., & Darby, C. L. (1967). Social facilitation of eating behavior in armadillos. *Psychological Reports, 20,* 1136.

Plomin, R., & Caspi, A. (1998). DNA and personality. *European Journal of Personality, 12,* 387–407.

Plomin, R., & Caspi, A. (1999). Behavioral genetics and personality. In L. A. Pervin & O. P. John (Eds.), *Handbook of personality: Theory and research* (2nd ed., pp. 251–276). New York: Guilford Press.

Plous, S. (1985). Perceptual illusions and military realities. *Journal of Conflict Resolution, 29,* 363–389.

Podratz, K. E., Halverson, S. K., & Dipboye, R. L. (2004). Physical attractiveness biases in ratings of employment suitability: Tracking down the "beauty is beastly." Manuscript submitted for publication.

Polak, M. (1993). Parasitic infection increases fluctuating asymmetry of male *Drosophila nigrospiracula:* Implications for sexual selection. *Genetica, 89,* 255–265.

Pollock, C .L., Smith, S. D., Knowles, E. S., & Bruce, H. J. (1998). Mindfulness limits compliance with the that's-not-all technique. *Personality and Social Psychology Bulletin, 24,* 1153–1157.

Porges, S. P. (1995). Orienting in a defensive world: Mammalian modifications of our evolutionary heritage. A polyvagal theory. *Psychophysiology,* 301–317.

Porter, R. H., Cernoch, J. M., & Balogh, R. D. (1984). Recognition of neonates by facial-visual characteristics. *Pediatrics, 74,* 501–504.

Porter, R. H., Cernoch, J. M., & McLauglin, F. J. (1983). Maternal recognition of neonates through olfactory cues. *Physiology and Behavior, 30,* 151–154.

Postmes, T., & Spears, R. (1998). Deindividuation and antinormative behavior: A meta-analysis. *Psychological Bulletin, 123,* 238–259.

Postmes, T., Spears, R., & Cihangir, S. (2001). Quality of decision making and group norms. *Journal of Personality and Social Psychology, 80,* 918–930.

Pound, N., Penton-Voak, I. S., & Brown, W. M. (2007). Facial symmetry is positively associated with self-reported extraversion. *Personality and Individual Differences, 43,* 1572–1582.

Pratkanis, A. R., & Aronson, E. (2000). *Age of propaganda.* New York: Freeman.

Pratkanis, A. R., Breckler, S. J., & Greenwald, A. G. (Eds.). (1989). *Attitude structure and function.* Hillsdale, NJ: Erlbaum.

Pratkanis, A. R., Greenwald, A. G., Leippe, M. R., & Baumgardner, M. H. (1988). In search of reliable persuasion effects: III. The sleeper effect is dead. Long live the sleeper effect. *Journal of Personality and Social Psychology, 54,* 203–218.

Pratto, F. (1996). Sexual politics: The gender gap in the bedroom, the cupboard, and the cabinet. In D. M. Buss & N. M. Malamuth (Eds.), *Sex, power, and conflict: Evolutionary and feminist perspectives* (pp. 179–230). New York: Oxford University Press.

Pratto, F., & Bargh, J. A. (1991). Stereotyping based upon apparently individuating information: Trait and global components of sex stereotypes under attention overload. *Journal of Experimental Psychology, 27,* 26–47.

Pratto, F., & John, O. P. (1991). Automatic vigilance: The attention-grabbing power of negative social information. *Journal of Personality and Social Psychology, 61,* 380–391.

Prentice, D. A. (1990). Familiarity and differences in self- and other-representations. *Journal of Personality and Social Psychology,* 369–383.

Prentice, D. A., & Miller, D. T. (1993). Pluralistic ignorance and alcohol use on campus: Some consequences of misperceiving the social norm. *Journal of Personality and Social Psychology, 64,* 243–256.

Prentice-Dunn, S., & Rogers, R. W. (1989). Deindividuation and self regulation of behavior. In P. Paulus (Ed.), *The psychology of group influence* (2nd ed., pp. 87–109). Hillsdale, NJ: Erlbaum.

Preston, C. E., & Harris, S. (1965). Psychology of drivers in traffic accidents. *Journal of Applied Psychology, 49,* 284–288.

Preston, S. D., & de Waal, F. B. M. (2002). Empathy: Its ultimate and proximate bases. *Behavioral and Brain Sciences, 25,* 1–72.

Preuschoft, S. (1992). "Laughter" and "smile" in barbary macaques (*Macaca sylvanus*). *Ethology, 91,* 220–236.

Profet, M. (1992). Pregnancy sickness as adaptation: A deterrent to maternal ingestion of teratogens. In J. H. Barlow, L. Cosmides, & J. Tooby (Eds.), *The adapted mind* (pp. 327–366). New York: Oxford University Press.

Pronin, E., Berger, J., & Molouki, S. (2007). Alone in a crowd of sheep: Asymmetric perceptions of conformity and their roots in an introspection illusion. *Journal of Personality and Social Psychology, 92,* 585–595.

Pronin, E., Gilovich, T., & Ross, L. (2004). Objectivity in the eye of the beholder: Divergent perceptions of bias in self versus others. *Psychological Review, 111,* 781–799.

Pronin, E., Lin, D. Y., & Ross, L. (2002). The bias blind spot: Perceptions of bias in self versus others. *Personality and Social Psychology Bulletin,* 369–381.

Ptacek, J. T., & Dodge, K. L. (1995). Coping strategies and relationship satisfaction in couples. *Personality and Social Psychology Bulletin, 21,* 76–84.

Puts, D. A. (2005). Mating context and menstrual phase affect women's preferences for male voice pitch. *Evolution and Human Behavior, 26,* 388–397.

Pyszczynski, T., Abdollahi, A., Solomon, S., Greenberg, J., Cohen, F., & Weise, D. (2006). Mortality salience, martyrdom, and military might: The great satan versus the axis of evil. *Personality and Social Psychology Bulletin, 32*, 525–537.

Pyszczynski, T., & Greenberg, J. (1987). Toward an integration of cognitive and motivational perspectives on social inference: A biased hypothesis-testing model. In L. Berkowitz (Ed.), *Advances in experimental social psychology* (Vol. 20, pp. 297–340). New York: Academic Press.

Pyszczynski, T., Greenberg, J., Solomon, S., Arndt, J., & Schimel, J. (2004). Why do people need self-esteem?: A theoretical and empirical review. *Psychological Bulletin, 130*, 435–468.

Quattrone, G. A., & Jones, E. E. (1980). The perception of variability within in-groups and out-groups: Implications for the law of small numbers. *Journal of Personality and Social Psychology, 38*, 141–152.

Quigley, B., & Tedeschi, J. (1996). Mediating effects of blame attributions on feelings of anger. *Personality and Social Psychology Bulletin, 22*, 1280–1288.

Rajecki, D. W., Bledsoe, S. B., & Rasmussen, J. L. (1991). Successful personal ads: Gender differences and similarities in offers, stipulations, and outcomes. *Basic and Applied Psychology, 12*, 457–469.

Rajecki, D. W., Ickes, W., Corcoran, C., & Lenerz, K. (1977). Social facilitation of human performance: Mere presence effects. *Journal of Social Psychology, 102*, 297–310.

Raskin, R., & Terry, H. (1988). A principal-components analysis of the Narcissistic Personality Inventory and further evidence of its construct validity. *Journal of Personality and Social Psychology, 54*, 890–902.

Raz, N., Gunning, F. M., Head, D., Dupuis, J. H., McQuain, J., Briggs, S. D., et al. (1997). Selective aging of the human cerebral cortex observed in vivo: Differential vulnerability of the prefrontal gray matter. *Cerebral Cortex, 7*, 268–282.

Razran, G. H. S. (1940). Conditioned response changes in rating and appraising sociopolitical slogans. *Psychological Bulletin, 37*, 481.

Read, A. W. et al. (1978). *Funk and Wagnalls new comprehensive international dictionary of the English language.* New York: Publisher's Guild Press.

Read, S. J. (1984). Analogical reasoning social judgment: The importance of causal theories. *Journal of Personality and Social Psychology, 46*, 14–25.

Read, S. J. (1987). Similarity and causality in the use of social analogies. *Journal of Experimental Social Psychology, 23*, 189–207.

Read, S. J., & Urada, S. I. (2003). A neural network simulation of the outgroup homogeniety effect. *Personality and Social Psychology Review, 7*, 146–159.

Reber, R., Schwarz, N., & Winkielman, P. (2004). Processing fluency and aesthetic pleasure: Is beauty in the perceiver's processing experience? *Personality and Social Psychology Review, 8*, 364–382.

Reber, R., Winkielman, P., & Schwarz, N. (1998). Effects of perceptual fluency on affective judgments. *Psychological Science, 9*, 45–48.

Reed, J. (1981). Below the Smith and Wesson line: Reflections on southern violence. In M. Black & J. Reed (Eds.), *Perspectives on the American South: An annual review of society, politics, and culture.* New York: Cordon and Breach Science Publications.

Reed, J. S. (1990). Billy, the fabulous moolah, and me. In J. S. Reed (Ed.), *Whistling Dixie* (pp. 119–122). San Diego: Harcourt Brace Jovanovich.

Reeder, G. D., Monroe, A. E., & Pryor, J. B. (2008). Impressions of Milgram's obedient teachers: Situational cues inform inferences about motives and traits. *Journal of Personality and Social Psychology, 95*, 1–17.

Reeves, R. A., Baker, G. A., Boyd, J. G., & Cialdini, R. B. (1991). The door-in-the-face technique: Reciprocal concessions vs. self-presentational explanations. *Journal of Social Behavior and Personality, 6*, 645–658.

Reeves, R. A., Macolini, R. M., & Martin, R. C. (1987). Legitimizing paltry contributions: On-the-spot vs. mail-in requests. *Journal of Applied Social Psychology, 7*, 731–738.

Regan, D. T. (1971). Effects of a favor and liking on compliance. *Journal of Experimental Social Psychology, 7*, 627–639.

Regan, D. T., & Fazio, R. (1977). On the consistency between attitudes and behavior: Look to the method of attitude formation. *Journal of Experimental Social Psychology, 13*, 28–45.

Regan, D. T., & Kilduff, M. (1988). Optimism about elections: Dissonance reduction at the ballot box. *Political Psychology, 9*, 101–107.

Regan, D. T., Williams, M., & Sparling, S. (1972). Voluntary expiation of guilt: A field experiment. *Journal of Personality and Social Psychology, 24*, 42–45.

Regan, J. W. (1971). Guilt, perceived injustice, and altruistic behavior. *Journal of Personality and Social Psychology, 18*, 124–132.

Reifman, A. S., Larrick, R. P., & Fein, S. (1991). Temper and temperature on the diamond: The heat-aggression relationship in major league baseball. *Personality and Social Psychology Bulletin, 17*, 580–585.

Reis, H. T., & Downey, G. (1999). Social cognition in relationships: Building essential bridges between two literatures. *Social Cognition, 17*, 97–117.

Reis, H. T., Nezlek, J., & Wheeler, L. (1980). Physical attractiveness in social interaction. *Journal of Personality and Social Psychology, 38*, 604–617.

Reis, H. T., Wheeler, L., Speigel, N., Kernis, M. H., Nezlek, J., & Perri, M. (1982). Physical attractiveness in social interaction: 2. Why does appearance affect social experience? *Journal of Personality and Social Psychology, 43*, 979–996.

Reisenzein, R. (1983). The Schachter theory of emotion: Two decades later. *Psychological Bulletin, 94*(2), 239–264.

Remley, A. (1988, October). From obedience to independence. *Psychology Today*, 56–59.

Rentfrow, P. J. & Gosling, S. D. (2003). The do, re, mis of everyday life: The structure and personality correlates of music preferences. *Journal of Personality and Social Psychology, 84*, 1236–1256.

Rhee, E., Uleman, J. S., Lee, H. K., & Roman, R. J. (1995). Spontaneous self-descriptions and ethnic identities in individualistic and collectivist cultures. *Journal of Personality and Social Psychology, 69*, 142–152.

Rhine, R. J., & Severance, L. J. (1970). Ego-involvement, discrepancy, source credibility, and attitude change. *Journal of Personality and Social Psychology, 16*, 175–190.

Rhodes, G., Yoshikawa, S., Clark, A., Lee, K., McKay, R., & Akamatsu, S. (2001). Attractiveness of facial averageness and symmetry in non-Western cultures: In search of biologically based standards of beauty. *Perception, 30*, 611–625.

Rholes, W. S., Simpson, J. A., & Orina, M. M. (1999). Attachment and anger in an anxiety-provoking situation. *Journal of Personality and Social Psychology, 76*, 940–957.

Richards, Z., & Hewstone, M. (2001). Subtyping and subgrouping: Processes for the prevention and promotion of stereotype change. *Personality and Social Psychology Review, 5*, 52–73.

Riggio, R. E., & Friedman, H. S. (1983). Individual differences and cues to deception. *Journal of Personality and Social Psychology, 45*, 899–915.

Riggio, R. E., & Woll, S. B. (1984). The role of nonverbal cues and physical attractiveness in the selection of dating partners. *Journal of Social and Personal Relationships, 1,* 347–357.

Risen, J. L., & Gilovich, T. (2007). Another look at why people are reluctant to exchange lottery tickets. *Journal of Personality and Social Psychology, 93,* 12–22.

Risen, J. L., & Gilovich, T. (2008). Why people are reluctant to tempt fate. *Journal of Personality and Social Psychology, 95,* 293–307.

Risen, J. L., Gilovich, T., & Dunning, D. (2007). One-shot illusory correlations and stereotyping. *Personality and Social Psychology Bulletin, 33,* 1492–1502.

Robberson, M. R., & Rogers, R. W. (1988). Beyond fear appeals: Negative and positive persuasive appeals to health and self-esteem. *Journal of Applied Social Psychology, 18,* 277–287.

Roberts, B. W., & DelVecchio, W. F. (2000). The rank-order consistency of personality traits from childhood to old age: A quantitative review of longitudinal studies. *Psychological Bulletin, 126,* 3–25.

Roberts, D. F., Foehr, U. G., Rideout, V. G., & Brodie, M. (1999). *Kids & media @ the new millennium.* Menlo Park, CA: Kaiser Family Foundation.

Roberts, T. A., & Pennebaker, J. W. (1995). Gender differences in perceiving internal state: Toward a his-and-hers model of perceptual cue use. In M. Zanna (Ed.), *Advances in experimental social psychology* (Vol. 27, pp. 143–176). New York: Academic Press.

Robins, R. W., & Beer, J. S. (2001). Positive illusions about the self: Short-term benefits and long-term costs. *Journal of Personality and Social Psychology, 80,* 340–352.

Robinson, E. A., & Price, M. G. (1980). Pleasurable behavior in marital interaction: An observational study. *Journal of Consulting and Clinical Psychology, 48,* 117–118.

Robinson, J., & McArthur, L. Z. (1982). Impact of salient vocal qualities on causal attribution for a speaker's behavior. *Journal of Personality and Social Psychology, 43,* 236–247.

Rodriguez Mosquera, P. M., Fischer, A. H., & Manstead, A. S. R. (2000). The role of honor-related values in the elicitation, experience, and communication of pride, shame, and anger: Spain and the Netherlands compared. *Personality and Social Psychology Bulletin, 26,* 833–844.

Rodriguez Mosquera, P. M., Fischer, A. H., & Manstead, A. S. R. (2004). Inside the heart of emotion: On culture and relational concerns. In L. Z. Tiedens & C. W. Leach, *The social life of emotions* (pp. 187–202). New York: Cambridge University Press.

Roesch, S. C., & Amirkhan, J. H. (1997). Boundary conditions for self-serving attributions. Another look at the sports pages. *Journal of Applied Social Psychology, 27,* 245–261.

Roese, N. J. (1997). Counterfactual thinking. *Psychological Bulletin, 121,* 133–148.

Roese, N. J., & Olson, J. M. (Eds.). (1995). *What might have been: The social psychology of counterfactual thinking.* Mahwah, NJ: Erlbaum.

Rogers, R. W., & Mewborn, C. R. (1976). Fear appeals and attitude change: Effects of a threat's noxiousness, probability of occurrence and the efficacy of coping responses. *Journal of Personality and Social Psychology, 34,* 54–61.

Rogers, T. B., Kuiper, N. A., & Kirker, W. S. (1977). Self-reference and the encoding of personal information. *Journal of Personality and Social Psychology, 35,* 677–688.

Rohrer, J. H., Baron, S. H., Hoffman, E. L., & Swander, D. V. (1954). The stability of autokinetic judgments. *Journal of Abnormal and Social Psychology, 49,* 595–597.

Rolls, E. T. (2000). The orbitofrontal cortext and reward. *Cerebral Cortex, 10,* 284–294.

Roseman, I. J. (1991). Appraisal determinants of discrete emotions. *Cognition and Emotion, 5,* 161–200.

Rosenberg, L. A. (1961). Group size, prior experience, and conformity. *Journal of Abnormal and Social Psychology, 63,* 436–437.

Rosenblatt, A., & Greenberg, J. (1988). Depression and interpersonal attraction: The role of perceived similarity. *Journal of Personality and Social Psychology, 55,* 112–119.

Rosenblatt, A., Greenberg, J., Solomon, S., Pyszczynski, T., & Lyon, D. (1989). Evidence for terror management theory I: The effects of mortality salience on reactions to those who violate or uphold cultural values. *Journal of Personality and Social Psychology, 57,* 681–690.

Rosenthal, R., & Jacobson, L. (1968). *Pygmalion in the classroom: Teacher expectation and student intellectual development.* New York: Holt, Rinehart, and Winston.

Ross, L. (1977). The intuitive psychologist and his shortcomings. In L. Berkowitz (Ed.), *Advances in experimental social psychology* (Vol. 10, pp. 173–220). New York: Academic Press.

Ross, L. (1988). Situationist perspectives on the obedience experiments. *Contemporary Psychology, 33,* 101–104.

Ross, L., Amabile, T. M., & Steinmetz, J. L. (1977). Social roles, social control, and biases on social-perception processes. *Journal of Personality and Social Psychology, 35,* 485–494.

Ross, L., Bierbrauer, G., & Hoffman, S. (1976). The role of attribution process in conformity and dissent: Revisiting the Asch situation. *American Psychologist, 31,* 148–157.

Ross, M. (1989). Relation of implicit theories to the construction of personal histories. *Psychological Review, 96,* 341–357.

Ross, M., & Sicoly, F. (1979). Egocentric biases in availability and attribution. *Journal of Personality and Social Psychology, 32,* 880–892.

Ross, S., & Ross, J. G. (1949). Social facilitation of feeding behavior in dogs: I. Group and solitary feeding. *Journal of Genetic Psychology, 74,* 97–108.

Roszell, P., Kennedy, D., & Grabb, E. (1989). Physical attractiveness and income attainment among Canadians. *Journal of Psychology, 123,* 547–559.

Rothbart, M., Evans, M., & Fulero, S. (1979). Recall for confirming events: Memory processes and the maintenance of social stereotyping. *Journal of Experimental Social Psychology, 15,* 343–355.

Rothberg, J. M., & Jones, F. D. (1987). Suicide in the U.S. Army: Epidemiological and periodic aspects. *Suicide and Life-Threatening Behavior, 17,* 119–132.

Rotton, J., & Frey, J. (1985). Air pollution, weather, and violent crime: Concomitant time-series analysis of archival data. *Journal of Personality and Social Psychology, 49,* 1207–1220.

Rozin, P. (1996). Towards a psychology of food and eating: From motivation to module to model to marker, morality, meaning, and metaphor. *Current Directions in Psychological Science, 5,* 18–24.

Rozin, P., & Kalat, J. (1971). Specific hungers and poison avoidance as adaptive specialization of learning. *Psychological Review, 78,* 459–486.

Rozin, P., Lowery, L., Imada, S., & Haidt, J. (1999). The CAD triad hypothesis: A mapping between three moral emotions (contempt, anger, and disgust), and three moral codes (community, autonomy, divinity). *Journal of Personality and Social Psychology, 66,* 870–881.

Rozin, P., & Royzman, E. B. (2001). Negativity bias, negativity dominance, and contagion. *Personality and Social Psychology Review, 5,* 296–320.

Rozin, P., & Singh, L. (1999). The moralization of cigarette smoking in America. *Journal of Consumer Behavior, 8*, 321–337.

Rubin, Z. (1973). *Liking and loving: An invitation to social psychology.* New York: Holt, Rinehart, and Winston.

Ruch, W. (1995). Will the real relationship between facial expression and affective experience please stand up?: The case of exhilaration. *Cognition and Emotion, 9*, 33–58.

Rudman, L. A., & Ashmore, R. D. (2007). Discrimination and the IAT. *Group Processes and Intergroup Relations, 10*, 359–372.

Rudman, L. A., & Borgida, E. (1995). The afterglow of construct accessibility: The behavioral consequences of priming men to view women as sexual objects. *Journal of Experimental Social Psychology, 31*, 493–517.

Rudolph, U., Roesch, S. C., Greitemeyer, T., & Weiner, B. (2004). A meta-analytic review of help giving and aggression from an attributional perspective: Contributions to a general theory of motivation. *Cognition and Emotion, 18*, 815–848.

Rusbult, C. E. (1980). Commitment and satisfaction in romantic associations: A test of the investment model. *Journal of Experimental Social Psychology, 17*, 172–186.

Rusbult, C. E. (1983). A longitudinal test of the investment model: The development (and deterioration) of satisfaction and commitment in heterosexual involvements. *Journal of Personality and Social Psychology, 45*, 101–117.

Rusbult, C. E., & Martz, J. M. (1995). Remaining in an abusive relationship: An investment model analysis of nonvoluntary commitment. *Personality and Social Psychology Bulletin, 21*, 558–571.

Rushton, J. P., & Bons, T. A. (2005). Mate choice and friendship in twins: Evidence for genetic similarity. *Psychological Science, 16*, 555–559.

Rushton, J. P., Russell, R. J. H., & Wells, P. A. (1984). Genetic similarity theory: Beyond kin selection altruism. *Behavioral Genetics, 14*, 179–193.

Russell, J. A. (1991). Culture and categorization of emotion. *Psychological Bulletin, 110*, 426–450.

Russell, J. A. (2003). Core affect and the psychological construction of emotion. *Psychological Review, 110*, 145–172.

Russo, J. E., Medvec, V. H., & Meloy, M. G. (1996). The distortion of information during decisions. *Organizational Behavior and Human Decision Processes, 66*, 102–110.

Russo, J. E., Meloy, M. G., & Medvec, V. H. (1998). Predecisional distortion of product information. *Journal of Marketing Research, 35*, 438–452.

Sabini, J. (1995). *Social psychology* (2nd ed.). New York: Norton.

Sacks, O. (1985). *The man who mistook his wife for a hat and other clinical tales.* New York: Summit Books.

Saegert, S., Swap, W., & Zajonc, R. B. (1973). Exposure, context, and interpersonal attraction. *Journal of Personality and Social Psychology, 25*, 234–242.

Sagar, H. A., & Schofield, J. W. (1980). Racial and behavioral cues in black and white children's perceptions of ambiguously aggressive acts. *Journal of Personality and Social Psychology, 39*, 590–598.

Sakai, H. (1981). Induced compliance and opinion change. *Japanese Psychological Research, 23*, 1–8.

Salancik, G., & Meindl, J. R. (1984). Corporate attributions as strategic illusions of management control. *Administrative Science Quarterly, 29*, 238–254.

Salovey, P., & Rodin, J. (1989). Envy and jealousy in close relationships. *Review of Personality and Social Psychology, 10*, 221–246.

Salovey, P., & Rothman, A. J. (1991). Jealousy and envy: Self and society. In P. Salovey (Ed.), *The psychology of jealousy and envy* (pp. 271–286). New York: Guilford Press.

Samuels, C. A., & Ewy, R. (1985). Aesthetic perception of faces during infancy. *British Journal of Developmental Psychology, 3*, 221–228.

Sanchez-Burks, J. (2002). Protestant relational ideology and (in)attention to relational cues in work settings. *Journal of Personality and Social Psychology, 83*(4), 919–929.

Sanchez-Burks, J. (2004). Protestant relational ideology: The cognitive underpinnings and organizational implications of an American anomaly. In B. Staw & R. Kramer (Eds.), *Research in organizational behavior* (Vol. 26, pp. 265–305). San Diego: Elsevier, JAI Press.

Sanchez-Burks, J., Bartel, C. A., & Blount, S. (2009). Performance in intercultural interactions at work: Cross-cultural differences in response to behavioral mirroring. *Journal of Applied Psychology, 94*, 216–223.

Sanchez-Burks, J., Nisbett, R. E., & Ybarra, O. (2000). Cultural styles, relationship schemas, and prejudice against outgroups. *Journal of Personality and Social Psychology, 79*, 174–189.

Sanday, P. R. (1981). The socio-cultural context of rape: A cross-cultural study. *Journal of Social Issues, 37*, 5–27.

Sanday, P. R. (1997). The socio-cultural context of rape: A cross-cultural study. In L. L. O'Toole (Ed.), *Gender violence: Interdisciplinary perspectives.* New York: New York University Press.

Sanders, G. S. (1981). Driven by distraction: An integrative review of social facilitation theory and research. *Journal of Experimental Social Psychology, 17*, 227–251.

Sanders, G. S., & Baron, R. S. (1975). The motivating effects of distraction on task performance. *Journal of Personality and Social Psychology, 32*, 956–963.

Sanna, L. J. (1992). Self-efficacy theory: Implications for social facilitation and social loafing. *Journal of Personality and Social Psychology, 62*, 774–786.

Sanna, L. J. (2000). Mental simulation, affect, and personality: A conceptual framework. *Current Directions in Psychological Science, 9*, 168–173.

Sansone, C., & Harackiewicz, J. M. (Eds.). (2000). *Intrinsic and extrinsic motivation: The search for optimal motivation and performance.* San Diego, CA: Academic Press.

Sapolsky, R. M. (1982). The endocrine stress-response and social status in the wild baboon. *Hormones and Behavior, 16*(3), 279–292.

Sapolsky, R. M. (1994). *Why zebras don't get ulcers.* New York: Freeman.

Sastry, J., & Ross, C. E. (1998). Asian ethnicity and the sense of personal control. *Social Psychology Quarterly, 61*, 101–120.

Satterwhite, R., Feldman, J., Catrambone, R., & Dai, L.-Y. (2000). Culture and perceptions of self-other similarity. *International Journal of Psychology, 35*, 287–293.

Saucier, D. A., Miller, C. T., & Doucet, N. (2005). Differences in helping whites and blacks: A meta-analysis. *Personality and Social Psychology Review, 9*, 2–16.

Saulnier, K., & Perlman, D. (1981). The actor-observer bias is alive and well in prison: A sequel to Wells. *Personality and Social Psychology Bulletin, 7*, 559–564.

Savin-Williams, R. C. (1977). Dominance in a human adolescent group. *Animal Behavior, 25*, 400–406.

Savitsky, K., Epley, N., & Gilovich, T. (2001). Is it as bad as we fear? Overestimating the extremity of others' judgments. *Journal of Personality and Social Psychology, 81*, 44–56.

Savitsky, K., Medvec, V. H., Charlton, A., & Gilovich, T. (1998). "What, me worry?": Arousal, misattribution, and the effect of temporal distance on confidence. *Personality and Social Psychology Bulletin, 24,* 529–536.

Schachter, S. (1951). Deviation, rejection and communication. *Journal of Abnormal and Social Psychology, 46,* 190–207.

Schachter, S., & Singer, J. E. (1962). Cognitive, social and psychological determinants of emotional state. *Psychological Review, 69,* 379–399.

Schacter, D. L. (2001). *The seven sins of memory: How the mind forgets and remembers.* Boston: Houghton Mifflin.

Schaller, M., Simpson, J. A., & Kenrick, D. T. (2006). *Evolution and social psychology.* New York: Psychology Press.

Schanie, C. F., & Sundel, M. (1978). A community mental health innovation in mass media preventive education: The alternative project. *American Journal of Community Psychology, 6*(6), 573–581.

Schank, R., & Abelson, R. P. (1977). *Scripts, plans, goals, and understanding: An inquiry into human knowledge structures.* Hillsdale, NJ: Erlbaum.

Scheib, J. E., Gangestad, S. W., & Thornhill, R. (1999). Facial attractiveness, symmetry and cues of good genes. *Proceedings of the Royal Society London B, 266,* 1913–1917.

Scheier, M. F., & Carver, C. S. (1977). Self-focused attention and the experience of emotion: Attraction, repulsion, elation, and depression. *Journal of Personality and Social Psychology, 35,* 625–636.

Scheier, M. F., & Carver, C. S. (1987). Dispositional optimism and physical well-being: The influence of generalized outcome expectancies on health. *Journal of Personality, 55,* 169–210.

Scheier, M. F., Fenigstein, A., & Buss, A. H. (1974). Self-awareness and physical aggression. *Journal of Experimental Social Psychology, 10,* 264–273.

Schelling, T. C. (1978). *Micromotives and macrobehavior.* New York: Norton.

Scherer, K. R. (1997). The role of culture in emotion-antecedent appraisal. *Journal of Personality and Social Psychology, 73,* 902–922.

Scherer, K. R., Johnstone, T., & Klasmeyer, G. (2003). Vocal expression of emotion. In R. J. Davidson, K. R. Scherer, & H. H. Goldsmith (Eds.), *Handbook of affective science* (pp. 433–456). New York: Oxford University Press.

Schick, T., & Vaughn, L. (1995). *How to think about weird things: Critical thinking for a new age.* Mountain View, CA: Mayfield.

Schimmack, U., Oishi, S., & Diener, E. (2002). Cultural influences on the relation between pleasant emotions and unpleasant emotions: Asian dialectic philosophies or individualism-collectivism? *Cognition and Emotion, 16,* 705–719.

Schlenker, B. R. (1980). *Impression management: The self-concept, social identity, and interpersonal relations.* Monterey, CA: Brooks/Cole.

Schlenker, B. R., & Leary, M. R. (1982). Social anxiety and self-presentation: A conceptualization and a model. *Psychological Bulletin, 92,* 641–669.

Schmitt, B. H., Gilovich, T., Goore, N., & Joseph, L. (1986). Mere presence and social facilitation: One more time. *Journal of Experimental Social Psychology, 22,* 242–248.

Schmitt, D. P. (2003). Universal sex differences in the desire for sexual variety: Tests from 52 nations, 6 continents, and 13 islands. *Journal of Personality and Social Psychology, 85,* 85–104.

Schnall, E., Wassertheil-Smoller, S., Swencionis, C., Zemon, V., Tinker, L., O'Sullivan, J., et. al. (2008). The relationship between religion and cardiovascular outcomes and all-cause mortality in the women's health initiative observational study [Electronic Version]. *Psychology and Health,* 1–15. Retrieved December 2, 2008, from http://dx.doi.org/10.1080/08870440802311322

Schoeneman, T. J., & Rubanowitz, D. E. (1985). Attributions in the advice columns: Actors and observers, causes and reasons. *Personality and Social Psychology Bulletin, 11,* 315–325.

Schroeder, C. M., & Prentice, D. A. (1998). Exposing pluralistic ignorance to reduce alcohol use among college students. *Journal of Applied Social Psychology, 28,* 2150–2180.

Schroeder, D. A., Penner, L. A., Dovidio, J. F., & Piliavin, J. A. (1995). *The psychology of helping and altruism.* New York: McGraw-Hill.

Schulz-Hardt, S., Frey, D., Luthgens, C., & Moscovici, S. (2000). Biased information search in group decision making. *Journal of Personality and Social Psychology, 78,* 655–669.

Schwartz, G. E., Weinberger, D. A., & Singer, J. A. (1981). Cardiovascular differentiation of happiness, sadness, anger, and fear following imagery and exercise. *Psychosomatic Medicine, 43,* 343–364.

Schwartz, J. (2004, May 6). Simulated prison in '71 showed a fine line between "normal" and "monster." *New York Times,* A14.

Schwartzwald, J., Bizman, A., & Raz, M. (1983). The foot-in-the-door paradigm: Effects of second request size on donation probability and donor generosity. *Personality and Social Psychology Bulletin, 9,* 443–450.

Schwarz, N. (1990). Feelings as information: Informational and motivational functions of affective states. In E. T. Higgins & R. M. Sorrentino (Eds.), *Handbook of motivation and cognition* (Vol. 2, pp. 527–561). New York: Guilford Press.

Schwarz, N., & Bless, H. (1992). Constructing reality and its alternatives: An inclusion/exclusion model of assimilation and contrast in social judgment. In L. L. Martin & A. Tesser (Eds.), *The construction of social judgments* (pp. 217–245). Hillsdale, NJ: Erlbaum.

Schwarz, N., Bless, H., Strack, F., Klumpp, G., Rittenauer-Schatka, H., & Simons, A. (1991). Ease of retrieval as information: Another look at the availability heuristic. *Journal of Personality and Social Psychology, 61,* 195–202.

Schwarz, N., & Clore, G. L. (1983). Mood, misattribution, and judgments of well-being: Informative and directive functions of affective states. *Journal of Personality and Social Psychology, 45,* 513–523.

Schwarz, N., Strack, F., & Mai, H. P. (1991). Assimilation-contrast effects in part-whole question sequences: A conversational logic analysis. *Public Opinion Quarterly, 55,* 3–23.

Schwarz, N., & Vaughn, L. A. (2002). The availability heuristic revisited: Ease of recall and content of recall as distinct sources of information. In T. Gilovich, D. W. Griffin, & D. Kahneman (Eds.), *Heuristics and biases: The psychology of intuitive judgment* (pp. 103–119). New York: Cambridge University Press.

Searle, J. R. (1983). *Intentionality: An essay in the philosophy of mind.* Cambridge, England: Cambridge University Press.

Sears, D. O. (1986). College students in the laboratory: Influences of a narrow data base on social psychology's view of human nature. *Journal of Personality and Social Psychology, 51,* 515–530.

Sears, D. O. (1988). Symbolic racism. In P. A. Katz & D. A. Taylor (Eds.), *Eliminating racism: Profiles in controversy* (pp. 53–84). New York: Plenum Press.

Sears, D. O., & Henry, P. J. (2005). Over thirty years later: A contemporary look at symbolic racism. In M. P. Zanna (Ed.), *Advances in experimental social psychology* (Vol. 37, pp. 95–150). San Diego, CA: Elsevier.

Sears, D. O., & Kinder, D. R. (1985). Whites' opposition to busing: On conceptualizing and operationalizing group conflict. *Journal of Personality and Social Psychology, 48,* 1141–1147.

Sedikides, C. (1995). Central and peripheral self-conceptions are differentially influenced by mood: Tests of the differential sensitivity hypothesis. *Journal of Personality and Social Psychology, 69,* 759–777.

Sedikides, C., Olsen, N., & Reis, H. T. (1993). Relationships as natural categories. *Journal of Personality and Social Psychology, 64,* 71–82.

Sedikides, C., & Skowronski, J. J. (1997). The symbolic self in evolutionary context. *Personality and Social Psychology Review, 1,* 80–102.

Segal, M. W. (1974). Alphabet and attraction: An unobtrusive measure of the effect of propinquity in a field setting. *Journal of Personality and Social Psychology, 30,* 654–657.

Segal, N. L. (1984). Cooperation, competition, and altruism within twin sets: A reappraisal. *Ethology and Sociobiology, 5,* 163–177.

Seibt, B., & Forster, J. (2004). Stereotype threat and performance: How self-stereotypes influence processing by inducing regulatory foci. *Journal of Personality and Social Psychology, 87,* 38–56.

Select Committee on Intelligence. United States Senate. (2004). Report on the U.S. intelligence community's prewar intelligence assessments on Iraq. Ordered reported on July 7, 2004. 108th Congress.

Seligman, M. E. P. (1975). *Helplessness: On depression, development, and death.* San Francisco: Freeman.

Seligman, M. E. P. (1988). Boomer blues. *Psychology Today, 22,* 50–53.

Seligman, M. E. P. (1991). *Learned optimism.* New York: Knopf.

Seligman, M. E. P., Maier, S. F., & Geer, J. H. (1968). Alleviation of learned helplessness in the dog. *Journal of Abnormal Psychology, 73,* 256–262.

Semin, G. R., & Manstead, A. S. R. (1982). The social implications of embarrassment displays and restitution behavior. *European Journal of Social Psychology, 12,* 367–377.

Seta, C. E., & Seta, J. J. (1992). Increments and decrements in mean arterial pressure levels as a function of audience composition: An averaging and summation analysis. *Personality and Social Psychology Bulletin, 18,* 173–181.

Sethi-Iyengar, S., Huberman, G., and Jiang, W. (2004). How much choice is too much? Contributions to 401K retirement plans. In O. S. Mitchell & S. Utkus (Eds.), *Pension design and structure: New lessons from behavioral finance* (pp. 83–95). New York: Oxford University Press.

Shah, J., & Higgins, E. T. (2001). Regulatory concerns and appraisal efficiency: The general impact of promotion and prevention. *Journal of Personality and Social Psychology, 80,* 693–705.

Shah, J. Y. (2003). Automatic for the people: How representations of significant others implicitly affect goal pursuit. *Journal of Personality and Social Psychology, 84,* 661–681.

Shapin, S. (2006, January 16). Eat and run. *The New Yorker,* 76–82.

Shapiro, D. H., Schwartz, C. E., & Astin, J. A. (1996). Controlling ourselves, controlling our world. *American Psychologist, 51,* 1213–1230.

Shaver, P. R., & Brennan, K. A. (1992). Attachment style and the "big five" of personality traits: Their connections with each other and with romantic relationship outcomes. *Personality and Social Psychology Bulletin, 18,* 536–545.

Shavitt, S., Sanbonmatsu, D. M., Smittipatana, S., & Posavac, S. S. (1999). Broadening the conditions for illusory correlation formation: Implications for judging minority groups. *Basic and Applied Social Psychology, 21,* 263–279.

Shearn, D., Bergman, E., Hill, K., Abel, A., & Hinds, L. (1990). Facial coloration and temperature responses in blushing. *Psychophysiology, 27,* 687–693.

Shearn, D., Bergman, E., Hill, K., Abel, A., & Hinds, L. (1992). Blushing as a function of audience size. *Psychophysiology, 29,* 431–436.

Shedler, L., & Manis, M. (1986). Can the availability heuristic explain vividness effects? *Journal of Personality and Social Psychology, 51,* 26–36.

Sheley, J. F., & Askins, C. D. (1981). Crime, crime news, and crime views. *Public Opinion Quarterly, 45,* 492–506.

Shelley, H. P. (1965). Eating behavior: Social facilitation or social inhibition. *Psychonomic Science, 3,* 521–522.

Shelton, J. N., & Richeson, J. A. (2005). Intergroup contact and pluralistic ignorance. *Journal of Personality and Social Psychology, 88,* 91–107.

Shelton, J. N., Richeson, J. A., & Salvatore, J. (2005). Expecting to be the target of prejudice: Implications for interethnic interactions. *Personality and Social Psychology Bulletin, 31,* 1189–1202.

Shepperd, J. A. (1995). Remedying motivation and productivity loss in collective settings. *Current Directions in Psychological Science, 4,* 131–134.

Shepperd, J. A., Ouellette, J. A., & Fernandez, J. K. (1996). Abandoning unrealistic optimism: Performance estimates and the temporal proximity of self-relevant feedback. *Journal of Personality and Social Psychology, 70,* 844–855.

Shepperd, J. A., & Taylor, K. M. (1999). Social loafing and expectancy-value theory. *Personality and Social Psychology Bulletin, 25,* 1147–1158.

Sherif, M. (1936). *The psychology of social norms.* New York: Harper.

Sherif, M., Harvey, O. J., White, B. J., Hood, W., & Sherif, C. (1961). *Intergroup conflict and cooperation: The Robbers Cave experiment.* Norman, OK: University of Oklahoma Institute of Group Relations.

Sherman, D. K., & Cohen, G. L. (2002). Accepting threatening information: Self-affirmation and the reduction of defensive biases. *Current Directions in Psychological Science, 11,* 119–123.

Sherman, D. K., & Cohen, G. L. (2006). The psychology of self-defense: Self-affirmation theory. In M. P. Zanna (Ed.), *Advances in experimental social psychology* (Vol. 38, pp. 183–242). San Diego, CA: Academic Press.

Sherman, J. W., Gawronski, B., Gonsalkorale, K., Hugenberg, K., Allen, T. J., & Groom, C. J. (2008). The self-regulation of automatic associations and behavioral impulses. *Psychological Review, 115,* 314–335.

Sherman, P. W. (1985). Alarm calls of Belding's ground squirrels to aerial predators: Nepotism or self-preservation? *Behavioral Ecology and Sociobiology, 17,* 313–323.

Sherman, S. J., & Gorkin, L. (1980). Attitude bolstering when behavior is inconsistent with central attitudes. *Journal of Experimental Social Psychology, 16,* 388–403.

Sherman, S. J., Mackie, D. M., & Driscoll, D. M. (1990). Priming and the differential use of dimensions in evaluation. *Personality and Social Psychology Bulletin, 16,* 405–418.

Sherman, S. J., & McConnell, A. R. (1995). Dysfunctional implications of counterfactual thinking: When alternatives to reality fail us. In N. J. Roese & J. M. Olson (Eds.), *What might have been: The social psychology of counterfactual thinking.* Mahwah, NJ: Erlbaum.

Shermer, M. (1997). *Why people believe weird things: Pseudoscience, superstition, and other confusions of our time.* New York: Freeman.

Shiller, R. J. (2000). *Irrational exuberance.* Princeton, NJ: Princeton University Press.

Shook, N. J., & Fazio, R. H. (2008). An experimental field test of the contact hypothesis. *Psychological Science, 19,* 717–723.

Short, R. V. (1979). Sexual selection and its component parts, somatic and genital selection, as illustrated by man and the great apes. *Advances in the Study of Behavior, 9,* 131–158.

Showers, C. (1992). Compartmentalization of positive and negative self-knowledge: Keeping bad apples out of the bunch. *Journal of Personality and Social Psychology, 62,* 1036–1049.

Shrauger, J. S., & Shoeneman, T. J. (1979). Symbolic interactionist view of self-concept: Through the looking glass darkly. *Psychological Bulletin, 86,* 549–573.

Shweder, R. A., & Bourne, E. J. (1984). Does the concept of the person vary cross-culturally? In R. A. Shweder & R. A. LeVine (Eds.), *Culture theory: Essays on mind, self, and emotion* (pp. 158–199). Cambridge, England: Cambridge University Press.

Shweder, R. A., Jensen, L. A., & Goldstein, W. M. (1995). Who sleeps by whom revisited: A method for extracting moral goods implicit in practice. *New Directions in Child Development, 67,* 21–39.

Sidanius, J. (1993). The psychology of group conflict and the dynamics of oppression: A social dominance perspective. In S. S. Iyengar (Ed.), *Explorations in political psychology.* Durham, NC: Duke University Press.

Sidanius, J., & Pratto, F. (1999). *Social dominance: An intergroup theory of social hierarchy and oppression.* New York: Cambridge University Press.

Sigall, H., & Landy, D. (1973). Radiating beauty: Effects of having a physically attractive partner on person perception. *Journal of Personality and Social Psychology, 28,* 218–224.

Sigall, H., & Ostrove, N. (1975). Beautiful but dangerous: Effects of offender attractiveness and nature of the crime on juridic judgment. *Journal of Personality and Social Psychology, 31,* 410–414.

Silk, J. B., Alberts, S. C., & Altmann, J. (2003). Social bonds of female baboons enhance infant survival. *Science, 302,* 1231–1234.

Silke, A. (2003). Deindividuation, anonymity, and violence: Findings from Northern Ireland. *Journal of Social Psychology, 143,* 493–499.

Silverstein, B., Perdue, L., Peterson, L., & Kelly, E. (1986). The role of the mass media in promoting a thin standard of bodily attractiveness for women. *Sex Roles, 14,* 519–532.

Simon, D., Krawczyk, D. C., & Holyoak, K. J. (2004). Construction of preferences by constraint satisfaction. *Psychological Science, 15,* 331–336.

Simon, D., Pham, L. B., Le, Q. A., & Holyoak, K. J. (2001). The emergence of coherence over the course of decision making. *Journal of Experimental Psychology: Learning, Memory and Cognition, 27,* 1250–1260.

Simons, D. J., & Chabris, C. F. (1999). Gorillas in our midst: Sustained inattentional blindness for dynamic events. *Perception, 28,* 1059–1074.

Simpson, G. E., & Yinger, J. M. (1985). *Racial and cultural minorities: An analysis of prejudice and discrimination.* New York: Plenum Press.

Simpson, J. A. (1987). The dissolution of romantic relationships: Factors involved in relationship stability and emotional distress. *Journal of Personality and Social Psychology, 53,* 683–692.

Simpson, J. A., Ickes, W., & Grich, J. (1999). When accuracy hurts: Reactions of anxious-ambivalent dating partners to a relationship-threatening situation. *Journal of Personality and Social Psychology, 76,* 754–769.

Simpson, J. A., & Kenrick, D. T. (1998). *Evolutionary social psychology.* Hillsdale, NJ: Erlbaum.

Simpson, J. A., & Rholes, W. S. (1998). *Attachment theory and close relationships.* New York: Guilford Press.

Simpson, J. A., Rholes, W. S., & Phillips, D. (1996). Conflict in close relationships: An attachment perspective. *Journal of Personality and Social Psychology, 71,* 899–914.

Sinaceur, M., & Tiedens, L. Z. (2006). Get mad and get more than even: When and why anger expression is effective in negotiations. *Journal of Experimental Social Psychology, 42*(3), 314–322.

Sinclair, L., & Kunda, Z. (1999). Reactions to a black professional: Motivated inhibition and activation of conflicting stereotypes. *Journal of Personality and Social Psychology, 77,* 885–904.

Singer, J. E., Brush, C. A., & Lublin, S. C. (1965). Some aspects of deindividuation: Identification and conformity. *Journal of Experimental Social Psychology, 1,* 356–378.

Singh, D. (1993). Adaptive significance of female physical attractiveness: Role of waist-to-hip ratio. *Journal of Personality and Social Psychology, 65,* 293–307.

Singhal, A., Rogers, E. M., & Brown, W. J. (1993). Harnessing the potential of entertainment-education telenovelas. *Gazette, 51,* 1–18.

Singh-Manoux, A., Adler, N. E., & Marmot, M. G. (2003). Subjective social status: Its determinants and its association with measures of ill health in the Whitehall II study. *Social Science & Medicine, 56*(6), 1321–1333.

Sistrunk, F., & McDavid, J. W. (1971). Sex variable in conforming behavior. *Journal of Personality and Social Psychology, 17,* 200–207.

Skov, R. B., & Sherman, S. J. (1986). Information-gathering processes: Diagnosticity, hypothesis-confirmatory strategies, and perceived hypothesis confirmation. *Journal of Experimental Social Psychology, 22,* 93–121.

Slater, A., von der Shulenburg, C., Brown, E., Badenoch, M., Butterworth, G., Parsons, S., et al. (1998). Newborn infants prefer attractive faces. *Infant Behavior and Development, 21,* 345–354.

Slavin, R. E. (1995). *Cooperative learning: Theory, research and practice* (2nd ed.). Boston: Allyn & Bacon.

Sloman, S. A. (2002). Two systems of reasoning. In T. Gilovich, D. W. Griffin, & D. Kahneman (Eds.), *Heuristics and biases: The psychology of intuitive judgement* (pp. 379–396). New York: Cambridge University Press.

Slovic, P., Fischoff, B., & Lichtenstein, S. (1982). Facts versus fears: Understanding perceived risk. In D. Kahneman, P. Slovic, & A. Tversky (Eds.), *Judgment under uncertainty: Heuristics and biases* (pp. 463–489). New York: Cambridge University Press.

Smith, A. (1776/1998). *The wealth of nations.* Washington, DC: Regnery Publishing.

Smith, A. E., Jussim, L., & Eccles, J. S. (1999). Do self-fulfilling prophecies accumulate, dissipate, or remain stable over time? *Journal of Personality and Social Psychology, 77,* 548–565.

Smith, C., & Ellsworth, P. (1985). Patterns of cognitive appraisal in emotion. *Journal of Personality and Social Psychology, 48,* 813–838.

Smith, E. R., & Miller, F. D. (1979). Salience and the cognitive mediation of attribution. *Journal of Personality and Social Psychology, 37,* 2240–2252.

Smith, E. R., & Zarate, M. A. (1990). Exemplar and prototype use in social categorization. *Social Cognition, 8,* 243–262.

Smith, P. K., Jostmann, N. B., Galinsky, A. D., & van Dijk, W. W. (2008). Lacking power impairs executive functions. *Psychological Science, 19*(5), 441–447.

Smith, P. K., & Trope, Y. (2006). You focus on the forest when you're in charge of the trees: Power priming and abstract information processing. *Journal of Personality and Social Psychology, 90,* 578–596.

Smith, S. S., & Richardson, D. (1983). Amelioration of deception and harm in psychological research: The important role of debriefing. *Journal of Personality and Social Psychology, 44,* 1075–1082.

Smith, T. W. (2009). Loving and caring in the United States: Trends and correlates of empathy, altruism, and related constructs. In B. Fehr, S. Sprecher, & L. G. Underwood (Eds.), *The science of compassionate love: Theory, research, and applications* (pp. 81–120). Malden, MA: Wiley-Blackwell.

Smoski, M. J., & Bachorowski, J.-A. (2003). Antiphonal laughter between friends and strangers. *Cognition and Emotion, 17,* 327–340.

Smuts, B. B. (1985). *Sex and friendship in baboons.* Hawthorne, NY: Aldine.

Smyth, J. M. (1998). Written emotional expression: Effect sizes, outcome types, and moderating variables. *Journal of Consulting and Clinical Psychology, 66,* 174–184.

Snibbe, A. C., & Markus, H. R., (2005). You can't always get what you want: Educational attainment, agency, and choice. *Journal of Personality and Social Psychology, 88,* 703–720.

Snyder, M. (1974). Self-monitoring of expressive behavior. *Journal of Personality and Social Psychology, 30,* 526–537.

Snyder, M. (1979). Self-monitoring processes. In L. Berkowitz (Ed.), *Advances in experimental social psychology* (Vol. 12, pp. 85–128). New York: Academic Press.

Snyder, M., & Swann, W. B. (1978). Hypothesis-testing in social interaction. *Journal of Personality and Social Psychology, 36,* 1202–1212.

Snyder, M., Tanke, E. D., & Berscheid, E. (1977). Social perception and interpersonal behavior: On the self-fulfilling nature of social stereotypes. *Journal of Personality and Social Psychology, 35,* 656–666.

Sommers, S. R. (2006). On racial diversity and group decision making: Identifying multiple effects of racial composition on jury deliberations. *Journal of Personality and Social Psychology, 90,* 597–612.

Song, H., & Schwarz, N. (2008). If it's hard to read, it's hard to do. *Psychological Science, 19,* 986–988.

Sparacino, J., & Hansell, S. (1979). Physical attractiveness and academic performance: Beauty is not always talent. *Journal of Personality, 47,* 449–469.

Spellman, B. A., & Holyoak, K. J. (1992). If Saddam is Hitler then who is George Bush?: Analogical mapping between systems of social roles. *Journal of Personality and Social Psychology, 62,* 913–933.

Spencer, S. J., Steele, C. M., & Quinn, D. M. (1999). Stereotype threat and women's math performance. *Journal of Experimental Social Psychology, 3,* 4–28.

Sperber, D. (1996). *Explaining culture: A naturalistic approach.* Oxford, England: Blackwell.

Spiegel, D., Bloom, J. R., Kraemer, H. C., & Gottheil, E. (1989). Effect of psychosocial treatment on survival of patients with metastatic breast cancer. *Lancet, 2,* 888–891.

Spivey, C. B., & Prentice-Dunn, S. (1990). Assessing the directionality of deindividuated behavior: Effects of deindividuation, modeling, and private self-consciousness on aggressive and pro-social responses. *Basic and Applied Psychology, 11,* 387–403.

Sprecher, S., & Regan, P. C. (1998). Passionate and companionate love in courting and young married couples. *Sociological Inquiry, 68,* 163–185.

Srull, T. K., & Wyer, R. S. (1979). The role of category accessibility in the interpretation of information about persons: Some determinants and implications. *Journal of Personality and Social Psychology, 37,* 1660–1672.

Srull, T. K., & Wyer, R. S. (1980). Category accessibility and social perception: Some implications for the study of person memory and interpersonal judgments. *Journal of Personality and Social Psychology, 38,* 841–856.

Staats, A. W., & Staats, C. K. (1958). Attitudes established by classical conditioning. *Journal of Abnormal and Social Psychology, 57,* 37–40.

Stangor, C., & Duan, C. (1991). Effects of multiple task demands upon memory for information about social groups. *Journal of Experimental Social Psychology, 27,* 357–378.

Stangor, C., & Lange, J. E. (1994). Mental representation of social groups: Advances in understanding stereotypes and stereotyping. In M. P. Zanna (Ed.), *Advances in experimental social psychology* (Vol. 26). San Diego, CA: Academic Press.

Stangor, C., & McMillan, D. (1992). Memory for expectancy-congruent and expectancy-incongruent information: A review of the social and social developmental literatures. *Psychological Bulletin, 111,* 42–61.

Stanovich, K. E., & West, R. F. (2002). Individual differences in reasoning: Implications for the rationality debate. In T. Gilovich, D. W. Griffin, & D. Kahneman (Eds.), *Heuristics and biases: The psychology of intuitive judgment* (pp. 421–440). New York: Cambridge University Press.

Stapel, D. A., & Blanton, H. (2004). From seeing to being: Subliminal social comparisons affect implicit and explicit self-evaluations. *Journal of Personality and Social Psychology, 87,* 468–481.

Stapel, D. A., & Koomen, W. (2000). How far do we go beyond the information given? The impact of knowledge activation on interpretation and inference. *Journal of Personality and Social Psychology, 78,* 19–37.

Stapel, D., & Koomen, W. (2001). Let's not forget the past when we go to the future: On our knowledge of knowledge accessibility effects. In G. Moskowitz (Ed.), *Cognitive social psychology: The Princeton symposium on the legacy and future of social cognition* (pp. 229–246). Mahwah, NJ: Erlbaum.

Stapel, D. A., Koomen, W., & van der Plight, J. (1997). Categories of category accessibility: The impact of trait versus exemplar priming on person judgments. *Journal of Experimental Social Psychology, 33,* 44–76.

Stapel, D.A., & Suls, J. (2007). *Assimilation and contrast in social psychology.* New York: Psychology Press.

Stasser, G. (1999). The uncertain role of unshared information in collective choice. In L. L. Thomson, J. M. Levine, & D. M. Messick (Eds.), *Shared cognition in organizations: The management of knowledge* (pp. 46–69). Mahwah, NJ: Erlbaum.

Stasser, G., & Titus, W. (1985). Pooling of unshared information in group decision making: Biased information sampling during discussion. *Journal of Personality and Social Psychology, 48,* 1467–1478.

Staub, E. (1989). *The roots of evil: The origins of genocide and other group violence.* Cambridge, England: Cambridge University Press.

Steblay, N. M. (1987). Helping behavior in rural and urban environments: A meta-analysis. *Psychological Bulletin, 102,* 346–356.

Steele, C. M. (1988). The psychology of self-affirmation: Sustaining the integrity of the self. In L. Berkowitz (Ed.), *Advances in experimental social psychology* (Vol. 21). Orlando, FL: Academic Press.

Steele, C. M. (1997). A threat in the air: How stereotypes shape intellectual identity and performance. *American Psychologist, 52*, 613–629.

Steele, C. M., & Aronson, J. (1995). Stereotype threat and the intellectual test performance of African Americans. *Journal of Personality and Social Psychology, 69*, 797–811.

Steele, C. M., Spencer, S. J., & Aronson, J. (2002). Contending with group image: The psychology of stereotype and social identity threat. In M. P. Zanna (Ed.), *Advances in experimental social psychology* (Vol. 34, pp. 379–440). San Diego, CA: Academic Press.

Steele, C. M., Spencer, S. J., & Lynch, M. (1993). Self-image resilience and dissonance: The role of affirmational resources. *Journal of Personality and Social Psychology, 64*, 885–896.

Stemmler, G. (1989). The autonomic differentiation of emotions revisited: Convergent and discriminant validation. *Psychophysiology, 26*(6), 617–632.

Stemmler, G. (2003). Methodological considerations in the psychophysiological study of emotion. In R. J. Davidson, K. R. Scherer, & H. H. Goldsmith (Eds.), *Handbook of affective sciences* (pp. 225–255). New York: Oxford University Press.

Stephan, W. G. (1986). The effect of school desegregation: An evaluation 30 years after Brown. In M. J. Saks & Saxe, L. (Eds.), *Advances in applied social psychology* (Vol. 3, pp. 181–206). Hillsdale, NJ: Erlbaum.

Stephan, W. G., & Stephan, C. W. (1996). *Intergroup relations.* Madison, WI: Brown & Benchmark.

Sternberg, R. J. (1986). A triangular theory of love. *Psychological Review, 93*, 119–135.

Stevenson, H. W., & Lee, S. (1996). The academic achievement of Chinese students. In M. H. Bond (Ed.), *The handbook of Chinese psychology* (pp. 124–142). New York: Oxford University Press.

Stevenson, H. W., Lee, S. Y., Chen, C., Stigler, J. W., Hsu, C. C., & Kitamura, S. (1990). Contexts of achievement: A study of American, Chinese and Japanese children. *Monographs for the Society for Research in Child Development, 55*, 1–2, Serial No. 221.

Stevenson, H. W., & Stigler, J. W. (1992). *The learning gap: Why our schools are failing and what we can learn from Japanese and Chinese education.* New York: Summit Books.

Stewart, D. (1988). Fleece chief. *Omni, 10*(4), 56–61.

Stewart, J. E. (1980). Defendant's attractiveness as a factor in the outcome of criminal trials: An observational study. *Journal of Applied Social Psychology, 10*, 348–361.

Stone, J., Lynch, C. I., Sjomeling, M., & Darley, J. M. (1999). Stereotype threat effects on Black and White athletic performance. *Journal of Personality and Social Psychology, 77*, 1213–1227.

Stone, J., Perry, Z., & Darley, J. (1997). "White men can't jump": Evidence for perceptual confirmation of racial stereotypes following a basketball game. *Basic and Applied Social Psychology, 19*, 291–306.

Stoner, J. A. F. (1961). *A comparison of individual and group decisions involving risk.* Unpublished master's thesis, MIT, Cambridge, Massachusetts.

Storms, M. D. (1973). Videotape and the attribution process: Reversing actors' and observers' points of view. *Journal of Personality and Social Psychology, 27*, 165–175.

Storms, M. D., & Nisbett, R. E. (1970). Insomnia and the attribution process. *Journal of Personality and Social Psychology, 16*, 319–328.

Strack, F., & Deutsch, R. (2004). Reflective and impulsive determinants of social behavior. *Personality and Social Psychology Review, 8*, 220–247.

Strack, F., Martin, L. L., & Stepper, S. (1988). Inhibiting and facilitating conditions of the human smile: A nonobtrusive test of the facial feedback hypothesis. *Journal of Personality and Social Psychology, 53*, 768–777.

Strack, F., Martin, L. L., & Schwarz, N. (1988). Priming and communication: The social determinants of information use in judgments of life satisfaction. *European Journal of Social Psychology, 18*, 429–442.

Strahan, E. J., Spencer, S. J., & Zanna, M. P. (2002). Subliminal priming and persuasion: Striking while the iron is hot. *Journal of Experimental Social Psychology, 38*, 556–568.

Strauman, T. J., & Higgins, E. T. (1987). Automatic activation of self-discrepancies and emotional syndromes: When cognitive structures influence affect. *Journal of Personality and Social Psychology, 53*, 1004–1014.

Strobel, M. G. (1972). Social facilitation of operant behavior in satiated rats. *Journal of Comparative Physiological Psychology, 80*, 502–508.

Strohmetz, D., Rind, B., Fisher, R. & Lynn, M. (2002). Sweetening the till: The use of candy to increase restaurant tipping. *Journal of Applied Social Psychology, 32*, 300–309.

Studd, M. V. (1996). Sexual harassment. In D. M. Buss & N. M. Malamuth (Eds.), *Sex, power, and conflict: Evolutionary and feminist perspectives.* New York: Oxford University Press.

Suh, E., Diener, E., Oishi, S., & Triandis, H. C. (1998). The shifting basis of life satisfaction judgments across cultures: Emotions versus norms. *Journal of Personality and Social Psychology, 74*, 482–493.

Sulloway, F. J. (1996). *Born to rebel: Birth order, family dynamics, and creative lives.* New York: Pantheon Books.

Sulloway, F. J. (2001). Birth order, sibling competition, and human behavior. In H. R. Halcomb III (Ed.), *Conceptual challenges in evolutionary psychology: Innovative research strategie: Studies in cognitive systems* (Vol. 27, pp. 39–83). Dordrecht, the Netherlands: Kluwer Academic Publishers.

Suls, J., Martin, R., & Wheeler, L. (2002). Social Comparison: Why, with whom and with what effect? *Current Directions in Psychological Science, 11*(5), 159–163.

Suls, J. M., & Wheeler, L. (2000). *Handbook of social comparison: Theory and research.* New York: Kluwer Academic/Plenum.

Summers, G., & Feldman, N. S. (1984). Blaming the victim versus blaming the perpetrator: An attributional analysis of spouse abuse. *Journal of Applied Social and Clinical Psychology, 2*, 339–347.

Surowieki, J. (200). *The wisdom of crowds.* New York: Random House.

Svenson, O. (1981). Are we all less risky and more skillful than our fellow drivers? *Acta Psychologica, 47*, 143–148.

Swann, W. B., Jr. (1992). Seeking "truth," finding despair: Some unhappy consequences of a negative self-concept. *Current Directions in Psychological Science, 1*, 15–18.

Swann, W. B., Jr., De La Ronde, C., & Hixon, J. G. (1994). Authenticity and positivity strivings in marriage and courtship. *Journal of Personality and Social Psychology, 66*, 857–869.

Swann, W. B., Griffin, J. J., Predmore, S. C., & Gaines, B. (1987). The cognitive-affective cross: When self-consistency confronts self-enhancement. *Journal of Personality and Social Psychology, 52*, 881–889.

Swann, W. B., Jr., & Read, S. J. (1981). Self-verification processes: How we sustain our self-conceptions. *Journal of Experimental Social Psychology, 17*, 351–372.

Swann, W. B., Jr., Wenzlaff, R. M., Krull, D. S., & Pelham, B. W. (1992). The allure of negative feedback: Self-verification strivings among depressed persons. *Journal of Abnormal Psychology, 101,* 293–306.

Sweeney, P. D., & Gruber, K. L. (1984). Selective exposure: Voter information preferences and the Watergate affair. *Journal of Personality and Social Psychology, 46,* 1208–1221.

Swim, J. K., Aikin, K. J., Hall, W. S., & Hunter, B. A. (1995). Sexism and racism: Old-fashioned and modern prejudices. *Journal of Personality and Social Psychology, 68,* 199–214.

Swim, J. K., & Sanna, L. (1996). He's skilled, she's lucky: A meta-analysis of observers' attributions for women's and men's successes and failures. *Personality and Social Psychology Bulletin, 22,* 507–519.

Tajfel, H., & Billig, M. G. (1974). Familiarity and categorization in intergroup behavior. *Journal of Experimental Social Psychology, 10,* 159–170.

Tajfel, H., Billig, M. G., Bundy, R. P., & Flament, C. (1971). Social categorization and intergroup behavior. *European Journal of Social Psychology, 1,* 149–177.

Tajfel, H., & Turner, J. (1979). An integrative theory of inter-group conflict. In W. G. Austin & S. Worchel (Eds.), *The social psychology of intergroup relations.* Monterey, CA.: Brooks/Cole.

Tajfel, H., & Wilkes, A. (1963). Classifications and quantitative judgment. *British Journal of Social Psychology, 54,* 101–114.

Tan, D. T. Y., & Singh, R. (1995). Attitudes and attraction: A developmental study of the similarity-attraction dissimilarity-repulsion hypotheses. *Personality and Social Psychology Bulletin, 21,* 975–986.

Tangney, J. P., Miller, R. S., Flicker, L., & Barlow, D. H. (1996). Are shame, guilt, and embarrassment distinct emotions? *Journal of Personality and Social Psychology, 70,* 1256–1264.

Tapias, M., Glaser, J., Vasquez, K. V., Keltner, D., & Wickens, T. (2007). Emotion and prejudice: specific emotions toward outgroups. *Group Processes and InterGroup Relations, 10,* 27–41.

Taubman-Ben-Ari, O., Florian, V., & Mikulincer, M. (1999). The impact of mortality salience on reckless driving—A test of terror management mechanisms. *Journal of Personality and Social Psychology, 76,* 35–45.

Taylor, D. M., & Jaggi, V. (1974). Ethnocentrism and causal attribution in a South Indian context. *Journal of Cross-Cultural Psychology, 5,* 162–171.

Taylor, S. E. (1983). Adjustment to threatening events: A theory of cognitive adaptation. *American Psychologist, 38,* 1161–1173.

Taylor, S. E. (1989). *Positive illusions: Creative self-deception and the healthy mind.* New York: Basic Books.

Taylor, S. E. (1991). Asymmetrical effects of positive and negative events: The mobilization-minimization hypothesis. *Psychological Bulletin, 110,* 67–85.

Taylor, S. E. (2002). *The tending instinct.* New York: Holt.

Taylor, S. E., & Brown, J. D. (1988). Illusion and well-being: A social psychological perspective on mental health. *Psychological Bulletin, 103,* 193–210.

Taylor, S. E., & Brown, J. D. (1994). Positive illusions and well-being revisited: Separating fact from fiction. *Psychological Bulletin, 116,* 21–27.

Taylor, S. E., Burklund, L. J., Eisenberger, N. I., Lehman, B. J., Hilmert, C. J., & Lieberman, M. D. (2008). Neural bases of moderation of cortisol stress responses by psychosocial resources. *Journal of Personality and Social Psychology, 95,* 197–211.

Taylor, S. E., & Crocker, J. (1981). Schematic bases of social information processing. In E. T. Higgins, C. P. Herman, & M. P. Zanna (Eds.), *Social cognition: The Ontario Symposium* (Vol. 1, pp. 89–134). Hillsdale, NJ: Erlbaum.

Taylor, S. E., & Fiske, S. T. (1975). Point of view and perceptions of causality. *Journal of Personality and Social Psychology, 32,* 439–445.

Taylor, S. E., Kemeny, M., Aspinwall, L. G., Schneider, S. G., Rodriguez, R., & Herbert, M. (1992). Optimism, coping, psychological distress, and high-risk sexual behavior among men at risk for AIDS. *Journal of Personality and Social Psychology, 63,* 460–473.

Taylor, S. E., Klein, L. C., Lewis, B. P., Gruenewal, T. L., Gurung, R. A. R., & Updegraff, J. A. (2000). Biobehavioral responses to stress in females: Tend-and-befriend, not fight-or-flight. *Psychological Review, 107,* 411–429.

Taylor, S. E., & Lobel, M. (1989). Social comparison activity under threat: Downward evaluation and upward contacts. *Psychological Review, 96,* 569–575.

Taylor, S. E., & Thompson, S. C. (1982). Stalking the elusive "vividness" effect. *Psychological Review, 89,* 155–181.

Taylor, S. E., Wood, J. V., & Lichtman, R. R. (1983). It could be worse: Selective evaluation as a response to victimization. *Journal of Social Issues, 39,* 19–40.

Teger, A. I., & Pruitt, D. G. (1967). Components of group risk taking. *Journal of Experimental Social Psychology, 3,* 189–205.

Tesser, A. (1980). Self-esteem maintenance in family dynamics. *Journal of Personality and Social Psychology, 39,* 77–91.

Tesser, A. (1988). Toward a self-evaluation maintenance model of social behavior. In L. Berkowitz (Ed.), *Advances in experimental social psychology* (Vol. 21, pp. 181–227). San Diego, CA: Academic Press.

Tesser, A. (1993). The importance of heritability in psychological research: The case of attitudes. *Psychological Review, 100,* 129–142.

Tesser, A., Campbell, J. D., & Mickler, S. (1983). The role of social pressure, attention to the stimulus, and self-doubt in conformity. *European Journal of Social Psychology, 13,* 217–233.

Tesser, A., Campbell, J., & Smith, M. (1984). Friendship choice and performance: Self-evaluation maintenance in children. *Journal of Personality and Social Psychology, 46,* 561–574.

Tesser, A., & Conlee, M. C. (1975). Some effects of time and thought on attitude polarization. *Journal of Personality and Social Psychology, 31,* 262–270.

Tesser, A., Martin, L., & Mendolia, M. (1995). The impact of thought on attitude extremity and attitude-behavior consistency. In R. E. Petty & J. Krosnick (Eds.), *Attitude strength: Antecedents and consequences.* Mahwah, NJ: Erlbaum.

Tesser, A., & Smith, J. (1980). Some effects of friendship and task relevance on helping: You don't always help the one you like. *Journal of Experimental Social Psychology, 16,* 582–590.

Tetlock, P. E., Peterson, R. S., McGuire, C., Chang, S., & Feld, P. (1992). Assessing political group dynamics: A test of the groupthink model. *Journal of Personality and Social Psychology, 20,* 142–146.

Thakerar, J. N., & Iwawaki, S. (1979). Cross-cultural comparisons in interpersonal attraction of females toward males. *Journal of Social Psychology, 108,* 121–122.

Thaler, R. H. (1980). Towards a positive theory of consumer choice. *Journal of Economic Behavior and Organization, 1,* 39–60.

Thaler, R. H. (1988). Anomalies: The ultimatum game. *Journal of Economic Perspectives, 2,* 195–206.

The price of beauty. (1992, January 11). *The Economist,* p. 25.

Thomas, S. L., Skitka, L. J., Christen, S., & Jurgena, M. (2002). Social facilitation and impression formation. *Basic and Applied Social Psychology, 24,* 67–70.

Thornhill, R., & Gangestad, S. W. (1993). Human facial beauty: Averageness, symmetry, and parasite resistance. *Human Nature, 4,* 237–269.

Thornhill, R., & Gangestad, S. W. (1999). The scent of symmetry: A human sex pheromone that signals fitness? *Evolution and Human Behavior, 20,* 175–201.

Thornhill, R., & Gangestad, S. W. (2005). Facial sexual dimorphism, developmental stability, and susceptibilty to disease in men and women. *Evolution and Human Behavior, 27,* 131–144.

Thornhill, R., Gangestad, S. W., Miller, R., Scheyd, G., McCollough, J., & Franklin, M. (2003). MHC, symmetry and body scent attractiveness in men and women (*Homo sapiens*). *Behavioral Ecology, 14,* 668–768.

Tice, D. M. (1993). Self-concept change and self-presentation: The looking glass self is also a magnifying glass. *Journal of Personality and Social Psychology, 63,* 435–451.

Tiedens, L. Z. (2001). Anger and advancement versus sadness and subjugation: The effect of negative emotion expressions on social status conferral. *Journal of Personality and Social Psychology, 80*(1), 86–94.

Tiedens, L. Z., & Leach, C. W. (2004). *The social life of emotions.* New York: Cambridge University Press.

Tiedens, L. Z., & Linton, S. (2001). Judgment under emotional certainty and uncertainty: The effects of specific emotions on information processing. *Journal of Personality and Social Psychology, 81,* 973–988.

Todorov, A., & Bargh, J. A. (2002). Automatic sources of aggression. *Aggression and Violent Behavior, 7,* 53–68.

Todorov, A., Mandisodza, A. N., Goren, A., & Hall, C. C. (2005). Inferences of competence from faces predict election outcomes. *Science, 308,* 1623–1626.

Todorov, A., Said, C. P., Engell, A. D., & Oosterhof, N. N. (2008). Understanding evaluation of faces on social dimensions. *Trends in Cognitive Sciences, 12,* 455–460.

Todorov, A., & Uleman, J. S. (2003). The efficiency of binding spontaneous trait inferences to actors' faces. *Journal of Experimental Social Psychology, 39,* 549–562.

Tomkins, S. S. (1962). *Affect, imagery, consciousness: I. The positive affects.* New York: Springer.

Tomkins, S. S. (1963). *Affect, imagery, consciousness: II. The negative affects.* New York: Springer.

Tooby, J., & Cosmides, L. (1992). The psychological foundations of culture. In J. H. Barkow, L. Cosmides, & J. Tooby (Eds.), *The adapted mind: Evolutionary psychology and the generation of culture.* New York: Oxford University Press.

Torrance, E. P. (1955). Some consequences of power differences in decision making in permanent and temporary 3–man groups. In A. P. Hare, E. F. Bogatta, & R. F. Bales (Eds.), *Small groups: Studies in social interaction.* New York: Knopf.

Tourangeau, R., Rasinski, K., & Bradburn, N. (1991). Measuring happiness in surveys: A test of the subtraction hypothesis. *Public Opinion Quarterly, 55,* 255–266.

Tracy, J. L., & Matsumoto, D. (2008). The spontaneous display of pride and shame: Evidence for biologically innate nonverbal displays. *Proceedings of the National Academy of Sciences, 105,* 11655–11660.

Tracy, J. L., & Robins, R. W. (2004). Show your pride: Evidence for a discrete emotion expression. *Psychological Science, 15,* 94–97.

Tracy, J. L., & Robins, R. W. (2007). Emerging insights into the nature and function of pride. *Current Directions in Psychological Science, 16,* 147–150.

Trafimow, D., Triandis, H. C., & Goto, S. G. (1991). Some tests of the distinction between the private self and the collective self. *Journal of Personality and Social Psychology, 60,* 649–655.

Travis, L. E. (1925). The effect of a small audience upon eye-hand coordination. *Journal of Abnormal and Social Psychology, 20,* 142–146.

Triandis, H. C. (1989). The self and social behavior in differing cultural contexts. *Psychological Review, 96,* 269–289.

Triandis, H. C. (1994). *Culture and social behavior.* New York: McGraw-Hill.

Triandis, H. C. (1995). *Individualism and collectivism.* Boulder, CO: Westview Press.

Triandis, H. C., McCusker, C., & Hui, C. H. (1990). Multimethod probes of individualism and collectivism. *Journal of Personality and Social Psychology, 56,* 1006–1020.

Triplett, N. (1898). The dynamogenic factors in pacemaking and competition. *American Journal of Psychology, 9,* 507–533.

Trivers, R. L. (1971). The evolution of reciprocal altruism. *Quarterly Review of Biology, 46,* 35–57.

Trivers, R. L. (1985). *Social evolution.* Menlo Park, CA: Benjamin/Cummngs.

Trope, Y. (1986). Identification and inferential processes in dispositional attribution. *Psychological Review, 93,* 239–257.

Tsai, J. L. (2007). Ideal affect: Cultural causes and behavioral consequences. *Perspectives on Psychological Science, 2,* 242–259.

Tsai, J. L., Knutson, B., & Fung, H. H. (2006). Cultural variation in affect valuation. *Journal of Personality and Social Psychology, 90,* 288–307.

Tsai, J. L., & Levenson, R. W. (1997). Cultural influences on emotional responding: Chinese American and European American dating couples during interpersonal conflict. *Journal of Cross-Cultural Psychology, 28,* 600–625.

Tsang, J., McCullough, M. E., & Fincham, F. D. (2006). The longitudinal association between forgiveness and relationship closeness and commitment. *Journal of Social and Clinical Psychology, 25,* 448–472

Turnbull, C. (1965). *Wayward servants.* New York: Natural History Press.

Turner, C., & Leyens, J. (1992). The weapons effect revisited: The effects of firearms on aggressive behavior. In P. Suedfeld & P. E. Tetlock (Eds.), *Psychology and social policy* (pp. 201–221). New York: Hemisphere.

Turner, M. E., & Pratkanis, A. R. (1998). Twenty-five years of groupthink theory and research: Lessons from the evaluation of a theory. *Organizational Behavior and Human Decision Processes, 73,* 105–115.

Tversky, A. (1977). Features of similarity. *Psychological Review, 84,* 327–352.

Tversky, A., & Kahneman, D. (1974). Judgment under uncertainty: Heuristics and biases. *Science, 185,* 1124–1131.

Tversky, A., & Kahneman, D. (1981). The framing of decisions and the psychology of choice. *Science, 211,* 453–458.

Tversky, A., & Kahneman, D. (1982). Evidential impact of base rates. In D. Kahneman, P. Slovic, & A. Tversky (Eds.), *Judgment under uncertainty: Heuristics and biases* (pp. 153–160). New York: Cambridge University Press.

Tversky, A., & Kahneman, D. (1986). Rational choice and the framing of decisions. *Journal of Business, 59,* 5251–5278.

Tversky, A., & Shafir, E. (1992). Choice under conflict: The dynamics of deferred decision. *Psychological Science, 3*(6), 358–361.

Twenge, J. M. (2002). Birth cohort, social change, and personality: The interplay of dysphoria and individualism in the 20th century. In D. Cervone & W. Mischel (Eds.), *Advances in personality science.* New York: Guilford Press.

Twenge, J. M., Baumeister, R. F., Tice, D. M., & Stucke, T. S. (2001). If you can't join them, beat them: Effects of social exclusion on aggressive behavior. *Journal of Personality and Social Psychology, 81,* 1058–1069.

Twenge, J. M., & Campbell, W. K. (2001). Age and birth cohort differences in self-esteem: A cross-temporal analysis. *Personality and Social Psychology Review, 5,* 321–344.

Twenge, J. M., Konrath, S., Foster, J. D., Campbell, W. K., & Bushman, B. J. (2008). Egos inflating over time: A cross-temporal meta-analysis of the Narcissistic Personality Inventory. *Journal of Personality, 76,* 875–901.

Tyler, T. R. (1984). Assessing the risk of crime victimization: The integration of personal victimization experience and socially transmitted information. *Journal of Social Issues, 40,* 27–38.

Uchino, B. N., Cacioppo, J. T., & Kiecolt-Glaser, J. K. (1996). The relationship between social support and physiological process: A review with emphasis on underlying mechanisms and implications for health. *Psychological Bulletin, 119,* 88–531.

Uematsu, T. (1970). Social facilitation of feeding behavior in freshwater fish. I. *Rhodeus, Acheilognathus* and *Rhinogobius. Annual of Animal Psychology, 20,* 87–95.

Uleman, J. S. (1987). Consciousness and control: The case of spontaneous trait inferences. *Personality and Social Psychology Bulletin, 13,* 337–354.

Umberson, D., & Hughes, M. (1987). The impact of physical attractiveness on achievement and psychological well-being. *Social Psychology Quarterly, 50,* 227–236.

United Nations. (2002). *Small arms survey.* New York: United Nations.

Uranowitz, S. W. (1975). Helping and self-attributions: A field experiment. *Journal of Personality and Social Psychology, 31,* 852–854.

Vaes, J., Paladino, M. P., Castelli, L., Leyens, J. Ph., Giovanazzi, A. (2003). On the behavioral consequences of infra-humanization: The implicit role of uniquely human emotions in intergroup relations. *Journal of Personality and Social Psychology, 85,* 1016–1034

Valenti, A. C., & Downing, L. L. (1975). Differential effects of jury size on verdicts following deliberations as a function of the apparent guilt of a defendant. *Journal of Personality and Social Psychology, 32,* 655–663.

Vallacher, R. R., & Wegner, D. M. (1985). *A theory of action identification.* Hillsdale, NJ: Erlbaum.

Vallacher, R. R., & Wegner, D. M. (1987). What do people think they're doing? Action identification and human behavior. *Psychological Review, 94,* 3–15.

Vallone, R. P., Ross, L., & Lepper, M. R. (1985). The hostile media phenomenon: Biased perception and perceptions of media bias in coverage of the Beirut massacre. *Journal of Personality and Social Psychology, 49,* 577–585.

Van Baaren, R. B., Holland, R. W., Kawakami, K., & van Knippenberg, A. (2004). Mimicry and pro-social behavior. *Psychological Science, 15,* 71–74.

Van Baaren, R. B., Holland, R. W., Steenaert, B., & van Knippenberg, A. (2003). Mimicry for money: Behavioral consequences of imitation. *Journal of Experimental Social Psychology, 39,* 393–398.

Van Boven, L., Kamada, A., & Gilovich, T. (1999). The perceiver as perceived: Everyday intuitions about the correspondence bias. *Journal of Personality and Social Psychology, 77,* 1188–1199.

Van de Ven, P., Bornholt, L., & Bailey, M. (1996). Measuring cognitive, affective, and behavioral components of homophobic reaction. *Archives of Sexual Behavior, 25,* 155–179.

Van Dort, B. E., & Moos, R. H. (1976). Distance and the utilization of a student health center. *Journal of the American College Health Association, 24,* 159–162.

Van Kleef, G. A., De Dreu, C. K. W., Pietroni, D., & Manstead, A. S. R. (2006). Power and emotion in negotiation: Power moderates the interpersonal effects of anger and happiness on concession making. *European Journal of Social Psychology: Special issue on social power, 36,* 557–581.

Vandello, J., & Cohen, D. (1999). Patterns of individualism and collectivism across the United States. *Journal of Personality and Social Psychology, 77,* 279–292.

Vanneman, R. D., & Pettigrew, T. F. (1972). Race and relative deprivation in the urban United States. *Race, 13,* 461–486.

Vasquez, K., Keltner, D., Ebenbach, D. H., & Banaszynski, T. L. (2001). Cultural variation and similarity in moral rhetorics: Voices from the Philippines and United States. *Journal of Cross-Cultural Psychology, 32,* 93–120.

Vaughan, P. W., Rogers, E. M., & Singhal, A. (2000). Entertainment-education and HIV/AIDS prevention: A field experiment n Tanzania. *Journal of Health Communication, 5,* 81–100.

Vescio, T. K., Gervais, S. J., Heidenreich, S., & Snyder, M. (2006). The effects of prejudice level and social influence strategy on powerful people's responding to racial out-group members. *European Journal of Social Psychology, 36,* 435–450.

Vescio, T. K., Gervais, S. J., Snyder, M., & Hoover, A. (2005). Power and the creation of patronizing environments: The stereotype-based behaviors of the powerful and their effects on female performance in masculine domains. *Journal of Personality and Social Psychology, 88*(4), 658–672.

Vescio, T. K., Snyder, M., & Butz, D. (2003). Power in stereotypically masculine domains: A social influence strategy X stereotype match model. *Journal of Personality and Social Psychology, 85*(6), 1062–1078.

von Hippel, W., Sekaquaptewa, D., & Vargas, P. (1995). On the role of encoding processes in stereotype maintenance. In M. P. Zanna (Ed.), *Advances in experimental social psychology* (Vol. 27, pp. 177–254). San Diego, CA: Academic Press.

Vonk, R. (1999). Effects of outcome dependency on the correspondence bias. *Personality and Social Psychology Bulletin, 25,* 382–389.

Vonk, R. (2002). Self-serving interpretations of flattery: Why ingratiation works. *Journal of Personality and Social Psychology, 82,* 515–526.

Wagner, R. C. (1975). Complementary needs, role expectations, interpersonal attraction and the stability of work relationships. *Journal of Personality and Social Psychology, 32,* 116–124.

Walker, I., & Pettigrew, T. F. (1984). Relative deprivation theory: An overview and conceptual critique. *British Journal of Social Psychology, 23,* 300–310.

Wallach, M. A., Kogan, N., & Bem, D. J. (1962). Group influences on individual risk taking. *Journal of Abnormal and Social Psychology, 65,* 75–86.

Wallerstein, J. S., Lewis, J., & Blakeslee, S. (2000). *The unexpected legacy of divorce: The 25-year landmark study.* New York: Hyperion.

Walster, E. (1966). Assignment of responsibility for an accident. *Journal of Personality and Social Psychology, 3,* 73–79.

Walster, E., Aronson, E., & Abrahams, D. (1966). On increasing the persuasiveness of a low prestige communicator. *Journal of Experimental Social Psychology, 2,* 325–342.

Walster, E., Aronson, V., Abrahams, D., & Rottman, L. (1966). Importance of physical attractiveness in dating behavior. *Journal of Personality and Social Psychology, 4,* 508–516.

Walton, G. M., & Cohen, G. L. (2007). A question of belonging: Race, social fit, and achievement. *Journal of Personality and Social Psychology, 92,* 82–96.

Wansink , B., Kent, R. J., & Hoch, S. J. (1998). An anchoring and adjustment model of purchase quantity decisions. *Journal of Marketing Research, 35,* 71–81.

Ward, R. (1994). Maternity ward. *Mirabella,* 89–90.

Waterman, C. K. (1969). The facilitating and interfering effects of cognitive dissonance on simple and complex paired associates learning tasks. *Journal of Experimental Social Psychology, 5,* 31–42.

Watson, D. (1982). The actor and the observer: How are their perceptions of causality divergent? *Psychological Bulletin, 92,* 682–700.

Watson, D., & Pennebaker, J. W. (1989). Health complaints, stress, and distress: Exploring the central role of negative affectivity. *Psychological Review, 96,* 234–254.

Watson, R. I. (1973). Investigation into deindividuation using a cross-cultural survey technique. *Journal of Personality and Social Psychology, 25,* 342–345.

Waugh, C. E., & Fredrickson, B. L. (2006). Nice to know you: Positive emotions, self-other overlap, and complex understanding in the formation of a new relationship. *Journal of Positive Psychology, 1,* 93–106.

Weber, M. (1947). *The theory of social and economic organization* (A. M. Henderson & T. Parsons, Trans.). New York: Oxford University Press.

Weber, R., & Crocker, J. (1983). Cognitive processes in the revision of stereotypic beliefs. *Journal of Personality and Social Psychology, 45,* 961–977.

Wegener, D. T., & Petty, R. E. (1994). Mood management across affective states: The hedonic contingency hypothesis. *Journal of Personality and Social Psychology, 66,* 1034–1048.

Wegener, D. T., Petty, R. E., & Smith, S. M. (1995). Positive mood can increase or decrease message scrutiny: The hedonic contingency view of mood and message processing. *Journal of Personality and Social Psychology, 69,* 5–15.

Wegner, D. M. (1994). Ironic processes of mental control. *Psychological Review, 101,* 34–52.

Wegner, D. M., Ansfield, M., & Pilloff, D. (1998). The putt and the pendulum: Ironic effects of the mental control of action. *Psychological Science, 9,* 196–199.

Wegner, D. M., & Bargh, J. A. (1998). Control and automaticity in everyday life. In D. T. Gilbert, S. T. Fiske, & G. Lindzey (Eds.), *The handbook of social psychology.* New York: McGraw-Hill.

Weiner, B. (1986). *An attributional theory of achievement and motivation.* New York: Springer-Verlag.

Weiner, B., Graham, S., & Reyna, C. (1997). An attributional examination of retributive versus utilitarian philosophies of punishment. *Social Justice Research, 10,* 431–452.

Weinstein, N. D. (1980). Unrealistic optimism about future life events. *Journal of Personality and Social Psychology, 39,* 806–820.

Wellman, H. M. (1990). *The child's theory of mind.* Cambridge, MA: MIT Press.

Wells, G. L., & Gavanski, I. (1989). Mental simulation of causality. *Journal of Personality and Social Psychology, 56,* 161–169.

Wells, G. L., & Petty, R. E. (1980). The effects of overt head movements on persuasion: Compatibility and incompatibility of responses. *Basic and Applied Social Psychology, 1,* 219–230.

West, S. G., & Brown, T. J. (1975). Physical attractiveness, the severity of the emergency and helping: A field experiment and interpersonal simulation. *Journal of Experimental Social Psychology, 11,* 531–538.

Wetzel, C. G. (1982). Self-serving biases in attribution: A Bayesian analysis. *Journal of Personality and Social Psychology, 43,* 197–209.

Weyant, J. M. (1984). Applying social psychology to induce charitable donations. *Journal of Applied Social Psychology, 14,* 441–447.

Whatley, M. A., Webster, J. M., Smith, R. H., & Rhodes, A. (1999). The effect of a favor on public and private compliance: How internalized is the norm of reciprocity? *Basic and Applied Social Psychology, 21,* 251–259.

Wheatley, T., & Haidt, J. (2005). Hypnotic disgust makes moral judgments more severe. *Psychological Science, 16,* 780–785.

Wheeler, L., & Kim, Y. (1997). What is beautiful is culturally good: The physical attractiveness stereotype has different content in collectivistic cultures. *Personality and Social Psychology Bulletin, 23,* 795–800.

Wheeler, L., & Nezlek, J. (1977). Sex differences in social participation. *Journal of Personality and Social Psychology, 35,* 742–754.

White, G. L., & Kight, T. D. (1984). Misattribution of arousal and attraction: Effects of salience of explanations of arousal. *Journal of Experimental Social Psychology, 20,* 55–64.

White, H. (1997). Longitudinal perspective on alcohol and aggression during adolescence. In M. Galanter (Ed.), *Recent developments in alcoholism: Alcohol and violence: Epidemiology, neurobiology, psychology, and family issues* (Vol. 13, pp. 81–103). New York: Plenum Press.

White, L. K., & Booth, A. (1991). Divorce over the life course: The role of marital happiness. *Review of Personality and Social Psychology, 12,* 265–289.

White, P. A. (2002). Causal attribution from covariation information: The evidential evaluation model. *European Journal of Social Psychology, 32,* 667–684.

Whitely, B. E. (1990). The relationship of heterosexuals' attributions for the causes of homosexuality to attitudes towards lesbians and gay men. *Personality and Social Psychology Bulletin, 16,* 369–377.

Whittlesea, B. W., & Leboe, J. P. (2000). The heuristic basis of remembering and classification: Fluency, generation, and resemblance. *Journal of Experimental Psychology: General, 129,* 84–106.

Whyte, W. H. (1956). *The organization man.* New York: Simon & Schuster.

Wicker, A. W. (1969). Attitudes versus actions: The relationship of verbal and overt behavioral responses to attitude objects. *Journal of Social Issues, 25,* 41–78.

Wicklund, R. A. (1975). Objective self-awareness. In L. Berkowitz (Ed.), *Advances in experimental social psychology* (Vol. 8, pp. 233–275). New York: Academic Press.

Wieselquist, J., Rusbult, C. E., Agnew, C. R., & Foster, C. A. (1999). Commitment, pro-relationship behavior, and trust in close relationships. *Journal of Personality and Social Psychology, 77,* 942–966.

Wigboldus, D. H. J., Sherman, J. W., Franzese, H. L., & van Knippenberg, A. (2004). Capacity and comprehension: Spontaneous stereotyping under cognitive load. *Social Cognition, 22,* 292–309.

Wiggins, J. S., Wiggins, N., & Conger, J. C. (1968). Correlates of heterosexual somatic preference. *Journal of Personality and Social Psychology, 10,* 82–90.

Wilder, D. A. (1984). Predictions of belief homogeneity and similarity following social categorization. *British Journal of Social Psychology, 23,* 323–333.

Wilder, D. A. (1986). Social categorization: Implications for creation and reduction of intergroup bias. In L. Berkowitz (Ed.), *Advances in experimental social psychology* (Vol. 19, pp. 291–355). San Diego, CA: Academic Press.

Wiley, M. G., Crittenden, K. S., & Birg, L. D. (1979). Why a rejection? Causal attribution of a career achievement event. *Social Psychology Quarterly, 42,* 214–222.

Wilkinson, G. (1990, February). Food sharing in vampire bats. *Scientific American,* 76–82.

Willer, R. (2004). The effects of government-issued terror warnings on presidential approval ratings. *Current Research in Social Psychology, 10,* 1–12.

Williams, D. R., & Collins, C. (1995). U.S. socioeconomic and racial differences in health: Patterns and explanations. *Annual Review of Sociology, 21,* 349–386.

Williams, J. R., Insel, T. R., Harbaugh, C. R., & Carter, C. S. (1994). Oxytocin administered centrally facilitates formation of a partner preference in female prairie voles (*Microtus Ochrogaster*). *Journal of Neuroendocrinology, 6,* 247–250.

Williams, K. D. (2007). Ostracism. *Annual Review of Psychology, 58,* 425–452.

Williams, K. D., Harkins, S., & Latané, B. (1981). Identifiability as a deterrent to social loafing: Two cheering experiments. *Journal of Personality and Social Psychology, 40,* 303–311.

Willis, F. N., & Hamm, H. K. (1980). The use of interpersonal touch in securing compliance. *Journal of Nonverbal Behavior, 5*(1), 49–55.

Willis, J., & Todorov, A. (2006). First impressions: Making up your mind after a 100-ms exposure to a face. *Psychological Science, 17,* 592–598.

Wilson, M. I., & Daly, M. (1996). Male sexual proprietariness and violence against wives. *Current Directions in Psychological Science, 5,* 2–7.

Wilson, M. I., Daly, M., & Weghorst, S. J. (1980). Household composition and the risk of child abuse and neglect. *Journal of Biological Science, 12,* 333–340.

Wilson, M. I., Johnson, H., & Daly, M. (1995). Lethal and nonlethal violence against wives. *Canadian Journal of Criminology, 37,* 331–361.

Wilson, T., & Brekke, N. (1994). Mental contamination and mental correction: Unwanted influences on judgments and evaluations. *Psychological Bulletin, 116,* 117–142.

Wilson, T., Centerbar, D., & Brekke, N. (2002). Mental contamination and the debiasing problem. In T. Gilovich, D. W. Griffin, & D. Kahneman (Eds.), *Heuristics and biases: The psychology of intuitive judgment* (pp. 185–200). New York: Cambridge University Press.

Wilson, T. D. (2002). *Strangers to ourselves: Discovering the adaptive unconscious.* Cambridge, MA: Belknap Press of Harvard University Press.

Wilson, T. D., Centerbar, D. B., Kermer, D. A, & Gilbert, D. T. (2005). The pleasures of uncertainty: Prolonging positive moods in ways people do not anticipate. *Journal of Personality and Social Psychology, 88,* 5–21.

Wilson, T. D., & Dunn, D. S. (1986). Effects of introspection on attitude-behavior consistency: Analyzing reasons versus focusing on feelings. *Journal of Experimental Social Psychology, 22,* 249–263.

Wilson, T. D., Dunn, D. S., Bybee, J. A., Hyman, D. B., & Rotondo, J. A. (1984). Effects of analyzing reasons on attitude-behavior consistency. *Journal of Personality and Social Psychology, 47,* 5–16.

Wilson, T. D., & Gilbert, D. T. (2008). Explaining why. A model of affective adaptation. *Perspectives in Psychological Science, 3,* 372–388.

Wilson, T. D., Lisle, D., Schooler, J. W., Hodges, S. D., Klaaren, K. J., & LaFleur, S. J. (1993). Introspecting about reasons can reduce post-choice satisfaction. *Personality and Social Psychology Bulletin, 19,* 331–339.

Wilson, T. D., & Schooler, J. W. (1991). Thinking too much: Introspection can reduce the quality of preferences and decisions. *Journal of Personality and Social Psychology, 60,* 181–192.

Wilson, T. D., Wheatley, T., Kurtz, J., Dunn, & Gilbert, D. T. (2004). When to fire: Anticipatory versus postevent reconstrual of uncontrollable events. *Personality and Social Psychology Bulletin, 30,* 1–12.

Wilson, T. D., Wheatley, T., Meyers, J. M., Gilbert, D. T., & Axson, D. (2000). Focalism: A source of durability bias in affective forecasting. *Journal of Personality and Social Psychology, 78,* 821–836.

Winch, R. F. (1955). The theory of complementary needs in mate selection: A test of one kind of complementariness. *American Sociological Review, 20,* 52–56.

Winch, R. F., Ktanes, T., & Ktanes, V. (1954). The theory of complementary needs in mate-selection: An analytic and descriptive study. *American Sociological Review, 19,* 241–249.

Winch, R. F., Ktanes, T., & Ktanes, V. (1955). Empirical elaboration of the theory of complementary needs in mate selection. *Journal of Abnormal and Social Psychology, 51,* 508–513.

Windhauser, J., Seiter, J., & Winfree, T. (1991). Crime news in the Louisiana press. *Journalism Quarterly, 45,* 72–78.

Wink, P. (1991). Two faces of narcissism. *Journal of Personality and Social Psychology, 61,* 590–597.

Winkielman, P., & Cacioppo, J. T. (2001). Mind at ease puts a smile on the face: Psychophysiological evidence that processing facilitation increases positive affect. *Journal of Personality and Social Psychology, 81,* 989–1000.

Winter, D. G. (1973). *The power motive.* New York: Free Press.

Winter, D. G. (1988). The power motive in women and men. *Journal of Personality and Social Psychology, 54,* 510–519.

Winter, D. G., & Barenbaum, N. B. (1985). Responsibility and the power motive in women and men. *Journal of Personality, 53,* 335–355.

Winter, L., & Uleman, J. S. (1984). When are social judgments made? Evidence for the spontaneousness of trait inferences. *Journal of Personality and Social Psychology, 47,* 237–252.

Wiseman, C. V., Gray, J. J., Mosimann, J. E., & Ahrens, A. H. (1992). Cultural expectations of thinness in women: An update. *International Journal of Eating Disorders, 11,* 85–89.

Wisman, A., and Goldenberg, J. (2005). From the grave to the cradle: Evidence that mortality salience engenders a desire for offspring. *Journal of Personality and Social Psychology, 89,* 46–61.

Witkin, H. A., Lewis, H. B., Hertzman, M., Machover, K., Meissner, P. B., & Karp, S. A. (1954). *Personality through perception.* New York: Harper.

Wittenbrink, B. (2004). Ordinary forms of prejudice. *Psychological Inquiry, 15,* 306–310.

Wittenbrink, B., Judd, C. M., & Park, B. (1997). Evidence for racial prejudice at the implicit level and its relationship with questionnaire measures. *Journal of Personality and Social Psychology, 72,* 262–274.

Wittenbrink, B., & Schwarz, N. (Eds.). (2007). *Implicit measures of attitudes.* New York: Guilford Press.

Wolf, S. (1985). Manifest and latent influence on majorities and minorities. *Journal of Personality and Social Psychology, 48,* 899–908.

Wolfe, T. (1979). *The right stuff.* New York: Farrar, Strauss, Giroux.

Woll, S. (1986). So many to choose from: Decision strategies in videodating. *Journal of Social and Personal Relationships, 3,* 43–52.

Wood, J. V. (1989). Theory and research concerning social comparisons of personal attributes. *Psychological Bulletin, 106,* 231–248.

Wood, J. V. (1996). What is social comparison and how should we study it? *Personality and Social Psychology Bulletin, 22,* 520–537.

Wood, W. (1982). Retrieval of attitude relevant information from memory: Effects of susceptibility to persuasion and on intrinsic motivation. *Journal of Personality and Social Psychology, 42,* 798–810.

Wood, W., & Eagly, A. H. (2002). A cross-cultural analysis of the behavior of women and men: Implications for the origin of sex differences. *Psychological Bulletin, 126,* 699–727.

Wood, W., & Kallgren, C. A. (1988). Communicator attributes and persuasion: Recipients access to attitude-relevant information in memory. *Personality and Social Psychology Bulletin, 14,* 172–182.

Wood, W., Lundgren, S., Ouellette, J. A., Busceme, S., & Blackstone, T. (1994). Minority influence: A meta-analytic review of social influence processes. *Psychological Bulletin, 115,* 323–345.

Wooley, S. C., & Wooley, O. W. (1980). Eating disorders: Obesity and anorexia. In A. M. Brodsky & R. T. Hare-Mustin (Eds.), *Women and psychotherapy: An assessment of research and practice* (pp. 135–158). New York: Guilford Press.

Woolger, R. J. (1988). *Other lives, other selves: A Jungian psychotherapist discovers past lives.* New York: Bantam.

Worchel, S. (1974). The effects of three types of arbitrary thwarting on the instigation to aggression. *Journal of Personality, 42,* 301–318.

Word, C. O., Zanna, M. P., & Cooper, J. (1974). The nonverbal mediation of self-fulfilling prophecies in interracial interaction. *Journal of Experimental Social Psychology, 10,* 109–120.

Wright, R. (1995, March 13). The biology of violence. *New Yorker,* 68–77.

Wright, R. (2000). *Nonzero: The logic of human destiny.* New York: Pantheon Books.

Wyer, R. S., & Srull, T. K. (1981). Category accessibility: Some theoretical and empirical issues concerning the processing of social stimulus information. In E. T. Higgins, C. P. Herman, & M. P. Zanna (Eds.), *Social cognition: The Ontario symposium* (pp. 161–197). Hillsdale, NJ: Erlbaum.

Wyer, R. S., Srull, T. K., Gordon, S. E., & Hartwick, J. (1982). Effects of processing objectives on the recall of prose material. *Journal of Personality and Social Psychology, 43,* 674–688.

Yang, M. H., & Bond, M. H. (1990). Exploring implicit personality theories with indigenous or imported constructs: The Chinese case. *Journal of Personality and Social Psychology, 58,* 1087–1095.

Yuchida, Y., & Kitayama, S. (2009). *Happiness and unhappiness in East and West.* Kyoto, Japan: Kyoto University.

Yudko, E., Blanchard, D., Henne, J., & Blanchard, R. (1997). Emerging themes in preclinical research on alcohol and aggression. In M. Galanter (Ed.), *Recent developments in alcoholism: Alcohol and violence: Epidemiology, neurobiology, psychology, and family issues* (Vol. 13, pp. 123–138). New York: Plenum Press.

Zadny, J., & Gerard, H. B. (1974). Attributed intentions and informational selectivity. *Journal of Experimental Social Psychology, 10,* 34–52.

Zahavi, A., & Zahavi, A. (1997). *The handicap principle.* New York: Oxford University Press.

Zajonc, R. B. (1965). Social facilitation. *Science, 149,* 269–274.

Zajonc, R. B. (1968). The attitudinal effects of mere exposure. *Journal of Personality and Social Psychology, 9* (monographs), 1–27.

Zajonc, R. B. (1980). Feeling and thinking: Preferences need no inferences. *American Psychologist, 35,* 151–175.

Zajonc, R. B. (2001). Mere exposure: A gateway to the subliminal. *Current Directions in Psychological Science, 10,* 224–228.

Zajonc, R. B. (2002). The zoomorphism of human collective violence. In L. S. Newman & R. Erber (Eds.), *Understanding genocide: The social psychology of the Holocaust* (pp. 222–240). New York: Oxford University Press.

Zajonc, R. B., Adelmann, P. K., Murphy, S. T., & Niedenthal, P. M. (1987). Convergence in the physical appearance of spouses. *Motivation and Emotion, 11,* 335–346.

Zajonc, R. B., Heingartner, A., & Herman, E. M. (1969). Social enhancement and impairment of performance in the cockroach. *Journal of Personality and Social Psychology, 13,* 83–92.

Zak, P. J. (2003) Trust. *The Capco Institute Journal of Financial Transformation, 7,* 13–21.

Zanna, M. P., & Cooper, J. (1974). Dissonance and the pill: An attribution approach to studying the arousal properties of dissonance. *Journal of Personality and Social Psychology, 29,* 703–709.

Zanna, M. P., Kiesler, C. A., & Pilkonis, P. A. (1970). Positive and negative attitudinal affect established by classical conditioning. *Journal of Personality and Social Psychology, 14,* 321–328.

Zanna, M. P., & Rempel, J. K. (1988). Attitudes: A new look at an old concept. In D. Bar-Tal & A. W. Kruglanski (Eds.), *The social psychology of knowledge* (pp. 315–334). Cambridge, England: Cambridge University Press.

Zarate, M. A., Uleman, J. S., & Voils, C. I. (2001). Effects of culture and processing goals on the activation and binding of trait concepts. *Social Cognition, 19,* 295–323.

Zebrowitz, L. (1997). *Reading faces: Window to the soul?* Boulder, CO: Westview Press.

Zebrowitz, L. A., Andreoletti, C., Collins, M. A., Lee, S. Y., & Blumenthal, J. (1998). Bright, bad, babyfaced boys: Appearance stereotypes do not always yield self-fulfilling prophecy effects. *Journal of Personality and Social Psychology, 75,* 1300–1320.

Zebrowitz, L. A., & McDonald, S. M. (1991). The impact of litigants' babyfacedness and attractiveness on adjudications in small claims courts. *Law and Human Behavior, 15,* 603–624.

Zebrowitz, L. A., & Montepare, J. M. (2005). Appearance DOES matter. *Science, 308,* 1565–1566.

Zebrowitz, L. A., Olson, K., & Hoffman, K. (1993). Stability of babyfaceness and attractiveness across the life span. *Journal of Personality and Social Psychology, 64,* 453–466.

Zebrowitz, L. A., Tenenbaum, D. R., & Goldstein, L. H. (1991). The impact of job applicants' facial maturity, gender, and academic achievement on hiring recommendations. *Journal of Applied Social Psychology, 21,* 525–548.

Zebrowitz, L. A., Voinescu, L., & Collins, M. A. (1996). "Wideeyed" and "crooked-faced": Determinants of perceived and real honesty across the life span. *Personality and Social Psychology Bulletin, 22,* 1258–1269.

Zhu, Y., Zhang, L., Fan, J., & Han, S. (2007). Neural basis of cultural influences on self-representation. *Neuroimage, 34,* 1310–1316.

Zillman, D. (1978). Attribution and misattribution of excitatory reactions. In J. H. Harvey, W. J. Ickes, & R. F. Kidd (Eds.), *New directions in attribution research* (Vol. 2, pp. 335–368). Hillsdale, NJ: Erlbaum.

Zillman, D. (1988). Cognitive excitation interdependencies in aggressive behavior. *Aggressive Behavior, 14,* 51–64.

Zillman, D. (1989). Effects of prolonged consumption of pornography. In D. Zillman & J. Bryand (Eds.), *Pornography: Research advances and early policy considerations.* Hillsdale, NJ: Erlbaum.

Zimbardo, P. G. (1970). *The human choice: Individuation, reason and order versus deindividuation, impulse and chaos.* Paper presented at the Nebraska Symposium on Motivation (1969), Lincoln, Nebraska.

Zimbardo, P. G., & Leippe, M. R. (1991). *The psychology of attitude change and social influence.* New York: McGraw-Hill.

Zuber, J. A., Crott, H. W., & Werner, J. (1992). Choice shift and group polarization: An analysis of the status of arguments and social decision schemes. *Journal of Personality and Social Psychology, 62,* 50–61.

Zuckerman, M. (1996). The psychobiological model for impulsive unsocialized sensation seeking: A comparative approach. *Neuropsychobiology, 34,* 125–129.

Zuckerman, M. (1998). Psychobiological theories of personality. In D. F. Barone, M. Hersen, & V. B. V. Hasselt (Eds.), *Advanced personality* (pp. 123–154). New York: Plenum Press.

Zusne, L., & Jones, W. H. (1982). *Anomalistic psychology.* Hillsdale, NJ: Erlbaum.

Zuwerink, J. R., & Devine, P. G. (1996). Attitude importance and resistance to persuasion: It's not just the thought that counts. *Journal of Personality and Social Psychology, 70,* 931–944.

Zweig, J. (2007). *Your money and your brain.* New York: Simon & Schuster.

Credits

Eric Nguyen/Jim Reed Photography/Corbis; **(B)** MGM/Photofest. **p. 184:** **(A)** Bettmann/Corbis; **(B)** AP Photo/Al Golub, Pool, The Modesto Bee. **p. 187:** **(A)** Charles & Josette; **(B)** Ed Quinn/Corbis. **p. 188:** Blank Archives/Getty Images. **p. 192:** The New Yorker Collection, 1977 Dana Fradon, from cartoonbank.com.

Chapter 6

p. 196: Michael Siluk/The Image Works. **p. 198:** (**top, A**) Bettmann/Corbis; (**top, B**) AP Photo; (**bottom**) Reuters/Corbis. **p. 199:** Natalie Fobes/Corbis. **p. 201:** Timothy A. Clary/AFP/Getty Images. **p. 203:** Paul A. Souders/Corbis. **p. 206:** **(A)** Hulton-Deutsch Collection/Corbis; **(B)** Julio Donoso/Corbis C6 Sygma. **p. 207:** Hunter Martin/Corbis. **p. 208:** 1982 Karen Zebuion, Courtesy New School Public Relations Department. **p. 209:** (**top**) Rob Rogers, © 1994 The Pittsburgh Post-Gazette/Distributed by United Feature Syndicate, Inc.; (**bottom**) Kevin R. Morris/Corbis. **p. 211: Figure 6.2:** **(A)** Photo courtesy of Terp Weekly Edition. **p. 215:** DILBERT, © 1999 Scott Adams/Distributed by United Feature Syndicate. **p. 218:** Kitayama, et al. From "Is there any 'free' choice? Self and dissonance in two cultures," *Psychological Science* 15.8 (August 2004) 527-533. Reprinted by permission of Wiley-Blackwell Ltd. **p. 219:** Courtesy of Daryl J. Bem. **p. 223: Figure 6.5:** (**top photo**) David Young-Wolff/Photo Edit. **p. 225: Figure 6.7:** Photos courtesy of Neil Hoos. **p. 229:** Romilly Lockyer/Getty Images. **p. 230:** The New Yorker Collection 1997 Bill Woodman from cartoonbank.com. **p. 231: Figure 6.9:** (**left photo**): AP Photo/Mike Derer.

Chapter 7

p. 234: Kpzfoto/Alamy. **p. 236:** **(A)** Corbis; **(B)** Detail from Eadweard Muybridge's photograph of Falls of the Yosemite.From Glacier Rock (Great Grizzly Bear) 2000 feet fall, No.36. Courtesy of The Bancroft Library, University of California Berkeley. **p. 239:** **(A, B)** ©Ekman 1975–2004. **p. 240:** **(A)** From The Expression of the Emotions in Man and Animals by Charles Darwin, fig. 5; **(B)** From The Expression of the Emotions in Man and Animals by Charles Darwin, fig. 6. **p. 241:** (**top**) Bettmann/Corbis; (**bottom**) All photographs courtesy Professor Dacher Keltner. **p. 242: Figure 7.1:** (**top photos**) from WEITEN 7e, fig. 10.22, p. 403; (**bottom photos**) © Ekman 1972–2004. **p. 243:** **(A)** Brand X/Getty Images; **(B)** Courtesy Dacher Keltner. **p. 245: Figure 7.2:** Photos from Haidt & Keltner, 1999. **p. 247:** Joe Giron/Corbis. **p. 251:** (**top**) AP Photo; (**bottom**) ImageState/Alamy. **p. 251:** Courtesy Library and Archives, Canada. Photograph by Yousef Karsh.

PART THREE

p. 272: Richard Carroll/Ambient Images.

Chapter 8

p. 274: Jeff Morgan social issues/Alamy. **p. 276:** The Granger Collection. **p. 278:** **(A)** M.N. Chan/Getty Images; **(B)** Mitchell Layton/Getty Images. **p. 279:** The New Yorker Collection, 2000 Mick Stevens, from cartoonbank.com. **p. 280:** Barbara Kinney/William J. Clinton Presidential Library and Museum. **p. 282:** Courtesy of Swathmore College. **p. 283: Figure 8.4:** photos from Asch, 1956. **p. 284:** Karl Prouse/Catwalking/Getty Images. **p. 288:** Getty Images. **p. 292:** **(A)** Bettmann/Corbis; **(B)** Bettmann/Corbis. **p. 293:** Courtesy Alexandra Milgram. **p. 294:** **(A, B)** From the film *Obedience*, © 1965 by Stanley Milgram and distributed by Penn State Media Sales. **p. 295:** From the film *Obedience*, © 1965 Stanley Milgram and distributed by Penn State Media Sales. **p. 296:** Photo by Jordon R. Beesley/U.S. Navy /Getty Images. **p. 299:** **(A, B)** Courtesy of Jerry

Burger. **p. 301:** **(A, B)** From *Obedience to Authority: An Experimental View* by Stanley Milgram, Harper & Row, Publishers, © 1974 by Stanley Milgram, p. 67. **p. 305:** Le Segretin Pascal/Corbis Sygma. **p. 307:** Yuriko Nakao/Reuters/Corbis. **p. 309:** Stephane Reix/ For Picture/Corbis. **p. 310:** Bettmann/Corbis. **p. 313:** Time Life Pictures/Getty Images.

Chapter 9

p. 316: The Photo Works. **p. 318:** **(A)** Lee Snider/Photo Images/Corbis; **(B)** Viviane Moos/Corbis. **p. 320:** David M. Dennis/Photolibrary. **p. 323:** (**top**) Imaginechina/AP Photo; (**bottom**) The New Yorker Collection, 1928 Carl Rose, from cartoonbank.com. **p. 324:** Gary Crabbe/AgeFotostock. **p. 325:** **(A)** PAVEL WOLBERG/epa/Corbis; **(B)** Kayte Deioma/Photo Edit. **p. 331:** Reuters/Corbis. **p. 332:** Hulton-Deutsch Collection/Corbis. **p. 334:** AP Photo/Daily Sentinel. **p. 335:** Debbie Noda-Pool/Getty Images. **p. 337:** **(A)** Swim Ink 2, LLC/Corbis; **(B)** Courtesy U.S. Army. **p. 338:** **(A)** Corbis; **(B)** Emmanuel Dunand/AFP/Getty Images. **p. 341:** (**top, A**)Organizing for America.com http://my.barackobama.com; (**top, B**) Courtesy of info@friendsofmccain.com / http://www.johnmccain.com; (**bottom**) Courtesy of Tom Calton. **p. 244:** The New Yorker Collection, 2003 Mick Stevens, from cartoonbank.com.

PART FOUR

p. 352 SuperStock/AgeFotostock.

Chapter 10

p. 354: Jeremy Horner/Panos. **p. 356:** Dave Allocca/Time Life Pictures/Getty Images. **p. 358: Figure 10.1:** (**photo**) ipnstock/StockPhotoFinder.com. **p. 359: Figure 10.2:** (**photo**) AP Photo/Kevin Rivoli. **p. 363:** **(A)** Natalie Fobes/Corbis; **(B)** Craig Lovell/Corbis. **p. 364: Figure 10.3:** (**photos**) AP Photo/Rick Bowmer. **p. 368:** Rob & Sas/Corbis. **p. 371:** The New Yorker Collection, 1999 Barbara Smaller, from cartoonbank.com. **p. 373:** The New Yorker Collection 2005 Marisa Acocella Marchetto from cartoonbank.com. **p. 375:** Jerome Tisne/Getty Images. **p. 379:** **(A)** Photo: Erich Lessing/Art Resource; **(B)** Nimatallah/Art Resource, NY; **(C)** Sunset Boulevard/Corbis; **(D)** Frank Trapper/Corbis. **p. 380:** AFP/Getty Images. **p. 381: Figure 10.6:** (**photos**) courtesy of Professor Judith Hall Langlois, University of Texas at Austin. **p. 382** (**top, A**) Archivo Iconografico, S.A./Corbis; (**top, B**) Evan Agostini/Getty Images; **Figure 10.7:** **(A, B, C)** Copyright 1994 Macmillan Publishers, Ltd. Photos courtesy of Professor David Perrett, University of St. Andrews, Scotland. **p. 384:** Glowimages/Getty Images. **p. 386:** Getty Images. **p. 390: Figure 10.9** (**top photos**) From "Menstrual cycles alters face preference," I. S. Penton-Voak, D. I. Perrett, D. L. Castles, T. Kobayashi, D. M. Burt, L. K. Murray & R. Minamisawa, *Nature* 399, 741–742 (24 June 1999), Fig.1. **p. 393:** The New Yorker Collection, 1997 Frank Cotham, from cartoonbank.com.

Chapter 11

p. 396: Mark Henley/Panos Pictures. **p. 400: Figure 11.1** (**photos**) Nina Leen/Time Life Pictures/Getty Images. **p. 401:** **(A)** Gallo Images/Corbis; **B)** Courtesy Barbara Smuts/Anthrophoto. **p. 402:** **(A)** David Katzenstein/Corbis; **(B)** Eleonora Ghioldi/Corbis; **(C)** Ralph Reinhold/Photolibrary. **p. 403:** The New Yorker Collection, 1976 Ed Koren, from cartoonbank.com. **p. 405:** **(A)** Kennan Ward/Corbis; **(B)** Corbis; **(C)** Dan Guravich/Corbis. **p. 406:** **(A, B, C)** Courtesy the Estate of Mary Ainsworth. **p. 409:** (**top**) The New Yorker Collection, 2002 Michael Maslin, from cartoonbank.com; (**bottom**) Mike Powell/Getty Images. **p. 410:** Reuters/Corbis.

p. 413: The New Yorker Collection, 1991 Mischa Richter, from cartoonbank.com. p. 417: (A–D) George Tames/The New York Times Photo Archives. p. 422: The New Yorker Collection, 1995 Leo Cullum, from cartoonbank.com. p. 423: (A) Wally Herbert/AgeFotostock; (B) R. Matina/AgeFotostock; (C) Tao Images/AgeFotostoc. p. 428: The New Yorker Collection, 1996 Robert Weber, from cartoonbank. Com. p. 430: Figure 11.9: (photos) Thinkstock/AgeFotostock. p. 433: (A, B) Redchopsticks Collect/AgeFotostock.

Chapter 12
p. 440: Courtesy of We Are Part Of You.org. p. 442: Stapleton Collection/Corbis. p. 444: (A) Yellow Dog Productions/Getty Images; (B) Phelan M. Ebenhack/ Washington Post. p. 451: (A–C) Archives of the History of American Psychology, University of Akron. p. 453: Scott Olson/Getty Images. p. 456: (A) Scott J. Ferrell/Congressional Quarterly/Getty Images; (B) David Stoecklein/Corbis. p. 457: RICHARD CLEMENT/Reuters/Corbis. p. 460: Steve Grayson/WireImage.com. p. 463: The New Yorker Collection, 2000 David Sipress, from cartoonbank.com. p. 464: Photo by Jesse Grant/WireImage.com/ABC. p. 468: Curtis Means/NBC NewsWire/AP Photo. p.: 469: Scott Olson/Getty Images. p. 473: Figure 12.7: (photos) Courtesy of Keith Payne. p. 475: Sygma/Corbis. p. 477: Figure 12.9: (photo) Corbis. p. 479: Alan Howden/Alamy.

Chapter 13
p. 484: Courtesy Boys and Girls Clubs of Greater Dallas. Ad Agency: Commerce House. p. 486: (A) Bettmann/Corbis; (B) Scott Peterson/Getty Images. p. 488: Michal Czerwonka. p. 491: (A) Sunset Boulevard/Sygma/Corbis; (B) AFP/Getty Images. p. 492: (A) IGN Entertainment, Inc.; (B) Reuters/Corbis. p. 497: Figure 13.5: (A) Focus on Sport/Getty Images. p. 499: (A) Robert van der Hilst/Corbis; (B) Dr. Napoleon A. Chagnon; p. 500: The New Yorker Collection, 2003 Frank Cotham, from cartoonbank.com. p. 502: (A) Leonard de Selva/Corbis; (B) Bettmann/Corbis. p. 505: Carlo Allegri/Getty Images. p. 506: AP Photo/Peter Kramer. p. 507: (top, A) Alan Levenson/Time Life Pictures/Getty Images; (top, B) Courtesy Debra DiPaolo; (bottom) Blaine Harrington III/Corbis. p. 508: The New Yorker Collection, 1989 Danny Shanahan, from

cartoonbank.com. p. 510: Courtesy The New York Times Picture Archives. p. 514: Gideon Mendel/Corbis. p. 515: The New Yorker Collection, 2004 Michael Crawford, from cartoonbank.com. p. 517: (A) Ed Kashi/CORBIS; (B) Vario images GmbH & Co. KG/Alamy. p. 520: Michael and Patricia Fogden/Corbis. p. 521: (A) Corbis; (B) Tom Brakefield/Corbis. p. 522: Illustrated London News/Bridgeman Art Library. p. 524: Melanie Stetson Freeman/The Christian Science Monitor/Getty Images. p. 527: (A) Loren McIntyre/Photolibrary; (B) Michael Patrick O'Neill/Alamy.

Chapter 14
p. 532: Derek Love-Art Director/Copywriter; Kristopher Blake-Copywriter; Agency-Adhouse NYC. p. 534: (A) Courtesy Press Office of John McCain; (B) AFP/Getty Image. p. 536: Andreas Rentz/Bongarts/Getty Images. p. 537: Hazel Markus. p. 539: Rubes cartoon by permission of Leigh Rubin and Creators Syndicate, Inc. p. 540: Figure 14.2: Zajonc, et al., Figure from "Social enhancement and impairment of performance in the cockroach," *Journal of Personality and Social Psychology* 13.2, 83-92. Copyright © 1969, American Psychological Association. Reproduced with permission. p. 545: Charles Gupton/Corbis. p. 546: (A) Roger Ressmeyer/Corbis; (B) John Storey/San Francisco Chronicle. p. 547: Reuters/Corbis. p. 548: Peter Turnley/Corbis. p. 549: Chris Graythen/Getty Images. p.: 551: Doug Steley/Alamy. p. 554 Corbis. p. 559: AP Photo. p. 561: The New Yorker Collection 1994 Mike Twohy, from cartoonbank.com.

Chapter 15
p. 568: AP Photo//Pat Auckerman. p. 570: (A) AP Photo; (B) AP Photo/Clarence Hamm. p. 571: The London Art Archive/Alamy. p. 575: (A) Spencer Grant/Photo Edit; (B) Craig Lovell/Eagle Visions Photography/Alamy. p. 578: Figure 15.3: (photo) Paula Lerner / Aurora Photos. p. 580: Figure 15.3: (photo) Dennis MacDonald/Alamy. p. 582: Spencer Platt/Getty Images. p. 590: Figure 15.6: (photo) Courtesy Nicholas Epley. p. 591: (A, B) Courtesy Sheena Iyengar. Iyengar, S. S., & Lepper, M. R. (2000). "When choice is demotivating: Can one desire too much of a good thing?" *Journal of Personality and Social Psychology*, 79, 995–1006. p. 596: Vanni/Art Resource, NY. p. 601: AP Photo/Gregory Bull.

Name Index

Page numbers in *italics* refer to figures, illustrations, and tables.

Subject Index

Page numbers in *italics* refer to figures, illustrations, and tables.

marriage (continued)
  positive focus in, 432
  "postromantic" feelings and, 437
  as transaction, 436–37
  types of, 37, 436–37
  see also marital dissatisfaction
marriage transactions, 436–37
Marshall Plan, 559
Maryland State Police Training Academy,
    359, 359, 360
Mbuti Pygmies, 502
measurement validity, 58
Mechanism of Human Facial Expression, The
    (Duchenne de Boulogne), 239
media, 163
  conceptions of social reality in, 342–43
  copycat suicide and, 490
  distortion in, 161–62, 162, 181
  hostility seen in, 343
  and persuasion, 339–43
  violence in, 489–90, 491, 505
  weak effects of, 340–41, 349
  see also advertising
meditation, 268, 577
memory:
  biases in, 156–59, 156, 158
  control and, 580
  flashbulb, 158, 158
  recovered, 156–57, 156
  schemas and, 173–74, 178
  self-knowledge and, 83–84
mental accounting, 588–89, 590, 594
mental health, social psychology and,
    571–81
mere exposure effect, 362–66, 363, 364, 365
mere presence, 541–43, 543, 545
message characteristics, 333–36, 337, 339
Michigan, University of, 588
Mideast Peace Accord (1995), 280
Mikulincer, Mario, 409
Milgram obedience experiments, 12–14, 12,
    16, 57, 60–61, 122, 131, 287, 293–304,
    294, 510
  Burger obedience experiments vs., 298–
    99, 299
  "empathy tests" in, 297–98
  indecisive disobedience in, 300–301, 313
  legitimacy and, 301–2, 301
  opposing forces in, 295–97, 295, 297, 304
  release from responsibility in, 301–2, 304
  setup of, 293–95, 293
  step-by-step involvement in, 302–3, 307,
    313
military, U.S., 337, 556
Mille Collines Hotel, 505, 505
mimicry:
  cultural differences and, 250
  emotion and, 249–50
  friendship and, 250
  see also automatic mimicry
mind, theory of, 26–28, 29
minimal group paradigm, 455
misattribution of arousal, 261, 489
MIT apartment study, 357–58, 358, 360
mobs, psychology of, 545–55, 546
  deindividuation and group mind in, 548–
    53, 548, 549

emergent properties of groups and,
    547–48, 547
  see also deindividuation
modern racism, 444–46
Modern Racism Scale, 448, 471
modern sexism, 444–46
monogamy, 503
monozygotic (identical) twins, 70–71, 70,
    347
mood:
  negative, in compliance, 309–12, 310, 312
  persuasive messages and, 336–37, 338
  positive, in compliance, 308–9, 309, 314
  see also emotion
mood maintenance, 309
Moonies, 318
mortality salience manipulations, 230–31,
    231
motivational perspective, on prejudice and
    discrimination, 454–61
  evaluation of, 460–61
  frustration-aggression theory in, 459–61,
    460
  minimal group paradigm in, 455
  social identity theory in, 455–59, 456
Müller-Lyer illusion, 281, 281
murder:
  serial, 151–52, 152
  see also homicide
mutual funds, 593
My Fair Lady, 598

N

narcissism, self-esteem and, 100
narratives, self-, social self and, 80
National Basketball Association (NBA),
    277–78, 278
natural experiments, 53–54
naturalistic fallacy, 28–29
natural selection, 24–25
nature or nurture, 493
Nazi Germany, 11, 61, 175–76, 298, 300,
    302–3, 336, 338, 415, 486, 486, 496,
    569, 589
  see also Holocaust
need for cognition, persuasive messages and,
    336
negative state relief hypothesis, 309–12, 310,
    312
neighborhoods, health and stress and,
    574–75, 575
neo-associationistic account of aggression,
    494–95, 495
neuroscience, social, 29
neuroticism, 69, 70, 71
  marital dissatisfaction and, 428
New Age beliefs, 189
New York Yankees, 129
NFL, 496, 497
NHL, 496, 497
Nightline, 343
Nirvana, 268
nonverbal displays, 251, 251
normative social influence, 281–85, 282,
    283, 289, 293
norm of reciprocity, 304–5, 305
nurture, nature or, 493

O

obedience, 12–14, 287, 293–304
  Burger's experiments on, 298–99, 299
  definition of, 277
  indecisive disobedience in, 300–301, 313
  legitimacy and, 301–2, 301
  Milgram's experiments on, 12–14, 122,
    131, 293–304, 293, 295, 297, 301, 307,
    313, 510
  in Nazi Germany, 298, 300, 302–3
  opposing forces and, 295–97, 295, 297,
    304
  release from responsibility in, 301–2,
    304
  step-by-step involvement in, 302–3, 307,
    313
observational research, 47, 48, 56
observer-participant, 220
OCEAN (Big Five traits, five-factor model),
    69–70
off-record communication, 105, 107
Olympic Games, 125, 126, 187, 251, 251
on-record communication, 105
On the Origin of Species (Darwin), 73
optimism:
  breast cancer and, 581
  construals and, 580–81
  in explanatory styles, 117
  health and, 579–81
  HIV and, 581
  unrealistic, 88, 89
orbitofrontal cortex, 236
order effects, 164–65, 166
Organization Man, The (Whyte), 357, 367
others, understanding of, 111–49
ought self, 87, 90
outgroup homogeneity effect, 464–65, 464,
    476
outgroups, 32
  accentuation of ingroup difference and
    similarity of, 463–64
  homogeneity effect of, 464–65, 464, 476
  stereotyping of, 442, 457–59
  see also intergroup hostility
overjustification effect, 222–23
oxytocin:
  love and, 248–49, 436
  marriage and, 248
  "tend-and-befriend" approach and, 579
  trust and, 248–49
  see also hormones

P

paired distinctiveness, 466–68, 468
palio experiment, 469–70
parental investment, 28, 29, 383–87
Park Forest study, 367, 367
participant observation, 47, 48
payoff matrix experiment, 290, 291
payroll deduction, 593
Pearl Harbor, bombing of, 556
"perceiver-induced constraint" paradigm,
    133
perceptual salience, 136, 136
perceptual vigilance, 163
peripheral route to persuasion, 328–30, 328,
    330, 333, 336, 338, 339

relationships (*continued*)
   health and, 577–78
   importance of, 400–404
   investments in, 425–28
   origins of relating to others in, 405–12
   power and hierarchical, 415–23
   relating to others in, 412–23
   romantic, 399, 423–37
   sacrifice and, 435
   sense of self and, 410–12
   social, 247–53
   social rejection and, 403–4
   three models of, 423
   see also attraction; social connection
reliability, 58
   research, 58, 59
representativeness heuristic, 184–91, *184, 185, 191, 193*
   and base-rate neglect, 184–86, 193
   and causality, 188–93
   definition of, 179
   joint operation of availability and, 191–93
   planning fallacy and, 186–88, *187*
reproductive fitness, 380–87, *386*, 388–91
   see also parental investment
research, 44–62
   applied, 59–60, *60*
   archival, 47–48, 56
   basic, 59–60
   bias and, 48
   convenience sample and, *49*
   correlational, 50–53, *51, 54, 55*
   debriefing and, 58, 61
   deception, 61, *62*
   ethics and, 60–62
   experimental, 50, 53–58
   hindsight bias and, 45
   hypotheses and, 47, 50
   informed consent and, 61
   institutional review boards and, 60–61, 62
   interventions and, 59–60
   observational, 47, 48, 56
   participant observation and, 47, 48
   prediction and, 45, 46, 47
   probability and, 59
   random sample and, 48–49, *49*
   reliability, 58, 59
   scatterplots and, 51, *51*
   surveys and, 48–50
   theories and hypotheses in, 47, 50
response latency, 321
reward perspective, on attraction, 391–93
rewards, in relationships, 416, 426
rhesus monkey experiment, 399, 400, *400, 402*
rioting, *see* mobs, psychology of
risk, biased assessments and, 181–82
risk aversion, 585–86
   definition of, 585
risk seeking, 587
risky shift, 561
ritualized displays, *245*
R. J. Reynolds Company, *318, 334*
Robbers Cave experiment, 450–53, *451, 454*, 479–80
Rod and Frame test, 143
role models, 600–601

Roman Catholicism, 313
Romans, 552
romantic relationships, 97, 130, 399, 423–37
   arranged marriages and, 436–37
   commitment in, 424, 425–28, *426*
   creating stronger bonds in, 432–37
   hormones and, 424
   illusions and idealization in, 434–36
   intimacy and, 424
   marital dissatisfaction in, 428–32
   sacrifice and, 435
   see also attraction
rumination, 572–73
Rwanda genocide, 298, 302, 485–86, *486, 505, 524, 524*

S

sacrifice, relationships and, 435
sadism, 10
sadness, 241, *241*
Saving Private Ryan (film), 125
scatterplots, 51, *51*
Schachter and Singer's two-factor theory of emotion, 259–61
schemas, 19–20, *20, 21*
   definition of, 19, 171
   information as mapped onto preexisting, 174–78
   self-, 84–85
   social judgment influenced by, 171–74
schematic participants, 84
secondary appraisal stage, 238
secondhand information, 159–63
   ideological distortions in, 161
   and impressions of other people, 160–61
   media distortion and, 161–62, *162*, 181
   sharpening and leveling of, 159–60, *160, 163*
secure attachment style, 407–9, *407*
selective attention, 171, *172*
selective evaluation, 344–45, *345, 349*
self:
   nature of, 68, *68*
   as social perception standard, 85–86
   see also social self
self-adaptors, 251
self-affirmation, dissonance and, 217
self-assessment:
   brain and, 83
   construal processes and, 80–81
self-awareness theory, 553–55, *554*
self-censorship, 558
self-complexity, 93
self-concept, 97, 408–9, 410
   context as defining of, 76
   cultural differences in, 30–33, *30, 31, 37*, 74–76, *75*
   gender and, 76
   and individualism vs. collectivism in the workplace, 33–34, *34*
self-consciousness:
   embarrassment and, 246, 247, 252
   shame and, 246, 252
self-construals, *see* self-concept
self-control, 87–88
self-definition, *see* self-concept
self-discrepancy theory, 86

self-distancing, 573
self-esteem, 68, 90, 91–100, *91, 92*
   contingencies of, 92–93
   cultural changes and, 98–99, *99*
   cultural differences and, 98–99, 100
   death and, 231
   definition of, 91
   education and, 603
   motives to elevate, 94–96, 100
   narcissism and, *100*
   possible dangers of high, 99–100, *100*
   prejudice used as bolstering, 457–59, *458, 459*
   self-evaluation model and, 94–98, *95*
   social acceptance and, 93–94
   task force on, 91
self-evaluation, 68, 91–100
   maintenance model of, 94–95
   motives of, 94–98, 100
   see also self-esteem
self-fulfilling prophecies, 176, 374, 599
   definition of, 374, 465
   effect on behavior, 176, 465–66
   in maintaining stereotypes, 465–66, 476
self-handicapping, 103–5, *104*, 107
self-image, 364, *364*
   see also self-concept
self-image bias, 80–81, 85
self-interest:
   persuasion and, 333–34, *334*
   wealth and, 582
self-knowledge, 68, 82–90
   cultural differences in, 90
   illusions and biases in, 88–90
   motivational function of, 86–88
   organizational function of, 82–86
   as standard in social perception, 85–86, 90
self-monitoring, 103, *103*
self-narratives:
   cultural differences and, 80
   social self and, 80
self-perception theory, 219–28, *219*
   body over mind in, 225
   inferring attitudes in, 219–20, 228
   movement and, *226*
   overjustification effect and superfluous rewards in, 222–23
   reconciling cognitive dissonance theory with, 224–28
   self-directed inference in, 220–21
   testing for arousal in, 221–24, *224*, 228
self-presentation, 68, 100–107, *101*
   definition of, 101
   and effect on health, 104
   public vs. private self-consciousness in, 102
   self-handicapping in, 103–5, *104*, 107
self-reference effect, 83–84, *84*, 85
self-schemas, 84–85
self-selection, 52, 54, 399, 536
self-serving bias, 128–31, *129*, 141
   attributions and, 129
self-verification theory, 96–97
Seminarian study, 14, 53, 61, 511
Senate Intelligence Committee, U.S., 557

September 11th, 2001 terrorist attacks, 158, *158*, 267, 281, 286, *313*, 450
  see also terrorism
Serbs, 298
serviceable habits, principle of, 240
SES, *see* socioeconomic status (SES)
sex, sexual relations, 37
sexism, 444–46
sexual harassment, 421
sexual identity:
  cultural differences in, 36–37
  evolutionary basis of, 28
  self-concept and, 75–76
  see also gender
sexuality:
  cultural differences in, 37
  evolutionary basis of, 379–81, 383, 385–86, 388–91
  homosexuality and, 37, 257, 303, 325
  intersex attraction and, 385
  intrasex competition and, 385
shame, 246, 252, 257, 259
sharpening, of information, 159–60, *160*, 163
Sherif:
  conformity studies, 280–81, *282*, 283, 289
  Robbers Cave experiment, 450–53, *451*
shyness, 10, 69
sibling dynamics, 72–74, *72, 73*, 81, 96
similarity, 366–72, *368*
  appearances and, 368, *368*
  complementarity vs., 369–70
  as facilitating smooth interactions, 371
  studies on attraction and, 367–69, *367*
  as validating own beliefs, 370–71
situation, health and, 576–79
situation, power of, 11–16, *12*
  channel factors in, 14–15
  fundamental attribution error in, 16
  Milgram experiment on, 12–14, *12*, 16
  Samaritan experiment and, 14, *15*
situational attributions, 121, 127, 131
  see also fundamental attribution error
situationism, 76–78
  social self and, 76–78
60 Minutes (TV show), 298
60 Minutes II (TV show), 7, 8
skill acquisition, 22
SLA (Symbionese Liberation Army), 67–68
Slave Market with Disappearing Bust of Voltaire (Dalí), *17*
slavery, 6, 441–42, *442*
sleeper effect, 333
smiles, felt vs. false, 239, *239*
smoking:
  consumer advertising and, 317–18, *318*, 334, 349
  persuasion and, *334, 335*, 349
snap judgments, 112–15
  accuracy of, 114–15
social acceptance, 93–94
social bonds, emotions and maintenance of, *243*
social cognition, emotion and, 253–58
social comparison theory, 79–80, 563–64
  self-esteem and, 94–96, *95*

social connection:
  breast cancer and, 578–79, *578*
  cortisol and, 577
  health and, 576–79
  longevity and, 577
  measures of, 576, *576*
  stress response and, 576
  see also relationships
social context, 76, 77, *77*
  cultural differences in attending to, 142–43, *142, 143*
Social Darwinism, 24
social dominance orientation, 419
social exchange theory, 393
social facilitation, 535–45
  competitive performance and, 536–37, *536*
  current perspectives on, 543–44
  initial research on, 536–37
  mere presence vs. evaluation apprehension in, 541–43, *542, 543*, 545
  practical applications in, 544–45
  of prejudice, 538
  Zajonc's theory in, 537–41, *539, 540, 541–43*
social identity theory, 455–59, *456*
social influence, 274–315
  bulimia and, 284
  compliance in, 277, 304–12
  conformity in, 277–93, *278, 288*
  definition of, 276–77
  obedience and, 277, 287, 293–304
  resisting, 313, *313*
social interaction, mimicry and, 278–79
social judgment, 150–95, *152*
  availability heuristic in, 179–83, *180, 181, 182*
  confirmation bias and, 167–70, *169*
  firsthand information and, 153–59, 163
  framing effects in, 165–66
  information biases in, 153–63
  joint operation of availability and representativeness in, 191–93
  order effects in, 164–65, *166*
  positive and negative information and, 162–63
  presentation of information in, 163–67
  prior knowledge and knowledge structures in, 179–78
  reason, intuition, and heuristics in, 178–93, *179*
  reasons for studying, 152–53
  representativeness heuristic in, 179, 184–91, *184, 185, 191*
  schemas as influence on, 171–74
  secondhand information and, 159–63
  serial killing and, 151–52, *152*
social loafing, 544
social neuroscience, 29
  behavior and, 29
  brain function and, 29
social psychology:
  characterizing, 7–11
  definition of, 7
  health, wealth, wisdom and applied, 568–606
  mental and physical health and, 571–81

propaganda and, 569, 570
  wisdom and education and, 594–604
social rewards, 506, 521
social science methodology, 602–4
social self, 67–109
  brain and, 83
  construal processes and, 78–81
  nature of, 69–81
  self-esteem and, 91–100, *91, 92*
  self-narratives and, 80
  self-presentation in, 100–107, *101*
  situationism and, 76–78
social self-beliefs, 82
socioeconomic status (SES):
  education and, 574
  health and, 574–75, 581
  IQ and, 599
  marital dissatisfaction and, 429
  stress and, 574–75, *575*, 577
sociology, 10
sociometer hypothesis, 93–94
sociometric survey, 357
Socratic method, education and, 603
source characteristics, 332–33
South, culture of honor in, 498–500, *499*, 505
spin framing, 165–66, *166*, 167
split-brain patients, 226–28, *227*
spotlight effect, 554
Stanford University, 8, 18, *19*, 525, 603
state self-esteem, 91–92, 100
statistical significance, 58–59
statistics, 602–4
status, 416
  boosting of ingroup, 456–57
  conformity and, 287–88, *288*
step-by-step involvement, 302–3, 307, *313*
stepchildren, 502–3, *502*, 505
stepparents, 502–3, *502*
stereotypes, stereotyping, 20–21, *21*, 23, 440–83, *442, 444*
  assessing true attitudes and, 446–49, *447*
  attributional ambiguity and, 476–77, 479
  automatic and controlled processing in, 470–75, *473, 475, 476*
  biased assessments and, 45, 462–68
  cognitive perspective on, 461–76
  and conservation of mental reserves, 461–62, *462*
  construal processes and biased assessments in, 462–68
  definition of, 20, 443
  disidentification and, 478
  harm of benevolent, 446
  immunity to disconfirmation and, 468–70, *470, 476*
  power and reliance on, 419
  reducing, 479–80
  self-esteem bolstered by use of, 457–59, *458*
  stigmatized victims of, 476–78
  subtyping and, 469, *469*
  see also discrimination; prejudice
stereotype threat, 477–79, *477*, 596–98, *598*, 604
  blocking of, *598*